W9-CQI-402

Foundations of Contemporary Psychology

Foundations
of Contemporary
Psychology

EDITED BY

Merle E. Meyer
The University of Florida

New York
OXFORD UNIVERSITY PRESS
1979

Library of Congress Cataloging in Publication Data

Main entry under title:
Foundations of contemporary psychology.
  Bibliography: p.
  Includes index.
  1. Psychology. I. Meyer, Merle E.
BF121.F63   150   77-16153
ISBN 0-19-502327-7

Preface

The general rationale for this book is that an introductory text in psychology should fully reflect the contemporary scientific theories and principles, as well as the psychological issues of our time. This text has not been reduced to a major theoretical approach, but rather describes the current thought that has been useful and helpful to the discipline, and to those important contributors to the future of psychology. While this book stresses the science of psychology, both cumulative and open-ended, it also incorporates the application of these principles to human problems.

Each chapter of this text is a contemporary statement of a basic scientific area in psychology. Today, no single author can marshal the erudition required for a broad inventory of the theories and principles. In order that an excellent text be fully developed, it was clear that the collaborative efforts of area specialists were required. While there may be minor limitations on the number of topic chapters, significantly greater depth has been achieved in the basic areas covered.

Foundations of Contemporary Psychology was so designed that each chapter is a comprehensive statement in its own right. By employing such a tactic, we have developed a text that allows maximum flexibility for the development of an individual instructor's course. The course could be developed where the emphasis was biological, or social-personality, or experimental, or any combination of tactics. While all the chapters may not be covered in a given course, the student has the essential materials all together in one source.

We express our gratitude to our colleagues, secretaries, artists, and publishers for their expert assistance. Fuller credits for illustrations appear in the captions.

Merle E. Meyer

Gainesville, Florida
January 1979

Contents

Contributors

Baldridge, Barbara
   formerly Assistant Professor of Psychology
   University of Florida

Bonnet, Michael H.
   Assistant Professor of Psychology
   Department of Psychiatry
   University of Cincinnati Medical School

Brackbill, Yvonne
   Graduate Research Professor of Psychology
   University of Florida

Branch, Marc N.
   Associate Professor of Psychology
   University of Florida

Brown, Judson S.
   Professor of Medical Psychology
   University of Oregon Health Sciences Center

Cunningham, Christopher L.
   Assistant Professor of Medical Psychology
   University of Oregon Health Sciences Center

Dawson, William W.
   Professor of Physiology, Psychology
   and Ophthalmology
   University of Florida Medical School

Dewsbury, Donald A.
   Professor of Psychology
   University of Florida

Eaton, Newell K.
   Research Psychologist
   Army Research Institute for the Behavioral
   and Social Sciences

Ellis, Henry C.
   Professor and Chairman of Psychology
   University of New Mexico

Epting, Franz
   Associate Professor of Psychology
   University of Florida

Goggin, Judith P.
   Professor of Psychology
   University of Texas, El Paso

Hake, Harold W.
   Professor of Psychology
   University of Illinois at Urbana-Champaign

Isaacson, Robert L.
   Professor of Psychology
   State University of New York at Binghamton

Landsman, Ted
   Professor of Psychology and Counselor
   Education
   University of Florida

Lippman, Marcia Z.
   Associate Professor of Psychology
   Western Washington University

Matarazzo, Joseph D.
   Professor and Chairman
   of Medical Psychology
   University of Oregon Health Sciences Center

McClearn, Gerald E.
   Professor of Psychology and Director of the
   Institute for Behavioral Genetics
   Institute of Behavioral Genetics
   University of Colorado

Meyer, Merle E.
    Professor and Chairman of Psychology
    University of Florida

Parenté, Frederick J.
    Assistant Professor of Psychology
    Towson State University

Plomin, Robert
    Assistant Professor of Psychology
    Institute for Behavioral Genetics
    University of Colorado

Schlenker, Barry R.
    Associate Professor of Psychology
    University of Florida

Severy, Lawrence J.
    Associate Professor of Psychology
    University of Florida

Shaw, Marvin E.
    Professor of Psychology
    University of Florida

Simon, Thomas W.
    Assistant Professor of Philosophy
    University of Florida

Suinn, Richard M.
    Professor and Head of Psychology
    Colorado State University

Sundberg, Norman D.
    Professor of Psychology
    School of Community Service
    and Public Affairs
    University of Oregon

Thorndike, Robert M.
    Professor of Psychology
    Western Washington University

Triandis, Harry C.
    Professor of Psychology
    University of Illinois at Urbana-Champaign

Van Hartesveldt, Carol
    Associate Professor of Psychology
    University of Florida

Watson, Robert I., Sr.
    Emeritus Professor of Psychology
    University of New Hampshire
    and Adjunct Professor of Psychology
    University of Florida

Webb, Wilse B.
    Graduate Research Professor of Psychology
    University of Florida

Yost, William A.
    Associate Professor of Psychology
    Parmly Hearing Institute
    Loyola University of Chicago

Foundations of Contemporary Psychology

Methodological and Philosophical Foundations of Psychology

Thomas W. Simon and Merle E. Meyer

Introduction

Philosophy and psychology have been closely allied throughout history. Before the nineteenth century, psychology was considered a branch of philosophy. Aristotle regarded psychology as an attempt to discover the nature of the soul and its attributes. The soul, according to Aristotle, was the principle of life. Gradually, Aristotle's notion of the soul was replaced, and more refined ideas of the mind became the proper domain of psychology. Finally, in the twentieth century, behavior became the focal point of psychology.

As psychology refined its subject matter from soul, to mind, to behavior, it broke away from philosophy correlatively—and psychology became an independent science. Many of the sciences followed this same pattern of general development. There is some association between how soon the science broke away from philosophy and the maturity of that science today. Physics, now one of the most advanced sciences, was one of the first sciences to separate from philosophy. The science of psychology is not as advanced as physics, because only within the last one hundred years has psychology been a separate independent science. A similar pattern has evolved within the science of psychology; some areas are more advanced, while others are relatively new.

What happens when a science liberates itself from philosophy? Basically, some philosophical questions are redefined to a point where they are legitimate material for the scientific method. Philosophers and scientists engage in very different activities. Through the use of rational argumentation, philosophers seek to answer very general and basic questions, examining the most fundamental assumptions. For example, a philosopher tries to construct a consistent theory that will fit coherently into an overall philosophical framework. The philosopher's main subject matter of study is concepts and ideas. The scientist, on the other hand, is primarily concerned with studying empirical phenomena according to the standards of the sciences (such as research, replication of results, experimental control), thereby explaining and predicting the phenomenon under investigation. Let us now look at psychology more specifically as a science and as a technology, and then examine its philosophical issues.

Methodological Foundations of Psychology

The word *psychology* originally came from the early Greek terms *psyche* and *logos,* psyche meaning "the mind," "the soul," or "life principles," and logos meaning "the discourse of." Hence, psychology was defined as "the study of the mind." Over its formal scientific history during the past one hundred years, the definition of psychology has been remarkably varied. Psychology has been described in a wide variety of ways, such as, the science of the "mind," "the self," "the psyche"; the study of private experiences, both conscious and unconscious; the science of "mental" activity; and the scientific study of behavior. In a very general way, the history of psychology is a history of a discipline seeking a definition of its subject matter (as more fully described in Chapter 2). Fundamentally, the various definitions have altered the given direction of the discipline and the type or kind of questions that psychology has asked.

Most contemporary psychologists will initially describe their discipline as a science of behavior and some would prefer to add the phrase "and experience." A few psychologists would go so far as to argue that the discipline cannot be defined because it is not a unitary subject matter, and therefore, it is meaningless and even misleading to attempt a single definition. In the last analysis, however, the subject matter is *behavior,* for if there is a unity in psychology, it is the scientific study of behavior and behavioral change, as behavior can be directly observed, measured, and studied. Behavior provides a basic paradigm for all psychology. Some may study behavior in order that they might attempt to infer "experience," the nature of the "mind," or (other) internal inferred processes or events. These theoretical terms are said to be inferred, because they are not directly observable or measurable. For the majority of psychologists, however, the scientific study of the behavior of organisms, including how it changes, *is* of major and significant interest in its own right.

Behavior

In a general way, we are all observers of behavior. When we look at humans or animals behaving, we all attempt to verbally describe their behavior and to "understand" it. On the other hand, when we make a scientific observation, the scientist looks at the behavioral event and measures or records it in such a way that given the same situation another scientist could make the same measurement or record.

The factual information in the science of psychology has been derived primarily through observational and experimental research. Most contemporary psychologists prefer experimental research where, in the simplest case, all of the conditions or variables are held constant except for one that is systematically varied in known and specified ways. When the variables under scientific investigation are controlled and systematically manipulated, the researcher can infer causal relationships between the variables. In the language of science, the variable(s) that is independently controlled and varied by the investigator is referred to as the *independent variable* and the subsequent behavioral changes that are measured are the *dependent variables*.

In our quest for comprehensive laws of behavior, three components of interest in most research are the stimulus, the organism, and the response, which must be described in some detail. We will begin with a discussion of our dependent variable, or the response, then our independent variable, the stimulus, and lastly the organism.

Response Analysis.   The classification of behavior encompasses all of the continuous flux of activity of an organism in time and in space. The complexities of these activities are enormous and may defy complete scientific description. For study, psychologists select segments of activities and those segments of behavior are called *responses.* But what is such a unit of behavior? Two psychologists could observe the same behavior of an organism over the same time-space frame. The "raw" data are the same, but the two observers may discover different facts or make different descriptions of that behavior. The point here is that the analysis of responses of what is essentially a continuous flux of behavior is often arbitrary. Nevertheless, the response constitutes the phenomenon that psychologists attempt to describe and understand, and to predict and control.

Within our contemporary history, two somewhat different conceptions or paradigms of the level of response analysis have been suggested, one *molecular* and the other *molar*. At the molecular level, it is suggested that the responses are to be analyzed in terms of glandular and muscular activity. Guthrie (1946) has argued that all the organism can do, in the last analysis, is secrete a gland and move a muscle, and that the appropriate response analysis is at this molecular level. Some psychologists have further reduced the level of analysis to electrical patterns and to biochemical actions of muscular contractions and activities of a neuron or a gland (Mpitsos, et al., 1978).

At the level of molar analysis, the emphasis is placed on the outcome of glandular and muscular activity. These larger and often gross responses are specified in terms of what changes they produce in the environment or the relation of the organism in time and space. Examples of this molar analysis are such responses as the present reader reading this text, a young child having a temper tantrum, or a food-deprived pigeon pecking a key that is followed by the presentation of food. The total flux of behavior could be broken down to minutiae but at this level, all molecular responses are conceived as irrelevant as compared to the single response of reading and page turning, having a tantrum or pecking a key. Furthermore, all the differences in detailed movements or patterns from one occurrence to the next are completely ignored and all responses are treated as a single response class.

There is no restriction on the magnitude of the response that psychologists study. The largest amount of present research, however, is at the more molar level of analysis. The total flux of behavior would remain an unanalyzed flux were it not for the psychologist's prior structuring of behavior into response categories for analysis based on the psychologist's best guesses as to what response units are worth studying and classifying. From these response analyses, we may come to better explain, predict, and control behavior.

Typically, the responses that are investigated are the relatively simple behaviors that repeatedly occur over time. With repeated responses it is possible to determine the immediately preceeding conditions that are associated with the responses. Science is not particularly interested in a phenomenon that occurs only once. With a single event occurring once, no functional relationship can be ascertained, we may simply never know "what caused that event to happen." Laws cannot be constructed to apply only to single events.

Response Measurement. As responses are the observable data for the scientific study of psychology, it is assumed that at least in principle, responses are measurable. Measurement is a prerequisite for scientific research regardless of the magnitude of the response, and all psychologists attempt to measure behavior in some way. When the response category is relatively simple, such as the pigeon pecking the key, the response can be measured in terms of the frequency of that response over a specific period of time. When the response is the electrical activities of the brain, the responses can be measured in the quantitative terms of the latency and magnitude of voltage changes. When a person is given a psychological test, the responses are only those answers given to specific questions and to the performance of the motor tasks.

These illustrations of response measurements are relatively simple ones. To some, measurement might seem to remove the subject matter into an abstract level. There is no question, however, that measurement is a fundamental issue in the science of behavior. To fully investigate complex behaviors, psychologists depend wholly on their abilities to solve the response-measurement problem. Behaviors must be categorized into relevant responses which in turn can be measured reliably. You will come to realize the genuine ingenuity of psychologists in selecting complex behavior for study and in measuring these responses as you progress through the various chapters of this book.

Once the response has been defined and measurement determined, a further concern is with the reliability of our measurement. The issues of measurement and the reliability of response measures are discussed in detail in Chapter 3. Reliability is central to the whole of the science, for without a reliable response measure, scientific study is not possible. To say that a response is reliable is to say that it is reproducible, and it is assumed that it is consistent. With consistency, science can attempt to describe and discover reproducible phenomena.

Response Dynamics. The behavior of an individual organism is in constant flux and yet it is assumed by psychologists that behavior is not random or spontaneous, but rather behavior is orderly and lawful. That is, there is a relationship that holds and exists between some antecedent conditions or *independent variables* and behaviors or *dependent variables*. It is assumed that every behavior has a "cause" or a set of antecedent conditions, and if that causal situation could be exactly duplicated, then that same behavior would occur. This assumption is paradoxical, however, in that the "causal situation" cannot be exactly replicated, because we cannot go back and duplicate time. This notwithstanding, the task of psychology is to apply the methods of the science and to discover the orderliness of behavior over time.

Within the analysis of behavior, particular experiments may be designed to study behavior in a *stable-state* or in a state of *transition*. Stable or steady state behaviors are those responses, such as eating, drinking, sleeping, that show relatively little variability in their characteristics over time. On the other hand, transitional responses are those that do systematically change over a period of time, such as learning, emotional changes, or mood changes. Stable and transitional states are not completely separate and independent but are characterized by the amount of variability of the response measure. To illustrate these points, two studies will be briefly described. Ferster and Skinner (1957) describe a study where a 23-hour food-deprived pigeon is trained to peck a key which was followed by the presentation of food for a few seconds. During the first session, the bird pecks the key, when the food tray is presented the bird eats, the food tray is removed and the bird again pecks the key that results in the presentation of the tray, and so forth. The next day, the 23-hour food deprived pigeon is again placed within the chamber, but now the experimenter has adjusted the food delivery apparatus such that the bird must peck 40 times (fixed-ratio 40) before the food tray is presented. Figure 1-1 demonstrates the transition from the pigeon having been continuously reinforced with food at the beginning to the fixed-ratio of 40 to which it was transferred. The responses following *d* are very stable and would remain so with very little variability, whereas, the responses at points a, b, and c show systematic transition states. In a second example, Solomon and Corbit (1974) describe the case where a dog is restrained in a harness and is given a series of 10-second elec-

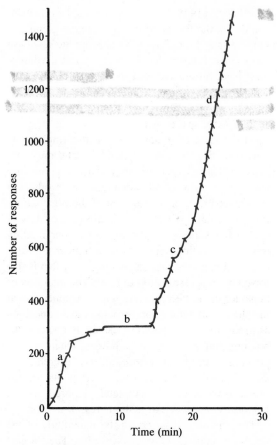

Fig. 1-1. An illustration of the transition of response (continuous reinforcement to a fixed ratio 40) and the development of stable-state responding (see d above). (C. B. Ferster and B. F. Skinner, *Schedules of reinforcement*, © 1957, p. 44. Adapted by permission of Prentice-Hall, Inc., Englewood Cliffs, N.J.)

tric shocks over a number of daily sessions. Figure 1-2 is a stylized illustration of the electrocardiograph responses of such a dog. As shown in the figure, during the first few stimulations there is a slow deceleration. What is most striking is the transition of this response. After many sessions of stimulation there is a small acceleration while being stimulated, but a quick and rather large deceleration once the stimulation is terminated. On a gross behavioral or molar level "the dog appeared to be terrified during the first few shocks. It screeched and thrashed about, its pupils dilated, its hair stood on end, its ears lay back, its tail curled

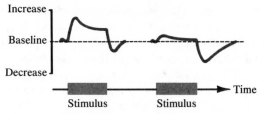

Fig. 1-2. Stylized illustration of the transition of heart rate responses to electric shock. The figure on the left illustrates the responses during the initial sessions; the right figure describes the response some days later. (R. L. Solomon & J. W. Corbit, An opponent-process theory of motivation: I. Temporal dynamics of affect. *Psychological Bulletin*, 1974, 81, 119–145. © 1974 by the American Psychological Association. Adapted by permission.)

between its legs. Expulsive defecation and urination, along with other symptoms . . . were seen (p. 121)." On the other hand, once released the dog seemed subdued, cautious and hesitant. After many such daily sessions, when stimulated, the dog appeared to be "annoyed" and "anxious" but when released was "euphoric," "active," and "joyful."

While the above examples are drawn from research, there are numerous observations from daily life which suggest both stable and transitional behavior. During the early development of an interpersonal love relationship between two people, typically, both persons feel a great and significant amount of joy and happiness when in the presence of the other person. If that relationship is suddenly terminated, one or both persons may feel lonely for a ·relatively short duration. On the other hand, if this relationship develops into a long term one, the individuals can come to express their feelings as one of contentment. However, if the relationship is ended by death or prolonged separations, the individual may experience grief and loneliness for a prolonged period of time (Solomon & Corbit, 1974). The data from such experiments and observations simply show some general aspects of the dynamics of behavior as a function of time within a given environment. Such behaviors, while stable or in transition, all show high predictability and reliability.

Stimulus Analysis.   Behavior does not occur in a vacuum; rather, behavior occurs in response to various *environmental conditions.* While the term environment is often used in general, the term *stimulus* refers to a specifiable change in part of the environment that is related to or associated with some specific response. The stimulus as the independent variable is, therefore, determined empirically from the organism's behavior and cannot be so defined or specified in advance of research. Once identified, stimuli may be manipulated independent of the behavior.

To briefly illustrate this definition of the stimulus, we will draw from a paper by Kagan (1972). He has reported the relationship between the age of young children and their attention (the response) to a series of mask-like representations of the human face (the stimulus). Attention was measured by the duration of time that the child looked at the various "faces" when these were presented one at a time. Looking-time was observed to decrease in children 4 months of age to 10–12 months and then increased dramatically up to 36 months of age. Once the stimulus variable has been identified as being associated with a reliable response, then the stimulus can be manipulated such as the various configurations of the "face." On the other hand, if there were no differences in looking time among the "faces" over the various ages, it would be argued that the "faces" were not functional stimuli.

The term stimulus, however, has not been restricted to the definition as described above. We have, within the theoretical and experimental literature a multitude of other definitions. It may be unfortunate that psychologists have used the single term, stimulus, for a broad array of concepts. However, the choice of the usage of this term, stimulus, is indicative of the conceptual or theoretical preference of the researcher rather than confusion (Turner, 1965). For example, a *physical stimulus,* such as a tone or a light, has been defined as relative "raw" physical energy (*distal* or *distant stimulus*) capable of exciting an appropriate sensory receptor (*proximal stimulus*) of an organism. At best these initial descriptions are for potentially effective stimuli. Then there are *current situational stimuli,* such as the "faces" in the example above that are specified independently of the responding organism and are under the direct control of the experimenter. The term, within this context, is simply a label given by the researcher for a set of experimental procedures and are at best referred to as *potential stimuli*. However, if these situational stimuli actually function as effective stimuli and are correlated with some response, then these stimuli will come to have a behavioral history and are *historical situational stimuli*. Lastly are the *intraorganic stimuli*, such as neuro-chemical changes, which are those stimulus events within the organism. Thus, from an eclectic point of view, stimuli can be external or internal to the organism and potential or actual in the current or historical situation.

A further feature of the stimulus analysis is the classification of stimuli based upon their temporal relationship to the response. In one class of operations, stimuli temporally *precede* the response or S→R. An electric shock to the finger is such a stimulus. This class of stimuli typically functions as a setting condition for the response to occur or as an eliciting condition (in this case finger withdrawal). In a second class of operations, stimuli are those that temporally follow the response R→S. This class of stimuli can function as a reinforcing or strengthening condition of a response, that in turn may increase the frequency of the response. To illustrate this class of stimuli, let us observe the "begging behavior" of a toddler for candy. If the parent gives the candy to the begging child, the candy (the stimulus) can, in the future, increase the fequency and the intensity of begging (the response).

Quantification of Stimuli.   At least in principle, a stimulus may be measured and analyzed in terms of its physical and/or behavioral dimensions, and by the behavioral changes produced by, or associated with, the stimulus. The greater the precision in the quantification of the stimulus, the better our prediction and control of behavior. Stimulus, then is a quantitative term.

In some research situations, a stimulus can be measured very precisely by the instruments of the physical sciences. For example, the visibility curves as described in Chapter 4 are related to the physical dimensions of the stimulus on the one hand and to a simple response on the other. The physical dimensions of the stimulus, light, can be quantified in terms of its electromagnetic spectrum (wavelength), its luminous intensity (candle power), and the like. Once quantified, these physical dimensions can be independently manipulated and differences in response magnitude observed. On this general basis, various psychophysical functions have developed and been elaborated as will be discussed in Chapter 3.

Within other situations, research may be carried out with extremely crude "quantification" where the stimulus is simply a verbal description of the experimental situation to which the organism is exposed or one which follows the response. An animal that is placed within a standard experimental chamber is, therefore, exposed to various visual, auditory, tactile, and olfactory stimulation. Typically, these stimuli are not quantified; rather the investigator simply describes the environmental apparatus. There is a great deal of variability in stimuli simply as a function of the movement of the animal within the chamber. Likewise, the investigator may only describe the stimulus that follows a specific response such as presentation of food. While the physical stimuli are not quantified, variation and manipulation of these stimuli can have systematic effects upon behavior and the behavior can be replicated.

Organism Analysis.   The *raison d'etre* for the scientific study of behavior is the organism itself. Involved in every research situation is an individual organism and its own unique characteristics that can and usually do differ from every other such organism. Each organism comes into a research setting with its own behavioral history as well as other differences such as height, weight, age, species, race, status, abilities, and health. Some research strategies place relatively little emphasis on the individual differences of the organism and others place a significant importance on the differences and maximize the use of these organism variables within their behavioral research.

The Kagan study that was described in the prior section is a good example of an organism analysis. It may be recalled that the looking-time reponse for the various configurations of a human face was also a function of the age of the children. In addition to the American children, Kagan also reported similar findings in Indian children in rural areas of

Guatemala as well as in the Bushman children of the Kalahari Desert of Botswana. Thus, the cross-cultural variable, as well as age, was also included to demonstrate the generality of the observations. The organism variable is of major interest in such research.

Experience. Psychology began, essentially, with a discourse regarding the individual person's inner life and conscious experiences. Thus the term, *experience,* has been historically a part of psychology in the sense that the person receives information from both external and internal stimuli, and that the person acts on this information in terms of personal motives, private motives, thoughts, and feelings. However, the concept of experience has been expanded recently. Experience is the awareness of the way the person attends to, perceives, integrates, and organizes information about the internal and external interpersonal and physical world (Holdstock & Rogers, 1977), "in simple or organized form of a specific response or organized form of states or conditions such as anxiety, emotion or the self" (Landsman, 1973). The person, therefore, is not only a behaving organism but is an active observer of the person's own behavior and is also consciously aware of "self" as a behaving, experiencing being. Thus, behavior may be thought of as less mechanical, less a function of the general environment and more dependent upon experience.

The study of private, subjective experience is, however, difficult to investigate with full objectivity and reliability. Often lacking explicit grounding in hard, rigorous data, experience is difficult to test scientifically. In order to investigate how a person looks at and interprets a given environmental situation, the researcher must attempt not only to examine the individual's behavior but also the person's verbal description of it. The person may be unwilling or even unable to describe the experiences. And even if the person is able and willing, the experiences may not be fully nor adequately described or labeled, primarily as a function of language. The typically vague use of a standard language is very limiting and makes it most difficult to fully communicate the fullness of a rich experience accurately to others.

Certain psychologists who have specific research interests in the experiencing person, have developed conditions and techniques that in part overcome these difficulties, as illustrated in Chapter 19. For example, Rogers (1942), in a counseling situation, reported the verbal reports of his clients in somewhat different ways and thereby allowed the persons to correct or to restate verbally their experiences. Jourard (1971) developed systematic methods of inquiry in his exploration of self-disclosure. Landsman (1973) and his associates have explored the study of experience through questionnaires. Reliable methods have been developed for the ratings of experiences from positive ones when the experiences are judged such as pleasure, satisfaction, fulfillment of hopes and aspirations, exhilaration, and ecstacy, to negative experiences as hopeless, despair, grief, and agony. These ratings can then be correlated with behavioral measures. For example, for those persons who rate their experiences as negative, those experiences may be associated with physical illness or trauma, attempted suicide, the loss of interpersonal relationships, or the suspension of striving. On the other hand, for those individuals who rate their experiences as very positive, ratings may be associated with good physical and emotional health, and the reaching of the fullest individual potential.

Psychological Research

Psychology is further defined as that subdivision of scientific inquiry that specializes in describing and in analyzing the interactions among the organism, the organism's responses, and environmental events. Neither the properties of the organism, the organism's environment, nor its behavior are of major interest in themselves. Rather, it is the associations or relationships that exist among the organism, the stimulus and the response, how these interactions and relationships come about that are our primary foci. The primary function of psychological research is to obtain objective answers to various questions. The questions or *hypotheses* are typically derived from theories, observations, or even from hunches about behavior. Essentially, the task of psychological research is to discover behavioral phenomena, to isolate the relevant variables that affect them, and to determine the relationships among the variables.

The Form of Relationships. Within contemporary psychological literature, there are various programmatic and conceptual structures around which psychologists tend to order their thinking and research. Three such structures or scientific paradigms will be discussed below.

S→R. Perhaps one of the simplest is the Stimulus→Response or S→R conception. That is, a stimulus leads to and is followed by a response. This model does not suggest or imply a specific theoretical bias, but, rather, the researcher's primary concern is with the relationship between the stimulus and response variables without specific reference to the organism per se. If the dependent variable shows systematic changes as the direct result of variation in the independent variable, it is said that a dependent variable is a function of the independent variable.

Functional relationships may not be fully determined simply by observing the organism's behavior. Rather, the researcher, in an experimental study, typically intervenes by the manipulation of the stimulus or independent variables. Through the *operations* or experimental procedures that are employed, the investigator can ascertain whether or not the systematic manipulations of the stimulus resulted in specific response differences.

The one basic principle that must be considered is to design the research in such a fashion that the effects of the manipulation of the stimulus or the antecedent conditions upon the behavior, can be evaluated unambiguously. The investigator attempts to design the research so that, hopefully, the study is not open to numerous and ambiguous interpretations. One of the common designs is to use *experimental* and *control* conditions. The operation is to manipulate a specifiable amount of the specific stimulus under the experimental conditions and a "zero amount" under the control conditions, and also to try to maintain all of the other variables constant. The general experimental-control, stimulus-response research paradigm is given as:

(Experimental)   Stimulus manipulation→R
(Control)   No stimulus manipulation→R

If the manipulations of the stimulus variable did, in fact, result in differences in the specific responses, *simulus manipulation→specific response differences* when compared to the control condition, the investigators may well be on the way to isolating the relevant stimulus variables and to determining the functional relationship between the stimulus and response variables. On the other hand, there is no assurance that the basic operations will, in fact, result in the specific response differences. This is an empirical question, and is answerable only by experimentation or observation.

To demonstrate this general procedure we will use the following illustration.

	learn A	learn B
Experimental	yes	yes
Control	no	yes

The subjects within one experimental condition learn task A (for example, a poem) and then they learn task B (another poem), whereas, the control subjects learn only task B. The question may be related to what effect, if any, has the learning of one poem upon the learning of the second one. If the results show that the control subjects learn task B faster than the experimental subjects, it may be concluded that learning task A first interfered with the experimental subject's learning of task B. On the other hand, if the experimental subjects learned task B faster than the controls, then having learned task A just facilitated the learning of B. This is a classic example of what is broadly referred to as transfer of training which will be described further in Chapter 10. Numerous investigators have centered their attention to the kinds of materials learned in task A that will facilitate or interfere with various kinds of materials learned in task B. Students are often faced with this problem during final examination week, when they wonder if they study for one final, will this facilitate or interfere with the study for other final examinations. Once a reliable phenomenon has been demonstrated, then the researcher can in turn investigate systematic variations of the "amount" of the stimulus conditions with numerous experimental groups and with their appropriate controls.

An expansion of the S→R concept is the S→O→R where the symbols stand for the stimulus, the organism, and the response. Within this design, the researcher may intervene by the manipulation of both the stimulus variables and the organismic characteristics. For example, in addition to variations of the stimulus variable, the experimenter might "manipulate" such organismic variables as the age, status, sex, and culture of the subjects, or perform manipulations on the organism such as making brain lesions or injecting drugs with experimental animals. With the simultaneous manipulation of both the stimulus and organismic variables, the research design becomes somewhat more complex. However, it is possible to determine if the relevant variable is the stimulus variable or the organismic variable or both interacting in the accounting for possible differences in behavior.

$R \rightarrow S^R$. A second major conceptual structure is the response $\rightarrow$ stimulus model or paragidm, where the stimulus follows the response temporally. The stimulus, S^R, within this context is generally referred to as a *reinforcing stimulus,* a *reinforcer,* or *a reward.*

Two general types of experimental studies have developed, one may be termed a *descriptive study* and a second, a *manipulative study,* (Sidman, 1960). Within a typical descriptive study the basic operational procedures are unchanged and maintained over time, and the primary research interests are the behavioral characteristics under such a specified experimental condition. In Figure 1.1, point *d* illustrates the behavior maintained by the fixed-ratio 40 (the pigeon gets food following every 40 pecks on response) and, as we can observe, the behavior is very stable, highly reliable, and very predictable under this procedure. With repeated daily sessions, this behavior will remain very constant with little variability and is said to be under experimental control. It is this kind of stable behavior that can serve as a baseline for a manipulative study.

Once the baseline is established, the researcher can proceed to manipulate independent variables of interest such as hours of deprivation, magnitude of the reinforcing stimulus, and a different schedule of reinforcement. Behavioral changes are often the result of the manipulation. In order to account for these changes, the investigator is generally able to describe these from such a baseline.

In a general way, the organism can serve as its own control and some research designs incorporate a direct and systematic replication. For example, let us assume a stable behavioral baseline of a bird on a fixed-ratio 40. Then, a given dosage of a drug is administered. Let us assume that the drug results in an increase in the rate of the response (pecking the key). Following the manipulation, the animal can be returned to the baseline operations. Once a stable baseline is again achieved, the investigator can again give the same dosage of the drug and again observe changes in behavior. By means of such direct *replication,* the investigator can determine the functional relationship between the drug and its effect upon behavior. Such designs can be further expanded, for example, by systematically varying dosage levels, and also by incorporating a control group where a drug is not given.

$R - R$. The last conceptual structure to be described here is the $R_1 - R_2$ paradigm. The response R_1, is some behavior that is correlated with some other response, R_2. The research interest may be that of determining whether a relationship or association exists between the two response variables. Science does not go about studying possible relationships in a random fashion, but rather a good theory may suggest what relationship might be of major importance to the science and what variables might be meaningfully associated. Within the R-R framework, the various response measures are not manipulated. Some scientists argue that this type of research is primarily descriptive. For example, if a researcher obtained the responses (test scores) from a group of children to an intelligence test (R_1) and then measured how well this same group of children did in school (R_2), the results could show that high intelligence test scores were associated with high performance in school and that low test scores were related to low performance as will be discussed in Chapter 18. From this, we might conclude that there was an association between these two response measures.

Frequently the research is not only concerned with relationships, but, in addition, with making predictions. If we know that the two response variables are correlated, then having information about one response variable enables us to make predictions about the second variable. Therefore, knowing a given score made by a child on the intelligence test allows the investigator to make a prediction of that child's school performance.

Initially, it was stated that the two primary tasks of the science of behavior were the isolation of relevant variables and the discovery of functional relationships among variables. It may be apparent that all functional relationships have one common element—the *prediction* of behavior. If the scientists have established a functional relationship through research, then by knowing that relationship, the scientist can make predictions about future responses. For example, if we know the test scores on an intelligence test, we can predict school performance. On the other hand, if the scientist's primary interest is in the control of behavior then the interests are in the establishment of $S \rightarrow R$ or $R \rightarrow S^R$ relationships where the response may be under stimulus control.

Psychological Concepts and Definitions. An observation or a question about some behavior is the beginning point in the method of the science of behavior. All science is essentially a social enterprise; thus, the researcher attempts to describe the behavior in such a manner as to fully communicate the observations to others. The description must be specific enough so that other researchers can verify the original observations. To describe behavior is to define it. One of the most common forms of definitions in science is an *operational definition*. When a behavior is defined operationally, it is defined in terms of the measurable and observable operations. The definition would state precisely what operations or methods were used including the measurements that were made, in order to replicate the behavior that is being defined. If the investigator cannot measure the behavior and specify the operations, then that observation is not open to the science of psychology.

The establishment of a scientific concept is complex. For example, let us look at the concept of intelligence. Various investigators started with an observation that there are many individual differences in how people learn within similar conditions, such as at school, and that these differences can be contributed primarily to the organism variable. A concept was then suggested and called intelligence. The concept was cast into a literary-like

definition describing the observation. Wechsler has defined intelligence as ". . . the aggregate or global capacity of the individual to act purposefully, to think rationally and to deal effectively within his environment." (Matarazzo, 1972) The initial procedure by Wechsler, as well as others, was to construct a scale or a test believed to measure that concept. Following the construction of the scale, the scores were found to differentiate reliably among individuals. By the operational definition, intelligence was measured by this test. But, does this test really measure intelligence? This question is a research question and not a question of the operational definition. Intelligence, defined by the Wechsler scale as well as others, has been found to be related to other independent measures of behavior, further described in Chapter 18. As the operations have established, there is a reliable phenomenon called intelligence, and an operational definition is given to it. Then, intelligence can and has been brought into the science of psychology. On the other hand, if the concept of intelligence cannot be demonstrated by the operations, or is not in some other way linked to observation, that term would remain outside of the science as it would not have had any scientific meaning.

Within contemporary psychology, concepts that meet the scientific criterion of operationism are admitted to the science. On the other hand, there are terms that are not operationally defined. This does not mean that they are wrong, but simply means that such concepts have not been demonstrated by operational procedures.

For example, some of the Freudian terms such as ego, id, and libido, are used in some circles to describe differences in behavior. At present, it is difficult to state what the direct antecedent conditions are and to operationally define the phenomenon.

While many of our scientific concepts are operationally defined, relatively few psychologists would think of their concepts in strictly operational terms. Rather, for example, the score on a given test of intelligence would be used typically to infer a theoretical or hypothetical capacity or state within the individual that "causes" the response. Many psychological terms and concepts are "causal-naming" that are inferred from and imposed upon the basic operations of our S-R and R-R laws by the scientist. These terms are *intervening variables* and *hypothetical constructs,* shown diagrammatically in Figure 1-3.

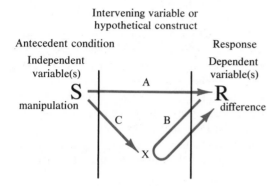

Fig. 1-3. A diagram illustrating the relationships among the variables. See text for discussion.

Within Figure 1-3, *A* would represent the basic operational definition where the response differences were a direct function of the manipulation of the stimulus or antecedent conditions. The bidirectional line *B* illustrates the scientist's inference of a process or a state, *X,* from the response differences, and may infer that this state or process results in the differences in behavior. Lastly, *C* states that *X,* our intervening variable or hypothetical construct, is directly related also to the independent variables or antecedent conditions.

In a reductionistic sense, the hypothetical constructs may be thought of as inferred concepts with physiological or neurological overtones. Such terms as memory trace, cell-assembly, reverberatory circuits, and central inhibitors state could readily fit our description of hypothetical constructs. These constructs may or may not be related to neural and physiological mechanisms but rather to the way the scientist thinks about the data. The intervening variables, on the other hand, are nonreductive concepts and are psychological and behavioral ones. Learning, attitudes, super-ego, frustration, and intelligence can be classified as intervening variables. In either case, the intervening variables and hypothetical constructs simply name a process, a function, or a state that the investigator hypothesizes or believes causes the response difference as a function relating directly to the antecedent conditions.

One of the chief advantages of the intervening variables and hypothetical constructs is the fact that they can be used as the foundation of theory and in explaining behavior. With the development of several independently-defined phenomena, it may be possible to hypothesize a single explanatory concept or principle that brings other concepts together. To illustrate this point, let's consider a concept from physics. From mechanics, it was possible to determine the laws of the inclined plane, of falling bodies, and of the pendulum, and from astronomy, the laws of planetary motion on the ebb and flow of tides. Each law could be operationally defined. However, Newton was able to bring these various independent variables under a single explanatory principle called gravity. While the intervening variables and hypothetical constructs are shorthand descriptions for behavioral relations in psychology, it is important to avoid confusing the name for an empirically-established relationship with the name given by our everyday language for an inner event or experience.

Psychology and its Practitioners

While psychology began as a branch of philosophy and then went on to establish its independence as one of the basic natural and social sciences, it has evolved, in addition, a modern psychological technology. Over the past few decades, with the growth in the foundations of basic principles of behavior, the discipline has significantly developed various areas of professional psychology (Peterson, 1976). These shifts have further demanded redefinitions of psychology to include applied psychology. The American Psychological Association (APA) states that:

As a *scholarly discipline,* psychology represents a major field of study in academic settings, with emphasis on the communication and explanation of principles and theories of behavior.

As a *science,* it is a focus of research through which investigators collect, quantify, analyze, and interpret data describing animal and human behavior, thus shedding light on the causes and dynamics of behavior patterns.

As a *profession,* psychology involves the practical application of knowledge, skills, and techniques for the solution or prevention of individual or social problems; the professional role also provides an opportunity for the psychologists to develop further his understanding of human behavior and thus to contribute to the science of psychology (1975).

Another way to describe psychology is to ask psychologists to indicate their primary scientific specialties, work settings, and work activities. The data from *Careers in Psychology* (1975) are shown in Figure 1-4. Section 1-4a of Figure 1-4 is a general summary of the primary scientific specialty as given by psychologists themselves.

Clinical and Community Psychology

Clinical psychologists specialize in the causes, diagnosis, and treatment of persons who show a broad range of maladaptive behaviors. Typically, a clinical psychologist draws upon psychological knowledge from personality (Chapter 19), behavioral assessment (Chapter 18), psychopathology, and psychotherapy (Chapter 20), as well as from physiological psychology, behavioral genetics, learning and motivation, and social and developmental psychology. In addition to their clinical services and activities, many psychologists conduct both basic and/or applied research, as well as service various community mental health agencies.

Developmental, Personality, and Social Psychology

Typically, developmental psychologists study the developmental processes covering the life span of organisms including such research topics as physical, cognitive, intellectual, language, social, and personality development, as well as issues such as individual and sex differences, the effects of early experience, abnormal development, and behavioral genetics. These and other related topics will be covered in Chapters 4, 5, 6, 7, 9, 11, specifically 14, 15, 18, 19 and 20.

Personality psychologists are concerned in their

basic research with the study of the normal and the maladaptive personality, individual differences, measurement of abilities and personal attributes, and personal growth. The basic principles and their applications are included in counseling, clinical, and community and school psychology. Topics in personality are discussed in Chapter 18, and specifically in Chapters 19 and 20.

The basic interest of social psychologists is the individual within an environment of significant other persons. Research in attitude development and change, social pressures, leadership, group decision-making, interpersonal attraction, communication, prejudice, group processes, conflict and accord, cross-cultural studies, and the importance of their social applications are all representative of the field. Discussions in Chapters 15, 16, and 17 are all basic to the area of social psychology.

Counseling and School Psychology

Counseling psychologists typically specialize in the normal personality and in its development and view their goals as remedial, preventive, supportive and developmental. In practice, they may work with individuals in groups in educational settings, community mental health centers, businesses, and industry. Chapters 15, 16, 18, and 19 cover topics related to this field.

The school psychologist functions as basic support to the teachers in the classroom. Some school psychologists' assignments are primarily in the assessment of individuals (Chapter 18), others work as school counselors (see discussion above), and others function as specialists in learning (Chapters 9, 10, and 11) and motivation (8).

Experimental and Physiological Psychology

In a general way, all psychologists are experimental or research psychologists. However, for the classification in the survey as shown in Figure 1.4A, it includes psychologists whose primary research concerns and identity are in the broad areas of animal behavior, behavioral genetics, sensation and perception, learning, motivation, memory, thinking and problem solving, language, concept formation, and sleep and dreams. The basic princi-

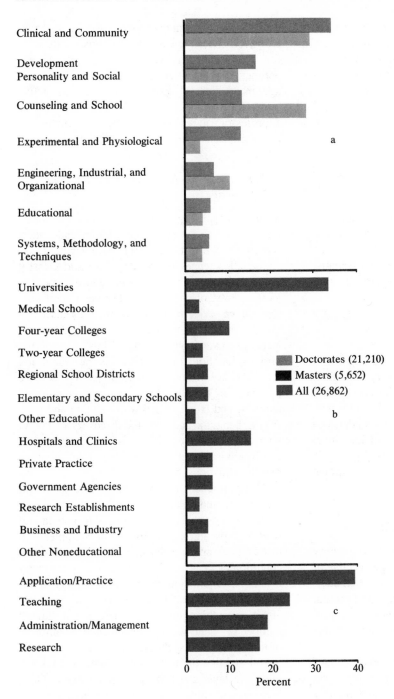

Fig. 1-4a.
Primary scientific specialty of 26,862 psychologists, given in percentages. (Data are taken from 1972 survey of psychologists in the United States and Canada who are members of the American Psychological Association.)

1-4b.
Employments settings of psychologists in percentages. (Data are taken from 1972 survey of psychologists in the United States and Canada who are members of the American Psychological Association.)

1-4c.
Primary work activity of psychologists in percentages. (Data are taken from 1972 survey of psychologists in the United States and Canada who are members of the American Psychological Association.) R. A. Kosschau, M. M. Johnson, and N. F. Russo, *Careers in psychology.* © 1975, p. 17, by the American Psychological Association. Adapted by permission.

ples of experimental psychology are discussed in Chapters 5, 6, 7, 8, 9, 10, 11, 12, and 13.

The basic research interests of physiological psychologists include the brain-behavior rela-

tionships related to such topics as the neural mechanisms of mental retardation, learning, memory, motivation, performance, and abnormal behavior; the relationships between neurochemistry, neuroendocrinology, drugs, and behavior; the sensory and the human autonomic nervous system; and, the development of the nervous system and behavior. Chapter 4 is the basic chapter for further discussion, but additional coverage is given in Chapters 5, 6, 7, 8, 12, 13, and 20.

Engineering, Industrial and Organizational Psychology

The design, the use, and the evaluation of various systems and environments where people live, work, and play are of interest to this specialty. As systems analysts, they may design work environments, equipment, and machines that meet the needs of persons who operate such systems. Chapters 3, 5, 8, 12, 15, and 18 cover research topics of interest to this area.

Educational Psychology

This branch of psychology may be concerned with a wide range of educational and training problems. Educational psychologists may work to design and evaluate various instructional methods and procedures, develop curricula, instructional media, and materials; and, evaluate the effects of individual differences in school. Chapters 3, 8, 9, 10, 11, 12, 18, and 19 are relevant to the area of educational psychology.

Systems, Methodology, and Techniques

This is a very broad array of interests from theory and theory construction, the historic perspective of psychological systems to experimental methodology, and quantitative measurements. The present chapter, Chapters 2 and 3, and in a general way all chapters in this text are the subject matter of this specialty.

In Figure *1.4B* you can see that about one-half of the psychologists are employed in colleges and universities, ten percent in schools and roughly forty percent in other employment settings such as hospitals, clinics, government, business, and industry. The largest primary work activity in Figure *1.4C* is in the practice and application of psychological principles, followed by teaching,

administration or management, and in research. However, most typically psychologists will function in combined activities. For example, an experimental psychologist may be a professor, manage an educational program, and have an active research program. A clinical psychologist may be a professor, a researcher, and also function in providing service in a psychological clinic.

A Summary of Methodological Foundations of Psychology

Science is typically viewed as a set of statements that attempt to achieve a description and understanding of the world about us. As a general foundation all sciences define, organize and classify objects, events, or phenomena. Once these objects, events, or phenomena have been described, the science seeks to understand them by discovering the functional relationships among these objects, events, or phenomena. Thus, one of the primary functions of all science is the search and the discovery of lawful relationships. The science of psychology studies the behavior of humans and animals, and is concerned with defining and classifying behavior and with the discovery of lawful interrelations among the organism, its behavior, and its environment, and with their applications to real life situations.

All of science assumes that nature is lawful rather than random or spontaneous. Science, therefore, assumes there are discoverable and lawful relationships among the events or variables and that every event is associated with some antecedent condition or "cause." It is also assumed that every event or phenomenon has a limited number of antecedent conditions. That is, everything does not affect everything else, that there are a limited number of "causes." A fundamental assumption of the science of psychology is that all behavior is lawful and that the task of this science is to determine the laws and principles of behavior. Once these relationships have been established, then that behavior can be predicted and controlled, and the basic laws can be utilized in various applied settings. In the next section, these assumptions are closely examined from a more philosophical standpoint in order to attain a broader perspective of the science of psychology. Because, as should be evident from the discussion so far, there are many different approaches to psychology, it becomes even more important to understand this philosophical or foundational approach.

Philosophical Foundations of Psychology

The philosophy of science is a means used to determine the ingredients needed to make a science. While concepts are needed, only a select group of them will be sufficient for a science. The kinds of concepts and the ways in which these concepts are organized are both important. So, not only must the proper bricks with which to construct the scientific building be found but also these bricks must be put together in a particular way. There are many ways to construct a theory, but only a few of these ways are scientific.

The first concern in this section is to obtain an overview of science. Once the overall structure of science is established, certain philosophical problems will be seen to arise. It is important to be able to tell the difference between a philosophical problem and a scientific one. This is particularly important when the science is psychology, because issues in philosophy and in psychology can easily become confused. But, before presenting these issues, let us examine the viewpoint of the philosophy of science.

Philosophy of Science

A scientist such as a psychologist, by concentrating on the facts, is primarily concerned with empirical issues. On the other hand, since the philosopher of science has more conceptual concerns, the philosopher is not as concerned with the facts as with the way one thinks about the facts. This is not to say that the scientist is not interested in concepts, nor is it to say that the philosopher ignores the empirical facts. The difference between science and philosophy is really a matter of degree.

Just as there are a number of different approaches used in science, so there are different viewpoints in the philosophy of science. Basically, these perspectives in philosophy of science are twofold: *prescriptive* and *descriptive.* An example will help illustrate this distinction. While scientists supposedly explain and predict events, philosophers try to determine what it means to explain and predict an event. When someone just happens to correctly guess what the weather will be tomorrow, is that a scientific prediction? Or, is it a scientific prediction when a fortune teller successfully predicts a marrigae from reading one's palm? These are philosophical questions. Moreover, the philosopher will examine the relationship between explanation and prediction. If the philosopher approaches these questions from the prescriptive viewpoint, he or she will not be so interested in describing explanations as they actually occur in science, but rather the aim will be directed more toward prescribing what the form of an explanation *ought* to be.

Other philosophers, taking a descriptive approach, are more concerned with how science actually operates. They are more interested in describing the social, political, and historical context within which science is carried out. Probably the most influential of these more descriptive approaches is the work of Thomas Kuhn (1970). Because Kuhn's analysis raises some interesting questions, both about science in general and psychology in particular, his position will be briefly outlined here.

According to Kuhn, scientific activity normally takes place within a hypothesized model, framework, or *paradigm.* It is difficult to precisely specify what a paradigm is, but roughly, a paradigm is a point of view shared by the investigators in a particular scientific discipline. For example, experimental psychologists and clinical psychologists may perceive the same situation differently, because they are viewing the situation from different paradigms or viewpoints. Even the mere fact that the experimentalist may refer to someone as a ''subject'' and the clinician may call that same person a ''patient'' or ''client'' is evidence of different paradigms at work. Experimentalists and clinicians have different ways of perceiving situations, different ways of determining what the problems are, and different ways of going about answering these problems. They operate from different paradigms.

A basic function of education is to instill this perspective or paradigm into students by using similar textbooks, having them solve model problems, and doing "classical" experiments. The student then learns that particular discipline's way of looking at things and that discipline's standards of success. For example, some experimental psychologists might determine success in terms of the ability to predict and control behavior, whereas many clinicians view success in terms of their ability to help patients.

Normally, the basic standards and other components of the paradigm remain unquestioned. In Kuhn's account, ordinary scientific activity consists of puzzle-solving, that is, further refining of the paradigm. Everyday scientific activity, then, is largely filling in the broad outline established by a paradigm. However, within any given paradigm there are unresolved and even unidentified puzzles. If these unresolved problems become too widespread, and if there is an alternative paradigm available, then a crisis results in which the paradigms compete for allegiances. An example drawn from astronomy is the view that the universe was earth-centered (Ptolemy) versus the view of the universe as sun-centered (Copernicus). It is interesting to consider whether or not psychology ever has or ever will undergo a revolution of the magnitude that radically altered astronomy. The analysis presented in Chapter 2 and in subsequent chapters will help answer that question.

Kuhn's analysis raises many interesting questions when applied to the sciences such as psychology. First of all, it is not clear whether psychology is pre-paradigmatic or multi-paradigmatic. In order for psychology to undergo a revolutionary change, it must have a paradigm. If psychology is pre-paradigmatic, this means that unlike a more mature science such as physics, no one model or exemplary way has been developed. As a pre-paradigmatic science, psychology would be at the same stage of development today as astronomy was hundreds of years ago. On the other hand, if psychology is multi-paradigmatic, then there are many competing models in psychology. After reading subsequent chapters in this book, a reasonable assessment can be made as to whether psychology is pre-paradigmatic or multi-paradigmatic.

Another claim that Kuhn makes is that the sciences, unlike the humanities (art, philosophy, and literature), are ahistorical. The sciences in contradistinction to humanities quickly forget their past. If one of the humanities is studied, the history of the discipline is generally an integral part of that study. Compared to textbooks in the humanities, those in the sciences seldom contain the original writings of their founders. But, in Chapter 2 an attempt is made to at least offset this trend in the sciences by presenting a history of psychology. It is certainly worth looking at history to see what advances were made, and even more importantly, to see what mistakes were made.

Finally, according to Kuhn's analysis, the social sciences (psychology, sociology, anthropology) differ from the natural sciences (physics, chemistry, biology) in that the psychologist, for example, is more influenced by the demands and concerns of everyday life. The natural scientist is supposedly much more insulated from society than the social scientist. The natural scientist can work on some strange particle within the isolation of the laboratory, free from the demands of the public. However, the public will keep a much closer eye on the social scientist who is working with human beings. But with today's concerns with nuclear energy, solar power, pollution of the biosphere and the like, this does not seem an accurate picture of science. Nevertheless, the relative effect of this isolation was and still is that problems are solved at a much more rapid rate in the natural than in the social sciences. Not only is psychology an infant science, but some might feel it may be condemned to infancy, because the psychologists allegedly cannot completely free themselves from social-political demands. For example, in physics almost anything can be done to a particle. This proves difficult for a variety of reasons when the subject of investigation is a human individual or even a human society.

In the next few sections, the basic structure of a scientific theory will be described. A building block approach will be employed starting with the basic components and building up to the theory itself. The analysis will combine the descriptive and prescriptive approaches.

Elements of Science

The basic building blocks of any scientific theory are *concepts*. Concepts can be looked upon as the words (ideas) used to describe and classify one's experiences. For example, as we have seen, certain human activities might be classified as a certain kind of response; in addition, certain environmental events might be classified as stimuli. The next task is to find ways of relating these concepts. Particular ways of ordering or finding interconnections among these concepts produce *laws*. A law consists of relating stimulus and response. Then, by means of these scientific laws, events can be explained, predicted, and even controlled. By finding connections among different types of explanations, a *theory* can be constructed. Finally, *models* can be used as a means of testing the theory.

Concepts (observational, theoretical, operational, quantitative)
↓
Laws (causal, functional, structural, universal, probabilistic)
↓
Explanation-Prediction
↓
Theory ← Models

The words in parentheses are not intended to be mutually exclusive but are simply used to indicate some of the different kinds of concepts and laws. Notice that order is the key relationship between the main components. Concepts order events; laws order concepts; explanations order laws; and, theories order explanations. Now, each of these elements of a science will be examined.

Concepts. Concepts are very important, for it is in terms of concepts that understanding is attained. Choosing concepts is no idle task. The types of concepts chosen affect the kinds of questions asked and the problems considered. The label attached to

a person (friend, acquaintance, or lover) affects another's understanding of that person. Similarly, in psychology, it is important to the understanding of human action whether the basic concepts are response, stimulus and response, experience, or something else. A stimulus-response formulation results in a very different analysis from a response-response one.

Psychologists acquire their concepts from a variety of sources. Some concepts are the result of intuitive hunches or creative acts on the part of the psychologist. In fact, at every stage of scientific development, creativity plays an important role. A machine would have difficulty imitating scientific activity.

Other concepts in psychology are borrowed from other sciences or from other areas of psychology. It is not uncommon for one science to borrow successful models from another science. Of course, there are dangers in this practice. A model borrowed from physics may be totally inappropriate when the subject matter is human behavior.

Still other concepts found in psychological theories are borrowed directly from everyday vocabulary. Examples include intelligence, drive, and motivation. This borrowing presents problems because the meanings of these words in science might be different from their ordinary meanings. The psychologist's definition of "intelligence" might be very different from the common definition of "intelligence," even though both use the same word.

Overall, the vocabulary used in psychology is becoming more technical and less comprehensible to the nonpsychologist. If someone is not trained as a psychologist, it is becoming increasingly difficult for that person to understand psychological theories. This development toward a more technical vocabulary is regarded as a sign of a maturing science. Physics has already followed this route, and it appears that psychology is headed in the same direction.

Although common vocabulary proves to be useful at the initial stages of theory construction for any science, using everyday words and concepts has distinct disadvantages. Lack of precision and lack of uniform usage pose difficulties when the psychologist attempts to incorporate common language into a scientific theory. For example, the word "intelligence" has a variety of meanings. Someone might label a person intelligent if that individual attains high grades in school, whereas another person might confine intelligence to those cases where the person can solve practical problems using common sense. But in order for concepts such as intelligence to be useful in a scientific theory, the psychologist must precisely define them and use them uniformly. Intelligence cannot mean one thing on one occasion and a completely different thing on another occasion. As will become evident in Chapter 18, psychologists have done a fairly good job defining intelligence in terms of IQ tests. Problems still arise, however, when the nonpsychologist (for example, a politician or journalist) uses the scientific definition of intelligence in terms of IQ tests as meaning the same thing as intelligence in the ordinary nonscientific vocabulary.

So, the psychologist either refines ordinary concepts or develops an artificial vocabulary. In either case, the aim is to attain precision and uniformity among the concepts by adequately defining them. "Define your terms!" is a command which the psychologist takes quite seriously. But "Define *all* of your terms!" is an impossible command to follow completely. Most of the key concepts of a theory should be precisely and uniformly defined, but not every concept in a theory can be defined without being circular. Definitions found in dictionaries are quite often circular; the first word is defined in terms of a second, which is defined in terms of a third word. The third word is then circularly defined in terms of the first. In order to avoid this circularity in developing a scientific theory, certain terms are regarded as primitive and they are taken as given or undefined. *Primitive terms* are left undefined within a theory and are used to define the other terms of the theory. For example, "well-adjusted person" might be taken as a primitive term in a theory of personality. This undefined term is used to define other terms such as "abnormal behavior."

In defining a concept there are at least two things that a psychologist will probably emphasize:

1. defining the concept in terms of observations;
2. providing measurements for these observations.

Observation and measurement are two critical ingredients of science. Defining in terms of observables and providing means of measurement are important methodological principles to follow. But idols should not be made out of these methodological principles; these principles should not become doctrines or dogmas. Ways of avoiding this type of problem will be presented in examining observation and measurement.

Observation. Observation through controlled experimentation is the cornerstone of the scientific enterprise. Common appeal to observable data ensures some degree of objectivity or intersubjectivity. When making a claim, the psychologist is not merely making a personal statement or assessment. If someone claims that females are smarter than males, then that person might simply be expressing his or her own bias. The psychologist would be more likely to propose the hypothesis: females are smarter, that is, they receive higher IQ test scores than males. If this claim is challenged, the psychologist can appeal to systematic observations. When reporting the results of an experiment, the psychologist is, in effect, claiming that if anyone else were to carry out the same experiment, he or she would find the same observations as reported. Therefore, the results can be replicated in science.

Even though observation is critical to science, it is not without its difficulties for there is no absolutely neutral way of describing what is being observed. Observation, never completely pure and unadulterated, is always contaminated to some degree or another by the beliefs, expectations, values, and even prejudices of the observer. If someone expects a person to be amiable, it is most likely that that person's behavior will be interpreted as amiable. The psychologist faces similar problems when expecting certain results from an experiment. If someone expects females to do better than males on an intelligence test, that expectation could influence the test results. The task of the scientist is to filter out these outside influences making the observations as pure as possible, at the same time realizing that observations are never completely pure.

When constructing a scientific theory, the number and quality of the observational terms should be maximized, but this does not mean that every term of the theory should be an observation term. To claim this would be tantamount to turning a useful methodological guideline into a doctrine. Two types of terms difficult to define in purely observational terms are *dispositional* and *theoretical* terms. Dispositional terms refer to hidden characteristics that can be evidenced under suitable conditions. A disposition such as being bad-tempered can manifest itself in observable behavior. But there is also a sense in which someone can be said to be bad-tempered, that is, a disposition can be said to be present, even though it is not presently being exhibited in behavior. The claim that someone has a great potential may well be true even if that potential has never been actualized. This is analogous to talking of the potential and kinetic (actual) energy of an object in physics. A rock atop a hill has a potential energy even though it is not moving. Dispositional terms are certainly related to observational terms, but they do not have to be completely defined in terms of observation. Theoretical constructs, like dispositional terms, are not directly observable. There have been a number of attempts at dispensing with theoretical terms altogether by defining all of the theoretical terms of a theory in terms of observational terms. Observational terms are important, but these attempts overemphasize their usefulness. Even though not completely definable in terms of observables, theoretical constructs such as unconscious wishes or the previously used example of gravity are very useful in science, because they help organize the concepts of a theory. The theoretical term "unconscious wish" may help explain how a conscious desire becomes distorted and manifests itself in bizarre forms of behavior.

Controlled systematic observation, one of the keys to a scientific psychology, is not the whole story. There are also nonobservational elements such as dispositional and theoretical terms. A strong theoretical foundation is as impotant as an observational base. Moreover, as will become evident in the next section, not every observation will qualify as a scientific one.

Measurement. Observation is a crucial element of any psychological theory. But if that were the only mainstay of psychology, the psychologist's task would not differ from any other investigation when the goal is to understand and predict human behavior. In general, people quite naturally try to understand and anticipate each other's actions. While the nonpsychologist observes behavior, the method of observation is probably different from the techniques used by the professional psychologist who tries to pinpoint the behavioral observations as precisely as possible by providing a means for measuring them.

There are two extreme positions that can be taken on this issue of measurement: a somewhat antimeasurement position, overemphasizing quality, and another promeasurement one, overemphasizing quantity. On the qualitative side of the coin it might be argued that measurement is very limited in psychology, because many "psychological facts" cannot be measured. A measurement provides some numerical standard, but allegedly these standards do not apply to everything such as human experience which is qualitatively unique to each person. Does it make any sense to talk about a .78 experience? Accordingly, these experiences cannot be measured.

On the quantitative side of the coin, it might be argued that in order for a concept to qualify as scientific there must be some method of measurement for that concept. Because there is no sense in talking about something like creativity unless an adequate means of measuring it can be provided, this type of concept would be scientifically inadmissible. But since intelligence can be measured in terms of IQ scores, then intelligence is an admissible concept for scientific psychology. So measurement is the filter through which only scientific concepts are allowed to pass.

Neither the extreme qualitative nor the extreme quantitative position is correct as a doctrine, but important lessons can be learned from each. The first position against certain applications of measurement serves as a warning of the difficult task that psychology has set for itself. Can something like happiness be adequately measured? The second position advocating the need for measurement provides a useful guideline, setting up an important goal for the psychologist. Physics, the most mathematical of the sciences, provides the most precise measurements, and, not coincidentally, is the most successful science. Psychology needs to avoid the extremes of both of these positions—the myth of quality and the myth of quantity (Kaplan, 1964), for qualitative terms to the exclusion of quantitative terms will leave a very imprecise science (or possibly even no science whatsoever), and a theory with exclusively quantitative terms results in an impoverished science. Both quality and quantity are needed.

Even though both qualitative and quantitative terms are needed, the direction of progress in a science seems to be toward increasing the quantitative terms. This can best be seen by first dividing up scientific concepts into the following types:

1. Classificatory
2. Comparative
3. Quantitative (Hempel, 1952)

Classificatory terms are generally thought to be qualitative in nature, enabling one to answer questions concerning what kind, for example, what kind of emotion, what kind of behavior, and so on. Behavior can be classified or categorized into different types, for example, voluntary and involuntary. In a sense, comparative terms are more refined classificatory ones in that the types of characteristics set off by classificatory terms are given gradations. Comparative degrees of voluntary behavior may include jumping out of the way of an oncoming vehicle which is less voluntary than pulling a voting machine lever for a political candidate. Or, the degree of emotional disturbance may be scaled according to whether the disturbance is absent, slight, moderate, or extensive. Comparative terms, enabling one to answer questions of degree ("Is Wilt taller than Bertha?") are capable of making differentiations of greater flexibility and subtlety than classificatory ones. This is even more true of quantitative terms which are more strictly called concepts of measurement, be-

cause they provide rules for assigning numbers to the properties being measured, enabling one to answer questions concerning how many or how much ("How tall is Wilt?"). For example, a precise measure might be provided for the intensity or force of an involuntary behavior like a knee-jerk or reflex response.

Although some psychologists may disagree, the development of a psychological theory can be viewed as progressing from classificatory to comparative to quantitative terms. Quantitative measurement should, however, not be blindly praised. Quantitatively measuring something is not necessarily the same as revealing the truth about or understanding that phenomenon. On the contrary, one of the drawbacks to using quantitative terms is that they sometimes cause these types of delusions. Nevertheless, the greater the degree of precision attained through measurement, the more testable the theory and the better the theory. But, as will become clearer in the next section, this refinement of a theory through measurement needs to be counterbalanced by increasing the scope of the theory.

Scientific Laws.   Observation and measurement are keystones to a science of psychology. To this list scientific laws must be added, because observation and measurement are not enough to guarantee scientific status since a science must also be systematic. The scientist attempts to find orderly systematic connections among the data in order to explain, predict, and control the phenomena. These regularities are expressed as scientific laws, a type of systematic relationship among concepts. If one assumes two classificatory concepts in a theory, certain environmental events categorized as stimuli and certain activities of the organism labeled as responses, then a functional relationship can be found between these two concepts. This regularity can be expressed in terms of the following scientific law:

> Whenever a specific kind of stimulus occurs, then a particular kind of response occurs.

The researcher then seeks evidence for the lawful regularities between stimuli and responses.

A number of important points should be noted about scientific laws. First of all, scientific laws are generalizations. If a specific instance of behavior is described (for example, someone slapping a friend), that description does not qualify as a scientific law. A scientific law, more than a mere description, is a generalization covering various descriptions.

A generalization can be either universal or statistical. While a claim that a large dog attacked a smaller dog is merely a description, another claim that all German shepherds attack smaller dogs is a universal generalization. Furthermore, a claim to the effect that 86 percent of all German shepherds attack smaller dogs is a statistical generalization.

But a generalized description still does not qualify as a scientific law even if a statement to that effect is always found to be true. If all the members (or even a certain percentage) of a psychology class are accurately described as having freckles, a scientific law has not been found. Having freckles is an accidental feature that the members of a particular psychology class happen to have, and it is not a lawful, scientific regularity. Whether or not a claim is a scientific law depends on the degree of generalization of that statement. To how many different kinds of things does the claim apply? A statement applying only to the confines of a single psychology class is of very limited scope. The first step toward making this into a scientific law involves extending the scope of the claim as far as possible to, for example, all psychology classes in the world. A way to determine the scope of a statement is to devise hypothetical test conditions, ascertaining whether or not the statement is true under those conditions. For example, if any student, say John the physics major, is chosen and placed in this psychology class, would he also have freckles? Chances are that John would not have freckles. This helps demonstrate that having freckles is an accidental feature of the psychology class and that finding a connection between these classmates and freckles does not uncover a scientific law.

Another important feature of scientific laws is the experimental or evidentiary support these laws receive. Evidence supports hypotheses used to test scientific laws. A form of an hypothesis is: Given that certain conditions are equal if a certain thing is done, then a particular result will follow. Notice the hypothetical, conditional nature of this formulation: *Assuming* _____, *if,* _____, then _____. Science, always open to debate, is tentative and conjectural.

Good factual support, needed for scientific laws, does not only refer to the quantity of the evidence collected in favor of the law but also to the quality of the evidence. At some time or another, most people are guilty of making generalizations on the basis of an insufficient quantity of evidence. Observing one instance of a person's behavior is generally not sufficient for drawing some general conclusion about that person's personality because the quality or variety of evidence is ignored. If a lawful connection is being sought between cigarette smoking and cancer, it is best to investigate a number of different types of people under a variety of circumstances—people who work around industry, people who work on farms, and so on.

The main points in this section can be summarized in terms of the basic characteristics of scientific laws:

1. Scientific laws are generalizations and not merely descriptions.
2. Scientific laws have a broad scope (the range of things that they cover).
3. Scientific laws need good evidentiary support (quantitatively and qualitatively).

Although the scientist focuses on the factual data through observation and measurement, she or he also projects these findings beyond the immediate data by proposing laws. Hence, science has conjectural, theoretical components. Since observing and measuring the data is not enough, some connections must be found among these observations and measurements in the form of laws. Using these scientific laws, it is now possible to see what a scientific explanation is.

Explanation and Prediction. When trying to "figure another person out" or understand another's actions, more than likely an explanation of that individual's behavior is being sought. By asking why certain people behave the way they do in particular situations, an explanation of that phenomenon is attempted. Explanations are answers to "why" questions.

Not every answer to a "why" question qualifies as an explanation. As an explanation for why a specific individual dropped out of school, someone might claim that it is because Jupiter aligned with Mars. Some people might be satisfied with an answer like this and think that they have an explanation for that person's behavior. But more than intellectual satisfaction is needed as a standard for an explanation, because there is too much variance between what different people psychologically accept as an explanation.

Nevertheless, this psychological state of intellectual satisfactions is an element of explanation. Explanation often seems equivalent to fitting the event to be explained into some familiar pattern which is already understood. If members of a different culture are seen kneeling with their hands folded, chances are that their behavior will be explained in terms of some familiar activity such as prayer.

Laws, the familiar patterns of science, have the virtue of being relatively uniform, whereas the familiar patterns used outside of science may not be so standard from one person to another. Remember that scientific laws are a certain type of generalization. Since generalizations without empirical support are not explanatory in themselves, scientific laws alone do not explain. Laws provide the broad scope of science and observations, the specifics. Combining general laws and specific observations results in explanations.

If someone wants to explain the occurrence of a certain kind of hallucination, she or he would search for scientific laws and the particular circumstances that produce hallucinations. Hallucinations would be explained by showing that they occurred according to certain laws (for example, those governing the effect of sensory deprivation on hallucinations) and as a result of certain particular circumstances (for example, sensory deprivation). An explanation shows how the event being explained fits under a pattern (laws) given certain circumstances (Hempel, 1966).

Although the examples so far have been of laws plus initial conditions explaining empirical facts, there are also cases where laws explain other laws. Lower level laws explaining behavior might also be explained in terms of some higher level neural laws about the central nervous system. This results in the following hierarchical scheme where a higher level law explains a lower level law, which in turn explains a particular fact:

NEURAL LAW
↓ Explains
BEHAVIORAL LAW
↓ Explains
EMPIRICAL FACT

However, it should be noted that a number of psychologists think that it is neither necessary nor fruitful to extend an analysis to this higher neural level.

Laws are used not only to help explain why an event did occur or is occurring, but also to help specify what will happen. Explanations are about the present, and predictions about the future. If a law is used to explain someone's present behavior, it seems reasonable to think that it could also be used to predict that person's future behavior, that is, what that person is going to do. But explanation and prediction do not always go together. There can be explanations without prediction. A person's present difficulties might be explained in terms of some traumatic experience she or he had as a child, but from that knowledge the individual's present dilemmas may not have been predicted. Yet, not all predictions are explanatory. The effects of marijuana on mood may be predicted without being fully explained. Soothsayers, mediums, and astrologers might make many successful predictions of various events but be unable to explain them. The ancient Babylonians were able to accurately predict the tides but could not explain them in terms of the moon's gravitational pull. Although successful predictions are important, science needs predictions that are based on scientific laws. These predictions, derived from laws and hypotheses, do not simply come out of thin air.

With a basic understanding of scientific concepts, laws, hypotheses, explanations, and predictions in the background, it is now time to examine theories.

Theories. Generally, a *theory,* regarded as a system of scientific laws, establishes the interconnections among the various laws. So, laws formulate the order and regularity among the empirical facts, and the theories do the same for laws.

It seems that most people have either explicit or implicit "theories" about the behaviors and personalities of other people. Someone may have a theory about why his or her friends always do better on tests. Here, theory means the same as an hypothesis, and scientists often use it in that way. But whether thought of as theory or hypothesis, these common sense views are probably not scientific. For one thing, a scientific theory is more systematic than a common sense one:

Science is not a substitute for common sense but an extension of it (Quine, 1966, p. 216).

. . . This increased care [by the scientist] is not a revision of evidential standards, but only the more patient and systematic collection and use of what anyone would deem as evidence (Quine 1966, p. 220).

One of the differences between the amateur's theory that people who watch violence on television are more prone to violence and the psychologist's theory about the same thing is that the scientist is probably more systematic than the nonscientist in explicitly deriving testable hypotheses from a theory and in gathering evidence to support the theory.

Theories are important in science not only for providing an explicit organization or a system but also for serving as the interpretative framework and guide for research. A scientist does not blindly search the world hoping to accidentally uncover a scientific fact. A neurologist does not merely probe the brain at random without a search strategy. Scientific search occurs within the context of a theory. Serving as a guide, a theory specifies the kinds of things to look for, and from a theory, testable hypotheses, focal points for scientific investigation, can be derived.

Theorizing, regarded as primarily a conceptual, mental activity, allows one to make conjectures and speculations about the world. Science progresses by bold theoretical conjectures. But a theory without good data to support it is only speculation, a crucial, but counterproductive activity when done in isolation. The mere accumulation of data without a good theory only yields a primitive understanding. Theories are the conceptual, and the data the empirical, components of science. Both theory and data are needed in order to increase knowledge through science.

Yet, a number of psychologists claim that psychology's goal ought not to be constructing grand theoretical structures but rather primarily to inductively describe the data. These commentators would presumably only climb the ladder to the level of laws, discounting any attempts to explain lower level laws in terms of higher ordered ones. Part of the motivation for this stems from a desire to keep the empirical basis of psychology intact. One could argue with this position, however, by claiming that there is a sense in which laws are theories whether it be the law or theory of gravitation or effect. Hence, almost every scientist would admit the importance of theories, but some would disagree about how important theories are.

Models. Models, like hypotheses, are sometimes used synonymously with theories or even paradigms. But models can also be used in senses distinct from theories. If a robot is built in order to simulate or imitate someone's behavior, this construction is a representational model. The aim in building models of this type is better understanding of the phenomenon in question. Representational models are generally easier to test than the actual thing being investigated. Although it may seem trivial to point out that the model is not the same as the object being modeled, it is important to remember that models make simplifying assumptions about the phenomenon being modeled. It is too easy to oversimplify using models.

Models may be of a pencil-and-paper variety, not necessarily being actual, concrete things. Mathematical models are good examples of these *abstract models.* But regardless of whether concrete or abstract models are being used, "the price of the employment of models is eternal vigilance" (Braithwaite, 1953).

Summary. Thus far the basic structure of science has been examined. Science has been viewed from the inside, determining what types of concepts, laws, explanations, theories, and models are needed for science. Next, when trying to determine what the general standards of science are, a more external perspective will be adopted.

Standards of Science

Although many theories have been and will be proposed, not all of these theories are scientific. While some of them compete and conflict with science, others try to attain scientific recognition. How is it determined whether or not a theory is scientific? Then once that question has been answered, how is a scientific theory evaluated? Not every scientific theory is as good as every other. Each of these important questions will be addressed separately.

Science and Non-Science. Since the relationships between science and religion are complex, we can only scratch the surface here. What are the differences between scientific and religious claims? What is the difference between an account of someone's action as being caused by certain environmental stimuli and an "explanation" of that same action in terms of the desires of a supernatural demon? One plausible answer is that the former claim is both testable and falsifiable, whereas the latter, religious claim is neither. What is meant by *testability* and *falsifiability?*

Since a scientific claim should be *in principle* testable or verifiable, some means should be proposed to empirically test the claim. In order to qualify, the tests need not have been actually performed, but the claim must be testable, that is, capable of being tested. In the 1950s, claims about the other side of the moon were testable even though they had not actually been tested. When testing an hypothesis a psychologist might manipulate an environmental stimulus and determine whether or not that stimulus results in a proposed response by the organism. It would presumably be impossible, even in principle, to manipulate the demon in a similar manner. While many religious

proposals are claimed to be necessarily true or known for certain, scientific claims are tentative and never certain, and are always subject to change.

Falsifiability is a related standard of scientific claims (Popper, 1968). Someone proposing a scientific thesis should be prepared to specify not only the conditions under which the claim is true but also the conditions under which the claim is false. For example, it might be claimed that whenever a friend laughs at another friend, the person being laughed at will sulk. Although it is fairly easy to specify the conditions under which this claim would be false—someone laughing at a friend where sulking does not result—it is difficult to envision under what conditions the demon hypothesis would be false, particularly if it is regarded as certain. While scientific claims are always open to being refuted, nonscientific claims are often regarded as irrefutable by empirical evidence.

There are at least three types of cases where proposals are nonfalsifiable, those claims that are (1) too vague, (2) too general, or (3) too *ad hoc.* When considering these three cases, nonreligious claims will be used. The first case of nonfalsifiability occurs when a claim is too general. An astrologist might try to explain that an individual is sensitive because he or she was born under a certain astrological sign. If by "sensitive" the astrologist simply means "capable of reacting to external stimuli," then every human is sensitive. No example of a human who would be insensitive on this interpretation can be found. The supposed explanation is so vague and imprecise that it is difficult to tell what would falsify or refute the claim.

Another category of nonfalsifiable claims occurs when the claim is not vague, but rather too general. For example, if every action that someone undertakes can be explained in terms of an inferiority complex, then there are no actions which that person can do that cannot be explained by an inferiority complex. There are no conditions under which attributing an inferiority complex to this individual would be false. Since the claim is overly general in covering too much, it is, in effect, nonfalsifiable.

In the third case, all the proposed refutations are taken care of by a catch-all, exception clause. The claim might be that eight-year-olds never engage in smoking cigarettes *except under certain circumstances*. Every time an instance of an eight-year-old engaging in smoking is discovered, the alleged counter-instance is never regarded as a refutation but is always placed under the exception clause. This is called *ad hoc reasoning* and means that every attempt is made to save the original hypothesis despite adverse evidence.

Testability and falsifiability, then, are two basic requirements of a scientific claim. It is interesting to apply these standards to various branches of psychology. Are the more clinical and applied branches of psychology scientific? Are the intuitions and clinical impressions of a practitioner testable and falsifiable in the same way that scientific hypotheses are? While a few commentators attack versions of psychoanalytic theory as being a pseudo-science incapable of being scientifically tested, others accuse parapsychology (the study of extrasensory perception, telepathy, and so on) of being nonscientific because it cannot be falsified. For example, psychic powers have a habit of not working when skeptical investigators are present. But before making a final judgment about any branch of psychology, one should become totally familiar with the theory in question. Now let us turn to the means of evaluating a claim once it has been established as being scientific.

Evaluative Standards of Science. Reference has already been made to some evaluative standards in the discussion of the elements of science. These are now combined with some additional ones, resulting in the following list: (1) scope and precision; (2) degree of empirical support; (3) experimental design and control; (4) simplicity or parsimony.

The better theories, having a broader scope and a greater degree of precision, cover a greater variety of items than their competitors. A theory applying to individual and group behavior has a broader scope than one which is confined to individual behavior. Scope also includes the connections a theory makes to other theories. One of the effects sought in evaluating the precision of a theory is the accuracy of the theory's predictions. A good theory, therefore, has the broadest possible scope (but not so general as to be nonfalsifiable) and yields precise measurements.

Notice that the second standard, empirical support, should be taken together with the first standard of scope and precision. If empirical support were taken alone, the result might be a theory with very high empirical support, but the support could be inaccurate and apply to a very narrow range of things. In this case, the theory would not be very good. Also, remember that it is the quantity *and* quality (variety) of the empirical support that is important.

Another important evaluative standard of a good theory is experimental control. When designing an experiment, there is a need to weed out extraneous or disturbing factors. In investigating a psychic's ability to bend forks with his or her mind, strict experimental controls are needed in order to prevent any trickery on the psychic's part. Outside influences might not only be a problem within the experiment, but the experiment itself may also create difficulties. The famous Hawthorne experiments, investigating the productivity of workers, resulted in productivity increasing during the experiment because the workers knew they were subjects of an investigation (Kaplan, 1964). The experimenter must make allowances for these factors. While these are not the only elements of experimental control, they should be sufficient to demonstrate its importance in assessing theories.

Finally, simplicity or parsimony can be used as an evaluative standard. Choose the theory with the simplest hypothesis; this does not mean choose the least complicated or the easiest to understand hypothesis, because the most complicated and most difficult to understand hypothesis may quite possibly be the simplest. The simplest theory is the one making the fewest assumptions. The following experience is not uncommon. A person is seated somewhere thinking of a friend in a distant city. Just at that moment a telephone call is received from that friend. The telephone call could be explained in terms of communication prior to the phone call between the two parties via some form of psychic, nonphysical energy. But it is much simpler to hypothesize that the friend had just received a letter from the other person which provoked the phone call, or some similar hypothesis. In order to accept the first hypothesis, the existence of a psychic, nonphysical source of energy would have to be assumed. The second hypothesis does not need this type of assumption and is therefore simpler.

So far, science in general has been the main subject with some references to psychology. In the next section, some issues in science particularly relevant to psychology will be examined providing a more exclusive treatment of psychology.

Problems in Science

There are obviously many problems within and about science. Two issues relating directly to the science of psychology are reductionism and free will. In addition to their intrinsic interest, these issues are being examined because they both raise specific philosophical questions. A clearer perspective concerning the differences between philosophical and scientific (empirical) questions is needed.

Reductionism.   What is the relationship between the various sciences? What, for example, is the relationship between physics and psychology? For many people physics is regarded as the best of the sciences. Physics, the first science to break away from philosophy, has made tremendous strides forward. Physics is the most precise, the most mathematical, and the most successful of the sciences. For example, the applications of physics to the world are far-reaching—from bridge-building to space exploration.

Allegedly, the most fundamental level of explanation has been reached when something can be explained in terms of physics. This belief has led some people to propose a thesis called *reductionism*. A reductionist claims that one science can be explained in terms of another more basic science. Eventually, the activity of groups (sociology) will be explained in terms of the behavior of each of the individuals constituting the group (psychology). Each individual's behavior can presumably be explained according to the physiology of that individual, and this physiology can in turn be explained by the laws of physics. A reductionist envisions the following hierarchal scheme:

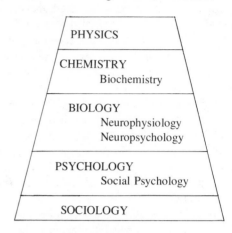

Theories lower on the pyramid are claimed to be reducible to or explainable in terms of the higher ones: sociology to psychology, psychology to biology, and so on.

Two positions that could be taken against reductionism emphasize the type of subject matter that psychology studies. First of all, it might be claimed that psychology studies mental activity that cannot be reduced to physical action. Thoughts, feelings, and emotions are regarded as more than some part of the brain being activated. The position regarding reductionism might depend on the view taken about the nature of the mind. The more important views in the philosophy of the mind are:

A. Dualism—the mental and the physical are irreducibly different.
   1. Interactionism—mental events cause bodily events and vice versa.
   2. Parallelism—mental and bodily events are correlated but do not causally interact.
   3. Eiphenomenalism—bodily events cause mental events but not vice versa.
B. Monism—the mental and the physical are basically the same.
   1. Identity thesis—the mental and the physical are two different ways of talking about the same material (physical) thing.
   2. Double-Aspect Theory—the mental and the physical are two aspects of the same thing which itself is neither mental nor physical.

Note that these positions taken on the nature of the mind are philosophical and not (except possibly obliquely) scientific.

A second way of arguing against reductionism is to claim a radical distinction between the methods used in the natural sciences and those in the social sciences. Natural sciences study objects such as atoms and chemical compounds. The study is very different when human activity is the focal point since humans have qualities such as beliefs, values, and experiences that differ in kind from those studied in the natural sciences. Moreover, the fact that humans are investigating humans must be taken into account. Understanding another person can mean empathisizing with that person or trying to have a similar experience. Certainly, this type of understanding is not available in the natural sciences. It seems ridiculous to talk of empathisizing with a rock. Moreover, it might be argued that psychology and not physics is the most fundamental science. Scientific activity consists of a subject investigating an object. Even if there is complete scientific knowledge of all the objects in the world, there will still be a need to explain the behavior of the scientific investigator, the subject observing the object. The final task of scientific investigation is then left to psychologists.

Regardless of the position taken on reductionism, the study of human behavior does present some philosophical problems peculiar to psychology. In the next section, a few of these philosophical issues relating to psychology will be addressed.

Free Will and Determinism. Are people free? Are they free to make their own choices and to act on those choices? These are important and difficult questions to ponder. Placing these questions into a specific context, imagine the implausible but possible situation where the psychologist is able to predict everyone's choices and actions. Furthermore, this imaginary psychologist can even accurately predict when and how a person might try to disprove the predictions if he or she knew them. Under these conditions, does it still make sense to say that a person has free will?

The psychologist in this scenario is a *determinist*. A determinist, as we have discussed, is one who believes that there is complete order in the universe. In other words, the determinist believes that there are scientific laws governing all aspects of the universe, including human behavior. Furthermore, the determinist believes that in principle each and every event that happens in the universe can be predicted. A science such as psychology seems to presuppose determinism, that is, the lawful and predictable nature of events. Yet, free will is cherished by almost everybody. There seems to be a short step from predicting someone's behavior to being able to control that person. There is, then, a conflict between scientific determinism and human freedom.

This scenario presupposes a sharp contrast between free will and determinism. Carnap (1966) suggests a way out of the quandary which reconciles free will and a deterministic science of psychology. Determinism is defined in terms of predictability; a completely deterministic system is one in which each successive state of the system is predictable from knowledge of the previous state. Defined in this manner, determinism should be contrasted with indeterminism (nonpredictability) and not free will. Free will is more properly contrasted with compulsion. If an individual is forced or coerced into performing an action, then that individual is not exercising free will. A psychologist predicting an individual's action is not coercing or compelling that individual. There can be free will or choice in a completely deterministic universe. Free will and determinism are perfectly compatible (Pap, 1962).

Many things could be said about the determinism and free will issue, but a more extensive discussion of it would take us too far afield. It is important, however, to see what type of issue is being examined. In the way it has been presented, the issue is a philosophical one and not an empirical issue within psychology. What is the difference between a philosophical and an empirical issue? The test for determining whether an issue is philosophical or empirical is to ask whether or not the scientific method could provide an answer to the question. If the scientific method can provide an answer, then the issue is empirical; if not, then it is philosophical.

Values. The fact/value dichotomy is so deeply entrenched in Western thought that it has been seriously questioned only recently. Questions of value and ethics were relegated to the emotive domain. These questions were thought to be subjective matters of taste which have little or no cognitive content. Scientists in attempting to be objective try to exclude these subjective matters of taste from science. This thesis does not try to make scientists out to be unethical. For, according to this view, scientists should certainly try to emulate the highest standards of moral conduct; but this is done in their role as citizens and not as scientists.

Attacking this hard and fast fact/value split, some (Rudner, 1953) argue that scientists in their role as scientists make value judgments. In accepting hypotheses, a scientist must decide how much evidence will be enough to accept an hypothesis. This decision is based on how much importance or value the scientist places on being wrong about that judgment. A greater amount of evidence will be required in order to accept an hypothesis concerning the purity of a polio vaccine than will be needed to accept an hypothesis concerning the purity of motor oil. A scientist places a greater importance on the risk of being wrong about polio vaccine than motor oil. This is because the scientist places a higher ethical value on human than on automobile welfare.

Regardless of where value judgments come into play, there is no doubt that psychology touches on many important and critical ethical issues that cannot be ignored. Psychologists experiment on living organisms, animal and human, and the rights of these beings cannot be overlooked in the name of science. Not only does the very experimental nature of psychology raise ethical issues, but psychologists are investigating matters that have important ethical ramifications. Is intelligence, for example, a matter of nature or nurture? Finally, the implementation of psychological knowledge in behavior control raises many old ethical questions in a new light.

A Summary of Philosophical Foundations of Psychology. More questions have been raised than answered in this section. Just as there is no sharp agreement about whether psychology is a preparadigmatic or a multiparadigmatic science, so there is no unanimity regarding the philosophical foundations of psychology. In fact, not having many of these issues resolved makes psychology an exciting discipline. Progress often comes at the price of controversy. Despite many lingering questions, one should have a better understanding of where psychology stands in "the bigger picture."

Glossary

Ad hoc reasoning: claims made in order to save a theory despite adverse evidence.

Behavior: a general term to describe the continuous flux of activity of an organism in time and space.

Circular definition: definition is given using the term being defined.

Controlled variable: the value of this variable is held constant or at a "zero amount" during an experiment.

Dependent variable: the variable that a science measures, predicts, or controls; in psychology it is the response.

Descriptive research: research where the independent variable is neither changed nor manipulated.

Determinism: assumption that all events can be explained and predicted; often contrasted with free will.

Dispositional term: term or concept that refers to a stated characteristic that can be manifested in behavior.

Environmental condition: often used synonymously with the stimulus variable or the independent variable.

Explanation: a means scientists use to understand events in terms of laws and observations.

Experience: the awareness of the internal and external interpersonal and physical stimuli.

Experimental research: research where the independent variable is manipulated in some specified amount.

Falsifiability: a specification of the conditions under which a theory would be false; a requirement of all scientific claims.

Hypothetical construct: an inferred concept with physiological or neurological overtones.

Hypothesis: a conjecture that a scientist tests through research.

Independent variable: the variable that a science uses for making a prediction; in psychology it is the stimulus or environmental variable.

Intervening variable: an inferred concept with psychological or behavioral overtones; may be used as an explanatory concept.

Law: generalizations concerning a broad range of phenomena and needing good empirical support; used to explain and predict.

Manipulative research: research where the independent variable is changed or manipulated in specified amounts.

Molar: an analysis of the response typically in terms of the outcome of the activity of the organism.

Molecular: an analysis of the response typically in terms of glandular and muscular activities.

Model: an abstract representation of something being investigated; often used synonymously with theory or hypothesis.

Operational definition: concepts that are defined in terms of the measureable and observable operations.

Operations: the specified experimental procedures employed in research.

Paradigm: common point of view adopted by various investigators.

Prediction: used to specify what will happen.

Primitive term: an undefined term used to define other terms of a theory.

Psychology: the science of behavior and its practical application.

Reductionism: thesis that some of the sciences can be explained in terms of a more fundamental or basic science.

Replication: the repetition of an experiment under the identical conditions of the independent variable.

Response: the dependent variable in psychology; the measured segment of behavior.

Simplicity: a way of evaluating a scientific theory according to the number of assumptions made.

Stable-state responses: those responses that show little variability over time.

Stimulus: the independent variable in psychology that is determined empirically from the dependent or response variable.

Testability: a requirement of a scientific claim that a theory is capable of being empirically tested.

Theoretical term: a term that helps organize the concepts of a theory.

Theory: an interrelated system of scientific laws.

Transitional responses: those responses that vary systematically over time; as opposed to stable-state responses.

Suggested Readings

deGroot, A. *Methodology: Foundations of Inference and Research in the Behavioral Sciences.* Belgium: Mouton & Co., 1969.

Eacker, J. N. *Problems of Philosophy and Psychology.* Chicago: Nelson-Hall, 1975.

Foder, J. A. *Psychological Explanation.* New York: Random House, 1968.

Hempel, C. G. *Philosophy of Natural Sciences.* Englewood Cliffs: Prentice-Hall, 1966.

Kosschau, R. A., Johnson, M. M., and Russo, N. I. *Careers in Psychology.* Washington: American Psychological Association, 1975.

Michalos, A. C., ed. *Philosophical Problems of Science and Technology.* Boston: Allyn & Bacon, Inc., 1974.

Suppe, F., ed. *The Structure of Scientific Theories.* Urbana: University of Illinois Press, 1974.

Turner, M. B. *Philosophy and the Science of Behavior.* New York: Appleton-Century-Crofts, 1967.

History and Systems of Psychology

Robert I. Watson, Sr.

Introduction

The history of a science, including that of psychology, is a psychological problem, because men and women have behaved and experienced in living that history. More specifically, the history of a field can be conceived as a problem in social psychology of the past, but most specific of all, as a problem in the psychology of attitudes that have characterized individuals in considering psychological problems (Watson, 1975). Psychologists like practitioners in any field have a predisposition to react in a relatively consistent way toward problems in their field at any particular period in its history.

These attitudes are referred to as "prescriptions" because, once established, they take on an imperative character (Watson, 1967). They are of a compelling nature so that often they are acted upon without psychologists having to devote thought to what they are doing. This imperative character may be illustrated by the positive commitment of contemporary psychologists to *quantitativism* (the "measurement" of Chapter 1) in carrying out a research investigation. They do not ask whether the problem in which they are interested should or should not be quantified; they just proceed to do so. It is the way a psychologist habitually behaves as a psychologist. Prescriptions are attitudes that serve to direct psychologists about what to do, about how to behave, and often are so thoroughly assimilated into their conceptions of their roles as not to need a weighing of alternatives.

As do all attitudes, prescriptive attitudes have both a cognitive and an affective component. As for the first component, when they stop to do so, they are quite legitimately able to articulate at least some aspects and some prescriptions so as to fit their conceptions of their role as psychologists. They have arguments with which to defend the essential correctness of their views. As for the second component, objects, problems and concepts of psychological import are viewed either favorably or unfavorably. Favorable disposition toward *quantitativism* is a case in point since it goes hand in hand with a simultaneous dislike, even an aversion for, *qualitativism,* the attitude that stresses differences in kind or quality.

The attitudes to be examined first are methodological rather than contentual. They concern how psychologists go about their task as scientists and not the attitudes they have about the contentual nature of their problems. It is appropriate to consider first methodological prescriptions, because they are shared with other sciences and philosophy and were borrowed from them. Although there is some overlap, scientists from different disciplines work on different contentual problems, but they share a common methodological outlook. These methodological attitudes were part of the thinking of psychologists when psychology emerged as a science. Only when the science of psychology emerges from the matrix of philosophy and the other sciences will its contentual prescriptions be examined.

Consequently, consideration of the methodological prescriptions that dominate psychology will set the stage for the historical account to follow.

Contemporary psychologists, besides favoring the already mentioned *quantitativism,* use methods of study that are open to verification by other competent observers (*methodological objectivism*); they regard the activities of the individuals they study as completely explicable by mechanical constituents (*mechanism*); they accept the study of nature without appeal to anything outside of nature (*naturalism*) they contend the events that they study are completely explicable in terms of antecedents (*determinism*); they emphasize the value of discovering general laws (*nomotheticism*); and they are predominantly interested in seeking knowledge from experience, especially experimental knowledge (*empiricism*).

It has been found that these and other attitudes have manifested themselves over extended periods of time. And this is a second distinguishing feature of both contentual and methodological prescriptions—recognizable continuity over a considerable temporal period. They have made their appearance at different points of time; some were lost from knowledge only to reappear again after a lapse of time. Prescriptive manifestations could be expected then to show many changes over the course of their history. Sometimes the very terms used to describe them differ at different times; they may be given varying degrees of emphasis; there are different patterns of relation with one another; sometimes they appear explicitly and verbally, other times are present only implicitly; at one time antagonistic, they may be synthesized at other times; they show different patterns of dominant or counterdominant status. These are but some of the dimensions of change possible. Through all of these varying guises, the prescriptions exhibit a tenacity that attests to their appeal to individuals of different times and places.

All prescriptions referred to as dominant in psychology today have been challenged during psychology's past and some are challenged at present by individuals who held opposing attitudes. Instead of holding a *quantitative* attitude, individuals have gloried in their emphasis upon the *qualitative*—that which is different in kind or essence. *Methodological subjectivism,* the use of methods open only to the specially adept, has had its defenders throughout all time. The appeal to *super-*

naturalism, as the final arbiter of true knowledge, was dominant over *naturalism* for 2,000 years. *Indeterminism,* the insistence that human events are not completely explicable in terms of antecedents, is a view which then and now has had its adherents within the sciences and elsewhere. Today, the dominant *nomothetic* view is challenged vigorously by a counterdominant *idiographicism,* the attitude that calls for explaining particular events or the behavior of particular individuals. Currently, *empiricism* does not simply dominate over *rationalism,* the appeal to reason as the source of knowledge, but rather empiricism has assimilated rationalism, a synthesis often referred to as logical (that is, rational) empiricism. In Chapter 1 there is a discussion not only of logical empiricism but also for an extended presentation of the interrelation of philosophy, psychology, and science.

It has been said that psychology has had a long past but only a short history. This is true in the sense that, until relatively recently, there was no science of psychology. Interest in the matters that were to become the concern of psychology were an inextricable part of the mother of all sciences, philosophy. Many contentual prescriptions were first conceived as relating to philosophical problems, and some still have contemporary, philosophical usages. Psychology, first drawing inspiration from philosophy, began to take further shape from its reactions to developments in the other earlier demarcated sciences.

Psychology's long past as aspects of philosophy extends from the beginning of the historical record and reaches high points of acuteness and scope among the ancient Greeks, during the period of the Church Fathers, in the late Middle Ages, and again at the beginning of the modern period of the seventeenth century. It was during these centuries that the events took place which fostered the development of the methodological attitudes which scientists possessed as they entered the period of psychology as a modern science. It is to its history in this narrower sense that we must confine our attention. Histories which present an account of these events before the modern period include Brett (1953) and Watson (1978).

Fig. 2-1.
Wundt, Fechner,
Helmholtz

Psychology in the Age
of Wilhelm Wundt

Although it is hazardous to try to specify priorities in the history of any field, the risk in identifying the first psychologist may be somewhat minimized by first specifying the criteria that are to be applied. The spirit of this chapter and of this book calls for this to be someone who (1) considered psychology as a science in the modern sense of the term, not as mental philosophy; (2) recognized a new scientific discipline was being founded; (3) identified with that discipline, and not some other; and (4) had a sufficient grasp of the nature of psychological science to interrelate some of its relevant problems into the beginnings of a reasonably complete system of psychology.

Wilhelm Wundt (1832–1920) was the first modern psychologist because he was the first individual to meet all four criteria. In his major book, *The Principles of Physiological Psychology,* which first appeared in two parts in 1873 and 1874, he stated unequivocally his intent to present psychology as a science. In its preface it is given for all to see, that the work was intended to "mark out a new domain of science" and, as a *science,* he goes on to say, cannot be based upon philosophical assumptions of any sort. He had succinctly informed us that he was founding a science of psychology.

The rest of his life and work was to bear out, not only his identification with it, but how he met successfully the other criteria as well. With Wundt, we begin that short history of psychological science that encompasses just about 100 years.

Wundt shared with his fellow scientists the then prevailing version of the methodological prescriptions of science. He was both strongly nomothetic and naturalistic in attitude and had no use for the study of the individual or for interpenetrating psychological with theological views. His reliance on other methodological attitudes will become evident as this account proceeds, but stress will be placed upon his particular adherences to prescriptive attitudes of a contentual nature.

Wundt began his career in physiological research in German universities. Even from the beginning, his particular choice of areas of research interest bore as much or more on psychological problems than it did upon the ostensible physiological bases from which he started. He accepted appointments as a professor of philosophy, since, in academic circles, psychology was still considered to be a branch of that field. In 1875 he became professor of philosophy at the University of Leipzig. This relationship was to continue over his remaining forty-five years.

Even before his arrival at the university, a room for his research had been set aside, so that in one sense at least, one of the two first laboratories in psychology was founded at the University of Leipzig in 1875, not 1879, the date "received opinion" calls for (Harper, 1950). (The other candidate for this honor is William James who equipped a small demonstrational laboratory at Harvard University in 1875.)

Important as it was to be as a fertile source of research, the laboratory's social-academic significance was equally as important. The maintenance of a laboratory as an ongoing entity made it possible for a considerable number of students to come study with him, to participate in the research of the laboratory, and to prepare research journal reports. With the founding by Wundt in 1881 of the *Philosophische Studien,* publication of research articles became possible because this was the first journal to be devoted primarily to psychology. The astonishing number of 116 individuals prepared their doctoral dissertations in psychology under his direction. No longer was psychology primarily a task for the solitary scholar preparing his books in his study. The psychologist was now a research worker collecting data in the laboratory and writing his results for publication in journals. Books did not disappear from the psychological scene. At Leipzig, it was inevitable that Wundt's task would be to synthesize the results from the laboratory. He did so in a torrent of books—in his lifetime Wundt published six psychology books in thirty-six editions.

Moreover, the presence of the laboratory setting had a considerable effect upon the method of research. Wundt took advantage of the situation to broaden and sharpen the introspective technique under a system of mutual collaboration. A continuing training program made it possible for the novices in introspection to be trained by those more expert. A tradition of what is meant by introspection emerged. Contemplation of one's mental content, or, perhaps better, meditation, had existed as long as recorded history. But there had been little awareness of it as a method. Meditation drew upon the everyday experience of a particular individual and reflected primarily the individual genius of the person involved in the contemplation. It was not necessary to draw upon the meditations of others.

Wundt firmly established the method of introspection as psychology's first characteristic task. Although he would make introspective experience the content of psychology, *contentual subjectivism* in prescriptive terms, he wanted it to be as *methodologically objective* as possible. He recognized that conscious contents are fleeting and in continual flux given to us in compounds, and it is the task of introspection to abstract the elements. In the service of *methodological objectivism* he took the step of uniting introspection with empiricism's sharpest tool, the experiment. The combined procedures of introspection and experiment may be illustrated by indicating some of the rules he laid down for experiments. Stimulation must not only be capable of repetition but also of variations in strength, hence making it an experiment. Manipulation by the experimenter of strength of the stimulus and recording the differences in introspective experiences reported means that this essential of an experimental procedure was being met.

Admirable as these rules may be to bring out the care in which *methodological objectivism* is sought, the introspective experience, as expressing *contentual subjectivism,* hardly becomes clear. Description of a procedural caution, avoidance of the so-called stimulus error, will bring us a little closer to the experience itself. In carrying out the process of introspection, introspectionists were warned that it is necessary to avoid the error of describing it in terms of the commonsense experience upon which meditation relied. An "orange" is not an orange so far as introspective report is concerned; it is the hues, brightnesses, and spatial characteristics of the sensation arising from the stimulus object. The introspectionist must describe the conscious content, not give the commonsense meaning to the object. To give the latter would be to commit the stimulus error.

Wundt's Heritage from Other Sciences

Since we have said very little about psychology's past, we must consider some of the historical contributions from other sciences which influenced Wundt. Wundt's explicit awareness of his debt to his predecessors is indicated in his choice of "physiological" as the qualifying term in the title of his most important work, *The Principles of*

Physiological Psychology (1873–1874). It would be wrong to infer that he chose it because he wished to stress the interrelation of physiological and psychological findings. Rather, the term was chosen in deference to the inspiration, the *methods* of physiology were to the fledgling science.

It so happens that the contributions of physiology that were open to his scrutiny in the 1870s and 1880s were being pursued by a second generation of physiologists. Some forty years earlier, in 1833, Johannes Müller (1802–1858) had been named at the University of Berlin to the first chair of physiology. Müller went on to write a systematic and exhaustive handbook of the physiology of man which drew together the scattered and unsystematic earlier reports of physiological research in a manner that is reminiscent of Wundt's later efforts in psychology. Without confining attention to the contents of Müller's book, what were some of the methods (and pertinent research areas) that Wundt had in mind in referring to psychology's debt to physiology?

Studies in reaction time that were to occupy Wundt, had originated in the eighteenth century astronomers' discovery that an observer sitting at the telescope had his own characteristic temporal speed in recording when a star passed the transit hairline of the telescope. Some observers were faster, others slower. In order to bring results of different observers in line with one another, a system of corrective constants called the "personal equation" was adopted by cooperating astronomers.

In 1868, the Dutch physiologist Fransiscus C. Donders (1818–1889), extended reaction time study by going beyond simple reaction time. Pressing a key, for example, when a light went on would give the simple reaction time as used by the astronomers. If this reaction were made more complicated, Donders reasoned, the increased time could be attributed to whatever was added. Simple reaction time had called for subjects to respond to stimulus *A* with response *a*. For discrimination time, Donders presented in irregular order several stimuli, A, B, C, D, but his subjects were to respond only to A, not to the others. As Donders predicted, his subjects took longer to make this discrimination than they did to make the simple re-

action. Subtracting simple reaction time from discrimination reaction time gave him the discrimination time. Choice reaction was even more complicated. Subjects now responded to A with a, B with b, C with c, and so on. This gave a still longer reaction time, and choice time was the total time minus the discrimination and the simple reaction time. The very time taken for mental events had been measured and thus, "mental chronometry" had been launched.

The contemporaneous physiological research, severely empirical in character, that Hermann von Helmholtz (1821–1894) carried on at various German universities, was so monumental as to have repercussions in various related fields, including the psychology of Wundt. Helmholtz's findings on the speed of neural impulse, indeed in showing that it could be measured at all, was directly related to psychological studies of reaction time. Moreover, Helmholtz offered experimental support of the theory of color vision which held that the retina of the eye is equipped with three kinds of receptors. The ingredients of the Young-Helmholtz theory of color vision are still accepted today as will be discussed in Chapter 5. His work on audition included his theory and demonstration that pitch was attributable to the particular place on the basilar membrane of the cochlea of the inner ear that resonated with the pitch frequency of the physical stimulus. Although too simple in itself since other factors must also be taken into consideration, Helmholtz' resonance-place theory is nevertheless the starting point from which current research proceeds.

It was, however, to a philosopher-physicist, not a physiologist, that Wilhelm Wundt paid the compliment of saying of his work that it was the first conquest in the field of experimental psychology. Over many decades of his long life, Wundt's older contemporary at the University of Leipzig, Gustav Fechner (1808–1887), had labored with a burning zeal to demonstrate that the mental and the physical are so functionally and inseparably interrelated as to be identical. He would find, he hoped, a unified view of body and mind through which he could demonstrate what to him was the fallaciousness of a materialistic view of life and nature, and would also solve the age-old philosophical mind-body problem. But there was another side to Fechner—that of the scientist. A former professor of physics, he appreciated the value of *quantification* and *methodological objectivity*. These philosophical and scientific strains were united on the morning of October 22, 1850 when, "before getting up," he had the insight that the law of the connection of body and mind was to be sought in the quantitative relations between increases in mental sensation and increases in bodily stimuli, not in simple proportion, but such that one-step increases in the former correspond to proportional changes in the latter. Thus, the idea basic to what was called psychophysics was born.

At the University of Leipzig in Fechner's early years, there was a very competent physiologist, Ernst Weber (1795–1878), who had already conducted some experiments in what at first might appear to be an unrelated problem—the relation of the muscle sense to touch. Weber had reasoned that if use of the muscle of the arm increased sensitivity of touching the skin alone, then allowing a person to make a judgment of heavier, lighter, or the same magnitude of a stimulus using *both* muscle sense and touch, would be more accurate than the same kind of judgments made using touch alone. To measure this, he chose comparative accuracy of judgments of heaviness of weights by comparing relative discriminatory ability in judging weights resting on the skin (touch alone) as compared to the fineness of discriminations made when actually lifting the weights (touch and muscle sense combined).

On each trial, the subject lifted two weights, one the standard, the other the comparison. His task was to say which one felt heavier (or the same). On the various trials, the comparison weight in relation to the standard weight might be very much heavier, much heavier, hardly heavier at all, identical, and with similar degrees, lighter comparison weights.

Weber found that for each standard weight there was a relation between the sheer heaviness of the weight and the subject's perception of differences between the weights. This is expressed as ratios of how much weight must be added to that of the comparison weight for the subject to consistently notice a difference. His experiments revealed that

it was one in forty, as far as the overall ratio was concerned. But it also held for other comparison weights, some heavier and some lighter than the initial one used. With the lighter weight, the ratio was .5 to 20, while with a heavier weight, the ratio was 2 to 80. Time and again, the ratio worked out to be about 1 in 40.

He now carried out this procedure with the identical weights but this time rested them on the skin. He now found the ratio to be 1 to 30, instead of 1 to 40. In other words, as much as one-thirtieth of the standard weight had to be added to it for a difference to be noticed. Since smaller differences in weight could be discriminated when the weight was lifted (1 to 40) compared to the discriminability when they rested on the skin (1 in 30) he concluded that adding the muscle sense to touch in the lifting procedure did make for finer discriminations when compared to touch alone.

Weber went on to study other sense modalities, for example, visual discriminations of difference of length of line. He martialed already available evidence of discrimination of pitch differences. Again and again, for each of the senses, he found constant ratios.

Fechner found in Weber's work the clue to his own problem of psychophysics. He went beyond Weber's many individual ratios to state what he called the Weber-Fechner law, a generalization of these results. Irrespective of sense modality, Fechner found he could state the relationship between the energy of the physical stimulus and the intensity of the perceived sensation by a logarithmic curve. This came about because his research showed that, as the intensity increased by steps of one (a just-noticeable difference), the stimulus must be increased geometrically by a constant multiple. Sensation had been measured, and he had found proof of his identity hypothesis of mind and body in a table of logarithms. His major work, bringing together the results of years of investigation, was the *Elements of Psychophysics* (1860). For contemporary illustrations of pyschophysical methods, see Chapter 3. What about Fechner's philosophical and mystical goals for psychophysics? In the excitement that his findings stimulated when considered as sensory research alone, it was forgotten by all but Fechner himself!

Wundt's System

This earlier work on reaction time, on sensation and on psychophysics, provided Wundt with research methods and problems. He had his rigorous introspective technique; he had students to carry out studies he would give them; he had a laboratory. With these tools he proceeded to fashion a psychology that was guided by systematic views that now can be summarized in terms of his contentual prescriptive allegiances.

Wundt was the great classifier and synthesizer of psychology's content as *conscious mentalism*—he was wholeheartedly preoccupied with that part of the mental life given in awareness. Nothing brings out more clearly his insistence that psychology concerns conscious phenomena and not the interrelation of the mental with the physical than his interpreation of psychophysics. He disagreed with Fechner. Instead of psychophysical procedures demonstrating a relation between the physical stimulus and the psychological experience, psychophysics gave the relation between sensation and judgment of that sensation, both psychological experiences. Psychology was clearly *contentually subjective* despite the *methological objectivity* that Wundt practiced. Moreover, it was a *molecular structuralism*—the search for the elements of the structure of mental life.

What, Wundt asked, are the dimensions of consciousness? They are twofold. There are qualities of experience, such as blueness, sweetness, not reducible to simpler events, and the varying intensities in which these qualities may be expressed. These two dimensions, quality and intensity, interrelate. For example, intensity (loud-soft) of a sound is never separable from some quality of pitch (high-low), but one can change the intensity alone or the pitch alone while maintaining unchanged the stimulating properties of the other. Moreover we may use two low notes and change the quality of the sound from that of either note alone.

In addition to sensation, another element of the mind was feeling. Feelings accompany sensations. Both are always present in immediate experience, although often the feeling component is so negligible that nontrained introspectionists do not notice

it. However, increase intensity of sensations and eventually every one would acknowledge the presence of feeling. The dimensions of feeling were threefold: pleasantness-unpleasantness, tension-relaxation, and exitement-depression. Feeling experiences were expressed in different, varying combinations, for example, pleauant, tense, excited.

When sensations and feelings are combined, they form ideas and perceptions. Principles of combination included not only that by associations in the way previously used, but also by "fusion," a different and separate principle necessitated by simultaneous combinations being so tightly knit as to require it. Combinations of feelings and ideas give rise to the emotions, some in which pleasure predominates such as joy and delight and others in which displeasure predominates such as anger and fear. Closely related to the emotions are the volitional processes in which the determining factors are the feelings. Feelings must reach a certain level of intensity if they are to produce volition. Volition culminates in action as when an angry person strikes the object of his anger. Without the volition, the experience would have been emotion alone.

At long last we have reached action as differentiated from reception as the final effect of a long chain of conscious experiences, all of which must occur before action. The mere sentence or two with which action is identified is appropriate to the relative significance that Wundt attached to action, the meager behavioral facet of psychology.

He used the principle of mental synthesis to account for the fact that a landscape did *not* add up to a series of specified visual sensations of variant hues and accompanying feelings of mild excitement, high pleasure and low tension, meaningfully perceived. Mental synthesis was, however, hardly anything more than a name for a gap in his system; he admitted that it existed, but he did relatively little about it than to call attention to it.

Despite the enormous detail of the many research studies and concepts, Wundt was working with a small canvas compared to the vast panorama of modern psychology. Aside from "association," as conceived by earlier philosophers, learning as a field hardly existed for him. Those areas of psychology that required a more dynamic view than his illustrated by motivation, intelligence, and thought, were hardly mentioned in the restriction created by his adherence to a *static* prescription. A conviction that was most important in mental life could be caught not in actions, but in enduring elements. For personality, a challenge to his system, he simply passed by with a plea that someday there would be a means for its study.

What may be said of the content of Wundtian psychology in short summary? It was *contentually subjective* in that its field was the mind; his psychology advocated *conscious mentalism* in that he rejected unconscious processes as irrelevant; it was *structural* in that the parts of the mind were stressed; it was *static* in that enduring, not changing or developmental, facets of mind were sought; it was *molecular* in that it sought to isolate and study the elements of the mind despite some attention to a molar principle of mental synthesis.

Wundt's Contemporaries

Although Wundt dominated German psychology of the last decades of the nineteenth and the first decades of the twentieth centuries, there were contemporary psychologists who worked independently. From a modern perspective, some of what was lacking in his point of view had beginnings in their work. Franz Brentano and Hermann Ebbinghaus are both important enough and sufficiently different in outlook to warrant consideration here.

Franz Brentano (1838–1917), for many years a Catholic priest and professor at the University of Vienna, drew his inspiration primarily from the work of Aristotle. In 1874, the same year in which Wundt completed his masterpiece, Brentano published his *Psychology from an Empirical Standpoint.* He promulgated what has come to be referred to as *act psychology.* In keeping with Aristotle, Brentano saw activity in mental life, or the *functional prescription,* as paramount. On seeing a color, the color itself is not mental, it is the *act of seeing* that is mental. The study of color, as such, belongs to physics; psychical phenomena on the other hand, while related to content, are not that content. Seeing, hearing, and so on, must

have some object, like blue, that they intend. "I see blue" *is* the act of the mental datum. When we see something, two things take place—the act of seeing and then, the seen object or content of seeing. Psychic phenomena consist of three kinds—ideating, judging, and feeling. These are the various types of relationships that a subject has to an object. The first is the ubiquitous relationship of having an idea of an object that, in itself, may be real, imaginary, past, present, or future. But in addition to the sheer diversity of relationships with objects, one may make an affirmation or denial of that relationship. Hence, there is judging. Attitudes taken toward these objects run the gamut from love (attraction) to hate (repulsion). Hence, there is feeling.

Brentano's system of act psychology stands in sharp contrast to Wundt's psychology of content. While both stood firm in acceptance of psychology's *contentual subjectivism,* Wundt saw the mind in terms of its static elements, and Brentano saw the mind in terms of its acts. Stated this way, the contrast serves to make clearer the distinction between the *structural* and *functional* which we will hear more about later.

Hermann Ebbinghaus (1850–1909) made his major contribution to psychology without benefit of teacher, a university environment, or a laboratory. He had chanced upon a copy of Fechner's master work, the *Elements of Psychophysics* (1860). The mathematical approach followed, and the research stirred him to the conviction that the methods with which Fechner had studied sensation and other simpler mental processes could be applied to memory, a higher mental process, that Wundt had specifically asserted in his recently-published *Principles of Physiological Psychology* to be impossible of experimental study.

Frequency was studied by Ebbinghaus because he regarded it as the essential factor in learning. The greater the frequency of presentation in the material, he theorized, the more one learns. Frequency was to be measured by the number of repetitions of material to be memorized to a specific degree of accuracy. Learning selections of poetry or prose would not be exact enough because prior learning would facilitate learning some selections and hinder others. He needed homogeneous, equally unfamiliar material. For this purpose he invented the nonsense syllable–consonants (for example, VUP, DOD, ZIT) with a vowel between. After construction, those that formed meaningful words were eliminated. Thus, *nuz* might be used, but not *bun*. After these eliminations, he had a reservoir of over 2,000 nonsense syllables from which to draw. In order to minimize the effect of variable errors attached to particular material, he would use the same procedure again and again, just like Fechner, until he had enough information to secure an average measure. For further control of extraneous matters, he behaved in an even more heroic fashion; he regulated his daily habits of living to precisely the same routine, day after day, year after year, during the course of his experiments.

A representative particular research task was for him to draw at random twelve nonsense syllables, read them through at the uniform rate of two-fifths of one second each, to pause fifteen seconds afterward to record the trial number, and to repeat again and again until he believed he could repeat them without mistake, at which point a trial without looking at the cards would be tried. If he failed, no matter now few the mistakes, he would record the number of errors, and then return to reading the list. This procedure would continue until he could give the complete list without error. This procedure, that of "complete mastery," allowed him to know the number of trials to learn. He then busied himself with learning other lists. After the lapse of a previously selected scheduled time, be it an hour, a day or a week, he would return to the originally learned list and ascertain the number of repetitions necessary to relearn to the same level of complete mastery. There would generally be a "savings" in that not as many readings were necessary for mastery. Hence, the "savings method" was conceived, which he calculated as a percentage of the number of trials originally necessary as compared to the number to relearn. If sixteen trials had been necessary for original learning and eight for relearning, the savings was $8/16$ or fifty percent. The very first relearning trial gave him still another measure of memory. Before relearning by rereading, he had found how many syllables he could recall *before* reading them again.

The number still known before rereading the list divided by the total learned was the measure of memory, as when four were remembered out of twelve, or thirty-three percent.

From years of its study, reported in his *Memory: A Contribution to Experimental Psychology* (1885), came the well-known Ebbinghaus curves of forgetting in which it is found that material is forgotten very rapidly at first and then more and more slowly. This is graphically shown by a curve that goes down very sharply at first and then gradually levels off. His results, while modified and enormously extended in many directions, have stood the test of time since, to this very day, some of his results are stated as if current in the contemporaneous review of research in human memory as described in Chapter 10.

Ebbinghaus' research has been a model for thousands of research studies. In stating the results in numerical terms of trials, accuracy, and time elapsed without recourse to introspections, he was using behaviors as *contentually objective* and *quantitative* an anything that was to come later from the behaviorists. Indeed, a major criticism leveled against his methods and results was by G. E. Müller (Müller, 1900), another psychologist independent of the Wundtian influence, who chided Ebbinghaus for not investigating the conscious experiences occurring while the learning was going on. Müller, who secured introspections in his study, while arriving at essentially the same curves of memory, found his subjects to make mental groupings, to give meanings to individual syllables, to express doubts felt about accuracy, and to experience an active sense of search for meanings that could be attached to the individual syllables.

The Beginnings of Psychology in the United States

Before the 1880s, mental and moral philosophy had been taught in American colleges. Characteristically, the teacher was the college president and usually a minister who did not fail to imbue his courses with the religious implications of the subject matter. A tradition of faculty philosophy was stressed that served not only as the philosophical psychology of the time, but also the basis of the then current educational theory of formal discipline. A faculty was a capacity or "power" of the mind, such as desire for knowledge, duty, memory, or moral taste, which could be strengthened by exercise.

Outside the college walls, in business and to some extent in medicine, another faculty philosophy flourished. This was *phrenology,* based upon impressionistic evidence that there was a correlation between the convolutions of the skull and the "powers" resident in the parts of the brain beneath the skull.

Before and immediately after the Civil War, higher education in the United States was confined almost exclusively to work at the undergraduate college level. The occasional master's degree was essentially nothing more than an extension of the undergraduate course. Graduate schools, as such, were just becoming established. In the 1870s and 1880s, the German university system began to attract favorable attention. American graduate students turned to training abroad to such an extent that in 1880, as many graduate students were enrolled in German and Austrian universities as there were in all of the United States. Over the next three decades, the reform of graduate education at Harvard University and in other places proceeded rapidly, and Cornell, Johns Hopkins, and Clark Universities, dedicated to graduate education, were founded.

In these educational changes, the "new psychology" was to occupy a strategic position. It was not only one of the new academic subjects introduced from Germany, but it would also supply the weapon to attack faculty philosophy.

Psychology enjoyed a tremendous upsurge in numbers and influence in the years after 1880. By 1895 twenty-four psychology laboratories, three journals, and a flourishing scientific society had been created. Only fifteen years before, none of this had existed (Albrecht, 1960).

Pioneers of the New Psychology

Many of these developments in psychology were due to the return of American students from abroad, particularly from Germany, and most specifically from those who had studied with Wundt. Three men were outstanding.

G. Stanley Hall (1844–1924), the first of these pioneers, is most important as organizer and administrator of the fledgling science. In 1882, he accepted an appointment at the newly founded Johns Hopkins University where he established a laboratory, and, in 1887, he founded the *American Journal of Psychology.* Shortly thereafter, he became the first president of Clark University which Hall modeled on the graduate schools of Germany. He assembled a brilliant faculty and did much to train large numbers of the first native-born generation of psychologists. In 1892, he called together a small number of the leading psychologists and proposed

Fig. 2-2.
Titchener and James

the founding of the American Psychological Association.

Hall was a man of great personal charm, open to widely varying interests, and given to a search for new developments in psychology which included arranging the occasion that gave rise to the first international recognition of the work of Sigmund Freud. His research marked him as a pioneer in many areas, particularly in studies of childhood, adolescence, and senescence. He made a gospel of childhood, insisting that its study was important for its own sake, not merely for the light it threw on the development to adulthood. At some point, he said that Wundt would rather have been commonplace than brilliantly wrong. It is possible that Hall would have reversed the statement for himself.

James McKeen Cattell (1860–1944), after taking an undergraduate degree, was first a student at Johns Hopkins and then went on to the University of Leipzig where he became Wundt's self-appointed first assistant. He insisted on working on a doctoral problem that involved individual differences in reaction time, contrary to the usual custom of having the problem assigned by Wundt. This self-independence combined with a dogged directness, marked his career. He, too, founded laboratories, first at the University of Pennsylvania and then at Columbia University where he spent the remaining years of his academic career. He actively continued research, but inevitably a large amount of his time as chairman was taken up with administering what soon became at Columbia University the largest graduate department of psychology in the United States, and which had in its department many other important psychologists.

It was two colleagues of Cattell at Columbia that showed experimentally the fallaciousness of the educational theory of formal discipline attributed to faculty psychologists. The theory of formal discipline held that memorizing material, irrespective of the material, strengthened memory in general. Cultivate any phase of memory and you have a better memory for everything. In a study of what came to be called transfer of training, Thorndike and Woodworth (1901) showed that transfer of improvement of memorizing ability depended mainly upon the degree of communality of the tasks. For

closely related activities, there was considerable transfer; for unrelated activities, none at all. Memorizing one kind of material did not aid in (transfer to) other kinds of material. Mental discipline did not work; memory for all kinds of material was not strengthened by practice with one kind of material.

Cattell was especially interested in studying the reasons for eminence in the sciences and edited many volumes of a series of biographical directories, *The American Men of Science,* which included all of the sciences. This, coupled with the editorship of the weekly journal, *Science* (which in 1900 became the official organ of the American Association for the Advancement of Science) and his vigorous defense of many causes, including psychology, made him the most prominent psychologist in the United States. His independence of spirit caused friction with the administration of Columbia University and, at the outbreak of World War I, because of his unpopular insistence on the rights of conscientious objectors, he was forced to resign. Despite his difficulty with Columbia, he continued to be a spokesperson for psychology and wielded considerable influence in the National Academy of Sciences to which he was the first psychologist elected. Youthful and vigorous to the end, in 1921 he organized the Psychological Corporation to promote the application of psychology. All of his activities gave to the beginnings of psychology in the United States much of its characteristic flavor.

The third and youngest major figure responsible for the beginnings of modern psychology in the United States was of a quite different stripe. This was Edward Bradford Titchener (1867–1927), an Englishman, and Wundt's most faithful pupil. He came to the United States in 1892 as Assistant Professor of Psychology and Director of the Laboratory at Cornell University. For the next few years, he was busy organizing the laboratory, buying and building equipment, carrying out the research, and writing articles. Gradually he attracted more and more students and so more of his time was spent in directing their activities and less time in the laboratory conducting research. During his lifetime, he directed fifty-eight doctoral dissertations as well as a host of minor studies.

Some of his time was spent in translating the

master but for many years he was frustrated in this endeavor because, before he could finish a translation, a new edition was published. Finally, he took no chances. He went to press, not with a translation of the entire book, but only of the first six chapters of the fifth edition of Wundt's *Principles*. The rest was never translated. Although Titchener wrote many books, by common consent, the most important are the four volumes which made up his *Experimental Psychology* (1901–1905). It was designed, not only for training, but also for drill and included two volumes as the student's manual and two volumes which were the instructor's manual. Another volume, *A Textbook of Psychology* (1910), is a more systematic statement of his views.

When most of Wundt's American students returned to the United States, they modified their views according to their particular temperament and made adaptation to the social setting in which they found themselves. Not so with Titchener. He gave to Wundt's psychology a systematic explicitness and expansion superior to that of his prolific master, but was faithful to it in all essential matters.

The *molecular* approach was carried by Titchener to its logical conclusion in one of his youthful efforts. Even though he did not take it too seriously even then, he calculated the number of sensory elements and found that the eye supplied somewhat less than 33,000, the ear, less than 12,000, and the rest of the senses, only about 18. In all, there were 45,018 conscious elements on which to build the mind.

He found it necessary to expand upon the Wundtian principles two attributes of quality and of intensity to include duration, clearness, and extensity (spread-outness). Taken together, these five classes were the attributes of the mind. All of these attributes became dimensions along which introspective reports were to be made. For example, "duration" may be long or short or medium.

It has already been stated that sensations were the elements of perception. But in his systematic overview, images became the elements of ideas and the affections the elements of the feelings and emotions. To summarize through the varying degrees of attention he paid to their investigation, Titchener stressed the study of sensation, mini-

mized the study of ideas, and placed the study of affections somewhere in between.

On the basis of introspective studies in the Cornell laboratory, Titchener did find it necessary to dissent from Wundt's tridimensional theory of affection. Tension-relaxation and excitement-depression turned out to be, in the introspective reports of his students, essentially muscular attitudes. This restored the traditional single dimension of pleasantness-unpleasantness to its position as the single dimension of affection or feeling.

Dictated by his unflaging dedication to molecularism, holding the elements of experience to its barest minimum, later work in his laboratory made him doubt that feeling was a class of conscious elements district from sensation. Under introspection, feelings turned out to be modes of pressure. Pleasantness was a bright pressure; unpleasantness was a dull pressure. He extended this concept so that affective experiences from every sense department were conceived as having an increment of bright or dull pressure. Feeling, too, had been reduced to sensation. It is not hard for one to infer that this way of regarding the matter seemed extravagant to his contemporaries, and his theory has been allowed to lapse into oblivion. It was one of the more unfortunate developments of an introspective approach that could be and was used as a basis of criticism of the use of introspection.

Titchener's system of psychology was faithful to that of Wundt in being *puristic* and *nomothetic*. The nearest approach he made to a utilitarian and ideographic study was one research excursion with psychological tests taken in his laboratory. The results were barren, confirming his opinion, and the matter was dropped. He did mention the study of the abnormal mind, but this was always in the context of *conscious mentalism,* except for a side comment that, when investigations of unconscious mental states had been tried, we leave the realm of facts for the sphere of fiction.

There was a fourth pioneer. The brilliantly inconsistent, provocative William James (1842–1910) refused to submit to neat summarization. He himself suggests what can be the appropriate analogy in one of the characteristics he attributes to consciousness. Experience, he said, in effect is a stream of consciousness which flows ever onward, not a mosaic of separate bits and pieces. Present are the more stable substantive states, the usual source of psychological study, but much neglected in our study of mental life are the vague, fleeting, unstable transitive states. "Like a bird's life, it seems to be made of an alternation of flights and perchings." (James, *Principles*, p. 158.) An intellectual hummingbird he was—here, there and everywhere, enriching, but never perching long enough in one place to be captured in a page or two. It is suggested that the reader join those many, many others who have read his, *The Principles of Psychology* (1890) for the fun of it.

The Decades of the Schools

The period dominated by the various schools of psychology extended from approximately 1910 to 1940. A school of psychology has been defined elsewhere (Watson, 1967) as adherence to a pattern of prescriptions by a group of psychologists, generally with an acknowledged leader. This formulation is expanded for this chapter to add that an important impetus to a school's origin came from the conviction of its pioneers that the prevailing dominant patterns of prescriptions was remiss in that it discouraged, neglected, or minimized certain significant prescriptions; and, that the nature of psychology would be set aright if the new prescriptive pattern being advanced by them was accepted instead. This expanded definition seems to apply to all schools except "structuralism" since Titchener and his supporters originally conceived of their approach as "psychology," and not as a school at all. This previously stated position became a "school" due to pressures from the newer opposing views. The other schools of psychology become more intelligible, if we first emphasize the dominant prescriptions that each school protested against. In this section, the historical background of the school in terms of individuals and events will be given and, lastly, some systematic views and methods that characterized the school in question will be summarized.

Both Wundt and Titchener had lived on into the era of schools which began around the second decade of the twentieth century, and they bore the brunt of criticism since their views of the nature of psychology was challenged by functionalists, behaviorists, and Gestalt psychologists. Titchener's views were the subject of criticism from the first two schools indigenous to the United States, while Wundt was more the target for the Gestalt psychologists whose concepts originated in Germany.

Structuralism

In his magnificent simplicity, Titchener saw his view of psychology *as* psychology, nothing more, nothing less. His complacency about the *status quo* of psychology, his psychology, was to receive a rude shock. Opposition came to the surface in the work of other psychologists not directly related to his tradition. In the United States, the pragmatic character of the prevailing climate of opinion did not accord with the Wundtian-Titchenerian denial of status to the application of psychology. Titchener's cavalier attitude toward contentually-objective work in animal behavior was galling to more than one student of behavior. To him, the study of animal behavior was a branch of biology and might be of some incidental interest provided its results were interpreted properly in inferred mentalistic, that is, contentually-subjective, terms.

Titchener's insistence that investigation of structure, psychic morphology as it were, took precedence over investigation of function did not accord with the interests of many American psychologists. They wanted to know how psychological life is related to the struggle to get ahead, to adapt to circumstances. In other words, they wanted to know more about the "how" and "why" of consciousness or its functions as contrasted to the stress that Titchener put on what mental life was like or its content. After the question was raised, grudgingly Titchener accepted structuralism as not too inept a term to describe his point of view. If others wished to attack his psychology, his structural emphasis seemed to him to be a position of strength. Titchener remained aloof, leaving to his faithful lieutenants the task of defense.

Many articles were written and whole books were devoted to the controversies among the schools. *The Psychologies of 1925,* and *The Psychologies of 1930* are titles of books characteristic of the period. Structuralism with its prescriptive allegiances and aversions was duly represented. But, structuralism was an idea whose time had passed. Why this was the case can be gleaned from the criticisms offered by the competing schools in the following discussion.

Functionalism

In a general, not too organized way, psychologists who expressed a functionalist view objected both to the primary position given to structure by Titchener and the others and to their insistence that psychology was a pure science. Functionalists agreed on the importance of the *functionalist* prescriptions, that psychological activities were more important than whatever structures carried them, and either a tolerance of or actual participation in *utilitarian* activities.

Antecedents of the functional view are not hard to find. The pragmatic climate of opinion in the United States has already been indicated. Although now discredited, the faculty psychology of the pre-experimental period was a contributory factor in that it had stressed functions, what the mind does, while phrenology of the same period was nothing more than a variety of faculty psychologies. Groundwork had also been laid for functionalism both by Brentano and his emphasis on acts as the basic psychological phenomena and by James and his insistence that mental life is expressed as a stream of conscious experiences. James had also argued that mind had survival value—if consciousness had no value, it would not have survived in the human species. James' position is an illustration of the most all pervasive intellectual influence that came from the assimilation into psychology of the implications of Darwinian evolutionary theory. Consider Darwin's contention that evolution is based on a struggle for survival in which those that make the most successful adaptations survive. Biological adaptation, translated into psychological terms, becomes psychological adaptation. In summary, how one functions psychologically, no matter the structure involved, becomes of paramount importance in psychologists' thinking.

The functionalists did not form a tidy, regimented group with mutually agreeable aspirations and goals. One is somewhat hard put to single out a particular person as the recognized leader. Because they wrote clear, expository articles and books advocating a functional psychology, one could say that James Rowland Angell (1868–1949) and Harvey A. Carr (1873–1954) can be so identified. Both of them were professors at the University of Chicago, a university which served as a central rallying point for the functionalists in the same manner that Cornell did for the structuralists. But even here the situation is not clear-cut. Another center for an even more vague advocacy of functionalism was at Columbia University, where, if one remembers the activities of James McKeen Cattell described earlier, one can see that they fell within the functionalist rubric.

One of the clearest statements was made in 1906 when Angell devoted his presidential address to "The Province of Functional Psychology" (Angell, 1907). He argued that functionalism is concerned with mental operations. The "how" and "why" of consciousness are contrasted to the "what" of structural psychology. Mind, moreover, mediates in relating the needs of the organism and the environment, a point inspired by the thinking of William James. Consciousness, he went on, helps to solve problems. The functional psychologist studies mental processes as a means of adjustment which in turn implies the mind-body relationship. In other words, functional psychology of his time was both *contentually-subjective* and *dualistic*. Its quarrel with structuralism was not over these attitudes but was directed against the static quality of the mind they saw as so evident in the work of Titchener and his followers.

As a school, functionalism was active before, during, and after the advent of behaviorism. Most early functionalists viewed psychology as *contentually subjective*. They thought in terms of mind and defended the adaptive nature of consciousness.

When faced with the full force of the behavioristic point of view, the functionalists found the transition quite easy, since the salient functionalist attitude could be preserved intact with adaptive functions of behavior the center of focus rather than those of the mind. Indeed, one of the Columbia functionalists, James McKeen Cattell, referred to psychology as the science of experience *and* behavior before John B. Watson wrote on the subject. It was Watson who was the psychologist most responsible for the rise of Behaviorism.

Behaviorism

John B. Watson (1879–1958) took his degree in psychology at the University of Chicago in 1903 with a dissertation on animal behavior, became professor at Johns Hopkins University in 1908, and was president of the American Psychological Association in 1915. In 1921, after a marital scandal, he left Johns Hopkins for a successful career in advertising.

It was in 1913 that Watson boldly offered a sweeping new definition of psychology. His manifesto was in an article that began with these striking sentences:

Psychology as the behaviorist views it is a purely objective experimental branch of natural science. Its theoretical goal is the prediction and control of behavior. Introspection forms no essential part of its methods, nor is the scientific value of its data dependent upon the readiness with which they lend themselves to interpretation in terms of consciousness (1913, p. 158).

Contentual objectivity for psychology was being demanded with banishment from psychological science of anything that smacked of *contentual subjectivity*. These ghosts and goblins of the mental life—the sensations, images, and affections of

the adaptive mind of Angell and Carr and the other functionalists—were to be thrust far into the outer darkness. Why? Because they could not be submitted to the rigors of *methodological objectivity*. They had no meaning for a scientist, no matter what private significance they might have for the individual experiencing them.

Many lines of already performed behavioral research could immediately be utilized in filling out the details of a behavioristic psychology. Provided one dismissed the introspective trappings as irrelevant excess baggage, the results of many human studies of reaction time, psychological testing, psychophysics, and learning were available. But Watson emphasized previous animal research. Watson already knew the pioneer work of Edward Lee Thorndike on learning in chicks and cats as well as other significant work on learning in animals done by several others in the United States and England. Above all, there was the work in Russia on so-called conditioning. A generation earlier than Watson's pronouncement, Ivan P. Pavlov (1849–1936), a Russian physiologist who won the Nobel Prize in Medicine in 1904, decided to spend the rest of his career (which spanned thirty-two years) in the investigation of conditioning, which he regarded not as psychological but as physiological in nature. The nature of conditioning will be illustrated a little later in a study Watson performed.

That the behaviorism of John B. Watson was *methodologically objective* is already evident. It is

Fig. 2-3.
Watson, Pavlov, Skinner

appropriate, however, to inquire—when using this attitude as the salient behavioristic attitude for psychology—just what methods are considered to meet this criteria. He explicitly states that he would have psychologists use observation with and without the aid of instruments, the conditioned response method, psychological testing, and the verbal-report method. This last merits special attention, because it will be found to express quite clearly his determination to be *contentually-objective,* and yet is the one on which he turned out to be most open to criticism. He argued that speech reactions are observable and open to the behaviorist, since they are similar in this respect to other motor reactions. Suppose the behaviorist is studying warm and cold responses when stimuli are applied to a given skin area of a subject. The subject is told to respond by the appropriate word when warm and cold cylinders are applied. He does so by saying "warm" and "cold." Watson argued that he had successfully by-passed the subjective dilemma. Sensation is not being investigated since we cannot observe the sensations of another person but we can observe that person's verbal report. The response is overt and is recorded as the result of the experiment.

Opponents were quick to point out that adherence to verbal report might be nothing more than mere verbal quibbling. They claimed that introspection, banished at the front door, was allowed to return by the back. This opportunity for criticism arose, because in his characteristically hasty way, his writings did not qualify his statements carefully enough.

The other methods he espoused did not excite as much opposition, in part because what is meant is seemingly more clear-cut, but also because they were already accepted, as in psychological testing, even by those who did not subscribe systematically to the behavioristic position.

Perhaps the central concept evident throughout all of Watson's writing is that of stimulus-response, terms which he had borrowed from the physiologists. Although he was not the first to use this manner of presentation of psychological theory and research, he used it in the services of a *contentual* and *methodological objectivism.*

Responses are ultimately reduced to two forms, motor and glandular. They may be overt and ob-servable or implicit and nonobservable. Responses are also categorized as either learned or unlearned.

It is the task of the psychologist to ultimately resolve matters psychological into its components; hence, Watson supported a *molecular* attitude. His emphasis upon describing psychological data in terms of relatively small units is noteworthy. Nowhere is this brought out more clearly than in his conception of personality. To Watson, personality was a straight-forward summation of the effect of stimuli and reactions upon the individual. It is the end product of an individual's habit systems which, in turn, are clusters of S-R units. A specific instance used by Watson to describe the personality of a particular individual was done by a list with the following order: shoemaking, (the man's trade), religious, patriotic, marital, parental, arithmetic, general information, special fear, personal, and recreational habit systems.

Somewhat more implicit in which has just been said about his view is that he was pledging himself to a strict *determinism.* Behavior, he argued, always involved a stimulus that brings about a particular response. It is not too great a simplification to say he used these terms where others before him had referred to cause and effect.

That research on the reflex used the terminology of S-R which made it possible for Watson to transpose the findings of the physiologists into aspects of behavioristic psychology. He simply disagreed with Pavlov who contended that study of conditioning was physiological in nature. Reflex study *is* psychological, not physiological, said Watson, since the response is behavioral. He did also insist that one must move on to investigate the reflex as it is involved in more complex reactions such as walking, talking, fighting, or eating. Watson would also leave the detailed analysis of the physiological substratum to the specialists in this area. Brain processes, as such, did not particularly interest him because of the sheer inaccessibility of the brain to behavioral study. He referred to it as the "mystery box" in a manner reminiscent of the current term, "black-box." This position brings out quite clearly Watson's adherence to a *peripheralistic* prescription—stress upon psychological events taking place at the periphery of the body, as contrasted to the *centralist* position which emphasizes psychological events within the body.

One of Watson's specific areas of research interest was emotional behavior of infants, and his most widely-known study was the search for the stimuli that produced objectively-observable emotional responses in infants (Watson, 1924, 1925). He found evidence for only three emotions: fear, rage, and love. Fear was produced only by the stimulus of a loud noise (striking a steel bar with a hammer) or loss of support (jerking the blanket). Objects traditionally assumed to produce fear—the dark, a snake, and the like—simply did not do so. Fear responses were described as catching the breath, followed by rapid breathing, changes in skin color, hand-clutching, puckering of the lips, and crying, and, if the child were old enough, crawling, walking, or running away. The only stimulus that Watson found to produce rage was hampering or restricting the infant's movements. The behavioral responses to rage were stiffening of the body, holding the breath, and slashing movements of the arms and legs. Love was found to be produced by stroking the skin, patting, and gentle rocking. Responses were smiling, cooing, and gurgling.

This study stimulated many others, including those offered in refutation. Generally speaking, confirmation of Watson's view was not forthcoming. The most telling blow was rendered by an ingenious study by Mandel Sherman (1927). He asked his observers to judge motion pictures of the emotions displayed by infants. In one of the phases of the study, observers viewed motion pictures, so spliced that the stimuli they saw and the emotional reaction of the infant that followed, were *not* related. To a considerable extent, they labeled the emotion, not in terms of the behavior of the infant, but by what they had been led to believe was the stimulating condition. That is, if they saw pictures of the infant being restrained followed by the emotional behavior, which was actually produced by a "fear" stimulus, they judged the emotion exhibited to be that of anger. The vaunted methodological objectivity of observation was not as valid as Watson had thought. Specific emotions had *not* been exhibited by young infants. Rather their generalized mass of random movements to any strong stimuli had been interpreted by Watson in line with expectations he had formed based on the nature of the stimulation.

As might be expected from his environmentalistic stance, Watson also studied conditioning in infants (Watson & Raynor, 1920). A study of an infant, "Albert," whose very name was to become a familiar part of the history of psychology, was the subject. Albert at that time was eleven months old and showed fear only to the expected loud sounds and loss of support. To almost everything else, including animals, such as the white rat, his response was to reach out, touch, and fondle. We now come to the experiment itself. When the rat was introduced, Albert reached toward it as expected, but just as he started to touch, an unseen steel bar was struck. In early trials of this combination, Albert jumped and after several stimulations, he jumped violently and whimpered. On the seventh day, the rat was presented *without* sound. Early in this day, Albert made no reaching movements, but later reached only to withdraw his hand as he touched the rat. On subsequent trials the same day, in which combined stimulation of rat and sound were given, the rat alone was introduced on the eighth trial. This time Albert turned and began to crawl rapidly away. Subsequent trials a few days later showed that the introduction of the rat alone produced whimpering, crying, and withdrawal. A conditioned fear response had been established, since a rat to which Albert had previously shown no fear, now brought forth fear. Other stimuli in the form of furry things such as a dog, a fur coat, or a rabbit, produced fear responses as well. To use Pavlov's terminology, the conditioned fear response had generalized. In Chapter 9 we will expand on Pavlov's concepts.

Directly as a result of his findings on emotion and learning in infants, Watson became very impressed with the pliability of human nature. He became an extreme *environmentalist*, perhaps never evidenced as strikingly as in the following quotation:

Give me a dozen healthy infants, well-formed, and my own specified world to bring them up in and I'll guarantee to take any one at random and train him to become any type of specialist I might select—doctor, lawyer, artist, merchantchief and, yes, even beggar-man and thief, regardless of his talents, penchants, tendencies, abilities, vocations, and race of his ancestor (1930, p. 104).

This quotation represents the final stage of his thinking on the matter. He had started as an avowed adherent to the theory of instincts and ended with a sweeping denial of their existence in humans.

In 1913, when he published the manifesto that opened this discussion, he had very little company in his behavioristic convictions. Before twenty years had elapsed, his view that psychology was a contentually-objective science was clearly predominant in the United States.

Gestalt Psychology

Gestalt psychology originated in Germany as a psychology of protest against the *molecularism* of the Wundtian tradition. Unlike the behaviorists in the United States, Gestalt psychologists did not question the existence and significance of consciousness. Rather, they doubted the reality of the contentually-subjective elements that other psychologists such as Wundt had used. The mistaken belief in *molecularism* which they wished to combat was referred to as the "bundle hypothesis." Sensory elements do not form a bundle, nor do associations serve to bind them together. Our field of vision is ordered and extended, forming a whole. We "see" unitary objects, a tree in a field with clouds above, not a bundle of sensations. The task of psychology is to explain these wholes by studying them and finding the properties of the whole, which was the psychological experience. Gestalt psychologists wished to revise psychology completely, not from the ground up but, as it were, from the figure down! A *molar* prescription that would be so all embracing as to make other aspects of psychology dependent upon it, and other prescriptions subsidiary to it, was their goal.

The experiment that Max Wertheimer (1880–1943) saw as founding Gestalt psychology, even before performing it, concerned the phi phenomenon (1912). What is phi phenomenon? It may be something of a letdown to be told that it was a new name for an already-known experience in vision—apparent movement when what is involved is actually an experience arising from a successive series of non-moving stimuli. A well-known commercial modification is so-called motion pictures; if a series of still photographs are flashed upon the screen at the appropriate speed, movement is attributed to the pictures. What Wertheimer and his assistants did was the following: Two lines were successively exposed for a given interval of time on two different places on the face of a tachistoscope. If there was too long a time between exposures, two lines that did not move would be seen separately and successively. If the time was too short, the subject would see the lines simultaneously. But, if the interval of time was optimal, the subject saw neither of these two experiences, but one line *moving* from one place to another. The experience, then, was one of a single line that visibly moved despite the physical fact that there were two stationary lines successively

Fig. 2-4.
Wertheimer, Koffka,
Köhler

exposed, separated by an interval of time. The perception did not correspond point-for-point with the physical stimulus.

It was not so much the experiment that was significant; it was the interpretation that Wertheimer offered that was to announce the call for a new systematic conception of psychology. A discontinuous visual stimulation yields the perception of continuous movement. Hence, the whole (the gestalt) is *not* just the sum total of the elements.

The traditional explanation of phi phenomena from the general theoretical *molecular* position is that each discrete stimulus gives rise to its own sensation and that on the basis of past experience, our perceptions of them are integrated. This explanation did not hold. Wundt, in dealing directly with apparent movement, interpreted it to be due to the kinesthetic sensations produced by the movement of the eyes. This, of course, required that the eyes move simultaneously in the same direction. Wertheimer neatly ruled out Wundt's explanation by arranging the experimental setting with suitable pairs of lines that required two simultaneous eye movements in *opposite* directions. The eyes could hardly move in both directions at the same time; therefore, Wundt's explanation was fallacious. In Wertheimer's opinion, the phenomena could only be explained by appeal to the principle of gestalt.

Gestalt psychology had a trio of leaders. Max Wertheimer was the oldest and indeed, in the first historic experiment on phi phenomenon, the other two were his subjects. They were not even aware of what Wertheimer conceived as the significance of the study until later. They were Wolfgang Köhler (1887–1967) and Kurt Koffka (1886–1941). They immediately set about working zealously in this newborn tradition.

Again there were antecedents. Most pervasive was a strong phenomenological trend in German psychological and philosophical work that dated back to the days of Goethe. The stress had been upon the study of immediate experience, not very different from the way experience as meditation had been interpreted by Descartes centuries before. It called for the faithful reporting in everyday global terms of the meaning of the situation, which stands in sharp contrast to molecular introspective analysis as promulgated by Wundt and the others.

Working in this molar tradition, Edgar Rubin (1886–1951), a Dane and a contemporary of Wertheimer, had emphasized the distinction between figure and ground—the object, and the generally more homogeneous environment in which the object is placed. Clear perception, he argued, formed the figure, the remainder gives the ground—the house against the sky, the word or picture on the white page, the recognized figure against the rest of the faces in the photograph, all have the relation of figure and ground. The Gestalt psychologist adopted this distinction, but considered that phenomenologists content with reporting the presence of some phenomena, did not go far enough. Gestalt psychologists would use phenomenology as a way step; a problem should be phenomenologically analyzed, and then one should proceed to experiment. In short, they advocated an experimental phenomenology.

An experiment by Köhler (1915) with hens brings out clearly what the Gestalt psychologists were trying to demonstrate. Hens were trained to take grains of food from a paper of a darker shade of gray and not from the adjoining lighter gray paper. If they pecked at a grain on the darker paper, they were allowed to eat it. If they pecked on a grain on the lighter paper, they were driven away. After several hundred trials, they learned to peck only at the grains on the darker paper. What had happened up to this point is essentially preliminary to the experiment itself. The darker gray paper of the learning trials was now accompanied by a sheet of still darker gray instead of the original, lighter sheet. Now, if the hens pecked on the original gray, they would have learned to respond to a specific shade of gray. They did not. Instead, they pecked at what was now the darker paper, despite the fact that the one to which they had learned was also present but was now the lighter of the two sheets. In other words, they were reacting to a total situation of Gestalt, a relation of lighter-darker, not to a specific element in the learning situation.

An even more well-known series of experiments by Köhler (1917) involved what is referred to as insight learning in chimpanzees, a major characteristic of which was that learning was a relatively sudden perceptual reconstruction of the field when the Gestalt was grasped. The chimpanzees were customarily fed within cages, and whatever experiments were conducted used this setting. One study involved placing sticks in the framework on the roof of the cage. The next morning, after being taken back to the cage, one of the chimpanzees found that there was a bunch of bananas outside of the cage. He was already familiar with using sticks to draw them in, but this time, there were no sticks in sight. He looked around, as Köhler put it somewhat anthropomorphically, as would a man seeking a tool, and after a few seconds his eyes went to where the sticks had been hidden the night before. He immediately climbed up to where they were hidden, brought one down, and drew in the bananas. Food outside the walls of the cage, too distant to be drawn in by hand, and sticks hidden in the rafters, came together into a Gestalt in which the parts now formed a whole. The chimpanzee had formed a Gestalt; he had so related the aspects of his situation to form a meaningful whole.

Gestalts are not only found within psychological processes; there are also patterned, organized Gestalts within the organism—physiological Gestalts. These Gestalts consist of the functioning of all aspects of the nervous system—afferent, central, efferent—as a unit. So, Gestalt psychologists did not neglect what went on within the organism. Their conception was a bold challenge to the prevailing conception that the nervous system was a neural hookup of isolated units that dominated much of previous physiological thinking.

It is apparent, then, that a *centralist* rather than a *peripheralist* prescription was held by these psychologists. A key Gestalt concept was *isomorphism*. Physiological Gestalts stand in a definite kind of relationship with psychological Gestalts in that psychological phenomena, and the brain processes underlying them, have a similar functional form.

As a psychology of protest, Köhler and Koffka were the more persuasive members of the trio while Wertheimer stood aloof from this phase of the struggle. Wertheimer, careful and meticulous researcher that he was, content that his scientific curiosity about some phenomena had been satisfied, would not bother to write up his results for publication. Consequently, he published relatively

little. He achieved a professorship at the University of Frankfurt in 1929, but Gestalt psychology had already received national recognition in Germany when Köhler had been appointed to a chair at the University of Berlin in 1921. Koffka had a long period of service at the University of Giessen. In 1927, he became a professor at Smith College where he remained until his death in 1941.

All three eventually came to the United States but took appointments at schools which either offered no or relatively little graduate work; therefore, they did not have the generations of students that would have resulted in a greater impact on the American scene. Others in the Gestalt tradition assumed leadership positions that resulted in some impress on the rest of psychology in the United States, especially in the psychology of perception.

Psychoanalysis

Throughout most of its history, psychoanalysis opposed many of the dominant attitudes characteristic of the rest of psychology. By presenting its opposing views, these other schools and scientific psychology in general are made to stand in sharper relief.

It is prophetic of the relative isolation of psychoanalysis from the rest of psychology to this very day that Sigmund Freud (1856–1939), the founder of psychoanalysis, spent most of his life in private practice in Vienna, and that even as late as the turn of the century, had few followers. It was during these early years that the basic outline of what ultimately was his mature position was established. Moreover, his theories, his approach to psychotherapy, and his method of research arose from interaction with his emotionally-disturbed patients and not from the laboratory or from the psychology that has been our present concern. To put it bluntly, he saw academic psychology as irrelevant. What he found in opposition were the prescriptive allegiances of other physicians, particularly psychiatrists, who held views comparable to, but not identical with, those previously considered by psychologists. Some of the major attitudes in medical settings that he opposed may be briefly identified. Their *staticism,* as expressed, for example, in preoccupation with diagnostic classification, their

Fig. 2-5.
Freud, Adler, Jung

rationalism (in the sense that it can be seen as polar to an irrationalism), and above all, their preoccupation with *conscious mentalism* ran counter to his experience with patients.

The isolation of psychoanalysis from the other schools is epitomized by its unique prescriptive allegiances. The strong, positive attitude toward *idiographicism* arising from interest in the individual patient was either absent or minimized in the other schools of psychology. Moreover, Freud was absorbed with *irrationalism,* since the patients were neurotic and psychotic, with *unconscious mentalism* especially when combined with *dynamicism* in unconscious motivation, and even with *developmentalism*. These also were relatively neglected among the other schools.

Freud gave a unique emphasis to those views which he shared with other psychiatrists and psychologists, for example, *determinism,* to which his allegiance was unswerving. Early in his career, at first without his urging, patients began to bring him accounts of their dreams. At first glance, it would appear that nothing could be more trivial. However, he had been trained in a strict deterministic tradition during his medical school days, despite the fact that his teachers thought of it primarily in terms of physical symptoms. Would not this credo apply to psychological phenomena,

even to dreams? Instead of seeing dreams as *curiosa,* serving no more than to illustrate a bizarre side of human nature, he reasoned that dreams must have some symptomatic causal significance. What, then, do they mean? At first he was only sure that somehow they represented, in a disguised fashion, wishes and feelings that the patient did not want to acknowledge consciously.

His patients were unaware of the significance of the symbols of their dreams until interpreted by Freud. They did not know what the dreams meant, and yet the dreams did have a meaning. There was the dream taken at its face value, its manifest content as understood by the patient, and the meaning behind the dream, its latent content inferred by Freud. Patently, the patients were not consciously aware of the significance of their dreams, and yet the problems they symbolized were both important and pervasive. The influence on mental life, of unconscious factors, *unconscious mentalism*—a prescription that hereafter was to be accepted with no doubt of its validity—was being manifested. Other forms of unconscious mentalism were identified. Patients showed an inability to accept interpretations of the significance of their dreams when they were faced with them. They struggled against accepting what, to Freud at least, seemed overwhelmingly clear; they stubbornly refused to see the "truth"; they became evasive and broke appointments. In other words, "resistance," as it came to be called, was exhibited. But they were not consciously aware that this was what they were doing—so again the influence of *determined unconscious mentalism* was being demonstrated.

Another significant finding began to emerge from what his patients told him. With what at first was to him an astonishing regularity, the traumas experienced by his patients in the past concerned sexual matters. Time and again, he found very upsetting childhood sexual experiences had occurred that were only very reluctantly revealed. A few years later he was to discover that many of these experiences never happened—instead they were sexual fantasies. Instead of letting this deter him in his exploration of the sexual roots of behavior of which he had become increasingly convinced, he faced the fact that they were fantasies. But why *sexual* fantasies? Why not some other form of fantasy? Fantasies or not, they did have a sexual basis. He concluded that the sexual instinct had ramifications in all areas of human experience.

There was a scattering of antecedents in earlier work but none of these grasped the crucial point that Freud had discovered—the importance in psychological life of unconscious motivation.

In his first writings, Freud referred to the phenomena under discussion as reflecting the influence of the unconscious as distinguished from the conscious mental life, which, to use an analogy he borrowed from Fechner, was but the tip of the iceberg with a great bulk of mental life beneath the surface. For the sake of greater precision in theory and therapy, and to make it more obvious that unconscious mental life was dynamic for the individual, he supplemented this view with a more detailed topographical theory.

The libido is the basic instinctual force of personality as well as the source of organization of personality structure. The id, the energy source, present at birth and fixed in the constitution, is the oldest of the personality structures. The libido's expression in the id is through tension-reduction. It obeys the pleasure principle, seeking pleasure and avoiding pain without any other considerations of decorum, morals, or modesty. The id is unconscious and never has a direct relation with the external world. The ego, the second personality mechanism, has the characteristic of being conscious. The id is known only through intrusions into the consciousness of the ego. Since in sleep (and during free association) the ego is at least partially relaxed, dreams are a means of mirroring in an indirect, distorted fashion, these id tendencies.

In contradistinction to the id, which is guided by the pleasure principle, the ego follows a so-called reality principle, that is, it takes into account the external world and its reality. The energies of the id press for satisfaction, and the ego modifies and channels them in keeping with the requirements of reality.

Since all libido was originally the id, it follows that the ego arises from the id's modification. In its constructive functions, the ego performs intellectual activities, considers alternatives, adapts, learns, remembers, and avoids. As a relative approximation, the ego represents "reason" while the id signifies the "untamed passions." In other words, the ego serves as an executive.

Despite what has just been said about the ego and consciousness, a portion of the ego is unconscious. This unconscious aspect results from repression. Material, once conscious, but unacceptable to the ego, is pushed back into the unconscious. Repression, then, is a means of the ego defending itself against unwelcome impulses. But this, of course, requires an expenditure of effort, and a continual effort at that, since id impulses continue to try to break through.

There are a considerable variety of other social-ego defense mechanisms in addition to repression. Just as in repression, they have the characteristics of demanding the expenditure of libido. For example, projection or the attributing of unwelcome impulses to others rather than to one's own personality dynamics, is one of the other ways the ego defends itself.

An important ego function that does not require the continual expenditure of energy is sublimation. Sublimations are socially-approved ways of discharging libido without anxiety. For example, oral pleasures may be sublimated by pleasure in speaking. A child experiencing this, may pursue a career as a politician or a professor. Many forms of sublimation, however, do not have such an obvious relation as that apparent in this illustration. In fact, they take on a whole host of socially-approved forms with areas of manifestations in respect for law, in social progress, and in friendly social relationships with others. Sublimation brings about a cessation of impulses without serving the continued defensive function of the other personality mechanisms.

The super-ego is the third of the personality structures arising from the libido and corresponds in some of its functions to the "conscience." It deals with the ego in a manner that might be compared to the situation obtained when a strict father admonishes his child. The tension this engenders in the child is guilt. It serves a special function of representing imperative demands for restriction and rejection. Sometimes, the ego and super-ego are in conflict; here, problems of adjustment arise. But in other situations they may function harmoniously and the pressure that the super-ego serves upon the ego may be relaxed. Speaking generally, the super-ego serves to control sexual and aggressive impulses that would otherwise endanger social stability.

Freud's original notion about there being stages of psychosexual development was initiated by the observation of infantile sexual strivings. Infants manifest sexuality in different ways than do adults. There must be, then, developmental differences between infants and adults. When examined more closely, Freud and his associates came to conceptualize a progressive series of areas of libidinal localization based on the manner that libidinal pleasure was found. First, there is the oral period, extending roughly through the first two years of life, where sucking and swallowing and later, biting, were the ways in which pleasure was found. This is followed by the anal stage, somewhat overlapping the previous one, but extending into the third year, in which first expelling and later retaining feces were the modes of pleasure-finding. The phallic period extends from ages three to five and centers on absorption in touching, looking at, and exhibiting the genitals. No new areas of libidinal localization were found between ages five to ten, so this was referred to as the latency stage since, while all previous modes of pleasure finding were exercised, there was a general drop in sexual inter-

ests. The genital period that followed was divided into a prepubertal phase at roughly 10 to 12 years of age in which there was revival of infantile modes of pleasure finding; and the pubertal or heterosexual-genital phase from about 12 to 14, in which the beginnings of adult modes of pleasure finding are attained.

The structural organization of personality in terms of the interrelation of id, ego, superego and environment were related to these stages. In the early oral phase, while id is present at birth, the ego, essentially passive in this period, emerges gradually into awareness. The ego of the infant is strengthened by mastery of walking and the beginnings of judgment during the oral period. Other developments follow, but considerations of space here demand mentioning but one other. Further reorganization of the various structures of personality into the adult form is attributed in large measure to the years of the prepubertal phases. In a sense, then, psychoanalysis claims that adult personality is hardly more than a footnote to childhood. The sophistication of the adult and the partial putting away of childish things takes place later, but the personality structures in large measure were set for all time by the experiences of childhood. Hence, personality, unlike the views taken in many other contemporary personality theories, is seen as more structured, less pliable, and less fluid.

Certain prescriptive attitudes are clearly being positively stressed in this, the mature formulation of psychoanalytic theory. There was soon emphasis on enduring aspects of personality (*statiticism*) but change, and factors making for change (*dynamicism*) was being emphasized even more. Moreover, *developmentalism,* the stressing of changes over the early life span, was being given prime importance. Along with his already discussed positive allegiance to *idiographicism, irrationalism, determinism,* and *unconscious mentalism,* these attitudes may be said to characterize Freudian psychoanalysis.

About the turn of the century, when Freud was in his mid-forties, and most of his greatest original contributions had been made, a new phase of his life began. That necessary ingredient for a school to emerge, attraction of adherents who shared his views, started when some young and relatively obscure individuals persuaded him to lead discussion groups of what he had recently begun to call "psychoanalysis." In 1907, a very different disciple came to visit him, Carl Gustav Jung (1875–1961), already a promising and potentially very important psychiatrist from Zurich. During the next five years, they were closely associated, even to the point of traveling together to the United States where both had been invited by G. Stanley Hall to address a convocation that was to celebrate the twentieth anniversary of Clark University. This trip was the first international recognition of psychoanalysis and did much to bring it to the attention of American academic psychologists, mainly because the papers they gave were published in American psychological journals.

Both organizations and specialized journals are means whereby a school is promulgated and other adherents attracted. These came in the first two decades of the century. Meanwhile, Jung, whom Freud had come to regard as his heir-apparent, had been developing in a gradual, not too readily discernible fashion an independent point of view concerning the nature of personality, psychotherapy, and general psychology. After premonitory clashes, the definitive final break came in 1914 when Jung resigned from the presidency of the newly formed International Association of Psychoanalysis. Jung had developed the position that libido referred to a general, not a sexual, tension. Freud saw this as bowing to popular opinion by minimizing the importance of sex; Jung saw this changed view as forced upon him by his investigations. Continued collaboration ceased.

Local organizations already present in Vienna and in a few other European cities began to be formed, not only on the continent but also in England and in the United States. Other psychoanalytically-oriented journals joined the pioneer ones established by Freud in Vienna. By the 1930s, Freud was a universally-recognized figure. In his last years, he was forced by the Nazi invasion to flee Vienna to London, where he died in 1939.

A tabular summary (see Table 2-1) of the contentual prescriptive allegiances of each school with the most salient listed first, will serve as a summarization. Not tabulated are either methodological differences of opinion (for example, the *idiographicism* of psychoanalysis and the *nomotheticism* of the other schools), or the methodological prescriptions against which they worked.

Striving for Integration in the Recent Past

The decades of the schools came to a close at about the end of the 1930s. From the 1940s on, there is a period marked by a striving for an integration of psychology into a coherent, unified science.

The views of Kuhn (1970), concerned with this

Table 2-1. Positive Contentual Prescriptive Attitudes in the Schools of Psychology

Structuralism	Functionalism	Behaviorism	Gestalt	Psychoanalysis
Structuralism	Functionalism	Contentual Objectivism	Psychology	Dynamicism
Contentual Subjectivism	Utilitarianism and Purism	Molecularism	Molarism	Unconscious Mentalism
Conscious Mentalism	Conscious Mentalism	Peripheralism	Contentual Subjectivism	Irrationalism
Molecularism	Contentual Subjectivism	Environmentalism	Centralism	Developmentalism
Purism				Contentual Subjectivism
Centralism				Centralism

problem of a comprehensive theoretical structure for the sciences, have received much attention recently and are described in the first chapter. A mature science is one that has a universally accepted *contentual model,* or *paradigm,* that serves to guide the activities of the science's practitioners at a given historical point in time. A paradigm gives scientists from a particular field a common core of agreement about contentual foundations, and thus defines the science. This agreement about content means that one can recognize a particular paradigm as applying to a particular science, be it chemistry, physics, or biology. Kuhn examines the history of the succession of paradigms that prevailed in particular sciences; in astronomy, the Ptolemaic (earth-centered) paradigm gave way to the Copernican (sun-centered) paradigm; in physics, the Aristotelian paradigm of "forces" gave way to the Newtonian view of absolute time and space; and, in turn, replaced by the paradigm of relativism with which the names of Einstein and Bohr are associated. Many of Kuhn's historical examples are devoted to accounts of events that occur when a new paradigm is emerging—what he calls a scientific revolution.

In this chapter, it is contended that psychology lacks an all-embracing, mutually acceptable contentual model or paradigm. Instead, psychology appears to be what Kuhn referred to as a preparadigmatic science, a state of affairs that prevailed in all science before they achieved guidance of their first generally accepted paradigm. The other possibility for psychology, that it is a multiparadigmatic discipline was pointed out in Chapter 1 but runs counter to the definition of a paradigm as a "universally accepted" model.

General, but nevertheless, convincing evidence of this lack of a generally accepted agreed-upon contentual model in psychology can be stated in a few sentences. Its history, as sketched herein up through the time of the schools, shows that patently it did not yet have this agreement about a model. If the recent past, after the period of the schools should be singled out as showing we now have arrived at a paradigm, there are two major arguments. There are still national differences among psychologists about the contentual problems on which they concentrate amounting to sev-eral national provincialisms that make it meaningful to speak of German psychology, Soviet psychology, and American psychology. Moreover, within a national framework, such as the United States, irreconcilable disagreements about what are acknowledged to be fundamental issues of content of psychology are not uncommon, of which the remnants of the schools' influences is an illustration. So, despite the certainty that some psychologists have about the overwhelming importance of their particular contentual view as proper to psychology as a whole, whether they call it a paradigm or not, it is not convincing in the face of this situation. This lack of a contentual paradigm in this particular Kuhnian sense means that psychologists have to continue to rely on their prescriptive attitudes to lead them to congenial research and theory.

It would seem that psychology is still a prescriptive science. Psychology is striving for, but has yet to find, the degree of contentual integration characteristic of the older, more mature sciences. A step in the direction of this integration, and perhaps the emergence of its first as yet unacknowledged paradigm, can be found in the gradual resolution (but not disappearance) of the schools. An examination of the contemporary status of the schools seems appropriate.

Structuralism as a school was fading away even before the 1940s. *Contentual subjectivity,* as the sole subject matter for psychology, was no longer a tenable proposition. Although the period of the schools showed a decline in allegiance to *contentual subjectivism,* more recent developments have shown a very marked resurgence of that which John B. Watson would have driven from the temple. Today, B. F. Skinner recognizes and accepts a "return to introspection" as a legitimate task in psychology. There are many lines of evidence that *contentual subjectivity* is considered a legitimate concern by at least some contemporary psychologists. There is the current intertwined interest in research and theory concerning "cognitive structure," certain approaches to perception, and continued utilization of Gestalt experimental phenomenology. In psychoanalysis, the study of conscious experience never lost its legitimate status, since their protest did not call for its elimination but what they considered to be an overemphasis on the conscious process at the expense of unconscious processes. There is even one segment of the psychological field that boldly insists on the primacy of consciousness to one's very existence as a psychological being. This is the so-called existential approach, which seems to have gained an increasing number of adherents in recent years.

The apparent paradox that structuralism has disappeared as a school and the argument that recently there has been increased interest in *contentual subjectivism* is easily resolved. Different methodologies are involved. The experimental phenomonology of the Gestalt psychologists, directed originally against Wundtian introspection, demonstrates this. The historical roots of these new developments are to be found not in structuralism, but in other sources, particularly phenomenology and existentialism which continues something similar to meditation (for which introspection was substituted by the structuralists).

The *contentually subjective* dominant aspect of functionalism quietly disappeared in the face of the dominance that behavioral aspects assumed in psychology. But the interest in function, salient to the school, did not disappear. Rather, functionalism was absorbed into general psychology so that, in this sense at least, practically all psychologists are functional in outlook even though they do not place upon it the label of a school. A rereading of the discussion of "functional relationship" in Chapter 1 will supply more background.

Gestalt psychology still serves as a healthy influence by reminding contemporary psychology of the necessity for considering molar as well as molecular aspects. Moreover, there has come the sobering realization that Gestalt psychologists never objected to analysis as such, and hence, considered molecular inquiries legitimate (although in the height of the emotionalism engendered during the decades of the schools, this was considered the major charge to be brought against them).

Today, psychoanalysis is the school least integrated into the general field of psychology and, therefore, requires a more detailed analysis. That most contributors to psychoanalysis are physicians with idiographic preoccupations, not psychologists, goes far to explain this lack of integration.

At the present time, there are hopeful signs of rapproachment. Some psychoanalytically-oriented psychologists have contributed to integration by helping to broaden the theoretical scope of the ego, epitomized by the expression "ego autonomy" which refers to the ego as being able to function in some measure independent of the id. In classical psychoanalysis, it was explained that the id was the *only* source of psychological energy. According to the newer position, the ego is now conceived as having its own energy source. This is, metaphorically speaking, the opening door that makes assimilation of nonpsychoanalytic psychological theory and research into psychoanalysis possible. There also has been a broadened appreciation on the part of most psychoanalysts of man's social relations as being in some measure freed from the effect of the so-called instincts, a now discredited concept among their ranks. Or, to say it in more positive fashion, they have recognized, as Freud did not, the crucial importance of social factors in shaping psychological events.

The continued influence of behaviorism on contemporary psychology is the most profound of all. Behavioral psychology, epitomized by the work of B. F. Skinner, has been reserved for discussion at this point because modern behaviorism still partakes most of all of the characteristics of the school outlines at the beginning of the section devoted to that topic. However, it is not a generally accepted contentual paradigm even though enthusiasts may consider it as heralding psychology's coming paradigm.

There has also been a gradual recognition that the extreme environmentalist position taken by Watson does not express something salient about behavioristic theory. To accept *environmentalism* as characteristic of behaviorism is to confuse his particular prescriptive allegiances with tenets essential to his theoretical position. His environmentalistic stance was not salient to behavioristic theory in that one can still be *contentually objective* as a modern behaviorist, and still hold to even a strong hereditarian emphasis.

During the decades of the schools and even more so now, many psychologists went about their psychological activities, perhaps a bit stimulated, but certainly neither hindered or directed by what was going on among the schools. Their major interests were the research that they were conducting in which they subscribed to the methodological prescriptions common to the sciences, but did not see contentual obligations as requiring systematic affiliation with the particular school or even with an overall integrating view of psychology as a whole. It may even be that contemporary psychologists have learned the lesson that absorption in the systematic details of specific research problems is a necessary preliminary step to later integration. In the long run, integration may be fostered by not striving too hard for it.

Psychology may lack a universally agreed-upon contentual paradigm, but it does share, in the unifying effect, a common adherence to the methodological prescriptions characteristic of all sciences.

The foundations of psychology are its scientific foundations, calling for an adherence to a *puristic* attitude. But, a word at least must be said about the increased contemporary respect for a *utilitarian* attitude. Many factors contributed to the development of the professional applications of psychology, not the least of which has been the widened and deepened relationship of psychologists to society outside of the academic world during the last fifty years. Indicative of what happened was the extensive demand by society for psychological services that occurred as an aftermath of World War II. Work in the military services served to broaden the outlook of the psychologists who participated. Characteristically, they had little professional experience before their participation; they came out of the conflict with an increased respect for the utilitarian attitude or even turned to professional activities themselves. In the post-war years, there occurred increased public pressure for psychological services, not only from within government agencies, such as the Veterans Administration, but also from the private sector, particularly in the health professions, and in business and industry. Moreover, governmental and private funding agencies, sensitive to the increased popularity of psychology, proved eager to support psychological research. Here again a problem-oriented eclecticism rather than school affiliation seemed natural and right.

But a potent source of conflict within psycho-

logical ranks was in the making. The *nomothetic* attitude, that science is a search for general laws, has given way to the work of many professional psychologists, especially clinical psychologists, and displaced by adherence to the *idiographic* attitude, a concern with explaining particular events and individuals. While these two attitudes are by no means irreconcilable, many psychologists behave as if they were. This clash of attitudes serves all too effectively, to delay the integration of psychology.

One of the fascinations of history is that it is a story that never ends. The student of psychology can guess, but cannot be even reasonably certain of what is to happen next. Your reading of the current foundations of psychology as a science, as expressed in the chapters that follow, will suggest some aspects of what your first answers will be and help you to conclude whether or not its foundations are sufficiently agreed upon to make it an integrated science.

Summary

The science of modern psychology, founded about one hundred years ago, has gone through three major shifts of its contentual nature. In the last half of the nineteenth century, it was founded by Wilhelm Wundt as the science of consciousness with introspection as its major method and the structural elements of mind its major goal. He also founded the first laboratory and a journal which meant that, instead of the solitary scholar of the past, there was a chance for training of a relatively large number of the next generation. Voices in opposition to his were raised, for example, that of Franz Brentano who insisted that psychology was concerned primarily with actions rather than with the structural elements that Wundt had favored.

When modern psychology reached the United States in the last decades of the nineteenth and first decades of the twentieth centuries, it was either structural and molecular (as it was in the thinking of Titchener) or, a little later, functional in the sense that some psychologists saw how the mind functions as the crucial issue, not its structure.

The second phase began in the United States in

the second decade of this century, with John B. Watson's proclamation and defense of psychology as contentually objective in that its goal was the study of behavior. In the following twenty years, behaviorism came to be accepted by many, if not most, psychologists.

In reality psychology as the science of experience never completely disappeared, although the structural school of Wundt and Titchener and its introspection as the method of choice did. Gestalt psychology used phenomenology as a means of preparation for experiment. It had been founded in Germany, but its major representatives came to the United States in the 1930s. It protested against the molecularism of both structural and functional psychology, and insisted that molar, rather than molecular properties were more significant to the content of psychology.

Psychoanalysis also was contentually subjective. It arose from the psychotherapeutic work of Sigmund Freud in Vienna, who departed from the characteristic search for general law (nomothesis) to devote concern to the individual (idiographicism).

Meanwhile, many psychologists are less concerned with affiliation with the tenets of any one of the schools than they are with their own research, particularly that in learning and physiological psychology.

In the recent past, there has been some evidence of an integration to the field but, nevertheless, contentual subjectivism expressed in terms of concern with experience, while not dominant over contentual objectivism, is still counterdominant. Psychology is the science of both behavior and experience.

Glossary

Conscious mentalism: An attitude emphasizing awareness of mental structure or activity in contrast to unawareness in unconscious mentalism.

Contentual objectivism: An attitude in which psychological problems are viewed as behavior of individuals in contrast to contentual subjectivism in which they are viewed as mental structure or activity.

Contentual subjectivism: See *contentual objectivism.*

Determinism: An attitude in which human events are seen as completely explicable in terms of antecedents as contrasted with indeterminism which views these events as not so completely explicable.

Developmentalism: See *staticism.*

Dynamicism: See *staticism.*

Ego: In psychoanalytic theory, that aspect of personality that gives awareness of self and carries out executive functions. While in the main conscious, it includes unconscious aspects which have been repressed.

Empiricism: An attitude in which the major, if not exclusive, source of knowledge is believed to be experience as contrasted with rationalism wherein the source is conceived to be reason.

Functionalism: An attitude in which psychological categories are viewed primarily as activities as contrasted with structuralism where they are seen as contents.

Id: In psychoanalytic theory, that aspect of personality that serves as the reservoir of psychic energy, and having the characteristics of being unconscious, innate, and desiring pleasure, regardless of consequence.

Idiographicism: See *nomotheticism.*

Indeterminism: See *determinism.*

Libido: In psychoanalytic theory, the source from which the dynamic manifestation of sexuality arises.

Methodological objectivism: An attitude that calls for use of methods open to verification by other competent observers as contrasted to methodological subjectivism which involves methods not open to verification.

Methodological subjectivism: See *methodological objectivism.*

Molarism: See *molecularism.*

Molecularism: An attitude in which psychological data are described in terms of relatively small units as contrasted to molarism where there is a preference for relatively larger or global units.

Naturalism: An attitude in which nature is seen as requiring for its operation and explanation only principles that are to be found within it, as contrasted with supernaturalism which calls for there to be transcendent guidance as well.

Nomotheticism: An attitude with emphasis on discovering general principles or laws as contrasted with idiographicism which stresses explanations of particular events or individuals.

Paradigm: An agreement about the content of a science

by its practitioners. Other meanings are also prevalent.

Prescription: The general term for the attitudes which
serves to direct psychologists in their views on the
contents and methods of their science, maintained
over large periods of time, although changing in manifestations at different historical periods.

Purism: An attitude that stresses seeking of knowledge
for its own sake as contrasted with utilitarianism
which stresses seeking of knowledge for its usefulness
in other activities.

Qualitativism: See quantitativism.

Quantitativism: An attitude that places stress on knowledge which is countable or measurable as contrasted
with qualitativism which stresses knowledge different
in kind or essence.

Rationalism: See *empiricism.*

Staticism: An attitude that places emphasis on a cross-
sectional view or on enduring aspects of psychological matters as contrasted with developmentalism
with an emphasis on changes with time or dynamicism which emphasizes changes and factors bringing
about change.

Structuralism: See *functionalism.*

Super-ego: In psychoanalytic theory, that aspect of the
personality which serves the function of the conscience and sometimes brings pressure on the ego; at
other times, is in harmony with the ego.

Supernaturalism: See *naturalism.*

Unconscious mentalism: See *conscious mentalism.*

Utilitarianism: See *purism.*

Suggested Readings

Marx, M. H., and Hillix, W. A. *Systems and Theories of Psychology.* 2nd ed. New York: McGraw-Hill, 1973.

Watson, R. I. "Psychology: A Prescriptive Science." *American Psychologist 11* (1967), 435–443.

Watson, R. I. *The Great Psychologists.* 4th ed. Philadelphia: Lippincott, 1978.

Statistics, Measurement, and Psychophysics

Robert M. Thorndike and William A. Yost

Introduction

People learn about their world by using information received through their senses. For centuries, people have accumulated information by observing the world around them and, in an activity that is largely peculiar to humans, have attempted to explain and understand the things which are observed. Every science that we now study is the result of a long period of observation and attempts to explain those observations.

The history of a science follows a predictable pattern. First, there is a period during which observations are made, recorded, and collected. Characteristically, two people looking at the same event or object will not see it in exactly the same way. If we may assume that the object or event is really the same for all who might observe it, then variation in reports by different people of what they have observed will hinder attempts to understand the object or event. (If you wish to prove for yourself that there is variation among people in their quantitative reports of the same thing, ask ten friends independently to guess your height.)

After a number of observations have been collected, someone will try to bring them together to arrive at an explanation or description of the class of events or objects which has been observed. It is usually at about this point that ideas of amount emerge. We see that different objects are different, because they possess varying amounts of some characteristic and that a single object possesses a (relatively) constant amount of that characteristic. Thus, the second stage in the historical development of a science is the invention of procedures for quantifying observations. In fact, we might say that until quantification of observations is possible, an area of study has not reached the point where it may be called a science.

Procedures for specifying the amount of something are extremely useful for a variety of reasons. One of these is that communication is much more accurate and efficient. Imagine trying to follow a recipe that called for "a moderate amount of flour, a smidgeon of butter, a little salt, and a fair amount of water." The result would probably not taste very good and might glue your mouth shut! We would also pity the poor carpenter who tried to build a house and had to cut and try each board. What is missing in both of these situations is a means of communicating how much of a thing is desired.

A second valuable result of obtaining information in a quantitative form is that it permits the use of mathematics in describing and interpreting the results of observations. Without quantification, none of our modern technological developments

The sections on statistics and measurement were contributed by R. M. Thorndike. The section on psychophysics was contributed jointly by Dr. Thorndike and Dr. Yost.

(which we now enjoy) would be possible. These practical benefits are a direct result of scientific inquiry which has made it possible to formulate precise mathematical predictions on the basis of quantified observations. When a science has reached a high level of development, it becomes possible to specify functional equations that permit accurate predictions about what will happen if certain conditions exist. Functional equations enabled the United States space program to land a man on the moon on the first attempt, because it was possible to predict exactly what forces would be acting on the spacecraft and what forces would be needed to counteract them.

Psychology, for the most part, has not developed to the point where it is able to make precise predictions about the objects and events which are its concern. However, methods for quantifying observations are a vital part of the development of psychology to its present level as a science and will play an increasingly important role in its future. In this chapter, we will discuss the ways in which numbers can be applied to observations, some of the techniques and terms which psychologists use to summarize their quantified observations, and two of the fields of inquiry in which quantitative methods are most directly applied.

Preliminary Measurement Issues

The word "data" refers to a set of observations, generally in quantitative form. These observations may be obtained in a variety of ways: for example, from tests such as those given to psychology students to determine how well they have understood a chapter on statistics, from census questionnaires sent out every ten years by the government, or from observation such as watching a rat run through a maze. These bits of information or data exist as numbers (items correct, number of children in the family, time taken to run the maze, and so on). The way that the numbers are obtained and the observations that they represent determine the meaning that they have, and meaning affects what can be done with the numbers as well as what can be concluded from them.

If numbers come from counting the number of

times an event occurred without reflecting differences in the amount of the event, they may have relatively little meaning. On the other hand, numbers such as those resulting from the measurement of length may contain a great deal of meaning and may be useful for a variety of purposes. For example, the numbers that physicists are able to obtain for the forces acting on a rocket have enabled us to put a man on the moon.

Scales of Measurement

Measurement is the act of assigning numbers to objects or events by comparison with a standard developed according to a set of rules. The rules for assignment of particular numbers constitute a *scale*. Thus, if we wish to measure the length of a board, we must assign some number to the board which characterizes its length. We get the number we need by comparing the board to some standard (a ruler) and reading off the number for the board. This is a nice, simple procedure because we have a well defined standard, and there will be high agreement about the number that describes the board's length among people who measure it. Or will there? Suppose one person measures the board in feet and inches and another uses the metric system. Each will use a different number to characterize the length of the board. There must be agreement as to the scale to be used. The problem is even more difficult when there is disagreement about the thing being measured, as there often is in psychology. For example, psychologists attempt to measure a characteristic of people that is called "intelligence," but there is disagreement among psychologists about what this characteristic is.

People who concern themselves with problems of measurement in science have identified several different types or classes of scales, depending on the amount of quantitative information that the numbers possess. Generally, four different types or levels of scaling can be identified (Stevens, 1951, 1968; Meyer, 1976).

Nominal scales use numbers to categorize objects or events or to name them. We may wish to use the number 1 to indicate that a person is male and 2 to indicate female. When numbers are used in this way, they contain no quantitative information at all but merely reflect group membership. (Some people argue that this use of numbers does not constitute measurement, but it does satisfy our definition.)

It is important to note that the numbers resulting from nominal measurement contain very little information. They may be used for counting purposes, but little else. [Consider, for example, how meaningless it would be to say that the average sex in a class is 1.38. In fact, ordinary arithmetic operations such as addition and division (which we used to find an average) make no sense with data that are nominal. The numbers do not indicate or represent ''amount'' of anything.]

The next level of scale is called an *ordinal scale*, because the numbers resulting from measurement can be used to order objects or events on the amount they possess of the thing being measured. The members of a class could be asked to stand in a line according to their height, and we could assign the number 1 to the shortest person, 2 to the next shortest, and so on up to the tallest. The person assigned the number 7 according to our rule is taller than the person who was given 6, but we do not know how much taller. Ordinal measurement, which often takes the form of ranks, permits comparison of individual observations but still gives relatively little information about amount, because the units along the scale are not known. For example, the difference in height between the shortest person in a class and the second shortest person might be 2 inches, while the difference between Person 6 and Person 7 might be ½ inch. In terms of an ordinal scale, both differences are called 1 unit, but the size of the unit changes from one place on the scale to another. Many measurements in psychology, such as tests of anxiety and other personality characteristics, are measured on ordinal scales.

In going from a nominal to an ordinal scale, we added some meaning to the numbers by saying that larger numbers meant more of the thing being measured. When the amount more from one number to the next is the same at any point in the scale, we say that we have an *interval scale*. Each unit on the scale is equal to every other unit. The most familiar example of an interval scale of measurement is the Fahrenheit thermometer. Here, the difference between 50° and 60° is the same as the difference between 90° and 100°. Of course, the change in your level of comfort may not be the same in both cases, but the change in molecular activity, which is what is really being measured, is equal in each instance.

Relatively few measurements of human behavior made by psychologists really form interval scales. This fact is frequently ignored, but it is rather important because such simple arithmetic procedures as addition and subtraction assume equal intervals throughout the scale. The importance of this assumption is still a matter of debate, but most of the statistics that will be discussed here are more properly used with interval scales.

The highest form of measurement scale is called the *ratio scale*. This is a scale that has equal intervals and a zero point which means exactly none of the thing being measured. Notice that the Fahrenheit scale has a zero point, but that this zero (the freezing point of benzene) does not mean ''no molecular activity.'' The temperature scale that is a ratio scale is the one developed by Kelvin. Zero on this scale is defined as the point where molecular activity stops, and equal interval units are marked off above this point to form the scale.

Ratio scales are common in physical measurement. For example, length, weight, and time may all be quantified as ratio scales (but do not have to be). Such scales have two properties in addition to having an absolute zero. First, they do not, in general, have negative values. We can speak of temperature of −50° Fahrenheit (on interval scale), but negative amounts of length are not very meaningful to most of us. Second, ratio scales permit statements of ''twice as much,'' ''one-third as much,'' and so forth. Ratio scales are the only ones with which all of the operations of mathematics are completely appropriate. The four levels of scales and the meaning conveyed by each type are summarized in Table 3-1. Notice that each higher level of scale contains all of the meaning of the lower levels plus something else.

There is an important difference between the scales that have been developed for measurement in the physical sciences (that is, those for length, weight, and so on) and the scales developed by psychologists to measure behavior. In addition to

Table 3-1. Four Types of Scales and the Information that they Contain

Scale	Information
Nominal	Numbers used to name thing Group membership
Ordinal	Nominal meaning + Larger numbers mean more of the trait Intervals not necessarily equal
Interval	Ordinal meaning + Equal differences on the scale mean equal increases in the amount of the trait
Ratio	Interval meaning + Rational or absolute zero

the fact that physical measurement scales are more likely to have the ratio scale properties of equal intervals and an absolute or rational zero, they can often be used for a variety of purposes. Length and weight are general properties of objects. In psychology, on the other hand, scales used to measure one type of behavior often cannot be used for any other purpose. Therefore, it has been necessary for psychologists to construct a wide variety of special-purpose measuring devices rather than to rely on a few general instruments such as rulers and equal arm balances.

Discrete and Continuous Scales

In addition to varying in the amount of quantitative meaning they contain (as summarized in Table 3-1), scales must also reflect the underlying nature of the characteristic being measured. The numbers used for the scale take on additional meaning when they are used in measurement, but the numerical values that can be used in the scale may be limited by the nature of the trait. It is possible to distinguish two kinds of traits. Some traits, such as sex, are an "either/or" proposition. You are either male or you are female, but you cannot be in between. Traits of this kind sort people into discrete categories and, therefore, scales used to measure them are called *discrete scales*. A scale is a discrete scale whenever it is not theoretically possible to divide the interval between two scale values.

In contrast, a *continuous scale* is a scale in which it is theoretically possible to divide any interval in the scale. The scale for length is a common example of a continuous scale. It is possible to divide an inch into half inches, halves into quarters, quarters into eighths, ad infinitum. It is possible, at least theoretically, to divide any unit of length in half, so length is a continuous scale.

Note that the definition of a continuous scale includes the term "theoretically." We must distinguish between things that are theoretically possible and those that are operationally possible. Many of the traits that psychologists measure are theoretically measurable on a continuous scale. However, the operations used to make the measurements result in discrete scale values. How this happens is apparent from the procedures often used to measure how much students have learned in introductory psychology courses. Student knowledge is probably a continuous trait. However, on a typical multiple choice exam, there are a limited number of possible scores. Each right answer adds one unit to your score, and it is not possible, *operationally*, to get 32½ items right.

All measuring procedures eventually reach the point where it is not operationally possible to divide the intervals further, even though it may be theoretically possible to do so. Thus, all measurement procedures eventually yield discrete scales. This is why the definition of discrete and continuous scales must be in terms of the nature of the underlying trait.

Approximation in Measurement

There is another distinction that may be made between discrete and continuous measurement. When the underlying trait is truly discrete, the number used to characterize it is exactly accurate. If we use the number 1 to refer to males and the number 2 to refer to females, a 1 accurately conveys the information that a person is male. There is no *error* involved in using discrete scales.

Measurements of continuous traits *always involve some error*. The number never exactly reflects the amount of the trait. Consider again the example we used above of the multiple choice exam. If knowledge is a continuous trait, some people's actual amounts of knowledge will be between the values of the scale. One person might have 27.1638 units of knowledge. The test would give him a value of 27 because that is the closest scale value available.

The accuracy of measurement of continuous traits depends on the size of the scale units available. In general, when a measurement is made, the scale value closest to the object is used. The finer the gradations on the scale, the more accurate the measurement will be; however, complete accuracy is never possible. For example, suppose that we have a board that is 63.69537 inches long. If our ruler is marked off in whole inches, the board would be called 64 inches long. With this ruler, all objects between 63.5000 inches and 64.4999 inches would be called 64, because they are closer to that scale value than to any other. Now, suppose our ruler is marked off in half-inches. Then the board would receive a value of 63½, because it is closer to that value than to any other. If the ruler had quarter-inch markings, the scale value for the board would be 63¾. We could obtain other rulers with finer and finer gradations and obtain more and more accurate scale values, but we would never have a completely accurate measurement of the board. All measurements of continuous traits involve approximation. The closest operational scale value is the one that is used.

Statistics

We noted earlier that quantification is an important part of all sciences. Mathematical procedures are applied to the numbers resulting from measurement in an attempt to describe relationships and to predict the outcome of future events from these known relationships. The particular branch of mathematics most frequently and fruitfully applied to psychological measurements is known as *statistics*. In this section, two classes of statistical procedures will be presented. The first class, descriptive statistics, includes methods for summarizing large groups of numbers and describing them so that their meaning may be more readily understood. The second class, inferential statistics, involves procedures for drawing conclusions from sets of data.

It is necessary to distinguish between "statis-

tics," which is a branch of mathematics, and "a statistic," which is a numerical value that characterizes a group of measures. The study of the procedures outlined in this section is the study of statistics, while each of the various numerical indices which we will develop is a statistic.

Descriptive Statistics

Psychological research often results in a very large number of measurements. Either many people are measured on one trait or many traits are measured, or both. In extreme cases such as Project TALENT (Flanagan, 1962), in which several hundred pieces of data were collected on the abilities, interests, and motivations of many thousands of high school students, we may be dealing with millions of numbers. However, even in much more modest situations, it is generally necessary to use the tools of descriptive statistics to summarize the data and put them into a form that can be more easily understood. There are several ways in which we can do this.

Organizing the Data.   Suppose that we have conducted an experiment in which 25 subjects were asked to memorize two lists of 100 words each. After learning the first list, the subjects listened to music and then were asked to recall the words they had learned. Next, they memorized the second list, listened to poetry being read, and then attempted to recall the second list. From a study such as this, we might get data such as those in Table 3-2. Even with only 25 scores for each list, it is difficult to make much sense out of the data.

Frequency Distributions.   One way to reorganize these scores so that they are more comprehensible is to form what is called a *frequency distribution*. To do this we find the highest and lowest scores (93 and 78 for List 1). We place the highest score at the top of the page and write each possible score below it (including ones no one received, such as 90), until we reach the lowest score, as shown in the first column of Table 3-3. Next, we make one check next to a score for each time that it appears in the list of scores. This is done in Column 2. The frequency distribution is completed by writing the

Table 3-2. Number of Words Recalled by 25 Subjects on Two Word Lists

Subject	List 1	List 2
1	78	81
2	84	80
3	82	77
4	92	86
5	83	89
6	78	80
7	86	84
8	85	90
9	83	77
10	79	78
11	84	84
12	89	84
13	93	89
14	88	88
15	86	75
16	81	81
17	84	84
18	84	82
19	92	80
20	89	85
21	88	83
22	80	76
23	87	85
24	79	75
25	78	83

lowing the progression $0 + 3 = 3$, $3 + 2 = 5$, $5 + 1 = 6$, and so on. Cumulative frequency distributions are often used for describing where a person falls in a grade distribution, because the distribution shows how many people scored below a given point or score.

Graphs. It is also possible to summarize a body of data in the form of pictures called *graphs*. Everyone is familiar with the graphs that appear in newspapers and magazines showing what part of government income is spent for defense, welfare, transportation, and so on. Graphs can also be used to show the data from psychological studies.

Two different types of graphs are shown in Figure 3-1. Both are graphs of the frequency distribution of scores from List 1 in Table 3-2, and they give the same information in slightly different form. The top graph, which is called a *histogram,* is formed in much the same way as Column 2 of the frequency distribution. The possible scores are marked out on the horizontal line or axis (called the *abscissa*) and an X is made above the score for each person who obtained it. Often squares are

number of checks for each score in Column 3. The frequency distribution shows at a glance which are the highest and lowest scores and which score (84) is most common. It also provides a more compact way of presenting the data, particularly when a large number of subjects have been measured and many have obtained the same score. (In practice, only Columns 1 and 3 would ordinarily be presented.)

Another type of frequency distribution, the *cumulative frequency distribution,* is shown in Column 4 of Table 3-3. This distribution shows the number of people whose scores fall *at or below* a particular score value. It is formed by starting with a zero for the first value below the lowest actual score and adding the frequency of the next higher score, then repeating the process for each score in turn. The values in Column 4 are obtained by fol-

Table 3-3. Frequency Distributions for the Scores from List 1

	FREQUENCY DISTRIBUTION		
Column 1 Score (x)	Column 2	Column 3 (f)	Column 4 (cf)
93	X	1	25
92	XX	2	24
91		0	22
90		0	22
89	XX	2	22
88	XX	2	20
87	X	1	18
86	XX	2	17
85	X	1	15
84	XXXX	4	14
83	XX	2	10
82	X	1	8
81	X	1	7
80	X	1	6
79	XX	2	5
78	XXX	3	3
77			0

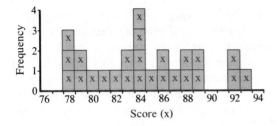

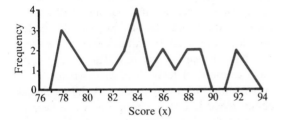

Fig. 3-1. Two ways of graphing the frequency distribution of scores from List 1 in Table 3-2.

dot or small x above each score at the level of its frequency. The graph is completed by connecting the dots. Note that in the frequency polygon only the midpoints of the intervals are given. Although the measurements are still approximate because we are dealing with a continuous trait, the interval limits are left unspecified. Notice also that the line is brought back down to the abscissa at the scores immediately above and below the highest and lowest actually obtained scores. Although the histogram and frequency polygon convey the same information, the histogram is generally used when there are relatively few subjects providing data, whereas the frequency polygon is more often used when there is a large number of subjects.

A third type of graph that is quite useful for some purposes is the *cumulative frequency curve*. As its name implies, it is a graph of the cumulative frequency distribution. It is formed by laying out the score values on the abscissa, as usual, and placing the frequencies from 0 to N (N = the total number of subjects) on the ordinate, as shown in

used instead of Xs (both forms are presented in Fig. 3-1). In either case, the result is a column above each score that indicates how frequently the score occurred in the data. The vertical axis, which is called the *ordinate,* is marked off in frequency units to make it easier to read the graph.

The histogram graphically shows the point that was made earlier about approximation in the measurement of continuous variables. The abscissa is marked off in intervals, and the value for each interval is given. However, the precise value given (that is, 78.00000) is the *midpoint* of the interval from 77.50000 to 78.49999 on the theoretically continuous underlying trait. On the underlying continuous trait of memory, the three people who received scores of 78 probably did not remember exactly the same amount, but they were closer to that scale value than any other and so obtained scores of 78. It is a general property of histograms that they represent intervals on the trait being represented and that the scale values given are the midpoints of these intervals. The bars in the histogram cover each interval from its lower limit to its upper limit.

The second graph in Figure 3-1 is called a *frequency polygon,* because it is a many-sided figure (polygon) showing frequencies. In the frequency polygon, the graph is formed placing a

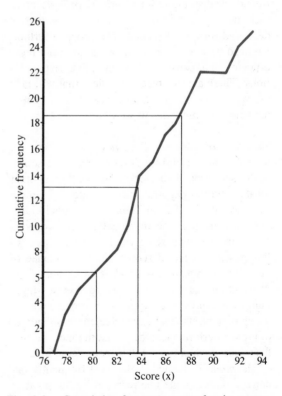

Fig. 3-2. Cumulative frequency curve for the scores from List 1.

Figure 3-2. Then each cumulative frequency is indicated by placing a dot over the score value at the height of its cumulative frequency, and the dots are connected. Notice that the curve rises most rapidly where the frequencies in the histogram are greatest (from 83 to 84) and is flat between score values which have 0 frequency (90 and 91).

Frequency distributions and graphs are fine for describing sets of data in general terms, but they have two serious drawbacks. First, they are rather cumbersome and take up a lot of space. It is not too unusual for psychological studies to include 10 or more variables with dozens of score values. If it were necessary to use graphs or frequency distributions to describe the data, readers of a study would have to wade through many pages for relatively little information. The second drawback, which is more serious than this inefficiency, is that frequency distributions and graphs are not in themselves quantitative. We cannot add or subtract them (although we may be able to add and subtract the scores of which they are made). Thus, although frequency distributions and graphs provide complete descriptions of data, they are a quantitative dead end for most situations. To proceed further, we need ways of handling data that are both more efficient and capable of quantitative manipulations. There are two types of indices that will give us what we need. These are measures of central tendency and measures of variability.

Statistics of Central Tendency. One type of number that is useful for describing a set of scores is the score that indicates in one way or another what is the most typical score. In the experiment that gave us the data in Table 3-2, it would have been possible to get scores from 0 to 100. An index of the most typical score would tell us where, in this possible range of scores, the performance of our subjects centered. A score at the center of the distribution makes it possible to use a single number to represent the typical performance of the group of subjects. There are three common indices of typical performance: the mode, the median, and the mean. Each of these will be considered in turn.

The *mode* is defined as the most frequently occurring score, or the one received by the greatest number of subjects. For the distribution we have been considering, the mode or *modal score* is 84.

This score has a frequency of 4 and is readily identified in either a histogram or a frequency polygon, because it is the highest point in the graph.

Although the mode is easy to find and has the simple meaning of being the most common score, it is not a particularly useful index of the center of the distribution. This is so for several reasons. First, the mode is found by counting. It is a function of the frequency of scores, not their actual value. Thus, it is a nominal statistic and cannot be used in further computations. Second, the mode is not necessarily a unique value. Two or more scores may have the same frequency. Thus, it is possible for a distribution to be *bimodal* (two modes) or even *multimodal* (many modes). A third weakness of the mode is that it may be nowhere near the center of the distribution. Looking at Figure 3-1, we see that a change .of one score from 84 to 78 would make 78 the mode, and this score is all the way out on one end of the distribution.

The *median* is a more useful measure of central tendency than the mode. It is defined as the point which divides the distribution in half, so that 50% of the scores are above the median and 50% are below. The median is found most easily from the cumulative frequency curve. Since we have 25 subjects, the 13th subject falls in the middle of the distribution (12 above him and 12 below). If we cut him in half (poor person!), we will divide the distribution in half. Looking at the cumulative frequency curve in Figure 3-2, we see that we can draw a horizontal line across from the 13th person on the ordinate to the curve. Dropping a line straight down to the abscissa, we can read off the median as approximately 84. An exact value can be found by using the information in Table 3-3 and a formula.[1]

The median has two advantages over the mode

---

1. The formula is $Mdn = LL + \dfrac{.5N - cf_{i-1}}{f_i}$

where LL is the lower limit of the score interval containing the median (*Mdn*), N is the sample size, cf_{i-1} is the cumulative frequency in the interval below the one containing the median, and f_i is the frequency in the interval which contains the median. The interval for the score 84 is from 83.5 to 84.5, so the median is

$Mdn = 83.5 + \dfrac{.5(25) - 10}{4} = 83.5 + \dfrac{12.5 - 10}{4} = 83.5 + \dfrac{2.5}{4} = 83.5 + .625 = 84.125.$

as an index of central tendency. First, it is unique. There can be only one median for any distribution. Second, the median will always be in the middle of the distribution because it must cut the distribution in half. The median cannot be out on one end of the distribution the way the mode can. However, the median only makes use of the order of scores. So long as the middle scores remain where they are, the top and bottom scores can move around without affecting it. The median would not change if the bottom three scores were 0 rather than 78. Thus, the median is an ordinal statistic.

The *mean* is the statistical name for the arithmetic average. It is found by adding up the scores for all the subjects and dividing by the number of subjects. The formula for the *mean(M)* is

$$M = \frac{\sum\limits_{i=1}^{N} X_i}{N}$$

where $\sum\limits_{i=1}^{N}$ (the capital Greek letter sigma) means to add up all of the scores which follow from 1 to N, X_i is the symbol for the score of each individual, and N is the number of individuals. The mean of the scores of our 25 subjects on List 1 in Table 3.2. is 84.48.

$$\sum\limits_{i=1}^{N} X_i = 2112; \qquad M = \frac{2112}{25} = 84.48.$$

Because it involves adding scores, the mean technically requires that the data be obtained on an interval scale of measurement. Since the mean itself is an interval scale number, it can be used for further computations and is an interval statistic. It is generally the most useful and stable measure of central tendency.

Statistics of Variation. Once we know where the middle of a distribution is located, we need to have some index of how the set of scores spreads out around that point before we have an adequate summary of the distribution. There are three commonly used indices of the spread or variation in scores. They are the range, the interquartile range, and the standard deviation.

The *range* is just what its name implies, the distance between the highest score and the lowest

score that were obtained. It is easily determined from the frequency distribution by the formula:

Range (R) = highest score − lowest score.

For the scores in Table 3-3, the value of the range is: $R = 93 - 78 = 15$. The range provides a quick and approximate index of the variation of a set of scores. However, because it is based on only two scores, it may change greatly from one ·set of measurements to another. (Think what would happen to the range of heights in your class if a professional basketball center or a midget were added to the group.)

The *interquartile range* provides a more stable index of variation than the range. *Quartiles* refer to quarters of the distribution. The first quartile (Q_1) is the point that separates or cuts off the bottom 25% of scores in the distribution. The second quartile (Q_2) cuts off the bottom two quarters (½) of the distribution and is the same as the median. The third quartile (Q_3) cuts off the bottom three quarters (or top ¼ depending on your point of view) of the distribution, and the interquartile range (Q) is the distance from the first quartile to the third quartile.

The values for the quartiles are found in the same way that the median was determined. With 25 subjects, the bottom quarter must include 6.25 subjects (¼ × 25) and the bottom ¾ must include 18.75 (¾ × 25) subjects. Marking off horizontal lines on the cumulative frequency curve at these frequencies and dropping lines down to the abscissa, we find that Q_1 is approximately 80.5 and Q_3 is about 87.5.[2] This gives us an interquartile range

---

2. Exact values for Q_1 and Q_3 may be determined by a slight modification of the formula for the median.

$$Q_1 = LL_{.25} + \frac{\frac{1}{4}N - cf_{i-1}}{f_i} \text{ and } \qquad Q_3 = LL_{.75} + \frac{\frac{3}{4}N - cf_{i-1}}{f_i}$$

The intervals change to those which include Q_1 and Q_3, respectively, and the appropriate changes are made in cf and f. Thus,

$$Q_1 = 80.5 + \frac{6.25 - 6}{1} = 80.75 \text{ and}$$

$$Q_3 = 87.5 + \frac{18.75 - 18}{2} = 87.875,$$

and the interquartile range is $87.875 - 80.75 = 7.125$. The graphic method using Figure 3-2 is an approximation. However, when used carefully, it works quite well, as in the present example, where the error from using it was only .125.

of 7. Stated another way, the seven score units between 80.5 and 87.5 include the middle 50% of our subjects, while 25% fall below 80.5 and 25% fall above 87.5. Like the median, the interquartile range is an ordinal statistic. It has the same weaknesses as the median: it is not based on all the scores and it cannot be used in later operations.

The *standard deviation* is the statistic of variation that overcomes the weaknesses of the interquartile range. The standard deviation uses the distance from the mean to each score in the distribution to provide an index of the variation of the scores. It tells us how much the scores vary or spread out around the mean.

The distance from a subject's score (X_i) to the mean is called his deviation from the mean and is found by subtracting the mean from the score [deviation $= X_i - M$]. Each subject's score deviates from the mean, but some scores are above the mean and some are below it. For scores below the mean, the deviation is negative. The sum of all the deviations from the mean

$$\left[\sum_{i=1}^{N} (X_i - M) \right]$$

is always 0, so that does not provide a useful measure of variation. We can overcome this problem by squaring each deviation before summing. If we then take the mean of these squared deviations (that is, add them up and divide by N) or

$$\frac{\sum_{i=1}^{N} (X_i - M)^2}{N}$$

we get an index of variation called the *variance*. The square root of the variance is the *standard deviation* or SD:

$$SD = \sqrt{\frac{\sum_{i=1}^{N} (X_i - M)^2}{N}}$$

The standard deviation is a very useful statistic of variation. It uses each score in the distribution and, like the mean, it is in the same interval scale as the original measurements. It reveals directly how much spread there is in a set of scores by using the distance between each person's score and the mean. One of its most common uses is in computing what are called standard scores.

Standard scores are special scores that express a subject's score in terms of the number of standard deviations his original score is above or below the mean. For our data in Table 3.2, we find that $\Sigma (X_i - M)^2 = 512.75$. The variance is 20.51 and the standard deviation is 4.53. Using the mean and standard deviation, we can find a standard score for each individual. Standard scores are given the symbol z and are found by the formula

$$z = \frac{(X_i - M)}{SD}.$$

With this formula we find that the first person in Table 3-2 has a standard score, or z-score, of -1.43.

$$z = \frac{78 - 84.48}{4.53} = \frac{-6.48}{4.53} = -1.43.$$

In other words, his score is 1.43 standard deviations below the mean for his group.

The most valuable feature of standard scores is that they provide a way of expressing scores from different distributions so that they are all on the same scale. If we were to compute standard scores for each individual in Table 3-2 (on List 1), we would find that the mean of the z-scores is 0 and their standard deviation is 1. This will be true for any distribution of z-scores. This property of the standard score distribution provides a common base to which scores may be converted for comparison. For example, a common problem in educational psychology is to compare a student's scores from tests in two different subjects. Little Johnnie got a score of 60 on a reading test and 45 on a math test. On which test was his performance better? If we know that the mean of the reading test is 50 and its standard deviation is 20 and that the mean and SD of the math test are 40 nd 5, respectively, we find that Johnnie's two z-scores are $+.5$ for reading $[(60 - 50)/20 = +.5]$ and $+1.0$ for math $[(45 - 40)/5 = +1.0]$. We come to the conclusion that he did a better job, relative to the others in the distribution, in math than he did in reading, even though his original or *raw score* in reading was higher. Standard scores of this general type are commonly used in psychology for comparing measurements of intelligence, personality, and other traits.

The use of standard scores is very common in psychology and education but not in other sciences. The reason for this is that physics, chemistry, and biology, for example, measure things for which there are well defined standards that are independent of the specific objects being measured. The "things" psychologists measure in people, such as intelligence and creativity, take on meaning only in comparison to the distribution of these "things" in other people. A physicist (or a carpenter) can measure an object using a ruler. The units of the ruler are defined independently of the object. Psychologists have not been able to devise scales with standards that are independent of the objects being measured, and have therefore developed scales that reflect a person's relative position in a group. The group is the standard for standard scores and other similar scales.

Frequency Distributions Revisited. Now that we have discussed two types of statistics that may be used to summarize frequency distributions, measures of central tendency (the mean, median, and mode) and measures of variation (the range, standard deviation, and Q), it will be useful to consider some of the other characteristics of distributions. Figure 3-3 reviews what we have covered so far. It shows distributions that differ in their means and in their standard deviations and what each will look like after the scores are converted to z-scores.

Each of the distributions in Figure 3-3 has the property called symmetry; that is, both sides have the same shape, and if the graphs were folded at their means one side would lie exactly on top of the other. However, it is possible to have other symmetric distributions, such as those in Figure 3-4. The distributions in Figure 3-3 are called unimodal symmetric distributions and are the ones most frequently found in psychology. One of the nice features of a distribution that is unimodal and symmetric is that the mean, median, and mode all fall in the same place.

Not all distributions are symmetric. When the scores all tend to fall at one end, the distribution is said to be *skewed*. Scores clustering at the low end of the curve give us a *positively skewed* distribution, while a large group of scores at the high end yields a *negatively skewed* curve. As is shown in

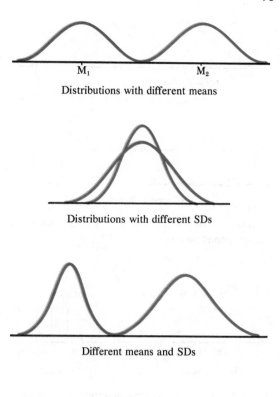

Distributions with different means

Distributions with different SDs

Different means and SDs

M=0   SD=1

All convert to this distribution with Z scores

Fig. 3-3.   Effects of differences in means and standard deviations on the location and shape of frequency distributions. Converting distributions to z-scores equates their means and standard deviations.

Figure 3-5, skewed distributions do not have the mean, median, and mode at the same point. In a positively skewed distribution, the mean will be higher than the median and the median will be higher than the mode. The reverse is true when the distribution is negatively skewed.

Correlation.   It frequently happens in psychology that a study will involve obtaining measurements of more than one variable in a group of subjects. For example, the study of memory for words de-

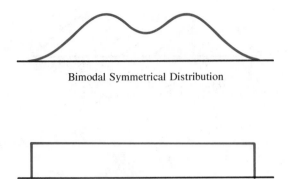

Bimodal Symmetrical Distribution

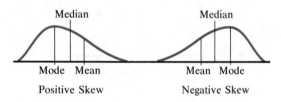

Rectangular Distribution

Fig. 3-4. Two symmetric frequency distributions that are not normal curves.

Median   Median

Mode   Mean   Mean   Mode

Positive Skew   Negative Skew

Fig. 3-5. Two nonsymmetric frequency distributions.

scribed earlier in this chapter included two lists of words. The investigator might feel that there is a relationship between the subjects' ability to recall the first list and the second list. We would say that there is a relationship between two variables if people who receive extreme scores on one measure (either extremely high or extremely low) tend to earn extreme scores on the other measure.

One way to examine the degree of relationship between two variables is to prepare what is called a *scatter plot*. Using graph paper, we put the possible scores for one variable on the abscissa and the possible scores for the other variable on the ordinate, as shown in Figure 3-6. Then a mark is made on the graph to represent each subject by taking his score on the first variable as one coordinate and his score on the second variable as the other. The sixth subject in Table 3-2 had scores of 78 and 80, so his point would be found by finding the intersection of 78 from the abscissa and 80 from the ordinate. This has been done in Figure 3-6, and his X is

circled. The point for every other subject has been plotted in a similar way.

Just as the frequency distribution is not a very efficient or useful way to describe a set of scores, so also the scatter plot is a cumbersome way to show relationships. We can see from Figure 3-6 that there is a tendency for people who got low scores on List 1 to get low scores on List 2, while high scorers on one list tend to be high scorers on the other. It would be very useful to have a statistic that would indicate this fact and, at the same time, show how strong the relationship is.

The *product moment correlation coefficient* (or *r*) provides both of these pieces of information. It is an index that has a range from -1.0 to $+1.0$ and is computed directly from the two sets of scores. The sign of the correlation coefficient tells the direction of the relationship, and its absolute size disregarding the sign indicates the strength of the relationship. A positive correlation will be found when the scatter plot goes from the lower left to the upper right of the graph. Scatter plots which run from the upper left to the lower right yield negative values for the correlation coefficient. Long skinny scatter plots yield high correlations and short fat ones give low correlations. Some typical correla-

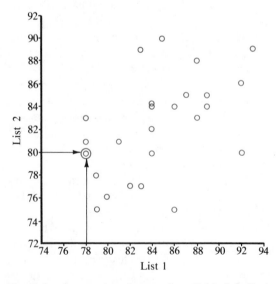

Fig. 3-6. Scatter plot of scores from Table 3-2. Each circle represents an individual. See text for explanation.

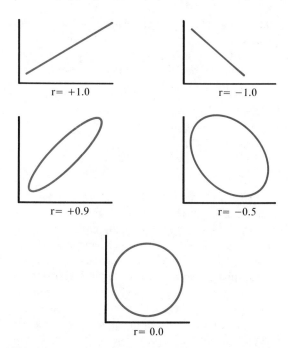

r= +1.0   r= −1.0

r= +0.9   r= −0.5

r= 0.0

Fig. 3-7. Scatter plots yielding different strengths and directions of correlation.

tions and the scatter plots which they describe are shown in Figure 3-7. The correlation between the two sets of scores in Table 3-2 is +.50.

Computation of a correlation coefficient is a fairly complex process. There are several formulas that can be used. The formula that shows most clearly how a correlation coefficient works uses standard scores. If we call the scores in List 1 Xs and the scores in List 2 Ys, then we can compute a z_X for each score in the X-list and a z_Y for each score in the Y-list. Multiplying each z_x by its corresponding z_Y, summing these products, and dividing by N gives the correlation coefficient. Expressed as a formula,

$$r = \frac{\sum\limits_{i=1}^{N} z_{X_i} z_{Y_i}}{N}$$

Standard scores that are above the mean are positive numbers, while z-scores below the mean are negative. If we multiply two numbers that have the same sign (either plus or minus), the result is a positive number. Multiplying numbers

with unlike signs yields a negative number. Therefore, if both of a person's scores fall on the same side of the mean, his product ($z_{X_i} z_{Y_i}$) will be positive. When this tends to be true for most people, the average of the products will be positive, the sign of the correlation coefficient will be positive, and high scores on one variable will go with high scores on the other (and low scores will go with low). A negative correlation will occur when people tend to have scores on one side of the mean for X and on the other side of the mean for Y.

Correlation and Prediction. In addition to describing the strength and direction of a relationship, the correlation coeficient can be used to help make predictions. If we know that the correlation between two variables, say intelligence scores and reading achievement scores, is +.60, we can use this information to make more accurate predictions of how well individual children will read knowing their intelligence. To do this we need to know the correlation between the two variables and the standard scores on one variable of the people for whom we wish to make predictions. If Suzie has an intelligence score of 110 on a test with a mean of 100 and a SD of 15, and the correlation between this test and our reading test is +.60, then her predicted standard score on the reading test ($z_{reading}$) is $\hat{z} = r z_{intelligence}$

$$\hat{z} = +.60 \, (+\, 2/3) = +.4;$$

that is, we would expect her to score about $4/10$ of a standard deviation above the mean in reading.

Predictions using the correlation coefficient are seldom exactly accurate. The lower the correlation, the less accurate will be the predictions made using it. This fact has caused many people to complain about the use of statistics to forecast behavior. It is claimed that statistics is a tool used to discriminate against racial groups and ethnic minorities. However, it is not the statistics that discriminate but the people who use them. The correlation coefficient is color-blind, and its use will yield the most accurate possible prediction if appropriate statistical values are used *with relevant measures*. There are some measures that are relevant for whites and not for blacks, and there are some occasions when the correlation between two variables is different for one group than another. When this occurs, it is up to the people involved to use the right measures and the right values for the statistical indices. Saying that statistics discriminate against certain groups is like calling the automobile a murderer, because there are bad drivers.

Inferential Statistics

We have seen that descriptive statistics provides means for describing and summarizing sets of data. Psychologists also use statistics to answer questions about the nature of behavior or to draw inferences about the causes of the results obtained in an experiment. The group of procedures used for these purposes is given the label of *inferential statistics*.

Probability and the Normal Distribution. Chance events occur very frequently in our lives. A person who is playing poker takes a chance when he draws to an inside straight. Assuming that none of the people at the table is cheating, he knows that the odds are against his drawing the card he wants, but, he can also determine what the odds are. If the deck has been well shuffled, the outcome of his draw will be governed by chance. Many of the early developments in inferential statistics took place because people wanted to be able to determine the odds in gambling situations.

Suppose a friend of yours asks you to play a game. He has 10 pennies that he will toss in the air. If there are six or more heads showing when they land, you will give him a dollar. If there are four or fewer heads, he will give you a dollar, and if there are five heads and five tails (we will assume none of them stays on edge), neither pays the other. Should you play the game?

On the surface this game looks like a fair gamble. However, your friend is not known for his honesty, so you decide to test him out by asking him to throw the coins once for no bet. You suspect that he has weighted the coins in his favor. He throws the coins and nine of them come up heads. Should you play?

Starting with the assumption that the coins are fair and that chance determines whether any one of them comes up heads, the probability that a single coin will be a head is ½ or .5. If two coins are tossed, there are four possible outcomes, but they are of three unique kinds.

Coin 1	Coin 2	
Head	Head	2 Heads
Head	Tail	
Tail	Head	1 Head, 1 Tail
Tail	Tail	2 Tails

With 10 coins there are 1024 different things that can happen, but they are of 11 general kinds, as shown in Figure 3-8. The histogram in the figure shows the frequency with which you should get 0 through 10 heads by chance from tossing 10 coins 1,024 times. It shows that the likelihood of getting nine or more heads on a single toss of 10 coins is not very great. There are only 11 ways this could happen (10 ways of getting nine heads and one way of getting 10 heads). The probability of this happening on any given toss is $^{11}/_{1,024}$ or .0107. It looks like your friend is cheating and you should not play his game.

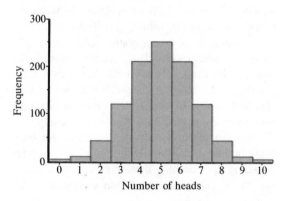

Fig. 3-8. Frequency distribution and histogram showing the number of heads expected in 1,024 tosses of 10 unbiased coins.

In reaching a decision not to gamble with our friend, we used inferential statistics in very much the same manner as it is used by psychologists to evaluate the outcomes of experiments. First, we started with a hunch that our friend had some loaded coins. Then, we made an assumption that the coins were fair and that chance would govern the outcome of a toss. This is called setting up a *null hypothesis*. The null hypothesis states what we would expect on the basis of chance. It is the opposite of what we think is really going on. The opposite of the null hypothesis is called the *research hypothesis* or *alternate hypothesis*. The process of statistical inference involves determining the likelihood that the null hypothesis is true. In our experiment we found that there were only 11 chances in 1,024 that we would get nine or more heads on a single toss of 10 coins if the null hypothesis that the coins are fair is true. This would lead us to question the truth of the null hypothesis. (Who wants odds of 100 to 1!) We would probably conclude that the null hypothesis is false and that its opposite, the research hypothesis, is true (that is, that the coins were loaded). Be careful to note that the research hypothesis states that the coins are not fair, not that our friend is a cheat. To conclude the latter would involve generalizing beyond the data at hand. We would have to perform additional experiments to conclude that our friend was cheating, because one could have gotten those 10 biased coins by chance.

There are two features of the use of inferential statistics that are very important to understand. First, we always test the likelihood that the null hypothesis is true. We never test the research hypothesis directly. Second, *statistics never prove anything*. Statistical inference may lead us to conclude that it is very unlikely that the null hypothesis is true, but there is always a chance that it is. When the results of an experiment are sufficiently unlikely to have occurred by chance under a true null hypothesis (most researchers use 1 chance in 20 or 1 in 100), we conclude that the null hypothesis is false and the research hypothesis is true. Saying that some result is *statistically significant* means that the probability that it occurred by chance is small. We may translate the term "statistically significant" to mean "unlikely to be due to chance."

In practice it is seldom possible or necessary to figure out the possible outcomes of an experiment. This is so because of some special properties of most frequency distributions. Many of the traits studied by psychologists yield frequency distributions that are unimodal and symmetric. Truly random events, such as the tossing of fair coins, yield a special unimodal symmetric distribution known as the *normal distribution*. If we run a smoothed curve through the histogram from Figure 3-8, we would get the curve shown in Figure 3-9.

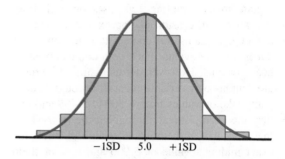

Fig. 3-9. Normal curve approximation to the frequency distribution of heads in Figure 3-8.

This bell-shaped curve is the normal distribution, and it is a very good approximation to the histogram with which we started.

The advantage of the normal distribution is that we can determine the proportion of total frequency that falls under any part of the curve. We can express any given point along the abscissa in terms of a standard score for that point (its distance above or below the mean divided by the standard deviation). In Figure 3-10 we have a normal curve, marked off in SD units above and below the mean. About 34% of the scores in the distribution fall be-

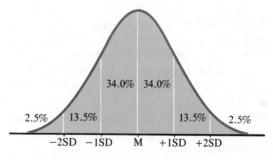

Fig. 3-10. Proportions of area under the normal curve.

tween the mean and +1 SD. Another 34% are between the mean and −1 SD. Going out to + or −2 SDs adds about another 13.5%, and 2.5% fall beyond 2 SDs on either side.

We will use Figure 3-9 to see how the normal distribution allows us to determine proportions. The mean of the distribution of coin tosses is 5.0 and its standard deviation is 1.58. Since the mean is 5.0, it splits the middle category of the histogram in half, putting 126 cases on each side. (Recall our discussion of approximation and the use of histograms. Of course, tossing coins produces discrete events. Each coin comes up either heads or tails. However, let us assume that these are continuously variable events that could theoretically take on values from 4.500 to 5.499 and that they are evenly spread throughout the interval. In that case, half of them would really fall below the exact midpoint value of 5.000 and half of them would fall above it. We will continue to assume these properties of continuous events and even distribution for the rest of this discussion.) At +1 SD, we are at 6.58, which includes the 126 cases of five heads above the mean, the 210 cases of six heads, and about 10 of the cases of seven heads (8%). This gives us 346 cases between the mean and +1 SD, and $346/_{1,024}$ is 33.7%. The result is not perfect due to smoothing to get the normal curve, but it is pretty close to the 34% given above.

It would have been possible to use the normal distribution to test our null hypothesis that our friend's coins were fair. First, we must note that the abscissa under the normal curve is infinitely divisible; it can be broken into an infinite number of very small parts. However, the outcome of a coin toss can only give one of 11 different results. Therefore, we will use the point 8.5 as the bottom or lower limit of the interval which includes nine or more heads. What we now must do is determine what proportion of the observations under a normal curve is in the area beyond 8.5. We find that the z-score of 8.5 is +2.21 [(8.5 − 5.0)/1.58]. There are tables (available in any of the statistics books listed at the end of this chapter) that give the proportion of the normal curve beyond a given z-score. Going to such a table, we would find a value

of .013553 and conclude that about 1.4% (100 × .013553 and rounding off) of the area lies beyond a z-score of +2.21. We would give odds of 14 to 1,000 that the coins were fair and probably say that the result was statistically significant. Thus, we would reject the null hypothesis that the coins were fair and accept the research hypothesis that they were not. Note that this result is not very different from the exact probability of $^{11}/_{1,024}$ obtained earlier.

Populations and Samples.   It is unusual for a scientist who is running a study to measure all of the subjects in which he is interested. A chemist performs his analyses on a small amount of the substance of interest, but he wishes to generalize his findings to other pieces of the same substance. A physicist studying hydrogen fusion is not interested in the particular hydrogen atoms at hand but in all hydrogen atoms. Likewise, the psychologist who studies human learning is interested not only in the subjects whom he measures but in a larger group. The large group to which we wish to generalize the findings of an investigation is called the *population,* and the smaller group that is actually observed and measured is called the *sample,* which is a subgroup of that population.

Populations come in many shapes and sizes. All people now living on the earth constitute a population. All male children attending public school and in the third grade in the State of California are another population. The definition of the population in any study is up to the investigator.

In order to make accurate statements about the population from a sample, the sample must be representative of the population. It must have individuals in it who are like those in the population. Inferential statistics uses samples to draw inferences about the nature of populations. Unless the sample is representative of the population, the inferences are likely to be wrong. (The most famous case of a wrong inference drawn from an unrepresentative sample was the Roosevelt-Landon election. Public opinion pollsters sampled telephone subscribers. Since these people tended to have more money and to be Republicans, the polls gave a false picture of the mood of the voting population.)

Procedures for statistical inference are based on the assumption that a *random sample* has been drawn from the population. A sample is defined as being random if each individual in the population has an equal chance of being chosen for the sample. Where large populations are concerned, particularly of people, random sampling is seldom possible. A useful alternative sampling technique and the one used in opinion polling is called the *stratified random sample*. In stratified random sampling, groups are chosen for the sample because they are like the population in various ways (for example, age, sex, and economic level) and sampling within strata is random. In this way, chance still determines which particular people are in the sample but stratification on important variables ensures that the sample will be representative of the population on these variables. Whatever the sampling procedure used, the inferences drawn from it will only be good if the sample is representative of the population.

Sampling Distributions. The data which we discussed earlier in this chapter and which were presented in Table 3-2 might have come from a group of introductory psychology students. Let us assume that they did, and that the sample we obtained was a random sample from a very large class. Our population, then, is really all members of the psychology class (no one who was not a member of the class could have appeared in the sample). It would have been possible to measure every member of the class (that is, the entire population) and compute descriptive statistics, for example, the mean and standard deviation, for the distribution of scores of the population. The descriptive statistics of a population are called *parameters*. A parameter, such as the mean, has a single value which is true of the population.

We have said that samples are used to represent the populations from which they are drawn. Therefore, the descriptive statistics computed for samples should be representative of the population parameters. However, no sample will exactly represent its population. Chance will make some sample statistics higher than the parameter and others lower. If we were to draw two samples from a population and compute their means and standards deviations, those sample means and SDs would probably not be exactly equal to each other or to the parameter values.

If we were to take a large number of samples from a population and compute the mean of each sample, it would be possible to make a frequency distribution of these means. The frequency distribution of the means of samples from a population is called the *sampling distribution* of the mean. In fact, the term "sampling distribution" refers to the frequency distribution we would get for any statistic if that statistic were computed for each of a large number of samples. There is a sampling distribution of the mean, of the median, of the standard deviation, and even of the correlation coefficient. Each of these sampling distributions may be used to make statistical inferences.

The *standard error* of a statistic is *the standard deviation of its sampling distribution*. The standard error of the mean is the standard deviation of the distribution that we would get if we took a large number of samples of a particular size from a population. In the example above, all members of the psychology class made up the population. It might be possible to draw several samples from the class, measure each sample, and find the mean of each sample on the measurement. Then, assuming that we know the mean of the population (the value of the parameter), it would be possible to calculate the standard deviation of the sample means around the population mean in exactly the same way that we calculated the standard deviation of individual scores around the sample mean. This standard deviation of the sample means around the population mean is the standard error of the mean.

In reality, we never know the exact parameters of a population, and we seldom take more than one or a few samples from the population. Therefore, we do not know precisely what the sampling distribution or the standard error of a statistic is. However, we do know that as the size of our sample or the number of samples gets larger, the sampling distribution of the mean comes very close to the normal distribution in shape. Statistical theory also shows that the mean of a random and representative sample is a good approximation to the population mean, and that the standard error of the mean may be estimated from a sample by the formula

$$SE_M = \frac{SD}{\sqrt{N}};$$

that is, the standard error of the mean will be equal (approximately) to the standard deviation of the sample divided by the square root of the sample size. As N gets larger, the approximation gets better and, in general, the standard error of the mean gets smaller.

Inferences about Means. A large part of the use of inferential statistics by psychologists involves making inferences about the means of samples. In the typical psychological experiment, two or more samples are drawn from a population and exposed to different sets of conditions. Each subject's performance on some task is then measured, and statistical inference is used to draw conclusions about whether the different treatments had different effects. The two conditions of the memory experiment described earlier are examples of the kinds of conditions that psychologists might use.

The data presented in Table 3-2 can be used to illustrate the process of drawing inferences about means. Since these data are from a hypothetical study, not a real one, we can arbitrarily change the conditions under which they were collected to suit our needs. (It is cheating to arbitrarily change the data from a real study.) Earlier, we assumed that both sets of numbers came from the same 25 people. We made this assumption in order to be able to compute a correlation coefficient, which shows the relationship between two measures taken on the same subjects. Now, let us assume that we have two groups of 25 each. One group memorized 100 words, listened to music, and then attempted to recall the words. The second group learned the same words and listened to poetry, and their recall was tested. Our research hunch might be that listening to poetry will interfere more with recall than will listening to music. The *null hypothesis* then would be that the mean recall score after listening to music will be less than or equal to the mean score after listening to poetry. Note that the null hypothesis is the opposite of what we expect to

happen. Our research hypothesis, which we will accept if we reject the null hypothesis, is that the mean recall after music will be greater than the mean recall after poetry. We will use essentially the same procedure to test this null hypothesis that we used to test our friend's honesty.

There is one major difference between our previous situation with the coins and our present one: we have two samples rather than one. Nevertheless, we still use the same basic approach to test our hypothesis. Suppose that we draw a pair of samples from the population and compute the means and the difference between the means. Suppose further that we repeat this procedure many times, each time drawing two samples, computing the mean of each sample, and finding the difference between the pair of means. Eventually, we can prepare a frequency distribution of the differences between pairs of means. This distribution is called the *sampling distribution of the difference between means,* and it has a standard deviation known as the *standard error of the difference between means.* Of course, we never actually draw all of these samples, but only one pair. The standard error of the difference between means (SE_D) is estimated by the formula

$$SE_D = \sqrt{\frac{SD_1{}^2}{N_1} + \frac{SD_2{}^2}{N_2}},$$

that is, we square the SD of each sample, divide it by its sample size, add the two together, and find the square root of this sum. The samples are separated to account for possible differences in SDs and the possibility that the samples may be of unequal size.

The null hypothesis says that the mean score for music listeners (M_1) is less than or equal to the mean for poetry listeners (M_2). Calling the difference between means D_M ($D_M = M_1 - M_2$), we may state our null hypothesis as $D_M \leq 0$ (D_M is less than or equal to zero). The alternate hypothesis, which we will accept if we find that the null hypothesis is unlikely to be true in light of our experimental results, is that D_M is greater than zero ($D_M > 0$).

This null hypothesis is tested in exactly the same way as our other null hypothesis, by computing the z-score of the obtained D_M. We find the z of D_M on the sampling distribution of the difference between means by the formula

$$z = \frac{D - M_D}{SE_D}$$

where M_D is the mean of the sampling distribution. However, the mean of the sampling distribution of differences between means is zero, so we need not consider it. Therefore, we may find the needed z by

$$z = \frac{D}{SE_D} = \frac{M_1 - M_2}{SE_D} = \frac{M_1 - M_2}{\sqrt{\dfrac{SD_1{}^2}{N_1} + \dfrac{SD_2{}^2}{N_2}}}$$

The data from our experiment yield the following results:

$$M_1 = 84.48 \qquad M_2 = 82.24$$
$$SD_1 = 4.53 \qquad SD_2 = 6.03$$
$$N_1 = N_2 = 25.$$

Therefore, we find z to be

$$z = \frac{84.48 - 82.24}{\sqrt{\dfrac{20.52}{25} + \dfrac{36.36}{25}}} = \frac{+2.24}{\sqrt{.821 + 1.454}} = \frac{+2.24}{\sqrt{2.28}} =$$

$$\frac{+2.24}{1.51} = +1.48.$$

Approximately 7% of the area of the sampling distribution lies beyond a z of $+1.48$, so the difference between the means of these two samples would not ordinarily be considered to be statistically significant. Our conclusion would be that, on the basis of these data, we do not have sufficient grounds to reject the null hypothesis. This does not mean that the null hypothesis is true, only that we are not willing to say that it is false.

The effect of sample size on inferential statistics is substantial. If we had obtained the same means and standard deviations from samples of 100, the value of z would have been 2.97. There is only about 0.145% of the distribution which lies beyond this z, and we would have concluded that the null hypothesis is false. There is only slightly more than one chance in 1,000 that we would obtain a difference this large by chance when the true difference is zero. The same difference between means may be statistically significant with one sample size and not with another.

Hypotheses Revisited. Up to this point in the discussion, we have been interested only in certain differences. In our coin example, we were not concerned about those situations in which there were more tails than heads, because outcomes at that end of the distribution were in our favor. We were only interested in the possibility that the coins were biased against us. Likewise, in the hypothetical experiment, we stated our hypotheses in such a way that we would reject the null hypothesis only if M_1 was greater than M_2. Hypotheses of this type are called *one-tailed hypotheses,* because the region where the null hypothesis will be rejected falls in one tail of the sampling distribution. One-tailed hypotheses predict the direction of the difference between means.

There are many cases in psychological research where the investigator is unable or unwilling to predict the direction of difference that will occur. When this is the case, he will phrase his hypotheses as *two-tailed* hypotheses. That is, the null hypothesis will state that the two means are equal, and the alternate hypothesis will state that they are not equal. Table 3-4 lists the one-tailed and two-tailed forms of the null and alternate hypotheses. The sampling distributions and rejection regions for these three hypotheses are pictured in Figure 3-11. A difference, expressed as a z-score, which falls in the rejection region of the appropriate distribution, leads to rejection of the null hypothesis.

Table 3-4. Comparisons Between Means in One- and Two-Tailed Hypotheses

	Null Hypothesis	Alternate Hypothesis
	$M_1 \leqslant M_2$	$M_1 > M_2$
One-tailed	or	or
	$M_1 \geqslant M_2$	$M_1 < M_2$
Two-tailed	$M_1 = M_2$	$M_1 \neq M_2$

An investigator who chooses a one-tailed hypothesis is putting all of his eggs in one basket. If the difference comes out in the wrong direction, he cannot reject his null hypothesis, no matter how

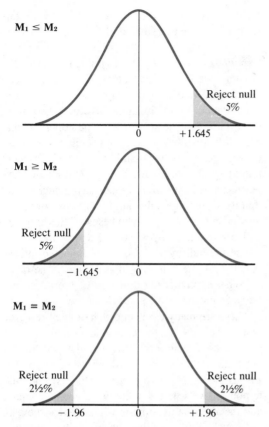

Fig. 3-11. Use of the normal curve in stating null hypotheses.

of 5%) is 1.96. Thus, for a SE$_D$ of a particular size, D_M must be larger to reject a two-tailed null hypothesis than to reject a one-tailed null hypothesis at a given level of statistical significance. The choice of which type of hypothesis to use depends on the nature of the study; however, the two-tailed hypothesis is used more frequently.

Psychological Measurement and Testing

The terms "psychological measurement" and "psychological test" are often used interchangeably and usually bring to mind measures of personality, such as those which may be used by clinical psychologists. The famous Rorschach Ink Blot Test, in which the person supposedly reveals his inner thoughts by expressing verbally what he sees in the ambiguous stimuli, is an example of such a test. In fact, as described in Chapter 18, psychological tests are used to measure abilities as well as personality. Any set of procedures that measures what a person can do, as well as those instruments designed to measure a person's attitudes, how he feels, or what he is likely to do, is rightfully called a psychological measuring device. Since psychology is the science of behavior, the term "psychological measurement" includes any procedure that yields a measure of behavior. The term "psychological test" generally includes those procedures that involve responses to written or pictorial material. The psychophysical procedures described in Chapter 5 yield psychological measurements, but they are not psychological tests. Chapter 18 includes descriptions of most of the types of psychological measurement that would be called psychological tests.

In this section, we will consider some of the principles and problems encountered when psychological measurements are used to make statements and forecasts about behavior in the "real world." The discussion will focus on problems of psychological testing, because this is the area of psychological measurement where the problems are most acute, most obvious, and have received the greatest attention. It is important to remember, however, that other types of psychological measurements, such as those dealing with learning in

large the difference is. (It is not legitimate to change one's one's hypothesis after looking at the data.) There are two reasons why one might choose a one-tailed hypothesis. The first case is the one in which the investigator is interested only in differences in one direction, and the second case is when the investigator is confident on the basis of prior research that the difference will be in a particular direction. Otherwise, it is best and safest to use a two-tailed hypothesis.

In those situations where a one-tailed hypothesis is appropriate, it will be easier to find a difference to be statistically significant, because the point marking off the rejection region is closer to the mean. The z which marks off 5% of the distribution in one-tail is 1.645, while the z which marks off 2.5% of the distribution in each tail (for a total

animals, with human sensation, and so on, are also subject to the same difficulties.

Problems in Psychological Measurement

There are three broad problems that confront the psychologist when attempting to measure behavior. These are: (1) the *accuracy* or *dependability* of the measure; (2) the *appropriateness* of the measurement procedure for making the desired measurement; and (3) the *interpretability* of the results of the measurement. The terms psychologists use for these three problems are: (1) *reliability,* (2) *validity,* and (3) *interpretability* or *norms.*

These problems are not unique to psychological measurement. They are potential factors in any measurement situation. For example, the physicist must be careful to maintain constant temperature, pressure and humidity to obtain accurate measures of length, the physician must use the right laboratory test to arrive at the correct diagnosis of a patient's illness, and each of them must have known standards with which to compare the results of measurement in order to arrive at appropriate interpretations of the results. However, in the measurement behavior, particularly human behavior, a person is more likely to have difficulty solving these problems than are users of most other types of scientific measurements. In the remainder of this section, each of these problems will be considered in turn.

Reliability.   One of the prominent features of behavior, especially of human behavior, is its variability. Using the definition of measurement (the assignment of numbers to objects according to a set of rules), we find that psychological measurement involves assigning numbers to behavior. The set of rules usually includes a standard situation, some standard stimuli, and a set of rules for assigning numbers to the behavior we observe. For example, measurement with a psychological test may include a standard situation (a quiet room, good lighting, a uniform set of directions given to all examinees, and so on), standard stimuli (the set of test items), and a set of rules (one point for each item answered correctly according to the scoring key).

In a situation such as the one just described, we will find considerable variation in behavior. This variation is of two kinds. The first kind is variation among people and the second is variation in the behavior of a single individual. To the extent that this second type of variation occurs, the measures will not be dependable because they will yield different numbers for a single person from one time or stimulus to another.

The basic principles of the reliability of measurement can best be seen using a physical example. Suppose that we wish to measure people's golfing ability. It would be possible to set up a standard situation in which the type of golf club, the ball, and the environmental conditions were all constant. If we then bring a group of people into this standard situation, we may measure each of them a large number of times. Each person might be asked to hit 100 golf balls with a particular club and our measure of that person's ability might be the distance that the ball is hit.

The "True Score" Model.   The results of our measurements will reveal two things. There will be variations among people in their "scores" and there will be variation within each person's scores from one shot to the next. We might say that each person's true golfing ability is the mean of that subject's scores on the separate "items" of the test and that the subject's variability around this mean is the *error of measurement.* The term that psychologists use to refer to the standard deviation of errors of measurement is the *standard error of measurement.*

Figure 3-12 shows what the results of our measurements might look like. Each of the little normal distributions contains the scores for a single person, and the large normal distributions gives the results for the group as a whole. The variance of the total group's results (the big distribution) is made up of variance between individuals (the variance of the individual means around the mean for the whole group) and the variance in scores within each individual (the square of the standard error of measurement). Thus, calling each person's mean that subject's *true score,* we can get an index of the relative consistency or stability of individual performances by noting that

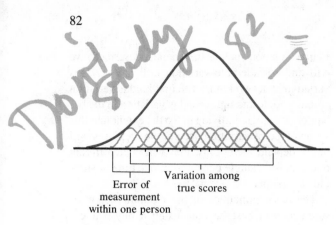

Fig. 3-12. Distributions of scores for individuals (small curves) and for the total sample (large curve) on the golfing test.

$$\text{Variance}_{\text{total}} = \text{variance}_{\text{true score}} + \text{variance}_{\text{error of}\atop\text{measurement}}$$

One definition of the reliability of a measuring instrument is the proportion of total variation that is true score variation:

$$\text{Reliability} = \frac{\text{variance}_{\text{true score}}}{\text{variance}_{\text{total}}}$$

The example that we have considered so far involves behavior that is very simple and has directly observable consequences. As the type of behavior being measured becomes more complex, the problem of consistency in the measurement of that behavior is of increasing concern. Not only is there variation among people in their responses to stimuli but there is also increasing variation within a single person in responses to the same or similar stimuli. This is the reason why psychologists have spent so much time and energy on the problem of reliability.

The Model Applied to Tests. The true score model may also be applied to behavior as measured by tests. In the golfing example above, each shot could be considered a test item. Because of the nature of the behavior, it was possible to use the same "item" for each observation. In the more conventional testing situation, it is necessary to use different items for each observation of behavior. Unless a variety of items is used, people will simply mark the same answer each time and will not provide any additional information. The items are stimuli, and the subject is asked to select a re-

sponse to each stimulus. In some cases, such as ability measurement, the subject is asked to select the response which correctly answers the question posed by the item. In others, the subject may be asked to select the response most accurately reflecting his or her feelings or attitudes about something.

A second way in which a test is different from the golfing example is that the items of the test vary in difficulty. In some types of psychological measurement, such as the time required to learn a maze, the rules for assigning numbers yield several levels of behavior directly. That is, a single observation yields a continuous measurement directly (within the limit of the size of the units). In other situations, such as tests, each observation (item) divides behavior into two categories, pass and not pass. A more or less continuous scale is formed by counting the number of times a person's behavior is "pass."

Let's consider a single individual from Figure 3-12 and isolate that performance as shown in Figure 3-13. Assume that our test "item" requires a shot of 150 yards to be considered a "pass." This person has a true score of 155 and should therefore pass the item. However, each shot is made up of the subject's true score plus some error, the error of measurement that causes that subject's performance to vary from one time to another. On about one-third of the attempts, the error of measurement will be sufficiently large (and in the right direction) to result in a shot of less than 150 yards. The true score model predicts that random variations in behavior will cause people to not pass some items they should be able to pass and to pass some items

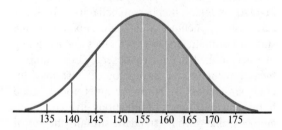

Fig. 3-13. Frequency distribution of responses for an individual on the golfing test. The shaded area indicates those responses on which the individual would "pass" an item of 150-yard difficulty.

they should not be able to pass because of errors of measurement.

In general, we may say that, if the items of a test lie along the continuum of some trait (for example, arithmetic ability or friendliness), the person whose distribution of possible responses (his true score plus errors of measurement) overlaps the item will sometimes give a ''pass'' response to the item and sometimes give a ''not pass'' response to the same item or a highly similar one. When a person's distribution of possible responses does not overlap a particular item, that person will always pass it or always fail it.

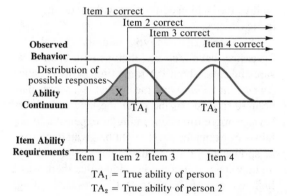

Fig. 3-14. Probability of passing each of four test items of differing difficulty for two individuals of different levels of ability.

A situation such as the one just described is shown in Figure 3-14. If person 1 with true ability TA_1 is taking a test that includes Items 1 through 4, he will get Item 1 correct because no response from his/her distribution of true ability plus error can be below the ability requirement of Item 1. Likewise, person 1 will always miss Item 4 because its ability requirement is above her/his distribution. However, person 1 might get Item 3 right and Item 2 wrong, even though Item 3 is more difficult than Item 2. This would happen if he/she responded at X to Item 2 and Y to Item 3, the differences in response being due to chance errors. Person 2 would pass Items 1, 2, and 3 and might pass the 4th item also.

This model accounts for inconsistency in responding, but it assumes that we could ask the same items over and over again to get a proportion of correct responses. Of course, we cannot do this because people remember items. Therefore, we try to use several different items of approximately the same difficulty. If a person's distribution of responses overlaps the ability requirements of the items, that person will get some of them right and some of them wrong. It is necessary to have items of varying difficulty so that the full range of human behavior may be measured. In Figure 3-14, all people whose distributions fall completely below Item 1 would receive a score of 0 and all those falling completely above Item 4 would get a score of 4. It is necessary to have easier and more difficult items to differentiate these people.

The true score model assumes that we can get a direct observation of inconsistency in behavior. This is seldom possible. In practice the way the reliability of a test is determined is by giving the test to a group of people twice and computing a correlation coefficient on the two sets of scores. The resulting reliability coefficient is called the *test-retest reliability*. If each person gets the same score on the retest that she/he got on the first testing, the reliability coefficient will be 1.0, indicating that the measurement is perfectly consistent. The reliability of a test is never this high, but some tests do show reliabilities of about .95.

There are two other ways in which reliability is determined. *Parallel forms reliability* may be determined when there are two equivalent measures of the same thing. For example, it is possible to prepare two arithmetic tests that are equally difficult but have different items on them. The parallel forms reliability of these tests is the correlation between them. (This type of reliability is sometimes called equivalent forms reliability.)

It is often possible to get two sets of scores when a single test has been given only once. This is done by dividing the test in half, usually putting the odd-numbered items in one half and the even-numbered items in the other, scoring the two halves separately, and computing the reliability as the correlation between the two sets of scores. Reliabilities determined in this way are known as *split half* reliabilities.

Validity. Reliability refers to the consistency or stability of measurement. We may think of reliability indices as indicating the relationship a test has with itself. However, we are seldom interested in test scores by themselves. Rather, we use tests to tell us something about people in nontest situations. Scores on an intelligence test are supposed to be related to other things, such as ability to do well in school. The relationship of test scores to things other than the test is known as the *validity* of the test. These "other things" may include scores on other tests; nontest measurements of behavior, such as teacher or supervisor ratings; domains of subject matter, such as the content of an introductory psychology course; and many other things. In the case of the golfing test described above, the validity of the test might be judged on whether it was related to actual scores made on the golf course.

Types of Validity. A test may be related to many things other than itself, and this fact has led psychologists to consider several different types of validity.

It is very important for the accuracy of test scores that the people taking the test believe it is a measure of what they have been told it measures. Otherwise, they will see no purpose to the test or may feel that they have been lied to; this may cause them to not try their hardest or to give false answers. In either case, the test scores may not be accurate. The quality of a test that it *looks like* it measures what the people taking it are told it measures is called *face validity*. A test that does not have face validity is unlikely to produce scores with other types of validity.

There are many situations in psychology where we are concerned with what we might call a domain of behavior. This is most apparent in the case of ability measurement, where we are interested, for example, in the ability to spell. We wish to generalize from a sample of test items to the population of items which might exist in the ability domain. In order to make this generalization, our test must include items which are a representative sample from the population of possible test items. The requirement that the test items be a representative sample of the behavior domain is referred to as *content validity*. Unless a test has content validity, it cannot be called a measure of the domain of behavior.

Content validity may be a simple matter, as in the case of a spelling test where the words in the test are a representative sample from the domain of words the students have studied. In other cases, where the behavior domain is complex and hard to define, content validity may be difficult to achieve. For example, what is the domain of behaviors that would indicate anxiety? The content validity of our golfing test would probably be improved if we included "test items" using a variety of clubs.

The type of validity with which people are most often concerned is called *empirical validity*. A test is said to have empirical validity if scores on the test show high correlations with other measures of behavior. For example, a test of arithmetic achievement would be considered valid if scores on it yielded a high correlation with grades in arithmetic courses.

There are really two types of empirical validity. Tests may have high correlations with other measures taken at about the same time. This is called *concurrent validity* and means that test scores may be used in place of the other measures which are perhaps more time consuming or expensive to obtain. For example, a test might be given to a group of applicants for a job rather than giving each one an interview, if it could be shown that there was a high correlation between test scores and ratings from the interview.

When test scores are correlated with other measurements made at some later date, the resulting coefficient is called the *predictive validity* of the test. This term refers to the ability of the test scores to forecast or predict future behavior. Predictive validity is involved when test scores are used to select students for college or employees for a company, because in each case we are interested in how well the individuals will do in the future.

The final kind of validity that concerns psychologists is called *construct validity*. Scientific theories always involve things called constructs that cannot be observed directly, and scientists devise ways to measure these things indirectly. We can measure the length of a table or the speed of light directly, but we have no direct measure of gravity. It is a construct. We infer that it exists because apples fall from trees and the planets move around the sun, but we must measure gravity by its consequences, not by direct observation. The same thing is true of most measurements in psychology.

Psychologists talk about and have theories about intelligence, personality, and learning, but they can never observe them directly. No one has ever seen "intelligence," only its manifestations in what is called intelligent behavior. We infer that learning takes place, because we observe changes in behavior.

Psychologists attempt to account for their observations by formulating theories that include constructs such as learning or intelligence. According to a particular theory, a measure of a construct should show certain relationships with other measurements. Measures of the same construct should show high relationships with each other, while measures of constructs that are not related should have no correlation with each other. A test is said to have construct validity if it has high correlations with measures of the same or similar constructs and low or negative correlations with measures of constructs that are supposed to be unrelated with or opposite to it. In other words, a measure has construct validity if it shows those relationships that are predicted by the theory from which the measure was derived.

The Need for Validity Information. Psychological tests, particularly of ability but also of personality, are widely used by schools, industry, and government to select future students and employees. In recent years, there has been a growing criticism by spokesmen of minority groups that the tests should not be used for these purposes because they are not sufficiently valid. In fact, many claim, with some justification, that the tests are systematically biased against anyone who is not from middle or upper class white society.

When a test is used to select or reject people for an occupation, we are primarily concerned with the empirical validity of the test. Face validity and content validity, which are evaluated by having measurement experts and potential users of the test review the test and its items, are necessary features of a good test, but they are not sufficient to ensure empirical validity. Before a school or employer can justify using a test to select people, there must be convincing evidence that test scores are substantially related to school or job performance.

The most difficult aspect of the validity problem is that a test does not have one level of validity but many. If two different schools perform validity studies of the same test, it is very likely that they will get different results. A single test may be valid for predicting employee success in one company but not in another or valid for one type of people but not for another. *To justify using a particular test in making selection decisions about people, we must be confident that the test has empirical validity for this particular job or school situation for people of this type.* Developing the necessary evidence requires a much more thorough program of research with the test than is typically undertaken. The often heard question "Is this test valid?" must be answered with another question, "Valid for whom and for what purpose?" When the answer to this question is known *and* the appropriate studies have been conducted, the first question can be answered. Only when the final answer is definitely affirmative can use of the test be justified.

Test Norms. Frank obtained a score of 46 on a test of arithmetic ability. What can we tell about Frank's performance? The answer is that we know very little about how well Frank did on the test. We do not know whether a score of 46 is very good, average, or very bad. When we measure Frank's height and find that he is 67 inches tall, we have a fairly good idea of what that means. The difference between these two measurements is that, in the case of height, we have a well defined standard, the ruler, whereas in the case of test scores, we do not have an agreed upon standard.

The process of defining standards with which to compare the results of psychological measurement is called establishing *norms*. The ruler provides a standard or norm for the measurement of length, and we measure a person's height by comparing that person to this norm. We must also have norms for behavior in psychological measurement in order for the measurement to have meaning. The test or other measuring procedure provides a standard sample of behavior, and comparison of the resulting score with norms for that type of measurement gives meaning to the score.

In interpreting a person's test score, we are usually interested in the position of that score relative to the scores of other people on the same test. Is the score above average or below average, and how far above or below? To determine this, we must obtain scores from other people. The people who are used to form the norms for a test are known as the *norm group*. The scores of the people in the norm group provide a standard against which we can compare the score of a given individual. In order for the scores to have meaning, the norm group should be a representative sample from the population of people with whom the test might be used. Consider, for example, how meaningless it would be to compare the scores of high school freshmen on a math test with those of college freshmen. The two groups come from different educational populations. One cannot be both a high school freshman and a college freshman, so attempting to compare numbers of one group with norms for the other would be a little like comparing apples and oranges. It is very important when using norms to add meaning to a person's scores that the scores be compared to norms for a population of which the person can be considered a member.

The necessity of having norms can be further illustrated by considering again the fact that Frank is 67 inches tall. In an absolute sense, this "score" has meaning. We know, for example, that Frank could stand up straight in a room with a 6-foot-high ceiling. However, we do not know whether we should consider him to be short or tall. In order to make this judgment, we must have measures of height from a group of people who are like Frank in other ways. If Frank is 10 years old or is a pygmy, then he would probably be considered tall. If he is an adult American male, then he would be considered short. The nature of the norm group adds meaning to Frank's score.

Types of Norms. Norms are developed in a variety of ways, all of which involve representative samples. One common type of norm is the *standard score norm*, which is essentially a z-score. The norm group is given the test and the mean and standard deviation are computed. The z-score of each obtainable test score is computed and recorded in a *table of norms*. Then, when a new individual takes the test, we can find in the table of norms the z-score that the individual's obtained score had in the norm group.

The z-scores may be converted into a more convenient form without changing their meaning. For example, the College Entrance Examination Board scores used by many colleges are z-scores that have been converted to have a mean of 500 and a standard deviation of 100. A 'College Board'' score of 650 is equivalent to a z-score of $+1.5$ $[(650-500)/100]$ and a score of 450 is a z-score of $-.5$. Even intelligence quotients (IQs), which were originally reported as mental age (MA) divided by chronological age (CA) multiplied by 100 $[(MA/CA) \times 100]$, are now generally standard scores with a mean of 100 and a standard deviation of 15.

Percentile norms are another frequently used norm. They are developed by forming a cumulative frequency distribution of the scores of the norm group and calculating the percent of the distribution falling below each obtained score.

Two other forms that norms commonly take are *grade norms* and *age norms*. These are specialized kinds of norms, used primarily in the lower school grades because their value and meaning come from the facts that children all develop in much the same way (but at different rates) and have a continuous progression of school subjects during this period of their lives. Test scores are converted to *age equivalents* and *grade equivalents*. An age equivalent of 6-3 years means that the child's score on the test was equal to the mean score obtained by children in the norm group who were 6 years and 3 months old when they took the test. If the child we are considering was 5 years old when taking the test, that child's performance was above average, while if the child was 7 years old, that child's performance was below average. Grade equivalents have the same type of interpretation, but the reference scale is years and months of schooling completed. Obviously, grade norms are useless outside of the school setting, and age norms usually lose their value when adulthood is reached.

Types of Psychological Tests

There are literally thousands of psychological tests that have been developed and published in the last seventy-five years. Tests have been designed to measure almost every aspect of human behavior, which will be discussed further in Chapter 18.

However, each test in this vast array of measuring devices may be classified as being one of two general types. Those tests composed of items for which there are "right" answers ask the question "How much can this person do?" and are called *tests of maximum performance*. Tests of intelligence and of special abilities are maximum performance tests. In general, we may say that any test in which a higher score is always preferred over a lower score is a test of maximum performance.

For many tests, there are no "right" answers to the items. The person is asked to describe feelings about something, likes and dislikes, or which of several alternatives she/he would prefer. Instruments of this type are called *tests of typical performance* and are used to answer questions such as "What does this person usually do?" Measures of personality traits, interests, and attitudes fall in this category. They are used to describe the person's normal mode of functioning, preferences, and values.

These two broad categories may each be subdivided into types depending on the use which is to be made of the scores or the degree of specificity in the stimuli presented. *Aptitude tests* are maximum performance measures that are used to predict future success, while *achievement tests,* which are also measures of maximum performance, are used to assess accomplishment. An arithmetic aptitude test is designed to predict how well individuals will succeed in learning arithmetic. An arithmetic achievement test is used to measure how much people have learned about arithmetic.

Typical performance measures vary greatly in the extent to which the items in the test call for interpretation by the person who is taking it. *Objective tests* present relatively unambiguous stimuli and ask the person to mark, for example, whether the statements are true of him/her or not. The *Minnesota Multiphasic Personality Inventory* is an objective personality test that yields several scores which supposedly describe a person's personality. *Projective tests* such as the *Rorschach Ink Blot Test* and the *Thematic Apperception Test* present highly ambiguous stimuli, often pictures, and ask the person to describe or make up a story about the stimulus. The assumption underlying projective

tests is that the respondent will "project" his/her own unconscious feelings and motivations into the stimuli and that these will be revealed by the responses. The distinction between objective and projective tests rests on the ambiguity of the stimuli and the method of responding rather than on the accuracy of the resulting scores. An objective test yields numerical scores for the individual based on responses to the particular items with which that individual indicated agreement or which the individual marked as like him. Projective test responses in the form of stories or descriptions of the content of ambiguous stimuli must be interpreted by a trained psychologist who understands the test. Any numerical information that comes from the test is the result of the psychologist's professional judgment.

Who Should Use Tests

The assertion is sometimes made that psychological tests are an invasion of privacy. As it stands, this statement is false. Psychological tests no more constitute an invasion of privacy than does the national census. What is true is that the data from either source, tests or the census, may be used for purposes that are an invasion of privacy. To prohibit the use of psychological tests is absurd. To restrict their use to people who are qualified to administer, to score, and, especially, to interpret them and who have need of the information they contain makes good sense.

Measures of maximum performance are less subject to misinterpretation than are typical performance instruments. The meaning of scores is more straightforward. They may be used with benefit by people with modest amounts of training such as teachers, school counselors, and personnel managers.

Some objective typical performance measures, such as attitude and vocational interest inventories, may also be used by people other than professional psychologists. However, personality measures, particularly the projective ones, should be restricted in their use to people with professional level training. This usually means that the person should have a doctor's degree in clinical psychology and supervised experience with the type of instrument involved.

The question of whether scores from tests should be revealed to the people who have taken the tests is very difficult to answer. On one hand, the person has a right to know what information others have obtained. On the other hand, the person may not be qualified to understand the meaning of those scores. Probably the best answer is that a qualified person should carefully interpret scores for the individual, making every effort to ensure that their meaning is understood. Under no circumstances should test scores be given or made available to people who do not have a bona fide need to know them.

Psychophysics

The first parts of this chapter have dealt with the need for quantification in psychology and with some of the methods that psychologists use to aid in the interpretation of data that are collected as part of a research study. In this section, we will discuss some of the very fundamental procedures that have been used to study psychological processes in humans.

As we saw in chapter 2, the term "psychophysics" was coined by Gustav Fechner, in the middle of the nineteenth century. Fechner was searching for a solution to the problem of the relation between the physical properties of stimuli and the psychological attributes of those stimuli. In his studies, he was attemping to develop a "physics of the mind" as a solution to the philosophical mind-body problem. The methods of psychophysics have had a major influence on the psychological study of human sensory processes (which will be discussed in detail in a later chapter).

Thresholds and Limens

Imagine that you are sitting in a room that is completely dark. If someone were to light a candle, you would immediately be aware of the substantial increase in illumination. The change in stimulus would result in a change in your perceptions. You would be aware or have a psychological experience of the change in stimulus. Now imagine that

you are in a brightly lit room. Again, someone lights a candle. Unless you could see the candle, you would not be aware that one had been lit. In each case, the change in illumination would be the same, but you would be aware of it in one case and not in the other. Phenomena such as this were studied by Ernst Weber, a contemporary of Fechner.

Weber focused his attention on two fundamental aspects of the relationship between the physical properties of stimuli and psychological responses to them: the smallest intensity of a stimulus that will elicit a response, and the smallest difference between two stimuli that can be perceived. The first of these properties is called the *absolute threshold,* or *limen,* and is the point at which the stimulus comes into awareness. The second is known as the *difference limen* and is the point at which two stimuli are recognized as different.

Ask a friend to hold a watch at a distance from your ear so that you cannot hear the watch ticking. Have that person gradually move the watch closer to your ear. At some point you will hear the watch, but the minute before you did not. The intensity of the watch when you first heard it is an estimate of your absolute threshold for hearing such sounds as the ticking of the watch. If you repeat this procedure several times, you will find that the distance at which you can hear the watch will vary from one trial to another. (Since the distance of a sound source from your ear is related to the intensity of the sound, distance provides a rough measure of intensity.) The absolute threshold for a particular type of stimulus is often defined as the stimulus intensity perceived 50% of the times it is presented. Thus, the intensity of the tick of the watch (as measured by sensitive physical measuring instruments) at the distance at which you can hear it just half of the time is your estimated absolute threshold for this type of stimulus.

Weber's Law

Weber's most important contribution was in the area of the difference limen. Suppose we start with a sound that you can hear all of the time and call this sound our standard stimulus, or S_0. Now we present a series of sounds, some louder, some softer, and some the same as S_0, and we ask you to indicate when you hear a sound that is louder than

S_0. There will be a particular sound intensity—call it S_1—which you will correctly perceive as louder than S_0 50% of the time. The difference in intensity between S_1 and S_0 is the difference limen at intensity S_0. The difference is also called the *just noticeable difference,* or JND.

If we repeat the experiment we have just conducted using a new and louder standard stimulus, S_{10}, we will find that there is another stimulus, S_{11}, which is just noticeably different from the new standard. The difference in intensity, $S_{11} - S_{10}$, is also 1 JND, and Weber claimed that these two differences were psychologically equal. According to Weber, the JND provides an interval scale of measurement of the psychological response to stimuli. However, Weber also found that the difference $S_{11} - S_{10}$ was greater than the difference $S_1 - S_0$ in terms of the physical scale used to measure intensity. The JND is actually a constant function of the standard stimulus such that:

$$\frac{S_{11} - S_{10}}{S_{10}} = \frac{S_1 - S_0}{S_0} = \frac{\text{JND}}{\text{standard stimulus}} = K.$$

In experiments with many types of stimuli, Weber found that the ratio of the JND to the standard stimulus was a constant. K is called the Weber constant, and the fact that JND/standard stimulus $= K$ is called Weber's Law. Weber's Law accounts for the fact that we notice when a candle is lit in a dark room but not in a brightly lit one. Another example is to consider descriminating between two weights. Suppose that for a standard 1-lb. weight, the JND is 0.01 lb. (1/100 of a lb.). That is, the subject can just tell the difference between a standard 1-lb. weight and a 1.01-lb. weight. The Weber Law is 0.01 lb./ 1 lb. $= 0.01$, so the Weber constant, K, is 0.01. The Weber Law predicts that if the standard weight was changed to 10 lbs., then the JND must be 0.1 lb., that is, JND/10 $= 0.01$; JND $= 0.01 \times 10 = 0.1$ lb.; or, at 100 lbs., the JND is 1 lb. (1/100 $= 0.01 = K$), etc.

Psychophysical Methods (Absolute Thresholds and Difference Thresholds)

For many years, psychophysicists have been studying methods (psychophysical procedures) of measuring sensitivity to sensory stimulation. Many of these psychophysical procedures have also been used to study other psychological phenomena.

Psychologists have recognized that there are problems in obtaining an estimate of sensory sensitivity by using behaviorally determined measures of absolute and difference thresholds. These will be discussed further in Chapter 5. In general, the subject in a psychophysical procedure is asked to make a decision as to whether or not a particular stimulus (absolute threshold) or a particular change in the stimulus (difference threshold) was detected. Many variables in addition to the subject's sensory sensitivity might influence that subject's decision in a particular experiment; that is, many aspects of the experimental situation or of the subject might cause the subject to have a bias toward saying that a detection of a stimulus or a change in a stimulus was experienced. Of course, the subject's sensory sensitivity will determine when a positive detection response is made. The psychophysicist tries to use procedures that will maximize the experimenter's ability to show that the subject's sensitivity, not bias, affected the detection decision.

For example, imagine that subjects A and B were presented a series of sounds at different intensities and each subject was asked after the presentation of each sound if a tone was "heard." Assume that Subject A interpreted these instructions to mean that he/she should say "yes, I heard a tone" if a "clear pure tone" was heard. Subject B thought that the instructions meant to say "yes, I heard a tone" if *anything* that sounded like a tone" was heard. Subject A will probably require a more intense tone before saying "Yes," while subject B will say "Yes" for tones of much less intensity. In this case the subjects' different biases for saying "yes," based on their interpretation of the instructions, might yield a difference in their detection decisions which is much greater than the difference in their auditory sensitivities.

Method of Limits

One of the methods used to estimate absolute and difference thresholds is diagrammed in Table 3-5. In the method of limits, a stimulus, such as a light, is presented in a descending or ascending series of intensities. Each time the stimulus is presented, the experimenter asks the subject to decide if that sub-

Table 3-5.   Example of the Method of Limits Psychophysical Procedure

Stimulus Intensity	Descending	Ascending	Descending	Ascending	% of Yes
100	Y				100
95	Y		Y	Y	100
90	Y	Y	Y	Y	100
85	Y	Y	Y	Y	100
80	Y	Y	Y	Y	100
75	Y	Y	N	Y	75
70	Y	N	N	Y	50
65	N	N	N	Y	25
60	N	N	N	N	0
55	N			N	0
Thresholds	67.5	72.5	77.5	62.5	

Over-all mean $\left(\dfrac{67.5 + 72.5 + 77.5 + 62.5}{4} \right) = 70.00$

Over-all threshold $= 70.00$

Note. Y, the subject said "yes;" N, the subject said "no."

ject detected the presence of a light (yes) or did not detect the light (no). For each series, the intensity midway between the intensities at which the subject changed the response from "yes" to "no" is used to estimate a threshold for that series. The overall threshold for the stimulus (absolute threshold in this case) is the average of the thresholds computed for each series.

The same procedure can be used to estimate a difference threshold. In this case two stimuli are presented, a standard stimulus and the standard plus some change in the standard. For instance, the standard might be 70 units of intensity, and the change from 70 units might be 5, 10, 15, or 20 units. In this case the subject receives on each presentation the standard (70 units) and either 75, 80, 85, or 90 units and is asked to respond "yes, the two stimuli are different" or "no, they are not different." Ascending and descending series are presented to obtain difference thresholds for each series, and the overall difference threshold is the mean of the series thresholds.

Although the method of limits does not ensure that the thresholds are unaffected by bias, many aspects of the procedure can be altered to decrease the influence of response bias on the estimated thresholds. These controls include the following:

both ascending and descending series should be used, the series should begin at different values and be of different lengths, and the subject should not be told which series is being presented.

Method of Adjustment

In the method of limits, the experimenter controls the stimulus. The method of adjustment is similar to the method of limits, except that in the former case the subject controls the stimulus. The subject is asked to vary some value of a stimulus, such as intensity, in order to "bracket" her/his absolute or difference threshold; that is, the subject is instructed to adjust the intensity of a tone until the tone is clearly detected and then to reduce the intensity until the tone cannot be detected. The subject then adjusts the intensity until he/she is fairly certain of detecting the tone, and so on. The subject eventually is asked to set the intensity to the level at which that subject is just barely able to detect the tone. This final intensity value is the absolute threshold. The difference threshold is obtained by asking the subject to adjust a comparison stimulus until it is just barely different from a standard stimulus.

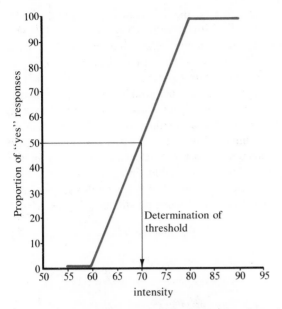

Fig. 3-15. A psychometric function for the data shown in Table 3-5. The absolute threshold is an intensity of 70 estimated at 50 percent proportion of yes responses.

Method of Constant Stimuli

Notice that in Table 3-5 the proportion of times the subject said "yes" for each value of intensity is shown on the right. We could plot the portion of "yes" responses as a function of the stimulus intensity. This plot, shown in Figure 3-15, is called a *psychometric function*. In general, a psychometric function is a plot of the subject's performance versus a measure of the stimulus. In this case, we could have obtained our threshold value of intensity by determining the intensity level required for a 50% proportion of "yes" responses.

The method of constant stimuli rather than the method of limits is usually used to obtain a psychometric function. In this procedure, many values of the stimulus are present approximately 20 to 50 times each in a random order of presentations, as is shown in Figure 3-16. In this figure, four stimulus intensities are presented four times each in a random order. The subject was asked on each trial to decide either "yes," the signal was detected or "no," the signal was not detected. The absolute threshold is obtained after plotting a psychometric

function by determining the intensity level which yields a proportion of "yes" responses of 50%. A difference threshold can be measured by presenting a standard and comparison stimulus on each trial and asking the subject to decide if the two stimuli are different or the same.

Quite often "catch trials" are inserted into a series of trials in the method of limits in order to ascertain the subject's bias toward saying "yes." A catch trial is a trial during which no stimulus (for estimates of absolute thresholds) or no stimulus difference (for estimates of difference thresholds) is presented.

Since there is no stimulus or no difference in the stimulus to detect, the subject should respond "no." However, in most cases the subject will sometimes respond "yes" during catch trials. The more times the subject responds "yes," the stronger the bias for saying "yes." Subjects with a strong bias for saying "yes" or whose bias changes a great deal throughout an experiment present a problem when determining a threshold; that is, the threshold will depend to some degree on the subject's bias, and thus not just on sensitiv-

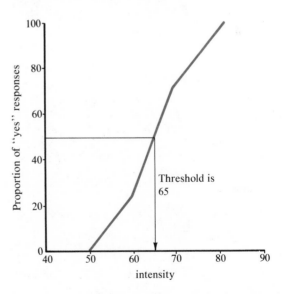

Fig. 3-16. An example of the method of constant stimulus is the psychometric function obtained from the data.

ity. However, at least in the method of constant stimuli, unlike the method of limits or the method of adjustment, we can estimate response bias.

Theory of Signal Detection

The theory of signal detection (TSD) was developed in the 1950s as an extension of work during World War II to evaluate radar and sonar observers (Green and Swets, 1974). In these psychophysical methods, one stimulus or one stimulus difference is presented on many trials and no stimulus or no stimulus difference is presented on the remaining

trials; that is, the TSD method is similar to the method of limits with many "catch trials" and only one stimulus value being presented. In most TSD procedures, half of the trials contain a stimulus or a stimulus difference and the other half of the trials contain no stimulus or no stimulus difference. The subject is asked on each trial to state "yes, I detect a stimulus" or "no, I do not detect a stimulus." Thus, there are four stimulus-response interactions that can occur, as is shown in the stimulus-response tables in Figure 3-17. The subject can say "yes" when a stimulus is presented (Hit), or "yes" when no stimulus is given (False

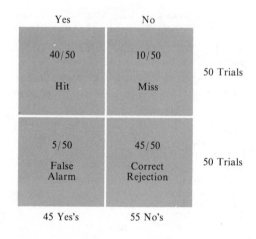

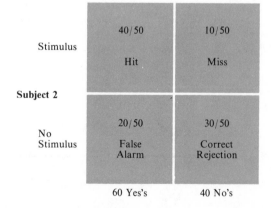

Fig. 3-17.   Four stimulus-response tables from the method of TSD. Stimulus A is less intense than Stimulus B and both are presented to each subject. Subject 1 has a bias toward saying "no" and Subject 2 has a bias toward saying "yes."

Alarm), or "no" when no stimulus is given (Correct Rejection), or "no" when a stimulus is presented (Miss). Figure 3-17 shows hypothetical data from two subjects, Subjects 1 and 2, who were presented two stimuli, A and B. Subject 2 was instructed to say "yes" on each trial when *anything* which sounded like a tone was heard. Subject 1 was instructed to say "yes" on each trial when a *clear* tone was heard. Stimulus B was more intense than stimulus A.

Let's first examine the Hits and False Alarms for the two subjects when the stimulus intensity was increased (Stimulus A to Stimulus B). Notice that the proportion of Hits increased and the proportion of False Alarms decreased as the stimulus intensity was increased. Now let's analyze the change in Hits and False Alarms from Subject 1 to Subject 2 for each stimulus. Notice that, for both stimuli, Subject 2 said "yes" more than Subject 1; that is, Subject 2's proportion of both Hits and False Alarms increased.

Increasing the intensity of sound should affect the subject's sensitivity, while the instructions should affect the subject's response bias. Thus, with changes in sensitivity, the proportion of Hits increases (or decreases) as the proportion of False Alarms decreases (or increases). For changes in response bias, the proportion of Hits increases (or decreases) while the proportion of the False Alarms also increases (or decreases).

The Receiver Operating Characteristic (ROC) curve is usually used to display these interactions. The ROC curve is a plot of proportion of Hits versus proportion of False Alarms, as shown in Figure 3-18. Notice that conditions representing changes in response bias (Subject 1 versus Subject 2) fall along a particular curve, whereas conditions representing changes in sensitivity (Stimulus A versus Stimulus B) form a new curve. Thus, the ROC curve allows one to determine if an experimental manipulation affects the subject's sensitivity or response bias. If the data fall along the same curve, response bias was altered; data forming a new curve represent a change in sensitivity. Thus, TSD allows the psychophysicist to separate response bias from sensitivity.

To measure sensitivity, one can use the area under a particular ROC curve. As sensitivity increases, the area under the curve on the ROC graph

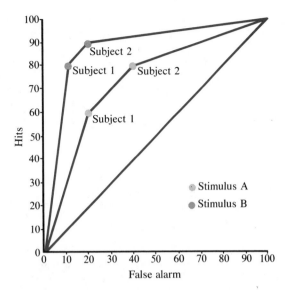

Fig. 3-18. The receiver operator characteristic (ROC) obtained from the results shown in Fig. 3-17.

increases. Changes in bias do not change the area, because the data fall on a curve and do not form a new curve. Thus, area under an ROC curve is a measure of sensitivity that does not change as response bias changes.

Another measure of sensitivity is the percent of correct responses [$P(C)$]. $P(C) = P(H) \times P(S) = P(CR) \times P(NS)$, where, $P(H)$ is the proportion of hits; $P(S)$ is the proportion of trials on which a signal is given; $P(CR)$ is the proportion of correct rejections; and $P(NS)$ is the proportion of trials on which no signal is given. If the number of stimulus presentations equals the number of non-stimulus presentations, then

$$P(C) = \frac{P(H) + P(CR)}{2}.$$

Figure 3-19 shows the $P(C)$ for the four conditions shown in Figure 3-17. Since the $P(C)$s for Subjects 1 and 2 are the same, one psychometric function is drawn for these conditions. The stimulus value which yields 75% $P(C)$ can be used to define an absolute threshold for this experiment. In this case, the value of the threshold does not depend on the subject's response bias. In general, $P(C)$ depends only slightly on changes in response bias. Therefore, TSD yields a measure of threshold that either

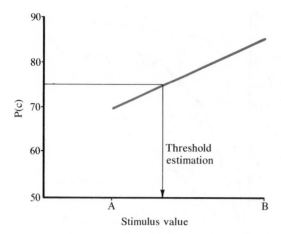

Fig. 3-19. The P(C) values for each subject and stimulus shown in Fig. 3-17. The psychometric function is also shown.

does not depend on response bias (area under an ROC curve) or depends only slightly on response bias [$P(C)$]. This is not true for measures of sensitivity obtained with the method of limits, method of adjustment, and method of constant stimuli.

Psychometric Functions and Thresholds

Although the psychophysical procedures we have discussed are used to study many different psychological phenomena, they have been used primarily to study sensory sensitivity. For many years, psychophysicists viewed these methods as a means for obtaining thresholds; that is, there was the belief that the sensory systems responded only after a certain level (threshold) of stimulation was reached and failed to respond if this threshold level was not obtained. Ideally, this would imply a very steep psychometric function and would not allow for any false-alarm-type responses in detection experiments. Since psychometric functions are usually not steep and subjects do respond "yes" when there is no stimulus (false alarms), the concept of a threshold has been continually discussed. Recall that a psychometric function is obtainable from all the psychophysical procedures described in this chapter.

After the introduction of the theory of signal detection, psychologists began to change their no-

tions about thresholds. Most present-day psychophysicists believe that sensory systems, with their remarkable sensitivity, actually respond to stimuli along a continuum, with an increase in level increasing the probability that the system can correctly report the presence of the stimulus; that is, there is no single level above which the system responds and below which it does not respond. Thus, according to this view, there is no threshold.

Although the concept of a sensory threshold may be incorrect, it is still used to characterize a psychometric function obtained with one of the psychophysical procedures. Psychologists still call that single number a threshold. It should be remembered, however, that the threshold is only one point on a psychometric function. Convention dictates that the threshold is obtained at a proportion of "yes" responses of 50% or $P(C)$ of 75%, but there is nothing to prevent an experimenter from deciding that a threshold will be obtained at a $P(C)$ of 80% or 65%, and so on. Thus, the threshold values obtained from a psychometric function are arbitrary numbers, chosen by the experimenter.

Psychophysical Methods (Scaling)

Fechner's major contribution to psychophysics was his development of a variety of methods for studying the relationship between stimuli and their psychological responses. In the typical psychophysical experiment, a large number of stimuli are presented many times to a single individual or perhaps to a few people. The object is to develop a psychological scale for the stimuli and to specify exact relationships between the physical scale for the stimuli and the psychological or subjective scale for responses. If such relationships exist, they would be true for all people and, therefore, in many psychophysical experiments only a single subject is used. Fechner was his one and only subject in many of his experiments, and he considered differences among people to result from errors of measurement.

Ordinal Scale Methods

One of the methods frequently used by Fechner in his psychophysical studies, and by many others since then for various problems in psychological measurement, is the method of *paired comparisons*. The subject is presented a large number of pairs of stimuli and is asked to state which stimulus of a given pair has more of the attribute being judged. For example, the stimuli may be pairs of objects all of the same size and shape but differing in weight. The subject is asked to lift each pair and judge which one of the pair is heavier. This procedure is still commonly used to measure people's preferences and values.

Another commonly used method for measuring a subject's responses is the method of *successive categories*. The subject is given a series of stimuli, such as 100 statements about the Catholic Church, and is asked to place each statement in a category which reflects, for example, the degree to which the statement is favorable toward the church. There might be nine categories ranging from "extremely favorable" through "neutral" to "extremely unfavorable." This procedure yields an ordinal scaling of the statements. It is also possible to measure people's attitudes by asking them the degree to which they agree with such statements. People who say they agree with statements which have been judged favorable to the church would be said to have a positive attitude toward the church.

Interval Scale Methods

In addition to the ordinal scale methods described above, several psychophysical methods have been devised to provide interval scales of the psychological responses to stimuli. Perhaps the most frequently used of these procedures is the method of *equal-appearing intervals*. This method is similar to the method of successive categories, except that the person doing the judging is asked to sort the stimuli so that the difference between the average of stimuli in adjacent categories is psychologically equal; that is, the difference between the average of stimuli in Category 1 and the average of stimuli in Category 2 should be equal to the difference between the average of stimuli in Categories 2 and 3.

Another type of interval scale method is called the *fractionation method*. In the simplest case, the method of *bisection,* the subject is given two standard stimuli and a stimulus which can be varied.

The subject is then asked to adjust the variable stimulus so that it is halfway between the two standards. Variations of this method call for the subject to adjust the variable stimulus to a point which is some other fraction of the distance between the standards, for example, one-third or one-fourth. Another variation is to present the two standards and a number of stimuli between them and ask the subject to select the stimulus which bisects the interval. The common element in all of these methods is that the subject is asked to determine intervals which are "psychologically equal."

Ratio Scales

S. S. Stevens (1975) believed that one could obtain a direct estimate of the psychological scale using procedures that would yield ratio scales. Stevens and his students and colleagues have spent the last thirty to forty years establishing ratio scales of psychological attributes of physical stimuli.

In one type of procedure, *magnitude estimation,* subjects are asked to assign a number to a psychological dimension of a stimulus such as loudness. The number is to be assigned such that if Stimulus A appears to be twice as loud as Stimulus B, then the number assigned to the loudness of Stimulus A should be twice that assigned to Stimulus B.

Data such as those shown in Figure 3-20 represent a scale of loudness versus sound intensity using the magnitude estimate procedure. Notice that the data are plotted on the y axis on a logarithmic scale. Decibels, the x axis, are logarithms of pressure; thus Figure 3-20 is a log-log plot of magnitude estimation versus sound intensity.

Another procedure used to obtain a psychological ratio scale is *direct ratio scaling*. In this method, a subject is asked to adjust one stimulus so that it appears to double in sensation along a psychological dimension. For instance, the subject might adjust the intensity of one light so that it appears twice as bright as a standard light. The standard intensity is assigned a scale value of 1 and the comparison intensity a scale value of 2. The comparison becomes a new standard, and the subject adjusts a new comparison light until it is twice as bright as this new standard. The new comparison brightness becomes 4 on the scale, and the procedure is continued in the same way in order to obtain the psychological scale (again the scale is a ratio scale).

In recent years, *cross-modality matches* have been used to obtain psychological scales. In the cross-modality matching procedure, the subject is asked to manipulate one stimulus in order to scale the psychological attribute of another stimulus. For instance, a subject might adjust the intensity of a tone so that it appears as loud as a light appears bright. After the intensity of the light is changed, the subject adjusts the intensity of the tone again so that it is as loud as the light is bright. Figure 3-21 shows the relationship between the intensity of a tone and the intensity of various criterion stimuli in cross-modality matching experiments.

Power Law

In the ratio experiments, Stevens has shown that the data, when plotted on log-log coordinates, are fit by a straight line. This implies that the psychological scale is related to the physical stimulus by a power function: $\psi = aS^p$, where ψ is the psychological scale, S is the physical stimulus, a is a constant, and p is the power constant. Thus, Ste-

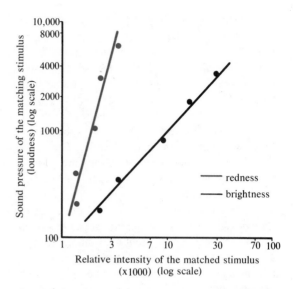

Fig. 3-21. The data from a cross-modality matching study. The data are plotted as the log of the intensity of tone whose loudness was judged equal to the criterion stimulus in brightness (Curve A) or redness (Curve B) versus log of the stimulus intensity for a light or log of the amount of red color in a mixture of colors.

vens has concluded that psychological scales are power functions; that is, the Power Law describes the relationship between a subject's psychological or subjective sensation of an attribute of a stimulus and a measure of a physical property of the stimulus.

Thurstone's Psychophysical Model

The person who was primarily responsible for providing a link between the classical psychophysics of Weber and Fechner and the measurement problems of other areas of psychology was Louis Thurstone. In the late 1920s, Thurstone was interested in a variety of scaling problems ranging from preferences for vegetables to attitudes toward the church. Earlier work in psychophysics had dealt mainly with the relationship between the physical dimensions of stimuli and their psychological counterparts. It was Thurstone who showed how psychophysical procedures might be applied to problems in the measurement of attitudes, pref-

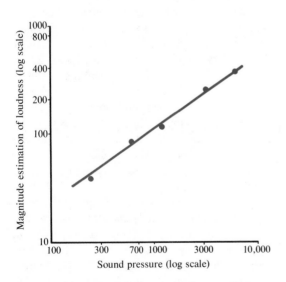

Fig. 3-20. The data from a magnitude estimation study plotted as log of the magnitude (in this case in units of loudness) versus log of stimulus intensity.

erences, values, and a variety of other dimensions of human functioning.

The Thurstone Model postulates that there is a physical *stimulus continuum,* which can be measured directly, and an *overt behavior* or *judgment continuum,* which can be observed in the form of the subject's statement that the stimulus is or is not present. Between these two observable events there is a *response continuum,* which represents the subject's psychological reaction to the stimulus which has been presented. The model illustrated in Figure 3-22 shows these three continua. The point *DP* on the stimulus continuum represents the decision point.

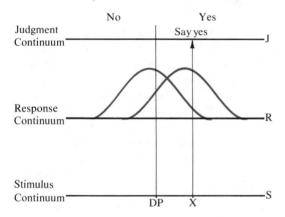

Fig. 3-22.   The three continua of the Thurstone Model showing that if a stimulus value, ×, falls above the decision point, DP, then the response would be "yes".

Any stimulus which is presented to the subject will cause a response on the response continuum (*R*), but this response, which Thurstone called a *discriminal process,* is not observable. However, the same stimulus will elicit different discriminal processes at different times. If we postulate that the set of discriminal processes which might occur for a particular stimulus has a normal distribution, called a discriminal dispersion, with a mode at the true value of the stimulus for the person, then, because the mean, median, and mode are all the same value in a normal distribution, 50% of the discriminal processes will fall below the *modal discriminal process* or true response value for that

particular stimulus. Assume further that the judgment continuum is divided at a point directly above *DP,* such that the part to the left results in a judgment of "no, the stimulus is not present," and the part to the right yields a judgment of "yes, the stimulus is present." Thurstone's model says that, on any given presentation of the stimulus, a response or discriminal process occurs at random from the discriminal dispersion. If the stimulus is a stimulus greater than the decision point (for example, at X), the subject will respond "yes" more than 50% of the time. Any stimulus below DP will be judged present less than 50% of the time.

The Thurstone Model has several advantages. It provides an explanation for inconsistent responses to the same stimulus. How the model can handle inconsistency in paired comparison judgments, for example, is shown in Figure 3-23. Stimuli S_1 and S_2 are fairly close together psychologically, while S_3 is substantially higher on the continuum than either of them. J_{12} is the judgment continuum for the comparison of S_1 with S_2. If, by chance, the discriminal process to S_1 happens to come from region *a* of the R_1 discriminal dispersion, S_2 will be judged greater than S_1, regardless of the response to S_2. Likewise, if the response to S_2 comes from region *b*, S_2 will be judged greater than S_1. However, if both discriminal processes come from the middle portion of the figure, there may be in-

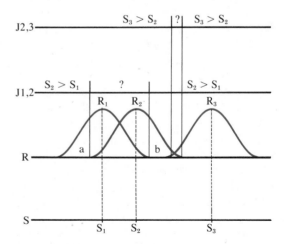

Fig. 3-23.   The use of the Thurstone Model to account for inconsistent responses.

consistency in judgment from one trial to the next. Sometimes S_1 will be judged greater, and sometimes S_2 will be judged greater. As the stimuli move further apart, the likelihood of confusion and inconsistency decreases. There is relatively little chance that S_2 will be judged greater than S_3 and none at all that S_1 will be judged greater than S_3, because their discriminal dispersions do not overlap. Notice that the Thurstone Model is the same as the model of reliability diagrammed in Figure 3-14.

Thus, the procedures of psychophysics can be used to study a variety of psychological phenomena. All of the procedures rely on the concepts of measurement, and the description and interpretation of the results involve the use of statistics. These factors play a dominant role in the study of experimental psychology.

Summary

The progress of a science partially depends on the degree to which numbers can be used to represent and organize the observations that scientists make. *Measurement* is the process of representing objects or observations by numbers, while a *scale* is a set of rules for assigning the numbers. Nominal, ordinal, interval, and ratio scales are the four basic types of scales. Few measurements are exact unless the characteristic being studied is discrete.

Statistics is the branch of applied mathematics that assists science in summarizing and drawing conclusions from sets of numbers. *Descriptive statistics* are procedures for organizing and summarizing data. These procedures include *frequency distributions* and *graphs* such as the histogram, indices of central tendency such as the *mode, median,* and *mean,* and indices of variability such as the *range,* the *interquartile range,* and the *standard deviation.* The *correlation coefficient* is a descriptive statistic that indicates the degree of relationship between the variables and may be used to make more accurate predictions about people's scores on one variable from their scores on another variable.

Inferential statistics deals with probability. The investigator has a *null hypothesis* that there is no difference between the groups in the experiment. If the difference found in the experiment is quite unlikely to have occurred by chance, the difference is said to be *statistically significant,* and the investigator concludes that the two samples represent different populations.

The quality of the conclusions drawn from experiments can only be as high as the quality of the measurements that produced the data. Behavior varies from moment to moment. The psychologist attempts to measure behavior in such a way that consistent aspects are revealed. The variation in a person's behavior is represented by the *standard error of measurement,* while the stability in the observations of a group of people is called *reliability.* The degree to which a test relates to things other than itself is called *validity.* Unless a test is valid it should not be used for making predictions or for describing people. Test *norms* present the scores of a large number of people on the test and are used for interpreting the score of an individual by showing where the score falls within a larger group of scores.

Psychophysics and the psychophysical methods are used to deal with the problems of relating properties of physical stimuli to the psychological attributes of these stimuli. Measurement of *absolute* and *difference* thresholds are an integral part of psychophysics. The *Method of Limits, Method of Adjustment, Method of Constant Stimuli,* and *Theory of Signal Detection* (TSD) are all used to obtain these threshold estimates. TSD offers the advantage of separating measures of *sensitivity* from measures dealing with *response bias.* The *Psychometric function* is used to obtain an estimate of both absolute and difference thresholds, while the *Weber fraction* is often used to discuss the results of measures of difference thresholds.

Scaling methods such as *ordinal scales, interval scales,* and *ratio scales* allow psychologists to relate physical properties of stimuli to their psychological attributes. Ratio scales usually yield a *power law* relationship between the physical properties and psychological attributes of stimuli. With *Thurstone's Psychophysical Model,* psychophysical procedures are applied to variables other than physical stimuli (that is, attitudes, values, preferences, and so on).

Glossary for Statistics and Measurement

Correlation: The degree of relationship between two variables. The *correlation coefficient* is the statistical index that reflects the amount of relationship and its direction. It may take any value from -1 to $+1$.

Cumulative frequency curve: The graph that shows the cumulative frequency distribution.

Cumulative frequency distribution: A method for summarizing the scores for a group. For each possible score the number of individuals whose scores are less than or equal to that score is reported.

Descriptive statistics: Methods used to summarize a group of measurements for more convenient and compact presentation. Includes measures of central tendency, variability, and relationship.

Frequency distribution: A listing of all obtained score values together with the number of individuals who received each score.

Frequency polygon: A graph representing the frequency distribution. The possible scores are listed along a horizontal line and a point is placed above each score value to represent the number of individuals receiving that score. The points are connected by straight lines.

Histogram: A graph representing the frequency distribution. The possible scores are listed along a horizontal line and a bar or column representing the number of individuals receiving each score value is placed above each score.

Hypothesis: A hunch or educated guess about something stated in such a way that it is possible to test the truth of the guess.

Inferential statistics: Methods used to test the probability that a null hypothesis is true.

Mean: The arithmetic average of a group of scores. This measure of central tendency is computed by adding up all of the scores and dividing the total by the number of individuals. It is the most generally useful index of central tendency.

Measurement: The assignment of numbers to objects or events to reflect different amounts of a trait. The numbers are assigned by comparing the object to a standard.

Median: The point in a frequency distribution below which fifty percent of the scores fall.

Mode: The most frequently occurring score in a frequency distribution.

Norms: The standards with which test scores are compared to give them meaning. Norms are usually established by testing a representative group of people and forming a frequency distribution of their scores.

Null hypothesis: The opposite of the research hypothesis. The null hypothesis usually says that a difference between groups is due to chance. The likelihood that the null hypothesis is true is tested with inferential statistics.

Parameter: A numerical value such as a mean or standard deviation that is computed for a population.

Population: All of the individuals who are of interest to a researcher. The total group to which one wishes to generalize a finding.

Range: A measure of variability which is the distance between the highest score and the lowest score. It is computed by subtracting the lowest score from the highest score.

Reliability: A measure of how consistent or stable the scores obtained from a test are.

Sample: That portion of a population from which data have been collected.

Sampling distribution: The frequency distribution of a statistic computed from independent samples from a population. For example, the sampling distribution of the mean is a frequency distribution of the means of samples.

Scale: A set of rules for applying numbers to objects.

  Nominal scale: A scale in which the numbers indicate group membership or are used to identify individuals. The numbers do not reflect the amount of a trait.

  Ordinal scale: A scale in which larger numbers mean more of the trait being measured but the units of the scale are unequal or unknown.

  Interval scale: A scale in which equal numerical differences between individuals mean equal differences in amount of the trait. Each unit is equal to every other unit.

  Ratio scale: An interval scale in which the scale value of zero means that there is none of the trait. Most ways of measuring weight and length are ratio scales.

Standard deviation: An index that reflects the degree to which the scores in a distribution spread out around the mean of the distribution. The square root of the variance.

Standard error of the mean: The standard deviation of the sampling distribution of the mean. This is an index of the degree to which the means of samples vary from the population mean.

Standard error of measurement: The standard deviation of the distribution of scores made by a person on repeated testings with the same test. An index of the consistency of performance.

Standard score: The difference between a person's score and the mean, divided by the standard deviation.

Statistic: A measure of central tendency, variability, or relationship computed for a sample.

Statistics: A branch of mathematics that deals with distributions of numbers. In psychology, statistics refers to a group of procedures for summarizing and drawing conclusions from data.

Validity: The relationship between scores on a test and things other than the test.

   Concurrent validity: The correlation between scores on a test and another measure of behavior taken at the same time.

   Construct validity: The extent to which a test measures a construct. The extent to which test scores show the relationships with other measures that are predicted by a theory.

   Content validity: The degree to which the items on a test represent a domain of behavior.

   Empirical validity: The correlation between test scores and other behavior. Includes concurrent and predictive validity.

   Face validity: The degree to which a test looks like it measures what it is claimed to measure.

   Predictive validity: The correlation between scores on a test and future behavior as measured at a later time.

Variance: A measure of variability which is the mean of the squares of the differences between the scores in a distribution, and their mean. The square of the standard deviation.

Z-score: A standard score. Z-score distributions always have a mean of zero and a standard deviation of 1.

Glossary for Psychophysics

Absolute limen: See *Absolute threshold.*

Absolute threshold: The smallest value of some physical variable which yields a threshold.

Correct rejection proportion: The proportion of times a subject responds that a stimulus was not present when it was not presented.

Cross modality matches: A scaling procedure in which a subject adjusts a stimulus in one sense to be equal in subjective strength to a stimulus presented to another sense. Used to obtain a ratio scale.

Difference limen: See *Difference threshold.*

Difference threshold: The smallest change or difference in some physical variable which yields a threshold. The same as the *Just noticeable difference* (jnd).

Direct ratio scaling: A scaling procedure in which a subject adjusts a stimulus until it is judged to be some integer multiple higher or lower than a standard stimulus along some subjective dimension. Used to obtain a ratio scale.

Equal-appearing intervals: A scaling procedure in which the subject is asked to sort stimuli so that differences between categories of stimuli are equal. Used to obtain an interval scale.

False alarm proportion: The proportion of times a subject responds that a stimulus was present when it was not presented.

Fractionation methods: A scaling procedure in which a subject adjusts a comparison stimulus so that it is some fraction of the distance between two other stimuli. Used to estimate an interval scale.

Hit proportion: The proportion of times a subject responds that a stimulus was present when it was presented.

Just noticeable difference (jnd): The smallest change or difference in some physical variable which yields a threshold. The same as the *Difference threshold.*

Limen: See *Threshold.*

Magnitude estimation: A scaling procedure in which subjects assign a number to a stimulus proportional to the strength of its psychological attributes. Used to obtain a ratio scale.

Method of adjustment: The psychophysical method used to obtain thresholds in which the subject adjusts the stimulus to bracket his threshold.

Method of constant stimuli: The psychophysical method used to obtain thresholds in which a series of different (random order) stimulus values are presented. A psychometric function is obtained from the method of constant stimuli.

Method of limits: The psychophysical method used to obtain thresholds in which the experimenter varies the stimulus in ascending and descending series and observer's response is "yes, I detect a stimulus" or "no, I don't detect a stimulus."

Miss proportion: The proportion of times a subject responds that a stimulus was not present when it was presented.

Paired comparison: A scaling procedure of presenting stimuli in pairs for judgment. Used to obtain an ordinal scale.

Power law: States that the psychological attribute of a stimulus (ψ) is proportional to the physical magnitude of the stimulus (S) raised to a power (P).

Psychometric function: A plot of the subject's performance in a psychophysical task in terms of percent detection versus a measure of the physical stimulus.

Psychophysics: The scientific study of the interaction between physical stimuli and psychological or subjective attributes of the physical stimuli.

Psychophysical methods: Research procedures used to estimate thresholds or to obtain scales of sensation.

Receiver operating characteristic (ROC): A plot of the *Hit proportions* versus the False alarm proportions obtained from a *theory of signal detection* experiment.

Successive categories: A scaling procedure of presenting stimuli and asking subjects to place them in categories. Used to obtain an ordinal scale.

Theory of signal detection: The psychophysical method used to estimate detection performance. The observer's *hits, false alarms, misses* and *correct rejections* are used to estimate a measure of detection sensitivity.

Allows experimenter to separate sensitivity from response bias.

Threshold: The level of a physical variable which yields a specified value of performance by a subject in a psychophysical task; usually the level of the physical variable required for 50% detection. Thresholds are often obtained from psychometric functions.

Thurstone's psychophysical model: A model used to account for discriminations made by subjects in psychophysical and other related psychological tasks.

Weber's law: States that the just noticeable difference or difference threshold (jnd) is proportional to the magnitude of the stimulus being discriminated (*S*).

Suggested Readings

Statistics

Chase, C. I. *Elementary Statistical Procedures*. New York: McGraw-Hill, 1967.

Edwards, A. L. *Statistical Analysis*. 4th ed. New York: Holt, Rinehart and Winston, 1973.

Klugh, H. E. *Statistics: The Essentials for Research*. 2nd ed. New York: John Wiley & Sons, Inc., 1974.

McCall, R. B. *Fundamental Statistics for Psychology*. 2nd ed. New York: Harcourt Brace Jovanovich, Inc., 1975.

Weinberg, G. H., and Schumaker, J. A. *Statistics: An Intuitive Approach*. 3rd ed. Monterey, Calif.: Brooks/Cole Publishing Co., 1974.

Measurement

Cronbach, L. J. *Essentials of Psychological Testing*. 3rd ed. New York: Harper & Row, 1970.

Helmstadter, G. C. *Principles of Psychological Measurement*. New York: Appleton-Century-Crofts, 1964.

Nunnally, J. C. *Introduction to Psychological Measurement*. New York: McGraw-Hill, 1970.

Thorndike, R. L., and Hagen, E. *Measurement and Evaluation in Psychology and Education*. 4th ed. New York: John Wiley & Sons, Inc., 1977.

Psychophysics

Kling, J. W., and Riggs, L. A. *Woodworth and Schlosberg's Experimental Psychology*. Vol. 1. Sensation and Perception. New York: Holt, Rinehart and Winston, 1972.

Egan, J. P. *Signal Detection Theory and ROC Analysis*. New York: Academic Press, 1975.

Marks, L. E. *Sensory Processes: The New Psychophysics*. New York: Academic Press, 1974.

Neural Basis of Behavior

Robert L. Isaacson and Carol Van Hartesveldt

Introduction

Why should someone interested in psychology study the brain? One reason is for the sheer enjoyment of discovering how the brain works. People are inherently curious. What better to be curious about than the organ responsible for the creation of skyscrapers, computers, poetry, atomic bombs, rocket ships, and music?

But curiosity, while a legitimate motive, is not a compelling one. There is a better reason for studying how the brain relates to behavior—to allow students to understand how the world is affecting them. Today, direct biological intervention with our brains is a commonplace event that should be understood. Alcohol, drugs, environmental pollutants, and dietary fads affect the operation of the brain. Mental disturbances may be treated more effectively with drugs than by the majority of strictly behavioral methods. Chemical treatments will become even more common in the future for a very simple reason: they work. How do they work? This is a goal of the scientist studying brain-behavior relations. What about some of the universal problems? Overproduction of people (which will be discussed further in Chapter 16) and underproduction of food are two of the major ones. What about those children born without enough food? Are their brains starved into permanent malfunction? What are the effects of malnourishment on brain growth and development? How can a starved child be helped to recover normal brain function in later life?

What about the problems of drug addiction? Why do people become addicted to heroin? Do changes take place in their brains? How can these changes be reversed to release that person from unwanted slavery to this drug? How does the alcoholic differ from other drug users? How can some people develop such a tolerance to alcohol that they seem only mildly intoxicated after consuming amounts of whisky that would make most people severely ill? Why is there a concentration of so many alcoholics in Scandanavia and certain parts of England? Why are so few Jews alcoholics? We do not know the answers to some of these questions, but when we do learn them, they will be based at least in part on explanations of how the brains of people have been changed by drugs, environment, or heredity (see Chapter 7 on Behavioral Genetics). To understand these answers, or to participate in finding them, it is necessary to learn about the brain and its fundamental principles of operation.

Perhaps it is more interesting to ask why most people know so little about such an indispensable organ as their brain. Nearly everyone has at least a rudimentary knowledge of the heart, lungs, and liver, yet the brain remains somewhat of a mystery. Is it because the brain is so much more complex than other organs? Are we reluctant to accept the fact that our thoughts, beliefs, and feelings are all generated by biological mechanisms? Is it because "mental disorders" (reflecting aberrant brain activity) have been considered shameful, and terribly frightening by society for so many years? Whatever the reason, students who do not seek knowledge about the brain and its functions deprive themselves of a fascinating adventure.

How should a student start to learn about the brain? We want to emphasize the theme that the brain is an exciting, dynamic organ of the body. We will discuss the dynamic nature of the brain in three different contexts: *the evolution of the brain, brain development,* and the *adaptive nature of the brain's activity.*

The Evolution of Brains

Many animals with one or few cells manage to get along nicely without any nervous system at all. One-celled animals are able to respond to many forms of environmental stimulation, demonstrating their ability to detect environmental events and to make appropriate responses to them. Often the responses are simple ones, as when an amoeba surrounds a particle of food by portions of its membrane, but single-celled animals can make differential responses to stimuli. They can retreat from strong stimuli but approach weaker ones. Because animals are made up of many cells, some method had to be found to communicate what is happening to the surface of one cell or a small group of cells to all of the others that make up an animal. In the case of animals made up of but a few cells, communication among cells can occur through the physical transmission of activity or movement in one cell to the next.

However, as more and more cells join together to form a complicated and larger organism, this process of physical communication, whereby one cell affects the next, becomes inefficient. Distances are large and the process of conducting reactions to environmental stimuli by waves of activity moving across the surfaces of the cells become too slow for rapid, adaptive reactions. A new kind of cell becomes necessary for better communication. Nerve cells are capable of conducting information rapidly from one part of the organism to another and for coordinating the actions of individual cells into meaningful acts of the entire organism. There are three fundamental activities performed by the nervous systems of all animals:

1. The evaluation of environmental changes (sensory systems).
2. The execution of behavior (motor systems).
3. The evaluation of the effects of behavior on the environment.

The detection of environmental changes depends on *receptors* in the periphery of the body, and sensory nerves, which carry information about the world to a central location for processing. In mammals, most receptors are sensitive only to certain types of physical stimuli. The eyes are sensitive to electromagnetic radiations while the ears are sensitive to rapid changes in air pressure. Other receptors are responsive to chemical stimuli like smell and taste. Certain animals, such as electric fishes, have evolved receptors that detect electrical currents in the water. Some birds may have the ability to detect gravitational fields when unable to use other, more common sensory modalities, as when they are flying in dense fog. In any case, these specialized receptors are coupled with the sensory nerves going to a central location which, in turn, is connected to other regions of the brain controlling the actions of the body. (For a further discussion of sensory systems, see Chapter 5.)

A second aspect of all nervous systems is concerned with the control of motor movements. In most animals, some nerve fibers run to individual muscles and muscle groups. When "activated," these nerve fibers cause the muscle to contract. The regulation of motor activity requires the integration of the actions of many muscle groups. The end-product must be coordinated activities of the organism that are useful in achieving goals, for example, consumption of food and water, escape, aggression, and so on. Since every animal must exhibit a wide variety of motor acts at different times and under different conditions, their nervous systems must have the ability to produce and store many such integrated patterns of muscle movements.

In all animals that have even very primitive brains—maybe even just a collection of a few nerve cells—there is the ability to organize different types of motor acts. These motor behaviors can be elicited by appropriate environmental stimuli. They can be thought of as being "on tap," waiting for the appropriate environmental conditions for release.

Brains can be thought of as the meeting point of sensory information and the beginning of motor actions. However, the brain is far more than the point of connection between sensory and motor events. If it were this simple, each and every time a particular sensory input occurred, the same motor response would follow. There would be a permanent invariant correspondence between sensory input and motor actions. The system would be "hard wired," to use computer terminology.

The fact is that all nervous systems and brains have cells interposed between the sensory input and the motor output systems. These interposed cells are called *interneurons*. There are more interneurons than cells that conduct information from receptor organs, or cells that reach out to the individual muscles. Thus, brains are primarily collections of interneurons. This fact gives us a new perspective on the role of brains. The interposing of interneurons between the sensory and motor systems allows differential responses to be made depending on a host of factors other than the immediate sensory event. They allow different reactions to occur to the same stimuli and, indeed, allow the same reactions to occur to a wide range of different environmental conditions. They are the means responsible for our flexibility in behavior. Interneurons allow the animal to operate with a freedom from environmental stimuli, and allow the organism to make responses contingent on past experiences, on states such as hunger or thirst, and on predictions of future consequences of present actions.

Why Large Brains?

Brains organized with interneurons between sensory and motor systems allow the individual to have freedom over direct and permanent dominance of behavioral patterns by immediate input from the environment. As evolution continued, the central nervous system proceeded to enlarge, adding millions of interneurons. In humans, there are roughly ten billion interneurons in the brain. The human brain should not be considered as the ultimate in the evolutionary development of inter-

neurons, however, since the number of cells in the brains of certain elephants and whales is undoubtedly greater than in the human brain.

It is unlikely that the enlargement of the brain adds greatly to the ability of the animal to detect signals from the environment or to have elaborate types of motor patterns. Selective destruction of the brains of mammals has shown that basic patterns of behavior often remain unaltered by such damage. Study of the sensory abilities of certain insects and other animals with very primitive brains has shown elaborate and fine-grained sensory abilities. Therefore, the enlargement of the brain is not necessarily associated with advances in motor capabilities or with greater sensory abilities. The advantage that animals with huge brains have is in their ability to calculate and anticipate consequences of actions. More contingencies can be considered when making decisions and long-range forecasts can be made about the effects of certain behavior or actions. We shall return to these problems after considering the basic units comprising the nervous system and the basic organization of the brain.

The Nature of the Nerve Cell

The brain and the central nervous system are made up of two kinds of cells. These are the nerve cells called neurons, and supportive cells called *neuroglia,* or *glia,* for short. The glia cells of the brain are of two major types. One type is called *astrocytes*. These are found throughout the brain, and their cell membranes are often wrapped around the nerve cells in a very intricate and intimate fashion. These cells are thought to "support" the activity of neurons by providing appropriate levels of nutrients and other substances needed for their sustenance. The other major type of glia cell is the *oligodendroglia,* whose function is to produce a fatty coating around the axons of some cells, which speeds up the rate of transmission of the nerve impulse. This fatty outer covering is called myelin. Neither type of glia cell transmits nerve impulses.

While nerve cells have many of the characteristics of all living cells, they also have one special characteristic: they can transmit excitation from one place to another in a very rapid fashion. This is a consequence of an excitable membrane that makes up the entire outside of the cell and its processes. It is remarkable, also, that nerve cells in most living animals are very similar. Nerve cells in cockroaches, squid, sharks, whales, and people share many similar functional and structural characteristics. They are usually thought to have three main portions: a *dendrite,* a *cell body,* and an *axon.* Actually, there are many dendrites coming from the cell body of most nerve cells, but usually only one axon leaves the cell, although it may branch to form several "collateral axons" reaching hundreds of other cells. Figure 4-1 illustrates the neuron and its parts.

In theory, excitation from another nerve cell or receptor cell reaches the dendrites or cell body of the receiving cell. This initiates activity in the cell body which may be transmitted along the axon to other cells. This common view of the flow of excitation is oversimplified but represents the standard, textbook view of the flow of information from dendrite to cell body, to axon, to other cells.

Sensory neurons are cells that have dendrites which can either act as receptors, or can be activated by the receptor cells specialized for the transformation of some environmental event into electrical or chemical changes affecting the membrane of the sensory cell. This excitation is then transmitted from the sensory neuron to other neurons in the nervous system. Motor neurons, the neurons directly controlling muscles, are located in the brain or spinal cord. They have a long axon that runs directly to the muscle. When the motor neuron is activated, the activity is transmitted along the membrane of the axon, and the muscle contracts.

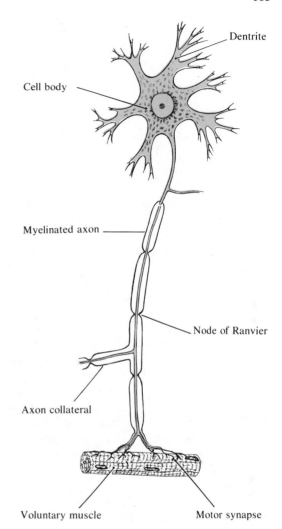

Fig. 4-1. A motor neuron and its parts. The dendrites receive information from other neurons. The axon conducts activity from the cell body to the muscle. The axon has collateral branches that will synapse on different muscle fibers. The axon is myelinated and has nodes of Ranvier which have no myelin.

The Activation of Nerve Cells

As mentioned earlier, the special characteristic of nerve cells is their ability to transmit excitation from one place to another by propagating changes along their membranes. The membrane of the nerve cell is composed of protein, lipids (fats), and a small amount of carbohydrates. The membranes of nerve cells are electrically charged, and it is the

rapid change in this electrical charge that represents the "discharge" of the nerve cell.

In the resting state, the nerve cell membrane is relatively *impermeable* to sodium ions (Na+) and to organic cations (A−), and partially *permeable* to potassium (K+) ions. (An ion is an electrically-charged atom or group of atoms.) Also, at rest, the

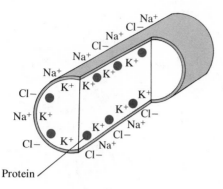

Fig. 4-2. Cross-section of an axon showing the differing concentrations of ions on the outside and on the
inside of the membrane. More Na$^+$ and Cl$^-$ are on the
outside of the axon than on the inside. More K$^+$ is on the
inside than on the outside. In addition, there are proteins
with negative charges inside the axon.

nerve cell has a high internal concentration of the
potassium and organic cations but a relatively low
internal concentration of the sodium ions. On the
outer surface of the membrane, there is high concentration of sodium and chloride ions, as illustrated in Figure 4-2. These differences in the distribution of ions produce a condition in which the
interior of the cell is electrically negative with respect to the outside. The magnitude of the electrical difference between the inside and the outside
of the cell is about 70 thousandths of a volt, or 70
millivolts. This resting condition is said to be the
polarized condition of the nerve cell membrane.
The same type of membrane polarization is also
found in the axons; indeed, the electrical difference between the inside and the outside of the
axon is somewhat greater than that in the cell body
(from 80 to 90 millivolts difference). When the
cell changes from a resting to an excited state, the
electrically-charged particles, or ions, are allowed
to flow across the membrane. When this occurs,
the membrane is *depolarized* (see discussion below
for further definition).

The segregation of the ions across the cell membrane that is found in the resting state, as well as
the changes which occur when the cell becomes
active, require the use of energy. Membrane
changes are not passive events but ones in which
the ions are moved at the *cost of energy*.

When an event occurs that excites the cell membrane, the permeability of the nerve cell membrane
to sodium is increased. Sodium ions rush into the
interior of the cell and as a result the electrical potential across the membrane decreases. This alteration in the membrane of the cell is called *depolarization;* it can be partial or complete. A partial
depolarization is when some of the segregation of
ions found in the resting state is partially abolished
for a short period of time. A complete depolarization is when the segregation of Na$+$ ions is totally
abolished for a moment. After either form of depolarization, the cell membrane begins to restore the
polarized state once again by pumping out sodium
ions from the inside of the cell and bringing back
potassium ions from outside the membrane. Depo-
larizations of the cell membrane are called *excitatory* actions. When events occur that produce a
greater degree of ion segregation than is normally
found, or *hyperpolarization,* the effect is called
inhibitory. Inhibitory events produce an increase in
electrical difference between the inside and the
outside of the cell.

At any given moment in time, every nerve cell is
subjected to some influences that tend to depolarize the membrane and others that tend to hyperpolarize the membrane. If the excitatory influences
on the cell or its dendrites reach a critical point,
then all of the nerve cell membrane begins to
depolarize. This depolarization runs down the
axon to its points of termination. The reaction of
the nerve cell is an *all-or-none* event.

It is generally accepted that there is at least one
place on the cell body near the beginning of the
axon which is a triggering mechanism for the reaction of the entire cell membrane, the all-or-none
response. Local excitatory or inhibitory changes in
the cell membrane that do not reach sufficient intensity to trigger the all-or-none response are
called *graded potentials*. Once the threshold for
discharge is reached, however, the depolarization
that occurs in the cell body and axon is always the
same size. This reaction is called the nerve impulse
or *action potential* (see Figure 4-3).

In the brain and in the periphery of the body,
many nerves that have long axons are covered by a
fatty substance called *myelin*. This fatty matter is
formed by supportive cells (oligodendroglia in the
central nervous system and by Schwann cells in the

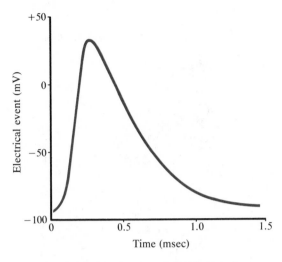

Fig. 4-3. Schematic drawing of the changes in nerve cell polarization during an action potential.

periphery of the body). The supportive cells extend their surfaces around the axon, wrapping it in ever-increasing layers. Lipid molecules accumulate inside these wrappings; the cross-section of a mye-

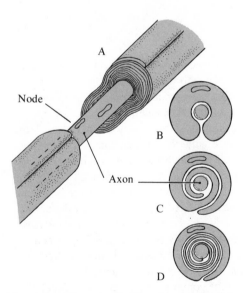

Fig. 4-4. Diagram showing the myelination of an axon. Part (a), a fully myelinated axon. The node of Ranvier has no myelin. Parts (b), (c), and (d) indicate the process of myelination shown in cross-sections of the axon. The myelin sheath is wrapped around the axon until several layers are formed.

linated axon is shown in Figure 4-4. The myelin is not laid down in one long, continuous coating but is broken into links. The axon is essentially bare between the links, and these bare spots are called *nodes*. The membrane depolarization that is the nerve impulse acts as if it jumps from one node to the next; this produces much more rapid transmission of the nerve impulse than would occur without a myelin wrapping.

Some diseases can affect the supportive cells that make myelin or the lipid deposit of which myelin is made. A destruction of myelin produces a devastating effect on behavior by disturbing the speed and coordination of movement; when there is a complete degeneration of myelin, death ensues.

Myelin has a distinctive white appearance. When looking at a brain or spinal cord through which a cut has been made, there is a clear difference seen between parts that look pinkish and those that look much whiter. The whiter parts are bundles of myelinated fibers traveling over long distances, such as from the interior of the brain to the spinal cord or from the spinal cord to the brain. The pinkish areas are mostly collections of nerve cells and unmyelinated fibers. These pinkish areas are usually called grey matter for the following reason. Most brains are immersed in solutions (like formaldehyde) to prevent their deterioration before they are subjected to anatomical study. In this process, the pinkish areas turn a grey color, while the myelinated areas remain white. Thus, the brain and spinal cord are often described as having grey matter (mostly nerve cells) and white matter (mostly myelinated fibers). It should be remembered, however, that the grey matter of the brain is not actually a grey color but only becomes grey after the tissue has been processed.

Transmission and Synapses

When a nerve impulse reaches the terminal portions of the axon, the activities occasioned by its arrival most often evoke the release of chemicals at the axon terminals. Chemicals are released into the space between the axon terminals and the membranes of adjacent cells. (In rare instances, transmission of the impulse from one cell to the other is accomplished electrically. These contacts between cells are called *gap junctions* or *electrical synapses*. They are probably rare in mammalian nervous systems.)

The chemicals released at the axon terminals by the nerve impulse are called *neurotransmitters* or *neurochemicals*. They have been produced originally in the cell body and transported down the axon to its terminals, although some are made locally in the axon terminals themselves. At the axon terminals, these chemicals are usually stored in small globular packages called *synaptic vesicles*. When the depolarization reaches the axon terminals, some of these stored neurochemicals are released into the gap between the terminal and the membrane of the next cell. There are molecules on the membrane of the nerve cell that are sensitive to the neurochemicals being released. They are called receptor molecules. Only those regions of the cell membrane containing the receptor molecules are sensitive to a particular transmitter. Usually the locations of the receptor molecules are called *receptors* or *receptor sites*. It is the activation of the receptor molecules that initiates the depolarizing or hyperpolarizing influence on the membrane. The synapse is illustrated in Figure 4-5.

The chemicals do not just disappear after acting on the cell membrane. Some neurotransmitters are quickly broken down into fragments by enzymes present in the gap between the cells. Fragments of the neurotransmitters are taken up into the axon

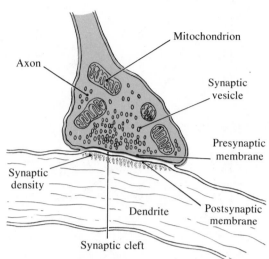

Fig. 4-5b. Diagram of a synapse. The presynaptic region is the axon terminal, which contains synaptic vesicles where the transmitter is stored. The transmitter will be released through the presynaptic membrane, pass across the synaptic cleft, and act on the postsynaptic membrane of the dendrite of another cell. Beneath the cleft there is often, but not always, an area of the membrane that is relatively dense to electrons, of the electron microscope. This area is called the "subsynaptic density," but its function is unknown.

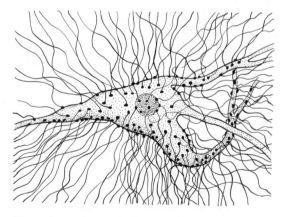

Fig. 4-5a. Numerous synapses on the cell body of a neuron. Based on drawings of the famous anatomist, S. Ramon y Cajal.

terminal once again, where the original neurotransmitter can be reformed by still other enzyme systems. Other neurotransmitters are taken up into axons intact and used again.

Nerve impulses that reach the muscles of the body cause muscle contractions. This is accomplished by much the same mechanism as the communications between neurones. Where the axons make contact with muscles, there is a small gap between the axon termination and the surface of the muscle. In the case of muscles that move the skeleton of the body (skeletal muscles), when the axon has been depolarized a chemical called *acetylcholine* is released by the axon terminal. The acetylcholine combines with receptor molecules on the muscle to produce electrical changes on the surface of the muscle fiber and its subsequent contraction. Under normal conditions, the surface of the muscle is only sensitive to acetylcholine at the

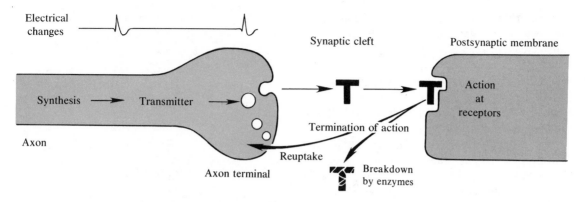

Fig. 4-5(c)   Schematic representation of neurotransmitter action. At least some portion of the transmitter substance released at the axon terminal is produced (synthesized) in the cell body and transported down the axon to the terminal. Other portions are synthesized in the terminal itself and taken up from the synaptic space. Electrical changes in the axon (see line above axon) that reach the terminal cause the release of transmitters (T) into the synaptic cleft, probably by changing the membrane so as to allow Ca^+ to enter the terminal. These ions then cause the vesicles in which the transmitter is stored to contract and rupture. Some of the transmitter is degraded by enzymes in the synaptic cleft but some reaches specific receptor sites on the postsynaptic membrane. Other portions of the released transmitter are taken up directly by the axon terminal from which it was released. When the transmitter reacts with the specialized receptor for it, this induces reactions in the postsynaptic membrane that alter the permeability of the membrane to different ions, thus producing depolarization (an excitatory reaction) or hyperpolarization (an inhibitory reaction). After it has acted on the postsynaptic receptors, it is either broken down by degradative enzymes or taken up into the terminal from which it was released.

place of contact under the axon terminal. The application of acetylcholine to any other part of the muscle fails to produce a depolarization or a contraction. These events are very similar to those changes that occur between nerve cells. Transmission between nerve cells requires a gap between the processes of two cells, usually the release of a chemical, specialized receptors for the chemical, and a membrane change on the receiving cell.

It was through the intensive study of the activities of nerve fibers on muscle that the *quantal* nature of neurochemical transmission was first discovered. Each vesicle of acetylcholine that is stored in an axon terminal produces a similar amount of depolarization on the muscle membrane. The amount of muscle contraction is determined by how many packets of transmitter are released. Each molecular packet contains one quantum of transmitter substance. It is believed that all neurochemical systems operate in this quantal fashion and that the contents of each vesi-

cle of neurochemical in an axon terminal produces an equivalent response on the adjacent membrane, whether it be of another nerve cell or of a muscle.

How Many Transmitters?

It is not known just how many neurochemicals act as transmitters in the central nervous system. However, there is good evidence that acetylcholine, the biogenic amines (noradrenalin, dopamine, serotonin), gamma-aminobutyric acid (GABA), glycine, glutamic acid, and aspartic acid can all function as neurotransmitters or neurochemicals. It is by no means certain how many others remain to be discovered.

Development of the Brain

During the course of development, the basic units of the nervous system are formed; as they migrate to their final locations, they give the brain its shape and pattern of organization. At the beginning of life there is but a single cell. This cell divides again and again, and as this proliferation of cells goes along, particular cells become "specialized" and produce a thin layer of cells on the surface of the organism. The cells making up this thin layer keep dividing and ultimately come to form a thin tube on the surface of the embryo. The core of this tube will become the fluid-filled ventricular system of the brain.

All of the structures of the mature brain, including some twelve billion individual cells in the human, start out from this hollow tube of cells. New cells are made just inside the lining of the tube and migrate out to other places. When a neuron arrives at its final destination, its axons and dendrites grow out to make contact with other neurons. Over time, the dendrites of each cell are reached by axons of other cells, and synapses are formed on them.

The human brain begins to take recognizable shape near the end of the first trimester of pregnancy as illustrated in Figure 4-6. Rudiments of the three major subdivisions of the brain—the *forebrain, midbrain,* and *hindbrain*—can be observed in the human embryo as early as the third week of life. The hindbrain becomes divided through the course of development into the *medulla oblongata,* the *pons,* and the *cerebellum.* The cerebellum appears as an outgrowth of the dorsal portion of the hindbrain; it is one of the few regions of the human brain whose development is completed after birth. The midbrain is generally divided into the *tectum* and the *tegmentum.* The tectum is on the *dorsal* aspect (the side toward the back) and the tegmentum, on the *ventral* aspect (the side toward the stomach).

Well before birth in mammals, the forebrain differentiates into a *telencephalon,* which ultimately comes to be the cerebral hemispheres, and a *diencephalon* which will contain the *thalamus* and *hypothalamus.* As the telencephalon develops, different structures appear at different times. The neurons that are arranged in a layered fashion (are called *cortex*) are formed near the time of birth. Because these cells are in layers (at least six of them), and because their arrangement is the most

3 week embryo

7 week embryo

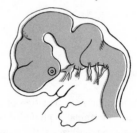

6 month fetus

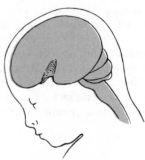

Newborn infant

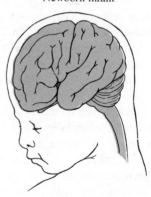

Fig. 4-6. Schematic representations of the development of the human brain at different ages.

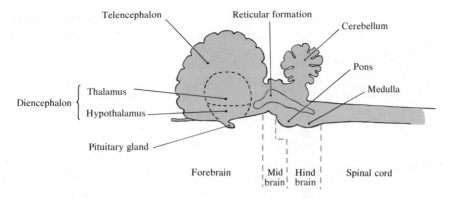

Fig. 4-7 Schematic representation of major brain subdivisions.

complex of the brain, they are called *neocortex* (evolutionarily new, layered tissue). Also developing from the telencephalon are the structures of the *basal ganglia* which lie deep in the brain anterior to the diencephalon. The basic organization of the brain is shown in Figure 4-7. The basal ganglia are thought to be primarily involved in the regulation of motor activities, but they also are involved in the expression of species-specific behaviors (see Chapter 6). Another group of structures that develops from the telencephalon is the *limbic system.* This is a collection of structures lying around the thalamus in most mammals, and all of the structures of the limbic system are strongly interconnected with the hypothalamus. Since the hypothalamus is the part of the brain most directly concerned with the regulation of the internal environment of the body, the limbic system has been thought to also participate in the control of the internal affairs of the body, especially those of an emotional nature.

In some ways, the hindbrain and deepest portions of the diencephalon and basal ganglia represent a common denominator among most vertebrate nervous systems. These basic structures occur in all the brains of living vertebrates. They are found in reptiles in a form with many similarities to the deep structures of mammalian brains. Collectively, they have been called a *protoreptilean brain.* It has been suggested that this

protoreptilean brain would be considered as containing the systems that play crucial roles in species-typical behaviors, such as the establishment of territories, the finding of food and shelter, reproductive acts, and the like. The telencephalic structures making up the limbic system come to add regulatory influences on the protoreptilean brain. This regulation would be based on the evaluation of the internal conditions of the body and the emotional state of the individual. The great elaboration of the telencephalon into the neocortical surface represents the achievement whereby the brain comes to have the ability to calculate elaborate contingencies in regard to planned actions. The neocortex would be the mechanism that acts to control and regulate both the limbic and protoreptilean portions of the brain.

This view of the mammalian brain, as being made up of three ''sub-brains'' with different functions, is shown in figure 4-8. As a model, it represents only a convenient way to look at and remember the functions of different parts of the brains of all advanced animals. It should not be taken to mean that there is an exact copy of a lizard brain in each of us or that all reptiles have nearly identical brains. In addition, it should not be taken to mean that the limbic brain is the same in all species either. What it should be taken to mean is that all animals share a common plan of brain structure that, within limits, has many behavioral,

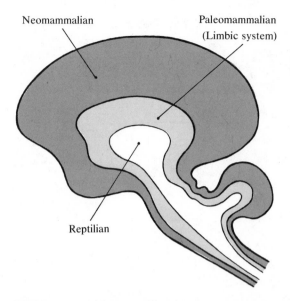

Neomammalian

Paleomammalian
(Limbic system)

Reptilian

Fig. 4-8. Three conceptual subdivisions of the mammalian brain.

species-typical acts represented by neural systems in the brain stem and along the base of the forebrain, many emotional and internal-organ control systems represented in limbic system structures, and neocortical system imposed on these first two components. Each species has its own environmental and behavioral idiosyncracies and has come to have rather its own specialized neural systems. All have somewhat different anatomical systems but these special arrangements always occur in the context of a protoreptilean, a limbic, and a neocortical brain.

The sequence of brain development is very similar in all mammals. In general, the parts of the brain which are phylogenetically older develop before those parts that have evolved more recently. For example, the spinal cord and brain stem form first, while the neocortex and cerebellum are among the last parts of the brain to mature. Looked at from a different perspective, it is the components of the protoreptilean brain that mature earliest, followed by those of the limbic system. This results in the birth of an animal with the basic mechanisms for all necessary behavior and internal adjustments completed. At later times, other systems develop related to the neocortex with its more complicated role in governing behavior.

The timetables of brain development differ considerably from one species to another. For all species, there is a period of time during which the brain grows at its most rapid rate. In the human, the brain begins to grow rapidly at the beginning of the second trimester of pregnancy. This period of growth continues through birth and slows down only about two years after birth. This period of high rate of growth is called the *brain growth spurt*. During this time, the cells of the brain are dividing and growing at their most rapid rate. The brain continues to enlarge, but at a markedly slower rate until it reaches its adult size and weight in the early teens.

There are a number of fascinating questions about the process of development that are still unanswered; some are rather basic questions. For example, when does the brain stop developing neurons? Some people believe that in humans, all of the neurons are made before birth and that only supporting cells (neuroglia or glia cells) are formed after birth. Others believe that some neurons, as well as glia cells, are made after birth. Other unresolved questions include: What guides nerve cells to their final destinations after they are formed? Is every cell predestined to go to a specific place? Are plans made for the formation of each and every synapse? Why do so many nerve cells divide and die before birth? What starts and what stops the division of nerve cells? How does the environment affect brain growth and development? More specifically, what kinds of environmental influences are important, and at what times during development, both before and after birth?

Disturbances of Brain Development

From the time that sperm and egg meet, the developing fetus is influenced by its environment. In fact, from the time of the union of the sperm and the egg, all solely hereditary influences have ended. Before birth, the environment is largely the conditions established by the nutrients and chemistry in the bloodstream of the mother. The developing fetus needs a continuous flow of oxygen and nutrients in order to develop properly. Interference with the flow of these essential materials or the introduction of toxic agents is likely to have detrimental effects on brain development. Many kinds of drugs and diseases have effects on the developing fetus that they do not have on the adult. For example, German measles contracted during the first trimester of pregnancy can cause a number of defects in the fetus including blindness, heart anomalies, and gross distortions of brain activity.

In many ways, the developing fetus is more vulnerable than the adult. Many poisons and infections readily cross the placental barrier to the fetus, and, if they do, produce disorders of development that often are permanent. Indeed, there are certain times during development when vulnerability is greatest. For the nervous system, the most vulnerable time is during the brain growth spurt, that is, between the second trimester of pregnancy to about two years of life. Disruptions of the baby's environment will have the greatest effects if they occur at this time. Consequently, these disruptions are most likely to lead to permanent brain changes. Temporary disruptions of the baby's environment have the greatest effect on the brain systems that are growing most rapidly. Each part of the brain is most susceptible to interruption at a slightly different time during its own particular growth spurt.

Malnutrition. The growing infant needs nutrients with which to build new cells and to provide materials for further development, and a lack of nutrients has disastrous effects on brain development. While starvation beginning in adulthood has little effect on the size and weight of the brain, malnutrition of the baby during the brain growth spurt, either before or after birth, results in an abnormal brain in terms of both its structure and function. No matter how much nourishment is provided later on, the brain will never reach its proper size and weight. Malnutrition after the brain growth spurt may cause a delay in the development of the brain, but this can be reversed by a return to a proper diet at some later time. These observations underline the need to provide mothers with an adequate diet throughout pregnancy as well as after birth, to prevent permanent debilitation from malnutrition.

What is the significance of malnutrition for behavior? Does a smaller, lighter brain lead to less intelligent behavior? The answer is not easy to obtain. Malnourished people usually have histories of poverty, disease, poor education, and many other problems as well. All of these factors influence performance on intelligence tests, and, consequently, it is difficult to isolate the effects of malnourishment, *per se*. Research on laboratory animals might seem to be a way to identify the behavioral effects of malnutrition, but on closer inspection, problems exist here as well. An animal can be malnourished in many ways. Some of the ways that have been used with laboratory rats include starving the mother, removing the mother from the cage for most of the day so the pups can nurse for a limited time, and increasing the litter size by providing a large number of foster pups. As a consequence, each infant gets less milk. However, all of these methods change the relationship between the mother and the pups and among the pups themselves. These differences could be the cause of behavioral changes as well as the malnourishment. In animals, as in humans, it is difficult to create a situation in which the developing infant is malnourished without any other differences in its environment. With these difficulties in mind, it can be said that malnourishment early in life seems to affect the animal's or person's interest in the world, the ability to adjust to stress and uncertainty, and to have normal emotional reactions to others. Malnourishment may also predispose people toward seizure disorders (such as epilepsy).

Sensory Deprivation. Malnutrition is only one kind of environmental influence that affects the development of the brain. After birth, the infant must receive stimulation of its sensory systems for them to achieve proper structure and function. Depriving a rat, cat, or mouse of light or of patterned visual stimuli for a period of time after birth will result in abnormalities of vision that are usually permanent. If the visual deprivation lasts long enough, the animal will be blind. Even though most of the pathways in the visual system have developed in these species well before birth, they must be stimulated in order to thrive. This is another example of the extreme sensitivity of the infant brain to abnormal conditions, since the same degree and duration of visual deprivation will not produce permanent structural changes in the brain of the adult.

Even relatively minor changes in experience

early in life may result in long-lasting effects on brain function and behavior. It has been found that young rats that are handled by humans, reared in groups with toys to play with, and exposed to a wide variety of sensory stimuli will mature faster and have somewhat larger and heavier brains than rats reared only with their littermates. The handled rats' secretion of hormones from the adrenal glands after stress will be changed. This change lasts a lifetime. Dogs raised in isolation become hyperactive and never interact properly with other dogs or people. Some nonhuman primates do not thrive if separated from their mothers and from peers in the colony. Similarly, human infants placed in orphanages where they receive little attention often tend to become apathetic and "fail to thrive." However, it would be a mistake to think that enhanced sensory stimulation is always the best thing for a developing organism. Rats and mice differ in their reactions to being with others of their species, and some types of monkeys do not exhibit any behavioral disturbances when separated from mothers and peers. For the human, sensory stimulation can be too intense as well as too little. Babies develop best when exposed to an appropriate amount and type of stimulation. They fail to do well if there is too little or too much.

Another problem exists for the interpretation of sensory stimulation experiments. Usually, the benefits are described as a more rapid development of the individual in terms of size, weight, or the attainment of some ability. But, is more rapid development a good thing? Are there advantages to the slow development of humans? Are larger, heavier brains better than smaller, lighter ones? These are important questions, and the answers are not entirely known. It is clear, however, that the brain matures according to a timetable that dictates when environmental influences will have their greatest effect on brain development and on later behavior.

The Interplay of Heredity and Environment

What is the relative importance of heredity and environment in regulating brain development? This question is impossible to answer. All behavior, as will be described in Chapter 6, reflects the joint ef-

fects of nature (heredity) and nurture (the environment). Genes create tendencies in the organism that may be expressed in a particular environment or under certain conditions.

One example of the relationship between heredity and environment is in the rabbit. Under most circumstances, the color of the rabbit's hair is genetically determined. However, if a baby rabbit with genes for white fur has a small patch subjected to cold by having an ice cube placed on it, the adult rabbit will have a patch of black fur there (see Figure 4-9). This shows that while the genes contain information about tendencies toward characteristics that will usually be exhibited these characteristics can be altered by environmental circumstances. The characteristics of the adult are determined by heredity and environment interacting with each other and not by either one alone.

Fig. 4-9.   A result of the interaction between heredity and environment. This adult rabbit with genes for white fur has a patch of black fur where it was subjected to cold during infancy.

About ten million people are thought to be "alcoholics" in the United States today. There is evidence of a genetic component in the tendency toward alcoholism, but it is also clear that no matter how strong such a disposition might be, the person will not become an alcoholic if there is no alcohol available or if total abstinence is practiced.

Therefore, while there is a genetic tendency for alcoholism, an environmental component is also essential, namely, the alcohol itself.

Another example of the interchange between genes and the environment in the human is a hereditary disorder called phenylketonuria (PKU). PKU is an inherited disorder of metabolism. In PKU, the enzyme that metabolizes a particular amino acid (phenylalanine) is missing. This defect has no effect on the infant before birth, since up to this time phenylalanine is metabolized by the mother. In the normal infant, this enzyme becomes active shortly after birth, when the mother's system cannot be used to break down the infant's phenylalanine. In the phenylketonuric infant, phenylalanine cannot be metabolized beginning at birth. It accumulates and interferes with many different kinds of biochemical processes in the body and brain. This interference disrupts brain development and inevitably results in children with low intellectual abilities. Once the damage is done, the effects on brain and behavior are permanent.

Although the enzyme is missing due to a genetic disorder, the disruption of brain development can occur only in a particular environment, that is, one in which there is plenty of phenylalanine. If the amount of phenylalanine in the diet is severely limited, the brain malfunction and the drop in intelligence can be minimized. Fortunately, children with PKU can be identified by a simple test of their urine and can be put on a low phenylalanine diet shortly after birth. If this is done, the disastrous consequences of a hereditary disorder can be greatly reduced.

Basic Gross Anatomy of the Brain

If a brain is considered to be those interneurons interposed between sensory fibers coming from receptors and motor fibers going to muscles, then all of the neurons in between would have to be considered as the brain. However, a further distinction is made between the brain and the spinal cord. In humans, the spinal cord is a collection of nerve cells and fibers (axons and dendrites) that lie within the bony vertebral columns. At the top of the spinal cord, there are enlargements representing the brain stem and cerebellum, those areas of the brain that arose from the hindbrain. Ahead of these regions is the major development of the brain as we generally think of it. The brain and spinal cord together are called the *central nervous system*. Cells and axons going outside these regions, such as nerves going to muscles, are in the peripheral nervous system.

To make clear how the human central nervous system is assembled, additional details must be added to the basic anatomical features described earlier.

The Spinal Cord

The spinal cord is the lower continuation of the hindbrain. It is made up of neurons and glia cells, cell processes, and fiber tracts (mostly axons). It has very prominent grey and white matter regions with the grey portions taking the shape of an H (or butterfly) in the center of the cord (see Figure 4-10). The white matter around the H is made up of long ascending and descending tracts of axons. By and large, axons going toward the brain go along the *dorsal* (toward the back) aspects of the spinal cord, while descending axons run along the *ventral* (toward the belly) portions of the cord. The cells whose axons run out to the muscles that move the skeleton are located in the ventral parts of the grey matter H and are called *ventral horn* cells, because of this location. Another name for these cells is *motoneurons*.

The motoneurons in the ventral horns of spinal cord grey matter are regulated by nerve impulses reaching them from cells of the neocortex, from the basal ganglia, from the cerebellum, and from various groups of cells in the upper regions of the spinal cord and midbrain. They also are contacted by some axons of sensory nerves from muscles, skin, and tendons related to the muscles they contact and by interneurons of the spinal cord that are, in turn, part of reflex mechanisms in the spinal cord itself. Thus, the control of muscle movements is controlled by many diverse influences extending from the neocortex on the one hand to local sensory input in the cord itself on the other.

The ways in which information from skin, muscles, and tendons reach the spinal cord is of special

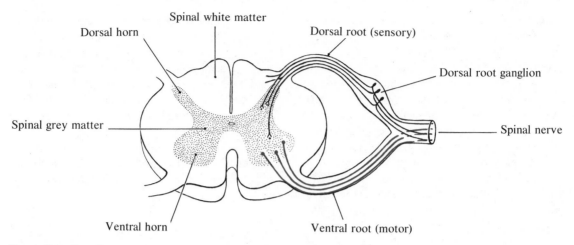

Fig. 4-10.   Cross-section of the spinal cord and peripheral nerves. The spinal grey matter contains larger numbers of cell bodies; the spinal white matter contains a preponderance of myelinated axons. Sensory fibers enter the cord through the dorsal root. Their cell bodies are in the dorsal root ganglion. The cell bodies of motor neurons are in the ventral horn of the spinal cord. Their axons exit through the ventral root. Peripheral nerves have both sensory and motor fibers.

interest. Lying just outside the spinal cord are clusters of cell bodies grouped together to form the *dorsal root ganglia*. (*Ganglion* is a term used to describe any collection of nerve cells outside the central nervous sytem; inside the central nervous system, clusters of neurons are called *nuclei*.) These cells are unique in the nervous system, since they have a very long process that runs to the skin or muscle on the one hand and into the spinal cord on the other (see Figure 4-10). Both components are myelinated. Is this process an axon or is it a dendrite? The name probably does not matter, but this long process conveys information from the periphery of the body to the spinal cord and toward the brain.

The processes (whatever they should be called) of the dorsal root ganglia and the axons of the ventral horn cells that go to the muscles enter and leave the spinal cord in the spaces between the *vertebral column*. This outer covering of the spinal cord is made up of rings of bone. It serves to protect the delicate spinal cord from damage, although by accident or disease the bony rings of the vertebral column can come to interrupt the spinal cord or the nerves that pass between them. If the vertebral column is compressed or broken to the extent that the spinal cord is severed, the brain cannot

receive sensory information from any part of the body whose sensory nerves are below the point of severance. Thus, the person has no feelings or sensations from these regions. By the same token, any muscles served by motoneurons below the break in the spinal cord can no longer be moved voluntarily and a permanent paralysis results.

The Brain Stem

At the top of the spinal cord, there are enlargements of the neural tissue that are called the medulla, pons, and cerebellum. As in the spinal cord, the ventral portions of the medulla and pons are made up of descending axons and the dorsal portions in these areas are largely axons ascending from the cord. In this region, there are several groups of nerve cells that receive axons from cells in the dorsal root ganglia and can be thought of as "relay stations" for sensory information on the way toward the brain (see Chapter 5 on sensory systems for further discussion). Also in these regions are groups of cells that act to regulate simple motor movements.

In the middle parts of the hindbrain and in the midbrain, there is a diffuse collection of nerve cells whose axons project both toward the brain and back down into the spinal cord. Many of these cells have very long axons. The arrangement of their cell bodies, however, does not seem to be too orderly and the result is a net-like appearance of the tissue when viewed in the microscope. Because of this, the area has been called the *brain stem reticular formation*. For many reasons, it seems likely that this system exerts regulatory influences on all other regions of the brain, altering the general excitability of nerve cells through the central nervous system. Some level of activity in this system is thought to be necessary to maintain consciousness and some drugs used to induce sleep (for example, the barbiturates) are thought to act by suppressing the activity in brain stem reticular formation.

The cerebellum is a large mass of brain tissue that sits above the pons in the hindbrain. Its anatomical configuration varies from one animal to another, but the role of the cerebellum in behavior is always to organize and coordinate motor movements, taking into consideration the position of the body in the environment. Most likely, over the course of evolution, the cerebellum developed out of more primitive neural systems related to maintaining balance and posture, but in animals with more complicated brains, it is a place where influences from many sensory systems converge with information coming from the forebrain through the pons. The consequence of cerebellar activity is coordinate movements under all conditions. The primary sign of cerebellar damage or disease is the loss of coordinated motor movements.

The Midbrain

This is the portion of the brain that connects the brain stem with the diencephalon. The dorsal portion is called the *tectum* (roof), the ventral part the *tegmentum* (covering). In the human, the tectum is made up of two pairs of elevations or lumps that are called the *superior* and *inferior colliculi*. The pair closest to the spinal cord are the inferior colliculi and receive information from the auditory system. The pair closest to the diencephalon are the superior colliculi and receive visual information. Both sets of colliculi are important for the localization of objects or sounds in the environment. The

tegmentum of the midbrain contains many ascending and descending fiber systems and several nuclei for *cranial nerves,* the nerves that serve sensory and motor functions of the head. The middle portions of the midbrain contain the forward extension of the reticular formation of the brain stem. At this region, it is called the midbrain reticular formation.

The Diencephalon

The diencephalon is composed of the *thalamus,* above, and the *hypothalamus,* below. It is like an egg in shape, situated in the middle and bottom of the brain. The hypothalamus runs along the base of the brain from the midbrain forward until the frontal lobes of the brain are reached. It is not very large in any species but is packed with a number of different nuclear groups. Moreover, a number of ascending and descending fiber systems, including the *medial forebrain bundle,* course through the hypothalamus. There are great differences between those hypothalamic nuclei near the middle of the brain (*medial*) and those on the outer edges (*lateral*). (See p. 126.) The lateral hypothalamus is the region through which the medial forebrain bundle passes. The hypothalamus is directly involved with the regulation of the internal organs and glands. This is accomplished through the autonomic nervous system which will be discussed separately below.

The thalamus is often considered as having two separate subdivisions: *dorsal thalamus* and *ventral thalamus*. The dorsal thalamus contains cell groups that receive information from all of the sensory systems (except olfaction) and send axons to limited neocortical areas. The ventral thalamus is made up of a set of nuclei that are involved with the regulation of motor movements and whose function is closely related to the activities of the basal ganglia.

All of the activities of the cells that make up the dorsal thalamus are closely tied to the neocortical surface of the brain. Some transmit sensory information to the neocortex but others are on the receiving end; that is, they are the recipients of nerve impulses originating in the neocortex. These regions then send axons back to other neocortical regions. All nuclei of the dorsal thalamus are in constant interchange with smaller or wider neocortical areas. This interchange is vital to the normal function of the neocortex.

The Basal Ganglia

This term is often used to refer to three major masses of cells located in front of and around the sides of the diencephalon. These cell groups are the *globus pallidus,* the *caudate nucleus,* and the *putamen*. (There are other structures of the basal ganglia but, because of space, they will not be considered here.) All three of these structures are involved with the execution of motor movements. The basal ganglia receive a great deal of input from the neocortex, from parts of the ventral thalamus, and from cells in the brain stem and midbrain. The exact nature of the behavioral contribution made by the basal ganglia is not well understood, but diseases that strike this system (for example, Parkinson's disease) produce tremor and an inability to initiate or maintain movements.

The Limbic System

The major structures of the limbic system are the *amygdala, septal area,* and *hippocampus*. All have strong connections with the hypothalamus and with each other. The hippocampus has its major interconnections with the septal area over a band of axons running in both directions called the fornix. The fornix pathway also reaches the hypothalamus and fibers from other parts of the brain besides the hippocampus pass through it to reach the hypothalamus. The amygdala has its own special pathways to the hypothalamus.

In humans, the hippocampus and the amygdala are tucked into bulges of neocortex along the sides of the brain called the temporal lobes. The septal area is located in the middle of the brain just ahead of the hypothalamus.

The Neocortex

The neocortical surface of the brain is divided into lobes as shown in Figure 4-11. The usual designa-

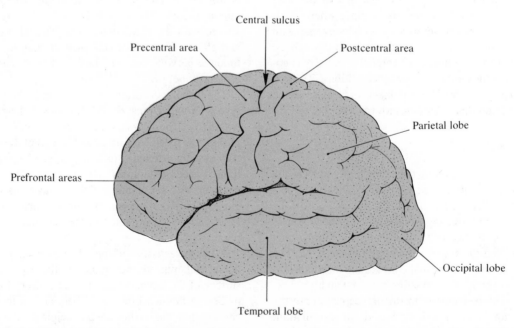

Fig. 4-11 Drawing of human brain with its major lobes and areas. The central sulcus separates the primary motor (precentral) and somatosensory (postcentral) regions.

tions of these lobes are (1) a *frontal lobe,* beginning with the central sulcus in the middle of the brain and continuing forward throughout the mid-anterior regions of the brain, (2) the *prefrontal lobes* which are the most anterior portions of the hemispheres, (3) the *parietal lobes* just in back of the central sulcus, (4) the *occipital lobes* at the back of the brain, and (5) the *temporal lobes* off on the right and left sides of the brain. To some extent, different behavioral functions depend on activity in these lobes. For example, the frontal lobes are thought to be primarily concerned with motor activities, because many cells in this region have axons that run into the spinal cord and end on cells concerned with the regulation of muscle movement. Damage to these regions produces a deficit in the ability to make very fine movements, such as the movements of the fingers when playing the piano. The parietal lobes receive afferent (sensory) information from receptors in the skin, muscles, and tendons of the body after they have been relayed through the dorsal thalamus. The occipital lobes receive nerve fibers that carry information arising in the visual system. Regions along the upper parts of the temporal lobes receive information arising in the auditory system. Once again, the neocortex only receives this information after relay in the dorsal thalamus. The activities of neurons in these various lobes are not restricted to the functions of mediating sensory information. It seems clear that all the neocortical regions in both hemispheres are involved in very complex intellectual activities.

Because the brain is a paired organ, there are right and left neocortical lobes. In many animals, the right and left lobes serve identical functions. In humans, however, the left and right hemispheres have some different functions. These differences have been dramatically demonstrated in patients with epilepsy in whom the two hemispheres have been disconnected from each other by surgically cutting the band of myelinated axons which interconnect them. (This operation was performed to reduce the debilitating spread of seizure activities.) By the use of clever testing techniques, it is possible to present stimuli of a visual or tactual nature to one side of the brain or the other, and thus to determine the abilities of the two hemispheres. Language, as well as the ability to manipulate symbols and abstract concepts seems to be a special property of the left hemisphere in most people and especially in the area where the temporal and parietal lobes meet. The ability to organize the environment in terms of spatial arrangements seems to be a special property of the right hemisphere.

Transmitter Anatomy

A relatively new way of studying anatomy has been developed in recent years. This is the study of cell bodies and axons containing specific transmitter substances. This has been done through the use of special stains applied to brain tissue that react with enzymes associated with specific transmitters that exhibit fluorescence when ultraviolet light reaches them (Falck, 1962). A complete description of transmitter system anatomy is beyond the scope of this chapter but some important details will be presented. This knowledge is useful in understanding how different parts of the brain are regulated and controlled by specific neurochemical systems. This not only allows us to understand the effects of drugs that alter these chemical systems, but also to predict ahead of time the effects of new drugs on behavior and mental activities.

Neurons containing *noradrenalin* are located in several groups of cells found in the brain stem (midbrain, pons, and medulla), and one large collection of such cells is in a region called the *locus coeruleus.* These cells project to the cerebellum, the spinal cord, the hypothalamus, the limbic system (especially the hippocampus), and the neocortex.

Cells that produce *dopamine* arise from three cell groups, two of which lie in the midbrain and one in the hypothalamus. These cells project to the basal ganglia, the septal area, the neocortex, as well as to some hypothalamic regions. *Serotonin*-containing fibers arise from cells in the *raphe nuclei* of the brain stem. Fibers from all of the biogenic amine systems (that is, noradrenalin, dopamine, serotonin) travel to the forebrain along the base of the forebrain, through the general area of the lateral hypothalamus. The medial forebrain bundle passes through this area, and it contains many of these fibers. This is the area which, when electrically stimulated, seems to be positively rewarding and which has been associated with neural systems related to eating and drinking.

The distribution of acetylcholine has been localized through the use of stains that mark the enzyme that degrades it. All of the chemicals used as transmitters must have enzymes that help form them and, after their use, degrade them. It is assumed that the presence of enzymes more or less specific to forming or degrading a particular transmitter implies the presence of the transmitter itself. In the case of acetylcholine, the identification of the degrading enzyme is far easier, technically, than the identification of the transmitter. It is found throughout the brain but is heavily concentrated in the basal ganglia, the septal area, and parts of the limbic system. It differs from the biogenic amines in that it appears to be made in cells found widely throughout the brain, whereas the biogenic amines are made only in selected sites and transported over long distances over axons of these cells.

Cerebrospinal Fluid and the Ventricular Systems

The brains of all mammals are hollow. Every brain develops from a neural tube formed very early in the embryo, and this tube is present in the adult as fluid-filled cavities in the brain and spinal cord. These spaces are called *ventricles*. The ventricles of the human brain are shown in Figure 4.12. There is a small slit-like ventricle in the area of the hypothalamus (third ventricle), and wide and extended spaces in the temporal lobes (lateral ventricles) which continue in a forward direction over the top of the basal ganglia. The ventricular system runs through the spinal cord as a central canal. The fluid that fills the ventricular spaces is called *cerebrospinal fluid*. It is clear and colorless, is virtually free of cells, and has little protein. It is a very special fluid of the body that is secreted by specialized cells in the ventricles. It flows constantly through all of the ventricular spaces. It also circulates around the brain and spinal cord underneath the several membranes (the meninges) that enwrap all of the central nervous system.

The role of cerbrospinal fluid in normal brain function is poorly understood, but it may have an important role in allowing certain chemicals and hormones to reach widespread areas of the brain. Disruption of the ventricular system or the circulation of cerebrospinal fluid can result in the development of *hydrocephaly* in which the cerebrospinal fluid builds up great pressure in a ventricular space and compresses the brain tissue to such an extent that it cannot function. In such cases, a tube can be placed into the brain to relieve the pressure and reduce the swollen ventricular cavity.

The Adaptive Processes of the Brain

Describing the structure of the brain can be misleading, because the description may obscure the constant activity of the cells of which it is made. Within all areas of the brain, there is constant change, both in the electrochemical activity of individual cells and in the actual physical locations of many of the fine dendritic and axon processes. The cells of the brain are alive and in motion. Usually, the distances of movement in axon and dendrites are microscopic so that there are no major changes in brain structure. However, the brain is alive and in constant activity, and all of the cells in it share these qualities of movement and life.

Sleep and Wakefulness

Even during sleep, the brain is active, although its activities during sleep are different from those when it is awake, as will be further described in Chapter 13. In humans, the activities of the outer rind of the brain, the neocortex, can be recorded through electrodes pasted to the scalp. This record is called an *electroencephalogram* (*EEG*). The rhythms recorded by the EEG represent the electrical activity of the neurons, axons, and dendrites of the brain, although there is no precise relationship between the EEG and the electrical activity in any one of these three anatomical components of the brain. However, the EEG can reveal things about the general state of brain activity. When a person is mentally active, the EEG is comprised mostly of fast waves of small voltage

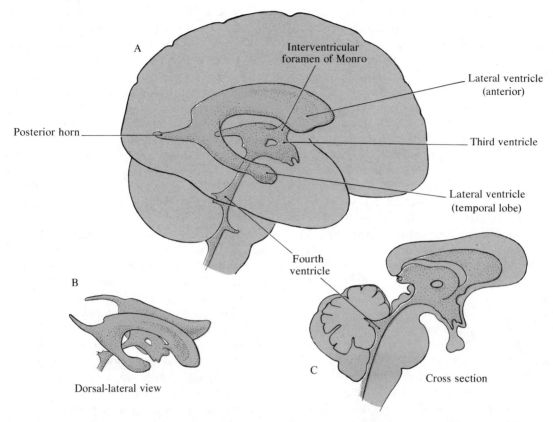

Fig. 4-12 Drawings showing the location of the human ventricular system. A shows the general position of the major ventricles in the brain while B provides a three-dimensional perspective without other brain areas represented. C illustrates the continuation of the ventricular system into the brain stem.

(low amplitude). At such times, the activity of the neocortex is said to be "desynchronized." As a person begins to be bored or drowsy, the electrical rhythms of the neocortex become more synchronized and the strength of the waves becomes greater (high amplitude). During most periods of sleep, the waves become even slower in frequency.

What causes sleep? Years ago, scientists thought that sleep occurred simply as a result of a decrease in sensory stimulation. If you wanted to go to sleep, all you had to do was go to a quiet, dark room with a comfortable bed. It soon became clear that this explanation of sleep was inadequate. Research on animals indicated that even if all the nerves carrying sensory information to the brain

were cut, the brain did not sleep perpetually. It is now clear that sleep is not a passive, resting state of the brain.

Both sleep and waking are active processes. The difference between sleep and waking is a difference in the kinds of activity which occur in special structures and systems of the brain. The activity of the brain is being regulated constantly by anatomical systems that influence many or all of its various regions. The reticular formation of the midbrain and brain stem is one important source of such general or diffuse influences but it is not the only one. Other systems providing general influences on the brain and behavior can be found in the thalamus and hypothalamus. Probably the biogenic amine systems (noradrenalin, dopamine, and serotonin) also play roles in regulating levels of activity in widespread regions of the brain.

How close is the relationship between the electrical rhythms represented by the EEG and the behavioral state of a person? Two kinds of evidence indicate that the answer to these questions is "not very." First, drugs can change the electrical activity of the neocortex, so that activity recorded from the brain no longer correlates with sleep or wakefulness. Drugs can be given which desynchronize the activity of the cortex even though the person may be able to sleep under the drug. Other drugs induce regular slow waves in the EEG even though the subject may be wide awake. Beyond this, however, is the fact that every now and again the EEG resembles that of an awake, alert person during the middle of sound sleep (see Chapter 13).

Sensory and Motor Systems

The details of organization of the sensory systems of the body will be discussed in Chapter 5. Only certain additional details will be presented here, those that relate to the actions of sensory information on the activities of the brain. To start with, it must be recognized that the effects of activity in the sensory systems are always superimposed on the ongoing activity of the brain. When a sensory stimulus is introduced, changes are produced in this prior activity. These changes occur in a variety of different places, including the parts of the brain stem, thalamus, and neocortex.

Sensory stimulation does far more than provide the means of obtaining information about the outside world. A certain amount of sensory input is necessary to maintain normal behavior. It contributes to the behavioral activation of the individual probably by influences reaching the diffusely projecting systems, such as the reticular formation. The disorganizing effect of too little sensory input has been dramatically illustrated in experiments on *sensory deprivation*. In a typical experiment, a person is placed in a sound-proofed room, blindfolded, and cotton wadding wrapped around his arms and legs. He or she is instructed simply to lie still. The longer the subject remains in this situation, the more bizarre his thoughts become. At first

it may be difficult to concentrate; later, thoughts become confused and disorganized. Rapid changes in emotion, and even hallucinations, are reported. This suggests that the brain does not simply receive external stimulation in a passive manner. It requires external stimulation in order to anticipate, plan, and experience life normally.

Sensory stimulation leads to activation of the motor systems both in direct and indirect ways. However, the brain and central nervous system have many "motor systems," and parts of many different brain regions ranging from the spinal cord to the neocortex participate in the regulation of motor movements.

Axons from sensory neurons from the skin and muscles are in direct contact with motoneurons and they are responsible for reflexes such as jerking the hand away from a painful stimulus. Many parts of the brain and spinal cord also send signals to the motoneurons. Furthermore, the motoneurons receive a constant bombardment from the cerebellum and the vestibular systems that help adjust the body's movements to its position in space and relative to the pull of gravity. There is constant activity in all of these systems even though no gross bodily movements are seen. An important point to be noted is that the "higher regions" of the brain can override the reflexive adjustments of the spinal cord mechanisms. For example, through conscious effort, the familiar knee jerk reflex that occurs when the lower front of the knee is tapped with a rubber mallet can be inhibited. The reflexive act of dropping a hot object can be suppressed if the object is known to be of great value even if holding the hot object is at the cost of tissue damage to the fingers. This probably is due to the action of cells in the neocortex that act to inhibit the reflex circuitry in the spinal cord.

Frontal regions of the neocortex have fairly direct connections with motoneurons in the spinal cord. For well over one hundred years, it has been known that an electrical current passed through anterior neocortical regions could elicit movements when the animal is in a drug-induced deep sleep. The region of the cortex from which movements can be elicited by electrical stimulation in this drugged state is called the *motor cortex*. Like the sensory areas of the neocortex, the motor cortex seems to contain a "map" of the muscles in the periphery of the body. Stimulation in different regions of the cortical motor map causes movement in different parts of the body as can be seen in Figure 4-13. This shows that the neocortex has cells that participate in the control of the specific muscles of the body. Under normal, undrugged conditions, muscle movements are under the control of more regions of the brain than when the animal is drugged and asleep. The neocortex is only one such source of this motor control.

Some of the regions beneath the neocortical surface add very special characteristics to movements. The importance of the continual activity of these parts can be dramatically demonstrated in people who have experienced damage to them. Diseases affecting some areas of the brain beneath the cortex can cause movements that the person does not intend and cannot control. Other kinds of subcortical brain damage cause a tremor if any movement is attempted, while other types of damage produces a tremor if no movement is taking place. Still other kinds of brain damage or disease make it difficult to begin or to stop movements. The types of motor disturbances that can occur as a result of subcortical disease or damage are large and varied. Almost all forms of motor disturbances commonly found in people are due to subcortical difficulties.

Complex motor acts are built-in to the spinal cord and brain stem. These are the instinctive acts and movements from which all more elaborate goal-directed acts are compiled. These fundamentals of action are controlled, regulated, and synthesized into sequences of behavior by neural systems originating in the forebrain, namely, the neocortex, limbic system, and other subcortical regions. It is as if these higher centers play on a brain stem key board of primitive, instinctive behaviors to produce behavioral results useful to the individual, based on opportunities in the environment detected by the sensory apparatus.

Autonomic Nervous System

Not only does the brain have systems that evaluate the outer world, the sensory systems, and control the muscles that move the skeleton, the motor systems; it also has separate sensory and motor systems for the internal organs and glands. The brain influences all of the internal organs, the blood ves-

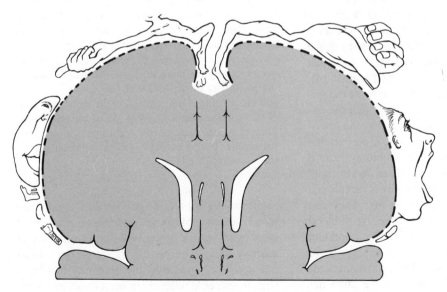

Fig. 4-13.
Schematic drawing of a cross-section through the middle of human brain. A sensory "Homunculus" is shown in the left and a motor "Homunculus" on the right. The amounts of areas of the body shown represent the relative degree to which different portions of the neocortical surface are related to these portions of the body.

sels, and salivary glands, and many of the endocrine glands.

The brain's regulation of the internal organs is
accomplished by nerve cells that are collectively
known as the *autonomic nervous system*. The autonomic nervous system has two major components or ''branches'': the *sympathetic* and the
parasympathetic. In general, the sympathetic
branch of the autonomic nervous system is
concerned with the organization of the body for
emergency reactions such as fighting or running
away from an enemy. It produces changes in the
activity of the organs directly concerned with the
emergency activities while, at the same time, it
mobilizes the metabolic activities of the body to
sustain the activity. The parasympathetic branch of
the autonomic nervous system is most active during resting conditions. At any moment the state of
the inner body is a result of the balance between
parasympathetic and sympathetic activities.

Most of the internal organs receive axons from
cells of both the sympathetic and parasympathetic
branches of the automatic nervous system. The
functional contributions of the two branches are
often antagonistic to each other. For example, in
the control of the iris of the eye, the activation of
the sympathetic branch opens the iris so that the
pupil is large; activation of the parasympathetic
branch reduces pupil size by closing the iris. The
two influences play on the muscles of the iris to
produce a size of opening reflecting the balance of
the two opposing inputs. Anatomically, the nerves
associated with the parasympathetic branch of the
autonomic nervous system come off the spinal
cord at its upper and lower ends (see Figure 4-14).
Nerves of the sympathetic branch come off the spinal cord at the middle regions. Although the autonomic nervous system is influenced by the activities of certain regions of the brain, especially the
hypothalamus and parts of the limbic system, it
was thought for a long time that these nerves could
not be controlled voluntarily. However, people can
learn to control their internal organs. They can
increase and decrease heart rates, the size of blood
vessels, and other bodily processes. An important
aspect of learning to do any of these things is for
one to come to know whether he or she is succeeding. Unlike motor movements, we are often not

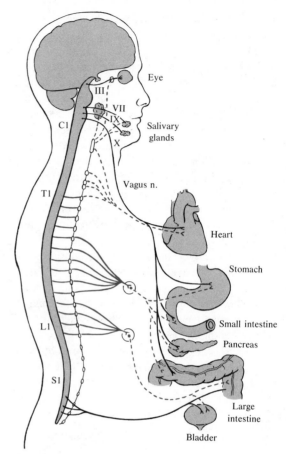

Fig. 4-14 Diagram of the human autonomic nervous
system. Fibers from the sympathetic division are shown
in red; fibers from the parasympathetic division in
black. The number of the cranial nerves are given in
roman numerals. C1 refers to the first pair of nerves
leaving the cervical area. T1 refers to the first pair of
nerves leaving the thoracic region. L1 and S1 indicate
the position of the first pairs of nerves leaving lumbar
and sacral portions respectively, of the spinal cord. The
X cranial nerve (vagus) is given special prominence because of its importance to the regulation of many internal organs. It also conveys sensory information from
these organs to the brain.

aware of the actions of our internal organs and
blood vessels. Machines have been made that
show heart rate or blood vessel size by visual or
auditory signals (*biofeedback*). A person's heart
rate could be signaled by the frequency of a tone.
High tones could reflect high heart rates, low tones

low rates. The person then can try to lower the tone and consequently, the heart rate. However, while using mechanical means of letting a person know what the internal organs are doing is useful in teaching people how to control them, it probably is not essential. Some yogis and other Oriental mystics seem to have learned how to control their internal reactions by other, largely unknown ways.

Hormones

Another way the brain regulates the internal organs is by use of the *endocrine glands*. The endocrine glands are glands which release their chemical contents or hormones directly into the bloodstream. Because the chemicals go wherever the bloodstream leads, their effects are generalized throughout the body. The master gland for many of the other endocrine glands is the *pituitary gland*. It is attached to the base of the brain directly below the hypothalamus. Neural and chemical messages from the hypothalamus cause the pituitary gland to secrete hormones which control the efficiency of the kidneys; hormones which cause contraction of the muscles of the uterus; growth hormone; and several hormones which must travel to other organs such as the thyroid gland, adrenal cortex, and gonads to stimulate the release of hormones in these glands.

However, the relationship between the brain and the endocrine glands is not a one-way street. Hormones circulating in the bloodstream are detected by cells in the brain, particularly by cells in the hypothalamus, and if levels are high, further hormone secretion is inhibited. In addition, circulating hormones act on the brain and help to regulate activity in some of its systems. For example, in many species mating behavior is highly dependent on the gonadal hormones. While these hormones are required to maintain the sex organs, they also act on the brain to facilitate reproductive behavior.

The importance of hormone action on the brain is clearly shown in the behavioral changes that accompany many kinds of endocrine gland disorders. For example, a decrease in thyroid gland activity can lead to feelings of depression, fatigue, and rapid swings of emotion; overactivity of the thyroid gland can lead to excitability, irritability,

and outbursts of rage. "Adrenal insufficiency," a disease in which there is a decrease in the hormones produced by the adrenal cortex, is often associated with personality changes like apathy, indifference, and negativity. Too great a production of these hormones is often associated with severe psychotic problems. The exact nature of the symptoms depends on the personality of the person before the endocrine disorder began.

Emotion and Motivation

Ideas about the biological basis of emotion and the nervous system have been based on the relationship between the activities of the organs of the inner body and their interactions with the brain. While experiencing emotions such as fear, anger, or joy, there are changes in pupil size, heart rate, respiration, the circulation of the blood, and many other factors. At one time it was thought that the perception of these bodily changes constituted the experience of the emotion. This theory cannot be true, since people with severed spinal cords still experience emotion. The brains of people with such damage cannot receive information from their bodies, either muscles, skin, or internal organs. Despite this, however, these peripheral changes in the body may contribute some relatively minor influences on the perception of emotion in normal people.

The study of the neural mechanisms underlying motivated behavior is complicated by the question of what motivated behavior really is. Behaviorally-oriented psychologists use "motivation" in many different ways and not all psychologists agree on a definition (see Chapter 8). Motives for achievement, power, and security are often discussed by social psychologists, but physiological psychologists have restricted their attention to very simple examples of physiologically-motivated behavior such as hunger, thirst, and sex. In defense of this procedure, at least these behaviors are examples of motives essential to individual life and the future of the species.

In the area of hunger, feeding behavior has been studied extensively both with respect to the kinds of internal signals which start and stop eating and the places in the brain important for such behaviors. The most important signals for eating are chemical in nature and are carried through the bloodstream to the brain. Certain cells in the hypothalamus are sensitive to changes in the amount of glucose, fat, and enzymes from peripheral organs associated with the conversion of sugar to starch and starch to fats, as well as the reverse processes. These cells then send messages to other areas of the brain that control feeding behavior. Within the hypothalamus, two regions have been identified that are of major importance for feeding. The *lateral hypothalamus* is important for feeding, since destruction of it results in an animal that will neither eat nor drink (Teitelbaum and Epstein, 1962). On the other hand, the *ventromedial nucleus of the hypothalamus* is important for satiation and the termination of feeding, since destroying it results in an animal that overeats and becomes obese (Miller, Bailey, and Stevenson, 1950). However, the anatomical story is not quite as simple as a feeding "onset mechanism" in the lateral hypothalamus and a feeding "offset mechanism" in the ventromedial hypothalamus. The first complication is that if the damage is restricted to the lateral hypothalamus itself, the animals will eventually begin to eat if they can be force-fed for a week or two. For a variety of reasons, it now seems that the lesions of the lateral hypothalamus interrupt a system of fibers that originate below the hypothalamus in the brain stem, go through lateral hypothalamus, and terminate in the basal ganglia. These fibers are catecholaminergic (they contain and use dopamine as a tramsmitter at their endings). Injury of a physical or chemical nature that interrupts these fibers produces a disturbance of eating behavior. It produces alterations in other behaviors, too. Animals with such damage pay little attention to environmental signals (vision and smell) that normally trigger food-oriented responses and, in addition, have a great reduction in their interest in undertaking almost any kind of activity (Wolgin, Cytawa, and Teitelbaum, 1976). This represents a decrease in arousal normally caused by sensory stimuli. Behavioral arousal is related to the amount of neural impulses reaching the brain over diffusely projecting systems like the brain stem reticular formation.

Another complication is the fact that destruction of the ventromedial nucleus leads to overeating only if the food tastes good. If the food is not tasty, animals with such damage will only eat enough to survive. In addition, they will only overeat if they do not have to do work for the food. It must be noted that the regulation of feeding, one of the most basic requisites for life, is highly complex. Both chemical signals in the bloodstream and neural signals from the internal organs play a part. Beyond this, however, damage to any of the forebrain structures involved with eating produces changes in the use of sensory information and the general arousal levels that have impact on a wide range of behavioral abilities of the animal or person.

One of the most exciting discoveries in the area of motivation, and, indeed, for brain research in general, was that a *"reward mechanism"* could be identified in the brain. In 1954, James Olds and Peter Milner discovered that electrical stimulation of certain parts of the brain could serve as reinforcement; that is, this stimulation increased the probability that the responses occurring before it would occur again. If it is arranged that an animal can press a bar that delivers electrical stimulation to the brain through permanently implanted electrodes, the animal will press the bar frequently. Because the animal can stimulate its own brain by pressing a bar, the phenomenon has come to be called *intracranial self-stimulation* (ICS) or just "self-stimulation." This kind of electrical reward generates high rates of bar pressing that last for hours or days. Self-stimulation can be most easily obtained from stimulation of a pathway in the brain called the *medial forebrain bundle* (MFB), a tract which interconnects groups of neurons in the midbrain with many parts of the hypothalamus and limbic system. As mentioned earlier, part of the medial forebrain bundle is made up of catecholamine-containing neurons, and it has been suggested that these neurons are the ones responsible for the rewarding nature of stimulation of the MFB. The evidence for this theory is primarily from experiments using drugs which alter the action of noradrenalin and dopamine in the brain. Drugs that increase the action of these transmitters markedly increase rates of responding for ICS, while drugs which block their action decrease rates of responding for ICS.

Because of the reinforcing nature of stimulation of the MFB, some have called it a "pleasure center" in the brain. Of course, it is impossible to determine the emotions experienced by animals. Electrodes have been implanted in people for a variety of reasons, ranging from attempts to relieve pain to attempts to identify the location of epileptic seizures. Stimulation of electrodes in the MFB (or places reached by axons traveling through it) has led to a variety of different experiences described by the subjects as a tickling sensation, a pleasant feeling of warmth, or the impression that an idea was about to come to mind. Because of the impossibility of defining subjective states in both animals and people (other than one's self), it is probably best to avoid terms such as "pleasure center" and define the effects of MFB stimulation as primarily in terms of their behavioral consequences.

What function does the reinforcement system of the MFB have in normal behavior? ICS is a most unusual circumstance, but it is possible that rewarding events of any kind, such as food, drink, sex, may all activate the MFB system. But what can be said beyond this? Very little, unfortunately.

Learning and Memory

Learning and memory are universal characteristics of animal life. From the single cell to the most complicated of animal organisms, the ability to alter behavior on the basis of past experience is observed. It is a characteristic that is not even dependent on a nervous system. Single-celled animals and multi-celled animals without a nervous system exhibit behavioral capacities generally known in higher animals as learning and memory.

The mechanisms responsible for learning and memory are too often thought of as a special property of the neocortical surface of the brain. However, learning and memory are *not* dependent upon the neocortex or even a nervous system, as mentioned above. This can be demonstrated by the ability of animals that are essentially without neocortex (such as reptiles and amphibians) to learn and remember. Furthermore, animals in which most of the neocortical mantle has been destroyed

by experimental surgery can also demonstrate learning and memory. Furthermore, many people with severe mental deficiencies and gross disruptions of the neocortical surface have substantial abilities to learn and remember despite substantial inability to cope with the problems of everyday life.

Research trying to find the anatomical locations of memories has been singularly unsuccessful. One of the foremost investigators of brain activities in the early portions of this century, Karl Lashley, even gave up the search for the locations of memories that he called engrams (Lashley, 1950). For many years he had attempted to find the locations of memory by removing different parts of the neocortex in the rat. He found that no one particular region was of any greater importance than any other for basic capacities to learn and to remember, implying that the changes made in the nervous system during learning are probably widespread rather than localized.

Epilepsy and Memory

The disease processes responsible for convulsions have been of special interest to those interested in memory. Of special interest are people with epileptic tissue in the temporal lobe region. Epileptic tissue refers to portions of the brain in which a disease process or damage has altered the nerve cells so that they have a tendency for simultaneous and repetitive discharges. This tendency for simultaneous discharges can spread from the point of disease or damage to many brain regions and the consequence of this spreading of epileptic activity is the behavioral convulsion seen in the person called an epileptic. When patients with one form of epilepsy, *temporal lobe epilepsy,* have their temporal lobes exposed for surgery, electrical stimulation of these exposed areas will often produce various kinds of memory experiences. Some patients report a series of memories on stimulation that resemble what might be found on a tape recorder. However, this release of memories is only found when the temporal lobes of epileptic patients are stimulated. They are not found when the temporal lobes of patients without epilepsy are stimulated. In some way the disease processes underlying epilepsy must affect the temporal lobes in such a way as to allow memories to be retrieved and feelings about memory elicited by electrical stimulation. This does not indicate, however, that memories are normally stored in the temporal lobes.

Some patients with temporal lobe epilepsy have an apparent inability to remember recent events. This behavioral disorder is also shared by people who have been alcoholics for many years and are suffering from degeneration of portions of their brains (Korsakov's syndrome). Such patients cannot remember recently-acquired information but do have reasonable memories of events that happened long ago. However, the interpretation of these memory deficits is difficult. For example, many memories that seem to have been lost can be restored if appropriate hints are provided. In a typical test, a patient is asked to try to remember a word and cannot. But if the first letter or first two letters of the forgotten word are provided, the person can remember the word (Butters and Cermak, 1975). This would indicate that the memory problem is best described as a difficulty in retrieving the word from some neural storage system than with the storage system itself. Additional support for such a view comes from the fact that the patients are sometimes able to recall general things about the items they are asked to remember even though they cannot seem to recover the specific items. For example, even though one of the affected patients could not remember the name of a visitor who had left the room for fifteen or twenty minutes, he was able to remember certain vague characteristics of the visitor. In this case the visitor was from Florida and the patient recalled that the person was from a "warm climate" but did not recall his name.

Interference with Storage of Information

Interference with the storage of information only occurs after some form of widespread disturbance of brain function. This is accomplished by the use of *electroconvulsive shock* (ECS) or the administration of drugs that affect many areas of the brain. With a general interference with brain function, memory for events occurring just prior to the disrupting procedure seems lost.

ECS has been used rather extensively for the treatment of people with depression. *Usually,* electrodes are placed on the head in such a way that an electrical current can be passed between them, stimulating the brain in a diffuse fashion. In most cases, the patient is treated ahead of time with tranquilizing agents or sedatives to minimize the psychological distress of the treatment. Some patients seem to be much less depressed for days or weeks after the ECS treatment. At times, however, a series of electroconvulsive shock treatments is necessary to alleviate the depression. For the present purposes, the observation that most patients are unable to recall events occurring just prior to the ECS treatment is important. Apparently the electrical disruption of brain activity has made it impossible for the patient to remember things occurring just prior to the treatment.

In animal studies, the same sort of effect is found. If an animal is trained to do something just prior to ECS, the animal is often unable to do it again when tested a day or two later. On the other hand, responses that were learned a long time before the ECS treatment are retained perfectly well. Among the techniques that can be used to produce a general disruption of brain activity is the administration of drugs that inhibit protein synthesis throughout the brain. This is of interest because of the possibility that information is stored by a change in substances (proteins) made by cells in different regions of the brain. In other words, this approach suggests that information storage is chemical in nature (Dunn, 1976).

These observations on the chemistry of memory are related to theories that suggest that memories must be *consolidated* for them to become permanent. According to such theories, memories can be stored by *short-term* or *long-term* memory processes. Short-term memories are thought to be mediated by transient neural changes, maybe the reverberation of nerve impulses among loops of nerve cells in various places of the brain; while long-term memories are permanent alterations, possibly changes in proteins made by nerve cells in the brain. The transition from a short-term system to a more permanent type of storage system is called *consolidation*. Even when generally disruptive treatments are given to animals after a learning experience, only short-term or recent memories are disturbed. Long-term memories are resistant to all types of disruptions. When a disrupting agent like ECS is given to animals that have learned something and memories for recent events is reduced, this only demonstrated that there is a period in which memories are "fragile." Whether or not memories are in a temporary form initially after learning and slowly become "consolidated" into a more permanent structure, remains to be proven. Also unproven is the hypothesis that all memories pass through a short-term process before entering a long-term process. There is evidence from both human and animal research that there are many systems of memory storage and that information enters all systems at the same time and is processed simultaneously but at different rates. (Human memory will be discussed in more detail in Chapter 10.)

The time after which a generally disrupting agent can affect newly acquired information (that is, the *fragile period*), varies with the type of task required of the animal, the familiarity of the animal with the training situation, the nature of the rewards or punishments used in training the animal, and various other factors. There is no one period of time in which memories are fragile. It can extend from as short a period of time as one-half second to sixty minutes, or longer, depending on the ways in which the experiment is being conducted. Therefore, it would be a mistake to think some neural events related to memory require a fixed period of time for the memory of a learned event to become consolidated. It can happen quickly or slowly depending on the circumstances.

Another type of experiment that is often used to study the biology of memory is the administration of excitatory or stimulant drugs after a learning experience. In this type of task, the animal is trained to make a response and at different times after the learning event, the animals are given a stimulant drug. Then, one or more days afterwards the animals are tested for retention of the learned response. With certain drugs this procedure produces

much greater retention of what has been learned than giving nonstimulant drugs to the animals after the learning trial. This indicates that it is possible to enhance the memory mechanisms initiated by a learning experience. Similar to the application of disrupting agents, treatments that improve memory must be applied shortly after the learning experience (for example, see Dawson and McGaugh, 1973).

In summary, it can be said that very little is known about biology underlying the phenomena called learning and memory. It would seem that these capacities are quite common throughout the animal world and are even being found in animals without a nervous system. The greatest emphasis has been on studies in which disruptive agents have been employed just after a learning experience. In such cases, retrieval of the knowledge obtained during the learning experience is impaired. Special use of hints or reminders can, however, allow for the retrieval of this information in the future. The suggestion arising from the experiments that have been done is that memories of the past are stored in a diffuse fashion or perhaps in many different ways in the brain but that the ability to gain access to this information for use in the future is more limited and subject to disturbance.

The subject of learning has not been discussed to this point. The reason is that very little is known about the ability to acquire information apart from the ability to use this information at later times (memory). It is known that damage in certain portions of the limbic system seem to allow the animals to learn some responses faster than normal animals, while damage in other portions of the limbic system produce animals that have great difficulty in learning these responses. However, careful examination of the behavior of the animals reveals that what has been changed by the damage is not an ability to learn but the ease with which the animal makes the response. Those with brain damage who seem to learn quickly seem to be able to give up old ways of behaving quickly, thereby executing the new requirements of the task before normal animals. Those with the seeming learning impairment are not able to give up old responses, those which occur as part of their heredity (species-typical behaviors) or those learned in similar situations in the past, or have difficulties in undertaking new behaviors generally. What has been changed by the brain damage is the performance capabilities of the animals and not their learning abilities (see Isaacson, 1974).

Beyond the Limits of Adaptation

While the brain is remarkable in its ability to adapt to changing conditions both inside and outside the body, it has its limits. The brain depends on materials carried by the bloodstream for a constant supply of oxygen, glucose, and other materials for its normal metabolism. Decreasing the supply of any of the necessary items leads first to temporary disruption of brain function, and if the deprivation continues, to permanent damage. The brain is also sensitive to the presence of many other chemicals carried by the blood, such as hormones. At appropriate levels, hormones from glands such as the adrenal cortex, the thyroid, and the gonads play a part in normal behavior through their action on the cells of the brain. If too little or too much of any hormone is produced, highly abnormal behavior may result. In fact, almost *any* change in the chemical milieu of the brain that alters the brain's metabolism, whether resulting from a disease process in the body or a foreign substance from outside the body, can result in psychotic behavior, that is, a *toxic psychosis*. This is often expressed by states of confusion or delirium, usually accompanied by amnesia (loss of memory) for the period of time when brain metabolism was interrupted. Toxic psychoses usually last only as long as the period of time while the brain's chemical milieu is changed, although permanent change may result, depending on the substance producing the alteration.

Continued exposure of the nervous system to some drugs leads to changes in brain function and behavior that are of considerable social importance. If one consumes large amounts of alcohol, barbiturates, or narcotics over a long enough period of time, the nervous system adjusts to their presence, and greater quantities of the drug are required to have the same behavioral or mental effect. This phenomenon is called *tolerance*. If one

stops (withdraws) the use of one of these drugs after the nervous system has adjusted to its presence, *withdrawal* symptoms may appear. This indicates that the nervous system can not readjust to the sudden absence of the drug. For some drugs, these withdrawal symptoms may be quite dangerous and even fatal. Sometimes it is possible to avoid many of these problems by withdrawing the person gradually from the drug, but even if this is possible, the nervous system of the withdrawn person is probably not the same as before the use of the drug. It is a well known fact that cigarette smokers, alcoholics, and narcotics addicts all crave their particular drug. They feel anxious and irritable without it for years afterward. At a behavioral level, this can be thought of as due to the loss of an enjoyable event, but it also represents a lasting change in the nervous system resulting from the prolonged exposure to the drug.

Drugs induce peculiar states in the people or animals taking them. With some drugs, behaviors learned under the drug will not be demonstrated unless the animal or person is tested under the drug. If tested without the drug, there is no sign of memory. This type of drug effect is called *state-dependency*. It is also related to observations made with people suffering from mental disorders, such as schizophrenia. Patients may learn more acceptable and satisfying patterns of behavior under a tranquilizing drug (like chlorpromazine), but these new behaviors are not exhibited by the people when they are not under the influence of the drug.

Suppose the brain itself is physically damaged as a consequence of an automobile accident or disease. Is there any adaptation to the lost neurons? Most of the neurons of the human brain are formed before birth. Once formed, they are not replaced if damaged or destroyed. Therefore, any damage caused by the death or destruction of neurons is permanent. This is not to imply, however, that no *changes* in the structure of the adult brain are possible. After nerve cells are destroyed, their axons degenerate, leaving empty the synapses they once made with other cells. Nearby normal axons may then "sprout" making collateral or branching axons that fill the empty synapses. This sprouting of axons has been repeatedly demonstrated by anatomical methods, but it is not yet known what effect *sprouting* has on the function of the damaged brain. Furthermore, not all neural systems have the capability to show sprouting. Whether or not sprouting occurs depends on both the system damaged and the age at which the damage occurs.

What happens to behavior after brain damage? Usually after a part of the brain is destroyed, there is a change in behavior. The particular behavioral change depends on what part of the brain is injured. Sometimes these behavioral changes are temporary. This probably is due to the fact that the brain damage has affected a host of regions well beyond the site of primary destruction. Some of these regions are affected in ways that are reversible, for example, a temporary reduction in blood supplies. As better circulation is established, the activity of the affected regions can be restored to normal. Therefore, after any brain damage, the greatest behavioral effects will be seen right after the accident with a progressive reduction of symptoms continuing for months or years until only the "hard core" deficits resulting from the direct loss of cells remain.

In cases of brain damage due to accident, it is fortunate that many of the symptoms seen immediately after the trauma disappear over time. However, when parts of the brain are destroyed for therapeutic purposes, recovery of function is not desirable. A prime example of this problem is the procedure of alleviating pain by destroying the neural pathways to the brain through which pain signals are transmitted. While these surgical procedures often provide relief from pain, it is unfortunate that the relief often lasts for only a few months. If the mechanisms underlying the return or recovery of function were known, it might be possible to enhance it in those patients suffering from the debilitating effects of brain damage and retard it in those patients for whom loss of a particular brain function may be beneficial.

If the brain is damaged and behavior is disrupted, and if no recovery of function occurs, what can be done? Unfortunately, for most kinds of brain damage, very little can be done at the present time. However, there are some brain disorders whose underlying mechanisms are understood well enough so that effective therapy has been devised.

One of these disorders is Parkinson's disease. In Parkinson's disease, an important group of cells which make dopamine and use it as their neurotransmitter degenerate, leaving the areas in the basal ganglia to which their axons project, relatively deficient in the input from dopaminergic neurons. The symptoms of this deficiency are disturbances in motor function and include muscle rigidity, tremor, an inability to initiate movements easily, and a lack of emotional expression of the face. An effective way to reduce the severity of these symptoms is to increase the amount of dopamine in the brain. Since dopamine itself does not easily enter the brain from the bloodstream, the substance from which it is made, L-DOPA, is given. Of course, the therapy must be given continuously since the disease has not been cured as yet; the dead cells have not been restored to life nor have new ones taken their place. The symptoms have been decreased because the chemical effectiveness of the remaining cells of the dopamine system has been enhanced. Even here, however, the benefits of L-DOPA treatment are not usually permanent because the unknown disease process causing the degeneration of the dopamine system continues causing more and more behavioral symptoms.

There are several mental disorders *not* associated with brain damage which can be effectively treated using drugs that change brain chemistry in particular ways. For example, depression can be lifted using drugs which increase the activity of the neurotransmitter noradrenalin in the brain; the symptoms of schizophrenia can be decreased by the use of drugs that block the action of the neurotransmitter dopamine. It is possible that the immediate biological cause of depression may be an insufficiency of noradrenalin transmission, and that of schizophrenia may be too great an activity in some systems utilizing dopamine as their transmitter. Both of these theories are speculative and the former is not well supported by current evidence, but they do focus attention on the role of the central nervous system on the origin of emotional disorders. There is strong presumptive evidence for a genetic contribution toward some emotional disorders, and this could be mediated by the genetic determination of activity in certain transmitter systems. Of course, it is important to remember that even though a disorder may have a genetic component, this does not mean that it will always occur. Behavior is always expressed in some environment. Genes can dispose a person toward disease, but depending on the environment, this may or may not result in the actual occurrence of the disease. The individual's internal chemistry is determined by the environment as well as by genetic instructions. Environmental conditions leading to stress, anxiety, pain, pleasure, or happiness all produce substantial and prolonged changes in body and brain chemistry as well as in the activity of many of the brain's subsystems. The brain is a meeting place of both genetic and environmental influences.

Sometimes the brain is damaged before or near the time of birth. Damage early in life can produce profound permanent effects on the person's ability to deal with the complex problems of everyday life. This is what is referred to as mental deficiency (retardation). Sometimes mental deficiency is described as an impaired ability to learn and remember, but this is not altogether accurate. Often mentally defective people can learn simple things just as easily as normal people. They remember them well, too. Their problems are of a different nature. They have problems of reasoning, using abstract concepts, planning for the future, and an enhanced tendency to perseverate previously learned responses. Brain damage later in life does not lead to these sorts of problems but rather to much more specific behavioral problems.

When the development of the brain is disrupted, specific systems are disrupted, but there are widespread alterations throughout the brain. These widespread changes usually involve the neocortical systems which are most involved in analyzing the complexities of the environment and finding abstract principles and generalities. Impairment of these abilities lead to practical difficulties such as errors in telling time, making change, or realizing the importance of insurance. The practical problems can lead to doubts about the person's own value. Many of the mentally defective are made fun of by other people. They are called "dummies" and "weird." This lowered self-evaluation

often leads to further maladaptive behavior due to emotional problems.

At the present time, there is little that can be done to help restore reasonable mental competencies to those who are born with prominent brain damage. However, this need not be true in the future. If we can gain further understanding of those processes initiating the damage and those causing the widespread nature of the damage, it may be possible to detect the initial damage and to reduce the generality of the secondary reactions.

Drugs

The tremendous success of the drugs used to treat depression and schizophrenia over the past two decades has led to the search for drugs to alleviate the symptoms of other kinds of mental disorders. By far, the psychiatric symptom most commonly treated today is anxiety. At any one time, approximately half of the adult population of the United States has a prescription for a drug to combat anxiety and unhappiness! Thus, a large proportion of our population is being treated for unwanted feelings by intervention at the level of their biology. Does half the population of our country have brain disorders requiring treatment at this level, or is it merely easier to treat behavioral symptoms of a problem with a drug than to get at the causes of the problems? Since no drug can *cure* a mental or emotional disorder but only temporarily relieve the symptoms, using drugs in treatment can prevent discovery of the source of the problem.

A major challenge for the future is discovering the contributions of biological and environmental factors to the expression of behavioral disorders. Certainly anxiety, unhappiness, frustration, guilt, and other feelings frequently associated with minor mental disorders can be created by family, school, or job environments, and can be relieved by changing those environments. On the other hand, many behavioral disorders do not respond to changes in the social environment or psychotherapy. For the most effective treatment of each particular mental or behavioral disorder, the appropriate types of intervention must be found.

Modern society is not only marked by an extensive use of drugs prescribed by physicians to change mood or for the alleviation of behavioral problems but also by the great use of "self-prescribed" drugs, namely, those purchased on the street. People buy and take these drugs for many different reasons, and there is no one overwhelming reason for drug use or drug abuse. Probably the problems and complexities of modern day life have led some people to see drugs as a means of escape to a fantasy world. Others take drugs for curiosity, for a new experience, for a "turn-on," or to relieve boredom. In a sense, this is the easy way since drugs can provide new experiences to a passive person, one who is unwilling to fashion a different lifestyle or obtain new experiences through individual effort. For whatever reasons, the use of both prescription and nonprescription drugs exists today as a common way in which people adapt to the world in which they live.

The use of drugs is not new. Alcoholic beverages have existed for as long as most cultures have been able to record their histories. Almost every culture found ways to brew or distill grains or fruits to make ethyl alcohol. Other types of drugs that alter mental states have had wide use in different cultures, such as the use of peyote in Mexico, but the use of these more unusual drugs has not greatly influenced Western industrial cultures until recently.

Probably the most widely used "self-prescribed" street drug is marihuana. This plant is widely and easily grown in many parts of the world and produces a large number of different effects on its users. It has many active ingredients which produce different behavioral and mental reactions. Probably each active component has its own time course of behavioral effects. Each of these effects lasts for a different period of time. The precise effects of this drug and its many components depend, in large part, on the environment in which the drug is used and the expectations the user has about the effects that will occur. What the user believes will happen usually does, a self-fulfilling prophesy.

The effects of marihuana last for a long time after the last use of the drug. Various components are stored in the body's fat supplies and can be re-leased for a month or more. These stored drug components add to the drug levels produced by taking another amount of the drug, partly explaining why repeated use of the drug often produces ever greater effects.

Another common type of drug illegally available in parts of the country is "speed." Actually, most "speed" is amphetamine, a drug that releases the catecholamines from their storage containers in the terminals of axons. It also potentiates the effectiveness of the catecholamines in other ways. The most common result of the drug is to mobilize the body and brain for action, producing profound effects on the heart and cardiovascular system. It activates the user, creating a greatly excited condition and, for this reason, is called an "upper."

"Downers" refer to drugs that produce sedation and a loss of action and interest in what goes on around the person. Such drugs are often barbiturates that are thought to reduce activity in the brain stem reticular formation but others are also found. One other "downer" is methaqualone (Quaalude) (in some street vocabularies "vitamin Q"). This drug depresses the activity of the brain through unknown mechanisms. When taken in large amounts the person becomes like a sleep walker and that person may lose control of motor behaviors. All central nervous system depressants have the ability to suppress breathing and the beating of the heart, actions necessary to life.

The "hard drugs" of the street are those with a morphine base. Starting with the milky substances derived from unripe seeds of certain poppies, chemical processes of distillation are carried on to purify the morphine component. Opium is from the Greek name for juice and today refers to the juice from the poppy seed. Smoking the dried juice was popular in the Orient, after it was imported into the area as a substance to be traded for tea. As a result of this introduction of opium into China and other oriental countries, millions of addicts were produced and it has not been until recently that the Chinese have been able to eliminate opium addiction through absolute elimination of opium importation.

The most severe addiction to morphine and compounds related to it comes about when it is introduced into the body in a relatively pure form by hypodermic. Changes in mood, sometimes a euphoric state, and mental clouding result from the drug along with a marked analgesic (pain-relieving) effect. In fact, the greatest behavioral or mental effect of morphine is that of reducing pain. It is the standard against which all other pain-killers are measured. The problem with morphine and related compounds (including heroin) is that the person using it develops *tolerance* to the drug and a physical *dependence* on it. Tolerance means that more and more of the drug is required to achieve the same mental reactions. Physical dependence means that when a person stops taking the drug, sufficient physiological distress is produced that almost any action seems justified to obtain more of it thereby reducing the withdrawal symptoms.

Dependence on any drug presents a very serious problem to the person and to society in which the cost of obtaining the drug is both high and illegal. Large amounts of money can be made through supplying and selling illegal "hard drugs" (and some "soft" ones) and as a result many people are willing to traffic in them. The person addicted to the drug cares little about how money is obtained to buy the drug, and, as withdrawal symptoms become more intense, will rob or kill to obtain the drug. Many young women turn to prostitution to obtain money to support their habits.

Current treatments for the addiction to morphine-related drugs in some states include the changing of the addiction from the illegal heroin or other morphine-related drug to methadone. Methadone is a drug with less behavioral actions than morphine but that prevents signs of withdrawal. More important, when used in drug rehabilitation programs, it can be given legally and at low cost. This enables addicts to change their lifestyles away from a preoccupation with obtaining money to support their drug habits. Physiologically, it is merely the substitution of one drug for another, and ultimately the addict must be weaned away from any drug dependence to have a full and complete life. Hopefully, as more is learned about the actions of morphine and related compounds in the brain, this may become an easier, less painful process.

Summary

While much of the current interest in the biological foundations of behavior stems from potential practical benefits of this information relative to mental illness and drug abuse, these practical gains will never be fully realized until the more fundamental riddles of the brain and its function are known. To help people live happier fuller lives, the most intense efforts must be directed toward research into basic problems of brain action. There will be no immediate panaceas, but as we learn each new secret of the organization of the brain, we have moved one additional step toward solving the practical problems of society.

We need to know a great deal more about how single cells work, how they produce their own transmitters, and how they are affected by the transmitters that are released on their surfaces by axons from other cells. We need to know about how the brain anticipates changes in its environment and how this anticipation influences receptors and other components of the sensory system. The more difficult investigations will be in those fields that represent interactions among different types of systems. For example, how does hunger influence sensory systems to enhance selectively reactions to food or food-related objects? How does the brain create illusions, hallucinations, and dreams? How do memories of the past, however they are stored in the brain, influence present behavior? These questions that are more closely related to behavior and mental activity are difficult ones, because there is no theory of sufficient breadth to relate cellular activity, anatomical systems, and neurochemical alterations to behavior. Yet, such theories cannot be made without a greater base of information about fundamental operations of the nervous system. Therefore, advances both in the solution of social and personal problems and the development of more adequate theories depend on an ever-increasing base of information about how the brain and body work.

Glossary

Acetylcholine: A transmitter substance liberated by many nerve cells in the brain and periphery of the body. It is the agent at the neuromuscular junction in the periphery of the body.

Action potential: The all-or-none spike discharge that travels down the axon of the cell and involves the soma of the cell as well.

Amphetamine: A stimulant drug that acts by several different mechanisms to enhance activity of the catecholamine systems and the serotonergic systems of the brain.

Amygdala: A collection of nerve cells organized into many different nuclear groups, some of which are related to the basal ganglia and others to the limbic system. Some portions of the amygdala have strong interconnections with the hypothalamus.

Astrocyte: A type of neuroglial cell.

Autonomic nervous system: Nerve fibers that innervate glands and smooth muscles of the body, as contrasted with somatic nerve fibers that innervate the striped muscles that move the skeleton. It has two branches, the sympathetic and the parasympathetic, which act in an antagonistic fashion much of the time.

Axon: The process arising from the nerve cell body over which the action potential is carried.

Basal Ganglia: These are collections of nerve cell bodies in the forebrain; including the caudate nucleus, the putamen, and the glubus pallidus.

Biofeedback: Techniques for providing an individual with information about the ongoing bodily activities of which he or she is not usually aware; for example, the use of auditory or visual indicators of brain electroencephalogram (EEG) activities.

Brain stem: In this chapter, this term is defined as referring to all of the neural tissue lying below the hypothalamus reaching to the beginning of the spinal cord itself.

Caudate nucleus: A nuclear group of the basal ganglia located in the medial forebrain area; it is thought to be important for the coordination of motor movements.

Cerebellum: The "little brain" sitting on the brain stem that is most concerned with organizing bodily movements relative to time and space.

Cortex: The outer or superficial parts of the brain but actually refers to any tissue that has a laminated character due to the presence of different layers of nerve cells.

Dendrite: Part of a neuron thought to be a place of contact for axon terminals from other cells. Dendrites are small branching processes arising from the nerve cell body.

Depolarization: A change in the potential across a nerve cell membrane that moves from about minus 70 mV towards 0.

Diencephalon: The brain areas connecting the telencephalon with the midbrain. It is made of two major portions: the thalamus and the hypothalamus.

Dopamine: A catecholamine found in certain nerve cells in the central nervous system and in sympathetic ganglia of the autonomic nervous system. It is believed to be a neurochemical transmitter with special importance in the basal ganglia.

Dorsal root ganglion: A collection of nerve cells that lie outside the spinal cord toward the back of the person or animal. The cell bodies in the dorsal root ganglion are connected with processes running from peripheral areas such as skin and muscles into the spinal cord. These neurons convey information about sensory activities stimulating receptors on the body surface and muscles.

Electroencephalogram (EEG): A term used to describe the recording of minute electrical potentials generated by brain cells and fibers. In the human, it is recorded through electrodes placed on the scalp according to certain standard locations.

Endocrine gland: Gland that releases hormones into the bloodstream to act on distant target organs.

Gamma-aminobutyric acid: An inhibitory transmitter at crustacean neuromuscular junctions. It is also likely to be an inhibitory transmitter in both the central and peripheral nervous systems of vertebrates.

Ganglion (plural ganglia): Group of nerve cell bodies located outside the brain or spinal cord, in the periphery of the body.

Gap junction: Area of contact between nerve cells at which the intercellular space between the membranes is exceedingly small (about 2mm). It is the presumed site of electrical coupling between cells.

Gene: Functional unit of heredity, the portion of chromosome that regulates synthesis of specific enzymes and proteins.

Globus pallidus: A nuclear group of the basal ganglia located in the central forebrain. It is thought to be related to the coordination of motor activities.

Graded potential: A change of the cell membrane potential whose amplitude is related to the intensity of the stimulus.

Hippocampus: A cortical (layered) tissue lying as a

ridge in the lateral ventricle of most mammals. It is strongly interconnected with the overlying neocortex, the septal area, and the hypothalamus, and is a part of the limbic system.

Hormones: Chemicals secreted by glands of the body released into the blood stream that act on target organs at a distance from the glands. Hormones are secreted by "ductless" glands (endocrine glands) as opposed to glands that have ducts and deposit their contents through these ducts on specified target tissues.

Hypothalamus: The lower portion of the diencephalon.

Interneurons: Neurons with processes that neither arise from receptor organs nor connect with muscles or glands.

Limbic system: A collection of nerve cells and processes with strong interconnections with the hypothalamus. Groups of cells usually included in the limbic system are the septal area, hippocampus, the amygdala, and the cingulate cortex.

Locus coeruleus: A nucleus of the brain stem which has a blue appearance. It is located just anterior to the cerebellum and contains nerve cells and processes that project both into the forebrain area and into the spinal cord. It is thought to be the major source of neurons using norepinephrine as their neurotransmitter.

Medial forebrain bundle: A collection of nerve fibers running between the forebrain and brain stem areas that pass through the lateral hypothalamic areas. Many regions of the forebrain and brain stem contribute fibers to these bundles, thought by some to be the area in which electrical stimulation produces rewarding effects in animals.

Medulla (oblongata): The most caudal part of the brain stem just above the spinal cord.

Motoneuron: Nerve cell in the ventral horn of the spinal cord whose axon innervates muscle fibers.

Neocortex: Cortical tissue of the brain which has, or has had during the course of development, six distinguishable layers of nerve cells and processes.

Nerve cells (neurons): These are the specialized cells of the brain and nervous system that conduct impulses through membrane changes.

Neuroglia (glia): A type of cell in the brain and spinal cord that has a supportive role in brain function but does not conduct impulses.

Neurotransmitter: A chemical released at a synapse by one neuron that affects the membranes of a second neuron, inducing a graded potential that may either depolarize or hyperpolarize the receptor site.

Node of Ranvier: Small unmyelinated segments along axons.

Noradrenalin: A catecholamine that is the transmitter liberated by most sympathetic nerve terminals in the periphery of the body and also is liberated by certain groups of nerve cells in the central nervous system. Also known as norepinephrine.

Nucleus (plural nuclei): Group of nerve cell bodies located inside the brain or spinal cord.

Oligodendroglia: A type of neuroglia cell that manufactures the lipid covering myelin around some axons in the brain and spinal cord.

Parasympathetic division (of the autonomic nervous system): Branch of the autonomic nervous system active in the maintenance of bodily functions of the normal variety (as opposed to emergency reactions to stressful stimuli).

Pituitary gland: Gland that secretes a variety of hormones into the blood stream. The secretion of many of its hormones are regulated by the hypothalamic areas immediately above it.

Pons: Area made up of fibers that bridge across the brain stem from the cerebellum on one side to the cerebellum on the other.

Protoreptilean brain: A term used to describe systems of the brain reaching from the basal ganglia through the hypothalamus and into the brain stem regions. Mechanisms of the protoreptilean brain are thought to be responsible for many unlearned, species-specific acts of most animals.

Putamen: A nuclear group of the basal ganglia located in the medial forebrain areas which works with the caudate nucleus in the coordination of motor activities.

Receptor site: The area of a cell membrane, perhaps even a single molecule on the cell membrane, that combines with a specific chemical transmitter or other chemical to produce a change in the membrane of the receiving cell.

Reticular formation: A mixture of nerve cells and fibers located primarily in the brain stem, but having extensions to the thalamus, which give rise to fibers thought to be important for maintaining arousal in the neocortex and other forebrain areas.

Schwann cell: Glial cell that myelinates nerves in the periphery of the body.

Septal area: A collection of nuclei in the middle anterior region of many mammalian brains that is strongly interconnected with the hypothalamus and the hippocampus. It is usually considered a portion of the limbic system.

Serotonin (5-hydroxytryptamine): A neurotransmitter present in the central nervous system and other body tissues.

Sympathetic division (of the autonomic nervous system):

Portion of the autonomic nervous system responsible for emergency reactions of the smooth muscles and glands, mobilizing the body to deal with sudden stressful situations.

Synapse: Place where neurons interconnect, comprised of axon terminal, synaptic cleft, and receptor site on another neuron.

Tectum: The roof of the midbrain, which is made up of the superior and inferior colliculi in higher animals.

Tegmentum: The ventral portion of the midbrain.

Telencephalon: The most anterior portion of the brain.

Thalamus: The upper portion of the diencephalon.

Thyroid gland: A paired gland in the neck which secretes hormones that regulate growth and metabolic activities.

Tolerance: When used in relation to drugs, tolerance refers to the fact that progressively higher doses of the drug must be given to provide the same effect.

Withdrawal effects: These are bodily reactions, usually of an adverse nature, that occur when an individual no longer takes or receives drugs that had been taken for a prolonged period of time.

Suggested Readings

Deutsch, D. and Deutsch, A. J. eds. *Short-Term Memory*. New York: Academic Press, 1975.

Dunn, A. and Bondy, S. C. *Functional Chemistry of the Brain*. Hollinswood, N.J.: Spectrum Publications, 1974.

Gardner, E. *Fundamentals of Neurology*. *6th ed*. Philadelphia: W. B. Saunders, 1975.

Isaacson, R. L. *The Limbic System*. New York: Plenum Publishing, 1974.

Isaacson, R. L., Douglas, R. J., Lubar, J., and Schmaltz, L. W. *A Primer of Physiological Psychology*. New York: Harper and Row, 1971.

The Nature and Nurture of Behavior: Developmental Psychobiology. Readings from Scientific American. San Francisco: W. H. Freeman & Co., 1973.

Progress in Psychobiology. Readings from Scientific American. W. H. Freeman & Co., San Francisco: 1976.

The Sensory Basis of Experience

William W. Dawson

Introduction

Because of the extent of the unknown just over each new scientific hill, it is difficult to predict exactly where science will be in the next decade or in the next century. However, some measure of the relative progress of science can be obtained by looking at the present amount of scientific knowledge in any area with respect to the early beginnings of knowledge development within that specialty. The present developmental position of the sensory sciences can be appreciated by such a comparison.

It is almost traditional to identify the beginning of sensory studies with the writings of the early Greek philosopher, Aristotle. Aristotle recognized the existence of five senses which he called the sense of seeing, the sense of hearing, the sense of smelling, the sense of taste, and the sense of touch. If this beginning, almost 2,000 years ago, had been the start of a smooth, continuous development, the picture of sensory development today would be quite different; but this development was not smooth nor continuous. During the long period between Aristotle and 1750 A.D., there were flashes of new knowledge, punctuated with long periods with no progress. About 200 B.C., the Roman, Lucretius, proposed that chemicals stimulated the smell sense by a structural interaction or a "lock and key" relationship. Leonardo da Vinci proposed a completely inaccurate concept of the eye's function about 1500 A.D. that was not corrected until 1604 by Johannes Kepler. Until the

eighteenth century and the discovery by Galvani that muscle and nerve tissue were electrically excitable, it had always been proposed that the nerves served to conduct fluid or "spirit" codes between the peripheral sense organ and the brain. A major advance in the philosophy of transmission of information through the body was contributed by Johannes Müller, who formalized the idea that there were particular neurons carrying visual, auditory and other sensory information, and that the stimulation of any of these systems would produce an experience unique to that particular sensory system. That is, stimulation of the eye by any means (electrical, mechanical, or light) could produce only a visual experience. This *Doctrine of Specific Nerve Energies* was modified later by Herman Helmholtz, who further proposed that each sensory subexperience (color as a subexperience of light; cold as a subexperience of touch; any specific tone as a subexperience of hearing) has its own set of characteristic nerve fibers. Therefore, Helmholtz proposed that, in the optic nerve, there were separate nerves that dealt with blue information, green information, or red information. It was at about this time that Sir Charles Bell, an English physician, discovered that the motor and sensory systems of the spinal cord of humans were entirely separate. These important, but basic, principles were the legacy of a very limited amount of anatomical experimentation and the philosophic approach to biology which had been traditional during the 2,000 year period from Aristotle until the beginning of the eighteenth century. No real progress in the understanding of the sensory systems was achieved until the beginning of the quantitative experiments in the late nineteenth century. The beginning of quantification emerged out of serendipity. Early astronomy, prior to the twentieth century, required a great deal of human judgment in the timing of the "movement" of the stars. It was discovered that individual observers in the same observatory showed marked differences in their measurements. Prior to this time, it had been generally assumed that all individuals had virtually identical sensory and motor capabilities. Quantitative measures in the astronomical laboratories clearly identified the factor of *individual differences* in the measurement of astronomical events.

In the mid-nineteenth century, technology for the accurate measurement of sensory phenomena was totally lacking. The earliest quantification of sensory phenomena began in the mid-nineteenth century in an innovative group at Leipzig under Wilhelm Wundt. Wundt had determined that orderly, quantitative information could be obtained by the accurate evaluation of human experience. Wundt became the founder of modern psychology, which he developed as an inquiry into the functioning of the sensory systems. The major tool was the new psychophysics (see Chapter 2).

A logical question at this point would be, "Why the delay of scientific growth between 1000 B.C. and 1750 A.D.?" There are several reasons. During the early part of this period, the world's population was relatively small and cities were small. In many areas there was a migratory population. Centers for education were few and often limited to the upper class. The technology needed to answer questions about biological problems was largely absent. But, perhaps, most important were the basic differences in the way that scientific questions were handled at that time, compared to those with which we are familiar. Before the fifteenth century, the manual manipulations and work required for experimentation carried a certain stigma and association with common labor. In distinction, intellectual pursuits were considered the highest level of human activity and were therefore appropriate means of developing biological knowledge. This philosophic framework is often referred to as the "rational" or "rationalistic" method and is

an extension of the methods advocated by Plato. The treatment of questions about the sensory systems by way of the purely rationalistic method contains numerous, obvious flaws. There was also a good deal of spiritualism in all thinking about the functions of living organisms. Mystical control of behavior was more generally accepted, while the possibility of a lawful relationship between function and anatomy was a foreign concept except to a very few. Although these problems were largely conceptual, perhaps even frivolous by today's standards, they were a formidable barrier against the development of new knowledge.

In the mechanical age of the seventeenth and eighteenth centuries, simple machines that had the capability of performing actions without supervision, at least for short times, gradually began to "leach out" the mysticism associated for thousands of years with movements of all kinds. Separately, the English physician, Henry Power, and the French philosopher, René Descartes, called attention to the similarities between mechanical activities and biological activities. Carefully confining their discussion to animals to avoid conflict with the Church, they pointed out that animal inferiority to humans provided for a mechanistic biology where structure could be related to function. The mysticism of "consciousness" or volitional activity was still reserved for humans. The consideration of the sensory functions and biological activities in general as mechanical processes, simultaneously (1) provided material for study in which hypotheses could be advanced and tested from an empirical rather than rational viewpoint, and (2) separated animals from spiritualism or mysticism, essentially as biological machines, providing material for research without fear of the Church. These concepts may seem very basic today, but are almost completely responsible for the rapid growth of information about sensory function in the 200 years between 1750 to 1950. Within this perspective of time, our actual total knowledge about sensory function is surely less today than it will be in another quarter century. Since knowledge accumulates in a multiplicative rather than a linear way, it is likely that more information will be provided in the next two decades than has been provided in the last century. It is surprising, but

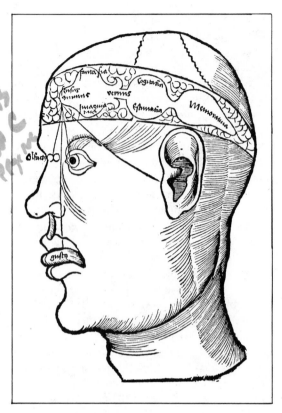

Fig. 5-1. Sensory pathways and brain divisions as conceptualized in 1504.

true, that the levels of knowledge availabe on sensory functions, in many respected academic circles during the period of the American Revolution, was of roughly equal quality to the levels of knowledge available today in the most rudimentary, aboriginal cultures of Western Australia and New Guinea. Although the science of sensory function has come a long way during the last two centuries, the frontiers still expand endlessly on all sides.

Current Concepts

In the previous section, the rapid growth of science was discussed, and it was made clear that there is little knowledge, older than 200 years, about the function of sense organs. The past 10 years have been very fruitful in the addition of new informa-

tion and the modification of old ideas about the sense organs. In this section, there will be a brief description of several of these new ideas from a very general viewpoint. The reader may wish to identify them early so that they can be recognized in the discussion of individual sensory systems.

Until very recently, the classical and "proper" idea of the nervous system, including its sensory components, was an unchanging, genetically determined network where elements were laid down early in development and, with good luck, served trouble free for a lifetime. It has been found recently that portions of the neural components of several sense organs have a renewal rate under normal conditions. That is, portions of cells in some systems may be "used up" and renewed in a regular cycle. In other cases, it has been found that some cells grow, mature, age, die, and are replaced on regular cycles over a period of days or weeks. In both of these conditions, the cell, or some part of it, changes continuously. There is a third case which provides for cell replacement when there has been damage. These concepts offer a much more dynamic picture of the sensory organs and peripheral nervous system than was true two decades ago. When the sections on specific sense organs appear, you will see which systems display the attributes described above. Some do and some do not.

The contemporary concept of neural organization views function, as initiated at the sensory receptor structure, as a change in electrical potential. When that electrical potential (the generator), caused by the external stimulus, becomes large enough, it in turn stimulates the axon of the first neuron and produces "spike" unit, or regenerative potential (see Chapter 4). These terms all mean the same thing and refer to a transient change in electrical properties of the axon, which moves from the region of the receptor toward the central nervous system at various speeds depending on the properties of the neuron. When the spike potentials reach the terminal of the first neuron, they have the ability to cause a liberation of chemicals which may then produce a change in the local electrical potential of the nerve of the next higher level, subsequently causing a depolarization of the beginning of the axon section of the nerve, and the onset of new spike potentials moving again toward the central nervous system. This is a brief and incomplete description of what has almost become a law of nerve conduction. Recent experiments have succeeded in obtaining data directly from different portions of the nerves in sense organs. It has been discovered that the receptor potentials produced by stimulation are not always the same; they may be hyperpolarizing (cell, negative inside) or depolarizing (cell, positive inside). The potential may travel from one neuron to the next without the production of unit or spike potentials. The transmission of information between neurons may be accomplished by electrical rather than entirely chemical means.

There is a gradual swing in thinking from the older ideas of rigid organization of sensory systems. It has recently been found that the events during the period of neural development may have great effects on the final functional nature of that particular sense organ system. These periods of "critical" development may be very short and occupy a very specific time period in the life of the organism. Abnormal stimulation of the receptor system during that period may alter the function of the whole sense organ system in an irreversible way. Several "diseases" of humans may be related to alterations of normal "critical" period development.

"Feedback" is a concept that is normally reserved for engineering systems, and is used in many sophisticated electronic circuits. A good example of feedback control can be found on many tape recorders. Modern tape recorders have no user control for amplitude of the voice being recorded. Only the amplitude of the playback signal is controlled by the user. The microphone element in the tape recorder is attached to an amplifier module, which is eventually attached to the recording heads. The recording head requires a minimum amount of signal in order to properly imprint the magnetic tape. When it does not get sufficient signal, it, in turn, signals the amplifier, which is "turned up." Conversely, if the signal is too large, the amplifier is "turned down." Feedback gets its name because of the routing of information, which is shown in Figure 5-2. When feedback is used in sensory system control, it is almost always "nega-

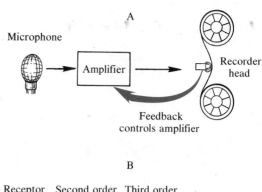

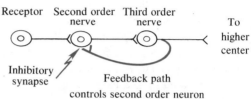

Fig. 5-2. Two simple feedback loop examples.

tive." Negative feedback would tend to decrease the sensitivity of the second order neuron as shown in Figure 5-2. In biological systems, feedback control is usually exercised by an inhibitory synaptic (negative feedback) connection.

The five senses of Aristotle no longer seem adequate to describe the multiple sensitivity found in humans. As knowledge has been gathered, separate receptor and processing systems have been described for the subdivisions of almost every sense modality. *Sense modality* refers to a general sensory system which may be subdivided into various sensory qualities. (An example for modality would be the "cutaneous" system, subdivisible into several sense qualities such as warm, cold, contact, and so on.) Aristotle's classification was based on separate anatomical organizations. As the knowledge of anatomy developed in the last 2,000 years, both discrete anatomical and functional processing systems have been described within many of the classical senses. For instance, within the classical modality of vision, one may now identify three separate receptor types for color vision, and a fourth receptor type which functions at low light levels. Segregation of these four separate qualities at the next physiological way station (lateral geniculate nucleus) further suggests that each system enjoys some functional independence.

Dynamic or ''change'' *sensitivity* is the final concept to be introduced before discussing specific sense modalities. As the various senses are discussed, you will see that absolute sensitivity of each system is high. However, you will also see that some systems approach the maximum sensitivity that is allowed by the laws of physics. That is, maximum visual sensitivity approaches the detection of a single light quantum and maximum auditory sensitivity approaches movements of near-atomic dimensions. When discussing systems with such innate sensitivity, it is easy to see the difficulty of providing a truly stable stimulus. Such a sensitive system should be able to detect relatively small changes in the environment, which would be seen as a variation around the steady state condition. Most of the basic sensitivity values that will be quoted are not based on continuous, steady state stimulation, but involve abrupt changes in the environment. The fact is, all sensory systems are set up to efficiently detect changes in the environment. In some, when the steady-state stimulus condition is achieved, the system gradually loses ''sensitivity'' and the stimulus effectiveness fades (habituates) out (see Chapter 1). This concept holds, as do most of the concepts discussed above, for all sensory systems. As we proceed through the discussion of each sensory system, look for the appearance and development of these concepts and take particular note of exceptions where they can be found.

The following sections are intended to integrate contemporary theory, recent research findings, and give a coherent view of sensory system function. Consequently, more depth is provided than is required in many beginning courses. Subsections are written so that many may be omitted at the discretion of the instructor. However, you may find these useful in later years.

Cutaneous Senses and Pain

Peripheral Anatomy

The identification and mapping of skin surface areas sensitive to warm, cold, pressure, and pain were among the first experimental undertakings in sense research. As early as 1925, reference grids were marked in ink on the human skin, and positions sensitive to warm, cold, or pressure were being stimulated so as to discover their *field* properties. A field is an area within which two stimuli interact in terms of the sensory result. As the stimuli diverge along the surface of the skin (or any other receptor area) the point at which they have no interaction is the point at which more than one field has become involved. The concept of field assumes a receptor or receptor organs under the stimulus influence, and that data is being obtained either physiologically or subjectively at some point in the neural pathway. The area ''seen'' by the site giving the information is the field and may vary with the place from which the data is taken.

It was shown early that the fields for warm, cold, and cutaneous pressure were surprisingly separate in most areas of human skin. Further, the number of sensitive sensory spots on any one surface varied considerably. For instance, the number of touch sensitive spots are much greater on the fingertips than on the back of the arm. In many laboratories, over a great number of years, spots sensitive to the various cutaneous stimuli were cut from human volunteers, and the neural structures contained beneath the spots were prepared for microscopic examination (histology). Figure 5-3 shows the consensus of the anatomical contents of two types of skin region. Figure 5-3B is a drawing of the major components in the glaberous (hairless) skin. The skin surface is shown to a depth of approximately 2 mm. The inner layers are a very active cellular area. Most of the non-neural and vascular cells arise from a continuous replacement action in the lower region of the reticular dermis. These gradually push their older sister cells out toward the surface. As the cells reach the limit of the papillary dermis and epidermis, they die and form the dead cell layer, sometimes called the stratum corneum. Immediately below the stratum corneum is the major area that receives nerve terminals. These are *''free''* *(unspecialized or uncovered) nerve endings* that also protrude into the epidermis. Meissner's corpuscles, Krause endbulbs, Merkel's discs, Ruffini

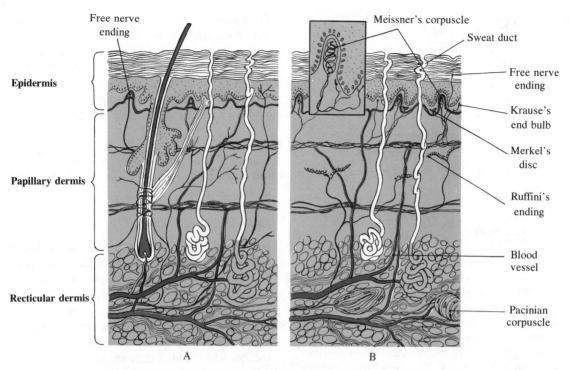

Fig. 5-3.   Sections of two types of human skin. A (left) hirsuit (hairy). B (right) glaberous (hairless). Major structures are shown. (After, Kenshalo and Nafe, 1963; Mountcastle, 1974)

endings, and Pacinian corpuscles are not true nerve endings but are a specialization of non-neural tissue wrapped around the nerve terminal, which is elaborately convoluted in some ending classes. In each case, the nerve itself is similar to the free nerve ending. The diameter of the free nerve ending gradually gets smaller and ends. This group of specialized end-organs is drawn in more detail in Figure 5-4. Aside from endings within these complex structures, cutaneous nerves terminate in the papillary dermis and epidermis as free endings. They terminate also at various levels of the deeper dermis and on the surface of small blood vessels. The largest of the encapsulated endings is the Pacinian corpuscle, which lies at the inner surface of the reticular dermis. Figure 5-3A shows the considerable difference between the organization of the glaberous and the hirsuit (hairy) skin. The most

obvious difference between Figure 5-3A and Figure 5-3B is the presence of the hair shaft. More close examination will show that the encapsulated endings, ranging from simple Meissner's corpuscles to the complex Pacinian corpuscles, are not found in Figure 5-3A. Indeed, it is generally agreed that such corpuscles are not present in hairy skin, and although they have been reported in outdated textbooks, it is widely accepted now that evidence of their presence was based on artifacts of the histological preparations. The nerve endings in the hairy skin are all of the unmodified, free type. These endings are in three places at various layers between the dermis and epidermis, around the shafts of the hairs, and in the vicinity of the junction of the venous and arterial components of the vascular network. The human hand and forearm contain both hairy and glaberous tissue areas.

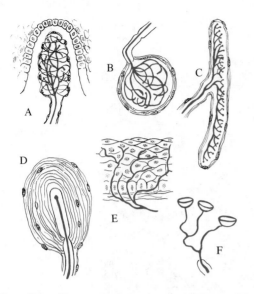

Fig. 5-4. Characteristic cutaneous nerve ending sketches. These are found in the glaberous skin and are listed with the classically associated sensory experience. A. Meissner's corpuscle (touch). B. Krause's end bulb (cold). C. Ruffini's end organ (warm). D. Pacinian corpuscle (deep pressure). E. Free (bare) nerve endings (pain). F. Merkel's discs (touch). (After Brown, 1973)

Although many nerve terminals, both encapsulated and unencapsulated, may be served from one stem or trunk axon, these axons gather together and form *peripheral sensory nerves*. The peripheral sensory nerve, which conveys information about the human hand, is the medial cutaneous nerve. Within the medial cutaneous there are a variety of axon sizes. These are classified by diameter in Figure 5-5, which is essentially a frequency by diameter histogram. That is, the numbers of axons with diameters of various dimensions are plotted against a group of diameters. Nerve axons are classified by sizes, the A, B, and C fiber diameters. But only A and C fibers have sensory function. B fibers are motor elements. A fibers are of larger diameter and are represented in the medial cutaneous nerve in the diameter range 4–14 microns (1 micron = 10^{-6} meters). A fibers also have a fatty sheath or *myelin* deposit which provides for a relative increase in the speed of conduction. C

fibers have very little or no myelin, and are generally in the range of 0.5–8 microns. The speed of conduction of the nerve impulse along the axon is directly related to its diameter and the extent of myelination. Conduction velocity or speed of nerve impulse transmission from one place to another may be approximated by a simple formula:

$$CV = 9D$$

where CV is conduction velocity in meters/second and diameter (D) is cross-sectional diameter of the axon in microns.

Touch and Pressure

It has been shown that there is a wide range of nerve ending types to be found in the human skin. The broadest range is in the glaberous skin. The largest ending is the Pacinian corpuscle, which occasionally is as large as 0.5 mm across its longest axis. There is a range of smaller nerve ending encapsulations. In the hairy skin are the free nerve endings which end at different places and on (in) different types of tissue. There is no direct knowledge about the function of any of the smaller nerve ending types or free nerve endings. These are so small that it has been impossible to record electrophysiological data from them in animals. However, some excellent research has been done on the Pacinian corpuscle by Loewenstein (1960). Very large Pacinian corpuscles may be found in the tissue supporting the gut of cats. An important experiment produced the results shown in Figure 5-6

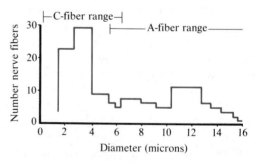

Fig. 5-5. Size distribution of nerve fiber (axon) diameters in the human medial cutaneous nerve. (After Gasser, 1935)

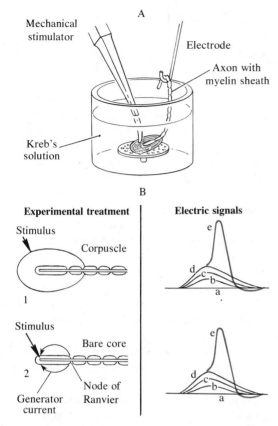

Fig. 5-6. Experiments on the pressure transducer properties of the Pacinian corpuscle. A. The experimental set-up; B. Experiments, (1) with whole capsule, (2) with capsule removed. Electrical signals to gradually increasing stimulus strengths (a–e) under experimental conditions 1–2. (After Loewenstein, 1960)

which shows how the experiment was arranged. A mechanical stimulator driven by an electrical signal was placed in contact with the ending capsule or outer layer. In the figure, part of the outer layers (capsule) have been cut away to show the position of the nerve ending. In life, the outer layer is continuous and is organized very much like an onion with a nerve ending in its center. The nerve ending could be contacted directly with microelectrodes or the nerve fiber could be draped over a small electrode so its signals could be recorded. B (right) shows that with increasing stimulus strength, the

generator potential (a, b, c, d) gradually increased until threshold was reached and an action potential was produced (e). Current flowed out of the first node of Ranvier and externally into the depolarized area. This current lasted as long as the stimulus was applied when the outer layer was removed and is called the generator current. With the outer layer intact, the generator current is transient and occurs only when the stimulus is first applied. Steady pressures do not produce a maintained generator current so long as the outer layers are intact. The capsule outer layers then function something like a balloon where inner pressures equilibrate immediately following the application of external pressure to the balloon skin. The mechanism for stimulating the nerve ending appears to be the application of an uneven pressure to the terminal. When a generator current increases to the *threshold level,* the node of Ranvier becomes depolarized and an action potential is produced. Normally the action potential would continue down the axon towards the central nervous system. Variations on this process are responsible for the excitation of all sensory nerve endings in the skin, encapsulated or free. The sequence is: stimulus → local change in membrane permeability → generator current → threshold → depolarization of the first node → conduction of the action potential. Nodes are not found in unmyelinated fibers. Consequently, in totally unmyelinated fibers, the generator current would serve to depolarize the axon near the point of stimulation and the action potential would arise in that region. Because of the reduced diameter and absence of myelin, conduction toward the central nervous system would be much slower.

It has been established that more than one nerve terminal may arise from a single-stem fiber. Generators produced in several nerve terminals may then *sum* to produce action potentials where each generator potential, separately, is below threshold. Recordings from axons at a distance from the cutaneous receptors show that receptor response can be divided into two categories, rapid adapting and slow adapting. In Figure 5-7 is shown the relationship between mechanical stimulation of the skin, the resulting generator potentials, and the action potentials produced by the generators for these

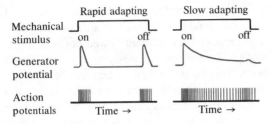

Fig. 5-7. Relationships between stimuli and the effect on generator potential production and subsequent action potentials on the stem axon for slow and rapid adapting receptors. Mechanical stimulus indents skin at "on" and is removed at "off".

two types of receptors. Clearly, the rapid adapting receptors are of little value in the evaluation of a steady stimulus but are excellent for detection. More information about stimulus quantity (deformation of tissue) is provided by the slow adapting receptor, but it will be noticed that its response also contains a transient that contributes relatively more information to the action potential train. In both cases, the early transient component of the stimulus and the rate of tissue displacement is very important in determining threshold.

The threshold for direct excitation of the receptor may be as small as 0.5 microns (0.5×10^{-6}, meters) if the movement is rapid (Gray and Malcolm, 1950). The sensitivity to such small displacements makes quantitative judgments by humans (*psychophysics*) very difficult. Nafe and Wagner (1941) showed that movement rates into human skin must be 3 microns per second or greater to achieve threshold. With carefully controlled stimulation, humans detect a cutaneous stimulus during the rapid phase of its movement into the tissue and during the rapid phase of its removal. If the stimulus is stable and tissue movement is not present, awareness of the presence of the mechanical stimulus ceases when the movement rate approaches zero. This is essentially what would be expected from the Figure 5-7 description of the effects of a stimulus on rapid adapting receptors.

Cutaneous sensory adaptation has been defined as a loss of awareness of the presence of stimulation when tissue contact and deformation is main-

tained. The rate sensitivity of some cutaneous receptors would account for some instances of adaptation. But since the skin is most often moving at relatively high rates (pulse, respiration), adaptation must also occur central to the receptor terminals. This type of adaptation is present both in the sensory areas of the spinal cord and the brain. A good example would be the loss of awareness of a wristwatch whose presence can be brought back into "consciousness" voluntarily by asking the individual to pay attention to this stimulus.

One means of measuring relative skin sensitivity in the absence of the exceedingly elaborate mechanical equipment which is necessary to control movement rates to better than 10 microns/second can be obtained by a simple two-point stimulator. The stimulator is similar to the pencil compass where the distance between the two points is variable. To measure sensitivity by this method, the points are applied to the skin and the distance between them gradually reduced until they are felt as one. This measure is distinct from a measure of absolute sensitivity, but deals more with the extent of overlap and density or "grain" of the cutaneous sensory fields. So long as the two stimulus points are affecting only one field, they are felt as a single point. There is a wide variation in sensitivity to two point stimulation on various cutaneous areas

Table 5-1. Two-Point Discrimination Thresholds for Various Human Body Surfaces in Mm. Numbers Are Stimulus Separations in Mm.*

Threshold (mm)	Surface
3.5	fingers
6	upper lip
8	nose
10	palm
10	large toe
17	forehead
22	foot sole
30	breast
37	belly
38	forearm
45	thigh
48	calf

*From Weinstein, 1968.

of the human body. Threshold for the discrimi-nation of two points ranges from approximately 3.5 mm on the fingertips to 48 mm on the calves of the legs (see Table 5-1).

It is rare when the neural concepts generated through experiments with animals are tested in humans. There has been one such experiment in cutaneous sensitivity (Hensel and Boman, 1960). German medical students volunteered for dissec-tion of the radial nerve, which is available in the dorsal portion of the forearm. Single nerve fibers were dissected from these nerves in the absence of long term general anesthesia. The skin of the fingers was stimulated with indentation by cali-brated weights, and the impulses produced in the radial nerve fibers were recorded. Figure 5-8 shows the results plotted as impulse frequency against duration of the presence of the 13 gm stim-ulus. This response has the characteristics de-scribed for a slow adapting receptor. Before deliv-ery of the stimulus, the impulse frequency was approximately 12/second. During the phase of rapid stimulus movement into the tissue, the frequency increased to over 120/second, falling to a relatively steady rate of about 70/second at the end of 5 seconds. Immediately after removal of the stimulus, the response rate fell to zero. Although this falls into the slow adapting receptor category, notice how the stimulus "on" and stimulus "off" events are selectively emphasized in the neural

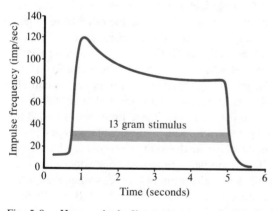

Fig. 5-8. Human single fiber response rate from radial nerve. Stimulus delivered to dorsal side of thumb. Stimulus was a 1 mm diameter plastic rod. (After Hensel and Boman, 1960)

response. C fibers outnumber A fibers in cutaneous nerves about 20 to 1. But the C fibers are small and very difficult to record, and they have never been recorded in humans. But Bessou and Perl (1969) studied 147 C fibers which supplied the cat's hairy skin. Eighty percent of these responded to mechan-ical stimulation. Thirty-six percent were extremely sensitive, responding to weights between 0.01 and 0.045 grams. The majority of C fibers which re-sponded to mechanical stimulation did not respond sensitively to thermal change.

In the introduction to this chapter, a major early advance called the "Doctrine of Specific Nerve Energies" was described. Restated, this Doctrine requires that every sensory experience (vision, hearing, cutaneous sensation, and so forth) is the result of arrival of information at the central ner-vous system over a particular set of nerve fibers originating in the appropriate sense organ. Stimu-lation of that sense organ and nerve fibers by any means will produce only one class of sensory expe-riences. Later, this theoretical system was modi-fied by Herman Helmholtz for hearing and vision. This modification is sometimes called the "Doc-trine of Specific Fiber Energies" and requires that particular sense qualities (red, blue, green, for vision; various pitches for hearing) are the result of excitation of specific groups of nerve fibers within the overall set of fibers unique to that particular sense organ. Max von Frey applied this scheme for quality discrimination to the cutaneous senses. He proposed that each discriminable experience or quality arising from stimulation of the skin was the result of excitation of a particular nerve ending type and subsequent transmission to the brain through very specific groups of nerve fibers serv-ing those endings.

The "Doctrine of Specific Nerve Energies" was a major advance in the analysis of the anatomical system responsible for sensation. However, the Doctrine did not recognize quality subsets. Further modifications by Helmholtz and later by von Frey were required to account for these (that is, blue, green, warm, cold). There is a compelling and sat-isfying order in the idea that a particular receptor type with its own peculiar morphological and func-tional organization is responsible for the pro-cessing and transmission to some brain site of all information about each unique sensory quality for each separate sense modality. Such a simple encoding and transmission relationship has great advantages for identification, tracing, and experimentation required for a complete description of any sensory quality and its physiology. Von Frey did not know how elaborate are the various nerve terminals in the skin nor the wide variation in nerve fiber diameters. It is unlikely that C fibers were known in his time, since they approach and pass the size limit resolution of the light microscope. More serious, however, are the problems of subjectiveness of the cutaneous sensory experiences. It is difficult to firmly establish that warm or cold or pressure, or even pain, with all of the connotations of that human experience, can be felt in nonverbal, lower animals. The best that can be hoped for is to deal with the functional properties of the peripheral neuron and to attempt to relate the activity of particular nerve axons (units) to the physical stimuli that are delivered to the region of their terminals in the skin, then to identify the configuration of the terminals and where in the skin the terminals may lie. Once that information is obtained, the response characteristics of the neurons to various stimuli may be correlated with human subjective, psychophysical results to derive a comparison if, indeed, one exists. The technology for achieving these goals has only been available about twenty years. The progress which has been made indicates that the modifications of the nerve terminals do not provide for classification into various types of quality specific sense organs. Rather, the modifications act as "filters" to vary the capability of the nerve terminals for detecting various aspects of tactile or pressure stimuli. The role of the numerous C fibers is more obscure. It is assumed that they end as free nerve endings. Clearly, C fibers may be excited by stimuli of many types.

Warm and Cool

The background of information for the sensations warm and cool is similar from both an experimental and theoretical point of view to that for touch and pressure. The transducer processes for pressure and touch are nicely modeled by the func-

tion of the Pacinian corpuscle (see Figure 5-6 on p. 145). It is fairly easy to see how mechanical deformation of the nerve ending might alter the membrane properties to the extent that a generator potential could be produced. It is more difficult to see how a small temperature gradient could produce the same membrane changes. In fact, Loewenstein showed that temperature changes of reasonable sizes have no effect on the excitation of the Pacinian corpuscle. Nevertheless, warm and cold are common human sensory experiences.

Physically, the stimulus for warm and cool is quite distinct from all other stimuli which produce human sensory experiences. For all other sense modalities, the stimulus can be described in terms of increments above zero. That is, weights may be applied to the skin, ranging from large to zero. Sounds may be applied to the ear with pressures from zero to some large value, and lights may be shown into the eye from extremely bright to zero. Zero temperature is very difficult to achieve and its physical correlate is the condition of no molecular motion. This occurs at about $-273°C$. This is an impractical baseline upon which to build temperature studies, since long before this temperature is reached, the tissue is dead. In life, the human skin has a varying temperature level. Skin temperature may vary several degrees depending on the environmental temperature, level of exercise, vascular condition, sex, and other factors. A man working outside in the winter where the air temperature is 10°C would feel warm if he went inside where the air temperature is 18°C. On the other hand, a person adjusted to a room temperature of 22°C will feel distinctly cold if that person goes into an environment where the ambient temperature is 18°C. The subjective experience warm or cold is entirely relative to the speed of adaptation of the skin, within certain limits. These limits are bounded by temperatures at which irreversible changes begin taking place in the skin. Irreversible changes in cell proteins begin to take place at about 43–45°C, while cell walls begin to leak ions when their temperature is depressed below about 10°C. "Comfortable" adapting temperatures are associated with skin surface temperatures in the region of 30 to about 36°C.

As was shown in Figure 5-3 on p. 143, there are

large areas of the human skin that have few or no specialized endings. Only free endings are to be found, and these are found at different places in the skin. Since the hairy skin has a single nerve ending class, and since hairy skin has been demonstrated to be as sensitive to temperature change as the nonhairy skin, Nafe proposed in 1934 that the transducer for temperature change was the smooth muscle of the microvascular system of the skin on which free nerve endings terminate. The movement of the smooth muscle in response to temperature change served to mechanically stimulate the nerve endings. Such a mechanism provided a convenient transducer for temperature to mechanical motion. It has never been demonstrated that smooth muscle responses to temperature change are large enough to provide an adequate transducer mechanism. Further, it has never been demonstrated that those neurons which are responsive to thermal change in the skin are the ones which have been seen to end, histologically, on the surface of smooth muscles. But, the only place in the human skin where nerve endings exist in the absence of vascular tissue is in the cornea of the eye. The cornea is highly sensitive to touch, and there is no general agreement as to whether stimulation with thermal change will produce a clear experience of warm or cold. Animal studies (Dawson, 1963; Maurice, 1975) indicate that corneal neurons respond to stimuli representative of all cutaneous sensory qualities including warm and cold. But, as in all other animal studies, the sensory quality interpretation which is available only from humans cannot be brought to bear to settle the argument.

Animal nerve responses to cold stimuli (reduction in temperature, from the resting adaptation level) have been reported by many authors. These are not noticeably different in characteristics from the "cold" fibers reported by Hensel and Boman (1960) dissected from the human radial nerve where cool stimulation was applied to the finger. Figure 5-9 shows that there is a "background" discharge rate of the radial nerve unit prior to temperature change. This rate increased rapidly after the beginning of cooling. As the rate of cooling slowed and stopped after about 50 seconds, the unit discharge rate also decreased. With the onset of rewarming, there was a cessation of all unit ac-

tivity which resumed a background rate once again, after the rewarming was complete to the initial adapting temperature of approximately 34°C. This particular fiber was not responsive to tactile stimulation. However, many "cold" fibers have been reported that do respond to touch or pressure. "Warm" fibers that respond actively to elevations in local temperature are very rare. They have been reported by only a few research workers. They do not appear to be uniformly distributed over the body as are "cold" fibers. The response characteristics of the warm fiber is similar to the cold fiber. That is, there is a transient response to temperature elevation, the rate of the responding of the fiber drops after the skin temperature is stabilized, and there is often a drop in response rate to zero when the skin is cooled to the original level. Figure 5-10A shows the time characteristic of such a fiber recorded by Hensel and Kenshalo (1969). This unit was recorded from the infraorbital nerve of the cat where it was not possible to find a significant number of warm fibers in several other body areas. Figure 5-10B shows the characteristic steady-state response of both cold and warm fibers. The steady-state is the unit response rate which occurs during the period that the skin temperature is held at a new (elevated or reduced) level relative to the initial adapting temperature. The values shown in Figure 5-10B are average values for approximately 20 fibers. The maximum fiber discharge rate for cold fibers occurs at about 23°C. Warm fiber maximum occurs at about 43°C. Temperatures this high are very near the levels required for tissue damage.

As with the detection of pressure, human tem-

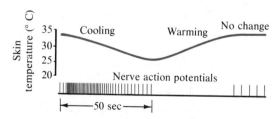

Fig. 5-9. "Cold" fiber response from axon dissected from human radial nerve. Record A shows temperature and nerve response in record B. Temperature begins at 34° C., falls to 26° C. and recovers. (After Hensel and Boman, 1960)

perature stimulus detection depends on the size of the area stimulated. As area increases, threshold decreases. There is no comprehensive comparison of temperature sensitivities over many body areas as there is for two-point threshold cutaneous touch stimulation. Temperature sensitivity of the dorsal part of the human forearm has been well described by Kenshalo and Nafe (1963). The stimulus area was about 2.5 square centimeters. Figure 5-11 shows (see upper curve) that, as the adapting temperature increases from 30 to 45°C, the temperature change required for the experience "warm" decreased to about 0.1°C. The adapting temperature is the stable level of temperature impressed on that skin area and which is no longer detected. The stimuli were imposed upon these "adapting" levels. The lower portion of Figure 5-11 can be considered almost the reverse of the upper section. As the adapting temperature was reduced from 45°C, temperature reduction required for the experience "cold" gradually became less, to thresholds of approximately 0.1°C. The temperature elevation (warm) curve describes the experiences for both females and males. However, there is a distinct difference in thresholds for females and males for cold stimuli. In a later publication, Kenshalo

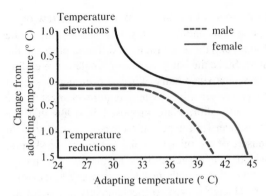

Fig. 5-11. Human thresholds for temperature change from various adaptation temperatures. (After Kenshalo and Nafe, 1963)

(1966) showed that temperature sensitivity in females is closely related to the ovulatory phase of the menstrual cycle. It was demonstrated that at high adapting temperatures, the preovulatory threshold was less by almost ½°C than the postovulatory threshold. Kenshalo showed that this correlated nicely with an increase in the peripheral volume-pulse and vasodilitation which correlated

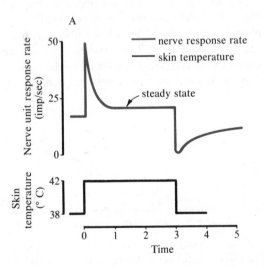

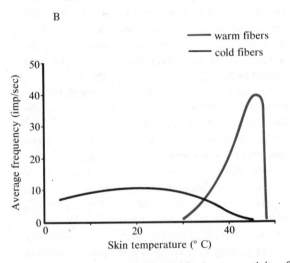

Fig. 5-10. Nerve unit response to skin temperature change and steady state. A. "Warm" unit. B. Average activity of several "cold" and "warm" response nerve units during several thermal steady state conditions. (After Hensel and Kenshalo, 1969)

also with the increase in the hormone progesterone, which is found during the postovulatory phase of the female menstrual cycle. The "male" portions of Figure 5-11 for humans correlate well with data published for both monkeys, responding behaviorally, and cats responding neurophysiologically. Thermal thresholds of males can also be influenced by vasodilitation or constriction. Dawson (1964) used adrenaline chloride to constrict the superficial blood vessels in a small area of the human male's forearm. Although the temperature change produced by the vasoconstriction was compensated, there were still significant changes (depression) of the experimental subject's thermal threshold compared to his opposite arm where there was no experimental vascular change.

The neurophysiological studies which have been cited have dealt only with large fibers in the peripheral nerves. Bessou and Perl (1969) studied 147 unmyelinated fibers in the cats' skin. Of these, only eight were responsive to either thermal elevation or depression in the absence of excitability to mechanical stimulation. One of the eight was positively responsive to thermal increase. Of 47 mechanoreceptors, most were stimulated by cooling but not warming. These are probably comparable to the human cold fibers response shown in Figure 5-9 on p. 149. Kenshalo and Hensel felt that the small number of elements sensitive to temperature in the cats' skin is indicative of a relatively low sensitivity of cats to temperature change and cannot support the conclusion that there are relatively few temperature sensitive fibers in mammals in general.

As with the data from the cutaneous touch or mechanoreceptors discussed earlier, we are confronted with the difficulty that, even though animal nerves may respond to warm and cold change, it is possible that their sensory experience is not the same as that which is excited in humans by the same stimulus. The data on warming and cooling does seem complete enough to conclude that von Frey's adaptation of Müller's Doctrine of Specific Fiber Energies is only partially correct. Peripheral nerves do transmit information about warm and cold. Although "warm" fibers are hard to find in animal preparations, "cold" fibers are plentiful. "Cold" fibers may signal the presence of warmth,

not by responding actively by the production of neural discharges, but by a relative decrease in activity during warming. This contingency was not predicted by the von Frey theory. Nafe's proposal that vascular tissue may act as a temperature transducer cannot be rejected either. There is sufficient reason to believe that changes in the mobility of peripheral blood vessels affect temperature sensitivity in that area. Of course, there is no reason why overall temperature sensitivity cannot be a joint undertaking between nerve terminals which are inherently temperature transducers and nerve terminals which end on thermally sensitive smooth muscle of the microvascular system.

Pain

Classically described, pain is one of the most easily understood and one of the most straightforward of sensory mechanisms. It is a response to tissue damage, it has survival value by forcing withdrawal and avoidance, and therefore should not be subject to adaptation. If von Frey's theory holds, "pain" information should be mediated by specific nerve ending types and specific tracts and connections to the central nervous system. The particular nerve ending type proposed by von Frey was the unencapsulated, free nerve ending. Depending on the seriousness of the damage and the particular nerve type, the high discharge rate of the surgically damaged nerve may continue for a few seconds or minutes and then suddenly stop, indicating irreversible damage. A cut of one's finger undoubtedly causes this type of damage in numerous peripheral nerve fibers, and the first information interpreted in the central nervous system, almost surely, is a result of such a "scream" of nerve discharge. Those circumstances that produce long-term pain in the peripheral nervous system are usually associated with swelling and redness of the tissue. This is called, clinically, the "inflammatory reaction" and is almost always associated with tissue and cell damage. When cells are damaged, complex chemicals are released. One such chemical, bradykinin, has the capability of exciting nerve endings to vigorous response. When bradykinin is presented to normal (undamaged) human tissue, the result is very painful. Con sequently, it is not always possible to determine whether the cause of pain is damage to the nerve endings themselves or stimulation of the nerve endings by a chemical liberated from nearby damaged tissue. Some earlier workers have proposed that for many types of pain tissue movement is required.

Stimulation of tissue for purposes of experimenting with pain is extremely difficult. Most painful stimuli are difficult to quantify. Hardy, *et al*. (1940), devised a quantitative method for studying pain. Infrared energy was used to raise the temperature of skin areas to levels judged painful by subjects. This procedure gave reliable quantitative results. It was found that thermal pain occurred at a tissue temperature of approximately 44°C where the threshold for pain was with an infrared energy input of approximately 180 millicalories/second/centimeter^2. A calorie is the amount of energy required to raise the temperature of one cc of water 1° on the centigrade scale. When subjects are stimulated by infrared energy for the production of pain, very lawful and regular results may be obtained if the stimulus is not left on too long. Figure 5-12 shows the estimation of pain magnitude from seven subjects, where several intensities of infrared were delivered to the skin. It may be seen here that the logarithm of the pain "magnitude" is almost a linear fit with the logarithm of the intensity of the infrared radiation.

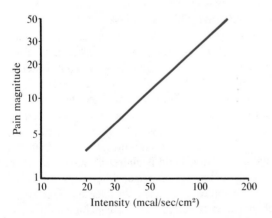

Fig. 5-12. Estimated magnitude of pain produced by infrared stimulation of the human skin. (After Adair, 1968)

Such a relationship is called the "power law" and has been found to hold between stimulus magnitude estimations and physical stimulus magnitude for many sensory systems (see Chapter 3). Subjectively, burning pain is quite different from "aching" pain, which more frequently arises from deeper tissues of the viscera (lungs, gut, and so on) and the bones and joints. There is very little known about the physiology of aching pain.

Some estimations of which fibers in peripheral nerves contribute to the pain experience may be made by blocking the larger fibers that are more sensitive to ischemia (reduced blood flow and consequent lack of oxygen). In an ischemic block, the smaller C fibers remain functioning for 30–40 minutes after the A fiber function ceases. In humans with only C fibers active, the sensation of pain may be consistently evoked. The resulting experience is excruciating.

The picture painted so far is that pain is an extremely stable sensory phenomenon across individuals. This may be true so far as the peripheral nervous system is concerned. However, when complex situations arise, pain becomes more labile. Pain or stimulation elsewhere in the body regularly elevates the threshold for pain at a test site. Many individuals are completely insensitive to pain during a hypnotic trance. The lability of pain is also documented by Figure 5-13, which shows that under laboratory conditions many pharmaceuticals which reliably affect the level of pain produced naturally seem to have little or no control over pain in some experimental conditions. The subjects contributing data to Figure 5-13 knew that there was a control (non pain killing) medication, but they did not know if they received it or a more potent treatment. The result indicates that none of the "analgesic" (pain killing) compounds had any measurable effect on the detection of pain by the subjects. It is well documented that the nature of reaction to painful stimuli varies greatly from individual to individual. Incapacitation by pain depends greatly on the sociological circumstances at that moment in time. Battlefield reports show that serious injuries are often ignored and appear to cause little inconvenience, while on other occasions an identical injury would be expected to be completely incapacitating. Melzack and Casey

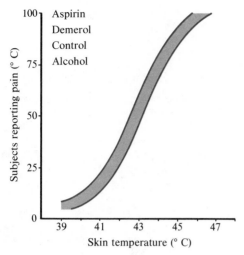

Fig. 5-13.   Reports of pain from subject groups receiving several oral chemical treatments. (After Chapman, et al., 1965)

(1968) questioned whether the reaction is a result of the sensation of the pain or involves an interpretive step. Patients with frontal lobe lesions of the brain or those who have been given morphine, are aware of the presence of painful sensations, but are no longer "concerned about them." The lability of pain and its susceptibility to many influences detract from its survival value and claims of specific stimulation → specific neural pathway → and the automatic nature of the response.

Melzack and Wall (1965) identified a large number of surgical procedures (to cut "pain nerves") which are performed on humans with intractable pain. These are usually cancer patients. Such surgical procedures are performed at almost all levels of spinal cord and brain. The only common feature among them is that no single procedure can be expected to permanently eliminate the painful experience. This argues strongly against a single pathway for the transmission of painful information. An interesting theory has been generated from experiments by Melzack and Wall. The *Gate Control Theory* of pain utilizes a balance between activity in small fibers (mostly C) and large fibers (mostly A) and their inputs into several regions of the spinal cord. Large fiber activity is

transmitted more rapidly and tends to "turn off" the control system reducing the effect of small fibers on the perception and the motor system which resides in higher brain centers. Essentially, the control of perception is a result of the balance between large and small fiber activity. Small fiber activity biases the gate control towards outflow into the perception system and a consequent experience of pain. The overall outflow of the gate control system (see Figure 5-14) is also under the influence of feedback from higher brain centers which can hold the gate closed even in the face of an overbalance of small fiber input. As we have already seen, mechanical (tactile or pressure) stimulation of the skin tends to activate large fibers. Minor wounds or tissue damage tends to activate

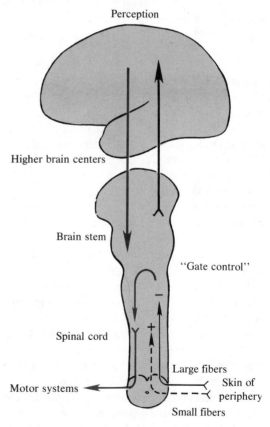

Fig. 5-14.   Basic elements of the gate control theory of pain. + signifies a cause of relative increase in subjective pain, − a relative decrease. (After Melzack and Wall, 1965)

small C fibers. A simple experiment will demonstrate how this works. If a straight pin is grasped in one hand so that only 2 or 3 mm of tip is protruding, one can jab (gently) the upper portion of the hand and feel a distinctly painful (C fibers) experience. If, however, the area to be jabbed is rubbed (not vigorously) (A fibers) for about 10 seconds before the pin is jabbed into the skin, the pin prick is frequently not felt (A fibers block C fiber activity), or if felt, it is usually not painful. This experiment has been tried on hundreds of students and is generally about 90 percent successful. An explanation can be made by the gate theory. Rubbing of the tissue produces volleys of large fiber sensory activity into the gate control. If this is followed immediately by the "painful" stimulus, the pin jab, the gate is already closed by the large fiber activity and the painful information is not transmitted into the perception and motor systems.

Central Projections

The brain and the pathways (spinal cord and brain stem) into it will be described for the cutaneous senses. Later other senses will be taken up. The cross-sectional appearance of each central nervous system locale is different and may be used as a "finger print." For your later assistance, the major characteristic shapes are pictured in Figure 5-15.

Cutaneous sensory information reaches the brain through many pathways (Figure 5-16). Those receptors above the torso communicate by way of the cranial nerve sensory components while those from the somatic segments of the body enter the spinal cord through the *posterior spinal roots*. After they enter the cord, they separate into *medial* and *lateral* divisions. The medial fibers enter the dorsal columns of the cord and ascend the entire length, while lateral fibers travel upward one to six segments and then downward one to two segments, and then synapse with dorsal horn cells that give rise to the *ventral* and *lateral spinothalamic tracts*. These tracts ascend to the brain in the *anterior* and *lateral columns* of the spinal cord. The majority of the dorsal column is made up of large myelinated (A) fibers with intrinsic rapid conduction velocities. The spinothalamic system is mainly made of small (C) fibers, which transmit at

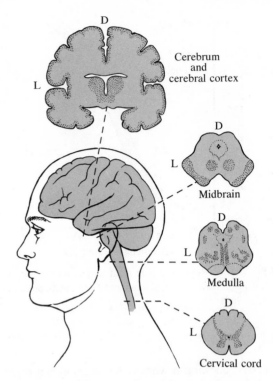

Fig. 5-15. Shape of sections through the central nervous system made at the major levels. L, lateral; D, dorsal. These will help in tracing pathways later in the chapter.

low velocity. The dorsal column system projects to the ventro-basal column of the thalamus, which is a major relay system for many types of sensory information. Fibers then pass to the cortex of the same side. Note that somatic areas on the right side of the body are innervated by dorsal column elements which synapse at the dorsal column nuclei of the spinal cord and cross to the opposite side of the spinal cord before ascending to the left thalamus and cortex. Consequently, the right side of the body is represented in the left thalamus and sensory cortex of the brain. Both the dorsal column and the spinothalamic systems are used for the transmission of information relative to pain stimuli. The pathway becomes much more complex for "pain" fibers once the information has risen to the brain stem. According to Melzack, surgery at various levels of the mid brain has different effects, depending on the particular pain

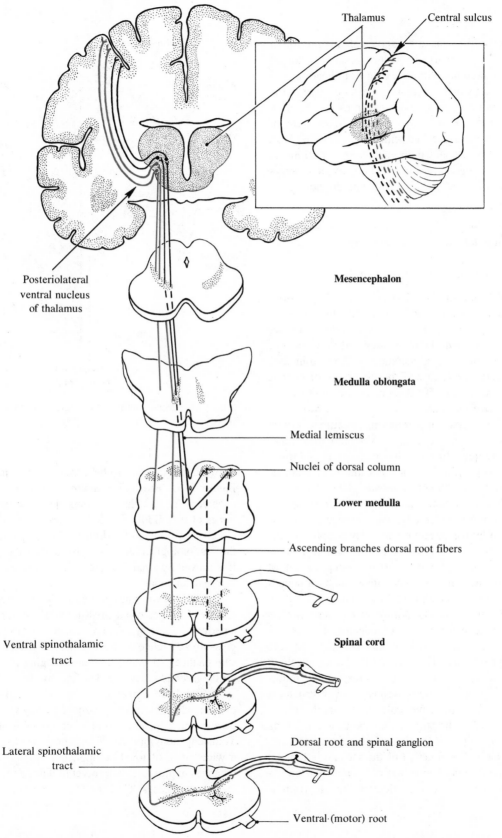

Thalamus

Central sulcus

Posteriolateral
ventral nucleus
of thalamus

Mesencephalon

Medulla oblongata

Medial lemiscus

Nuclei of dorsal column

Lower medulla

Ascending branches dorsal root fibers

Ventral spinothalamic
tract

Spinal cord

Lateral spinothalamic
tract

Dorsal root and spinal ganglion

Ventral·(motor) root

Fig. 5-16.   Pathways for transmission of sensory data from somatic areas to sensory cortex. (After Guyton, 1971)

"quality." Lesions of the spinothalamic portion of the mid brain markedly reduce sensitivity to pin prick, but do not eliminate pain from heating. Lesions nearby in the central tegmental portion of the mid brain accentuate pain responses to pin prick but reduce pain responses to heat. Many areas of the brain are associated with pain, including both sensory cortex and prefrontal cortex. Lesions of any one of these areas alter the quality of sensitivity to certain classes of pain but do not affect others.

Hearing and the Vestibular System

The Stimuli and Organ Anatomy

The function of the *auditory* system is *hearing*. The terms audition and hearing are the same for practical purposes. The *vestibular* system provides knowledge about the orientation and movement of the body in space. Orientation is meant to include both static position and the directions of change during movement. The vestibular and auditory systems share the same bony housing, the *labyrinth*. There are gross similarities in structures serving the two sensory processes. Although their functions are quite different, it is convenient and traditional to present them at the same time. Humans are provided with symmetrically placed labyrinths which are embedded in each *temporal* bone (see Figure 5-17). Externally, the entrance to each is marked by the structure which lay people call the ear. Correctly, this is the *pinna*, a floppy cartilaginous structure which serves to keep rain out of the ear canal and has some minor value for sound-gathering and detection of directionality. The stimulus for the vestibular portion of the inner ear has both static and dynamic components. That is, the sense organs in the *semicircular canals* respond to movement only. They are active during acceleration and deceleration but fail to respond even during constant velocity movement. Other structures at the base of the semicircular canals are the *utricle* and *saccule*. The stimulus for the utricle is tilting of the head out of the vertical plane and linear acceleration. The function of the saccule is thought to be detection of vibration but is not fully understood. The auditory portion of the labyrinth is

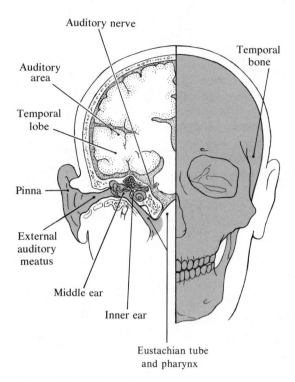

Fig. 5-17.   Major auditory structures and their locations.

shown in relationship to the semicircular canals in Figure 5-18. The major auditory structure is the cochlea. The cochlea is connected through the bones of the middle ear to the *tympanium,* a large circular membrane (ear drum). The tympanium is the first biological element in the auditory system. It is moved by small changes in air pressure in the external ear canal.

There are two common causes for air pressure change. Changes of air pressure which occur over a period of hours or days are changes in barometric pressure and relate to the weather. When air pressure changes are more frequent, ranging from 20-20,000/second, they are detected by the auditory system and are perceived as sound. Audible air pressure changes can be produced by any vibrating device and appear as simple or complex tones. Transient, nonvibrating disturbances (clicks) have a wide range of tonal components. Sound waves (changes in pressure) will travel in fluids and solids as well as in gases. They travel at a constant veloc-

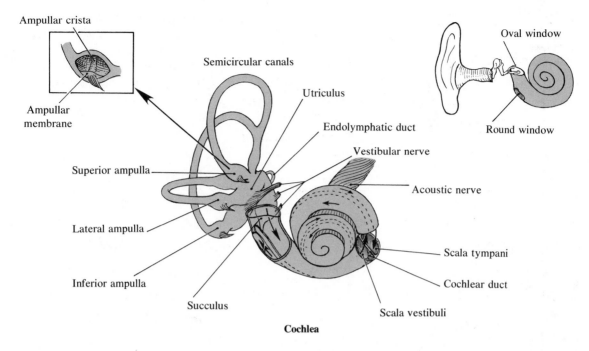

Cochlea

Fig. 5-18.   Gross anatomy of the human labyrinth (vestibular and auditory) systems.

ity (C). $C = \sqrt{b/p}$, where b is the modulus of elasticity and p is the density of the medium. For a sinusoidal sound, as in Figure 5-19, the distance between the air pressure peaks is called the *wavelength*. Wavelength and frequency in Hertz (Hz) are related by way of a constant (for air or other media) by the formula $\lambda = C/F$, where $C =$ velocity, $F =$ frequency in Hz, and λ is the wavelength.

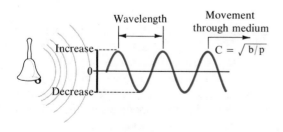

Fig. 5-19.   Some physical aspects of a sound front from a source at the left. Frequency (f) is the number of pressure change cycles that occur in one second. C is the velocity of sound (see text).

The normal range of the auditory system is very wide. The range between the threshold for hearing and the acoustic (pressure) levels which are uncomfortable is approximately one million, million (10^{12}). To deal with such a wide range of stimulus energies, a special system has been developed to describe auditory stimuli. This measure is a *decibel* (db). If sound pressure is the stimulus, the decibel would be equal to $20 \log_{10} p/pr$ (p = sound pressure). The usual reference pressure (p_r) is 0.0002 dynes/cm². This pressure is near the human threshold for detection of a signal at 1000 Hz. When pressure measurements are used, the notation db, SPL (sound pressure level) is used. Using this measurement system, a just detectable whisper would be about 0 db (SPL), while the sound of a rock band nearby would equal approximately 90 db (SPL). Sensitivity of the auditory system varies with frequency. In fact, sensitivity in humans is greatest in the region of frequencies used in human speech. These range from approximately 500 to 3000 Hz (see Figure 5-20). The full auditory range is experienced only by young people. By age 50, frequency range is reduced, but most significantly

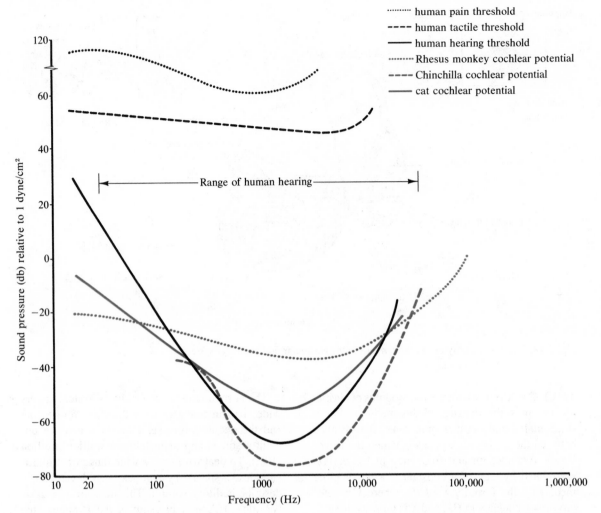

Fig. 5-20.   Sound pressure thresholds (db-spl) for hearing vary with frequency. At higher intensities tactile and pain experiences can occur. Below 20 Hz, sounds are not heard.

at the high end. The typical upper limit for a person age 55 is 8000 Hz. As sound intensity increases above hearing threshold, high intensities may produce tactile or painful experiences. There is evidence for inner ear damage at pressure levels above 100 decibels. Such levels are encountered in subways, near jet aircraft, and near rock bands with amplifiers. Sounds with frequencies below 20 Hz are not heard but are felt. In hearing, movements of the inner ear and the middle ear structures are very small at threshold. The movement of the tympanium at threshold for a 2000 Hz tone is no

greater than about 10^{-9} cm. The diameter of the hydrogen atom is 10^{-8} cm. It is reasonable to ask how these small movements are measured.

The Nobel prize winner, von Békésy, mechanically stimulated excised fluid filled ear structures while observing their movements with water immersion microscope. Using a high speed stroboscope, it was possible to "freeze" the motion of the various structures while examining them with the microscope. A good quality optical microscope can resolve about 10^{-4} cm. Consequently, relatively large movements were required. The pressure levels were measured and movements expected from the much lower pressures around the threshold for hearing were calculated. Figure 5-20 shows hearing threshold is minimal at around 2000 Hz. This sensitivity bias in the center of the range for human hearing appears to be produced by the mechanical structure of the external auditory meatus. Values are species dependent. The physical dimensions of the human auditory meatus conducts pressure changes most efficiently in the 1000–5000 Hz range. The human perceptual correlate of frequency is *pitch*. But Figure 5-21 shows that equal increments in frequency do not produce equal increments in subjective pitch. If pitch is plotted as a psychophysical scale against the logarithm of frequency, the result is quite nonlinear. The pitch unit, the *mel*, increases one unit for every discernable change in frequency. It can be seen that over the full frequency range of hearing the number of possible pitch discriminations does not exceed about 4000. The most rapid rise in the curve in Figure 5-21 is in the region of about from 1000 to 8000 Hz. This indicates that pitch discrimination is finer in this region which, as did threshold, correlates with the frequency band for the frequency contents of human speech. The biasing factor here is not only the external auditory me-

atus. Pitch discrimination begins on the basilar membrane of the cochlea, and it is probably here that the major bias exists.

Physiology of Hearing

Pressure changes in the air are converted to mechanical movement by the tympanium. This mechanical movement is transmitted through the three bones of the middle ear and coupled directly to the tissue of the *oval window* of the cochlea. As pictured in Figure 5-18, the cochlea appears as a coiled structure similar to a snail's shell. The structure is partitioned by a major sensory structure called the *organ of corti*. One section of the organ of corti is a relatively stiff membrane, the *basilar membrane*. These structures are shown schematically in Figure 5-22. The entire volume of the middle ear of humans is approximately 2 cc. Therefore, the bones are small. The oval and round windows are flexible and allow for the transmission of motion to the fluids of the cochlea without significant change in pressure. The fluid filled cavities of the upper portion of the cochlea (*scala vestibuli* and *scala media*) communicate with the lower cavity (*scala tympani*) through an opening in the apex of the cochlea called the *helicotrema*. The scala vestibuli and scala tympani are filled with *perilymph,* which differs in salt concentration from the fluid in the scala media which is *endolymph*. Both have similarities to blood serum but have no proteins. Disturbance of the fluid in the upper chambers caused by movement of the oval window causes movement of the basilar membrane. The place of maximum movement varies with sound frequency because of the membrane's mechanical properties. High frequency movements of the stapes tend to cause basilar membrane displacements near the oval window. Medium frequencies tend to displace the basilar membrane in the middle, and low frequency sounds move most of the membrane (see Figure 5-23). Essentially, the mechanical characteristics of the basilar membrane provides a rudimentary frequency analysis of the mechanically excited, hydraulic disturbances of the fluid inside the cochlea. The multichamber arrangement of the internal regions of the cochlea may be misleading. They have no direct rela-

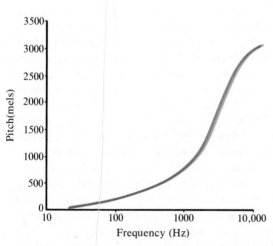

Fig. 5-21. Relationship between pitch (subjective experience) and sound frequency (a physical quantity).

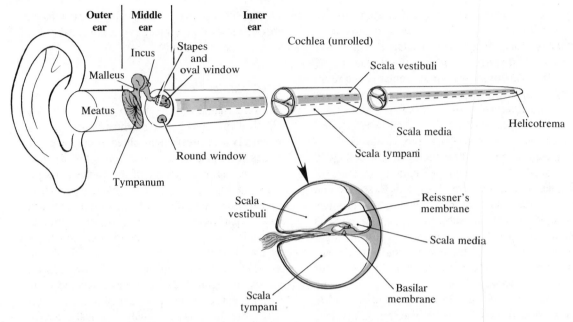

Fig. 5-22.   Schematic of major structures involved in hearing.

tionship to frequency analysis on the basilar membrane which functions as though it is in a very large volume of fluid. If this were true, disturbances of the fluid initiated at almost any position would have relatively little effect upon the resonant characteristics of the membrane. As it turns out, some surgical procedures which replace the middle ear ossicles in humans make a connection between the round window (rather than oval) and the tympanium. When this is done, the frequency analysis capability of the basilar membrane is not changed.

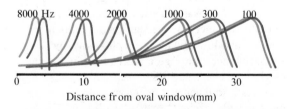

Fig. 5-23.   Position of displacement of basilar membrane by tones of various frequencies. (After Guyton, 1971)

The receptor function for hearing occurs in the *organ of corti*. Figure 5-24 shows a section of the organ of corti which contains the *basilar membrane,* its *hair cells,* the *tectorial membrane* above and the hairs upon the hair cells which rest upon the under-surface of the tectorial membrane. As the basilar membrane is deflected by disturbance of the cochlear fluid, it bows upward or downward much as a tablecloth being shaken between two people. When this occurs, the structure at the base of the hair cells, called the *reticular lamina,* moves back and forth. This movement tends to cause a bending or *shearing* action of the hairs relative to the stable tectorial membrane. The movement of the hairs is the event of reception, since the hairs are portions of the receptor cells. The receptor cells connect synaptically to dendrites of the *cochlear nerve,* whose cell bodies rest in the spiral ganglion inside the cochlea. Thus, the primary axons are the cochlear nerve fibers, but the receptors and sources of generator potentials are most probably the hair cells and are separate. There are two sets of hair cells, inner and outer. In persons with hearing losses in specific frequency bands, it has been

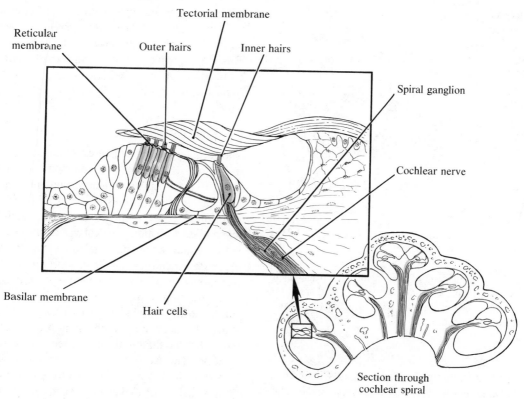

Fig. 5-24. Section through the organ of corti. (After Guyton, 1971)

demonstrated frequently that the hairs at certain places in the cochlea are missing. This is most often the case when the hearing loss is due to the exposure of very loud narrow frequency band sounds. There are 15,000–20,000 *outer hair* cells and about 3,500 *inner hair* cells in each cochlea. These provide for the stimulation of approximately 30,000 neurons in the cochlear nerve which is one division of the auditory branch of the eighth cranial nerve. The different functions for the inner and outer hair cells are not clear, but it is likely that they contribute to the detection of approximately 5,000 different pitches by the average human in the presence of the relatively gross mechanical frequency analysis carried out by the basilar membrane (refer to Figure 5-23). The shapes of the inner and outer hair cells are distinct. Each cell type synapses not only with *afferent* (nerves conducting towards the central nervous system)

neurons, but also with *efferent* neurons (conducting information from the central nervous system toward the hair cell), which are a portion of the *olivo cochlear bundle*. Each nerve fiber branches and contributes information to or from more than one type of hair cell (Figure 5-25). Single elements in the cochlear nerve divide repeatedly and contact more than one hair cell (Davis, 1961). The full functional significance of multiple neural representations of hair cells at various positions on the basilar membrane for a particular nerve fiber is not clear. However, it is probable that this multiple representation and the efferent input tend to sharpen, neurophysiologically, the relatively gross tuning of local areas of the basilar membrane to specific frequency bands. If one records neural impulses from afferent elements of the cochlear nerve, frequency sensitivity or "tuning" curves may be generated. Figure 5-26 on p. 162

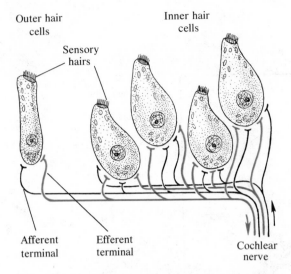

Outer hair cells

Inner hair cells

Sensory hairs

Afferent terminal

Efferent terminal

Cochlear nerve

Fig. 5-25. Hair cells of the organ of corti and their innervation by the cochlear nerve, radial and spiral afferent fibers and efferent olivocochlear bundle. (After Wersäll, et al., 1965)

shows that, although at high stimulus intensities the tuning curve may be relatively broad, the cochlear nerve fibers have a maximum sensitivity in a very narrow frequency range. If tuning curves are recorded at the same time that the olivo cochlear (efferent) bundle is electrically stimulated, the tuning curves become still sharper. Each of the eight single fiber tuning curves shown in Figure 5-26 display a "best" frequency or

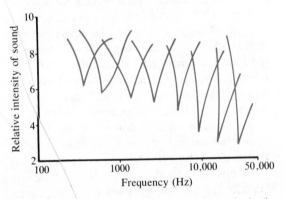

Fig. 5-26. Tuning curves for eight nerve units in the cats' cochlear nerve. Note increase in selectivity as frequency increases. (After Kiang, 1970)

critical frequency. Fibers with critical frequencies greater than two kiloHertz (kHz) are more sharply tuned than those with lower critical frequency. This is in agreement with the improved pitch discrimination above 1000 Hz found in humans (refer to Figure 5-21).

The Vestibular System

The receptors in the semicircular canal, as shown in Figure 5-18 have much in common with the hair cells of the cochlear structure and innervation. Yet, the functional roles are quite different. As mentioned earlier, the semicircular canals are tubes filled with fluid. An enlargement in each of the three tubes contains a gelatinous organ called the *crista ampullaris*. The crista serves to block the free movement of fluid through the system. In the crista are embedded vestibular sensory hair cells similar to those found on the basilar membrane. When the head moves, the bone of the canals move, but the fluid in the canals tends to retain its position. The base of the crista ampullaris is attached to the bony wall but is surrounded by the fluid, which tends to make the unattached portions flex in response to fluid pressure. The result is a bending of the crista. This bending of the hairs in the crista is the receptor stimulus. Depolarization of the hair cells occurs and stimulation of the vestibular nerve follows. These hair cells are not the cell bodies for the primary nerves but are much like the auditory hair cells, in that the sensory nerves synapse upon the receptor cells. The vestibular sensory cells also appear to receive efferent neurons, whose function is not understood at this time. Bending of the hair cell in one direction causes excitation (depolarization) of the afferent nerve fiber. Bending in the opposite direction causes a *hyperpolarization* of the sensory cell and "turns off" the afferent nerve fiber. Two sets of semicircular canals are in humans. One canal of each set is oriented in such a way that it is either inhibited or excited by movement in any plane. Consequently, changes in position are readily detected. Since the response of the sensory cell depends upon the inertial influences between the crista and the semicircular canal fluids, it can be seen that, once the individual reaches a constant velocity, the crista will gradually return to its initial position and movement will no longer be detected. It is more correct, then, to call these receptors *acceleration* receptors than movement receptors. The threshold for rate of acceleration in humans is about 0.5°/second for rotatory movements. Much psychophysical research has been done on this system in conjunction with the space exploration efforts, where accelerative forces change rapidly.

Buried in the base of the bone that supports the semicircular canals are two other receptor organs. One structure is called the *utricle* and the other the *saccule*. Both contain hair cells similar to those found on the basilar membrane and in the ampular crista of the semicircular canals. The structure of the utricle, which corresponds to the crista, is called the *macula*. The hair cells of the macula are oriented in numerous directions in distinction to those on the basilar membrane and the semicircular canals. In conjunction with the hair cells, there are densely packed otoliths which are "stones" or calcite crystals. These crystals press on the hair cells whose orientation is varied to the extent that any tilting of the head will result in bending of some hairs in the direction of excitation. Because of the varied orientation of these hairs and their supporting cells, it is probable that they are excited also by linear acceleration as well as tilting of the head. Since terrestrial creatures are continuously subject to gravitational forces, some cells in the otolithic organs would respond continuously in any given position. In this respect, the otolithic structures are the static counterparts to the dynamic informational system provided by the semicircular canals.

Auditory Control Mechanisms

There is more evidence for central control of the auditory than for the vestibular system. The olivo cochlear bundle has been described as a method used for feeding information from the central nervous system to the cochlea for control of some hearing functions, primarily pitch discrimination. A second control mechanism exists in the motor innervation of the muscles of the middle ear. The bones of the middle ear (refer to Figure 5-22) and tympanium are connected to the temporal bone by the tensor tympani muscle. Immediately following very loud sounds, the tensor tympani muscle constricts and reduces the mechanical freedom of the ossicles and the tympanium. This restriction in the movement of the ossicles effectively attenuates the amplitude of the transmitted auditory signal by about 10 db. Within a few minutes, the tensor tympani releases the ossicles and normal hearing is possible. This protective reflex is most effective immediately after the onset of very loud sounds and declines in effectiveness (habituation or adaptation?) after the sound has been present for an extended period of time. Following very loud noises (greater than 100 db), there is a measurable hearing loss in most people. This hearing loss is called temporary threshold shift (TTS) and is experienced for a number of hours. Davis (1950) showed that TTS may last as long as 71 hours after exposure to loud sounds which existed for only a few minutes at 120 db. The frequency discriminations affected by TTS are almost always higher than the content of the inducing sounds. If sounds of sufficient intensity to produce TTS are continued for extended periods of time, permanent damage follows.

Theory

Several firsts have occurred in the study of auditory function. In the mid eighteenth century, Duverney obtained the first government research grant from the French Academy of Science for the investigation of hearing. His major purchase was two lutes on which he demonstrated the principle of "sympathetic vibration," or resonance. The demonstration showed that when one lute string was plucked, the equivalent string on the nearby instrument resonated at the same frequency although it had not been plucked. He proposed that the spiral lamina of the cochlea, which includes the basilar membrane, resonates sympathetically with sounds induced from the exterior. Later, Helmholtz extended the notion of sympathetic vibration to account for the detection of all frequencies and their analysis through the action of tuned resonating structures (bands) on the basilar membrane. This notion of individual element resonance was later modified as a result of von Békésy's (1960) work to incorporate the findings that the acoustic disturbance of the basilar membrane moved from the region of the stapes towards the helocotrima. The distance of the disturbance from the stapes and the amount of membrane excited by it are the components of the "traveling wave" theory. The traveling wave and *resonance theory* positions differ in that the traveling wave moves along the basilar membrane and excites the membrane maximally in a region depending on the resonant characteristics of the membrane as a whole. The resonance theory, on the other hand, requires the presence of specific resonators which respond selectively to frequency components in the absence of general movement. As recognized today, this body of theory is classified as "place" theory.

The major competing theory was initiated by Rutherford and is sometimes called the "telephone" theory. The telephone theory predicts that the membrane moves at the same rate or frequency as the content of the incoming pressure disturbance. The associated neural structures then are stimulated at that frequency and transmit at that frequency. As presently accepted today, this basic body of theory is classified as "frequency" theory. As is frequently the case in science, both the frequency and place theorists appear to be correct. A crucial experiment was performed by Wever and Bray about 45 years ago. Wever and Bray (1930) recorded electrical impulses from the auditory nerves of cats. The nerve discharge was amplified and led into an audioamplifier unit and speaker whose output could be heard. At frequencies below 4 kHz, the sounds into the cat's ear were reproduced faithfully by the amplified nerve signals. Above 4 kHz the quality deteriorated rapidly,

and above 5 kHz there was only noise. It appears then that the peripheral auditory system acted as a microphone at frequencies below 4 KHz. However, it is well established that *single* sensory nerves do not respond when stimulated above 200–300 Hz. To handle this fact, Wever proposed the "*volley*" hypothesis. Figure 5-27 illustrates the function of the volley. Beginning with an acoustic stimulus of 400 Hz, auditory nerves one and two respond to each second change in sound pressure. Consequently, each nerve is operating only at 200 Hz. The total input to the brain, however, is *summed* so that the representation is 400 Hz. In this way, the burden for following high frequencies is "rotated" among the representative nerve fibers whose individual frequency of response limits cannot exceed 200–300 Hz.

To account for the known facts of auditory perception, all theoretical points must be used. That is, at low frequencies, the majority of the basilar membrane is displaced and the system operates as Rutherford would have predicted, something like a telephone. The movement of the basilar membrane is encoded directly as a frequency analog into the synchronous discharges of the auditory nerve fibers. As the frequency increases, excitation of the basilar membrane becomes more specific and certain numbers of nerve fibers are excited selectively. These respond at high stimulus frequencies as described in Wever's volley theory and there is rotation of the discharge among the adjacent neurons. Finally, for very high frequencies (greater than 10 KHz), an exclusive place theory probably comes into function. That is, relatively few nerve fibers are involved and subserve a par-

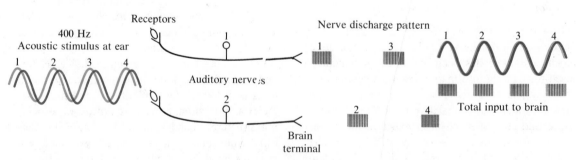

Fig. 5-27.   Volley theory of frequency encoding above 200 Hz.

ticular location from the basilar membrane very near the stapes, which is displaced selectively at very high frequencies. Stimulation of the specific neurons signals "high frequency" to the brain. The theoretical basis of intensity coding and transduction at the hair cell is less easy to explain. It has been demonstrated that individual auditory neurons have approximately a 25 db sensitivity range. Some of these have very high sensitivities and some very low sensitivities. Since, under ideal conditions the overall range of auditory signal detection is 160 db, a type of "volley" theory must be used to account for this wide range. Galambos and Davis (1943) proposed that there is a distribution of sensitivities among the auditory nerves, where activity in certain fiber groups indicate high levels of stimulation and others indicate very low levels of stimulation. Around the threshold of sound detection, the movements of the basilar membrane do not exceed 10^{-8} cm. These movements are smaller than can be detected by the electron microscope. Some very sensitive mechanism exists to allow for the initiation of a generator potential dependent upon this motion. It has been suggested (Flock, 1965) that movements of the hairs of the hair cells cause a generator potential within the cell and the subsequent liberation of a chemical transmitter which initiates activity in the terminals of the auditory nerves. Doubtless, activations of many hair cells and the summation of generator potentials must occur before the nerve is excited.

There are many adaptations and uses for hearing among the various animal species. A most typical use for hearing among animals is the localization of sound and possible survival benefits from it. This localization is made by virtue of slight differences in *time of arrival* (phase difference) at the ears. If the human nose is pointed toward a clock-like coordinate system reading from 1 to 12 o'clock and a sound occurs at 3 o'clock, there will be a very slight (microseconds) delay between the arrival of the sound at the right ear and the arrival of the sound at the left ear. There will also be a slight difference in loudness because of the shadowing of the left ear by the head. Delay and shadowing cues are very easily used by humans and other mammals to accurately determine the

spatial location of the sound source. A very elaborate neural network involving the cerebellum and superior colliculus of the brain are involved in an "almost" reflex system relating detection of sound and the rapid movement of the eyes toward the source. Snakes, on the other hand, have much less sensitive auditory systems in which the bones of the middle ear are fused together and there is no external auditory canal. In these animals, the auditory system is developed primarily for the detection of small vibrations of the earth rather than airborne sounds. Both aerial and aquatic mammals use sound for the precise location of objects. Bats and dolphins emit high frequency clicks that travel to objects in the environment and bounce back, giving cues about both position and the physical character of the object. The auditory systems of these species are highly elaborate and function well in detections of sound frequency in excess of 150 KHz. It is easily understandable why bats, which travel at night, and dolphins, which frequently hunt for fish in dark or turbid waters, could make use of such a "sonar" system. A dolphin with suction cup "blinders" over its eyes can use sounds to discriminate between two fishes of roughly equivalent size and shape where one is normally its preferred food and the second is normally rejected by him when visual cues are available. In the absence of the visual cues, the dolphin appears capable of making many discriminations based on sound reflection. Smell is not a factor here since dolphins appear to have no external mechanism for the detection of odors.

Central Pathways

The major afferent pathways from the left ear are shown in Figure 5-28. It should be remembered that an equivalent representation passes from the organ of corti of the right ear. Information from the organ of corti travels through the cochlear nerve bundle of the auditory nerve into the medulla section of the brain stem. The larger portion of the auditory information passes then from the ventral cochlear nucleus to the superior olivary nucleus on the contralateral side. As in most sensory systems, the major fiber pathways cross to the contralateral side and ascend toward the cortex. In the auditory

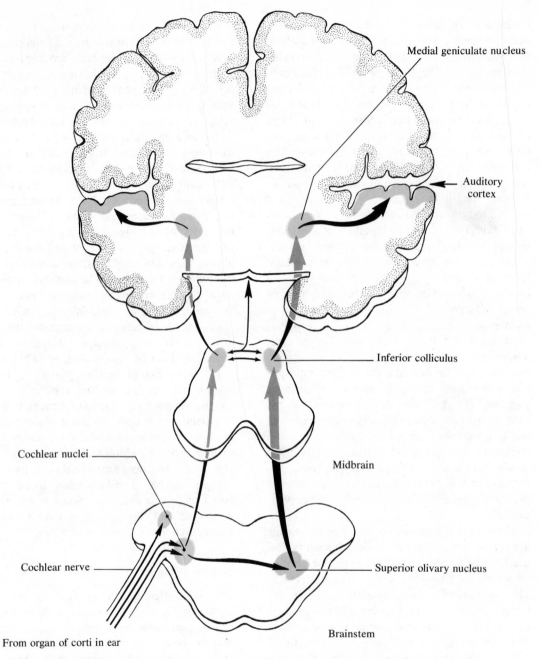

Fig. 5-28.   Major afferent pathways from the ear to the auditory cortex. Major pathway is emphasized.

system, two way stations are encountered between the olivary nucleus and the auditory cortex. These are the *inferior colliculus* and the *medial geniculate* nucleus. The medial geniculate nucleus is a

portion of the thalamus which is a processor for most of the major sensory systems. Here, there is an exchange of information between the right and left superior colliculus. At this level the *acoustico-*

optic tract branches off and eventually provides information for the visual-auditory "target seeking" reflex, which is important in the binaural localization of targets. A smaller representation of the left ear travels through the left side of the medulla and midbrain and reaches the left auditory cortex. Consequently, both ears are represented in each auditory cortex. The contralateral ear provides the strongest input.

The Chemical Senses—Appreciation of Flavor

One of the main attributes of living cells is irritability. Irritability can be understood as a change of membrane characteristics and ion distribution in response to external stimulation. This stimulation may be thermal, mechanical, electricial or chemical. Phylogenetically, one of the earliest specializations was the elaboration of cells particularly for the detection of chemicals in the environment. In simple animals, chemicals with nutritional value generally result in movements toward, and injurious chemical substances result in movements away. In humans, the complex result of chemical stimulation is *flavor*. This is neither the result of *gustation* (taste) or *olfaction* (smell) taken separately. But, as can be attested to by anyone with a cold serious enough to cause upper respiratory congestion, flavor is remarkably reduced in quantity and quality when the olfactory receptors are no longer available for stimulation. With upper respiratory congestion, onion bits may be confused with apple if the "taster" has no information about what is being eaten.

Gustation

Physiology. Receptors for the gustatory or taste sense are located primarily on the tongue but are found elsewhere in the oral cavity. The receptors are found in specialized organizations of tissue called *papillae*. There are three types of taste papillae having sensory capabilities on the human tongue. These are the *circumvaliate* papillae, which are in an intermediate position on the tongue, the *fungiform* papillae which are the most

numerous type and are found all over the tongue but alone on the leading edge, and the *foliate* papillae which are furthest to the rear of the tongue (see Figure 5-29). These papillae receive sensory nerve terminals from the *glossopharyngeal* nerve and from the *corda tympani* branch of the *facial* nerve. The anterior two-thirds of the tongue are served by the corda tympani, and the posterior third are the glossopharyngeal. The presence of

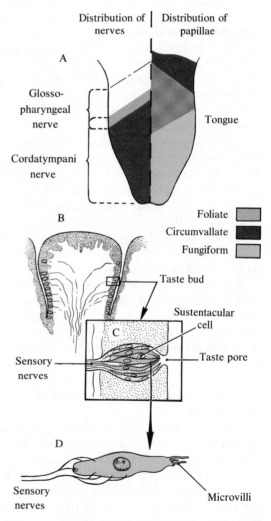

Fig. 5-29. Taste surfaces and cells. A. Distribution taste papillae and sensory nerves on the tongue. B. Receptive organs in the papilla. C. The taste bud, receptive organ. D. The receptor, taste cell.

taste organs (buds) is the difference between functional and nonsensory papillae. There may be as many as 500 taste buds on one papilla. About 10,000 buds are found in the young human, but the number is sharply reduced with aging. Each taste bud contains two classes of cells, the *taste cells* themselves and the *sustentacular cells*. The taste cells are the receptors for the sensory experience and receive innervation from the glossopharyngeal or corda tympani nerve. Each stem nerve axon may send processes to several taste cells. Surrounding the taste cells in the buds are the sustentacular cells, which are of non neural origin. The taste cell is set aside from other cells in the buds because it possesses *microvilli*. The microvilli are hair-like extensions which protrude into the *taste pore* of the bud. The taste cell is not the cell body for the sensory nerve and is similar in structure to the hair cells of the cochlea. The cell bodies that provide nutrition for the corda tympani nerve are located in the geniculate ganglion. Fiber diameters for the corda tympani nerve range from 8 microns to less than 0.5 microns. There are about 2,500 axons in the corda tympani. Of these 530 are myelinated larger fibers and approximately 2,000 are unmyelinated. If a cross section is taken at the base of a single taste papilla, typical fiber counts at that point would demonstrate about 172 unmyelinated and 42 myelinated fibers.

The generator potential for activation of fibers of the glossopharyngeal and corda tympani nerves are produced in the taste cells. Typical synapses connect with the sensory nerve terminals. However, the transmitter chemicals produced at the synapses are unknown. When taste solutions are washed over the taste buds, approximately 20 to 25 milliseconds are required before the sensory nerve fibers respond.

If the glossopharyngeal or corda tympani nerves are cut, the taste cells die. But the taste cells return when the nerves regenerate. It has been discovered recently that the normal taste cells "turn over" or are renewed periodically. That is, each taste cell has a finite life span. As sustentacular cells mature in the periphery of the taste bud, they move toward the center, develop microvilli and are innervated by the sensory nerve terminals. At this point, they become taste cells and function as receptors. In

humans, after about 12 days of life, the taste cell dies, degenerates, and its debris is extruded through the taste pore. Rates of taste cell renewal vary between animals.

The profile of chemical sensitivity for any taste cell is highly variable. Typically, taste cells that respond vigorously to sour substances do not respond well to sweet substances. Most of the research on taste cell sensitivity has used chemicals which typify the four *primary taste* experiences which are found when the human tongue is stimulated. Any pure taste experience in humans may be duplicated with fair accuracy by the mixture of the *primary tastes*. These tastes are *sour, salty, bitter,* and *sweet*. Chemicals typical to these taste primaries are sour—hydrochloric acid, salty—sodium chloride, bitter—quinine, and sweet—sucrose. Figure 5-30 shows the response profiles from the excitation of nerves from four different taste buds on the rat tongue measured with microelectrode recording techniques. Békésy electrically stimulated individual taste papillae in humans and found that the responses were subdivisible into the four taste primary categories. This would tend to suggest that taste papillae are organized around specific sensitivities and that there is a relatively homogeneous population of taste buds in each papillae (Békésy, 1966).

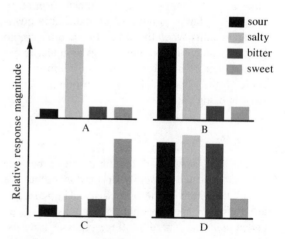

Fig. 5-30. Relative responsiveness of four rat taste buds (A–D) to chemicals with taste characteristics similar to those producing the four "primary" taste experiences in humans. (After Guyton, 1971)

In human taste, all substances must be soluble in saliva. Humans taste a wide range of chemicals whose consituents are potential cell poisons. These include both cyanide and hydroxyl ($^-$OH) bearing molecules. Further, taste experiences can change rapidly. These facts suggest that the taste substances do not find their way into the cell but are effective as stimuli when *"adsorbed"* to the surface of the microvillae. In this position, they do not alter cell content and they may be readily displaced by other stimulating molecules. The subjective tastes of substances are partially under control of factors other than chemistry. Temperature, texture and the concentration of the tasted material have a definite effect upon the subjective human experience. At very high concentrations saltiness becomes bitter. For instance, Figure 5-31 shows how the subjective nature experience varies and how "pleasantness" falls off at very high concentrations of all materials, except sweet ones. There is good agreement between the neural outflow along the corda tympani nerve and the subjective estimation of stimulus concentration. An interesting experiment was performed by Borg *et. al.* (1967), who were able to record from the corda tympani nerve in human subjects who were simultaneously able to evaluate the subjective magnitude of various taste stimuli concentrations flowed over the tongue. Figure 5-32 shows that both neural and subjective functions when plotted on a

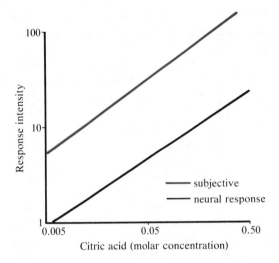

Fig. 5-32.   Comparison of human subjective and neural response magnitude to concentrations of citric acid flowed over the tongue. (After Borg, et al., 1967)

log–log axis produce a straight line with the subjective response being slightly more sensitive to the taste substance concentration than the neural response. Several other taste primary substances were evaluated during Borg's experiment and showed similar relations between subjective and neural response characteristics. There was a variation in the slope of the curves, indicating that relative sensitivity to change in *molar* concentration was not identical across the primary taste substances. The molar concentration of compound is equal to its molecular weight divided into the weight of the amount of the compound (grams) contained in one liter of the final solution.

Taste *preference* means the tendency of an animal to choose certain foods more often than others. Most species including humans (in the absence of purely social control) tend to regulate the intake of certain foods according to body requirements (Fregly, 1967). It has been demonstrated frequently that animals with the adrenal glands removed, and who consequently excrete high quantities of sodium, will selectively drink water with the highest concentration of salt when there is a range of concentrations available. Further, humans injected with excessive amounts of insulin, which

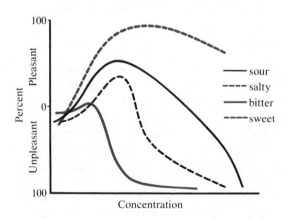

Fig. 5-31.   Affective nature of concentration of materials producing "primary" taste sensations in humans.

reduces blood sugar, will select foods that have high sugar concentrations. There is some indication that the taste cells themselves are at least partially sensitive to the concentrations of compounds in the circulatory system. If quinine is injected intravenously in the human, it may be tasted within a few seconds. It has never been clearly demonstrated whether a taste preference arises in the central nervous system or in the taste buds. We know now that the taste cells are produced from the sustentacular cells, whose chemical compositions must be influenced by the prevailing body chemistry at time of development. This would seem to offer one mechanism for the establishment of taste preferences at the cellular level.

The theoretical systems for control of taste stimulus intensity and taste quality are relatively more firmly established than the theoretical backgrounds relative to the cutaneous senses. If Békésky's findings were entirely correct, each taste papillae has its own primary chemical propensity, and the anatomical basis for quality discrimination is fairly clear. That is, it is established at the periphery. However, there is evidence for genetic control of peripheral sensitivity. Some persons cannot taste phenylthiocarbamide, which has a very strong taste for others. We have already seen that the mechanism for stimulation of the taste cell probably is adsorption of taste stimulating molecules onto the surface of the microvilli. This type of binding is weak and the molecules tend to leave the receptor surfaces rapidly. Beidler (1954) has proposed a theory of taste intensity encoding which is consistent with the adsorption of chemicals to the microvilli membranes and the resulting conformational changes of the membrane, which can result in permeability changes and eventually nerve excitation. He has shown that if the taste cell membrane has a finite number of equivalent but independent sites for the absorption of chemical molecules, a simple formula will describe both the psychophysical and electrophysiological data.

$$R = \frac{CKR_s}{1 + CK,}$$

where R is the magnitude of the response to the stimulus, C is the concentration of the stimulus, the maximum response is R_s and K is a constant which describes the strength of the binding of the chemical to the site on the microvillus. The response magnitudes predicted by this equation have held very well for numerous animal species so long as simple (monovalent) chemicals like sodium chloride are used. However, the equation does not hold well for substances with large molecular size such as proteins and complex sugars. This is the *fundamental taste equation.*

Central Pathways. The pathways from the tongue to the cortex of the brain begin in the anterior two-thirds of the tongue, where terminals of the corda tympani nerve are found. The posterior portion of the tongue is similarly innervated but from branches of the glossopharyngeal nerve. Both of these nerves course toward the tractus solatarious of the brain stem where they synapse with secondary fibers to form a portion of the major tract known as the *medial lemniscus.* The medial lemniscus travels to the thalamus and the taste elements then pass on to endings in the insular cortex of the brain (see Figure 5-33). This set of pathways closely follows the traditional pathways for sensory information from all body surface areas up to the thalamus. It was mentioned earlier that taste papillae exist at other places in the oral cavity. Taste papillae are found on the walls and the roof of this area. Most of these papillae receive innervation from the vagus nerve, which also contributes to the medial lemniscus after synapsing in the tractus solitarious. The vagus nerve contribution to the experience of taste appears to be minor.

Olfaction

Physiology. *Olfaction,* or the sense of smell, is the second of the three sense components required to produce the sensation called flavor. Unlike gustation (taste), where the potential food substance is brought directly in contact with the tongue, partially dissolved by the saliva, the olfactory stimulus source is usually at a distance. Molecules of the odorous substance which can be carried by the air are taken into the nose during breathing or active "sniffing." Substances which have no vapor pressure (not partially air soluble) have no odor. When the odorous molecule reaches the internal portion

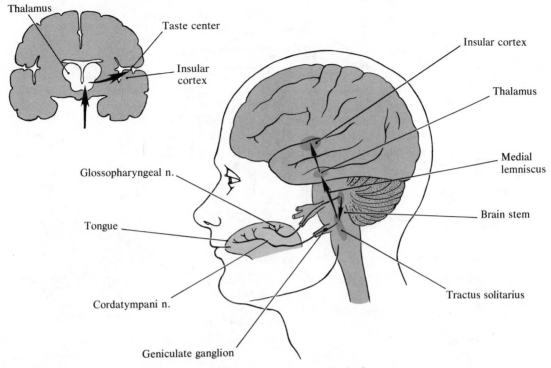

Fig. 5-33. Major pathways for taste information from the tongue to the brain.

of the nasal cavity it may not reach the sensory area. The direct path for air through the nose bypasses the upper respiratory, sensory area. Sniffing and the production of eddy currents are necessary for ordorous molecules to reach the upper regions. The roof of the nasal cavity consists of a perforated bone, the *cribriform* plate. On the inner surface of the cribriform plate rests the *nasal mucosa*. The nasal mucosa consists primarily of three functional cell types in the olfactory sensory region (Figure 5-34), *supporting cells, receptor cells, basal cells* and complex structures called *Bowmans* glands. The Bowmans glands participate in the secretion of the *mucous* layer, which is found on the innermost portion of the olfactory area. In the mucous layer are the cilia of the receptor cells. The cilia are extensions of the receptor cell bodies much as were the hair cells of the cochlear receptors. Extensions of the supporting cells also rest in the mucous layer. The supporting cell extensions are microvilli, which are also relatively long but

are somewhat smaller than the cilia of the receptors. The supporting cells appear to separate the receptor cells. Internal to the supporting and receptor cells is a third cell type, the basal cells. The receptor cells are the cell bodies of the primary neurons of the olfactory area. These primary neurons gather near each opening in the cribriform plate, form a bundle, and exit. As one goes central from the olfactory area, these bundles coalesce into a larger bundle called the *olfactory nerve*. Each separate bundle is encased in a sheath that arises from the basement membrane of the olfactory epithelium.

The olfactory sensory area is distinct from other areas of the nasal epithelium. The cilia of the receptor cells are randomly oriented in the mucous and, upon microscopic examination, appear much like a bowl of spaghetti. In nearby areas, where there is no sensory function, there are respiratory cilia which are constantly moving in the live animal. These cilia move foreign bodies, picked up in

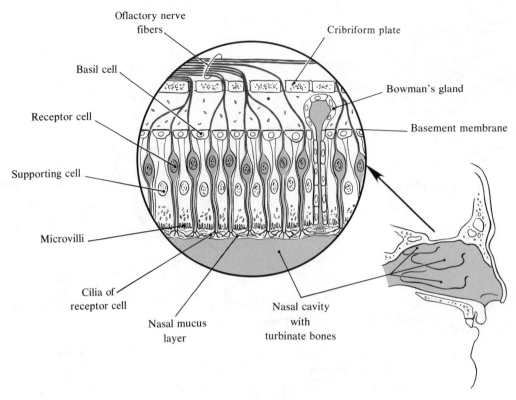

Fig. 5-34. Olfactory epithelium of nasal region. Scale is distorted to illustrate small detail. (After Andres, 1966)

the air stream, toward the periphery. They are not randomly oriented and move in a wave-like fashion.

In many mammals there are in excess of 150 million olfactory receptor cells. Among mammals, olfactory receptors are very numerous in dogs, slightly less numerous in rabbits (about 100 million receptors), while the olfactory area is somewhat smaller in humans. Since each receptor produces one axon, there should be about 100 million nerve units in the two olfactory nerves. Since the olfactory epithelium is a bilaterally arranged structure, the two olfactory nerves travel separately to the olfactory bulb regions which are the next higher centers. Consequently, the mammalian olfactory nerves provide the greatest number of information channels of any single sensory neural structure. Action potentials may be recorded in the olfactory nerve when odors are blown through the

olfactory region in such a way that they can reach the olfactory mucosa. It is very difficult to record potentials from single olfactory nerves. These axons are some of the smallest in the mammalian body and average 0.2 microns in diameter. Consequently, it may be predicted that the movement of the nerve signal toward the olfactory bulb is slow. Coupled with the production of unit potentials in the olfactory nerve is the development of a slow ("generator like") potential which may be recorded from the surface of the olfactory mucosa. As pictured in Figure 5-35A, the relationship between the slow potential and the unit potentials is quite good. This slow potential has been called the electroolfactogram and is thought to be the equivalent of the receptor potential in other receptor systems. It is undoubtedly the net result of the simultaneous excitation by many thousands of cells in the region of the recording electrode. There is also a good relationship between the logarithm of stimulus intensity and the logarithm of the response amplitude for electroolfactograms (EOG). Figure 5-35B shows this relationship (over a relatively small concentration region) where n-butanol was used to stimulate EOG production in the frog olfactory muscosa.

Psychophysically, a large variety of odorants produced perceived odor intensities which conform to the power function (''Psychophysical Power Law''), which states that $R = ks^b$, where R is perceived intensity, s is the intensity of the stimulus and k and b are constants that refer to the intercept and slope of the function respectively, when the results are plotted on double logarithmic coordinates. In logarithmic terms, the function becomes $\log R = b (\log s) + \log k$. The exponent b seems to distinguish most often between the various sense modalities. For example, its value is about 0.33 for visual brightness compared to 0.60 for odor intensity. Figure 5-36 shows the perceived

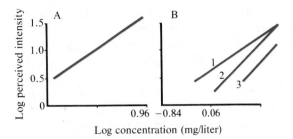

Fig. 5-36. A. Subjective intensity and concentration of pentanol samples sniffed. (After Cain, 1968). B. Effects of olfactory adaptation on perception of intensity as in A. Adaptation to pentanol was increased by a factor of four between each set of records, in sequence 1–3. Concentration is in milligrams of pentanol dissolved in a liter of air.

odor intensity of pentanol of various concentrations (here, b = 0.58). It is particularly interesting to notice that the exponent *b* has been shown to be very nearly related to the water solubility of the odorants. Cain (1968) has obtained almost a perfect rank order correlation between the size of the exponent *b* and the water solubility of several odors which have been subjectively scaled by other investigators. Really, it is not surprising that water solubility is an important attribute of odorant chemicals, since the receptor cell cilia are bathed in mucous. The solubility of chemicals in water allows the mucous to act as a ''filter'' in the selection of chemical stimulants. Adaptation to chemical stimulation affects the sensitivity and perceived intensity of later responses to the chemical. Figure 5-36B shows how controlled sniffing of pentanol prior to testing for subjective intensity, alters the intensity function. In curves 1, 2, and 3 there was increasing adaptation to pentanol and a consequent reduction in perceived intensity for equivalent concentrations of stimulus. However, there was no great change in the shape of the intensity-stimulus concentration function.

The structure of olfactory receptors in mammals is similar to that described above for humans. Unlike many other sense systems, the sensitivity of some animals to chemical odorants is generally accepted as greater than in humans, but some of the highest sensitivities have been demonstrated in in-

A

Olfactory unit neural discharge

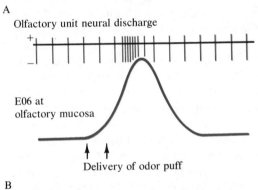

E06 at
olfactory mucosa

Delivery of odor puff

B

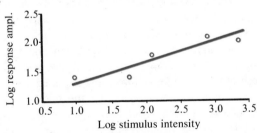

Log stimulus intensity

Fig. 5-35. A. Records of unit activity and slow potential response at the olfactory bulb and mucosa, respectively, after a puff of odor. (After Döving, 1966) B. EOG response relationship to stimulus (n. butanol) intensity. (After Ottoson, 1956)

sects. The insect olfactory apparatus is similar at the cellular level to that found in humans. However, its gross anatomy is quite different, as shown in Figure 5-37. The receptors are of many different shapes and sizes in insects. One major type is called the *sensilla*. A typical sensillum is shown in Figure 5-37. In insects, the sensory cell (sensillum) protrudes through the thick cuticle of skin and resides in a fluid filled extension of the cuticle. Chemicals reach the sensory cell's outer segment by penetrating to the sensillum fluid through pores in the cuticle. The sensory cell is the cell body for the nerve axon. It is supported as in humans by epithelial (sustentacular) cells. There are literally thousands of insect species. But only a few of these have been studied for olfactory sensitivity. Probably the most data is available on the moth (*Bombyx mori*). The sexual attractant liberated by the female moth has been chemically duplicated in the laboratory. This chemical is bombykol. It is possible to record nerve activity from the antenna sensilla of the moth. Figure 5-38 compares the behavioral response (flying) of the male moth with

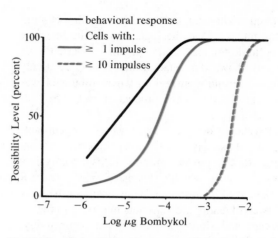

Fig. 5-38. Behavioral and receptor cellular response of the moth (*Bombyx mori*) to the sex chemical Bombykol. (After Kaissling and Priesner, 1970)

the probability of chemosensory cells firing to various levels of stimulation with the artificial compound, bombykol. Several hundred cells were recorded. It should be noted that the behavioral response is slightly more sensitive than the response indicated purely by nerve activity. The behavioral response probability reaches the 50 percent level at about 10^{-5} micrograms of bombykol. Kaissling *et. al.,* (1970) has calculated that this is approximately equivalent to the 520 molecules distributed randomly over the 25,000 receptor cells on the moth capable of responding to bombykol. The curve shows that in order for the probability of the cellular response (one nerve impulse or more) to exceed 50 percent, the concentration of bombykol would need to rise to 10^{-4} micrograms. As it turns out, this particular sensitivity is to only one type of bombykol. Most large organic chemicals have an organized structure of carbon and hydrogen and other atoms. The specific placement of these atoms in the structure can be altered (as a mirror image) without changing the number or type of atoms present. Such alteration in position is called *isomerization*. When this is done, the atomic composition of the molecule has not changed. However, the configuration of the molecule has changed. When bombykol is changed to an isomer (mirror image), the sensitivity of the sensillium to it falls off by approximately 10,000

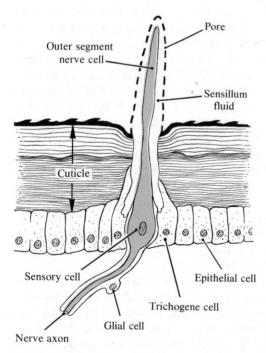

Fig. 5-37. Insect sensillum schematic anatomy.

times. This suggests very strongly that the antennae olfactory receptors of insects may be sensitive to not only chemical composition but to the architecture (*stereo chemical structure*) of the particular compound.

There is evidence that in lower mammals, odors experienced in development have an effect on adult food preferences. LeMagnen and Tallon (1968) demonstrated that rats, provided with the odor of citral during infancy and the early days of nursing, later showed preferences toward diets containing citral, where normal animals actively rejected the citral flavored diet. Olfactory effects on other behavior has been reported in the human female. It was demonstrated (LeMagnen, 1950) that the female may have a reduction in threshold (elevation in sensitivity) to the chemical Exaltolide during a particular 48 hour period surrounding the time of ovulation during the menstural cycle. Sensitivity in some women increases by a factor of approximately 10,000. Exaltolide is similar to the steroid musk (androstan), which is present in the human male urine. As we will see in the section on central anatomy of the olfactory system, it is one of the most extensive sense systems in the whole human brain. But, the complete effects of olfactory response, sensitivities developed during youth, and the control of olfactory sensitivity by hormonal secretions are poorly understood in humans.

There is a third system contributing to the experience, flavor. This system is probably the least known of the three present in humans and discussed earlier in this chapter. This system is the *trigeminal nerve network,* which is found in the upper nasal cavity. Recent data by Tucker (1963) and several others (for example, Dawson, 1962) have shown that the trigeminal nerve endings, which have no receptor organs associated with them and which terminate freely (much like their cutaneous counterparts), are very sensitive to chemical odorants. Up until about ten years ago, it was thought that trigeminal sensitivity extended only to chemical irritants. It has been demonstrated since that trigeminal responding occurs for chemicals both in the "irritant" category and those previously considered typical of "pure" olfactory stimuli. The extent and subjective impact of trigeminal stimulation in humans, in contrast to stimulation of the olfactory mucosa, is not at all clear. It appears that there has been no satisfactory separation of olfactory and trigeminal responses in human subjects.

Lower animals (from mammals to frogs) have trigeminal, free nerve endings ending on the nasal mucosa. In addition, all vertebrates above fishes have specialized structures called the *vomernasal system* (organ of Jacobson) which has also been shown to have chemical sensitivity. But, the work on it has not proceeded very far.

A summary of the peripheral anatomy of the upper nasal cavity would suggest that in mammals the chemically sensitive area is much greater than that typically assigned to the olfactory region. If one includes the trigeminal endings and the possible functions of the vomernasal organs, it would appear that the majority of tissue known as the nasal mucosa probably serves to transmit information about chemical odorants. Some texts have discussed the possibility of efferent control of the olfactory mucosa from the central nervous system. Structures which could have been efferent nerve terminals in the olfactory mucosa probably were endings of the trigeminal neurons, which end also among the epithelial cells. At this time, there is no demonstrated, efferent supply system to the olfactory periphery. Like the taste cells, it has been recently demonstrated that the olfactory receptor cells are capable of renewal or replacement. Graziadei and Metcalf (1970) demonstrated with both light and electron microscopy that proteins which are taken up only during cell division can be located in the olfactory neurons of frogs and rats at various times during adult life. The best estimate at this time is that the olfactory receptor cells and their neural processes can differentiate from the basal cells of the epithelium. This is probably more frequent when there is damage to the olfactory system. Recent work has demonstrated in birds that sectioning of the olfactory nerve results in near total degeneration of the olfactory epithelium with subsequent recovery, replacement of the olfactory receptors and regrowth of the olfactory nerve.

The theoretical basis for olfactory intensity discrimination contains concepts similar to those discussed for taste. Depolarization of the peripheral receptors causes a generator potential and, subsequently, action potentials along the primary neurons. We have seen that the rate of action potential production is closely correlated with the psychophysical judgment of stimulus intensity. For any particular chemical, the activity of those responsive receptors (within the 100 million or so present on the mucosa) is summed as an "estimate" of activation level at the olfactory bulb and higher centers. The situation is not so clear for the discrimination of the quality in the olfactory system. Where taste has four "primary" sensory experiences and chemicals, in olfaction several conflicting primary sets have been listed. One of the most successful quality theories is that of Amoore (1967). Amoore originally identified seven primary odor-chemicals, based on their gross molecular profiles (size and shape) and experimentally determined that he could in this way account for many variations in odor quality. He proposed several specific shapes of cell receptor sites into which suitable odor molecules could fit. Chemists call this a "lock and key" arrangement. It was first proposed by the Roman philosopher Lucretious, around 300 B.C., to have relevance to the olfactory system. Amoore's seven primary theory presently does not seem to fully account for the range of odor qualities. However, the lock and key concept still seems to be one of the most promising in the determination of odor quality. Within this framework, the molecular shape would fit into a receptacle of an equivalent size and shape upon the cell surface of the receptors. This would be by the process of adsorption as described for taste. A generator could result if the fitting to the specific receptor site produced a temporary, local penetration of the receptor membrane, which would allow for a flow of ion current. Such a theoretical proposal was made by Davies and Taylor (1957). Since the molecules would be lightly bound by adsorption to the surface of the receptor, their stay in that position would be transient and their removal, perhaps due to movement of the cilia or the mucous, or both, could result in restoration of the normal state of the receptor membrane. The process of adsorption was first proposed by Lord Adrian in England during the third decade of this century. Adrian blew odors through the nasal area of freshly slaughtered sheep, after decapitation, and found that the odor was attenuated (retained) in passage through the head. Adsorption could be proposed if the odor was picked up by subsequent pure air injections through the nasal cavity, and this is precisely what was found.

The surface characteristics of the wet mucosal membrane may provide another mechanism for separation of odorants by quality. One helpful method of chemical analysis used in the laboratory is called paper chromatography. In this procedure, chemicals migrate from one end of a wet sheet of paper and travel various distances, depending on their weight and/or charge characteristics. Mozell (1970) has suggested that the wet mucosa may act for odorant molecules in a way similar to the paper chromatograph. That is, molecules may travel along the wet mucosal sheet for distances, depending upon their weight and charge characteristics. Using the frog mucosa, Mozell recorded from bundles of afferent olfactory nerve fibers originating at different places on the mucosa. He found that there was a gross separation for molecular size by place and time at which the stimulus arrived. This gross separation is not incompatible with the "lock and key" concept which is specific for receptor excitation.

Central Projections

A typical peripheral and central olfactory system is presented in Figure 5-39. This schematic system does not include the trigeminal system which classically is not included as part of the olfactory region. Figure 5-39 shows the peripheral olfactory system to the right, as seen from above. The olfactory region of the mucosa and the olfactory bulbs, connected to the mucosal receptors by the olfactory nerves, are shown as paired and bilaterally symmetrical. The 100 million olfactory receptors send a total of 100 million olfactory nerves into the olfactory bulbs. The bulbs are, in many respects, like small brains moved out to the periphery for the handling of a particular data processing problem. This is true also in the retina, as we will see in the next section. The lateral commissure is an interconnection for information transfer between the two olfactory bulbs. Indicative of the amount of

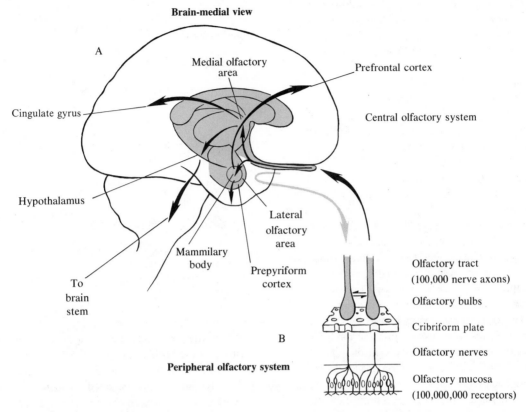

Brain-medial view

Medial olfactory area

Prefrontal cortex

Central olfactory system

Cingulate gyrus

Hypothalamus

Lateral olfactory area

Mammilary body

Prepyriform cortex

To brain stem

Olfactory tract (100,000 nerve axons)

Olfactory bulbs

Cribriform plate

Olfactory nerves

Olfactory mucosa (100,000,000 receptors)

Peripheral olfactory system

Fig. 5-39.   Olfactory system of the brain, left (as seen cut in half, from the right side). Right, peripheral olfactory system. Arrows indicate direction of information flow.

data processing which has gone on in the olfactory bulbs is the number of nerve axons which leave the bulbs in the olfactory tracts. These total approximately 100,000.

In the left half of Figure 5-39, one half of the brain is shown. This is the left half of the brain, drawn as though the brain were cut in two and viewed from the right (medial) aspect. Traditionally, the brain is divided into the new and old sections (neo and paleo cortices). The large majority of the paleocortex and the adjacent structures compose the rhinencephalon or ''smell'' brain. In animals with relatively little neocortex, the rhinencephalon is the major brain area and appears to have extensive connections with the peripheral olfactory apparatus. In higher mammals, large areas of the brain still receive input from the olfactory

bulbs through the olfactory tracts. The tracts terminate at two brain areas, the medial olfactory area and the lateral olfactory area. Each, in turn, sense projections to several other important areas which include the brain stem, the prefrontal cortex and the hypothalamus. In contrast to lower vertebrates, the degree of commitment of the mammalian brain to olfactory functions is poorly understood at this time. A full coverage of the extensive olfactory interconnections is not within the scope of this book chapter. However, it is safe to say that almost all of the vegetative functions of the brain plus appetitive motivational, autonomic control, hormone secretory functions and even the gross activation systems are at least in partial interaction with the olfactory tracts through one or another relay system. In contrast to the known anatomy of other sensory systems, there are clearly established feed-back (efferent) paths between the symmetrical peripheral systems. Each olfactory bulb receives an efferent bundle (Fig. 5-39) from its counterpart.

Vision

Humans are highly, but not totally, visually dependent for information about the external environment. Because of its extensive practical use to humans, vision has received relatively more attention as a physiological and psychological process than any other sensory system. In many terrestrial mammals, two eyes are the basis for binocular vision which provides for the enhanced contrast at the edges of objects viewed binocularly. Binocular viewing also provides for visual cues which give the impression of depth or stereovision. In addition to the systems that provide for monocular or binocular vision, each eye contains two largely separate neural systems, one operating in the daylight and one under dark or nighttime conditions. These are called the *photopic* and *scotopic* systems, respectively. The eye is frequently referred to as a "camera." This is a remarkable oversimplification and is roughly similar to explaining a major computer by using finger counting as an analogy.

Optics

The stimulus for vision comes from a narrow segment of the continuum of energies called the *electromagnetic spectrum*. Physically, visible light is no different in its basics from *radio waves* or *cosmic rays*. In fact, it lies in the middle of the electromagnetic spectrum approximately halfway between the cosmic ray wavelengths and those wavelengths which are associated with radio waves. Figure 5-40 shows this continuum expressed in centimeters of wavelength. As in the auditory system, wavelength is the distance from any single point on a wave to the next identical point. The portion of the electromagnetic spectrum which can be seen by humans, under most conditions, ranges from 0.4×10^{-4} to 0.75×10^{-4} centimeters in wavelength. Contrary to popular opinion, other wavelengths can be seen if they reach the sensitive

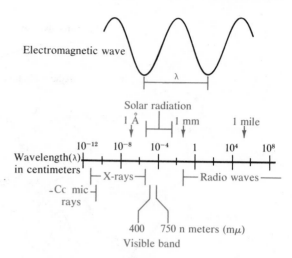

Fig. 5-40. The electromagnetic spectrum with commonly used regions identified. Å = Angstrom, μ = micron (10^{-6} meters), mm = millimeter, n = nano = 10^{-9}, λ = wavelength.

receptor structures and are present in sufficient intensity. *Infrared* radiations ($1 - 2 \times 10^{-4}$ cm) can be seen in the dark if sufficient energy is present and x-rays are readily detected by persons who have dark adapted for an extended period of time. The range of wavelengths in the *visible spectrum* contributes the experience color to persons with normal eyes. Short wavelengths, around 400 *nanometers* (0.4×10^{-4} cm) are seen as deep blue, while long wavelengths (700 nanometers) are seen as deep red. Between these lie the yellows and greens.

Before color or any other visual detection can be made, the electromagnetic energy (in this case visible light) must pass through the various structures (*intraocular media*) of the eye. Whenever light travels from a medium of one density through a surface of a medium with a second density, the light ray is bent, unless it strikes the surface perpendicularly. This bending of light traveling through a surface is called *refraction*. Figure 5-41 shows two rays of light traveling initially through air, then through a more dense, transparent material and back again into the air. Beam 1 strikes the dense medium perpendicular to the surface, travels in a straight line through the medium and exits in a straight line into air. Beam 2 strikes the surface at an angle, is bent (refracted) and is bent again as it leaves the second surface. The dense medium may be anything more dense than air (it may be glass, or it may be the cornea of the eye). Of course, if the material was less dense than air there would be refraction also, but the angles would change. Refraction is caused by the slowing down or speeding up of the light wavefront as it passes through the medium. Light travels in a vacuum at approximately 186,000 miles/second. In any other medium, the velocity is reduced by a factor equal to $1/n$ where n is the *refractive index* of the medium. It follows that refraction, or the amount of bending of the light ray, is dependent upon the angle of the

light ray relative to the surface and the speed of light in that medium, which is directly proportional to its density or refractive index. Bending of light at the surfaces of various media is the basis of all optical systems whether they be glass or eye tissue. Objects which control light rays are called lenses. *Spherical lenses* are the most common used in optical systems. As shown in Figure 5-41, there are two basic types, the *convex* spherical lens and the *concave* spherical lens. The surface curvature of the convex lens (Figure 5-41B) is arranged so that parallel light rays striking one surface are bent inward at the first surface and again inward at the second surface. Since perfectly parallel rays are

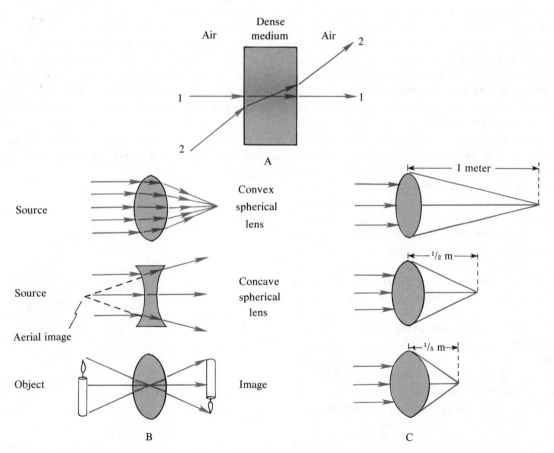

Fig. 5-41. Refraction and image formation. A. Refraction of light rays in a dense medium. B. Convergence of light rays by a convex lens, divergence of light rays by a concave lens, and image formation by a convex spherical lens. C. Power of lens changes with curvature.

usually obtained only from very small spots of light at great distance, these are brought to a focus or image which is also a small spot. For parallel rays, the distance between the center of the lens and the point of focus (the image) is the *focal length* of the lens. Concave spherical lenses have surfaces which tend to cause divergence of an incident, parallel beam of light rays. An image is not formed, but an *aerial image* can be located by tracing the diverging rays backward (dash lines, Figure 5-41B) until a focal point is reached. This focal point may also be calculated, or it may be located with a second, spherical lens of known power. It may be seen, intuitively, that the combination of a concave spherical lens and a convex spherical lens of exactly the same *power* will produce a net refractive result of zero. That is, the convergence of the spherical lens will precisely cancel out the divergence of the concave lens. The only change in the parallel light rays will be those due to losses of light from reflection from the lens surfaces and scatter of light within the lenses. Therefore, lens powers may be added or subtracted in a lens system. Convex lenses are positive in sign and concave lenses are negative in sign. These may be used in mathematical operations. That is, a +5 (convex) lens and a −2 (concave) lens = +3 (convex) lens. When an image is produced by a single lens such as in the lower illustration (Figure 5-41B), tracing of rays from the object (candle in this case) indicates that the resulting image will be upside down and reversed. (Accounting for a right side up visual world gave early theorists a lot of trouble.) The result is the same regardless of the number of concave or convex lenses used close to one another. These simply add or subtract to produce a net "complex, concave, or convex" lens. Lens power is a measure of the ability to bend parallel light rays. Power (diopters) = 1/f where f is the focal length in meters. Focal length is measured from the center of the lens to the "focal" or *image plane*. In Figure 5-41C, the three lenses are shown with increasing curvatures. Power increases with curvature. It may be seen that for these three lenses the power in diopters for the top lens equals 1, the second equals 2 diopters, and the power of the third lens is 5 diopters. *Convex* lenses are called positive lenses because of the convergence

of light rays produced by them. Similarly, *concave* lenses are called negative lenses because of the divergence of light rays. If one begins with parallel light, the angles of convergence for a convex lens of one diopter will be complementary to the angles of divergence for a negative (concave) lens of equal power. This relationship holds true for all lens powers whether they are positive or negative.

There are surfaces on or within the human eye which refract light and contribute to the overall optical effectiveness of the eye. One purpose of each of these refractive surfaces is to provide an image of good quality at the rear of the eye. You have already learned that as a light ray passes from one medium into another, it is bent if the two media have different densities. As light passes through from the front of the eye toward the rear, there is first the relatively thin medium, air. Then there is a refraction at the surface of the cornea (see Figure 5.42). As light passes through the cornea, it encounters a second refractive surface at the junction of the cornea and aqueous humor. The aqueous humor is slightly less dense than the cornea. After passing through the aqueous humor, a third refractive surface is encountered at the surface of the lens which is more dense than the aqueous humor. The lens has several density gradients in it, but

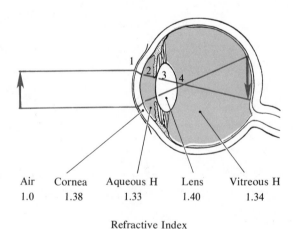

Air	Cornea	Aqueous H	Lens	Vitreous H
1.0	1.38	1.33	1.40	1.34

Refractive Index

Fig. 5-42. Refractive surfaces of the eye and indexes of refraction of the structures (B–E). The object is at infinity and produces parallel light rays.

their discussion is outside the scope of this text. At the rear surface of the lens there is a final refractive function as the light ray passes from the dense lens to the somewhat less dense vitreous humor. The optics of the eye then function together as a compound lens with an overall, light converging (positive) power. The major question in dealing with this compound positive lens is "Where does its center lie"? Obviously, it is placed between the front of the cornea and the rear of the lens. If one takes a point someplace near the front surface of the lens, the distance to the retina is about 19 mm from the center of the eye's compound lens. If a focus can be formed under these conditions, one may estimate the approximate power of the eye optics as a single compound positive lens. If the focal length is 19 mm from the center of the lens, what is the power of the lens? A second important question is "considering the information you have about refractive surfaces and power, which element of the eye's 'compound' lens system is the most powerful?" That is, which contributes the most to the overall power of the system? It is the one with the greatest refractive power or ray bending potential. It is the cornea. Why not the lens?

There are several natural, refractive errors which are encountered in the human eye. The "normal" condition is called *emmetropia* (Figure 5-43). A light at a distance from the eye (greater than 7 meters) will produce nearly parallel light rays. The optics of the eye are such that these light rays are brought to a sharp focus on the retina. A most common eye refractive defect is *myopia*. In myopia, the eye is as though it were too long for its optical system. That is, the image of the distant object is brought to a focus before it reaches the retina and the rays have started to diverge again. The reason for this condition may be that the eye is indeed too long. It is equally possible that the power of the lens system is too great. The second common refractive defect in humans is called *hypermetropia* (hyperopia). In hyperopia the image of the object, at a distance, is formed as though the eye is too short for its lens system. Indeed, it may be shorter than normal, but the same effect would be realized if the lens system was of insufficient power. In both cases, the image of the distant object would fall behind the plane of the

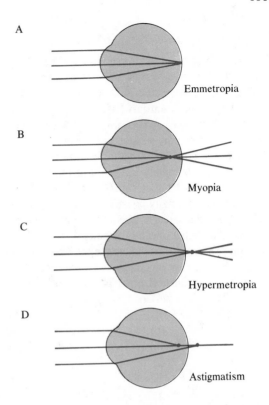

Fig. 5-43. Common human refractive errors. Focal points of objects at infinity (practically 20 ft.) are shown with reference to the rear of the eye.

sensitive retina. The fourth cause for image focus defects in humans is *astigmatism*. Astigmatism may be combined with any of the other conditions. That is, one may have astigmatic "emmetropia," astigmatic myopia or astigmatic hypermetropia. Astigmatism means that the image of the object at the distance is in focus in one retinal region and out of focus on another region of the retina. That is, the image has more than one focal plane. This may be caused by a nonsymmetry of the refractive surfaces of the eye. It would be as though one portion of one of the lens surfaces (or cornea) had a greater or lesser curvature than its remaining surface. Astigmatism is corrected by the use of complex additional lenses which are ground into the surface of the typical spherical lens which we have already discussed. This additional lens surface is called cylindrical or a cylinder lens.

Gross Anatomy of the Eye

The gross anatomy of the human eye and the anatomy of the eyes of all terrestrial mammals are very similar, except for some "relatively" small details. The gross anatomy of the mammalian (human in this case) eye is shown in Figure 5-44. The distance from the surface of the cornea to the surface of the sensitive retina in the central part of the eye is approximately 22.3 mm in the average human. The diameter of the cornea is about 10 mm, and the maximally constricted iris never produces a pupil that exceeds about 8 mm in diameter. The eye is held in a pouch of bone, which is called the orbit. The eye is attached to the orbit by a set of extraocular muscles which provide it with mobility in the vertical and horizontal planes and a small amount of torsional mobility. The eye is also attached to the skin of the exterior by a relatively frail tissue (conjunctiva) which attaches to the eye at the edge of the cornea. This tissue was referred to as the "white of the eye" by the early American revolutionary hero, Colonel Prescott, at the Battle of Bunker Hill. The iris, in normal humans, is a muscular structure which partially covers the forward surface of the lens. It is pigmented and gives the eye its "color." The iris serves to provide a small amount of regulation of the amount of light entering the eye. Its effect must be necessarily small, since the surface area of the opening (the *pupil*) can only vary by a factor of about 16, while the sensitivity of the eye varies over a range of approximately 12 million.

Between the cornea and the iris is a chamber

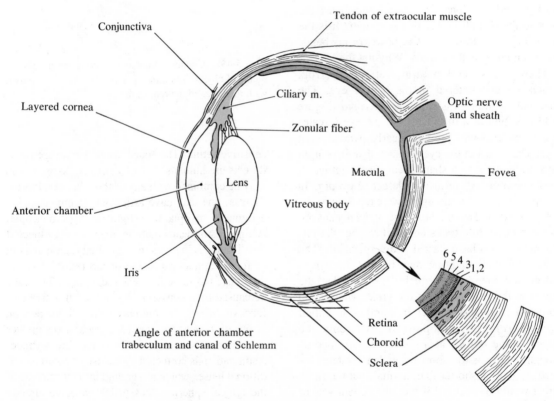

Fig. 5-44.   Section through the human eyeball. Inset : 1 and 2. receptors and their cell bodies, 3. horizontal cells, 4. Bipolar cells, 5. amacrine cells and interplexiform cells, 6. Ganglion cells and optic nerve fibers.

filled with a fluid. The anterior chamber is filled with the *aqueous humor,* which is secreted by cells on the inner layer of the iris. This secretion pours (100 microliter/hour) out of the posterior of the iris (the *ciliary processes*), circulates between the iris and the lens, and fills up the anterior chamber. The fluid then drains through the angle of the anterior chamber, first through a "strainer-like" system of tissue called the *trabeculum* and drains into the *canal of Schlemm,* which eventually communicates with the venous system. The function of the aqueous humor is important. It provides for a major portion of the nutrition of the cornea by diffusion of materials from the anterior chamber into the posterior cell layers of the cornea called the *endothelium.* It also provides for the regulation of the internal pressure of the eye. The active control of secretion of aqueous humor and its drainage through the angle determine the *intraocular pressure.* Since the eye is little more than a poorly elastic structure filled with fluid, one can see that excessive pressures would tend to alter or turn off the vascular supply to the rear of the eye. This is precisely what happens when the pressure control is lost in a common disease of humans called *glaucoma.*

The diameter of the human lens is controlled by the muscles of the *ciliary* body. The ciliary muscles are attached to the lens through a series of fine ligaments called the *zonular fibers.* As the lens thickness becomes less, the total refractive power and curvature of the lens becomes less, and the focal length of the optical system becomes greater. In young people about 18 years of age, the range of adjustment of lens power (accommodation) is about 16 diopters. This gradually decreases with age, and lens hardness increases until about age 50, when the range is no more than 2 or 3 diopters. When the degree of accommodation reaches a minimum with age, the person is said to be *presbyopic,* and it is no longer possible for the eye to adjust internally for major distance differences between objects.

The vitreous body is probably the largest and the most passive structure in the eye. The vitreous body is composed primarily of transparent *collagen* (protein) *fibrils* which are maintained and secreted by *hyalocytes,* small cells on the outer zones of the vitreous body near the equator of the eye. The internal pressure of the eye is transmitted from the vitreous body to the surface of the retina. In some respects, the vitreous body keeps the retina attached to the surface of the *choroid* and *sclera.* This is important because the retina receives a majority of its nutrition from the epithelium of the choroid, a highly vascular structure, and the retinal attachment to the choroid is weak.

The Retina and Eye Function

The *retina* is the light sensitive region of the eye and contains both receptors and neural elements. Primary, secondary, tertiary, and quartenary neurons exist in the retina which, embryogically, is an extension of the brain. In humans, the most highly used retinal region is composed of the *macula* and *fovea,* which rests in its geometric center. The macula is a specialized retinal region because of its dense receptor population and its slight pigmentary coloration. In the center of the macula, the fovea is a small depression in the surface of the retina which contains a dense population of receptors, specialized for the processing of fine optical detail. Image processing is confined almost entirely to these areas in humans. The enlarged area from Figure 5-44 is developed schematically in Figure 5-45A which shows the relative organization of the retina, the vascular choroid, and the outer scleral shell. The receptor cells of the retina have their sensitive processes imbedded in a pigment layer (pigment epithelium) which lies on the inside of the choroid. Nutrition is transferred through this layer into the *receptors.* Below are the *horizontal* cells which serve to shunt information back and forth across the plane of the receptors. The *bipolar* cells communicate information to the deeper parts of the retina and encounter a second set (oriented perpendicular to them) of information carrying cells, the *amacrine* cells. The interplexiform cells provide a feedback path across the amacrine cell and bipolar cell layers (Dawson and Perez, 1973; Boycott, 1976). The final information pathway is constituted by the *ganglion* cells. The ganglion cells accept the information processed by layers 1–5 and send it out over the neurons which are collected together and become the *optic nerve.*

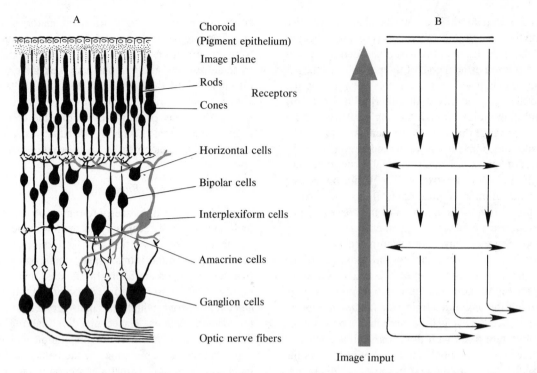

Fig. 5-45. A. Schematic diagram of major cell and layer types of the retina. B. Directions of information transfer within the retina.

In the adult human there are approximately 1 million nerve fibers in the optic nerve ranging from approximately 0.1 micron to about 8 microns in diameter. The directions of information transmission are shown schematically in Figure 5-45B, along with the names of the participating cell types. The choroid and pigment epithelium provide for another function aside from nutrition. In most humans, the pigment epithelium is dark and serves to absorb light from the image which may not be necessarily utilized by the receptors. If this light were not absorbed by the pigment, it would become scattered and distort the quality of the image. Albino humans have no pigment and have very poor visual acuity. A diagram of the cellular structures found in the peripheral retina is shown in Figure 5-45. Peripheral retina is any retinal region outside of the macular area (Figure 5-44). The midperipheral retina is used, neither wholly in dark adaptation nor wholly in daylight vision. It contains both *rod* and *cone* receptors. Retinas which have both rod and cone receptor types and their associated neural systems are classified as *duplex* retinas. This means they are capable of functioning both in relatively high and low light conditions and that there is a physiological shifting from one system to the other. This shifting process from light to night vision is called *dark adaptation*.

The process of seeing begins when light strikes the receptors. The receptor tips (*outer segments*) are literally embedded in the pigment epithelium (Figure 5-45). The process of night vision which uses "rod" receptors is fairly well understood. The cones in Figure 5-45 are the larger of the receptor types in layer 2 (Fig. 5-44). The rods are the longer, slimmer structures. The receptive *outer segments* of these cells lie largely in the upper portions of layer 2. Rod outer segments are about one micron across and about 50 microns long. The receptor outer segment is a vessel for the photopigment *rhodopsin* which is arranged with other cell organs in layers. The photopigment layers are generated at the inner portion of the rod outer segment. The photopigment layers age and are gradually pushed to the apex of the cell by the production of new pigment layers. It eventually leaves the top of the receptor and is carried away. Each rod outer segment in most mammals is completely renewed about every few weeks. The visual receptors (rods and cones) are the primary neurons for the visual sensory system. The photosensitive pigment rhodopsin chemical structure is altered rapidly in the presence of light (Figure 5-46). Immediately on a receipt of light, the rhodopsin liberates calcium ions which cause the closing of channels in the membrane of the receptor outer segment. This, in turn, reduces the membrane current and causes a *hyperpolarization* (increase in outside positive charge). This is contrary to the typical depolarization which is seen in other activated receptor cells (as in the cutaneous sense receptors). The rhodopsin changes color (bleaches) when exposed to light and then breaks down into other chemicals. The process of sensitivity increase when one goes from a high light level into a dark room is the restoration (regeneration) of high levels of rhodopsin which is accomplished through the cycle described in Figure 5-46. The reconstitution of the photopigment rhodopsin is brought about by vitamin A1, which is provided to the receptor endings from a store in the pigment epithelium. Long durations of vitamin A deficiency can produce reduced sensitivity in dark adaptation

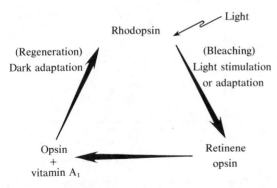

Fig. 5-46.   Bleaching and dark adaptation products in the rhodopsin cycle. (After Wald, 1959)

and/or eventual night blindness. A family of related photopigments may be found in the cone receptors which are used when the eye is adapted to high light levels. The cone photopigments are also stored in disc shaped structures (*saccules*) which are stacked up in the receptor outer segment, much as is the case for rods (Figure 5-45). This group of pigments has a different overall characteristic light absorption than rod photochemical. If visual thresholds for pure lights (containing few wavelengths) from the blue to the red are measured in the dark adapted human, a *luminosity function* similar to that in the upper left of Figure 5-47 will be produced. This curve peaks at approximately 505 nanometers (in the green). As the human eye becomes less dark adapted, its sensitivity shifts toward longer wavelengths and the peak sensitivity is found at 560 nanometers (yellow). The shift in color (wavelength) sensitivity between dark and light adaptation is called the *Purkinje shift*. The lower section of Figure 5-47 shows the density (light absorbance) at various wavelengths of the photochemical rhodopsin and of three cones from the human retina analyzed by microspectrophotometric techniques. It can be seen that the wavelength peak for light absorption by rhodopsin or rods if very close to the peak sensitivity shown by the dark adapted human. The spectral absorption of the cone receptors, where several cones were measured separately, shows a family of curves indicating three different pigments. These have absorption peaks at 445 nanometers (blue), 535 nanometers (green) and 570 nanometers (red-yellow). These three peaks and associated curves, if summed together with appropriate weighting, can account for the subjectively measured luminosity curve (above right, Figure 5-47). The important aspect of these research findings is that the color sensitivity curves for both dark adapted and light adapted humans appears to be determined by the spectral absorption characteristics of the photopigments of the visual receptors themselves. In the duplex retina, the rod system operates under low light conditions, with a single maximal sensitivity point at 505 nanometers. The rod system conveys information only about shades of gray. The cone system operates in light adapted conditions and is made up of recep-

A

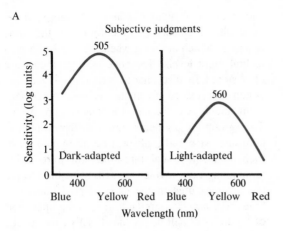

Fig. 5-47. Subjective brightness "luminosity" curves for humans judging threshold at various spectral wavelengths under dark and light adapted conditions. (Below). Light absorbance spectra of rod receptor pigment and individual human cones. (After Adler, 1965; Marks, W., Dobelle, W., and MacNichol, E., 1964)

B

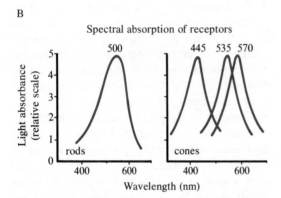

pected, the cones which function during daylight vision, provide color vision and high image resolution, are most dense at the foveal center of the retina. However, this density drops off rapidly and the rod density becomes heavy. The width of the central area of vision is approximately 1.6 millimeters and is roughly equal to 6° of visual angle. If cones are responsible for daytime vision, it can be easily seen from Figure 5-48 that the majority of vision in humans must go on in the central retina very close to the point of fixation. On the nasal side of each retina is the head of the optic nerve (see Figure 5-44 on p. 182). There is no receptor or retinal structure immediately upon the optic nerve. Therefore, an image formed at that point cannot be seen. This is filled in perceptually by people and is not noticed except under special conditions. It is called the *blind spot* because objects imaged on it are not seen.

Figure 5-45 on p. 185 shows that there is no direct pathway from a single receptor to a single optic nerve fiber. In fact, each optic nerve fiber "looks" at a variety of receptor areas, from very small (but densely packed) surface areas near the fovea to relatively large areas in peripheral retina. Each optic nerve fiber and its ganglion cell body produces a neural output message which is representative of the visual excitation in the receptors in its *field* organization. Figure 5-49 shows how these fields interact. The fields of ganglion cells and the numbers of receptors represented in them are con-

tors of different types which are maximally sensitive individually to red, green or blue light. With these three "primary" color sensitivities, mixtures which will produce any other color experience can be generated. The number of rods and cones varies as the retina is examined at distances from the central *point of fixation*. This is the point towards which one brings one's eye when maximum resolution is required. Fixation locates the center of the object of interest directly on the retina's fovea. Figure 5-48 shows how the receptors are distributed at varying distances from the fovea. As ex-

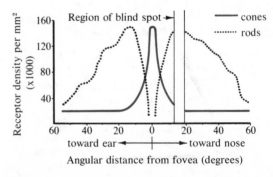

Fig. 5-48. Receptor types and density at various points on the horizontal plane of the human retina. (After Pirenne, 1948)

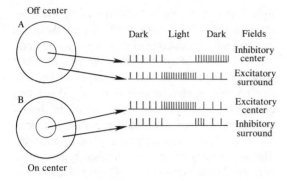

Fig. 5-49. Ganglion cell concentric field concept for "on" and "off" center cell types and for various sequential illumination conditions described on the diagram.

trolled by the lateral interconnections of the neurons between the ganglion cells and receptor layers (Figure 5-45B). The neurons of these interlayers serve to process information about the visual image in several ways. In primate retinas, they serve to sharpen images by means of *lateral inhibition,* they contribute to the dark and light adaptation process by increasing or decreasing sensitivity and improve movement detection by sharpening the contrast at image edges. The receptive fields control the retinal output which is transmitted through optic nerve fibers. At any time, there is a background of neural activity (resting level) in visual fields which as part of the eye, are constantly in micro motion and are scanning the visual environment which consists of light and dark areas. Then there will be a rate of varying output from the optic nerve fibers. The presence of the output at one optic nerve fiber could indicate illumination of the center (Figure 5-49B) of its field. The same illumination of a different fiber's field could tend to reduce output as a result of the lateral inhibition caused by the interaction of these fields in the neural "wiring" of the intermediate retinal layers. When viewed from above, the fields of the retina are circular and overlapping. For the retina, a field may be defined as the amount of retinal surface which has an effect on ganglion cell output. There are two typical types of fields in higher mammals.

These are the *"off center"* fields and the *"on center"* fields. When the off center cell's center is illuminated, the steady state (background) discharge rate of the ganglion cell is reduced. But when the off center illumination is turned off, there is a vigorous (rebound) discharge of the off center ganglion cell. When the periphery of the off center field is illuminated, the ongoing discharge rate is highly elevated until the illumination turns off. Then the steady state rate returns slowly. Illumination of the on center cell's center causes a rapid change from the background or resting rate to a high rate of ganglion cell discharge (Figure 5-50, cell b). But if the on center cell's periphery is illuminated, the background discharge is turned off until the light goes off. Then there is a vigorous discharge. You can see how movement of a line edge or other segment of an image across the field A or B would cause changes in the discharge of the ganglion cells and act as an efficient means for signalling detection of a moving object. Field properties are demonstrated easily in light adapted retinas. When the retina becomes dark adapted, the field properties are much less clear. This is one reason why acuity is so low in the dark adapted eye.

If an object is brought into a field, it can be seen that a rapid change in neural outflow would occur. But if the object remains stationary, then it is also easy to see that a balance would be struck between the *center* and *surround* properties of the field and that the neural discharge would strike a medium someplace between "off" and a high rate. This level of excitation mimics the resting or background state and is probably why images held stationary upon the human retina rapidly fade from view. Several experiments have been done using elaborate optical systems to prevent the image from moving on the retina even though the human eye is constantly moving. When the retinal image becomes truly stabilized, a human observer can no longer see it. Micro eye-*saccades* (scanning movements) are the result of very small muscular tremors and occur regularly. There is no voluntary way to suppress these eye movements.

The important lateral interactions that occur in the intermediate retinal layers are the major distinction between image processing eyes (as in vertebrates) and simple light detectors. Elaboration of these lateral inhibitory functions provide for some highly sophisticated image detection systems (rabbits, frogs) which selectively respond to objects with particular orientations, some moving at particular velocities, some which are new (have not been seen recently) and so forth. All of these specific types of sensitivities have been found in various mammalian retinas. The processing system of the intermediate retinal layers was diagrammed schematically in Figure 5-45 on p. 184.

Until a few years ago, it was assumed that these retinal neural cells interacted by means of spike (all or none) neural potential production as is assumed to take place in most other processing centers of the nervous system. Recent technical advances have made it possible to record from the inside of the very large retinal cells which can be found in some vertebrates (such as salamanders). When one records from individual cells and has the ability to identify them, it is found that the cells of the intermediate retina do not produce spike (all or none) potentials. Indeed, they process, manipulate, or summate graded potentials much like those produced in receptors. If other vertebrate retinas are similar, the system then works very much like an analog computer where potentials are added, subtracted, and divided depending upon the particular network. The result of this manipulation of signals is the discharge of the ganglion cells into the optic nerve fibers. At this point, the first spike, or "all or none," potentials occur in the optic nerve fibers of the eye. It is tempting to propose that many other areas of the nervous system may process in the same way and that information is moved from one processor to another (over fairly long distances) by "all or none" potentials (Werblin and Dowling, 1969; Dawson, 1973).

Color and Pattern Vision

It has been shown that there is selective absorption of various wavelengths of light by different receptors and these correlate well with the three primary colors blue, green, and red. Mixtures of these colors as lights can produce all other known colors. The *trichromatic* theory of color vision states that mixture of these colors as spectral hues (colored

lights) and their selected absorption by the three receptor types (see Figure 5-47 on p. 186) would consequently produce the other subjective colors. The full story of neural encoding of chromatic (color) information is not known. However, the first processing step of several occurs (depending on species) in either the retina or in the lateral geniculate nucleus, in which many of the optic nerve terminals synapse with secondary neurons. This first color encoding mechanism begins in the horizontal cells (second retinal layer) in lower vertebrates like frogs and turtles, while in primates an analogous process occurs in the lateral geniculate nucleus (De Valois, 1965). It has been shown above that the retinal cells respond to stimulation by graded changes in intracellular electrical potential. When the horizontal cells of teleost (fishes and amphibians) are penetrated, two cell response types are found. Responses of type "L" cells are indicated by an increase in internal negativity (hyperpolarization). The degree of hyperpolarization is proportional to the amount of light received, relatively independent of color. Type "C" cells may hyperpolarize or depolarize depending upon the color of the stimulus. Figure 5-50 shows the relative intracellular response magnitude for cells that are excited (hyperpolarized) by red stimulation and inhibited (depolarized) by green stimulation. This cell would be called a red excitatory-green inhibi-

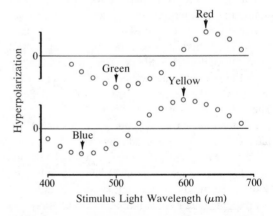

Fig. 5-50. Graded responses of "C" type horizontal cells of the teleost fish at 18 different wavelengths of light. (After Svaetichin and MacNichol, 1958)

tory cell. These are occasionally referred to as "opponent" cells in the literature. The other typical "C" type of cell is shown in the lower Figure 5-50. It is a yellow hyperpolarizing-blue depolarizing cell. This encoding mechanism class of cell response is referred to as the *"opponent-response theory"* of color vision. It can be seen that within the C and L cell types, there is differential encoding for red, green, yellow, blue, and achromatic (gray) lights. In higher animals such as primates, the L-C encoding mechanisms are moved more central and appear first in the cells of the lateral geniculate nucleus where the encoding appears as modulation of the rate of action potential (spike discharge) production. The representation of color in the optic nerve of primates is poorly understood because of the large number of optic nerve elements.

As with most of the sensory systems we have discussed, the receptors seem to have a major portion of the known control over subjective experience. This is not surprising, since they are the first element in the physiological chain. Light detection threshold (jnd) appears to be largely receptor in origin. Figure 5-51 compares the light level of a stimulus required to produce a subjective threshold experience or a 10 microvolt receptor potential.

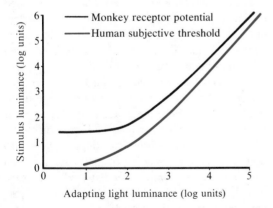

Fig. 5-51.   Threshold for detection of light by subjective report and by cone receptor potential. Human had 1.1 mm foveal test stimulus; monkey had 1.1 mm foveal test stimulus. Receptor threshold (monkey) was taken at 10 microvolts. (After Boynton and Whitten, 1970)

The full range of visual sensitivity (like auditory sensitivity) is very difficult to measure directly. This is because the minimal thresholds approach the limits imposed by physics. For vision, the minimal threshold approaches a few light quanta (5–9 delivered to the eye in a few seconds) for an observer deeply dark adapted (Hecht, *et. al.,* 1942). The upper limits of light sensitivity border on stimuli which literally burn holes in the receptor layer. Such a stimulus is the direct view of the sun. Direct viewing of the sun for more than a few seconds will produce a permanent retinal lesion, called a *scotoma*. An extensive system of standards have been established so that the specification of illumination levels can be made. These standards have been established by the *International Commission on Illumination* (ICI Photometric Standards) and are based on a standard illuminant, or source, the *international candle*. The unit of light produced by the international candle is one *candela*. The apparent brightness of newly fallen snow in full sunlight is about equal to the luminance of the same snow when the light falling upon it is produced by a source equal to 10,000 candelas held one foot from the surface. At the other end of the visibility scale, a source equal to .02 candela can be seen clearly at two miles on a very dark night by fully dark adapted observers.

The major feature of the sensitivity change of the eye in darkness is the transition from color (day or *photopic*) vision to night (dark or *scotopic*) vision where there is no color sensitivity. Today, humans rarely use their scotopic system since, even in darkness, they carry artificial sources which bring the level of stimulation above the cone threshold. The rate of dark adaptation depends on the previous level of light adaptation. When the adapting light is turned out, an orderly temporal increase in sensitivity occurs (Figure 5-52). If a test light is provided in the center of the visual field, the shape of the curve will depend on the size of the test light. If only a small area of the central field is tested, a "mainly cone" curve will be obtained. This is the 2° function shown in Figure 5-52. As the size of the test spot is increased and more rods are brought into use, the sensitivity becomes greater and an increase occurs over a longer period. An important feature of Figure 5-52

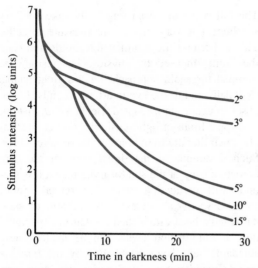

Fig. 5-52. Thresholds during human dark adaptation for stimuli of various sizes fixated in the center of the visual field.

important function, the detection of patterns. The resolution of repeating patterns or discrimination between edges and lines is most commonly thought of as *acuity*. Although there are many types of acuity as there are many objects to see, the most common acuity is called *Snellen* acuity, from the inventor of the Snellen eye chart. The ability to resolve differences in small letters is the basis of the eye chart whose elements begin subtending 0.5 minutes of visual angle. These then double in size in each line of larger letters. The average eye without optical error will faithfully see the second from the smallest line, where the elements subtend 1 minute of arc. Since the eye chart is viewed at 20 feet in order for the retinal angle to equal one minute of arc, the notation 20/20 is used for that line. This indicates that the individual reading that line at 20 feet is seeing what the normal individual would see at 20 feet. Most Snellen charts have one or two very large letter lines which would be seen by the normal individual at 200 or 400 feet. Consequently, a person who can read only one of these lines would have a Snellen acuity equal to 20/200 or 20/400. Legal blindness, in most states, requires a Snellen acuity of 20/200 or worse. Obviously, legal blindness is not total blindness.

Even if the optical system of the eye refracts the light rays properly, there are many other intraocular phenomena which tend to reduce visual acuity by producing *blur*. These are *scatter, diffraction*, and *chromatic aberration*. As presented earlier, the refractive power of a lens is dependent upon the wavelength and speed of light. Since wavelength and speed vary together, it can be seen that the red component of white light does not fall at precisely the same focal point (is not refracted identically) as the blue component of white light. For white light then, the image is spread out over the retina more than it would be if the object was illuminated by monochromatic (single wavelength) light alone. This spreading of the image is called *chromatic aberration*. Scatter also tends to blur the image. As the light strikes the not totally transparent intraocular media, it tends to be scattered. It is scattered further by the structures of the retina and behind the retina. Finally, light rays passing through the openings interact with the edge of these openings much as water passing through an

is the event that occurs at approximately seven minutes after the beginning of dark adaptation. Note how the curve becomes slightly flattened before additional increases in sensitivity occur. This is called the Purkenji shift and is the transition from cone to rod vision. Subjectively, the Purkenji shift is seen at dusk when red colors and yellow colors begin to fade and blue colors take on an increased emphasis. This transition from long wavelength to shorter wavelength sensitivity marks the shift in color sensitivity shown in the upper part of Figure 5-47 on p. 186. If the Purkenji shift signifies the shift from cone to rod vision and if cones are the predominating receptor in the central 10° of the retina as was shown in Figure 5-48, one would predict that the dark adapted person would see dim lights best "off center" or on the peripheral part of the retina. This is precisely what happens. Observers in military units are trained early that detection of dim objects at night should be done by looking slightly away from where they are expected to be seen. This is easily verified by looking for high flying aircraft at night.

Aside from its ability to resolve colors and the presence or absence of lights, the retina has a third

opening produces eddy currents. These edge effects (diffraction) serve to further spread the image on the retina producing blurred images. You may wonder how good visual acuity is obtained in the face of so many negative influences. The system which serves to rescue acuity in mammals is pictured in Figure 5-45 on p. 184 and is contained in the sharpening effects of the neural retinal fields. The amount of improvement can be appreciated best by considering the size of the image which would be produced by an ideal eye (without scatter, diffraction, or aberration) at the retinal surface. Many young people can see an object with a visual angular subtense of 0.5 minutes of arc (20/15 Snellen acuity). It can be shown that such an object would cover an area approximately 2.4 microns wide on the retinal surface. If each foveal cone receptor is about 1.5 microns in diameter, this object which is seen well by young people covers no more than two cone cells at any time. Reflection on this will suggest that this is amazing resolution. However, one must remember that the eye is constantly moving and that the object is being seen sequentially, by many cones or pairs of cones. By some process which is not understood, a type of analysis of all of the bits of information provided as the image moves over an area of many microns in diameter is reassembled into a continu-

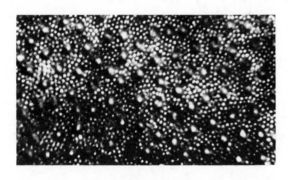

20 micrometers

Fig. 5-53. Mosaic of human retinal receptor cells as seen from above. Twenty-one-year-old male, paracentral retina 20° from the fovea. Large round receptor outer segments (cones) are surrounded by smaller rod receptor outer segments. (Courtesy of Dr. C. A. Adams)

ous, stable image somewhere between the receptors (Fig. 5-53) and their final points of projection in the central nervous system.

Central Projections

Figure 5-54 shows the major visual pathways with the human brain as model. The location of the visual cortex of the brain varies between mammalian species. If the retina were divided vertically into two halves for the right eye, it would be split into a left and right (nasal and temporal visual field) area. Each half of the visual field is represented in the optic nerve and retains its spatial identity until it reaches the optic chiasm. At the chiasm, the nasal field fibers cross into the optic tract and join the temporal field fibers from the opposite eye. The optic tract then continues to one of the major brain areas for preliminary processing of sensory information. This area is the *thalamus*. The visual thalamus is called the *lateral geniculate nucleus*. It can be seen that information about the left visual field (from each eye) travels through the optic tract, the lateral geniculate nucleus and reaches the right visual cortex by way of neurons originating in the lateral geniculate nucleus called the *optic radiations* or the *genoculocalcarine tract*. The left and right hemispheres of the brain exchange information through the *corpus callosum*. In humans, the visual cortices are at the rear most aspect of the brain called the *occipital pole*. This region is further divided into *striate* and *prestriate cortex*. The primary input from the optic radiations (Figure 5-55) is to the striate cortex. But information from the radiations also passes directly to the *superior colliculus* and to the *prestriate cortex*. In turn, the striate cortex also sends information to the superior colliculus and to the prestriate cortex. Pathways exist which connect the striate cortex directly to the *frontal eye fields* and by way of the prestriate cortex to the *inferotemporal cortex*. The prestriate cortex is directly connected to the frontal eye fields and the inferotemporal cortex receives and sends information into the frontal eye fields. The visual fields of the retina are faithfully reproduced at the striate cortex, and it is here that responses to images are particularly strong. Prestriate cortex cells respond to images and movements in particu-

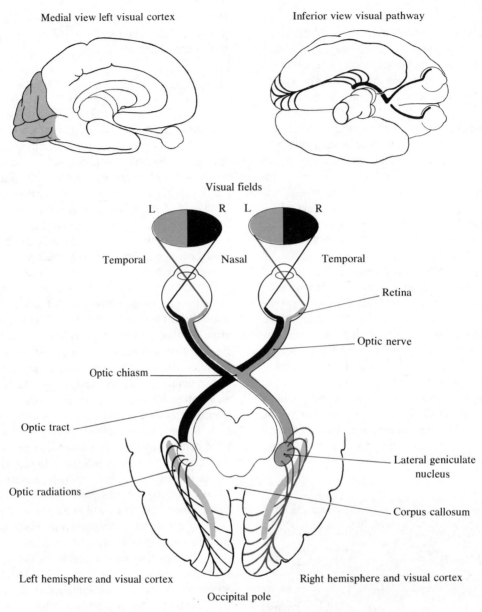

Medial view left visual cortex

Inferior view visual pathway

Visual fields

L   R   L   R

Temporal   Nasal   Temporal

Retina

Optic nerve

Optic chiasm

Optic tract

Lateral geniculate
nucleus

Optic radiations

Corpus callosum

Left hemisphere and visual cortex   Right hemisphere and visual cortex

Occipital pole

Fig. 5-54. Schematic of the main visual pathway. Note the representation of the visual field of each eye in the crossing of the nasal portions of the optic nerves (temporal fields). (After Sperry, 1968)

lar directions or to images with elements of a particular orientation. Without the striate or prestriate cortex, monkeys have a great deal of difficulty learning pattern discrimination tasks. Although, a few workers have found that, with extensive training, monkeys may discriminate simple patterns and differences in illumination level when the majority of the striate and prestriate cortex is removed. When the inferotemporal cortex is removed, simple visual acuity and brightness discrimination are not changed, but learning of some difficult types of tasks are disturbed. The

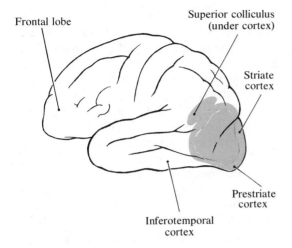

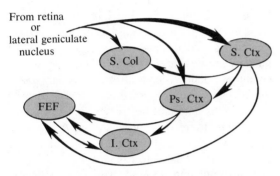

Fig. 5-55. Major higher brain centers involved in the processing of visual information. Human brain as seen from the left side. Direction of information flow is shown below. FEF frontal eyefields; I. Ctx, inferotemporal cortex; S. Col, superior collicus; Ps. Ctx, prestriate cortex; S. Ctx, striate cortex.

frontal cortex and superior colliculus are involved in the positioning of the eyes in space. In humans, lesions of the frontal lobe interfere with movements of the eyes together, and there is frequent production of paralysis of the eyes. However, there is recovery from this condition after several weeks. Neurons in the frontal eye fields respond vigorously when the eyes move, and most vigorously at the initiation of eye movements. The superior colliculus is part of the "old brain," or tectum, which served the majority of eye functions prior to the phylogenetic development of the neocortex. In mammals, the superior colliculus cells receive information about visual input and also data from several other sensory systems. Stimulation of the superior colliculus causes movement of the eyes in space, as though an object were seen in the retinal field representing that particular superior collicular site. The superior colliculus appears to play a major role in the development of "target" acquisition behavior which moves the eye position toward a target so that foveal, fine resolution can be brought to bear (Stryker and Schiller, 1975).

The characteristics of neural cell responses in the brain are quite distinct from those reported in the retina. Earlier, it was explained that most of the retinal cells appeared to respond in the absence of action potentials. The intracellular response of the retinal cells is "graded" depending on its level of activation. This type of recording is not available for cells in the mammalian central nervous system. Extracellular recordings from some cells in the visual area of mammals indicate that there are three major types of cell action potential response. In the superior colliculus, cells respond to both brief flashes of light and to the presence of moving slits and objects of other shapes presented to the retina. As described in Figure 5-56, the superior colliculus cells would correspond to the "simple" cell response type. Simple cells are also found in the striate cortex. *Simple cells* respond to bars or slits of light presented to the retina and moved in various directions. They are not particularly directional sensitive, nor are they sensitive to the size of the stimulating bar of light, unless it becomes large enough that it exceeds the limits of the "excitatory" region of its retinal field (Fig. 5-50). The *complex cell* type is similar to the simple cell, except that the movement of the slit is most exciting in a particular direction. In some directions, the slit's movement produces no excitation at all. Complex and simple cells are found in the striate areas of the cortex. Some complex cells are also found in the prestriate cortex. The *hypercomplex cell* type is sensitive both to direction of movement and to the size of the moving object. If the preferred direction is not provided, the cell may not respond; or if the size becomes larger than the preferred size, it may not respond. Hypercomplex cells are not found in the striate cortex but are common in the superficial and deeper cortical areas of the prestriate regions.

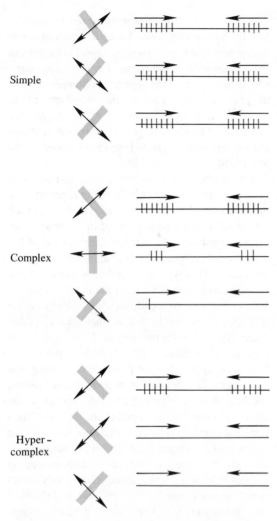

Simple

Complex

Hyper-
complex

Fig. 5-56. Some attributes of cells in the visual areas of the brain. Arrows on slits indicate direction of movement of light slit on retina. Spike potentials are drawn to represent amount of activation. Note influence of size and direction on cell activation. (After Hubel and Wiesel, 1965)

Effects of the Environment

The consequences of environment, experience, and their influences on early development have been of great interest in developmental psychology for many years. Alterations in adult behavior have been clearly demonstrated, but the mechanisms in-

volved at the neural level have not been clear. Recent research in the visual system has illustrated how important experience during development can be and has begun to explain the cellular mechanisms involved. Several years ago, it was shown that stimulation is required for the normal development of the retina and the visual system (Riesen, 1961). Using infantile monkeys, Riesen demonstrated that rearing in total darkness produced blind adult behavior and atrophy of neural cells in the retina and visual pathway. Equal times in the dark had much less serious consequences in adult animals. Abnormal development is also seen in some eye conditions in humans. In *strabismic amblyopia* (squint), one eye in the child will track its counterpart incorrectly. If the incorrectly aligned eye turns inward (*esotropia*), the individual is said to be cross-eyed. If it turns outward (*exotropia*), the individual is said to have divergent squint. When humans grow with one or the other of these eye conditions, adult vision is affected. In many cases, the deviating eye is "turned off," and if surgical correction is not made before age six, it is almost impossible to recover normal function (acuity) even after surgery and training. In these cases, the cause for the visual defect is most certainly not a lack of stimulation. At most, the images falling on the retinas are "out of registry." Misalignment of the eyes of adults causes *diplopia* (double vision). Diplopia may be demonstrated by pressing gently on the outside of one eye so that it is moved with respect to its normal position. When viewing an object binocularly, two images may be easily seen. The cellular consequences of misalignment have been demonstrated by a group of excellent papers written by Hubel and Wiesel (1965). In kittens, the muscular balance of one eye was altered so as to produce asymmetry or the optical conditions necessary for diplopia. In normal kittens and cats, cells of the visual cortex are excited more by binocular stimulation than by stimulation of each eye separately. The number of cells driven by stimulation of the eye, contralateral (opposite) and ipsilateral (same side) to the visual cortical area being studied do not respond well normally. But when both eyes are stimulated simultaneously, by objects which fall in the same visual field, the number of responding cells increases by well over

100 percent. In the kittens that had eye misalignment during visual development, the preference toward cellular response is almost reversed. That is, there is very little excitation of the cortical cells by simultaneous stimulation of the same retinal fields in both eyes. Hubel and Wiesel showed that if the deviation was surgically produced after about three months of life, the binocular loss was much less or nonexistent. From this and other related research, they conclude that the anatomical connections between the retinal and striate cortex are determined genetically. However, there is a critical period in cats during the first three months of life, when these connections are highly susceptible to the effects of deprivation, and that alteration of normal input leads to a severe decline in the ability of that eye to influence cortical cells. More recently, Von Noorden (1975) has demonstrated similar results in monkeys. The major difference is that the critical period was longer and began at a different developmental time. Abnormal stimulation may be considered a type of deprivation. If kittens are exposed to stripes moving clockwise during weeks 2–5 of life, their cortical cell responsiveness later will show a distinct bias toward clockwise movement. Normally, cortical cells which are unidirectionally sensitive show no special directional bias (Daw *et. al.,* 1978). Consequently, alternation of the "normal" environment during a critical period can have drastic effects on neural organization.

It is clear at this time that, for humans, almost any deviation from normal vision during the period of one to six years has the potential for producing permanent, visual defects (amblyopias) in the adult. This is particularly unfortunate, since many children do not have eye evaluations until they begin school at six years of age. At this time, the period of visual development is almost over, and it is almost always too late.

Visual development may be seen in an entirely separate dimension as development across the animal kingdom (*phylogenetic development*) is studied. In contrast to the human eye, which has been described in this chapter, there is a rich and highly varied sequence of eye types to be found in animals ranging from humans to one-celled organisms. An introductory text cannot hope to give a reasonable account of such a divergent group of methods of dealing with the visual stimulus. Each eye configuration is governed by the complexity of the organism which supports it and is adapted in many ways for the particular visual and physical problems confronted in its environment. Consequently, there are almost as many eye types as there are animals and environments. As a single example, many burrowing animals (snakes and alligators, and such) have developed a second cornea (spectacle or brille) which serves to protect the eye's cornea when the animal is underwater or is burrowing through sand or other relatively abrasive materials. There are equally ingenious adaptations of retina, lens, extraocular muscles, and most other visual structures. The most comprehensive treatment of eye adaptation with species is presented in a volume by Gordon Walls (1942).

Summary

The sensory systems used by various animals appear to be designed to serve a particular group of necessary functions in that animal's natural environment. The sensory experiences that may result from stimulation of the receptors of any sense organ are highly influenced by the physical interactions which occur between the stimuli and tissue prior to reaching the sensory receptor. In general, sensory receptors are exceedingly sensitive detectors of the particular forms of energy to which they normally respond. But, the receptors or neural processing elements nearby are organized in such a way that even relatively large amounts of unchanging stimulation results in a loss of sensitivity to that stimulus type. All sensory systems are most sensitive to changes in stimulation from the environment rather than from steady-state stimulus conditions. Sensory receptors are all associated with nerve cells and their networks. In most sensory systems, a great deal of processing information occurs before the nerve messages reach the central nervous system. From examining this relatively more simple processing system, many new discoveries about how nervous system processing works have been made in the last few years. Several sensory systems receive and act upon information from the central nervous system. These feedback loop control circuits appear to control the peripheral processing of central information dependent on the condition of the central nervous system. The development of normal sensory processing and

normal sensory brain areas in humans and many lower animals is altered by unusual sensory experiences during "periods of critical development." The application of modern, quantitative techniques to the study of sensory processes is only 50 to 75 years old. Much remains to be learned.

Glossary

Acceleration: An increase in speed of an object from a steady rate.

Acuity: Measures of degree of visual resolution. (There are several types.)

Adsorption: A low energy bonding of a chemical to a membrane. Adsorbed materials do not pass through membranes into cells.

Aerial image: An image which may not be formed on a surface but which may be treated optically as though it were present in air.

Afferent: Nerves conducting from the periphery to the central nervous system.

Analgesic: A drug that reduces pain sensitivity.

Astigmatism: An optical error most commonly seen in humans with slight defects of their cornea (departure from symmetry).

Aqueous humor: The fluid of the front chamber of the eye. Aqueous humor provides nutrition for the cornea.

Auditory system: All anatomical structures both peripheral and central nervous which process information about sound.

Basilar membrane: A structure in the cochlea that acts as a rudimentary frequency analyzer and serves in the transducing of movement to nerve impulses relative to auditory function.

Blind spot: The area of the retina occupied by the head of the optic nerve. A light insensitive region.

Blur: The loss of resolution of image edges due to optical error.

Candela: The international standard of illumination—the international candle.

Chromatic abberation: Errors in focusing of white light caused by simple lenses. Focal plains for different colors fall in different positions due to differences in the speed of light across the spectrum.

Cilliary processes: Specialized cells on the rear of the iris which secrete aqueous humor.

Cochlea: That portion of the bony labyrinth devoted to auditory function.

Collagen: Gel-like organizations of protein fibers as found in the vitreous body of the eye.

Columns, anterior/lateral: Major divisions of the spinal cord serving sensory functions.

Cribriform plate: The bony perforated roof of the olfactory area of the upper nasal passageway.

Crista: The vestibular analog of the basilar membrane. A gelatinous structure in which are embedded the hair cells of the vestibular receptors.

Critical frequency: The frequency or frequency band which maximally excites a nerve fiber.

Depolarization of nerve: An increase of the negativity of the nerve's exterior with relative positive increase of the nerve's interior; the condition necessary for neural excitation.

Diffraction: Alteration of light rays by interaction with edges such as the pupil.

Doctrine of specific nerve energies: A formal doctrine published by Johannes Müller. It established unique peripheral pathways for each sensory system and firmly joined the sensory function with the nervous system (*ca.* 1840).

Dynamic sensitivity: Selective sensitivity to changes in incident energy (environmental stimuli).

Efferent: Neurons that conduct information originating in the central nervous system toward the periphery.

Endothelium-cornea: The inner cellular lining of the cornea.

Field properties: Properties of the field or tissue regions whose sensory stimulation may serve to excite a cell at any place in the nervous system.

Flavor: A complex experience determined by several sensory systems including warm, cold, touch, olfaction, and gustation.

Free nerve endings: Nerve terminals that end without any identifiable special structure.

Gate theory: A formal theory of pain perception that involves balance of action of nerve fiber types and processing both in the spinal cord and central nervous system.

Generator potential: A potential in a receptor or other place in the nervous system which, on growth in amplitude, can initiate a spike (propagated) action potential.

Hair cells: The auditory receptor cell.

Hearing: The detection of sound pressures in the air.

Hyperpolarization: An increase of positivity (reduced negativity) of the nerve's exterior. A condition required to inhibit nerve excitation.

Individual differences: Differences in functional ability for any activity can be demonstrated between any human individuals.

Inferior colliculus: A major way-station for auditory information in the mid-brain.

Inferotemporal cortex: Functions in the processing of color information and in controlling eye movements.

Intraocular media: Those structures inside the eye through which light must pass in order to strike the retina.

Intraocular pressure: The pressure built up by the secretion of aqueous humor.

Ischemia: A condition of tissue resulting from an abnormally low availability of oxygen.

Isomerization: A chemical change in configuration of a molecule without alteration of the atomic components of the molecule.

Labyrinth: The bony structure housing the receptor organs for the vestibular system.

Lateral geniculate nucleus: The main intermediate nucleus between the eye and the visual cortex. A portion of the main sensory relay site, the thalamus.

Lateral inhibition: The inhibitory effect on adjacent cells produced by activation of cells excited by normal means.

Luminosity function: Relative sensitivity of the eye to various wavelengths of light.

Medial: Referring to the middle, central area of a structure, usually middle of the brain.

Medial geniculate nucleus: Part of the thalamic system devoted to the routing of auditory information toward higher brain centers.

Microvilli: Hair-like extensions of cells, usually into noncellular areas.

Nasal mucosa: The region of the olfactory area lined with the sensitive, receptor regions and a region of mucous secreting cells.

Occipital pole: The most posterior portion of the human brain devoted to the primary processing of visual information.

Olivocochlear bundle: A nerve trunk that transmits information from the central nervous system into the cochlea; an efferent fiber bundle for the auditory system.

Opponent response theory: Cells that respond actively to one color are negatively influenced by its complement.

Optic radiations: The pathway operating between the lateral geniculate nucleus and the visual cortex.

Organ of corti: Structure on the interior of the cochlea which responds to changes in air pressure.

Outer segments: Outer portions of the visual receptor cells containing photopigment chemicals.

Peripheral sensory nerves: Bundles of sensory axons or single axons which convey information of a sensory nature from the periphery toward the spinal cord or brain.

Photopic: Referring to the portion of the visual system that operates under high light conditions.

Plato: A famous Greek philosopher-teacher (*ca.* 2,500 B.C.).

Posterior spinal roots: Same as dorsal roots; large bundles or sensory nerve fibers which enter only in the dorsal (posterior) portion of the spinal cord.

Presbyopia: A visual defect of older people caused by limited accomodation and solidification of the lens.

Prestriate cortex: Region surrounding the striate cortex; receives information from the striate cortex and some input from the lateral geniculate nucleus.

Primary (sensory): The basic, most simple stimulus conditions from which all sensory experiences of a particular class can be built.

Psychophysics: A research methodology designed to convert human experiences into a quantifiable data form.

Pupil: The opening in the iris which admits light to the rear of the eye.

Purkinje shift: The shift in relative color sensitivity as the eye proceeds from light to dark adaptation.

Refraction: Changes in the direction of light travel caused by entering or leaving a surface.

Resonance: A vibrating object will induce vibration in a nearby object of similar mechanical properties.

Resonance theory: A theory of hearing based on frequency analysis requiring sympathetic resonance of many sites along the basilar membrane, selectivity sensitive to particular frequencies.

Retina: The neural-sensory layer of the eye; contains receptors and neural information processing elements; also produces the optic nerve.

Saccade: Typical eye movement during scanning of a field. (There are fast and slow components.)

Scatter-light: Diffusion of dispersion of light rays due to interaction with imperfections or nontransparent regions of the intraocular media.

Scotoma: A regional loss of sight in the visual field.

Scotopic: Referring to the portion of the visual system which operates under very low light conditions.

Semicircular canals: "Pretzel" shaped canals that are part of the labyrinth and that compose the acceleration-deacceleration sensing system of the vestibular system.

Spinothalamic tracts: Large bundles of neurons of the spinal cord which rise to the sensory area of the brain called the thalamus. These function as a communication system between the brain and some sensory areas which communicate to the spinal cord by way of the dorsal (posterior) root system.

Strabismic amblyopia: A visual defect caused by improper vision during the period of eye development; usually associated with reduced acuity in one eye during visual development; also occurs with eye misalignment.

Stereochemical structure: The overall shape of a complex organic molecule.

Striate cortex: Site of projection of the optic radiations.

Superior colliculus: Center for coordination between visual information, eye movement and other sensory modalities.

Sustentacular cells: Supporting (non-neural) cells which serve to maintain the taste cells in place.

Taste cells: The receptor cells for the gustatory (taste) sensory system.

Temporal bone: A section of the human cranium in which the peripheral portions of the auditory and vestibular systems are embedded.

Threshold level: The amount of stimulation that is just barely perceptible.

Trebeculum: A filter-like meshwork of cells which close the entry of the canal of Schlem and act as a straining device for the aqueous humor.

Trichromatic theory: Three color receptor types and systems are adequate to account for perception of all colors; usually red, green and blue primaries.

Trigeminal nerve: A sensory nerve trunk (one of the major cranial nerves) which provides for nerve terminal, ending in most tissue of the head and neck.

Tympanium: The ear drum, the first biological structure in the auditory system.

Ventral: Reference to a position generally below some other object or structure.

Vestibular systems: Neural and non-neural structures in the periphery and central nervous system which respond to changes in the position of the body or its movements.

Volley hypothesis: A mechanism proposed to account for the transmission of very high frequency information through the auditory nerve system. The rotation of "responsibility" for firing among groups of nerve fibers.

Vomernasal system: Chemoreceptive structure found in the nose of many lower vertebrates.

Zonular fibers: The ligaments that suspend the lens.

Suggested Readings

Brown, J. L. *Sensory Systems*. In Brobeck, J. ed., *Best and Taylor's Physiological Basis of Medical Practice*. Baltimore: Williams and Wilkins, 1973.

Cornsweet, T. *Visual Perception*. New York: Academic Press, 1973.

Boudreau, J. and Tsuchitani, C. *Sensory Neurophysiology*. New York: Van Nostrand Reinhold, 1973.

Geldard, F. *The Human Senses*. 2nd ed. New York: John Wiley, 1972.

Cristman, R. J. *Sensory Experience*. Scranton, Pa.: Intext Press, 1971.

Animal Behavior

Donald A. Dewsbury

Introduction

Most people are interested in the behavior of animals. The keeper of tropical fish, the visitor to the zoo, and the television viewer tuning in a favorite weekly animal program are all expressing their interests in the lives of animals. At a more professional level, the study of animal behavior constitutes the primary endeavor of thousands of scientists of varying interests and backgrounds, who represent a wide array of disciplines. Included are not only psychologists but zoologists, endocrinologists, anthropologists, wildlife researchers, agriculturists, and many more. Together, these scientists have created a discipline notable for its activity, excitement, and diversity.

Strictly speaking, all psychology—except for the efforts of the few psychologists interested in the behavior of plants—is the study of animal behavior. By convention, however, only a small part of this total endeavor is usually treated under the rubric of the discipline of "animal behavior." When either the species or the behavior studied falls outside of the range studied in all other branches of psychology, the research will usually be dealt with as "animal behavior." Figure 6-1 is one way of portraying the range of material studied in animal behavior and other branches of psychology.

There are over one million recognized animal species. Yet the vast majority of studies in psychology are restricted to but a few common species: humans, white rats, white Carneaux pigeons,

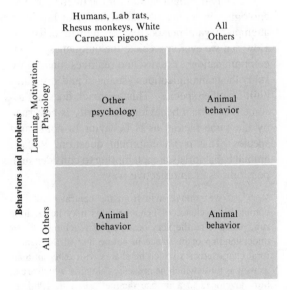

Fig. 6-1.   A conceptualization of the subject matter of the study of animal behavior relative to that of the rest of psychology.

and so on. Similarly, there are many kinds of behavior and kinds of questions that can be asked about behavior. Most studies in psychology, however, are restricted to such problem areas as learning, motivation, and physiology. We shall consider here only studies in which either the species or problem studied falls outside the range just described.

Many would define psychology as the study of *human* behavior. One may legitimately ask why it is that psychologists should be interested in the kinds of animal behavior studies we shall discuss. There are a variety of reasons. Often a particular problem can be studied only in a nonhuman animal. This may be for ethical reasons, such as the convention against making unnecessary brain lesions on humans, or for scientific reasons, such as the relative ease of work with the nervous systems of simple organisms. Often, comparative studies are undertaken to test the generality of principles derived from the study of a limited number of species. Further, studies of animal behavior have sometimes led to applications of relatively short-term economic import having some tangible "pay off," as in the training of animals to perform designated tasks.

Probably the main reason for the interest of psychologists in studies of animal behavior lies in an attempt to gain perspective on human behavior. How can we ever appreciate the uniqueness of our communication systems and edifices unless we study the communication systems of and structures built by other species? This approach does not assume that human behavior necessarily is governed by the same factors as is behavior in nonhuman species. That is an empirical question. Rather, animal behaviorists are attempting to consider such possibilities in an objective way:

". . . if we remove man from the central point in a comparative science of behavior, this may in the long run, prove to be the very best way of reaching a better understanding of his place in nature and of the behavioral characteristics which he shares with other animals as well as those which he possesses alone or which are in him developed to a unique degree" (Beach, 1960, p. 17).

The Problem Areas of Animal Behavior

A distinguished European ethologist, Niko Tinbergen, has provided a framework for the study of animal behavior which we shall also use as the framework for the major portion of this chapter. According to Tinbergen (1963a), animal behaviorists must begin their study with careful *observation* and *description* of behavior. Observation and description are followed by systematic research

designed to answer four classes of questions— those relating to *behavioral development, immediate causation, evolution,* and *adaptive significance.* As these are important concepts, they merit further discussion.

Observation and Description

In their rush to find answers to the interesting questions of development, causation, and so on, many scientists rush through the phases of observation and description. However, it is important to remember that observation and description provide the bases for all subsequent research. If the description of a behavioral pattern is incomplete or inaccurate, years of subsequent research may be wasted, as these workers misinterpret behavioral phenomena. Animal behaviorists have been leaders in a "return to the basics." As a result of their efforts, comprehensive, objective descriptions of behavior now are available for a variety of behaviors in a variety of species.

Whenever an observer classifies and records behavior, he or she is by necessity imposing preconceived notions as to the structure of behavior. It is impossible to classify and report without using measures and words that force a certain structure upon the final data. Animal behaviorists generally try to use terms that are as neutral and descriptive as possible and that carry minimal surplus meaning. Thus, animal behaviorists often prefer to describe motor patterns such as the tail wag of a dog or the exact movements that comprise a pattern presumed to be related to courtship before making inferences regarding the function of the behavior under observation. Photographs, motion pictures, and videotapes are very helpful in minimizing the bias involved in making observations. Such aids have the additional advantage of allowing one to go back and reexamine permanent records to search for details of behavior that may have been missed the first times through.

Development

The first of the four classes of questions discussed by Tinbergen is that of behavioral development, or *ontogeny.* When dealing with developmental questions, one is typically concerned with behavioral changes over the total life-span of the individual. A primary interest in this domain has centered about he ways in which the genes and the environment act and interact in producing behavior. Increased attention has recently been devoted to the other end of the developmental continuum— changes in behavior that are a part of the aging process.

Immediate Causation

The search for immediate causes of behavior can be undertaken at many levels. Often, this entails a search for physiological mechanisms correlated with behavior. Usually, the search for such mechanisms entails study of hormones and activity of the nervous system. Questions of sensory processes and stimuli, of motivation, and of a variety of environmental determinants of behavior all fall within the realm of questions of immediate causation. Questions of immediate causation have been the primary concern of most psychologists.

Evolution

Most psychologists and biological scientists believe that the organisms living on the earth today are the products of many centuries of evolutionary history. There is good evidence to support the view that the behavior of animals has evolved just as their structure has. The search for evolutionary roots and changes in behavior relates to the third class of questions in the study of animal behavior.

Function

When biologists or biopsychologists raise questions of function, they are asking about the role that the behavior plays in promoting survival, adaptation, and reproduction. Animals are marvelously adapted to the environments in which they normally live. Behavior provides a critical part of this adaptation. A study of the ways in which behavior promotes survival and successful reproduction rounds out a comprehensive analysis of behavior and an understanding of both its immediate and ultimate causation.

Historical Roots of the Contemporary Study of Animal Behavior

The historical roots of the study of animal behavior have been traced well back into the history and prehistory of *Homo sapiens*. Cave paintings of animals reveal specific knowledge that early humans possessed regarding animal habits.

The views of the ancient Greeks were important in the formulation of Western culture. In the fourth century B.C., Heraclitus, a Greek philosopher, proposed that there were two types of creation. Only men and gods were the products of rational creation and possessed souls. All other brutes were in a class by themselves. This approach set the tone for many views of the relationship between human and nonhuman behavior that still persist today. Aristotle was somewhat more enlightened and actually proposed a graded scale of intelligence in which humans were placed at the top, directly above the Indian elephant.

Much of the history of the study of animal behavior, from the time of the Greeks until the present, lies in philosophy and natural history. It was not until the writings of Darwin that comparative studies of human and nonhuman behavior received substantial impetus. The theory of evolution and the view that different species had common origins provided important impetus for studying human behavior on terms similar to those on which nonhuman behavior might be studied. In addition, Darwin wrote an important book, *Expression of the Emotions in Man and Animals,* which actually considered human and nonhuman behavior from a comparative perspective. Facial expressions and other means of communicating emotions were compared across species in considerable detail.

Around the turn of twentieth century, a group of important early animal behaviorists flourished. In 1882, George John Romanes wrote a book entitled *Animal Intelligence.* Although it laid much groundwork for comparative studies of learning, its value was limited by Romanes' repeated reliance on anecdotes rather than careful objective observations of animal behavior. C. Lloyd Morgan sounded a warning against explanations of behavior using complex, higher-order concepts when simple explanations would suffice. Jacques Loeb was even more extreme, and viewed behavior as the result of tropisms, simple physico-chemical responses directed toward or away from specific stimuli. In William James' *Principles of Psychology* published in 1890, much space was devoted to discussions of animal behavior.

The development of the study of animal behavior in the 20th century can best be understood by contrasting the development of the two major disciplines from which it has been formulated, ethology and comparative psychology. The story is one of relatively independent development through the early part of the century, interaction and controversy in the 1950s, and a gradual unification resulting in the contemporary science of animal behavior.

There is no simple definition of ethology. Basically, classical ethology was an approach to the study of animal behavior, developed among a group of European zoologists during the first half of the twentieth century. The classical ethologists stressed the importance of careful observations made in the natural habitat in the belief that only with such observations could one avoid distortions of behavior believed to occur as a result of laboratory living. Classical ethologists were very much interested in the study of evolutionary questions and relied heavily on the "instinct" concept in their explanations of behavior. Their primary subjects were insects, fish, and birds. Classical ethology is personified in the work of Konrad Lorenz and Niko Tinbergen, two scientists who, along with Karl von Frisch, shared the Nobel Prize for Physiology and Medicine in 1973. Their research on egg rolling in the greylag goose, imprinting in geese, reproductive behavior of stickleback fish, and the behavioral patterns of gulls became classics of ethological literature. Tinbergen's *The Study of Instinct,* written in 1951, provided a theoretical integration of much ethological material and represents a high watermark for classical ethology.

As ethology was developing among European zoologists, a very different science of animal behavior was developing among American psychologists. In the early part of the twentieth century,

animal psychology represented a fairly broad-based approach, the subject matter of which was a great variety of behavior in a great variety of species. Throughout much of the twentieth century, however, animal psychology became progressively focused on more and more restricted problems. Most studies came to be done on mammals, particularly albino rats. Research became restricted to the controlled conditions of the laboratory and elaborate statistical methods were used to tease out experimental effects. The study of learning became the major endeavor and the development of comprehensive theories was a major goal. While a few psychologists, such as Karl Lashley, C. P. Stone, Norman R. F. Maier, T. C. Schneirla, C. R. Carpenter, and Frank A. Beach were engaged in a broader-based comparative psychology, the overwhelming majority of animal psychologists were concerned with the study of learning in white rats.

Both ethologists and animal psychologists had developed what each regarded as "the objective science of behavior." Each discipline had developed in relative isolation, using different kinds of animals and different methods. It was natural that when ethologists and animal psychologists recognized one another in the 1950s, some rather bitter controversies occurred. Ethologists were critical of the narrow approach of animal psychologists with regard to their choice of subjects and methods. Animal psychologists were intolerant of the lack of control and experimental manipulation in the work of ethologists. Utilization of the concept of *instinct,* a notion used by ethologists but discarded by animal psychologists, became a focus of disagreement.

A few signs of the discord between animal psychologists and ethologists that existed in the 1950s still remain today. For the most part, however, a synthesis of the two approaches has been achieved. Indeed, it is now often difficult to tell a contemporary ethologist from a contemporary comparative psychologist. Each has been influenced by the other. Ethologists have recognized the value of quantitative methods and laboratory research. Psychologists have become more mindful of distortions of behavior that can occur as a result of the removal of animals from their natural habitat to the artificial environment of the laboratory, and have broadened the range of species that they study. The rapprochement is best illustrated in Robert Hinde's 1970 book, *Animal Behavior, A Synthesis of Ethology and Comparative Psychology;* in the formation of the Animal Behavior Society, bringing together American zoologists, psychologists, and others interested in the study of animal behavior; and, in the mutual representation of individuals from different backgrounds in today's animal behavior journals. The input from psychology and zoology, together with that from other areas such as anthropology and various agricultural and wildlife sciences, has created a discipline that, although difficult to define, represents a large and exciting area of contemporary research activity.

Patterns of Behavior

The major portion of this chapter will be structured about Tinbergen's proposed organization for the study of animal behavior. We will begin with a general description—a discussion of some of the things animals do and animals behaviorists study. This will be followed by a consideration of each of the four main classes of questions asked by animal behaviorists: development, immediate causation, evolution, and adaptive significance. Finally, one type of behavior, copulatory behavior, will be viewed from each of these standpoints, in an attempt to illustrate the approach animal behaviorists take toward a comprehensive understanding of animal behavior.

Nonsocial Behavior

While there is considerable overlap and interaction between behavioral patterns that might be labeled "social" and "nonsocial," this dichotomy provides a convenient basis for discussing patterns of animal behavior. Included as primarily nonsocial behavioral patterns are locomotor patterns, activity cycles, sleep, shelter-seeking, orientation, ingestive behavior, thermoregulation, elimination, maintenance behavior, exploratory behavior, play, and tool use.

Each species has a characteristic set of patterns of *locomotion.* Different species are adapted primarily for flying, burrowing, walking, or swimming, depending on the environment in which the species has evolved. While the patterns of flight of insects, bats, and birds involve quite different motor activities and control, all can be recognized as serving a similar function, that is, propulsion through air.

Most species display a characteristic *activity cycle,* usually based on a 24-hour day. Commonly, animals are diurnal (active during the day), nocturnal (active at night), or crepuscular (active at dawn, dusk, or both). The nocturnal habits of owls, many rodents, and cockroaches and the diurnal habits of most primates are highly reliable characteristics of the species in question.

Sleep represents an extreme of motor inactivity in diurnal activity rhythms. Accurate determination of sleeping patterns involves examination of behavior, electrical activity of the brain [as measured by the electroencephalograph (EEG)], muscle potentials, and eye movements. The three primary states that can be distinguished for virtually all mammalian species are illustrated in Figure 6-2. In the waking state, the animal is behaviorally active, showing normal muscle tension and eye movements. The EEG, taken from cerebral cortex, shows low voltage, fast activity. In the first major sleep stage, so-called *slow wave sleep,* there is a loss of both muscle tension and eye movement. The EEG record becomes "synchronized" with higher voltage, slower activity. The final state of

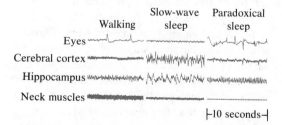

Fig. 6-2. Electrical recordings from a cat during waking, slow wave sleep, and paradoxical sleep. From T. Allison and H. Van Twyver, "The Evolution of Sleep," *Natural History,* 1970, 79(2), 56–65.

sleep is one with renewed eye movement associated with reduced muscle tone. The EEG again shows the "desynchronized" pattern of low voltage and rapid activity. This final state is known as either *Rapid Eye Movement,* or REM, sleep, because of the concurrent eye movements, or *"paradoxical" sleep,* because of the waking-like activity of the brain at a time when the animal is behaviorally quiescent and difficult to arouse. Paradoxical sleep in humans appears generally associated with dreaming. Animals fluctuate between slow wave and paradoxical sleep in orderly patterns throughout their sleep periods, which will be discussed further in Chapter 13.

Many species seek or construct some form of *shelter*. For some species, as for many birds and fish, a nest may be built as a temporary structure used only for a single breeding season. Chimpanzees construct new sleeping nests each night. For other species, such as beavers and many burrow-dwelling species, the next may provide a home for a considerable period of time well beyond the breeding season.

Ingestive behavior includes eating, drinking, breathing, and associated activities. Diets vary greatly from species to species, with different species being primarily carnivorous, herbivorous, or omnivorous. Some species have a very restricted diet. Koala bears, for example, eat only eucalyptus leaves. Other species, like most rodents, are omnivorous, accepting a considerable range of diverse food. Within these general categories, there are many subdivisions. For example, among herbivores, there are grass eaters, seed eaters, fruit eaters, and grazing and browsing species.

The elaborate motor patterns involved in *predation* have been a favorite topic in ethological studies. Many species *hoard* food, gathering it in times of plenty and eating it in times of need. Classical ethologists emphasized studies of the hoarding behavior of many species in their natural habitats, while animal psychologists have emphasized the effects of physiological and environmental manipulation on the hoarding behavior of white rats.

Ethologists have been interested in the motor patterns used by different species when they drink, while psychologists and physiologists have emphasized studies of the physiological bases of thirst. Breathing is often taken for granted but can be crit-

ical in some species. Dolphins, which live in water but breathe air, must surface periodically in order to breathe.

As most species can live effectively only within a relatively narrow temperature range, *thermoregulation* is critical to survival. Much shelter-seeking behavior and many diurnal activity cycles represent adaptations which permit animals to avoid those parts of their environments that reach intolerable temperatures during part of the day. In the laboratory, fish and rats can be trained to emit an arbitrarily-selected response, such as a bar press, when the consequence is a temperature change.

One might think that patterns of *elimination,* that is, urination and defecation, would be of little interest to the animal behaviorist. However, such patterns provide the basis of several interesting analyses. For example, there is a decided difference in defecation patterns correlated with nest usage. Species that build permanent nests generally avoid contaminating them by leaving the nest in order to urinate and defecate, while wandering species, such as many primates, generally eliminate wherever they happen to be. Elimination patterns are sexually dimorphic (differ between male and female) in some species such as dogs, and provide research material for the study of the development of sex differences. Some psychologists regard the amount of defecation in an unstructured environment, the open field, as an index of "emotionality" in rats. Urine and feces are a rich source of *pheromones,* chemicals which function in communication between individuals of a species. Such eliminative products may be used to mark a territory or to provide information as to the estrous state of a female. Young rats may orient toward their mothers or learn which foods to eat as a result of cues contained in their mothers' feces.

Many behavioral patterns function in the general *maintenance* of the organism, especially for care of the fur or skin. A variety of grooming, scratching, bathing, and sand bathing patterns function in this way.

Exploration of the environment and of objects in the environment is an important activity for many species, especially among the young. Many complex vertebrates are attracted to novel objects and will devote much time to their exploration, although such attraction may be preceded by a "neo-phobia," (the fear of new and strange places). Exploration provides the animal with knowledge of its environment. Thorough knowledge of the environment is important in revealing the location of resources and of protected sites that can be used in times of danger.

Play is difficult to define. It generally entails the reordering, exaggeration, and repetition of normal behavioral sequences, often in contexts that do not provide the normal setting for such behavior. Like exploration, play is especially characteristic of young organisms and can be highly social.

Orientation is easily overlooked. Almost all species have sensory mechanisms which keep them oriented in their environment and enable them to tell "which way is up." The topic of orientation also includes the manner in which animals find their way about the environment. The orienting mechanisms of simple invertebrates have been the topic of much laboratory research and theoretical consideration. The analysis of orientation in migratory species, such as birds and sea turtles, has provided some of the most impressive feats and difficult puzzles in the study of animal behavior.

Tool using, defined as "the manipulation of an inanimate object, not internally manufactured, with the effect of improving the animal's efficiency in altering the position or form of some separate object" (Alcock, 1972), is common in many species. Sea otters use rocks to crack open eggs; archer fish propel water at insects, knocking them off vegetation and into the water; and, chimpanzees transform leaves into sponges which are useful in soaking up drinking water from inaccessible locations.

In this brief survey of "nonsocial" behavior, we have done little more than mention the various functional categories of behavior. At the least, such a catalog should provide an indication of the array of behavioral patterns that different species display and that are fair game for the animal behaviorist.

Social Behavior

Social Organization. To the casual observer, there may appear to be little order to the spacing and interactions of animals in the field. However, careful observation reveals that virtually all complex species display some form of social organization. The bee hive, fish school, wolf pack, monkey troop, and human community all represent different types of social organization. Organized societies can be characterized as having: (1) permanence of individual composition; (2) cohesion based on a social response toward conspecifics; (3) individual recognition; (4) complex systems of communication; and (5) a structured division of labor based on specialization.

The most common forms of social organization are based on *dominance* and *territoriality*. Dominance generally refers to the ability of one animal to take precedence over another with respect to access to resources, be that food, water, space, or even a sexual partner. Many species form stable dominance hierarchies in which all individuals of a group appear to recognize their status relative to that of each other member of the group. Typically, overt fighting is limited to brief periods when there is an alteration in the hierarchy. Orderly, simple dominance hierarchies can be found in small flocks of chickens. Each animal has a position in a simple linear order of rank. Dominance is expressed through delivery of a peck to the subordinate animal. The term "pecking order," is derived from observations on fowl. More complicated dominance hierarchies, in which alliances between animals may increase the effectiveness of certain individuals, can be found among primates and carnivores.

There are many forms of animal territoriality. Most have in common an active defense of a specific area against conspecifics. In some cases, territories may be defended only against others of a given sex or age class. All seem characterized by a privileged access to resources that is space-dependent. Animal A may have privileged access to food when in his territory, but the relationship is reversed in the territory of Animal B. Many species are territorial for just part of their annual cycle. For example, Uganda kob, a species of antelope native to Africa, stake out limited territories in which the males collect harems solely for breeding. By contrast, many diurnal songbirds stake out relatively large territories within which they nest and feed. Most marine birds have small territories that extend only a short way beyond the nest. Such species must travel over substantial distances in order to feed. The mode of social organization is but one part of the total adaptation of the species to its environment and must evolve in conjunction with patterns of feeding, activity, and so on.

Reproductive Behavior, Agonistic Behavior, and Communication. There are many different kinds of social behavior. Particular attention has been devoted to the study of reproductive behavior, agonistic behavior, and communication. *Reproductive behavior* includes a complete cycle, often beginning with a seasonal onset of reproductive activity and continuing through the processes of mate location and selection, courtship, copulation, and, in many species, pregnancy and parental behavior. Patterns of courtship and copulation can be quite intricate and have provided a favored subject for ethological analyses. The nature and extent of parental behavior can range from prolonged care by both parents to very minimal provisioning by one partner.

Patterns of *agonistic behavior* are those which function in situations of conflict between members of a species. Agonistic behaviors are divided into two categories: approach, such as threat gestures and overt fighting; and withdrawal, such as fleeing. In the early ethological literature, it was often assumed that there was a unitary aggressive drive which was responsible for all of the aggressive behavior of an individual. However, Moyer (1968), a physiological psychologist, has argued that there may be many forms of aggression, each with its own environmental determinants, motivational characteristics, and physiological bases. Moyer's initial list included predatory, intermale, fear-induced, irritable, territorial defense, maternal, instrumental, and sex-related aggression. While such a formulation is complex, it may provide a more realistic view of the nature of the diverse collection of behaviors that tend to be lumped together under the label of "aggression" in simpler formulations.

In a sense, communication is virtually equivalent to social behavior, as there can be no social behavior without communication and virtually all communication is social. There are many spectacular examples of animal communication. When foraging honeybees return to the hive, they engage in a complex dance. Karl von Frisch received the Nobel prize for his research that indicates that, at least under some circumstances, new foragers are recruited by the dance and determine the direction and distance to the food source from it. Recent research has indicated that communication of the location of feeding sites may be even more complex than that proposed by von Frisch. The songs of birds and calls of frogs, which are familiar to most of us, often function in repelling conspecific males and attracting females. Some signals are quite prolonged and powerful. The songs of humpback whales can last up to thirty minutes before the unit is repeated and, under favorable conditions, may be transmitted over many miles.

Virtually any sensory channel can be used in communication. We have already mentioned chemical communication via pheromones and auditory communication as in birdsong. Communication via the tactile and visual modalities is also quite common. The exact modality favored by different species is a function of habitat and lifestyle. Visual signals are ineffective over long distances for species that live in dense forests; chemicals are more effective than sounds if the signal must persist, as is the case with trails that lead ants to food. Many signals are composites of different modalities and contain considerable redundancy.

Animal Social Psychology. Much of the research on animal social behavior that has been conducted by psychologists has been done in the laboratory. Animal social psychologists have been interested in the modes of interaction between animals when tested under carefully controlled conditions. Typical studies have dealt with social facilitation, imitation, competition, and cooperation. The phenomenon of *social facilitation* refers to the fact that many behaviors are performed more readily or at a higher rate when an animal is in the presence of a conspecific, than when it is in isolation. Rats, chicks, and dogs will eat more, rats will copulate faster, and humans will turn a fishing reel more rapidly in the presence of a conspecific than when alone. A variety of species, including rats and rhesus monkeys, have been shown to learn by observing conspecifics; they *imitate*. Competitive situations can facilitate performance in some situations. Studies of cooperation have been particularly successful. It is an easy task for a monkey to learn to press a bar on signal to avoid shock. It is more difficult when two monkeys must cooperate; one animal sees the signal and the other must press the lever. Such tasks have been mastered by rhesus monkeys even when the only communication between them lies in the facial expression transmitted over a closed-circuit television screen (Miller, 1967).

Development of Behavior

Having surveyed descriptive material relating to the kinds of behaviors that animals display, we are now ready to consider the four classes of questions with which animal behaviorists deal: development, immediate causation, evolution, and adaptive significance. We shall begin with the development of behavior.

Nature-Nurture and the Problem of Instinct

The development of any individual organism represents the joint product of the interaction of genes with the environment. If an organism lacks either a viable set of genes or a benign environment, it will be unable to sustain life. The interactions of genes and environment are so complex and so intricately entwined that it is unlikely that any characteristic of an organism, be it behavioral or structural, can be said to be totally dependent on either the genes or the environment. Despite the thousands of pages that have been written in attempts to answer questions such as "Is this behavior learned or innate?" or "Is this behavior due to nature or nurture?," it is apparent that no behavior is exclusively dependent on one or the other.

While all behaviors appear to be a product of gene-environment interaction, the relative contribution of the two factors varies greatly. As a result, different behavioral patterns may appear either highly plastic (that is, vary greatly as a function of variations in the environment in which an animal is reared) or well buffered from environ-

mental effects (that is, develop along very similar lines even in very different environments). This contrast is well illustrated with examples relating to the development of song patterns in birds. European blackbirds and ring doves have been reported to sing their normal, species-typical song even when reared in total isolation from either other birds or the sounds of other birds. By contrast, the songs of chaffinches which are reared in isolation are quite distorted when compared with the songs of animals given the opportunity to learn from conspecifics. Thus, the development of birdsong in the European blackbird is well buffered from environmental variation, while that of the chaffinch is quite plastic.

If one could obtain a distribution of behaviors quantified with respect to the relative contribution of genes and environment, the resulting distribution would be continuous; that is, rather than finding just two categories of behavior (for example, learned and innate), one would find a multitude of gradations with respect to the relative role of genes and environment. Many individuals prefer to label behaviors that would fall at one end of the continuum as "learned" and those at the other end as "instinctive" or "innate." There seems little harm in this, so long as one recognizes that there may be important genetic and environmental influences on both kinds of behavior. The bird that is reared in isolation has many opportunities to learn, despite the lack of conspecifics. The ability to learn in and of itself must have a genetic basis. This complicated state of affairs led one animal behaviorist (Hailman, 1969) to choose as a title for one of his papers, "How an Instinct is Learned."

Rather than engaging in endless debates of the nature-nurture problem and fruitless attempts to classify behavior as learned or innate, most contemporary animal behaviorists choose to study the ways in which both genes and environment act to influence behavior.

Genetic Influences on Behavior

There is much evidence to support the view that genes are one important influence on the development of behavior. Genetic influences are most clearly seen where a single gene has primary influence and where a trait is discontinuously distributed (that is, where individuals fall into clearly defined classes that do not overlap). The ability of humans to taste a chemical called phenylthiocarbamide (PTC) is such a trait. Although PTC tastes quite bitter to some people, others taste nothing at all. The ability to taste PTC appears inherited according to expected Mendelian ratios. The inheritance of audiogenic seizure proneness in mice appears to have a similar basis. When exposed to a loud bell, the mice of some strains go into a seizure pattern, whereas those of other strains show no such response. A single gene seems critical to the development of the tendency to show convulsions on first exposure to a loud bell. In both of these examples, there are known or presumed environmental influences on the behavior as well as known effects of other minor genes. However, the major influence of the single gene is clear.

Unfortunately, most behaviors in which psychologists are interested are continuously distributed and appear to be influenced by many genes, each having a relatively small influence. This has forced behavior geneticists to use more complicated and sophisticated techniques in teasing out the ways in which genes influence behavior. Different approaches include studies of specially inbred and selected strains and the application of complex mathematical models to the results of experiments in which animals of differing genotypes are bred according to particular patterns. The results reveal an array of differing forms of influence and interaction of genes and the environment.

A particularly clear example of the ways in which genes influence animal behavior can be seen in the work of Dilger (1962) on lovebirds of the genus *Agapornis*. These birds cut strips of nesting material, such as leaves or paper, before carrying them to their nest site. The peach-faced lovebird (*A. roseicollis*) normally tucks strips into its rump feathers in order to carry them to the nest. Fischer's lovebird (*A. personata fischeri*) carries nesting material in the bill. Dilger crossbred the two species to see what the hybrids would do. They acted confused. Hybrids showed movements appropriate to both tucking strips under their feathers and to carrying them in their bills. They were unable to use either method consistently for effective transportation of nesting materials. With practice, the hybrids eventually came to carry nest strips in their bills and to build appropriate nests. However, signs of abortive tucking movements were still evident after two years of practice of carrying nesting material.

Ontogeny of Behavior

Sensitive Periods.   As it matures, the young organism is continuously exposed to a myriad of environmental stimuli. However, the responsivity of the organism to particular stimuli changes as it develops. Thus, there are *sensitive periods,* times at which stimuli are maximally effective in producing long-term developmental changes in behavior, as well as periods of comparative insensitivity.

The best known example of a sensitive period phenomenon is that of *imprinting*. It is well known that newly hatched fowl tend to follow the first moving object that they encounter. If the stimulus is appropriate and the animal is of the appropriate developmental stage, the animal may come to follow that stimulus in preference to any other; it has become imprinted to the stimulus. In nature, the first moving object encountered is usually the mother. Thus, the following response is directed at the mother and normal development ensues. However, animal behaviorists have succeeded in imprinting young fowl to a bewildering array of objects: green cubes, red balls, models of female and male ducks, and indeed, even to the experimenters themselves. While it is true that imprinting can be achieved with a great array of different objects, those objects vary in effectiveness. There appear to be perceptual preferences, as, for example, for relatively complex stimuli, which are independent of specific learning.

The sensitive period for imprinting in ducklings reaches a peak during the first day posthatching, typically at about thirteen to sixteen hours. The reasons for this maximal sensitivity are not entirely clear, although reasonable hypotheses are available. Before this age, the abilities of young ducklings to walk are not sufficiently developed to permit effective following. After this period, ducklings often react to novel objects with fear responses that interfere with imprinting.

Many psychologists have become interested in the imprinting phenomenon, as they think that they see certain parallels between avian imprinting and pervasive effects of early experience in other species, particularly humans. Implicit in such thinking is the view that imprinting in birds is a relatively simple and well understood phenomenon. Nothing could be further from the truth. New complexities of the imprinting processes are being revealed on a regular basis. It is now apparent that young birds have a preference for the maternal call of their own species and that this preference appears in birds that have never heard the call. In some situations, the preference for species-typical maternal calls can override effects of visual imprinting. As mother and young appear to carry on a dialogue around the time of hatching, including the prehatch period, it is likely that these auditory preferences play an important role in the identification of the parent in the natural habitat.

A major reason for the interest of psychologists in imprinting is the belief that its effects are irreversible and persist into adulthood, so that a duck that was imprinted on a red ball would attempt to mate with a red ball in preference to a normal conspecific. However, there is little evidence to support this belief. The limited imprinting experience that characterizes most laboratory research appears not to produce long-lasting, irreversible effects. Pervasive lifelong alterations in mate preference appear to require much more prolonged contact and may even be the result of the operation of a second, entirely different sensitive period (Hinde, 1970). Indeed, it now appears that "sexual" imprinting may be a totally different phenomenon from "filial" imprinting (Dewsbury, 1978).

"Imprinting" and the general problem of identification of the mother in precocious birds is a fascinating problem in the overall study of animal behavior. However, it represents a very complex and poorly understood process and should not be used as a model for the complex and poorly understood processes that occur in humans and from which it appears to differ substantially.

The study of sensitive periods in mammals has also received much attention. A vast array of effects have been demonstrated. Young rats and mice have been handled, removed from their mother, shocked, cooled, or shaken during the first ten days or so of life. Persistent effects of such manipulations, often seemingly beneficial, are usually detected when, as adults, treated animals are compared to untreated controls. The stimulated animals have often been shown to be more active and to defecate less when tested in an open field, to show more appropriate patterns of adrenal steroid secretion in response to stress, and even to learn more rapidly than controls.

In another series of experiments, the brains and behavior of rats and mice reared after weaning in complex and impoverished environments have been compared. Typically, one group is raised in isolation in bare wire cages, while the other group is reared in a complex environment with many toys on which to climb and with other animals with which to play. Reliable differences have been found in the weights of either whole brains or of specific parts of brains, in the concentrations of enzymes associated with neural transmission, and in various other measures of the anatomy and physiology of the brains of such animals. These alterations in brain anatomy and biochemistry are probably of great behavioral importance.

It should be clear that the experiences encountered by young organisms, particularly during sensitive periods, can be of pervasive influence on adult life. However, these processes are very complex, even in nonhuman animals, and great care is needed in generalizing from one species to another.

Changes in Behavior as a Function of Age. An alternative approach to the study of effects of specific experiences occurring during sensitive periods is to study the normal course of behavioral development in young organisms. Just as human infants show a normal ontogenetic progression through crawling, walking, talking, and so on, the development of behavior in nonhuman subjects follows orderly progressions. The most characteristic activity of the newborns of many species is sleep. Newborns not only sleep more than adults, but they spend a higher proportion of their sleep time in paradoxical sleep. Given the high percentage of time that infants spend in paradoxical sleep, together with the existence of paradoxical sleep in the fetus, one is left with the fascinating question of the phenomenology of such activity. Do the fetus and the newborn experience dreams and, if so, what might be the content of those dreams?

The ability to learn also changes with age, with young organisms generally being less efficient in learning and remembering than adults. This creates a certain paradox in that young organisms are poor learners, but experiences encountered early in life have particularly pervasive and long-lasting effects on the organism. How are such experiences remembered? One suggestion is that a process of *reinstatement* maintains the memory of important early experiences. Reinstatement refers to "a small amount of partial practice or repetition of an experience over the developmental period which is enough to maintain an early learned response at a high level, but is not enough to produce any effect in animals which have not had the early experience" (Campbell and Jaynes, 1966). In a manner very much like the prolonged experience which influences mate selection in birds, repeated experiences encountered through reinstatement may maintain effects of experiences that otherwise would have been forgotten by young organisms.

Developmental changes in feeding patterns, orienting abilities, sexual behavior, agonistic behavior, and a host of other behaviors have revealed orderly developmental patterns.

Immediate Causation

In moving from questions of behavioral development to those of immediate causation, we shift time scales from those dealing with the long-term development of organisms to processes immediately preceding and concurrent with the behavior of interest. The material within this area can be divided into that related to environmental influences, to internal factors, and to their integration.

Environmental Factors

Effects of Environmental Factors. Events in the environment affect behavior in many ways, some of which are relatively simple whereas others are quite complex. Ethologists have found that many of the

responses that they have studied are triggered by *sign stimuli*, relatively simple objects in the environment. Territorial defense by European robins is normally triggered in response to the presence of a rival male in the territory of another male. Ethologists have constructed a number of "models" in attempting to determine which aspects of the conspecific are critical. They have found that the intruding object can look very little like a robin as long as it has a red "breast"—a bunch of red feathers will do. A very accurate model of a robin which lacks a red breast is relatively ineffective in eliciting territorial defense.

A favorite subject of ethological research has been a small freshwater fish, the stickleback. Sticklebacks become territorial during the breeding season, at which time the male's belly turns red. Ethologists have found that the presence of objects with a red belly in a male's territory elicits territorial defense. As with the European robin, models

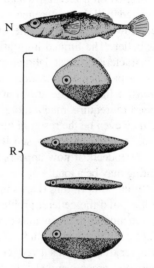

Fig. 6-3. Models constructed by ethologists to study sign stimuli releasing attack behavior in sticklebacks. Model N resembles a stickleback, but lacks a red belly, and is relatively ineffective in releasing attack. Group R models do not closely resemble sticklebacks, but have red undersides, and were relatively effective in releasing attack behavior. From C. N. Tinbergen, *The Study of Instinct*, (Oxford: Oxford University Press), 1951.

which look very much like a stickleback but which lack the red belly are comparatively ineffective. However, a variety of objects having red undersides are effective (see Fig. 6-3). If the base of the model is swollen rather than red, a configuration that resembles a female ripe with eggs, courtship behavior is released.

Many environmental determinants of behavior appear much more complex than sign stimuli. The many manipulations utilized by students of learned behavior fall within this category. These manipulations include a variety of environmental changes and center about schedules of reinforcement—programs that determine when the responses that an animal makes are rewarded and when they are not. Although the effects of schedules of reinforcement on behavior appear quite similar across the range of species studied thus far, this represents a rather small sample of available species and further research is needed. For example, there are already indications that the reinforcement processes of fish may differ from those of most mammals (Bitterman, 1975).

Sensation and Perception. Environmental factors have their influences on behavior as a result of changes in the organism that are initiated through stimulation of sensory-perceptual processes (see Chapter 5). It is important to remember that each species is equipped with its own sensory apparatus and hence has its own phenomenal world, or *Umwelt.* Animal behaviorists have often erred because of their failure to recognize the degree to which the sensory worlds of nonhuman species differ from their own. Many species can hear sounds of much higher pitch than we can. If we try to study behavior in these species without devices permitting us to detect such sounds, we may miss important aspects of animal behavior solely because of our own sensory limitations. Bees can respond to the polarization of light and can see "colors" in the ultraviolet part of the spectrum. A variety of species of fish possess electrical sensory systems whereby they actively generate electrical currents from electric organs and are able to detect the presence of objects in the water as a result of the effects of such objects on the resulting electrical field. Bats have an analogous echolocation system, in

which high frequency sounds are emitted and objects are detected as a result of their reflections of these sound waves. Investigators must be prepared to encounter a range of sensory-perceptual responsivities which differ substantially from their own.

The processing of sensory information differs greatly among different species. The octopus provides good examples of the difficulty of understanding species-specific patterns in the processing of sensory information. Although the octopus is quite good at detecting irregularities in the surface of objects, such as grooves on the surface of a cylinder, it is unable to determine the direction of these irregularities or grooves. Although the octopus is able to respond to differences in the weights of different objects, as in compensating for different weights when lifting them, it is unable to use this information to learn to select one or the other of two objects differing only in weight. It seems odd to us as humans that an animal should be able to use such information in one context but not in another. Yet, patterns of the processing of sensory information may be as characteristic of a species as are the batteries of sensory receptors themselves.

Internal Factors

The immediate determinants of behavior include both external or environmental factors, and internal or physiological factors. Among the most spectacular examples of regulation of behavior by internal factors are *biological clocks.* The daily diurnal rhythms (called *circadian rhythms* because they last "about a day") of many species appear internally or "endogenously" controlled. Thus, a flying squirrel kept under conditions of constant light or constant darkness will continue to show alternating periods of activity and inactivity in a pattern very close to the 24-hour cycle the squirrel shows in a more normal environment. A variety of experimental controls have virtually eliminated any possibility that uncontrolled external factors are providing a time cue.

Neural Determinants. Physiological psychologists and neuroethologists are engaged in extensive programs in which they are attempting to relate overt behavior to the physiological processes with which they are correlated (see Chapter 4). By employing techniques such as electrical stimulation of the brain, electrical recording of neural activity, chemical stimulation of the brain, and destruction of particular parts of the brain, these researchers are making rapid strides in this endeavor. For example, the neural bases of several of the forms of aggressive behavior are under investigation. The lateral hypothalamus, a structure implicated in feeding behavior, is also involved in predatory aggression. The ventromedial hypothalamus seems particularly important in the control of irritable aggression. Fear-induced, irritable, and predatory aggression may each be influenced by activity in different parts of the amygdala, a structure in the forebrain (Moyer, 1968).

Hormonal Determinants. Hormones are also important regulators of behavior. Adrenal hormones, for example, play important roles in stress responses; in adaptive behaviors, including learning; in metabolic function; and ultimately in food preferences. The sex hormones are important in the regulation and timing not only of sexual behavior but of parental behavior and aggression. Intermale aggression is highly dependent on the presence of sex hormones; castration produces a marked reduction in intermale aggression in a wide range of species.

The familiar Mongolian gerbil provides an interesting example of hormone-behavior relationships. Gerbils have a prominent sebaceous gland on the underside of the body. This gland secretes a scented substance, a pheromone, that is used in scent marking of the environment. Gerbils have a stereotyped pattern in which they lower their abdomens and drag them across prominent small objects in the environment, thus depositing pheromone and "marking" the objects. Both the size of the scent gland and the behavioral pattern itself are under the control of androgens, male sex hormones. Castration results in a marked reduction in both the size of the gland and the frequency of the marking response; replacement therapy with androgen injections will result in a restoration of both (Thiessen, 1973).

Integration

We have discussed the effects of various kinds of external and internal determinants of behavior in isolation, because it is with such stepwise treatment that each kind of effect is most clearly understood. In fact, all of these influences interact to produce integrated patterns of behavior. External stimuli trigger behavioral and physiological responses, which may in turn alter behavior, the environment, the behavior of conspecifics, and other aspects of the internal milieu. A comprehensive understanding of any complex behavioral pattern requires some appreciation of the ways in which these different factors influence each other and produce orderly, biologically appropriate, sequences of responses. A summary of known influences on the reproductive behavior of canaries is illustrated in Figure 6-4. The stimulative and inhibitory interactions among stimuli, hormones, and neurally based responses result in the normal reproductive cycle.

Evolution of Behavior

Questions relating to the evolution and adaptive significance of behavior deal with time spans much longer than the order of lives of individual organisms—on the order of millions of years and many, many generations of animals.

Evolutionary Processes

After almost a century of debate regarding evolutionary processes, there is now widespread agreement among biologists with respect to the fundamental soundness of the so-called modern synthetic theory of evolution. Evolutionary processes work by taking genetic variability and shaping it to meet environmental demands. Within any population made up of animals not derived from the same germ plasm, there is variability in the complement of genes possessed by different individuals. This genetic variability contributes to the structural and behavioral variability of the population. It is the forces of natural selection that work

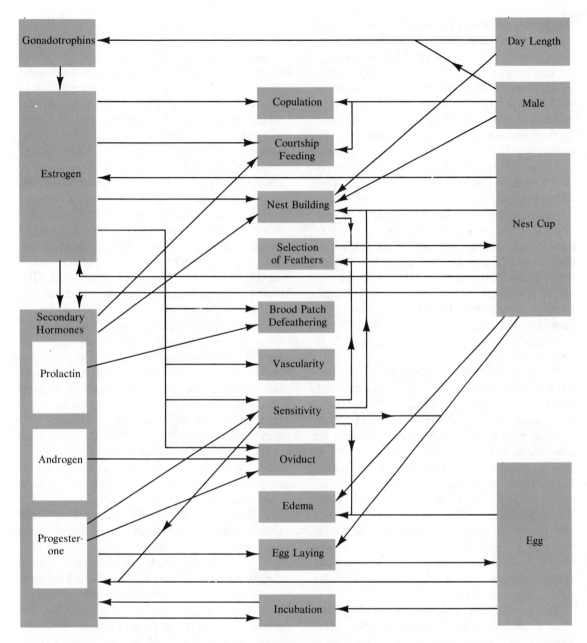

Fig. 6-4. Interaction of factors in the control of the reproductive cycles of canaries. From "Interaction of Internal and External Factors in Integration of Canary Reproduction." In F. A. Beach (ed.), *Sex and Behavior* (New York: John Wiley), 1965.

with genetic variability and shape the genetic, and thus, structural and behavioral nature of the population. Some animals are more *fit* than others; they are better able to survive and to produce viable, fertile offspring. Increased fitness can come about in a variety of ways. An individual may be better at avoiding predators, at finding food, or in reproducing than others in the population. In extreme cases, an individual's fitness may be increased by sacrificing its own life in order to save a number of close relatives. The representation of genes possessed by such an animal in the "gene pool" of the next generation may actually be increased by such an act. Over generations of the action of forces of natural selection, the gene pool of the population changes and the animals in the population become better adapted to the environment in which they are evolving. Random processes have created variability; natural selection has shaped that variability by permitting the more fit animals to make a disproportionately large contribution to the gene pools of successive generations.

The actions of natural selection can be mimicked in the laboratory. In a typical experiment, two groups of fruit flies, which are recognizable but capable of interbreeding, are permitted to breed at random. The experimenter removes the offspring of hybrid matings. Over the course of several generations of such artificial selection, fewer hybrids are produced. The courtship patterns and responses of the two groups are altered, so that the likelihood of crossbreeding is reduced. Selection against crossbreeding, accomplished by removing the offspring of such matings, can create a change in courtship behavior which reduces the chances of hybrid matings, thus increasing fitness under these conditions.

The gradual accumulation of small genetic changes, usually in association with geographical isolation, can produce differences so great as to result in speciation, the creation of species. One large group of animals may have become separated into two isolated groups, and each group then adapts to its own habitat. If the two groups encounter each other after many generations of such adaptation in isolation, it will be unlikely that the animals will interbreed.

Animal Species

A *species* may be defined as a group of individuals that are capable of breeding among themselves under natural conditions but are reproductively isolated from other groups. Thus, species are defined in terms of their breeding patterns in the natural habitat. As the result of the reproductive isolation from other groups, members of one species come to look different from members of other species. It is through such differences that we normally identify members as belonging to one species or another. "Keys" are available which permit us to take an unknown specimen, consider certain of its characteristics, often bones and teeth, and classify it appropriately as belonging to one or another species. As a result primarily of contributions by the ethologists, it is now recognized that behavioral characteristics can be as reliable as guides to the correct identification of species as are many structural attributes. Indeed, the classification of several species has been revised on the basis of behavioral data (Mayr, 1963). Some species of fireflies cannot be distinguished on the basis of any known structural differences but have different flash patterns and do not interbreed in nature. Hence, they are "good" species.

Each species has a two-word Latin name (for example, *Rattus norvegicus*), and all species are arranged in a hierarchical taxonomic system. As one goes from species to progressively broader classifications—genus, family, order, class, and phylum—the number of animals included in the category (or taxon) increases.

The appropriate means for representing evolutionary history is as a tree, not as a unidimensional, progressive evolutionary chain (see Figure 6-5). Many species evolved but later became extinct, and hence are no longer available for study. When we consider living species, we are looking only at the most recent evolutionary endpoints, the newest twigs on a vast tree. While it is virtually certain that there were fishes and amphibians in the evolutionary lineage leading to mammals, such animals were quite different from the goldfish and frogs common today. Although we may have had a monkey-like creature as a relatively recent ances-

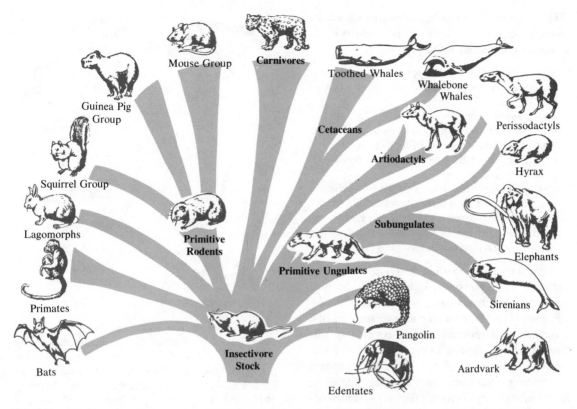

Fig. 6-5. A schematic representation of the evolution of placental mammals. From *A Shorter Version of the Second Edition of The Vertebrate Body* (Philadelphia: W. B. Saunders), 1956.

tor, that creature may have looked very little like those swinging from trees in the jungles today.

If we are to understand evolutionary history, it is necessary that we make inferences about many species including those that are extinct. This is a difficult but important undertaking.

Studies of the Evolution of Behavior

Studies of the evolution of behavior can be divided into those conducted at the species level and those at the phyletic level. In studies at the species level, one works with a relatively small group of closely related species, usually in an attempt to determine the probable course of evolution of discrete mea-surable behavioral patterns. At the phyletic level, one works with a much wider range of species in an attempt to understand the broad sweep of evolutionary history.

Studies at the Species Level. Ethologists have stressed studies of the evolution of behavior at the species level, primarily through studies of the displays that different species show in courtship and agonistic interactions. Typically, ethologists work with a group of species so similar to each other as to be classed in a single genus. By using widely accepted taxonomic relationships based primarily on structure, inferences can be made about behavioral evolution.

The origins of the display movements studied in ethology can often be traced to one of three kinds of sources (Hinde and Tinbergen, 1958):

1. *Intention movements*—incomplete or preparatory movements that occur at the beginning of a behavioral sequence.
2. *Displacement activities*—seemingly "out-of-context" behaviors displayed by animals in situations of conflict (for example, a bird in conflict over whether to fight or flee might suddenly preen its feathers or peck at the ground).
3. *Redirected activities*—when direction of a behavior at the object eliciting it is somehow blocked, the behavior may be directed elsewhere (for example, aggressive behavior may be redirected from a dominant animal to a less dominant, innocent bystander).

As such relatively variable behaviors evolve into courtship or aggressive displays, they become quite rigid and stereotyped, or "ritualized." Certain components may become exaggerated, and the coordination of movements may become so different that it is difficult to recognize the original behavior. The motivational bases also change. Conspicuous structures, such as wing patches or areas of brightly colored feathers, sometimes evolve along with the behavior, making the display even more dramatic.

Examples of ritualized behaviors can be seen in the displays of the green heron (see Figure 6-6). The "snap display" signals a readiness of the male to accept female courtship, but evolved from a displacement pattern of twig gathering. The "stretch display" was derived from intention flight behavior, but now signals that the male is motivated to pair bond (Alcock, 1975 and Meyerriecks, 1960). In both cases, ethologists have been able to trace the evolutionary origins of elaborate displays according to the principles just outlined. Similar evolutionary histories have been determined for a variety of behaviors in different species.

It is in comparisons using closely related species and clearly defined behavioral patterns that demonstrations of the evolution of behavior become most convincing.

Studies at the Phyletic Level. Psychologists often have been more interested in the broad sweep of the evolution of behavior than in study at the

Fig. 6-6. Four display patterns of the green heron: A, the aggressive full-forward display; B, the snap display of courting males; C, the stretch display; D, the flap-flight display. From *Animal Behavior—An Evolutionary Approach* (Sunderland, Mass.: Sinauer), 1975 and A. J. Meyerriecks, "Comparative breeding of four species of North American herons," Nuttall Ornithological Publications, 1960, 2, 1–158.

species level. They have sacrificed some of the precision of studies at the species level in an attempt to gain greater generality. By studying the behavior of interest in a variety of diverse species, they have attempted to delineate the broad course of evolutionary history.

For example, Allison and Van Twyver (1970) studied sleep in a wide range of species. There is little systematic evidence of sleep in fishes, amphibians, and reptiles. All species of birds that have been studied show both slow wave sleep and paradoxical sleep. Most mammalian species also display both patterns. The sole exception is the spiny anteater, an egg-laying mammal native to Australia. Allison and Van Twyver proposed that sleep evolved independently in birds and mammals and that, in the mammalian line, slow wave sleep evolved first. They believe that the egg-laying mammals and the more common "therian" species had common ancestors among the first true mammals. Slow wave sleep may have evolved in those ancestors, whereas paradoxical sleep evolved at a later time and only in the therian line of descent.

The dominant interest of comparative psychologists studying the evolution of behavior has been in the evolution of learning abilities. Often implicit in this undertaking is a belief that species differ in a measurable ability referred to as "intelligence." With estimates of the "intelligence" of different species, we should be able to order species along a single scale from the smartest to the dullest of creatures.

Attempts to produce such a hierarchy have generally been unsuccessful. There are few orderly species differences to be found when performance on relatively simple tasks (for example, classical conditioning, avoidance learning, and so on) is considered. Species A may outshine Species B at learning in one context, while Species B may excel in another.

Their lack of success with simple problems has led comparative psychologists to study more complex problems. A favorite task has been that of "learning sets," or "learning to learn." An animal is presented with a choice between two "junk" objects, such as a fountain pen and a spoon. If it selects the one designated by the experimenter as correct, it gets rewarded; there usually is no reward if the animal chooses incorrectly. After a number of trials on this problem, the animal is presented with a second problem in which it must learn to discriminate between two new objects. As it is faced with additional problems, the animal may improve in solving them; that is, it learns to learn. When performance levels are at their peak, the animal may err only on the first trial of a problem, and then only half of the time. Once that animal can determine which response is correct for a given problem, it may make no further errors. The performances of a number of mammalian species on learning set problems are compared in Figure 6-7. The data show a reasonable ordering of species with the highly evolved old-world primate, rhesus monkeys, learning best, while the rodent species are much slower.

There are a number of problems inherent in the learning set data and method. Recent comparisons

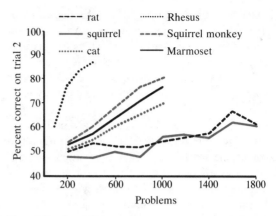

Fig. 6-7. Learning set formation in six species of mammals. From "Primate Learning in Comparative Perspective: by J. M. Warren. In A. M. Schrier, H. F. Harlow, and F. Stollnitz (eds.), *Behavior of Nonhuman Primates: Modern Research Trends* (New York: Academic Press), 1965.

have suggested that the learning set method, with its traditional reliance on differently-colored junk objects, has been differentially biased in favor of highly visual species, such as primates. Birds have been shown to perform much better in learning set situations than one would expect on the basis of their "bird brains." This may be because they are highly visual animals. When rats are given learning set problems based on smell rather than on vision, they score about as well as primates do on visual learning sets. Thus, while the learning set methodology and other similar methods may produce systematic orderings of species, they appear biased for and against certain species and may not really reflect the evolution of "intelligence" (see Warren, 1973).

As sensory demands, motivational levels, and so on, can never be equated across species, an alternative approach is to vary them systematically for each species. The hope is that there will be meaningful qualitative species differences in learning rather than the quantitative differences of the sort discussed above. Somes successes have been achieved with this method. For example, the conditions under which fish show improved performance following partial reinforcement of correct responses (that is, when they are rewarded for some but not all responses) and the responses of fish to changes in the amount of reward given in learning tasks seem to differ from the characteristic responses of many mammalian species (Bitterman, 1975). Despite these successes, we have a long way to go before any systematic "evolution of intelligence" can be written.

Comparisons of different species in learning tasks are quite difficult. Not only is it difficult to equate the sensory demands, motivational levels, and amounts of reward for different species, but different species appear to have evolved specific learning abilities appropriate for survival in their particular niche. Such specific abilities are difficult to encompass within the rubric of a general "intelligence." The utilization of animals from diverse species groups exaggerates not only the magnitude of the species differences of interest but also those which need to be controlled or equated. Despite these difficulties, such phyletic comparisons have such potential for producing conclusions of great generality that it appears likely that these attempts to generate meaningful phyletic comparisons will continue.

The Adaptedness of Behavior

The fourth and final set of questions asked by animal behaviorists concerns the adaptedness of behavior. Questions of adaptive significance are essentially evolutionary questions, and thus represent the other side of the coin discussed above under the heading of evolutionary history. As species evolve, they often become progressively better adapted to the environments in which they live. The behavioral patterns that they display are not random but are rather finely tuned to their particular habitat. It is these specific adaptations, appropriate to particular lifestyles in particular habitats, that form the subject matter for the study of adaptive significance. In studies of evolutionary history we attempt to uncover continuing patterns of evolution through phylogeny, but in the study of adaptive significance we study the specific adaptations of each species. Analogous adaptations may occur repeatedly in different groups of animals. Thus, insects, birds, and mammals all show certain similar

adaptations for flying, although each group has evolved flight independent of the other.

In studies of the adaptive significance of behavior, we are interested in "why" a particular behavioral pattern evolved, that is, how the behavior in question functions in the adaptation of the species to its environment. There is no indication that the animal comprehends these adaptive relationships. Rather, natural selection has shaped organisms which respond appropriately in particular situations.

There are three primary methods for the study of these ecological adaptations: the experimental method, the behavior-genetic method, and the method of adaptive correlation.

The Experimental Method

The most convincing evidence of the function of a behavioral pattern comes from studies using the experimental method. Generally, the experimenter gains some insight into the probable function of a behavioral pattern through systematic observations. The experimental method is used to confirm and extend such hunches. The method is quite simple. Where one believes that a given characteristic functions in a particular way, one conducts an experiment in which the characteristic is varied and measures the consequences. If the consequences appear deleterious (that is, that fitness would be reduced), one has relatively good evidence of the function of the characteristic in question.

In practice, the experimental method is often not applicable, and there are few really good studies using this method. Among the best studies are those of Tinbergen and his associates on eggshell removal in gulls (for example Tinbergen, 1963b). Soon after hatching, the gulls of most species remove the broken eggshells from recently hatched chicks and deposit them away from the nest. The Tinbergen group thought that this behavior might be an antipredator adaptation. The conspicuous white insides of the shells might make it easy for certain predators to locate the nest and thus prey upon its occupants. The experimenters constructed some nests near gull breeding sites and placed broken eggshells near some nests but not others.

As expected, those nests with conspicuous eggshells were preyed upon more frequently than those nests that lacked eggshells. The behavioral pattern of eggshell removal thus would appear to have evolved because birds showing such behavior had a greater chance of leaving viable, fertile offspring, in this case because of decreased risk of predation.

Many species of moths and butterflies have dark spots on their wings. These spots are hidden when the animal is at rest but are exposed when the wings are moved. The wing spots closely resemble the eyes of much large species. It was hypothesized that they may function in scaring off potential predators. Normal moths and moths from which the eyespots had been removed were placed in a large cage containing predatory birds. The displays of the moths with eyespots were more effective in avoiding predation than those of moths lacking their normal spots.

The Behavior-Genetic Method

A number of animal behaviorists have used behavior-genetic methods in an attempt to understand behavioral adaptation. The method rests on some fairly sophisticated theory derived from population genetics. While the theory is difficult, the resulting experiments are straightforward. One begins with several inbred strains of a given species. An inbred strain is a strain that has gone through at least twenty generations of brother-sister matings. The result is a group of animals that are almost as alike as identical twins; genetic variability is almost nonexistent. The many inbred strains of mice, first created for use in cancer research, have become popular subjects in behavior-genetic analyses. After measuring the behavior of interest in the inbred strains, one crossbreeds them to produce all possible hybrids among the different inbred strains. The behavior of the hybrids is then compared with that of the parents. If the behavior of the hybrids is not intermediate between the inbred strains, one has presumptive evidence for an adaptive function for the behavior.

For example, in a wide array of learning tasks, it has been found that the hybrids created from inbred strains are better learners than the inbred

animals. This is presumptive evidence that the ability to learn is adaptive.

Given the opportunity, mice will do a lot of running. Psychologists have built running wheels on which mice can run continuously, and psychologists are able to measure fully the amount of running. Typically, the hybrids run more than do their inbred parents. It would appear that the tendency to run in such circumstances has an adaptive correlate functioning under natural conditions.

The hybrids produced by crossing inbred strains of mice have bigger brains than inbred animals. This suggests that big brains may be adaptive. If one raises mice under conditions of environmental enrichment, one finds that hybrid mice show greater increases in brain weight as a result of environmental enrichment than do inbred mice. Thus, the ability to respond to environmental enrichment with increased brain weight may be adaptive (Henderson, 1970).

The Method of Adaptive Correlation

Although it may not produce the most precise information regarding behavioral adaptation, the method of adaptive correlation has been the most common method used. This is because it is relatively easy to apply. Generally, there is a "target" pattern in question as one wishes to understand the function of a particular behavior. One studies variations in both the target behavior as well as various other attributes (for example, structure, ecology, and other behavior) for a variety of species. If the behavioral pattern in question is generally associated with a particular kind of lifestyle or some other characteristic, one has evidence that the behavior is an adaptation associated with that lifestyle or other characteristic. For example, a number of adaptations have evolved among and only among species that live in aquatic environments or that fly. Such characteristics can be understood as adaptations for the aquatic environment or for flying. One advantage of such correlations is that they are testable. Once a correlation has been proposed, it can be tested by studying additional species. If the correlation continues to hold, one's confidence in the validity of the proposed correlation may be increased.

A classical usage of the method of adaptive correlation is that of Cullen (1957). Cullen was interested in the reproductive behavior of kittiwakes, a species of gull that is atypical in that it nests on cliffs. Most species of gulls nest on level ground. Cullen found thirty-two differences between the reproductive behavior of kittiwakes and other species. These differences appeared to be adaptations appropriate to cliff nesting. For example, kittiwakes build more elaborate nests than ground-nesting birds, presumably because of the dire consequences that would result if an egg should roll out of the nest. Subsequent studies have shown that other cliff-nesting species show adaptations similar to those of kittiwakes. This confirmation increases confidence in the conclusion that these reproductive patterns are indeed adaptations for cliff nesting.

In their comparative studies of sleep, Allison and Van Twyver found that some species are "good" sleepers (that is, they sleep readily, for long periods, and have much paradoxical sleep), while others are "poor" sleepers. Moles, ground squirrels, and cats are good sleepers, while rabbits, sheep, and donkeys are poor sleepers. Allison and Van Twyver suggested that sleep patterns are correlated with safety from predators. All of the good sleepers are species which either are predators themselves or which have relatively safe places to sleep. Poor sleepers lack such protection. Similar patterns can be seen in the ways in which animals explore objects. For example, small rodents, which face considerable danger from predation, are much less bold in exploring new objects than are large carnivores, which are relatively safe from predation in their natural habitats.

The sensory systems and brains of different species can be seen as adaptations for particular modes of living. In general, animals that are susceptible to predation have their eyes located at the sides of their heads. This permits them to scan wide portions of their environments without moving their heads. The price they pay is a loss of convergence necessary for fine visual discriminations. Predatory species and species that live in trees need finer visual acuity, and generally have eyes located nearer to each other and more in the front of their head rather than on the side. Nocturnal species often have large eyes and a structure called a tapetum, located behind the retina, reflecting light back through it, and increasing sensitivity to dim light.

The brains of different species also are a reflection of the lifestyle they have adopted. The thalamus, sensory cortex, and motor cortex of different species vary in size in ways that correlate with the uses that the animals make of the associated sensory modalities. Thus, the sensory areas associated with the hands of monkeys and the snouts of cats are disproportionately large. The brain areas responsible for fine manipulation are much larger in a species like raccoons, with fine manipulative ability, than in cats or dogs, in which there is less fine manipulation of objects.

The method of adaptive correlation has been important in increasing our understanding of the manner in which behavior is adapted to the environment. While the relationships produced by this method are less precise than those that can result from more experimental approaches, such proposed relationships are testable and have greatly increased our understanding of behavioral adaptation.

Adaptation and Learning

Each species represents a collection of specific adaptations all of which must work in conjunction to produce a total animal that is viable in its particular habitat. Often, there is value in viewing particular behavioral patterns in relation to the total adaptation of the species rather than in attempting to study it in isolation. The recognition of the specificity of adaptations in different species has recently had a substantial impact on the study of the "laws of learning." An increasing number of comparative psychologists are recognizing that learning processes are part of the total adaptation of the species to its environment. In many instances, animals may be adapted to learn certain things rather than others. Imprinting, discussed earlier, provides an excellent example. The apparent existence of specific learning abilities in different species further complicates the search for a characteristic of animal "intelligence."

It now appears that animals may be "prepared"

to make certain associations and "contraprepared" to make others. Usually, if an animal is to associate a response with a particular consequence, the consequence must immediately follow the response. However, there are some notable exceptions to this rule. Rats that have tasted a novel substance and then been made sick as long as four hours later will associate the taste of the novel substance with getting sick and will be reluctant to drink it again. This learned tasted aversion has been called the *Garcia effect*. The rats show no association over long-time delays between illness and visual or auditory stimuli. The readiness with which rats learn to avoid substances whose taste is associated with illness, even after long delays, suggests that such preparedness may have adaptive value. Wild rats that ingest poison in sublethal doses avoid the taste of poisoned food in the future, even if there has been a long delay between ingestion and illness (see Garcia et al., 1974).

The organism does not enter learning experiments as a blank slate but rather comes equipped with a whole collection of species-characteristic response tendencies. Thus it may be very difficult to condition a pigeon to peck a key or to train a rat to press a bar in order to avoid shock. By contrast, it may be easy to train them to move from the location of shock and to peck or bar-press for food. Such learning is more compatible with species-characteristic response tendencies.

The comparative study of learning has been greatly influenced by the recognition that the "laws of learning" may differ from species to species and from response system to response system within a given species.

Copulatory Behavior: An Attempt at Synthesis

Thus far, we have progressed through discussions of description and the four basic classes of questions asked by animal behaviorists, and we have discussed a variety of different behavioral patterns in so doing. We shall now reverse this approach in an attempt to solidify an understanding of these approaches. We shall work with one form of behavior, copulatory behavior in mammals, and con-

sider it from each of the perspectives discussed in the main body of this chapter.

Patterns of Behavior

All species of mammals engage in copulatory behavior, but the details of copulatory patterns vary greatly from species to species. We can start with the familiar laboratory rat. In laboratory tests of copulatory behavior in this species, one typically starts with an experienced male and a female that is known to be receptive. Female rats become receptive about every fourth day, in association with changes in their estrous cycles. The male pursues the female and mounts her from behind. The female stops as the male mounts. The female then adopts a stereotyped posture of *lordosis,* in which the head and tail regions are elevated and there is a concave arching of the back. Adoption of this posture facilitates penile insertion. The male shows two kinds of insertions. On most occasions, the penis remains in the vagina for just one-quarter of a second before the male dismounts; no sperm are transferred. These insertions are called *intromissions*. On other occasions, the duration of the insertion is somewhat longer and sperm are transferred. These are called *ejaculations*. Typically, the first intromission occurs about one minute after the animals are paired. There then follows a "series" of about ten intromissions, spaced about one minute apart. Finally, an ejaculation occurs. The pair then rest for about five minutes before engaging in another ejaculatory series. About seven ejaculatory series may be completed before the rate of copulation becomes so slow that we can regard the animals as "satiated."

Not all species copulate the way rats do. We can specify four major dimensions along which copulatory patterns vary. As each of the four characteristics of copulatory patterns has two alternatives, there result 2^4 or sixteen possible patterns of copulatory behavior, as can be seen in Figure 6-8.

Locking. In some species, such as dogs, there is a mechanical tie or lock formed between the penis and the vagina during copulation which prevents male and female from separating. Other species, such as rats, do not lock.

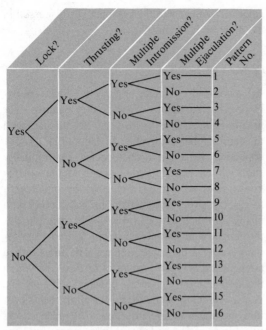

Fig. 6-8. Patterns of copulatory behavior in male mammals. From D. A. Dewsbury, "Patterns of Copulatory Behavior in Male Mammals," *Quarterly Review of Biology*, 1972, 47, 1–33.

Thrusting. In laboratory rats, there is but a single brief pelvic thrust on each insertion. Most primates, by contrast, show repetitive thrusting during their insertions.

Multiple Intromissions. Whereas many species, such as dogs and many primates, are able to ejaculate the first time that the penis is inserted into the vagina, others require multiple intromissions before ejaculating.

Multiple Ejaculations. While many species, such as rats, continue copulating until they have attained several ejaculations in a single episode, others, such as some large ungulates, cease copulating after attaining one ejaculation.

Using this system, as illustrated in Figure 6-8, we can classify the copulatory pattern of each mammalian species. Rats display Pattern 13 (no lock, no thrusting, multiple intromissions, and multiple ejaculations); dogs display Pattern 3

(lock, thrusting, ejaculation on a single insertion, and multiple ejaculations); and, humans often display Pattern 11 (no lock, thrusting, ejaculation on a single insertion, and multiple ejaculations).

While this is a convenient system for classifying species, it should be remembered that such patterns vary in other ways as well. Different species show courtship patterns of varying complexity, differing postures assumed during copulation, and different behavioral patterns associated with copulation. There are important quantitative differences within each of the sixteen possible patterns.

Development of Behavior

The development of copulatory behavior, like that of all behavior, involves interaction of the genotype and the environment. Many of the species differences discussed above appear to be of genetic origin. Attempts to produce substantial qualitative alterations in the copulatory patterns of different species have been largely unsuccessful. There are substantial quantitative differences in the copulatory behavior of inbred strains of mice, rats, and guinea pigs, and behavior-genetic analyses have helped to establish the ways in which genetic differences influence the behavior.

Environmental factors are critical to normal behavioral development. Rats and guinea pigs reared in isolation from their conspecifics have generally been found deficient in their copulatory behavior. The most famous examples of such effects come from the studies of Harry Harlow (for example, Harlow et al., 1971) on rhesus monkeys. Monkeys raised from birth on an artificial "surrogate" mother made of wire and terrycloth were totally ineffective in their reproductive behavior.

The actions of hormones in development provide one of the clearest examples of a sensitive period. Animal behaviorists have conducted a large number of experiments, primarily in rats, in which the kinds and amounts of hormones circulating in the systems of young rats are altered. Around the time of birth, males have relatively large concentrations of androgens (male sex hormones), whereas females have lower levels of sex hormones. This difference is critical to later development, as can be seen from experiments in which hormone levels are manipulated. Any rat, male or female, that has androgens present during the sensitive period around the time of birth will show an adult pattern typical of the male, with mounting, intromissions, and ejaculations, but no lordosis in response to mounting. By contrast, rats that have had no hormone present during the sensitive period, be they genetic males or females, typically show lordosis when mounted but little male copulatory behavior. These effects appear irreversible; the presence or absence of hormones later in life cannot compensate for tendencies established by the presence or absence of hormones during the sensitive period. In humans, there appears to be a sensitive period as well, but it is prenatal, and behavioral differences are more subtle. Females exposed to androgens during the sensitive period are likely to show tomboy-like behavior, but not to show the complete male syndrome as in rats (Money and Ehrhardt, 1972).

Immediate Causation

The stimuli responsible for eliciting and controlling copulatory behavior come through many modalities, the relative importance of which varies from species to species. In rodents, olfaction seems particularly important; pheromones play an important role in the onset of mating. Visual signals are of particular importance to primates, although some pheromonal influences have been reported. Many rodent species communicate during copulation using ultrasound, high-frequency sound to which the unaided human ear is insensitive. Scientists studied the copulatory behavior of laboratory rats for many years before realizing that they were missing one of the most important means of communication because of their own sensory limitations.

Hormones are important determinants of behavior in both males and females. Females of most species mate only when in the appropriate stage of their estrous cycles. If the ovaries, the source of sex hormones, are removed, sexual behavior will cease. It can be restored with appropriate hormone injections.

Of course, the central nervous system is critical to the integration of copulatory behavior. Many of the reflexes which comprise copulatory behavior are organized in the spinal cord. The total in-tegrated copulatory pattern is a function of activity in the brain itself. Brain structures appear to exert a tonic inhibition on the activity of lower structures. Many areas of the brain have been implicated in the control of copulatory behavior, but certain areas of the hypothalamus appear to play a particularly central role, both in the direct control of behavior and in the control of hormonal secretions, which in turn affect behavior.

As neural activity is largely a chemical process, there has been much recent interest in drugs and their effects on copulatory behavior. It appears that there may be a general inhibition of the reflexes that constitute copulatory patterns, and that this inhibition may be maintained by certain chemical transmitters in the brain, especially serotonin. Depletion of levels of serotonin results in a facilitation of copulatory behavior.

Evolution of Behavior

In studies of the evolution of copulatory behavior, one would search for orderly patterns in the evolutionary development of species-typical copulatory patterns. Unfortunately, the search for orderly evolutionary patterns in mammalian copulatory behavior has, thus far, been largely unsuccessful. Copulatory patterns, which appear to be rather unmodifiable developmentally, appear easily altered by evolution. Thus, one may find substantial differences among even closely related species as they adapt to differing habitats and lifestyles. Copulatory patterns may show ecological adaptations, with no clear evolutionary progression.

The Adaptedness of Behavior

Each of the three major methods for the study of the adaptedness of behavior has been applied to the problem of the adaptedness of copulatory behavior. One question that has been asked experimentally is that of the function of the multiple intromissions that precede ejaculation in laboratory rats. Why should males display a pattern of brief intromissions over the course of ten minutes or longer instead of simply transferring sperm on their first insertion? The answer lies in the effects of the male's behavior on the female. If pregnancy is to be successful, certain neuroendocrine reflexes must be triggered in the female. These reflexes alter her hormonal milieu and stimulate sperm transport. It is copulatory behavior that initiates these responses in the female. The pre-ejaculatory intromissions are necessary for the elicitation of the responses in the female that are important for successful pregnancy. Experiments have shown that females receiving ejaculates without prior intromissions rarely become pregnant, while those receiving the full copulatory pattern usually do become pregnant.

Behavior-genetic methods have also been used in attempts to understand the adaptive significance of copulatory behavior. Such methods have indicated an adaptive value to rapid copulation with relatively few irrelevant responses.

The method of adaptive correlation can be used to relate copulatory patterns to other species characteristics. The copulatory patterns of carnivores, such as bears, wolves, and lions, tend to be quite prolonged. Locking and thrusting patterns have been reported in some species. By contrast, plains-dwelling ungulates, such as antelopes, tend to have very brief copulations, with no thrusting and ejaculation on a single insertion. Pressure from predation appears to be an important determinant of copulatory pattern. Among rodents, locking patterns are found only among species with relatively safe nest sites, such as the elaborate houses of wood rats, the arboreal nests of golden mice, and the burrows of grasshopper mice. Again, pressures from predation appear to be important.

While this survey has been quite brief and incomplete, it illustrates the ways in which each of the four classes of questions can be asked of a single kind of behavior. The ultimate result of a broad-based inquiry using all four kinds of questions should be progress toward a comprehensive understanding of the behavioral pattern in question (see McGill et al., 1978).

Humans in the Study of Animal Behavior

Many animal behaviorists look forward to the day when humans can be more completely included in studies of animal behavior. They hope that results gathered on nonhuman species will generalize to humans.

A number of popular and semipopular writers, such as Konrad Lorenz, Robert Ardrey, and Desmond Morris, have attempted to extrapolate results of studies of nonhuman species to the human species. In general, most animal behaviorists seem to feel that these attempts have been unsuccessful.

An alternative approach to that of extrapolating results from nonhuman species to humans is to extrapolate methods. There is a rapidly growing discipline, called human ethology, in which scientists are attempting to utilize many of the methods studies of animal behavior using humans as subjects. This appears to be a fruitful approach which is already paying dividends, particularly in the study of development in young humans and in the study of nonverbal communication.

Summary

The first tasks in the study of animal behavior are to observe the behavior and to provide a thorough description thereof. Observation and description are followed by a consideration of four classes of questions: questions of development, immediate causation, evolution, and function.

The contemporary study of animal behavior is the result of the interaction of ethologists, comparative psychologists, and animal behaviorists from other disciplines.

The development of behavior is the product of the continuing mutual interaction between genes and the environment. Events experienced early in life can have pervasive influence on the developing young animal.

Immediate determinants of behavior include environmental factors, the operation of sensory-perceptual mechanisms, and such internal factors as the activity of the nervous system and of hormones.

Behavior evolves much as does structure. Natural selection works through differential survival and reproduction so that some genes will be better represented than others in future generations.

Ethologists have made such progress in the study of behavioral evolution through systematic comparison of groups of closely related species. Other animal behaviorists have attempted to understand the broad sweep of evolutionary history at the "phyletic level."

Through the actions of natural selection, behavior has become adapted to the lifestyle adopted by each species. Behavioral adaptation can be studied using the experimental method, the behavior-genetic method, or the method of adaptive correlation.

The study of patterns of behavior, development of behavior, immediate causation of behavior, evolution of behavior, and the adaptive significance of behavior can be illustrated through a consideration of the study of patterns of mammalian copulatory behavior.

Glossary

Adaptive correlation: A method of studying the function of behavior in which adaptive significance emerges from a comparative study of variations in several characteristics in a variety of species.

Agonistic behavior: Behavior that occurs in conflict situations in animal behavior, including approach, threat, overt fighting, and withdrawal.

Circadian rhythm: A rhythm lasting about a day and producing systematic daily fluctuations in a physiological or behavioral phenomenon.

Dominance: The ability of one animal to gain privileged access to resources (for example, food, space, sex partners) that is not strictly dependent on location.

Ethology: An approach to the study of animal behavior developed by a group of European zoologists who emphasized the study of the evolution of instinctive behavior in a variety of species in the field.

Garcia effect: The tendency for rats to learn readily to associate illness with novel tastes from substances which they ingested, even though ingestion may have occurred some time before the illness.

Imprinting: The tendency for young precocial birds to follow the first moving objects which they encounter.

Inbred strain: A strain of animals that is the result of at least twenty generations of brother-sister matings so that virtually no genetic variability remains.

Learning set: A task in which an animal is presented with a series of different discrimination learning problems wherein the animal often shows improvement with successive problems or "learning to learn."

Lordosis: A stereotyped receptivity posture in mammalian copulatory behavior in which the head and tail regions are elevated creating a concave arching of the spine.

Pheromones: Chemicals that serve to mediate communication within a species.

Reinstatement: The supplementation of initial learning with a small amount of additional practice which, in and of itself, would not result in detectable changes in performance.

Sensitive period: A period in the lifetime of an organism in which environmental events have maximal effects on the subsequent development and behavior of the organism.

Sign stimulus: A term coined by ethologists to describe a relatively simple object in the environment that is capable of eliciting a fixed action pattern.

Social facilitation: An improvement in the rate, probability, or some other index of behavior, occurring as a function of the presence of another organism.

Species: A group of individuals that are capable of breeding among themselves under natural conditions, but that are reproductively isolated from other such groups.

Territoriality: Alternatively an active defense of space against conspecifics, often of the same sex, or a privileged access to resources in a particular area.

Tool using: The manipulation of inanimate objects, not manufactured internally, that results in an improvement in the efficiency with which an animal alters the position or form of an object.

Umwelt: The unique sensory-perceptual world of an animal.

Suggested Readings

Alcock, J. *Animal behavior: An Evolutionary Approach.* Sunderland, Mass.: Sinauer, 1975.

Dawkins, R. *The Selfish Gene.* Oxford: Oxford University Press, 1976.

Dewsbury, D. A. *Comparative Animal Behavior*. New York: McGraw-Hill, 1978.

Hinde, R. A. *Biological Bases of Human Social Behavior*. New York: McGraw-Hill, 1974.

Hinde, R. A. *Animal behavior: A Synthesis of Ethology and Comparative Psychology*. 2nd ed. New York: McGraw-Hill, 1970.

Tinbergen, N. *The Study of Instinct*. Oxford: Oxford University Press, 1951.

Behavioral Genetics

Robert Plomin and Gerald E. McClearn

Introduction

During the latter part of the nineteenth century, in the intellectually turbulent times following the publication of Darwin's theory of evolution, a dispute developed concerning the importance of heredity and of environment in determining behavior. This "nature-nurture" argument became an active and acrimonious scientific, philosophical, social, and political controversy. The social and behavioral sciences became increasingly polarized over the matter, and many people came to accept the view that there were only two tenable positions: one was either a champion of hereditary determinants or an advocate of environment. Each position claimed complete and exclusive determination for one's own "team" and scorned the arguments of the opposition. Although this is no doubt an excellent way to encourage intercollegiate athletics, it is a most inappropriate way to approach an important scientific question. In point of fact, a more open view, explicitly acknowledging the possibility that heredity and environment work together, has been expressed throughout the controversy. This integrative view, supported both by theoretical developments and by the accumulation of empirical data, is now increasingly accepted, even though the outmoded extremist views are still heard occasionally.

Genetic Introduction

Gregor Mendel, the father of modern genetics, described his experimental results on the crossing of pea plants and provided a theoretical explanation in 1865 for the transmission of traits from one generation to another. The units of heredity that he postulated were simply hypothetical "factors" or "elements," and Mendel did not and could not know where they were located or how they were constituted. Indeed, it was not until 1909 that these units of inheritance were given the name "genes."

Among the many questions addressed in early genetic research was that of location of the genes. It was discovered that the hereditary factors were located on very small, string-like objects, called *chromosomes* ("colored bodies") because of the way these chromosomes responded to dyes applied for microscopic examination. Chromosomes are found in the nuclei of the cells of the body, and they differ from one another in terms of length and certain other structural characteristics. They are paired, with one member of each pair of chromosomes in a given individual having originated in each parent of that individual. They are present in all body cells, and they occur in a number that is typical for the particular species. For example, the fruit fly, *Drosophila melanogaster*, one of the most commonly investigated organisms in genetic

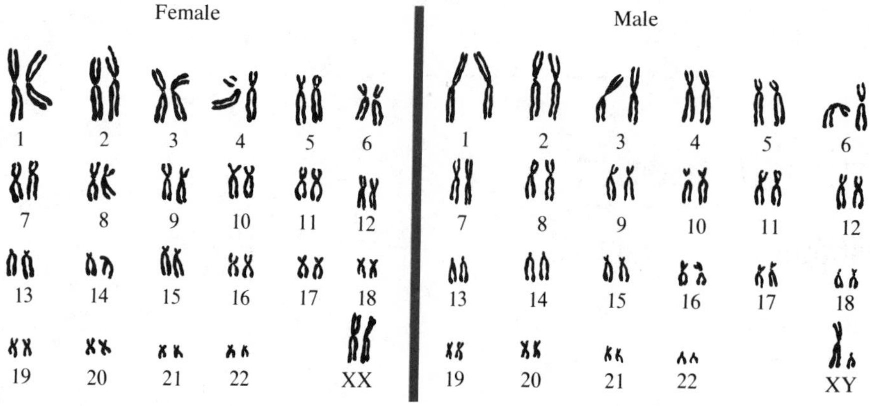

Female   Male

Fig. 7-1. Karyotypes of a normal human female and a normal human male.

research, has only four chromosomes, the mouse has forty, and man has forty-six. The *karyotypes,* or chromosomal constitutions, of a normal human female and a normal human male are shown in Figure 7-1. It may be seen that, with respect to twenty-two of the chromosome pairs (called *autosomes*), there is no difference between the sexes. With respect to the twenty-third pair (the *sex chromosomes*), a difference exists between the sexes. Females have a pair of rather long chromosomes, designated as X-chromosomes; males have only one X-chromosome which is paired with a small Y-chromosome.

Sophisticated research, much of it conducted with *Drosophila melanogaster,* revealed that the genes are located in serial fashion along the chromosomes. This linear arrangement is very systematic. There appears to be a particular spot, or *locus,* on a given chromosome where a particular gene is located. By virtue of the paired nature of the autosomal chromosomes, therefore, two forms of each gene are present in every body cell of an individual. For females, the same is true for genes on the X-chromosome pair. For males, however, the genes on the X-chromosome do not have pairmates on the Y-chromosome, because there are very few genes on the Y-chromosome.

One important observation is that there are only half as many chromosomes in the germ cells, or *gametes* (the sperm and the ova), as there are in the body cells. Furthermore, this half is composed of

one member of each pair. The chromosome number in the germ cells is described as *haploid,* as distinct from the *diploid* number in the body cells. When a sperm and an ovum unite at conception, the two haploid sets combine and the diploid number is restored in the *zygote.* Ordinarily, the process of reduction of chromosome number during gamete formation and restoration of the diploid condition upon fertilization proceeds reliably and without error. When an error does occur, however, some serious consequences can ensue. For example, through a mistake in gamete formation, an ovum can contain both members (rather than just one) of a small chromosome pair identified as number 21. When an ovum of this sort is fertilized by a normal sperm containing one chromosome number 21 (and, of course, one of each of the other chromosome pairs), the result is a zygote that contains two of each chromosome pair except number 21, which has three. This condition is sometimes descriptively referred to as *trisomy* (three-body) *21.* The excess of hereditary material in this case, for reasons not yet understood, interferes with normal developmental processes and results in a distinctive combination of symptoms called *Down's syndrome.* In addition to certain anomalies of the face, hands, and other physical features, persons with Down's syndrome have greatly reduced IQ scores.

Just as an excess of genetic material can have a disruptive effect, chromosomal absence can be very deleterious. Another kind of accident at the time of gamete formation can result in an ovum or sperm with no X-chromosome. When such a gamete joins a normal X-bearing one, the result is a zygote with only one X-chromosome. These individuals also display a distinctive syndrome, including retarded sexual development and reduced stature, among other symptoms. Behaviorally, these "Turner's syndrome" patients appear to have a specific deficit in spatial abilities, with an otherwise reasonably intact cognitive capability.

These and similar chromosomal anomalies occur at a frequency of about one in 200 newborns. Most chromosomal anomalies have even more serious consequences. Trisomy for chromosome 18, for example, produces a syndrome with multiple congenital defects, and the average survival of such patients is only about three months. Many other anomalies cause such extensive disruption that early spontaneous abortions occur.

As already mentioned, each gamete contains one-half of the genetic material of the organism that produced it. It is important to note that the haploid number of chromosomes in each gamete is not a random set of half of the full diploid complement; rather, one member of each chromosome pair is included. The number of possible different ways in which these chromosomes can be combined may be very large, indeed. With the twenty-three pairs of chromosomes in man, for example, there are trillions of different possible arrangements for the offspring from one set of parents. The fact that the child gets half of its genetic material from each parent can account for the resemblance between children and parents; the differences between them can be attributed in part to the fact that chromosomal pairing in the offspring represents a unique combination of genetic material.

A given gene may exist in two or more alternative forms called *alleles*. Let us symbolize an allele of a particular gene as *A* and another allele as *a*. There are three possible arrangements of these two alleles (*AA, Aa,* and *aa*); these are referred to as *genotypes*. Now observe that a parent with the *AA* genotype can generate only *A* gametes. Similarly, a parent with the *aa* genotype can generate only *a* gametes. Individuals with either an *AA* or an *aa*

genotype are referred to as *homozygotes*. The mating of an *AA* individual with an *aa* individual will give rise to a *heterozygote* (*Aa*) offspring. (In this and similar discussions, when the genotype with respect to a particular locus is being considered, it is important to remember that a gamete would also contain alleles of all of the other loci of the total genotype.)

The possibilities are more varied for a mating of two heterozyotes (*Aa x Aa*). *Each parent will generate both A* and *a gametes, in equal numbers.* Thus, in the female, an *A* egg will be produced half of the time, and half of the time an *a* egg will be produced. It is a matter of chance whether a particular egg is fertilized by an *A*-bearing or an *a*-bearing sperm. Therefore, half of the *A* eggs will be fertilized by *A* sperm, producing a zygote with an *AA* genotype; half of the *A* eggs will be fertilized by an *a* sperm, producing a zygote with an *Aa* genotype. Similarly, upon fertilization, half of the *a* eggs will generate an *Aa* genotype and half will generate an *aa* genotype. Thus, we expect equal numbers of *AA* and *aa* genotypes and twice as many that are *Aa;* that is to say, the expected ratio is 1 *AA* to 2 *Aa* to 1 *aa* in the offspring of a mating of this type. In any particular family, the outcome might deviate substantially from this ratio, but the expectation is closely met when a number of similar families are considered.

One of the most important of Mendel's discoveries was that an *aa* individual produced by a mating of *Aa × Aa* did not differ phenotypically from one produced by a mating of *aa × aa*. In the former case, the *a* allele had existed for a time in the same cells with an *A* allele. However, when the *a* allele separated from its *A* partner in the process of gamete formation, its nature was unchanged by this association. Naturally, the same applies to the *A* allele.

Various relationships may exist between genotypes and the *phenotypes,* or observable characteristics, that they influence. For example, for some loci, the heterozygote is halfway between the homozygotes with respect to the trait in question. This situation is described as an *additive* one. For other loci, the phenotype of the heterozygote is just like that of one of the homozygotes. A good example is the color of hair pigment in mice. A mouse with the *BB* genotype is black. The *bb* genotype results in a brown mouse; whereas the heterozygote, *Bb,* is just as black as the *BB* homozygote. In cases such as this, the mode of inheritance is described as *dominant-recessive*. The *B* allele is said to be dominant, and the *b* allele, recessive.

Numerous examples exist of single loci that influence behavior. In humans, the best known single-locus condition is probably *phenylketonuria* (PKU). The "normal" allele, which is dominant, may be represented by *P* and the recessive allele by *p*. Homozygotes for the recessive allele, *pp,* are mentally retarded unless they are provided with a special diet. It is fortunate that the *p* allele is relatively rare. Only about one in 25,000 births is a *pp* individual. However, it is interesting to note that about one of every seventy-five individuals is a heterozygote, carrying the *p* allele hidden because of the dominance of the *P* allele which they also possess.

Another, more familiar condition due to a single locus is red-green color-blindness. The locus involved happens to be on the X-chromosome, and this location results in a special pattern of transmission known as sex linkage. For females, there is no difference from autosomal inheritance. Color-blindness is due to homozygosity for a recessive allele, which is designated by *c;* heterozygotes are normal, as are individuals homozygous for the dominant allele, *C*. For males, however, since they possess only one X-chromosome, the usual considerations of dominance and recessiveness do not apply. If a male's X-chromosome has the *c* allele, there is no possibility of its effect being masked by a dominant *C* allele, and the individual will be color-blind. There are, therefore, many more males who are affected than females. Note that an affected son can only have received the *c* allele from his mother; in order to be a male, he must have received a Y-chromosome, and that can only have been provided by the father. Very often, though not always, the mother will have received the *c* allele from her father, who would therefore have been color-blind. Thus, traits that are inherited in a sex-linked fashion often show a pattern of "skipped generations."

The foregoing discussion was concerned with loci considered one at a time. In the real world, of course, the whole packet of loci from one parent unites with the whole packet from the other parent to form the zygote. This fact leads to the consideration of several additional phenomena. First, it may be noted that each chromosome must have many loci. Although there are only twenty-three pairs of chromosomes in humans, it is estimated that there are perhaps hundreds of thousands of loci. Loci on different chromosomes are said to display independent assortment. That is to say, alleles that come into a zygote in one gamete need not be associated in the gametes produced by the mature individual who develops from that gamete. For example, consider a mating in which one parent is homozygous *AA* and (at another locus) *bb,* while the other parent is homozygous *aa* and *BB*. This mating can be represented as *AAbb × aaBB*. In this case, the one parent could produce only *Ab* gametes, the other only *aB* gametes, and the offspring would be double heterozygotes (*AaBb*). Half of the gametes produced by one of these offspring will possess *A* and half will possess *a;* furthermore, half will possess *B* and half *b*. If the loci are on different chromosomes, whether a gamete receives *A* or *a* has no influence on whether it receives *B* or *b*. Therefore, equal numbers of *AB, Ab, aB,* and *ab* gametes will be formed.

As a consequence of their location on the same chromosome, some loci tend to be transmitted together. Let us suppose that the loci are immediate neighbors on the same chromosome. When the chromosome containing *A* is allocated to a particular gamete, the *b* allele will necessarily have gone to the same gamete; similarly, *a* and *B* will be allocated together. The loci are said to be *linked*. In such cases, only two kinds of gametes can be formed: *Ab* and *aB*. These are in the same configuration as that of the chromosomes received by the individual at his or her conception.

During gamete formation, there is an opportunity for an exchange of material between chromosome pairs to occur. Basically, the chromosomes come into contact, break, and rejoin in such a way that sections of the chromosomes have been exchanged. If two loci are on the same chromosome, but not immediately adjacent, such *crossing over* can occur between them. Thus, in our example, an *A* can occasionally get a new partner, *B*, while the *a* becomes newly paired with the *b*. Under these circumstances, four gamete types are again possible, although typically in unequal numbers. Some *recombinant AB* and *ab* gametes will be generated, but there will be many more of the *nonrecombinant Ab* and *aB* gametes.

For many loci, the phenotypic expression of the genotype is independent of the genotypes of other loci. However, there are situations in which different loci interact. In addition to the black-brown coat color locus in the mouse, which was mentioned above, there is another locus affecting coat color. This is called the albino locus. If the animal is *CC* or *Cc,* it has full color; if it is *cc,* regardless of its genotype at the black-brown locus, it will be white. In a sense, the *cc* genotype overrides the expression of the other locus. This type of interaction between loci is called *epistasis.*

The examples cited to this point have been dichotomous, that is, the phenotypes were of one type or another—PKU or normal, color-blind or not color-blind, and so on. Many of the phenotypes that are of particular interest to behavioral scientists, however, do not lend themselves to such categorization. These phenotypes are continuously and more or less normally distributed (see Chapter 3). For some time in the history of genetics, there was considerable debate concerning whether different rules applied to inheritance of such *quantitative traits* than to inheritance of the categorical Mendelian traits. It was eventually shown that the patterns of inheritance of quantitative traits could be reconciled with Mendelian rules by assuming that many single loci have small effects on the same phenotype. This *polygenic* model can best be understood by considering the simplest case of two unlinked loci, each having equal influence on the phenotype and each acting additively (without dominance or epistasis).

All possible combinations of genotypes for the two loci are shown in the first column of Table 7-1. In accordance with the simplifying assumptions just mentioned, we may arbitrarily assign a value of 1 for each capital letter in the genotype. (The reader should confirm that such scoring does, in fact, comply with the assumptions.) These geno-

Table 7-1. A Model of Genotypic Values and Relative Frequencies of Genotypes of Offspring from the Mating of Double Heterozygotes

Genotype	Genotypic Value	Relative Frequency
AABB	4	1
AABb	3	2
AAbb	2	1
AaBB	3	2
AaBb	2	4
Aabb	1	2
aaBB	2	1
aaBb	1	2
aabb	0	1

typic values are shown in the second column of Table 7-1.

For further illustration, let us consider the mating of two double heterozygotes, *AaBb* × *AaBb*. A convenient way of displaying the results of this mating is illustrated in Table 7-2. Because we are assuming the absence of linkage, each parent will produce equal numbers of four kinds of gametes (*AB, Ab, aB,* and *ab*). These possibilities are shown along the side of the table for the male parent and across the top for the female parent. The intersection of these four rows and four columns provides sixteen cells, with genotypes as shown. All of the possible genotypes identified in Table 7-1 occur in this mating and, by counting the genotypes in the cells in Table 7-2, it can be seen that their relative frequencies are as shown in the third column of Table 7-1. Of all sixteen combinations of gametes, one produces an *AABB* genotype, two produce *AABb,* one produces *AAbb,* and so on. For convenience, all of the sixteen out-

Table 7-2. Types of Gametes and Zygotes from the Mating of Double Heterozygotes

		Female Gametes			
		AB	Ab	aB	ab
	AB	AABB	AABb	AaBB	AaBb
	Ab	AABb	AAbb	AaBb	Aabb
Male Gametes	aB	AaBB	AaBb	aaBB	aaBb
	ab	AaBb	Aabb	aaBb	aabb

Table 7-3. A Model of Genotypic Values, Randomly Assigned Environmental Effects, and Phenotypic Values

Genotypes	Genotypic Value	Environmental Effect	Phenotypic Value
AABB	4	−1	3
AABb	3	+1	4
AABb	3	0	3
AAbb	2	+1	3
AaBB	3	0	3
AaBB	3	0	3
AaBb	2	−1	1
AaBb	2	+1	3
AaBb	2	+2	4
AaBb	2	0	2
Aabb	1	0	1
Aabb	1	+1	2
aaBB	2	−2	0
aaBb	1	−1	0
aaBb	1	−1	0
aabb	0	0	0
Mean:	2	0	2
Variance:	1	1	2

comes are given, along with their genotypic values, in the first two columns of Table 7-3. The mean of the genotypic values is 2.0, and their variance (V_G) is 1.0.

To this point, nothing specific has been said about the influence of environment. In classical Mendelian inheritance, environment can affect a trait, but the influence is usually not sufficient to cause any ambiguity about the category to which an individual should be assigned. With the respect to polygenic traits, however, consideration of environmental influences is an integral part of the analysis. To depict the role of environment in the present example, varying magnitudes of environmental influence, either positive or negative, have been randomly assigned, as shown in the third column of Table 7-3. The mean of these effects is 0, and their variance (V_E) is 1.0. If we assume that these environmental effects simply summate with the genotypic values, the phenotypic values would be as shown in the fourth column of Table 7-3. The phenotypic mean is 2.0, and the variance (V_P) is 2.0.

The distributions of the genotypic values, environmental effects, and final phenotypic values are illustrated in Figure 7-2. An important outcome is that the genotypic and environmental variances sum to give the phenotypic variance:

$$V_G + V_E = V_P.$$

Fig. 7-2. Distributions of genotypic values, randomly assigned environmental effects, and resulting phenotypic values.

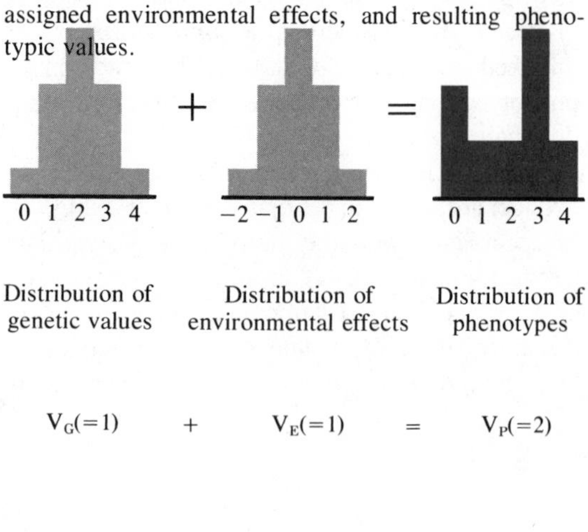

Distribution of genetic values	Distribution of environmental effects	Distribution of phenotypes
$V_G(=1)$	$V_E(=1)$	$V_P(=2)$

This relationship permits an approach to evaluating the relative contributions of genetic differences and environmental influences to the overall phenotypic variability displayed in a population. The index that is used for this purpose is called *heritability* (symbolized h^2) and is defined as the proportion of the phenotypic variance that is attributable to genotypic variance:

$$h^2 = \frac{V_G}{V_P}.$$

In our present example, $h^2 = 0.5$, reflecting the equal contributions of V_G and V_E (each of which is 1.0). We are, of course, able to measure only the phenotype; thus, only V_P is directly assessable. There are, however, various strategies for estimating V_G, V_E, and h^2, and these will be discussed in some detail later.

It is important to recall that a number of simplifying assumptions were made in generating our example: two unlinked loci, no dominance, no epistasis, and no interaction of genes and environment (their effects were simply additive). Even though real-life situations are more complex, this simple model does provide a starting point. By generalizing to more than two loci, by considering a large population with many matings of various types, and by taking into account the effects of complicating interactions (between alleles, between loci, and between genotype and environment), an appreciation of how genes can influence continuously-distributed characteristics may be obtained.

Of particular importance is the observation that heritability is a statistic descriptive only of the state of affairs with respect to a particular phenotype in a particular population with a particular array of environmental factors at a given point in time. It must not be taken as indicating an eternal verity concerning the phenotype, for heritability can vary from population to population and, within a population, from time to time.

So far, our discussion has described, in an elementary manner to be sure, how genes work in the sense of formal rules relating genotype to phenotype. Exciting research discoveries in the past couple of decades have also informed us about the mechanisms through which genes work. Rather early in the history of genetics, it was discovered

that genes could influence biochemical properties of organisms just as they could influence more immediately observable phenotypes. Results of further research prompted the suggestion that genes might *always* exert their primary effects on enzymes. Different enzymes are critical to different metabolic processes; thus, the effects of genes on enzymes could influence traits dependent upon these processes. This hypothesis is quite a different conceptualization from the notion that there are genes for eye color, genes for height, genes for intelligence, and so on. All genes are seen as acting similarly at the level of their basic effects.

As yet, the details of the biochemical and physiological mechanisms of genetic influence are not well worked out for many behaviors. Best understood in this respect are several conditions of mental retardation. The classic example is phenylketonuria, already mentioned in another context. Homozygotes for the recessive allele (*pp*) have a defective form of the enzyme, phenylalanine hydroxylase. The metabolism of phenylalanine is grossly impaired, and a variety of metabolites accumulate in abnormal amounts. Although the reason why this abnormality often results in mental retardation is not yet completely understood, an understanding of the general mechanism in this case led to the development of a rational therapy. The early and consistent administration of a diet containing no phenylalanine to a child with the *pp* genotype avoids retardation.

More recently, the chemical nature of the genes themselves has been discovered, and the chain of molecular events leading from gene to phenotype has been described. The genes are composed of deoxyribonucleic acid (DNA). A molecule of DNA is composed of phosphoric acid, deoxyribose sugar, and four bases (nitrogenous compounds)—adenine, guanine, thymine, and cytosine. The phosphoric acid and sugar form two strands that coil around each other to form a double helical structure. These strands are held at a fixed distance apart by pairs of the bases, as shown in Figure 7-3. Adenine pairs only with thymine, and guanine only with cytosine.

In the process of cell reproduction, the strands separate and each takes one base of each pair with it. Since the chemical constituents of DNA are available in the intracellular environment, new

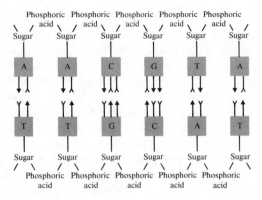

Fig. 7-3. Flat representation of the strands and bases of a molecule of DNA. A, adenine; T, thymine; C, cytosine; G, guanine.

bases can attach selectively to the bases of the separated strands. Thus, as illustrated in Figure 7-4, two replicas of the original DNA come to exist. This discovery explains how the genes in the

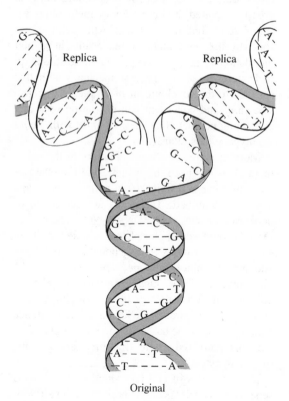

Fig. 7-4. Duplication of DNA.

single-cell zygotes can be duplicated in a sufficient number to provide a complete set of genetic material for the many cells of an adult.

In addition to being capable of self duplication, DNA can also transfer the ''information'' it contains to a single-stranded ribonucleic acid (RNA) by the process of base pairing. Thus, the RNA formed against the DNA will have cytosine paired with guanine on the DNA, or vice versa; since uracil substitutes for thymine in RNA, adenine-uracil pairs are formed. The RNA is then involved, along with other cellular structures, in the synthesis of proteins—of which enzymes are a class.

The genetic information is coded in triplets, or sequences of three bases. Thus, three uracils in a row on RNA (derived from three adenines in a row on DNA) specifies the insertion of a particular amino acid, phenylalanine, in the formation of an enzyme molecule. Other amino acids are specified by other triplets. Chemically speaking, we can now see how one allele can differ from another. They differ in base sequence, and this difference is reflected in the enzyme that is produced.

This brief discussion of molecular genetics is, of course, greatly oversimplified. However, it is sufficient to permit an appreciation of how genes can indeed influence behavior. Through specification of enzymes, all bodily parts and processes are influenced by the genes. These include the nervous system and the endocrine system, both of which are critically involved in behavioral determination.

Methods of Behavioral Genetics

It is now generally agreed that nature and nurture play complementary roles in determining behavior. There can be no behavior without both genes and environment. Because genes and environment are intertwined in the development of behavior, the mistaken notions of the ''nature-nurture'' argument have too often been replaced by the equally mistaken idea that the individual effects of heredity and environment cannot be analyzed. If we took this view seriously, it would mean that we cannot study the effect of genetic factors on behavior, because they are hopelessly enmeshed with the effect of environment. It would also mean that we cannot isolate environmental effects, because they are inseparable from genetic effects. Few psychologists would be tempted to agree with the latter statement, however, because it contradicts decades of experimental research in psychology aimed at investigating environmental influences on behavior. As a matter of fact, we can study the effect of the environment independent of genes, and we can also study the effect of genes independent of environment.

Because we have already said that there can be no behavior without both genes and environment, it may seem paradoxical to say that they can be studied independently. An analogy may be helpful. A sailboat needs both sails and a hull. The "behavior" of a sailboat (speed, turning, ability to "point" into the wind, "planing" ability, and so on) depends on the design of its sails and the design of its hull. The aerodynamic shape of the sails, their number and size, and their positioning are important; equally important are the depth, width, length, and shape of the hull. Obviously, for sailboats, there can be no behavior without both sails and hull, but this does not restrict us from asking about the independent contributions of sail design and hull design to the behavior of sailboats. That these two factors may interact is shown by the fact that certain hull designs are useful only with particular sail designs. However, this interaction does not prevent us from finding independent contributions of sails and hulls. For example, regardless of the design of their sails, we know that flat, broad-beamed boats plane better and that catamarans go faster but do not turn as easily.

In the same way, we can say that behavior requires both genes and environment, that these influences may interact, and that we can determine their independent contributions to behavior. The contributions and interactions of genes and environment can be determined empirically, just as we can analyze the effects of sail design and hull design on the behavior of sailboats.

The sailboat analogy is useful to make another general point about behavioral genetics. How would you determine whether hull design or sail design affected the behavior of sailboats? You would try different designs and see if they made a *difference* in the boat's behavior. All experiments

study *differences:* an independent variable is manipulated to produce differences between groups. In other words, we study things that make a difference. Behavioral genetics is the study of genetic and environmental influences that make a difference in behavior. Just as hull design is more important than sail design for turning and sail design is more important for straightaway speed, genetic differences may be more important for some behaviors and environmental differences may be more important for others.

Thus, even though there can be no behavior without both genes and environment, we can ask whether it is the genes or the environment that make a difference in a particular behavior. For example, people differ in intelligence (see Chapter 18). What causes these differences? Environmental hypotheses come to mind. Families differ in the stimulation they offer for cognitive growth. Environments differ in motivating people toward intellectual goals. Educational experiences differ. However, genetic hypotheses should also be considered. As we shall see, evidence suggests that genetic factors are at least as important as environmental influences in producing individual differences in intelligence.

How would you untangle genetic and environmental influences in behavior? You might say that if a particular behavioral trait, such as intelligence, is inherited, then children ought to resemble their parents. Children do, in fact, resemble their parents in intelligence. However, a shared environment as well as shared genes may be responsible for the resemblance. What we need are situations, or "experiments," that control the influence of genetic factors in order to study the influence of the environment. Conversely, we need to control the environment to study the effect of genes.

Animal Studies

The necessary control conditions are more easily arranged for animals other than humans. If animals which are nearly identical genetically are reared in different environments, we can be quite confident in attributing any behavioral differences among the animals to environmental differences. On the other hand, if genetically-diverse animals are reared in the same environment, behavioral differences among them are presumably caused by their genetic differences. The species that have been the focus of attention in such studies are mice, rats, and fruit flies (*Drosophila melanogaster*). Their genetic variability can be controlled through specific breeding procedures, and their environments can be controlled in the laboratory.

Animals can be bred to be very similar genetically by a method called *inbreeding*. For example, many different highly inbred "strains" of mice have been established by brother-sister matings over several generations. Inbreeding reduces genetic variablility within a strain, and continued inbreeding for a score of generations produces animals that are essentially identical in their genetic constitution. Different inbred mouse strains can often be distinguished by their coat color or morphology; they also can differ behaviorally. If different strains are reared in the same laboratory environment (for example, standard laboratory cages, food, temperature, lighting, and so on), differences among the strains can be ascribed to their genetic differences. In other words, we know that behaviors that show strain differences are influenced by genetic factors. A single gene, a few genes, or many genes may be involved. For more complex behaviors, it is more likely that many genes are involved.

Differences among inbred mouse strains have been found for nearly every behavior that has been investigated. For example, strains differ in activity in running wheels, "emotionality" in a lighted open field (which is noxious for most rodents), exploratory activity in a novel environment, aggression, sound-induced seizures, sexual behavior, social behavior, learning, memory, alcohol preference, susceptibility to the effects of injected alcohol, and even the extent to which they squeak when they are picked up by their tails (Sprott and Staats, 1975). Thus, genes influence many behaviors in mice. Strain differences in learning will be discussed in some detail later.

Environmental factors are implicated if mice of a single inbred strain reared in different environments are shown to differ in behavior. Studies of this kind have investigated the behavior of mice under various environmental conditions, including

"enriched" environments with playthings and lots of room for running, crowded environments, and environments made stressful by shock or other aversive stimuli. Results of such studies often indicate that these environmental circumstances do indeed influence behavior.

Some investigations have employed different strains *and* different environmental conditions to determine the relative importance of genes and environment. For example, DeFries (1964) studied the effects of prenatal stress in two inbred mouse strains. Female mice in the last half of pregnancy were forced to swim for three minutes and were also subjected to visual and auditory stresses (such as bright lights and loud noises). Control groups were not stressed in these ways. The offspring of the experimental and control females of the two inbred strains were tested for activity in an open-field apparatus. Figure 7-5 shows that one of the strains (designated BALB/c) was much less active than the other (C57BL), indicating that genetic factors affect activity in an open field. The environmental condition (stressful versus nonstressful) made little difference in activity when all of the animals were considered together. The environment did have an effect, but it was in opposite directions in the two strains. In the BALB/c strain, the mice stressed prenatally were slightly more ac-

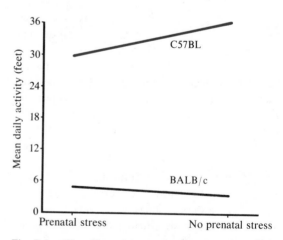

Fig. 7.5.   The effect of a stressful prenatal environment on the activity of two inbred strains of mice. (After DeFries, 1964)

tive than the controls, while the stressed C57BL animals were less active than controls. This example illustrates genotype-environment interaction, which refers to either the differential response of genotypes to environments or the differential effect of environments on genotypes. It is an important concept to which we shall return later.

Inbred strains are also used to elucidate the relationship between genes and behavior. If members of two inbred strains differing in a particular behavior are mated (that is, if the strains are "crossed"), the behavior of their offspring (known as the first filial generation, the F1) tells us something about the mode of inheritance of the behavior. For example, we know that mice of some inbred strains will almost invariably have a seizure when exposed to a loud noise and that other strains never have such seizures. This strain difference suggests that genetic factors are important in susceptibility to sound-induced seizures. We can then go on to determine whether a single gene is responsible for seizure susceptibility and, if so, whether it operates in a recessive or dominant manner. If susceptibility to sound-induced seizures is due to recessive alleles, then the F1 offspring of a cross between a strain that never has seizures and a strain that almost always has seizures should *not* be susceptible to seizures. If seizure susceptibility is due to one or more dominant alleles, all of the F1 offspring of such a cross should exhibit this behavior. Different modes of inheritance also lead to different expectations for the second filial generation (F2) produced by random mating of F1 animals and by other crosses between the F1, F2, and parental populations. For all of these crosses, a single-gene recessive hypothesis is in agreement with the actual proportion of offspring susceptible to sound-induced seizures (Collins and Fuller, 1968).

Although inbred strains can also be used to explore the contribution of genetic factors to a behavioral trait which is influenced by many genes, there is a more direct way to test the inheritance of such a trait. Rather than comparing inbred strains, we could begin with a foundation population derived from crosses between many inbred strains (a "heterogeneous stock") and then attempt to breed selectively for the trait. Such a *selective*

breeding program is conducted by mating mice high in the trait to establish a "high" line and mating mice low in the trait to establish a "low" line. If there is some influence of genes on the trait, the behavior of the high and low lines will become increasingly different when mating within lines is continued over several consecutive generations. Also, the rate of separation between the lines provides a direct estimate of the heritability of the trait. If the heritability is found to be 1.0 (that is, if there are no environmental contributions to differences in the trait), the selection response will be complete in one generation. . On the other hand, a trait that is not influenced by genes will not respond to selective breeding. Successful selection has been accomplished for several behaviors, including preference for and susceptibility to alcohol, activity, learning, and rearing behavior in mice and emotionality, speed of maze learning, and avoidance learning in rats. Both inbreeding and selective breeding procedures will be discussed again when we consider behavioral genetic studies of learning.

Human Studies

Obviously, we cannot (nor do we wish to) selectively breed people, randomly assign them to environments, or produce genetically identical groups analogous to inbred strains of mice. We can, however, find naturally occurring situations in which, on the one hand, genetic influences are controlled so that the effects of the environment can be studied and, on the other hand, environmental influences are controlled so that the effects of genes can be studied.

As mentioned earlier, when genetically-related individuals share the same environment, an observed similarity between them can be due to their shared environment as well as their shared genes. Although family studies of this kind do not untangle genetic and environmental influences, they are useful for setting limits for genetic and environmental effects. For example, if children do not resemble their parents at all in a particular trait, neither their genetic similarity nor their shared family environment influences that trait. Other, nonfamilial environmental factors must be important. Family studies are also useful in analyzing the relationship between genes and behavior. Construction of a "family tree," known as a pedigree, can suggest the mode of inheritance of a particular trait. For example, if a single-gene trait is due to one or more dominant alleles, the offspring of two affected homozygous individuals should all be affected, and no affected offspring should be produced by two unaffected individuals.

The major family relationships of use in genetic analyses are those between parents and offspring, siblings, identical twins, fraternal twins, and half-siblings. Individuals who are related in these ways normally share both genes and environment, so both genetic and environmental hypotheses would predict that they should resemble each other. For example, with respect to IQ, it is true that each of these relationships shows a significant correlation (which is an index of resemblance, as was discussed in Chapter 3). But what is the relative contribution of genetic and environmental factors? An answer to this question can be approximated, because individuals in these different relationships do not share genes to the same extent. Identical twins have the same genes because they come from the same fertilized egg. Fraternal twins (and all full-siblings other than identical twins) share half of their genes on the average, although any particular pair may share more or less than 50 percent of their genetic material. Half-siblings are individuals who have only one parent in common (as, for example, the relationship between a child that a divorced parent brings into a new marriage and a child of the new marriage); they share a quarter of their genes on the average. In each of these relationships, the individuals also share environmental influences characteristic of that type of relationship.

Table 7-4 lists these family relationships and describes their genetic and environmental similarity. The essence of the twin method, which is an example of a naturally occurring "experiment," can be gleaned from the table. Pairs of identical and fraternal twins develop in the same womb, are reared in the same family, and are the same age. Thus, the environmental influences that they share are roughly the same. However, identical twins are identical genetically, while fraternal twins are not. If many pairs of twins are studied and identical

Table 7-4. The Genetic and Environmental Similarity of Family Relationships

Relationship	Genetic Similarity	Environmental Similarity
Parents and their children	½	Yes
Full-siblings	½	Yes
Identical twins	1	Yes
Fraternal twins	½	Yes
Half-siblings	¼	Yes

twins are found to be no more similar than fraternal twins in a particular trait, then genetic factors cannot be important in determining variability for that trait. On the other hand, if identical twins are more similar, we know that the trait is influenced by genetic factors. Fraternal twins may be of the same sex or opposite sex, while identical twins are always of the same sex. Because of the sex chromosome differences between males and females, and because of the differing environments to which males and females are exposed, twin study analyses are better if we compare only same-sex fraternal twins to identical twins.

The twin method has often been subject to criticism. One problem was the precise determination of whether a particular twin pair is identical or fraternal. It is now possible, however, to perform highly accurate blood analyses in which the members of each pair of twins are compared for genetic markers in the blood. If any of these genetic markers is different in the twins, they must be fraternal; if the markers are exactly the same, the twins are identical. It is, of course, difficult to obtain blood samples from many pairs of twins. A fortunate turn of events is the finding that twins can be classified as identical or fraternal on the basis of physical characteristics such as eye color, hair color and texture, and height. Using blood analysis as the criterion, this method of diagnosis has an accuracy greater than 90 percent (Nichols and Bilbro, 1966).

Another problem with the twin method involved what is usually referred to as the "equal environments assumption." As described above, the twin method assumes that the identical-twin and fraternal-twin relationships differ only in degree of genetic similarity——that is, that they do *not* differ in similarity of environment. However, it is known that identical twins tend to be dressed somewhat more alike, to spend more time together, and to be treated a bit more similarly by their parents than fraternal twins (Loehlin and Nichols, 1976). (At least, this was true in the past, although there is a current trend to dress them differently and treat them more as individuals.) Even if it is true that identical twins are treated more similarly, does this mean that the twin method is invalid? The answer, as we shall see, is ''no.'' The small differences in treatment, such as being dressed somewhat more similarly, are unlikely to be able to account for the considerably greater similarity of identical twins than fraternal twins in the behaviors that we shall consider. Actually, the proper question is: Does the slightly greater environmental similarity of identical twins make a difference in behavior? There is evidence that it does not. Studies by Scarr (1968) have shown that twins whose zygosity [that is, monozygous (identical) or dizygous (fraternal)] is mistaken by their parents or by themselves are treated and behave according to their true zygosity. For example, true identical twins whose parents thought they were fraternal are treated as similarly and behave as similarly as identical twins who are known to be identical. Thus, the classification of twins as identical or fraternal did not affect their behavioral similarity.

Another test of the equal environments assumption is even more direct. Because identical twins are identical genetically, differences within pairs of identical twins can be caused only by environmental factors. Some identical twin pairs are treated more similarly than others; also, for any trait, some identical twin pairs are more similar behaviorally than others. Thus, we can ask whether similarity of treatment is in fact related to similarity in behavior. This is a direct test of the crucial question. Does a greater similarity in the environments of identical twins make a difference in their behavioral similarity? The answer is resoundingly negative (Loehlin and Nichols, 1976). There is no correlation between similarity of treatment (being dressed alike, spending more time together, and so on) and behavioral similarity in personality or cognitive abilities.

Looking again at Table 7-4, you might be able to think of some naturally occurring ''experiments'' other than the twin method. For example, we could compare full-siblings (who share half of their genes on the average) to half-siblings (who share only a quarter of their genes on the average). Thus, a genetically-influenced trait should show higher correlations for full-siblings than for half-siblings. This comparison is not as good as the comparison between identical and fraternal twins, however, because full-siblings are likely to experience considerably more similar environments than half-siblings (who usually have been reared for some period of time in different homes).

Correlations for IQ can be used as an example of such considerations. Table 7-5 lists the median correlation for each of the family relationships given in Table 7-4, with the exception of half-siblings (for which no data yet exist). An IQ correlation of 0 would mean that there is no resemblance at all between the individuals who are being compared, and a correlation of 1.00 would mean that they are identical. The data in Table 7-5 show that identical twins are considerably more similar than fraternal twins, indicating that genetic factors

Table 7-5. Family Relationships and IQ

Relationship	Genetic Similarity	Environmental Similarity	Median Correlation for IQ
Parents and their children	½	Yes	.48
Full-siblings	½	Yes	.49
Identical twins	1	Yes	.88
Fraternal twins	½	Yes	.53

Note. Adapted from Jarvik and Erlenmeyer-Kimling (1967).

seem to have an important influence on IQ. Furthermore, the fact that the correlations for the other family relationships are about the same as their genetic similarity also supports (but does not prove) the suggestion that there is a substantial genetic component in IQ.

Family studies are not the only approach to the study of genetic and environmental influences on human behavior. An even more powerful method is the adoption study. Through adoption, genetically-related individuals may live in unrelated environments, and genetically-unrelated individuals may live in the same environment. Similarity between the former individuals assesses genetic influences, while similarity in the latter case assesses the influence of environment. In this way, the adoption study accomplishes our goal of untangling genetic and environmental contributions to behavior.

As an example of the usefulness of the adoption study, let us consider the situation when unwed parents relinquish their child for adoption immediately after birth. These biological parents give their child genes but no postnatal environment. On the other hand, parents who adopt the child provide an environment but no genes. Thus, the correlation between biological parents and their children who are relinquished for adoption measures the influence of genetic factors, while the correlation between adoptive parents and their adopted children assesses the influence of environmental factors. These two correlations should roughly add up to

the correlation between parents and offspring when the parents rear their own children, since both genes and environment are shared in this situation.

This example illustrates the power of the adoption design as a natural "experiment." It randomizes (that is, controls) environmental influences in order to study the effect of genes, and it randomizes genetic influences to study the effect of the family environment. Similarly, siblings (including twins) are sometimes adopted into different homes. If the home environments are unrelated, any correlation in behavior between the siblings must be a function of their genetic similarity. In a case where genetically-unrelated children are adopted into the same home, similarities in behavior must be a function of the home environment. Table 7-6 summarizes the features of adoption studies and compares them to family studies. It can be seen that the adoption design separates the genetic and environmental components of family relationships.

What, then, do we find for adoption studies of IQ? The median correlations for each relationship in family studies and adoption studies are listed in Table 7-7. Because adoption studies are much more difficult to conduct, they are much more rare. For the genetic estimates (second column), there are only three studies relating the IQ of biological parents and their children who were relinquished for adoption, three studies of separated siblings, four studies of separated identical twins, and no studies of separated fraternal twins. For the envi-

Table 7-6.   Adoption Designs

| | FAMILY STUDIES | | ADOPTION STUDIES | | | |
| | (Individuals share genes and environment) | | Randomizing environment to study genetic influences [a] | | Randomizing genes to study environmental influences [b] | |
Relationship	Genetic similarity	Environmental similarity	Genetic similarity	Environmental similarity	Genetic similarity	Environmental similarity
Parents and their children	½	Yes	½	No	No	Yes
Full-siblings	½	Yes	½	No	No	Yes
Identical twins	1	Yes	1	No	(unrelated children reared in same family)	
Fraternal twins	½	Yes	½	No		

[a] Genetically-related living in *un*related environments.   [b] Genetically-*un*related living in related environments.

Table 7-7. Median IQ Correlations for Family Studies and Adoption Designs

Relationship	FAMILY STUDIES (Individuals share genes and environment)	ADOPTION STUDIES	
		Genetic influences [a]	Environmental influences [b]
Parents and their children	.48	.32	.18
Full-siblings	.49	.46	(unrelated children
Identical twins	.88	.75	reared in same family:
Fraternal twins	.53		.17)

Note. Adapted from Jarvik and Erlenmeyer-Kimling (1967) and Jencks (1972), with newer data included.
[a] Genetically-related living in unrelated environments.
[b] Genetically-unrelated living in related environments.

ronmental assessments (third column), there are four studies relating IQ of adoptive parents and their adopted children and seven studies of unrelated children reared in the same family. By comparing the columns of Table 7-7, we can see that the IQ correlations in family studies are primarily due to genetic similarity rather than environmental similarity. Keep in mind that each column of data in Table 7-7 corresponds to different genetic and environmental components, as noted in Table 7-6. Note that full-siblings reared apart are almost as similar (.46) as siblings who have lived together with their biological parents (.49). Genetically-unrelated children who are adopted into the same family are much less similar (.17). Thus, these data suggest a strong genetic component and indicate that the environmental similarity involved in living in the same family is not as important as genetic similarity in influencing IQ.

Quantitative Estimates of Genetic and Environmental Influences

Data from behavioral genetic studies can do more than point to the possible influences of genetic and environmental factors. Quantitative estimates of the relative contributions of the two types of effects can also be derived. It seems apparent from Table 7-7 that genetic factors account for more of the individual differences in IQ than do environmental influences, and such general information is often sufficient. However, scientists have a penchant for more precise description. As mentioned earlier, a statistic called "heritability" is the proportion of individual differences (phenotypic variance) due to genetic factors. Similarly, although it is a rather clumsy term, "environmentability" can be used to refer to the proportion of individual differences not explained by genetic factors. Let us emphasize again that heritability (or environmentability) must not be thought of as a constant value. These statistics *describe* individual differences in a particular population with that population's genetic and environmental differences at that point in time. Heritable does not mean unalterable. If new genetic or environmental factors are introduced into the population, the description of the relative roles of genetic and environmental influences can change.

It is also important to remember that these descriptive statistics apply to a population rather than to an individual. If we say that height has a heritability of .80, that is shorthand for saying that 80 percent of the differences in height observed in this population at this time are genetic in origin. It does not mean that an individual who is five feet tall grew to the height of four feet as the result of his genes and that the other twelve inches were added by the environment. It means that people differ in height and that 80 percent of this variation is due to inherited differences. The same reasoning, of course, applies to behavioral traits.

Animal Studies. There are three methods used to establish heritability and environmentability in studies of animals: classical analysis, selection, and family resemblance. To conduct a *classical analysis,* inbred strains (called parental populations) are crossed to produce an F1 generation. As we noted earlier, members of each of the inbred strains are identical genetically, so any differences within strains are due to the environment. The hybrid F1 generation also has no genetic variability. For example, considering a particular locus with two alleles (*AA* in one parental strain, and *aa* in the other), we may see that crossing the two parental strains yields offspring who are all *Aa*. Thus, variability within each of these three groups estimates environmental impact (because there are no genetic differences). When we cross F1 animals at random to produce an F2 generation, genes segregate according to Mendelian laws. The F2 generation, therefore, has genetic as well as environmental variability. Because the F1 shows only environmental variability and the F2 shows both environmental and genetic variability, the difference between the variances of the F1 and F2 generations is the amount of genetic variability. Heritability, as we have said, is the proportion of the total variability (genetic plus environmental) that is attributed to genetic variability. Thus, one estimate of heritability from a classical analysis can be derived as follows:

$$\text{Heritability} = \frac{\text{Variance F2} - \text{Variance F1}}{\text{Variance F2}}$$

$$= \frac{(\text{V genetic} + \text{V environmental}) - \text{V environmental}}{(\text{V genetic} + \text{V environmental})}$$

$$= \frac{\text{V genetic}}{\text{V total}}.$$

The second method for estimating heritability comes from the selective breeding procedure described earlier. Suppose that we wish to use the *selection* method to determine the influence of genetic factors upon activity in an open field. We would establish a ''high'' activity line and a ''low'' activity line by mating like extremes over consecutive generations, and then we would test the activity of their respective offspring. If open-field activity is completely determined by genetic factors, offspring ought to be exactly like their parents in this behavior; that is, offspring of high-active mice should be as highly active as their parents. If open-field activity is not at all influenced by genetic factors, the mean activity level of the high-active offspring should not be different

from the mean of all animals in the previous generation. When a difference is found between these means, it is referred to as the *response to selection*. In other words, the response to selection is the change in the mean that accompanies one generation of selective breeding. We would also determine the difference between the mean activity level of those extreme individuals chosen to be parents and the mean of all animals in that generation. This difference is known as the *selection differential;* it is a measure of the strength of selection pressure.

The quantitative estimate of heritability resulting from this method is expressed as follows:

$$\text{Heritability} = \frac{\text{response to selection}}{\text{selection differential}}.$$

Thus, the meaning of a particular response to selection depends on the size of the selection differential. Let us say that the response to selection for open-field activity was found to be 5. A relatively high selection differential of 20 would result in a heritability of .25 while a more moderate selection differential of 10 would result in a heritability of .50. In a large-scale selection study, the actual heritability of open-field activity in mice was found to be .26 (DeFries et al., 1974).

The third method for estimating heritability in animal studies is to measure the similarity of parents and their offspring, of full-siblings, and of half-siblings (offspring who have only one parent in common). This procedure is similar to the method used to estimate heritability in human studies, and it will be described in detail in the following section. At this point, however, it is interesting to note that a parent-offspring analysis of mouse open-field activity yielded a heritability estimate of .22 (DeFries and Hegmann, 1970), which is very close to the estimate derived from the selection study. On the other hand, the heritability estimate from a classical analysis of open-field activity was .43 (McClearn and DeFries, 1973), because estimates from highly divergent strains are likely to show a large amount of genetic variability.

Human Studies. Estimates of heritability and environmentability can be derived from both family studies and adoption studies. The most intuitively-obvious estimate of heritability comes from adoption studies of identical twins who are placed in different homes immediately after birth. As indicated in Table 7-6, any similarity in behavior (phenotypic similarity) between such twins can be due only to genetic factors, if their environments are uncorrelated. Because they are identical genetically, their phenotypic similarity directly estimates the heritability of the trait. Consider that a correlation is the proportion of the phenotypic variance that is shared by the individuals being compared (in this case, by identical twins) and that heritability is the proportion of phenotypic variance due to genetic variance. Thus, because their shared phenotypic variance is completely attributed to genetic variance, the correlation for separated identical twins *is* the estimated heritability of the trait. Referring to Table 7-7, the median IQ correlation for identical twins living in unrelated environments suggests a heritability of .75. In other words, this suggests that about 75 percent of the individual differences in IQ observed in this population was due to genetic factors. Since the environment is given credit for individual differences that are not genetic in origin, environmentability in this case was about 25 percent.

Although the estimation of heritability from studies of identical twins reared apart is appealingly direct, this method is no better than other estimates of heritability, and it is limited by the rarity of separated identical twins. In adoption studies of genetically-related individuals living in unrelated environments, correlations between individuals who share half of their genes estimate half of the heritability of the trait. For example, the correlation between biological parents and their children who are relinquished for adoption estimates half of the influence of genetic factors, and doubling this value yields another estimate of heritability. Doubling the correlation of .32 given for this relationship in Table 7-7 suggests that the heritability for IQ is .64. Doubling the correlation of .46 obtained in adoption studies of full-siblings suggests a heritability of .92. Heritability may also be estimated from family studies using the twin method. Because identical twins are twice as similar genetically as fraternal twins, we may subtract the fraternal twin correlation from the identical twin correlation to estimate half of the heritability of the trait. Referring again to Table 7-7, the difference between the identical and fraternal twin correlations for IQ is .88 minus .53, or .35. Doubling this difference suggests a heritability of .70. If heritability is about .70 in this case, then environmentability is about .30. Although these estimates vary somewhat, they consistently point to significant genetic influence.

There are several complicating issues that would demand consideration in a more detailed treatment of these quantitative methods for estimating heritability and environmentability. One such complication is the fact that there are two kinds of heritability, "broad" and "narrow." Broad heritability (which, for example, is estimated by twin studies) includes all genetic variance. Narrow heritability (as estimated, for example, by the selection method) includes only "additive" genetic variance, that is, it excludes genetic variance caused by interactions between alleles and between loci. Details of such complicating factors are discussed by McClearn and DeFries (1973). None of these complications, however, would prevent us from concluding that genetic factors play a major role in the etiology of IQ.

Genotype-Environment Interaction. In our earlier discussion of behavioral genetic methods used in animal studies, we described an experiment in which a particular environmental condition (prenatal stress) had an opposite effect on activity of two inbred mouse strains (see Figure 7-5 on p. 236). The C57BL animals were less active when stressed prenatally, while the BALB/c mice were more active. This is an example of genotype-environment interaction. In other words, the two strains (genotypes) responded differently to the environmental stress condition (or, alternatively, environmental stress affected the two strains differently). From our previous discussions of the tremendous variability of human genotypes, we know that marked genetic differences exist among men as well as mice. Thus, the above example serves as a reminder that we must not expect a particular environmental variable to have the same effect on all people all of the time.

As a useful illustration of the effect of genotype-environment interaction on human behavior, let us again consider the condition of severe mental retardation known as phenylketonuria (PKU). Back in the 1930s, as now, there were many retarded individuals, and there were many attempts to alleviate retardation by modifying the environment in various ways. It was noticed that certain retarded individuals emitted a distinctive odor. This odor was found to be caused by an excess of phenylalanine, and it turned out that individuals affected by PKU have a defective form of an enzyme involved in phenylalanine metabolism. This defect results in the abnormal accumulation of various metabolites which are severely damaging to the developing brain. The development of a treatment for the condition was made possible by this understanding of its biochemical and physiological mechanisms. A special diet containing no phenylalanine, when administered early in life, very substantially reduces retardation in children affected by PKU.

The moral to the story of PKU is that a researcher who thought that a special phenylalanine-free diet would alleviate all conditions of mental retardation would be sadly disappointed. Individuals suffering from PKU constitute only a very small proportion of the retarded. If the special diet were administered to all retarded individuals, there would be no noticeable beneficial effect on the population as whole. Nevertheless, this environmental intervention has an extremely powerful influence on a *particular type* of retardation. Of course, the moral also applies to the study of many kinds of environmental effects on many types of behavior, and it emphasizes the importance of recognizing the presence of genotype-environment interactions. It has recently been shown (Plomin et al., 1977) that the adoption study method can provide a searchlight to scan for possible interactions between genotypes and environments.

Behavioral Genetics and Psychology

Behavioral genetics provides the methods needed to untangle genetic and environmental threads woven into the fabric of behavior. These methods are potentially applicable to any area of psychology—perception, information processing, learning, cognition, language, personality, psychopathology, development, and social behavior. However, most of the work in human behavioral genetics has focused on intelligence, psychopathology, and personality. We have already discussed research that points to a significant genetic component in intelligence. In this section, we shall describe behavioral genetic research with respect to learning, specific cognitive abilities, psychopathology, and personality. First, however, let us speculate for a moment about the potential contribution of behavioral genetics to other areas of psychology.

Individual Differences and Psychology

We must wonder why behavioral genetic analyses in areas other than intelligence, psychopathology, and personality have been so rare. The answer lies in the traditional typological approach of psychology to the study of behavior. Psychologists interested in learning became accustomed to thinking of *the* organism; that is, even differences *among* species were not recognized. For example, one of the classic books in the area of learning is entitled *The Behavior of Organisms* (Skinner, 1938), even though only one species (rat) was studied. Although some of these findings do generalize across species, there are important differences as well. It is obvious that some variables (for example, language) which are essential to an understanding of human learning do not apply to learning in lower organisms. Such differences, of course, have been recognized by comparative psychologists, whose major concern is describing differences among species. Unfortunately, many psychologists have continued to ignore differences *within* species—to think of *the* mouse or *the* human being. Our earlier discussion of strain differences in mice makes clear the hazards of a typological approach to the study of behavior in that species, and we also know that there are marked individual differences among people.

Psychological experimentation has often supported typological thinking by treating individual differences as "error." The essence of the experimental method is the random assignment of subjects to groups so that the only differences between the groups are created by the independent variable. Individual differences within these groups are considered as "errors" that detract from the statistical significance of the intergroup differences. Results of such an experiment can be interpreted by saying that the independent variable did or did not cause a difference between the groups in this experimental situation. However, it remains to be determined whether the results generalize to the world outside the laboratory. In this sense, experiments suggest *what could be* the effects of the independent variable on the behavior of people in the real world.

In contrast, approaches that consider individual differences (sometimes called correlational methods) describe *what is* observed about behavior in a particular population. Behavioral genetic studies are an example of such an approach; they describe genetic and environmental differences that produce differences in the behavior of people in the real world. Actually, the two methodological viewpoints should be considered as complementary. Sound speculations about *what could be* are best derived from descriptions of *what is*.

The importance of individual differences in traditionally experimental areas of psychology may be seen in studies of information processing. The goal of most of these studies has been typological, to find *the* model of how people process information. Hundreds of researchers and thousands of studies in this flourishing research area have not converged on a single model. What has become most apparent is the fact that people differ greatly in how they encode and retrieve information.

Once the spotlight is shifted to individual differences, the stage is set for behavioral genetics. As we have said, behavioral genetics is the study of genetic and environmental influences that make a difference in behavior. Since behavioral differences have always been the focus of research on intelligence, psychopathology, and personality, it is no accident that the methods of behavioral genetics were first applied in these areas. One general lesson to be learned from these studies is that genetic factors must be considered in any attempt to explain complex human behaviors. This lesson

will no doubt increase the application of behavioral genetic methods to other areas of psychology. At this point, we shall turn to a description of the results of behavioral genetic studies in our four chosen areas.

Learning

Chapter 9 will be devoted to a detailed discussion of learning; in this chapter, we shall discuss the contributions of behavioral genetics to research in this key area. In the past, learning was studied typologically, with little consideration of differences within species or even among them. Although it is now quite common to recognize the importance of the latter, variation within species still tends to be neglected. Nonetheless, behavioral genetic analyses have shown that nearly every type of learning is influenced by intraspecific genetic variability. For example, studies of inbred mouse strains have shown genetic differences in active avoidance learning, passive avoidance learning, escape learning, reversal learning, discrimination learning, maze learning, and even heart-rate conditioning.

Active avoidance learning will serve as an example. This type of learning is commonly studied in an apparatus known as a "shuttle box," which is a box with two compartments and an electrified floor. An animal is put in one compartment and a light is flashed on, followed by a shock which continues until the animal moves to the other compartment. Animals learn to avoid shock by moving to the other compartment as soon as the light is turned on. We should say that *some* animals learn to avoid the shock. There are wide individual differences in learning, and studies of inbred mice suggest that the differences are genetic to some extent. The left side of Figure 7-6 shows avoidance learning for three inbred strains of mice on five days of training with one hundred trials each day (Bovet et al., 1969). It can be seen that none of the strains avoided on the first day; animals received shock on more than 90 percent of the trials. The DBA strain, however, learned quickly and avoided the shock 85 percent of the time by the fifth day. On the other hand, the CBA strain never learned at all; even on the fifth day, these animals avoided the shock only

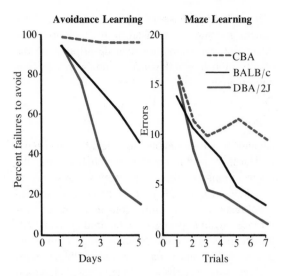

Fig. 7-6. Avoidance learning and maze learning for three inbred strains of mice. Avoidance learning consisted of five consecutive daily sessions of 100 trials. Each point in the maze learning illustration represents the average number of errors made by 16 mice given one daily trial. (After Bovet et al., 1969)

tered and is referred to as *hybrid vigor,* or *heterosis.* The term is used in the same sense when we speak of hybrid corn or other hybrid vegetables and fruits. As we have already seen, the process of inbreeding, if continued for a sufficient number of generations, results in a strain all members of which are essentially identical genetically. All animals of the strain will be homozygous for each locus and, at any particular locus, all animals will be homozygous for the same allele. Some of the alleles that are fixed are recessive, resulting in the expression of recessive traits that are often deleterious. For this reason, inbred strains often show "inbreeding depression," which is a reduction in vigor. When two inbred strains are crossed to produce an F1 generation, recessive alleles from one strain are likely to be masked by dominant alleles from the other strain. Thus, in comparison with the parental strains, F1 animals are likely to show increased vigor if recessive and dominant alleles are involved in the trait under consideration. The fact that hybrid vigor is apparent for avoidance learning supports the suggestion that genetic effects are present.

The selection method has also been used to show that avoidance learning is influenced by

4 percent of the time. The BALB strain was intermediate between the DBAs and the CBAs.

Figure 7-6 also shows that strain differences are not peculiar to aversive learning (that is, learning to avoid an unpleasant event such as shock). Performances of the same three strains on an appetitive task, learning to run through a maze to obtain food, are shown on the right side of the figure. Once again, the DBA strain learned quickly, the CBA strain was slow in learning (although they learned a bit this time), and the BALB strain was intermediate.

The suggestion that avoidance learning has a significant inherited component has been supported by results of classical genetic analyses. One such study (Collins, 1964), for example, included the DBA and BALB strains, noted above as being fast and intermediate learners, respectively. The F1 animals produced by crossing these strains were even faster in learning than their DBA parents. This genetic phenomenon is commonly encoun-

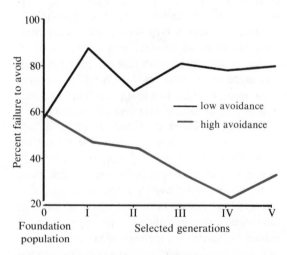

Fig. 7-7. Avoidance learning during selection for high and low avoidance in rats. The number of animals represented by each point ranges from 18 to 95. (After Bignami, 1965)

genes. Two lines of rats, the Roman High Avoidance (RHA) and the Roman Low Avoidance (RLA), have been developed by selective breeding for differences in speed of acquisition and retention in learning to avoid shock in the shuttle box. The results are presented in Figure 7-7. Before selection, the animals avoided shock on 42 percent of the trials; after five generations of selection, the RHA and the RLA avoided shock on 68 percent and 20 percent of the trials, respectively.

It can be seen that the inbred strain method and the selection method concur in suggesting a major role for genes in the determination of individual differences in avoidance learning. This is only one example of the potential application of behavioral genetic analyses to the study of learning.

Specific Cognitive Abilities

The evidence from family studies and adoption studies summarized in Table 7-7 (on p. 241) indicates that a substantial portion of individual differences in IQ is caused by genetic factors. However, IQ does not tell the whole story of intelligence. Underlying intelligence are specific cognitive abilities such as verbal ability, spatial ability, perceptual speed, and memory. The fact that these specific abilities are modestly correlated with one another lends some support to the notion of "general intelligence," but they are sufficiently different to provide a more fine-grained analysis of cognitive functioning.

Behavioral genetic analyses have begun to focus on specific cognitive abilities rather than on intelligence in general. In a recent study in Hawaii, fifteen tests of cognitive ability were administered to approximately 1,500 families (over 5,000 individuals) of two ethnic groups, Americans of European ancestry (AEA) and Americans of Japanese ancestry (AJA). Four factors (clusters of related tests) emerged from an analysis of the fifteen tests: verbal (vocabulary and fluency), spatial (visualizing and rotating objects in two- and three-dimensional space), perceptual speed (simple arithmetic and number comparisons), and memory (short- and longer-term recognition of line drawings). The factors were nearly identical in the two ethnic groups, suggesting that cognitive processes are

organized in much the same way in these two populations (DeFries et al., 1974).

Correlations between parents and their children (averaged for father-son, father-daughter, mother-son, and mother-daughter) in the two ethnic groups for the four factors and a "general" factor (an index of "general intelligence") are presented in Table 7-8. Because parents share half of their genes with their children, doubling these correlations provides an upper-limit estimate of heritability. (We say that it is an "upper-limit" estimate, in this case, because environmental influences are also shared by parents and their children.) For the general factor, these estimates of heritability (.76 for the AEA sample and .58 for the AJA sample) are in line with the previously mentioned estimates of heritability for IQ. Correlations for the four specific cognitive factors indicate substantial heritability, although less than for general intelligence. It is interesting to note that the data suggest greater heritability in both ethnic groups for the verbal and spatial factors than for perceptual speed and memory.

Table 7-8. Single-Parent, Single-Child Correlations for Specific Cognitive Factors in Two Ethnic Groups

	Americans of European Ancestry (1,744 pairs)	Americans of Japanese Ancestry (536 pairs)
Verbal	.32	.31
Spatial	.32	.25
Perceptual speed	.24	.17
Memory	.15	.13
"General"	.38	.29

Note. Adapted from DeFries et al (1976).

There have been about a dozen twin studies of specific cognitive abilities. Two of the larger of these (including 346 pairs of twins and 493 pairs, respectively) were conducted in Finland (Brunn et al., 1966) and in the United States (Schoenfeldt, 1968). Although the studies used different tests, they each included two tests measuring each of the four cognitive ability factors. The correlations for identical twins and for fraternal twins and the es-

Table 7-9. Identical and Fraternal Twin Correlations and Twin Study Heritabilities for Four Cognitive Ability Factors in Two Twin Studies

| | DATA FROM BRUUN ET AL. STUDY[a] | | | DATA FROM SCHOENFELDT STUDY[b] | | |
| | Correlations | | | Correlations | | |
	Identical (157 pairs)	Fraternal (189 pairs)	Heritability	Identical (337 pairs)	Fraternal (156 pairs)	Heritability
Verbal	.78	.53	.50	.80	.48	.64
Spatial	.59	.36	.46	.67	.41	.52
Perceptual speed	.73	.50	.46	.67	.51	.32
Memory	.64	.32	.64	.43	.19	.48

[a] Bruun et al., 1966.
[b] Schoenfeldt, 1968.

timated heritabilities for each factor are presented in Table 7-9. (Remember that heritability is estimated by doubling the difference between identical and fraternal twin correlations.) Again, these studies point to a substantial inherited component in specific cognitive abilities. They also suggest that heritability for the specific factors is somewhat less than for general intelligence. Finally, although results of these studies and of the family study in Hawaii do not agree completely as to which cognitive abilities are most highly heritable, there is the same hint that verbal and spatial abilities may be more heritable than perceptual speed.

Now that the influence of genes on intellectual functioning has been established, considerably more information on the genetic and environmental determinants of specific cognitive abilities can be expected in the near future.

Psychopathology

In this section, we shall briefly summarize behavioral genetic studies of the two major types of psychoses, schizophrenia and the manic-depressive syndrome. Behavioral descriptions of these conditions will be given in Chapter 20. Traditionally, schizophrenia has more often been the subject of behavioral genetic studies. Results of many of these studies have indicated that schizophrenia runs in families. Because schizophrenia has been viewed as an either-or phenomenon (either an individual is schizophrenic or not), correlations are not the appropriate statistic to describe

familial resemblance. Instead, the data are reported in terms of "risk" that the condition will appear in various relatives of schizophrenic individuals. Risk is the *expected* incidence for various relationships, and it takes into account the fact that not all relatives will have passed the age range in which schizophrenia usually appears (from fifteen to at least forty-five years of age). Although there is considerable variation from study to study, the median risk for parents of schizophrenics in fourteen studies was 4.2 percent; for siblings of schizophrenics, it was 7.5 percent; and the children of a schizophrenic parent in five studies had a median risk of 9.7 percent (Rosenthal, 1970). Because the incidence of this condition in the general population is about 1 percent, these results suggest that first-degree relatives of schizophrenics (those who share half of their genes) are four to ten times more likely to be schizophrenic than an individual randomly chosen from the population. There also is evidence that second-degree relatives of schizophrenics, such as grandparents, grandchildren, and uncles and aunts (who share a quarter of their genes), are about twice as likely to be schizophrenic as the average individual.

Since these data were obtained by the family study method, they indicate that genes have an important effect, but they could also be compatible with environmental influences. Twin studies or adoption studies are necessary to put genetic and environmental hypotheses to the test. Results of eleven twin studies in seven countries have been reported in terms of concordance for schizophrenia in groups of identical and fraternal twins (Kringlen, 1966). Members of a twin pair are said to be *concordant* if they both possess or both are free of a particular trait, and the relative frequency of concordance in identical and fraternal twins can be used to compare the groups. Like correlation, concordance is a measure of resemblance. In the studies reported by Kringlen, the median concordance for identical twins was 42 percent, while that for fraternal twins was 9 percent. Although these concordances do not conform to a simple genetic model, they do clearly support the genetic hypothesis. However, because they are far below concordances that would be expected if the environment had no influence, they also suggest that environmental factors are important. Results of adoption studies are consistent with these conclusions. Of fourteen pairs of identical twins who were reared apart from the first year of life, ten pairs were concordant for schizophrenia (Gottesman and Shields, 1972). Although a situation of this kind is obviously rare, and the sample is accordingly small, the observed concordance of 72 percent strongly supports the hypothesis that genes have an important effect on schizophrenia. The fact that four pairs were not concordant suggests that environmental influences are also pertinent.

More adequate sample sizes come from adoption studies in which children of a schizophrenic parent are reared by adoptive parents who suffer from no known psychopathology. The first study of this type was conducted by Heston (1966). He studied forty-seven adults who had been relinquished for adoption by their schizophrenic mothers within the first few weeks of life. A group of fifty adults who had also been adopted but whose biological parents had no known psychopathology was used as a control group. The average age of the adults was over thirty-five years (toward the upper end of the age range in which schizophrenia usually appears). The startling finding was that five of the adults in the experimental group were diagnosed schizophrenic, while not one of the control group was so diagnosed. This landmark study has since been replicated twice, and a total of 137 adopted persons born to schizophrenic mothers has been studied. The frequency of schizophrenia among these subjects was 10.2

percent, which is nearly the same as the rate found when children are reared by schizophrenic biological parents (Crowe, 1975). In all three studies, none of the adopted children in the control groups was schizophrenic.

While an overall view of the adoption data suggests that both genetic and environmental factors are involved in schizophrenia, results of the latter studies indicate that the *family* environment does not have a very important effect. If such environmental influences are important, the frequency of schizophrenia among children born to schizophrenic parents should be noticeably greater when schizophrenic parents rear the children than when they are reared by nonschizophrenic adoptive parents. The conclusion that the family environment is not very important is endorsed by a study that employed a modification of the adoption design. Wender et al (1974) studied the "schizophrenic spectrum" (a broader category of psychopathology sometimes called "schizoid") in adopted children and their biological and adoptive parents. In agreement with previous studies, these investigators found that adopted children whose biological parents were schizoid were significantly more likely to be schizoid than adopted children whose biological parents were normal. The study also included twenty-eight "cross-fostered" children, that is, children whose biological parents were normal but who were reared by schizoid adoptive parents, and a control group of children whose biological and adoptive parents were normal. If the family environment contributes to schizophrenia, we would expect a greater incidence of schizoid disorders among cross-fostered children than among the controls. The results, however, showed no difference between the two groups and this important finding has been replicated in another study by the same investigators (Wender et al., 1978).

Rather than starting with schizophrenic parents and determining whether or not their children are schizophrenic, one study (Kety et al., 1976) reversed the procedure. Adopted schizophrenic individuals and a control group of nonschizophrenic adoptees were located, and the incidence of schizoid disorders in the biological and adoptive relatives of these individuals was determined. The frequency of schizoid biological relatives of the schizophrenic adoptees was 12 percent; for the nonschizophrenic adoptees, it was only 4 percent. The two groups did not differ in the incidence of schizoid disorders among their adoptive relatives. Once again, the evidence suggests that genes are more important than family environment in the etiology of schizophrenia.

Taken together, these behavioral genetic studies point to a major role for inherited factors in schizophrenia. A recent survey of adoption studies of schizophrenia (DeFries and Plomin, 1978) found 211 biological relatives of schizophrenics (who never lived with these relatives) and 192 matched "control" individuals. Even though the biological relatives did not live with the schizophrenics, 13 percent of them were schizophrenic. Only 1.5 percent of the control relatives were schizophrenic. However, the degree of genetic influence and the mode of inheritance are not fully understood. Part of the problem arises from questions about diagnosis. For example, should schizophrenia be strictly defined, or should it include the whole "schizophrenic spectrum"? Most investigators have noted increased psychopathology short of actual psychotic episodes in biological relatives of schizophrenics. Even though the concordance for clearcut schizophrenia is only 42 percent for identical twins, it is unusual to find a completely "normal" identical twin of a schizophrenic individual. Studies of the broader category of psychopathology referred to as the "schizophrenic spectrum" indicate an even greater degree of genetic influence, and one researcher (Heston, 1970) suggests that the data implicate a single dominant gene in the transmission of schizophrenia. Most investigators, however, opt for polygenic inheritance with some environmental influence.

Although much remains to be learned about schizophrenia, attention has recently turned to the other major type of psychosis, the manic-depressive syndrome. The incidence of manic-depressive psychosis in the general population is slightly less than the incidence of schizophrenia, and persons suffering from it are less likely to be hospitalized because the symptoms are less severe. Nevertheless, it is an important societal problem if for no other reason than most suicides are thought to be precipitated by depression. Like schizophrenia, manic-depressive illness shows increased risk in affected families. In the studies reported by Rosenthal (1970), the risk for parents of manic-depressive psychotics was 7.6 percent, that for siblings was 8.8 percent, and that for children was 11.2 percent. The risk in each of these relationships is slightly higher than analogous risks for schizophrenia. Twin studies strongly suggest that genetic factors make an important contribution to familial resemblance. In seven such studies (with a total of ninety-nine pairs of identical twins and 252 fraternal twin pairs), the concordance for identical twins was 71 percent and that for fraternal twins was 19 percent. There are as yet no adoption studies of manic-depressive psychosis.

Research on the manic-depressive syndrome may be used to illustrate the fruitfulness of an analytical approach to the behavioral genetic study of complex behaviors. The clinical observation that there are two distinct types of manic-depressive psychosis led to many important discoveries. Some so-called manic depressives actually alternate between depression and normality, not between depression and mania. This type has been labeled "unipolar depression." The type that exhibits episodic bouts of mania and depression is called "bipolar manic-depressive psychosis." Evidence from three sources suggests that the unipolar and bipolar types are etiologically distinct. First, three studies have demonstrated that the types tend to be inherited separately. Unipolar depressives tend to have unipolar relatives, and bipolar depressives tend to have bipolar relatives (Perris, 1972). Second, evidence is mounting that a dominant sex-linked gene is involved in the bipolar type but not in the unipolar type (Mendlewicz and Fleiss, 1974). The third indication that the types are distinct comes from biochemical studies in which bipolars, but not unipolars, responded to lithium treatment (Baron et al., 1975).

In addition to the division of manic-depressive psychosis into two different types, there are indications that each type may be further divided. Although a sex-linked mode of inheritance for the bipolar condition was demonstrated by Mendlewicz and Fleiss (1974), they also found some cases of father-to-son inheritance. This could not have occurred if the bipolar condition is always inherited in a sex-linked fashion. Biochemical studies by Taylor and Abrams (1975) showed that some bipolars respond to lithium treatment and some do not. Although they do not differ in onset or duration of illness, the responders tend to be more euphoric in their mania and the nonresponders frequently exhibit auditory hallucinations. Unipolar depressives have recently been divided into two types on the basis of their response to tricyclic antidepressants (Kupfer et al., 1975). The tricyclic responders, unlike the nonresponders, tend to be chronically anxious and obsessive. Another categorization divides unipolar depression into a "pure depressive disorder," with onset after the age of forty and an equal number of affected males and females, and "depression spectrum," with an early onset and a preponderance of affected females (Winokur, 1974).

It can be seen that analysis has been the key to progress in research on psychopathology. Before 1900, no distinction was made between schizophrenia and the manic-depressive syndrome. The differentiation of psychosis into these two major types gave impetus to research, especially with respect to schizophrenia. Recently, the division of manic-depressive psychosis into bipolar and unipolar types stimulated a burst of research, and yet another boost is likely to come from further analyses of the bipolar and unipolar conditions. The genetics and biochemistry of psychopathology, as well as the role of environmental influences, have become more clearly defined by the use of an analytical approach in behavioral genetic research. There is no doubt that this approach will be important in the study of other complex behaviors as well.

Personality

We have noted that activity, "emotionality," and social behavior in mice are influenced by genetic factors, and it is reasonable to suppose that basic aspects of personality in humans may also be affected by genes. However, partly because of problems of measurement, there have been very few behavioral genetic studies in this area. Nearly all of these have been twin studies using self-report personality questionnaires. Even though a great deal of confusion has resulted from the fact that few of the studies have used the same measures, genetic factors have been implicated in most personality traits, perhaps as much as in the case of cognitive abilities.

The largest twin study of personality was conducted by Loehlin and Nichols (1976). More than 300 pairs each of identical and fraternal twins, all of high-school age, answered the 480 items (eighteen scales) of the California Psychological Inventory. As an exception to the unfortunate rule that most twin studies of personality have used different questionnaires, Horn et al. (1976) also used the California Psychological Inventory in a study of 200 pairs of adult male twins (fifty-five years old, on the average). The twin data for the high school boys in the Loehlin and Nichols study and for the adult males in the study by Horn and his colleagues are presented in Table 7-10.

It is clear from these data that personality is to some extent inherited. For the high-school boys, the average correlations for the eighteen scales were .51 for the identical twins and .24 for the fraternal twins, yielding a heritability estimate of .54. The average correlations for the adult males were .44 for identical twins and .19 for fraternal twins, suggesting a heritability of .50. It is particularly interesting to note that high-school twins living together are only slightly more similar in personality than adult twins who have been living apart for at least three decades. Thus, both studies agree in suggesting a strong genetic component in personality. This suggestion is supported by the results of other twin studies.

There is little agreement, however, concerning which aspects of personality are most highly heritable. Again, the lack of consensus has been caused in part by the use of different measures of personality in different studies. However, even when two studies using the same personality inventory are compared, Table 7-10 shows that there is only slight agreement between them. Both studies did find that Communality was one of the least heritable scales and that Achievement via Conformance was one of the most heritable. The rank-order correlation between the two sets of heritabilities was only a modest .22.

Table 7-10. Identical and Fraternal Twin Correlations and Twin Study Heritabilities for the 18 Scales of the California Psychological Inventory in Two Twin Studies

	HIGH SCHOOL MALES[a]			ADULT MALES[b]		
	Identical twin correlations (202 pairs)	*Fraternal twin correlations (125 pairs)*	*Heritability*	*Identical twin correlations (99 pairs)*	*Fraternal twin correlations (99 pairs)*	*Heritability*
Dominance	.57	.13	.88	.53	.28	.50
Capacity for status	.54	.35	.38	.54	.25	.58
Sociability	.51	.25	.52	.51	.18	.66
Social presence	.51	.15	.72	.54	.21	.66
Self-acceptance	.42	.14	.56	.47	.23	.48
Sense of well-being	.54	.33	.42	.43	.13	.60
Responsibility	.57	.29	.56	.44	.33	.22
Socialization	.53	.15	.76	.43	.25	.36
Self-control	.56	.26	.60	.45	.12	.66
Tolerance	.59	.28	.62	.47	.17	.60
Good impression	.49	.28	.42	.42	.13	.58
Communality	.31	.23	.16	.22	.06	.32
Achievement via conformance	.48	.05	.86	.41	.01	.80
Achievement via independence	.57	.39	.36	.49	.25	.48
Intellectual efficiency	.57	.29	.56	.49	.30	.38
Psychological-mindedness	.47	.28	.38	.36	.18	.36
Flexibility	.41	.23	.36	.49	.10	.78
Femininity	.41	.27	.28	.27	.15	.24
Average	.51	.24	.54	.44	.19	.50

[a] Loehlin and Nichols, 1976.
[b] Horn et al, 1976.

One reason for this lack of agreement is that the California Psychological Inventory suffers from considerable item overlap; that is, nearly 200 items are scored on more than one scale, and some are scored on as many as seven of the eighteen scales. For this reason, most of the scales are difficult to differentiate in terms of heritability. When overlapping items were eliminated, two of the scales (Responsibility and Femininity) showed zero heritability and Achievement via Conformance remained highly heritable (Horn et al, 1976). Another method used in the same study was to analyze individual items rather than scales. By the application of rather complicated statistical procedures, the researchers identified forty-one reliable "genetic" items among the 480 items of the California Psychological Inventory. Similarly, seventy-four environmental items (items showing no heritability) are selected. Results of a factor analysis of the genetic items revealed a large cluster of items related to conversational poise (for example, "It is hard for me to find anything to talk about when I meet a new person."). Many studies converge on the conclusion that sociability is to some extent inherited, and these results suggest that the underlying inherited component in sociability may be an ability to interact with strangers. The other clusters of genetic items and the clusters of environmental items were not large. The largest environmental cluster dealt with leadership (for example, "I think I am usually a leader in my group"). The use of item analysis is a promising method for revealing genetic and environmental influences on personality.

In addition to problems of measurement, another hindrance to the behavioral genetic study of personality has been the lack of a theory to guide the search for inherited components of personality traits. Although this difficulty also applies to the study of intelligence, the problem with respect to personality may be more severe. Each personality trait (sociability, for example) may prove to be as complex as the whole range of cognitive abilities included within "general intelligence." Researchers can be overwhelmed by the complexity of personality.

Buss and Plomin (1975) have recently presented a theory of personality development based on "temperaments," which they defined as inherited personality dispositions. The theory includes four traits: emotionality, activity, sociability, and impulsivity. (Although activity is not often considered in studies of personality, those that have included it usually found evidence of a genetic effect.) Evidence for the heritability of these traits has been obtained in studies in which parents rated their young children on items related to these aspects of personality. An exception to the use of ratings is a recent study of sociability in one- and two-year-old twins (Plomin and Rowe, 1978). The social response of infants to a stranger and to their mother was objectively measured in standardized situations. The results indicated that social responding to a stranger is heritable but that social responding to the mother is not. Although more research is needed, particularly research using objective measures of behavior, this theory of temperament may serve as a theoretical focus for the study of personality.

Behavioral Genetics, the Behavioral Sciences, and Society

From the examples that have been cited in the foregoing, it is apparent that behavioral genetics has many points of relevance to psychology. Because so much of the data of behavioral genetics has been obtained from animal studies, it could be regarded as a specialty within animal behavior or comparative psychology. From another perspective, parts of behavioral genetics could be identified as within the domain of physiological psychology; genes have been used essentially as tools, either in the form of inbred strains or selectively bred lines, to manipulate behavior and study related physiological processes (such as endocrine function, brain biochemistry, or liver enzyme activity) or to manipulate these physiological processes and study concomitant behavioral changes. Yet another view, taking note of the extensive information on the genetic basis of individual differences in cognitive and personality processes, could describe behavioral genetics as a branch of psychometrics or of differential psychology. Those areas of behavioral genetic research that have revealed the ontogenetic unfolding of hereditary influence and the interaction of genotype with environmental factors during development have obvious relevance to developmental psychology. Behavioral genetics is brought into the realm of clinical psychology by the accumulation of evidence concerning the role of genetic factors in schizophrenia and other psychoses.

Furthermore, to take a broader view, behavioral genetics is more than just a bridge between genetics and psychology. Psychology has no corner on the behavior market, and the possible pertinence of genetics to the behavioral perspectives of anthropologists, economists, political scientists, sociologists, and others is gradually being recognized.

Regardless of the particular lens through which behavior is viewed, probably the most important single implication of behavioral genetics is in respect to individuality. As we have seen, each of us (excepting identical twins and other identical multiple births) is genetically unique. It is really quite astonishing to consider that the probability is essentially zero that the exact genetic constitution of the reader of this paragraph has ever appeared before in the entire history of humankind or that it will ever appear again in the future.

Genetic influence on behavior has now been demonstrated for such a wide variety of traits and in such a wide variety of species that we may make the *a priori* supposition that there will be some genetic and some environmental influences on any behavioral trait. This certainly represents an advance over previously held views that regarded any trait as innocent of genetic influence until clearly proven guilty of it. The way is now open for quite a different view of human behavioral individuality than the widely held one that all human beings would behave alike if they were exposed to the same environment. The evidence shows that expectation to be not just simplistic, but naive. There is no question of the importance of the environment as a shaper of people, but we should not regard the raw material of a developing individual as being passively responsive. The system is much more dynamic than that, with constant interaction between the genotype of the individual and the environmental forces to which he or she is exposed.

Such a perspective on human behavioral diversity has some apparent conflicts with various social and political philosophies. By something of an historical accident, the issues have been drawn largely in the context of racial differences in intelligence. Briefly stated, evidence has been presented that the average IQ of American Blacks is lower than that of American Caucasians, although the distributions overlap extensively. Some have argued that this *phenotypic* difference is due to *genotypic* differences (for example, Jensen, 1969), and a few (for example, Shockley, 1972) have urged action programs based on this assumption. However, many behavioral geneticists have pointed out that, in consideration of the grossly unequal environmental conditions under which the Blacks and the Caucasians have lived, there is no way to draw strong genetic conclusions from the phenotypic differences (Loehlin et al., 1975). If equality of opportunity were to become a reality, the distributions might remain the same, or they might come to overlap completely, or they might change relative positions. We champion this view, and we particularly deplore the race-IQ issue as a red herring that has diverted attention to alleged *group* differences from the important contributions of behavioral genetics to the understanding of *individual* differences. If an assessment of an individual is required, it must be made on that individual; it cannot be inferred from his or her group, class, or racial membership.

Dobzhansky (1964) has warned about confusing the political, ethical, or religious notions of equality or inequality with the facts of biological diversity. It can be argued that the best way to approach the goal of equal opportunity is by careful attention to individuality, and that an approach likely to frustrate that goal is to proceed upon the counterfactual assumption that all people are biologically equivalent. Behavioral genetics, we believe, can and will contribute to the elaboration of an ethic of individual worth.

Summary

Behavioral genetics is part of the new wave of biopsychology that studies the biological bases of behavior. It focuses on the contribution of genes to behavior and provides methods to untangle genetic and environmental influences on behavioral traits. In this chapter, basic concepts of genetics were introduced, behavioral genetic methods for the analysis of animal and human behavior presented, and the impact of behavioral genetics on psychology discussed using examples from the areas of learning, cognitive abilities, psychopathology, and personality. The chapter is concluded by a discussion of the social implications of behavioral genetics.

Glossary

Adoption study: Comparing the similarity of genetically-related individuals living in unrelated environments and genetically-unrelated individuals living in the same environment.

Allele: An alternate form of a particular gene.

Chromosomes: Very small, string-like objects (DNA) in the nucleus of every cell. Genes are functional units of chromosomes.

Gene: A functional unit of DNA that produces or controls the regulation of proteins. There are thousands of genes on each of the twenty-three pairs of chromosomes in humans.

Genotype: A particular set of alleles at a locus (for example, Aa or AA alleles at a particular locus) or at several loci (for example, AaBb or AABB).

Genotype-environment interaction: The differential response of genotypes to environments, or conversely, the differential effectiveness of environments for particular genotypes.

Heritability: The proportion of phenotypic variance that is due to genotypic variance. It describes genetic influences on individual differences in a particular population with that population's genetic and environmental differences at that point in time.

Inbreeding: Matings of genetically-related individuals. Inbred strains (which are essentially identical in their genetic constitution) of animals have been established by brother-sister matings over several generations.

Karyotype: An orderly arrangement of the chromosomes. In humans, the twenty-three pairs of chromosomes are ordered from largest to smallest in a karyotype.

Locus: A place on a chromosome where a particular gene is located.

Phenotype: An observable characteristic, such as an IQ score.

Polygenic: The influence of many genes. Many of the phenotypes that are of interest to behavioral scientists are likely to be polygenic rather than influenced by a single gene.

Selective breeding: Mating animals high in a trait and also mating animals low in a trait. If there is genetic influence on the trait, the "high" and "low" lines will become increasingly different over several generations of such selection.

Twin method: Comparing the similarity of identical twins (who share all genetic factors) and fraternal twins (who share only half of the genetic factors) to determine the relative contribution of genetic and environmental influences on a trait.

Suggested Readings

Ehrman, L. and P. A. Parsons. *The Genetics of Behavior*. Sunderland, Mass.: Sinauer Associates, 1976.

McClearn, G. E., and DeFries, J. C. *Introduction to Behavioral Genetics*. San Francisco: W. H. Freeman, 1973.

Rosenthal, D. *Genetic Theory and Abnormal Behavior*. New York: McGraw-Hill Book Company, 1970.

Motivation

Judson S. Brown, Newell K. Eaton,
Christopher L. Cunningham

Introduction

Although the word *motivation* and its many synonyms have been part of our everyday language since ancient times, the study of motivation is still in its scientific infancy. Psychologists are not yet sure how motivation should be defined or how it should be measured. They cannot agree as to the physiological or psychological mechanisms by which it might affect behavior, and they differ widely in their ideas concerning its causal antecedents. Many of them doubt that our understanding of behavior will be improved by appealing to motivation, and some have even urged us to expunge the word entirely from our psychological vocabulary.

Given this willingness to acknowledge how little we know about motivation, one may wonder why we feel that a chapter on motivation is nevertheless worthwhile. Part of the answer is that the student stands to profit from exposure to a conceptual area in which the ideas are still in the process of evolution and change. The field of motivation is presently in a state of considerable flux; hence, it provides us with many examples of the problems that behavioral scientists face in seeking to bring order into a confused and nebulous domain. Another part of the answer is that some knowledge of present-day motivational conceptions and research findings is helpful in comprehending related areas of psychology, such as learning, personality, physiological psychology, and social psychology.

Because our treatment of motivation, especially our "Theoretical Preface," departs somewhat from tradition, a brief outline of what will be presented may be helpful to the reader. First of all, we have adopted the position that motivation is best construed as an attribute or property of the individual organism, a property having some of the dimensions of personality characteristics. The word motivation is thus a concept in a scientific language, a concept being a name for a property or character that different individuals have in common. Second, the initial, and most essential, step in the study of motivation is the development of objective laboratory testing procedures by which individuals can be ranked with respect to the degree of the property of being motivated. Third, the development of a standardized ranking procedure must be followed by detailed descriptions of the test, of the rules for its administration, and of the responses a subject must make in order to get a specific rating. Such written descriptions constitute the essence of a definition of the concept of motivation. Thus, the articulation of a formal definition depends on the prior development and implementation of practical procedures for rank-ordering the motivational levels of individuals. Fourth, those who have been assigned different ratings may also differ systematically with respect to other properties or with respect to the performance of other tasks. Consequently, empirical laws can be developed that relate motivational level to other characteristics or other activities of the individual. If a number of such laws emerge, the retention of the test and its associated definition is justifiable, regardless of how arbitrary the test may appear to be or how unlike common sense notions it is. Fifth, a standardized test also serves the important function of providing a kind of ''meter'' by which any condition or state can be appraised as to its motivational relevance. Thus, any condition whose presence affects test scores, whether by increasing or decreasing them, qualifies as a motivational variable. The use of a test in this way as a motivational gauge helps to minimize debate over which variables are to be labeled ''motivational.'' Sixth, some of the conditions that appear to qualify as motivational variables are relatively discrete external stimuli, while others are biochemical, physiological, or neural states of the organism. Still others are more complex conditions, such as inherited predispositions or cultural endowments. Finally, some of the characteristics of motivational variables (for example, whether they are due to learned or innate processes) provide useful topical headings for the presentation of empirical findings. Accordingly, the second and third major sections of this chapter will deal with unlearned (basic) and learned (derived) motivational variables, respectively.

Theoretical Preface—Motivation as a Concept Based on Observable Properties

Despite the many uncertainties that surround the topic of motivation, we can be sure that the word *motivation,* as an element in the language of a science of behavior, is a *concept.* But exactly what, you may ask, is a concept? A concept is a name for an attribute or characteristic that different individuals (or things) have in common. *Motivation is thus a name for a characteristic that some individuals may have more of than others and that any individual may have more of at one time than at another time.* Intelligence, anxiety, honesty, and rigidity are also names for properties of organisms and are thus also concepts. The only reason for trying to study the presumed property of motivation is that the effort may enrich our under-

standing of human and infrahuman behavior. If, from a knowledge of that property, we can predict how well people will do in school or in business, or how well animals will perform in mazes, then our efforts will have been worthwhile. A confirmed relation between degree of being motivated and some other character or activity is a simple *empirical law.* As noted in Chapter 1, the formulation of such laws, and the making of predictions from them, are major goals of the behavioral scientist.

Although we can easily see that a man is tall or short, we cannot see, in the same simple way, how highly motivated he is. Being motivated is not a characteristic to which we can point; it is more abstract than such properties as the color of one's hair, or the number of fingers on someone's hands. Because of this, those who attempt to rate levels of motivation often disagree considerably. One may claim that a losing football team was poorly motivated, whereas another may argue that it was too highly motivated.

Progress in the scientific study of motivation depends on our being able to rate the motivational levels of individual organisms in reliable ways. But how can we do this if motivation is not a characteristic like height or eye color that we can observe? The answer is that our ratings must be based on properties or actions that *can* be seen (or heard or felt, and so on). This same tactic is followed when we make decisions about other unobservable attributes such as anxiety, embarrassment, and intelligence. We say a man is anxious, not because we see anxiety as such, but because we see that he is perspiring excessively. A young girl is said to be embarrassed because we see her blush, and a boy is regarded as intelligent if we see him check the right answers to certain questions on an intelligence test. Both as laymen and as scientists, we make judgments about personality traits or other such properties, not by observing them directly, but by recording actions or characters that *are* directly detectable.

Therefore, to study the property of being motivated, we must first devise testing procedures through which reliable ratings of motivation can be made in terms of the visible features or actions of individuals. The animal psychologist might decide, for example, to assign rats to differently motivated groups on the basis of their running speeds in mazes. Speeds could be accurately measured with a stopwatch, and the investigator could assert quite arbitrarily, that any animal that runs faster than, say, 1 meter per second is highly motivated, and that any animal that runs slower than this is not highly motivated. Other observers, by following the same procedures, could easily reach agreement as to which rats are highly motivated and which are not. Two (or many) levels of motivation could thus be identified by using running speed as a criterion, even though motivation is not directly observable. Once the rats have been divided into differently-motivated sets, one can determine whether those sets behave differently in other situations or exhibit other properties in different degrees. If so, new empirical laws can be articulated. In addition to sorting populations into differently-motivated groups in this way, one can also determine whether individuals are more highly motivated at one time than another. This can be done by testing them on two (or more) occasions, either when their bodily states are different or when environmental conditions are different.

Motivational Criteria and Common Usage

In constructing a test of motivation, the psychologist may use criteria that fit with commonsense notions or may ignore them. In principle, one is free to use any tests and any criteria whatsoever, no matter how peculiar they may appear to be at first sight. The quality of any testing procedure is properly judged by its utility in predicting other behaviors and in leading to clearer conceptions, not by its accuracy in reflecting the ideas of the common person.

Why arbitrary ranking techniques are acceptable can be made clear by supposing that a scientist has chosen to rate individuals who sneeze frequently as being more highly motivated than individuals who seldom sneeze. Rating motivation in this way may seem idiotic, since we have not been told that sneezing is indicative of level of motivation. But sneezes *can* be accurately counted by different observers, and if performance in a wide variety of tasks can be predicted from number of sneezes, the procedure will soon lose its apparent stupidity.

Palmists claim that the length of human life can be predicted from the length of certain lines on the palm. This may strike most of us as bizarre. But the reason it seems bizarre is that the predictions are, in fact, very poor. So, no matter how strange our selection procedures may appear to be, they are worth retaining if, but only if, our success in predicting performance in other situations can be improved by using them to define motivational levels.

Making Selection Criteria Explicit

After new procedures have been developed for assigning individuals to different motivational levels, difficulties may be encountered in applying those procedures consistently from time to time. This situation can be partially remedied, and the reliability and utility of the ratings can be improved by preparing a written record of the kinds of tests that are administered and of the kinds of responses that must be made thereto to attain specific ratings. Such descriptions are especially important when the selection procedures involve complex tests and many measurements. Under such conditions, reliance upon an experimenter's fallible memory, in place of clearly stated rules, can lead to highly variable and unreliable results.

Defining "Being Motivated"

Written descriptions of testing procedures also serve the useful function of helping others to understand what we mean when we say that a person is or is not motivated. If the statements are grammatically and logically correct, and clearly describe the test and the scoring procedures, *they comprise the essence of a definition of the property of being motivated.* (We speak here, and subsequently, of "being motivated" rather than of "motivation," since this form of expression fits better with the idea that we are dealing with a characteristic of an individual.)

To see why a procedural description is a necessary part of a good definition, consider the possibility that the author of the description is asked, "How do you define 'being highly motivated' "? To such a question the author can reply, "As my written document shows, my motivation test contains five questions relating to the ways in which people spend their spare time, five questions concerning their work habits, and five questions concerning their hopes and aspirations. People who take this test and get scores of 75 or higher (by scoring methods I describe) are *defined* as being highly motivated." Moreover, the questioner, by reading and following the directions can administer the same set of questions and get similar results.

Sentences describing the empirical operations and actions that must be carried out to administer a test, along with the required results and scoring procedures, may be used in what are called *operational definitions* (see Chapter 1). For example, an operational definition of "being highly motivated" might look like this:

Matt is highly motivated ($\equiv$) (if) Matt takes the 15-item test (described separately), and (then) Matt gets a score of 75 or above.

In this definition, the words "highly motivated" in the sentence at the left of the three-bar sign ($\equiv$) are defined by, or equated to, the two phrases at the right of the sign. The sign itself means "means the same thing as." Since the short sentence at the left means the same thing as the long one at the right, the left-hand sentence with "highly motivated" as its predicate, can be true only if *both* the statements on the right are true. Thus, we can say it is true that "Matt is highly motivated" only if it is also factually true (1) that we have given Matt the 15-item test and (2) that Matt has obtained a score of 75 or better. A definition such as this leaves little room for ambiguity, provided the test has been described clearly, has been administered under the prescribed conditions, has been carefully scored, and the stipulated levels of performance have been attained. A property defined in this way may be said to be "real" provided it enters into many different lawful relations with other properties or activities. As Boring (1933) has noted, "There is no other scientific meaning for reality" (p. 7).

It is important to add that operational procedures like these have been used with great success in defining intelligence. Thus, when we say that

"Mike has an intelligence quotient (IQ) of 130" we mean that he has taken a certain objectively described test under stipulated conditions, has obtained a certain raw score, and that the raw score has been transformed into an IQ score by clearly stated mathematical operations. The description of the test, of the procedures for its administration, and of the computations performed in obtaining the IQ score constitute the operations in the definition of "Mike has an IQ of 130."

Although the procedures used to define degree of intelligence are well standardized, this is not at all true of motivation. Thus, all of the following criteria (and more) have been used in rating the motivational levels of animals: persistence in overcoming obstacles, general activity level, rate of learning, goal-object preference, rate of extinction, terminal performance level, speed of locomotion, and body weight loss. Attempts to measure motivation in human subjects have involved the use of imaginative stories, reactions to stress, physiological measures of arousal, and responses to a variety of questionnaires. As we shall see later on, some limited successes have been obtained with a few of these criteria.

For expository purposes we have spoken, up to this point, of only one property, that of "being motivated." However, at their discretion, behavioral scientists may *define* as many different properties or characteristics as they wish. Conceivably, they might choose to formulate operational definitions of properties such as being motivated to eat, to sleep, to drink, to gamble, to seek power, to paint pictures, or anything else. Such a proliferation of motivational concepts can be defended only if each is unambiguously defined in terms of empirical operations, and if each enters into different and fruitful relations with other concepts or activities.

Between- and Within-Subject Differences in Motivation

In studying motivation, an investigator may be concerned with both between- and within-subject differences in motivation. Since these involve distinctive procedures and assumptions, comments on each are appropriate.

Between-subject differences in motivation may be studied by first administering a motivation test to a randomly selected group of individuals. On the basis of the resulting scores, one can then pick out two (or any other number) of subgroups that are then defined as differing in motivation. Next, one can evaluate the usefulness of this procedure by asking whether the subgroups also differ with respect to other properties or in their performance in learning situations, in athletics, in business, or whatever. If, for example, the groups are found to have different grades in school, the investigator can articulate a simple lawful relation between degree of (test-defined) motivation and scholastic achievement. Such a relation would be useful since it would enable one to predict scholastic achievement from motivation scores.

An experiment by Taylor (1951) exemplifies this approach to the study of between-subject motivational differences. In the first phase of her investigation, two groups of subjects were chosen out of a larger group on the basis of scores on a test designed to measure anxiety or drive (these two terms are used synonymously by Taylor). Those who had high scores were defined as anxious (high-drive) subjects, those with low scores as nonanxious (low-drive) subjects. The two groups were then tested in an eyelid-conditioning situation to determine how rapidly they would learn a new conditioned response (see Chapter 9 for a description of such conditioning procedures).

The data obtained during the conditioning session are plotted in Figure 8-1, where one can see that the anxious subjects acquired the conditioned response much more rapidly than did the nonanxious individuals. This exemplifies an empirical law, because an instance of one concept (drive level) is associated with an instance of another concept (conditionability). The success of the testing procedure in predicting differences in rate of eyelid conditioning was sufficient to justify the provisional retention of both the test and of the concept (drive or anxiety) defined by its use.

Within-subject motivational differences can be

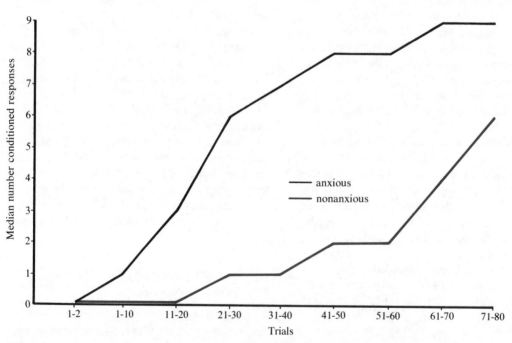

Fig. 8-1. Curves showing the acquisition of a conditioned eyelid response by anxious and nonanxious groups. With successive blocks of trials, the increase in number of conditioned responses is faster for the anxious subjects. Adapted from Taylor (1951) and reproduced by permission of the author and publisher.

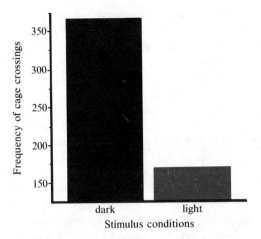

Fig. 8-2. Mean level of cage activity as a function of conditions of illumination. Adapted from Isaac and Reed (1961) and reproduced with permission of the author and publisher.

studied by comparing the motivational test scores of any individual who has been tested on two or more occasions with the same test. If differences are encountered, they may be due to variations in the subject's physiological condition or to changes in the social or physical environment. An example of the effect of different physical environments on the behavior of Siamese cats is provided by an experiment by Isaac and Reed (1961). As part of a more involved study, these investigators recorded the number of times cats moved from one side of a cage to the other when in the dark and when in the light. Figure 8-2 shows that the animals were much more active in the dark than in the light, a finding consistent with the assertion that cats are nocturnal animals. Although Isaac and Reed did not view frequency of cage crossings as a motivational test, had they done so they could have used their data to define within-subject differences in motivational levels. They might have asserted, that is, that cats are more highly motivated in the dark than in the light.

Strength of Motivation and Performance

The fact that motivation can be defined in terms of scores obtained from a standardized test does not mean that the relation of motivation to the perfor-

mance of other tasks will either be simple or congruent with common sense. Indeed, there is reason to expect that the relation of motivation to the performance of criterial tasks will vary greatly with the way in which motivation is defined and with the kind of task under study. In some cases, the higher the motivation, the better will be the performance of the reference task; that is, performance and motivation will be *directly* related. In other instances, however, the higher the motivation, the poorer the performance, so that the relation will be an *inverse* one. A possible example of the latter is provided by the athlete who is so "eager to win" that he "chokes up" and performs poorly.

There are also numerous instances in which progressive increments in (defined) motivation are accompanied by improvements in performance up to a point, beyond which further increments in motivation result in performance decrements. The outcome, in such an instance, is an inverted U-shaped curve such as that shown in Figure 8-3, in which the rising portion of the curve indicates a *direct* relation between performance and motivation, whereas the falling portion depicts an *inverse* relation. This figure also makes it clear that, for the two members of some *pairs* of motivational values, such as 1 and 3, 1.5 and 2.5, and so on, *performances are identical*. Thus, changes in motiva-

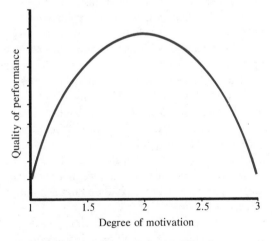

Fig. 8-3. An inverted U-shaped relation between performance and motivation. Here the effect of changes in motivation differs dramatically depending on where, in the range of motivational values, the changes occur.

tion from one value to the other of any such pair, in either direction, would have no effect on performance.

We must conclude, therefore, that unless we know what kinds of tests or procedures have been used, what the reference tasks are, and what specific motivational changes are involved, we cannot say how motivational shifts or differences will affect the performance of other tasks. It may get better, it may get worse, or it may not change at all.

Identifying Motivational Variables

A major problem facing the student of motivation is that of deciding which conditions or events are capable of affecting level of motivation. Any condition that does is usually called a *motivational variable,* and until such conditions are identified, experimental manipulations of level of motivation are impossible. Traditionally, those who have tried to identify motivating conditions have relied primarily on intuitive or common-sense ideas, placing special emphasis on the notion that variables should be energizers to be motivating. Unfortunately, this approach has not worked well, partly because the intuitions of different investigators differ enormously. Moreoover, conditions that seem as though they should lead to more vigorous action sometimes lead to immobility and poor performance. Fear-arousing cues, for instance, often inhibit movements, despite the common-sense expectation that they should lead to violent activity.

Most of the difficulties surrounding an intuitive approach can be circumvented by employing a standard motivation test as a kind of "meter" against which variables can be gauged as to their motivational relevance. If this procedure is followed, *a variable qualifies as a motivational variable if, but only if, it is associated with test-score differences.* This is a logical procedure, because changes in the measure that defines motivation are taken as evidence that the condition under scrutiny affects motivation.

In implementing this procedure, it makes no difference whether the condition under evaluation produces an increase or a decrease in test scores. It also does not matter whether a variable that elevates (or depresses) motivational level turns out to

depress (or elevate) performance in some other nontest situation. Thus, this technique for deciding which conditions are motivating frees us from the constraints of intuition. We no longer need be troubled by the finding that a condition defined as motivational sometimes leads to more vigorous responding and sometimes to less.

This procedure for categorizing a variable as motivational can be illustrated by referring back to Figure 8-2 on p. 261. Illumination level, since it affected cage-crossing, would qualify as a motivational variable if cage-crossing were the standard test of motivation for Siamese cats. Thus, the results of the Isaac and Reed study could be used to define both within-subject motivational differences due to changes in light intensity and to define light intensity as a motivational variable. If some other test had been used as the basis for saying that light intensity is a motivational condition, one could conclude from Figure 8-2 that cage-crossing frequency is affected by a known motivational variable.

Conditions that are alike in having been identified as motivational variables may nevertheless differ in many ways. A major difference is that some of them seem to function motivationally because of innate characteristics, while others seem to depend on what the organism has learned. Hereafter, variables of the first kind will be called *basic,* and those of the second kind will be called *derived.*

Basic Motivational Variables

Any condition of an organism, or any external or internal stimulus, or any specific treatment applied to it that demonstrably affects its motivational test scores qualifies as a motivational variable. Moreover, any such variable that is effective despite the lack of opportunities for learning to occur is a basic variable. For instance, if a loud noise is heard by an individual just before or just as that person is taking a motivation test, and if the subject has never heard such a noise before, and if the test scores are altered thereby, then the noise is a basic motivational variable. Other examples of such basic variables are electric shocks, brain lesions, acrid odors, bitter- or sweet-tasting substances, dietary deficiencies, extreme temperatures, genetic predispositions, sensory characteristics, and injurious stimuli. The terms *primary, biogenic* (having its genesis in the biological nature of the organism), and *physiogenic* (having its genesis in the physiological complex) are widely used as alternatives to *basic*. In the ensuing discussion of basic variables, genetic endowment will be considered first, followed by discrete stimulus conditions such as electric shocks, and by changes in life-support systems and in neural (brain) systems.

Genetic Endowment

The hereditary background of the organism, its genetic endowment or *genotype,* is an important determinant of its behavior over a wide range of circumstances (see Chapter 7). Genotype is properly regarded as a motivational variable by our criteria, provided individual differences in motivation can be ascribed to genetic diversity. Hence, if the high and low scorers on a motivation test can be identified as genetically different, genotype can be listed as a motivational variable; and if learning can be ruled out, the variable is *basic*. Genotype can also be varied, in a sense, by picking out populations or groups that are known to have different genetic structures.

Many students of animal behavior who have encountered individual differences in performance have searched for genetic correlates of those differences. Through the use of various procedures, especially that of selective breeding, genotype has been shown to be related to open-field behavior, food-hoarding, alcohol consumption, audiogenic seizures, affiliation, and aggression, in studies involving mice, rats, chickens, and dogs (Lindzey, Leohlin, Manosevitz, and Theissen, 1971; Theissen, 1971). An experiment on social dominance by Lindzey, Winston, and Manosevitz (1961) provides an appropriate example.

These investigators first trained hungry mice to run through a small tube to obtain food rewards. Tests for social dominance were then administered in which two animals were introduced simultaneously into the two ends of one tube. Whichever animal forced the other to back out was defined as

the more dominant. Levels of dominance proved to be related in an orderly manner to the strains of the mice being tested. If level of dominance had been used to define motivation, a not unreasonable possibility, the conclusion could have been drawn that motivational differences are related to genetic differences.

In another study by Theissen, Owen, and Whitsett (1970), the effects of single genes in mice were examined in a variety of behavioral tasks. The genes that were studied significantly affected open-field behavior, water-escape response latency, and running activity in a wheel. In Figure 8-4, open-field activity (in terms of number of grid squares crossed) is shown as a function of genetic background (genotype). Were one's test of motivation to include open-field activity, water-escape latency, or running wheel activity, genetic background would qualify as. a basic motivational variable.

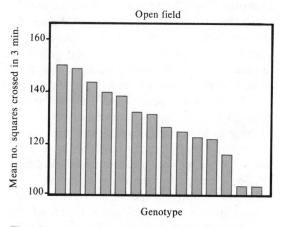

Fig. 8-4. Three-minute activity scores of fourteen groups of mice with different genotypes. Activity was measured in terms of the number of different squares of an open-field arena that were entered during the three-minute period. Adapted from Theissen, Owen, and Whitsett (1970) and reproduced with permission of the author and publisher.

Almost nothing is known about the effects of genetic background on human motivation, primarily because this variable has received little systematic research attention. Presumably, procedures could be followed like those used to study the relation of genetic background to intelligence. In such studies, the similarity of the IQ scores of identical twins reared apart has been compared to the similarity of scores for fraternal twins reared apart. Genetic endowment is then invoked to account for any greater similarity between scores of identical twins than between fraternal twins. In contrast to the expanse of data on IQ and genetic endowment, however, there is little to suggest that personality characteristics, possibly including motivation, might have some heritable component.

Under the general heading of genetic endowment, we may also include such attributes as sex, intelligence, sensory capacities, motor capacities, and others. To the degree that motivational differences might be related to these characteristics, the latter would become motivational variables. Studies could then be made of relations between them and other performance levels or other characteristics.

The development of motivational tests that are comparable for different species or strains entails difficulties, largely because of the wide range of sensory, structural, and motor capacities that would be involved. If a motivational test required responses of flying from one point to another, then insects, birds, butterflies, and bats could all be tested, but people, whales, and many other animals would be excluded. Structural differences as extreme as those represented by the animals of these groups might prevent one from developing any single test for interspecies comparisons of motivation. Attempts to measure the comparative intelligence of different species have run afoul of similar problems. Nevertheless, it might still be possible to make meaningful comparisons among organisms with similar motor and sensory capabilities.

Although motivational differences attributable to genetic endowment are assumed to be relatively stable over time and relatively independent of the momentary situation, they can be modified by specific kinds of training. The speed of the thoroughbred horse improves with practice, and rats that have been reared with kittens do not exhibit the fear of cats that rats normally manifest.

It is well to remember that apparent differences in motivation in different species may be due to unrecorded differences in training conditions, in fatigue, or in other factors instead of, or in addition to, genetic endowment. The possibility that the several strains have been differentially exposed to damaging environmental conditions (poor diets, radiation, drugs, and so on) may also require evaluation. When information concerning individuals' past histories is not available, it is impossible to estimate the relative contributions of genetic constitution and training to motivation.

Discrete Conditions

We turn now to basic motivational variables that take the form of discrete events or stimuli. The motivational relevance of such events can be determined either by introducing them on only one of two occasions when the same individuals are tested or by introducing them to the members of one group but not the other. In either case, if test scores are affected (either increased or decreased) and if prior experience can be ruled out, the conditions become basic variables. Some of the conditions, especially bitter substances, air blasts, raucous noises, and electric shocks, are traditionally said to be aversive or noxious. Others, such as the odors and tastes of some foods, the sound of the mother's heartbeat to the neonate, and parental caresses, illustrate attractive or pleasant variables. In addition, it should be noted that, though they are not external stimuli like electric shocks, some semidiscrete states such as hunger and thirst, which can be produced at will by an investigator, are traditionally included among the discrete motivational conditions.

Whether a given event is to be described as attractive or aversive depends on how individuals behave with respect to that event in specific situations. Events are attractive or repulsive *to organisms*. Typically, events or conditions are described as attractive or appetitive if they are approached or tolerated by organisms. The labels *aversive* or *noxious* are applied to events from which organisms escape. But conditions or stimuli that are judged to be aversive in one setting may be deemed attractive in another. One might think that poisonous substances would always be aversive, yet human beings sometimes deliberately consume them. The aversiveness or attractiveness of stimuli or events, whether they are motivationally relevant or not, is thus *relative* to the kinds of organisms, the specific situations, and the kinds of behaviors that are used in defining attractiveness or aversiveness. In the following sections, we shall discuss several variables that seem to fall into these categories. For our purposes, the accuracy of the classification is less important than the demonstration of motivational effects and the search for lawful relations between them and other activities or properties.

Before considering specific conditions, however, we must comment on the ways in which research studies of such variables are usually arranged. First, a previously identified variable may be manipulated in such a way that its presence or intensity is unrelated to the subject's behavior. This procedure is sometimes described as a *noncontingent* manipulation, since the variable's presence is *not dependent on* (not contingent on) the occurrence of any specific response. Our earlier example of the effects of illumination on activity in cats was of this kind. Second, circumstances may be arranged so that if a chosen response is exhibited at a certain time, the variable is then introduced or eliminated. This procedure is called a *contingent* manipulation, since the change in the variable depends on the occurrence of the selected response. Behavior may be either weakened or strengthened by the contingent introduction or removal of a motivational condition. The outcome depends on the nature of the variable and on its relation to the response in question. As we have noted, a motivational variable is a condition that either increases or decreases test scores and that may either enhance or degrade performance in other situations.

Electric Shock.   When an organism first experiences an intense stimulus such as an electric shock, its reactions are often immediate and violent. As Solomon and Wynne (1954) have pointed out in the case of the dog, strong shocks elicit vigorous visceral reactions, diffuse and intense skeletal responses, some of which may enable the animal to escape the shock, and neuroendocrine discharges

that produce widespread hormonal secretions. In addition, secondary, response-produced stimuli are fed back to the central nervous system from the viscera, musculature, and joints, there to interact with higher nervous system activity arising from chemical feedback and from intense afferent and efferent discharges. Adult humans exposed to relatively weak, brief shocks report tremoring, heart palpitation, and a sinking feeling in the pit of the stomach (Nisbett and Schachter, 1966). Clearly, such descriptions suggest that the reactions of these organisms to a concurrently administered motivational test would be dramatically affected by electric shock. Shock is, therefore, widely regarded as a basic motivational variable capable of producing immediate changes in level of motivation. The aversiveness of many stimuli can nevertheless be weakened by pairing them with appetitive events (Pavlov, 1927), by stimulus deprivation early in life (Thompson and Melzak, 1956), and by specialized training procedures (Miller, 1960; Terris and Wechkin, 1967). A weak shock can also be made more aversive by pairing it with a stronger shock (Crowell, 1974).

The effects of electric shock on the behavior of infrahumans have been widely studied and have been found to depend on such conditions as the electrical characteristics of the shock, its intensity and duration, the part of the body to which it is applied, the situation in which it occurs, the number and type of previous exposures to shock, and whether its onset or offset is contingent upon the organism's response. In studying these factors, psychologists have considered shock both in terms of its capacity to function as a stimulus and in terms of its ability to elicit various skeletal and "emotional" responses. At present, however, it does not appear that we know enough to use this distinction as a means of separating shock's motivational effects from its nonmotivational effects. [See Brush (1971) and Campbell and Church (1969) for more detailed considerations of the various effects of aversive stimulation on behavior.]

In one type of experiment, a stimulus is presented in such a way that the organism can escape from it by making an appropriate response. For example, rats can quickly learn to escape from shock on the floor of an alley by running into a safe goal box. Data obtained by Nation, Wrather and Melgren (1974) in an experiment of this kind are presented in Figure 8-5. Here it can be seen that the stronger the shock, the greater the increase in response speed over trials. If Nation et al. had previously related degree of motivational change to shock intensity, they could have gone on to formulate a tentative law relating such changes to speed of escape from shock.

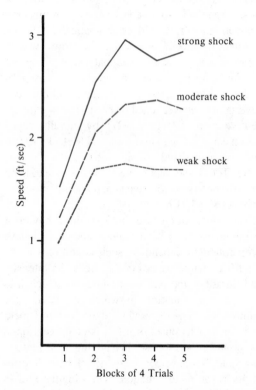

Fig. 8-5. Mean total running speeds in escaping from shocks of three different intensities over blocks of four trials each. Adapted from Nation, Wrather, and Mellgren (1974) and reproduced by permission of the author and publisher.

Many studies have also been made of the behavioral outcomes of response-contingent presentations of shock. In these, investigators have examined the effects of electric shocks that are introduced immediately after the completion of some response, such as running down an alley, pressing a lever, or licking a drinking tube. As

might be expected, this procedure generally results in a weakening or suppression of the response. Occasionally, however, it produces facilitation of the response (Cunningham, Brown, and Roberts, 1976; Fowler, 1971; Hartlep and Bertsch, 1974; McKearney, 1969). Although such findings will undoubtedly complicate the types of laws that we ultimately derive concerning the effects of shock, it is possible that both outcomes can be related to the motivational character of shock.

It should be noted that the suppressive and facilitative effects of response-contingent shock may be due in part to the presence of cues that have been paired with shock (for example, the apparatus) as opposed to shock itself. In such instances, the behavior observed would be attributed to a *derived* motivational variable, that is, to a variable that had *acquired* its ability to function motivationally.

Electric shock that is presented noncontingently also has many surprising effects. Myer (1971) has suggested that the predominant response during shock is increased skeletal activity, whereas the reaction to situational cues (visual and auditory) that have been paired with shock is diminished activity. If we focus just on behaviors that occur during shock, we see that the type of "active" response that occurs depends on the nature of the situation and the organism's previous experiences in that situation. Given the right circumstances, moderate intensities of shock facilitate fighting behavior ("boxing," biting, and attack), copulation, eating, and drinking in rats (Myer, 1971). Such findings suggest that there may be an important relation between the motivational nature of electric shock and the most likely "active" behavior in any given situation.

Imprinting Objects. One example of an external stimulus event that is usually said to have intrinsic attractive motivational properties is the "imprinting object" (Hoffman and Ratner, 1973; Hoffman and Solomon, 1974). An imprinting object is one that an immature animal appears to "attach" itself to (and will follow) during a limited period in its development. Normally, it is the animal's mother, but it may often be any object that moves in the presence of the animal during a "critical" period.

Previous practice is not necessary for the attachment to occur.

Hoffman and his colleagues have reported several instances in which the response-contingent manipulation of an imprinting object (a moving block of white foam rubber) affected the behavior of ducklings soon after hatching. For instance, ducklings learned to peck a pole to produce brief presentations of the imprinting stimulus and learned to refrain from following the stimulus when its removal was contingent upon following. Noncontingent manipulations of the imprinting stimulus also affected the duckling's behavior. Ongoing "distress calls" decreased when the imprinting object was presented after its removal. If the duckling had learned to peck a pole to produce the object but had temporarily stopped pecking, a brief presentation of the imprinting object induced the duckling to resume its pecking.

Given that we have designated the imprinting object as a motivational variable, it is clear that we can point to a number of behaviors that might be related to its motivational character. Of some interest is the fact that its effect varies with such factors as the frequency and duration of previous exposures to the object and with the animal's age. These are the types of variables that must be delineated in the formulation of lawful relations between the motivational change produced by the imprinting object and other behavioral consequences.

Food and Water, and the Behaviors of Eating and Drinking. Food and water have often been described as attractive external events having effects similar to other variables thought to be motivational, and they significantly affect behaviors other than eating and drinking. Much of the information we have about these variables comes from experiments in which food and water have been presented contingently upon the appearance of some response. It is well known, for example, that food can be used to increase the frequency and vigor of such responses as running and lever-pressing, and that the magnitude of these effects depends on the amount and kind of food that is presented (Mackintosh, 1974). In general, although the effect of reward size often disappears with extended practice,

the larger the reward, the more vigorous the responding. Psychologists differ as to whether this is due to the action of food itself on the strength of the response or to the effect of cues that have been paired with food (Bolles, 1967). If the latter were true, changes in behavior might more properly be attributed to a derived motivational variable. However, when food can be unambiguously identified as a motivational variable, its motivational properties can be related to those of the deprivation condition and to the occurrence of the instrumental response.

In only a few instances have observations been made of behavior while organisms are actually eating or drinking. In studies of the response-contingent effects of these variables, attention is usually focused on the behavior that precedes the delivery of food or water, and the amounts given are generally so small that little time is spent in consumatory activity. In a recent investigation, however, emphasis was placed on the potential motivational effects of consumatory behavior (specifically, drinking water from a tube) on the rat's unconditioned startle response to a brief, intense tone (Ison and Krauter, 1975). In this study, rats that had been deprived of fluid for varying amounts of time (8, 24, 96 hours) were permitted to lick water from a tube for short periods. Occasionally, while the rat was drinking, or between drinking bouts, the startle-eliciting tone was presented. A special recording system enabled the experimenters to measure the vigor or amplitude of the startle response. The results were expressed in a relative amplitude measure and are shown in Figure 8-6. Two things are apparent. First, the startle response was greater while the rat was drinking water than while it was sitting still. Second, the overall amplitude of the response decreased with increases in the number of hours of fluid deprivation. Another experiment indicated that the magnitude of the enhancement during drinking depended on the nature of the fluid being consumed (water produced a greater effect than evaporated milk), suggesting that the effect depended on the substance itself and not just on the skeletal activity involved in drinking.

Had Ison and Krauter identified the act of consuming water as a motivational variable, that is, as

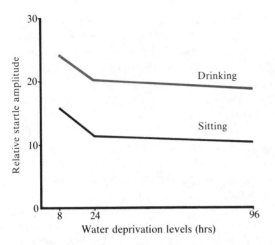

Fig. 8-6. Relative startle amplitudes during and between drinking bouts at three degrees of water deprivation. (Experiment 4) Adapted from Ison and Krauter (1975) and reproduced by permission of the author and publisher.

a condition affecting motivational test scores, they could have asserted that the magnitude of the startle response was a function of the animal's drinking-induced level of motivation.

Drugs. Many of the variables that might qualify as motivational are events or conditions that produce changes in the organism's "internal" as opposed to its "external" environment. Generally speaking, events in this category consist of chemicals (drugs) or electrical stimuli applied to internal sites. Studies involving such internal events are often difficult to conduct, especially in the case of drug stimulation, since one may not be able precisely to control the onset, intensity, or duration of the internal condition. Nevertheless, if the administration of a drug can be shown to produce changes in motivation, the effects of those changes on various activities can be assessed in much the same way as with external stimuli.

Some users of such substances as alcohol, cocaine, mescaline, and marijuana strive to obtain the drugs and claim that the internal states produced by them are "attractive." But nonusers who have tried the drugs often avoid them and assert that the drug states are aversive. Many studies have been designed to assess the alleged "attractive" nature of certain drug conditions by arranging the environment so that the organism can gain access to the drug by performing some response. In an experiment by Davis, Lulenski, and Miller (1968), rats that were given brief, unavoidable shocks were able to inject a barbiturate (hexobarbital) directly into their own bloodstreams by pressing a lever. Such drugs are often prescribed for humans to relieve anxiety and tension. The bar-pressing rates of these rats became reliably greater than those of control rats that received the same amount of shock and drug, but with the drug being administered independently of their responses. Since the effect did not appear in the absence of shock, a law relating instrumental performance to drug-produced level of motivation would have to include reference to the presence of shock.

The response-contingent administration of a drug may also lead to a decline in behavior. Recent studies of "bait-shyness" and "taste aversion" provide good examples of this. It has been shown in several experiments that if the ingestion of a salt or saccharine-flavored solution is followed by an illness-producing drug, such as lithium chloride or apomorphine, rats will subsequently drink much less of the solution and show a decreased preference for it (Garcia, McGowan, and Green, 1972) (also, see Chapter 9).

The effects of the noncontingent administration of drugs on performance have also been studied extensively. In one experiment involving humans, Schachter and Wheeler (1962) gave different groups of subjects injections of epinephrine (adrenaline), chlorpromazine (a tranquilizer), or a "placebo" (a harmless saline solution). The use of the placebo is an important control condition in drug research, because it enables the experimenter to assess those effects of the injection procedure that do not depend on the particular substance being injected (for example, simply being pricked by a needle may itself be a motivational variable). As an additional control in this experiment, all of the subjects were told that they were receiving a harmless injection of a vitamin C derivative so that all groups would have similar expectations about the effects of the injection.

During a test phase of the study, the subjects watched a slapstick comedy chase scene from a movie. Two independent observers scored the subjects' reactions to the film every 10 seconds by categorizing their behavior according to this scheme: (a) neutral (straight-faced); (b) smile; (c) grin (teeth showing); (d) laugh; and (e) belly laugh. The observers were ignorant of the drug condition of the subject but were able to agree on their behavior ratings 90 percent of the time.

The epinephrine group showed the greatest amount of "amusement," followed in order by the placebo group and the chlorpromazine group. Schachter and Wheeler viewed this outcome as consistent with a theory of emotional behavior that stresses the interaction between level of physiological activation (in this case, produced by drugs) and the individual's cognitive interpretation of the arousing situation. Within the present framework, to the extent that these drugs qualified as motivational variables, we could assert that level of motivation was related in a particular way to behavior in an amusing situation.

There are many more experiments in which the effects of drugs on the performance of particular responses have been studied. For instance, Cappell and Herman (1972) have reviewed a variety of studies designed to assess the alleged tension-reducing properties of alcohol. These authors and others seem to be agreed on one thing in the area of drug research, namely, that the behavioral effects of any given substance depend on a variety of factors: dosage, mode of administration, previous experiences with the drug, type of task, the nature of the other motivational variables that are present, and so on. Consequently, the task of relating the motivational character of any given drug to behavior is far from simple.

Brain Stimulation. Some of the more dramatic examples of the effects of internal events on behavior have stemmed from the application of direct chemical, thermal, and electrical stimulation to the brain. As with electrical stimulation of the skin, contingent and noncontingent stimulation of the brain induces a variety of behavioral changes that depend on the following: the locus of stimulation; its type, intensity, and duration; the situation in which it is given; and previous experience with it. If brain stimulation is identified as a basic motivational variable, lawful relations between it and various behaviors can be sought. The following are examples of outcomes often thought to be related to the motivational properties of brain stimulation.

Response-contingent presentations of brief, low-voltage shocks to different parts of the brain have been shown both to increase and decrease the frequencies of many behaviors. In one of the earliest of these experiments, Olds and Milner (1954) surgically implanted chronic (permanent) electrodes in the brains of anesthetized rats in such a way as to cause them no discomfort during the course of their normal daily activities. By means of flexible wires that could be connected to the exposed ends of the electrodes, electric currents could be delivered to precise locations deep within the brain whenever the rat pressed a lever. When certain areas were stimulated (especially the septal region), the rats learned to press the lever to *produce* stimulation and often responded at extremely high rates, sometimes in excess of 100 per minute. In other areas of the brain, stimulation had no effect, while in still different ones it appeared to be aversive; that is, the rats would give up lever-pressing when responding was followed by brain stimulation.

Reinforcing and punishing effects of response-contingent brain stimulation like these have been replicated many times with different species and with different responses. Miller (1969) has even shown that curarized rats (rats that have been temporarily paralyzed by a drug) can learn to make specific autonomic responses (for example, increases or decreases in heart rate, intestinal contractions, vasoconstriction, and vasodilation) either to escape or to produce certain types of brain stimulation. Much effort has gone into attempts to "map" the rewarding and punishing electrode sites within the brain and to compare behavioral changes produced by brain stimulation with changes produced by contingent external events [see Deutsch and Deutsch (1973) for a recent view of this research].

Noncontingent electrical brain stimulation has been found both to inhibit and to enhance ongoing behavior. In addition, it often appears to be responsible for initiating specific kinds of allegedly motivated behaviors. Valenstein, Cox, and Kakolewski (1969) cite studies showing that stimulation of various parts of the hypothalamus will produce the following behaviors: eating, drinking, gnawing, hoarding, stalking-attack, coprophagia (eating of fecal matter), and male copulatory behavior. These behaviors occur despite the absence of external conditions that would normally elicit the behavior in the absence of brain stimulation. In one of these experiments, Steinbaum and Miller (1965) electrically stimulated the lateral portion of the hypothalamus of nondeprived rats in the presence of wet food mash. In comparison to nonstimulated control rats and rats stimulated at other times in the absence of food, these rats eventually ate 2.5 times the normal amount of mash and showed dramatic increases in weight. They overate to such an extreme that, in the absence of stimulation, they were completely inactive and spent most of their time on their backs with their limbs in the air.

Thermal stimulation of the anterior region of the hypothalamus has been shown to lead both to increased fluid intake and to a wide range of other behaviors, suggesting that this area is involved in thermoregulation. In support of that contention, local anterior hypothalamic cooling has been reported to decrease fluid intake, and to lead to the complex of behaviors (vasoconstriction, shivering, and so on) associated with adaptation to a cold environment (Hokanson, 1969). Interestingly, these adjustments do not necessarily take the form of elicited reflex responses, but appear to entail well-coordinated sequences of learned behaviors evoked by both internal and external stimuli.

Some physiological psychologists suggest that brain stimulation produces an increase in a specific "drive" which evokes a corresponding behavior (Deutsch and Deutsch, 1973). Others speculate that the effects of brain stimulation may not be so specific, since stimulation at one point can produce different behaviors depending on conditions in the external environment (Valenstein et al., 1969). Albeit much more research will be needed to resolve this issue, it seems clear that brain stimulation has several effects that might be indicative of motivational properties.

Changes in Life-Support and in Neural Systems

Under this broad heading we shall consider some potentially motivating consequences of (1) chronic dietary deficiencies, (2) short periods of food, water, or air deprivation, and (3) localized brain damage. These diverse conditions may all be viewed as essential to life, since any in the extreme, eventuates in death.

Prolonged Dietary Deficiencies. The behavioral and physiological effects of diets containing inadequate amounts of substances such as protein, sodium, thiamine, fat, and sugar are so dramatic that it would be difficult to imagine they would not also have marked motivational consequences. Empirical demonstrations of such outcomes, however, await the development of motivational tests of established utility. If such tests were to involve opportunities to discriminate adequate from inadequate diets, evidence for the motivational properties of deficient diets would doubtless be forthcoming.

It has long been known that under normal conditions, when organisms are allowed to choose from a wide variety of food substances, they tend to select balanced diets. In a classic study by Davis (1928), newly weaned infants were allowed to choose their own diets, and, over a period of months, selected foods that provided nutrients essential to good health and normal growth. In 1943, Richter conducted a study of dietary selection in rats under well-controlled laboratory conditions. As in Davis' study, Richter's subjects chose well-balanced diets. Moreover, their ability to do so was found to be related to the integrity of their taste mechanisms. When Richter severed the pathways innervating their taste receptors, his rats no longer selected adequately balanced diets.

It is interesting to note that although organisms can alleviate specific nutritional deficiencies by choosing diets containing needed components, preferences for certain nonessential substances can be changed by following their ingestion with essential substances. For example, Garcia et al. (1967) demonstrated that rats deficient in thiamine, a substance required for the metabolism of most foods, increased their preference for foods which were followed by thiamine.

Rozin and Kalat (1971) have suggested that two basic mechanisms govern the specific hungers resulting from the lack of particular dietary elements. The first is a specific, apparently unlearned, taste for sodium. Thus, sodium-deficient rats select a sodium-enriched diet immediately upon contact with it. This has been noted under a number of conditions, but only when the substances have a salty taste (Strickler and Wilson, 1970; Nachman, 1962).

The second mechanism accounts for the learning of preferences for diets containing essential vitamins and minerals. Rozin and Kalat suggest that a diet deficient in thiamine has unpleasant consequences, such as weight loss and *anorexia* (loss of appetite for food). Diets associated with these consequences acquire aversive properties, and are rejected, while novel diets, even if also deficient, are initially preferred. If the new diet contains the needed substance, the preference for the diet continues, and the subject satisfies its dietary need, demonstrating its "specific hunger." On the other hand, if the new diet is also deficient, it too acquires aversive properties relative to other novel diets. Thus, it would seem that a specific hunger may be reinterpreted, in many cases, as a specific aversion to nutritionally deficient diets, and a general initial acceptance of novel foods.

Not all dietary deficiencies are remedied through the selection of appropriate foods. In some animal experiments, sugar is chosen over protein, even when protein is needed. Lower animals are not alone in sometimes failing to correct dietary deficiencies. In certain eastern countries, for example, white, rather than brown, rice is the chosen foodstuff, despite the deficiency of nicotinic acid in white rice, the lack of which can lead to a disease called pellagra.

Short-Term Deprivations.   It is now time to look at the effects of short-term deficiencies of substances or conditions that are essential to the organism's life, the absence of which may produce both between- and within-subject differences in motivation.

Individuals whose access to these life-maintaining commodities or conditions is blocked, manifest obvious changes in behavior, and along with them, altered motivational test reactions. Depriving the individual of food, water, or oxygen; or of the opportunity to urinate, defecate, and maintain normal body temperatures, are instances of altered life-support conditions that would probably qualify as

motivational variables. Perhaps such conditions as physical restraint (deprivation of movement), altered day-night cycle patterns, sensory deprivation, sleep deprivation, social isolation, and overcrowding, might also be included here.

Food and Water Deprivation.   These are probably the most widely studied variables of this kind, with many hundreds of published experiments dealing with their effects on performance in multifold test situations. Traditionally, the deprivation condition has been specified (defined) either in terms of hours of deprivation or in terms of percentage weight loss from some initial or standardized level. Bolles (1967) has endorsed the percentage weight-loss definition, because it appears to give a better indication of the organism's need. Others argue that behavior appears to be jointly determined by weight loss and the maintenance schedule (Weinstock, 1972). Unfortunately, the correspondence between these different defining operations and the various consumatory and instrumental behaviors to which they are related is far from perfect.

Generally speaking, in experiments with infrahumans, as the length of food or water deprivation is increased, there is an increase in the amount of food and water consumed, even if the animal has never been deprived before (Dufort and Wright, 1962; Siegel, 1947). In such studies, however, consumatory behavior eventually reaches a maximum, with further increases in deprivation producing no increase in consumption. Extended deprivation ultimately results in a decline in behavior, largely as a result of general bodily weakness.

Another relation between deprivation and consumatory behavior generally appears to be true. Namely, once a deprivation period has ended, the latency to resume eating or drinking is negatively correlated with the length of deprivation. That is, as Figure 8-7 shows, the longer the deprivation time, the shorter the latency to respond.

Although consumatory behavior following food and fluid deprivation has been studied most extensively in infrahumans, a few investigators have recently looked at consumatory behavior in humans, following deprivation. For example, Hill (1974) studied the eating responses of normal (nonobese) adults during a dinner meal either 1 or 18 hours after the previous meal. As might be ex-

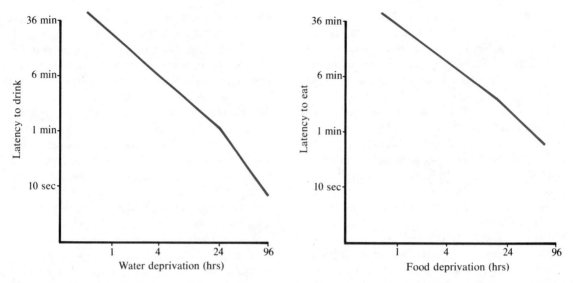

Fig. 8-7. Times required for rats to resume drinking and eating when permitted to do so following water- and food-deprivation periods of various durations. Both scales in logarithmic units. Adapted from Bolles (1962) and reproduced by permission of the author and publisher.

pected, at the longer deprivation, the subjects ate more. Detailed analyses of videotape recordings, however, revealed a number of other facts about the eating behavior of the hungry subjects: they took more bites, required more time to eat, spent less time per bite, and "sampled" (made a series of bites on the same food item) more often. Amount per bite, amount per sample, and time per sample, however, were no different than in the 1-hour condition.

Deprivation of food and water also affects instrumental (operant) behavior in animals (for example, running down a straight alley, pressing a lever). In learning situations of these kinds, the speed, amplitude, and resistance to extinction of the response tend to be enhanced by increases in food deprivation (up to a limit). In more complex learning situations (for example, discrimination learning), however, the relation between deprivation and performance is less uniform. Thus, increased deprivation may facilitate learning only if the problem involves an easy discrimination, and some kinds of training procedures (for example, *forcing* in which experiences with both alternatives are provided) tend to diminish the effect (Mackintosh, 1974). (See Chapter 9 for further discussion.)

There are also many studies of the effects of deprivation on a variety of "noninstrumental" behaviors. We have already noted that water deprivation appears to depress the rat's startle response to an intense auditory stimulus (Ison and Krauter, 1975). Moreover, the facilitative effect of deprivation on level of general activity (for example, Jakubczak, 1973) has long been regarded as supporting the idea that deprivation energizes any and all behavior indiscriminately. Recent reviews of the data on the relation between deprivation and general activity, however, suggest that this apparent energization may be a phenomenon unique to hungry rats in activity wheels (Valle, 1975). When activity is tested in other devices (for example, a stabilimeter or tilt-floor cage), the relation becomes less clear. Many studies of deprivation and activity are also difficult to interpret because of the possibility that cues are present that have been closely associated with food. In such instances, activity levels may reflect the influence of the cues rather than the deprivation condition. Although the role of deprivation as a motivational variable may not be as universal as has sometimes been suggested, it is undoubtedly an important determinant of many types of behaviors.

Air Deprivation. Most of us would not need to

hold our breaths for very long to be convinced that being deprived of air has dramatic, perhaps motivational effects. Broadhurst (1957), for example, has shown that increasing durations of air deprivation enhance the swimming (escape) speed of rats submerged in a water tank. Punzo (1974) has recently replicated these findings with an aquatic insect (water beetle), an organism that is more likely to encounter air-deprivation conditions in the normal course of its activities. These insects spend most of their lives in and under water, but depend on air inhaled at the water's surface for their survival. Punzo restrained the insects below water for periods of time ranging from 1 to 25 minutes. In order to reach the surface, they were required to traverse a 12-inch horizontal tube. The results, depicted in Figure 8-8, show an orderly positive relation between what Punzo called "running time" and minutes of deprivation. Punzo noted that at deprivation durations of approximately 30 minutes, the insect's behavior became extremely disorganized, suggesting that the upper limit of its endurance had been reached.

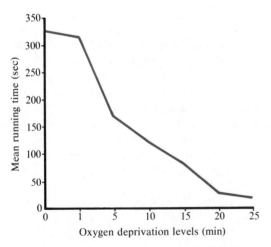

Fig. 8-8. Mean time taken by water beetles to traverse an underwater passageway as a function of deprivation time prior to release. Adapted from Punzo (1974) and reproduced by permission of the author and publisher.

Brain Lesions. In an earlier section, we examined some investigations in which electrical, chemical, and thermal brain stimuli were found to be related to differences in the performance of a variety of tasks including possible motivation tests. We shall now look at changes in performance resulting from lesions (localized areas of destruction) experimentally produced in the brains of laboratory animals. Such lesions might well qualify as basic motivational variables.

Numerous studies have demonstrated that a portion of the brain, the *hypothalamus,* is closely associated with the endocrine system, the autonomic nervous system, and higher cortical areas, and serves to modulate many biologically important functions such as food and water intake, temperature regulation, and much more. One topic that we have chosen to discuss here is the relation between the hypothalamus, food-related behaviors, and motivation. (See Chapter 4 for further discussion.)

Many relations between hypothalamic nuclei and food intake are well understood (Novin, Wyrwicka, and Bray, 1976). For example, lesions of the ventromedial hypothalamus (VMH) lead to a condition called *hypothalamic hyperphagia.* Subjects with such lesions eat considerably more than normals and show marked gains in body weight. One function of the VMH is believed to be that of "telling" the individual when to stop eating. Not only do subjects with VMH lesions eat too much, as if the normal processes that terminate eating are no longer working, but chemical or electrical stimulation of the VMH leads to the immediate rejection of food. Analogous relations, though opposite in direction, have been noted between the lateral hypothalamus (LH) and food-related behaviors. Lesions in the LH produce *aphagia,* a condition such that an organism will not eat, and may starve to death even when surrounded by food. Contrariwise, stimulation of the LH has the effect of augmenting eating and food-related behaviors.

Because of the close relation of the VMH and the LH to behavior, it has been suggested that they are associated with an organism's level of motivation, perhaps functioning as motivational "centers." Rats and monkeys with VMH lesions perform food-getting tasks more vigorously than normal animals. Likewise, LH stimulation has been shown to lead to marked improvement in the performance of various food-reinforced learning tasks. A report by Hamilton and Brobeck (1964) provides an example of these effects of VMH

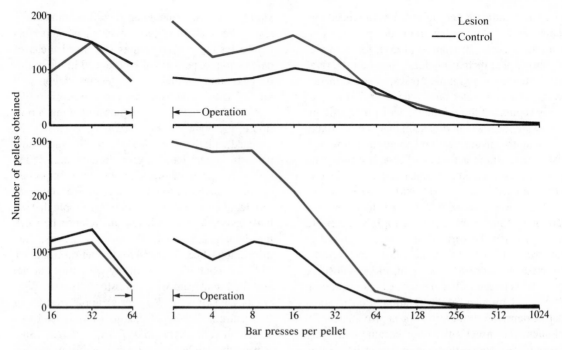

Fig. 8-9.   Number of pellets obtained by two hyperphagic Ss (heavy lines) and their controls (light lines) before and after the operation. Adapted from Hamilton and Brobeck (1964) and reproduced by permission of the author and publisher.

lesions. Seven rhesus monkeys were trained to barpress for food on a variety of fixed-ratio (FR) reinforcement schedules. Following surgically produced VMH lesions in four of these animals, two exhibited clear signs of hyperphagia. Compared to unoperated controls, the two hyperphagic monkeys ate substantially more food when permitted to earn it by pressing a lever. This was true with fixed-ratio schedules up to FR 64, where only every 64th barpress produced a food pellet. Figure 8-9 shows the performance of subjects with and without lesions.

An experiment by Singh (1972) further illustrates the effects of VMH lesions on the performance of a food-reinforced task. Rats with VMH lesions were compared with normal rats in a test where they could either receive "free" food, or could work for food on a fixed-ratio schedule. (See Chapter 9.) Several previous studies had shown that rats (and children) preferred to work for reinforcement even when food could be obtained without working. Singh proposed that if the VMH

lesions lead to a reduced motivation level, then rats with lesions should work less than normal rats. On the other hand, if the VMH lesions lead to increased motivation, the VMH rats should work more than the normal control subjects. As the data in Figure 8-10 show, rats with VMH lesions, spent more time working and received a larger percentage of their reinforcements through work than normal subjects. These relations held at fixed-ratios of 1, 3, and 11.

Finally, an experiment by Kent and Peters (1973) provided further evidence of the effects of VMH lesions on food-related learned behaviors. Rats with VMH lesions performed better on both food-reinforced barpress and runway-traversal tasks than control subjects at the same degree of food deprivation.

In connection with this topic, two additional considerations are worthy of note. First, in some older studies, subjects with VMH lesions worked to obtain more reinforcements than normals only at low fixed-ratio schedules, if at all. The notion that

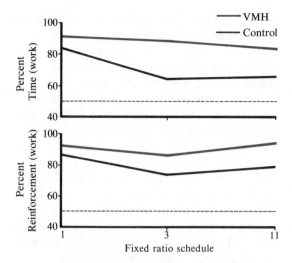

Fig. 8-10. Percentage of time spent working and percentage of food reinforcements (pellets) obtained for working by rats with VMH lesions and by controls. Adapted from Singh (1972) and reproduced by permission of the author and publisher.

hyperphagic subjects are more "motivated" than normals was questioned, and the "hypothalamic hyperphagic paradox" was suggested: namely, VMH subjects eat more food than normals, but are less willing than normals to work for food. More recently, however, those results have been attributed to interference due to heightened emotionality and decreased frustration tolerance in the subjects with lesions. Second, in physiological research, the possibility exists that when one tries to stimulate, or make lesions in, a particular *area* or "center," one actually stimulates or destroys a *pathway* between areas, thus having direct effects only on areas in distant portions of the brain. Recently this thesis has been cogently defended by Grossman (1975) with respect to studies of the role of the hypothalamus in the control of food and water intake.

Derived Motivational Variables

In this, the third major section of this chapter, we shall be concerned with events and conditions that are presumed to be related to motivational level and which have attained that status through the mechanisms of conditioning and learning. In short, the motivational relevance of these conditions is *derived* rather than basic. Perhaps the most significant instance of a derived motivational variable is the individual's educational background or cultural endowment. Clearly, what we have been taught by the many diverse agencies in our societies has a strong likelihood of affecting level of motivation, no matter how it may be defined. The following analysis begins, therefore, with the topic of cultural endowment, continues with a discussion of stimuli that become derived variables when they evoke conditioned aversive emotional reactions, and concludes with a look at environmental conditions that have attained motivational relevance through associations with pleasant events. The idea that initially neutral events can be derivatively motivational is expressed in other writings through the use of the terms *sociogenic* (originating in social processes), *psychogenic* (produced by psychological mechanisms), *learned, secondary,* and *acquired.*

Cultural Endowment

The term *cultural endowment* refers to the educational and socializing experiences provided for individuals by teachers, parents, ministers, peers, mates, and others. Cultural endowment has been chosen to parallel the term *genetic endowment,* used in the previous section on basic variables, and to underscore the idea that individual differences in motivation may be produced by exposures to different cultural environments. If differently-motivated groups are found to differ with respect to the cultures from which they spring, then we can predict that other sets of individuals, with similar cultural histories, will have comparable levels of motivation. In addition, subjects with different cultural backgrounds and with correspondingly different levels of motivation would also be expected to differ in meaningful ways in the performance of other tasks or in other characteristics. Such relations subserve the formulation of behavioral laws relating derived variables to between-individual differences in motivation and to other performance differences or other properties.

Examples of cultural differences that might affect motivation are plentiful. Children who have been reared in very orthodox religious homes react quite differently to matters of honesty, sex, tobacco, adult movies, material wealth, alcohol, drugs, television, and such, than do children of nonreligious homes. The endowments provided for their offspring by pacifists, racists, sexists, Republicans, agnostics, Catholics, Baptists, Communists, Fascists, and other groups, vary along multitudinous dimensions. The dogmas and doctrines that each group seeks to imprint on its children through carefully designed educational programs and repetitive rewards and punishments have profound effects on their entire lives. The habits, attitudes, concerns, beliefs, ideas, convictions, and values acquired during the early years of acculturation are derived antecedents of between-subject differences in motivation.

To make this point clear, let us look at two examples, one fictitious, the other genuine. First, consider the possibility that two individuals have obtained quite different scores on the same motivation test, despite the fact that, being identical twins, their genetic endowments are equal. Suppose also that one of the twins grew up in the home of his or her parents and the other in a foster home in a different community. Such a finding would surely lead us to suspect that the motivational difference might be due to dissimilar cultural endowments provided by the two homes. If those environments were indeed very different, cultural heritage could be identified as a motivational variable associated with test-score differences. Quite probably, the performance of the twins in other situations would also differ, as would some of their other characteristics. The other differences might also correlate with the (defined) differences in motivation.

Our second example, is provided by the work of McClelland, and his associates (1953, 1955). These investigators have conducted extensive studies of the need to affiliate, the need for power, and, especially, the *need for achievement*. The last of these, which we will discuss here, has been described as a tendency for individuals to strive to achieve success or to perform well in situations where they expect to be judged as to the quality of

their performance. The McClelland group first addressed itself to the problem of how to measure or evaluate the need for achievement (abbreviated *n Ach* or *n Achievement*). Toward that end they employed a test, patterned after Murray's Thematic Apperception Test (TAT), in which somewhat ambiguous pictures were presented to subjects who were asked to tell imaginative stories about what was happening to the people in the pictures. (See Chapter 18 for further discussion.) For several groups the telling of the stories occurred *after* they had performed simple scrambled-words tasks (anagrams). Some individuals were told that these tasks were unimportant, on the supposition that relaxed, "don't care" attitudes would be adopted. For others, the instructions were calculated to have an entirely neutral effect; for still others, the instructions were designed to be intensely "ego-involving" and to elicit concern with performing well. In short, qualitatively different instructions were used for different groups on the common-sense assumption that different levels of achievement need would be aroused in the groups and would persist during a subsequent TAT session. It was hoped that the contents of the TAT stores told by the different groups would differ so that a relation would be obtained between achievement motivation, as induced by instructions, and references in the stories to topics of success, trying hard, and the like. Consistent with these expectations, the stories of the relaxed, "don't care" group contained fewer achievement references than the stories of the neutral group; these, in turn contained fewer such items than the stories of the ego-involved (achievement-oriented) group. This outcome supported the conclusion that the TAT test might serve to detect differences in achievement motivation, and, with changes in the scoring system, to detect other kinds of motivation (for example, hunger, power, affiliation) as well.

The important point, in the context of this discussion, is that differences in TAT scores were also found to depend on the attitudes and child-rearing practices of the subjects' parents. In particular, McClelland *et al* reported that their data supported the hypothesis that strong achievement motives tend to develop in families and cultures where the independent development of the individual is emphasized. By comparison, achievement motivation tends to be low in children of families who encourage dependence on the parents and the adoption of subordinate roles. This example underscores the idea that cultural endowment may significantly affect motivation ratings.

A pivotal question related to these conceptions is how the educational practices of different societies can produce between-subject differences in motivation. It seems reasonably certain that individuals are not taught to be motivated in any simple or direct manner. Instead, they are taught to make many different specific responses to a broad range of conditions. If a motivation test is sensitive to the kinds of responses acquired in different societies, individuals with different learning histories will get different scores and will be assigned different (defined) motivational levels. Persons who have been taught that it is sinful to be lazy, and that hard work is virtuous, will give different answers to questions about the value of work or tell different TAT stories than those who have had other teachings. Those who have been taught to want commodities they do not have, react differently than do those who have been taught that material wealth is the root of all evil. At a later point, we shall comment again on this matter of the mechanisms through which cultures can affect motivation.

Evidently then, between-subject differences in motivation may be traced not only to genetic (basic) factors but also to cultural (derived) differences. Individuals bring to test situations rich repertoires of attitudes, beliefs, skills, values, habits, and ways of reacting that may affect their motivation scores. When those scores vary in some regular way with differences in cultural backgrounds, cultural endowment becomes a derived motivational variable. However, the construction of the test is of great significance and some forms will be more sensitive to cultural influences than others.

The importance of social stimulation for the fullest development of the organism is dramatically illustrated by the Harlows' (1962) experiments with monkeys. What they observed was that if young monkeys were denied the typical opportunities to interact with other youngsters they would fail to perform normal mating functions at maturity. Moreover, female monkeys raised in isolation were deficient in their mothering skills at adulthood. The Harlows concluded from this, and from other studies, that intimate social and tactual contacts between the infant and other monkeys, including its mother, are of great significance to the normal development of a wide range of behaviors. In so far as any such activities might be tapped by a so-called test of motivation, it is evident that social deprivation would markedly affect ratings of levels of motivation.

Discrete Conditions as Derived Variables

We shall be concerned in this section with discrete environmental conditions or events, primarily conditioned stimuli, that seem to qualify as derived motivational variables. Of such events, those that have become motivationally changed through association with basic noxious events will be discussed first, followed by events that have been associated with basic pleasant events.

Derived Variables Based on Noxious Stimulation. An early demonstration of the way in which neutral events may be transformed into noxious stimuli through associations with aversive events was provided by Watson and Reyner (1920). (See Chapter 9 for further discussion.) In their investigation, the sight of a white rat, though originally neutral to a child, became a fearsome stimulus after the rat had been paired with a painfully loud sound. Although some attempts to replicate the experiment have failed, it has been widely cited as an instance of *classical emotional conditioning,* wherein the sound was an unconditioned stimulus (UCS) and the white rat was a conditioned stimulus (CS). In the present context, the UCS would stand as a basic motivational variable, and the sight of the rat, after it had been paired with the US, as a *derived* motivational variable.

Some theorists maintain that derived variables do not function motivationally unless they elicit conditioned emotional reactions. This belief is based, in part, on the fact that training does not change physical stimuli; training only changes organisms. When it is said that a stimulus becomes transformed into a derived variable, what is intended is that the *organism* becomes transformed and hence reacts in new ways to that stimulus.

Conditioned Fear. The idea that a conditioned emotion (fear) may serve as an important determinant of various kinds of behaviors has been widely held over the years. Freud, early in this century, was among the first to stress the idea that fears or anxieties have motivating and other functions. Mowrer (1939) also argued that an acquired fear or anxiety evoked by a CS might be motivationally significant. One of his criteria for classifying such stimuli as "motivators" is that they must energize or potentiate other responses such as those of escaping from fear-eliciting environments. Another criterion is that reductions in fear, following responses which eliminate a fear-arousing CS, must strengthen or reinforce those responses.

These two ideas, that fear is an energizer and that fear-reduction is reinforcing, have been used to interpret avoidance learning, masochistic behavior, the effects of punishment, and the abnormal behavior of compulsives and neurotics. If the organism is free to retreat from a place where it has been hurt, it will do so repeatedly even though no further primary pain is experienced there. If a particular environment is viewed as a CS that elicits an aversive reaction of fear, it makes sense to suppose that escape from that environment would be rewarding. Similarly, the compulsive handwashing of a mental patient may be viewed as an action that diminishes acquired apprehensions or fears (see Chapter 20).

The concept of anxiety reduction as reinforcement has also been applied to the problem of how individuals acquire self-control (Dollard and Miller, 1950; Hefferline, 1950). When one is punished for the performance of a particular response, the internal (proprioceptive) stimuli produced by that response will be paired with an aversive UCS. On subsequent occasions, when one starts to respond again, the cues arising from the earliest phases of the response can serve as conditioned stimuli to elicit a fear reaction. If one then inhibits the response, the cues are eliminated, fear is reduced, and the tendency to refrain from responding is strengthened. This process may be involved to

an important degree in our learning to inhibit responses having a high probability of being followed by aversive consequences.

The property of "being fearful," like the property of "being motivated," cannot be directly observed. Hence, it too must be defined in terms of behaviors and procedures that *are* observable. Traditionally, individuals have been described as fearful if they exhibit exaggerated startle responses under certain conditions, if they learn responses that eliminate alleged fear-arousing stimuli, and if repetitive avoidance responses are enhanced by the introduction of stimuli that have been paired with aversive events. Estimates of fearfulness provided by these and other criteria, though not in exact agreement, are sufficiently covariant to support the belief that similar processes are involved in all.

To indicate how studies of fearfulness are actually conducted, we turn to an experiment by McAllister and McAllister (1962) which was concerned with the reinforcing effects of CS termination on a locomotor response in rats. In that study, rats were first given several paired presentations of a light (CS) and a shock (US). For one group, the CS was presented *before* the US, and for another (control) group the CS *followed* the US. These procedures are called *forward* and *backward* conditioning, respectively. It was expected that the CS would come to elicit conditioned fear in the forward group, since the light was always followed by shock, but not in the backward group. The effectiveness of these procedures in producing fearfulness was evaluated by seeing how quickly the two groups would learn to run from one box to another to escape from the light. On each learning trial the light was turned on and a measurement was made of the speed with which the rat jumped over a hurdle into the other box, a response that caused the light to go off.

The results of these measurements are plotted in Figure 8-11. There it will be seen (upper curve) that the animals in the forward group showed progressive increases in response speed over successive blocks of trials. The members of the backward group, however, showed no improvement in performance (lower curve). Getting away from the lighted side of the box was reinforcing for one group but not for the other. This performance dif-

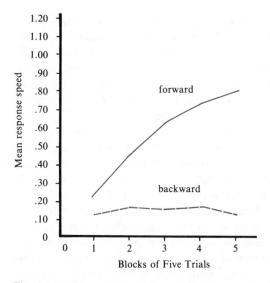

Fig. 8-11. Mean speeds with which rats given forward or backward fear conditioning trials jumped over a barrier to escape from the conditioned stimulus that had been previously paired with shock. Adapted and reproduced with permission of the author and publisher from McAllister, W. R. & McAllister, D. E. Role of the CS and of apparatus cues in the measurement of acquired fear. *Psychological Reports*, 1962, **11**, 749–756.

ference supports the idea that the light (CS) was fear-arousing only for the forward group.

In a similar experiment, the McAllisters have shown that under some circumstances, even rats given backward conditioning trials learn to escape from a place where shocks have been administered. This occurs when opportunities have not been provided for fear of the environmental cues, the box, to become extinguished. Such an opportunity, incidentally, was provided in the experiment just described. The possibility that the cues of the apparatus can become conditioned elicitors of fear is of considerable importance to the interpretation of various studies. Whenever a determination is to be made of the degree to which a discrete CS such as a light has become capable of eliciting fear, it is necessary to extinguish fear of the place where light and shock have been presented. Children learn to fear rooms such as a dentist's office where they have been hurt, as well as the sight and sound of the specific object, the drill, that is the source of pain.

The literature bearing on conditioned fearfulness and the variables that affect its growth and maintenance is too vast to review here. It is sufficient to note that many of the conditions and arrangements that affect the strength of conditioned reactions, in general, are of significance for the development and maintenance of fearfulness. Thus, fear increases with number of CS-US pairings, is stronger the more intense the US, is weakened by CS-alone presentations, and so on. (For a review of these findings see McAllister and McAllister, 1971).

Conditioned Emotions and Human Behavior. The conditioning of emotional reactions to specific stimulus patterns is one way in which societies develop derived variables capable of affecting changes in motivation. In industrialized nations, children are taught to fear onrushing cars, precipitous heights, uncontrolled fires, whirling lawnmower blades, exposed electrical wires, danger signs at railroad crossings, the skull-and-crossbones on bottles of poison, and much more. But in primitive cultures, they may be taught to feel afraid when signs portend the actions of evil spirits, when animals howl in unusual ways, and when the sun is occluded during an eclipse. Presumably, any of these signs or cues, if presented during the taking of a motivation test would significantly affect test performance and thereby (defined) levels of motivation.

Discussions of human motivational phenomena often stress the idea that people are taught to need various material possessions or experiences and that these needs have motivational overtones. Murray (1938), for example, compiled a list of almost thirty psychogenic needs including needs for achievement, aggression, dominance, deference, recognition, order, and play, to name but a few. A careful examination of the ways in which societies might teach an individual to have needs suggests that what is often involved is the formation of derived variables based on aversive stimulation. Let us see how this might be effected.

To begin with, consider what it means to say that one has a psychological (derived) need. Perhaps the best answer is that an *individual has a derived need for something whenever the lack of that something is accompanied by learned aversive emotional responses*. A woman has a psychological need for a new dress provided she is unhappy without it. People who are not appreciated by their peers may have a psychogenic need for recognition; if they are distraught without it, they need it. In addition, if we have learned to be unhappy when we do not have certain material things, or when we have not performed in certain ways, then when we get those things or do perform satisfactorily, we will necessarily be happier and more assured. If our culture teaches us to have needs such as these, along with their feelings of disquietude, then there is every reason to suppose that the evocation of such (conditioned) feelings, at or about the time a motivation test is being administered, will affect the resulting scores.

The aversive emotional reactions characteristic of learned needs cannot be elicited by the things or conditions that are needed, since those are not present. However, such reactions *can* be evoked by immediately present events that have previously accompanied the distress produced by the lack of an object. Consider, for example, the learned need for money that is characteristic of many, though not all, Americans. Among the cues that evoke apprehension about lack of money are the following: an empty mailbox on the day when a paycheck is expected to arrive, a notice from the bank that an account is overdrawn, the feel of empty pockets when it comes time to pay the bill in a restaurant, or a notice from one's boss that one has been fired. In many cases, these stimulus patterns have been followed by punishments or unpleasant consequences and have thereby acquired the power to evoke aversive emotional reactions. Such cues clearly exemplify derived variables whose presence may affect motivation. To *develop a need for money is thus to learn to be discontented when cues are present that denote a lack of money*. If such cues do not have an aversive effect, as may be true for the hobo, then a need for money has not been acquired.

One also learns, of course, to respond in unique ways to money itself, or to cues indicating that adequate supplies of money are available. One learns the differential responses of being apprehensive to no-money cues and of being relaxed in the presence of have-money cues. Society arranges the contingencies so that punishments or nonrewards tend to follow one set of cues and rewards follow the other. Money in the hand provides stimuli that counteract apprehension-eliciting, no-money cues, thereby reinforcing whatever behavior produced the money. For many persons, striving for money is associated with the acquired apprehension-arousing action of signals that denote a relative lack of money. People work for money because they have learned to become upset in the presence of cues which tell them that they have less money than they need or than others do. Horney (1937) has described this as a "fear of impoverishment" and has suggested that it is this fear that drives humans to work for money. (See Chapter 19.)

Similar processes may be involved in the development of many other psychological needs. As we have previously noted in respect to the achievement motive, cultures that stress individual achievement and personal enterprise teach their members to be worried, concerned, or distraught when they have failed to reach prescribed levels of attainment. Religious organizations teach children to feel anxious or guilty in the presence of cues denoting failures to pray at the proper times, to attend church services, to partake of communion, or to contribute in financial or other ways. Parents try to make their children feel uneasy if they fail to brush their teeth, to say "thank you," or to behave in compliance with the mores of the parents' culture. Signs of having failed to act according to rules and expectations stand as derived variables that elicit reactions of guilt, apprehension, inferiority, or regret. Such reactions doubtless have motivational significance.

This general characterization of psychological needs is consistent with the ideas of Veroff and Veroff (1972) concerning *power motivation*. From a careful appraisal of research with the Thematic Apperception Test (TAT) they have concluded that the power incentive, defined as "concern with attaining or maintaining control of the means of influence" should be construed as a *negative* rather than a positive goal. That is, those who score high on a test of power motivation are those who seek to avoid feelings of weakness or inferiority rather than those who actively enjoy influencing others. High scorers tend to be those who are low in income, who have had little formal education, and who are of low social standing. Such individuals, it seems, are those who are most likely to be bombarded by signals indicating a lack of the power to affect others. And such a power deficit may produce aversive feelings of inferiority and weakness. Striving for power thus becomes *a striving to escape from aversive feelings of weakness or inadequacy.* A similar stance was taken some years ago by Adler (1927), who held that feelings of inferiority with respect to one's search for status and achievement underlie power motivation. (See Chapter 19.)

A little reflection will indicate how pervasive and powerful are the propaganda directed toward the creation of derived needs in our society. Many Americans, who already have adequate automobiles, are taught to become unhappy when their neighbors acquire newer and more expensive vehicles. The sight of a new car in a neighbor's driveway, as it contrasts with our older car, elicits feelings of unhappiness in many of us. This is largely the result of a relentless assault from TV commercials and other ads in which we are repeatedly told that we should envy our neighbor's new car and should buy a better one if possible. The atmosphere of the large university is such that its professors learn to become anxious when they see that their lists of publications are shorter than those of others. The implied threat, that one will perish if one does not publish, is calculated to arouse anxiety, an aversive state that can be eliminated by the act of publishing. Creative artists too, often report that their anxiety levels are high during periods of low productivity and that the apprehensive state is dissipated when inspiration returns. Such anxieties must be acquired, since people are not born to become anxious when nonproductive.

From this line of reasoning, it follows that individuals can acquire multiple needs. They can learn to need power, approbation, affection, new cars, very old cars, TV sets, and much more. They can even acquire *a need to induce needs in others,* as may be true of entrepreneurs who spend millions to make others feel dissatisfied with not having bought the entrepreneurs' products. In many instances, it is possible to identify specific external (or internal) events that elicit the feelings of dissatisfaction underlying each need. The needs are descriptively unique, but uneasiness is clearly involved in behaviors that result in the transformation of "not having" into "having" states of affairs. In the last analysis, psychological needs appear to be essentially aversive conditions: one has a psychological need for something when one does not have that something, when cues indicate that the something is not present, when those cues elicit aversive reactions or feelings, and when receiving the object or condition negates the aversive state and replaces it with feelings of satisfaction or relaxation. As individuals develop, the degree of "not having" that is aversive may change dramatically. For a small boy, not having 10 cents for candy can be aversive; for the same individual, when he becomes a successful business man, not having a million dollars may be equally aversive. One learns to be unhappy or to feel inferior with levels of achievement or possession that were once entirely satisfying.

Before leaving this topic we must note that when stimulus events are transformed into derived aversive variables, other events may gain in *relative* attractiveness. If unpleasant consequences attend not having money, then having money becomes pleasant by comparison. As we shall see shortly, the opposite may also be true: if pleasant consequences attend having money, then not having it acquires an aversive cast relative to having it. The sets of stimuli denoting both "having" and "not having" can perhaps become derived variables through the agency of either aversive or attractive consequences.

Derived Variables Based on Pleasant Stimulation. In the previous section, we have seen that neutral events, after they have been associated with noxious conditions, may be reacted to as though they have become aversive. In this section, we turn to instances in which neutral events, following associations with attractive or pleasant events, are reacted to as though they have become *attractive.* An event is motivationally neutral provided it has no effect on motivation ratings. Neutral events become motivational variables of the *derived* class if, following associations with either aversive or attractive conditions, they then *do* affect test scores.

An example of a derived variable based on pleasant or attractive associations is provided by the effects of food reward on the behavior of the rat in the simple straight runway. After the hungry animal has traversed the alley and has been fed at the goal, the cues in that region lose their neutrality and gain motivational loading by virtue of having been linked with food. According to Spence (1956) the goal-box cues function as conditioned stimuli that elicit conditionable portions of the final consummatory complex of eating, salivating, chewing, and swallowing. Such a conditioned reaction appears in anticipation of reaching the goal and is regarded as a behavioral correlate of an "expectancy" of food. Goal-box cues thus become *derived* variables to the degree that they elicit conditioned responses like those evoked by food itself. Note that conditioned anticipatory consummatory reactions are the conceptual counterparts, in positive situations, of conditioned fear reactions, in aversive situations. In both cases, of course, it is the organism that changes, not the physical stimuli.

As an aside, it may be observed that if the animal is punished rather than fed in the goal box, the nearby cues become more aversive, and by contrast, the cues as the other end become *relatively* more attractive. Either aversive or pleasant goal events may, in this way, generate gradients of conditioned affect in which one end is attractive (or aversive) relative to the other.

A major use to which Spence's conception has been put is in explaining the results of "magnitude of reward" experiments with animals. In general, rats that have received large rewards run faster toward a goal box than rats given small rewards. Such performance differences cannot be explained by saying that the food incentive "pulls" the animal toward the goal and that the "pull" is stronger the larger the amount of food. Such a "pull" notion is inappropriate in nearly all cases since the food is seldom visible to the animal until the food cup is actually reached. Resort must be had, therefore, to explanations involving stimuli that act on the animal *before* it arrives at the goal. According to Spence, the larger the reward, the better the conditioning of the consummatory goal reaction to the environmental cues at or near the goal. The cues of the runway, being similar to those near the goal, elicit generalized anticipatory reactions, whose strength or vigor, varies directly with the size of the reward. Since Spence believed that locomotor reactions were "energized" or "potentiated" by the conditioned goal reaction, it followed that the larger the reward (and hence the better the conditioning), the speedier the approach toward food.

An alternative interpretation might be that the larger the reward the better the conditioning of a positive emotional reaction to the cues of the goal box and the greater the *difference* in relative attractiveness (or relative aversiveness) of start- and goal-box stimuli. Provided speed of running is determined by the magnitude of that difference, it follows that the larger the reward, the better the performance.

A striking example of a derived variable based on pleasant tactual stimulation is provided by Harlow's (1958) experiments on *"contact-comfort"* in infant macaque monkeys. For these animals, the tactual cues of feeling and clinging to a real mother or to a terry cloth substitute mother have innately rewarding and comforting properties of great potency, more so, indeed, than does food. When fear-arousing stimulus objects are presented to an infant, it immediately turns to a mother, whether real or artificial, capable of providing the warmth, softness, and clingability that are the essential elements of the contact-comfort complex. An infant macaque clinging to a terry cloth mother is illustrated in Figure 8-12.

In this context, it is significant to note that other stimuli, especially the visual cues provided by the mother's face and form, acquire tranquilizing, emotion-reducing charcteristics from repeated associations with the contact-produced tactual and thermal cues. For example, infant monkeys that have been "raised" by a terry cloth mother will press a lever to get to look at her far more frequently than to look at a different mother or at a blank wall. Moreover, if the infants are placed in strange surroundings which make them very apprehensive, the mere sight of the cloth mother, even though physical contact with her is prevented by a transparent barrier, is comforting. The visual cues are not innately comforting, however, since the first sight of a cloth mother to a 250-day-old infant raised under other conditions evokes screams, emotional reactions, and persistent avoidance. Nevertheless, with repeated exposures to a cloth

Fig. 8-12. This is the typical response of the infant macaque monkey to the cloth mother when frightened. Adapted from Harlow (1958) his Fig. 14, p. 679 and reproduced by permission of the author and publisher.

mother, the animals soon come to accept it and to cling to it, in preference to wire mothers that do not provide contact comfort. When opportunities to cling are provided, strong attachments develop and the sight of the mother becomes highly rewarding. The data plotted at the left of Figure 8-13 show that infants given this type of training do not, at first, press a lever to look at either a cloth mother, a wire mother, or a blank chamber. The tendency to make responses that are followed by those visual stimuli increases with age, however, and with continued comforting by the cloth mother. In the second test session, shown in the figure, the cloth mother was not looked at as frequently as were the wire mother and the blank room, but by the third and fourth sessions, the cloth mother had clearly come to be the preferred visual object. These data strongly suggest that neutral, or even aversive, visual stimuli can be transmuted into positive, rewarding stimuli by repeated

associations with highly rewarding tactual cues. The sight of a comforting mother is a *derived* motivational variable.

Our final example, from the field of applied psychology, provides another illustration of the motivational impact of sociocultural processes as well as a case study in the construction and use of motivational tests. Traditionally, the job performance of employees is said to depend on such factors as wages, vacations, rank, and social approval. But this holds true only for those for whom such consequences of good performance have acquired reward value through the processes of learning and acculturation. If one has not learned to value money, or values it but has plenty, or values it but does not expect to get it by working harder, then the promise of money is unlikely to affect one's level of motivation. Reasoning along these lines, applied psychologists (for example, Vroom, 1964; Lawler, 1973) have suggested that the motivational levels of employees can be measured by determining the values they place on the monetary rewards, promotions, and so on, that may accompany good performance. By means of a questionnaire, which may be construed as a motivation

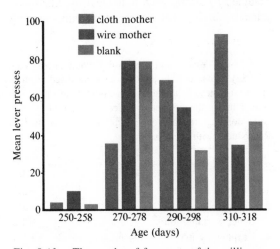

Fig. 8-13. The results of four tests of the willingness of infant macaque monkeys to press a lever for the opportunity to look at a cloth mother, a wire mother, or a blank chamber. The ages of the monkeys at the time of the tests are shown on the base line. The monkeys had never seen any of the objects prior to the tests. Adapted from Harlow (1958) and reproduced by permission of the author and publisher.

defining test, estimates are obtained of the degree to which each potential job outcome is valued by an employee. The test also yields estimates of the workers' expectations (subjective probabilities) that such outcomes will follow good performance, plus estimates of the degree to which employees believe that working hard will lead to better task performance. Indices of *value, subjective probability,* and *effort* are combined by means of different formulas, depending on the situation and the investigator, to yield motivation scores. Ultimately, the composite motivation rating is related to some index of task performance.

In a recent investigation, Orpen (1975) has followed these procedures in measuring the motivational levels of assembly-line workers in a machine-tending task. Orpen first determined some of the possible outcomes, for the workers, of good performance on the task. These are listed in the first column of the accompanying table. Each worker then indicated the *value* of each outcome on a scale of 10 (-5 = very low, $+5$ = very high), as well as his expectation of the *probability* (chances in 10) that each outcome would actually follow good performance. *Effort* ratings were also obtained by asking each individual the likelihood (chances in 10) that improved machine-minding

performance would result from the expenditure of greater effort. Each person's ratings of the value of each outcome were multiplied by the probability rating for that outcome. The value-probability products were then added together and their sum was multiplied by the individual's effort rating. The numerical result served as the workers' motivation score.

The mean value and probability ratings obtained for 82 workers for each of the outcomes are shown in Table 8-1. As the means indicate, the values ranged from neutral to moderately valued, and all outcomes were judged to have a reasonable chance of occurring, given good performance. In addition, the standard deviations indicate that there was a good deal of variation in the values individuals placed on the various outcomes, and in their beliefs that the outcomes would follow good performance.

When Orpen compared an operator's motivation score with a supervisor's rating of job performance, he found that there was a strong positive relation as shown by a correlation of $+.62$. Thus, the higher the individual's motivation score, the better his performance (as indexed by the supervisor's rating). Orpen also calculated the relations between performance and motivation scores based

Table 8-1. Means and Standard Deviations of Value and Probability Estimates ($N = 82$). Nine possible job outcomes are listed at the left of this table, and workers' mean estimates of the value of each outcome and of the probability of attaining it are shown under the columns headed with an M. Columns headed with SD are the corresponding standard deviations of those estimates. (Adapted from Orpen, 1975. Reproduced with permission.)

	VALUE		PROBABILITY	
Job outcome	M	SD	M	SD
1. Getting a pay rise	+2.34	3.36	4.16	3.60
2. Getting promotion	+2.21	2.69	4.76	3.32
3. Better working hours	+0.22	4.18	4.28	3.17
4. Keeping my job (not being fired)	+1.81	2.71	5.11	3.47
5. Working with others I really like	+0.81	2.61	5.91	2.81
6. Getting more responsible jobs to do	+0.61	3.21	6.10	2.93
7. Receiving compliments and praise from my boss	+0.4	4.01	5.73	2.98
8. Gaining respect from other workers	− .01	4.21	4.55	3.29
9. Getting a feeling of accomplishment from my work	+ .11	3.53	6.71	2.76

on single factors, like mean outcome value, and between performance and motivation based on other combinations of these factors. This can be viewed as an empirical comparison of Orpen's original motivation test with a number of other motivation tests. Such a comparison tells us which test works best, that is, which one proves most useful in predicting behavior. In this case, Orpen's original scoring system yielded the highest correlation with performance, and that system was retained as the best motivational test for use under those conditions.

Summary

We began this chapter with the comment that the word *motivation* and its many synonyms have been part of our everyday vocabulary for ages. Nevertheless, the phenomena which this term purportedly describes are still poorly understood, perhaps because they are covert and impalpable, or perhaps because the scientific study of behavior is itself so recent.

Our theoretical preface, which outlined our strategy for studying motivation, stressed the point that motivation is best construed as a *concept,* that is, as a name for a characteristic or property that different individuals may possibly have in common. In this respect, it is like other psychological concepts such as intelligence or anxiety. To investigate this property, one begins by devising practical testing procedures for rating both the motivational levels of different individuals and changes in the motivational level of any one individual. Such tests may be based on common-sense notions of motivation, but that is not necessary, and may even be harmful. What *is* essential is that the tests involve objective procedures that can be communicated to, and followed by, other scientists. The necessary communication can be effected by accurately describing the tests and the rules for their administration. When such descriptions have been prepared they can be incorporated into formal (operational) definitions of the concept of the property of "being motivated." Formal definitions must stipulate the nature of the test and the kinds of responses that must be made to it, if a particular motivational rating is to be attained.

The most important step, after the production of a test, is to determine whether the test-defined attribute of "being motivated" is lawfully related to other attributes or activities. If so, these activities can be predicted and explained from a knowledge of (defined) level of motivation, and the test, along with the concept it helps to define, can be said to be *significant* or *useful.* Lacking such laws, the concept must be discarded, a new test must be developed, and a new concept defined. Examples of the development of successful tests in the manner suggested are found in the work of Taylor and Spence, McClelland and his associates, Orpen, and others.

Any test that proves to be useful in this way can serve importantly as a "meter" by which various conditions can be appraised as to their motivational relevance. Thus, any event (environmental, organic, hereditary) that is found to be associated with either increases or decreases in test performance (and hence in motivational level) qualifies as a motivational variable. The study of motivation is, in large part, the study of the effects of such variables on the performance of a variety of tasks. Intense external stimuli (electric shocks, loud noises, acrid odors), emotional states, biochemical (drugs and hormones) and physiological states, inherited predispositions, and cultural backgrounds, serve as examples of possible motivational variables. Of these, some appear to have an intrinsic capacity for affecting motivation whereas others have acquired that capacity via specific kinds of learning or conditioning experiences. The former are termed "basic" variables and the latter "derived."

In our discussion of basic variables we have noted that genetic endowment can affect the performance of animals in simple situations, and that discrete, manipulable stimuli such as electric shocks, imprinting objects, appetitive goal objects, drugs, and electrical-chemical brain stimuli all have pronounced effects on many facets of behavior. A well-developed motivational theory will doubtless be able to show that these variables are motivationally relevant, by virtue of their effects on test scores. Both short- and long-term food and water deprivations have been found to affect performance dramatically and, for many investigators, serve as prime exemplars of motivational variables. The experimental introduction of lesions of the brain has also served to increase our understanding of the central mechanisms that control ingestive, maternal, and other regulatory behaviors.

Finally, our treatment of derived (psychogenic) variables has emphasized the idea that the more significant of these are stimulus patterns that, as a consequence of learning, tend to elicit reactions of uneasiness or disquietude. Events that signal a lack of money, power, affection, success, or approbation, all seem motivationally relevant. In significant ways, therefore, actions that produce, as their consequences, additional power, money, affection, and so on, are actions that diminish negative affective states. Actions may also be influenced, however, by cues (motivational variables) denoting the imminent appearance of pleasant events. These incentive signaling stimuli often seem to work in combination with stimuli that evoke negative affective states.

Historical Footnote

An examination of the historical antecedents of contemporary interpretations of behavior reveals the continuous influence of two competing conceptions of the determinants of action. One of these, the rationalistic view, holds that the behavior of humans is determined by processes of thinking and reasoning. A human being is seen as a calculating organism able to choose freely from among alternative courses of action and to assume moral responsibility for those choices. Plato, Aristotle, St. Augustine, and Thomas Aquinas were among many who advocated such a view. Because, on this conception, humans move themselves and initiate their own actions, little room was left for a motivating or driving force capable of producing action by moving people against their will or without their awareness. The second view, sometimes characterized as deterministic or naturalistic, emphasizes the notion that behavior is controlled by the individual's environment and by agencies beyond one's voluntary control. This conception is more sympathetic to the possibility that organisms may be moved or pushed by forces within and without them in opposition to purely rational processes.

While a few of the early Greek philosophers adopted deterministic views such as the second, it gained advocates slowly prior to the seventeenth century. At that time, Descartes suggested that human beings exemplified the operation of both deterministic and rationalistic processes. Animals, he believed, were not rational creatures; lacking both mind and soul they were little more than machines. In contrast, humans, though machine-like in certain ways, possessed minds or souls which enabled them to reason and thereby to override the mechanistic processes.

A more complete break with the rationalistic tradition came from the British philosophers, especially Hobbes, Locke, Hume, and John Stuart Mill and his son. For them, inborn ideas were deemed less important as determinants of behavior than what is learned through experience. Moreover, humans were regarded as seeking pleasure and avoiding pain, their actions being interpreted as natural phenomena. It is worth noting that these views developed in the era when the physical laws of nature were being mapped out and power driven machines were starting to appear.

The intellectual revolution occasioned by Darwin's "The Origin of Species" in 1859 was clearly of enormous significance for the rationalistic and deterministic views. In particular, Darwin made a convincing case for the conclusion that humans and animals are alike both structurally and functionally and that there is an essential continuity between them. After this, humans could no longer be viewed as specially-created creatures with divine characteristics, but simply as a distinct species in a continuum of species. The biological continuity of human beings with animals quite naturally suggested a continuity as to the determinants of behavior, and it soon became fashionable to search for rational or intellectual processes in animals and for instinctive behavior patterns and motivational urgings in humans.

Thorndike (1898) was among the first to study the intelligence levels of animals by subjecting them to problem-solving tasks whose solutions demanded the acquisition of adaptive behavior. His findings led him to abandon the view that successful performances were due to ideational processes. Instead, it appeared that rewards and punishments served automatically to strengthen or weaken associative bonds between stimuli and responses. The focus thus shifted from learning by cognitive insights and decisions to learning by trial and error and the consequences of successful performance. Moreover, Thorndike was quick to discover that the animals would not exhibit a rich repertoire of initial reactions, from which the correct ones could be selected by rewards and punishments, unless they had been deprived of food or water.

Seriously weakened by the Darwinian revolution, the rationalistic conception was further threatened by the arguments of McDougall (1908) and Freud (1915). McDougall held that humans are not essentially rational or good, that rational actions are the exception rather than the rule, and that one's behavior is actually governed by powerful instinctive forces. Such appeals to the instinctive activation of behavior are consonant with a deterministic philosophy that provides room for driving or energizing agencies. Freud's analysis served further to erode the conception of the uniqueness of humankind by firmly documenting the irrationality of many human actions. In his psychiatric practice, Freud found many instances in which the cause of a patient's behavior was unknown to the patient, and when revealed, could even be abhorrent to the patient. Freud concluded, therefore, that much of the working of the human mind is unconscious, and hence beyond rational control. Further, his conception of humans incorporated an energizing or driving, motivation-like component, the libido, which exerted a powerful effect on psychological thought.

The idea of instinctive control seemed at first to have real merit, but it soon waned under the attack of those who believed that complex behaviors are more learned than inherited. Watson (1913), the founder of the behavioristic movement, was in the forefront of the anti-instinct program, along with Kuo and Bernard. One of the weaknesses of the instinct view was that the nature of the instinct was usually inferred from the same behavior its introduction was designed to explain. Thus, the observation that sheep gather together in groups led to the postulation of a gregarious instinct which was used, in turn, to explain why sheep gather together in groups. Additionally, instincts were introduced uncritically in almost unlimited number to account for even the most trivial actions. William James, for instance, maintained that men spit because they have a spitting instinct. The instinct idea was generally abandoned during the second decade of this century, but its driving or moving aspects were retained in the newer concepts of drive, and its behavior directing functions have recently been reemphasized by such ethologists as Lorenz and Tinbergen.

Woodworth (1918) has been credited with popularizing the term drive as it applied to behavior. For him, movements of an organism cannot be explained simply by reference to initiating stimuli. Other organic processes contribute importantly, especially those involving the release of stored energy. Just as the trigger of the gun does not propel the bullet, but serves only to release the latent energy in the powder, so stimuli produce movements by unlocking stores of energy. The direction of the movement is controlled by other processes called mechanisms. Woodworth thus distinguished between drive, as a kind of nonspecific activator, and the mechanisms through which the drive is channeled into coordinated motions. The mechanism is the structure that is made to go by the power that is applied. In Woodworth's theories and in Freud's, we find the beginnings of the idea of a nonspecific drive, an energy that is blind until guided by a directing process, the mechanism. The analogy to automotive mechanisms is obvious: the motor pushes the vehicle and makes it go, but the motor does not want, so to speak, to go in any particular direction. It is the steering system that controls the direction in which the energy will be dissipated. Thus, although drive became one of the substitutes for instincts and was endowed with many of their properties, the substitution of a single source of nonspecific drive for a multiplicity of drives further widened the gap between instincts and drive.

Despite Woodworth's suggestions, the drive

concept was not immediately accepted by experimental psychologists. Boring's *History of Experimental Psychology* (1929) contains neither the term drive nor the term motivation in its index of subjects. Nevertheless, experiments explicitly directed toward the study of animal drives appeared shortly. Prominent among them were Moss's (1924) attempts to measure hunger motivation by means of an obstruction box technique. In this two-compartment apparatus, the food (or other incentive) that was placed in one chamber could be reached only by crossing over an electrified grid floor between the two compartments. The strength of the drive was expressed in terms of the intensity of shock that would just counterbalance the approach or in terms of the number of times an animal would cross over a fixed intensity of shock. Richter (1927), noting that food-deprived animals tend to become active, used amount of random activity as an index of hunger. From records of activity and of stomach contractions, he concluded that the stimuli provided by the contractions were the cause of the overt activity. Hunger and thirst thus came to be construed as intense and persisting goads whose noxious influence could be terminated only by the adaptive act of seeking and ingesting food.

The most explicit and highly developed motivational theory of modern times was undoubtedly that of Hull (1943, 1952). For him, conditions such as food and water deprivation and external noxious stimulation all contributed to a common pool of drive (*D*), which, like Freud's libido, was nonspecific and which was, thereby, endowed with the capacity to activate any specific habit or reactive predisposition whether learned or unlearned. For Hull, performance was thus dependent on the multiplicative combination of nonspecific drive and habit. This idea that performance is determined by some combination of steering and driving agencies is obviously reminiscent of Woodworth's distinction between drives and mechanisms and is an idea that continues to exert a powerful influence on present-day thinking. For Hull, the operations (for example, deprivation) that produced the multiplicative drive were also ones that generated internal stimuli to which specific responses could become associated through learning. Moreover, Hull held that the growth of associations was contingent upon the reduction in drive attending the making of the final consumatory response. In this and in other ways, Hull sought for interpretations that were physicalistic and did not require the addition of mentalistic or rational processes.

Although Hull distinguished between drive and habits, others such as McClelland and Atkinson, have combined the energizing and directing of behavior. According to their formulations, an organism is motivated or energized *toward* some particular goal or class of goals. In short, goal direction is involved in the motivational process, and it is appropriate to speak, as in everyday language, of specific drives *for* particular goal objects. Both the nonspecific and specific drive views are present in varying degrees in contemporary theories and are based on both learned and unlearned sources of motivation.

Finally, we must note that not all contemporary psychologists have chosen completely mechanistic or deterministic models of behavior. Some have retained many of the elements of older rationalistic theories. Men such as Allport, Maslow, and Rogers have built their conceptions of behavior more on reason and on the intrinsic goodness of man. While biological sources of motivation are included, primary emphasis is placed on *self-actualization,* a motivational concept that incorporates a driving force tending to bring about the most effective utilization of the individual's capacities and the attainment of the highest levels of achievement.

Glossary

Audiogenic seizure: A relatively violent, erratic behavioral outburst induced by loud high-pitched sounds in rodents, especially rats and mice.

Basic motivational variable: Any variable that qualifies as a motivational variable by virtue of some intrinsic biological characteristics of an organism. To be distinguished from *derived motivational variables.*

Biogenic: Arising in, and mediated by, the biological characteristics of the individual.

Conditioned taste aversion: A learned tendency to avoid

foods or liquids that have been associated with unpleasant or painful consequences.

Contingent: Causally dependent upon. A food reward is contingent upon the occurrence of a particular response if the apparatus is so designed that when the response occurs, the food is inevitably delivered.

Derived motivational variable: Any event to which an organism is sensitive, whether internal or external, that has attained the status of a motivational variable through the operation of the processes of conditioning and learning.

Drive: Used frequently and interchangeably with "motivation." In several theories, drive is a nonspecific energizer of a wide assortment of response tendencies.

Hyperphagia: A tendency to consume excessive amounts of food.

Imprinting object: An object, usually the mother, to which young animals become strongly attached, thereafter following it closely. Under artificial experimental conditions, animals may also become attached to inanimate objects or to human caretakers.

Incentive motivation: The presumed behavior-augmenting effects of to-be-attained rewards or of the expectations of such rewards.

Motivation: Traditionally, a force or process that "moves" the organism. Also, a property or characteristic of organisms akin to personality characteristics. Commonly distinguished from specific tendencies to perform particular responses.

Motivational variable: Any external event, genetic characteristic, or internal state associated with differences or changes in scores on tests used to define level of motivation.

Placebo: A neutral substance such as a sugar pill often administered in drug experiments to the members of a nondrugged group to control the effects of expectancy or suggestion.

Proprioceptive: Of, or pertaining to, the sensory consequences of movements arising from receptors in muscles, joints, tendons, and the nonauditory systems of the inner ear.

Psychogenic: Having its genesis or origin in the learning experiences of the organism rather than in its biophysical structures, functions, or relations.

Sociogenic: Stemming from an individual's cultural-social experiences. (Compare psychogenic and biogenic).

Vasoconstriction: A diminution in the size of small peripheral blood vessels. Often accompanied by changes in skin temperature, electrical conductivity, and so on.

Suggested Readings

Buck, R. *Human Motivation and Emotion.* New York: John Wiley and Sons, 1976.

Ferguson, E. D. *Motivation: An Experimental Approach.* New York: Holt, Rinehart and Winston, 1976.

Haber, R. N. *Current Research in Motivation.* New York: Holt, Rinehart and Winston, 1966.

Levine, F. M. *Theoretical Readings in Motivation: Perspectives on Human Behavior.* Chicago: Rand McNally Publishing Co., 1975.

McClelland, D. C. and Steele, R. S. *Human Motivation: A Book of Readings.* Morristown, N.J.: General Learning Press, 1973.

Wong, R. *Motivation: A Biobehavioral Analysis of Consummatory Activities.* New York: McMillan Publishing Co., 1976.

NOTE: The preparation of this chapter was supported in part by grants from the National Institute of Mental Health (MH 23607), from the National Institute of Alcohol Abuse and Alcoholism (AA 07074, AA 01229), and from the National Institute of General Medical Sciences (GM 01495).

Learning

Marc N. Branch and Merle E. Meyer

Introduction

Usually "learning" refers to unobserved changes within an organism that are inferred from the behavior of that organism. In many situations, the performance of an organism is thought to reflect the concurrent, ongoing process of learning, but there are also situations in which "learning" is thought to occur in the absence of any observable behavior. Although this chapter is entitled "Learning," we will not try to define the term, but instead, devote our efforts to describing various procedures or operations that are used to produce changes in behavior from which "learning" is inferred.

As pointed out in Chapter 1, two of the main functions of science are prediction and control of events, and many psychologists try to predict and control behavior. When we say an organism has "learned" something, it allows us to make predictions about its behavior, and when we also specify the conditions that produce "learning," we can control behavior. By specifying the conditions needed to produce a certain behavioral outcome, then, we can both predict and control behavior without need of referring to some unobserved process or processes called "learning."

The term "learning" has been applied to a myriad of relationships between environment and behavior, and virtually all changes in behavior-environment relationships can be attributed to "learning." However, such indiscriminate use of the term has robbed it of meaning. It is probably

quite unlikely that a single physiological process, called "learning," is correlated with the wide range of procedures that produce changes in behavior-environment relationships.

The procedures for modifying behavior that will be described in this chapter are fundamental, and the processes involved operate continuously time a rat presses a lever a small pellet of food is delivered. If the frequency of lever-presses increases, then lever-pressing is an operant. In the example of going to New York, suppose that each behavioral phenomena described in the other chapters of this text.

Respondent Behavior

There are various paradigms or operations for modifying or changing behavior. Within this section, we shall be interested primarily in those behavioral effects that are a function of the procedures or operations associated with *respondent* behavior. Respondent behavior is behavior that is defined in terms of the stimuli that elicit it. That is, it is reflexive behavior.

The Functional Reflex

Perhaps the simplest behavioral operation is the presentation of a stimulus, which in turn produces responding by an organism. This basic paradigm is shown in Figure 9-1. In this paradigm, the *unconditional stimulus* (US) regularly *elicits* (pulls out or

Fig. 9-1. The basic paradigm for the functional reflex. An unconditional stimulus, US, elicits an unconditioned response, UR.

evokes) a measurable "reflexive-type" response or *respondent*. The *unconditioned response* (UR), or respondent, is a reliable and measurable response produced by the unconditional stimulus.

A number of reflexes are familiar, such as food in the mouth producing salivation, a bright light eliciting pupillary contraction, electric shock eliciting withdrawal reactions, and smog in the eyes causing tearing. The reflex is neither the unconditional stimulus nor is it the unconditioned response, but rather the reflex is the functional relationship or correlation between them. For example, salivation by itself is not a reflex in that there is no specification of an eliciting stimulus. Rather, a salivary reflex is the *relationship* between food in the mouth and the flow of saliva.

Some Characteristics of the Reflex

An unconditional stimulus (e.g., food), by definition, reliably elicits the unconditioned response (e.g., salivation). However, the topography (that is, the physically measureable characteristics) of the response will be functionally related to the properties of the stimulus. For a response to be elicited, the stimulus intensity must reach or exceed a certain *threshold* value. A very weak, or *subliminal,* stimulus will not elicit a response. Thus, for a response to occur the stimulus must be above the critical threshold value. A second relationship is that for stimuli above threshold, the intensity of the stimulus is positively related to the *magnitude* or size of the response up to a limit where the strength of the response is maximal. That is, up to a point, the stronger the stimulus the greater the response. Lastly, there is a brief interval of time, referred to as *latency,* between the onset of the stimulus and the onset of the response.

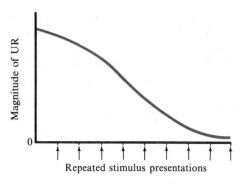

Fig. 9-2. Graphic illustration of habituation. The arrows indicate the presentation of the US. With repeated presentations of the US the magnitude of the UR diminishes.

In general, the latencies are shorter with more intense stimuli.

With repeated presentations of the unconditional stimulus, the respondent may be *habituated* or may be *facilitated*. In habituation, the strength of the response declines or becomes weaker with repeated presentation of the stimulus as shown in Figure 9-2. Alternatively, repeated presentation of

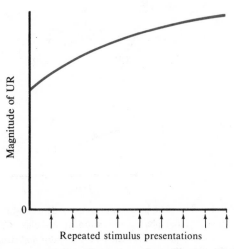

Fig. 9-3. Graphic illustration of sensitization. The arrows indicate the presentation of the US. With repeated presentations of the US the magnitude of the UR increases.

the unconditioned stimulus may result in an increase in respondent strength; this effect has been called facilitation or sensitization. This phenomenon is illustrated in Figure 9-3. For our point here, it is sufficient to say that the response topography of a reflex can be a function of the stimulus and of prior exposure to that stimulus.

Respondent Conditioning and Associated Phenomena

Respondent conditioning (often referred to as *Pavlovian conditioning* or *classical conditioning*) involves the presentation of a previously neutral or *conditional stimulus* (CS), which temporally precedes an unconditional stimulus. One of the major characteristics of the respondent-conditioning paradigm is that the conditional stimulus and the unconditional stimulus are presented independent of the organism's behavior. That is, stimulus presentations do not depend on any behavior by the subject.

Basic Paradigm. The general operation for respondent conditioning is shown in Figure 9-4. By definition, a stimulus that does not elicit the unconditioned response is a *"neutral" stimulus* with respect to that specific unconditioned response. This *"neutral"* stimulus is referred to as a condition*al*

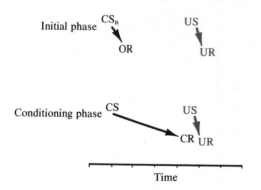

Fig. 9-4. The basic paradigm for respondent conditioning. In the initial phase, a conditional stimulus, CSn, occurs and is followed in time by a unconditional stimulus, US. The CSn elicits an orienting response (OR) and the US elicits UR. In the conditioning phase, after a number of CS-US pairings, the CS becomes associated with the US and elicits the conditioned response, CR.

stimulus. However, when it comes to elicit the respondent through repeated pairing with the unconditional stimulus, it then can also be called the condition*ed* stimulus. A response elicited by a conditioned stimulus is called a *conditioned response* (CR).

Within the initial phase of respondent conditioning, the conditional stimulus is "neutral" with regard to elicitation of the conditioned response. However, this stimulus may elicit another reliably-measured response, the *orienting response* (OR). For example, if an auditory stimulus is presented, it initially results in an increase in heart-rate. This functional relationship is referred to as an "investigatory reflex" or an "orienting reflex." One characteristic of the orienting response that distinguishes it from other respondents is that it *habituates,* or decreases, rapidly but may reappear as soon as changes in the stimulus occur.

After conditioning, the conditioned response is elicited by the conditional stimulus. The conditioned response resembles the unconditioned response but usually is not identical to it. As we shall see, the two responses differ in form, in latency, and in reliability.

For an example of "appetitive" conditioning of a respondent, we will briefly describe one of Pavlov's (1927) classic respondent conditioning studies in dogs. In 1904, Pavlov was awarded the Nobel Prize for his significant findings on glandular and neural aspects of digestion. However, he had noted prior to that time that various stimuli, such as the sight of a food pan, or the approach of the animal caretaker, which regularly preceded the presentation of food came to elicit the flow of saliva in his dogs. He called these "psychic" secretions. He believed these "psychic" secretions were the gateways to the study of the central nervous system and, for the remainder of his life, he turned his research efforts to the study of these responses. In a typical experiment, as shown in Figure 9-5, a dog was placed in a restraining harness in order to keep the dog properly oriented and free from extraneous influences. After a few minutes for habituation to the test environment, the experiment proper began. (Prior to the experiment, Pavlov had made a small incision in the dog's cheek and attached a tube to the salivary gland so

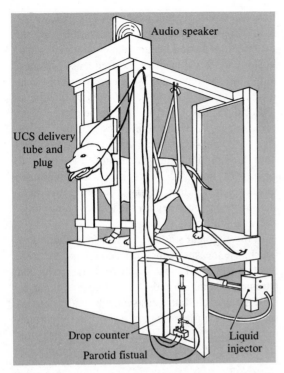

Fig. 9-5.   A view of a dog in a restraining and conditioning apparatus prepared for salivary recording. (Courtesy of D. W. Lauer and M. M. Shapiro)

that he could measure directly the amount of salivation in drops outside the mouth.) Initially, a tuning fork was sounded (CS) for a few seconds followed by the presentation of meat powder (US) in the dog's mouth, whereupon the dog salivated (UR). Pavlov noted that initially the sound did not elicit salivation, while food in the mouth did. On the other hand, the sound was associated with head turning and picking up of the ear, all of which he labeled the "investigatory reflex." After pairing the sound of the tuning fork and the meat powder for a few trials, Pavlov noted that when the tuning fork was sounded alone a small number of drops of saliva appeared. After thirty or so trials, the dog salivated a great deal when the sound was presented. Thus, it was apparent to Pavlov that the dog was conditioned to salivate in response to the sound of the tuning fork and that a new reflex was formed, which he called a conditional reflex.

A second classic example of respondent condi-

tioning, using a human subject, is a study reported by Watson and Rayner (1920). This study differs from Pavlov's in at least one major way. The unconditional stimulus used to elicit the behavior was aversive and the organism made "defensive" or "fear-like" responses. Albert, an eleven-month-old child was observed to be happy and played with a white rat prior to conditioning. Next, during the conditioning phase, a loud noise (US) was paired with the rat (CS). The noise elicited startle and fear-like responses such as the child falling forward from a sitting position, whimpering and crying, and showing other signs of "defense." After several pairings of the noise and the rat, Albert showed all of the distress responses and attempted to crawl away from the rat when it was presented to him in the absence of the noise. This example is not a "pure" case of respondent conditioning, since stimuli were not presented independently of Albert's behavior.

Respondent conditioning can be characterized by the operations involved, but some have also tried to characterize the process on the basis of the nature of the observed responses. The responses have been described as autonomic, "involuntary," or diffuse emotional responses. Changes in salivation, digestion, heartrate, galvanic skin response (changes in electrical resistance of the skin), constriction of blood vessels—can all be affected through respondent conditioning. These smooth muscle or glandular responses are associated with emotional behavior, and malfunctioning of internal body processes within the natural environment may be a function of the stimulus situations in which the organism finds itself. While these responses are subject to respondent conditioning, they are also modifiable by different operations (Miller, 1969; Kimmel, 1974). Respondent conditioning is not limited to autonomic nervous system responses, as several skeletal responses such as limb-movements, eyelid responses are easily conditioned using the respondent conditioning paradigm.

Measurement of the Conditioned Response.   To examine acquisition of the conditioned response, it is of fundamental importance that the response be accurately and reliably measured. Following Pav-

294

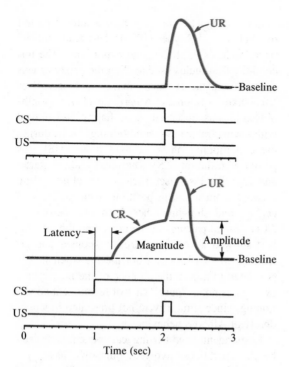

Fig. 9-6. Schematic records of the eyelid responses of a single subject. Part A shows the functional reflex, UR, when the US is presented. Part B illustrates both the CR and UR and the latency, amplitude, and magnitude measurements.

lov's procedure, one strategy is to use test trials where the conditional stimulus is presented and the unconditional stimulus is omitted. A second method is to measure the conditioned response during the presentation of the CS and before the presentation of the unconditional stimulus. This latter procedure is referred to as the *anticipation method*. Both methods utilize the same fundamental measurements of the conditioned response: *frequency, latency, amplitude,* and *magnitude.* The frequency measure is simply the number of conditioned responses divided by the number of trials; the latency is the time between the presentation of the conditional stimulus and the beginning of the response; the amplitude is the absolute size of the response prior to the onset of the unconditional stimulus; and the magnitude is the total con-

tinuous response, such as the total number of saliva drops, during the presentation of the unconditioned stimulus and the conditional stimulus. Figure 9-6 illustrates the frequency, latency, amplitude, and magnitude measurements of a conditional eye-blink response followed by the unconditioned response to an air-puff to the cornea of the eye. In part A of the figure, the conditioned response did not occur, the latency is maximum, and both the amplitude and magnitude measures are zero. Part B of the figure shows a conditioned response, hence the response occurred and measurements can be taken on the latency, amplitude, and magnitude.

In most typical studies, the researcher settles on a response measure which has been found to be the most reliable and most sensitive to the particular parameters being investigated. Of course, it is possible to make all four measurements, and when this is done, these measures are not perfectly correlated. Therefore, it is apparent that these measures are not all measuring exactly the same thing.

Acquisition of Conditioned Responses. With repeated pairing of the conditional stimulus and unconditional stimulus, the strength of the conditioned response gradually increases until the response reaches some upper limit (*asymptote*). With repeated pairing following this asymptotic level, the strength of the conditioned response remains constant. Figure 9-7 typifies the acquisi-

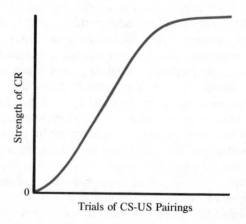

Fig. 9-7. The course of respondent conditioning with repeated pairings of the CS and US.

tion of respondent conditioning in a generalized laboratory study. The rates of acquisition and the asymptotic levels depend on the various parameters of variables of the experiment.

From general laboratory research, it appears that respondent conditioning takes place in increments over the course of several trials. This assumption, however, is often challenged by the human clinical literature. For example, within a very traumatic situation, after a single pairing with an intense aversive stimulus previously neutral stimuli can elicit a whole constellation of fear responses. While these are not controlled experiments in the usual sense of the term, some theoretical notions suggest that one can observe asymptotic behavior after a single trial.

Experimental Controls. In order to specify more fully the conditioned response obtained with the pairing of the CS and US, various experimental control groups become essential in order that we eliminate possible alternative explanations. In general, the control procedures are those that provide the control organisms with the same experimental conditions as the experimental organisms except for the contiguous, that is, temporally close, CS-US presentations. Rescorla (1967) has recommended the following control-procedures—present CS only, present US only, present CS and US randomly, present US first followed by CS (backward conditioning) and present CS-US simultaneously. Each control procedure has certain functions as well as limitations. Some investigators (Beecroft, 1966) argue that simultaneous CS-US presentation is the best control procedure.

The control groups are utilized in respondent conditioning studies to illuminate the possible behavioral changes that are not a function of the contiguous CS-US pairing. Two nonassociative behavioral changes that occur often in respondent conditioning studies are *pseudoconditioning* and *sensitization*. Each can mimic true conditioning. If only the US is presented for several trials and then the CS is presented, a response may occur which resembles a conditioned response. This is referred to as pseudoconditioning. This phenomenon is common when the US is aversive (Kimble, 1961) and is probably based on a startle reaction. On the

other hand, sensitization is an increase in the response elicited by the CS as a function of US presentation.

Extinction and Spontaneous Recovery of Conditioned Respondent Behavior. The basic operation for eliminating a conditioned respondent is to present the conditional stimulus repeatedly over trials without the unconditional stimulus. When only the conditional stimulus is presented, both the magnitude and amplitude of the conditioned response gradually become less, and the latencies become longer. After a sufficient number of trials, the conditional stimulus will no longer elicit a response, and *extinction* of a conditioned respondent is said to have occurred. Extinction, however, is not permanent. If sufficient time elapses and the conditional stimulus is again presented to the organism, a conditioned response will be elicited. This reappearance of the conditioned response is called *spontaneous recovery*. Spontaneous recovery is regularly observed in extinction testing when the subject is presented with a fixed number of trials per day. Typically, the magnitude and amplitude will be larger and latencies shorter at the beginning of a session than they were at the end of the prior session. Figure 9-8 illustrates a generalized acquisition curve with control conditions, extinction, and spontaneous recovery of a conditioned respondent.

Inhibition and Disinhibition of Respondent Behavior. If a "novel" stimulus, different from the conditioned stimulus, is presented before or during

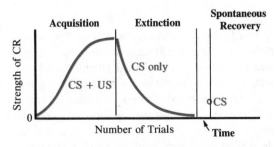

Fig. 9-8. A schematic illustration of acquisition (CS + US), extinction (CS only) followed by a lapse of time and spontaneous recovery when the CS is presented.

presentation of the conditioned stimulus, that stimulus can disrupt or *inhibit* the conditioned response. Similarly, if a "novel" stimulus, different from the unconditional stimulus, is presented simultaneously with the onset of the unconditional stimulus, that "novel" stimulus can likewise inhibit the unconditioned response.

The phenomenon of *disinhibition* has essentially the opposite effect as inhibition, where a "novel" stimulus is presented before or during the conditioned stimulus, which in turn increases the magnitude of the conditioned response. Disinhibition is usually demonstrated during the extinction of a conditioned response. If a "novel" stimulus is introduced before or during the conditioned stimulus, this may result in a temporary increase in an extinguishing conditioned respondent. These effects are illustrated in Figure 9-9.

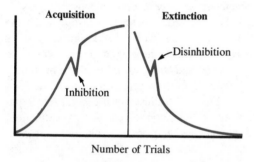

Fig. 9-9.   An illustration of inhibition and disinhibition of the CR. During acquisition a novel stimulus is presented, as indicated by the arrow, that comes to inhibit the CR. In extinction, the novel stimulus is presented (arrow) that comes to disinhibit the CR.

Generalization and Discrimination of Respondent Behavior.   If a conditioned response can be elicited by a specific conditional stimulus, and if a stimulus *similar* to the original conditional stimulus is then presented, this new stimulus will often elicit the conditioned response. The strength of the response, however, will usually be less, and the decrement is a function of the relative difference between the original conditioned stimulus and the second stimulus. This defines the process of *gener-*

alization. Generalization to stimuli along common dimensions such as frequency, hue, or intensity is called *stimulus generalization,* and the decrement of the conditioned response as the differences between stimuli increase is referred to as *generalization decrement* or a *generalization gradient*. As seen in Figure 9-10, which represents a hypothetical gradient of generalization, the greater the stimulus differences, the greater the decrement. Basically, the procedure to test for generalization involves the conditioning of the organism to a specific stimulus (CS) and then, on successive trials, presenting varied but physically-similar stimuli without pairing those stimuli with the unconditional stimuli.

In the experiment where little Albert was conditioned to fear a rat, the conditioned fear response to the rat also generalized to other furry-objects such as a rabbit, cotton, a fur coat, a dog and even a mask of Santa Claus. Prior to the original conditioning to the rat, these stimuli had all been shown to Albert. None elicited a generalized fear response. Unfortunately, no exact measurements of

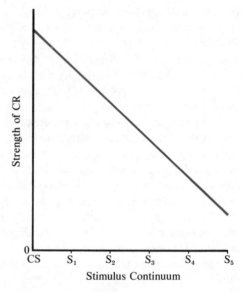

Fig. 9-10.   An illustration of a hypothetical gradient of respondent generalization. The CS is the original conditioned stimulus that results in the greatest strength of the CR. As the stimuli become different, S_1 to S_5, the CR diminishes in strength.

the strength of the response were taken. In extreme cases, these generalized fear responses are seen clinically as phobic reactions, and variations of extinction procedures are utilized in behavioral therapy to control them.

While it is biologically significant that an organism generalizes, it is also adaptive that an organism discriminate among stimuli. An organism is said to discriminate if it responds differentially to two different stimuli. In respondent discrimination, if a stimulus (CS+) is paired with an unconditional stimulus on random trials, and if on the other trials another stimulus (CS−) is not associated with the unconditioned stimulus, then the organism, after numerous trials, will discriminate between the stimuli. That is, the CS+ will elicit a conditioned response, whereas the CS− will not. The acquisition of discriminative responses is illustrated in Figure 9-11. In this study CS+ was a tone of 700 Hz and CS− was 3500 Hz. A mild electric shock to the finger served as the unconditioned stimulus and the respondent elicited by the shock was a galvanic skin response (a change in skin resistance). Respondent discrimination is the result of both acquisition and extinction.

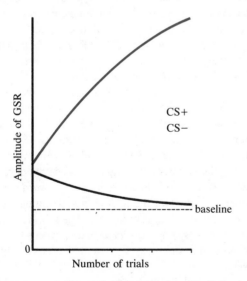

Fig. 9-11. An illustration of respondent discrimination of the galvanic skin response. The figure demonstrates the discrimination when the CS+ (700 HZ tone) is associated with the US (shock) and when the CS− is a 3500 Hz tone.

Higher-Order Conditioning A logical extension of respondent conditioning suggests that if a conditional stimulus (tone) elicits a respondent (salivation), then another neutral or conditional stimulus (light) could be paired with the original conditioned stimulus (tone) and after a number of pairings, this stimulus (light) would elicit the conditioned response. This is called higher-order conditioning, and the paradigm is illustrated in Figure 9-12.

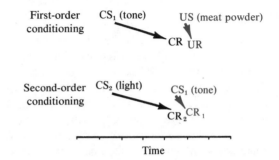

Fig. 9-12. A paradigm for second-order conditioning.

Second- and even third-order conditioning (that is, two CSs or three CSs) have been reported in the experimental literature; however, the conditioned responses extinguish rapidly (Rescorla, 1973). In order to maintain the conditioned response, the unconditional stimulus is occasionally paired with the original CS. In an analysis of complex emotional behavior, it is often difficult to trace the behavior back to the original conditioning situations as respondents can have various conditioning histories associated with a broad array of stimuli.

Some Variables Influencing Respondent Conditioning

Today, there is substantial experimental literature relating different variables to various effects on respondent conditioning. In the following section, a few of the major variables that influence respondent conditioning will be discussed.

Characteristics of the Unconditional Stimulus. Many investigators have studied the functional relationship between the intensity of the unconditional stimulus and the conditioned response. In general, at least with aversive unconditional stimuli, the more intense the stimulus (up to some limit) the greater the conditioned response (Prokasy et al., 1958). Little research with positive unconditional stimuli has been reported.

Although the intensity of aversive stimuli has an affect on respondent conditioning, numerous studies have shown little or no relationship between the duration of the unconditional stimulus and the conditioned response.

Characteristics of the Conditional Stimulus. The results of various studies on the relationship between the intensity of the conditional stimulus and the conditional response are contradictory. Some experiments have found no fixed relationship between intensity of the conditional stimulus and the conditioned response. However, Gormezano (1972) has reported that more intense conditioned stimuli result in greater respondent conditioning. On the other hand, if the conditional stimulus is so intense that it elicits an orienting response that does not habituate, respondent conditioning may be difficult, if not impossible, to obtain (Sokolov, 1963).

In the original Pavlovian experiments, intermittent stimuli, such as the sound of a tuning fork or buzzer, running water, flashing light, and the like, were used as conditional stimuli. Few studies have compared the dynamic characteristics of these stimuli to the typical, static ones. It appears from the reported research, however, that the intermittent conditional stimuli are more effective than static stimuli in the acquisition of respondent conditioning.

Temporal Relationships of the CS-US. The temporal relationships between the conditional stimulus and the unconditional stimulus are significant determinants in the acquisition of a conditioned respondent. The major operational procedures, as shown in Figure 9-13, involve different temporal relationships between the two stimuli.

A *simultaneous conditioning* procedure, by tradition, is one in which the onset of the conditional stimulus is presented within five seconds of the

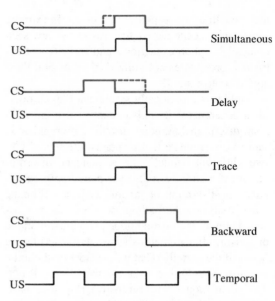

Fig. 9-13. Five respondent conditioning procedures that differ in temporal relationships between the CS and US.

onset of the unconditional stimulus. However, onset of both stimuli occurring at precisely the same time is also called simultaneous conditioning. It is this latter method that is called simultaneous conditioning in contemporary experimental literature, and that usage will be employed here. The two other most typical operations are the *delay* and the *trace* procedures. For delay, as the figure illustrates, the conditional stimulus precedes the unconditional stimulus in time and can overlap temporally the unconditional stimulus. By contrast, in the trace procedure, both the onset and offset of the conditional stimulus precede the onset of the unconditional stimulus. In the *backward conditioning* operation, the unconditional stimulus precedes the conditional stimulus. The last procedure illustrated is *temporal conditioning* where the unconditional stimulus is presented at fixed intervals.

In general, little, if any, respondent conditioning occurs with the simultaneous and backward conditioning procedures. Delayed, trace, and temporal conditional stimuli can all result in respondent conditioning. Apparently, for conditioning to occur, the conditional stimulus must temporally precede the unconditioned stimulus.

Of special concern is the temporal relationship separating the onsets of the conditional and unconditional stimuli, or the *interstimulus interval* (ISI). It is that interval of time that defines the CS-US contiguity. Much early research suggested that the optimal interval is 0.5 second between the onset of the two stimuli, and longer or shorter intervals result in poorer conditioning. However, there is probably no fixed optimal interstimulus interval, as the optimal interval varies with the nature of the responses and species of animals. For example, in eyelid-conditioning, 0.5 second is optimal in humans in contrast to 0.02 second in rabbits, and for heartrate conditioning 2.5 seconds is best in dogs, but 12 seconds is best in humans. As Figure 9-14 reveals, respondent conditioning will reach its greatest level if the conditional stimulus precedes the unconditioned stimulus by a short interval of time generally measured in seconds or parts of a second. If the interval is shortened or lengthened, the CS-US contiguity is weakened, and with longer interstimulus intervals, respondent conditioning often will not occur at all.

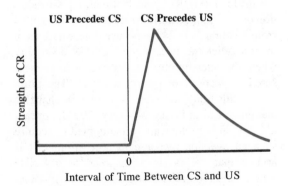

Fig. 9-14. A schematic illustration of the effect of the interstimulus interval (ISI) on respondent conditioning.

The *intertrial interval* (ITI) has also been found to affect respondent conditioning. When the time between trials is short, the number of trials neces-

sary for maximum or asymptotic conditioning is far greater than if the time interval between trials is longer. Most studies show that massing (using short intertrial intervals) results in poorer conditioning than spacing trials.

Intermittent Presentation of the Unconditional Stimulus. There are some interesting questions as to the behavioral effects of intermittently presenting the unconditional stimulus, that is, not presenting it on all trials. Of particular concern is whether intermittent presentation of the US results in slower respondent acquisition rates or in lower asymptotic levels of the conditioned respondent. Research literature is not conclusive in answering these questions.

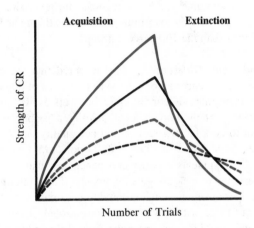

Fig. 9-15. The acquisition and extinction of respondent conditioning with intermittent presentation of the US. The 100 percent US presentation group is illustrated by the solid line, the 75 percent group by the filled circles, the 50 percent group by the hatched lines, and the 25 percent group by the open circles.

Figure 9-15 illustrates four experimental groups where each group had the same number of CS-US pairings but not the same number of trials. For the 100 percent group, the two stimuli were paired on each trial; for the 75 percent group, the unconditional stimulus was omitted randomly on one of every four trials; for the 50 percent group, the US was randomly omitted on half of the trials; and for the 25 percent group on one of every four trials, on the average, both the conditional and unconditional stimulus were presented. As the figure shows, all intermittent presentations resulted in slower rates of respondent conditioning. As this study did not involve enough trials, little can be said about the asymptotic level of the respondent. However, if we were to extrapolate the curves, it would appear that lower asymptotic levels would result. It should be pointed out, however, that there is a substantial number of studies in the comparative animal literature suggesting little or no difference in either the rates or levels of acquisition as a function of degree of intermittency of pairing of CS and US.

Of additional interest in Figure 9-15 is the fact that in spite of slower rates of acquisition, the effects of intermittent presentations of the unconditional stimulus yielded a reversal during extinction. That is, the intermittent groups extinguished slower than the 100 percent group.

Individual Differences. Pavlov noted that there were differences among the various breeds of dogs in their rates of conditioning, as well as within breeds. At the human level, intelligence appears not to be a factor, but age and personality do. As described earlier in Chapter 8, Taylor (1951) gave college students a paper and pencil test that was designed to measure general anxiety. Then, taking subjects from those who scored high (anxious) and from those with low scores (nonanxious), Taylor conditioned the two groups in an eyelid-conditioning experiment. As can be seen in Figure 9-16, the "anxious" group conditioned faster and reached a higher asymptotic level than the "non-anxious" group.

Constraints. Various limits or constraints on respondent behavior exist. Many of these pose no significant problem for describing respondent behaviors, as these constraints can be explained by differences among species in the sensory or motor capacity of the organism. These biological constraints do not violate the generality of the behavioral principles, for they can be explained in terms of differences in species-specific behaviors. It is apparent that for members of species, that certain respondents are more readily conditionable than

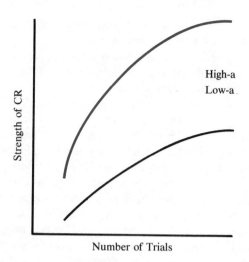

Fig. 9-16. A schematic illustration of respondent conditioning with high-anxious subjects (high-a) and with low or nonanxious subjects (low-a).

for members of other species (Seligman and Hager, 1972). The acquisition of taste aversion in the rat is a dramatic case (Garcia, et al. 1975; Kalat and Rozin, 1971). Rats acquire an aversion to a distinctive taste in their food (CS) if the animals are made sick (UR) by such stimuli as X-irradiation or by lithium chloride injection (US) presented from 30 minutes to 24 hours later. These data seem to contradict the necessity of CS-US contiguity where the interstimulus intervals are usually measured in seconds or part of seconds. The time-course function, however, is similar in shape to that illustrated in Figure 9-14 on p. 299. It appears that the rat is biologically programmed to acquire such an aversion response to taste stimuli. It is argued that the rat is predisposed to associate illness with food-related stimuli but not with other stimuli such as tones and lights. Biologically, the taste stimuli have greater survival significance to the rat within its natural environment than do the visual and auditory stimuli (Barker et al., 1977).

Up to this point, we have been discussing behavior that is elicited by stimuli and is considered "reflexive." While humans and other animals certainly have many reflexes, respondent conditioning allows us to influence only a small portion of an organism's behavioral repertoire. Many behaviors we observe seem to occur in the absence of any specific eliciting stimuli. Such behaviors constitute a large portion of the repertoire of most organisms, and are said to be *emitted* rather than elicited. We turn now to a discussion of emitted behavior.

Operant Behavior

The Operant

Although most psychologists agree that psychology is the study of behavior, there is less agreement about how to identify behaviors to be studied. In order to study any event scientifically, including behavioral events, it is usually necessary that the event be a repeated one; that is, it is quite difficult to study the variables that affect an event that occurs only once. Thus, scientists generally group events into classes for study. The problem is in choosing which characteristic(s) of a class of events ought to be used in assigning events to categories. This problem has been especially prominent in the study of behavior. For instance, let us say that you are interested in studying fishing. In order to study fishing, it is necessary to identify reliably when fishing has actually taken place. A first approach might be to try to identify episodes of fishing by the physical form, or *topography,* of the behavior. It might be decided that if someone is near water and has fishing equipment, that person is engaged in fishing. There are, of course, problems with this approach. For example, a person might be on a boat with fishing equipment, even with a fishing line hanging over the side of the boat, and yet that person may be out getting a suntan, rather than fishing. Thus, trying to identify repeated instances of behavior on the basis of the topographical characteristics of the behavior is often not successful in cases where the topography may vary widely. From one point of view, it seems that it is the purpose of the behavior that really identifies it. This creates a problem for the behavioral scientist. Since the notion of purpose generally implies that behavior occurs because of some future event, the scientist is temporarily left in the uncomfortable position of identifying behavioral

units on the basis of events that have not yet occurred. Of course, there is a solution, and it lies in the notion of *the operant,* first elaborated by B. F. Skinner (1935).

Operants are so called because they operate on the environment, and they are defined by their effect on the environment. A typical laboratory example of a simple operant is lever-pressing. A rat, for example, may press the lever with its left paw, right paw, both paws, elbows, snout, head, and so on. In all cases, it is the fact that the lever has been depressed, not what the behavior looks like, that tells us that the behavior has occurred. Thus, an operant is a *class* of behaviors that all have *a common effect on the environment.* An example of a more complex operant might be the behavior of going to New York. You can go to New York by walking, flying, taking the train, hitchhiking and by other means. You also might go to New York *via* Chicago, over the pole, or directly. All these seemingly diverse behaviors might be part of a single operant that we would label "going to New York," since they all result in your arriving in New York.

Operants are behaviors that produce a common effect on the environment. Applying a mild electric shock to the upper leg of a dog results in flexion of the dog's leg; this is clearly a behavior that produces a consistent change in the environment, that is, the dog's lower leg gets closer to its body. Yet, we would not consider leg flexion in this instance an operant. This apparent paradox leads us to a second defining characteristic of an operant. Behavior is considered to be operant in nature if, and only if, the behavior can be *modified by its consequences.* Suppose it is arranged that each time a rat presses a lever a small pellet of food is delivered. If the frequency of lever-presses increases, then lever-pressing is an operant. In the example of going to New York, suppose that each time you go to New York there is a reliable consequence, for example, you get mugged. If the frequency of your going to New York decreased, then we would consider going to New York an operant.

Reflexes are often referred to as *involuntary* behavior. Behavior that is modifiable by its consequences (operant behavior) is usually referred to as ''voluntary'' or ''purposive'' behavior. It is easier to understand the notion of an operant if you consider operant behavior as being defined by its purpose. ''Fishing'' is a label we give to behaviors that have the ''purpose'' of obtaining fish. The frequency of fishing can be modified by whether or not any fish are caught.

In summary, the two criteria for identifying operants are, (1) operant behavior operates on the environment, and (2) operant behavior is affected by its consequences. Operants may be very small pieces of behavior, or extremely complex and/or abstract units of behavior. The range of operants that have been examined experimentally range from the behavior of single muscle fibers to such abstract classes of behavior as imitation, but most of the operants studied in the laboratory are fairly

simple. The use of simple, rapidly repeatable operants allows the experimenter to ''compress time.'' That is, many repetitions of the operant are possible within a short period of time, something that would not be possible with larger units of behavior. Most researchers investigating operant behavior are concerned with studying variables that alter the frequency (responses/time) of behavior, so by using rapidly repeatable operants a relatively wide range of frequencies may be observed in a relatively short period of time. Thus, the use of simple operants is largely a matter of experimental convenience. Researchers assume that data generated from studying simple operants will be generalizable to more complex cases. Whether this assumption is justified, of course, will be determined by further research on large, complex operants.

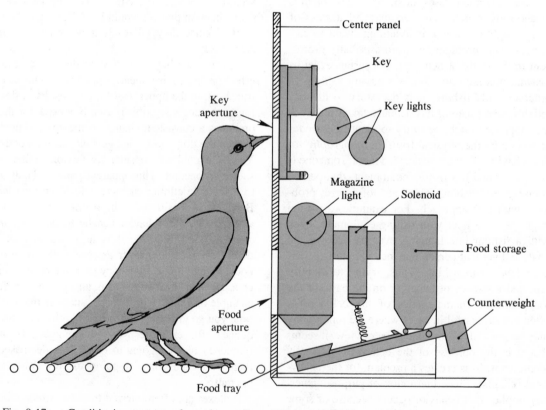

Fig. 9-17a.   Conditioning apparatus for a pigeon. From Ferster and Skinner, 1957.

Operant Conditioning and Associated Phenomena

Before proceeding to discuss operant behavior in some detail, let us familiarize ourselves with some typical experimental arrangements and some basic experimental results. Displayed in Figure 9-17 are two sets of apparatus, one for a rat and one for a pigeon. These schematized drawings show the kind of equipment typically used to study operant behavior in these two species. Both sets of apparatus have several features in common. In each case, the subject is restricted to a relatively small amount of space in which there is a device that the subject may manipulate. In the apparatus for the rat, there is a lever that may be depressed, and for the pigeon there is a circular disk (or key) mounted on one wall that the pigeon may peck. Also common to both of the sets of apparatus is a device by which food can be made available. In the apparatus for the rat there is an automatic feeder that can deliver food pellets into a small cup near the lever, whereas in the apparatus for the pigeon, there is a somewhat different device that can present grain to the pigeon through an aperture below the key. Not shown in Figure 9-17 are two other important parts of the typical experimental apparatus for studying operant behavior. The chambers shown are usually enclosed in a sound-attenuating and light-tight enclosure that blocks out unwanted stimuli. Also not shown in Figure 9-17 is the automatic control equipment almost invariably employed in the study of operant behavior. Automatic equipment is employed to ensure that the operation of the experiment proceeds smoothly and in a consistent fashion that would not be possible if all the experimental arrangements were directly controlled by human experimenters who occasionally make errors.

Measurement of Operants. Many aspects of operants can be studied using these kinds of apparatus. For example, the duration of each operant, the intensity, the latency between some event and the emission of an operant, and a host of other

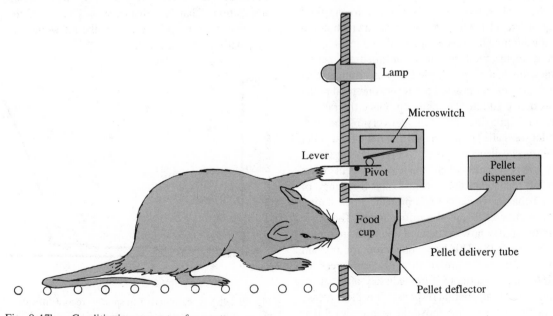

Fig. 9-17b.   Conditioning apparatus for a rat.

aspects of the behavior can be investigated. The most studied aspect of operant behavior, however, has been its *frequency*, or *rate*, of occurrence. Rate of responding (responses/time) has been studied for many reasons, but one reason stands out in importance. *All* behavior occurs with some rate, so rate is a basic property of all operant behavior. Thus, rate is the preferred dependent variable in the study of simple operants such as lever-pressing, because it increases the likelihood that we will be able to generalize our findings to other classes of operant behavior.

The Basic Paradigm. To describe a simple operant conditioning experiment, we shall use one of Skinner's classic experiments with a rat as the subject. The rat was deprived of food until it weighed about 80 percent of its normal weight. Then the rat was placed in a small chamber with a lever, such as the one shown in Figure 9-17 and allowed to spend some time in the chamber without any special happenings. This allowed the rat to adapt to the chamber, and also allowed determination of the *operant level* of lever-pressing. The operant level is defined as the frequency of occurrence of an operant when the operant does not have, and never has had, any special consequence. Next, food pellets were dispensed into the food cup at irregular intervals. Soon Skinner observed that each time the feeder operated, the rat went directly to the food cup and consumed the pellet. Once this had been achieved, it was arranged that each time the rat pressed the lever, one food pellet was delivered into the food cup. Once the rat was regularly pressing the lever, delivery of the food pellet was called *reinforcement*, and the food pellet itself was called a *reinforcer*, or *reinforcing stimulus*. Any event, when made contingent upon operant behavior, that increases the frequency of that behavior is called a reinforcer. Presentation of a reinforcer is called reinforcement. The basic paradigm may now be defined and is diagrammed in Figure 9-18. The basic operation for operant conditioning is the presentation of a reinforcer, or reinforcing stimulus (S^R) immediately after an organism emits an operant response. It is the increase in rate of the response above the operant level that defines operant conditioning.

$$R \rightarrow S^R$$

Fig. 9-18.   The basic paradigm for operant conditioning. A member of an operant class, R, is followed by a reinforcing stimulus, S^R.

Acquisition.   In Figure 9-19, the results of Skinner's experiment are shown. The graph is called a *cumulative response record*, and is a continuous record of lever pressing over time. The way such a graph is made is by having a pen move at a constant speed from left to right across the paper as time passes and each press on the lever moves the pen up slightly. Thus a flat horizontal line indicates no lever-pressing, and a line that goes up indicates that the lever was pressed. The steeper the line is, the faster lever-pressing is occurring. Thus, you can determine the rate of responding just by looking at the slope of the graph. The steeper the slope of the line, the faster the responding. The graph in Figure 9-19 shows that about 50 minutes after the beginning of the test session, the rat pressed the lever once, and then pressed once again after another 40 minutes. After about an additional 20 minutes, the rat pressed the lever again and thereafter pressed the lever at a high constant rate. These results define the process of free-operant acquisition. That is, advantage was taken of the fact that, without prior training, the rat would occasionally press the lever.

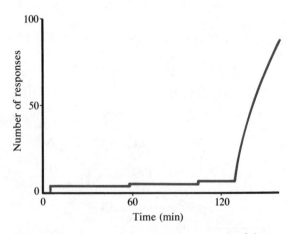

Fig. 9-19.   A cumulative response record of lever pressing by a rat during free-operant acquisition (Skinner, 1938).

Extinction and Spontaneous Recovery. Suppose that after acquisition the rat is placed in the chamber but lever presses no longer result in presentation of the food pellet. This procedure—discontinuing reinforcement—is called *extinction.* The effect of extinction on lever pressing is illustrated in Figure 9-20. The steep slope at the left side of the graph indicates that the rate was high at the beginning of the test session in which extinction began. Over the course of time, the graph becomes less steep and eventually becomes flat, indicating that the rat stopped pressing the lever. The curve in Figure 9-20 is *negatively accelerated,* and is very typical of a record from a subject whose behavior has been subjected to extinction. Such a cumulative response record is often called an "extinction curve," and the behavioral result of the extinction procedure is often called extinction, too.

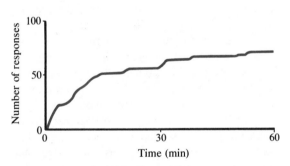

Fig. 9-20. A cumulative response record of lever pressing by a rat during extinction (Skinner, 1938).

Not shown in Figure 9-20 are other effects of extinction. When extinction begins, it is likely that the rat will begin pressing the lever vigorously, biting the lever, defecating, and, in general, engaging in what might be called "emotional" or "aggressive" behavior. Also, there tends to be an increase in the variability of response topography. That is, during conditioning, the physical form of the lever press usually becomes relatively stereotyped. That is, the rat presses the lever the same way almost every time. By contrast, during extinction, the form of the response usually varies widely.

By the end of the test session with extinction in effect, the rat completely ceased pressing the lever. If the rat is returned to the test chamber sometime later, with extinction still in effect, it will begin pressing the lever again and generate another extinction curve. This extinction curve, however, will have fewer responses in it. This phenomenon, a resumption in responding after extinction, is called *spontaneous recovery,* and is analogous to the spontaneous recovery of conditioned reflexes.

Spontaneous recovery may appear to be very mysterious, but in fact there is a very logical explanation for its occurrence. Many experiments have shown that extinction progresses most slowly when conditions during extinction are as similar as possible to those that were in effect during conditioning. For example, extinction proceeds much more slowly, that is, it takes longer and more responses to complete extinction, if during extinction the feeder mechanism continues to operate making its clicking sound, than if the feeder is completely disconnected and makes no sound after each lever press. During the first extinction session the rat stopped responding some time well after the session had begun. There are many aspects about the beginning of a session which are not present near the end of the session, so a rat that has stopped responding at the end of a session does so in different stimulus circumstances than those present at the beginning of the session. "Spontaneous recovery" tells us that behavior at the beginning of the session has not yet extinguished. If the rat were exposed to several test sessions of extinction, it eventually would stop pressing the lever during the entire session.

Satiation. In Skinner's experiment the rat was allowed to obtain only 50 pellets per day. Suppose that instead of allowing the rat to obtain only 50 pellets during a test session, it is allowed to obtain 500 pellets. Figure 9.21 displays the results of such an experiment. Behavior begins at a high constant rate, but over the course of time the rate of the behavior declines, as indicated by the decreasing slope of the cumulative response record. This decline in response rate as a function of repeated presentation of the reinforcer is called *satiation.*

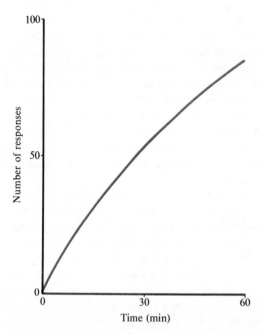

Fig. 9-21. A cumulative response record of a rat pressing a lever during the course of satiation (Skinner, 1938).

Although satiation produces effects somewhat similar to those produced by extinction, its effects can be differentiated from those of extinction on the basis of their permanence. If the rat were exposed to 10 daily sessions in which 500 pellets were available, and then on the eleventh day exposed to extinction, the rat would emit a large number of lever presses during extinction. If the same rat were exposed to 10 successive daily sessions of extinction and then exposed to extinction again on the eleventh day, it it highly probable the rat would not press the lever at all. Thus, satiation temporarily reduces the rate of operant behavior, whereas extinction can permanently reduce the rate of operant behavior. Extinction, then, is an operation that can be used to eliminate some behavior permanently.

An example of the use of extinction in the elimination of a child's tantrums is provided in a report by Williams (1959). The child engaged in tantrums when being put to bed; he would scream and fuss if his parents left the room before he went to sleep. The usual consequence of a tantrum was that the parents would return to the bedroom and try to calm the child. Williams assumed that it was possi-

ble that the attention given by the parents by going in to soothe the child was serving to reinforce the tantrum behavior. A program was arranged whereby the parents did not enter the child's bedroom until a tantrum had stopped. Thus, the tantrum no longer produced the attention of the parents that it previously had. Tantrums were completely eliminated in a very short amount of time.

"Superstitious" Behavior. In Skinner's experiment, it was arranged that each time the rat pressed the lever a pellet was immediately delivered to the food cup. This fixed dependency between a response and reinforcement is not necessary for operant conditioning to occur. Accidental relationships between behavior and reinforcers can result in operant conditioning. This fact was dramatically demonstrated by Skinner (1948) in an experiment with pigeons. Skinner placed food-deprived pigeons in a chamber and arranged that grain be presented for 3 seconds every 15 seconds. The pigeons were required to do nothing. Nevertheless, each pigeon soon developed a very stereotyped set of behaviors between each food presentation. The process involved is best described by Skinner himself: "The conditioning process is usually obvious. The bird happens to execute some response as the hopper appears; as a result it tends to repeat this response. If the interval before the next (grain) presentation is not so great that extinction takes place, a second 'contingency' is probable. This strengthens the response still further and subsequent reinforcement becomes more probable" (p. 169). You can surely identify many of your own behaviors that are not instrumental in producing reinforcement but that occur nonetheless before reinforcers. For example, consider the "body English" employed by a bowler releasing the ball. The body contortions have no effect on the path of the ball, but they do sometimes occur just before a reinforcing event such as a strike. Skinner's experiment shows us that even though "body English" does not produce a well-bowled ball, it can be affected by the consequences of a good roll.

Shaping. In Skinner's experiment, training a rat to press a lever was accomplished by arranging that as soon as the lever was pressed a food pellet was delivered. Note that advantage was taken of the fact that the rat would occasionally press the lever. However, suppose we wanted to train a rat to engage in some behavior that it had never emitted before. The technique that has come to be known as *shaping* allows us to produce new behaviors in our rat. For example, we may wish to train the rat to stand up on its hind legs and press a panel in the ceiling of the chamber. The rat, of course, would probably never engage in this behavior if we were not to intervene. But how to intervene? We do so by making delivery of a food pellet (reinforcement) depend on the rat emitting *successive approximations* to the desired response. Let us proceed through a possible sequence that would eventually lead to the rat pressing the panel on the ceiling. We first make reinforcement depend on the rat being right underneath the panel. After a few pellet presentations, the rat returns to the same spot regularly. At this point we stop delivering food for merely being beneath the press panel in the chamber. We then begin taking advantage of the effects of extinction, that is, that variability of topography increases during extinction. Thus, it is likely that the rat will rear up on its hind legs. As soon as the rat emits this behavior, we reinforce it, and we continue to reinforce rearing beneath the press-panel. Of course, soon the rat is rapidly rearing beneath the press-panel. Next we make our criterion for the delivery of a food pellet more stringent. For example, we now only reinforce rearing in which the rat straightens its back entirely (thus getting it closer to the ceiling). Once this behavior is well established, we change our criterion again, now reinforcing only movements directed towards the panel while the rat is standing up underneath it. By then reinforcing ever closer approximations to a panel press, we naturally induce the rat to press the panel. Thus, we have trained the rat to emit an entirely new response. To summarize, shaping makes use of both the process of conditioning and the process of extinction. We reinforce a first approximation to the desired terminal behavior, and this increases the frequency of this behavior. Next we change our criterion for reinforcement to a closer approximation to the desired behavior, and this generally results in extinction being in effect for many of the behaviors that were reinforced earlier. Extinction

increases the variability of the behavior. The temporary increase in variability makes it more likely that behavior meeting the new criterion will occur and be reinforced.

Shaping makes use of a more general procedure known as *differential reinforcement*. Differential reinforcement simply means that some responses are reinforced and others are not, and the procedure can be used to produce many behavioral effects. Differential reinforcement has often been used to modify topographical properties of behavior. Suppose, for example, in the illustration of a rat pressing a lever, most lever presses had a force of about 25 grams. The range of forces was from 10 to 50 grams, but the average force was 25 grams. We could introduce differential reinforcement in the following way. We could arrange that only those lever presses with a force of more than 35 grams be reinforced. The typical outcome of such a procedure would be that the rat would soon be making most presses with a force exceeding 35 grams. When such a result is obtained, we say that *response differentiation* has occurred.

The use of differential reinforcement and shaping in applied settings is exemplified by the work of Wolf et al. (1964). These experimenters were working with a severely emotionally-disturbed boy, one of whose problems was that he would not wear his eyeglasses. They began by first training the boy to wear glasses without lenses. Several empty glass frames were placed around the room, and the child was given small pieces of candy or fruit when he picked up, carried around, or otherwise handled the frames. Successive approximations to bringing the frames nearer his eyes were next reinforced. After a few weeks of daily sessions the child was eventually trained to wear his regular glasses. Note that in this example, as well as in the example of the rat pressing a ceiling panel, a key feature is the gradual way in which the terminal behavior is approximated. Shaping and other response differentiation procedures require gradual rather than abrupt changes.

Reinforcement

The word reinforcement currently is used in two ways. The first and most simple definition of the term is that reinforcement is the operation of presenting a reinforcer. The second definition of the word is that reinforcement is the effect of the operation of reinforcement. This is somewhat confusing; an example may clarify the situation. In the example of the rat pressing the lever, we would say that reinforcement occurred each time a pellet was presented. It occurred in the first sense simply because a reinforcer, the pellet, was delivered. It occurred in a second sense because the frequency of lever pressing was increased.

There are two main types of reinforcement—positive and negative. It is important to remember that the words reinforcer and reinforcement apply only to situations in which the frequency of behavior is *increased*. Thus, both positive and negative reinforcement result in an *increase* in the frequency of behavior. Positive reinforcement is said to have occurred when presentation of a stimulus following a response results in an increase in the frequency of that response. Negative reinforcement is said to have occurred when the removal of some stimulus immediately after a response increases the frequency of that response. For example, a husband may be yelling at his wife. If she emits the response of leaving the room, leaving the room is immediately followed by removal of the loud, offensive noises. In this case, leaving the room is negatively reinforced by removal of the noise. This distinction between positive and negative reinforcement is somewhat artificial, since removing a stimulus presents its absence and presenting a stimulus removes its absence. It was hoped, however, that once a negative reinforcer had been identified for a particular response, that it could be used also as a punishing stimulus. This hope, however, has not been realized.

An example of the difficulty of identifying a consequent operation as negative reinforcement or positive reinforcement is provided by an experiment by Weiss and Laties (1961). In their experiment, rats were shaved of their fur and placed in a small chamber that was inside a refrigerator kept at about 4° c. Mounted above the chamber was a heat lamp, and inside the chamber there was a lever. Each time the rat pressed the lever, it received a brief burst from the heat lamp. The rat soon began to press the lever regularly. The procedure and results are straightforward enough. The problem comes when we try to decide if we have witnessed positive reinforcement or negative reinforcement. Was it the presentation of the heat, or was it the removal of the cold that was responsible for the increase in frequency of lever-pressing? The problem, of course, is currently without solution. The example merely serves to show that the distinction between positive reinforcement and negative reinforcement is not always an easy one to make.

Table 1 below provides a guideline for classifying consequent events. Presenting an event immediately after an operant can either increase the rate of the operant (positive reinforcement) or decrease the rate (positive punishment. Punishment will be discussed later in this chapter.). Removing a stimulus immediately following an operant can also increase (negative reinforcement) or decrease (negative punishment) rate.

Psychologists have expended considerable theoretical effort on trying to explain why reinforcers reinforce, or to be able to identify reinforcers in advance of their demonstrated ability to be used as reinforcers. An early suggestion was that anything that satisfied a basic need could be used as a reinforcer. A basic need was defined as any need related to the survival of the organism or its genes,

Table 9-1.

		CONSEQUENT OPERATION	
		Present stimulus	*Remove stimulus*
	Increase frequency	Positive reinforcement	Negative reinforcement
Effect on Behavior			
	Decrease frequency	Positive punishment	Negative punishment

for example, food, water, sex, and so on. One of the problems with this notion was the acknowledged long delay between presentation of a reinforcer and eventual satisfaction of a need. For example, the delay between drinking water and any appreciable effect on the water-electrolyte balance in the body is considerable. And during this delay, many other behaviors occur that apparently are not influenced as much as the behavior that occurred immediately before the water was drunk. A modification of the need-reduction theory consisted of postulating that there are drive states within an organism that are immediately affected by the intake of some reinforcer. This type of approach has been called a drive-reduction theory. An experiment by Sheffield et al. (1951) pointed to a conceptual weakness of the drive-reduction type theory. Sheffield and his associates showed that the opportunity to mount a female and intromit but not ejaculate would serve as a reinforcer for male rats. It certainly seems unlikely that any drive was reduced in this situation. Nevertheless, a reinforcing effect was observed.

Occurring concurrently with the attempt to define why reinforcers reinforce, has been the attempt to identify reinforcers in advance of their demonstrated utility as reinforcers. As noted above, reinforcers are stimuli which, when made dependent upon responses, increase the frequency of those responses. Thus, a reinforcer is initially defined as such by its ability to function as a reinforcer, so, if one were to say that a response were increased *because* it was reinforced, one would engage in circular logic. It is circular to say that a reinforcer is the cause of an effect when we cannot identify the reinforcer until after it has "caused" the effect. It was once hoped that once a stimulus had been identified as a reinforcer for one response, that it could then be predicted that the stimulus would reliably reinforce other responses. This would remove the circularity involved in describing the reinforcer as a cause of behavior. This approach, too, has proved to be inadequate. The fact that a stimulus will serve as a reinforcer for one response, two responses, or ten responses, is no guarantee that it will serve as a reinforcer for all responses. Thus, we are currently left with a state of affairs in which a reinforcer may not be used as an explanation of behavior. Rather, the terms reinforcer and reinforcement merely describe a functional relation between behavior and stimuli.

One rule that has emerged from research on defining characteristics of reinforcers is what has come to be known as the Premack principle (Premack, 1959). Premack's approach is that reinforcing states of affairs deal with the opportunity to engage in some behavior. Premack proposed that if you observe two behaviors, A and B, then the behavior that occurs with the higher probability can be used to reinforce the behavior with the lower probability. In the example of the rat pressing the lever, behavior A would be pressing the lever, and behavior B would be eating the food pellets. If we were to observe the rat in a situation where it has the opportunity both to eat or to press the lever, eating would most likely be the higher probability behavior. Thus, by making the opportunity to engage in the high probability behavior, eating, depend upon emission of the lower probability behavior, pressing the lever, we can arrange a situation in which reinforcement is observed. Premack's principle has proven to be a powerful tool. For example, in the laboratory it has been shown that it is possible to reinforce licking a water tube with the opportunity to run in a wheel, and with appropriate deprivations, it has been shown possible to reinforce running with drinking. Thus, either running or drinking could be used as the reinforcer for the other response, depending on which had the higher current probability. Premack's principle seems less appropriate when discussing reinforcers that seem to involve virtually no behavior on the part of a subject such as intracranial brain stimulation or delivery of food directly to the stomach. Premack has argued, however, that his formulation can deal effectively with such reinforcers.

Premack's principle has been used in the natural environment as well. An example is provided in the work of Homme et al. (1963). These experimenters noticed that in a nursery school, children often spent a lot of time "running around the room, screaming, pushing chairs." These behaviors were labeled as high probability and were then made contingent upon desired behaviors. For example, sitting quietly in a seat would be intermittently followed by instructions to "run and scream.'' By providing occasional opportunity to engage in the high probability behaviors, Homme and his colleagues were able to increase the frequency of the desired behaviors.

Conditioned Reinforcement

So far, in the discussion of reinforcement, we have discussed events that appear to be natural reinforcers, for example, food, for a food-deprived organism. A quick look at the natural environment, however, shows that many behaviors have consequences that probably are not naturally reinforcers. For example, someone may engage in some work where the consequent event is the presentation of money. Money is hardly a substance that could be expected to be reinforcing for everyone. In fact, money cannot be a reinforcer without some prior conditioning history with respect to it. Clearly, a printed green piece of paper has little intrinsic value of its own to most people. Reinforcers that have obtained the power to reinforce through some conditioning history are usually called *conditioned reinforcers,* or secondary reinforcers. The general method or operation for establishing some neutral stimulus as a conditioned reinforcer is to pair it with a primary reinforcer. For example, if we wished to make the word ''good'' a conditioned reinforcer for a child, we could say the word ''good'' as we presented the child with another reinforcer, such as food.

While conditioned reinforcement plays a strong explanatory role in describing the everyday behavior of people, it has been an ephemeral phenomenon in the laboratory. There are few convincing demonstrations of conditioned reinforcement in the laboratory, suggesting that we are still far from understanding the exact way in which it is established.

Parameters of reinforcement

There are two main parameters of reinforcement that have been studied. The first parameter that has been studied experimentally is the magnitude, or amount of reinforcement (Logan, 1960). Generally speaking, larger magnitudes of reinforcement will lead to greater resistance to extinction, that is,

more responses are emitted during extinction. Also, however, larger magnitudes of reinforcement result in more rapid satiation, so few total responses can be generated at any one time with large magnitude of reinforcement. The other parameter that has been studied is delay of reinforcement, that is, the time between a response and delivery of a reinforcement (Grice, 1948; Dews, 1960). Again speaking generally, for there are always exceptions to rules, the greater the delay of reinforcement, the slower conditioning will progress.

Schedules of Reinforcement

One of the most important, if not the most important, factors influencing a reinforcer's effect is the schedule according to which the reinforcer is presented. A schedule of reinforcement specifies which responses will be reinforced and when they will be reinforced. In the natural environment, it is probably the exception rather than the rule that each response produces a reinforcer. When fishing, it is usually not the case that each cast of the line results in a fish being caught. Rather, fish only occasionally are caught. Nevertheless, we continue to fish, and as many of us can testify, you can get a lot of fishing for not very many fish!

In the laboratory, schedules of reinforcement have been divided into two main types: time-based schedules, and response or number-based schedules. Number-based schedules are the simplest to understand. They are usually referred to as *ratio schedules,* since they specify the ratio of responses to reinforcers. There are two main types of ratio schedules, *fixed-ratio* (FR) schedules and *variable-ratio* (VR) schedules. A fixed-ratio schedule specifies that every *n*th response will be reinforced. For example, a fixed-ratio 10 (FR10) schedule would specify that every tenth response would be reinforced. In a variable-ratio schedule the ratio of responses to reinforcement varies from one reinforcement to the next reinforcement. One time it might take five responses to produce a reinforcer, the next time 15 responses to produce a reinforcer, and the next time 10 responses to produce a reinforcer. This schedule would be a variable-ratio 10 (VR10) schedule, since the value of the schedule is usually specified as the *average* number of responses required for reinforcement. Time-based schedules are usually called *interval schedules*. Under a *fixed-interval* (FI) schedule the first response that occurs after a fixed period of time has passed is reinforced. Under *variable-interval* (VI) schedules the first response that occurs after varying periods of time since the last reinforcement are reinforced.

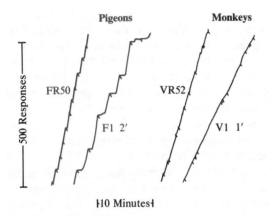

Fig. 9-22. Cumulative response records made by pigeons pecking keys and monkeys pressing levers under four different schedules of reinforcement. Shown are records from a fixed-ratio schedule (FR), a fixed-interval schedule (FI), a variable-ratio schedule (VR), and a variable-interval schedule (VI).

Each of the four basic types of schedules generates a particular pattern of emission of the reinforced operant. Figure 9-22 shows cumulative response records generated by four different schedules: fixed-ratio, fixed-interval, variable-interval, and variable-ratio. Note the similarities and differences in the cumulative response records. In each record, the small diagonal mark indicates food delivery. Under both the fixed-interval schedule and fixed-ratio schedule, there is a period of not responding following each reinforcement. Under the variable schedules, however, responding is continuous throughout the time period shown. There are no pauses either after reinforcement or at any other time. Thus, variable schedules generate constant rates of responding, whereas

fixed schedules generate periods of nonresponding and responding. Note also that response rates are generally higher under the ratio schedules. Also notice the large number of responses produced by the interval schedules. Interval schedules require only one response after the end of the interval to produce reinforcement, yet thousands of unreinforced responses may be emitted.

Examples of ratio schedules abound in the natural environment. The fixed-ratio schedule is analogous to a piece-work regimen, that is, a regimen that requires a fixed amount of work be done in order to get paid a certain amount. Variable-ratio schedules appear when we think of gambling. For example, consider playing a slot machine. Each pull of the arm on the one-armed bandit has an equal probability of producing the reinforcer, money. This arrangement results in a variable number of responses being required for *each* payoff. Thus, we have a variable-ratio schedule. In Figure 9-22, we saw that a variable-ratio schedule of food presentation to a food-deprived subject yields high, constant rates of responding. Anyone who has seen people playing slot machines will testify that slot machines also can generate high constant rates of lever pulling.

Examples of interval schedules are not as common in a natural environment but do exist. A bus that runs on a proper schedule represents a fixed-interval schedule of bus presentation. Looking for the bus will only be reinforced (by sight of the bus) if you are looking when the bus arrives. An example of a variable-interval schedule can be found in our much-used example of fishing. The person fishing is not likely to catch a fish until it swims near the bait. No matter how fast the person fishing casts a line and then reels it in, there will not be much of a chance to catch a fish until the fish enters the area in which the person is casting. Note that in our example of an animal pressing a lever that occasionally presents food on a variable-interval schedule, moderate constant rates of responding were generated. Now think of someone casting a line while fishing. Rarely do you see anyone madly casting, reeling in, casting, reeling in, casting, reeling in, and so on. Instead, you see moderate constant rates of casting and reeling the line in.

These examples point to a feature of ratio and

interval schedules that allows them to be differentiated in the natural environment. It is true that in ratio-schedules, the faster one responds the more frequently one will get reinforcement. For example, if you were exposed to a fixed-ratio 10 schedule, and it took you five minutes to make the 10 responses, you would get reinforcement once every 5 minutes. If it took you five seconds to make the responses, then you would get reinforcement every five seconds. This is not true of interval schedules. If the next interval in the schedule is ten minutes it does not matter whether you make 1,000 responses in the 10 minutes or 1 response in the 10 minutes, you will not get a reinforcer until a response is made after the 10 minutes has elapsed.

As mentioned at the beginning of this section, the schedule according to which the reinforcer is delivered is an extremely important determinant of its effect. Schedules may be thought of as motivational variables, because they can determine the "vigor" with which responding occurs. A subject exposed to a relatively short variable-ratio schedule would be described as extremely motivated, since such a schedule produces responding that occurs at a high constant rate. The same subject under a long variable-interval schedule would appear somewhat lackadaisical, occasionally emitting the operant. Thus, the demeanor with which an animal behaves can be determined by the schedule of reinforcement.

Schedules of reinforcement usually specify that responding produces reinforcement only intermittently. One of the most profound effects of such intermittent reinforcement is the greatly increased resistance to extinction. A rat given one reinforcer for each of 50 lever presses will usually make about 100 responses during extinction that immediately follows this conditioning experience. A rat that receives 50 reinforcers under a short variable-interval schedule will probably make around a 1,000 or more responses during extinction. This extremely powerful effect of intermittent reinforcement can be ascribed partly to the role that "similarity" plays in extinction. It was pointed out earlier that extinction proceeds most slowly when conditions during extinction are most like those that prevailed during conditioning. Consider the example of a rat getting 50 reinforcers, one for

each press, *versus* the rat getting 50 reinforcers on a variable-interval schedule. When the first rat encounters extinction, that rat emits its first unreinforced lever press. The rat that had been responding under the variable-interval schedule, however, has emitted many unreinforced responses during conditioning, and, thus, when extinction begins for this rat, there is not as great a change. In the first situation, then, the rat immediately encounters a novel situation, whereas in the second, the rat does not.

Schedules also have other effects. For example, they can determine the accuracy of complex performance. Ferster (1958) trained a chimpanzee to press one key three times and then another key once in order to obtain a food pellet. Under these conditions the chimpanzee made about 70 percent correct responses. That is, about 70 percent of the time the chimpanzee made exactly three responses on the first lever before emitting a response on the second lever. The other 30 percent of the time, it either made too few or too many responses on the first lever. Ferster next changed the situation so that only every 33rd *correct sequence* of presses resulted in the presentation of food (FR33). Under these conditions the chimpanzee made about 99 percent correct sequences. Thus, the schedule improved the accuracy of performance on this complex task.

Schedules of reinforcement can also affect behaviors other than those for which the reinforcer is being scheduled. As an example, consider a rat pressing a lever that produces food according to a fixed-interval schedule. Suppose that the rat also has available a drinking tube from which it can drink at any time. If the fixed-interval schedule is relatively short, for example, 10 seconds, the rat spends most of its time pressing the lever and drinks very little water. If the fixed-interval schedule value is changed to about 2 minutes, the rat continues to emit characteristic fixed-interval controlled behavior, that is, there is a period of not pressing the lever after food is delivered followed by a transition to a relatively steady rate of lever-pressing until the next pellet is delivered. Under these conditions, however, the rat may drink nearly half its body weight in water in the space of two hours of exposure to such a schedule! If we further increase the fixed-interval to, say, eight minutes, the rat still continues to respond on the lever appropriately, but, in this case, the rat drinks virtually no water. So by varying the schedule of food presentation, we can determine whether the rat drinks a little water, an enormous amount of water (more than it would generally drink in five days), or virtually no water at all. The drinking in this situation is usually described as schedule-induced polydipsia, and several other behaviors besides drinking have been shown to be schedule induced (Falk, 1971).

Schedules of reinforcement are also strong determinants of the effects of psychoactive drugs. Suppose a pigeon is injected with a relatively large dose of a barbiturate (a "downer" in current parlance), and this pigeon has been trained that when a response key is blue that a fixed-interval 5 (FI5-min) minute schedule food presentation is in effect, and when a response key is red that a fixed-ratio 30 (FR30) response schedule is in effect. The nearly anesthetized pigeon is placed in a chamber where it can peck the response key. The pigeon will appear to be virtually asleep. When the blue (fixed-interval) light is turned on, the pigeon will

remain immobile. When the color of the key is changed to red, the pigeon will get up and peck the red key at an extremely high response rate, often higher than that seen when the animal is not drugged. If the blue key light is reinstated, the animal ceases pecking and appears to go to sleep. This powerful demonstration shows the importance of the scheduling of reinforcement in determining the effects of drugs. In one case, when the blue light is on, we would classify the barbiturate as a sedative, yet when the red light is turned on the barbiturate appears to be a stimulant. This serves to emphasize the danger of classifying behaviorally-active drugs simply as depressants or stimulants, since the effect of drugs can be modified greatly by environmental circumstances.

An even more powerful, and yet much more puzzling, effect of scheduling is displayed in some recent findings by Kelleher and Morse (1968) and McKearney (1968). (See also Morse and Kelleher, 1977.) These investigators have been able, through certain scheduling of events, to get squirrel monkeys to press a lever when the *only* consequence of pressing the lever is to produce a painful electric shock. This is an electric shock that the subject ini-

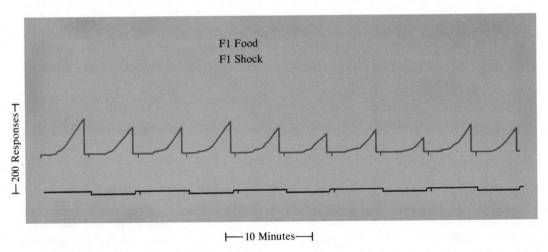

Fig. 9-23. Cumulative response record from a squirrel monkey pressing a lever alternately under a schedule of food presentation and under a schedule of electric shock presentation (5 mA). Downward deflection of the event pen indicates that the interval ended with electric shock. The pen reset to the baseline at the end of each fixed interval, and one minute timeout periods occurred after each fixed interval. The end of a timeout period is indicated by the hatchmark on the record. (Printed by permission of J. W. McKearney)

tially is trained to avoid, and if presented on other schedules, would serve to suppress behavior. Figure 9-23 shows cumulative response records from a squirrel monkey that responded alternately under a fixed-interval 5-minute (F15-min) schedule of food delivery and fixed-interval 5-min (F15-min) schedule of electric shock delivery. Whether the last lever press in the interval presents food or presents shock apparently made little difference in the temporal patterning of behavior.

Several powerful demonstrations of the importance of schedules of reinforcement have been described, but the study of schedules of reinforcement is really just beginning. We do not know what it is about schedules of reinforcement that allows them to interact to such a great degree with other kinds of behavioral variables. Suffice it to say that the student should be well aware that perhaps the most important aspect of reinforcement is the schedule according to which it is presented.

Motivation

In the description of the basic experimental paradigm for operant conditioning, we specified that the subject (a rat) was deprived of food so as to maintain it at 80 percent of normal weight. In most operant conditioning experiments, some kind of deprivation is employed to establish a stimulus as a reinforcer. Usually the deprivation is as severe as that described above, and severe deprivation is employed for a very important experimental reason. Severe deprivation magnifies the effectiveness of a reinforcer, so that the experimenter can observe more easily the direct effects of reinforcement and also observe more easily the interactions between reinforcement and other variables. Severe deprivation, then, serves as the behavior analyst's microscope.

In the example of the basic experimental paradigm, the deprivation operations were held constant (that is, the rat was kept at 80 percent of normal body weight) throughout the experiment. In most experiments on operant conditioning, deprivation procedures are held constant. The fact that the subject's deprivation level is held constant does not mean that the deprivation is without effect. Deprivation with respect to some reinforcer usually produces diverse effects, and may be considered as an operation that, by itself, has relatively nonspecific effects. If the reinforcer in question has been used to strengthen operant behavior, the probability of *all* behaviors that have been strengthened by the reinforcer will increase. Motivational variables then, do not necessarily have a specific behavioral effect, but rather serve as general "energizers" of behavior.

Perhaps the most common error made by prospective psychologists is the utilization of motivation as the sole explanation for some behavior. For example, it is common to hear descriptions such as "she got a hamburger from the hamburger stand because she was hungry." This sentence implies that the major cause of the behavior was a motivational state called hunger. Note, however, that she did not eat the wrapper and throw the burger in the trash, nor did she go to a clothing store to get it! Her experience with respect to hamburgers was an important determinant of her behavior. The motivational state induced by food deprivation was *not* the sole determinant of her behavior. However, once operant behavior has been established through reinforcement during some deprivation state, that behavior can be produced merely by increasing the deprivation. Consider the example of the rat pressing a lever. If we allowed the rat to return to 100 percent body weight and then placed it in the conditioning chamber, the probability of lever-pressing would be quite low. By depriving the rat of food again, however, we can immediately increase the frequency of lever-pressing. Thus, once operant behavior has been acquired, it can in essence be "turned on and off" by motivational operations. Perhaps it is this latter feature that has made it common to ascribe to motivation such a powerful role in the explanation of behavior. Another factor is probably also involved. Consider the hamburger eater. When she goes to get her hamburger, discriminable stimuli are present (most of them inside her skin) that are correlated with the label "hunger." Thus, stimuli correlated with her motivational state are present just before she goes to get her hamburger, whereas there are no (or few, at best) stimuli correlated with the behavioral history that determined that she go to a hamburger stand instead of a car wash, and that she not eat the wrapper instead of the hamburger.

The student should be reminded that it is not always the case, in fact, that behavior can be "turned on" via a motivational operation. The schedules of reinforcement just described can override, to a great extent, the effects of deprivation, and another behavioral principle, that of stimulus control, can also override deprivation effects. Let us turn now to a discussion of stimulus control.

Stimulus Control

Up to this point we have been speaking as if behavior occurs in a virtual vacuum, that is, we have not paid any attention to the immediate surroundings in which behavior occurs. We all know, of course, that the surroundings that we are in influence our behavior. In the study of operant behavior, experiments designed to examine how the environment influences operant behavior are called experiments on stimulus control of behavior. Return to the example of a rat in a chamber with a lever and a feeder (see p. 302). Suppose that the rat has been trained to press a lever that results in the occasional presentation of a food pellet. Assume that this training has taken place with a light on in the chamber. Now the situation changes slightly so that for variable periods of time the light in the chamber is on and for variable periods of time it is off. It is further arranged that when the light is off extinction is in effect, that is, presses of the lever do not result in the presentation of a food pellet. What we will reliably observe in such a situation is that soon the rat comes to press the lever only when the light is on and does not press it when it is off. When this result is achieved, it is said the rat's lever-pressing behavior is under stimulus control of the light, because whether or not the rat presses the lever can be controlled merely by turning on the light. It is important to note that this outcome is not a necessary one for the rat to obtain all the available reinforcers. The rat could get all of the pellets simply by continuously pressing the lever, both when the light is on and off, although no pellets will be delivered when the light is off. In this situation we call the light a *discriminative stimulus* (S^D). A discriminative stimulus can function in a manner similar to the way a conditional stimulus does. That is, when the stimulus is presented, the response immediately follows. In the case of a conditional stimulus we say that the stimulus *elicits* the response. In the case of a discriminative stimulus, however, we say that the stimulus *sets the occasion* for the response to occur. The paradigm for establishing stimulus control is diagrammed in Figure 9-24. In the presence of one stimulus, S^D, the response can produce a reinforcer, and in the absence of that stimulus, S^Δ, the response does not produce a reinforcer.

$$S^D : R \rightarrow S^R$$
$$S^\Delta : R \nrightarrow S^R$$

Fig. 9-24. Basic paradigm for establishing stimulus control of an operant. In the presence of one stimulus class, S^D, responses are reinforced, whereas in the presence of another stimulus class, S^Δ, responses are not reinforced.

A natural-environment example of stimulus control of behavior is provided in the work of Redd and Birnbrauer (1969). The two stimuli in their situation, rather than being a light on and a light off, were two different adults. One of the adults dispensed food and praise to children only when they played. The other adult dispensed food and praise at fixed intervals of time regardless of whether the children were playing or not. After a short amount of exposure to these two different adults, whenever the adult that dispensed food and praise for playing behavior entered the room the children began to play, and when the adult who dispensed the food independently of the children's behavior entered the room play behavior was not affected. Thus, the playing of the children in this study came to be controlled by the different stimuli, one adult versus another.

The two examples above lead to a definition of stimulus control. Stimulus control is said to exist when there is *differential responding in the presence of different stimuli*. In the first example, the rat pressed the lever when the light was on and did not press the lever when the light was off. In the second example, playing occurred when one adult entered the room but did not occur when the other adult entered the room. These examples also point to the standard way of establishing stimulus control of behavior. One simply arranges different contingencies of reinforcement in the presence of different stimuli.

The standard procedure for establishing stimulus control, that is, establishing different contingencies of reinforcement in the presence of different stimuli, usually results in many "errors" occurring during the development of stimulus control. For example, in a simple discrimination procedure with an S^D and an S^Δ, during the development of stimulus control, many responses are usually made to S^Δ. Terrace (1963) developed a procedure in which stimulus control can be achieved with very few, and sometimes no, errors. The procedure takes advantage of an existing discrimination to produce a new discrimination. For example, suppose a pigeon has been trained to peck a key when it is red (S^D) and does not peck a key when it is green (S^Δ). To establish a discrimination between a circle and a square on the key the following procedure could be employed. First, the circle would be superimposed on the red key and the square on the green key. Then, the intensity of both the red and green key lights would be gradually reduced until only the circle or square was left. If the elimination of red and green from the stimulus complexes were accomplished gradually enough, then a new stimulus control relation with the circle as S^D and the square as S^Δ, could be established with no pecks on the square ever occurring. Thus, an errorless discrimination may be established by building from an existing discrimination and by gradually changing the stimuli. The key to the procedure is the gradual changing of S^D and S^Δ, and such a procedure is called *fading*. Fading has been used successfully in a wide variety of situations, including applied settings with humans, and appears to have widespread generality. A purported advantage of establishing stimulus control without errors is that the normal emotional concomitants of extinction do not arise because no responses are emitted in S^Δ. That is, those behaviors that are usually labeled as "aggressive" or as reflecting "frustra-

tion" are absent during errorless discrimination acquisition.

In all these examples, the discriminative stimuli were presented one at a time, or successively. Such procedures are referred to as *successive discrimination* procedures. It is also possible to have two responses available, for example, two keys for a pigeon and to present two stimuli simultaneously. One stimulus would be correlated with reinforcement and the other with extinction. Typically, the pigeon's task would be to peck the key that had the stimulus correlated with reinforcement on it. Such procedures are called *simultaneous discrimination* procedures.

In the examples above, different behaviors were emitted in the presence of different stimuli. In this situation we say that a *discrimination* exists. Thus, the term discrimination refers to the case in which there is stimulus control of behavior. There is, of course, the other possibility. It might be the case that the same behavior is emitted in the presence of two or more different stimuli. When that is the case, we say that *generalization* has occurred. Generalization is a typical result of reinforcing an operant in the presence of a single stimulus. If, after such training, we examine the frequency of emission of the behavior in the presence of other, similar stimuli, we often see the behavior emitted. For example, after training a pigeon to peck a key that has a vertical line on it, we can then expose the pigeon to keys with lines at angles other than vertical upon it. The result of such an experiment is shown in Figure 9-25. Note that as the key becomes more and more different from the originally trained stimulus configuration, that less and less pecking of the key occurs. The graph shown in Figure 9-25 is often called a *generalization gradient,* or a *stimulus control gradient.*

The concepts of discrimination and generalization can be used to deal with those relationships between stimuli and behavior that are called *concepts* and *abstractions.* An example of a concept is the concept of a dog. When a child is young it may call all small four-legged animals "dog" after having been trained to identify a single dog, but after some training the child learns to identify dogs reliably and to classify other animals into other categories. When this happens we say that the child

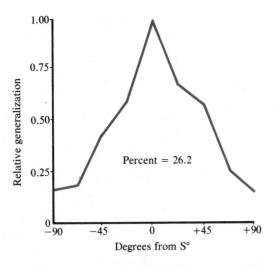

Fig. 9-25. A stimulus control gradient, or generalization gradient. Response rates are expressed as a proportion of the rate to the original S^D (a vertical line). 26.2 percent of the responses during the generalization test were made to S^D. (Hearst *et. al.,* 1964)

has the concept of a dog. Using technical terms, we say that at this point the child generalizes among those stimuli that are dogs and discriminates between dogs and other animals. Thus, a concept is usually a stimulus control relation in which there is generalization within the category and discrimination between categories. An abstraction is closely related to the notion of a concept; in fact, some argue that they are identical. An abstraction refers to a relation between stimuli and behavior in which a single property of a wide variety of stimuli comes to control a certain aspect of behavior. As an example, take the abstraction red. The behavior that is controlled is the emission of the word "red," and it comes to be controlled by all stimuli that have the property of reflecting long wavelengths of light that we generally call "red."

Even more complex abstractions are possible. Harlow (1949) trained a monkey in a simultaneous discrimination, where on successive trials two inverted cups were presented. One had a "+" on it and the other had a "−" on it. The monkey's task was to pick up the cup with the "+," and this cup had a food pellet under it. Once the monkey had mastered this problem (usually taking 50–100

trials), a new problem was presented. Now one cup had a "□" on it and the other had a "△," and the monkey had to pick the cup with the "△" on it. Soon the monkey solved this problem. The experiment was continued, always introducing a new pair of stimuli when the monkey solved a problem. After a few hundred such problems, Harlow observed a startling phenomenon: it never took the monkey more than two trials to solve a problem! If the monkey chose the correct cup on trial one, then it made no errors at all, and if it chose the wrong cup on the first trial, it immediately switched to the other cup on the second trial and never made another error on that problem. This phenomenon, an increase in the efficiency with which related discriminations are acquired, is called learning to learn or *learning set.* Over the course of the many discrimination problems, a complex stimulus-control relation evolves, one that is dependent on the result of the subject's own behavior. The entire sequence "pick up cup, get food" serves as a stimulus for continuing to pick up that cup, and the sequence "pick up cup, get no food" serves as a stimulus to pick up the other cup.

Conditional Discrimination

There is a complex type of discrimination that plays an extremely important role in the analysis of language or verbal behavior. This type of discrimination is called a *conditional discrimination.* Returning to the simple discrimination problem in which a rat is trained to press a lever when a light is on and not to press the lever when the light is off, we can establish a conditional discrimination in the rat by arranging the following circumstances. To the experimental apparatus, we add the possibility of delivering a tone to the rat. Next the situation is changed slightly, so that when the tone is *off* the circumstances are identical to those described earlier. That is, when the light is on the rat can press the lever and occasionally get food and when the light is off presses have no effect. However, when the tone is *on,* then presses when the light is on have no scheduled effect and presses when the light is off can produce food. In this case, what the light signifies is conditional, that is, depends on the state of the tone. Under such conditions, the rat comes to press the lever when the tone is on and the light is off and when the tone is off and the light is on, but does not press the lever in the other two possible stimulus configurations.

The study of conditional discrimination is important, especially in the study of human verbal behavior, because so much of verbal behavior is under conditional stimulus control. As a simple example, consider the sentence "Look out!" In most situations these two words signify a warning, but suppose you were inside a building and someone first said to you "Look at that!," whereupon you start looking around the room for what. Next, the person says "Look out!" which will probably signify to you to look out a window. As this simple example shows, the meaning of "Look out!," that is, the behavior the sentence controls, depends on the context. This is analogous to the conditional discrimination described for the rat. In that case, the "meaning" of the light also depended on the context (tone).

In the laboratory the most common method of studying conditional discrimination is the procedure known as matching-to-sample, which is diagrammed in Figure 9-26. In such a procedure a subject is required first to make a response in the presence of a sample stimulus. Once this response is made two other stimuli appear, each of which is associated with a different response. One of the two stimuli matches the first stimulus, whereas the other stimulus does not. In a matching-to-sample experiment, the subject is required to make a response to the stimulus that matches the original stimulus in order to obtain reinforcement.

Attention. Of course, when we operate in our normal environment there are many stimuli around, and these stimuli are around when certain behaviors are reinforced. Nevertheless, it is only certain of these stimuli that come to control behavior reliably. In the laboratory, such conditions can be simulated (and also simplified) by arranging a situation such as the following. We arrange that a rat's lever-presses are intermittently reinforced when both a tone and light are on, and that presses do not produce reinforcement when both the tone and light are off. After a short amount of training under such a procedure the rat will come to press

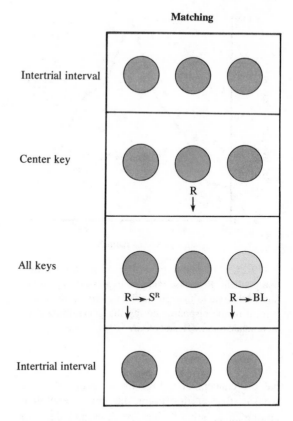

Matching

Intertrial interval

Center key

All keys

Intertrial interval

Fig. 9-26. A schematic representation of a matching-to-sample procedure for pigeons. (Cumming and Berryman, 1961)

the lever when tone and light are on and not press it when they are off. Suppose now, however, the rat is tested with the tone alone and then the light alone. If we discover that, for example, the rat only presses the lever when the tone is on, and not when the light is on, we say that the rat was paying attention to only the tone. It is important to note that we do not say that the rat responds only in the presence of the tone and not in the presence of the light *because* of attention. It is the fact that differential responding did occur in the presence of the two different stimuli (tone and light) that leads us to say that attention was observed. It is important to remember, as pointed out in Chapter 1, that giving a name to a behavioral phenomenon does not explain it nor tell us how to change it. Attention as a concept has often been improperly used as an explanation of the behavior that it, in fact, names. The variables that influence the relationship between stimuli and behavior that are called attention have not been well delineated. Of course, there are the obvious kinds of data that show that blind subjects' behavior will generally not be well controlled by visual stimuli when they are presented jointly with auditory stimuli, but in-depth analyses of the variables responsible for one stimulus having precedence over another have not been conducted very often.

Complex Behavior Sequences

We have been speaking of relatively small, simple units of behavior such as pressing a lever or pecking a key. Obviously, behavior can be considerably more complex. Long sequences of behavior occur that lead to a single reinforcer. The study of the phenomenon of *chaining* of behavior helps to analyze such long sequences. Figure 9-27 shows the actual sequence of behaviors involved in pressing a lever that produces a food pellet each time it is pressed. The lever press produces a click of the feeder, which serves as a discriminative stimulus for looking in the food cup, which in turn results in the sight of the pellet which serves as a discriminative stimulus for grabbing the pellet. Grabbing the pellet results in stimulation of the pellet in the paws which then may serve as a discriminative stimulus for placing the pellet in the mouth. Pellet in the mouth may serve as a stimulus for chewing, and chewing precedes swallowing, the stimuli arising from which might serve as the discriminative stimulus for approaching the lever and pressing

again. Thus, even a simple situation involving only a press of a lever and the presentation of a single pellet can be considered as quite a long sequence of behaviors. To study sequences of behavior experimentally, however, arbitrary long sequences must be established. Suppose a rat has been trained to press a lever only in the presence of a light, that is, the light is established as a discriminative stimulus. Next a chain can be suspended from the ceiling. If the rat pulls the chain, the light is presented in the presence of which a lever press produces a food pellet. Soon the rat will be emitting the sequence, pull the chain, press the lever, quite regularly. A small tunnel may then be added inside the chamber. Then the rat could be required to crawl through the tunnel before pulling the chain, thus establishing a sequence of behavior that includes crawling through the tunnel, pulling the chain, and pressing the lever. Note that the entire sequence terminates with a single pellet of food. If you think that the sequence just described is a complicated sequence to train a rat, consider the following sequence of behaviors. Climb a spiral staircase, cross a narrow bridge, climb a ladder, pull a toy car near via a chain, get in the car, pedal the car to a second staircase, ascend the staircase, squirm through a tube, climb onto an elevator that descends to a platform, and press a lever. This sequence represents an actual sequence trained to a rat named Barnabas, at Brown University. Barnabas was trained this entire sequence in the space of a few training sessions (Pierrel and Sherman, 1963).

In establishing a chain, the last member of the sequence is trained first, the second to the last be-

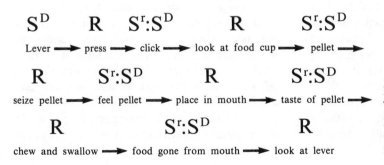

S^D R $S^r:S^D$ R $S^r:S^D$

Lever → press → click → look at food cup → pellet →

R $S^r:S^D$ R $S^r:S^D$

seize pellet → feel pellet → place in mouth → taste of pellet →

R $S^r:S^D$ R

chew and swallow → food gone from mouth → look at lever

Fig. 9-27.
The sequence of behaviors involved in pressing a lever and eating a pellet, denoting reinforcing (S) and discriminative (S^D) functions of stimuli.

havior in the sequence is trained second, the third, third, and so on. Laboratory studies have shown that complex sequences of behavior are acquired much more quickly when trained in this fashion, as opposed to training the first behavior in the sequence first, the second, second, and so on. It is interesting to note that most sequences of behaviors taught to humans are not taught by training the last response first, the second to the last second, and so on, but rather are trained with the first response in the sequence being established, then the second, and so on. An example is teaching a child to tie his shoe. Usually the child is trained first to cross the strings then to pass one of the strings around a finger, and so on until the child finally pulls the two loops to tighten the bow. It usually takes a considerable amount of time to train a child to tie a shoe. The data from laboratory experiments on sequences of behavior, however, would suggest that training a child to tie a shoe should proceed in the opposite way. You could begin by tying the knot almost all the way and letting the child pull the loops to finish the knot. As soon as the child does this well, the knot could be tied somewhat less completely and the child could pull the loop through and then pull it tight. By proceeding in this seemingly "backward" fashion, shoetying can be taught quite rapidly.

Analyzing sequences of behavior as we did with simple lever pressing, points to an important consideration. That is, a single stimulus may have more than one behavioral function at a time. The press of the lever produces a click which then serves as a discriminative stimulus for approaching the food cup. The clicks might also be considered as the immediate reinforcer of the lever press. In the example of the sequence of crawling through the tunnel, pulling the chain, and pressing the lever, we could say that presentation of the chain served both as the reinforcer for crawling through the tunnel and as the discriminative stimulus for pulling the chain. Likewise, presentation of the light serves as a reinforcer of chain pulling and as a discriminative stimulus for lever pressing. When analyzing any behavior, it is always important to consider the possible functions of a stimulus. A stimulus may be a reinforcer, a discriminative stimulus, or an eliciting stimulus, and a single stimulus may have *all three* of these functions *simultaneously.*

Aversive Control of Behavior

Punishment. Punishment is the label given to the following relationship between behavior and stimuli. If some event is made dependent on the emission of an operant, and the operant *decreases* in frequency, then it is said that punishment has occurred. The stimulus that was presented dependent on the behavior is called a *punisher.* Punishment in this sense is very similar to the definition of punishment used in everyday life. The major difference between the definition given above and an everyday definition of punishment is that the scientific definition given here is a functional definition, that is, whether or not a stimulus is a punisher depends on its effect on behavior and cannot be determined in advance of its operation. Just because an event "seems" to be noxious does not mean that it can be used as a punisher under all circumstances.

For many years punishment was thought to be an ineffective mode of behavioral control, both in the laboratory and in other settings. Most of the early research on punishment showed it to be not a particularly effective method of suppressing behavior and a method that did not produce permanent changes in behavior. These experiments, however, employed relatively mild punishment. In the late 1950s, Azrin (1956) embarked on a long series of experiments on punishment and discovered conditions under which punishment could be extremely effective at reducing the frequency of behavior, and sometimes reducing the frequency to zero permanently.

Of course, the experimental study of punishment requires that there be some behavior that is punished. Most experimental investigations of punishment have employed schedules of positive reinforcement to maintain behavior that is later punished. Such investigations have revealed several aspects of punishment that are important in determining its effect. The most powerful parameter of punishment in determining its effect is the intensity or duration of the punisher. Most experimental studies employ electric shock as the punishing stimulus, but other stimuli such as loud noises, blasts of air, pinches of the tail, and presentation of periods of time out from positive reinforcement have also been employed. In all cases the intensity and/or duration of the punishing stimulus is an important determinant of its effect, with more intense or longer duration punishers being more effective in suppressing behavior. The history of the subject with respect to the punishing stimulus is another variable that has been shown to be of considerable importance in the study of punishment. Several experiments (for example, Church, 1969) have shown that early exposure to intense punishment results in greater effectiveness of lower intensity punishers later. These investigations have also shown that a history of mild punishment with a particular punishing stimulus makes later use of higher intensity presentations of that stimulus less effective. Thus, if we can extrapolate these results to other situations, it would imply that gradually increasing the intensity of a punisher will not result in the most effective use of the punisher. Abrupt introduction at a high intensity is more effective. A third important parameter of punishment is the delay between the behavior to be punished and the presentation of the punisher. Punishment is by far the most effective when presented immediately after the response to be punished.

The degree of suppression observed under a punishment procedure where every response is punished depends a great deal on the schedule of reinforcement maintaining the behavior that is punished. Speaking generally, it is more difficult (that is, it takes a more intense or longer duration punisher) to suppress behavior maintained by ratio schedules than it does to suppress behavior maintained by interval schedules of reinforcement. Another important variable in determining the effect of punishment is the schedule according to which the punisher is delivered. Most reliable suppression of behavior occurs when every response is punished. Other schedules of punishment, however, have been employed and it has been shown that punishment is still effective when presented intermittently. However, when presented intermit-

tently, punishment must be of a greater intensity to produce an equivalent amount of suppression that would be seen if every response were punished (Azrin and Holz, 1966).

A final, extremely important determinant of the effect of punishment is illustrated in a simple experiment performed by Azrin and Holz (1966). They trained food-deprived pigeons in a chamber where there were two response keys that the pigeon could peck according to a fixed-ratio schedule. Under such conditions pigeons reliably come to peck only one of the keys since the fixed ratio is in effect on either key and moving between keys yields no increase in the amount of reinforcement that the pigeon can obtain. In the first condition of the experiment, the key that the pigeon usually did not peck was covered, and then responding on the remaining key was punished with electric shock. Each peck on that key produced an electric shock. Next, the intensity of the shock was varied. The graph in Figure 9-28 shows the results of this experiment by the curve labeled A. As the intensity of the punishment was gradually raised, behavior first started to decrease when the punishment intensity was 60 volts and was completely eliminated when the intensity was 120 volts. In the second phase of the experiment, the second key was un-

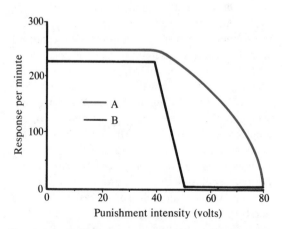

Fig. 9-28. Response rate as a function of punishment intensity when no alternative response was available (curve A) and when an alternative was available (curve B) [Azrin and Holz, 1966]

covered, providing an alternative source of reinforcement. Once again the intensity of punisher was gradually increased from day to day. This time, however, pecking the key that produced punishment was completely suppressed at 60 volts. Thus, a less intense punisher was needed to suppress the behavior when an alternative means of obtaining the reinforcer was available.

Punishment has not been used extensively in applied settings, but Lovaas and his colleagues have made considerable use of the technique (for example, Lovaas and Simmons, 1969), combined with reinforcement of appropriate behaviors, of course, in the treatment of autistic children. Lovaas's results with punishment procedures have been spectacular, to say the least. Children who have been thought to be totally incorrigible and uncontrollable have been trained using some punishment procedures to stop damaging themselves, to pay attention, and so forth. However, the effects may not be permanent. Lovaas et al. (1973) reported the results of an eight-year follow-up study that revealed that most of the children returned to their former autistic behavior unless their parents continued the treatment approach.

Escape and Avoidance Behavior. Behavior that results in the *termination* of a stimulus and is thereby increased in frequency is called *escape* behavior. Thus, escape behavior is, by definition, equivalent to behavior maintained by negative reinforcement. Escape behavior is often confused with avoidance behavior. In order for behavior to be considered escape behavior, it must be behavior that results in the termination of a stimulus. *Avoidance* behavior involves the *prevention* of the presentation of the stimulus not its removal. For example, you can escape from the rain when you are being rained on. That is, you can make a response such as going under some shelter that terminates the rain from hitting. By contrast, you can avoid the rain by going under the shelter before the cloud bursts.

Escape behavior has not been extensively studied. The most likely reason for this is that it is often difficult to pick an arbitrary response as an escape response. For example, to train a rat to escape an electric shock to its feet by pressing a lever, one might use an apparatus similar to that shown in Figure 9-17 on p. 302, with the added provision that electric shock could be delivered through the grid floor. The shock could then be turned on, and one could wait for the rat to press the lever, or to approximate a press of the lever before terminating the shock. A problem quickly arises, however, since electric shock to the feet elicits many behaviors in the rat, virtually all of which are incompatible with pressing a lever. Many rats will freeze when shocked. Others will jump up and down and lick their paws. Obviously, if they are doing this, they will not be pressing a lever. Thus, the study of escape behavior using arbitrary responses is often quite difficult.

Avoidance behavior has been much more extensively studied, and history of the study of avoidance provides an interesting lesson in the progression of theoretical thought and experimental procedures. Early avoidance experiments were usually conducted in what is known as a shuttle box (see Figure 9-29). The subject, usually a rat, would be placed in one side of the shuttle box and the door in the center would be closed. At some point, a warning tone would be sounded in the side of the box where the rat was, and simultaneously

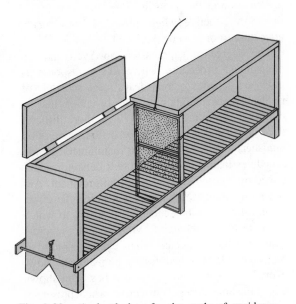

Fig. 9-29. A shuttle box for the study of avoidance. (Miller, 1948)

the door would be opened. A short period of time after the tone had been sounded, an electric shock would be delivered to the rat's feet. Usually, the rat would run to the other side of the shuttle box where no shock was being delivered. So, in the beginning of such an experiment the rat would escape from the shock by running to the other side of the shuttle box. After several repetitions of this, however, the rat would run to the "safe" side of the shuttle box as soon as the tone was sounded and thus avoided being shocked. This procedure lent itself to a very plausible explanation of avoidance behavior, elaborated by Mowrer (1960), called the *two-factor theory* of avoidance. He presumed the two factors were respondent conditioning of "fear" and escape responding. It was assumed that the sounding of the tone before the shock was presented represented a forward-pairing, respondent-conditioning paradigm, and that the result of this pairing was that "fear" was aroused by the tone. Thus, the rat would escape from the tone and the reinforcer for such behavior was supposed to be fear reduction.

In the early 1950s, Sidman (1953) devised a new avoidance procedure. In his procedure, an apparatus similar to that shown in Figure 9-17 was employed, with the addition that electric shock could be presented to the rat through the grid floor. In Sidman's avoidance procedure, two clocks controlled when brief shocks could be delivered to the rat. One clock, called the shock-shock timer, determined how often shocks occurred if the rat did not press the lever at all. If the shock-shock timer were set at 10 seconds, then the rat would get a brief shock every 10 seconds as long as it did not press the lever. The other timer was called the response-shock timer, and this timer specified how long a response postponed a shock. A press of the bar in this situation, then, stopped the shock-shock timer and started the response-shock timer. If the response shock timer were set at 20 seconds, then each time the lever was pressed it would give the rat a 20-second period of safety. If the rat then went 20 seconds without pressng the lever, a shock would be delivered and the shock-shock timer would be started. In this situation, the rat could avoid all shocks by never allowing 20 seconds to pass without a lever press. Sidman found that his

rats would all press the lever under these circumstances and eventually avoid nearly all shocks. In this procedure there is no explicit warning stimulus that can signal the impending shock. Thus, there is no stimulus that can be conditioned to arouse fear. Sidman's results, then, were damaging to the two-factor theory. However, proponents of the two-factor theory, proably because of its simplicity and plausibility, suggested that there could be an unobserved stimulus that served as the warning stimulus in Sidman's avoidance procedure (Anger, 1963). It is true that there is the fixed relationship between lever press and the amount of time that will pass before a shock can be delivered (as specified by the response-shock timer). It was suggested that there was an internal stimulus that grew in intensity as the time since the last shock increased, and that internal stimulus was the one that served as the warning stimulus in Sidman avoidance. Of course, postulation of internal stimuli presents considerable difficulty for an experimenter trying to validate such a theory, because it is difficult to measure such stimuli accurately. Other experiments (for example, Herrnstein and Hineline, 1966), however, have reduced the generality of the theory by showing that a fixed temporal relationship between a response and the delivery of a shock is not a necessary condition to produce avoidance behavior. The time by which a response postpones a shock can be quite variable, and behavior will still be maintained.

Recently, it has been shown that the acquisition of avoidance responding can be influenced by prior experience with the stimulus to be avoided, even though the stimulus is presented in a context much removed from that in which the avoidance conditioning takes place. Specifically, dogs were exposed to brief electric shocks that occurred randomly in time. The dogs had no control over the occurrence of these shocks, that is, they could neither escape from them nor avoid them. After such exposure, acquisition of shock avoidance responding was greatly retarded. This phenomenon was labeled "learned helplessness" (Seligman, 1968, 1975).

Extinction of avoidance and escape behavior can be conceptualized as involving either of two procedures. In the first procedure, all shock is discontinued, that is, responses have no consequences and no shocks are delivered. Under such a procedure it often takes a very long time for behavior to reach low levels. The other method of extinction is to continue to present shocks but to make responses ineffective in preventing or escaping from them. Under this procedure diminution of responding is often more rapid.

Operant-Respondent Interactions and Overlap

We have been speaking up to this point as if operant and respondent behaviors are independent entities that never interact. There are many situations, however, in which both operant and respondent properties of behavior do interact (Davis and Hurwitz, 1977). One of these interactions was alluded to in our discussion of escape behavior. If the stimulus to be escaped or avoided elicits certain reflex-like patterns of behavior, such patterns of behavior could be incompatible with the desired avoidance or escape behavior. When this is the case, of course, it is difficult to establish avoidance or escape behavior. Recently some attention has been given to these elicited patterns of behavior, and their role in avoidance conditioning. It has been suggested that in order for avoidance conditioning to proceed rapidly, the avoidance response must be compatible with the animal's species-specific defense reactions that are elicited by the aversive stimulus (Bolles, 1970). Thus, to be able to predict properly whether or not a particular response can be conditioned as an avoidance response when a particular aversive stimulus is employed, one needs to know the subject's usual species-specific reactions to the stimulus to be avoided. It is possible to train responses that are probably not species-specific defense reactions as avoidance behaviors. For example, many investigators have trained rats to press levers to avoid electric shocks, and it is quite clear that pressing a lever is not one of the rat family's species-specific defense reactions to electric shock. However, it is important to note that conditioning a rat to press a lever usually takes quite a long time.

A recent discovery also serves to point out the possible overlap between operant and respondent behaviors. One of the most well-studied behaviors in a pigeon is pecking a lighted disk, or key. This behavior has been shown to have many of the same properties as operants. That is, key pecking may be brought under stimulus control by operant methods, and conforms appropriately when different schedules of reinforcement are employed. It is also subject to punishment. However, consider the following purely classical conditioning procedure. A food-deprived pigeon is placed in a chamber such as that shown in Figure 9-17 on p. 302. Next, it is arranged that about every minute, on the average, the key is lighted for 8 seconds. At the end of the 8 seconds, the key light is extinguished and the food magazine is moved into position so that the bird can eat for a few seconds. The pigeon has never been trained to peck a key, nevertheless, after a few occurrences of the key light-food presentation pairing, the pigeon will come to peck the key while it is lighted. This phenomenon is called *auto-shaping* (Brown and Jenkins, 1968). Note that the procedure is one that would be labeled delayed classical conditioning. Nevertheless, the result of the procedure is that pigeon pecks a key—a response that for many years was considered to be purely operant behavior. Here then, is another example of how operant and respondent behaviors may overlap. It has only been within the last several years that researchers have begun to pay attention to these interactions. The area remains a fruitful one for research.

Historically, respondent conditioning and associated phenomena were assumed to be restricted mainly to the behavior of smooth muscles and glands, whereas operant conditioning and its associated phenomena were assumed to be restricted to behavior involving skeletal muscles. The restriction on respondent conditioning is obviously unwarranted since leg flexion, eyeblinks, and even key pecks by pigeons have been classically conditioned, and these behaviors involve skeletal muscles. Recent research has shown that behavior of smooth muscles and glands can be operantly conditioned. The initial demonstration of operant conditioning of behavior of smooth muscles was reported by Miller and DiCara (1967) who showed that the blood pressure of paralyzed rats (so they could not "cheat" and use their skeletal muscles) could be increased or decreased by the use of reinforcing electrical stimulation of the brain. Since that initial demonstration, many investigators have shown that blood pressure, heart rate, gastric motility, brain-wave activity, and other internal behaviors are subject to operant conditioning. The study of operant conditioning of internal behaviors is usually called "biofeedback," and practitioners of biofeedback are examining the utility of operant conditioning techniques in the alleviation of headache, high blood pressure, gastric hyperactivity, and assorted other maladies. Some rather extravagant claims about the efficacy of these procedures have appeared in the popular press, but it is quite clear that the use of such procedures is still in the early stages of development. Much more research needs to be done before definitive statements about the therapeutic utility of biofeedback procedures can be made.

Summary

Psychologists engaged in basic research on those processes we normally call "learning" have made extensive use of two classes of procedures to produce and study "learning" in animals. The first class of procedures, usually called respondent or classical conditioning, involves "pairing" (that is, presenting in a fixed temporal relationship) two stimuli. One of the stimuli, the unconditional stimulus, usually results directly in (elicits) measurable behavior; the other stimulus, the conditional stimulus, does not elicit the behavior in question. If a temporal sequence in which the conditional stimulus predicts the unconditional stimulus is arranged, the conditional stimulus comes to elicit behavior that is usually similar to that elicited by the unconditional stimulus. The second class of procedures, usually called operant or instrumental conditioning, involves arranging consequences for behavior. Behavior that is emitted by an organism may be followed by consequences that increase the likelihood that the behavior will occur again (reinforcement) or by consequences that reduce the probability of the behavior subsequently (punishment).

Using respondent and operant conditioning principles, psychologists have established accounts of abstraction, concept formation, discrimination, problem solving, and many other complex phenomena, and have also discovered ways of producing behavior that would normally be called neurotic or even psychotic.

The principles of operant and respondent conditioning are continuously challenged by new experiments and new conceptualizations in the hope of providing ever better prediction and control of behavior.

Glossary

Abstraction: A relationship between behavior and environment characterized by discriminative control of responding by a single property of stimuli, independent of other properties.

Avoidance: The name given to behavior that is maintained because it prevents or postpones the occurrence of a stimulus.

Conditional stimulus (CS): A stimulus that can elicit a reflex-like response as a result of being paired previously with an unconditional stimulus.

Conditioned reinforcement: A behavioral process in which probability of responding is increased by contingent presentation of a stimulus, and the stimulus is effective in increasing the probability because of a specific conditioning history. The stimulus is called a conditioned reinforcer.

Discrimination (also stimulus control): A relationship between environment and behavior characterized by differential responding in the presence of different stimuli.

Discriminative stimulus (S^D): A stimulus in the presence of which responding can be reinforced. A discriminative stimulus sets the occasion for a response. Usually an S^D is contrasted with a stimulus in the presence of which responding is not reinforced (S^Δ).

Escape: The name given to behavior that results in the termination of a stimulus, and, as a consequence, becomes more frequent. Such a relationship between behavior and environment defines the stimulus as aversive.

Extinction: 1) In operant conditioning, the discontinuation of reinforcement that results a reduction in response probability. 2) In respondent conditioning, no longer presenting the unconditional stimulus, (no longer pairing a neutral stimulus with the unconditional stimulus), that results in a weakening of the conditioned reflex.

Fading: Gradually changing a stimulus configuration.

Generalization: The spread of effects of conditioning to stimuli similar to those present during conditioning but not actually present during conditioning. Similar responding in the presence of different stimuli.

Learning: 1) Acquisition of new behavior. 2) A process inferred from changes in behavior, distinguished from performance. Learning can occur in the absence of any observable change in performance, but ultimately must be manifested by a change in performance (that is, what happens to you now may not produce any immediately noticeable effects, but your behavior later may be changed). The term is usually reserved for those situations in which behavior changes as a function of experience.

Operant: A class of responses, the probability of occurrence of which can be modified by the consequences for individual responses in the class.

Operant conditioning (also *Instrumental conditioning*): The modification of the probability of members of an operant by consequences.

Punishment: A behavioral process in which the probability of occurrence of members of an operant class is decreased via contingent presentation or removal of a stimulus. The stimulus is called a punisher. The operation of presenting a punisher.

Reflex (also *Respondent*): The reliable production of a response by a stimulus. An unconditioned reflex is characterized by production of a response by a stimulus that does not depend on prior conditioning. A conditioned reflex depends on conditioning for its existence. See *Respondent conditioning.*

Reinforcement: 1) A behavioral process whereby the probability of occurrence of members of an operant is increased by contingent presentation (positive reinforcement) or removal (negative reinforcement) of a stimulus. Stimuli which have this function are called reinforcers. 2) The operation of presenting a positive reinforcer or removing a negative reinforcer. 3) In respondent conditioning, the presentation of an unconditional stimulus contingent on presentation of a conditional stimulus.

Respondent conditioning (also *Classical conditioning, Pavlovian conditioning*): 1) A behavioral process by which a previously neutral stimulus comes to elicit a reflex-like response. 2) Repeatedly pairing (that is, presenting regularly prior to) a neutral stimulus with an unconditional stimulus.

Schedule of reinforcement: A specification of which responses within an operant class will be reinforced and when.

Unconditional stimulus: A stimulus that reliably elicits a response and does so in the absence of any specific conditioning history.

Suggested Readings

Honig, W. K. and Staddon, J. E. R. (eds.) *Handbook of Operant Behavior.* Englewood Cliffs, N.J.: Prentice-Hall, 1977.

Hulse, S. H., Deese, J., and Egeth, H. *The Psychology of Learning,* 4th ed. New York: McGraw-Hill Book Company, 1975.

Reynolds, G. S. *A Primer of Operant Conditioning.* rev. ed. Glenview, Illinois: Scott, Foresman, 1975.

Skinner, B. F. *About Behaviorism.* New York: Alfred A. Knopf, 1974.

Tarpy, R. M. *Basic Principles of Learning.* Glenview, Illinois: Scott, Foresman, 1975.

Human Memory and Learning: The Processing of Information

Henry C. Ellis, Judith P. Goggin,
and Frederick J. Parenté

Introduction

The topics of human memory and learning are of central importance in contemporary psychology. The range of events that can be learned is vast and complex. Indeed, even the simplest behaviors exhibited by very young infants come to be modified because of their ability to learn and their capacity to retain the products of learning experiences. Our daily activities regularly involve learning and memory. As we read a book, listen to a lecture, or engage in conversation, we try to organize the information into some meaningful, reasonably coherent pattern. We reflect on the information, impose structure where none is obvious, and attempt to relate what we are currently learning to prior knowledge. We try to apply or generalize our learning to new situations, sometimes successfully.

The processes of learning and memory are so commonplace in our daily lives that we may fail to recognize their pervasiveness. Examine for a moment a small block of time in your daily routine such as meeting friends for coffee and conversation. Much of the conversation focuses on activities over the past few days, plans for the future, and concerns for momentary issues. In discussing these plans and activities, you recall information and bring it forward in your immediate consciousness. As you prepare to relay an anecdote, you organize your thoughts so that the story will interest your audience and sustain their attention.

Our conceptions of learning and memory have volved over a number of years and are in a state of flux today. The traditional view of learning was that of the formation of stimulus-response associations. Thus, learning was viewed as an *association* between events, which means learning when and/or where to execute a response. With this conception of learning, memory was relegated to a relatively minor role in the state of affairs. It was simply the product of learning and was seen as a secondary process. Since learning was the formation of associations, memory was regarded as the retention of these associations. The principal focus of interest was on the fate of learned associations, that is, how their strength changed over time and how they were weakened as a result of new learning.

Early in the history of learning and memory, as was discussed in Chapter 2, critics attacked this view as much too simplistic. The foremost critics were the Gestalt psychologists who viewed learning and memory in a substantially different manner. There were two important assumptions of the Gestalt psychologists which distinguished their approach from that of stimulus-response associationism. The first was that learning was an active process rather than the passive registration of associations. The assumption was that the organism actively engaged in dealing with information to-be-learned and looked for ways to make material more easily understood. The second important assumption was that learning and memory involve *organizational* processes. Information was assumed to be organized in memory on the basis of structured perceptual processes. Perception involved the fusion of discrete events into some kind of meaningful, organized whole, whose representation was then stored in memory. For instance, in learning the word pair DOG-BICYCLE, the pair was not thought to be learned as a rote stimulus-response pair. Rather, the subject was believed to have images of the words as they were related to an organized, interacting unit. Related to the Gestalt reaction was the work of Bartlett (1932) who argued that memory involved *reconstructive* processes. The idea was that our memory of events consisted of reconstructing past experience on the basis of partial information abstracted from that experience.

Contemporary psychologists view memory as an information processing system, and share with Bartlett and the Gestalt psychologists the belief that memory is far more than the passive registration of information. The human is seen as a processor of information in which stimulation from the environment is actively processed by the organism.

Studying Human Memory and Learning

A number of procedures for studying human memory and learning have been developed. The particular method used depends on the objective of the researcher and the particular set of processes that are of immediate interest. These procedures include recall, recognition, reaction time, and serial and paired-associates learning.

Recall

Memory and learning may be studied simply by requiring a person to produce the correct response.

Being able to produce your date of birth or your address are obvious examples of recall. If the information consists of visual patterns, such as a face, then recall is tested by having the person reproduce (draw) the face.

Recall may be tested in two general ways. In *free recall,* a person is asked to produce the information learned in any order one wishes. For instance, if presented a list of words to memorize, free recall requires only that the person recall the words without regard to the order in which they were presented. The second type of recall is called *cued recall* because a specific cue is presented during the recall test. The cue may be explicitly presented with the material to be remembered. For example, a subject may be given a series of items such as TRAFFIC JAM with instructions to learn each word and its preceding cue. Later, the subject is presented the cue word TRAFFIC and asked to recall the appropriate word. In contrast, the recall cue may be information that was not presented at training but that bears some relation to the to-be-remembered word. Cued recall is an important technique for studying retrieval processes in memory because the cue guides the retrieval or search process.

Recognition

Another procedure for studying memory is the recognition memory task. A person is required to select items previously learned or experienced from a larger set of items containing both old items which were experienced and new items which were not actually presented.

Two general procedures are used. In a *forced-choice* recognition test, a person is shown an array of items, say four or five, and asked to pick out the correct item, that is, the one previously experienced. This is essentially like taking a multiple-choice examination where you pick out the correct answer from several alternatives. Another example is a photographic array of suspects of a crime from which a witness attempts to identify the alleged criminal.

In the *single-stimulus* procedure a person is shown one item at a time and asked to respond "old" or "new." Here the measure of recognition must include the number of old items correctly recognized and the number of new items falsely recognized; this is the case because the number of correct recognitions can be influenced both by the person's actual memory of the items and by his response bias, his tendency to say "yes" or "no." For instance, a subject who said "yes" to *all* items presented would get a perfect recognition score, but would falsely select all new items. Thus valid measurement of recognition memory requires that the subject's response bias or criterion for responding be separated from the actual memory of the items.

Reaction Time

Another measure of memory that has become increasingly popular in recent years is reaction time. Reaction time is a useful measure because it is assumed that the various processes in memory require some time to perform. Thus, the speed at which certain memory tasks are carried out is thought to reflect their complexity or difficulty. In studies using reaction time, the general procedure involves probing (testing) for well-memorized information and measuring the time elapsed between presentation of the test probe and the subject's response. For example, Sternberg (1966) used reaction time measures to study retrieval processes in memory. Subjects were given a short list of digits, ranging from one to four, and asked to remember them. Thus the memory set was well within the subjects' memory span. The test stimulus (probe) was a single digit, and the subject had to indicate whether or not the digit was a member of the original set presented. The time needed by the subject to make this decision and respond was the measure taken.

Sternberg was interested in the way a person reaches this decision. On the one hand, the subject might compare the probe to all of the stored digits on a one-by-one basis, that is, successively; on the other hand, the subject might compare the probe to all of the stored items simultaneously. In deciding whether or not the test probe is in the memory set, the subject must process the information presented, and this processing may be divided into three stages: the test probe must be encoded in memory; the probe must then be compared with the memory set; and finally, a response must be

made. It seems reasonable to assume that the time required for the first and third stages does not vary with the size of the memory set. Therefore, increasing the size of the memory set from one to four digits should require a corresponding increase in reaction times only *if* the subject makes each comparison singly, that is, on a one-to-one basis. In contrast, no increase in reaction time should occur if the subject processes all items simultaneously. The results of Sternberg's study indicated a linear increase in reaction time with increasing set size, thus allowing him to interpret these results as evidence for a successive or serial-search process. This is just one example of how reaction time measures are used in contemporary memory research.

Serial and Paired Associate Learning

The first three measures described are used primarily to study memory. They may, however, also be used in the study of learning. For example, if one examines how free recall changes over trials, then interest is in free recall learning (Tulving, 1968). Similarly, repeated trials in a recognition task are used when the interest is in recognition learning itself.

In this section, we shall examine two traditional methods in human learning. In *serial learning* the task of the subject is to learn a series of items in a particular order. Learning your social security number or a telephone number is an instance of serial learning. As an example, Bower and Winzenz (1969) presented subjects with digit strings auditorially; the strings were broken into groups by pauses such as 783-4652-828, where the dashes represent pauses, and the subject then attempted to recall the digits in order.

Paired associate learning refers to the association formed between pairs of items. In the laboratory task, the subject is given pairs of items to learn, such as words, with the first item in the pair regarded as the stimulus and the second as the response. In everyday life, associating names with faces would be an instance of paired associate learning. Another example is the learning of foreign language equivalents to English words.

With this brief review of major procedures in memory and learning, we shall now turn our attention to memory as an information processing system. First, we will examine the structure of the memory system.

Structure of Memory

For convenience, the human memory system can be divided into three different stores or components: sensory memory, short-term memory, and long-term memory. These different components are thought to be necessary for storage of information. The fact that there are different stores refers to the *structure* or the "architecture" of the memory system. Memory structures are the permanent part of the human memory system and thus set the boundaries within which memory processes operate (Atkinson & Shiffrin, 1968). On the other hand, there are important *processes* in memory such as rehearsal and selective attention. For example, you may rehearse a telephone number in order to remember it for future use or selectively attend to your professor's lecture and ignore the conversation going on behind you.

Sensory Information Store

The first stage in the human memory system is the sensory information store (SIS). The SIS is a system that holds sensory representations or images of events impinging upon the sense organs for very brief durations. These images may be *iconic* referring to sensations in the visual modality, *echoic* (auditory), or they may come from any of the other sense modalities. In any case, the sensory store is characterized by situations in which a stimulus continues to produce an effect after it has been terminated. We have all experienced our sensory memories at work. Looking into the sun for a short period of time leaves a solar spot in our visual field that eventually fades. Try this as a demonstration: First, close your eyes and keep them closed for about a minute. While your eyes are closed, hold your hand approximately 12 inches in front of your face. Now blink once and be sure to keep your eyelids closed after you blink. The icon (image) of your hand will persist after your eyelids have closed and will immediately begin to fade.

What is important to note about the fading iconic representation is that its brief persistence allows us to scan the image and to extract information from it if necessary. The SIS is capable of retaining far more information than can be efficiently processed (Sperling, 1963). Since we do not remember all of the information held in iconic storage, the SIS may be described as a transition zone where we shift from perception, the reception of information, to memory, the retention of information. The information in the SIS decays very rapidly and may be effectively scanned for about one-half second. That portion of the information that we attend to is then passed on to the short-term memory system for further processing. Figure 10-1 illustrates the basic components of the memory system, showing the relationship between the sensory information store, short-term memory, and long-term memory.

Short-Term Memory

The short-term memory store is the center of activity in the information processing system. Since information in the short-term store can come from either the SIS or the long-term memory store, it is probably accurate to characterize the short-term memory store as the *crossroads of our information-processing system*. For example, we are usually able to remember a new telephone number for at least as long as we need to dial it. Similarly, the study of mathematics requires us to learn specific formulae, and procedures for solving problems; we can then recall each formula for as long as is necessary to work the problem at hand. These examples illustrate two of the three functions of short term memory (STM). First, the short-term store holds information for immediate use. Second, we may process information in STM for efficient storage in long-term memory. Finally, long-term memories may be retrieved and updated in the short-term store.

If information is to be held in short-term memory for any length of time, it must be rehearsed or mentally repeated. In the absence of rehearsal, it is more likely to be forgotten. In contrast, if rehearsal continues, the information may be transferred to long-term memory and permanently stored.

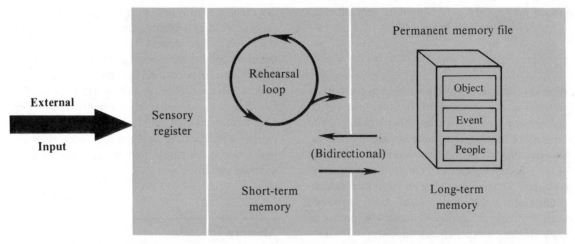

Fig. 10-1. Basic information processing system: Sensory information store, short-term memory with rehearsal loop, and long-term memory. External information enters the sensory information store where it is selected and passed on to the short-term store. In the short-term store, it is processed for immediate use and/or permanent storage in long-term memory. Note the bidirectionality of information flow between the short-term and the long-term storage areas.

To illustrate the workings of the rehearsal mechanism, try this simple exercise: Have a friend write down five telephone numbers with which you are unfamiliar. Then have your friend read these numbers to you, one at a time, followed by a three-second pause. During the pause, try to remember each number by rehearsing it and, after the three seconds is up (but before your friend reads the next number), write the numbers down on a piece of paper. Repeat the process until you have recalled all five of the telephone numbers. Now, write five new telephone numbers and test your friend's memory; however, during the three-second interval, have your friend recite the alphabet backwards from the letter Z prior to recall of each of the numbers. You will probably find that you were able to recall all of the numbers, while your friend was able to remember only portions of each. The difference in recall is due to the fact that your friend was prevented from rehearsing the numbers and was thus unable to retain them in short-term memory.

Perhaps the most important characteristic of short-term memory is that it is a *limited-capacity* system. In other words, we are capable of retaining approximately seven pieces of information in the short-term store at one time. If our STM is restricted to seven bits of information, you may wonder how we can retain strings of more than seven digits or, for that matter, sentences of more than seven words. The answer is both simple and intuitive. Short-term memory is facilitated by our ability to "chunk" or group information into larger units (Miller, 1956). Indeed, one very effective way to remember telephone numbers is to rehearse the number as a series of chunks rather than as a series of single digits. For example, the number 277-4239 is more easily retained if it is rehearsed as two-seventy-seven, forty-two, thirty-nine as opposed to a string of single digits: two, seven, seven, four, two, three, nine. Regardless of the procedure, processing is always going to be limited to about seven pieces of information. The chunking procedure allows you to easily process the seven numbers, because the unit of information has been shifted from a single digit to chunks of two or three digits. Without skills in chunking or grouping, the amount of information that can be processed at any one time is quite limited and is bound by the single element chunk. Typically, people who have "good memories" have an increased facility for grouping or organizing information into chunks, which permits very efficient storage of information in memory.

Long-Term Memory

Whereas the information in short-term memory is present for only a brief period of time, information in long-term memory is relatively permanent. The capacity of the long-term store is virtually infinite, although this fact is sometimes overlooked because of our frequent failures to recall information. Nevertheless, anyone who has ever been to a demonstration of hypnosis has probably been impressed with the subjects' ability to recall the details of early childhood experiences. Such demonstrations suggest the permanence and immense capacity of our long-term store. Some of this information is always accessible, such as the name of your parents or your hometown. Other information, such as the name of your high school English teacher, may be recalled only under certain conditions.

Information in long-term memory depends on the action of the short-term system for updating and reorganization. One feature of the long-term store is that memories may be reorganized on the basis of new information coming into the system. Since the information is always present in long-term memory, we can gain access to it and begin reorganizing it again.

As mentioned earlier, the distinction between the memory systems is one of convenience and is not meant to imply that our short-term memories are located in one portion of the brain and our long-term memories are located in some other portion. It may be more accurate to say that the physiological mechanisms underlying short-term mem-ory involve a form of continuous electro-chemical process within the brain, whereas long-term memory involves a permanent change in the structure of the brain cells or their interconnections. This conception does not require that the memory stores have a different physiological locus; indeed, the fact that we can retrieve information from our long-term memories, and that this information can exist in both the long- and the short-term store simultaneously, suggests that there exists a single memory system.

Memory Processes

It was noted in the introduction to this chapter that memory is assumed to be much more than the passive registration and storage of information about environmental events. As a processor of information, the human actively processes stimulation from the environment through the memory system. The memory system consists of three basic processes: encoding, storage, and retrieval. These are shown in Figure 10-2. *Encoding* is the process by which information in the form of physical energy from the environment is transformed into some state suitable for memory storage. For example, as you listen to a lecture you normally do not remember everything verbatim, but encode the gist or essential features of the talk. This process of focussing on the essence of the lecture while ignoring nonessential detail is encoding. *Storage* refers to the maintenance of information over time. The fact that events are remembered for days, weeks, or years seems to require that some representation of these events be held in memory; thus, the idea

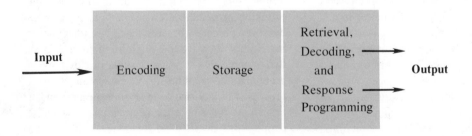

Fig. 10-2.
Processes in memory: encoding, storage, retrieval.

of memory storage is important. Finally, *retrieval* refers to the means by which we access and use information in memory. Retrieval involves an active search for stored information and logically follows encoding and storage. We will now examine these processes in greater detail.

Encoding

We have all been faced with situations that require us to transform or convert information into a form that is meaningful or easily retained. This transformation involves encoding the information into a form compatible with the structure of memory. Examples of encoding operations include elaborating on the information contained in an external stimulus, selecting only a portion of the external stimulus, or verbally labeling a visual form (Ellis, 1973). For example, encoding occurs when we recognize a word from a pattern of auditory stimuli. At a more general level, college students often underline the relevant aspects of an assigned chapter in the hope that their memory for the highlighted material will suffice as preparation for an upcoming examination.

Many aspects of our physical and social environment do not find their way into our experience. One form of selectivity is regulated by features of our sense organs and our nervous system. Many kinds of stimulation, such as radioactive bombardment or certain spectra of the sun's rays, are imperceptible to us. Another type of selectivity concerns the ability to control our sense receptors so as to reduce incoming sources of input that are irrelevant or distracting. For example, intensive concentration on an important or long-awaited letter from a loved one does not require the use of our ears, and it is usually the case that we will "tune out" distracting auditory messages while processing the letter visually. Finally, sensory selection can occur within a particular (auditory, visual) system. Reading an interesting novel while watching our favorite television program illustrates the frustration that usually accompanies selective processing of information in the same sensory modality. The two types of selectivity are examples of "sensory gating" and are studied by psychologists interested in

perception and sensation. The third type of selectivity is a pure case of "selective attention" and is of interest in the study of human learning, memory, and cognition.

Selective Attention. We have all been to crowded parties where our ears are bombarded by a vast array of extraneous information. Beside the conversation in which we are engaged, we also hear those of other guests, boisterous laughter, the sounds of ice cubes in glasses, and the crunch of potato chips and pretzels. It may seem to you that you hear all of these extraneous noises in the course of conversing with your friends. However, the total amount of information in the party situation almost always exceeds our processing capacity, and we must constantly select which information will be processed and which will not.

The problem of how we are able to attend to one conversation in the midst of others has been addressed rather directly in the laboratory in a series of "shadowing" experiments (Cherry, 1953). These experiments mimic the cocktail party situation and provide a more controlled way of studying selective attention. The subjects wear earphones and hear two different messages presented simultaneously, one to each ear. The task requires the subject to "shadow" or repeat one of the messages as it is received by one ear; while the listener hears and shadows the one message, a second message is received by the other ear. Later, the subject is required either to recognize or to recall the information from the unshadowed message. Usually, only the gross characteristics of this information are remembered, such as whether it was delivered in a male or female voice. However, if the listener perceives particularly relevant information (for example, a name or words that are relevant to the shadowed message), then the shadowed message will be temporarily disrupted and the words encoded. Therefore, we do not screen out all of the information from "unattended" messages that reach our ears.

Serial and Parallel Processing. It should be clear from our discussion that even though we do not attend to all of the information we receive, we are able to handle large amounts of the information impinging upon us at one time. In other words, stimulation can be processed simultaneously although such processing is incomplete; this means that information may be received in *parallel* (at the same time) but is not encoded all at once. Often, we are forced to switch back and forth between inputs that occur simultaneously. Such sequential encoding is called *serial* processing. In serial processing, the most important information may be chosen for further processing. Whether or not the human information processing system is parallel or serial is a topic of some theoretical controversy; however, it is probably most accurate to say that elementary or superficial processing of information occurs simultaneously (in parallel) whereas information that is to receive careful processing at considerable depth is handled sequentially.

Laboratory investigations of serial and parallel processing in humans usually involve a task that is similar to proofreading. Subjects are required to scan lists of letters in search of specific letters that have been designated as "target" items, and the experimenter measures the amount of time it takes the subject to find the target item (for example, Neisser, 1964). The task is roughly analogous to looking in a telephone directory for the name of a specific individual or to searching the classified section of the daily newspaper for a particular type of used car. Although these tasks appear simple, they are actually rather complex and are affected by a number of different variables. For example, the similarity of the target and non-target items influences search times. Very short search times occur when non-target letters are very dissimilar to the targets; in general, the more similar the letters, the longer the search time.

A human being does not necessarily encode all features of the stimuli presented in a visual search task. For instance, if your task is to scan a list of letters and identify only a subset, such as C, O, G, J, Q, S, and so on, you would abstract the relevant or essential features of this set and ignore other features. All these letters contain curved lines, which is the essential aspect for detection. In this instance, only those features of the nontarget letters which are sufficient to distinguish them from the target letters are encoded for purposes of serial processing.

The parallel aspects of visual search tasks are most obvious when we must search for more than one target or when the target is quite complex. For instance, proofreading a manuscript requires a simultaneous search for a variety of errors in punctuation, grammar, spelling, and so forth. The skilled proofreader is quite proficient in this task.

Nature of the Memory Code. It should be clear by now that the coding of information in memory not only is a complex process but also is essential if we are to reduce the information load to manageable proportions. Still another area of interest concerns the *nature* of the memory code or the manner in which information is represented in memory. At least four types of memory codes may be identified: physical-image codes, verbal-name codes, symbolic codes, and motor codes.

1. *Physical-Image Codes.* As we mentioned earlier, our sensory information store is a large-capacity system that is capable of retaining the physical resemblance of a stimulus object for a brief period of time. Such a representation bears a close correspondence to the actual physical event and is called a *physical-image code*. Information in short-term memory is sometimes retained in an image-like or physical state that is similar to what is held in the sensory store (Brooks, 1968). For example, describing the face of a bank robber to a policeman requires the witness to hold the visual trace of the felon's face in short-term memory while the physical characteristics are described. In a similar vein, all of us are capable of bringing to mind the image of our home town. The process usually involves the production of a few detailed scenes such as our residence or neighborhood. These two examples suggest the range and level of detail which may appear in physical-image codes.

That form of short-term memory image that bears the closest direct correspondence to the physical experience is called *eidetic* and has been popularly referred to as "photographic memory." As the name implies, photographic memory refers to an uncanny ability that some of us have to remember objects and events exactly. Eidetic memorizers seem to process information the same as normals although the capacity of their physical-image codes appears to be significantly greater than normal (Leaks et al., 1969). They can describe a stranger's dress and facial features in minute detail and recall selected passages from textbooks verbatim (Stromeyer and Psotka, 1970). Whether this ability is due to superior visual rehearsal strategies, and is therefore a matter of practice, or reflects an innate capacity difference is currently unknown.

2. *Verbal-Name Codes.* The letter "A" comes in a great many shapes and sizes, but all seem to mean the same thing. This is simply to say that the letters "A," "a," or *"a"* are identical in meaning even though they differ in size and script. Similarly, the word "dog" is representative of a vast array of canines from toy poodles to great Danes. Verbal-name codes are important to us in that they integrate related but different events in memory.

It is possible to distinguish the use of physical-image codes and verbal-name codes in the laboratory with a matching task that requires the subject to respond as quickly as possible to letter pairs (Posner, 1973). The subject is first shown a single letter, such as A, for as long as it takes to identify it. Immediately following identification, a second letter is presented, and the subject must indicate by pressing a key whether the second letter is the same as, or is different from, the first. The results of this type of experiment depend on the nature of the second letter. If the second letter is physically identical to the first, as in AA, the match process occurs quite rapidly; if the letters are the same, but the first is upper case and the second is lower case, such as Aa, the match is slower. This difference in matching time occurs only when the interval between the letters is very brief. At longer intervals, the amount of time required for a match is the same, regardless of the case of the second letter. These findings suggest a difference in coding at the short and long interval. At longer intervals, the verbal or name code is used as a basis of the response, whereas at the shorter intervals, the physical-image code is more efficient than matching on the basis of name.

3. *Symbolic Codes.* Every college student is familiar with the peace symbol. The red, white, and blue cloth that sways in the breeze above most civic centers has meaning for every citizen in the United States. Such symbols play an important part in our lives and relate to our experience by suggesting something other than a mere physical resemblance of an object or event. Symbols are abstract codes and represent events of considerable complexity.

Laboratory investigations of symbolic codes are typically restricted to verbal materials. For example, the words "love" or "justice" may be conceived as symbols for a vast array of different experiences. Such abstract or symbolic codes rarely take on a specific form but may represent characteristics of the events that are common to all forms of the event. The exact nature of abstract or symbolic codes is unclear, and you may wonder how symbolic codes differ from verbal-name codes. The answer to this question is incomplete, although you will not be far from the mark if you note that verbal-name codes usually entail some form of visual image. For example, the word "dog" will usually bring to mind some specific mental image of a four-legged, furry creature. Symbolic codes are less specific or concrete, and the things they represent usually cannot be remembered easily. In addition, symbolic codes may vary considerably between individuals.

4. *Motor Codes.* Getting into our car, placing the key into the ignition, releasing the safety brake, and buckling the seat belt are activities that we rarely think about and can be performed while our thoughts are on something else. They are motor behaviors and are typically not easily prone to disruption. Motor behaviors are thought to be stored as motor codes, and motor codes control the majority of our daily physical activity. We are usually too busy with processing physical-image and verbal codes to pay much attention to them. Once a motor pattern is learned, its motor representation in memory can be maintained with only a minimum of conscious attention (Posner and Konick, 1966).

It is difficult to isolate examples of motor codes that do not involve aspects of other memory codes. Perhaps an example will, nevertheless, make the concept clear. A skilled guitarist in a rock-and-roll band can produce a variety of chord patterns on a fret board in a matter of seconds, providing the guitarist is allowed to use his guitar for demonstration. However, if this same guitarist is given a diagram of the fret board of the guitar and required to label the appropriate fingering of the various chords, the guitarist may find it necessary to go through the motions of forming the chords with an imaginary guitar prior to filling in the various positions on the diagram. What is significant to note about this example is that the motor code serves as a mediator or "go between" between the diagram and the verbal-name code, such as A-flat. Clearly, motor codes are important, illustrated by the fact that some very competent musicians are blind or are unable to read music and must depend solely on the "feel" of the instrument.

Much of our thinking is dependent on the development of motor codes, and there are some psychologists who postulate that our perception is based on the motor tracing of objects and events into the memory store. This type of thinking has been furthered by Jean Piaget and other developmental psychologists as well as by physiological psychologists in the Soviet Union. Piaget believes that many of a child's cognitive abilities arise out of his early tactile and motor experiences with the environment (Piaget and Inhelder, 1969). For example, a child's depth perception is highly influenced by the motor operations of crawling amongst the various objects in the playpen and on the floor of the house. Similarly, a good part of language acquisition is dependent on the use of facial movement to add particular emphasis to our communication. The Soviets have extended these ideas, formalizing them into what they call the "Soviet motor copy theory" of perceptual learning. The gist of the theory is that, when we initially perceive an object, the mental representation of the object is based on certain motor movements that occur during the perception. For example, when presenting a person with a simple visual pattern to be learned, the movement of that person's eyes corresponds to the outline of the pattern. Once the mental representation (motor copy) of the object is established (the object is learned), there is no longer any need for the motor tracing and these muscular activities disappear in the course of recognizing the shape as either "old" or "new" (Epstein, 1967).

Encoding Variability. It has been proposed that our perception and subsequent encoding of environmental stimuli can vary from presentation to presentation of stimuli (Martin, 1968). The basic idea is that an encoded version of an environmental stimulus is not necessarily identical on subsequent presentations and that encoding variability has important consequences for learning and memory. This idea is quite simple. To illustrate, the encoding variability hypothesis assumes that the encoded representation of some stimulus might be symbolized as e_1 in one situation but as e_2 in another. You might, for example, encode the face of a stranger you see in a jewelry store in a particular fashion, e_1, but if the stranger produces a hand gun and demands a tray of rings from the jeweler, your perception of this stranger would change radically, and hence you would encode a new representation of the stranger, e_2.

Martin has argued that certain environmental stimuli can be expected to produce more variable encodings than other stimuli. Specifically, stimulus events that are low in meaningfulness are assumed to be encoded more variably than stimuli high in meaningfulness. For example, the nonsense syllable XFL might have several different encodings whereas the word DOG is likely to be encoded in one way. The importance of the encoding variability hypothesis is the recognition that the encoded version of a stimulus can differ from the actual environmental (nominal) stimulus and that our encoded representation can change on subsequent presentations of a stimulus.

Short-Term and Long-Term Memory: Dual Storage Systems?

For convenience, we have described memory as consisting of three different functional systems. We have also indicated that this description is not entirely accurate, since the human information processing system is probably better conceived of as continuous. Whether or not our memory system is continuous or stage-like was, until quite recently, an issue of theoretical interest and hot debate. The basic question was whether STM and LTM represent two different memory systems, which function according to different principles, or whether they represent a continuum, which functions according to the same principles. First, we will discuss the evidence concerning a dual memory system followed by evidence favoring a continuous memory system. Then we shall outline a "levels of processing" approach to memory, which allows us to view memory as an essentially continuous process.

Evidence: Pro and Con. A variety of evidence has been offered in support of a dual process theory of memory. Some of this evidence is consistent with the early physiological speculations of psychologists such as Hebb (1949), whose contention is that there are at least two stages of neural activity that underlie the development of memory. During the first stage, "reverberating circuits" are established. This means that one neuron excites the next which, in turn, excites the next, and so on. The neurons function as a network or circuit, and the activity of the neural network proceeds in a continuous fashion so long as the excitation is maintained. After some period of time, these neural networks develop permanent structural changes as a result of repeated stimulation and are stored as permanent memories. Therefore, the difference between short- and long-term memories is thought to be related to the permanence of the connective bond between memory cells. Whether or not our short- and long-term memories develop in the same or different places of the brain is unclear; however, the notion that memory involves the establishment of connective networks among memory cells is both intuitively reasonable and has been incorporated in many current computer models of memory and cognition.

The belief that short-term and long-term memory are localized in different areas of the brain has received some experimental support. Severe memory deficits may result if there is damage to a certain area of the brain called the hippocampus. If the hippocampus is destroyed, subjects have great difficulty learning new information. However, these same subjects can recall information that they learned prior to the destruction of the hippocampal region. It is also important to note that the patients' performance on intelligence tests involving primarily short-term memory functions is not diminished. The patient can retain information in short-term memory if allowed to rehearse it. What appears to be lost is the ability to process

new information into a state whereby it may be placed into long-term memory. These patients show no memory for prior information, repeating questions they had asked five minutes earlier or failing to recall the names of individuals to whom they have recently been introduced. Their inability to retain information for more than a brief period of time is consistent with the notion of dual memory stores.

Several additional sources of evidence that support the dual process memory notion may be cited. The first concerns capacity differences between the two systems. There is little contention about the fact that short-term and long-term memory have vastly different capacities. The capacity of STM is roughly seven chunks of information. These items may be words, digits, letters, practically anything, but we are still restricted to about seven. On the other hand, the capacity of LTM is virtually unlimited.

The second kind of evidence supporting the dual process notion concerns the types of information that appear to be processed in one system to the exclusion of the other. Some researchers have noted that STM and LTM appear to differ in terms of the type of encoding that may occur in the two systems. More specifically, some experiments indicate that acoustical features of items are encoded in STM, whereas semantic (meaningful) features of items are encoded in LTM. The proposal is that STM is essentially an auditory storage system in which acoustic information is maintained but no interpretation of the information is made. Meaning is thought to develop in LTM.

Finally, the rapid forgetting in STM relative to the slower rate of forgetting in LTM led some researchers to believe that the mechanisms for forgetting in the two systems differed. It was hypothesized that forgetting from STM occurred because of time-dependent decay of the memory trace. On the other hand, forgetting from LTM was assumed to occur because of interference among similar memory traces.

In contrast to the dual process view, many psychologists argue that memory is best conceived as a continuum rather than a dichotomy. For example, consider a memory system that resembles a long conveyer belt in an automobile factory. The parts on the conveyer belt before you are analogous to our short-term memories. We can easily recall the specifics of parts that pass before us, their shapes, sizes, and even their serial numbers. As the parts travel down the conveyer belt, their details fade from view. In order to check on the specifics of any of the parts we must enter the warehouse, find the part, and examine it. In this example, the warehouse is analogous to our LTM, and the conveyer belt illustrates the continuum of memory (see Murdock, 1974, p. 266f).

The position of the single-process theorist is that interference operates in both STM and LTM and that there is no need to posit a decay process that is unique to the short-term store alone. Although the rapid forgetting in STM obtained by Peterson and Peterson (1959) led some to believe that forgetting in STM was due to a decay process, it was quickly shown that interference occurs in STM (Keppel and Underwood, 1962). Investigations of short-term memory have shown that forgetting of information progressively increases with increases in proactive interference, that is, interference due to prior learning. The importance of this finding is that it suggests that memory is basically a continuous process and the STM and LTM are both affected by interference. In addition, single-process theorists contend that the existing physiological evidence does not necessitate a dual storage system. For example, although destruction of the hippocampus (an area deep in the temporal lobes of the brain) leads to severe memory disruption, it is also the case that similar disorders can be induced with destruction of other brain areas such as the entorhinal cortex, which is located directly adjacent to the hippocampus (McLardy, 1970). Thus, it does not appear that any one area of the brain can be regarded as a specialized locus for particular kinds of memories.

The fact that STM and LTM differ in capacity is indisputable. However, it may be legitimately argued that this does not require two different storage systems and may only reflect differences in the operation of the same mechanism. Finally, the division of memory on the basis of acoustic and semantic variables is inadequate on intuitive grounds. If LTM were primarily a semantic store, how is it that we often are confused by seemingly well-learned acoustic features, such as the British and Australian accents? Moreover, some laboratory evidence shows that short-term memory confusions can occur with semantically related materials. In short, what was once a strong case for a dual-memory store is now seriously weakened.

Levels of Processing: A Resolution. Probably the most useful approach toward resolving the issue of dual versus single storage systems has been proposed by Craik and Lockhart (1972). These researchers suggested that data which appear to support the notion of a dual memory may just as easily be explained in terms of what they call levels of processing. The gist of their idea is that the learning of anything requires a series of processing stages that vary along a *continuum of depth*. In the initial stages of processing, stimuli are analyzed for their gross physical features such as contours, lines, angles, as well as characteristics such as brightness and loudness. Intermediate stages of processing include the storage of information in memory and the matching of new input against these stored representations, which is the process of stimulus recognition. After a stimulus is recognized, it is processed further by association and by integration with the existing information that is stored by long-term memory. This final stage requires a great deal of semantic organization, and the entire process involves a series of stages in which information is processed at progressively greater depths. Consider, for example, the processing that might occur when the word DOG is presented. As a superficial level of processing, you might note that the word contains three letters, with a vowel between two consonants. A somewhat deeper level of processing would occur if you were to note that the word rhymes with HOG. Finally, the item's meaning (that is, a four-legged animal that barks) and its relationship to other items in your memory (it makes you think of CAT) represent a still deeper level of processing. Thus, coding of items becomes progressively more complex or deeper as the lexical, acoustic, and semantic characteristics are processed in order.

The levels of processing approach to the study of memory is important, because it apparently resolves the controversy of a single versus a dual or multistage storage system. If we adopt the levels of processing approach, a multistage conception of memory is no longer necessary to account for the discrepancies in processing between our sensory, short-term, and long-term memory systems. The variables that appear to affect these memory systems differentially may be explained in terms of processing differences at the various levels. Extending this notion to its limit, the primary factor that determines how long information will be remembered is the *depth* at which the information is processed.

Retrieval

It is staggering to think about the number of facts that are available to us at any given point in time. This information ranges from the most trivial of events to important information. Although there appears to be no limit to the number of facts that we can store away for future use, our ability to access that information when we need it is limited. To illustrate this point, think about the popular party game called "trivia." In this game, we are asked any number of questions dealing with unimportant facts such as "What was the name of Roy Rogers' dog?," "What was the name of the Cisco Kid's comrade?," or "What type of bullets did the Lone Ranger shoot from his pearl-handled revolver?" Those of us who have engaged in this pastime have been amazed at some people's ability to recall these seemingly irrelevant facts without hesitation. For others, there is an embarrassing delay that usually ends in our recognizing the correct answer after someone else has correctly recalled it. (Roy Rogers' dog's name was "Bullet." The Cisco Kid's comical sidekick was called "Pancho." The Lone Ranger shot "silver" bullets.) When we encounter such questions several distinguishable, but interrelated processes occur before an overt reply can be made; these processes compose our retrieval system. *Retrieval* is the process of search and location of specific information required by the memory system.

The first stage of the retrieval process is the search of available information in memory. Often, this process is immediate and direct. For example, if we are introduced to a new person and are told the person's name, it is usually no trick to maintain the name in STM for immediate access throughout the course of the conversation. Some information such as our name and social security number, appears held in abeyance in LTM for ready usage. On the other occasions, the search process is less direct and immediate, as in the "trivia" game. We cannot readily predict how difficult it will be or how long it will take to recall a specific fact. It is probably the case that retrieval from the SIS or STM will generally be more rapid than from LTM, although not necessarily so. After extensive practice, some or all of the search process occurs so quickly that it is hardly noticed. Regardless of which information store is searched, the final stage of retrieval is always the same, namely, to guide and direct an appropriate verbal and/or motor response.

Retrieval from the Sensory Information Store. Information in sensory memory is apparently "read" directly from the store. In other words, search of iconic or echoic memory is a matter of *scanning* the image or repeating the verbal message before the information fades from memory. Laboratory investigations of iconic scanning indicates that iconic images consisting of letter arrays are scanned at approximately 10 milliseconds per letter (Averbach, 1963). The scanning rate is even higher when the letters are combined into meaningful sequences such as words. The most interesting aspect of the sensory search process is the question of what scans the iconic image. Recall that the duration of an iconic image is too brief for us to scan it with movements of our eyes. Still we are able to process these images as if we were able to continually regulate our eyes' fixations before the image fades. Although it is tempting to suggest that our "mind's eye" is responsible for the search, such an explanation is next to useless. Our best conclusion at present is that the human information processing system seems to be capable of scanning visual displays internally, that is, with nothing but direct fixation of the eye.

Retrieval from Short-Term Memory. Perhaps the best examples of search operations in short-term memory are concerned with immediately perceived information. Such information is held in memory and scanned either visually or rehearsed auditorily for as long as is necessary to reproduce the information in its entirety. This maintenance and searching of information in short-term memory is what has been generally referred to as memory scan. If the memory involves acoustic or auditory information, it is clear that some form of rehearsal will be involved. On the other hand, if the information in STM is a physical image of some kind, our scanning will be similar to that involved in sensory memory. For example, eidetic (visual imagery retained in the memory) imagers usually report that they are able to retain a visual image of an object "somewhere before their eyes" for extended lengths of time. This ability allows the eidetic imager to scan and process the image for greater lengths of time and provides an excellent example of retrieval of scanned information from the short-term store.

It is interesting to note that visual images in short-term memory can be processed at approximately four times the rate at which auditory information can be rehearsed. In addition, the time required to process a single bit or unit of information in short-term memory is approximately 40 milliseconds (Sternberg, 1969). This latter finding comes from experiments that systematically vary the number of elements that are present in short-term memory and consequently the time required to process all of the elements in order to decide whether a particular element is "old" or "new." The procedure usually involves presenting from one to six random digits to subjects to be memorized. After this display is learned, a single test digit is presented, and the subject is required to indicate, as quickly as possible, whether the test digit was among the set that was originally studied. The time required to identify the test digit as "old" or "new" increases by about 40 milliseconds for each additional item that must be searched in the memory set. The task is analogous to entering a party and immediately taking note of the guests present, going to the bathroom, and upon your return, taking a rapid survey of the guests who arrived in your absence. In this example, each new guest would require approximately 40 milliseconds to process.

Retrieval from Long-Term Memory. Consider the following question: "What did you wear to school last Tuesday?" To find the answer, the search process proceeds according to at least two stages. The stages entail a variety of different questions, and each question allows us to eliminate information on the basis of its reasonableness. For example, you may initially answer, "I wore Bermuda shorts, tennis shoes, a sport shirt, and a tweed coat." This type of answer would probably be rejected immediately if it were too warm for a tweed coat. Such possibilities can be eliminated without extensive search of long-term memory.

Continuing your memory search you might then ask, "Let's see, on Tuesday, what did I do?" A reasonable starting point, which is the first stage of the search process, begins with this general context. This simply means that the first level of long-term memory search usually entails an examination of a variety of information that surrounds the desired fact. Additional facts such as, "Tuesday I had only one class and in the morning I washed my car," may be recalled. Once the general context is recalled, a more detailed search of the specific aspects of the scene is possible. For example, "I wore my old tennis shoes because I didn't want to get my new boots wet." Eventually, the entire memory is recalled, "I wore my tennis shoes, my old jeans, and a T-shirt with holes in the sleeves."

As the example indicates, search of long-term memory involves at least two distinct stages. The first stage eliminates impossibilities as well as calls up related information that surrounds the to-be-recalled fact. Thus, the first level of search entails a broad survey of possibilities, some of which may be processed further. When one general episode or aggregate of facts is identified, the second level of search is initiated. At this point, we scan the restricted information until we eventually locate an answer that is reasonable; the reasonable answer usually involves additional information that is extracted from the constellation of facts that surround the answer. The answer is then verified against the contextual information.

The process is roughly analogous to searching the yellow pages of the phone book for a specific ice cream store. We may remember that the store sold particularly good ice cream, but cannot remember the name of the store or its phone number. In the first level of our search, we disregard all restaurants except those that sell ice cream. That is, we turn to the portion of the phone book entitled "ice cream vendors." We then search that information and in searching we recall a number of specifics about the location and the store. "It was on the east side of the city on a major street." We then limit our search to those stores that conform to our restrictions and limit the set further. In the process, we remember something about "31 Flavors." Finally, we locate a "Baskin-Robbins" located on East Central Avenue and respond accordingly.

Working Memory

Earlier, we described the short-term store as a crossroads of our memory system. By crossroads we meant that information from either the sensory or long-term store could be held in short-term memory for further processing. Such memories are in an "active" state; that is, they are being retained for encoding and storage in LTM or they are memories that have been retrieved from long-term memory and "operationalized" in the short-term store. As an example of an operationalized long-term memory, shut your eyes (so as to screen out any new input) and think about your social security number. These digits will then be in an operational or active state. With little effort, you can even scan the imaged display. This operationalized information shares many similarities with the information that is received from the sensory store. For example, it is an experimental fact that information in short-term memory can be examined at about the same rate whether or not it is coming from the sensory store or is operationalized from long-term memory. There are also ways in which the processing of new and long-term memories differ. For example, if you are unable to rehearse new information in short-term memory, the information is lost. However, operationalized memories are not affected by rehearsal-prevention activities. Information in this state can usually be recalled simply because the memories are always present in the long-term store.

Working memory is related to the two levels of long-term memory search that we discussed earlier. In the first level of search, a broad class of information is operationalized for retention and scanning. The second level of search may then be restricted to this smaller, more available, operationalized memory. Often, the search process leads to frustration in that the operationalized (first-level) memory is too broad, and we are unable to extract the specifics of the information that we need. The frustration stems from the feeling that the information is "right on the tip of the tongue."

The "tip of the tongue" phenomenon has been thoroughly investigated in the laboratory (Brown and McNeil, 1966). In these experiments, subjects were read dictionary definitions of unfamiliar words and asked to produce the word. For example, a definition might be "the act or practice of spying on others;" the word is "espionage." Another definition might be, "A military post with troops stationed on a permanent basis;" the word is "garrison." Some of the subjects were frustrated by these definitions. They "knew" what the word was but they could not produce it; it was on the tip of their tongue. The tip-of-the-tongue state is interesting because of the variety of responses that it produces. Subjects would offer words that either sounded like the word or had similar meanings. Others were able to produce the first letter of the word or other details, such as how many syllables the word had, even though they could not produce the word itself. In any case, the tip-of-the-tongue phenomenon is important, because it lends support to the notion of a two-level search process that we described earlier. If the second-level search is unable to produce the correct information, then the response must be based on the first-level search; in other words, the answer is based on whatever information has been operationalized and is currently maintained in working memory.

Response Programming

A final stage in the information processing system is concerned with response programming, which is the "hookup" of information in working memory to an appropriate response. The response may be as gross as a spoken word or the pushing of a button. It may be as delicate as the slicing of the surgeon's knife in a brain operation or as finely controlled as the movement of a ballet dancer. Although a mechanism for generating responses is necessary, most memory theorists have not addressed this issue in any detail. The ones that have note that there is not enough evidence available to describe the workings of a "response generator" in meaningful detail. Regardless of specifics, the response generation mechanism probably involves some form of "feedback system."

Recall this childhood game. A friend hides something in a room and you try to find it. As you approach the place where the object is hidden your friend says, "You're getting warmer;" as you get further from the place you are told, "You're getting colder." Working memory probably guides our overt responses in a similar fashion. Motor or verbal responses are selected for their appropriateness and matched against our working memories. The match process involves selection ("You're getting warmer") and may be based on the strength of past associative connections between the response and the working memory. In other words, the matching of responses to working memories may amount to little more than the identification of which response has occurred most frequently with a specific memory in the past.

The fact that all of us respond inappropriately at one time or another suggests that a variety of responses are considered and a single response selected. The fact that an inappropriate response is usually somewhat similar to the correct one supports the notion of a feedback mechanism that is employed in the selection process. Aside from these rather gross statements, the details of the response programming process will have to remain unspecified.

Organization and Memory

A striking feature of human memory is that it involves organization. The idea of organization in memory is not new, having long been emphasized by Gestalt psychologists. As we saw in the introduction to this chapter, Gestalt psychologists were quick to object to associationistic conceptions of learning and memory, conceptions that emphasized the importance of contiguity and frequency of experience in strengthening associations. In contrast, Gestalt theory viewed contiguity and frequency as important *only* insofar as they permit the operation of organizational processes in memory. What is important in the organizational approach to learning and memory is the emphasis on the active mind of the learner. The learner is viewed as actively processing the information to be learned, not merely passively registering the information. It is assumed that the learner is trying to organize the information in some meaningful fashion, to devise strategies, to think, to plan, and to formulate hypotheses about the information being placed in memory (Ellis et al., in press). We will now examine some of the evidence for organization in memory.

Clustering in Free Recall

One type of evidence for organizational processes is *clustering* in free recall. Clustering refers to the fact that the order in which we recall words differs from the order in which they were presented. For example, Jenkins and Russell (1952) presented subjects a list of 48 words consisting of known associatively related pairs, such as "dog-cat;" the words were presented in scrambled order so that the members of the related pairs did not occur together during input. Even though the words were not presented together at input, the subjects tended to recall them in clusters of pairs. This describes one type of clustering in free recall known as *associative* clustering.

If the study list is composed of groups of words related to categories, then the order of recall will tend to reflect the category relationships. For example, Bousfield (1953) asked subjects to study a list of words representing several categories including birds, vehicles, and so on. The words were randomly mixed on the study list, yet, at recall, subjects tended to recall words that belonged to a given category in clusters. This type of clustering is called *category clustering* in free recall. A subject's recall protocol, which describes the order of output, might appear as follows: *bus, train, automobile, plane, robin, bluejay, sparrow, finch*, and so forth. Thus, a clustered sequence in recall is objectively defined in terms of consecutive items that are all members of a predetermined category.

Subjects who cluster more show better recall. But is it clustering that actually causes the improved recall? Here we are not so sure. Thompson, Hamlin, and Roenker (1972) conducted a study in which they had subjects recall categorized lists on three successive trials. They then divided their subjects into two groups of high and low clusterers and examined the relation between degree of clustering and amount of recall. Beginning with the first trial, high clusterers recalled substantially more words than did low clusterers, a finding which suggests, but does not prove, a causal relationship.

Subjective Organization

Humans will also impose their own organization on lists of words when no obvious or predetermined categories are present. This type of organization is called *subjective organization* and was first clearly demonstrated by Tulving (1962). He found that, in repeated free recall trials of a list of completely unrelated words, each subject gradually recalled the list in a progressively more consistent fashion. In other words, humans tend to impose their own organization on the material to be learned even though no evident organization is present. In this situation subjects do differ from each other in their idiosyncratic organization; the important thing is that a given subject becomes more consistent with respect to the subject's own order of recalling the words.

Natural Language Mediation

Another type of organizational strategy used by humans is called *natural language mediation*. Natural language mediation refers to the ability of people to use their own language as an aid in learning and remembering new information. This usually involves verbal elaboration of the to-be-learned material into a phrase or sentence (Montague, 1972). If asked to remember the words "cat" and "television," you may make up the sentence, "The cat slept contentedly in front of the television." Since the two words are placed in the con-

text of your language, the process is referred to as natural language mediation. The items to be learned might be less meaningful events such as nonsense materials. For example, suppose you had to remember the items DEY and LAZ; these could be thought of as "day" and "lazy" and further elaborated as the sentence, "This is a good day for being lazy."

But do natural language mediators really help us to remember? Montague, Adams, and Kiess (1966) conducted a convincing experiment on this question. They gave their subjects a single presentation of 25 pairs of syllables and asked them to report the natural language mediator used, if any. Twenty-four hours later, the subjects were asked to recall the pairs and the mediators used. The result of interest was the relation between the ability to recall the pairs and the ability to recall the mediators. They found that when the mediator was correctly recalled, 72 percent of the pairs were correctly recalled. In contrast, when the mediator was forgotten, only 2 percent of the pairs were recalled. Thus, the mediator clearly contributes to our ability to recall information.

Imagery

Our ability to use mental images is a powerful factor in learning and memory. You can intuitively recognize the significance of imagery as you try to answer the following question: "Where was the kitchen located in the house you lived in when you were eight years old?" You first try to recall the house you lived in when you were eight; this is an easy task if you have lived in only a few houses. Next you would try to recall a visual-spatial arrangement of the house and then locate the kitchen. Perhaps the kitchen overlooked a porch, which overlooked a backyard patio.

The use of imagery as a mnemonic device was known to the ancient Greeks and Romans (Yates, 1966), and is richly illustrated in a story reported by the Roman Emperor, Cicero. According to history, a Greek poet, Simonides, was commissioned to read a poem at a banquet in honor of a wealthy Roman nobleman. After reading the poem, Simonides was called outside the banquet hall by a messenger; in his absence the roof caved in killing all those at the banquet table, crushing them beyond recognition. Simonides was nevertheless able to identify each person for purposes of separate burial, because he was able to recall the place of each guest reclining at the table. The explanation of this unusual feat of memory is quite simple; Simonides formed a mental image of each person coupled with the place each person reclined so that a compound image of each person and place was stored in memory. This procedure is called the method of *loci* (location), because it requires the development of an image which is related to a specific location.

You can try the method of loci the next time you are in a small group of, say, ten or twelve people who are seated in specific locations. Fix your attention on each person and the specific seat the person occupies; visualize an image of the two together. Later, try to recall the location of each person by recalling the image as a cue for recalling each person. Similarly, you can apply the method of loci to remembering a grocery list. For instance, each item on the list, such as bread, milk, meat, lettuce, tomatoes, soft drinks, and so on, is visualized in connection with some spatial location. Imagine walking from your house to the grocery store so that you pass a number of objects. As you pass a grove of trees imagine that loaves of bread are hanging from the tree, that cartons of milk are on the porch, and so forth. Again, each object is associated in memory with a specific location.

There is no doubt that the effects of mental imagery in learning and memory are quite powerful. One explanation of these effects is that images may serve jointly with, or as an alternative to, verbal codes as a way of representing information in memory. If you have *both* image and verbal codes then the representation would be more powerful. This idea is known as the *dual-coding hypothesis* of memory (Paivio, 1971). The basic idea is that we have at least two coding systems, one dealing with verbal, linguistic information and the other dealing with nonverbal information.

Mnemonic Devices

Another way of organizing information for efficient storage in memory is through the use of *mnemonic devices*. Natural language mediators represent one type of mnemonic device. More generally, mnemonics refer to techniques or devices used to relate material being learned to some previous knowledge or structure (Norman, 1969). One of the most frequently used mnemonics is the rhyme. Rhymes are especially effective as mnemonic devices because if we make a mistake in recalling information, we will destroy the rhyme. Consider the rhyme used to remember when Columbus discovered America: "In 1492 Columbus sailed the ocean blue." The rhyme establishes an organization which is easy to remember; as long as you remember blue you can remember the digit 2 since no other final digit rhymes.

What makes a rhyme effective? Apparently what a rhyme does is to restrict the number of response alternatives you must search. Bower and Bolton (1969) have shown that rhymed pairs of words, such as *bat-hat,* are no easier to learn than pairs such as *bit-bin,* which are related by an assonance rule. The pairs are equally easy to learn because the first word restricts the search for the second word; that is, the subject knows that the first two letters of the words are identical. Thus, given *bit* your search is restricted to words beginning with *bi*.

Constructive Processes

So far, we have stressed the organizational character of human memory, noting a number of processes that attest to the importance of organization. Another type of organizational process refers to *constructive processes* in memory. In general, constructive processes mean that we somehow are able to integrate information in memory into a more or less coherent structure; this structure is sometimes called a *schema* (Bartlett, 1932). Once we have acquired a schema, it can determine whether or not a person will judge information such as sentences, prose passages, and so on, as having been previously encountered. In short, our ability to recognize or recall previously presented information is influenced by the schema which we have acquired. Thus, a schema is some kind of structural framework into which information may be integrated.

Bartlett's (1932) early work provides a concrete picture of schema formation. He presented subjects with prose passages of folktales and later they recalled the passages. Bartlett found that subjects tended to remember certain details, pass over others, and recombine or reconstruct information so as to come up with new interpretations of the passages.

In an important study, Bransford and Franks (1971) have shown that information will be recognized even though it is *not* presented explicitly. They gave subjects a list of simple sentences which, if combined, would represent a complex sentence containing several ideas. For example, the complex sentence, "The scared cat running from the barking dog jumped on the table," can be broken down into four simple ideas: (1) "The cat was scared," (2) "The cat was running from the dog;" (3) "The dog was barking;" (4) "The cat jumped on the table." During the study phase of the experiment, the subjects heard a list of sentences containing only one, two, or three of the ideas. For example, they would hear, "The cat was scared" (one idea), "The scared cat jumped on the table" (two ideas), and so on. Never did they hear four-idea sentences in the study phase.

During the recognition test, the subjects were presented several kinds of sentences. Some were actually presented in study (old sentences), some not heard during study but were consistent with the ideas presented (new sentences), and others were inconsistent with the ideas presented. During the test the subjects were presented with one-, two-, or three-idea sentences they actually heard, plus *four*-idea sentences they had not actually heard. Two things are noteworthy in this study: First, subjects were just as confident that they had heard the new sentences as the old sentences, and second, subjects were more confident that they had heard the four-idea sentences than the three-, two-, or one-idea sentences! These results are striking because they indicate that humans are quite willing to believe that they have heard something even when it was never actually said. It is this type of finding that lends strong support to the idea of constructive processes in memory (Cofer, 1973).

These findings have very important implications for practical affairs such as eyewitness testimony

and eyewitness identification. They raise serious doubts about the credibility of eyewitness testimony and should lead us to the realization that such testimony is not necessarily valid. Indeed, Loftus and Palmer (1974) have shown that eyewitness identification of automobile accidents is subject to constructive processes in the witnesses' memory. Witnesses will vary their reports of the extent of automobile damage based on the way questions are put to them. Use of phrases like, "How badly was the car smashed?" will lead to higher estimates of damage than if more neutral terms are used.

Perceptual Grouping

One of the important ideas of Gestalt theory was that the way things are grouped perceptually will determine the way they are eventually organized in memory. The basic idea is that discrete stimuli are not responded to as such but are organized in some form. Bower (1970) has summarized some recent studies of perceptual grouping where subjects are asked to memorize strings of digits. The digits are presented auditorially and broken up into groups by pauses. For instance, a subject might hear the sequence 365-21-843-7594, where the dashed lines represent pauses. Only when the digits are grouped identically on successive trials does the subject learn the sequence of digits. If the grouping structure varies on successive presentations, such as 36-5218-4375-94, subjects show no improvement in recall. This is the case where the series to be learned has no obvious or inherent "higher-order" structure.

In contrast, if the series to be learned does have a "higher-order" structure, then varied groupings actually facilitate recall (Ellis et al., 1975). They used word pairs such as BANCOW and CUPNET, and divided the pairs spatially into groups of letters such as BA NC OW. One group of subjects was presented the sequences with the identical grouping on successive presentations and the other saw different groupings on successive presentations. Subjects never saw the intact words, such as BAN or COW. Their task was to recall the letter string. Under these conditions, subjects in the varied input condition recalled substantially more word pairs than did the constant input group. These findings indicate that varied input allows the subject to organize more effectively the information for memory *if* there is some overall structure (meaningful words) to be detected. In effect, subjects will regroup the letters into words, which are much easier to remember, and are more likely to regroup if the letter sequences are varied. Apparently, varied input leads us to ignore the specific groupings and to "chunk" the letters into a word.

Semantic Memory

A final illustration of organizational processes in memory is seen in the area of *semantic memory*. In contrast to investigations of search processes using material learned in the laboratory, studies of semantic memory concern the search processes applied to our natural memories, that is, the memories that we all acquire naturally during our lifetimes. One issue in semantic memory is simply how humans store the enormous number of words they use in speaking and comprehending a language. More specifically, the questions are: What

is the structure of semantic memory, what kind of organization exists among words in memory, and how is this semantic knowledge used in various tasks?

One view, put forth by Quillian (1966) and recently elaborated by Collins and Loftus (1975), is that the various senses of particular words or phrases are best represented by nodes in a network. Such a network is illustrated in Figure 10-3. Each node, such as RED, is linked with other concept nodes that define the properties of the concept. Not all these links are equally important to the meaning of the concept and, as a consequence not all are equally accessible; that is, not all are used or thought about equally often. As Collins and Loftus point out, the concept "human" probably has links to "lungs," "hands," and "warts," but they are not equivalent as defining properties of "human."

Several tests have been made of these and other assumptions of this model of semantic memory. One such test is the inference task (Collins and Quillian, 1969) in which subjects are asked questions like, "Are canaries yellow?" or "Do canar-

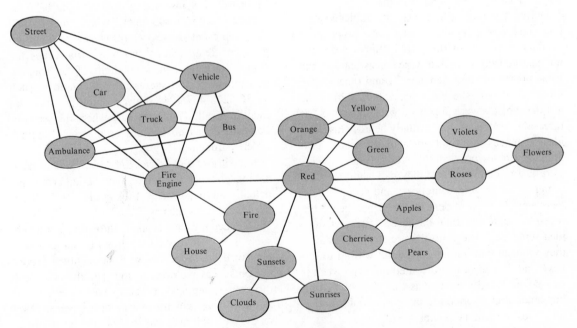

Fig. 10-3. A schematic representation of concept relatedness where a shorter line represents greater relatedness. (From Collins and Loftus, 1975)

ies fly?'' The time to respond either affirmatively or negatively is then considered to be a measure of the strength of the connection or the travel time between nodes. The search in memory for the answer to these questions requires activation of the nodes involved, such as CANARY and YELLOW, which then spreads throughout the network via the connecting links. If the activation from the two nodes eventually intersects, and if the path connecting the two fits the context of the question, an affirmative answer will be given. Under the assumption that the link between YELLOW and CANARY would be more accessible than that between FLY and CANARY, the reaction time to the first question should be faster than that to the second. This is precisely what happens.

Summary

In this section we have briefly examined some of the evidence which supports the view that memory is organized. In summary, our memory system is not simply a dumping ground of facts arranged in random fashion. We are constantly shifting, organizing, and reorganizing our memory representations. If indeed we are to store information effectively, it must be organized in some fashion (Ellis, 1978).

Forgetting

Forgetting is one of the most pervasive characteristics of human behavior. Is there any student who has not experienced the sudden panic of not remembering a fact in an examination that seemed to be firmly in mind the night before? Because the unpleasant or embarrassing results of forgetting are so noticeable, we usually fail to consider the more positive side of the phenomenon. For example, after a period of time has elapsed, we rarely recall experiences of pain or anguish at anywhere near their original intensity. And imagine how cluttered our minds would be if we retained all the trivia we learn during the course of our lifetime! Indeed, those rare subjects who have unusually good memories often encounter personal problems, because they do not know when to keep their mouths shut,

that is, to stop recalling information that may annoy or embarrass others.

Forgetting may be defined as the inability to recall learned material after an interval of time. Several things should be noted about this definition. First, this is an operational definition in that it specifies how to measure forgetting; it does not imply anything about the reasons why one forgets. Secondly, although the emphasis is on failure to recall learned material at the time of the test, this loss may not be permanent. A common experience is the inability to remember a name or a fact which can later be recalled with ease. Thirdly, in order for forgetting to occur, the material must have been learned in the first place in the same sense that one cannot lose something that one never possessed. Because forgetting is measured in terms of information lost, two estimates of retention are required: (a) the amount retained at the end of learning, and (b) the amount retained on a later test. The amount of forgetting is simply the difference between these two measures. This means that it is impossible to measure forgetting if one does not know how well the material was learned initially. Considerable difficulties in estimating the amount of forgetting frequently occur because of this.

Traditional Theories of Forgetting

Recurrent attempts have been made by psychologists to solve the riddle of forgetting. Many of these explanations have been variants of three traditional approaches to memory loss: decay theory, consolidation theory, and interference theory.

Decay Theory. Perhaps the oldest interpretation of forgetting is that memories decay over time. Plato likened memory to a wax tablet on which perceptions were impressed as a seal of a ring. We remember while the image lasts and forget when it is effaced. Other early thinkers believed that memory depended on movements or vibrations of body fluids and that forgetting occurred when these activities dampened and died out. The persistence to the present day of this conception of forgetting is evidence of its compelling nature. Although decay theories differ in their particulars, they have a common core. Memory traces are said to be laid down when a perceptual event occurs, and with the passage of time, this trace gradually fades. Forgetting proceeds as the trace decays.

One distinctive feature of this theory is the assertion that different kinds of activities that fill the retention interval do not differentially influence the rate of forgetting. Brown (1958), one of the leading advocates of decay theory, assumes that a trace begins to decay as soon as it is formed unless rehearsal is permitted. Rehearsal, he maintains, "is likely to counteract the effect of decay, either directly, or through the establishment of a new trace" (p. 14). If trace formation is followed by the presentation of other material, retention will decline because rehearsal is not permitted. In addition, other similar material may be confused with the trace material. This occurs because, as the trace decays, details or particular features of the trace are lost and the individual may not be able to distinguish one trace from another. Note, however, that confusion in recall is not regarded as the cause of forgetting but as the result of forgetting.

Although this theory has a certain intuitive appeal, it is difficult to test. Ideally, one would want to see if, in fact, memories do decay over time. But how can one vary *only* time? That is, how can one vary time without also varying the activities occupying the time interval? Unless this can be done, the time variable will necessarily be confounded with retention interval activity. Perhaps the closest thing to an "empty" time interval is an interval filled with sleep. Even though all activity does not cease during sleep, learning certainly must be nonexistent or at least at a minimum. One can therefore ask, "Do we forget while we are asleep?," and "Is there less forgetting during sleep than during an equal period of wakefulness?" Decay theory would answer "yes" to the first question, since memories are assumed to decay over time. The answer to the second question would be "no" since the time interval is the same. Sleep research shows that we do, in fact, forget while we are sleeping, but contrary to decay theory, we forget more when we are awake than when we are asleep. Interestingly, there is some suggestion that, while asleep, we forget more

while we are dreaming than while not (Ekstrand, 1972).

A second problem with decay theory concerns the assumption that trace decay involves a permanent loss of memory. Therefore, this theory cannot easily handle two phenomena. First, some memories may be reasonably permanent and seemingly decay little. We all have vivid recollections of some events that happened years ago; for example, you may recall in full detail your first day at school, and we are not likely to forget skills, such as bicycle riding, no matter how many years ago we were last astride one. Secondly, if memories are permanently lost, why are we occasionally able to remember things that we previously had been unable to recall? If you cannot remember the answer to a question during an exam, but suddenly remember the answer as you walk out of the room, how could your forgetting be due to a permanently decayed trace? In summary, then, memories may be lost through passive decay or disuse, but the evidence supporting this view is not compelling, and it cannot possibly account for all the phenomena of forgetting.

Consolidation Theory.   A second set of theories assumes that, given the right circumstances, memories may be fixated permanently and, for this reason, are called consolidation theories. Usually, a STM store of finite capacity is postulated, and forgetting is said to occur when additional material enters the store and either displaces an item in the store or disrupts the on-going process. Theories falling into this category generally do not discuss the relationship between the displaced items and the material which causes the displacement; thus, neither meaningful similarity nor formal similarity are considered to be variables of importance. Because memory may be lasting, the STM store must be supplemented by a more permanent component, the LTM store; these theories were discussed earlier in the context of dual store models of memory. Hebb (1949), for example, stated that if perseveration of a memory trace is allowed to continue uninterrupted for a sufficient length of time, or if the trace is repeatedly aroused, then structural changes take place in the brain and the trace becomes a permanent one. If the activity trace is disrupted, however, the necessary structural changes will not occur and the memory trace will not last. Although consolidation and decay could both occur, the assumed processes involved are quite different. Decay theory suggests that memories become weaker or decay as a function of time, whereas consolidation theory suggests that memory traces are fixated as a function of time.

Tests of this theory, for the most part, have been carried out in the animal laboratory where there has been an attempt to disrupt the consolidation of memory traces through the use of drugs or electroconvulsive shock (ECS). Nevertheless, some comparable work has also been done on people who are undergoing shock therapy (Cronholm, 1969). At least two kinds of memory disturbances occur after ECS. First, patients experience anterograde amnesia, which is the inability to retain information learned after the shock. Secondly, the patients suffer from retrograde amnesia; that is, they have difficulty recalling information learned just prior to the treatment. Similar retrograde effects occur as a result of concussion. These data suggest that there is a period of time after learning during which memory traces are particularly labile. If brain trauma occurs while consolidation is in progress, forgetting will occur.

Studies using ECS with humans are obviously difficult to perform, and with the decline in the use of this kind of therapy, they are quite few in number. To get around these problems, one group of researchers devised a procedure which they argue is an analogue to ECS (Ellis et al., 1971). They presented lists of fifteen line drawings to college students for free recall. On control trials, all of the pictures were of familiar objects, such as a hat, a train, and so on. On experimental trials, one critical item was inserted in the middle of the list. This critical item was a picture of a nude of either sex that had been obtained from a sunbathing magazine. The question was whether a nude suddenly appearing in the middle of a psychological experiment would also produce forgetting. As you might have guessed, it does. In comparison with recall of items on the control lists, there was "retrograde amnesia" for the two items immediately preceding

the nude and "anterograde amnesia" for the six items following the nude.

In summary, there are data that have been interpreted as support of consolidation theory, but one must be cautious in drawing conclusions because of the relative lack of human experimentation on the issue.

Interference Theory. Interference theory, which was alluded to in the earlier discussion of STM and LTM, has been a strong alternative to decay and consolidation interpretations of forgetting. Again, there are several variants of this theory, but all maintain that forgetting occurs because other material that we learn interferes with the recall of the to-be-remembered information. The more similar the interfering information is to the to-be-remembered information, the more interference it will provide. In its strongest form, this theory also suggests that information, once learned, is a permanent part of the organism. Let us see how this theory works.

There are two main sources of interference: information learned before and information learned after the test material. These two sources have been distinguished both experimentally and conceptually.

If the interference stems from prior learned material, it is said to proactively interfere with recall and is studied by means of a proactive interference (PI) paradigm. A schematic for this paradigm is:

Group	Phase 1	Phase 2	Phase 3
Experimental	Learn A	Learn B	Recall B
Control	Rest	Learn B	Recall B

The experimental and control groups differ in their treatment during Phase 1; the experimental group learns Task A while the control group rests or learns material that is unrelated to B. Both groups then learn Task B. If, in the later test of Task B, control subjects recall more than experimental subjects, we can conclude that learning Task A has had a detrimental effect on the later recall of Task B or, in other words, proactive interference has occurred.

The Brown-Peterson paradigm provides one of the most striking demonstrations of the interfering effects of prior learned material. A trial in this paradigm is as follows: (a) a ready signal is presented for 2 sec; (b) three words are presented for 1.5 sec, and the subject is asked to read them aloud; (c) a three-digit number then appears for 15 sec; the subject is told to count backwards from this number by 3s as fast as possible; (d) finally, a question mark is presented for 10 sec, during which time the subject is to recall the three words if possible. Thus, one has only to remember a few words for 15 sec, but rehearsal is prevented during the retention interval. Suppose that the words on the first test are CAMEL MULE TIGER and that the words on Tests 2 and 3 are also animal names. Performance on the first test is a measure of recall when there have been no prior interfering items in the experimental context. On the second test, however, the three words from Test 1 provide interference and there are six interfering items by Test 3. Typically, recall on Test 1 is nearly perfect. On later tests, however, the subjects have greater and greater difficulty in remembering the items. This rapid drop in recall has been attributed to a buildup of PI over tests. It has also been shown that one can get rid of the interference by simply presenting items from another category, say foods. Recall then increases to almost the same level that it was on the first test. This phenomenon is known as release from PI (Wickens, 1970).

Interference can also be produced by material that has been learned subsequent to the acquisition of the test material. In this case, we say that retroactive interference (RI) has occurred. This paradigm may be diagrammed as:

Group	Phase 1	Phase 2	Phase 3
Experimental	Learn A	Learn B	Recall A
Control	Learn A	Rest	Recall A

Here the experimental and control groups are identical in Phase 1 but differ in their treatment during Phase 2, with the experimental condition learning a second task that is generally similar to Task A and the control condition either resting or learning a second task that is quite distinct from Task A. If the control subjects recall more of Task A in the test than experimental subjects, it can be concluded that learning Task B had a detrimental effect on recall of Task A; that is, retroactive interference has been produced.

Retroactive interference can be very reliably produced in the laboratory. For example, the sleep studies mentioned in the discussion of decay theory showed that a period of wakefulness following learning resulted in more forgetting than an equivalent period of sleep. The assumption, of course, is that the learning that constantly goes on when one is alert interferes with recall.

Cue vs. Trace Dependent Forgetting

In the discussion of memory processes, encoding, storage, and retrieval mechanisms have been described in some detail. These processes are obviously just as important to forgetting as they are to learning. Explicit acknowledgement of this fact was made by Tulving and Madigan (1970) in their distinction between trace-dependent and cue-dependent forgetting. Certainly theories that describe memory loss in terms of decay or disruption are ones that postulate trace-dependent mechanisms of forgetting. It is possible, however, that forgetting is not due solely, or even primarily, to changes in memory traces. Memory loss can also occur because retrieval cues at the time of a retention test are inadequate for the recovery of the information. Since the information was recoverable immediately after learning, either the quality of retrieval cues has degenerated or their quantity has been reduced over the retention interval. Of course, to say that forgetting occurs because of a change in or loss of retrieval cues is, in a sense, unsatisfactory because it leaves us with another question: Why do we forget our retrieval cues? Nevertheless, this approach to the problem of forgetting has produced some helpful insights into the process.

Research on cue-dependent forgetting has consistently shown that memory depends on the similarity between how one encodes information during learning and how one encodes it during the test. The experiment of Light and Carter-Sobell (1970) is a good example of the phenomenon. They presented college students a series of sentences with adjective-noun phrases underlined. The adjectives were chosen to bias the meaning of the noun, for example SLICED HAM. On a later recognition test, adjective-noun phrases were again presented, and the task was to recognize whether or not the noun had been presented before. The experimental manipulation was the relationship between the adjective present during the test and the one present during learning. The adjective-noun phrase could be identical (SLICED HAM), have a similar meaning (SMOKED HAM), or have a different meaning (RADIO HAM). As expected, noun recognition was highest with the same adjective, intermediate with the similar adjective, and lowest with the dissimilar adjective. Since one can assume that the memory trace of the noun was identical in all cases, data such as these provide convincing evidence that some forgetting depends on the cue used for retrieval.

Models of Memory

It may seem to the reader that the concept of memory has been considerably advanced and refined since the time of the Greeks. Although psychologists may disagree about how much progress in understanding has been made, the greatest progress has been the realization that the workings of the mind can be described in some detail. Our minds are not the "black boxes" that the early behavioristic psychologists once thought they were. The behaviorist's approach to understanding memory was an attempt to arrive at a working description of the mind's functions through the use of a particular methodology. Stimuli go in, responses come out, and the task of the memory psychologist is to record which responses are associated to which stimuli and then to describe the relationship. The behaviorist shows little concern with the nature of the processes that are going on inside our black-box memories. They regard their task as one simply of specifying "input-output" relations, which are all that is necessary to specify and predict behavior; they also regard the description of the functioning of the various brain mechanisms as too microscopic to be of any psychological utility.

Clearly, behavioristic approaches are capable of describing behavior, but they appear less useful in the understanding of the complex processes of memory and thought. Nevertheless, at least one point in the behaviorist philosophy is worth reem-

phasizing. Attempts to understand human memory at a minute physiological level are perhaps too ambitious a task and are analogous to trying to understand the workings of a computer at the level of electron flow. Learning how a computer operates first requires an understanding of the machine's gross functions. Once these processes are understood, then a detailed knowledge of its circuitry is of considerable utility. The same is probably the case with human memory. It may be best to characterize the mechanisms and processes of memory before there is an attempt to understand the minute details of the system. Hopefully, this logic will help to place the description of models of memory that follow in its proper perspective.

The information processing approach to memory is basically a means of theorizing about the workings of the mind and of illuminating the mechanisms that underly perception, memory, and thought. Both of the memory models that we will discuss attempt to characterize the fate of information in terms of the various transformation mechanisms that handle it. The first of these models is the traditional "Buffer" model of Atkinson and Shiffrin (1968). The second model is called HAM, which stands for *Human Associative Memory*. HAM is representative of many of the more recent "propositional" memory models and has been proposed by Anderson and Bower (1973).

The Buffer Model

The Buffer model (Atkinson and Shiffrin, 1968) has been discussed throughout this chapter, since it is characteristic of many models of memory. Now we will describe its features in greater detail (as outlined in Figure 10-4 on p. 352). The memory system includes three storage systems: the sensory register, the short-term store, and the long-term store. The name "Buffer model" comes from the fact that information is maintained in an active state in the short-term store prior to use of storage in long-term memory. Therefore, the short-term store serves as a "buffer" between the sensory register and the long-term store.

The buffer model is composed of two basic features, *structural components* and *control processes*. The structural components are the permanent

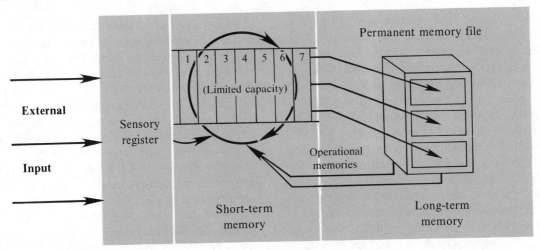

Fig. 10-4. The Buffer Model of Atkinson and Shiffrin: Sensory register, working memory (short-term) with rehearsal loop, long-term memory file. Note the limited capacity (7 unit maximum) working memory, the transfer of information from working memory into the long-term file, and the operationalized information from the long-term file back into the working memory.

features of the model (the sensory register, the short-term store, and the long-term store). In contrast, the control processes are transient and flexible and are under the control of the individual. As we mentioned earlier, when information enters the system, it is processed differently by each of the structural components. This transformation process is depicted in Figure 10-4. External information, which is almost always maintained in an image-like state, is immediately stored in the sensory register; those portions of the image that we do not attend to are lost from the register.

The second component of the system is the short-term store, which Atkinson and Shiffrin call "working memory." Working memory has two functions. One is to act as a buffer between the sensory register and long-term memory. Anything that gets through the sensory register must be rehearsed prior to storage in long-term memory; if this information is not rehearsed, it is lost. A second function of working memory is to accommodate the "operationalized" memories from the long-term store. Information in working memory is subject to decay, as well as to displacement from new information that enters the store from either the sensory register or the long-term store. An analogy may be useful here.

The buffer may be regarded as a private mail service with a limited number of mail boxes (approximately seven). Letters enter the mail service, fill up the boxes, and are processed for filing or action. That is, some of the letters may be responded to immediately, while others are filed away for further consideration. Since the mail service only has seven mail slots it can only handle seven letters for processing at one time. Which of the letters is processed first is completely under the control of the secretary; however, the secretary must work quickly since letters are continually entering the mail service, and these letters may displace the ones that are already there. The arrow from the sensory register to the short-term store indicates receipt of a new letter into the mail service. If the letters that are in the mail service have not been processed, they may be pushed from their slots upon receipt of the new letter. If the old letters are more important than the new letter, the latter may never gain entry into the mail service until the old letters are processed. The arrows going from the short-term store to the long-term store indicate that the secretary has prepared some of the letters for permanent filing. This information must be organized within the file cabinet and may be extracted later for updating or action. Once filed in the permanent store, the letter is in an inactive state. However, if the letter is extracted for further processing later, it is placed into the mail service and updated there. Depending on the extent of the additional processing, the letter may prohibit any new letters from entering the mail service until the update is completed. Although this analogy is oversimplified, it does serve to emphasize a number of points. First of all, our working memories are limited-capacity systems and processing at full capacity is difficult. Second, the processing of information in working memory largely determines which portions of the external world eventually become part of our permanent memories. Finally, the contents of working memory come from either the sensory register or the long-term store, and which information is to be processed is under the control of the individual.

Control processes regulate the flow of information from the sensory register to the short-term store and from short-term to long-term memory. In the sensory register, control processes function to select information for transfer to STM. The control processes in STM are concerned with rehearsal of information, coding, and the search and retrieval of the retained information. Organizational processes are the primary mechanisms of control in long-term memory. Since we have discussed each of these processes in detail earlier, we will not elaborate on them here.

The buffer model is one of the best developed models of memory. Its major limitation is a lack of specificity as to the workings of the various components, such as the organization or representation of information in long-term memory. In recent years, however, a number of models have appeared that provide a more detailed view of memory. One such model is the *Human Associative Memory* model of Anderson and Bower (1973).

Human Associative Memory (HAM)

The human associative memory model of Anderson and Bower is perhaps the most complete representation of memory available today. The basic unit of the model is the "proposition," which is a meaningful or grammatical connective relation between encoded informational units (called

"nodes") that are stored in long-term memory. In other words, all objects, events, and relationships are represented in memory according to a node that corresponds to that bit of information, and the proposition serves to add meaning and structure to this mass of information. The basic propositionalized memory structure consists of a simple relationship between two facts; however, the proposition can also be used to connect simple structures to form complex structures with the addition of higher-order propositions. The idea of simple and complex thought has been around since the time of John Locke, and the HAM model has revitalized the idea with the proposition serving as the integrative bond between stored information in memory. The model currently functions as a highly sophisticated computer program that is capable of duplicating human performance in a variety of learning tasks.

Components of HAM. The basic components of HAM's memory are outlined in Figure 10-5. External information enters the system through visual and auditory sensors and is stored in visual and au-

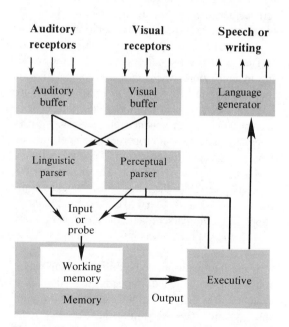

Fig. 10-5. Human associative memory (HAM) model of Anderson and Bower. (From Anderson and Bower, 1973)

ditory buffers. Each of these buffers is a limited-capacity system, and once information enters the buffer it is immediately transformed according to its relevant features prior to decay. This means that once the information is in the buffers, it is closely scrutinized by perceptual and linguistic parsers. The function of the parsers is to analyze the information and to produce a meaningful description for further processing in working memory. The function of the linguistic parser is to analyze symbolic information. This simply means that the linguistic parser translates linguistic or verbal descriptions into symbolic or conceptual statements. On the other hand, the perceptual parser is concerned with a physical description of the information in the buffer. For example, consider learning the following phrase, "Mick Jagger sings." The linguistic parser would probably report the fact that "a major rock star utters musical phrases" to the working memory. The perceptual parser would probably describe the same sentence as the object "sings" occurs to the right of the object "Jagger," which occurs to the right of the object "Mick." In each case, the descriptions of the phrase would be expressed in a propositional format. The basic difference between the two descriptions would be the nature of the propositions that relate the elements of the sentence.

The outputs of the parsers are sent to the working memory store where they are compared with the information in long-term memory. If the purpose of the task is to memorize the phrase, it is recorded in the permanent store according to its linguistic and physical properties. If the purpose is to recognize the phrase as "old" or "new," then a "Match" process is invoked. The match process involves a search of the long-term store and a comparison of what is found with the input that is supplied by the parsers. The match process is the way that HAM recognizes information as "old" or "new."

If the information is to be utilized in any way it must first be matched (recognized). After it is matched, it is then sent to the executive portion of the system. The executive has control over processing in the system and oversees the fate of the output of the working memory. The executive

may direct further scan of long-term memory or additional scanning by the parsers. If a response to the input is required, the executive may activate the language generator which will provide the appropriate response. This is the final stage of information processing and is used to output answers to questions or to request further information about the working memory output. The language generator, like so many decoding devices, is left only loosely described.

Propositional Memory Structures. Information in HAM's memory is stored in an encoded form. HAM represents each bit of information as a memory node and these nodes are connected into binary graph structures as presented in Figure 10-6. This structure corresponds to the sentence "In the book the knight slayed the dragon." The binary graph structure that represents the sentence has two parts, a context subtree and a fact subtree. The context portion of the sentence is labeled with a C and the fact portion is labeled with an F. Each of the numbers represents a subdivision of the proposition, and remaining capital letters represent certain meaningful relations that exist among the components of the sentence. Articles such as "A" and "the" are not maintained in the graph structure.

The sentence "In the book the knight slayed the dragon" is represented by a single node, 1, which stands for the total proposition. A second node, 2, stands for the context of the event, which is further subdivided into the location (L) and time (T) where the event occurred. Similarly, the fact node, 3, branches into a subject (S) node and a predicate, 4, which is further subdivided as a relation (R) and an object of the relation (O). This completes the binary divisions. The elements of the sentence (ϵ) are already stored in memory and are simply related into a meaningful expression by the propositional structure (Anderson and Bower, p. 139).

The propositional memory model of Anderson and Bower has received a great deal of recent interest, popularity, and predictive success. As a computer program, the model seems to mimic human performance with considerable accuracy; to date, HAM stands as the most complete conceptualization of memory available.

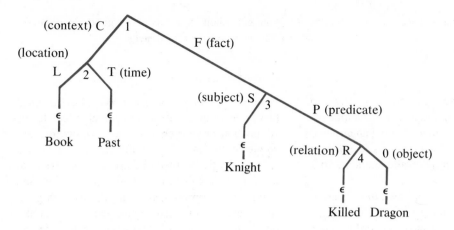

Fig. 10-6.
Propositional memory structure used in the HAM model. (From Anderson and Bower, 1973)

Human Learning

So far, we have described the major features of human memory as an information processing system. We have stressed this approach to problems in memory, because it has been the one adopted by most current researchers in this area. However, we will now turn briefly to a few, more traditional topics in human learning. These include concept learning, motor skills learning, perceptual learning, and transfer of training.

Concept Learning

Fortunately, we have the ability to generalize from specific situations and thus are able to abstract general ideas about events in our environment. Indeed, learning would be a burdensome affair if we have to learn each new situation from "scratch;" this would clearly be the case if we "rote" learned every new task. The fact that we can generalize from specific instances and form concepts is an important mental process. Concept learning refers to any activity in which we learn to appropriately categorize or classify events in accord with some rule. The fact that a young child learns the simple concept of "redness" means that he can classify a variety of objects, sorting out those that are red. Similarly, a child learning the concept of "dog"

learns to classify animals on the basis of particular features such as having four legs, a coat of hair, and being within some range of size and shape. Here we deal with a more complex concept which has multiple features. In either instance, the child must learn to *abstract* the relevant features in order to acquire the concept. If, for example, the child calls all four-legged animals "dogs," then he obviously has not learned the concept because he has failed to abstract the relevant features.

But what is a concept itself? A concept is the basis on which we appropriately classify events. More specifically, a concept refers to a set of features shared by various events which are connected by some rule. For instance, the concept of "red barn" refers to objects that are both red and barns; we call this a conjunctive concept because the two features must occur together. Similarly, the concept "registered voter" refers to someone residing in a particular area for some minimum time, being over eighteen, and in previous years in some places, a taxpayer. Concepts vary along a dimension ranging from concrete to very abstract. The concept "red barn" is very concrete; so are "ten-speed bicycles," "vegetables," "houses," and so on. In contrast, concepts like "justice," and "democracy" are instances of abstract concepts. Typically, abstract concepts are more difficult to learn because many more features must be abstracted.

The factors affecting concept learning will be described in Chapter 11.

Motor Skills Learning

Much of our learning, such as learning to drive, to play sports, and to repair and maintain equipment, involves motor skills learning. Piloting an airplane is an obvious example. This involves learning to carefully manipulate controls while attending to a variety of stimuli.

Motor skills learning is any learning situation which requires us to make a sequence of precise motor responses. Where we have to coordinate our motor responses with what we see or hear, we sometimes refer to the activity as perceptual-motor skills learning. Driving is an obvious example because you must learn to coordinate what you see and hear with your motor responses. You have to continuously adjust your behavior in accord with continuously changing input. You must slow down, accelerate, brake rapidly, turn, and so on, to a variety of events that appear in your visual field such as intersections, stop signs, speed regulations, and such. Similarly, most athletic skills such as swimming, tennis, skiing, basketball, and football require that you adjust your responses in accord to various stimulus conditions.

In the laboratory, motor skills are studied in a variety of ways. Typically two types of tasks are studied: those that consist of relatively discrete responses and those that are essentially continuous. Running, jogging, swimming are essentially continuous responses; kicking a football or shooting a basket are essentially discrete responses.

The most important factor influencing skill learning is feedback. Feedback can be of two kinds. One type is called *extrinsic feedback,* in which you are told by someone else how you are performing, or you may be told by a device. For instance, the "score" displayed by a pinball machine is an instance of extrinsic feedback. Similarly, being told "right" or "wrong" is an instance of extrinsic feedback. In contrast, feedback can be *intrinsic,* which is feedback we directly receive from our own body movements. The "feel" you get when you serve a tennis ball, or the feeling you get when you execute a good dive are instances of intrinsic feedback.

Perceptual Learning

Another type of learning is *perceptual learning,* that is, learning to attend and perceive features of stimulation in your environment. An obvious example is the task of proofreading. The skilled proofreader has learned to detect a great variety of errors including those of spelling, punctuation, and grammar. The proofreader can do this with great speed and accuracy, something the novice cannot do. Similarly, the skilled winetaster can make fine discriminations that are difficult or impossible for the novice. The fact that we do improve in our perceptions of the world is what is meant by perceptual learning. We can, of course, become worse as well.

One important type of perceptual learning is seen in the search task. Imagine, for a moment, trying to locate a friend at a busy airport terminal. You find yourself rapidly scanning a large number of unfamiliar faces looking for your friend. Similarly, scanning the want ads or looking for your car in a huge parking lot are other instances of searching behaviors.

Our ability to search for target stimuli can be improved with practice. In laboratory studies of search behavior, subjects show enormous improvement in searching for letter targets simply as the result of sustained practice. What apparently happens is that we learn to reduce the search down to a few critical features of the stimuli and thus need less time to scan the stimuli. The study of perceptual learning is an area that is receiving increasing attention by psychologists (Gibson, 1969).

Transfer of Training

As a final topic in learning, we turn to transfer of training. Transfer refers to the influence of prior learning on performance in a subsequent task. The effects of transfer may be positive where prior learning is seen to aid new learning. In contrast, negative transfer occurs when prior learning interferes with new learning. Situations where there is no effect of prior learning define zero transfer.

We frequently see instances of positive transfer when the learner first masters an easier task and then moves on to a more difficult one. For instance, young children are first taught to discriminate the easy letters of the alphabet before learning the more difficult ones such as "b" and "d." Similarly, modern training procedures in skiing use this principle. The method used in many ski schools is the graduated-length method (GLM) which is based on the principle of transfer from an easy to a more difficult task. The beginning skier starts out with a pair of short skis until the basics are learned. Once the skier has gained some degree of stability on the slopes, that skier is then advanced to a longer set of skis. This procedure is continued until the skier is eventually fitted with a set of skis appropriate for height and weight. The GLM method has been shown to facilitate learning for the beginner and has been adopted by many instructors throughout Europe and North America.

In contrast, negative transfer most frequently occurs when we must learn to make new responses which are incompatible with old ones, or when we must learn to make new responses to old stimuli. For instance, learning to play squash can seriously interfere with your tennis game, because squash requires that you move your wrist whereas tennis requires that you keep a stiff wrist. In this instance, incompatible responses are required. To illustrate the second situation, negative transfer can easily occur if you have to drive on the left-hand side of the road after driving on the right. American visitors to England frequently report this kind of interference (Ellis, 1965).

Summary

In this chapter, we have examined human memory and learning as the processing of information. Environmental stimuli enter the sensory registers of the memory system. Selected information may be further processed by short-term memory, and some information may be further processed for long-term storage. The distinction between the three stores was seen as one of convenience, as current evidence indicates that memory can be regarded as a single system, with capacity differences viewed as differences in levels of processing. Memory was seen as a three-stage process involving encoding, storage, and retrieval. Of major importance were the topics of memory organization and forgetting. The Buffer and HAM models of memory were examined in some detail as representative instances of integrative formulations of memory. Finally, several selected topics in human learning were examined.

Glossary

Attention: Process of focusing selectively on some parts of the environment while ignoring other features.

Buffer model: An information processing model of memory which assumes that information is held in an active state in the rehearsal buffer prior to being transferred to the long-term store.

Clustering: The tendency to organize or group items of information during recall in some sequence which is based on categories or mutual associates.

Constructive processes: The tendency of humans to construct or reconstruct information in memory, altering the information to make it more consistent with some schema.

Encoding: Process by which information in the form of environmental energy is transformed into some state suitable for storage.

Forgetting: Loss of ability to recall information after some interval of time.

Imagery: Process by which we represent information in some perceptual-sensory mode.

Levels of processing: A framework for viewing memory in which information placed in memory is a function of the depth at which the information is processed.

Long-term memory: Relatively permanent portion of the memory system.

Memory codes: The stored representation of some event in memory.

Mnemonic devices: Ways for efficiently organizing information for efficient storage in memory. Rhymes are an example.

Retrieval: Process of accessing information stored in memory.

Short-term memory: A limited-capacity system of memory in which items must be processed in some way in order to become more stable or permanent.

Semantic memory: Our memories of linguistic events.

Working memory: An active system of memory where information is assembled and organized prior to recall.

Suggested Readings

Adams, J. A. *Learning and Memory*. Homewood: Dorsey, 1976.

Anderson, J. R., and Bower, G. H. *Human Associative Memory*. Washington, D.C.: Winston, 1973.

Cofer, C. N. (ed.) *The Structure of Human Memory*. San Francisco: W. H. Freeman, 1975.

Crowder, R. G. *Principles of Learning and Memory*. Hinsdale: Erlbaum Assoc., 1976.

Ellis, H. C. *Fundamentals of Human Learning, Memory, and Cognition*. Dubuque: Wm. C. Brown, 1978.

Horton, D. L., and Turnage, T. W. *Human Learning*. Englewood Cliffs: Prentice-Hall, 1976.

Houston, J. P. *Fundamentals of Learning*. New York: Academic Press, 1976.

Hulse, S. H., Deese, J., and Egeth, H. *The Psychology of Learning*. New York: McGraw-Hill Book Company, 1975.

Marx, M. H. and Bunch, M. E. (eds.) *Foundations and Applications of Learning*. New York: Macmillan, 1977.

Cognition—Problem Solving, Concept Formation, Language

Marcia Z. Lippman

Introduction

One of the major tasks of the life long developmental process is that of gaining knowledge about our world. The adaptiveness of our interactions with the environment are directly related to the degree to which our conceptualizations of reality correspond with reality. Our map of reality is likely to lack correspondence if we do not have enough information, if we fail to attend to the relevant attributes, or if we do not make correct inferences on the basis of the information we have. The area of psychology called *cognition* is concerned with the ways in which knowledge about the world we live in is gathered, stored, retrieved, and utilized. Although the processes are numerous—sensation, perception, retention, recall, transfer, memory, language, concept formation, problem solving, and so on, we shall focus on only the latter three in this chapter. It should be kept in mind that these processes are interdependent; it is only for the purposes of exposition that they become separated. It would be difficult to think about or even correctly label a dog, for example, if we had never encountered a dog or a description of a dog by direct sensory experience. Likewise, the direct encounter would be of little value if we had no means of representing prior experience in memory.

Problem Solving

If a child's toy rolls under the couch and cannot be reached even by daddy's long arm, we would say that they have a problem—one of retrieving the child's toy before the child dissolves into a puddle of tears. This problem situation, like others, is characterized by the fact that (a) there is a goal to be attained, in this case two pronged, that of retrieving the toy and calming the child; (b) the initial attempts to solve the problem were unsuccessful in that neither the child nor the father could simply reach out for the ball; and (c) there are two or more possible courses of action. The father could try to pull the toy toward him using a broom or some other arm-extending tool or he could move the couch away from the wall to allow space for him to go behind it. The more usual response of simply walking over to an object and picking it up will not work in this case.

Three Views

There are three main views as to how problem solutions are reached. Each view emphasizes an aspect of problem solving and has typically confined its research efforts to a small subset of problem types. The result is that there is no one viewpoint that has systematically attempted to deal with the many types of problem situations that may be encountered. Each approach offers something to the understanding of problem solving, however.

Associative. The associative view of psychology (which includes Behaviorism) represents an attempt to apply the set of well-established principles of classical and instrumental conditioning to all aspects of behavior, including problem solving. See Chapter 2 for a general presentation of Behaviorism, and Chapter 9 for a review of these principles. One of the primary notions that associative psychologists apply in explaining problem solving is that of the response hierarchy. Particular responses become strongly associated with particular stimuli because of repeated pairings in the past or because the response has resulted in reinforcement. When the same stimulus or one similar is encountered later, it first elicits the response that has been most frequently associated or reinforced previously in that context. That response is said to have high response strength. For example, if you were asked to give the first word you could think of in response to the stimulus word *man,* you would most likely say *woman,* because it has been previously associated with man more frequently than other words. Suppose you were asked to continue giving words that *man* makes you think of. By the time you got to the fifteenth one and said, perhaps, *tree,* the response would be one that had been previously associated with *man* many fewer times than *woman, work, strong, tall, bald,* or *baseball.* When an individual's prior learning history is known, responses to a particular stimulus may be ordered in terms of their strength (or likelihood of occurring) from high to low.

Applying the notion of response hierarchy to problem solving, a problem is said to exist when the high strength responses resulting from an individual's prior learning history are inappropriate to a situation. If an object has previously been used in a particular way, for example, a nutcracker for breaking open nuts, using it to open a tight jar lid might not immediately occur to a ten-year-old. The problem would exist until that lower probability response had been aroused (or a stronger person came along to help).

Since problem solving involves thinking, an unobservable process, early behaviorists declared that problem solving was out of the perview of psychology. Later, thinking and problem solving were studied, but thinking was viewed as simply attenuated muscular activity, usually involving the vocal apparatus. In other words, it was assumed that minute unobservable muscular reactions in the arms and legs resulting from thinking about mowing the lawn were, in fact, thought. This emphasis on peripheral processes (muscular movements) as the medium of thought gave way to an emphasis on more central processes (central nervous system—brain). It was assumed that the processes mediating between the stimulus and response need not necessarily be accompanied by motor evidence of behavior, but are described as internalized representations of an overt response. In humans, it is assumed that these internal responses are often in the form of covert verbalizations. Such internalized responses are assumed to serve as a link between the stimulus situation and the final response, representing the working of the "mind."

The father's arrival at a solution to the child's problem of a ball lost under the couch might be conceptualized as follows. After unsuccessfully attempting to reach the ball, the father scans the room for an arm-extender. He sees a broom and notices the long handle. The handle (stimulus) elicits the internal response, stick or pole (mediator) which, in turn, triggers the correct response of reaching for the toy with the broom handle (response). Poles have previously been successful in retrieving objects beyond reach. Solution was reached when the father gave up the high strength response of reaching with only his arm, and resorted to the lower strength response (lower probability response to *object under couch* but not *pole*) of using the pole.

Gestalt. According to Gestalt theory, problems are encountered because people incorrectly perceive some situations. Incorrect perception of a situation occurs when a response is called for that is unusual in a given context. The child's problem in obtaining the toy exists because, the child perceives the couch as a part of a stationary configuration of furniture. That is, the couch is perceived as part of an organized whole or arrangement of furniture. Alternately, the problem could be conceptualized as existing because the child perceives brooms only as one set of tools used for cleaning. Gestalt theory maintains that solution of a problem requires an individual to reorganize his perception of a situation. This reorganization may be a change in a pattern (location of couch) or involve a change in perceived function of an object (change in perception of broom from cleaning tool to arm-extender). See Chapters 2 and 12 for a more complete presentation of Gestalt theory.

Information Processing. The information processing approach attempts to specify in considerably more detail than the associative approach the processes involved in problem solution. According to the information processing approach, a problem exists when there are a variety of alternative responses that could be made. Primary interest is to discover what procedures or strategies individuals use in selecting among those alternatives. The theorist attempts to write a step-by-step program of what an individual must do to arrive at a particular solution. Often these programs are then submitted to the computer to demonstrate that the hypothesized steps do in fact lead to a particular outcome. The computer, guided by the program, can simulate a variety of behavioral processes to the extent that it can make the decisions required in a game of chess or checkers. It is assumed that the steps outlined in the program *may* be a good model of the steps followed in the decision-making processes involved in problem solution by people. Although the information processing approach is often equated with computer simulation, many theorists have borrowed assumptions, concepts, and vocabulary from the computer analogy but apply them directly to human data rather than writing programs.

Types of Problems and Factors Affecting Performance

Several types of problems have been used by researchers in their attempts to understand the problem solving process. Generally, the problems have a single correct solution that is known to the experimenter. The subjects are infrequently requested to deal with problem situations that may have several possible situations or for which there is no known solution, requiring creative efforts. Typically the problem-solving process itself is studied indirectly. Experimenters look at what factors influence solution time in an attempt to draw inferences about the steps. These variables include the organization of the materials, instructions, hints, verbal labels, size of problem, previous experience, and solution familiarity.

Insight Problems. A Gestalt psychologist, Wolfgang Kohler (1925), reported an example of what he termed *insight* in the ape Sultan. Presented with what is now known as the two-stick problem, Sultan was faced with the problem of reaching a banana on the other side of the cage bars. In the cage with him were two hollow bamboo sticks which could be fitted together. Neither stick alone was long enough to reach the banana as Sultan discovered after several attempts. It was not until he was sitting on a box seemingly idly playing with the two sticks that he arrived at the solution. By chance, the two sticks were lined up in such a way that with only a push the smaller was inside the larger creating a single, long pole. This aspect of the solution was arrived at by trial and error, but the use of the newly formed tool to collect the banana was immediate. Sultan was described as jumping up and running to the bars to draw the banana towards him. Kohler suggested that the sudden shift in behavior was due to a change in perspective, or reorganization of the elements of the situation. The emphasis of the Gestalt explanation of the animal's solution on reformulation of the problem contrasts with the emphasis placed on overt trial and error in reaching solution by one associative psychologist, Thorndike. The Gestalt theorist focuses on the "ah-ha" experience of insight rather than the past experience (trial and error behavior) which leads to the correct response. It is certainly true that during observation of a particular period of the solution process, no reliance on overt trial and error will be evident. Does that necessarily imply that the correct response was not arrived at, at some prior time, through trial and error? Birch and Harlow would argue, no, the response simply may not have been applied in exactly the same situation.

The results of a study by Birch (1945) suggested strongly that past experience is relevant to problem-solving performance in the so-called insight situations. He found that only one of his six chimps could successfully solve the two-stick problem the first 30 minutes allotted to them. The one chimp, Jojo, who did solve the problem had been observed to play with sticks prior to the study while the other chimps never had. After three days experience with sticks, however, all six chimps solved the two-stick problem on the first try. Although we cannot rule out the interpretation that a perceptual reorganization occurred during play, the results clearly demonstrate that past experience does play a role in seemingly sudden problem solution.

The role of prior learning in problem solving has been shown in numerous other studies, in particular those by Harlow (1949). His experiments have shown that only after many problems, often as many as 200, does a chimp or monkey show a dramatic change in performance. Insight may often appear to be a sudden thing but when the past history is known, it is found that insight is the result of cumulative learning. Harlow would argue that the change in performance is not the result of sudden perceptual reorganization but the fact that the animal has learned what *not* to respond to. That is, the animal has learned to inhibit responses to inappropriate stimulus attributes which initially competed with the correct response.

Trial-and-error and insight behaviors in problem-solving situations had once been assumed to be totally independent. The research of Birch, Harlow, and others suggests this belief is unwarranted. Trial and error is necessary to eventually make the correct response resulting in problem solution. It is only after the animal or person has discovered what the correct response is in similar problems that the subject is capable of displaying insight behavior (absence of overt trial-and-error behavior) in a new problem situation.

Insight-type problems presented to human subjects resemble the two-stick situations in that there is no guarantee of solution and the subject is required to use materials in an unusual way. An ex-

ample of an insight problem is the candle problem (Duncan, 1961). The subject is in a room with a candle, some tacks, a small box, and some matches on a table, and is simply told to figure out a way to put the candle on the wall so that it will not drip wax on the table or floor when burning. This situation poses a problem for most individuals, because the box must be used in a rather unusual way as a platform for the candle. As shown in Figure 11-1, the solution is achieved by tacking the box to the wall, melting wax to provide a base for the candle, and then lighting the wick. The task

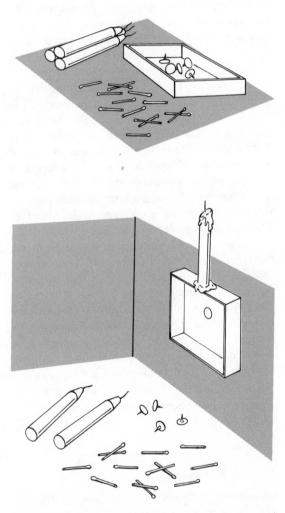

Fig. 11-1. Candle problem materials (upper square) and solution (lower drawing). (After Bourne, Ekstrand, and Dominowski, 1971)

proves sufficiently difficult that many subjects fail to reach a solution within the alloted time (usually 15 minutes). When a solution is reached, however, it is generally sudden, as was Sultan's, and is not a chance happening as a result of overt trial and error behavior. Often the subject will simply stare at the materials for a time (perhaps engaging in covert trial and error, that is, thinking, before the solution is reached).

Three important advances occur toward the end of the second year of a child's life which Piaget (1952) maintains underlie the shift from reliance on trial and error to so-called insight in problem solving in humans. First, the child becomes capable of internal representation which makes covert trial and error possible. Second, solution is speeded by the fact the child is increasingly systematic in solution-seeking behavior, no longer being reliant on hit and miss, trial and error. Third, the child's capacity for internal presentation allows for displaying deferred imitation. The child may covertly or overtly short-circuit the trial and error solution process by introducing new responses that the child has previously observed others perform. Interestingly, it is not until near the end of the second year that the human child has "caught up" with the adult ape with respect to problem solving capabilities.

Functional-Fixity Problems. The candle problem offers an example of another phenomenon known as *functional-fixity*. As already noted, some subjects failed to reach a solution within the allotted time. Duncker (1945) has proposed that these subjects may have had difficulty in arriving at the solution because they were fixed or set in their perception of the function of at least one of the materials required in the solution (hence the name functional-fixedness). This interpretation has been tested by manipulating the way in which task materials are presented. It has been found that procedures that draw attention to the key object will facilitate performance. For example, it has been shown that the candle problem changes markedly when the box is presented empty rather than with tacks in it (Adamson, 1952; Glucksberg, 1962). Less than half of the subjects were able to solve the problem when the box contained tacks, while

nearly all solved the problem when the box was empty. When the box was empty, it was apparently easier for subjects to perceive the box as something other than a container. Also, the presence of the empty box may have facilitated subjects' taking notice of the box as something separate from the tacks. Support for the second interpretation was found in an experiment by Glucksberg and Weisberg (1966). They found that solution was facilitated by printing a label (for example, BOX, MATCHES) on each item. The label BOX apparently drew subjects' attention to the box. This study also demonstrates the effect that language can have on thinking, a topic to be discussed in a later section.

Undoubtedly the verbal label served more than one function in the task, since the functional-fixity interpretation of the empty box result has also been supported. It has been found that the subject's set going into the experiment as to the use of the critical object or tool influences solution time. If the set arouses responses incompatible with the correct use, solution will be slow. One way of demonstrating the operation of set would be to have one group of problem solvers use the critical object in its normal way just prior to the experiment while a second group uses it in a novel way that would transfer to the problem situation. Those who used the object in a novel way should solve the problem with less difficulty. A part of this procedure was used in a situation where subjects were faced with the problem of connecting two strings suspended from the ceiling. The two strings could not be simultaneously reached. Solution required use of an unlikely object as a weight to create a pendulum. Birch and Rabinowitz (1951) found that the particular weight selected to create the pendulum was affected by the pre-experimental uses of the two weight choices. The two weight choices were an electrical relay and an electrical switch. Subjects who were asked to install the relay in an electrical circuit before solving the string problem chose the switch in solving the problem. Subjects who had installed the switch prior to the problem selected the relay. Control subjects with no previous installation experience were equally split in their selections of the two weights. As predicted, the installation experience apparently set subjects to perceive the one potential weight only in the function for which they had previously used it. Functional-fixity, the tendency *not* to use the object used in the installation experience, was found to decrease with time. When seven days fell between the installation experience and the two-string problem situation, selection of the two weights was again at chance level (Adamson and Taylor, 1954).

The operation of functional-fixedness is abundantly clear in our everyday lives. How often the solution to a problem is right in front of us, but we fail to recognize it because other responses associated with the object are much stronger than the required response. For example, how many people would think of using a plastic bag (which contained vegetables from the market) to temporarily mend a leak in the radiator hose of a car? With a small leak a plastic bag applied tourniquet-style serves the purpose nicely. The use of the bag in this manner is a very low probability response that most individuals would not consider. Previous uses tend to create a set difficult to overcome.

There are marked differences in ease of overcoming sets. The individual who can readily think of the less obvious uses of an object is said to be an *original* thinker. Mednick (1962) has hypothesized that the original individual has a flat association hierarchy (no responses have high strength; several are of low to moderate strength), tends to respond slowly, but can produce many responses. The unoriginal individual, in contrast, has a steep associative hierarchy (a few responses have very high strength; a few others are of very low strength), shows a high rate of response initially, but can produce only a few responses. For example, if we presented the word *plastic bag* to a group of subjects, a few (the original subjects) would be able to give us many possible uses, some of which would be unconventional or original. The unoriginal subjects, however, would be able to come up with only a few, highly conventional uses. Just as pre-problem use of an object in an unusual way may aid in problem solution, coming into a task with a set to give original uses for objects will facilitate problem solution.

Set-Inducing Problems. Subjects may come into the problem-solving situation with a set that inter-

feres with the subject's perception of the objects in a novel use or may acquire an interfering set *during* the course of the experiment itself. The effect of installation experience on the choice of weight in the two-string problem was an example of experimental manipulation of the set brought to the task. The Luchins' water jar problems (described below) represent a classic example of a case in which interfering responses are learned in the course of the experiment. In both cases, the results are interpretable in terms of negative transfer of training.

In a water jar problem, the subject is presented with three jars all of a specified capacity. These same jars are used in a series of six problems that are all solvable by the same equation: $B - A - 2C$. For example, the subject might be asked how to get 100 quarts using a jar having a capacity of 21 quarts (A), 127 quarts (B), and a jar of 3 quarts (C). After solving six different problems using the same solution equation, the subject is presented with a seventh problem that could be solved by the simple subtraction of C from A (subject is asked how to get 20 quarts using a jar of 23 quarts (A), 49 quarts (B) and a jar of 3 quarts (C). Over half of the subjects use the more complex solution equation on the seventh problem instead of simply A minus C.

As might be expected, the complex solution becomes a stronger response tendency and produces greater interference on a later simple problem as the number of set-inducing problems increases (Tresselt and Leeds, 1953). Strength of set has been shown to be a function of number of problems also for arithmetic problems and word problems.

Although most demonstrations of the effects of a problem solving set have been designed to show negative transfer to the final problem, a set need not necessarily result in poorer performance if the set adopted during the course of a series of problems is applicable to all problems. Certainly the set we have acquired to follow the same steps in solution of division problems in arithmetic is an example of the positive influence of development of a set or solution rule. Once the appropriate set or solution method has been learned, solution of subsequent problems is rapid and errorless (or nearly so). Recall the insight behavior shown by Kohler's apes and Harlow's monkeys, in which response was rapid and errorless once the appropriate solution method was found. The development of set will seem to indicate a debilitating rigidity in problem solving only when the set is inappropriate to the final goal behavior established by the experimenter, or in everyday situations, by the individual, teacher, or parent.

Word Problems. The anagram has been the most frequently used type of word problem, particularly by the associative psychologist. An anagram problem is one in which a series of letters are presented to the subject who is asked to arrange them in order to make an English word. For example, attempt to rearrange each of the following sequences to make words: NELIN, NEDOZ, HCWHI, ESTHE, KLSTA. The task is similar to some components of the familiar game of SCRABBLE. The game SCRABBLE is more difficult, however, since all of the letters available are not necessarily used in the solution. These irrelevant letters increase time to form a word.

The anagram is an especially useful medium for studying the variables that lead to positive and negative transfer, because we know a lot about words—their frequency of use, meaningfulness, allowable letter sequences, and so on. Many of the same variables that affect anagram solution time also affect solution time for nonverbal problems.

One of the most reliably demonstrated variables affecting anagram solution time is frequency of occurrence of the word in the language. High frequency words such as CHAIR, SUGAR, TRAIN, require less solution time than low frequency words such as PEONY, GROIN, TRIAD (Mayzner and Tresselt, 1958). If an anagram has two possible solutions for example, *stalk* and *talks* are both possible from KLSTA), the higher frequency word (*talks*) is given as a solution by most subjects.

Just as set was found to affect performance on other types of problems, establishment of a set has been shown to facilitate anagram solutions. If the same solution strategy can be used on all problems, the effect of the establishment of the set is positive. If the same strategy will not apply to all

the anagram problems, of course, the effect of the set will be negative. An example of the establishment of a set having a positive effect on solution time is available in the series of five anagrams presented at the beginning of this section. All five can be solved by simply reversing the first two letters and transposing them to the end of the sequence, for example, NELIN becomes *linen* and KLSTA becomes *stalk*. An interesting side-effect of the establishment of a set is that when an anagram has two solutions (KLSTA), the less frequent (*stalk*) will occur if it follows from the set. The influence of set is typically found to exert a stronger influence on response strength than the frequency of occurrence of the word in the language.

The letter order or the organization of the letters within the anagram has been shown to affect solution time. It takes longer to discover the correct solution, *ocean,* from a meaningful word, for example, CANOE, than from EANOC (Ekstrand and Dominowski, 1968). The meaningful word is more likely to elicit associates that delay the subject's producing the lower strength response, *ocean.* The inclusion of high frequency bigrams (two adjacent letters of a word) within the anagram also affect solution time. Solution is facilitated if the bigram is a component of the correct solution and inhibited if the bigram is not a component. For example, the solution, *poker,* should take longer for the anagram KPEOR than for KPOER.

Yet another organizational factor found to influence anagram solution difficulty is pronounceability of the anagram. The easier the anagram was to pronounce (for example, WIHEG vs. EHIWG) the longer subjects took to reach the solution (WEIGH). In short, any organizational pattern that elicits responses incompatible with the lower probability solution will affect solution time. This generalization, of course, holds true for any kind of problem situation.

As one might well expect, the number of letters in an anagram affects solution time. The more letters there are, the more difficult the problem. The increase in difficulty is most pronounced with an increase from 3 to 6 letters than from 6 to 8 (Kaplan and Carvellas, 1968). The difficulty with 5–6 letter words is probably due to the fact that there are more competing responses at that length. There are more words in our language of that length than of 3–4 or 6–8 letters.

Search Problems.   Tasks that have a clearly defined set of alternative responses, the number of which may be easily varied, are typically utilized by the researcher operating from an information processing point of view. The researcher is interested in studying the sequence of steps that the problem solver goes through in reaching the solution. Problems include such things as discovering which light in a series is defective, discovering which switches turn on a specified light pattern, completing a jigsaw puzzle, playing a game of chess, listing items satisfying specified criteria, or solving mathematical problems.

In some situations, the only way to arrive at a solution is to systematically search each possible alternative. Such a systematic search method is called an *algorithm*. An algorithmic search differs from trial and error behavior in that the algorithmic search is more systematic. There are many situations, however, when a systematic search of all alternatives is impractical because of the large number of alternatives (as with a 1,000 piece puzzle) or because it may not be necessary. There may be some basis, a rule or other device, to limit the search. Such a rule or device is called a *heuristic*. If the rule is appropriate to the situation, solution will be rapid and efficient. If, however, a judgment error is made in the selection of a heuristic, there may be no solution found. A heuristic is typically used when a person is putting together a puzzle. Instead of systematically trying every piece in a particular spot until the correct one is found, most puzzle workers start with edges so that initially their search can be limited to straight-edge pieces. Coloration may also serve as a cue so that for one spot the problem solver can specify that the piece must have a straight edge and be sky blue with bits of white clouds running through it.

An experiment by Detambel and Stolurow (1957) provides an example of the kind of study that is done to examine the information-seeking process. Two hundred devices were built, each of which consisted of three components, A, B, and C. One of the three components was out of order on each device. Component A was defective on

half of the devices, B on a third, and C on a sixth. The three components differed in the number of screws that had to be removed to determine whether the component was working. There were seven screws for Component A, four for B, and one for C. Given the work factor (number of screws) and the probability of trouble, the most efficient sequence would be CBA. You would only have to take out five screws versus seven by starting with C and B while still having the same likelihood (.5) of discovery of the source of malfunction as you would have if you started with A.

Most subjects began with the low-work lid, Component C, but shifted to A after they discovered the probabilities. Probability of a particular lid being the source of trouble proved to be a more important determinant of performance than effortfulness. Only one of the twelve college students stuck with the most efficient, CBA sequence.

As one might expect, there are individual differences in whether or not the optimal information seeking strategy is adopted. Generally, subjects who score high on intelligence tests also perform more efficiently on complex search tasks.

Problem Solving in Perspective

As we have seen, laboratory problem situations come in many forms, just as do real life problems. But what generalizations can we make about the factors that affect the ease of discovery of solution to a problem?

The most pervasive factor is the strength of competing responses, as an associative psychologist would put it. We have said that a problem exists when the initial attempts to reach a solution fail. In other words, when a high probability response fails, it is necessary to resort to those of lower probability or strength. (Recall that response strength is determined by prior conditioning history. Those responses that have been previously successful will be of high strength.) The difficulty of a problem is directly related to the number and strength of incorrect responses evoked by the task situation. The intereference caused by the higher strength responses can, in some cases, prevent the individual from reaching a solution within a reasonable amount of time. Any procedure that decreases the strength of incorrect responses and increases the strength of the initially weaker response will facilitate solution.

Task related variables which were found to affect the relative strength of correct and incorrect responses were:

1. *Prior learning or set* (for example, chimps having previous experience with sticks solved the two-stick insight problem more rapidly than those with no experience; prior installation of an electrical switch led subjects to select a relay in the two-string pendulum task; prior use of a complex equation in solution of water-jar problems led subjects to continue use of the complex equation when the problem could be solved by a simple one).

2. *Complexity* (for example, anagrams with 5–6 letters were more difficult than those with 3–4; number of pieces in a puzzle or the number of lights on a string of defective Christmas tree lights affected solution time).

3. *Embeddedness* (for example, subjects failed to perceive the box as a potential part of the candle-problem solution when it contained tacks; anagrams were more difficult to solve when they contained a common letter sequence such as *er* that was not a part of the solution).

Concept Formation

Probably one of the most commonly asked questions is, "What is it?" In asking this question, we are usually hoping to be able to find a pigeon-hole in our already existing knowledge into which to fit an unfamiliar object. Often when we ask such a question, we have already limited the possible answers. For example, we may know that the creature we have just seen has characteristics in common with birds. What we do not know is its more specific membership in the category (for example, blue heron). A system is beginning to show itself already. Knowing that what we have seen is a bird, automatically implies that it is living and in the animal rather than plant category. This type of organization of experience is derived from input through our senses. The resulting pigeon-holes are not an unrelated set of slots or boxes to which we relegate a particular aspect of our experience.

Rather, the system includes an intricate network of hierarchical relationships.

Each category is definable in two ways, by intension and by extension. To define by *intension* is to list the stimulus properties and functions common to all the members of a class. To define by *extension* is to list all the objects or events composing the category.

Typically, when an individual demonstrates that that person has made a categorization by giving the same response to several stimuli which share certain properties, we say that person has acquired a *concept*. A concept is in itself unobservable. It is an abstraction that has been agreed on by the members of a culture (Johnson, 1971). To facilitate communication among members of a culture, many concepts are represented by a vocabulary item in our language, for example, dog, cat, square, life, up, weight, husband, bird, and so on.

The formation and use of concepts serve a very important function in our everyday lives. One of the basic tasks of development is that of attempting to come to an ever increasing match between our knowledge of reality and reality itself. This task requires that we process a tremendous quantity of information each day. In fact, there is a great deal more information potentially available than we can ever hope to take in. As information processors, we humans leave much to be desired. We have limited apprehension spans and memory capacity. That is, we can only attend to and remember a limited number of informational units simultaneously. Simply put, we cannot see and hear everything available all at once.

To compensate for this inherent limitation, we are selective in what we attend to. Also we form coding rules that provide the basis for selection among the available stimulus dimensions. In so doing, we are able to respond to new instances of a class without having to start from scratch each time. Once we have discovered what the defining characteristic of *cats* are that distinguish them from other animals, we can immediately categorize each new instance of cat that we encounter. This saves a great deal of strain on memory. By contrast, the other alternative would be quite taxing. We could memorize that A is cat, B is cat, C is cat, D is cat, and so on, where A, B, C, and D are individual

Table 11-1(a).   A subset of positive and negative instances of the concept ZUF.

ZUFs
(Positive instances)

Others
(Negative instances)

cats. That could eventually result in our having to "carry around" a lot of cats in our heads. Instead we develop an abstraction that is independent of any particular cat. This code on reality saves having to repeatedly ask "What is that?" each time we encounter a new instance.

To put ourselves in the position of a child having to learn a concept, consider the positive and negative instances of ZUFs in Table 11-1a. The nonsense word ZUF is a concept name. The creatures labeled ZUF are a subset of ZUFs. Instances vary on several attributes: shape, number of legs, number of toes, and closeness of eyes. In attempting to discover the concept ZUF, the first task is to determine which attributes are relevant, that is, which attributes are systematically related to the name ZUF. The second task is to discover the coding rule that describes the relationship between the relevant attributes.

As you study the instances presented in Table 11-1a, ask yourself, (a) Is shape relevant? (b) Is number of legs relevant? (c) Is closeness of eyes relevant? (d) Is number of toes relevant? (e) Is shape of mouth relevant? Your answers should be "No" to the first three questions and "Yes" to the last two. Shape, number of legs, and closeness of

eyes were not systematically related to the correct category label, ZUF; hence they are irrelevant attributes. The shape of the mouth was related, however, as was the number of toes. We must now ask ourselves: Specifically, how are these attributes related to the concept label and to each other? The answer to this question gives us the rule defining the concept. If a smile *and* three toes are present, then the creature is a positive instance of a ZUF. Note the ease with which you can now respond to the new instances in Table 11-1b. You are able to respond ZUF with no hesitation to both instances, even though these particular instances were not encountered in the original set. You have no need to carry around specific instances in memory in order

Table 11-1(b).   New instances of the concept ZUF.

to identify old or new instances. All you need to remember is what to attend to and the rule defining the concept. It is in precisely this same manner that the class concepts we develop in our everyday lives allow us to respond adaptively and to exist without feeling continually bombarded by too much stimulation. As in the example, where we could ignore shape, number of legs, and distance of the eyes, we learn to ignore information that is irrelevant to our responding in a particular situation.

Factors Affecting Concept Learning

Number of Stimulus Attributes. Identification of the stimulus properties relevant and those that are irrelevant to the concept is one of the major tasks of concept learning. The difficulty of this abstraction process has been found to be related to the number of relevant and irrelevant dimensions of a concept (Bulgarella and Archer, 1962; Walker and Bourne, 1961). As shown in Figure 11-2, task difficulty increases as the number of relevant or irrelevant dimensions increases. For example, the ZUF concept was considerably easier in the form originally presented than if a ZUF had to have only two legs and eyes closely spaced in addition to a smile and three toes. The addition of two relevant dimensions would have increased the amount of time required to discover the relevant attributes. The task could also have been made more difficult by

adding irrelevant rather than relevant dimensions, for example, color, size, or arms. On the other hand, elimination of irrelevant dimensions would have facilitated acquisition. Suppose that all the creatures had been of the same shape and only had two legs. The task of discovering that shape of mouth and number of toes were relevant would have been greatly facilitated, since we would have had fewer bases for the development of misleading hypotheses.

Positive and Negative Instances. Typically concept learning situations expose the individual to many stimuli. Some of those will be examples of the concept or *positive instances*. Others will not be examples or *negative instances*. For example, a creature with a smile and three toes is a positive instance of a ZUF. Creatures with a circle mouth, two toes, a frown, or five toes are all negative instances of the ZUF concept. Similarly, a yellow Volkswagen and yellow Chevy are both positive instances of the concept, YELLOW CAR. Green, red, tan, blue, and black cars are negative instances.

Suppose that it were not possible to present both positive and negative instances of the concept CAT. There happen to be only cats in the neighborhood and no dogs or other animals. How would presentation of only positive instances affect concept learning? It has been found that when only positive instances (such as yellow cars, cats, ZUFs) are presented, the task proves to be much easier than if all negative instances are presented (Freibergs and Tulving, 1961). As shown in Figure 11-3, NO and YES are not equally informative opposites in the concept learning situation. With practice, however, the difference in utilization of positive and negative instances can be reduced.

There are three qualifications that need to be made with respect to the generalization that a concept is acquired more rapidly by exposure to only positive instances. First, the generalization holds only with concepts defined in certain ways (conjunctively). Negative instances have been found to be more informative than positive under some conditions (concepts defined disjunctively) (Chlebek and Dominowski, 1970).

A second qualification of the generalization regarding ease of learning concepts relates to the

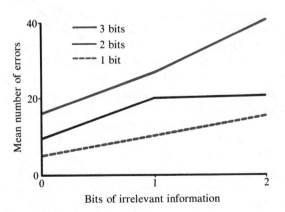

Fig. 11-2. Mean number of errors as a function of number of relevant and irrelevant dimensions. (From Bulgarella and Archer, 1962)

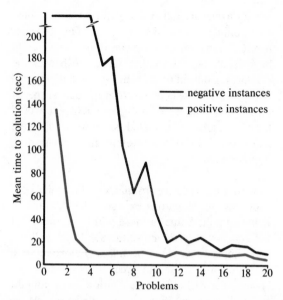

Fig. 11-3. Time to solution on 20 problems with only positive or only negative instances. (From Freibergs and Tulving, 1961)

amount of information the learner has about the nature of the concept and the range of values the dimensions may take. Concept formation would be totally impossible, not just slower, on the basis of all negative instances if the range of attributes were unknown. Learning of the ZUF concept would not be possible with only negative instances (non-ZUFs) if the learner did not know at the outset that there are two distances that eyes can be (close, far), two numbers of legs (two or four), two shapes of mouth (circle, smile), and so on. The impossibility of acquiring a concept without some knowledge of the nature of the concept at the outset is clear when we consider attempting to discover the concept CAT through exposure to only noncats.

A third qualification of the generalization that concept learning is easier when only positive instances are presented pertains to the transfer situation. Suppose a child has only been exposed to instances of cats, never other animals. In real life, a person is not always going to encounter positive instances. Sooner or later the child will come face to face with a dog. What happens to the accuracy of categorizations when the child is suddenly faced with negative instances? It has been found that a

child will often include some negative instances as exemplars of the concept. That is, the class formed on the basis of positive instances alone often proves to be too broad, or overextended, and a child is likely to call a dog by the concept label CAT. Exposure to negative instances is needed to rule out the relevance of some attributes (Johnson, 1971).

Redundant Information. Sometimes a combination of attributes will occur in all instances of a concept. For example, the ZUFs might also have been red while the other creatures might have been blue. When two or more dimensions overlap in this way, they are *redundant*. That is, they are related to the ZUFs in the same way. Classification could be made on the basis of either color or the mouth-toe attributes. Many children's toys include redundant cues to facilitate learning. Cups of graduated sizes may also be of different colors. Puzzle pieces may be positioned on the basis of piece edges or shape outlined on the cardboard base. When identification of a concept can be made on the basis of any one of such redundant relevant dimensions, concept learning occurs much faster than when no such redundancy exists. The only difficulty that might be encountered is again on transfer to a more general set of instances. For example, if red were redundant with shape of mouth and number of toes of the ZUFs during original learning, there would probably be some errors made when later ZUFs without the red cue were encountered.

Redundancy may occur among the irrelevant as well as the relevant attributes. However, the effect on performance is quite different. In general, it has been found that performance on a concept task improves as the number of redundant relevant dimensions increases, but deteriorates as the number of redundant irrelevant dimensions increases, assuming the individual detects the redundancy (Bourne and Haygood, 1959, 1961).

Salience. There are two characteristics of the human information processing system that can be capitalized on to facilitate identification of the relevant attributes of a concept: (1) the selective nature of our perception and (2) our tendency to select on the basis of saliency. The *salience* of a stimulus dimension refers to the extent to which it stands out relative to the other attributes. Picture, for example, the members of an orchestra dressed in traditional black, all except one. That one forgot and left on his plaid sports jacket. That sports jacket would prove to be a very salient stimulus in that setting by virtue of its deviance from the black worn by others.

The relative salience of dimensions in a concept learning situation has been found to affect concept learning performance. It has been found that the relevant dimension is identified more readily if it is more salient than the irrelevant dimension. Presenting the toes of only the ZUFs in red, for example, would not only result in a redundant cue, color, but one of great salience. Such a trick would draw attention to the toes and increase the likelihood that subjects would test hypotheses regarding its relevance to the problem.

Salience of a dimension may also be affected by the magnitude of the differences between the values of an attribute (Archer, 1962). Everyone has had the experience of counting out change to pay for an item, to find to their embarrassment that they mistook a penny for a dime. A quarter, is however, rarely mistaken for a dime. The reason for the lower likelihood of confusion of the quarter and the dime has to do with the greater salience of one relevant attribute, size. A relevant attribute of size is more likely to be singled out of an array in a concept learning task if the sizes presented are very different. Similarly, it would prove easier to grasp a concept if circles were presented as positive instances and squares were presented as negative instances than if hexagons were positive and octagons were negative instances of the concept.

Salience is a relative thing. Previous experience has been found to influence which dimensions are salient for a particular individual or group of individuals. It has been found that young children and some brain damaged subjects tend to classify a set of objects varying in color, form, or numerosity on the basis of color rather than putting all the objects of the same form together as do most adults. Research has also indicated that children have much more difficulty than adults in focusing their attention on attributes not initially salient for them. The result is that when irrelevant rather than the relevant dimensions prove to be salient for the concept learner, learning is very slow. Similarly, children encounter difficulties in acquiring concepts that require simultaneous consideration of two or more attributes.

Types of Conceptual Rule. The variables we discussed thus far have dealt with the influence of stimulus factors on the identification of the relevant attributes. However, discovery of the relevant attributes is not sufficient to define a concept. It is also necessary to determine in what combination those attributes that are relevant must occur before the concept applies. Recall that two attributes, shape of mouth and number of toes, were relevant for the ZUF concept. The presence of a smile alone was not sufficient to define the concept; number of toes (three) also had to be considered since only instances with both characteristics were correlated with the response ZUF. When a combination of two or more characteristics must be present as in the ZUF example, the concept is said to be *conjunctive*. An instance of a ZUF must have a smile *and* three toes. An everyday example of a concept defined by a conjunctive rule is HOUSE. At minimum, a foundation, walls, doorway, and roof must be present. If only one of these aspects is present, such as walls, we are not referring to a house, but perhaps a fence in this instance. Another example of a conjunctive concept is WIFE. To meet the criteria for this concept, an individual (instance) must be a woman *and* be married.

When only one of two or more options in dimensions must be present in an instance, the concept is said to be *disjunctive*. The key word is *or* as is evident in the following example. If the ZUF concept had been defined such that creatures with either a smile *or* three toes, but not necessarily both, were positive instances, the concept would have been disjunctive rather than conjunctive. Note that if the concept had been disjunctive (*or*) rather than conjunctive (*and*) with respect to the number of toes and shape of mouth, many more instances would have qualified as positive instances of the concept ZUF. Other principles for defining concepts are listed in Table 11-2.

Study of the effect of type of rule on concept learning has shown that concepts defined by con-

Table 11-2. Conceptual Rules Describing Binary Partitions of a Stimulus Population. (From Bourne, Ekstrand, & Dominowski, 1971)

Rule Name	Symbolic Description*	Alternative Symbolic Description	Verbal Description	Real-Life Examples
Affirmation	R	None	Every red pattern is an example of the concept	Any attribute will do
Conjunction	R S̄	None	Every pattern which is red and a star is an example	A *volume: large and book-ish*
Inclusive disjunction	R U S	None	Every pattern which is red or a star or both is an example	An eligible *voter: a resident and/or a property owner*
Conditional	R→S	R̄ U S	If a pattern is red then it must be a star to be an example; if it is nonred then it is not an example regardless of shape	A *well-mannered male:* If a lady enters, *then* he will *stand*
Biconditional	R↔S	(R∩S)∩(R̄ U S̄)	A red pattern is an example if and only if it is also a star; any red non-star or nonred star is not an example	An *appropriate behavior:* wearing an *overcoat if and only if* it *is cold*

*R and S stand for red and star (relevant attributes), respectively.

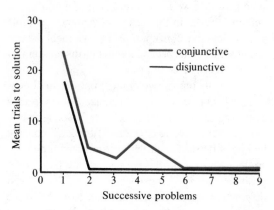

Fig. 11-4. Mean trials to solution of nine rule-learning problems based on conjuctive and disjunctive rules. (From Bourne, 1967)

junctive and disjunctive rules are acquired faster than those defined by other types of rules, such as, conditional or biconditional. As shown in Figure 11-4, this difference is only found on the first few

concept learning problems in a series. By the sixth problem, there is little difference in speed of concept formation. The initial advantage in learning concepts defined by conjunctive and disjunctive rules is undoubtedly due to familiarity and experience with such concepts. Most everyday concepts are defined by those two rules.

Feedback

Feedback is any form of information to the learner that indicates whether the learner's response was correct or incorrect. A father provides feedback when he tells his son that, no, the animal they just passed was not a horse; it was a cow. When the learner is not only told when that learner is incorrect, but is also provided with the correct response as did the father, learning is facilitated (Bourne and Pendleton, 1958).

It should be noted that information is also available to the learner directly from the stimuli experienced as the learner encounters instances of the concept. Individuals may come to develop class concepts solely on the basis of shared physical attributes or functions of objects but the resultant concept may not be identical to that formed by other individuals. There are usually numerous ways to categorize any set of stimuli, making it difficult to get consensus between individuals when there is not an agreed upon basis.

Experimental Paradigms

Most studies of concept formation are variations on two basic procedures: the *reception* and the *selection* paradigms. The reception paradigm has been employed in most studies. The learner is presented with a randomly selected stimulus (usually on a card) and told to place it in the positive or negative category (pile). Of course, initially the learner has no basis for categorization. The feedback received will provide the learner with information to use in categorizing the next stimulus card presented. With the reception procedure, the stimulus cards are usually presented one at a time, that is, successively.

The selection paradigm is typically used when the experimenter wishes to study the strategies employed by concept learners. Rather than the experimenters presenting stimuli in a predetermined successive order, the learner selects (hence the name, selection paradigm) cards from the total array. That is, all the positive and negative instances are laid out before the learner at the outset of the experiment. One card is designated as an example of the concept. From then on, the learner must make stimulus card selections alone. Typically, those selections are not random but follow one of several patterns or strategies. The task is somewhat analogous to that encountered in the parlor game CLUE in which the players ask questions to determine the weapon, place, and guilty person in a hypothetical crime.

Strategies in Selection Studies

Those who assume that the learner plays an active role in obtaining information about environment, view the concept learning process as one of formulating, testing, and eliminating hypotheses (for example, Bruner et al., 1956; Krechevsky, 1932; Levine, 1959, 1963). Hypotheses represent systematic attempts to eliminate or confirm the role of the many varying dimensions in a situation. A succession of hypotheses is typically needed to allow for confident decision about the relevance of particular attributes to the concept. The steps concept learners take in reformulating their hypotheses differ. Bruner et al. (1956) have identified four strategies.

One of the commonly used strategies is known as *conservative focusing*. The concept learner systematically checks out the relevance of each dimension by first hypothesizing that all the attributes present in the positive instance shown by the experimenter initially are relevant. To illustrate, we will follow a potential sequence of card selections and hypotheses (see Table 11-3). The learner would be presented with 16 cards which differ in shape (circle, square), number (one, two), color (red, green), and border (borderless, bordered). Each dimension has two values. The experimenter begins the task by presenting CARD 1, two red circles without a border, to the learner. The card is designated as a positive instance of the conjunctive concept, RED CIRCLE. Not knowing how many or which attributes are relevant, the learner hypothesizes any or all of the attributes may be relevant. Using the conservative focus, the learner proceeds to systematically select cards which vary from the original instance in one attribute. The first card choice might be, for example, CARD 2 based on the hypothesis that border may be a relevant dimension. The learner is told that the card is an example of the concept, allowing that person to rule out border as a relevant dimension. The next card choice is based on the hypothesis that number is relevant. Accordingly, CARD 3 is identical to CARD 1 except for the number of red circles. Since the learner is told that CARD 3 is an instance also, the learner's hypothesis regarding number disconfirmed. Since all the cards have been red and have been positive instances, the learner decides to test out the relevance of the color dimension. The CARD 4 choice is identical to CARD 1 in border, number, and shape, but the circles are now green. Feedback that the card is not a positive instance confirms the learner's hypothesis that color is a relevant attribute. But is redness

Table 11-3. Example of Stimulus Card Selections Using a Conservative Focus Strategy (Adapted from Pollio, 1973).

Card Selections	Hypotheses	Feedback	Conclusion
CARD 1 ⟨R⟩ ⟨R⟩	(positive instance selected by E)		
CARD 2 ⟨R⟩ ⟨R⟩	border relevant	+ instance	border irrelevant
CARD 3 ⟨R⟩	number relevant	+ instance	number irrelevant
CARD 4 ⟨G⟩ ⟨G⟩	color relevant	− instance	color relevant
CARD 5 R R	shape relevant	− instance	shape relevant

alone sufficient or must the figures be circles? To test out the relevance of shape, the CARD 5 choice is identical to CARD 1 except for the shape (squares rather than circles). Since this card fails to qualify as an instance, the learner now knows that shape, border, and number are irrelevant dimensions but that color and shape are relevant. The learner might now confirm his hypothesis that the concept is RED CIRCLE by selecting a couple more instances.

Following this conservative focusing strategy will lead to the problem solution efficiently, that is, with a minimum number of card selections. Not all concept learners operate as systematically as this, however, but attempt to select a card which varies in more than one attribute from the designated positive instance. The learner takes a gamble that the hypothesis about a combination of attributes is correct, hence, the name *focus gambling* for this strategy. It is obvious that this strategy will save time if the learner did indeed jump to the correct conclusion. If the learner is incorrect, however, that person will probably have to resort to a more conservative strategy.

The two focus strategies provide systematic procedures that minimize the load on memory. Two other possible strategies, *simultaneous* scanning and *successive* scanning are considerably more taxing to memory. Simultaneous scanning involves keeping track of which combinations of attributes have been previously viewed and whether each was a positive or negative instance. It is rather like trying to keep track of which cards (remembering suit, number, face, and who played it) have been played in a bridge game, who played each, and what effect its appearance had on other players' behavior. Successive or part scanning is more feasible because only the information from each stimulus card relevant to the subject's hypothesis need be scanned and remembered.

It should be noted that use of a stragegy may be temporary. Often a learner will be unsuccessful with one approach and switch strategies in the middle of the problem.

Individual Differences

Although task variables have important effects on performance, individual characteristics of the problem solver also interact to affect the efficiency of problem solving and conceptual behavior. It is to be expected that when there are alternative routes to solution, individual differences in strategy and solution time will be observed.

Intelligence. Individuals differ as a result of hereditary and environmental contributions in what they know and how rapidly acquisition occurs. Although there are many dimensions to intelligence, research has looked at the relationship between those indexed by the familiar IQ score and concept learning performance. In general, it has been found that higher intelligence is associated with better performance on concept tasks. That is, fewer errors are made, attribute identification is made faster, and the information provided by the experimenter is used more efficiently (Denny, 1966; Osler and Fivel, 1961).

There have been few attempts to determine what components of the IQ test performance are specifically related to conceptual behavior. Is memory, spatial abilities, inferential skill, or what, most related? Although the results are not based on IQ test memory subtests, nor do they directly assess the effects of individual differences in memory, studies have been made that do demonstrate the role of memory in concept formation.

Memory. The identification of relevant attributes and the rule of combination in a concept learning situation requires memory of information accrued from previous positive and negative instance of the concept. It is obvious that discovery of shared characteristics is dependent on the availability in memory of the characteristics of previously encountered instances of the concept.

The role of memory has been demonstrated by provision of artificial aids. When subjects are presented with a listing of all the instances rather than each singly, performance improves because the subjects have a record of what has occurred (Cahill and Hovland, 1960).

Anxiety. Performance on many types of tasks has been shown to be related to the level of arousal of the individual. State of arousal is typically indexed by recordings of heartrate, palm sweating, breathing rate, pupillary dilation, and so on. Specifically, it has been found that there is an optimal level of arousal for a given task. This generalization is known as the Yerkes-Dodson Law. But you may ask, what does arousal have to do with anxiety? One point of view is that arousal level is affected by need states such as hunger, thirst, boredom, social approval, the need to achieve, and so forth. When the need state for one or more needs is high, the individual is said to be anxious (Bourne et al., 1971). Since anxiety affects arousal, it is not surprising that it has been found that individuals who are chronically anxious perform differently on

concept learning tasks than high anxious individuals. The difference in performance is greatest on complex tasks, with high anxious subjects performing poorer than low anxious subjects (Romanow, 1958; Dunn, 1968).

Interestingly, anxiety does not affect the performance of high and low IQ individuals in a similar manner. As can be seen in Figure 11-5, high anxiety helps the concept performance of high intelligence subjects but hinders that of low intelligence subjects (Denny, 1966). This effect is undoubtedly due to the fact that what constitutes a complex task differs with the intelligence level of the individual.

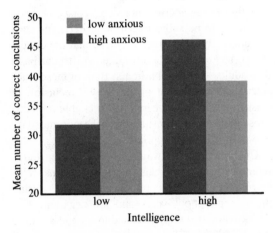

Fig. 11-5. Mean number of correct concept conclusions made by high and low anxious subjects of high and low intelligence. (From Denny, 1966)

Conceptual Development

The adult's tendency to organize the environment is evident in one's everyday interactions with objects and people as well as in one's language. What is perhaps most surprising is that all the adults within a culture tend to arrive at approximately the same kind of organization. The resulting organization allows for adaptive interaction with the environment. As noted earlier, the major advantage of organization, such as the development of conceptual categories, is to reduce the load on our limited memory capacity. Once we have figured out what physical and functional characteristics are common to washcloths, we respond to a new instance of a washcloth as if we had been using that particular one all of our lives.

Recognition of the shared characteristics of objects, people, events, relationships, and so on is not something that occurs automatically without learning. The many variables affecting concept learning have already been discussed. But, we might well ask, how does this all relate to conceptual development in children? Certainly the six-month-old has experienced washcloths while being cleaned up after a meal, but the child still may attempt to put it in its mouth, throw it onto the floor, or manipulate it as if it were a toy. This kind of behavior exemplifies the young child's tendency to initially be *overinclusive* in its concepts. The child also tends to be subjective in its criteria for classification. By subjective, we mean that the child's categorizations may be on quite a different basis than adults' or other children's. Both of these characteristics are evident in the baby's inclusion of washcloth in the category of suckable objects. Most adults would consider this behavior maladaptive or at least inappropriate.

Children are not always overinclusive or undifferentiated in their classification systems. *Underinclusion* is also common particularly during the late preschool years and kindergarten. Underinclusion is typically related to a child's failure to comprehend that objects, people, and events can belong to more than one category simultaneously and that categories are interrelated through hierarchical networks. The child's pet is at the same time, Fido, terrier, dog, pet, canine, mammal, animal, vertebrate, and so on. Each subsequent class in the list subsumes or is superordinate to all previously listed classes.

The young child's difficulty in grasping the notion of multiple classification is evident in the results of a study by Kooistra (1964). Children encountered two sets of dolls, the fathers and the doctors. One doll was then moved from the father set to the doctor set, while the child was told that this father had gone to school and is now a doctor. When the question, "Is he still a father?" was posed, most five-year-olds responded, "no." Nine-year-olds, however, saw that the father could

be both a father and a doctor, that is, belong simultaneously to two categories. Similar inflexibility in concept behavior is seen in young children if they are asked to first categorize a series of blocks on the basis of shape, then on color or some other dimension.

In our previous discussion of concept learning, it was emphasized that one of the basic tasks is that of discovering the relevant attributes defining a category. It was noted that the difficulty of the task was affected by the number of relevant and irrelevant dimensions present in the instances. A series of studies by Ricciuti and his associates examined the effects of redundancy and number of irrelevant dimensions on the categorization behavior of infants twelve to twenty-four months old (Ricciuti and Benjamin, 1957; Ricciuti, 1965).

The easiest task involved simply showing an infant eight objects and asking the infant to play with them. The objects could be sorted into two categories of four each. The two object groups differed in three attributes: color, texture, and shape. Since any one of the attributes could be used in making the categorization, the three attributes are said to be redundant. Although one-year-old infants rarely physically separated the objects into two piles, about half were observed to handle the objects of one group before touching the objects of another group. When the two groups of objects were much more similar, differing in one attribute (size), only 25 percent of the one-year-olds showed ordered handling of the objects. The increasing ability with age to identify objects with a common attribute without the aid of redundant cues was evident in that 50 percent of the eighteen month olds and 63 percent of the two-year-olds showed ordered handling of the objects.

Despite the fact that even infants show evidence of recognition of commonalities among objects, their classification skills are limited. Many concepts require the presence of a combination of attributes for identification. The infant and most preschoolers can only classify on the basis of a single attribute such as size, shape, or color. When two or more attributes must be present, they typically have difficulties. For example, both shape and size are relevant attributes of the concept, SMALL TRIANGLE. Similarly, the concept FA-

THER must meet at least two criteria, the individual must be male and have children.

Piaget and others have studied the child's increasing ability to deal with conjunctive concepts. The procedure typically used is quite different from the card sorting procedure frequently used with adult subjects. Instead children's ability to deal with conjunctive concepts has been studied using the logical multiplication procedure. This procedure emphasizes rule identification as opposed to attribute identification. The child may be shown a set of objects arranged in an organized fashion, for example, a 2×2 matrix representing the logical multiplication of two dimensions, each having two attributes, except that one cell is empty (see Figure 11-6 for an example of a completed matrix). The child's task is to select the correct set of stimuli to fill the empty cell from an assortment of possibilities. Smedslund (1964) has found that in such a task, only about 10 percent of the seven- and eight-year-olds could correctly complete the matrix. The results demonstrate the difficulty young children have in coordinating attributes conjunctively even though they can correctly perceive and identify the shapes, colors, sizes, texture, or other dimensions used in such experiments.

Interestingly, preschool children have acquired many concepts that require the application of a conjunctive rule in their everyday lives. The four-year-old rarely makes the toddlers' mistake of labeling all four-legged animals as dogs or all birds as chickens. The failure to demonstrate this ability in the logical multiplication type of tasks probably stems from an inability to *systematically* (logically rather than intuitively) apply the conjunctive rule. This change from intuitive thought to logical operations epitomizes the growth of intelligence for Piaget during the middle childhood period.

Language and Its Development

"More doggie," "Me need it," "Two doll," "Want go get it." These utterances of two-year-olds are music to parents' ears but often prove difficult for the uninitiated to interpret. Not only are some of the word sequences unusual to English, but also the pronunciation of certain sounds may leave something to be desired. However, it is well known that parents and siblings quickly learn to decipher the strange language code of the young child. Interestingly, they make few demands on the child to correct grammatical errors. How then does the child come to acquire grammatically correct forms of speech in just a few short years?

Research on language acquisition has focused on two questions, often separately: (1) what does the child know about language at various stages of development, and (2) how is language acquired? Each of these questions and their relationship to understanding language development will be discussed in turn. Before addressing the specific question of what the child learns about the language code, it is necessary to consider the characteristics of the final product.

Nature of Language

It is generally assumed that one of the prerequisites to understanding *how* language is acquired is the development of a good decription of *what* is acquired. Psychologists turn to the linguist for that description. There is disagreement among

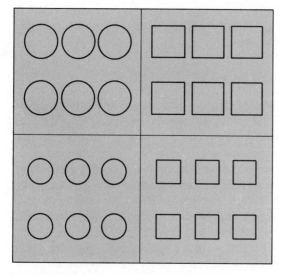

Fig. 11-6. Results of 2 x 2 logical multiplication of two shapes of two sizes.

linguists, however, as to the best description of the linguistic code.

Levels of Analysis. The description of the linguistic code is complex and open to alternative interpretations, in part because of the many levels at which language can be described. For example, consider, the sentence "The boy goes surfing on Wednesdays." We could look for commonalities with other sentences at the level of the individual sounds. This level is formally referred to as the phonemic level. A *phoneme* is the smallest unit of speech that makes a difference to the speakers of a language. For example, the sound difference in "pun" and "bun" signals a difference in meaning to English speakers, hence the /p/ and /b/ sounds are classified as phonemes.

We could also look for commonalities across sentences at the word level but we would quickly experience some difficulties. Some words are made up of more than one meaningful unit, for example, "black-berry" or "go-es." Description of language at one step higher than the phoneme is for that reason not at the word level, but takes place at the morphemic level. The *morpheme* is the smallest meaningful unit of speech. It cannot be broken down further and still retain meaning. In some cases, the meaningful units must occur joined to another morpheme. The /es/ in "goes" cannot occur alone, despite the fact that it conveys meaning, namely, tense.

Moving up the ladder one more rung, language can also be described at the phrase level. The *phrase* is an ordered cluster of words that go together. By "go together" is meant that they serve as a functional unit. The best way to clarify this level of language structure is by illustration. Consider the two strings of words that follow:

1. hole in put can brick girl the the
2. the girl can put the brick in the hole

There are clusters of words that we would all agree belong together in Sentence 2 that are not apparent in Sentence 1, even though it is composed of the same words. We would probably cluster the words in the second sentences in one of three ways:

2a. The girl / can put the brick in the hole
2b. The girl / can put / the brick in the hole
2c. The girl / can put / the brick / in the hole

In most sentences it is found there are alternate groupings that can be made. Note that each regrouping involves breaking a sequence of words into a smaller set. This characteristic of language, its hierarchical structure, is viewed as the key to its efficiency as a code on meaning.

Yet another level of analysis of the sentence deals not with the code itself, but with the meaning or semantic component. The *semantic* level refers to relationships between words as well as the meanings of individual vocabulary items within a sentence. It is one thing to know what the concrete referents of "dog" and "bark" are but quite another to know that "the barking dog" and "the dog barks" are expressing the same basic relationship between "dog" and "bark."

Grammar Models. Several types of grammar models have been proposed as representations of the regularities that exist in language at the word and phrase levels: finite-state, phrase structure, transformational, and case grammars. The major goal of these theories is to devise a set of rules that will generate all the possible (actually an infinite number) grammatical sentences and will never generate ungrammatical sentences. Some linguists have also added the constraint that the system must be simple enough to make it possible for a human to acquire such a set of rules. Grammar models are of interest to psychologists as theories of what it is the language user knows about the structure of language.

What Is Acquired

What a child or adult knows about the language code cannot be directly observed, but inferences can be drawn on the basis of what is said and comprehended. Deviations from what the adult would typically say provide one major source of information regarding children's knowledge of language. The types of errors that children make—overgeneralizations, simplifications, deletions, and substitutions—have been found to be systematic. That is, many children make the same types of errors at approximately the same point in their language development. Such findings have led to the conclusion that a child's speech is rule-governed, just as the adult's is assumed to be—not by an external grammar model but by one's own internalized implicit set of rules. Most of the errors or deviations a child makes from adult language forms are consistent with the child's "hypothesis" at that moment regarding the appropriate grammatical structure to use.

You all undoubtedly remember classes in grammar in your elementary and secondary schooling and probably are wondering how the psychologist studying language acquisition could suggest that the child is, in a sense, "making up" or inducing grammar rules that are then applied to the child's own production and comprehension. It makes more sense if you keep in mind that the grammar rules you studied in school were simply hypotheses generated by linguists as to the system or rules that the people speaking a particular language follow. Formal grammar rules such as those we learn in school to sharpen our knowledge of the rules can be thought of as models or theories of what adult speakers of a language know about the language code.

It should be noted that when we say a language user has acquired knowledge of the rules of language, this does not mean that the rules are necessarily known in any explicit way. Without formal schooling, language users cannot rattle off the rules to which their speech conforms. The rules are implicit. It has been shown that even adult subjects may learn an artificial language through exposure to some of the possible sentences of the language, but they are unable to say what rules they are following when they create new sentences which fit the rules. Another thing to keep in mind is that often there is a discrepancy between what a language user *knows* and what the language user produces. Just because someone usually speaks as if that person knows the rules of the language, it does not mean all productions will follow them. When a person is tired, distracted, overloaded, and so on, that person is likely to deviate. Because of this discrepancy, linguists and psychologists often distinguish between what a language user knows, *competence,* and what a language user says or comprehends, *performance.*

Evidence for the assumption that language users, both child and adult, behave as if they have acquired rules can be found at more than one level of language. At the phonological level (sound),

Messer (1967) has demonstrated that even three- and four-year-olds can identify which of two nonsense sequences of sounds could occur in English and which could not (for example, dwil vs. nwil). Since the children could have never encountered these nonsense words before, their judgments must have been based on some abstraction of what sequences can occur, an abstraction that is independent of particular words.

At the morphological level (smallest meaningful units of speech), it has been clearly demonstrated that children from three to five have acquired a functional knowledge of the rules for use of word inflections. Inflections are special sounds that are added to the ends of words to convey plurality, tense, and so on, such as plural endings /-s/, the past tense /-ed/, and progressive verb ending /-ing/. To determine whether children had productive, not just rotely acquired knowledge of word endings, Berko (1958) showed children pictures of imaginary creatures. Each child was told something about them. For example, "This is a wug. Now there is another one. There are two of them." The child was then asked to complete the sentence "There are two _____." The sentence was correctly completed with "wugs" by the children, even though "wug" was a word never encountered before. The child is assumed to be applying rules induced from hearing speech to the nonsense words presented in the Berko study. With English, as with nonsense words, when a case is encountered that does not follow the general rule, children typically overgeneralize. For example, the plural of "goose" is "geese" but most preschool children will maintain that it is "gooses" even when told the correct form. Such deviations from the adult model provide further evidence that the young child is creating forms that fit that child's current rule, not simply a repetition of what that child heard.

Several studies have focused on whether there is any psychological validity to grammar models representing the phrase structure of sentences. For example, Johnson (1965) reported that the probability of making errors in the recall of sentences is greater at the phrase boundaries than within a phrase. If an error were made in recalling the sentence "The house/across the street/is burning" (slashes not presented to subjects), it tended to occur between "house" and "across" and between "street" and "burning." Once a phrase was started, it was completed correctly. The difficulty came in getting the next phrase started. The subjects apparently were learning the sentences, not as a sequence of unrelated words, but in units corresponding to the phrase-structure.

In general, the assumption that the speech and comprehension of language users follow implicit rules has received considerable support. There is disagreement, however, regarding the best way (that is, the best grammar) to represent the rule knowledge attributed to the language user.

Early Language Development

Grammatical sentences do not emerge automatically at birth. They undergo a long developmental history. That history is the subject of this section. Unless there are anatomical or emotional problems, most children utter their first words somewhere around one-year-old. This event is found to occur with relatively little age variability despite great disparities in linguistic environment. The richness of the child's language environment has been found to affect the rate of progress once speech begins but to have little effect on age of onset. The regularity in age of onset has been interpreted by Eric Lenneberg (1967) and others as indicating that early speech behavior is under maturational control. As with walking and other motor milestones, opportunity to practice does facilitate acquisition once the child is physically ready but no amount of pushing will substantially speed up development before that point is reached.

Prelinguistic Period. In keeping with this notion that early language is maturationally controlled, we find that infants proceed through a predictable sequence of vocalizations prior to the utterance of the first words. During the first year, the child's prespeech vocalizations change markedly in the direction of closer and closer approximation to adult speech, yet some sounds used frequently by adults such as /s/ and /r/ may be used infrequently, if at all, by the infant.

The child's prespeech vocal repertoire is rather limited, being mainly the cry. Although a simple,

undifferentiated response, the cry serves an important communicative function. Because of the infant's immobility, it is the only means of initiating contact with the outside world. The basic role of vocalization as a means of communication is laid down during this period. Also infants may be learning something basic about their ability to have an effect on their environment—the beginning of competence.

Not all of the young infant's vocalizations during the first couple of months are produced while crying. A large proportion of the noncrying vocalizations, however, are similar in sound to crying. They are most similar to the vowel sounds we make in the middle and back of the mouth, for example, /e/, and /ae/. It is not long before these vowel sounds are joined by the front vowel sounds, for example, /o/ and /u/, made by pushing air through rounded lips.

Early appearing consonant sounds are usually made during periods of distress or in anticipation of feeding (Lewis, 1936). The back consonants, /h/, /g/, and /k/, are typically the first to be heard, followed by the front consonants, /m/, /p/, and /b/. Other consonants such as /t/, /d/, /l/, and /s/, make their appearance much later, because they require some interaction of the tongue with teeth. Most infants do not have upper front teeth until the last quarter of the first year, if then.

Noncrying vocalization gradually increases during the first three months and begins increasingly to be separated from distress. The nondistress vocalizations of the two- to six-month-old are typically referred to as *cooing*. By six months the nature of vocalization has changed qualitatively and quantitatively. Vocalization at this age is called *babbling*. Babbling includes a wider variety of sounds than cooing. Sound sequences involving the reduplication of consonant-vowel sequences begin to occur ("mamamama" or "babababa"). Unlike earlier vocalizations most babbling is clearly detached from stress. In fact, it often accompanies other expressions of happiness such as smiling or chuckling. One of the most interesting changes is the apparent autonomy of the babbling activity. It frequently occurs while the infant is absorbed in play or lying awake in the crib. Much of the infant's babbling seems to serve no apparent social function. It often ceases when the child becomes aware of the presence of mother or sibling in the room. One gets the impression that the sound of the infant's voice is self-reinforcing and that the child purposely varies sounds to hear the consequence.

Despite the apparent lack of social function, it is during this period of self-maintained play with sounds that the child also begins to become aware that the others can make the same sounds. Sometime around six months, the child may engage in *mutual imitation* with the parent. This kind of play must begin with a sound made by the child. If the parent imitates the baby, the baby will in turn imitate the parent. Variations in sounds will be initiated by the child. True imitation where a child reproduces a sound or behavior not already part of the child's repertoire comes toward the end of the first year.

The early vocalizations—crying, cooing, and early babbling—are unlearned responses that require little in the way of reinforcement or auditory feedback (hearing own speech) to become a part of the child's behavior repertoire. Of course, once the sounds appear, it is possible to increase the frequency of those vocalizations by systematically reinforcing with a social response such as adult vocalization and a pat on the tummy (Rheingold et al., 1959). It has even been shown that the frequency of specific vowel and consonant sounds can be increased by differential reinforcement (Routh, 1969). It should be mentioned that although parents may differentially reinforce a few early sound sequences such as "mama" or "dada," there is no evidence that the drift found in babbling toward adult speech patterns is due to differential reinforcement. The evidence suggests instead that parents reinforce their children for vocalizing in general, often with an adult vocalization. These adult vocalizations plus those occurring during routine caretaking and play provide many speech models. Probably it is in part from attempts to match the sounds produced by models in imitative play that the infant's vocalizations come to an ever closer match with the adult's during the prelinguistic period.

The importance of feedback and exposure to linguistic input increases after six months. It has been found that until that time, deaf children produce cooing and babbling that are not different from that produced by hearing babies (Lenneberg et al., 1965). After six months, however, the quality and quantity of the deaf child's babbling sounds are noticeably different from the hearing infant's babblings.

The role of the linguistic environment is evident when the babbling of children of different language groups is compared. The babbling of the Chinese infant is quite different from the babbling of the Anglo-American infant (Weir, 1966). Chinese babies show more pitch variation, a characteristic of the Chinese language. These differences are not evident until after six months of age, indicating the importance of maturation prior to that point and the role of environment thereafter in determining the form of vocalizations. Interestingly, it is the intonation rather than the specific sounds produced that is most different across infants of different language groups. There is surprising similarity in the predominance of certain sounds across such diverse languages as English and Japanese.

Speech Perception in Infancy. Language development involves learning to perceive and comprehend as well as produce speech. Typically, it is found that throughout childhood, speech comprehension is ahead of production. This has been found to hold true for infants as well as older children. Prerequisite to comprehension, however, is the ability to discriminate speech from nonspeech and to discriminate particular sounds used in speech.

There is some evidence that by the end of the first month the infant responds differentially to the human voice and other sounds (Wolff, 1966). The infant is more likely to orient to a voice, cease sucking, and be quieted by a voice than other sounds. As young as four months, the child will orient toward and smile at the mother's voice over an unfamiliar voice (Laroche and Tcheng, 1963).

Our grandmothers probably would not believe this, but recently it has been found that infants as young as one month have surprising sensitivity to the very small differences between some of the phonemes (sounds signaling differences in meaning) we use in our language, such as the /p/ in "pa" and the /b/ in "ba" (Eimas et al., 1971). Determining that the infant this young is capable of such discriminations requires very special procedures. Similar procedures are sometimes used to assess hearing in small children. These procedures take advantage of the fact that even very young infants will perform a response for stimulus change in their environment. In the Eimas et al. study, the stimulus change was a sound sequence such as /pa/. Presentation of the /pa/ was made contingent upon sucking (that is, presented only after a sucking response had been made). It is also well known that after many repetitions, individuals discontinue responding to an auditory stimulus; they habituate. When habituation occurs, the auditory stimulus is no longer able to maintain sucking and the rate decreases. Accordingly, Eimas et al. presented /pa/ after sucking responses until habituation set in and sucking declined. Then a new auditory stimulus, /ba/ was introduced. Sucking rate should increase only if the infant detects the difference between /pa/ and /ba/. In fact, it was found that when a change in stimulus occurred, sucking increased, indicating that the infants did discriminate the difference in sound.

These results suggest that the young infant is indeed capable of selectively responding not only to speech but to specific speech sounds. Armed with these capabilities, the infant may be able to detect similarities between its vocalizations and those of others.

Holophrastic Speech. In the course of babbling the infant produces some sound sequences which are singled out for reinforcement by the parent. These simple sound sequences, such as "mama," "papa," or "dada," take on the status of the baby's first words when the child begins to use them to name or refer to particular individuals.

Initially the child's words may be used simply as labels, but it is not long before the child is using words in an attempt to communicate wishes or describe an ongoing situation. A single word is often used to stand for a relationship such as possession ("Mary" for "Mary's jacket"), agent-action ("go" for "he goes"), action-object ("cookie" for "eat cookie"), and action-locative

("floor" for "sit floor"). When a single word stands for a phrase or sentence, it is referred to as a *holophrase.*

It has been observed that children may use the same word in several contexts, but in each context the word itself must be interpreted differently (Bloom, 1970). For example, "mama" may be heard in the following contexts: (a) child pointing to mother's purse, (b) child unable to reach cookie on shelf, and (c) child unable to locate mother. In each context the meaning of the single word, "mama," appears to be different; possession ("It's mama's purse"), help asking ("Mama, help me reach the cookie"), and attention or location seeking ("Where are you, mama?"), respectively. The main evidence we have that the child is using single words to express whole ideas is the child's reaction to our interpretation. The child may be quite indignant if mother says, "oh, isn't that nice," in response to his holophrase "cookie" if, in fact, the child had not just had a cookie but were asking for one.

There are some obvious limitations to such a simple communication system. It is only possible to get the point across if the listener is turned into the context at the moment the utterance is made. Others may have more difficulty.

Interesting evidence for the interpretation that single words may stand for whole ideas has been reported by Menyuk and Benholtz (1969). They found differences in the intonation of the same word depending on the context. Those which were interpreted on the basis of context as questions showed the rising inflection characteristic of questions. Those single words which were interpreted as statements or declarations of fact had the characteristic fall in frequency that occurs in adult speech. (Listen to what happens to your voice at the end of the sentence "Where is he going?" in contrast to the sentence "He is going.")

Two-Word Utterances. A few months after the first word appears, words begin to occur in combinations. Considerable communicative power is obtained, for now the child can express many relationships that were only implied in the child's holophrastic speech.

Several investigators have made in-depth analysis of the child's early utterances in an attempt to determine what, if any, system the child uses for combining words. It had been observed that words are not randomly combined; only a few of the possible combinations of words in a child's vocabulary actually occur. The assumption is made that the child must be operating under some constraints or rules in the same way that adults do in sequencing words.

This kind of reasoning led to several attempts to write a grammar (discover the child's rules of combination) for children's speech (Braine 1963a; Brown and Fraser, 1964; Miller and Ervin, 1964). These investigators arrived independently at basically the same description of the child's early two-word utterances. It was observed that the child uses a few words very frequently, called *pivot* words. Other words are used less frequently, usually in combination with a pivot word. This class has been called *open* words, because any new vocabulary items are likely to fall into this category rather than the pivot class.

Although little commonality of class membership across children was observed, there was considerable similarity across children in how these two classes were combined. Braine (1963a) and others observed that each pivot word had its own fixed position. That is, some always occurred first in utterances and others always occurred second in a particular child's speech as is evident in the following examples. (The pivot word is in italics). By representing the commonalities of each

See sock	Want *do*
See baby	Bunny *do*
See window	
	Boot *off*
More cookie	Water *off*
More taxi	Sweater *off*
There ball	Mommy *go*
There high	Me *go*

list symbolically, we can state the following two rules of combination (where S refers to Sentence, P_1 and P_2 refer to subclasses of pivot words, and O refers to open class words):

$$S \rightarrow P_1 + O$$
$$S \rightarrow O + P_2$$

These two simple rules were found to describe most of the recorded utterances of several children studied. Those that did not fit the two rules were sometimes combinations of open class words such as "mommy sleep," "want cookie," and "baby sweater." These could be represented by the rule:

$$S \rightarrow O + O$$

Braine (1976) has also identified two additional patterns in first word combinations: associative productivity and groping patterns. Associative productivity refers to word combinations in which a particular pivot word is used with several other words but *all* the resulting combinations with that pivot occur in adult speech. Since there are not "errors" to indicate that the child may be utilizing a general rule to construct these combinations, Braine prefers to regard them as imitated combinations. Groping patterns refer to combinations produced with great hesitancy and with no consistent word order. It is as if the child is searching for a means of expressing meaning before the child has acquired sufficient grammatical competence.

Further study of the same children by Brown and others led to attempts to demonstrate that gradually the pivot and open classes divided into subgroupings that eventually came to match the word classes used by adults. These attempts have not been particularly successful, probably because the pivot grammar is only a superficial representation of what children know about language.

Lois Bloom (1970) argues that the distributional analysis made by Braine and others it not an inaccurate description but is inadequate. It misses much of the richness of the meanings being expressed. The pivot grammar only describes the fact that certain words tend to occur in a fixed position and share context with a subset of other words. It does not represent relationships. Bloom suggests that the observer can be fooled or misled by only looking at the surface structure (utterances out of context) and not paying attention to what the child is attempting to express.

Bloom (1970), Brown (1973), and Schlesinger (1971) have analyzed children's early two-word utterances in terms of the functional relationship between words. The relationships were inferred from the context in which the utterances occurred.

This required careful recording, sometimes using video tape, of speech in context for later analysis. This type of analysis has revealed that words change function in two-word utterances even though they may retain the same relative position across utterances. For example, from the context in which "mommy iron" and "mommy busy" occurred, Bloom inferred that they expressed an agent-action or state of being relationship, that is "mommy is ironing" and "mommy is busy." In the utterances "mommy lunch" and "mommy slipper," however, the function of "mommy" differed from the preceding examples. The context revealed that "mommy" had become a possessor in a possessor-object relationship in these latter examples. Based on inferences from speech in context, a set of twelve relationships has been identified as occurring in early two-word utterances.

Although more adequate experimental techniques will have to be devised to test the existence of these inferred relationships, the evidence to date does suggest that at least from a semantic point of view, the child's early utterances are more complex than previously thought.

Three-Word Utterances. The next big step in language acquisition is the three-word utterance which quickly gives way to four- and five-word utterances. It is at this point that we are able to see considerable progress in the structural knowledge acquired by the child. This change in structural knowledge is evident in the elaborations made of the noun phrase and verb component of the verb phrase of utterances.

Initially the elaboration occurs in the noun phrases serving as objects at the end of sentences. For example, "That hat" may become elaborated into "That my hat," and later to "That my red hat." The formation of subclasses of noun modifiers (articles, adjectives, possessive pronouns) takes place during this period. For example, it becomes necessary to differentiate between these subclasses because possessive pronouns (such as, my, our, his) do not occur after articles as do other modifiers. We say "That is a car" and "That is a blue car," but we do not say "That is a my car."

Complex Structures. It is intuitively appealing to assume that children will master the least complex structural forms before moving onto the more complex question, passive, negative, relative clause, conjunctive, and so on. Accordingly, we might expect that a child would first master such basic sentences as "I am going to the store" before attempting to convey such notions as "I am not going to the store" or "Why can't I go to the store." The sentence "I am going to the store" would seem to be an essential frame that would have to be acquired first. There is no evidence, however, that children proceed in such a systematic way in their acquisition of structural knowledge (Bloom, 1970; Brown and Hamlon, 1970). They do not wait around for the simple sentence to become refined before asking questions or using the negative. It is just that the early forms of those more complex structures are far from adult sentence forms.

The acquisition of two types of complex structures has been studied in some detail: the negative and question. There are many commonalities in the early acquisition of the negative and question which will become evident as we trace the development of each.

The early instances of the use of the negative usually involve simply preposing a word or sentence with a special negative operator, *no*. The following examples of the early uses of *no* to negate an affirmative sentence are taken from the speech of children recorded by Klima and Bellugi (1966) and Bloom (1970).

> No drop mitten.
> No the sun shining.
> No want soup.
> No fall.
> No lollipop.
> No fire engine.
> No throw it.

Since these same utterances also occur without the *no* at the beginning, it appears that the child has simply preposed the negative to sentences already in the repertoire, *NEG + S*.

The next approximation to the adult use of the negative has been found to be inclusion of the negative contraction within sentences, such as, "He can't do it" or "She won't let me." The negative morpheme (not) also occurs without an auxiliary, such as, "That not blue one." During this period the auxiliary never occurs without the negative, however, suggesting that the negative contractions (such as *can't*) are simply imitated vocabulary items. There is no evidence yet that the child, during this period, can negate *any* sentence. It is not long, however, before the auxiliary appears separate from the negative and both appear to be used in a productive fashion. It should be noted that even after adult forms appear in a child's speech, the old forms often remain. Both a two-year-old and a five-year-old may say "I not do it" (Menyuk, 1969).

The sequence of development of the question is very similar to the negative except that there is one form that precedes the prepose. It is possible to ask a question simply through the use of rising intonation at the end of a sentence. For example, the sentence "I said that?" does not contain a question word (such as, what or why), yet we can communicate that we are in question. The young child uses this technique before beginning to use "whats" and "whys." The child simply raises its voice at the end of a word or phrase, for example, "Sit?" or "Me go too?" (Menyuk and Bernholtz, 1969). The use of rising inflection, however, only works for questions that can be answered by "Yes" or "No." If the child needs a more elaborate answer, that child must ask what is called a Wh-question using *where, when, what, who,* and so on (such as "Who is that?"). As most parents will attest, the early form of the Wh-question is frequently "What dat?" or "Who dat?" or "Where you go?" Sometimes it seems as if the child has forgotten how to say anything but "no," "What," and "Why?"

The next phase in the development of the Wh-questions parallels the negative prepose stage in the development of negatives. A question word is followed by a sentence in its usual word order. For example, the child may produce "How he can be a doctor?" Note that the auxiliary *can* and the subject *he* have not been inverted as is usual in the adult form, such as, "How can he be a doctor?" Interestingly, during the same period, word order is correctly inverted in the Yes-No type question but still not inverted in Wh-questions. Rather than using the earlier form "You can't fix it?," the child will ask "Can't you fix it?" When inversion of the auxiliary does occur in Wh-questions, it occurs first in affirmative sentences, followed

somewhat later by inversion in the negative. Children seem to be limited in the number of complexities that can be handled simultaneously.

It may take as long as four years for the adult forms of questions to predominate in the child's speech, despite the early appearance of question intonation and of the Wh-question words. Meanwhile, the complexities of tense, auxiliaries, and noun modifiers in the simple, active, declarative sentence have long before been nearly perfected. Apparently there is some relationship between structural complexity and the amount of time required to achieve the adult structural form of sentences. As noted earlier, no such relationship between structural complexity and age of first appearance of attempts at complex structures has been found to exist. Questions and negatives are attempted at the holophrastic stage.

Later Grammatical Development

Usually around three years of age, additional forms of grammatical complexity begin to appear in rudimentary form. For example, children begin to join related ideas with conjunctions such as *and* or *but;* they attempt to modify the main verb with adverbial clauses beginning with such words as *when, before, after,* and *because;* they begin to modify the noun phrase with relative clauses (for example, I know the boy *who did that*); and they begin to use complements following verbs (such as I want *to go home*.)

Despite their early beginnings, certain uses of these structures are avoided, misused, or misinterpreted sometimes as late as nine or ten years of age. One construction that does not appear in spontaneous speech until relatively late is the use of the relative clause as a modifier of the subject of the main clause, such as "The girl *who lives down the street* ran home crying" (Limber, 1973). Since children as young as four may use such clauses to modify objects (such as "I know the girl *who lives down the street*"), it appears that children operate on the general principle: do not interrupt the main clause with a relative clause.

Young children also seem to operate using a simple principle when interpreting and producing sentences with adverbial clauses, such as, *"After I finished gardening,* I washed up" (Clark, 1971;

Johnson, 1975). Three- and four-year-olds correctly comprehend such structures, only if the occurrence of actual events coincides with the order of mention in the sentence. Until five or six years of age, they have difficulty interpreting the same sentence given above with reversed clause order (I washed up *after I finished gardening*).

As late as nine or ten years of age, some children have difficulty interpreting complement structures which violate the general rule (minimal-distance principle) that the subject of any complement is the noun phrase nearest to it (C. Chomsky, 1969). For example, in the sentence "John asked Jill to do the work," *Jill* is the subject of the verb (*do*) of the complement, that is, *Jill* is the doer, not *John*. Because a sentence such as "John asked Jill what to do" is an exception to the general rule (*John,* not *Jill* is the subject of the verb *do* and hence, the sentence should be interpreted "John asked Jill what *he* should do"), it is frequently misintrepreted as if it meant "John asked Jill what *she* should do."

It is clear from these examples that although the basics of language structure are acquired in the first three or four years, it takes several more years before the structural code is perfected. Infrequently used structures and those that are exceptions to a general rule may cause difficulty, even into adulthood. Both semantic and syntactic development continue for many years.

The Process of Acquisition

Arriving at a description of what children are learning about language only brings us part way in the understanding of language acquisition. In fact, it only opens the way for many questions about the process of acquisition or *how* language is acquired. What role do specific environmental factors play in the development of language? How important is imitation as a mechanism of acquisition? What role does maturation play?

There is no argument among theorists that exposure to linguistic input is necessary for language acquisition, but they do differ in the relative importance placed on the role of differential reinforcement, child response in the form of imitation, and parental response in the form of expansion of the child's utterance (Child: "Me go?" Parent: "You want to go?").

The view identified with many psycholinguists and with the linguist Chomsky (1965) during the 1960s emphasized maturation as playing a dominant role in acquisition. It was postulated that the child brings to the task of language learning an innate propensity for acquiring phrase-structure and transformation rules (Chomsky, 1965; McNeill, 1966). Given at least minimal exposure to language, it was argued that there was no alternative but for the child to acquire language just as the child inevitably learns to walk (as long as there are no physical complications). How theorists have interpreted "propensity" has varied considerably, ranging from innate knowledge of linguistic universals (those aspects of rules common to all languages) to possession of the biological apparatus for processing input and producing speech.

On the other end of the continuum were theorists who emphasized the learned aspect of language and the role of environmental factors in determining actual speech (for example, Braine, 1963b; Staats, 1971). The primary vehicles for transmission of language have been commonly believed to be imitation (a form of operant conditioning) and shaping (reinforcement of successive approximations to adult speech) Sherman, 1971; Staats, 1971).

Imitation. During the preschool years, children are known for their tendency to imitate anything their parents do and say, often to the great embarrassment of the parents. Knowing the extent to which children imitate adults and older children, it seems only common sense to assume that they may add structural complexity to their speech through imitation. Certainly there are many good speech models available to a child. Why is it not possible that the child learns language simply by saying what the child hears others say?

Although most children do imitate the speech of others at times, there are some loopholes in the notion that imitation is a *necessary* process in the course of language acquisition. First of all, a few cases of children who cannot speak but who acquire functional, receptive language have been reported (such as Lenneberg, 1962). Apparently it is not necessary to have ever uttered a word to acquire knowledge of the semantic and structural aspects of language necessary for comprehension. Lenneberg has also reported instances where children have not been able to practice speech because of medical problems. When the problems were cleared up and the child was able to speak for the first time, it was found that his speech was not that of a child just learning his first words, but age-appropriate.

A second form of evidence is that children with normal speech typically show evidence of understanding the use of structures before they are able to actually produce them in speech. This lag in speech suggests that imitation may not be essential for gaining new structural knowledge.

Another argument against the primacy of imitation as a mechanism of acquisition is the fact that children make many errors in their productions that adults do not make, such as "There is a boy what is tall," "He hitted me," "All gone lettuce." The discovery that many of these errors are not simply omissions, but are substitutions or overgeneralizations, has led several investigators to assume that the child must be doing more than simply imitating adult speech. They argue that the child is "creating" utterances in keeping with a set of rules abstracted from the speech input heard. The child need never have heard or said a sentence before producing it.

Perhaps the most surprising evidence against the importance of the role of imitation is the finding that not all children are frequent imitators of their parents. At least, many do not imitate immediately following or within the next ten utterances following the model sentence. Ervin-Tripp (1964) examined the speech records of five children and found little evidence of imitation, particularly imitation more complex than spontaneous speech. A later study (Bloom et al., 1974) reported finding that *some* children imitated a great deal (as much as 40 percent of their speech) but others imitated rarely (less than 10 percent of their utterances). More important than the finding of variability in amount of imitation was information bearing on whether imitations were structurally more complex than spontaneous speech. While none of the children in the Ervin-Tripp study were reported to show developmental advances in structural complexity through their imitative speech, Bloom et al. reported that those subjects who did imitate did show some developmental advances in their imitations. The advances were typically on structures that were just beginning to emerge in spontaneous speech. Children did not bother imitating sentences containing structures they had already mastered, nor did they attempt to imitate sentences containing structures entirely new to them.

In summary, imitation is one means of adding structural complexity, but apparently not essential. Since most children are capable of imitating and have the opportunity to do so, we must assume that imitation does play some role in the language acquisition of most children. The next question we must ask, then, is what type of speech model do parents typically provide for their children? Does the complexity of parents' speech to children change with the age and linguistic sophistication of the child?

Parents' Speech to Their Children. One would expect that the optimal model would be one that is slightly more complex structurally than the child's speech. Listening to adults conversing or to an adult lecturing, you would hardly get the impression that the adult model could coincide with this ideal. It has been found, however, that mothers make considerable adjustment in their speech depending on the age of the child (Moerk, 1974; Nelson, 1973; Snow, 1972). Mothers do not talk "baby talk" to their children, nor do they talk over the heads of their children. Generally speaking, mothers greatly reduce both the length and complexity of their utterances to young children. For example, mothers of two- and three-year-olds use sentences about half as long as to adults. As the child's language improves, the complexity and length of the mother's speech increases. Most interesting is that the mother's speech has been shown to be just slightly more complex than the child's—probably the ideal model.

Optimizing learning conditions even more, the mother often produces these short, well-formed sentences as expansions of things the child has said (for example, Child: "Mommy soup" Parent: "Yes, that's mommy's soup";. Some middle-class mothers have been observed to expand as much as 30 percent of their children's utterances. During the two- and three-word utterance period, parents tend to repeat what the child has said in part as a check on interpretation. They are inadvertently providing a model which the child often does imitate. Part of the time the child's imitation is developmentally progressive as in the example below (from Slobin, 1968).

> Child: Pick'mato
> Adult: Picking tomatoes up?
> Child: Pick'mato up

Reinforcement.   Although it is clear that children often do imitate and may learn from it, the extent to which they rely upon this means of acquisition has not been determined. However, one thing is clear. Parents do not usually provide differential reinforcement for their children's early utterances. There is no evidence that parents gradually shape their young children's speech by reinforcing improvements in structure, and ignoring, or punishing inappropriate word usages. Such procedures would probably achieve the same end result but are apparently unnecessary. Parents may differentially reinforce speech productions at a later age to help refine the child's grammar but typically do not do so during the early acquisition stages. Parents are much more responsive to the factual accuracy of the message than how it is said. For example, Brown et al. (1969) report the mother of one of their subjects answering casually, "That's right," to the child's grammatically incorrect description of the mother, "He a girl." On the other hand, sometimes perfectly grammatical utterances will bring disapproval because of their factual inaccuracy.

In general, amount and quality of parent speech have been found to be more important determinants of advances in the child's language than reinforcement for the child's speech (Clarke-Stewart, 1973; Nelson, 1973).

Exposure.   Earlier we mentioned a view of language acquisition which emphasized the role of maturation. Proponents of this view maintain that exposure to language models in everyday, meaningful contexts is all that is critical for acquisition.

The child need say nothing. Expansions by mothers are viewed only as a valuable source of data about the regularities of language, not as a model to be repeated. Needless to say, it is difficult to obtain data relevant to this position, since most children do speak and they do imitate. Only those special cases of children who comprehend but do not speak would support this view that only exposure is essential.

Evaluation Attempts.   A few attempts have been made to experimentally determine the relative importance of mere exposure to speech, provision of expansions, and the child's imitation of modeled speech (Nelson et al, 1972; Cazden, 1965; Malouf and Dodd, 1972). With the exception of Cazden's study, children who were in groups that imitated model sentences or had their own speech expanded showed better performance on later measures of language progress than did children who were simply exposed to the same input. It is important to point out that children did make progress by merely being exposed to structured information such as sentences. Faster progress was made, however, when they took more active roles by imitating a model, producing a description that an adult could expand, or producing a sentence that an adult could comment on. It may not be so important whether the child's verbalization precedes (allowing for adult expansion) or follows the model sentence (imitation), as long as the child is actively involved in the communication process.

Two things are clear: Input is critical for language acquisition and rate of acquisition is related to amount and quality of input. It is less clear, however, what conditions of exposure to linguistic input are essential for acquisition. Active involvement by the child in actually producing meaningful speech appears to speed acquisition, although it may not be essential.

Thought and Language

We all assume that even though thoughts are not observable, they require some medium of representation. Because many of our thoughts are expressed in covert (internal) speech, it is easy to jump to the conclusion that thought and language are synonymous. But, can we think without language? Is language the only medium for internal representation? Does language control our thought? Is it true that a young child or a mute, deaf person cannot think without language? These and many other questions immediately come to mind when the relationship between thought and language is brought up. It is a question that has intrigued philosophers and psychologists since ancient times, but eludes a clear answer since both thought and inner speech are unobservable and may occur with minimal behavioral evidence.

Three major views regarding the relationship between language and thought have been proposed and widely accepted at various points in our intellectual history. These views are: (1) language determines thought, (2) thought is synonymous with language, and (3) thought determines language. It is only recently that psychologists have explored a fourth alternative, namely that all three views may be correct (Bourne et al., 1971; Jenkins, 1969). To aid in evaluating the question of the relationship between thought and language, the evidence for each view will be presented in turn.

Language Determines Thought. The most highly articulated hypothesis was put forth by Edward Sapir and Benjamin Whorf. It is known alternately as the Whorfian Hypothesis or the linguistic-relativity hypothesis. This linguistic-relativity hypothesis emphasizes the role of language in determining perception, understanding, the content of thought, and the very processes of thought. The strength of Whorf's convictions regarding the dependence of thought on language is evident in his claim that, "We dissect nature along lines laid down by our native language" (Carroll, 1956, p. 213).

Specifically, the linguistic-relatively hypothesis claims that our world view and nonverbal behavior such as perceptual discriminations are affected by the vocabulary and by the grammar of the language we speak. The kinds of observations which Whorf relied upon heavily were the differences between languages in the degree of differentiation in vocabulary for a particular type of object or event. For example, the Hanunoo in the Philippine Islands have been described as having ninety-two

names for rice, each referring to a different variety (Brown, 1965); and the Arabs as having hundreds of names for camels (Thomas, 1937). Whorf argued that a high degree of differentiation in our vocabulary influences how we perceive the world. That is, because of the many words for rice, the Hanunoo people will perceive small differences between rice grains and respond differentially, whereas we would not. The difficulty with this line of reasoning is that it is impossible to assess whether individuals have many names to represent what they know about rice and what they need to communicate to others, or whether the discriminations are made because the words are there. Although it seems most reasonable to assume that we develop words to convey the distinctions important in our everyday lives, there is evidence that the language code can influence an individual's perceptions independent of the importance of making a discrimination in everyday life (that is independent of his knowledge). It has been clearly demonstrated that having a verbal label for an experience may affect ones discriminations and recall of information.

In one demonstration, it was found that providing a label (or having the subject provide one) for a colored patch affected the subject's subsequent pattern of generalization in recognizing that color (Thomas and DeCapito, 1966; Thomas et al., 1968). Subjects were originally shown a blue-green stimulus (490 millimicrons in wavelength) and then exposed to additional stimuli similar but not identical to the original. They were instructed to press a key each time they thought they saw the original blue-green stimulus. Those subjects who had labeled the original blue-green as *blue* pressed the key when they saw stimuli in the blue range (below 490 millimicrons in wavelength). Those who had labeled the blue-green as *green,* however, tended to confuse the stimuli in the green range (about 490) with the original. The label, blue or green, biased perception, a result in keeping with the Whorfian hypothesis.

Another study consistent with the Whorfian hypothesis demonstrates the effect of verbal labels on memory. This classic study (Carmichael et al., 1932) required that subjects draw a set of twelve figures (see Figure 11-7) after having been exposed

Word List I		Word List II
Curtains in a Window	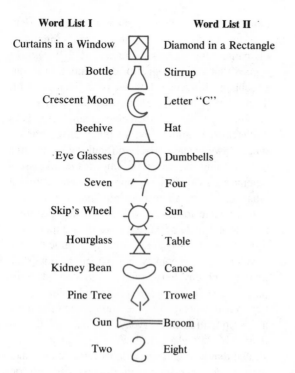	Diamond in a Rectangle
Bottle		Stirrup
Crescent Moon		Letter "C"
Beehive		Hat
Eye Glasses		Dumbbells
Seven		Four
Skip's Wheel		Sun
Hourglass		Table
Kidney Bean		Canoe
Pine Tree		Trowel
Gun		Broom
Two		Eight

Fig. 11-7. Stimulus figures and verbal labels presented to subjects. (From Carmichael, Hogan, and Walter, 1932)

to a name for each. The two groups of subjects received different labels for the figures. One group heard List I, while the other heard List II. Some of the labels were not entirely accurate codings of the figures. For example, the internal figure in the first drawing was not actually a diamond although one group received the label, "diamond in a rectangle." The effect of the verbal label in such instances was to distort memory for the figure. The errors in subjects' reproductions resulted in a figure that was more similar to the referent of the verbal label than to the actual figure presented in the list. The results suggest that subjects encoded the labels rather than an image of the shape so that the details of the original figure were not available to memory at the time the drawings were made. The subject has applied an information reducing category to his experience.

Although it is impossible in real life to determine the direction of influence—whether words are created to code experience or whether words affect our experience—there is clear evidence that words *can* influence our experience. That this is probably not the only direction of influence will become evident in the subsequent material.

Thought is Language. Although this view has few proponents currently because of its extreme form, it is historically and theoretically important. It has greatly affected the direction of research on thinking and the nature of representation. The view that there is no need to distinguish between language and thought became the accepted position of early behaviorists. Watson, the father of behaviorism, wrote, ". . . *what the psychologists have hitherto called thought is in short nothing but talking to ourselves*" (McGuigan, 1966, p. 10, italics in original). More specifically, Watson maintained that the muscular movements acquired and used during overt speech are the medium for internal speech, the primary form of thought. This view contrasts sharply with the view that thought is a central neural event requiring no motor responses, covert or overt.

The peripheral theory or motor theory of thinking, as the behaviorist view is referred to, is not without its intuitive appeal. We have all experienced the phenomenon of covertly talking our way through a difficult job or covertly rehearsing how we are going to explain the dent in the right fender to Dad. Certainly much of what we consider thought does take place as covert speech.

Before becoming too enamoured with the view, however, we might want to ask Watson a couple of questions to clarify our understanding of this motor theory of language. First, can thought occur without language? Watson did give his attention to this question and concluded that any bodily movement could serve as a medium for thought. For example, when we imagine "picking up a suitcase," a change in muscle potential occurs in the arm, not the speech apparatus. This peripheral response is thought according to Watson. Although he considered the possibility that we could think without words, his emphasis on subvocal speech as the primary mode of representation is evident in the closing section of his exposition, "What is Thinking?" He closes, ". . . we can say that *"thinking"* is largely *subvocal talking*—provided we hasten to explain that it can occur without words'' (McGuigan, 1966, p. 16, italics in original).

The second question we might ask Watson is whether thinking can occur in the absence of a motor response. To this question Watson would not equivocate; he would reply that responses are a necessary condition for thought and that usually these responses will be covert language. Whether we are reading a novel, doing an arithmetic problem, imagining a bikeride, or whatever, peripheral responses can be recorded. These peripheral responses are the substance of thought.

Attempts to support the motor theory of thinking before and after Watson's time have often consisted of the use of recording devices placed on various parts of the vocal apparatus or other muscles believed to be involved in thought (such as Jacobson, 1931). Most such studies have reported that following instructions to engage in some task (like arithmetic problems), there is indeed muscular contraction occurring in the speech apparatus or other peripheral muscles. Another method of study has been to record finger movements of deaf individuals whose exclusive mode of communication is sign language. Max (1935) found that there were changes in the action potential recorded from fingers during the dreams of the deaf. In other studies, he found that the presentation of language stimuli lead to finger activity also. It is interesting and somewhat compelling evidence for the motor theory of thinking that such finger movements would accompany the processes of thinking and dreaming for some signing deaf individuals.

Attempts to refute the motor theory of thinking have taken a curious form. For example, one enterprising researcher reported the absence of an effect on thinking while his tongue and lips were anesthetized. Others were more thorough in their attempt to eliminate the possibility of peripheral responding. Smith and his asscoiates (1947) administered a form of curare (d-tubocurarine) to one subject. The drug is known to result in paralysis of the skeletal muscles. Based on the report of the subject after the experiment and the EEG recording of brain activity, it was concluded that there was no interruption of consciousness. The subject was able to accurately remember the questions asked of him during the experiment and the various stimuli that had been presented. Although the testing procedure leaves much to be desired, the results do suggest that thinking may occur in the absence of peripheral responses.

Carryover from the motor theory of thinking is evident in the elaborate verbal mediation hypotheses offered by more recent psychologists as representations of thought. Although the notion that peripheral responses must accompany thought has been largely forgotten, the emphasis on covert language as a medium for thought has been retained. Consider, for example, the verbal-loop hypothesis of Glanzer and Clark (1962). It maintains that subjects translate all experience into a verbal form. This verbal code is stored until such time as retrieval is necessary. At that time the subject uses this verbal code as a basis for response. The possibility that nonverbal experience may be represented more directly by a nonverbal code, such as imagery, has only recently received attention (Paivio, 1971).

Thought Determines Language. This view too has its intuitive appeal. The phenomenon of having an idea we want to communicate but cannot seem to translate into verbal form fluently is all too common. This type of experience gives the impression that thought can exist independent of language. Both the Swiss genetic epistomologist Plaget (1967) and the Russian investigator Vygotsky (1962) argue that thought and language have independent origins but merge at a certain point in development. Their relationship then is mutual interdependence; that is, one serves the other. The result is that thought becomes increasingly verbal and speech becomes more logical. Plaget and Vygotsky diverge in their views regarding the exact nature of the influence of language on thought. Plaget maintain that nonlinguistic understanding of a concept must precede linguistic expression. That is, teaching children the appropriate language to use in a particular situation will not improve their performance as some have argued (see Bruner, 1964). According to Plaget, understanding must first come through nonlinguistic interaction with the real world. The concept must precede the label. Sometimes, however, that understanding requires the use of symbolic thought operations which may be aided by the use of language. As the individual matures, it is impossible to determine whether thought precedes language or language precedes thought.

During the preschool years especially, Piaget maintains that the child must base understanding of reality on the child's own interactions, that language cannot serve as the teacher. Support for this position has been supplied by one of Piaget's associates, Hermina Sinclair-de-Zwart (1967). She demonstrated first that the acquisition of a new concept or logical operation is accompanied (not preceded) by a modification in the child's language. Then she studied the effects of teaching the appropriate linguistic expressions used by those who had already attained the concept to those who had failed. She reasoned that if language determines thought, teaching the appropriate verbalizations should facilitate acquisition of the concept for younger children. For example, teaching a young child to discriminate the opposites *long-short* and *thin-fat* and to correctly apply the labels might be expected to facilitate the child's coordination of changes in length and thickness on a conservation of substance task. In this task, the child is asked whether two identical balls of clay still have the same amount of clay even after one has been shaped into a long, thin sausage. Even though the children watched this transformation take place, most preschoolers failed to recognize that there is still the same amount of clay. Although one is now longer, it is also thinner. There has been a compensation in thickness as a result of the change in length. Sinclair-de-Zwart found that linguistic training resulted in some improvement in verbal descriptions of task variables but had little effect on conservation performance, a finding consistent with the view that language does not determine thought, rather the thought precedes linguistic expression.

All of the Above.   As we have seen, support can be cited for each of the views regarding the relationship between thought and language. Given such circumstances, the most reasonable conclusion would be that all are true under certain conditions and at certain times in the developmental process. At the very least, we might conclude that

language and thought are interdependent, but not necessarily synonymous. Perhaps the most fruitful approach for researchers would be to discover more about how they interrelate (Jenkins, 1969).

Summary

Three major aspects of cognition were discussed: problem solving, concept formation, and language. Although problem-solving situations were found to come in many forms, three factors were found to affect the ease of solution of all types: prior learning set, complexity, and embeddedness. Even so-called insight problem solutions were found to be a result of cumulative learning. The way in which the three factors influence problem solving can best be summed up in the statement that the difficulty of a problem is directly related to the number and strength of incorrect responses elicited by the task situation.

Because of the human's limited information processing capabilities, it is impossible to respond to all the potential information given in the environment. To circumvent this limitation, humans organize their experience by giving the same response to numerous stimuli which share select properties. The resulting concepts are abstractions which allow for responding to novel stimuli as if they had been previously encountered.

Several factors affect formation of concepts. Concept identification is fastest when the number of relevant and irrelevant dimensions is small, only positive instances are presented, two or more relevant dimensions are redundant, relevant stimulus dimensions are salient, the conceptual role is conjunctive, and the learner is provided with feedback as to the accuracy of that person's response. The strategies concept learners use in the process of identification of the relevant attributes and rule defining the concept vary from the efficient and safe conservation focusing strategy to the more taxing scanning strategy.

Many concepts are represented in our language as vocabulary items. As such language provides a code for the communication of ideas and feelings. This code has been shown to both influence and be influenced by thought. For example, giving an inaccurate verbal label to an experience can distort the later recall of the experience. Acquisition of verbal labels is dependent on the prior understanding of the nonverbal concept.

The acquisition of the language code has been found to take place with surprisingly little specific training. Maturation and exposure to a rich linguistic environment in the context of a child's everyday experience are essential for normal language development. The role of maturation is evident in the similarity of vocalizations across children of similar ages and in the futility of attempts to train too early. The role of environment is evident even before the first word in the gradual drift of vocalizations toward the adult frequency of particular sounds, the adult sound sequences, and the adult intonation patterns. The result is babbling which sounds as if it were meaningful speech.

Evidence suggests that the child acquires structural rules that become increasingly differentiated. Long before adulthood, the child behaves as if its speech and comprehension are governed by rules that linguists represent by phrase-structure and transformation grammars. Analysis of the context of early utterances has revealed that the structural complexity of a child's speech lags behind the child's attempts to communicate complex ideas or relationships. Initially a child may use a single word to stand for a whole sentence with the grammatical function of the word changing with the situation. Contrary to expectations no relationship has been found between structural complexity and age of first appearance of attempts to produce complex structures. However, it does take longer for the complex structural forms to be perfected. Comprehension and production difficulties are demonstrated by some children on a few complex structures well into middle childhood.

Glossary

Conjunctive concept: A concept is said to be conjunctive when a combination of two or more attributes must be present. For example, a positive instance of the concept "red triangle" requires the presence of both redness and triangularity. The presence of either alone will not suffice. It contrasts with a disjunctive concept which requires that only one of the two (or more) attributes be present.

Functional-fixity: Concept proposed by Karl Duncker attributing subjects' difficulty in reaching some problem solutions to their tendency to be set or fixed in their perception of at least one of the materials required in the solution.

Holophrastic speech: Refers to the use of a single word to stand for the idea normally expressed in a phrase or sentence by adults. Contrasts with the use of a single word simply as a label or name for an object. Holophrastic speech is characteristic of the one- to two-year-old.

Insight: Term describing problem solving behavior characterized by an "ah ha" experience of apparent sudden discovery of the solution by covert means (thinking) rather than by overt trial-and-error.

Linguistic relativity hypothesis: View of relationship between thought and language advanced by Edward Sapir and Benjamin Whorf. Sometimes referred to as the Whorfian hypothesis. This view emphasizes the dependence of thought on language, claiming that the vocabulary and grammar we use determine the perceptual discriminations we make.

Peripheral theory of thinking: Alternatively known as the motor theory of thinking, this view of the relationship between thought and language maintains that there is no need to distinguish between the two. Thought is primarily subvocal speech. The major proponent of this view, Watson, claimed that any bodily movement can serve as a medium for thought.

Phoneme: The smallest unit of speech that signals a difference in meaning to the speakers of a given language. By itself, this unit is meaningless, but it can signal a difference in meaning when in combination with other phonemes. For example, /p/ and /b/ are phonemes in English because the sound difference between two words such as "pan" and "ban" signals a difference in meaning.

Relevant dimensions: Those stimulus features which are criteria for membership in a particular concept class. For example, color (redness) and shape (triangular) are relevant dimensions of the concept "red triangle." Size and orientation of the triangle are irrelevant dimensions, since they are unrelated to the concept definition or identification.

Syntax:: Rules governing the structure or ordering of words in utterances. Often used interchangeably with the word "grammar." Contrasts with semantics which refers to the rules governing the assignment of meaning to utterances.

Trial-and-error learning: Discovery of correct response in a problem situation from a set of alternative responses by actually trying out many or all of the alternatives until the correct response is tried and verified as correct. Sometimes contrasted with insight learning.

Suggested Readings

Dale, P. *Language Development: Structure and Function.* 2nd ed. New York: Dryden Press, 1976.

Johnson, D. M. *Systematic Introduction to the Psychology of Thinking.* New York: Harper & Row, 1972.

Posner, M. I. *Cognition: An Introduction.* Glenview, Ill.: Scott, Foresman, 1973.

12

Perception

Harold W. Hake

Introduction

The title of this chapter is a single word, an important word in psychology, although it has no precise definition. In an intuitive way, we understand perception to refer to all those processes involved in sensing and evaluating our environment. Although such processes must involve the action of the specific senses—vision, hearing, olfaction, gustation, and the skin senses—often the word *perception* is reserved for those processes that are not associated with any one sense alone. Many perceptual topics arose in philosophy originally and many predate much of our knowledge concerning sensory action. Hence, perceptual topics still tend to be discussed separately from the growing elaboration of sensory neurophysiology. The following discussion of perception is more perceptual than sensory, in those terms. It assumes some knowledge of the structure and function of the specific senses while often not concerned directly with any specific one.

Much specific information about sensory functioning can be found in Chapter 5. Other chapters in this text contain information about topics that we tend to think of as being "perceptual," and the student is referred to them in connection with the subjects of this present chapter. Chapter 2 on history, Chapter 3 on psychophysics, Chapter 11 on cognition, and Chapter 4 on developmental trends are especially relevant.

The reader should understand also that the word *perception* almost always refers to human perception. A true comparative study of the senses exists, but not of perceiving. A major reason is that when we speak of perception, we very often refer to the *experience* of perceiving. If animals are *aware* of their perceptual processes, as we are of ours, we have found it difficult to establish this as a fact, whatever we suspect the case may be.

Perceptual Experience

Not all psychologists are ready to grant scientific status to the concept of human perceptual awareness of experience, and a marked split in attitudes exists.

Two Points of View about Perceptual Experience

This split in attitudes about the importance of inner experience in the study of perception is the source of much confusion for students new to perceptual topics. On the one hand, some psychologists hold that the study of perceptual experience is the crucial topic for psychological study. Others reject that position and impose the requirement that only events that are open to public observation should be a part of the study of perception. They believe that the subjective experiences of perceiving are not.

Which of these two points of view dominates has varied from decade to decade. Early American psychologists, around the turn of the century, were interested strongly in perceptual topics. Much of this interest concerned concepts involved in one's own private perceptual experience—such things as *sensations, images,* and *percepts.* Much use of those mentalistic terms was involved.

In the second and third decades of this century, John B. Watson (1925) enthusiastically attacked this mentalism and advocated the outlawing of all topics for study that could not be publicly observed. Considerable enthusiasm for this point of view was expressed, an enthusiasm that did much damage to the early study of perceptual topics. The *behaviorism* of Watson, while outlawing all mentalism and concern with private, internal concomitants of seeing, hearing, smelling, tasting, and so on, outlawed really all of the perceptual topics of interest at that time. Behaviorism itself had little to say about the important perceptual questions, and so perceptual topics began disappearing from textbooks. Watson's own textbook had no perception chapter, for example, and did not mention the word.

However, chapters on perception were soon back in print. The new content of these chapters consisted mainly of the contributions of Gestalt psychology (see Köhler, 1947), brought to this country by persons fleeing Nazi persecution in Europe. And so perception chapters, which behaviorism had emptied, reappeared in American textbooks, this time full of a new treatment of perceptual topics that was exotic, alien, highly interesting to readers, and even more subjective than before.

The Gestalt point of view was very different from the treatment perceptual topics had received from the earlier American writers, but the earlier treatment and the Gestalt discussions of perceptual topics had in common the belief that the *experience* of perceiving was a crucial topic in its own right. In fact, to the Gestalt psychologists, no greater proof of the correctness of their beliefs was necessary than the proof a single observer could provide in examining private, inner experiences of seeing or hearing.

The upshot of all this is that two seemingly contradictory points of view exist side-by-side in American psychology. The first of these, representing a *positivistic* point of view, derives from the earlier behaviorism of Watson. Essentially, this point of view asserts that the concept of perceptual experience should be invoked as a scientific concept only when this is necessary in order to explain perceptual facts—relations between stimuli and responses. This is a *parsimonious* approach, invoking the complex concept of inner experience only where perceptual behavior cannot otherwise be explained. The opposing point of view holds that the domain of perceptual experience is the primary business of the student of perception, who is well trained to deal adequately and in a rigorous fashion with perceptual experience of the other person. Fortunately for students, these two points of view tend to treat different sorts of perceptual problems. Few confrontations exist, and, as a matter of fact, it is not easy to find instances where our understanding of perception rests on the assumption that someone is experiencing an inner perceptual event of a particular find. Some instances will be mentioned briefly.

Imagery and Subjective Reporting

Discussions of subjective aspects of perception often involve the concept of *images,* which the dictionary defines as mental pictures of things not actually present. Clearly, we mean something like that—the perceiver experiences and responds to something apparent only to him or her. Examples are after-images, reversible figures, and eidetic images.

Figure 12-1 provides examples of after-images and reversible figures. Both the experience of an after-image and of the reversibility of a pattern are very real, though private, and the behavior of viewers while experiencing either can be explained adequately only by accepting that obvious fact.

The case of eidetic imagery is more controversial. Persons with eidetic imagery are commonly said to retain a vivid image of a stimulus pattern, after it has been removed from view, and can examine the image at leisure and report on its details in the absence of the actual stimulus pattern. Most of us mortals lack this very convenient ability, and so persons with eidetic imagery have long been the subject of fascinating study.

The trick, however, is to discriminate between a true *Eidetiker,* who is examining an image of the now absent stimulus and is reporting the details of that image, and someone else who is a very quick

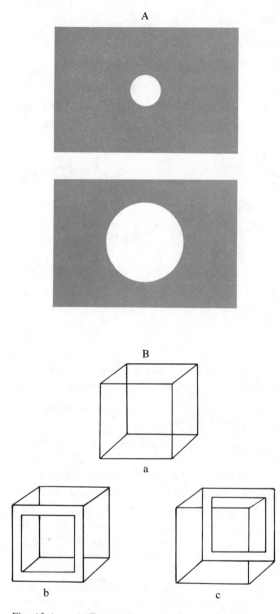

Fig. 12-1. (A) To experience an afterimage, close one eye and fixate the cross in the top rectangle for 30 sec. Then fixate the cross in the bottom rectangle. Very shortly a dark disc will be seen in the center of the white area. (B) The top outline cube can be seen in either of the orientations indicated in the bottom two cubes. Because its seen orientation tends to alternate, the top cube is known as a *reversible cube*.

study and was able to memorize quickly many details of the stimulus while it was still visible. In other words, the fact that a subject can report a lot of stimulus detail after the stimulus has been removed is not sufficient demonstration that an eidetic image is being viewed internally. The list of ways in which the *Eidetiker* can be distinguished from the subject who is a usually quick study and makes efficient use of the stimulus while it is present is still incomplete. A partial list of such ways has been provided by Ralph Norman Haber, whose work on eidetic imagery supports a belief in the important role of imagery in the behavior of eidetic children.

The list includes the observations that: (1) Nearly all the children judged to be eidetic report that images fade in a short time and that the fading follows a typical pattern; (2) The eidetic image resembles an after-image in that it appears to be projected onto a surface; that is, it is "out there" rather than in the head. Subjects judged to be eidetic appear unable to move the image from one surface to another. When such attempts to move an image are made the image is reported to "fall off" the surface and thereafter is not available to the child; (3) Children judged to be eidetic are capable of merging or superimposing pictures previously seen separately in order to produce a new visual affect. This is illustrated in Figure 12-2, taken from a report prepared by Haber (1974).

Notice that in all these examples the concept of internal, private perceptual experience is necessary to understanding the perceiver's behavior. We can explain his or her behavior in no other way. Only in the case of the Eidetiker are we still trying to demonstrate that there are no other sufficient explanations.

Two Basic Questions about Subjective Experience

The brief discussion of eidetic imagery suggests the point that questions involving someone else's subjective experience are not easily settled. Unfortunately, students striking up a first acquaintanceship with perceptual topics often have questions on that topic very much in mind. Such

Fig. 12-2.   In testing for eidetic imagery, children are shown the picture on the left. After it has been removed, the picture in the middle is exposed. The right-most picture depicts what children would see if the left picture persists as an image while the middle picture is being viewed.

questions tend to be related to one or the other of the following two basic questions.

> 1. Do we get information by way of our senses without being aware of it?

The question here is whether perception can occur unconsciously, without our being aware of it.

It has been suggested that several levels of perception occur, and that while we may be aware that we are perceiving on one level, perception occurs at the same time on another level without our being aware of it. Can the impact of advertising be *subliminal*, for example? The word *limen* means threshold; so the question asks whether stimulation below the threshold of awareness can have an impact.

This is a difficult question to answer, because it is difficult to demonstrate absolutely that a perceiver is truly unaware of stimulation that has affected him or her in some way. Stimulation, such as an aspect of a television commercial, may have been unnoticed at the time, but appropriate probing may still be able to elicit evidence of awareness of that aspect later on. Thus, we are always left with the possibility in any situation that just the right set of tests will show awareness of the nature of stimulation received earlier, and of its consequences. If so, the stimulus was not truly subliminal.

> 2. Are we aware of information we did not get through our senses?

One of the issues involved here concerns the sorts of perceptual information we possess at birth (see Chapter 14). Do we possess any information at all about our world at birth, or must we learn about it entirely in all its bewildering detail? The belief that certain types of "understandings" of our environment are present at birth, and therefore did not enter via our senses, is known as *nativism*. The *empiricist* position, on the other hand, emphasizes the lack of such inborn understandings and emphasizes the importance of perceptual experience and learning in the production of adult knowledge of our environment. The controversy described is the ancient *nature* vs. *nurture* controversy, about which we will provide some interesting and important detail later on (see also Chapter 6).

A second related question, which has appealed to generations of students, concerns the possibility that perception can occur without the use of any of the known senses. Is this really possible?

We do know that a wide variety of types of sensory functioning exists among animals. Many mammals are sensitive to very high frequency sounds that we cannot hear. Sensitivity to the polarized characteristics of light exists among some insects. Other examples can be found, so it is easy to speculate that we may have perceptual avenues not yet described.

By far, the possibility of greatest interest to students is that extrasensory perception (ESP) is a reality. Some persons take this possibility quite seriously, and attempts have been made to communicate by this means even over vast distances, from our moon to earth in one case.

What is ESP? In a typical demonstration, a communication from one individual to another is attempted while every possible precaution is taken to prevent the involvement of the known senses. For example, a "transmitter" located in Los Angeles and a "receiver," located possibly in New York City, both have in mind a definite set of message alternatives that are to be transmitted from city to city. The alternatives could be a set of geometric figures arranged in a random sequence, and at set moments carefully timed in both cities the transmitter looks at each figure and concentrates on it. For each such occurrence, the transmitter records what the figure was, and the receiver records what he or she "sensed" the figure to be.

After all figures have been "transmitted" from Los Angeles and recorded in New York City, the most important part of the process remains. This is the task of comparing the transmitted list of figures with the received list, noting the number of correspondences of figure sent with figure received. This number must then be compared with the number of correspondences that could have occurred by chance alone, as from time to time sheer coincidence could produce even an error-free set of transmissions.

How many correspondences could have occurred by chance? Figure 12-3 suggests that a dice game can provide that number. The ESP transmissions are simulated by rolling one die to simulate sending a figure and another to simulate receiving a figure. Correspondences occur when sending and receiving dice both show the same number. In the case of any one transmission, a correspondence

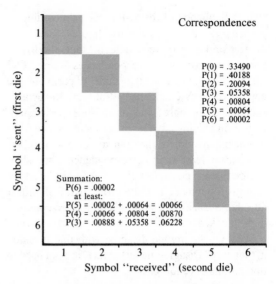

Fig. 12-3.   The matrix at the top suggests that if one die is thrown to represent the number (symbol) "sent" and another is thrown to represent the symbol "received," then correctly received symbols (correspondences) can occur in 6 ways and errors occur in the remaining 30 ways. Hence, the probability of a correspondence is $\frac{1}{6}$, and the probability of an error is $\frac{5}{6}$—which correspond to the probability of throwing any single number on a die ($\frac{1}{6}$) and the probability of not doing so ($\frac{5}{6}$). This analogy and the binomial theorem can be used to set out the probability of a given number of successes in throwing the same number in 6 throws of a die. By summation, we obtain the probability of obtaining exactly 6 successes in 6 throws, of at least 4 successes in 6 throws, and so on.

can occur in any one of 6 equally likely ways (rolling a 1 on both dice, or rolling a 2 on both dice, and so on). A noncorrespondence can occur in any of 30 ways (36 possible different outcomes minus the 6 possible correspondences). The likelihood of a correspondence occurring by chance then is 6 in 36 tries, or $\frac{1}{6}$; and the likelihood of a noncorrespondence is 30 in 36 tries, or $\frac{5}{6}$. The likelihood of a correspondence occurring, in other words, is the same as the likelihood of throwing a particular number in rolling a single die. Figure 12–3 capitalizes on this analogy and supplies the probability of successes in trying to roll a particular number in six rolls of a die.

We may conclude from Figure 12–3 that the

chance likelihood of the ESP receiver recording in proper order the six geometric figures "sent" by the transmitter is quite remote. In fact, the likelihood of *at least* four correspondences is only .087 (in 100 repetitions of the same experiment we could expect by chance to get at least four correspondences in only nine of those experiments). Hence, in judging any one experiment we can form the decision rule: if the transmitter and receiver produce at least four correspondences, we shall decide that the possibility that chance produced the result is too remote and, therefore, that ESP did, if all other avenues of communication were convincingly blocked.

Why would anyone disagree with that decision in that case? Disagreements, in fact, are not hard to find among psychologists.

a. Some would believe that the decision rule is too lenient. Perhaps we should require at least five correspondences. In that case, the likelihood of that result occurring by chance alone is even more remote (that is, less than 1 in 100 repetitions), and we would be less likely to accept a chance result as being truly ESP.

b. The dice game may be thought to be an inappropriate description of the effects of chance in this situation. For example, separate transmissions probably are not independent, in the way that separate rolls of a die can be. Hence, our estimate of the likelihood of chance effects will be inappropriate.

c. It often occurs that ESP experimenters do not stand pat with the sort of decision rule adopted above. For example, it is sometimes supposed that ESP ability may vary in a single person from day to day. Hence, all those occasions on which fewer than five correspondences occur in six transmissions may be taken only as evidence that ESP power was not present at *that* time, rather than as an indication that chance processes are indeed at work.

The point of all this is that an ESP experiment is easy to arrange and difficult to interpret. Psychologists tend to be unsympathetic to the concept, both because of a lack of consistency and rigor often evident in the interpretation of ESP results and because of the conviction that if ESP really occurs, it is an unreliable perceptual channel of little importance in the evolutionary history of mankind.

In summary, these paragraphs have described the concept of perceptual awareness (looking, seeing, feeling, and so forth) and two quite different approaches to the concept. One approach, *phenomenology,* accepts the subjective experience of perceiving as an important phenomenon for study in its own right. The other, *positivism,* uses such a mentalistic concept only when it earns its own way—only when it appears useful in explaining responses to stimulation. Both approaches exist side-by-side in American study of perceptual topics, and both have made important contributions. Irrespective of point of view, however, many highly interesting perceptual topics involve the concept of the *experience* of perceiving in one form or another, and we are never far from that concept in this chapter. Whether a perceiver is ever truly unaware of ongoing perceptual processes, however, or is aware of information not received via the usual sensory channels are difficult questions to answer rigorously in a public way.

Points of View

The study of perception involves strongly held points of view about *how* perceptual processes should be studied as well as *what* should be studied. First impressions are likely to be dominated by the controversies involved and to miss the fundamental contributions of each point of view.

In most of what follows, the major points of view and their contributions are described. This is done with the thought in mind that many readers may not have run across these concepts before.

The discussion begins with two points of view that are strongly *phenomenological* in character. That is, both accept subjective experiences of perceiving as appropriate topics for scientific study. *Perceptual psychophysics* is taken up first, as that discipline involves both useful methodology and a conception of perception that can be applied usefully in understanding other points of view. The subject of the second section is the *Gestalt* point of view, also strongly phenomenological in approach and clearly the most influential of all points of view. It will be evident to all readers that we are still working out in our own terms the fundamental principles underlying what the major Gestalt psychologists had to say about human perception.

Perceptual Psychophysics

Elsewhere in this text, psychophysics and the methodology involved, is considered in some detail (see Chapter 3). Psychophysics is considered briefly here as one of the basic conceptions of the human perceptual processes: simply that just as there are fundamental *physical* characteristics of stimulation, for example, physical ways in which lights and sounds can vary, so the *experience* of stimulation also has characteristics or dimensions. These characteristics of perceptual experience can be given scientific status and related to the corresponding physical characteristics of stimulation.

It is true, obviously, that perceivers can analyze experience, can, for example, listen to a complex musical tone and judge only its *loudness* or its *pitch*. A light can be described in terms of its *brightness*, its *hue*, or its *purity*. Our language contains many of these descriptive words, all of which we apply to things in the world around us. They refer specifically to how we experience those things, *not to the things themselves*.

The Psychophysical Scale. Psychophysics describes or measures stimuli in terms of their experiential effect. In Figure 12-4, a set of simple tones, which differ physically only in frequency, are described also in terms of their apparent pitch. The result is a *psychophysical function* or *scale,* the *mel* scale of pitch for pure tones. *Pitch* and *frequency* are not the same thing, as pitch increases faster than does frequency of pure tones at low frequencies and slower at high frequencies.

Note that in the production of such a scale, the perceiver is asked to serve as a kind of meter. While exposed to a stimulus under controlled conditions the perceiver is asked to make a judgment

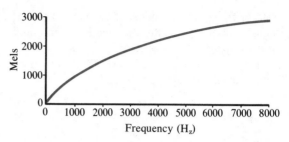

Fig. 12-4. The relationship between the physical measure, frequency of sound, and the judgment of pitch in mels. If the relationship were a straight line, would we need to distinguish between pitch and frequency? (Data from Stevens, S. S. and Volkmann, J., 1940)

about the experience of perceiving that stimulus. Only the perceiver can do this, that is, can describe the experiential characteristics "red" and "green" corresponding to long and medium wavelengths of light or can indicate which sounds are "loud" and which are "soft." The words used are those of modern English, but they refer to very ancient categories of perceptual experience. Without the perceiver, such terms have no meaning. Light differs in wavelengths; it is not in physical terms any color at all.

It is often mistakenly thought that the ways in which sounds or lights *appear* to vary are related in very simple ways to their physical characteristics. This sort of one-to-one correspondence is implied by Table 12-1 in which a correspondence is implied, for sounds and lights, between the experiential aspects on the left in each case and the physical characteristics of stimulation on the right. This correspondence suggests, for example, that *loudness* is the experiential correlate of the physical characteristic *intensity*, and that *pitch* is the corre-

Table 12-1. Misleading Correspondences Between Characteristics of Perceptual Experience and Physical Characteristics of Stimulation

LIGHT		SOUND	
Experience	*Physical Aspect*	*Experience*	*Physical Aspect*
Hue	Wavelength	Pitch	Frequency
Brightness	Intensity	Loudness	Intensity
Saturation	Homogeneity	Timbre	Homogeneity

late of *frequency* of sound. If so, we could dispense with the words that describe experience and use the physical characteristics instead. For example, we would not need to speak of both pitch and frequency of sound.

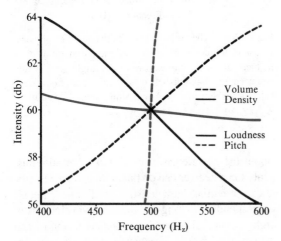

Fig. 12-5. Isophonic contours. The line marked "loudness" indicates all those combinations of intensity and frequency that sound equally loud. To sound equally loud, a tone must be made more intense as its frequency is decreased and less intense as frequency is increased. Similar relations are shown for the attributes of *pitch, tonal density,* and *tonal volume.* (From Boring E. G., 1942)

Figure 12-5 is quite convincing on this point. The curved lines in the figure are *isophonic* contours. The contour marked "loudness" indicates all those combinations of frequency (Hz) and intensity (dB) that sound equally loud. Obviously then, all those combinations on the center horizontal line that represents constant intensity and changing frequency would not sound equally loud. The other line, marked "pitch," indicates combinations of frequency and intensity that appear to have the same pitch. It is easy to see that pitch is not the same as frequency, as tones of the same frequency and varying only in intensity do not have the same pitch characteristic. So pitch and loudness are not simple experiential reflections of the physical dimensions of sound: frequency and intensity. Similar demonstrations indicate that the

visual experiences of hue, brightness, and saturation have quite complex relationships with the physical characteristics of light. The experiential dimensions, the *attributes,* have a reality of their own, and they are an important part of the terminology of perception.

How many such attributes are there? There was a time, just three or four decades ago, when the demonstration of a new attribute was an interesting event, like the discovery of a new star or comet. A new attribute, of course, had to have the characteristics implied in Figure 12-5, namely that experience of a particular sort remained constant while physical characteristics of stimulation varied. It could not have a simple one-to-one relationship with another attribute, and it had to have an intuitive appeal for perceivers and be easily used.

Currently, the demonstration of a new dimension of experience, a new attribute, is of minor interest. The types of stimulation of interest are much more complex now, and the suggestion of new dimensions of perceptual experience is commonplace. The importance of the attributes as explanatory concepts, however, has grown considerably.

A Descriptive System for Perceptual Experience. As an outgrowth of the psychophysical traditions described, a descriptive system for stimulation has evolved, a descriptive system based on how stimulation is perceived rather than how it can be measured physically. In this new system, we can recognize a characteristically psychophysical conception of perception itself. This is simply that the perceptual significance of stimulation is sufficiently supplied by the location of that stimulation in a conceptual space which has the attributes as its coordinates. Of course, Figure 12-5 is not such a space, since the physical characteristics of *frequency* and *intensity* are the coordinates. On the other hand, Figure 12-6, Part A, which has *pitch* and *loudness* as coordinates, is such a space. One can see at a glance that tones varying only in frequency and having identical intensities do not have the same loudness. Tones are plotted in the plane according to perceptual significance, not physical characteristics. Although physically only frequency is varied, the tones differ in both pitch

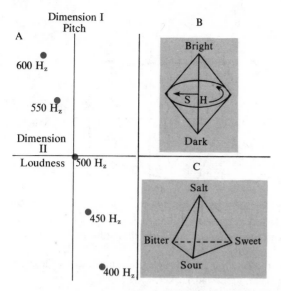

Fig. 12-6. Three conceptual spaces in which stimuli are located to represent how they are perceived relative to each other. (A) Pure tones varying frequency only. With increasing frequency, *pitch* increases and *loudness* decreases. (B) Colored surfaces plotted in three dimensions on the surface of or within a double cone. Colors plotted high in the cone are bright; those plotted low are dark. Hue (H) of the surfaces determines radial position around the central axis, and distance out from the central axis (arrow) indicates relative saturation (S) of colors. (C) Tastes plotted in three dimensions on the surfaces of a tetrahedron.

and loudness. Figure 12-6, Part B and 12-6, Part C provide other examples.

The coordinates of Figure 12-6, Part A are the arbitrary and quite ancient attributes of pitch and loudness, and the figure itself is quite arbitrary. The perceiver listening to the tones was told to judge the *pitch* or *loudness* of the tones, and we assumed that the perceiver understood what is meant by those terms. This *a priori* assumption about how stimuli will be perceived is unnecessary in the modern psychophysical approach to the problem. Two examples of a more acceptable method are considered in the next few paragraphs. This method represents the application of methodology derived by persons interested originally in the specification of "mental" and perceptual abilities, an area known commonly as the "measurement" area in psychology.

The Scaling of Color. In the first of these examples, we ask a perceiver to look at colored tiles, presented three at a time, and to arrange the three tiles on a neutral background so that the relative distances from tile to tile mirror the apparent *similarity* of the tiles.

This is a rather different way in which to judge the appearance of colored surfaces. Instead of being asked about the *hue,* or *brightness,* or *purity* of the colors the perceiver is asked only about the *similarity* of one surface to another. It is left to an analysis of those judgments to produce the ways in which the tiles apparently did vary in similarity as the perceiver saw them. This amounts to an attempt to make some geometric sense of the distances between tiles as the perceiver located them on the surface. In this attempt, it is assumed that the *similarity* of two tiles and their physical *distance* apart are related in a regular way.

In making sense of the distances apart, it is conceivable that those distances could be accounted for by assuming that each tile can be represented by a point on a straight line, as in Figure 12-7, Part A. We should expect this not to work out because of the circularity of hue similarities. The two end points, representing dark red and purple, are really quite similar. Therefore, the mapping of the tiles as points on a straight line would fail to account adequately for the mutual distances apart of the tiles as arranged by the perceiver. Red and purple are located too far apart and any rearrangement of the points on a single straight line will produce the same problem. Evidently, an arrangement of points representing tiles in a unidimensional space (a straight line) will not suffice. We conclude that the tiles appeared to vary in more than just one way.

An attempt to arrange points representing tiles in a plane will be more successful if we used care in preparing the tiles in the first place. In that case, the distances between tiles as produced by each subject should be accounted for quite well by plotting points to represent the tiles in two dimensions. Such a plot is shown in Figure 12-7, Part B. This is the familiar *hue circle,* and this conceptual schema would account quite well for the mutual similarities and dissimilarities of the tiles. Since two dimensions define a plane, we assume that the tiles

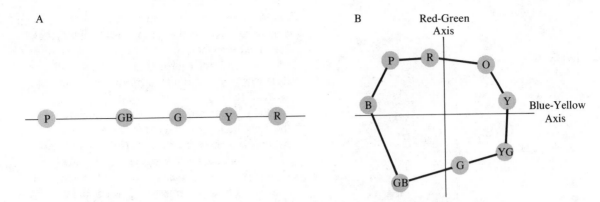

Fig. 12-7.   (A) We try to set out the colored tiles on a straight line to reflect the similarities perceived by observers. (Greater distance apart corresponds to greater dissimilarity.) The attempt fails, because the tiles at the ends of the line are always more similar than plotted distance apart suggests.
(B) We can make sense of all judgments by locating the colored tiles in a rough circle in a plane of two axes. (These are contrived results resembling actual results; for actual data, see Helm, C. E. and Tucker, L. R., 1972.)

apparently differed one from another, as the perceiver experienced them ("saw" them), in two basic ways. The two dimensions and suggested names for them are shown in the figure.

Figure 12-8 is the interesting scale configuration expected for a perceiver who confuses reds and greens. For such a perceiver, the experience of hue

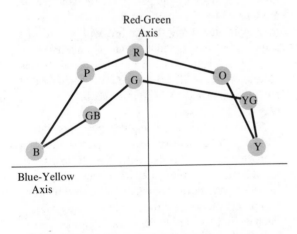

Fig. 12-8.   The scale configuration expected to result when the tiles are judged by a color-weak perceiver who confuses reds and greens. (Again, interested readers are referred to the work of Helm and Tucker.)

would be confined to blues, grays, and yellows, although life experiences would teach that other persons use the terms "red" and "green" for some of those colors.

The reader should note that this short and schematic presentation of the psychophysics of colored surfaces consists of two elemental parts.

1. A judgmental task that allows the perceiver to relate each of a set of stimulus objects to all others in the set in terms of experienced similarity of the objects. The basis for perceived similarity is left to the perceiver.
2. The derivation of dimensions of similarity: the underlying ways in which stimuli were judged to be similar or dissimilar. The dimensions of similarity become the axes of a conceptual space in which the stimuli are plotted as points, as in Figure 12-7, Part B. This plot of points provides the complete *psychophysical* conception of how the set of stimuli is perceived, including description of the *salient perceptual dimensions* and the extent to which the stimuli are related to each other in terms of those dimensions.

The way in which points representing stimuli do plot in a conceptual space defined by salient dimensions will vary from perceiver to perceiver, as a comparison of Figure 12-7, Part B and Figure 12-8 shows. Figure 12-7, Part B represents the color tiles as they would be seen by a perceiver with normal vision; Figure 12-8 represents the tiles as they would be seen by a color-weak perceiver who confuses reds and greens.

The Scaling of Faces. There are important applications of this methodology in case of quite complex stimuli where no simple or obvious physical description exists. An interesting example is that of the human face. Can the human face be specified psychophysically as a stimulus? If so, what are the salient dimensions and how are they related to facial features?

An important application was described by Jones and Wiggins (1975) at the University of Illinois, who asked thirty-two black and thirty-three Caucasian female subjects to judge the similarity of pairs of front-view, color-transparency photographs of nine black and nine white male college students. Each of the sixty-five subjects judged each pair of photographs using a numerical scale running from "very similar" (1) through "very dissimilar" (9). These judgments provided the similarity data, like those obtained for the tiles, needed for the multidimensional analysis. Subjects also judged the pairs of photographs in terms of which face was preferred.

The analysis of the similarity judgments indicated that the faces appeared to vary in at least six ways, that is, there were six salient dimensions of apparent variation from face to face. In the language used in connection with the tiles, the faces had to be plotted as points in a space with six dimensions.

Most ordinary mortals have trouble visualizing spaces with more than three dimensions, but this is no great handicap since the faces can be plotted with respect to a pair of dimensions at a time (on a plane), and the faces can be related to the dimensions by that means. For example, the nine white and nine black male faces are plotted with reference to two of the perceptual dimensions in Figure 12-9. The faces are sorted into separate groups by the *race* dimension, but black faces and white faces are spread out equally over the *maturity* dimension. The remaining dimensions included among others, *face shape* (long and narrow vs. broad) and *affect* (attractiveness of faces vs. degree of threat represented).

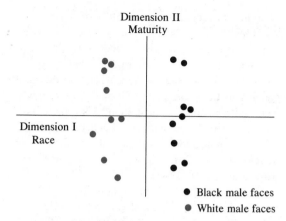

Fig. 12-9. Black male facial photographs and white male photographs were judged a pair at a time in terms of similarity within pairs. Judged similarity can be accounted for partly by plotting the faces in two dimensions. In that two-dimensional plot the two sets of photographs are separated with respect to the race dimension but not the maturity dimension. (From Jones, L. E., 1975)

The reader should keep in mind that an important, and perhaps quite new, conception of faces is implied. This conception is *psychophysical* in origin, coming from a tradition that has as its goal the description of the attributes of the experience of stimulation and the specification of stimuli in terms of these attributes. The attributes become the yardsticks by which stimuli are measured and specified. The assumptions are that a stimulus, whether or not it has known physical characteristics, can be specified in a system of experiential attributes and that the latter specification reliably predicts how perceivers respond to the stimulus. The experience of the perceiver in looking, hearing, touching, smelling, and tasting has a metric all its own, and a science is implied in the task of specifying that metric.

The Gestalt Tradition

The other major phenomenological approach very evident in modern thinking about perception is that of Gestalt psychology. Detailed discussions of the contributions of the major Gestalt psychologists are found in accounts of the history of psychological topics, where their work is described as it was presented in the early decades of this century (see Chapter 2). Such descriptions can be quite confusing to American students, because the language and the ideas of the Gestalt psychologists were quite abstruse, almost alien. Also, there was no single Gestalt psychology. Each of the major contributors–Köhler, Kaffka, and Wertheimer—treated slightly different topics in characteristic ways (see Köhler, 1947).

Many perceptual principles described by these men have become a part of our culture. For example, if students know anything about Gestalt beliefs, they know that: (1) *Good* stimuli are more easily perceived and remembered, and (2) A perceptual whole entity is more than the sum of its parts.

How stimuli can be good, bad, or indifferent can be a puzzle unless one knows that Gestalt beliefs are about several equivalent domains. These domains are shown in Figure 12-10 with domains stacked one above the other. They are *isomor-*

phic—any statement that applies to one applies equally to all. For the Gestalt theorist, the top, abstract layer was important, because the theoretical statements applied most readily there. These statements had to do with a type of *field theory,* involving an abstract field of forces in which points interacted and were influenced by force fields. Wolfgang Köhler had been trained as a physicist, and the analogy between perceptual principles and characteristics of electromagnetic fields is quite strong.

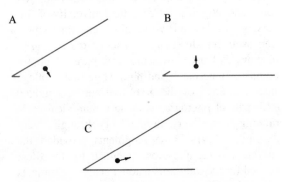

Fig. 12-11.   If in (A) and (B) the point is judged to be farther from the line than it actually is, then in (C) those effects must combine to make the point appear farther from the intersection of the lines than it really is, a case of vector addition.

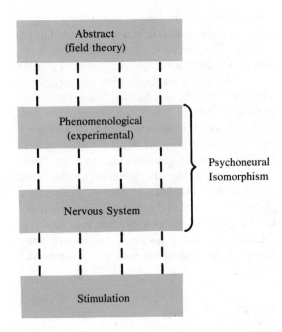

Fig. 12-10. The Gestalt isomorphic domains within which the same perceptual principles were thought to apply, a source of some discomfort to American students.

Figure 12-11 illustrates a type of perceptual distortion that can occur in the case of the interaction of a line and a point and provides a verifiable prediction about a more complex figure. To American students, the assumption that a drawn line and a drawn dot can interact on the page seems obvious nonsense. The forces that cause the interaction could not exist there; they must exist in another of the domains of Figure 12-10. We are likely to look for such forces in the domain of the central nervous system; the Gestalt psychologist was apt to think of those forces in any of the domains, and wrote of them as though they held true for the stimulus domain and the experiential domain as well.

It is useful to take note of a special case of isomorphism, *psychoneural isomorphism,* which was said to exist between the phenomenological (experiential) domains and the domain representing the central nervous system. This principle says, briefly, that a point-for-point correspondence exists between how stimuli *appear* and their representation in the sensory nervous system. Hence, whenever stimuli are distorted in perception, as in the case of visual illusions, their representations are also distorted in the nervous system.

Figure 12-12 provides an example of a visual distortion occurring because of the effect of something seen previously, the figural after-effect. The top set of squares can be thought of as affecting the nervous system such that the two equal squares at the bottom are seen as unequal when viewed after the top squares.

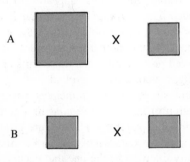

Fig. 12-12. The Figural After-Effect: First look as steadily as possible at the small x in (A) with one eye closed. Do this for 20 to 30 seconds and then look with the same eye at the x in (B). The two equal squares in (B) may then look unequal in size.

In what type of a nervous system would such effects occur? Omitting details, the answer of the Gestalt psychologist was simply that such distortions would occur in a nervous system that had field properties; the field produced by looking at the top squares affects the appearance of the bottom squares when they are viewed.

The remainder of this section is concerned with a fundamental Gestalt conception of human perception—and with how American psychologists have interpreted that belief in their own terms. This fundamental conception is that the perceptual process is an *active* process involving an active response of the perceiver to over-riding organizational properties of stimulation.

Perception: An Active Process. This principle says, first, that perception is not a passive affair in which the perceiver operates like a camera, recording all the minutia of stimulation in detail and with fidelity. Instead, perception is a very active process that processes stimulation in order to achieve a particular perceptual result—the experience of stimulation as a conceptually organized entity in which details may be lost but in which essential features are clearly represented.

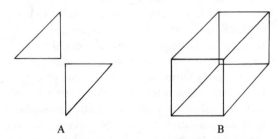

Fig. 12-13. An example of "hidden figures." The pattern of two triangles in (A) tends to be lost perceptually when (B) is seen as a three-dimensional figure.

The "hidden figures" of Gottschaldt (1926), illustrated in Figure 12-13, for example, are a common illustration of the compelling nature of an over-riding perceptual organization of a stimulus pattern, a perceptual result in which details may be lost, or can be seen only with great effort. Figure 12–14 makes the same point, again illustrating the

Fig. 12-14. The triangles may be seen as complex isosceles triangles lying flat on the page or as simple, equilateral triangles standing on one edge. (From Attneave, F., 1968)

compelling nature of a perceptual organization. The perceiver adds a dimension, experiencing simple triangles as existing in three-dimensional space rather than as complex triangles lying flat on the page.

Perceptual Organizations. The question of what such over-riding organizations achieve for the perceiver is a major one for contemporary psychologists. A simple answer, although not a complete one, is that perceptual organizations enable us to get along in a world that possesses such a richness of detail and potential for rapid change that no flesh-and-blood sensory apparatus could possibly encompass all in a usefully short period of time. In contemporary terms, we would say that perceivers suffer from *channel* limitation. We cannot be sensitive to, and attend to, all the details that assail our eyes and ears each moment of waking life. We cope with that by organizing stimulation so that only the essential character of stimulation is perceived and responded to.

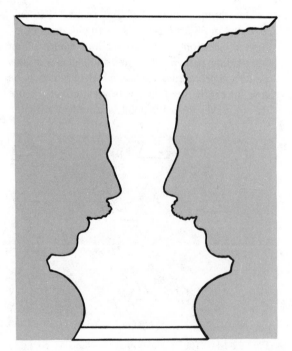

Fig. 12-15. A reversible figure. The profile is that of Albert Einstein. (Another reversible figure is Part B of Figure 12-1.)

Gestalt psychologists said this in a different way. Figure 12-15 contains a pattern like those of Rubin (1921) who used them to illustrate the *figure-ground organization* of perception. In this simple illustration, the distinction between the *figure,* which stands out clearly, and the *ground,* which appears homogenous and to exist behind the figure, seems quite apparent. This particular illustration was chosen because two alternative perceptual "organizations" are possible, either a central vase or two opposing faces in profile. It seemed to Rubin that without considerable effort the perceiver is limited to seeing either one organization or the other, and Rubin was convinced this must be so. Why is it not easily and ordinarily possible to see both?

For Rubin, the answer appeared to be simply that such *figure-ground organization* is a normal part of human perception. Parts of the visual field that have figural properties are selected out and perceived prominently, and those parts are seen as existing in a context, the ground.

Rubin suggested two principles governing the separation of *figure* and *ground* in a complex visual stimulus pattern. (1) The figure-ground organization that occurs when a pattern is first viewed is highly likely to be the one that occurs when the stimulus pattern is seen again. This is called *figural persistance.* (2) If in fact, a stimulus pattern is organized in one mode while first viewing it (such as the faces in Figure 12-15) and in another mode when it is viewed again (such as the vase in Figure 12-15), then during the second look, the pattern is not likely to appear familiar, that is, as a pattern seen before.

That second principle is a highly interesting one to psychologists, because it contains a very helpful clue about the nature of perceptual organization and its functions, as the Gestalt psychologist understood it. This has not been easy to come by, as Gestalt writers simply took the existence of perceptual organization for granted. They said, in effect, that the same God who made the world made the perceiver, and it seemed perfectly natural, since the world is made up mainly of objects, that our perceptual equipment meant to sense that world should be capable of organizing stimulation into objects and forms and to do this so that those aspects (figures) stand out from the remainder (ground).

Perceptual Channel Capacity. In the last two decades, psychologists have wondered whether we really understand in detail what that statement really means. They began to think about a new concept, which they called *perceptual channel capacity.* This is the capacity of the perceptual system to take in information and use it effectively. Obviously, we can conceive of the capacity of the *perceptual channel* as being either too small, as being just right, or as being too large for the informational demands that the world in which we live imposes upon us.

What is the perceptual channel? A complete answer to that question is necessarily technical, but a sufficient answer here is that the perceptual channel includes both the sensory receptors and associated neural structures and also the nature of the stimulation that elicits responses in those structures.

The sensory structures and functions have been described in Chapter 5. We know that our auditory channel is limited to sound frequencies between approximately 20 Hz. (cycles per second) and 20,000 Hz. This is a rather restricted spectrum of sensitivity when compared with the auditory sensitivities of some other mammals, such as the dog and dolphin, both of which respond easily to frequencies of sound far in excess of 20,000 Hz.

A most important auditory stimulus for the human listener is speech, which itself imposes further channel limitation because the definition of channel includes also all the constraints and restrictions involved in the perceptual stimulus. Speech sounds, in the case of English speech, are mainly in the range from 500 Hz to 1200 Hz, the range of frequencies produced by modifying in the mouth and throat the *laryngeal tone* produced in the larynx. But a far greater limitation upon the speech channel is imposed by the rules followed in producing the sounds we perceive as English speech. Only a limited number of sounds are produced, and these tend to follow each other in predictable ways. So, we say the perceptual channel in the case of English speech is defined and limited both by the constrained nature of the stimulus and

by the nature of auditory sensitivity. The greater limitation is imposed by the characteristics of speech as a stimulus.

A similar situation can be described in the case of visual perception. Visual sensitivity is limited also in terms of our lack of sensitivity to some types of stimulation. When we speak of *visual channel* limitations, however, we refer also to the constrained nature of visual stimulation. Not just any sort of visual stimulus is likely to occur. The visual channel, as is true of the auditory channel, is limited by all the constraints evident in the nature of visual stimulation, which is impressively predictable in time and pattern. We live in an orderly world in which those events that occur are organized in terms of objects moving from here to there, sometimes rotating and changing surface characteristics, but usually retaining their identities in a familiar terrain. And so the visual channel is limited also by very great constraints imposed upon the sorts of stimulation that ordinarily occur.

An important implication about perceptual functioning is implied by the previous paragraph. That implication is that a perceptual system that selects out certain aspects of stimulation for special attention can succeed so long as those aspects of stimulation are more crucial than others. A perceptual system that organizes input can succeed, that is, provide a valid and reliable representation of the world, only if the world itself is organized in the same way.

Organization in a Miniature Perceptual World. For the moment set aside thoughts about just what the organizational properties of the world may be, and consider a simple example of a miniature world of stimulation. This case was described by W. R. Garner (1962).

The miniature world is described in Figure 12-16, Part A. In this world, the only stimulus patterns that can occur are the cells of a 3 x 3 table. Each cell can be either filled or unfilled. Hence, there must be $2^9 = 512$ possible patterns that can appear. If each of the patterns is equally likely to occur as a stimulus, then we can specify the perceiver's *uncertainty* about which pattern will occur next, on the average. This would be

$$\text{Uncertainty (U)} = \log_2 512 = 9 \text{ bits}$$

in the language of *information theory*. Nine units of uncertainty are involved, where one unit is the uncertainty associated with predicting which of two equally-likely events will occur. That is, $\log_2 2 = 1$ bit. Also, $\log_2 4 = 2$ bits, implying that a choice among four alternatives is equal to two successive two-choice decisions. (Remember that $\log_2 4 = 2$ is the same as saying that $2^2 = 4$.)

This miniature world has a modest uncertainty associated with it, 9 bits, and we know this is the upper bound because only one of the 512 patterns described can occur, nothing else. So we need a modest perceptual capacity that is capable of sensing each of the 512 patterns as it occurs.

We suppose, however, that this miniature world was created so that not all of the 512 patterns do occur. Only those patterns that represent bar graphs, as shown in Figure 12-16, Part B can occur. In that case, only $4 \times 4 \times 4 = 64$ patterns are possible, and therefore the perceiver's uncertainty now would be

$$U = \text{Log}_2 \, 64 = 6.00$$

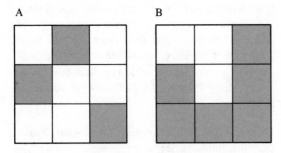

A   B

Fig. 12-16. (A) One of the 512 patterns of the miniature "world" of stimulation. (B) One of the restricted set of 64 patterns that result when a schematic rule (only bar graphs) is applied. Why is (B) a redundant pattern? (After Garner, W. R., 1962)

The restriction that only "organized" patterns can occur (bar graphs) has reduced the perceiver's uncertainty considerably. We say that this uncertainty reduction is associated with *redundancy* in the stimulus world. This redundancy (R) quantitatively amounts to

$$R = 9 - 6.00 = 3.00 \text{ bits.}$$

In ordinary terms, the redundancy is not hard to locate in the stimulus patterns, because only the cell at the top of each bar needs to be noticed. All cells under that must be filled. That is the rule, and so those underlying cells do not add anything. They are redundant. In fact, if one of those cells were inadvertently sensed as being empty, the perceptual system would be justified in filling it in. This would achieve what is known currently as *error suppression* and was known by the Gestalt psychologist as *closure,* making imperfect perceptions conform to organizational principles of the stimulus world. This type of redundancy is called *schematic redundancy,* meaning that a subset of patterns was chosen from a larger set, following a schematic rule (bar graphs only!).

By analogy, we can recognize that our real stimulus world is a redundant one. The number of stimulus patterns facing a perceiver is a much smaller number than the number that could exist in a truly chaotic world, not organized into related objects, and so on. So the perceiver can get along with a limited perceptual system, provided that system takes advantage of the *schematic redundancy* that exists in the world around us.

The Minimum Principle. The Gestalt point of view is that our perceptual systems do operate in that fashion. In fact, it is supposed that all perception involves the application of schematic rules in an effort to perceive stimulation in as simple a way as possible. Figure 12-17 contains a set of plane figures varying from quite regular and simple on the left to quite irregular and complex on the right. The one on the left appears to be a redundant figure, chosen from a small set of highly regular hexagons, for example. At first glance, the one on the right will appear to be chosen from a larger set of more complex patterns. Hence, we would say that the perceiver's uncertainty about the nature of the left stimulus is low; uncertainty about the right stimulus is high.

The reader may have noted, however, that in looking at the right-hand figure a *schematic principle* can be utilized to greatly decrease uncertainty about that figure's identity. The rule is that the figure is a three-dimensional view of a cube. Once that is realized, perceptual uncertainty is much

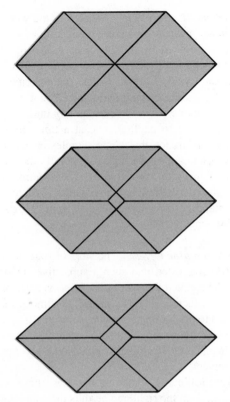

Fig. 12-17. Perceptual uncertainty associated with the right-hand figure can be reduced by seeing the figure in three dimensions.

reduced; the patterns, including the one on the left, are all seen as part of a constrained set: all are views of a cube.

Hochberg (1957) suggested that perceptual effort to reduce uncertainty about stimulation is the general case in perception and represents the *minimum principle* of perception, the principle that in perceiving we act to reduce our uncertainty about the nature of the stimulus. This is accomplished by the discovery and application of schematic rules that greatly reduce the possibilities associated with stimulus situations. Both Figure 12-14 and Figure 12-17 are often cited as applications of this principle. In both cases, purely two-dimensional patterns are simplified perceptually by the addition of a third dimension.

Stimulus Goodness. This brings us to stimulus goodness. Thanks to the work of W. R. Garner,

we are able to associate this concept with what he described as *stimulus possibilities*. In conceptual terms, the more schematic rules that apply to stimuli, and therefore the smaller the set of possible stimuli, the greater is stimulus goodness. Figure 12-18 provides illustrations from the work of Garner (1970). To those illustrations, the reader should add the suggestion of the Gestalt psychologists that the circle is the best example of a good figure. If we ignore size, then there is only one outline circle. If it is rotated or reflected, it is still the same figure. The schematic rules that generate the circle imply there is only one such figure.

Current Status. We may now restate in our own terms the current status of the contributions of the Gestalt tradition.

A

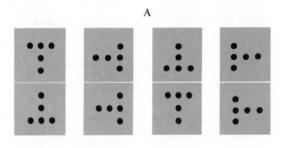

B

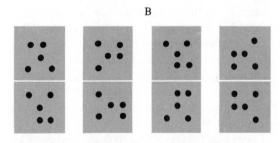

Fig. 12-18. The T pattern in (A) is *rotated* in the first row to produce three new patterns and each of these is *reflected* in the second row. Note that only three unique patterns exist among the variations produced by rotation and reflection of the T pattern. In contrast, in (B), *rotation* and *reflection* of the prototype pattern produce seven unique patterns. In Garner's review, this implies that figural goodness is higher in the case of the T pattern, which resists perceptual changes even though rotated and reflected. (See Garner, W. R., 1970)

1. Gestalt psychologists left a legacy of *phenomenology,* an unquestioned interest in immediate perceptual experience as one of the levels of discourse or one of the domains in which perceptual details may be studied.
2. The perceiver, being a part of the world and constructed following the same principles and utilizing the same materials, shows the same organizational properties. Those schematic rules involved in the construction of the world are represented in the perceiver also, and therefore the perceiver, in actively processing stimulation, easily takes advantage of the redundancies of the world of stimulation. The perceiver shows special sensitivities for stimulus patterns that conform to these schematic rules and special insensitivities for those that do not. Uncertainty about stimulation is always reduced by perceiving stimulation to be an example of the action of a simplifying or organizing rule, the *minimum principle* of perception.
3. The Gestalt point of view, and those in the next sections, are perhaps less a point of view about human perception than a point of view about the nature of the world, which as a source of stimulation is highly constrained (redundant).

A Third Point of View: Perception as a Reconstructive Process

The study of human perception has always stimulated controversy, and very strong positions on one side or the other of most perceptual issues are quite common. In the previous section, the point was made that perception is an active process. This idea is a pervasive one, and it is rather widely thought that the perceiver has a task to perform in achieving perceptual objectives. The task exists either because: (1) The perceptual channel has limited capacity, and some aspects or characteristics of stimulation must be emphasized at the expense of others, as the Gestalt psychologists believed; or (2) Perception is not a photographic process in which stimulation is directly registered in the nervous system and utilized in that registered form. Rather, what the perceiver experiences is the end product of a process operating on that stimulation, a process that *reconstructs* the source of that stimulation. One illustration of how perception is thought to be reconstructive in nature arises from consideration of how the perceptual system remains in calibration with the world.

Perceptual Calibration. What does the word *calibration* mean in this context? A simple illustration is provided by the customer in a paint store who wishes to buy a can of gray paint to match the gray on a wall at home. Unless the customer has brought a sample along that choice is not likely to be an accurate one. However, in looking from one paint sample to another, one at a time, the customer will notice that some samples appear light gray, some appear dark gray, and still others have a medium gray appearance. That seems commonplace. Yet how is that possible? Where does our standard for grayness come from? How is it maintained?

The Adaptation Level. The work of Harry Helson (1964) suggested that such a subjective standard, which he called the *adaptation level,* is determined by three factors: (1) The nature of stimulation attended to predominately *at the moment,* (2) The nature of background stimulation, and (3) Relatively unchangeable "residual" characteristics of the perceiver.

The following equation involves those three quantities on the right and permits the computation of the adaptation level for the grayness of surfaces at any moment.

$$\text{LOG (AL)} = \text{LOG K} + \frac{\text{LOG } \bar{R}_S + 3 \text{ LOG } R_B}{4}$$

In this equation, K is a constant, reflecting "residual" factors, LOG $\bar{R}_S$ is the logarithmic mean of the reflectances (grayness) of stimulation given primary attention, and R_B is the reflectance of background stimuli. From moment to moment, the adaptation level shifts such that at any given time, it equals approximately a weighted average of recent stimulation and the background grayness.

Note that this means that the gray paint samples in the paint store act to alter the remembered gray of the wall at home, that in fact perceivers do not have *absolute* recognition standards, at least for very simple sorts of stimuli. Instead, in the case of many sorts of more primitive sensory experiences we refer stimulation to an internal standard that fluctuates with the nature of recent experience.

It is also important to notice that it is *not* being suggested that the perceiver is aware of his internal standard and compares stimulation with it in an explicit way. Instead, the perceiver experiences only the result of the comparison. Grays lighter than the momentary adaptation level are experienced as light gray, grays darker than the adaptation level are experienced as dark gray, grays equal to adaptation level are perceived as neutral gray. In other words, the perceiver does not experience stimulation directly; the direct stimulus for perception is a reconstruction: the difference between stimulation and the adaptation level.

This is an important statement of belief, a statement that has so far weathered many serious challenges, the most serious of which is the suggestion that the nature of immediate stimulation (the grays seen in the paint store) does not change directly the nature of perceptual experience (how the grays in the paint store *look*). Rather, immediate experience changes merely what we are likely to *say* about our perceptual experience at the moment. Some evidence exists on both sides of that issue, but the majority of the evidence favors Helson's suggestion. Although his original formulation may be somewhat too simple, it appears true that perception itself is altered by the nature of recent stimulation.

In summary, for simple sorts of stimulation perceptual calibration is not absolute. We experience, not stimulation itself, but the relation between stimulation and a standard. This standard is determined by recent stimulation, background stimulation, and "residual" factors associated with the perceiver.

Usefulness of Shifting Standards. The suggestion that we are not in direct contact with stimulation can be somewhat disturbing, but even more troublesome is the notion that an internal standard, the adaptation level, is unstable and changes freely as a function of momentary stimulation. Intuitively, perception does not seem that unstable.

Note, however, that in some important perceptual situations, it is very useful to have a shifting internal standard. Indeed, it is the shifting standard that makes our perception *seem* stable. An important example is the case where we move from a sunny, out-of-doors environment into a room lighted rather dimly by incandescent lamps. A mechanical device, such as a light meter, will register a very large difference in the amount of light being reflected from surfaces indoors relative to light reflected from outdoor surfaces, and it will continue to do so indefinitely. That is, the meter will never *adapt* to the indoor lighting conditions.

Not so for the human perceptual system, which will soon adapt to the interior scene. Whereas out-of-doors, a neutral-appearing (gray) surface would have been one that reflected a great deal of rather blue (short wavelength) light, after a very short period indoors a neutral-appearing surface would be one that reflects less, and somewhat reddish (long wavelength) light. This perceptual shift has the effect of restoring surfaces indoors to a "natural" appearance for the perceiver. The interior scene will not appear to be uncomfortably dim nor noticeably red. That the light is red, however, can be verified easily by photographing the interior scene on color film.

Hence, a shifting neutral standard is a necessary and quite functional perceptual asset, that allows things to be seen as being relatively constant in their surface color characteristics even though the nature of illumination may change markedly in amount and kind.

It will occur to readers that in many sorts of perceptual situations recognition of patterns can be quite absolute and accurate. In fact, the recognition of shape, or pattern, of a stimulus represents the case where the perceiver is less dependent on internal standards, because one aspect of the stimulus can be judged against another aspect apparent in the stimulus itself.

An interesting experiment by Weintraub (1971) makes this point clearly. Stimuli like those used in his experiment are represented in Figure 12-19. The set of stimuli used by Weintraub actually had fifteen rectangles within each row and column, but a modified set is shown in the figure to better enable the reader to see the effects Weintraub found.

Sets of fifteen stimuli were used, one set at a time; each stimulus in the set appeared as a luminous rectangle in the dark, and the subject was asked to judge the height of each with the use of the numbers "One" (shortest) through "Fifteen" (tallest). Subjects were best able to judge the height of the fifteen stimuli varying, from one to another, as do the rectangles in the negative diagonal from upper left to lower right in Figure 12-19. They were less able to judge the stimuli in any one

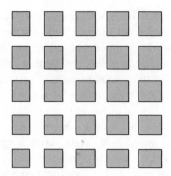

Fig. 12-19. A set of rectangles similar to those used by Weintraub (1971). When they saw each rectangle individually in the dark, subjects were better able to identify rectangles varying in shape, as do the five in the negative diagonal from upper left to lower right. The five squares varying in size from lower left to upper right were identified significantly less well. As you see them here, which set seems most distinctive from rectangle to rectangle?

row or column of the table. Performance was worst of all for stimuli varying in size, as do those along the positive diagonal from lower left to upper right in the figure. Note that in the case of those stimuli, no reference standard for judgment exists in the stimulus itself, since height and width varied together and the height/width ratio is the same for all. So, subjects could not improve judgment by comparing height with width within each rectangle and had to depend on an *internal* judgmental standard for height. Evidently, we are very much more judgmentally acute when we can use an external referent for judgment.

Weintraub concluded that another way of saying the same thing is to say that we are much better at the task of judging shape than in judging size of stimulus objects. The perception of shape involves comparison of pattern elements relative to each other. The perception of size throws us back on the less precise sort of internal standard that Helson described.

Perceptual Constancy. Our sensitivity to relations existing within stimulation leads to the stability of perception as an experience. Objects do not appear to change markedly in size as they recede, to change surface color when viewed under different illuminations, or to change shape when viewed from several angles. Notice that we must say that they do not change "markedly," as perceptual changes do occur to some extent under all those conditions. However, perceptual stability is the rule, not change.

This stability, or invariance, of perception has been called *perceptual constancy:* Apparent object characteristics (surface color, object shape, and object size) remain constant under varying conditions of viewing (changes in illumination, viewing angle, and distance). We are aware of many more sorts of perceptual constancy, of course, but these three types serve to illustrate study of the topic.

An understanding of the task involved in achieving constancy demands that we grasp the distinction between (1) characteristics of objects as they exist and (2) representation of those characteristics in the senses. Figure 12-20 makes that distinction in the case of color (A), size (B), and shape (C) constancy.

How well do we do in seeing object color, size and shape? To assess this we have needed measures of constancy. One such measure is defined for Figure 12-21. The concepts involved are depicted in rudimentary form in the figure. The measure is not easy to depict in a drawing, but suppose that we are in a small plane flying over cultivated fields in flat country. We see Field A close underneath the left wing and we try to pick out a field farther away that is of equal area. If we pay attention to the perspective lines in the drawing, we see that Field a occupies one unit of area, as does Field A. Field c matches the area of Field A, as both are drawn on the page, and in the context of the drawn perspective would be grossly too large. Field b matches neither the *perspective size* nor the *drawn size* of Field A, and is also an inappropriate choice. Hence, we conclude that Field a was intended by the artist to be of the same area as Field A, because it has the appearance Field A would have if Field A were located that far away. Conversely, when we get closer to Field a, it will appear just as Field A does now.

A measure of perceptual constancy is provided by:

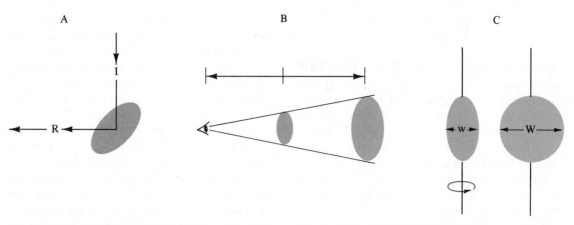

Fig. 12-20.   In (A) illumination (I) falls upon a gray disc, which reflects part of the light to the perceiver. The absolute amount of light reflected (R) depends on the amount of (I), while the ratio (R/I) depends on the grayness of the reflecting surface. It is that ratio that must be perceived accurately, since the ratio describes the object characteristic *grayness*. In (B) two discs of differing size both occupy the same proportion of the total visual field of the perceiver—who must respond to *real size*, by allowing for different viewing distances, rather than responding merely to visual angle occupied. In (C) the perceiver must not be deceived by the effect of rotation on the appearance of the circle shown on the right. The *real width* (W) must be seen, rather than merely the *projected width* (w).

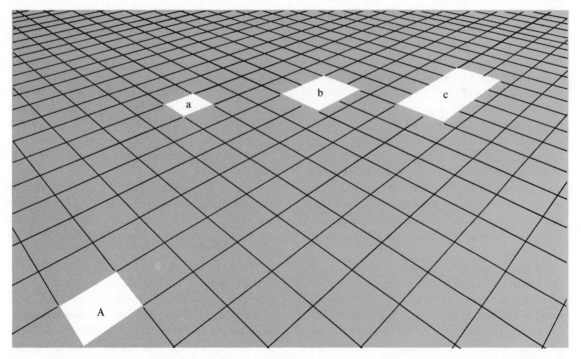

Fig. 12-21.   The drawing was prepared to depict cultivated fields being overflown in flat country. We look down and see Field A and try to see another field that matches Field A in area. Field a has been drawn to appear as A would if located at that distance from us, that is, it has the same *perspective size*. Field c has the same *drawn size* on the page as A, but in appearance at that distance suggests it is really many times larger than A. Field b matches A in neither *perspective* nor *drawn* size.

$$BR = \left| \frac{x - c}{a - c} \right|,$$

in which BR stands for Brunswik ratio. Note that if our choice is Field c, $BR = |(c - c)/(a - c)| = 0$, signifying no constancy at all. If we choose Field a, $BR = |(a - c)/(a - c)| = 1$, signifying perfect constancy. If we choose Field b, BR will have a value between 0 and 1. Note that the absolute value of the ratio is intended.

Similar measures of color constancy and shape constancy can be developed by referring back to Figure 12-20 on p. 415.

Much research on the subject of constancy has shown that constancy is usually attained in everyday perceiving, although not perfectly. Color constancy, usually explored as ''lightness'' or ''grayness'' of surfaces, depends on the appearance of illumination as it strikes more than a single surface. Color of surfaces will be independent of illumination if the effect of the illumination on each surface and on the background can be seen simultaneously (Wallach, 1948). If only one illuminated surface is visible, color constancy is usually lacking. As we should expect, size constancy tends to fail, when the true viewing distance is not perceived (Lichten and Lurie, 1950). Shape constancy deteriorates when the angle of view is not accurately perceived (Langdon, 1951).

A great deal of thought and comment has concerned just how the accurate perception of object characteristics is accomplished in spite of distortions introduced by the nature of viewing conditions. A major type of explanation is the Gestalt belief that the powerful relational characteristics of perception account adequately for the occurrence of constancy.

To many persons interested in constancy as a perceptual phenomenon, however, the *Gestalt* explanation is not a satisfying one, and appeal is made to another substantial tradition of thought on the matter. This is the traditional belief that all perceptions are *inferences* drawn about the nature of the objects from which stimulation comes. The supposition is that we cannot know the world directly. Stimulation from the world provides only *cues*, and from those cues our perception of objects and distances must be inferred.

Distance as an Inference. A considerable impetus for this belief was provided early by a substantial misunderstanding about the nature of distance perception. In the eighteenth century, Bishop Berkeley was impressed by the fact that while we have visual receptors that are impressively sensitive to the two-dimensional pattern of light falling upon them, there appeared to be no receptor apparatus directly sensitive to the distance between us and objects in our environment. Hence, the straight-line distance between us and an object was something that had to be inferred or derived from the two-dimensional portrayal of objects on the retinas of the two eyes. In those two-dimensional portrayals, it was suggested, there are certain *cues to distance* that can be utilized by the perceiver. Some of these cues are useful in the case of binocular viewing, and others are useful in the case of viewing with one eye only.

The most important binocular cue is associated with the fact that normal vision is *binocular* and *fused*. Because the eyes are separated, each has a distinct view of close-by objects, and the images on the retinas are slightly discrepant. This discrepancy provides a compelling experience of objects located in depth in normal vision. This is a marvelous achievement, for at one and the same time, the discrepant views of the two eyes are fused in the experience of a single view, while somehow the discrepancies are preserved and resolved as determinants of the apparent depth or distance away of objects viewed.

Figure 12-22 encourages the student to learn to prepare and to fuse discrepant views in home-made *stereograms*. Once learned, this skill provides an everlasting and enjoyable appreciation of *stereopsis*.

Another binocular cue is associated with double images. Figure 12-23 illustrates the concept of the *horopter,* the locus of all points in the visual field of the binocular perceiver that are imaged to *identical points* on the retinas of the two eyes. These are all points in the field that are fused in perception. Points farther away or closer than the horopter are seen as double images. Unless we try to see these double images, they are suppressed and unnoticed, but they can provide a cue to the distance of objects upon which the eyes *converge*

A

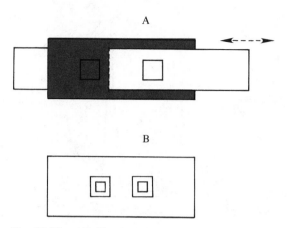

B

Fig. 12-22. (A) The device used to space properly the two elements of a *sterogram*. Prepare the shaded rectangle. Dimensions are about 20 cm. by 8 cm. The rectangle has the left square drawn on it and the vertical slit cut in it. A slide of white paper, containing the other square, is inserted in the slot as shown. While fixating with both eyes on a point between the squares convergence of the eyes is relaxed (Relax!). Soon the squares apparently begin to move towards each other. This can be encouraged by moving the slide until the two squares apparently coincide. This yields the crucial distance that must separate the elements of the sterogram in this "thousand-yard stare" technique. Then a stereograph like that shown in (B), with the squares separated by the crucial distance, will appear three dimensional when viewed as the device was viewed. Then many other patterns can be drawn to produce convincing depth.

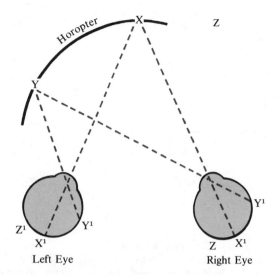

Fig. 12-23. With eyes converged on point, x, x is seen as a single object. So is point y, which is also located on the horopter. Any single point located at a distance given by the horopter arc is seen as single. Points not located on the horopter, such as point z, are seen doubly in vision (not fused).

and *accommodate* (focus). Obviously, objects seen clearly and singly are beyond some objects seen as fuzzy and double and closer than others also seen doubled.

Some of the *monocular* cues to depth can be quite compelling and can work together to produce a convincing experience of depth. A case in point is the viewing of a photographic print. Of course, no real depth exists in this situation, because all stimulus points in the print are equidistant from the viewer, and both eyes see the same view of the scene represented. Still, there can be a surprising degree of depth in certain photographs or drawings. The secret is revealed in Figure 12-24. Any photographic reproduction of a scene will appear to have a compelling appearance of three-dimen-

sionality or depth if the retinal angles subtended in the view represented in the reproduction are about the same as they would be if the view were seen directly. In most photographic reproductions, these relations do not hold because the reproductions are too small, as in most prints, or too large, as in most projected slides.

Other monocular clues have been suggested to include *interposition* (nearer objects overlap or partially cover farther objects); *size* (where object sizes are known, relative apparent angles subtended by objects can provide cues to distance), *linear perspective* (a special case of the size cue, perhaps: as distance increases parallel lines appear to converge); *aerial perspective* (object colors of distant objects appear less saturated or pure: examples are city buildings viewed from the distance of a few blocks or mountains viewed from a few miles).

The entire list of monocular cues to distance is quite long and well known to persons in the visual arts. We need not consider them all here. One of those so far omitted, *texture gradients* in the field of view, will be taken up a little later on.

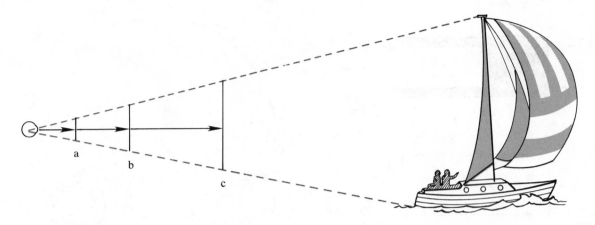

Fig. 12-24.   Life-like depth can be seen in photographs and drawings of the boat that preserve the size-distance relationships shown. A photograph at (a), for example, must cover the same visual angle as did the boat when viewed directly. Usually photographic prints are too small to achieve this at the normal viewing distance for photographs.

In summary, the many "cues to distance" have been reviewed. These are the cues that enable the perceiver to achieve accurate impressions of the distance of objects viewed. The word "achieved" creeps in here because of the belief of Bishop Berkeley that distance cannot be sensed directly and must be inferred from indirect monocular and binocular cues.

Perceptual Inference

The notion that perceived distance or depth is an *inference* can be another startling concept that does not seem to check out well with perceptual experience, but the *inferential* point of view about the fundamental nature of perception is an influential one.

The underlying supposition is that perceptual experience is an amalgam, a mixture of some parts coming from the senses at any moment and a larger part derived from stored information.

William James, the first influential American psychologist, stated the idea as follows:

Enough has now been said to prove the general law of perception, which is this: *That whilst part of what we perceive comes through our senses from the object before us, another part* (and it may be the larger part) *always comes out our own mind.* (James, 1962, p. 334)

James believed that on the basis of the stimulation activating the senses at any moment, we draw an inference about the nature of the objects (out there) that would most likely have given rise to that sort of stimulation. Inferences that we draw in this way are acquired habits. We perceive the actually more probable thing, based upon likelihoods derived from the learned implications of incoming sensory patterns experienced throughout our lives. The inferential process itself is not a conscious one; Helmholtz had suggested previously that perceptual inferences are automatic unconscious processes.

The conception of the perceptual process as being *inferential* is representative of a class of beliefs. The basic supposition is that momentary sensory information coming in is too rudimentary, ambiguous, or incomplete to specify exactly what the corresponding physical stimulus was "out there." Perceptual experience, on the other hand, is always regular and complete in the adult perceiver, because experience teaches us that this is true of the world in which we live. The process is assumed to be much like that experienced by the legendary blind child exploring an elephant. After touching as much of the elephant as can be reached, after learning about its limbs and trunk and tail, about its textures and movements, after smelling it and hearing it and after listening to descriptions of it, a whole entity is perceived. This is a living animal called an elephant. Thereafter, fragmentary stimuli from the elephant, a whiff of breath, the stamp of a massive foot, or a brush of abrasive skin, will no longer be perceived as isolated perceptual fragments. All come to mean "elephant" in its impressive entirety. If our blind child were blind at birth, his "elephant" will not correspond to ours exactly, but it will be as complete and plausible as anything else in his experience, even though he has experienced only fragments of it at any one time. That is the *inferential* point of view of the matter.

Two Inferential Theories of Perception

In contemporary psychology, two major types of inferential theories exist: *Probabilistic Functionalism* and *Transactional Functionalism*. The word functionalism occurs in these theories, because both emphasize the fact that an appropriate perception of a stimulus can achieve something useful for the perceiver. Where perception allows the perceiver to predict the nature of future stimulation arriving from the environment, perception to that degree is adaptive or functional.

Probabilistic Functionalism. The first of the theories named was described by Egon Brunswik. His "lens model" of perception in Figure 12-25 schematically describes the perceptual process (see Hammond, 1966). As in the case of all inferentialists, Brunswik supposed that the perceiver is not in direct contact with the environment, represented by an environmental event, the *distal event* (DE). Instead, the DE is represented in the senses as a pattern of *proximal cues* (x_1 through x_n), and from these cues a percept (p) is derived. It has been suggested that percepts can be derived to meet either of two *perceptual objectives,* or else a mixture of these.

1. The percept can be derived to be as veridical as possible. If that is the objective, then the perceiver strives to achieve as great a correspondence as possible between the percept (P) and the distal event.
2. The percept can be derived to be as *coherent* as possi-

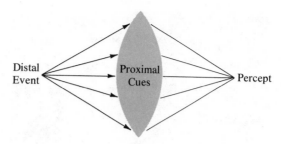

Fig. 12-25. The "lens model" of Egon Brunswik. An event in the immediate environment (Distal Event) is represented at the sense organs by *proximal cues,* from which the perception (Percept) of the Distal Event is derived. The Percept can be *veridical* if it corresponds well with the Distal Event. However, the percept can be quite complete and consistent with the nature of the proximal cues and yet be nonveridical. In that case, the Percept is *coherent.*

ble (Hake 1966a, 1966b). This objective is reached if the percept is complete, if it is plausible, and if it permits accurate predictions of perceptions yet to come. Note that these objectives can be reached even though the *veridicality* of the percept is low. That is, the correspondence between the percept and the cues (x_i) can be close even in cases where the distal event is imperfectly and unreliably represented by the cues. In brief, it is supposed that in many cases it is more important that the percept be complete and plausible than it it be entirely accurate. Much perceptual effort is devoted to achieving *coherent* perceptions, without question, and this is one major principle of belief about the nature of human perceptual processes.

Figure 12-26 provides an illustration. The faces are schematic, constructed by varying forehead length (features located low in the face) and nose length. Although they are crudely schematic, they do lead to coherent perceptions of faces to which human characteristics can be attributed. Usually, for example, it is not difficult to perceive the faces as being either "intelligent" or "unintelligent;" the face in the lower right usually is judged most intelligent while the one in the upper left is usually thought least intelligent.

In terms of Brunswik's "lens model," the facial features are the proximal cues, and the apparent intelligence of a face is the percept derived from the

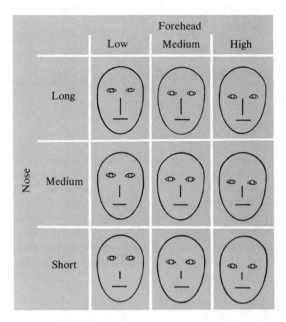

Fig. 12-26. Schematic faces, which can seem to possess "intelligence," or the lack of it.

cues. We may, if we wish, use this sort of experimentation to compute the relationship that exists between the cues and the percept.

Rodwan and Hake (1964) found that judgments of the "intelligence" of such actually-neutral, schematic faces could be predicted accurately from a weighted combination of the cues, such as:

$$-.2060X_1 + .6181X_2 - .0687X_3 + .7555X_4$$

in which X_1 is nose length, X_2 is length of chin, X_3 is distance between the eyes, and X_4 is length of forehead. A short nose, a long chin, and a long forehead—all of which produce a small face in the center of the head—tend to be taken as indicators of more intelligence.

Such perceived relationships are usually quite marked, perhaps indicating that the "intelligence" of others is an attribute that is readily and consistently inferred in the case of real as well as schematic faces. Other judgments of the schematic faces, such as "beauty," "likeability," "mood," "age," and "character" have been studied with similar results (see Brunswik, 1947, pp. 99–106).

The "lens model" is quite useful conceptually in exploring situations in which living persons are

perceptual stimuli. In viewing another person, we find ourselves often arriving at a conception of some personality trait or enduring characteristic. We do this not by perceiving that trait directly; rather, we arrive at the trait as an inference drawn from an accumulation of moment-by-moment actions and utterances of the other person. All of the specific things that individual does and says can be represented by the cues, the X_i, in the lens model. The inferred personality trait is the percept derived from those cues.

Such person concepts, to be veridical, demand a great deal of careful observation, but more often such concepts are formed on the basis of quite casual and brief observations. And so the interpretive aspect of the perception of other persons often predominates. Instead of an accurate perception of the other person, we produce a *perceptual stereotype:* a culturally-determined, simplified perception of a complex stimulus pattern, another person (see Lippmann, 1922).

A frequently studied example of stereotopy in social perception is the case of *ethnic identification:* the tendency to assign persons to ethnic groups in which all persons are perceived to have the same single set of traits. We know this tendency as racial bigotry, and the bigot, by common reputation, is said to be especially able in the self-assigned task of discriminating non-minority from minority persons. Early research showed, for example, that persons with high degrees of prejudice (as judged by other means) were more acute than others in the task of discriminating between Jews and non-Jews. This was later shown to be false; highly prejudiced persons are merely more confident of such judgments (Malpass, 1969).

The inferential process by which perceivers derive unitary, often simple conceptions of another person, or a group of persons, has been called *impression formation.* Asch (1946) described the defining experimental situation in which subjects are given a set of personality trait adjectives, supposedly descriptive of another person, and then asked to describe impressions of that person. The resemblance of that experimental paradigm to the perceptual process as conceived by Brunswik is obvious. Impression formation as a topic will be considered further in Chapter 15.

The emphasis on the interpretive functions in perceiving, which is characteristic of the inferential point of view, provides insights about individual differences in perceiving. We know these are quite marked and are most noticeable where stimulation is least definite. Such situations provide opportunities to learn about factors determining the outcomes of the perceptual inferential process.

Reported sightings of UFOs provide a good example. Without taking a stand on the issue of whether such objects exist really or not, we must acknowledge that the issue is an important one to many Americans. Polls have indicated that at least one-half of our population believes that UFOs are "real." About one in twenty claim to have seen one. At one point, official concern led to a full-scale investigation of these issues and a report (the Condon Report, 1968; see Hynek, 1972) that assigned all but a fraction of sightings to misperceptions of well known objects or meteorological events. The report by no means has quieted controversy about the meaning of UFO reports, but frequency of sightings diminished to some extent for a time after the report appeared.

The waxing and waning of UFO reports over time suggests that the frequency of sightings depends on a characteristic of the perceiver, namely the strength of belief in the possibility that UFOs are real. Perceivers with stronger beliefs, presumably, are more likely actually to see in an ambiguous, uncertain viewing situation that now characteristic shape and details of the classic "saucer," and perhaps its crew.

The study of persons who have reported UFO sightings has provided some insights about this, but the situation is complex. Certainly, UFO sighters are not characteristically from any particular part of the country. Nor are they of any particular level of education, age, or sex. However, they do tend to be what Donald Warren (1970) has described as *status inconsistents.* Sighters tend to have inconsistent rankings with respect to three *achieved statuses:* income level, education, and job classification. An example is a person with advanced degrees who has a low-status job and a meager income, or a very modest education combined with a high-status job. The result of status inconsistency is *social marginality,* a partial or complete, real or imagined exclusion from the social communities made up of status consistent persons. The cab driver with a Ph.D. may believe he really fits neither with other cab drivers nor with others holding advanced degrees. The female mechanical engineer may feel she possesses simultaneously the socially incompatible statuses of female and technical expert.

Warren suggested that *social marginality* of this sort should lead to behavior and beliefs that "break the system" or permit escape into new roles, new possibilities. Socially marginal persons, then, should be those who report UFOs, because such sightings both confound the "system," and open up breathtaking, new possibilities.

This suggestion is close to the mark. In the case of white males only, low income combined with advanced education and higher job classifications is associated with a rate of UFO sightings that is twice the national average. Status inconsistency for medium-income, white males is associated with a rate four times the national average.

Other investigators have asked whether both the sightings and the status inconsistency might not be the result of still other personality variables or aspects of personal history. In any case, an important point is made: A sizeable and identifiable group of Americans perceive and report occurrences in our world that others simply do not share. The role of interpretation in perceptual experiences can be considerable, and this role is related to perceiver variables, one of which is readiness to interpret ambiguous stimulus input in ways that satisfy social needs.

Transactional Functionalism. The second major inferential approach is *Transactional Functionalism* (Ittelson and Kilpatrick, 1951). The word "transaction" is used here to mean that perception results from a transaction occurring between the perceiver and his or her environment. In this the perceiver takes an active role and brings to perception a series of assumptions about our world based on experience with it. Perception as a process involves the apprehension of the probable significances of stimulation received. This is an uncertain process because the true, or objectively-described nature of the distal events in the world is not given completely by the proximal pattern of stimulation. For any pattern of proximal stimulation, it can be shown that there is an infinite variety of stimulating conditions that could have produced that pattern. So says the theory.

Transactional functionalism is best known for the interesting demonstrations devised to illustrate its principles. A well known example is the trapezoidal window shown in Figure 12-27A. The natural assumption is that the view is of a rectangular window rotated somewhat so that the right-most side is closer to the viewer. This assumption conforms to our *assumptive* world in which only rectangular windows usually occur, and windows usually look just like Figure 12-27A. when they are viewed so that the right side is closer.

If the window begins to rotate in the direction of rotation indicated in Figure 12-27B, perception may not conform to this direction of rotation (counterclockwise), especially if the scene is viewed monocularly or by means of motion-picture or television presentation, both of which suppress depth cues and heighten the illusion,

which is that the window is rotating in the opposite direction (clockwise). This is the perceptual outcome because of the *perspective assumption* that the apparently large side of the window is closer. Hence, the side marked L appears to rotate from right to left in *front of* the side marked S. Actually, the side marked L has moved from right to left *behind* the side marked S, and at (D), the two sides have exchanged places. At this point, the actual counterclockwise motion carries the large side L from left to right apparently *in front of* the small side S, this motion being consistent with the assumption that the large side is closer to the viewer. Hence, although the trapezoidal window rotates continuously in a counter-clockwise direction, it is seen to oscillate, to reverse its motion periodically, so that the large side L is always seen moving in front of the small side S. *Accuracy* of perception in this instance is sacrificed in favor of *plausibility*, conformance of what is seen with our assumptions about the nature of the action we are viewing.

This is an easy demonstration to produce using a painted window of trapezoidal shape, and a syn-

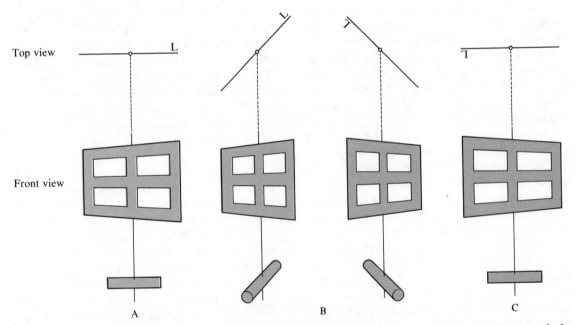

Fig. 12-27. Drawings show sequence of front perspective views of the *trapezoidal window* as it turns counterclockwise through the positions shown in the top views. Large end of the window L and actual direction of rotation is shown in the top views. (For further details see Ittelson, W. H. and Kilpatrick, F. P., 1951.)

chronous clock motor used to produce the rather slow rotation required.

A somewhat deeper understanding of the transactional approach can be achieved by the addition of a rod, suspended so that it penetrates one of the openings in the window. Different assumptions involve the bar and the window. The bar is free to rotate apparently in either direction, but perceptually the window is not for the reasons described. What is seen, then, as the window rotates counterclockwise with the rod suspended through one of its panes? The answer is usually that the window appears to oscillate back and forth, as before, while the bar rotates continuously and in so doing moves effortlessly through the solid mullions of the window.

This is a rather surprising perceptual result, because it does not conform to normal assumptions about the world in which we live. Solids do not easily pass through solids. Evidently, the perceptual process makes separate and independent meaning of the movement of the bar and the movement of the window. This is indeed what transactional functionalism suggests. We can be aware superficially of the existence and relationships among a wide variety of things, but when attention gets more penetrating, it also gets more restricted. The act of perceiving the complex behavior of the window in time, of being aware of the sequential significances of stimulation received from it, prevents us from attending fully to other sequential significances of stimulation received at the same time. A kind of attentional *zoom lens* is implied. More attention to detail in one part of the visual field tends to exclude other areas from detailed notice (Ames, 1953). The act of making sense simultaneously of the bar's movement and of the window's movement evidently exceeds the capacity of the system.

To summarize the inferential point of view briefly, Bishop Berkeley emphasized the need for indirect detection of the distance of objects from the perceiver, who lacks any sense receptors directly sensitive to that distance. Distance must then be inferred from indirect cues. Taking the matter further, the two functionalist positions described involve the belief that in any sort of perceptual process stimulation coming to the senses is always inadequate to describe completely events in our environment, and the nature of those events then must be inferred from those fragmentary inputs. Inputs are evaluated in terms of general knowledge of or assumptions about the nature of the world as well as the significance of such fragmentary inputs in previous experiences.

The reader should note again that statements about the nature of perception always involve important assumptions about the nature of the world in which we do our perceiving. Reconstructive theories, such as the two functionalist points of view described, assume that our world is an orderly, constrained, redundant place. Only in such a world could fragmentary inputs supply cues useful in inferring what the inputs come from or what the missing fragments of input may be. In a truly chaotic world, knowledge about a fragment of that world can provide no information at all about the rest of it. Knowledge of an event in the past does not help at all in predicting events to come or their significance when they do occur.

Perceptual Clean-Up Effect. In a very direct sense, the theorist puts the perceiver in the same position as the astronomer who has received a print of a photograph taken by a satellite at rest on another planet. The photograph may contain random irregularities and blurring, and in order to improve this view of the surface of the planet, the astronomer may wish to "clean up" the photograph a bit by removing the blurring and other irregularities. This separation of aspects of the photograph that appear to result from random noise processes, on the one hand, from aspects of the photograph that may genuinely represent terrain features of the planet, on the other, requires an act of faith. The assumption that must be made is that the orderly and patterned aspects of the photographs represent terrain features, while random inhomogeneities in the photograph do not. Given that assumption the random inhomogeneities can be filtered out, and the astronomer is then left with a photograph that appears plausible. Of course, that photograph is only as valid as the assumption made.

Similarly, the human perceiver may *reconstruct* an orderly perception of the world "out there," by assuming that the world is orderly. In that case, knowledge about that orderliness enables the perceiver to "fill in" missing parts of stimulation and to blot out those parts of stimulation that do not conform to the orderliness assumption. Such processes can work only in the case of orderly planets, as we believe our own to be.

Psychophysical Correspondence

The direct opposite to the *reconstructive* point of view, of course, is that stimulation is never, or almost never, fragmentary in nature and that perceivers are always, or almost always, in close and direct contact with the environment. This is the point of view of James J. Gibson, whose *hypothesis of psychophysical correspondence* states that for every aspect of perceptual experience, no matter how subtle, there is a corresponding aspect of stimulation arriving at the sense organs. In other words, stimulation is normally sufficiently complete in detail to account for our perceptual experience. No inferential process based on incomplete input need be supposed.

If that is correct, then Bishop Berkeley was wrong. Distance is not an abstract straight line stretching between the perceiver and object. Instead, the situation is as shown in Figure 12-28; the

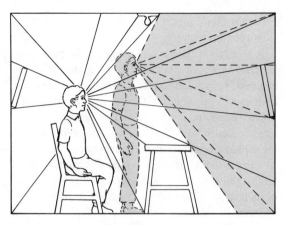

Fig. 12-29. The optic array of a seated and a standing observer in a simple environment. (From Gibson, J. J., 1966)

visual world is filled with textured surfaces, and the grain of that texture directly indicates distance.

Figure 12-29, from Gibson's *The Senses Considered as Perceptual Systems* (1966), illustrates what is meant by an *optic array* of light paths from objects to a perceiver's eyes. One particular array is characteristic of a seated perceiver; another is characteristic of the standing perceiver. Taken together, the two arrays serve to completely specify the room and its objects. If not, further move-

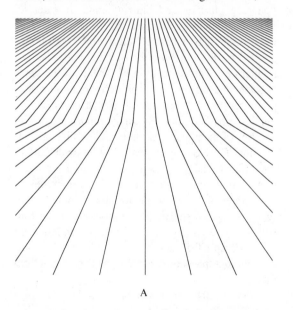

A

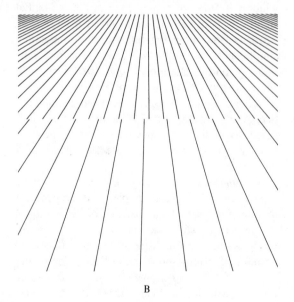

B

Fig. 12-28.   The textures that appear as surfaces, corners (A), and edges (B). (From Gibson, J. J., 1966)

ment of the perceiver, and consequent changes in the optic array, will serve to accomplish this.

The light ray paths drawn in Figure 12-29 represent only a small part of the actual set. When all are considered, both the slant of surfaces and the edges of surfaces are clearly specified. *Slant* is specified by gradients of texture, as in Figure 12–28, Part A; *edges* are specified by discontinuities in texture, as in Figure 12-28, Part B.

The Gibson point of view is a compelling one, especially when the dynamic character of the flow and movement of the optic array in time is considered. Figure 12-30 illustrates a situation that drew Gibson's attention early in the genesis of his ideas. This is the flow of an optic array apparent as a pilot approaches the threshold of a runway.

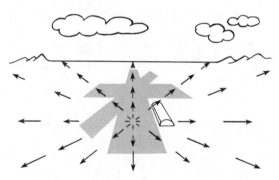

Fig. 12-30. The flow of the optic array as the pilot approaches the threshold of the runway. (From Gibson, J. J., 1950)

In this conception, the older idea that distance must be inferred from monocular and binocular cues receives quite a jolt. A wealth of indicants appear available to assure the pilot as to whether he is or is not on the proper approach path. In the process, the judgment of distance would not appear to be involved directly; the pilot responds instead to the pattern of texture that flows and enlarges with approach to the runway. The only part of the runway that enlarges and does not flow, for example, is that small portion of the runway threshold towards which the plane directly moves.

Certainly also, this point of view verifies the intuitive belief of many persons that momentary stimulation almost never appears inadequate to specify our environment. We are misled occasionally, but not often enough to suppose that the stimulus for perception is normally inadequate.

Students becoming familiar for the first time with the psychological study of perceptual topics may have some difficulty in understanding how points of view as far apart as those of the inferentialists and J. J. Gibson can remain unresolved. Such continuing divergency of concepts deserves a section of its own at the end of this chapter, but one obvious explanation lies in the fact that the sheer complexity of the topic of perception allows considerable choice in what it is we wish to study and to explain. We may either concentrate on all those instances in which contact with our environment is sure and adequate or on those instances in which this is less true, such as examples of perceptual distortions. The latter, of course, also serve to add a little interest to textbook pages.

Changes in Perceiving: Learning and Adaptation

To this point, we have considered four major points of view about the fundamental nature of human perception. This fifth section concerns an aspect of perception that is universally accepted by all points of view: perception of stimulation changes systematically as experience with that stimulation continues.

In describing those changes, we speak both of *perceptual learning* and *perceptual adaptation*. The first term is used to refer to relatively enduring changes in perceptual experience, subject to some forgetting, while the results of perceptual adaptation tend to persist only so long as the stimulus situation persists.

Perceptual Learning

Perhaps the most important sort of enduring perceptual change occurring with practice is the achievement of finer and finer distinctions among stimulus patterns. The practiced look through a microscope at a drop of pond water is a much more articulated, detailed, and familiar experience than was the first look. The night sky in winter with practice becomes familiar terrain charted in terms of easily recognizable constellations—an appearance entirely different from its appearance for the unpracticed observer.

This suggests that the usual result of perceptual practice with any set of complex stimulus patterns is the change from stimulus confusion and overgeneralization of response to specificity. An analogy useful in understanding this transition is provided by concepts from learning theory of an earlier time (Hull, 1943). In the case of a unidimensional stimulus dimension, such as a set of tones varying in frequency, one such tone, say 1000 Hz, can be selected as a conditioned stimulus. A specific response is conditioned to that stimulus during a series of conditioning trials (see Chapter 9). After the trial series, the occurrence of the 1000-Hz tone alone, without a reinforcing stimulus, will evoke a conditioned response, but so will a wide range of tones both lower and higher in frequency than 1000 Hz. This spread of responding to stimuli that had not occurred in the conditioning trials is known as *stimulus generalization.*

In subsequent conditioning trials, generalization can be reduced markedly by a technique in which three stimuli occur in random order. The 1000-Hz tone is reinforced whenever it occurs, but a 950-Hz tone and 1050-Hz tone are never reinforced. The result is decreasing generalization, or more *discrimination:* in the absence of reinforcement, the conditioned response is elicited by a much smaller range of tones above and below 1000 Hz.

A similar change from generalization to specificity of responding in the case of complex stimulus patterns is known as stimulus *differentiation* (see E. J. Gibson, 1969). As experience with a set of complex stimulus patterns progresses we learn to respond to stimulus distinctions not originally noted. Using the terms defined in the preceding section, we could say more precisely, with J. J. Gibson, that *psychophysical correspondences increase with practice.*

E. J. Gibson suggested two mechanisms underlying differentiation: *abstraction,* the discovery during practice of the fundamental ways in which stimulus patterns differ, and *filtering,* ignoring noncritical aspects of the patterns.

What sorts of experience with stimulation lead to differentiation? Gibson emphasized the fact that the process occurs in any sort of repetitive experiences with a set of complex stimuli, but usually the act of learning to discriminate among stimulus patterns, to learn their similarities and differences, involves the learning of descriptive labels for the patterns as well. And so a great deal of thought has been devoted to the possible role of the labels themselves.

When we have a set of very distinctive names, and we learn to associate each name with one of a set of confusable stimulus patterns, do the very great differences from name to name then help us avoid confusing one pattern with another? As a matter of fact, the result of practice in learning a unique name for each of a set of stimuli usually is increased ability to avoid confusing any one stimulus with another. But this result by itself does not demonstrate that the unique names attached to the stimuli have enhanced perceptual differences from stimulus to stimulus. Other factors may account for the result.

C. W. Eriksen and the author compared the effect of using a separate, unique label for each of twelve stimuli with the effect of using one label for more than a single stimulus. In an extreme case, subjects used just two labels, one for six of the stimuli and the other label for the remaining six stimuli. Subjects learned to discriminate among the stimulus patterns whether they used a unique label for each or the same label for several. The results have been confirmed generally, and so we conclude that it is not the learned association between a label and a stimulus pattern that is crucial; what is important is *looking at the patterns with a purpose.* The crucial element in differentiation is some sort of task that requires us to learn to discriminate each pattern from the rest (see Hake and Eriksen, 1955).

An important type of stimulus label is the numerical estimate (feet, yards, meter, and such). The performance of adults in learning to use such estimates was studied by Gibson and Bergman (1954). Two groups of subjects were asked to estimate eighteen different distances ranging from 52 to 395 yards over the ground out of doors. These estimates were made without correction, that is, without knowledge of the true distances. Following that, one of the groups, the experimental group, experienced trials in which ninety different distances ranging from 39 to 435 yards were estimated, with each estimate being corrected by the experimenter. Following that session, which the other group (the control group) did not experience, both groups then made another set of estimates of the original eighteen distances. With continued practice subjects in both groups reduced the amount of error in their estimates, but the intervening practice of the experimental group produced a greater reduction of error in the second set of estimates of the eighteen distances.

Subsequent work of Gibson and others suggests clearly, however, that in trying to understand this experiment and others like it we must distinguish between (1) a possible increased perceptual ability to see distances more accurately, and (2) a possible increased ability to use the verbal estimates more consistently. In the second alternative, practice in estimating distances would not change perception itself, but rather enables the perceiver to know what 100 yards, 50 feet, or 80 meters, for example, look like as distances over the ground. Research has favored the latter interpretation, and this has provided no surprises for hunters, yachtsmen, and other sorts of out-of-doors types.

Clearly, then, perceptual learning appears to involve two processes. One of these is the process of differentiation. The other consists of acquired skills in the use of appropriate descriptive labels for stimulus patterns. About a third possible process, we are less sure. This is the possibility that rewards and punishments can determine *what* is perceived—determine why, for example, one person sees the planet Venus in the evening sky and another sees a UFO.

In trying for an answer to that one, Solley and Santos (1958) tried to influence which alternative view of a reversible cube (such as that in Figure 12-1 on p. 397 was experienced by a subject. Three cubes occurred in random order in a series of trials. One cube was the standard, ambiguous cube, and the other two had additional emphasis of lines to increase the likelihood that the cube appeared in one orientation (front surface to left) or the other (front surface to right). The purpose of

the trials was to influence subjects to see the standard cube in a particular one of the orientations whenever it appeared in the series. This was accomplished by presenting the cube with that particular emphasis on the majority of trials and providing verbal reinforcement whenever the subject reported seeing that cube in the intended orientation.

As the experiment progressed, subjects more and more frequently reported seeing the standard cube, occurring on test trials, in the intended and rewarded orientation. Subsequent research has repeated this finding, but has raised a crucial question. What is the real result of this experiment, particularly of the verbal reinforcement given by the experimenter? What was changed? Was it how the subject saw the standard cube or was it merely the subject's report of what was seen? At this point, we do not have a way of choosing between those two alternatives.

The topic of perceptual learning extends beyond the concepts covered in this section to interesting questions about the role learning and experience, which occur in the young organism, plays in the attainment of adult perceptual achievements. That part of this topic is considered later on in this chapter as well as in Chapter 14.

Perceptual Adaptation

The subject of perceptual *calibration* was considered in an earlier section where it was suggested that exposure to a particular stimulus situation leads to shifts in the perceptual frame of reference, a *normalization* process in which there is a shift in the value of stimulation that appears neutral or normal. This is a common experience. We all share it, for example, when we enter a darkened theater. *Dark adaptation* proceeds as we sit in the dark, and soon we begin to perceive the interior of the theater. After that process is complete, a lighted surface that previously was judged neutral (neither very bright nor very dim) would now be judged intolerably bright. The new set of stimuli for which we are then calibrated, or adapted, are all quite dim.

Such adaptation effects have been described for the patterned characteristics of stimulation as well.

As much as four decades ago, it was known that if one viewed for a minute or so a slightly curved line, or a slightly tilted one, the curved line would be seen as becoming less curved, or the titled line as more vertical. Following that, a single, straight, vertical line would be seen as either curved in the opposite direction or tilted to the opposite side, depending on what had just been given prolonged fixation. Such an effect is called an *after effect*. The same sort of effect was discussed in connection with Figure 12-12 on p. 407.

Other more major adaptation effects have been studied extensively by psychologists. One early interest had its origins in knowledge of the optics of the eye. Since the eye resembles a camera—in that it has an aperture (pupil), shutter (lids), lens system (cornea and lens), and a light-sensitive surface (retina) on which an image is thrown—a major question, largely philosophically rather than physiologically phrased, concerns how the perceiver makes use of the images thrown on the back of the eye. The image back there is inverted, as in a camera, and so a question of much interest arose: Do we learn early in life to deal with this up-side-down image, and if so, how?

One important way to explore that question involved the use of an optical system (a set of mirrors or prisms) that inverts the image at the back of the eye so that it is right-side-up. The process of adjustment to that right-side-up image is then studied in detail. This experiment has been done several times. In each case, the subject is asked to wear the image-inverting device for many days, and during that time the subject's experience and visual skills are measured and recorded.

One such study, perhaps the best known, was conducted by G. N. Stratton in the late nineteenth century (see Epstein, 1967). Stratton wore the inverting device for eight days and recorded his experiences in some detail. His results have been of much interest to psychologists. Perhaps a primary reason for this interest involves basic curosity about the extent to which we must learn, beginning at birth, to perceive our environment. If we equate conceptually the sort of perceptual learning that occurs very early in an individual's lifetime with the perceptual learning that must occur when an adult begins to wear an optical image-inverting device, then the latter situation takes on a special importance. Many do equate those two situations, and so there has been persistent interest in the Stratton experiment and others like it.

Of all the questions asked about the Stratton study, perhaps the one of outstanding interest is the question of whether he ever adapted to the image-inverting device to such a degree that the optically upside-down world actually began to look right-side-up. Stratton wore the device for eight days, his eyes being blindfolded when the device was not worn, and his visually guided actions improved steadily during that period. As to whether the world ever began to appear right-side-up, no solid answer has appeared. His report suggests that he learned to accept an inverted world, even that part of it outside the range of vision at any moment appeared inverted; and if anything, he gradually began to feel that he himself was up-side-down in an inverted world. When the device was removed after the experimental period Stratton reported that what he saw was surprising and bewildering, yet recognizable as the world he had experienced before he began wearing the device. Certainly, this old, pre-experimental world did not itself look upside-down.

Variations of this basic experiment have been tried since Stratton's time, and are still being tried without providing solid answers to the question. We know that subjects wearing an image-inverting device do learn to get around in the visually distorted world that results. But when asked whether the world ever begins to appear right-side-up, the answer is usually that this question is irrelevant to what the subject experiences. After adapting to optical inversion, the world becomes familiar and manageable again. It begins to look "right" again, but even when that stage is reached, subjects report when asked that what they see is not the previous, familiar, right-side-up world.

It is certain, however, that while wearing an image-inverting device, subjects do undergo marked perceptual changes. Whether such changes should be called *adaptation* or whether they should be called *learning* is a bit of a problem since the effects are often quite enduring. It takes some time for perception to return to normalcy after several days' exposure to optically distorted vision. But once the return to normalcy is achieved, it is relatively easy to respond adequately again to distortion when the device is worn once more. New visually guided behaviors that develop during the use of the distorting device are quite quickly reinstated, suggesting that the perceptual effects produced are situationally controlled; whole complexes of new visual responses can be called forth by specific viewing situations, once those responses have been learned in that situation. Once one has learned to use a microscope, a pair of binoculars, or even new eye glasses, the perceptual adjustments required for competent use of such devices are enduring and easily reinstated each time they are used.

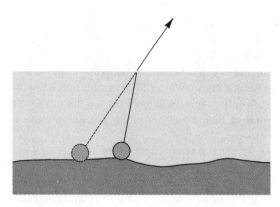

Fig. 12-32.   Image of a ball in shallow water is displaced by the refraction of light at the surface of the water.

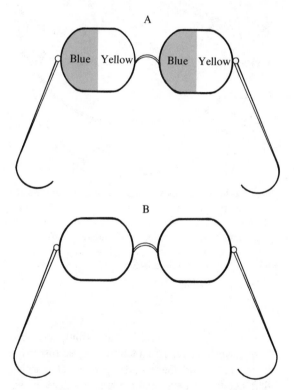

Fig. 12-31. The split-field spectacles are shown schematically in (A). The left half of each lens is blue; the right half is yellow. After continuous wear for several weeks perceived blue and yellow, depending on the direction of gaze, tends to disappear. If then the plain lens spectacles of (B) are worn instead, yellow tends to be seen with gaze left and blue with gaze right. (From Kohler, I., 1962)

This *situational* characteristic of visual adaptation is emphasized in Figure 12-31. Such situation-specific adaptation (eyes left vs. eyes right) illustrates the complexity and flexibility of the visual system, which not only adapts to new stimulation, but also restricts that adapted state to those perceptual situations for which the state of adaptation is appropriate.

Psychologists have been intensely interested in how adjustments to optically rearranged stimulation occurs, and much of the process is now understood. We can illustrate the process very simply in Figure 12-32. In that figure the optical displacement of a ball in shallow, clear water is represented. An observer wading in the water to the right of the ball reaches for the ball and reaches beyond it in an attempt to grasp the image of the ball, which is displaced away from the observer by light refraction at the surface of the water.

The attempt will fail, of course, as the observer is reaching for a phantom, and unless the distortion in the situation is detected and adjustment for it is made, the observer is doomed to frustration in repeated attempts to seize the ball. In fact, we know that the observer would adjust and with repeated attempts to touch the ball would come closer and closer to the real ball, finally touching and seizing it.

An error-correcting process occurs in this situation, because in reaching for the ball the observer adds his/her own arm to the scene, and it too is displaced by the distortion process. The observer, in effect, can notice the visual effect of moving the arm in a known way, with repeated trials learn that a distorting process is present, and discern the nature of that process. And so adjustments can be made.

The neural activity that arises in the central nervous system resulting from the visual stimulation received as the observer reaches for the ball is known as *reafferance*. That term refers specifically to sensory stimulation that is related systematically to *movements initiated by the perceiver*. Richard Held (1965) and his associates at the Massachusetts Institute of Technology have conducted a long series of experiments that tends to show that

adaptation to optic distortion can occur only when *reafferance* can occur, that is, when the observer can make active, self-initiated movements in the distortion situation. Figure 12-33 provides an example of a situation in which *reafferance* is minimized and little adaptation to the effects of image-displacing prisms occurs.

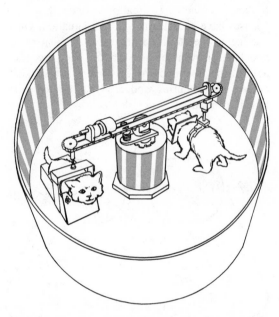

Fig. 12-34.   The *active* kitten in the harness makes self-initiated movements; the *passive* kitten in the carriage is moved by every movement of the *active* kitten, but cannot make major self-initiated movements. *Passive* kittens show measurable slowness in developing normal sensory-motor coordination. (From Held, R., 1965)

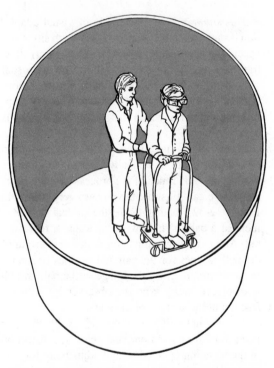

Fig. 12-33.   This illustration raises an interesting question. Will the observer being pushed adapt successfully to the distortions produced by the prisms he is wearing? Results suggest that he adapts less well than when he is permitted to walk around while wearing the prisms. (From Held, R., 1965)

Figure 12-34 emphasizes the analogy described here earlier between adaptation to optic distortion in the adult and the original perceptual learning that occurs in developing mammals. The *active* kitten in the harness is permitted a lot of self-initiated movement; the *passive* kitten in the carriage is moved by every movement of the *active* kitten, but does not initiate much movement itself. The lack of *reafferance* permitted the *passive* kitten leads to measureable slowness in the development of normal sensory-motor coordination after the kitten is freed from the apparatus.

The Physiological Basis for Perceptual Processes

Much of the material covered thus far derives from our philosophical origins; much of what follows is concerned with processes and mechanisms that are grounded in biology.

Much of the latter concerns the sense modalities themselves. Knowledge of structure and function of receptors and associated nervous systems has replaced or supported earlier concepts of how the receptors could or should function (see Chapter 5). The topics that are "perceptual," however, were defined earlier here as those that are not obviously associated with any single sense modality. These topics are more complex and subtle. They were slower in being closely associated with organic structure and function.

Still, a strong beginning has been made in the search for the physiological basis for perceptual processes, a beginning that has produced new concepts and new approaches to the study of perception.

Hebb's Conceptual Nervous System

In retrospect at this point, the dominant figure involved in the early expansion of interest into the biology of perception is D. O. Hebb of McGill University, who is not himself a biologist. Indeed, he described, at first, not a real central nervous system (CNS), but rather a "conceptual nervous system" that was unacceptable as a flesh-and-blood mechanism (Hebb, 1949). This conception contained within it several powerful ideas, however, and these quickly directed attention to crucial aspects of the real CNS.

Hebb's problem was a conceptual one at the outset, a problem posed by a contradiction between the facts of neurophysiology known at the time and the useful explanatory concepts of Gestalt psychology. Neurophysiology indicated strongly that perception must be associated with the excitation of spe-

cific cells in the nervous system, for the basic organization of the nervous system involves cells conducting impulses along well defined tracts. "Cross-talk" or spreading excitation beyond the confines of specific tracts was not then thought to be the rule in CNS functioning. On the other hand, the Gestalt principles implied that the *pattern* of excitation was crucial, not the specific cells excited. Their point of view emphasized the importance of the organization of force fields spreading beyond the confines of localized tracts; and a confrontation was implied between this field-type nervous system of the Gestalt psychologist, which appeared to require about as much structure as a bowl of oatmeal, and the switchboard type of nervous system in which transmission is confined to discrete tracts.

Hebb had been a graduate student in the laboratory of Karl Lashley, who was strongly influenced by Gestalt positions in the matter, and in that laboratory attempts were made to settle the specific question as to whether learned habits were stored in discrete places in the mammalian nervous system. Was there an *engram,* a specific storage locus for each specific habit or memory? Or, are habits stored as diffuse patterns or fields?

One research strategy involved teaching laboratory rats simple habits prior to creating lesions over the top surface of the brain. The effect of those lesions, which varied in size and location from animal to animal, was measured by the time taken to relearn these habits after recovery from surgery. From this work emerged the twin principles of *mass action* and *equipotentiality:* the location of surgical destruction of the cortex was not as important as its extent in affecting retention of habits acquired before surgery. This meant to Hebb that habits could not be stored in localized and well-defined areas of the nervous system, as conventional neurophysiology suggested they must be. Retention of perceptual learning was impaired seriously by large lesions that, perhaps, interfered with the massive organization of the brain that Gestalt conceptions demanded. And so the major problem was to understand how this could happen in a brain organized as conventional neurophysiology suggested it to be, with cells interconnected in a switchboard pattern and neural impulses conducted only between interconnected cells.

The Cell Assembly and Phase Sequence

Hebb suggested schematically some simple mechanisms that could make sense of this discrepancy. He suggested that the smallest unit of organization in the nervous system is the *cell assembly,* consisting of neuron pathways interconnected in complex ways and spread out within wide areas of the cerebral cortex, the top of the brain. It is a redundant network. Cuts in isolated parts of it do not prevent circulation of impulses in the remaining circuits. And, so long as activity occurred somewhere in the assembly, there was some experiential analogue of that activity. In other words, activity in a cell assembly provides the physiological analogue for the simplest instance of an image or an idea in the perceptual experience of the observer.

We must appeal to example on this, as Hebb did. In the developing perceiver, activity in a single cell assembly could correspond to the experience of seeing some small fragment, or feature of the world, a line or an angle formed by two lines, for example. In the adult this sort of isolated fragmentary perception would be unlikely because the cell assemblies by then are inner-connected in *phase sequences,* and activity in them would correspond to a more complex perception, of an entire form such as a face or a scene, and so on. Hence, the adult experience of seeing an object corresponds to activity in a diffusely located neural structure, the phase sequence, spread out widely in a complicated fashion within large areas of the brain. Because of the diffuse location of the cell assemblies and phase sequences Hebb's conceptual nervous system had the functional characteristics demanded by accepted *Gestalt* concepts while at the same time had structural characteristics that did not contradict known neurophysiology. The paradigm was too simple, of course, and others provided refinements to increase its plausibility as a model of what perceptually related central nervous system mechanisms could be.

Development of the Conceptual Nervous System.

The systems seemed to Hebb to be in-complete without some statement about the origins of the hypothetical structures he had described. He thought that the assembly, perhaps consisting of up to 100 or so neurons, would be built up by experience with stimulation. Some particular stimulating condition, some pattern of light or localized pressure on the skin, might lead to activity in a small set of neurons. Call them Set A. These neurons might have endings close enough to the endings of other neurons, Set B, to fire them. This event would then make more likely that the next activity in Set A aroused by the same or very similar stimulation would again lead to activity in Set B. In other words, a particular sort of stimulation occurring repeatedly would lead to the development of a lattice of sets of neurons whose firing becomes characteristic neural activity for that particular stimulating pattern. This lattice is the cell assembly, and Hebb was saying that it, and the phase sequence, require stimulation of the senses for normal development.

This important role of early sensory stimulation in developing children had been suggested to him by evidence indicating that crucial aspects of normal perceptual functioning are either learned or else develop very early in the child, and that in any case some minimal amount of normal stimulation from the environment is required. This evidence was in the form of case histories of young persons who had been born with cataracts (cloudy lenses), or else had developed them very early in childhood. Cataracts allow light to enter the eye but prevent imagining of patterns on the retina.

These histories were gathered in a monograph by von Senden in 1932, but were not widely known. In reading these protocols, Hebb was struck by what was reported to occur when the cloudy lens was removed and replaced by an adequate external spectacle lens. Although many of the protocols were quite old, and the report language of the physicians often archaic, it seemed clear that vision for patterned stimulation of even simple sorts was badly deficient and resisted training for considerable periods, perhaps for the lifetime of the individual, if surgery occurred after adulthood was reached. Even simple geometric patterns could be identified in some cases only after very lengthy practice, and even then was specific to the forms used in training. Ability to discriminate between a white circle and a white triangle could disappear, for example, when the color of the two forms was changed to yellow. The colors, on the other hand, could be correctly identified. In short, the results appear to emphasize two things: (1) That concepts of simple shapes and ability to respond differentially to them is not a native endowment, but rather must be learned by experience with them; and (2) This experience must occur before individuals reach adulthood.

Hebb was familiar also with the report of A. H. Riesen (1947) that infant chimpanzees raised in darkness showed similar inability to perceive and respond to even grossly patterned stimulation after the animals were released from the deprivation situation. Riesen's original report had to be qualified later when it was discovered that dark-raised chimpanzees show signs of degenerated neural tissues in the eye, but subsequent to that, similar behavioral effects were demonstrated in chimpanzees raised from birth with devices over the eyes that admitted diffused light but did not permit pattern vision. In the case of those animals, no retinal degeneration in the eye was noted, although, as we shall see, other serious damage probably did occur.

The Critical Period Hypothesis. Both types of evidence strengthened belief in the importance of sensory stimulation in the normal development of perceptual nervous system. The supposition is that during early development a *critical period* occurs. If adequate stimulation occurs during that critical period, normal perceptual development occurs. If not, then perceptual skills are acquired with difficulty, if at all.

Comparison with the Real Perceptual Nervous System

Developments in neurophysiology, occurring since Hebb described the conceptual nervous system, now permit us to explore these ideas more fully and to test the critical period hypothesis in a special way. The developments involve mainly an interesting new recording technique that led to a great expansion in interest in the specific activity of sensory nervous systems in response to specific types of stimulus inputs.

Single-Cell Recording. The development of single-cell recording techniques permitted electrophysiological changes within single nerve cells to be recorded. With ingenuity, these recordings could be made at various levels in the sensory nervous system all the way from primary receptor cells in the eye, for example, to cells in the cortex of the brain.

Figure 12-35 is a schematic view of the underside of the human brain and in it three major areas of the visual system are located—the retinas in the eyes, the lateral geniculate bodies, and the visual cortex. (Only that part of the visual cortex visible from below is shown.) These three areas are those in which single cell recording has been most important.

The procedure is easily described. The subject, usually a domestic cat, is anesthetized, but with eyes open, lies prone facing a projection screen. A very small microelectrode is then carefully placed

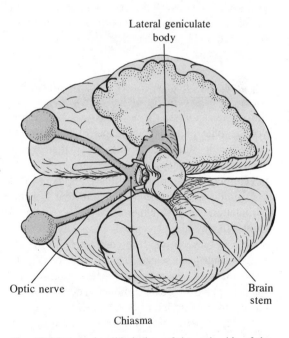

Fig. 12-35. A simplified view of the underside of the brain, showing the retinas, the lateral geniculate bodies, and the visual cortex.

in contact with a single cell in one of the three structures described. The experimental objective is to correlate a particular pattern projected on the screen "viewed" by the cat with a particular pattern of electrical activity picked up by the electrode.

Receptive Fields. In a simple case, with the electrode in the retina or the geniculate, *simple receptive fields* can be defined. The receptive field of a retinal nerve cell, for example, is defined as that area of the retina which when stimulated by light stimulates activity in that cell. The activity stimulated may be an augmentation of a base-rate activity or else a diminution of it depending on where in the receptive field the light falls. In the case of *complex receptive fields,* with the microelectrode in contact with a single cell in the visual cortex, more complex results have been reported. Some cortical cells respond to line stimuli oriented in a particular way or to edges with particular orientations and positions. Other, even more "complex" cells, respond only to the orientation of lines or edges, no matter where on the screen they are projected. Much work has been done in describing in detail the several types of cortical cells and their organization in the cortex of cats and monkey (Hubel, 1963).

The Specific Effect of Early Perceptual Experience. This specificity of knowledge concerning the organization of the visual systems has provoked some quite precise experimentation concerned with Hebb's early suggestion that experience with stimulation is a necessary part of the development of adult perceptual equipment. This precision involved the realization that sensory stimulation can have either of two effects: (1) As Hebb suggested, perceptual neurophysiological structures may not develop completely in the absence of adequate sensory stimulation; or (2) The structures may be present in the new organism and then atrophy if adequate stimulation does not occur during an early period of development.

Crucial experimentation involving newborn kittens quite definitely supports (2). It has been reported that cortical cells of young and visually inexperienced kittens strongly resemble cells of mature cats, except for some sluggishness in response. The evidence comes from the application of the single-cell recording technique, and the results suggest that the receptive field organizations of cortical cells are all present and similar to those of the adult cat. When, however, the eyelids of very young kittens were sutured together (which permits some illumination of the retina but not patterned stimulation) and the single-cell recording procedure applied some two or three months later, marked abnormality of response was noted. Failure to find the complex normal functioning typical of the adult cat was the rule, and the deficits described were more severe in the case of kittens with one eye sutured than in the case of kittens with both eyes sutured. Where just one eye had been sutured, more failures were reported in attempts to locate *binocular cells,* cortical cells that can be stimulated by light imaged in either eye (McCleary, 1970).

Although the work described does not include the perceptual development of human subjects directly, recordings from the intact human visual cortex allow us to infer that our own visual systems are not unlike those of other primates or the cat in any radical way and require patterned stimulation of specific kinds for normal development. A striking example of this is the parallel in the development of binocular functioning in kittens and human infants. If *strabismus* (misalignment of the two eyes so that they do not converge normally on a point) is induced surgically in kittens during a critical period beginning at four weeks of age and ending at twelve weeks, a significant failure of development of binocular cortical neurons results (Banks, Aslin, and Zeton, 1975).

Strabismus, unfortunately, occurs naturally in the human child, and although it has not been possible to examine cortical tissue in such cases, it is possible to measure binocularity or *steropsis* (stereoscopic vision) in persons who had abnormal binocular experience because of the occurrence of strabismus sometime in their lives. The measure used is the degree to which the *tilt aftereffect* transfers from one eye to another. Exposure to a tilted pattern occurs in one eye; testing for the effects of this exposure occurs in the other. The results for twenty-four subjects indicated that corrective surgery (adjustment of the extrinsic muscles that coordinate eye direction) occurring very early in life was associated with greater stereopsis later in life. The critical period during which normal binocular experience is crucial begins several months after birth and appears to end by four to six years of age.

It has been suggested that a similar effect occurs when astigmatic optics are not corrected in the very young (Freeman, Mitchell, and Millodot, 1972). When, for example, the optics of the eye introduce extensive blurring of horizontal lines, but not vertical lines, the normal development of neural systems sensitive to horizontally oriented lines and edges will not occur. Astigmatism can be corrected by the use of compensating contact lenses or spectacles; however, the suggestion is strong that if this correction occurs too late in development, an insensitivity to horizontal pattern elements is not correctable.

A *summary* of the meaning of these results can be made by reference to Hebb's notions about the development of perceptually involved neural structures. He appears to have been correct in supposing the existence of a critical, early period in the development of perceptual systems, but wrong with respect to what occurs during that period. He suggested that neural networks involved in the perception of patterns develop during that period only if patterned stimulation was experienced to support that development. The evidence points instead to the conclusion that perceptual structures develop in the very young, but then deteriorate if not supported by adequate, patterned stimulation during the critical period.

The Perceptual Stimulus.
Earlier, in connection with the *inferential* approach to the study of perception the distinction was made between the *distal* stimulus, in the environment, and the *proximal* stimulus, which is the representation of the distal stimulus at the receptors. In the case of vision, we understand this to be the distinction between an object in the environment—a human figure, for example—and the images of the object on the retinas in the eyes of the viewer. This distinction has interested psychologists very much, of course, because it demands an explanation of just how the perceiver is able to connect up the pattern of light making up the retinal image with the existence of an object out there in the environment.

The Physiological Stimulus.
The neurological conceptions of Hebb and the specific descriptions of the sensory nervous system permitted by the single-cell recording technique have served to emphasize another distinction among types of stimuli, as described in Chapter 1. This is the distinction between the *proximal* stimulus and the *physiological* stimulus. The physiological stimulus consists of those aspects of the proximal stimulus that actually stimulate neural systems.

One of the implications of that distinction is that the occurrence of the proximal and physiological stimuli in time can be quite different. The physiological stimulus, since it involves the action of physical systems, can be expected to show inertia, getting really under way after the onset of the proximal stimulus and continuing for a finite period after the proximal stimulus has disappeared.

The Critical Stimulus Duration.
The occurrence of the physiological stimulus also requires some minimum duration of the proximal stimulus. Before mid-century, research had explored this minimum by presenting complex patterns visually for quite brief durations and asking subjects to describe or to draw what they saw. Three *levels of development of the percept* were described. In the case of very brief stimulus durations, a tenth of a second or less, only gross sorts of descriptions of stimulation could be provided. Stimuli could be described as diffuse or compact, light or dark, large or small, and so on. During the second phase, for stimulus durations of up to one or two seconds, some contours and other details were described, and subjects reported, often erroneously, what the patterns seemed to be. The third phase, involving even longer durations, involved clear perceptions of the stimulus and its identity.

The critical durations determining these three stages depended upon the nature of the stimulus materials used. Those given here are from the work of Bridgen (1933) who used geometric figures. However, description of three stages was common in research of this type. Bridgen called them the stages of *gross differentiation, inaccurate perception*, and *differentiation*, corresponding to the shortest to longest stimulus durations.

Bridgen described reports of subjects that during brief exposure of a stimulus pattern they often felt they knew what the stimulus was but then lost this knowledge by the time they could respond after the termination of the stimulus. It is a common complaint in the perception laboratory, suggesting that during a brief stimulus exposure activity is getting under way in the sensory nervous system, activity that if continued leads to the confident identification of the stimulus. When the proximal stimulus ends, however, this activity begins to decay and decays quite rapidly in the case of briefly-presented stimuli. By the time the perceiver begins to describe what has been seen, little trace of the stimulus remains in the central nervous system, and the perceiver is unable to describe what the stimulus was.

However, even a brief stimulus leaves behind some sort of activity in the sensory nervous system, residual activity that can combine in complex ways with new neurophysiological activity aroused by a subsequently received stimulus. The perception of motion pictures supports this statement. In the usual presentation of motion pictures, a succession of static displays is involved, and these are perceived easily as continuous movements of objects and scenes. Obviously, the perception of each separate static display is being combined with and influenced by displays that precede and follow it.

Two-Flash Interactions.   An experiment by Eriksen and Collins (1967) provided some useful information about this phenomenon. Their work was an example of *two-flash tachistoscopy* in which the subject sees two briefly-presented stimulus patterns, one after the other. Both the first and the second stimulus patterns were apparently random collections of dots. When superimposed, however, a letter could be seen, thus providing an objective test of whether the two brief stimulus flashes were perceptually combined. Each dot pattern by itself provided no clues to the letter formed by the composite.

If we think about this situation in Hebb's terms, we should expect that when the first dot pattern

occurs the visual system should be stimulated into processes that result in the perception of that pattern as a random pattern of dots. If the second dot pattern commences after the processing of the first pattern is well under way and that first stimulus has disappeared, then a separate processing of the second pattern will occur, and it too will be seen as a random dot pattern. The work of Eriksen and Collins indicates that separate perception of the two-dot patterns occurs when offset of the first pattern precedes onset of the second by about 75–100 msec. (.075–.100 sec.). If this lag between offset and onset is shortened, subjects combine the two stimulus flashes to some extent and are able to report which letters are present in the combined pattern. With very short lags, presumably, the second pattern arrives in time to be processed in combination with the first. With lags longer than about 100 msec. the second pattern arrives too late to be processed with the first, and the subject perceives two separate patterns of randomly placed dots.

Masking.   Subsequent work has shown that any characteristic of either of the two stimulus patterns that makes it stand out in some way, such as greater intensity or duration, diminishes the tendency for the two stimuli to be combined. Tendency to combine patterns is diminished also when the two stimulus patterns cannot be combined perceptually into an easily resolvable pattern. In that case, especially when the second stimulus is perceptually unusual in some way, *retroactive masking* can occur. The subject perceives the second stimulus but not the first—as though the neural processes evoked by the first stimulus are halted or co-opted by stronger processes evoked by the second stimulus.

The term *retroactive masking* is used for the case where the first and second flashes are imaged on the same place on the retina. Another interesting situation occurs when the first and second stimulus flashes are not imaged to the same place. Figure 12-36 illustrates a first stimulus, a disk, and a second stimulus, a ring that just fits around the disk when superimposed. The term *metacontrast* has been applied to retroactive masking occurring in this situation. The ring, although it occurs after the

Fig. 12-36.   The lighted disk is followed in time by the lighted ring, which is presented so that it surrounds the area the lighted disk had occupied. With appropriate timing the ring may mask the disk, although the disk comes first in time.

disk, can effectively mask the disk. The subject reports not seeing the disk, although it can be seen plainly when it appears alone or when the ring follows the disk after a long delay.

Two conceptions of what occurs in retroactive masking have been suggested by psychologists. One of these assumes that a stimulus of adequate duration is placed in a short-term visual storage system. Placement of the stimulus in storage, and processing of it there, can be interfered with by a subsequent stimulus. When that occurs all trace of the prior stimulus is lost, and the result is that the prior stimulus has been erased or changed by the subsequent stimulus.

The second conception, Eriksen's *integration hypothesis,* is more *parsimonious* in that it does not suppose the existence of a short-term storage

system. Instead, the hypothesis states simply that the prior and subsequent stimulus patterns are combined if (1) they occur sufficiently close together in time, and (2) they form when combined a coherent pattern that is not too complex to be recognized.

In any case, the reader should note that both conceptions involve an important distinction between the *physical stimulus pattern* as it exists on a page or on a screen, or even as imaged in the eye, and the *physiological stimulus,* which is a series of complex neural physiological events evoked by the physical stimulus, which commences some time after the physical stimulus first appears and continues some time after the physical stimulus has disappeared. It is assumed that the perceiver's experience of the stimulus is a concomitant of the neural physiological processes. The nature of the neural physiological events associated with the physical stimulus depends upon stimulation preceding and succeeding the physical stimulus. And, finally, the implication is clear that ultimate understanding of our experience as perceivers waits on a more explicit understanding of the neurophysiological events evoked by stimulation.

Computer Analogies

The concepts of *storage* and *erasure* of items in storage, mentioned in the previous sections, are concepts borrowed from computer technology, a relatively recent source of ideas about human perception. Considerable interest exists in the possibility that the increasingly complex area of computer design will reveal something crucial about our own nervous systems, especially those aspects having to do with perceptual processes.

Although the analogy is tempting, real gains in understanding of human perception as a process have been slow in developing. Computers operate in a step-wise fashion processing inputs in ways that must be described in great detail. And so, when perception is described in those terms it tends also to be subjected to the same fine-grained analysis. Often the analogy breaks down in that process.

Recognition by Computers

A primary interest of persons who see perceptual analogies in the operation of high-speed, high-capacity computers is the process of recognition. This is a function that computers can perform quite well in well-defined and constrained situations, and the process can provide clues about the nature of human recognition. Students should be aware, however, that much of the speculation about this may be useful only because we know so little detail of the human recognition process.

Template Matching. Several different fundamental recognition processes have been described for computers. The first of these is *template matching,* in which the task of the system is to recognize each of a set of letters or symbols. Each letter or symbol to be recognized must always be the same size, style, and orientation because the recognition process consists entirely of testing to learn whether a presented letter or symbol matches exactly one or another of the stored templates or standards. This is a rather simple case, such as occurs in computer recognition of printed numbers on bank checks.

Analysis and Synthesis. This is a more demanding task in which the recognition of a particular pattern, such as a letter of the alphabet, involves an analysis of the pattern into elements (lines, angles, curves, homogeneous areas, contours, and so on.) and a detailed examination of the relations existing among those elements. This can be seen as a logical extension of template matching that permits a great deal more flexibility. Recognition can be of the *invariances* evident in patterns, for example those aspects of the letter A that must be present even though carelessly written, even though size of the letter and its style may vary over a wide range.

Computer systems capable of that sort of recognition performance have been devised. One such device has been very useful at the University of Illinois in scanning cloud chamber photographs for evidence of atomic particle trails, a task it performs quickly and tirelessly.

In its action, does that sort of computer processing mimic human recognition? This certainly may be the case, but we are a long way from knowing the facts in detail. We must keep in mind the truism that two functions can appear closely analogous without necessarily implying that the processes underlying those functions need be similar.

Perceptual Recognition

As to how human recognition occurs, an important act of recognition was described earlier in this chapter. The *adaptation level* was described as a sort of central value, or average, of recent stimulation of a particular sort viewed against a particular background. In the case of each new stimulus of that sort, the perceiver was suggested to experience the result of the comparison of that new stimulus with the adaptation level.

In an important sense, this is a recognition process, in that stimulation is referred to or compared with a *stored concept* or *standard*. The stored standard enables the perceiver to comprehend the new stimulation: it is greater than, less than, or just like the stored standard.

The work of Michael Posner *et al* (1967) enables us to apply the same sort of notion to the recognition of complex stimuli. A stimulus class was created by first choosing a single complex pattern, which was then systematically distorted in a stepwise, incremental fashion to create, one after another, a whole set of stimuli, all related to the original figure. For this new class the original complex pattern is the *prototype,* the most typical representative, or essence of, the class of stimuli created. Figure 12-37 shows a prototype and five instances created by a distortion process. (The numbers in the figure indicate the degree of distortion involved in producing each instance.) Four classes were produced in this way.

Subjects were asked to learn to classify into three classes a list of twelve patterns, seen one after the other in a random order. The list consisted of four distortion instances of each of three prototypes. This *learning* procedure was continued until subjects correctly classified by prototype all patterns in two successive appearances of the list. They then saw a *transfer list* of twenty-four patterns. Three of these were the prototypes, which the subjects had not seen previously; six were distortions seen in *learning;* six were new distortions of the original three prototypes; and six were distortions of a fourth prototype not used previously. Finally, three patterns were random patterns unrelated to the four prototypes. Subjects were asked to classify these twenty-four patterns according to the prototype to which they appeared to be related.

If the notions described above are generally correct, we should expect that in classifying the twenty-four patterns in the transfer task subjects should do this with few errors for the prototypes (even though they had not seen them before), because the concept of the prototype is essentially what is gained during the learning trials. Furthermore, the subjects should do better in classifying new instances of the same prototypes represented in the learning trials than in classifying new in-

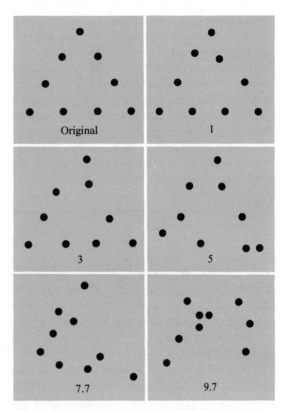

Fig. 12-37. A prototype and five instances created by allowing a chance process to determine dot locations. The numbers in the figure indicate degree of distortion of the prototype. (From Posner, M. I., Goldsmith, R., and Welton, Jr., K. E., 1967)

stances of a new prototype. Both of these outcomes did occur.

Evidently, as perceivers gain experience with instances of a class of stimuli, information about the prototype of all those instances is picked up quite efficiently. All patterns of that type are then perceived and recognized in terms of perceived relations with that prototype.

In summary, the recognition functions of computers were described and contrasted with perceptual recognition of complex patterns. The latter was described in terms of the *adaptation level* concept, developed by Helson to account for the recognition of simple stimuli. The *prototypical pattern,* in the case of complex stimuli, corresponds to the *adaptation level* in the case of simple stimuli. In either case, recognition of stimuli depends on their similarity to the stored standard, which is the adaptation level or prototypical stimulus.

Of course, this does not tell us much about how recognition of complex patterns occurs as a sensory or neurophysiological matter. It suggests strongly, however, that recognition of complex stimuli (faces, buildings, intersections, landscapes) is not different in kind from recognition of simple stimuli (grayness of surfaces, size of simple objects, intensity of simple tones).

Concluding Thoughts

This chapter has described several major points of view about the interesting experiences and behaviors that we call "perceptual." Familiarity with these points of view has an important advantage for readers, who are then able to place in proper context the great variety of facts and beliefs that make up this area of study.

This variety of subject matter reflects the fact that so much of what we do and experience is considered to be "perceptual," at least to some extent. Hence, perception as a topic cuts across most of the major topics in this book, and much material that is "perceptual" in nature has been left to other chapters, as frequent references to other chapters have indicated. This is particularly true of sensory action. Students should master the material in Chapter 5 before signing off on the topic of perception.

The study of perception, as described here, may also impress students as an unusually disputatious matter. Many major disagreements still characterize our attempts to understand and explain the processes involved. Before concluding, therefore, we need to deal with this disagreement itself.

One of the major reasons for continuing disputes about the fundamental nature of perceptual processes is the obvious one that we do not yet have the basis for deciding between basically different points of view, such as those represented by the inferential on the one hand and psychophysical correspondence on the other. We do not yet have, for example, a basis for deciding whether or not stimulation is fragmentary and incomplete typically, as

the inferentialists suppose, or is always complete or at least sufficient, as J. J. Gibson supposes. Without that basis we cannot seriously begin to determine what the role of an inferential process must be, if indeed it is needed at all. Nor do we yet know precisely what sort of world we live in, considered from a perceptual point of view. Is it as constrained in variety as Gestalt psychologists have suggested? What sort of perceptual load is imposed by our need to perceive our world in whatever detail is necessary for survival and enjoyment? All these remain for knowledgeable persons to answer.

Another source of disputes is an underlying disagreement about how perceptual events should be explained. The origins of psychology in the older disciplines of biology, philosophy, and physics were mentioned earlier in this chapter. Corresponding to those multiple origins are alternate types of explanations for perceptual phenomena. These types, all involved in this chapter, include the *physiological,* the *phenomenal,* and the *psychophysical* type of explanation.

For American college students, the most satisfying of these usually is *physiological explanation.* An event is thought explained when the physiology

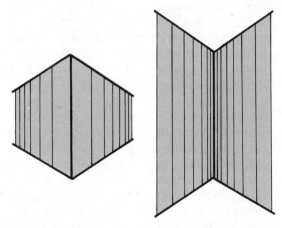

Fig. 12-38.   One explanation for the length distortion seen in the familiar Müller-Lyer illusion is a phenomenological one that says that the two patterns look just like outline drawings of two corners. Unequal apparent sizes result from the tendency of the outside corner and the inside corner to appear to be at different distances.

underlying it is described. Slowly but surely our understanding of neural mechanisms underlying human perception is increasing, and for many no further explanation is required.

On the other hand, an explanation that is *phenomenological* in character can be considered to be quite adequate. For example, Figure 12-38 emphasizes the parallels between the typical Müller-Lyer illusion and the usual perspective depiction of interior and exterior corners. The explanation of the illusion is simply that the Müller-Lyer pattern *looks just like* the outline drawing of a real situation in which the inside corner looks longer. It is one of a class of instances in which a perspective drawing introduces an impression of depth, an impression in which lines of equal length on the page appear to be at different viewing distances and hence of different real lengths.

Still others reject both the *physiological* and the *phenomenological* type of explanation and are content instead with a full *psychophysical* exploration of perceptual situations. In the case of the Müller-Lyer illusion, for example, "explanation" occurs when the relationships between each element of the pattern and the extent of the illusion have been worked out in detail. Such a *psychophysical* explanation involves a good deal of labor and patience, but when complete this work serves to provide a complete statement about the crucial pattern variables that evoke the illusion. To some, that is as much "explanation" as is ever required.

Obviously, depending on which type of explanation is most compelling, different approaches to the study of perception are taken and different experiments get done. These different approaches can leave little common ground to be explored by all. That, we suppose, adds to the interest and charm of the topic we know as "perceptual."

Glossary

Adaptation level: An internal standard with which incoming stimulation is compared. We perceive not stimulation itself, but stimulation as compared with such a standard. The adaptation level is not constant and varies with stimulation in predictable ways.

Coherent perception: Perception is coherent if it is complete, if it is plausible, and if it permits accurate prediction of stimulation yet to come. Perception can be coherent without being accurate (veridical).

Critical period hypothesis: Supposes a period in early perceptual development during which adequate stimulation is required to avoid the loss of neural structures and functions essential for normal adult perceptual experience and skills.

Cues to distance: Even in monocular viewing, or in viewing photographs with both eyes, there are certain cues to the location of objects relative to each other. These cues include relative size, texture gradients, overlap, clearness of outline and color, as well as others.

Distal stimulation: The characteristics of stimulus objects "out there" in the world.

Eidetic imagery: An unusually vivid image of a stimulus pattern retained after the pattern no longer can be seen directly. Persons with such imagery, Eidetikers, are identified by the use of a complex set of tests.

Extra sensory perception (ESP): Communication of information between persons using a channel other than the known perceptual channels. Probably of little biological usefulness, if it exists at all.

Feature analyzers: Organization of retinal and central nervous cells into hierarchies of cells with specific sensitivity to stimulus patterns and orientations. The supposition is that recognition of a complex stimulus pattern occurs by means of analysis of the component features of the pattern.

Figure-ground organization: The Gestalt distinction between aspects of a stimulus pattern that appear central, and to stand out clearly, and the ground, which appears as background for the figure.

Gestalt psychologists: Opposed the radical parsimony of the behavioristic approach to the study of perception. They were strongly *phenomenological* and stressed the active character of perception as a process that satisfies a *coherence,* rather than a *veridical* criterion of the adequacy of perception.

Images, percepts, and sensations: Mentalistic concepts referring to the content of perceptual experiences.

Minimum principle: The principle stating that in perceiving we act to reduce our uncertainty about stimulus possibilities, and perceive, if possible, each stimulus pattern as a representative of a small, constrained set of patterns.

Nativism: The belief that certain types of "understandings'' of our environment, and corresponding ability to adequately perceive it, are present at birth. The *Empiricist* point of view emphasizes the lack of such abilities at birth and emphasizes the role of active experience in the development of perceptual skills.

Perception: Those processes involved in looking, hearing, smelling, tasting, and feeling that usually involve more than a single sense. We also mean the *experience* of sensing stimulation.

Perceptual adaptation: Changes in perceptual experience or behavior that tend to persist only as long as conditions of viewing or listening persist. Those characteristics of perception that are determined by immediate stimulation and tend to shift with shifts in stimulation characteristics.

Perceptual channel capacity: The capacity of the perceptual channel to take in information and use it effectively. The implication is that this capacity has limits.

Perceptual constancy: The extent to which perceivers respond adequately to the constant characteristics of stimulus objects by penetrating and overcoming distortions introduced by viewing conditions.

Perceptual inference: Follows from the assumption that we do not sense our environment directly. Stimulation from the world provides cues only. From those cues our perception of objects and their locations must be inferred.

Perceptual learning: Relatively enduring changes in perceptual experience or behavior resulting from practice with stimulation.

Phenomenology and positivisism: The *phenomenologist* accepts perceptual experience as a necessary subject for study by proper methods. The *positivistic* point of view accepts experiential aspects of perceiving as scientifically respectable concepts only if that acceptance is necessary to our understanding of perceptual behavior. Watson's *Behaviorism* was an extreme example of the positivistic point of view.

Physiological stimulation: Those aspects of proximal stimulation that actually stimulate activity in the perceptual nervous system.

Probabilistic functionalism: A major *inferential* point of view about human perception, which asserts that the perceiver strives to achieve, by responding to *proximal* stimulation appropriately, a useful correspondence between the *distal* stimulus in the environment and his perception of it. This process is probabilistic in the sense that there is an uncertain relationship between proximal stimulation and the distal stimulus from which stimulation comes.

Proximal stimulation: The representation of distal stimulus patterns at the senses.

Psychoneural isomorphism: Gestalt psychologists

thought of this as a point-for-point correspondence existing between how stimulus patterns appear and the activity they produce in the central nervous system when viewed.

Psychophysical correspondence: The hypothesis that for every aspect of perceptual experience, no matter how subtle, there is a corresponding aspect of stimulation arriving at the sense organs. Hence, stimulation is always sufficient, and no inferential perceptual process is required.

Psychophysics: The study of the fundamental ways in which perceptual experience varies, the *attributes,* and the relations between those ways, or dimensions, and the characteristics of stimulation.

Reafferance: Sensory stimulation and neural activity arising specifically from actions initiated by the perceiver.

Receptive field: The precise description of the characteristics of a stimulus that augments or diminishes, from a base rate, activity in a single retinal or central nervous cell in contact with a microelectrode.

Retroactive masking: A second stimulus interferes with perception of a first stimulus preceding it in time. *Metacontrast* occurs in vision when retroactive masking results even though the first and second stimuli are not imaged to the same place on the retina.

Schematic redundancy: Stimulus patterns naturally existing in the world around us are redundant in the sense that they are very much constrained in possible variety and therefore partially predictable from their context. Patterns tend to be orderly and regular in appearance, as opposed to random and chaotic, thereby reducing and simplifying the task of the perceptual systems.

Stereopsis: Stereoscopic vision—the experience of objects in depth arising from viewing with two eyes, whose slightly different views are fused in a single impression.

Stimulus goodness: A good stimulus is highly redundant schematically—it is an example of a very small set of stimuli of the same sort. In the extreme case, such as a circle, the good stimulus is unique in that it remains unchanged even though rotated or viewed in a mirror.

Transactional functionalism: A major *inferential* point of view about human perception, which holds that adequate perception results from a transaction occurring between the perceiver and his environment. In this the perceiver utilizes a series of assumptions about our world. On the basis of these assumptions the significance of inadequate stimulation is derived.

Veridical perception: Perception is veridical if it is accurate, representing exactly the true stimulus from which stimulation came to the senses.

Suggested Readings

Christman, R. J. *Sensory Experience,* Scranton, Pa.: Intext, 1971.

Gregory, R. L. *The Intelligent Eye,* New York: McGraw-Hill, 1970.

Griffin, D. R. *The Question of Animal Awareness,* New York: Rockefeller University Press, 1976.

Hebb, D. O. *Organization of Behavior,* New York: John Wiley, 1949.

Köhler, W. *Gestalt Psychology,* New York: Liveright, 1947.

McCleary, R. A. *Genetic and Experiential Factors in Perception.* Glenview: Scott, Foresman, 1970.

Sleep and Dreams

Wilse B. Webb and Michael H. Bonnet

Introduction

The "other world" of sleep and dreams has been an intriguing subject throughout history. Probably the most widely used descriptive term to be associated with it has been "mysterious." While our knowledge today is far from complete, a surge of research in the past two decades has done much, however, to reduce the mystery of this dark kingdom.

Perhaps the most troublesome questions about sleep have centered around matters of consciousness. What is the nature of this gap in our perceiving being that we call sleep? The problems are further compounded by the enigma of dreams, since they present an unreal reality of possible impossibilities. The psychoanalyst describes dreams as the "royal road to the unconscious." On a philosophical level, the states of waking, sleeping, and dreaming are not easily separable. This led to Bertrand Russell's comment: "I do not believe that I am now dreaming but I cannot prove it."

The English essayist, Samuel Johnson said, ". . . and all lie down in the equality of sleep." However, the timing, the place, and the particular mode of the response is remarkably varied. Among humans, the changes from infancy through adulthood and into aging are great; from some six periods of sleep averaging some 16 hours per 24-hour period in the infant to a single episode, averaging about 8 hours at night, in the adult. Within one age group, the amount of sleep can vary among individuals within a normal range of some 6 hours in total amount—some individuals averaging less than 6 hours and others 12 hours. Across species the differences are yet more dramatic (see Table 13-5 on p. 465). Some animals sleep a few hours while others, such as the gorilla, sleep more than half of each 24-hour period. Some animals sleep only at night, others during the day. Some sleep solidly for hours on end and others intermittently in brief snatches of sleep.

Defining Sleep

To begin to know this apparently enigmatic and varied part of our lives, we must begin by defining and measuring it. There are essentially two behavioral components of sleep; the sleeper is less responsive to the world, and activity is sharply diminished. Less obvious are the facts that bodily functions and the pattern of the central nervous system activity change. All of the following have been examined as potential "definitions" of sleep.

Sensory Thresholds. The beginning of an experimental approach to sleep was done by a student of Fechner in the 1860s. It involved an attempt to judge the depth of sleep by the loudness of a tone necessary to awaken the sleeping subject. Sensory thresholds were found higher in sleep, but were extremely variable. Further research made clear that thresholds varied with the meaningfulness of the auditory stimulus, with modality of stimulation, with the procedure of stimulation (for example, time length or an ascending series of tones), and with the number of arousals per night, among other things. In short, although thresholds were elevated in sleep, they could not be good descriptors of the process itself.

Motility.   When a person goes to sleep, that person's activities are sharply decreased. As a result, activity, or as defined in research, *motility,* was probably the most widely used index of overall sleep "quality" in early sleep studies. The main problem with the use of motility to define sleep in humans is that a total of only about 3–5 minutes is spent in movement during the night. Therefore, motility is not often used by itself.

Physiological Measures.   When a person goes to sleep, physiological functions tend to decline in rate. Sleep is, in general, characterized by decrease in respiration, heartrate, and systolic blood pressure, although erratic fluctuations are noted. There is a slow regular change in body temperature. Temperature may drop as much as 1° C from sleep onset to late in the sleep period, when a temperature rise begins again. The bottom of the temperature curve normally precedes waking by about 2–3 hours. Unfortunately, all of these changes also occur in people in prone positions who are not asleep, and the changes are slow and different for each physiological function measured. This means that these measures cannot be readily used to distinguish sleep from merely lying down.

The Electroencephalogram (EEG).   As early as 1875, it was known that there were measurable electric currents in the brain. During the 1920s, a German psychiatrist, Hans Berger, made recordings from the scalp of an intact human brain. Such recordings were (and are) made by measuring changes in electrical potential between two small pieces of metal called electrodes attached to the scalp.

The findings of Berger were real and appreciated outside his native Germany. Brain activity began to be explored as a clinical indicator of central nervous system disturbances. In 1937, Loomis, Harvey, and Hobart reported striking differences in electrical brainwave activity in people who were asleep. Although measured currents of the brain are very small and are measured in terms of *micro-volts* (1 microvolt = 1 millionth of a volt), orderly changes in the activity allowed the designation of several stages within sleep.

Today, sleep is almost always measured by the electroencephalogram (EEG) with other concomitant measures. The original sleep characteristics discovered by Loomis, Harvey, and Hobart form the basis of modern sleep classification with one very important addition. Aserinsky and Kleitman reported in 1957 the observation that, occasionally during the night, the EEG of sleeping subjects would look very much like the EEG of an awake person. In addition, the subject's eyes would begin to dart around in the form of rapid eye movements under the closed lids. This EEG tracing and the *Rapid Eye Movements (REMs)* became the basis for another state or stage of sleep.

Patterns in Sleep

The monitoring of eye movements and EEG allows the differentiation of five stages of sleep. An EEG record (a 12-second example is shown in Figure 13-1) is a typical waveform pattern that can be described in terms of *amplitude*—how high each wave is when its voltage level is translated into pen movements on the page—and *frequency*—the number of cyclic up and down pen movements occurring during each second.

A large variety of normal waking motor and mental activities is represented by an EEG consisting of low amplitude, high frequency waves in seemingly random patterns. However, most people, when relaxing with their eyes closed, show a pattern of brain waves that is very regular at about 8-12 cycles (peaks) per second and is called *alpha* (see Figure 13-1A). This relaxed, waking, alpha state is also called stage O when it occurs during the night because people pass through this state in the process of moving from waking to sleeping. As sleep approaches, the alpha activity slowly disappears. Sleep onset is commonly defined as the point at which alpha activity occurs in less than half of each minute, and waking behavior such as eye blinks or body movement is not seen. These changes signal the beginning of stage 1 sleep (13-1B), which is seen to have a low voltage, irregular pattern, essentially indistinguishable from active

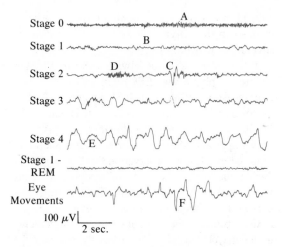

Fig. 13-1. Sleep stages as defined by the electroencephalogram (EEG). Note the similarities and differences in brain activity over the stages. Some stage-defining characteristics are labeled: A. alpha waves B. low voltage activity C. K-complex D. sleep spindle E. delta waves F. rapid eye movements (REM).

waking. Stage 1 is typically followed quite rapidly by stage 2. Stage 2 is characterized by the appearance of *sleep spindles* (13-1D) *and K-complexes* (13-1C). Sleep spindles, which are short, fast 14-16 cycles-per-second waves, received their name from their resemblance to thread wrapped around an old fashioned sewing spindle. K-complexes are low frequency, high amplitude waves which stand out very dramatically from the low amplitude activity seen during stage 2. However, as stage 2 continues, the EEG amplitude slowly increases and low frequency (1-2 cycles per second) high amplitude waves begin to appear. These waves, called *delta* waves (13-1E), define stages 3 and 4. Stage 3 is a transitional stage which usually lasts only a few minutes at a time (about 5 percent of the night) and most often serves to mark the entrance or exit from stage 4, in which the EEG record is covered with high amplitude, slow delta waves.

Although specific stages of sleep are labeled, and described as independent entities, each stage slowly changes toward, and merges into, the next so that the stage changes themselves also come to exhibit a wavelike pattern. The delta activity of

stage 4 will slowly die out resulting in stage 3, then stage 2. The spindles and K-complexes of stage 2 will eventually cease and the flat irregular record of stage 1 will appear. However, this irregular EEG record is accompanied by REMs (13-1F) (hence called stage 1—REM) as well as a host of physiological changes.

A Normal Night of Sleep

There is a wide range of individual differences in normal sleep behavior, and one should bear in mind that "average" amounts carry no connotation of good or bad. Sleep varies from person to person and from group to group of people. The most studied group and the one of primary interest here is the college student. For the average student, bedtime is 12:30 on weeknights and 1:30 on weekends (White, 1975). About 5 to 15 minutes are required to fall asleep, and the average student then sleeps for 7.4 hours (or 8.5 hours on weekends). There are few awakenings, perhaps one every other night, and these awakenings last less than 5 minutes.

Figure 13-2 traces the sleep of one such young adult over three nights as recorded by the EEG. Several things are worthy of note. One is the rather regular progression of the sleep stages. There is a tendency to move from stage 0 to stage 1 to stage 2 to stage 3 and to stage 4 and back again in an orderly manner. The effect is like a wave or a staircase with the sleeper usually moving up or down one step at a time throughout the night. A second important cyclic aspect of the sleep process is seen in the timing of the REM phase of sleep. If you will look again at Figure 13-2, you will see that REM occurs in about 90 minute intervals. Seldom in the regular process of sleep will a REM burst occur before about an hour. After the first occurrence, the average length between REM bursts will be between 90 and 100 minutes.

Figure 13-2 reveals two other important general trends in the sleep process. It can be seen that more time is spent in some sleep stages than in others during the night. Table 13-1 gives the percent of total sleep spent in each stage by a group of young adults. About half the night is spent in stage 2, perhaps because stage 2 acts as a sort of crossroad.

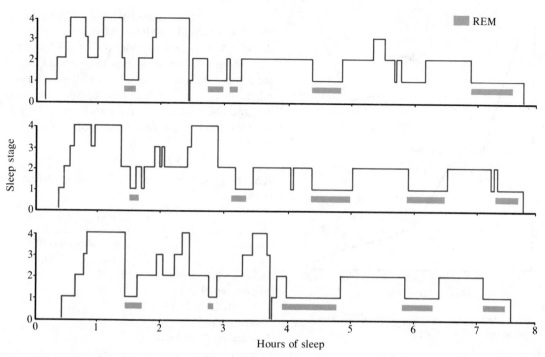

Fig. 13-2. Minute-by-minute display of the course of sleep in terms of sleep stages. Three nights of sleep are displayed for one subject.

One must pass through stage 2 to get to stages 3 and 4, and one must pass back through stage 2 to get to REM.

The average college student spends 22–25 percent of the night (about 100–120 minutes) in REM. The first REM period is typically the shortest,

about 5–10 minutes. REM periods get progressively longer as the night passes, with later periods occasionally reaching 50–60 minutes in length. In contrast, most stage 4 is seen in the early part of the night with almost all of it seen in the first four hours of sleep. This relation of time of stage 4 oc-

Table 13-1. Sleep Stage Percents and Characteristics in Young Adults

	Percent of Night	EEG Characteristics
Stage 0	1 percent	alpha 50 percent or more of record (8–12 cycles per second)
Stage 1	5 "	alpha drops out, less than 50 percent of record
Stage 2	48–50 "	sleep spindles and K-complexes (14–16 cycles per second)
Stage 3	5–7 "	Delta waves (.5–3 cycles per second) 20–50 percent of record
Stage 4	13–16 "	delta waves (.5–3 cycles per second)
Stage 1-REM	22–25 "	stage 1 EEG, REMS, loss of neck muscle tone

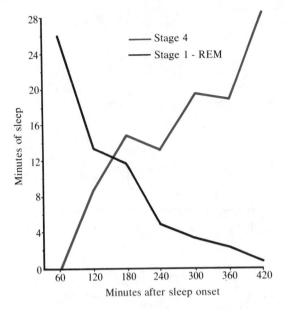

Fig. 13-3. Distribution of stages 4 and REM with respect to time during the sleep period.

currence and time of REM occurrence is shown graphically in Figure 13-3.

Quiet and Active Sleep

Many of the changes typically associated with falling asleep are the consequence of reclining and relaxing. The slow, regular breathing, general absence of body and eye movement, and the slow regular brain activity shown by the EEG, particularly in stages 3 and 4, have led stages 1, 2, 3, and 4 to be called "quiet" sleep as well as NREM sleep. On the other hand, REM sleep has also been called "active" or "paradoxical" or "dream" sleep. All of these names are appropriate. As REM begins, one may observe small twitches of the sleeper's face and fingertips, and breathing becomes irregular. The bulge of the cornea of the eye can be seen to dart back and forth more rapidly than eyes can be seen to move even during waking. Heartrate is variable and cerebral blood flow and brain temperature increase, but certain muscles lose their tonus. Penile and clitoral arousal responses occur in both adults and newborns.

The most exciting aspect of REM sleep has been the demonstrated relation between REM and dreams. As noted earlier, Aserinsky and Kleitman, on observing eye movements in their sleeping subjects, made the immediate guess that those subjects might literally be watching their dreams, and that an objective measure of the transitory half-conscious mental image called a dream might be at hand.

Table 13-2. Dream Recall as a Function of Definition of Dreams*

Dream Definition (various studies)	Percent of Awakenings in Which a Dream Was Recalled	
	REM	NREM
Definite recall of dream content	74	17
Vivid recall of content	88	0
Coherent, fairly detailed description	80	7
Detailed recall of complete drama	85	0
A dream recalled in some detail	69	34
Content recalled in some detail	62	13
Some specific content	86	23
Specific content	82	54
Not specified	60	3
Not specified	85	24

*After Snyder, (1963).

The obvious experiment then was to awaken people during REM and to ask them if they were dreaming. The initial results were quite gratifying in support of the hypothesis—74 percent of REM awakenings resulted in vivid dream recall while only 17 percent of NREM awakenings resulted in such recall. Further work has revealed that the probability of dream recall depends very much on the definition of a dream (Table 13-2). The evidence indicates that a substantial amount of cognition occurs in NREM sleep as well as in REM sleep. This means that when a dream is defined in terms of simple mental context or experience, dream recall is high from both REM and NREM. As more complex or vivid detail is required, fewer NREM reports are classed as dreams. Two dream reports from a subject, an English major, follow:

1) He is in a sleep laboratory, filling out a pencil and paper form. Someone passes by commenting that the task is a stupid one. (NREM)

2) In the first scene, he is standing on a street corner, holding his bicycle and talking to someone about a girl who wanted to be a striptease dancer.

In a second scene, he is in a doctor's study with two women and the doctor. They are discussing two books. The heroine in the first book was a striptease dancer, but is no longer this, but a nurse. The women are discussing how much hardship she has as a nurse. (REM) (Foulkes, 1975, p. 301)

These examples exhibit many of the characteristic differences between REM and NREM dream reports. NREM recall is generally more like thinking, less vivid, less visual, more possible, more concerned with actual people and events, less emotional, and more poorly recalled than reports secured from REM periods. REM reports correspond more closely to the classic vivid, hallucinatory experience called a dream. NREM reports correspond more closely to that part of our waking thought in which we let our minds wander or drift when we are not actively thinking or working on something.

Study of the timing and occurrence of REM had led to a greater understanding of dreams in several ways.

1. Dreams are typically made up of a montage of the previous day's events, but it is not uncommon for external stimuli during the REM period to be incorporated into the dream. Andre Maury, in an 1861 book on sleep and dreams, reported a dream set during the French revolution. The dream included his questioning, condemnation, and his travel to the place of execution. He climbed onto the scaffold, was bound, and the guillotine fell. He felt his head separate from his body and awakened to find that the top of his bed had fallen and had struck the back of his neck as the blade would have. The bedtop striking his neck had been incorporated as his execution.

2. Maury's dream has been used to support the contention that entire dreams take place in a second or less. Several REM studies indicated that this is not true. There is a positive correlation between the amount of time a person has been in REM and the length of his dream recall. Sleepers when awakened either 5 or 15 minutes after REM onset could correctly identify the time after REM onset (either 5 or 15 minutes) 83 percent of the time. It was presumed that the ability of the subjects to correctly identify their length of REM was based on the amount of dream recall. If so, dream time seems to correspond fairly well to waking time.

3. As mentioned earlier, the first observation of REMs led to speculation that the dreamer was watching his dream. This was called the *scanning hypothesis*. Attempts of experimenters to predict patterns of eye movements from dream reports, however, have resulted in negative findings, perhaps, because eye movement patterns are usually quite complex. The most pervasive evidence against the scanning hypothesis comes from kittens that had been functionally blinded by being raised in dark from birth. Although they had had no visual experience and were not able to see, their REM activity during sleep was normal. Humans blind for as long as 55 years also show eye movement activity, although it is not as easily detected as in others. The dreams of these subjects were auditory in nature.

4. The young adult spends about 2 hours each night dreaming, but may not remember any dream material the next morning. When asked during the day, only 37.5 percent (Webb and Kersey, 1967) of a large group of subjects reported recalling a dream when they awoke that morning. An analysis of the last hour of sleep of subjects in a laboratory revealed that the probability of waking up from REM in that hour was .45. Since the probability of recalling a dream from REM is about .80, one would expect a dream recall of about 36 percent ($.80 \times .45 = .36$), if subjects only recalled dreams if they happened to be awakened in the morning during them.

Variations in the Sleep Process

Having categorized sleep as a neat, average phenomena, we must now admit that few of us are really average. There are many influences on sleep that cause the typical patterns we have described to change whether by design or by imposition. We may, for example, vary our sleep to work, play, or study late; our sleep may suffer as a result of stress; and sleep changes with age. For all the complexities readily imaginable, sleep can actually vary only a few ways across each 24-hour period. The time of sleep onset, sleep length, the time of awakening, and the number of sleep periods per day may vary. There may also be changes in the amount and distribution of sleep stages. But, from these simple variations, we can become sleep deprived, take naps, become a shift worker.

Developmental Changes

The world of the infant is very different from the adult world in many ways, the sleep is no exception. A three-day-old infant may sleep anywhere from 12 to 22 hours per day (mean about 16). Figure 13-4 details the developmental aspects of sleep length in terms of REM and NREM amounts. The sleep of the newborn is spread over the day and

night in 5 or 6 sleep periods. By 12 weeks of age, the average baby in a group of infants is sleeping 10 hours between 8 PM and 8 AM and 5 hours between 8 AM and 8 PM. As the infant matures, the amount of sleep during the day slowly decreases while the length of night sleep remains at about 10 hours. The slow reduction in day sleep is seen by a decrease in the frequency and length of naps and accounts for the drop in total sleep length per 24 hours that is seen between the ages of 6 months and 5–7 years, when the last daily nap is usually given up. Reduction in night sleep length continues throughout adolescence, and sleep length tends to stabilize around 7 and one-half hours in adults. There is much variability in individual sleep patterns, though. About 3 percent of adults normally sleep longer than 9 hours per night, and an additional 3 percent sleep less than 6 hours per night.

In terms of the sleep stages, there are two particular graphic changes with development. As seen in

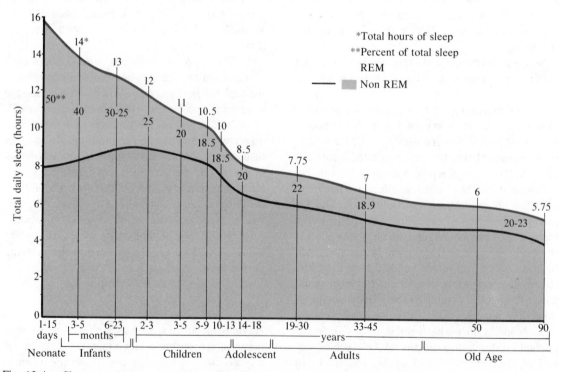

Fig. 13-4. Changes, with age, in total amounts of daily sleep, daily REM sleep, and in percentage of REM sleep. Note sharp diminution of REM sleep in the early years.

Figure 13-4 the neonate spends half of its sleep time per day (about 8 hours) in REM. In the first 5 years of life, the percentage of REM during sleep periods is rapidly reduced to around 30 percent, a change that is even greater when one realizes that the total amount of REM per day is reduced to a little over 2 hours, a fourfold drop. As the total sleep length continues to decrease on into the 20s, the amount of REM also shows a slow decrease.

The second well-documented developmental change is a reduction in the amount of stage 4. A two-year-old shows over 100 minutes of stage 4 sleep. A moderate decline is seen until the age range of 25-30, when major reductions in the amount of stage 4 are seen. On the average, by age 35, there is less than 40 minutes of stage 4 per night and by age 50 some subjects have no stage 4. As the amount of stage 4 decreases, there is a rise in the number of awakenings, with a group of 70-year-olds reporting an average of eight awakenings per night. (Williams, et al, 1974).

Personality and Sleep

Several studies have compared long sleepers (usually 9 + hours per night) with short sleepers (usually less than 6 hours per night) on a number of personality scales. Evidence of relationships is mixed. Webb and Friel (1971) screened over 4,000 college freshman to find 22 consistent short sleepers and 32 consistent long sleepers. A large number of personality inventories administered to the two groups showed no consistent differences between the two groups. However, Hartmann (1973) using the same personality inventories with a group of 11 long sleepers and a group of 18 short sleepers found that the long sleepers tended to score higher on nervousness-anxiety, and social introversion and to have less "social presence." Psychiatric interviews left the impression that the short sleepers as a group were more energetic and ambitious, and tended to worry less. Long sleepers were characterized as complaining and critical, perhaps with mild neurotic problems. To further confound the picture, Tune (1969), in his sample of 509 subjects, found no correlation between neuroticism and average sleep length. Moreover,

he found that his long sleepers were *less* introverted than his short sleepers, the opposite of the results obtained by Hartmann. These results suggest that the relation of personality to sleep is tenuous at best, at least in normal people. In very disturbed personalities, however, sleep disturbances may be seen. The clinically-depressed person has less stage 4 sleep, wakes up more often and spends more time awake during the night. The condition improves with treatment of the depression and may indicate some of the general effects of anxiety on sleep rather than personality factors. Schizophrenics may show disturbed sleep but often do not. This parallels the observation that schizophrenics may not be anxious, if they have constructed a stable private world.

Influence of Day-to-Day Activities

Sleep, like hunger and other biological activities, appears to be modified by many extraneous factors but only to a certain extent. Sleep can be put off, pushed aside for awhile, and broken up from within or without, but sleep always exists in the background and must ultimately occur. The many experiments looking for effects on sleep of very many activities have succeeded mainly in impressing us with the ability of sleep to continue in the face of severe demands and with the stability of that sleep process regardless of many influences. One must realize that sleep is both preceded and accompanied by a complex surrounding.

Six hours of concentrated reading, relaxing, or studying prior to bedtime have been found to have no effects on the distribution of sleep. Similarly, watching violent or stressful films prior to bedtime has been shown to have no effect on the various sleep stages. An early study of college athletes indicated that exercise in the afternoon resulted in increases in stage 4 sleep during the immediately following night, but that evening exercise did not result in increased stage 4, perhaps because the body was still "activated" at bedtime (Baekeland & Lasky, 1966). However, more recent studies have failed to confirm this finding. In terms of EEG results then, even the effect of strenuous exercise seems to have little effect on sleep.

The Surround of Sleep

The world does not sleep when we go to bed. Influences continue throughout the night, sensory input continues to be processed during all sleep stages. In one study (Oswald et al, 1960) a tape recording of a series of names was played throughout the night. Subjects were asked to clench their fists when they heard their own name or a second, designated name. Waking up to a name was also scored as a response. Responses were counted only when the subject was in sleep stages 2, 3, or 4. Subjects responded to their own name 25 percent of the time, to their second, designated name 12 percent of the time, and to other, control names less than 2 percent of the time. The results indicate that accurate sensory discrimination continues during sleep and that things to which we attach meaning will more easily awaken us. Persons asked to live in an environment with a very loud tone occurring every 22 seconds for 30 days showed only small and inconsistent changes in sleep parameters. Persons exposed to more meaningful sounds like truck noises or sonic booms showed only small sleep disruption, usually in the form of transient awakenings. An exception to this general rule is seen in some older people who appear to have very fragile sleep and are easily disrupted. As sounds become more personally important, such as the cry of a newborn to its mother, response probability increases.

We are, of course, influenced by more than sounds. Our total environment and our acceptance of that environment affect our sleep as well. If we take a vacation, we often find that on our first night we do not usually sleep as well as we do at home. We may not sleep as soundly and may awaken several times. Such an effect, commonly called the *First Night Effect,* is often seen on subjects on their first night in the sleep laboratory. The First Night Effect is characterized by more stage 0, stage 1, and awakenings, coupled with less REM. Subjects thoroughly familiarized with a laboratory or sleeping in a laboratory with rooms designed as much as possible like normal bedrooms show less First Night Effect. Subjects with anxiety increased by threats of electrical shock during the night usually show significant changes in those factors previously mentioned as seen in the First Night Effect. Even those changes, which might amount to an increase of 10 minutes of stage 0 or 10 minutes of stage 1 over an "average" night, are not large in comparison to the 450 minutes of normal sleep. Sleep, in normal subjects, is a powerful process that is not easily denied.

Drugs and Sleep

Throughout history, we can find attempts to directly bring sleep under our control by drugs. In our present culture, the use of drugs to modify many behaviors has increased greatly, and sleep is no exception.

An examination of the shelves of any drugstore will produce a number of products designed to give ". . . sleep, rest and peaceful sleep, sleep, sleep . . .". These "over-the-counter" medicines usually contain antihistamine and often additions of aspirin or even belladonna. There are two real problems with these medicines. The first is the problem of effectiveness. When recommended doses of a major brand were given in a laboratory, they had no more effect on the sleep of people with sleep problems than did sugar pills. If these substances are effective in the real world, it may be largely due to the *placebo* effect. The effectiveness is most likely based on purely psychological grounds; that is, the pills are bought in the belief that they will aid sleep. It is the belief, not the specific pill, that influences sleep. The second problem lies in the fact that the pills, not doing anything, often do not alleviate sleep problems, and higher than recommended doses are tried. Unfortunately, overdoses have various side effects varying from disorientation and hallucinations to coma.

Another common sleep inducer is the "nightcap," an alcoholic beverage taken at bedtime. The effects of a small dose of alcohol on the sleep pattern are unknown. Laboratory studies have focussed on much larger doses, comparable to drinking oneself into a "state of oblivion." One study, using the equivalent of three stiff drinks, found that it took subjects less time to fall asleep and that

REM was reduced during the first half of the night. The initial REM reduction was made up by an increase in REM during the second half of the night. Larger doses of alcohol result in a longer suppression, because REM does not usually occur until about 90 minutes after sleep begins, and the small amount of alcohol might be metabolized by then. Alcohol is a sedative and could aid sleep onset with occasional use. However, sleep-inducing effects tend to disappear with repeated doses.

People with problems in getting to sleep often go to a doctor, who usually prescribes sleeping pills. The most typical prescription is one of a class of drugs called barbiturates. About 250 different barbiturates (brand names include Nembutal, Seconal, and Eskabarb) have been synthesized, although only about a dozen are widely used. Barbiturates do, in fact, serve in aiding sleep. EEG studies (usually of Nembutal) have indicated that barbiturates temporarily give a reduction in sleep latency, more stage 4, less REM, fewer awakenings, less body movement, and a normal total sleep length. The latency and length characteristics may vary with particular barbiturates.

For occasional usage and at medically-prescribed levels, the barbiturates are effective in allowing sleep. But, barbiturates are easily abused and generally have deleterious effect on REM sleep. An experiment by Oswald and Priest (1965) illustrates the effects of repeated barbiturate use. After control nights, the subjects received a barbiturate preparation nightly for nine nights. During the first four drug nights, there was less than one-half the normal amount of REM. During the next five nights, percent of REM per night increased back to normal values. The return of REM to normal levels is evidence of a developing *tolerance* for the drug; that is, the drug began to become less and less effective in its soporific effects after four nights. At this point the dosage was increased by 50 percent, and REM suppression was again seen. However, tolerance to the new level of drug appeared in about three days. After the drug had been given for eighteen consecutive nights, it was discontinued. The drug withdrawal effects on body chemistry caused an immediate jump in the percent of REM sleep to abnormally high values, and

changes in the REM sleep pattern were noted for six weeks after drug withdrawal. Of more importance to the subjects, the withdrawal period was marked by insomnia, frightening nightmares, and a feeling of having slept very poorly. One subject averaged only three and a half hours of sleep on the first three nights after drug withdrawal, although he usually averaged about seven.

The rapid increase in tolerance and the unpleasant effects of barbiturate withdrawal have combined to make barbiturate use a hard habit to break. In addition, high levels of barbiturate intake or the use of longer lasting barbiturates means that all of the drug will not be metabolized by morning. The resulting grogginess may initiate the morning use of stimulants, particularly amphetamines. A vicious cycle of higher and higher doses of amphetamines during the day and barbiturates during the night ensues and leads to addiction and a very real drug problem.

Drugs, of course, can be used to limit sleep as well as to induce it. Caffeine is probably the most commonly consumed stimulant. Recent studies have indicated that consumption of a large amount of coffee (four cups) or its caffeine equivalent shortly prior to bedtime results in longer sleep latency, more awakenings, more time awake, more shifts from one sleep stage or another, and less total sleep time. Amphetamines are a stronger stimulant than caffeine. Taking them can eliminate the desire for sleep for longer periods than caffeine. Sleep after amphetamine administration is difficult, and there is a large reduction in REM when sleep is possible.

Sleep Disturbances

Most of us take sleep for granted much of the time, and as long as we feel and function well, there is no problem. However, on occasion, each of us has probably been plagued by a sleep problem of one sort or another. For most of us the problem is occasional insomnia—an inability to go to sleep or an inability to stay asleep. Several other sleep dysfunctions are also fairly common. Most of these occur in early childhood: sleep walking, enuresis (bed wetting), and night terrors. There are also the bothersome intrusions of sleep talking and snoring, and the somewhat more frightening problems of nightmares and narcolepsy. The pervasiveness and the time of occurrence of these conditions are summarized in Table 13-3.

Before discussing the particular disturbances, we will emphasize some problems in Table 13-3. Nearly all of the disorders are associated with age, all vary in intensity of manifestation, and all may vary in terms of occurring only occasionally or being persistent. For example, in one individual, "full-blown" episodes of sleep walking may occur with high frequency for a period of one or two years and never occur again. In another, limited sleep movements—sitting up in bed, for example, may occur intermittently throughout a lifetime and may never be recognized. The data reported in Table 13-3 were only those episodes that were "clear and present" manifestations of such persistence and intensity as to be recognized as a problem. The descriptions that follow must be seen in that context.

Narcolepsy

All of us have been "attacked" by sleep. Usually, however, such attacks occur under appropriate conditions. We have not gotten enough sleep, the book we are reading is dull, or the surroundings monotonous. However, as many as 100,000 Americans have *narcolepsy*, inappropriate and irresistable "sleep attacks," in varying degrees. These "sleep attacks" consist of periods of irresible sleep at inappropriate times such as while walking down the street. At these times, often with the forewarning of an *aura*, or unusual feelings or perceptions, the person briefly lapses into an overwhelming sleep. It may last from a few minutes to 15 minutes.

Because of the dramatic effects on the person, narcoleptic attacks have been popularly associated with epilepsy or psychopathology. However, recent sleep research indicates that the attacks are rather a disturbance in the sleep process. Specifically, the evidence indicates that narcoleptic attacks are characterized by REM sleep at their onset. Recalling several aspects of REM strongly supports the claim that these attacks are dysfunctions of REM. Normally, during the night, REM does not appear until some 90 minutes after sleep onset, and the appearance of REM at the very beginning of a narcoleptic episode is unusual. Further, REM, we have seen, is associated with dreams and the prewarning or aura of the narcoleptic may be a part of this pattern. Most critically, particularly in lower animals, REM is associated with a loss of muscle tone, that is, an inability to move.

The EEG in narcoleptic attacks (beyond the early REM onset) is normal and not like that seen in epilepsy. Also, no clear association has been

Table 13-3. Sleep Disturbances

	Age Range Primarily Affected	Usually Outgrown	Percent of Primary Age Range	Sleep Stage of Occurrence
Night Terrors	3–5	yes	2–5%	stages 3 and 4
Enuresis	4–7 (bedwetting considered normal before bladder control learned)	yes	15–25%	stages 3 and 4
Sleep Walking (Somnambulism)	5–12	yes	15%	stages 3 and 4
Nightmares	peak at 8–10	lessen	95%	REM
Narcolepsy	onset 15–25	no	.05%	awake
Sleep Talking	all ages, primarily less than 25	lessen	40–60%	Evenly distributed across
Insomnia	all	no	14–20%	awake

found with psychopathology. There is some evidence of a genetic background, since there is a strong tendency for these attacks to run in families.

Sleepwalking

Again, contemporary sleep research has shed a new light on sleepwalking, (also called somnambulism). Until quite recently, these episodes were thought to be an acting out of a dream or to indicate the presence of a personality "dissociation" in which the sleeper was acting out some deep-seated psychological problem. While this may be true in rare instances, laboratory recordings of a broad sample of sleepwalkers all found the walkers walking during stage 4 or deep sleep. From this it can be inferred that sleepwalking could not be associated with dreaming. Indeed, sleepwalkers on being awakened, do not report "dreaming" and seldom recall any aspects of the episodes. Since somnambulism is typically outgrown (although it may continue occasionally in adulthood) and has not been linked with any specific personality disturbances, it is now looked upon more as a developemental disorder rather than a psychological disturbance.

Enuresis (Bed Wetting)

While enuresis occurs during sleep, it is not, in fact, appropriately considered a sleep disorder. Enuresis typically occurs in the earlier part of the night. As such, it tends to occur in stages 3 and 4 but is not clearly dependent upon their presence, since it often occurs in other stages of sleep. Modifying sleep is unlikely to effect enuresis. More typically, enuresis is a complex interrelationship between maturational rate, parental expectancies, and training procedures. The picture may be compounded by emotional problems and physiological dysfunction.

Night Terrors

Night terrors (*pavor nocturnas*) refers to a sudden awakening from sleep with an appearance of extreme panic. There may be screams or groans, and the person may crouch in an appearance of terror.

Such attacks usually last only a few minutes. The appearance of terrors peaks between the ages of three and five years of age but is seen in rare instances in adults. It is natural to think of these as the result of particularly terrifying dreams. They are not. Laboratory studies show that they are abrupt awakening from very deep or stage 4 sleep. These studies went further and showed that they could actually be induced by abrupt awakening from this stage of sleep but not from other stages. The child seldom reports any particular disturbing mental content and almost inevitably does not recall the event in the morning. In short, it is essentially an unconscious reaction. Night terrors are probably caused by the very rapid shift of consciousness from the state of deep sleep to waking.

Other Sleep Dysfunctions

Nightmares can be differentiated from night terrors on several accounts. Almost everyone has had a terrifying dream at one time or another, and nightmares are truly dreams, for they arise from REM sleep. Nightmares, of course, are not confined to children, although their occurrence peaks between 8 and 10 years of age. It is much more difficult for children to shrug off a nightmare as a simple bad dream. Children do not have a reality that is as well defined as that of an adult, and the possibility of lions hiding beneath the sheets is still a very real one.

Sleep talking is a phenomena that has long been observed and commented on. It appears to be relatively common—up to 60 percent of a sample of college students were reported as having been told that they talked in their sleep, and half of those were still active sleep talkers. A recent laboratory study, in which subjects spent an average of six nights in the laboratory, found that 39 percent of the random sample spoke at least once in their sleep. Most sleep talking occurs in NREM sleep. Sleep talking may include single words, shouts, meaningless sequence of words, coherent speeches, or even conversation. Episodes may be quite lengthy (the sleep laboratory record was claimed as a 45-word speech in 1966), but not always related to the mental content which is reported if the sleep talker is awakened. Agreement of the talk to mental occurrence was 79 percent during REM but only 21 percent in stages 3 and 4 as observed by Arkin et al (1970). In general, the talking emerging from REM sleep tends to be more emotional and internally generated, whereas talking in stages 1 and 2 is more coherent and lifelike. The sleep talking at sleep outset, where we learn the "truth" about our roommates and when we can sometimes get responses to questions, is probably occurring in that borderline between sleep and waking during stage 1 (if the person is asleep at all).

Another sort of sleep utterance, of course, is snoring. One source estimates that there are 35 million snorers in the United States and that snoring is evenly divided between men and women. Although prescriptions, operations, and patented devices are as plentiful as theories of snoring, there is no proven cure, and very little work has attempted to relate snoring to the process of sleep. One recent study found that the amount of snoring did not differ in different sleep stages but that the amount of snoring was greatest shortly after sleep began and least near the end of sleep.

Insomnia

Insomnia is easy to define—difficulties in getting to sleep or maintaining sleep. However, it is difficult to classify. It may be episodic, occurring only occasionally, or it may be chronic, occuring night after night. Often the complaints do not match the degree of actual sleep disturbances; poor sleep may be tolerated and accepted by some, while only slight disturbances of sleep are accompanied by persistent complaints in others. And, as we shall see, the sources of insomnia are manifold. What is certain is the significant presence of insomnia. A number of surveys provide evidence of "frequent troubles in going to sleep or staying asleep." These surveys indicate that about 7 percent to 20 percent of a sample will voice such complaints.

The systematic diagnosis and treatment of insomniacs is too recent to give accurate figures about the sources and "kinds" of insomnia. However, sorting them out in terms of sources can give us a clearer picture of disturbed sleep.

Situational Insomnias. Any situation that leads to a continued response to the world around us can interfere with sleep. Simply, while we are doing something other than sleeping, we are not sleeping. Very often the world presses on us (or we feel compelled to press on the world) and sleep is disrupted. A dreaded examination tomorrow or a similar great project, and troubles or excitement left over from today follow us into our bed. When such factors are present, sleep has difficulty finding its proper place. When sleep does occur, such concerns may disturb the sleep process. As long as these strong pressures persist, sleep will be disrupted or evade us, and we will be "insomniacs." Naturally, these circumstances may be transient, or they may persist—the pressures of staying in school or living up to a goal, for example. It is certain, however, that as long as the pressures remain, sleep will be disturbed. That disruption will be characterized by long sleep latencies, many awakenings, and possible difficulty falling asleep after those awakenings. When the waking problems dissipate, normal sleep will return.

Sleep Disorders. We have seen earlier that, particularly in childhood, the sleep itself shows variations such as sleepwalking, enuresis, and night terrors. Sleep is disturbed while they are present, although most often outgrown.

Secondary Insomnias. Poor sleep is often an accompaniment of some primary disturbance such as an underlying pathology. Disturbed sleep is an almost inevitable concomitant of affective psychoses (depression) and also is a typical complaint among psychoneurotics. (See Chapter 20). In the former, sleep disturbances approximate 100 percent and in the latter, sleep complaints were reported in some 50 percent of a sample.

Aging. We noted earlier that stage 4 sleep declines and stage 0 (awakenings) and stage 1 (light sleep) increases as a natural consequence of age. In some individuals, this loosened control over the sleep process may be quite severe, and there is a consequent increase in night time awakenings or early awakenings. Figures taken from a large sam-

Table 13-4.   Sleep Complaints as a Function of Age

	Age Group		
	15–25	33–45	55–65
Less than five hours sleep	5 percent	7 percent	14 percent
Longer than an hour to get to sleep	2 "	4 "	14 "
Awaken before 5 A.M.	1 "	3 "	10 "
Frequently wake up	5 "	14 "	23 "

ple of subjects from three age groups concerning various sleep complaints are shown in Table 13-4. While the rise in complaints may not be entirely due to aging alone, certainly some of it is.

Sleep Timing.   Some portion of insomnia is due to our mismanagement of sleep. Again and again on questionnaires, we find a strong correlation between regularity of bedtime within a constant sleep environment and ease or "goodness" of sleep. While a part of this relationship may simply reflect a generally better organized life, a part is likely to be due to a more appropriate set of sleep habits. Sleep is a biological rhythm organized in time. If the time and place for sleep are highly variable—at bed at 3 A.M. on one night and at 10 P.M. the next night to "catch up"—sleep has no way of developing a systematic tendency to occur. This rhythmic aspect of sleep is also related to the typically reported problems of sleep in the shift worker, such as feeling tired or being unable to sleep for a prolonged period. Such workers often sleep during the time when their biological rhythm is set for waking activity.

Drug Related Insomnias.   This cause of insomnia is among the most frequently seen in sleep clinics. Unfortunately, many drug related insomnias are the direct result of attempts at "curing" or "containing" a sleep problem ending in creating a greater one. As we have seen, most depressants, which include alcohol and sedatives, distort the natural sleep process. As a consequence, the sleep period becomes a battleground between these distortions and the needs of the natural process. Almost inevitable, when the battle is prolonged, sleep becomes disturbed.

Impositions on the Sleep Process

Sleep and waking flow in a natural rhythm within the 24 hours of the day. However, people often intrude on or modify this rhythm. They stay up late. Sometimes people may stay awake for a day or two. Perhaps they just shorten their sleep. For example, going to sleep late but having to get up early the next day is a common occurrence. Most sleep variations cause changes in the usual time of going to bed. Shift work or jet travel cause dramatic shifts in sleep onset time. We have seen earlier that drugs modify the structure of sleep. All of these factors are impositions on sleep. We are beginning to know something about the consequences.

Going Without Sleep

One thing is certain to happen when we stay awake for increasingly long periods of time—sleep presses back in the form of increasing sleepiness. This is seen in Figure 13-5 which shows the relationship between the length of time awake and the strength of the sleep response as indicated by the latency of sleep (the length of time it takes to go to sleep) when the person attempts to sleep.

But what are the other effects? A number of experiments have deprived animals and people of sleep for varying periods of time. Humans have been experimentally sleep deprived for as long as 265 hours and animals for a good deal longer. To date, no permanent physiological damage has been attributable to the loss of sleep. The sensory modalities continue to function, reflexes are intact, and biochemical changes have been described as

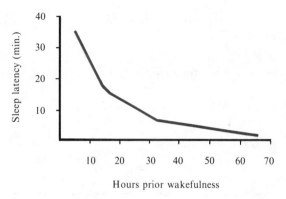

Fig. 13-5. Relationship between hours of prior wakeful ness and EEG sleep latency.

"modest and subtle." The only obvious effects in humans are an increased hand tremor and some difficulties in focussing the eyes ("double vision"). The sense of balance may also show some changes. Although there have been some reports of disturbed behavior such as hallucinations and delusions or uncontrolled emotional outbursts, these episodes have not been seen in less than three days without sleep and appear in individual cases rather than as a typical response to sleep loss. These individuals may have responded similarly to any stress- such as starvation, isolation, or continuous anxiety.

It is certain that everyone becomes more and more sleepy under the press of sleep loss, and this affects the way they feel and to some extent the way they perform. It is intriguing and more than a little puzzling that someone who looks exhausted and who reports being exhausted can generally perform most tasks when called upon almost as well as when rested. Only seven types of tasks have been shown to be to some extent affected by prolonged total sleep loss. They include: 1) Long tasks—the longer the task, the more likely it is to be performed more poorly after sleep loss. Errors become more and more frequent as the task continues. 2) Tasks in which subjects do not know and are not told how well they are doing. Giving knowledge of results may allow subjects to judge their behavior and try harder if they begin to do poorly. 3) Difficult tasks—performance on difficult tasks is much worse with sleep loss while simple tasks may be performed just as well as nor-

mally. 4) Timed tasks—any task which is speeded or which must be completed in a short period of time relative to the work required will show sleep deprivation effects. 5) Newly acquired skills—behaviors just learned, as a newly licensed driver on a driving task, will show more decrement than behaviors which have become habitual. 6) Complex tasks—the larger the number of mental or motor operations (regardless of any memory requirements), the more likely the task is to be affected by sleep loss. 7) Short-term memory tasks—any task which requires many elements to be put into short-term memory will be affected by sleep loss.

There are two non-task factors that can increase or decrease the effects of sleep loss on performance. Psychological factors such as interest, motivation, and prior experience with sleep loss have been shown to influence performance after sleep deprivation. Interesting tasks, such as games, generally are performed as well as ever. Motivation, such as being paid or being monitored by a supervisor, usually counteracts sleep deprivation effects. Situational factors also modulate performance after sleep loss. Physical activity before task performance and during breaks helps decrease sleep deprivation effects. Interspersing frequent breaks during which task performance is not required also helps eliminate performance decrements associated with prolonged work. Drugs can increase or decrease sleepiness. However, the amount of performance change that is due to an incapacity to perform and the amount that is simply the result of a losing battle with sleepiness has not yet been fully sorted out.

Shortening Sleep

Under pressures or pleasures we may get several hours less sleep than usual for a night or for months. In a study done at the University of Florida, the daily sleep time of a group of young adults was reduced from the normal 7 and one-half to 5 and one-half hours for 56 days. The subjects were able to maintain the 5 and one-half hour schedule. Performance decrements were minor, although EEG sleep characteristics differed to some extent. There was a slight enhancement of stage 4 sleep and a substantial reduction in REM sleep. This reduction in REM would be expected from the fact that REM occurs predominantly in the last part of the normal sleep period—the part of the period that was cut off when sleep length was shortened. The subjects reported that it was hard to wake up in the morning and that they felt drowsy during the day for the first two weeks of the experiment.

A few studies have tried to reduce sleep length gradually, usually reducing sleep by about 30 minutes every two weeks. Although very few subjects have been studied, it appears that few measurable problems appear in normal 7 and one-half to 8 hour sleepers until their sleep is reduced to 4 and one-half hours or less. After this point subjects begin to feel fatigued, irritable, and begin to feel an intense need for more sleep. The provocative finding of the long term studies, however, is that the subjects did not return to their normal 7 and one-half to 8 hours of sleep after the study but rather slept 1 or 2 hours less per night.

The problems associated with shortened sleep are the result of a "sleep debt." A recent study restricted sleep to only four hours or two hours. On the next night, the subjects were permitted to sleep as long as they could. They slept longer after the two hour sleep night than the four hour sleep night. A need for more than the normal amount of sleep can appear after a single shortened night.

Selective Stage Deprivation

The knowledge of sleep stages and particularly the association of REM with dreams has led many researchers to explore the need for the specific stages of sleep. One experimental way to study the need for a specific stage is to deprive subjects of that stage and to note the results. The studies of the effects of losing particular stages of sleep are very useful because drugs, as we have seen, reduce REM sleep. Further, because sleep stages are not evenly distributed across the night, partial sleep deprivation (simply sleeping fewer hours than normal) is, in fact, a form of selective deprivation.

The role of dreams in sleep has been of extreme interest because it was thought that the hallucinations and delusions, characteristic of schizophrenia, might be dreams that had broken into waking reality. Sleep deprivation, especially REM deprivation, was thought to be a possible trigger that would initiate waking hallucinations. With this possibility in mind, William Dement reported the first studies of dream deprivation in 1960. His method was simple. He watched individual subjects sleep all night for many nights. Each time the EEG pattern began to show a characteristic REM pattern, he woke the subject up for a few minutes. As the nights passed, the need for REM was seen in several ways. Dement noticed that with each succeeding night of deprivation, he had to awaken his subjects more often. As the pressure for REM built, the REM sleep attempted to enter sleep more frequently. The pressure for REM was also seen when the deprivation was ended. For as many as five nights following REM deprivation more REM than normal was seen in the sleep of the subjects. In fact, the REM "rebound" was sometimes as much as double the normal amount of REM.

A study of the need for stage 4 sleep showed results even more graphic than the studies of REM deprivation. Whenever a subject entered stage 4, that subject was given shocks. During the first night of stage 4 deprivation, more than 125 shocks were necessary to prohibit the occurrence of stage 4 while only about 15 were required to eliminate REM in other subjects. As deprivation continued over nights, the number of shocks necessary to deny stages increased rapidly. About 250 shocks per night were required to eliminate stage 4 and 55 to eliminate REM after five nights of selective deprivation. When the deprivation procedures were stopped, there was a definite rebound. An increase in stage 4 was seen only on the first night after deprivation ended, while REM rebounds continued for three nights. These results imply an increase in pressure or a need for these specific stages of sleep.

In the large number of deprivation studies which have now been done, a great majority of subjects have shown few behavioral ill effects, but the effects shown appear to be differential to the type of deprivation. The general consensus is that REM deprivation leads to a state of hyperactivity with some accompanying loss of "interpersonal effectiveness." Stage 4 deprivation, on the other hand, leads to a more hypoactive and depressed response state. The relation of these various sleep stage deficits and subjective feelings to behavior are certainly not obvious or substantial.

Sleep Onset Variation

In addition to prolonging wakefulness and shortening sleep, we vary when we go to sleep. We all stay up late or go to bed early. The grossest disruption of a stable bedtime is often seen when people go onto a shift work schedule or are involved in "jet lag," which results from flying across a number of time zones.

The effects of varying the sleep onset time are now well-known. When the period for sleep is moved to a normal waking period, the temporal ordering of sleep and waking is disrupted. REM sleep occurs much earlier than its normal time of about 90 minutes after sleep onset. The sleep period has more frequent awakenings and is often terminated early.

There are several factors that help account for problems encountered in attempts to sleep or to be awake at unusual times. Body temperature may be one of the largest factors. Body temperature shows a daily cycle with the lowest temperatures normally occurring at about 4:00 A.M. and highs occurring during late morning or the afternoon. Sleepiness and performance follow the same general curve. If we started working on the midnight to 8:00 A.M. shift or flew from New York to Tokyo, our "body time" would be out of synchrony with our periods of activity. In the middle of our shift (or during Tokyo afternoon), our body temperature would be falling, and our reaction time might slow a bit. We would not feel quite as sharp as usual. Over a matter of ten days or so, our body time would slowly shift to match our new waking pattern if our new pattern were consistent. Pilots, flying all over the world, would probably never adjust to Tokyo time. Similarly, shift workers who work a shift for only a few days at a time or who dramatically alter their sleep patterns on weekends would not adjust their body rhythms to their sleep patterns.

Obviously, travelers and shift workers are not the only violators of the natural rhythmicity of sleep/waking patterns. Take Joe College. As observed earlier, he normally sleeps from 12:30 A.M. to 8:00 A.M. But the zoology test, the chemistry lab, the Bogart movie, or more esoteric pleasures often keep Joe up until 4:00 A.M. This might be followed by an attempt to attend an 8:00 A.M. class, a "catch-up" nap from 2:00 P.M. to 4:00 P.M, and a bed time of 11:00 P.M. Several things can be predicted from this sleep pattern as it differs from normal. Joe's performance from 1:00 A.M. to 4:00 A.M. will be poor, for it is during his normal sleep time. He will be sleepy at 8:00 A.M. and although he could perform as well as ever, he probably would not. Both of Joe's sleep periods would be of a slightly different than normal quality, and one will fall when Joe is normally awake—an added trouble. Finally, Joe's prior wakefulness of only seven hours (4:00 P.M. to 11:00 P.M.) coupled with an attempt to try to sleep during a normal waking time will make the 11:00 P.M. bedtime much earlier than the time when Joe will finally fall asleep.

Dreams and Interpreters

The nature and meaning of dreams have puzzled, frightened, and delighted humanity across the ages. One of the earliest preserved pieces of writing is a series of dream interpretations done in Egypt about 2000 B.C. According to the Bible, the value of the ability to interpret dreams was so great in ancient Egypt that Joseph, by correctly interpreting the dream of seven years of plenty and seven years of famine, was elevated to ruler of all Egypt second only to the Pharaoh.

In our times, certainly the major interest in dreams has been stirred by Sigmund Freud. His book, *The Interpretation of Dreams,* published in 1900, reflected his belief that dreams were "the royal road to the unconscious." Freud saw dreams as having two functions. Dreams were on the one hand, the "guardians" of sleep, in that he believed people dreamed to keep from waking. Secondly, dreams served as wish fulfillments. Freud reports a young woman who dreamt she was having her menstrual period, from which Freud (correctly) inferred that the woman was pregnant (had in truth missed her period) and that she was more than a little hesitant about being tied down with a child. Freud's interpretation of her dream was that she *wished* she were having her menstrual period and therefore was not pregnant. Freud believed dreams operated on two levels. The actual dream report (of having the menstrual period, in our example) is called the *manifest content* of the dream. The manifest content is considered to be the transformation of unacceptable, unconscious, sexual urges into something more acceptable. Freud termed these unconscious urges the *latent content*. In the dream, those latent urges were a desire not to be "pregnant." According to Freud, the woman subconsciously did not want to have the child. The latent wish was transformed to be expressed as an acceptable manifest scene of having a menstrual period.

Freud found several ways that the unconscious urges were changed in dreams and he called the transformational process *"dream work."* Dreams are primarily visual. The expression of an abstract concept such as happiness or anger must be altered, so that it can be expressed in visual terms. For example, love may be represented by touching or physical proximity, hate by an overt attack. The dream work of condensation, displacement, and symbolization involves the use of imagery in expressing thoughts. *Condensation* follows from the fact that interpretations (that is, the latent content) are much longer than the dream itself. One dream may become a condensation of many latent concepts. For example, to dream of an orchestra leader may represent all of the complex relationships with one's father in which the elements of a guide, a leader, and an authority are multiply-fused into the single image. The process of *displacement* may result in emotional responses associated with one thing or person being transferred to another person or thing. Tearing the wings off a May-fly could easily represent the displaced wish to harm one's wife or brother or sister. Finally, Freud stressed the idea of *symbolism*. A symbol is the use of objects to represent a particular concept. Many common dream elements represented other less acceptable desires. For example, a woman might dream of a man breaking into her house and chasing her upstairs with his umbrella. Freud believed that sharp or elongated objects were phallic symbols—they represented the penis. Similarly cups, boxes, houses, or any container could symbolize the vaginal cavity. Freud also believed that any sort of rhythmic activity such as running, horseback riding, or climbing represented the sexual act.

Because Freud chose to base his theory of personality on primarily sexual grounds, Freud often found sexual desires in their latent content. Other dream analysts, not seeing either sex or wish fulfillment as the major driving force in personality and dreams respectively, have viewed the interpretation of dreams somewhat differently. Carl Jung, for example, proposed a compensatory theory of dreams in which the dreamer compensates in his dreams for things which he is lacking during waking. Because one cannot talk back to the boss or be overly rude to the neighbors during the day, aggression and violence become common dream themes. Further, Jung saw dreams as messages from the psyche. In this sense, dreams might serve as a thinly veiled warning to give up smoking or to get a medical checkup.

Freud's system and conclusions were based on the reports of his disturbed patients who may have learned to produce the dreams Freud wished to hear. Further, Freud used anecdotal methods. This means that he did not necessarily record, report, or analyze all of the dreams of a patient but tended to concentrate on the more "meaningful" ones; ones that could be meaningfully interpreted within his framework. Several later investigators used the approach of systematic observation. The method was simple. Each time a subject awoke, that subject wrote down any dreams he remembered. After a large sample was collected, the dreams were examined for common themes, characters, and emotions. This approach appears pedestrian in comparison to the emotion-charged hidden meanings unearthed by Freudian analysis. Moreover, the results are somewhat at variance with the usual conception of dreams, but they are representative of normal dreams of normal people.

The most voluminous collector of dreams in the past few years has been Calvin Hall, who has published several reports on some 10,000 dreams that he has collected from normal people. He classified his dreams into several categories including the setting, the characters, the plot, and the emotions expressed.

The most common setting was a dwelling or building or a conveyance such as an automobile. The most popular room in dreams set at home was the living room. This evidence contradicts what we have always been told about dreams—that they are exotic, bizarre, and nonsensical. Rather, they are commonplace and have a tendency to be constructed from familiar scenes. Yet they are not entirely representative of waking life. Places of work occupy a much lower percent of dream time than normal time, and recreational activities take up more than their normal waking percent.

Other people usually appear in our dreams. The dreamer is the only character in a mere 15 percent of dreams. Other characters are a mixture of strangers, friends, and family. Surprisingly, only 56 percent of people in dreams are known to the dreamer. Young adults tend to dream about people their own age but not about prominent people or current events.

The classification of dream actions shows them to be remarkably ordinary. The largest group of dreams involve movements such as walking, running, or riding. Other common themes include talking, sitting, watching, socializing, and thinking. Dreams of falling, floating, or flying were very uncommon in the sample. Perhaps, they are remembered because of their uniqueness rather than their frequency. Common activities such as swimming, playing games, and dancing are fairly frequent as are dreams of sex in adolescents and in young adults.

The emotional tone of dreams was primarily negative. Of emotions felt during dreams, apprehension was most common (40 percent of the sample). Hostile acts, such as physical attack or denunciation, outnumbered friendly ones by a ratio of almost 2.5 to 1. Yet, despite this, dreamers found 41 percent of their dreams pleasant and only 25 percent unpleasant.

Hall's approach to dream interpretation is almost as simple as his manner of collecting dreams. Simply put, Hall believes that "a dream is a personal document, a letter to oneself." There may be no more compelling reason for a dream than there is for a writer to write a short story, but the product, whether it be story or dream, is nonetheless an expression of the creator. It therefore tells about the creator. The story created is not an expression of objective reality and may reflect multiple conceptions of the world. Further, Hall advises that dreams are best interpreted by gathering a series of them. Similar themes usually run through a series of dreams and some dreams are easier to comprehend than others. An obvious dream can often serve to shed light on more complex symbolic dreams. Also, a series of dreams can serve to uncover several different traits of the dreamer. The several dreams can be put together like a jigsaw puzzle for an overall picture.

The Neurophysiology and Biochemistry of Sleep and Dreams

There has been a long search for a sleep center in the central nervous system. While modern brain research has shed light on the complexities involved in the central nervous system in the sleep process, the notion of a single sleep center has evaporated, primarily because very many brain areas have been found to play a role in the control of sleep. M. Jouvet, one of the foremost researchers in the neurophysiology and biochemistry of sleep, discusses his area in terms of "the errors of the past theories and the illusions of the present." We will present data here in the light that the future may bring many changes.

The brain stem has always played a prominent role in explanations of sleep and waking behavior (see Chapter 4). The middle area of the brain stem is called the reticular core or reticular formation. All information ascending to the brain or descending from the brain passes through this area. Stimulation anywhere in the body excites reticular cells. For this reason, the reticular system is called nonspecific. Theories of sleep, based on reticular activity, were based on the idea that reticular activation through large amounts of sensory input kept us awake. When sensory input decreased, the reticular system was less active, and when a critically small amount of activity was reached, the brain could no longer be kept awake and sleep followed. However, such theories had a particularly difficult time explaining why lesions in certain parts of the reticular formation that cut off much incoming sensory information resulted in animals that did not sleep. The ability of specific lesions of the reticular formation to give constant waking behavior also implies that there exists in the reticular formation an active sleep producing center and that sleep is an active process.

At present, two parts of the brain stem are heavily implicated in the production of sleep. One is the central group of nuclei extending from the upper edge of the medulla to the back of the midbrain. They are collectively called the *Raphé*. Their function is the mediation of NREM sleep. The second important brain stem site is the *locus coeruleus,* which is located at the level of the middle of the pons lateral to the Raphé system. The locus coeruleus plays a large part in the control of REM. Both of these areas are thought to be influenced by and operate through a series of specific neurotransmitter systems.

A schematic diagram of the brain stem area is shown in Figure 13-6. The system in the figure is a simplified version of that proposed by Jouvet (1969) and operates as follows. The onset of sleep is caused by the freeing of a transmitter substance, serotonin, from the Raphé system as a result of descending or ascending neurotransmitter activity. The serotonin triggers forebrain structures to give NREM sleep onset. Lesions in the anterior segments of the Raphé diminish NREM sleep, and the amount reduction is related both to the amount of the Raphé system destroyed and to the magnitude of the reduction of serotonin in the brain. The lower portion of the Raphé is thought to communicate with the locus coeruleus by complex connections, because lesions there, while resulting in only minor losses in NREM sleep, eliminate REM sleep. A certain amount of activity in the Raphé may serve to prime or excite the locus coeruleus, which then inhibits activity in the Raphé. Thus the locus coeruleus plays a dual role of signaling the end of NREM sleep and initiating either waking activity or REM sleep. Experimentally-produced selective lesions in the locus coeruleus have resulted in the following conclusions: 1) The anterior portion of the locus coeruleus appears involved in waking activity. 2) The middle section mediates

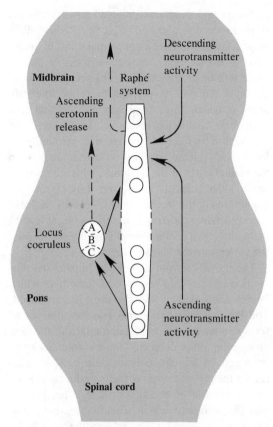

Fig. 13-6. Sleep mechanisms in the brain stem. The locus coeruleus can be divided into three sections in terms of its apparent functions: A. moderation of waking brain activity B. moderation of REM sleep C. control of muscular relaxation during REM. The interactive effects of the Raphé system and the locus coeruleus are indicated.

the brain rhythm characteristic of REM sleep with eye movements, and 3) The caudal section (the lower section towards the tail) of the locus coeruleus controls the total muscular relaxation seen in REM sleep. Lesions in the caudal portion result in animals who orient to stimuli not physically present during their sleep as if they may be acting out dreams.

Forebrain mechanisms are also certainly involved in the production of sleep, but the actual pathways and structures involved have not as yet been drawn into a coherent picture. While sleep may result from electrical stimulation in many parts of the forebrain, two major areas of importance will be discussed here. The preoptic area of the hypothalamus is perhaps the only forebrain area in which high frequency as well as low frequency stimulation results in sleep onset. The mechanism is likely to be through serotonin release. Such releases may act on frontal areas or on the medial areas of the thalamus, which is seen by many as a cortical pacemaker. Low frequency stimulation of the medial thalamus results in sleep. Also ascending reticular connections might lead to thalamic activity which would then serve to pace the cortex into the various stages of sleep.

The introduction of a drug that impairs the production of serotonin results in an insomnia which begins about a day after the drug is introduced. The lag may serve to signal that the reserves of serotonin have been used, and the lack of the new production limits sleep until more serotonin can be produced. In animals so treated, electrical stimulation of the preoptic areas of the hypothalamus is no longer capable of producing sleep. This implies that the serotonin which stimulation would normally release could not be released because it did not exist. Since the serotonin was not released, sleep did not occur. The administration of drugs which lead to serotonin, results in a rather rapid onset of sleep.

Most available evidence indicates that various brain stem structures play prominent roles in sleep. The importance of the brain stem is evidenced by lesions which cut the entire brain stem at different levels can result in an animal which is constantly awake or constantly asleep. After a period of time, however, these animals begin to show both waking and sleeping behavior as if some forebrain system has begun to take over for the lost reticular systems. This suggests that there are other forebrain mechanisms which can mediate the sleep/waking process. The brain is complex, modifiable, and certainly contains many redundant systems. A complete explanation of sleeping or waking on a neurophysiological or a biochemical level probably awaits a much more complete explanation of brain function as a whole.

Theories of Sleep

Why sleep? Is it a biological necessity or a luxury? Is it restorative, protective, an escape, or does it avoid exhaustion? As dream interpretations stretch to the earliest written records, attempts to explain the need for and the process of sleep stretch to antiquity. One of the earliest theories of sleep is credited to Alcmeon in the sixth century B.C. Alcmeon believed that sleep resulted from a retreat of blood into the veins and waking to its return.

The expansion of knowledge of anatomy, physiology, and chemistry during the 1800s and thereafter led to many hormone and blood chemical explanations of sleep and waking. Most of the theories were restorative in nature; that is, waking was thought to result in the building up of waste or fatigue-producing material which was toxic enough at some level that sleep began. During sleep, the toxic materials either dissipated or increased until they triggered waking. An example was a theory that a certain carbon dioxide level in the blood would result in sleep, and a higher level would result in waking. The problem with this theory and all theories that state that sleep is necessary to restore some chemical balance is that no one has been able to find the substance being built up and broken down. The common belief that sleep relieves, refreshes, and restores, lacks the central support of there being anything which is actually restored during sleep.

If sleep does not result from the accumulation of toxic substances, could it be an instinctual means of avoiding possible intoxication or exhaustion which might result from continued wakefulness? Sleep, according to this theory begins from a loss of interest in the environment and ends at some nonspecified time when one becomes tired of sleeping. Such a theory would predict that subjects placed in a dark, soundproof room with gloves on their hands to reduce tactile stimulation would sleep all the time. This experiment has been done, and subjects did not sleep constantly. In fact, they slept less than normal when they were in sensory deprivation.

Even the obvious explanation, "We sleep to rest" does not appear to be true. Studies of energy consumption have shown that human beings expend as much energy sleeping as they do lying quietly awake. The lack of support for the obvious explanations has been more than puzzling to sleep researchers. Some researchers have come to consider the possibility that sleep does not have a function at all and that it is the largest mistake ever made in the evolutionary process.

It is extremely hard to imagine that any function that produces vulnerability to attack, does not allow searching for food consumption, excludes procreation, and nonetheless occupies a good deal of our lives has no reason for existence. Webb (1974) has searched for the function of sleep across the wide range of the animal kingdom and evolution, and has evolved an adaptive theory described below.

The Adaptive Theory of Sleep

All mammals sleep, but different mammals sleep different amounts. Size is not the determiner of sleep length. Table 13-5 gives the average amounts of sleep that several members of the animal kingdom get each day. Predators, such as cats, dogs, and man, sleep a good deal more than their prey (sheep, rabbits, and so forth), except when the prey animals are burrowing animals like the hamster or mole. Deep burrows serve to protect some animals from predators. In terms of evolution, the sleep length and habits listed make good sense. A

Table 13-5. Sleep Lengths Among Mammals

Animal	Length per 24 hours
Bat	19
Hamster	14
Cat	14
Chimpanzee	11
Jaguar	11
Mole	10
Man	7.4
Cow	7
Sheep	6
Bottle-nose Dolphin	5
Elephant	4

sleeping sheep would soon be lost from the herd and would make easy prey. The jaguar, awake or asleep, is less likely preyed upon. The notion underlying an adaptive explanation of sleep is simply this: sleep evolved in relation to the ecological niche of each species. For "long sleepers" such as man, sleep aids in extracting the man from the hostile and unproductive world of darkness. For such animals as sheep or other grazing animals, sleep is "contracted" and shortened in duration under the continuous pressure of predators or the requirements of grazing.

An adaptive theory must explain why sleep occurs at all. The answer may lie in a very simple demonstration. Take a drive in the country on a cloudy night, pull off the road, stop your car, and turn off the lights. If the point is not made yet, open the door, get out, and walk a few steps—but be careful. Human beings cannot see well in the dark, and being primarily dependent on vision, tend to stumble and get lost. Such tendencies are clearly maladaptive, for they make routine actions dangerous and food gathering impossible. Lack of vision makes man easy prey. In these circumstances, the most adapative thing a man could do would be nothing. A man does not stumble if he does not move, and he uses less energy if not moving. However, in an organism built to respond, nonresponding is very difficult. Evolution might select for a mechanism that could insure nonresponding at the correct time; that is, when responding would be detrimental. Sleep is the perfect nonresponse. It can keep the curious quiet and the frightened still until daylight makes responding appropriate again.

Summary

Sleep as a state of consciousness has been variously discussed since the time of Aristotle. However, modern research has concentrated on changes in brain electrical activity as the defining characteristic of sleeping and waking, because this activity is similar from night to night and can be easily identified. Further, because the monitoring of brain activity causes relatively little sleep disruption, many topics are open to examination.

Sleep has been found to show striking changes with age and with the use of drugs. Sleep is also clearly dependent upon the length and placement of the previous sleep period. However, daily activities seem to have only minor influences on the sleep process. Several anomalies ranging from insomnia to enuresis, night terrors, and narcolepsy have been identified, examined, and where possible, treated.

Dreams have long been a fascination to mankind whether they were believed to be visitation by gods, curative, wish fulfillment, or a random collection of sensations. Their importance was under-scored with the discovery of their strong association with rapid eye movement (REM) sleep, a biological phenomenon. The importance of a biological tie is that REM sleep can be examined by physiologists as a central nervous system process. Such examination has led to the conclusion that, while there is no single sleep controlling center in the brain, several areas, primarily in the brain stem, are responsible for mediating sleep and waking and the stages within sleep. Unfortunately, even given such information, the function of sleep as a restorer, a protector, an escape, or a process to avoid exhaustion is still not known.

Glossary

Alpha: A brain wave with a frequency of 8–12 cycles per second which is produced when a person is in a relaxed, waking state.

Amphetamine: A stimulant drug.

Amplitude: The height of a wave from a reference zero point.

Condensation: In the Freudian system this refers to the fact that one dream symbol may represent several latent wishes.

Delta: High amplitude brain waves with a frequency of 1–3 cycles per second which are associated with deep sleep (stages 3 and 4).

Displacement: A process in which emotional responses associated with one thing or person are transferred to another thing or person.

Dream work: In the Freudian system, the means by which unconscious urges are transformed into dreams. Methods include condensation, displacement, and symbolism.

Electroencephalogram (EEG): A graphic record of the electrical activity of the brain found by placing electrodes on various parts of the scalp.

Enuresis: Bed wetting during sleep.

First night effect: Sleep on the initial night in a strange environment differs from normal sleep in that there is more stage 0, more stage 1, more awakenings, and less REM than normal.

Frequency: The number of cycles or repetitions per second of a wave.

Insomnia: The inability to go to sleep or to remain asleep. More specifically, a person is usually defined as an insomniac if that person normally takes longer than 30 minutes to fall asleep, awakes five times or more during the night, sleeps less than six hours, and would like to sleep more but cannot.

K-complex: A low frequency, high amplitude brain wave which is characteristic of stage 2 sleep.

Latent dream content: This is the Freudian term that refers to unconscious urges which are at the base of dreams but which are unacceptable to the conscious mind and must therefore be transformed into the manifest dream content by dream work.

Locus coeruleus: A nucleus located in the middle part of the pons lateral to the Raphé. The locus coeruleus is thought to play a large part in the initiation of REM sleep and concomitant bodily activities.

Manifest dream content: The Freudian term that refers to a dream as it is literally reported.

Narcolepsy: A disorder, possibly genetic, in which irrestible attacks of sleep occur at inappropriate times. In varying degrees, narcolepsy affects .05 percent of the population and may be characterized by a sleep onset REM period.

Raphé: A series of nuclei extending from the upper edge of the medulla to the back of the midbrain. The Raphé, is thought to control the onset of NREM sleep.

Rapid eye movements (REMs): Eye movements that are characteristic of human sleep and appear about every 90 minutes during the sleep period. Their occurrence is highly associated with the report of dreams.

Scanning hypothesis: An hypothesis that eye movements during REM sleep correspond to the dreamer actually "watching" his dream.

Sleep spindle: A brain wave of frequency 14–16 cycles per second, usually 1–2 seconds long that helps to characterize stage 2 sleep. It somewhat resembles a sewing spindle in appearance.

Symbolism: The use of one object to represent another object the latter of which might be objectionable to think about in itself.

Tolerance: A physiological process by which the body adjusts to a particular drug dosage, after repeated taking of the drug. The drug becomes ineffective, and increased amounts of the drug are then needed to be as effective as the original dose once was.

Suggested Readings

Dement, W. C. *Some Must Watch While Some Must Sleep*. San Francisco: W. H. Freeman, 1972.

Faraday, A. *Dream Power*. New York: Berkeley Publishing, 1972.

Freud, S. *The Interpretation of Dreams*. New York: Avon, 1965.

Kleitman, N. *Sleep and Wakefulness*. Chicago: University of Chicago Press, 1963.

Luce, G. G. and Segal J. *Insomnia*. Garden City, N.Y.: Doubleday, 1969.

Webb, W. B. *Sleep the Gentle Tyrant*. Englewood Cliffs, N.J.: Prentice-Hall, 1975.

Developmental Psychology

Yvonne Brackbill

Introduction

During the first 1,800 years of our history A.D., philosophers made occasional armchair forays into childhood, such as the role of the state in the upbringing of children (Plato, Aristotle), whether the child's nature is basically bad (Locke) or good (Rousseau). But it was not until a century ago that children became a special focus of empirical study rather than speculation. During these last one hundred years, several famous persons have made significant contributions to the study of childhood, both in terms of what they studied and the *methods* they used to study it.

The great naturalist, Charles Darwin, turned his attention to the young human animal after four decades of studying nonhuman animals. The object of this scrutiny was his infant son; the topic, the origin of emotions; and the method, that of *observation* under natural conditions. Darwin published his observations in 1877 as "a biographical sketch of an infant."

The *questionnaire* as a method of study was popularized by G. Stanley Hall, who is generally regarded as the father of American child psychology. Hall and his students collected questionnaire data about children on many topics ranging from children's prayers to children's fears. The first results of this prodigious effort were published in 1883 under the intriguing title, "The Contents of Children's Minds."

Sigmund Freud used *psychoanalysis* as a method of retrospectively studying the childhood antecedents of adult personality. Although this theory of psychological development is grounded in the significant events of infancy and childhood, Freud, himself, never psychoanalyzed a child. Rather, he constructed his account of childhood personality from the personal narratives of adult patients.

Testing as a method of studying children was introduced by Alfred Binet at the turn of the twentieth century. Binet's goal was the practical one of sorting out French school children in terms of their ability levels. His "Experimental Study of Intelligence" appeared in 1903, and in 1905, together with Simon, he published the famous treatise on "The Necessity of Establishing a Scientific Diagnosis of Inferior States of Intelligence."

Pavlov's early work on conditional reflex formation in dogs inspired many to use similar *laboratory-experimental methods* in investigating learning in other organisms. In 1907, Krasnogorskii in Russia and Bogen in Germany published accounts of classical conditioning in young children. In the United States, where Pavlov's techniques were becoming Americanized, Watson (with Rayner, 1920) published the first operant conditioning study of a child.

At the same time that rigorously controlled laboratory-experimental methods of research with children were getting under way in the United States, the Swiss scientist, Jean Piaget, began a long series of studies using a *"clinical"* technique of observation, interviewing, and the like that was far removed from the closely controlled standardization fashionable in contemporary American research. Piaget's theories have had considerable impact on our way of looking at the development of language, perception, and cognitive processes in children.

All of the systematic methods of child study just described are *cross-sectional* in nature. That is to say, they are methods by which children are studied once and not again so that any age comparisons involve different groups of children at the ages to be compared. In the 1920s, Lawrence K. Frank, then director of the Laura Spelman Rockefeller Foundation, made large sums of money available for *longitudinal* research in child development, that is, research in which the same children are seen repeatedly over a period of their development. Longitudinal research is essential, he argued, if we want to find out which psychological characteristics are stable and which change with age. Thus inspired and funded, many major universities in the United States initiated longitudinal programs (some of which are still viable two generations later) that have altered significantly and permanently the nature of psychological research with children.

With this introduction on methods of child study and the men who introduced these methods, we move on to consider *why* psychologists study children.

Why Psychologists Study Children

Scientists who study the psychological development of children do so for different reasons. Some are children-oriented. These investigators are primarily interested in children: their general development, their welfare, and so on. Other investigators are process- or function-oriented. They are primarily interested in a substantive area of psychology (such as personality or comparative psychology), and their interest in children stems from a desire to study this area at a simpler level than that represented by the complex adult. For example, as psycholinguists become more involved in a nature-nurture controversy—that is, whether language stems mainly from the unfolding of innate tendencies or is learned—psycholinguists look to the young child who is just beginning to speak as the most appropriate subject of research.

Thus forewarned, the reader will be prepared for different emphases within the typical conglomerate called "developmental psychology." In some areas, the child comes through clearly as a real, whole, developing person. In other areas, the developing process is the primary focus of study while the developing child provides the background. In this chapter, we will focus on processes, but only on those that are distinctly developmental (that is, that show outstanding changes with age). These areas include development of sensation and perception, cognition, language, and socialization. Before proceeding to describe developmental changes in these areas, we will consider some general principles of development.

Continuity of Development

We are in the habit of thinking of prenatal (before birth) and postnatal (after birth) states as two separate existences rather than as a continuous developmental process. Thus, we start assigning ages at the point at which an infant is born rather than at the time it is conceived. This way of referencing development to birth is inaccurate and misleads us in many ways. For example, we group together babies whose chonological (postnatal) ages are the same but whose prenatal ages were so different that the premature may never catch up with the full-term infant in structural and functional development. As another example, we use chronological ages in comparing infants of different species whose structural and functional ages are grossly unequal at the point in development when they happen to be born (see Figure 14-1). The timing of birth is an evolutionary outcome that reflects many circumstances of which development is only one, and it is developmental age that we are really interested in, not chronological age or birth date.

Development means literally the extent to which something unfolds or makes good its potential. Ideally, we measure it in terms of the degree to which present level of functioning approximates adult level. Developmentally speaking, the only way in which the postnatal state differs from the prenatal state is that the baby is no longer a passive recipient of events. The baby now must begin to cope for itself. It must do its own breathing in

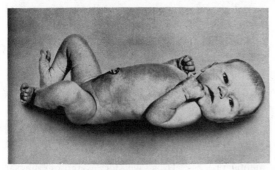

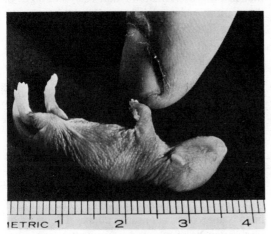

Fig. 14-1. These newborn animals—the guinea pig, human being, mouse, and opossum—are the same chronological age. Clearly, they are in different stages of structural development. They are also in very different stages of functional development. (Opossum, William Jurgelski, Jr., mouse and guinea pig, from Gottlieb, 1971, photos by Rainer Foelix; human infant, Maternity Center Assc., New York)

order to get air, and must start sorting out those incoming stimuli that have biological significance from those that have no significance. We use chronological age as an index of development because it is a convenient, easily calculated, readily verifiable index. But we must remember that it is also an inexact, imperfect index and that our real concern as students of psychology is with developmental age, not chronological age.

Structural Development

The course of physical development from conception to adulthood is not an even one. Figure 14-2 illustrates this in terms of weight gain from early prenatal development through adolescence. Clearly, the human body has two unusually fast periods of growth (growth spurts), one lasting from time of conception to about the end of the first postnatal year and the second occurring at adolescence. This unevenness in overall physical development is matched by unevenness in growth of different parts of the body. During its fetal-infant growth spurt, the most remarkable physical aspect of the human organism is its very large head relative to the size of its body. During the adolescent growth spurt, legs grow long before shoulders grow wide; feet and hands reach adult size while the rest of the body is still growing.

In neurological development, there is one major growth spurt, extending from early prenatal period to about 18 months of postnatal age. (See Chapter 4 for further discussion.) Here too, as is the case with physical development, different parts of the nervous system develop at different rates, as shown in Figure 14-3.

Growth spurts are more than just academically interesting. They are important because they represent *sensitive* or *critical periods* in development,

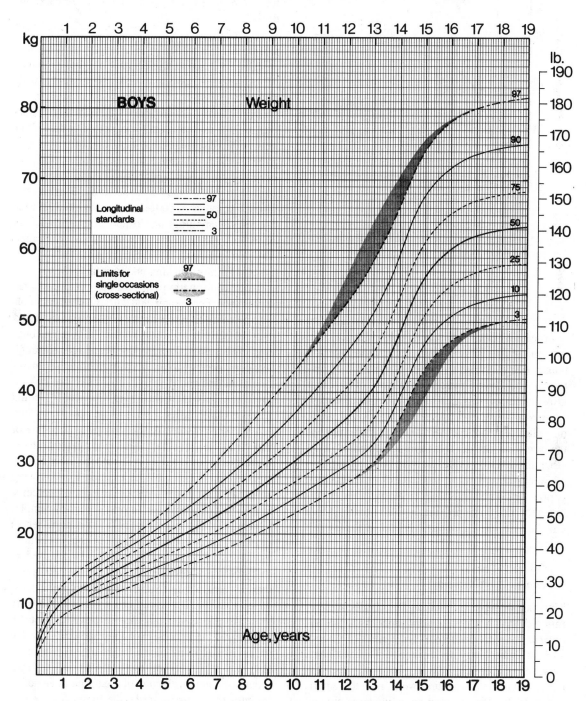

Fig. 14-2.   The uneven course of physical development from prenatal stage through adolescence. (J. M. Tanner)

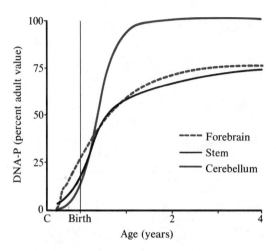

Fig. 14-3.   Growth of different parts of the brain. Notice that central nervous system development continues well beyond birth (Dobbing and Sands, 1973)

that is, periods during which a maturing function or process is maximally sensitive to influences that may modify its development permanently. In the human being, the sensitive period for limb formation is the first trimester (90 days) of prenatal growth; during this period teratogenic (literally, *monstrosity-forming*) agents such as thalidomide may alter development permanently. In the puppy, the sensitive period for forming attachments to other animals, to people, and to places is from 3 to 12 weeks of age while in the duck, the sensitive period for attachments begins shortly after hatching and ends in approximately 24 hours. (More will be said later about attachment in the human being.)

Functional Development

Thus far, we have been talking largely about maturation of structures. *Structural* (anatomical) *development* is a vital concern to some areas of science such as embryology and anatomy. Psychologists, however, are concerned with *functional development,* that is, how structures work, how these parts are used by the developing animal or human. Structure and function are not perfectly correlated. For normal children of the same age, brain struc-

tures are remarkably similar, whereas the behaviors of these same-aged children are remarkably diverse.

Obstacles to the Study of Functional Development.   To study and understand the development of behavior is no easy task, particularly with younger children. Consider the difficulties in studying infant development scientifically. First, the infant is unmotivated to cooperate or do well in any study. The infant may be afraid of the strange experimenter. It may interrupt investigations by crying, by frequent demands to be fed, or by falling asleep in the middle of the study. Further, the infant's response repertoire is very limited. It cannot tell us anything, and cannot use a pencil and paper to write down his or her answers. The range of motor responses is pretty much limited to kicking and flailing, sucking and turning its head.

To get information out of a baby requires a resourceful experimenter and an advanced technology. Seventy-five years ago, William James stated that the newborn's world was a "blooming, buzzing confusion." Twenty-five years ago, although less convinced of total chaos, psychologists maintained that newborn infants could not see colors, could not be conditioned (see Chapter 9), could not do a whole variety of things we now know they can do. The reasons for this change in our state of knowledge are twofold. First, psychologists have shifted from an interest in describing how behaviors develop "normally" to an interest in knowing how early an infant *can* do things or perceive things under optimal conditions (see, for example, Fitzgerald and Brackbill, 1976). Second, recent years have brought great improvements in technology, methodology, and in the hardware used to study behavior development. Of course, these two reasons are related. Some of psychology's most creative techniques have been created specifically to study and understand infant development. In any event, the net result of these advances is that we no longer think of the infant as either a blank slate or an object of total confusion. Instead, today, psychologists think of the infant as an active initiator of events, describe the infant for the first time in history as "competent," and take whole chapters or books to index its skills. Bearing this in mind, the reader should anticipate—should hope, in fact,—that today's accurate catalog of infant accomplishments will become tomorrow's obsolete list, of interest chiefly to the historian.

We will now go on to describe the results of research on psychological functions that show marked changes during the course of development.

Sensory and Perceptual Development: The Child Takes in the Environment

Psychologists have been interested in knowing whether some sensory functions develop sooner than others. The different sensory functions are linked to different brain structures. These structures mature during infancy, and they mature at different rates, as we saw in Figure 14-3. One would expect that those sensory modalities that are structurally linked to the most primitive, earliest developing brain structures would develop before those modalities that are structurally part of newer, later developing brain structures. This is true in general. At birth, or shortly thereafter, the baby is able to distinguish basic smells and tastes and is highly sensitive to tactile stimulation (touch) and to changes in bodily position (proprioceptive/vestibular stimulation), as well as pain. These are all sensory functions linked to "older" parts of the brain. Sensory functions mediated by "newer" parts of the brain are less fully developed at birth. The infant's auditory and visual capabilities (particularly the latter) must continue their development postnatally.

Development of Auditory and Visual Abilities. At birth, the infant can discriminate with surprising accuracy among a wide variety of sound stimuli. For example, the newborn infant can discriminate speech sounds from nonspeech sounds (Condon and Sander, 1974.) This is about the extent of the infant's ability to sort out auditory stimuli in terms of their importance or significance. The child must mature somewhat before it can use auditory stimuli skillfully, learning to respond to some stimuli but not to others.

The visual modality is probably the slowest to develop. This is not surprising since neither the

eye, the optic nerve, nor the visual cortex has finished developing at time of birth. All basic visual abilities—acuity, accommodation, tracking and scanning, brightness and color discrimination—show development and improvement postnatally. Much of this improvement takes place within the first six postnatal months. Some functions continue to develop beyond that age, however. Binocular vision does not finish developing until about three years of age (Banks et al, 1975). (Auditory and visual abilities were described in detail in Chapter 5. The interested reader is also referred to Appleton et al, 1975 and to Cohen and Salapatek, 1975.)

Requirements for Normal Sensory Development. The basic ingredient for normal sensory development is structural integrity of the receptors (sensory receiving apparatus). (These were described in Chapter 5.) There are requirements beyond structural integrity, however. For sensory and perceptual maturation to take place normally, the developing organism requires unrestricted sensory input, variation in that sensory input, and motor feedback from the sensory system itself and the body as a whole. For example, young chimpanzees and kittens who have been reared in darkness (no sensory input) suffer atrophy of essential parts of the visual apparatus, including retina and optic nerve. Even when they are reared in light but prevented from seeing patterned visual stimuli (as, for example, in a homogeneous visual surround made up of a room with walls of one color and no contrasts), they subsequently show visual deficits, particularly in form discrimination and depth perception. (See Figure 14-4.) Finally, young animals whose eyes are stimulated by both light and visual patterns but who are deprived of visually correlated motor feedback also show subsequent deficits in visual-motor behavior. For example, depriving the young organism of the opportunity to move its eyeballs or scan the stimulus, depriving it of the chance to see its own limbs (for example, by fixing a very wide collar around the neck), or simply by carrying it passively through a visual field rather than allowing it to locomote actively through that field, results in temporary or even permanent deficit in visually guided behavior, in perceptual

Fig. 14-4. A normal kitten, alert and tense, surveying the deep end of a visual cliff. Prior visual deprivation interferes with depth perception and hence the kitten's wariness of sudden dropoff. (William Vandivert and *Scientific American*)

motor coordination, and in ability to discriminate between self-initiated and externally-initiated movements. (The interested reader is referred to a review of this research in Riesen and Zilbert, 1975.)

The effects of deprivation on sensory and perceptual development have been most thoroughly studied in the visual modality. However, they are certainly not limited to that modality. Deprivation of auditory and tactile stimulation confirm the findings regarding the importance of early visual stimulation for subsequent normal development of perception and perceptual-motor function. Thus, for example, rats and ducks temporarily deprived of auditory input early on, experience later difficulties with auditory learning tasks under laboratory and natural conditions. (A recent review of the effects of early deprivation on later sensory development may be found in Riesen and Zilbert, 1975.)

To carry out similar experimental studies on

human beings is, of course, ethically impossible. Yet, there are some naturally occurring conditions that approximate those used in animal studies. Deafness is one such case. We can observe that deaf infants are not discernibly different in behavior or ability from their hearing counterparts as young infants. Nevertheless, they develop behavioral aberrations, particularly in the area of language, as they grow older. (See Chapter 11.) This is likely caused, at least in part, by the cumulative effects of auditory nonfeedback. Similarly, it is probable that the negative effects that institutionalization has on children are not wholly due to parental deprivation but stem in part from *sensory* deprivation, particularly insufficient variety of sensory input.

Response to Continuous Stimulation

When we talk about sensory abilities, we usually talk about the child's response to the onset or offset of a stimulus. What happens when a stimulus goes on and stays on continuously as a source of regular, unchanging, monotonous stimulation? Under these conditions, sensory stimulation affects more than just sensory functioning in the infant. It affects the whole state or basic level of functioning. Thus, for example, when one plays music (or any other form of continuous auditory stimulation) to an infant, the infant shows a marked decrease in heart rate, respiration rate, crying, and motor activity along with an increase in time spent asleep (Brackbill, 1971, 1975).

This pacifying effect of continuous stimulation is not restricted to the auditory modality, but occurs as well with visual stimulation, auditory stimulation, and so on. The proprioceptive-touch stimulation provided by swaddling (see Figure 14-5) is a very good example of the continuous stimulation effect. Further, the effect described above is more marked the greater the number of sensory modalities continuously stimulated. This pacifying effect of continuous stimulation is apparently a developmental one, depending in some way on central nervous system (CNS) maturation and integrity. That the effect can be seen in a rare experiment of nature, a baby born without a cortex, suggests that the pacification provided by con-

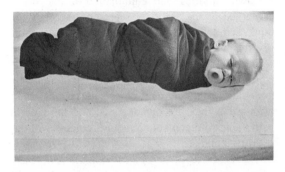

Fig. 14.5.   Effects of continuous proprioceptive-tactile stimulation through swaddling. Figure 5a shows an infant who has just been swaddled. The photograph in Figure 5b, taken a few seconds later, shows the infant already falling asleep. (Y. Brackbill)

tinuous stimulation is mediated at a primitive, subcortical level of the brain.

Preference for Certain Sensory Stimuli.   As a function of maturation, the infant not only comes to discriminate accurately among sensory stimuli, but also develops *preferences* for different types of sensory input. Since the infant cannot tell us whether it prefers one thing or another, we *infer* preference from behaviors indicating acceptance or pleasure (attention, smiling) as opposed to rejection and displeasure (turning away, crying). Considerable research has been done on the infant's visual preferences at successive chronological ages, particularly the preference for the human face over nonhuman visual stimuli, and preferences for one feature of the human face over another.

By the time an infant is two months of age, the face has become a compelling, powerful, and attractive stimulus for him. Within the following two months, the infant develops a definite preference for a face over a nonfacial stimulus of equal complexity. Although the infant prefers the facial features in their normal position, it does not pay attention to all features. Eyes are the first feature the infant attends to; later, it begins to pay attention to the mouth, then to the face as a whole (Gibson, 1969). Up to the age of about three months, a two-dimensional photograph of the face elicits smiling; thereafter, the face has to be three dimensional (Polak et al, 1964). By four months, not just any three-dimensional face will elicit smiling; the face has to be that of a parent or familiar adult. (Fitzgerald, 1968).

How such selectivity develops is an interesting question. As adult human beings, we like to believe that our offspring have preprogrammed, built-in preferences for humanoid sounds and objects and that they prefer as babies the same things we prefer as adults. Although preferences for sensory events do manifest themselves early on, the question of their origin, genetically based or shaped through learning, has yet to be clarified. Older babies who have always been fed warm formula prefer that to cold formula, but the newborn infant accepts refrigerated liquids as readily as warm (Holt et al, 1962). Similarly, as we have noted, babies develop a strong preference for the human face over nonfacial stimuli. Does this preference develop from an innate basis or from the fact that the face is the most frequently appearing stimulus in the infant's visual world? Does it come about through genetic determination or because facial stimuli signal the arrival of comfort and fulfillment of various biological needs? These and many more such unanswered questions are the domain of developmental psychology.

Cognitive Development: Intellect and Intelligence

Psychologists pursue the study of cognitive development in two ways. One approach is to understand the development of mental processes: thinking, problem solving, concept formation, and creativity (see Chapter 11 for a fuller discussion). The other approach is by testing mental abilities, chief among these being intelligence (see Chapter 18). We will examine these two approaches from a developmental framework.

Development of Cognitive Processes

Jean Piaget's theory and extensive research on cognitive development from infancy to adulthood dominate this area. Piaget's emphasis is on how we come to know what we do, not on how that knowledge is modified.

Four concepts are keystones to understanding Piaget's theory of cognitive development: *schemata, assimilation, accommodation,* and *equilibrium.* These concepts have to do with the way in which individuals process and store information and thoughts. *Schemata* are the inferred cognitive structures that change with development. Schemata have been likened to concepts, classification schemes, or segments of stored information (Wadsworth, 1971). Young children have but few schemata whose boundaries and contents lack precision and accuracy. Thus a child, having learned to call one man "daddy," is apt as well to categorize any other man as "daddy." With experience and development, the child's schemata change; they become more numerous, differentiated, and precise. *Assimilation* and *accommodation* are the processes that accomplish this change. Through assimilation, the individual sorts new information into already existing schemata (the non-daddy goes into the "daddy" category). Through accommodation, an existing schema is either modified to fit the new information, or a new schema is created (for example, a new category of non-daddy men). When the processes of assimilation and accommodation are in relative balance, Piaget speaks of that balance as *equilibrium.* Equilibrium is a kind of cognitive homeostasis—a state the individual tries to achieve when faced with imbalance or disequilibrium between assimilation and accommodation.

Schemata, assimilation, accommodation, and equilibrium are functions that describe cognitive processes at any age. They are not exclusive properties of childhood. What is distinctive about cognitive development?

Piaget sees cognitive development in sequential stages, with the child's progress through these being the result of a continuing interaction between the child's activity and environment. The first stage, which he calls the stage of *sensory-motor* intelligence, is marked initially by reflex functioning and lack of differentiation between self and objects in the environment. In this stage, which lasts from birth to about 2 years, the child is very action-oriented and cannot as yet pause to reflect on his or her own activities. The culmination of this period is marked by the ability to represent internally (to think symbolically). This inference is based on several behaviors making their appearance in the second year of life. Chief among these are the child's ability to imitate in the absence of a model; the child's behaving as if objects and people exist even when they are out of view; and the child's being able to reach solutions to problems without overt trial and error.

The next stage, *preoperational thought,* lasts from about 2–7 years. During this stage the child begins to use language and to think. However, this thinking is initially restricted in several important ways. Most notably, thinking is marked by (1) *egocentrism,* an inability to shift perspective from self to others; (2) *centering,* rigid attention to one aspect of a situation while resisting information input of a qualifying or contradictory nature; (3) *inability to comprehend transformations* from original state to end state; and (4) *inability to reverse* a train of thought from end state to original state. An example of the characteristics of preoperational thought is that the young child has not yet developed schemata to handle "conservation problems." "Conservation" refers to the fact that numbers, areas, volume, and weights remain the same despite changes in position or shape. For example, the preoperational child agrees that there are equal amounts of water in two beakers of the same size and shape. However, if the water from one of these is poured into another beaker of different size and shape, the preoperational child maintains that there is more (or less) water in the new beaker than there was in the old container.

The third stage of cognitive development, *concrete operations,* lasts from about 7–11 years. During this stage, the child is able to apply logical operations to concrete problems. He is now able to think about something from another's point of view, to consider more than one characteristic of a situation (decentering), to attend to the ways in which beginning states are transformed to end states, and to reverse his thinking from end to beginning state. The child at this stage is able to solve conservation problems, for example, it understands that changing the shape of containers does not change the amount of water they hold, or that placing five pennies in a long row does not make more pennies than five pennies placed in a short row. Note, however, that the effective operation of the child's logic at this stage is tied to concrete, tangible, visible problems.

The fourth state of cognitive development, *formal operations,* begins at about 11 years. The child's effective use of logical operations is no longer bound to concrete problems. It is now able to deal with abstractions, logical propositions, hypotheses, probabilities, and possibilities. When asked "If cows had three legs . . . ," the child is able to carry on and argue logically since its ability to analyze logically is no longer tied to concrete content.

The Growth of Intelligence

The measurement of intelligence began as a developmental problem when, in the late nineteenth century, the French government asked Alfred Binet to *assess* the current status of French schoolchildren and to *predict* their future potential for achievement. These two purposes of ability testing have remained the same over the years, although many other aspects have changed considerably, such as the content of tests, the methodology surrounding test construction, standardization, and so on.

Measurement of Ability During Infancy and Early Childhood. Psychologists have designed several tests to measure abilities at the infant and preschool levels. The most widely used of these is the Bayley Scales of Infant Development (Bayley, 1969) which may be used up to 4 years of age. Sample items from the Bayley scale are shown in Table 14-1. The reader will notice the very consid-

Table 14-1. Examples of Items from Bayley Scales of Infant Development

Age 4 months

Baby inspects own hands
Baby able to grasp red ring dangled in front of him
Baby turns head in direction of ringing bell
Baby reaches for a red cube placed in front of him

Age 10 months

Baby walks with help
Baby stirs with spoon in imitation of tester
Baby looks at pictures in a book
Baby imitates scribble

Table 14-2. Examples of Items from the Stanford-Binet Intelligence Scale

Age 4 years

Picture vocabulary. Child asked to name pictured objects such as hat, tree, umbrella.

Memory for objects. Child asked to name which one of 3 objects has been removed from display he just saw.

Picture completion. Child asked to finish an incomplete drawing of a man.

Comprehension. Child asked "why do we have houses?" "Why do we have books?"

Age 10 years

Vocabulary. Child defines correctly such words as scorch, muzzle, haste, and so on.

Cause-effect relationships. e. g. child asked to explain "Why should children not be too noisy in school"

Reading comprehension. Child asked to read a paragraph, then explain to tester what he has just read.

Memory for digits. Child must repeat from memory 6 digits which tester has just enumerated.

Word naming. Child asked to name as many words as he can in one minute.

erable difference in content between these items and those of tests for more mature children. This difference reflects the fact that the infant's behavioral repertoire is severely limited for testing purposes. The infant cannot read instructions or even understand them when presented verbally; it cannot write or use a pencil; and cannot respond verbally to the examiner's questions. Given these differences alone, one might suspect that the outcome of ability testing at the youngest ages would bear little relation to the outcome of intelligence testing at later ages. Indeed, this is the case. Predictability of later IQ from earlier scores is not feasible until about the fourth year of life.

Why this failure to predict? Among the most important reasons are these. First, infant ability tests do not measure what is conceptualized as intelligence in adults. As can be seen in comparing Tables 14-1 and 14-2, infant ability test items are largely sensory-motor in nature, whereas those of children's intelligence tests have a much broader base and more abstract nature. Second, infants have no "test-taking motivation." In other words, they do not yet desire to cooperate with an examiner, nor do they wish to do well on a test. A third reason for the failure to predict stems from the fact that infancy is a period of extremely rapid psychological as well as physical growth. During this period, the infant's emerging abilities often appear suddenly so that what the examiner does not find today, may very well emerge tomorrow. In addition, these newly emerging abilities are likely to be unstable with a consequent reduction in test reliability.

Intelligence During the School Years. Prediction to later IQ improves markedly by 4 years of age. The correlation between an individual's IQ measured at 4 years and again in adulthood is about .40. The size of this child-to-adult correlation increases to its maximum, about .90, by 10 years of age.

Prediction of school performance from IQ test scores alone typically has been reported as about .50. Predictability increases, however, when IQ is combined with a measure of motivation to achieve academically. When a child's IQ test score shows a higher level of ability than would be expected on the basis of his or her school achievement, educators speak of *underachievement,* meaning that the child is not living up to his or her potential. The converse situation is called *overachievement.* These are shorthand terms for describing the role of low versus high motivation as it interacts with measured intelligence.

Correlates of Intelligence Test Scores. Several variables show strong and consistent relationships to differences in IQ scores from early childhood onward. One such variable is family composition. Mean IQ decreases as the number of children in the family increases. Intelligence is also correlated with birth order, first-borns having the highest mean IQ, second-borns the next highest mean, and so on. Mean IQ is related as well to socioeconomic status, whether the latter is measured by prenatal occupation or income. Urban residents have higher mean IQs than do residents of rural areas. Race is also correlated with mean IQ, American blacks scoring 10 to 15 points lower than American whites, on the average (Shuey, 1966). Finally, although most childhood and adult IQ tests have purposely been constructed to eradicate sex differences, such have been found in a study of 27,000 4-year-old children, primarily from lower socioeconomic groups, in which mean Stanford-Binet IQ scores averaged 3 points higher for girls than for boys (Broman et al, 1975). It should be remembered that these differences are averages, that is, they are differences between group means. They do not hold for individual scores. For example, one cannot say that every 4-year-old girl has an IQ 3 points higher than every 4-year-old boy.

That the differences just described exist is an empirical fact and not open to question. However, the *interpretation* of such differences, that is, why they exist and how they develop, is open to question (see Chapter 18 for further discussion). Some arguments favor heredity as the principal factor in intelligence, whereas others favor environmental determinants. Additionally, in many such studies, methodological artifacts are allegedly responsible for the finding of differences. Currently a great deal of controversy is being generated over the issue of the relative contributions to IQ of heredity and environment, particularly with regard to racial differences.

Language: From Babbling to Speech

Language Precursors: The Development of Speech Sounds

At birth, the components of the vocal apparatus are present but their development and final structural configuration are not complete. Before the human infant can produce the sounds that adults agree are speech sounds, the oral cavity must grow, the larynx must descend into proper position, and the vocal tract must finish its general development. This does not take place until about 3–4 months of age.

Even before anatomical development is complete, however, the baby begins to produce a few vowel-like sounds. These steadily increase in variety. By about 2 years of age, the child can produce as many vowel sounds as can an English-speaking adult (depending on the classification system used). Mastery in the production of consonant sounds, of which there are 22 in English, takes longer—about 5 years. Generally speaking, vowels produced at the front of the mouth are mastered sooner than those produced at the back of the mouth, whereas back consonants are produced earlier than front consonants.

Two things should be noted about every speech sound development. First, the baby's phonetic production is not initially limited to speech sounds represented in the English language. The baby also produces sounds that do not occur in English but do occur in other languages. These gradually disappear from its repertoire—a phenomenon that has been called "phonemic contraction." A second interesting aspect of early speech, *sound production,* is that it lags behind speech, *sound recognition.* The newborn infant shows a remarkable ability to discriminate among speech sounds even though it will be some months before the infant can produce the same sounds. Similarly, in later years, the size of the vocabulary that the child actually uses lags behind the number of different words the child correctly recognizes. As a general rule, competence in language recognition precedes competence in langage production.

Developmental Milestones in Language

At birth, the outstanding vocal ability of the infant is its ability to cry; it can also cough, gurgle, sneeze, and breathe noisily. By 4–5 months of age, the infant begins to babble; these sounds are the first combination of vowels and consonants. From such "random" combinations, the infant's first word emerges by the end of the first year. During the lat-

ter part of the second year the child's vocabulary starts to increase very rapidly so that by the age of 5, a child uses over 2000 words.

Lateralization

The two hemispheres of the brain are not equally important for language development. It is generally believed that in most adults the left hemisphere receives, processes and stores speech sounds while the right hemisphere serves these functions for nonspeech sounds (see Chapter 4). This division of labor is called *hemispheric lateralization.* It is tested by presenting sounds separately to the two ears and noting whether differences in the behavioral or electroencephalographic (EEG) response are correlated with the differences in presentation. Recent evidence shows that lateralization begins to develop as early as the first year of life (Molfese et al, 1975). It has even been suggested that lateralization is greater in infancy than later, when the anatomical interconnections between hemispheres increase and mature.

Semantic Development: Meaning in Communication

Language is our means of communicating with other people. However, we are only able to communicate with those with whom our words and gestures share common meanings, that is, those having semantic commonality. How does this commonality develop? What is the relationship of language to cognitive processes; to perceptions, experiences, and thoughts? Do language and cognition develop independently? Do they develop in parallel or noninteractive fashion or does the development of one depend on and follow the development of the other?

The early German associationists believed that thinking and perception are independent of language and can occur without it. On the other hand, the early behaviorists downgraded the position of thinking, claiming that it is nothing more than internal representation of speech. Most theorists have adopted less extreme positions concerning the relation of language to cognition. Some hold that language and thought develop independently, whereas others hold that although language and thought are initially independent they later become one inseparable function. Still other theorists see langue and cognition as having a sequential, dependent order of development. An anthropological point of view holds that language precedes cognition, that it actually shapes what we see and how we think. An opposite point of view, held by Piaget and others, holds that language follows and depends on prior conceptualization. From this point of view, language is simply a medium for thought, the avenue by which thoughts are expressed. As one student of children's language put it, "By studying [speech], it is possible to discover the whimsical and elusive laws of childhood thinking" (Chukovsky, 1963, p. 15).

The reader may have concluded by now that the study of semantic development is an area richer in theory than in empirical evidence. There are, however, some general statements that can be made about the content of children's speech from Piaget's early investigations. Piaget found that early speech is *egocentric* in nature. That is, although the presence of another person may stimulate a young child to talk, the content of the child's speech is not purely conversational or communicative, because the child cannot yet adopt the point of view of the other person. At a later point in development, cognitive structures mature and communicative skills mature as a consequence. At this point, speech becomes *socialized*. A child now makes serious and increasingly successful attempts to take the point of view of its conversationalist counterpart; the child has graduated from the phase of "collective monologues" to true communicative interchange. (The reader is referred to Flavell, 1963, for a more detailed account of Piaget's theory.)

Syntactic Development

In addition to learning the meaning of words, the child must learn how to use them grammatically. The child must learn the grammatical rules that govern transformational changes in word usage (grammar, syntax) and that ultimately allow all the intricacy and accuracy in language that adult users demand. Chomsky's (1972) theory of "generative

transformational grammar" addresses itself to the question of linguistic competence and creativity, for example, how people come to use language innovatively, to understand and produce linguistic utterances that they have never heard or used before. According to Chomsky's followers (see, McNeill, 1970) children do not learn two sets of nouns, singular and plural, but rather one set of rules by which singular nouns are transformed into plural nouns. Similarly, they learn (generate for themselves through experience) rules by which simple sentences can be turned into complex ones, rules by which declarative sentences can be turned into passive voice sentences, and so on. In other words, language structure is said to develop by the child's acquiring a general set of rules from which that child subsequently and from then on generates particular, meaningful communications.

Correlates of Language Ability

Verbal skills show some strong and consistent correlations with demographic, social, and psychological factors. One such demographic factor is socioeconomic level. Statistically significant differences in verbal skills among children from upper and lower class homes appear shortly after the end of the first year and continue thereafter. Another factor strongly correlated with language ability is sex differences. It has been shown that, *on the average,* girls are consistently superior to boys in age of first speech, articulation, verbosity and verbal fluency, vocabulary, grammar, spelling, reading, and general verbal skills (Maccoby, 1966). Family composition also has a bearing on the development of language skills. Only children and firstborns score relatively higher than later-born children. Children born as singletons do better than twins, and twins better than quadruplets. Children from monolingual (for example, English only) homes generally have higher verbal ability than those from first generation immigrant and thus bilingual homes. The careful reader will note that these correlates of language skills are much the same as the correlates of tested intelligence. This should not be surprising, since verbal ability is the single largest component of intelligence test scores, so that when we talk about language ability and tested intelligence, we are talking about functions with considerable psychological overlap.

Language Acquisition: Learned or Innate?

We commonly talk about a child "learning a language." But do the laws of learning that apply in the laboratory and classroom hold as well for the nonlaboratory situation in which the child acquires the languge of those about? One major attempt to show that the laws of operant conditioning are sufficient to account for language development (Skinner, 1957) was roundly criticized by Chomsky (1959) who argued that mechanistic stimulus-response learning principles explain neither the complexities of language usage nor the intricate relation between language and cognitive variables. Chomsky holds that the child is preprogrammed for language in both its semantic and structural aspects. In other words, he believes that language is an innate process, that it is *generative* rather than learned as a long series of individual stimulus-response bonds, and that it follows laws of maturation rather than laws of learning.

Nevertheless, language development is modifiable through the experiences we commonly think of as learning. For example, Irwin (1960) showed that reading to infants from lower socioeconomic class homes for fifteen minutes a day significantly increased their vocalization rates, and that this increase was maintained as long as the reading program continued. Burtt (1941) showed that repeatedly exposing an infant to foreign language words made it easier for the child to learn those words for as long as a decade after their initial presentation. Moore (1967) has demonstrated that with proper management of the learning environment and motivational process, children as young as 3 years of age can learn to read and write. The process of phonemic contraction, whereby the child gradually loses the infantile ability to produce those sounds which are not part of its own native language, suggests that differential reinforcement plays an important role in acquiring a language. All such empirical evidence strongly suggests that language acquisition is not solely a matter of preprogramming and heredity, but is to a very considerable extent environmentally determined.

Social Learning

To socialize (v.t.): to render social, esp. to train for social environment. This Webster dictionary definition pinpoints the responsibility faced by parents and other members of the adult world—to turn the unsocialized infant into a civilized participant of society. We take this process for granted to such an extent that we forget the enormity of the task and its extreme importance. This can be judged, however, by considering the consequences of its absence. Imagine how negatively *you* would react to the appearance in your classroom of a classmate who, yelling and screaming, discards all his or her clothes, urinates on one student, hits another, and finally, thumb in mouth, plops down on the lap of a third. These are all behaviors that one finds in infants and very young children. Such behaviors are expected and tolerated at this age, but as the child grows older, tolerance for them decreases. What are the techniques that parents use to encourage more socially acceptable behaviors? What are the steps in the social learning process?

Attachment

Attachment is the basis for socialization. It is the cornerstone upon which social learning develops. By "attachment" we refer to two clusters of behavior. First, presumably because of the protection it ensures, the child seeks physical proximity or contact with the object of its attachment and resists being separated from that object. Second, the child seeks from that object attention and signs of approval.

Under normal circumstances, the first object of a child's attachment is the mother. Attachment soon extends to the father, then to other members of the nuclear (immediate) family, then to significant others in the extended family (grandparents and other relatives) as well as those outside the family. However, unusual circumstances show us that the object of early attachment does not have to be a mother or even an adult. Much stronger attachment to peers than to adults may occur if adults are not available and peers are. For example, Anna Freud and Dann (1951) have described the natural history of an unnatural grouping of six Jewish war refugee children who from birth were buffeted from one concentration camp to another, always as a group, but without any lasting contact with an adult. By the time they were brought to England in their fourth year of life, the closeness of their social and emotional ties to one another was as extraordinary as their disdain for any adult with whom they had contact.

Attachment is not restricted to one specie. A young rhesus monkey raised by a dog may show a stronger attachment to this foster parent than to another rhesus monkey (Mason and Kenney, 1974). Young geese raised by a human being attach themselves to and prefer that person to one of their own kind (Lorenz, 1937). Nevertheless, under normal circumstances the first object of attachment is generally the mother, and for the sake of convenience and brevity, we will speak exclusively of her in this role.

If the process of attachment tolerates so many variations, what are the minimum conditions for its occurrence? One condition certainly is that the object of attachment must be receptive to the formation of an attachment and be regularly available to the infant. Another is that there must be in the infant sufficient maturation of those sensory and response systems involved in attachment. Still another condition that interests psychologists and zoologists alike concerns age and time limits. It is generally thought that there are age/time constraints on the development of attachments, such that the infant-mother bond must be established during a *sensitive* or *critical period* and can be formed with difficulty or not at all when the infant is too young or too old. The lower age limit is set by the development of those sensory modalities that are a precondition to the development of attachment. The upper age limit can be determined experimentally by withholding an attachable object and seeing if attachments can be formed at a later age. Figure 14-6 shows the critical period for forming primary attachments in relation to other milestones in the puppy's development (Scott et al, 1974).

Whether there is an upper age limit to the establishment of early attachments is of great practical importance for human development. As mentioned earlier, the upper age limit can be determined by withholding an attachable object, but such an experimental procedure is restricted to nonhuman animal subjects. Ethical considerations deter us from such experimental manipulations with human beings. As a consequence, we are left with ethics intact but the question unanswered for human development. Among monkeys, depriving an infant of the chance to form a primary attachment to another monkey (mother or a peer) means that subsequent or secondary attachments may also be interfered with (Harlow, 1971). As an adult, the

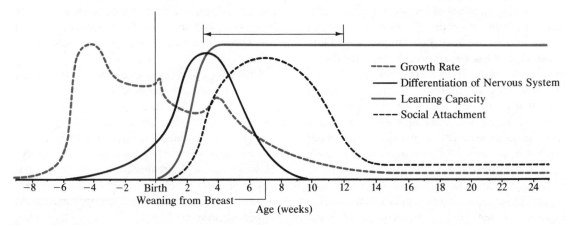

Fig. 14-6.   Critical periods in the dog's development. (Time is plotted in weeks.) The critical period for primary socialization extends from 3 to 12 weeks. (Scott et al., 1974)

deprived monkey may not develop a normal attachment to a mate or to its own offspring. Does the same hold true for human beings? Many psychologists claim that it does and cite for documentation such studies as those of parents who have battered their babies or studies of criminal repeaters, both populations of which show a high incidence of attachment failures during infancy. Sigmund Freud was probably the first to hold that socialized behavior depends on superego (conscience) formation, which, in turn, depends on attachment to a parent figure; and, once the human being has developed beyond the bounds of childhood, the strength of an overly developed or too rigid superego can be decreased through psychoanalysis but it cannot be increased through such treatment.

If the first step in social learning is becoming attached to significant figures in the socialized world of adults, the next step is building on that attachment a willingness to accommodate oneself to the demands of that socialized world. What are these demands? What does the young child do that is most at variance with societal standards?

For one thing, the infant demands to be fed at odd and inconvenient hours, he initially drinks his food rather than eat it, and plays with his food or throws it on the floor or at people. Thus, the infant needs to be weaned, to learn to restrain its desires to eat until others are ready for breakfast, lunch, or dinner, and then to eat in a civilized manner. Another set of uncivilized behaviors that the young child shares with young pets is the tendency to defecate whenever and wherever it pleases and, given the chance, to play with its feces or use these products of elimination in some way that society finds repellent and outrageous. Similarly, the infant is impulsive and aggressive; it engages in a variety of activities that are potentially harmful to itself and others; it plays with its genitals, it masturbates, and so on.

These then are the tasks of socialization, the behavioral reasons why the young child must be "rendered social," as Webster says. We will describe briefly when parents begin to modify and socialize these behaviors. Then we will go on to describe the ways in which they do it, that is, the disciplinary techniques they use.

Feeding and Elimination: Important Areas of Learning

In regard to feeding and weaning, most parents of today manage some sort of compromise with their babies so that they are fed neither rigidly by the clock nor completely on demand. In the United States, weaning typically begins during the second half of the first year; infants are able to complete the shift from sucking to drinking and eating by their first birthday. Many investigators have studied the possible relationship to later personality development of early feeding and weaning practices—principally the use of breast versus bottle to feed—and the earliness and abruptness of weaning (the transition from sucking to drinking). The results of these studies are inconsistent so that there is no clear evidence that feeding and weaning processes in and of themselves leave identifiable and lasting marks on the child's personality.

Weaning is not too difficult a task for the parent, since the child is hungry and the parent has what the child wants (food). In other words, the child's motivation to eat encourages acquiescence to parental demands. Toilet training is more difficult, because the child has what the parent wants. The relative distribution of power is not as one-sided as it is in weaning. Indeed, toilet training has been described by Freud as the first real power struggle between parent and child.

In the United States, the age at which parents initiate bowel training has increased gradually within the last few decades. In the 1940s, it was generally started before age six months. By the 1960s, the starting age had shifted toward the end of the first year. As is the case with weaning, there are wide variations in practices in other countries. For example, in the late 1950s, most English parents were beginning to "pot" their infants by age two weeks (Douglas and Blomfield, 1958). (Note that the muscles involved are not physiologically capable of control until the second half of the first year!) Generally speaking, the later the age of initiation the shorter the time required to complete bowel training. Bladder control is generally achieved after bowel training. (A review of studies on feeding, weaning, and elimination may be found in Caldwell, 1964.)

Consideration of the major tasks of early socialization leads us to ask how parents accomplish these goals, that is, what disciplinary techniques they use in socializing the child.

Disciplinary Techniques

Disciplinary techniques can be grouped along several dimensions, one of the most important being whether the parents use love-oriented or power-oriented methods. Cutting across this dimension is another important one—whether the technique is negative or punitive in nature as opposed to being positive or rewarding. Disciplinary techniques that are love-oriented and rewarding include the use of praise, distractions, and reasoning. Love-oriented, punitive techniques include isolation, withdrawal of love, and signs of disapproval (such as the "silent treatment"). Disciplinary techniques that are power-oriented tend for the most part to be punitive as well. Such techniques include physical punishment and verbal displays of force (such as commanding, screaming, threatening).

Disciplinary Techniques and Personality Development. Parents who are themselves loving and warm tend to use love-oriented techniques, whereas those who are cold, hostile, or outright rejecting tend to use power-oriented techniques. As far as the development of the child's personality is concerned, there are many investigators who believe that the use of love-oriented techniques is correlated with the development of internalized standards of control, morality, compliance, and responsibility. Conversely, power-oriented techniques are more closely associated with the development of responsiveness to external constraints rather than conscience (shame or fear of punishment rather than guilt) and higher levels of aggressiveness that are less adequately channeled into socially approved outlets.

Any account of disciplinary techniques may leave readers with the impression that all the child's behaviors are the result of directly applied rewards and punishments and that the laws of learning are sufficient to explain the acquisition of behavior. This impression would be incorrect. There are many things children do and many char-acteristics they display that have no apparent antecedents in directly applied rewards or punishments. For example, one of the best predictors of whether children and young adults will use drugs is whether or not their parents regularly smoke and consume drugs, such as alcohol, and sedatives (Blum, 1972). Parents serve not only as dispensers of reinforcement but also as models that their children imitate. The same can be said for peers as models in the child's later development. Recent research has proved what the church and village elders suspected all along, that parents serve as examples to their children. Thus, it has been found that exposing children to others' aggressive behavior subsequently increases their own aggression, that exposing them to altruistic, helping models increases their altruistic behavior, and so on.

Socializing Agents Shift from Family to Community

During infancy, the child's immediate family is ordinarily the exclusive focus of its affectional concern. The child's response at this stage to strangers is typically one of disinterest, apprehension, or fear. By the time the child reaches three to five years of age, the child usually meets other children of similar age (peers) who are neighbors or part of a preschool group. At this age there is very little in the way of real interaction. Instead, the children are most apt to engage in *parallel play,* that is, individual play in which the children have physical but not psychological proximity. For example, if you walk into a nursery school class you will see children sitting on the floor, next to others, but engaged in their own activity. By the time the child enters school, the child also enters the social world of peer interactions as well as relations with significant adults outside the nuclear family. The social horizons of childhood are broadening and will continue to do so up through adolescence. At the same time, the amount of contact the child has with parents is decreasing. This reciprocal relationship between family and nonfamily sources of socialization is shown graphically in Figure 14-7.

It is not surprising that along with a shift in amount of time spent within and outside the fam-

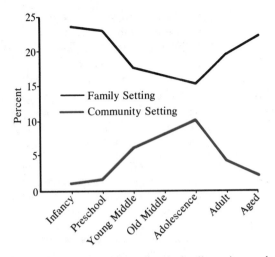

Fig. 14-7. Percent of time spent in family settings and community settings from infancy through old age. (After Wright, 1956)

ily, there is a shift in the psychological significance of these two influential spheres of the child's development. Peer groups gradually become a dominant force in the child's life until as an adult, the person settles down to form a family of his or her own. Note, however, that although the relative influences of family and community may be reciprocal, they are not in conflict unless the goals set by parents and peers conflict.

What we have been describing typifies middle-class, urban, American children. What happens under other conditions to the relative influence of family and peer groups? Although this is something we cannot manipulate experimentally in a laboratory, some other cultures provide us with "natural" experiments.

In urban areas of the Soviet Union, many preschoolers attend full-day nursery schools. For the school age child, peer group contact is even more extended. Soviet schools meet five and one-half days per week, and a rich program of extracurricular activities engage the child's after-school hours. Peer contacts are highly important for another reason: beginning with entrance to primary school and continuing throughout the life span, the peer group is empowered to evaluate each partici-

pant's behavior respecting conformance with the goals of the group in particular and the goals of the society in general. These evaluations are not incidental, random, or casual but are carried out at regular intervals under formal conditions in group meetings. Such group evaluations begin with school groups and Young Pioneers, then continue as part of all major groups to which the developing individual will belong, including professional or working group, multi-family dwelling group, and so on. Under such circumstances, the influence of the peer group relative to that of the nuclear family is greater in the Soviet Union than in the United States. (For a readable account of Soviet philosophy on monitoring morality, see any of the novels by A. S. Makarenko; for example, *Learning to Live*, 1953, or Bronfenbrenner, 1970.)

The Israeli living group, or kibbutz, provides another example of relatively strong peer group influence. In the kibbutz, children are cared for in residential groups from early infancy, only visiting their parents, both of whom work in the fields, briefly each day. Thus, in the kibbutz, the residential nursery is home base, while in the Soviet Union the child's home base is still the nuclear family. One consequence for children of both cultures is a high degree of conformity to peer values (Spiro, 1958). However, since both cultures have strong and explicit ideological values emphatically conveyed in peer groups, there is relatively little conflict between adult and peer values.

Relation of Child to Other Group Members. The extent to which the child is influenced by a peer group is one thing. Quite a different subject is the extent to which the child influences the group or is accepted by the group. What determines the child's social status within a group? Psychological research consistently finds several variables to be correlated with popularity. An averaged profile of the popular child shows one who is friendly and outgoing, cooperative and capable of seeing situations from another point of view, well-adjusted, one who is bright and does well in school, who is a later-born or only child, who is from the middle or upper class, and whose relations with parents is a good one (Hartup, 1970).

Sex Differences in Psychological Development

Biologically, there are many ways in which men and women differ, from overall physique to finest aspects of neurological structure. In most societies, including our own, there are also vast differences in social, economic, and political roles played by men and women. There are very few families in which husbands stay home to care for house and children; there are also very few industries or governmental posts in which women hold high executive positions. As psychologists, we are concerned to know whether there are such profound and varied sex differences in psychological characteristics as well. Child psychologists ask the further question: what is the developmental history of psychological sex differences?

The answer to the first question appears to be that psychological differences are not as profound and varied as biological differences or those imposed by the social, economic, and political systems. At least they are not as extensive as people tend to think they are. Maccoby and Jacklin (1974), who recently surveyed the research on sex differences, conclude that many of the psychological characteristics we think of as differentiating males from females are in reality myths or prejudices, unsupported by empirical evidence. Thus, Maccoby and Jacklin demonstrate from their careful review of the literature that, despite beliefs to the contrary, there are no differences between men and women in sociability, suggestibility, self-esteem, learning or achievement motivation, or in the relative contributions of heredity and environment to their behavior. There are other psychological characteristics that may prove to differentiate between the sexes but for which evidence to date is insufficient or conflicting. These include competitiveness; dominance; compliance; "maternal" behavior; fear, timidity and anxiety; activity level; and tactile sensitivity. Those behaviors that show real sex differences are relatively few: girls excel in verbal ability, while boys excel in aggressiveness and in visual-spatial and mathematical abilities.

It is the task of the *social* psychologist to explain the causes and origins of the myths that persist regarding sex differences (see Chapters 15 and 17). It is the task of the *developmental* psychologist, however, to explain the etiology of those sex differences in behavior that are firmly established by empirical evidence. Four theories have been put forward regarding the development of psychological sex differences. In brief, they are:

1. That sex differences in behavior are a direct reflection of biological differences, including genetic factors. According to Maccoby and Jacklin, this theory has some validity for differences in aggression and in visual-spatial ability.
2. That sex differences in behavior result from differential parental reinforcement for such behaviors. That is, parents reward "feminine" behavior in girls and "masculine" behavior in boys while discouraging sex-inappropriate behaviors. "Reinforcement" includes both overt, directly administered rewards and punishments as well as more subtle means of shaping behavior.
3. That sex differences in behavior result from modeling, identification, or the child's imitation of the behavior of the same-sex parent, other adults, and peers.
4. That sex differences in behavior result from "self-socialization" through which the child acquires a generalized set of rules and beliefs.

(The interested reader should consult Maccoby (1966) for more detail regarding each of these four theories.)

Androgyny

Until recently, femininity and masculinity have been thought of as opposite and mutually exclusive characteristics. By this traditional way of thinking, a woman is feminine only to the extent that she is not masculine and a man masculine only to the extent that he avoids "feminine" behaviors under all conditions. Lately, this conception has been challenged on grounds of both validity and social desirability. It has been proposed that not all human beings fit the traditional classification. Instead, it is proposed that many men and women are neither exclusively masculine nor feminine but are *an-*

drogynous, that is, they possess both sets of characteristics and bring each to bear under situationally appropriate conditions. Thus, the androgynous individual can resist pressures to conform (a "masculine" trait) yet be playful and nurturant (a "feminine" trait) under different, and appropriate, circumstances (Bem, 1975). Because their behavior is responsive to the demands of the situation, it is argued that androgynous individuals are more flexible and that androgyny is the most adaptable role for the changing needs of society and for the individual's mental health. What are the characteristics of parents and family life that foster androgyny in children? It has been speculated that androgyny is more likely to be cultivated in egalitarian homes where neither parent dominates the other or the family. [The interested reader will find a fuller discussion of this topic in Bem (1975).]

Summary

In this chapter, we have presented an overview of the history of developmental psychology, the methods used in developmental research, some general considerations regarding developmental research, and a description of some psychological areas that show marked developmental changes: sensation and perception, cognition, language, socialization, and sex differences. Discussions of some other very interesting developmentally related topics can be found in other chapters of this text.

Glossary

Adolescence: The period of life between onset of puberty and adulthood.

Androgyny: Possessing both male and female characteristics and bringing each to bear under situationally appropriate conditions.

Attachment: We infer that a child is attached to a person or object when (1) the child seeks physical proximity or contact with that person or object and resists being separated from it, and/or (2) the child seeks attention and signs of approval from that person.

Childhood: The period of life between infancy and adolescence.

Cross-sectional: Research design in which children are studied once rather than longitudinally and in which age comparisons involve different groups of children rather than the same children at different ages.

Development: Refers to both the process and extent of behavioral maturation or change through time. Usually indexed as age-related change.

Growth spurt: Period of unusually rapid physical development. Two such major periods are during (1) prenatal-infancy and (2) adolescence.

Infancy: The first few months of life; frequently, by convention, the first 12 months.

Longitudinal: Research design in which the same children are studied on repeated occasions, that is, at successive ages.

Socialization: The techniques and process of turning the child into a civilized participant of society, of imbuing the child with morals and manners.

Suggested Readings

Botwinick, J. *Aging and Behavior.* New York: Springer, 1973.

Bronfenbrenner, J. *Two Worlds of Childhood: U.S. and U.S.S.R.* New York: Simon & Schuster, 1970. (Available in paperback)

Lefrancois, G. R. *Adolescents.* Belmont, Cal.: Wadsworth, 1976.

Richards, M. P. M. *The Integration of a Child into a Social World.* Cambridge, England: Cambridge University Press, 1974.

Wadsworth, B. J. *Piaget's Theory of Cognitive Development.* New York: David McKay, 1971.

White, S., and Welsh, B. eds. *Human Development in Today's World.* Boston: Little, Brown, 1976.

15

Social Behavior

Marvin E. Shaw

Introduction

The preceding chapters have made it abundantly clear that human behavior is a complex phenomenon. Behavior is determined by a wide range of variables and appears in many diverse forms. When we consider *social behavior,* the phenomena become infinitely more complex. The term social behavior refers to all behavior that is influenced by human beings and their products. Consequently, social behavior includes not only behavior that is influenced by the presence and behavior of other persons, but also behavior that is influenced by the inventions of humans. And our products may be tangible objects such as buildings and machines or intangibles such as social roles, rules of conduct (norms), and social attitudes. It is not difficult to understand the wide-range effects of these products on behavior.

Social behavior falls into three broad classes or categories of behavior: (1) *Individual social behavior*—behavior that is essentially individualistic and idiosyncratic, but that is, nevertheless, influenced by social factors. Perception, motivation, and learning are examples of this class of social behavior. (2) *Shared individual social behavior*— behavior that is individualistic but is shared by most members of a social group. Social attitudes, concepts of personal space, and social norms are examples of this kind of social behavior. (3) *Interpersonal behavior*—behavior that occurs when two or more persons interact, either face-to-face or

less directly as through an exchange of letters or via the telephone.

Social behaviors vary widely with respect to acceptability by members of society. Some behaviors are viewed as appropriate and are accepted by almost everyone; other behaviors are acceptable to some and rejected by others. When the latter kinds of behavior are sufficiently important to members of the society, they become social issues (for example, racial prejudice, social aggression, political orientations, and so on.) See Chapter 16 for further discussion. Social issues will be considered in the next chapter; this chapter will deal with less controversial, but equally important, aspects of social behavior. Specifically, we will examine person perception, attitudes, interpersonal attraction and affiliation, personal space, and behavior in groups.

Person Perception

Perception, as we have seen, is a crucial aspect of psychological behavior. Our perceptions of the world around us exert a powerful influence on our orientation to it and on all aspects of our behavior. Social perception, which includes the effects of social factors on perception and the perception of other people, is perhaps the single most important part of perception, because it determines our behavior with respect to other persons and groups. It is, therefore, of great significance not only to our day-to-day interactions with others, but also to the very existence of society.

Basically, the process of *social perception* is the same as perception in general: it is *selective* and *organized*. The individual selects from a vast array of objects only those objects that are of interest and significance to that person, who then organizes the separate parts of these perceptions into meaningful wholes. Social factors often determine which parts of the individual's world he or she will choose to perceive and how the things that are selected become organized into unitary wholes. However, the perception of other persons involves one aspect that ordinarily does not occur in the perception of physical objects such as tables and chairs. Persons are perceived to have intentions, motivations, and attitudes, and the attributions of these characteristics may be the most significant determinant of person perception. For example, persons or groups may be forgiven for actions that produce bad effects, if they are perceived to have good intentions, and actions that result in good outcomes may be castigated if seen as arising from evil intentions.

Person perception is a multi-faceted phenomenon, and it is difficult to decide which facet should be examined first. Somewhat arbitrarily, we will ask first about processes of person perception (that is, impression formation, attribution processes), and then consider the question of accuracy of perceptions.

Impression Formation

When two persons meet for the first time, each seeks to learn as much about the other person as possible. How intelligent is the person? What does he or she do (occupation)? Is the person interesting or a bore? Dominant? Submissive? Aggressive? And much more. The person seeks this kind of information partly out of curiosity, but the information also serves a useful purpose. It enables each person to know how to behave in the presence of the other. This process of impression formation is an important event not only during the initial encounter, but also in every interaction between two individuals. Although the process of impression formation occurs most rapidly during the first meeting, it is a continuous process, and the first impression of another may not stand the test of time.

During an encounter, each person is not only trying to learn as much as possible about the other person, but at the same time, each is engaging in a process known as *self-presentation* or *impression management*. That is, each person is trying to create a particular impression on the other person. Sometimes this attempt is deliberate; for example, when the situation is a job interview. More commonly, however, the person is unaware that he or she is trying to create a particular impression; it is so habitual that the person acts without conscious thought.

An individual often forms an impression of another person on the basis of very limited information. This fact was demonstrated dramatically by Asch (1946) in a very simple fashion. Individuals were given a list of adjectives (for example, intelligent, skillful, industrious, warm, determined, practical, cautious) and asked to write a description of the person having these characteristics. The respondents were able to write rather detailed descriptions of the person, including much "information" not contained in the adjective list. Once the impression of the hypothetical person has been formed, it is difficult to change. When respondents were given two lists and described two hypothetical persons, and then told that the lists applied to the same person, they had great difficulty combining their impressions. Some traits seem to be more *central* than others in that they alter the interpretation or meaning of other traits. "Warm" and "cold" are examples; a warm and determined person is usually perceived as one who perseveres in the face of difficulty, whereas a cold and determined person is often seen as a ruthless individual who will stop at nothing to have his or her way. Which characteristics are central, however, depends on the particular other characteristics the person is believed to possess.

First impressions often dominate later impressions, but this is not always the case. If a list of traits like those used by Asch are given in reversed orders, those traits appearing early in the list exert stronger influences than those appearing near the end of the list. However, favorable first impressions are more easily changed by negative information than unfavorable impressions by positive information about the person. Unfavorable information about a person is less ambiguous than favorable information, since positive behavior may be explained either by social conformity or by dispositional characteristics of the individual.

The evaluative aspect of the impression that we have of another person is probably the most significant one for social behavior. If individuals are evaluated positively (favorable impressions), we are likely to want to affiliate with them, be willing to do favors for them, cooperate with them, and generally respond to them in congenial ways. On the other hand, negative evaluations (unfavorable impressions) often lead to avoidance, hostility, aggression, or other forms of antisocial behavior. Whether a given person is evaluated positively or negatively depends on the kinds of characteristics that person is perceived to have or that are attributed to him or her. This process will become more understandable after we discuss attribution processes.

Attribution Processes

The perception of personal characteristics and the attribution process are not entirely separate events. Those who study the perception of persons make the assumption (at least implicitly) that personal characteristics are actually present in the person and the problem is merely one of detection. Consequently, the question most often asked is how accurately one person can detect (perceive) the characteristics of others (such as, emotions, personality traits). In contrast, those who study attribution processes make no assumptions about the reality of that which is attributed to others; whether the attribution is "accurate" or not becomes an irrelevant question. Consequently, the study of perceptions involves both the perceiver and the thing perceived; the study of attributions emphasizes the attributor. However, it should be clear that when an individual believes that another has certain attributes, his or her behavior will be influenced in much the same way, whether or not the other person actually possesses these attributes.

Many readers already know a great deal about attributions, although you may not have given it much thought. Consider, for example, a university football team that wins an important game; stu-

dents who attend the university are likely to say, "*We* won the game." But suppose the team loses? Then, *they* lost the game. We tend to take credit for successful outcomes and deny responsibility for unsuccessful outcomes, even when we have not directly contributed to the action (Jones and Nisbett, 1976). But more importantly for social behavior are the attributions that are made to others. Generally speaking, when a person does something that has relevance for another person, the other wants to know the reasons for the person's actions. If a man does something that annoys you, did he intend to hurt you or was the effect an unintentional byproduct of an attempt to achieve another purpose? If a woman does you a favor, does she have ulterior motives? The attributions that you make about the person's intentions will determine how you react, and eventually how you will evaluate that person.

When an effect or outcome is produced that involves an individual, that cause of the effect may be attributed either to the individual (*personal causality*) or to the environment (*impersonal causality*) (Heider, 1958). The degree to which effects are attributed to the person or to the environment depend on *distinctiveness, consistency,* and *consensus* (Kelley, 1967). If a given effect occurs when the person is present and does not occur when he or she is absent (distinctiveness), the person is more likely to be seen as the cause of the effect. If the actions of a person are consistent over time, effects associated with that action will probably be attributed to the person. For example, suppose a male friend is late for an appointment and you know from past experience that he is usually on time. You probably will attribute his lateness to circumstances, such as the afternoon thunderstorm or the heavy traffic. On the other hand, if you know that he is usually (consistently) late, you undoubtedly will attribute his lateness to a personal characteristic.

In some cases, a person may have little objective basis for making the attribution. In such instances, one often relies on consensus. Suppose that you are a member of a group that is trying to select a leader, and the question is whether person *X* has the necessary skills to be an effective leader. Whether or not you attribute these skills to person

X may largely depend on consensus among members of your group. Do others agree that X has these skills? If so, you probably will attribute them to X; if they do not, you will most likely assume that X does not possess the needed skills to be an effective leader.

One of the more important aspects of attribution for interpersonal behavior is the *attribution of responsibility*. The question here is whether another person should be held accountable for the effects produced by his or her actions. If a person is responsible, then that person is open to sanctions by others. If the effects are judged to be good, praise and reward are in order; if the effects are bad, blame and punishment are appropriate.

The degree to which an individual is held responsible for his or her actions depends on the *developmental level* of the attributor, the *quality* and *severity* of the outcome of the action, and the *circumstances* in which the action occurs. Developmental level is a function, primarily, of chronological age; young children use fewer criteria for making attributions than do adults. The quality of the outcome may be either good or bad; generally, a person is held more responsible for bad effects than for good effects, presumably because good effects may be due merely to conformity to social norms, whereas bad effects reflect undesirable personal traits. Also, the more severe the outcome, the greater the attribution of responsibility. The circumstances in which the action occurs that are important for attribution of responsibility are *association, commission, foreseeability, intentionality,* and *justifiability*. The circumstances, relative to the actor, involve association when the actor is associated with the outcome in any way, whether or not his or her actions actually produced the outcome. A member of the Ku Klux Klan may be held responsible for the actions of the group, even if that person was not actually present when the actions occurred. Commission is involved when the person's own action produced the results in question, whether or not that person could have foreseen or intended the outcome. Foreseeability refers to the degree to which the actor might have foreseen that his or her actions would produce the outcome. Intentionality is operative when the actor acts purposively; the outcome is the goal of the ac-

tion. Finally, an action may be justified because the actor is coerced or made an offer that could not be refused. For example, a person who kills another person in order to save his or her own life is held less responsible than one who kills without provocation.

The degree to which each of these circumstances is considered in making attributions varies with developmental level. In general, young children consider only association and causality, whereas most adults consider primarily foreseeability, intentionality, and justifiability. For most adults, very little responsibility is attributed when only association and commission are involved; attribution increases when the outcome might have been foreseen and reaches a maximum when the outcome is intentional. Less attribution occurs when the action is justified, even when the outcome was intended by the actor.

Accuracy of Person Perception

Although the behavior of the perceiver or attributor will be the same regardless of the reality of the perception or attribution, the consequences for interpersonal behavior may depend markedly on the degree to which the person's beliefs about another are reasonably *accurate*. For this reason, it is important to know about the degree to which one can accurately perceive the feelings, motives, and behavioral tendencies of others. For example, if one member of a two-party interaction believes that the other is angry, that member's actions will be quite different than if the other were seen as being afraid. These actions will be appropriate or inappropriate, depending on the accuracy of the perceptions of the emotion being experienced by the other person. And the other person's reactions will depend on the appropriateness of those actions. Thus, the entire pattern of interaction may depend on the accuracy of perception.

Most of the time, we are able to interact with others with relatively little conflict, suggesting that perceptions of personal characteristics are reasonably accurate. Numerous studies of person perception have raised some question about this "commonsense" notion. Many years ago a series of studies was conducted to measure degree of accuracy of the perception of emotions in others. Photographs of actors and actresses who had been instructed to express various emotions were shown to others who were asked to identify the emotion being expressed. Accuracy was very low, and it did not improve greatly when photographs of persons actually experiencing the emotions were used. However, accuracy improved markedly when situational factors were included. At the time these studies were conducted, it was concluded that we are able to perceive the emotions of others with some accuracy only when we know the circumstances eliciting the emotional experience. We now know that the low accuracy obtained in the early studies was, at least in part, a consequence of the terms that are used to label emotions. For example, a given emotion may be called love, mirth, or happiness, but never labeled fear or anger. When data from the early studies of judgment of emotions from facial expressions were reexamined to take into account these differences in labeling (that is, when highly similar labels were treated as referring to the same emotion), accuracy increased.

It is also important to accurately perceive the personality characteristics of others, since this information serves as a guide for interpersonal behavior. Unfortunately, it is very difficult to measure this kind of perception. The usual procedure is to measure personality characteristics in a group of persons by means of a standard personality test. This same test is then given to a group of judges who are requested to respond to the test the way they think the other persons did. The degree of correspondence between the two sets of scores is taken as a measure of accuracy. Again, accuracy is usually poor. However, there are many problems with this type of investigation, the most significant ones being those related to the personality tests. Personality tests are often of questionable reliability and validity, so that it is not certain that personality has been measured accurately. Furthermore, most personality tests are disguised so that the respondent does not know what his or her responses mean about his or her personality. It is unlikely that the judges will have this knowledge, which is of course necessary if they are to validly report their perceptions of the other person.

Despite the problems of measuring accuracy of perception of others, most people usually do not make grossly erroneous judgments about the feelings, attitudes, and behavioral tendencies of those persons with whom they associate. These judgments make possible social interactions that are usually coordinated and relatively conflict-free. However, when judgments about others are inaccurate, interpersonal conflicts often occur.

Attitudes

A particularly important personal quality is *attitude*. Persons in every culture develop attitudes about the significant persons, groups, and objects in their world. These attitudes influence social relations in many important ways. For example, a particularly pernicious kind of attitude is *racial prejudice,* which may result in various forms of antisocial behavior directed toward the object of the prejudicial attitudes. These include unfavorable statements about members of the race (antilocution), avoidance, discrimination, aggression, and sometimes extermination (for example, Hitler's attempt to exterminate the Jews). Favorable attitudes usually produce more positive responses, such as attraction and affiliation.

The Nature of Attitudes

An attitude may be defined as *a relatively enduring system of affective, evaluative reactions toward a social object or class of social objects.* It is a generalized feeling, positive or negative, toward persons or things in our world. An attitude is the result of the *evaluative beliefs* that the person has about the attitude object. An evaluative belief is one that includes an *evaluative concept.* This process of attitude formation will become clearer after we consider the nature and acquisition of evaluative concepts and beliefs.

As individuals grow up in a society, they acquire a large number of evaluative concepts. They learn that some things are good, desirable, worthwhile, preferable, and so on, whereas other things are judged to be bad, undesirable, worthless, and the like. In our own culture, we can think of such positive evaluative concepts as honesty, intelligence, truthfulness, cleanliness, cooperativeness, and so on; negative evaluative concepts are exemplified by laziness, dishonesty, brutality, and similar "bad" characteristics. Such concepts are acquired as a consequence of direct and/or vicarious reinforcement. For example, children may observe that others who are truthful are rewarded and that they themselves are given positive reinforcements when they tell the truth. Therefore, they learn that truthfulness is regarded favorably by members of the group and eventually they too accept truthfulness as "good." When this happens, they have acquired an evaluative concept called "truthfulness."

Evaluative beliefs are of the form, "Manatusians are truthful." Evaluative beliefs are acquired in much the same way as evaluative concepts. Imagine a small boy who has acquired a negative evaluative concept: dirty. This boy is walking down the street with his mother when they encounter a dog. The mother shakes her fist at the dog and says, "You dirty dog, get out of here." This may be accompanied by other indications of distaste for the dog. On subsequent encounters with dogs, the boy very likely will imitate his mother's behavior and be rewarded for it. When he says, "dirty dog," the mother may very well smile at him, pat him on the head, and in other ways show her approval to this response to the dog. In a similar way, the boy may come to believe that dogs are dangerous, that dogs are unfriendly, that dogs are not to be trusted, and so on. Each of these beliefs incorporates a negative evaluative concept concerning dogs and these contribute to the emergent feeling that we refer to as attitude.

Thus, attitudes are a consequence of the beliefs that persons have about the attitude object. Beliefs have at least two dimensions that are important for attitudes: the *strength of the belief* and the *quality (goodness or badness) of the evaluative concept* embedded in the belief. In general, the stronger the belief and the more extreme the evaluative concept, the more extreme the attitude toward the attitude object. If a person considers honesty as highly desirable and believes strongly that members of group X are honest, the person will have a strongly positive attitude toward group X.

Attitudes have several important characteristics that must be considered. First, attitudes differ in *kind* just as do the objects in a person's psychological world. Individuals hold attitudes toward persons, things, social issues, and the like. Second, attitudes differ in *content,* depending on the nature of the attitude object. Third, attitudes differ in *precision;* that is, the evaluative beliefs about some attitude objects are more exact and definite than those for some other attitude objects and the person's concept of the attitude object may be more or less clearly structured. For example, a person may have clear notions about what makes his automobile go, but his or her notions about nuclear fission may be fuzzy, vague, and confused. Precision of attitudes will vary accordingly. Fourth, attitudes vary in *specificity.* Some attitudes are relatively isolated, nongeneralized, and/or not connected with any other attitudes. Others are highly generalized and interconnected with a whole body of related attitudes. Fifth, attitudes differ in *intensity;* some attitudes are held very strongly and others very weakly. Finally, attitudes differ in *saliency.* Some attitudes have special significance for the individual, whereas others play only a minor role in his or her psychological world.

The Measurement of Attitudes

It is sometimes important to know the attitudes of persons or groups concerning social issues or other attitude objects. For example, a government agency may want to know the feelings of the people about an issue in order to guide their actions, or manufacturers may need to know consumer attitudes toward their products in order to change negative attitudes or to capitalize on positive attitudes. In such instances, a method for measuring attitudes is essential. Similarly, scientists must be able to measure attitudes if they are to examine their formation, organization, and change.

Attitudes are commonly measured by *attitude scales* (Shaw and Wright, 1967). A typical scale consists of a series of evaluative statements about the attitude object; the respondent is asked to indicate agreement or disagreement with each statement. Positive attitudes are inferred from agreement with statements that reflect positive evaluative beliefs about the attitude object, such as "The only salvation of the human race is birth control." Agreement with negative statements like "The practice of birth control should be punishable by law," presumably reflects negative attitudes. The attitude "score" is determined by the number and strength of positive and negative statements agreed with.

Attitude Change

Suppose you are a citizen who wishes to change the general public's attitude toward air pollution. You know that this attitude is at best only mildly negative and you believe that it should be highly negative. How would you go about inducing this change? From our discussion of the nature of attitudes, it follows that an attitude can be changed in either of two ways: changing the person's evaluative concepts or changing the person's beliefs about the attitude object. Consider a belief such as "Air pollution is a necessary evil if we are to have a healthy economy." The evaluative concept here is that a healthy economy is good. Therefore, one might make at least a small change in a person's attitude about pollution if the person could be made to accept the idea that a healthy economy is bad. This is a very difficult task, since evaluative concepts are usually firmly entrenched as a result of a long history of reinforcement. The other way to try to change the attitude would be to convince the person that air pollution is not an inevitable consequence of a healthy economy; that is, to change the person's belief. This is not easy, but investigators have demonstrated several procedures that influence attitude change.

The most common attempt to change attitudes, in both the laboratory and in "real" life, is through some process of communication. We are exposed to this process daily via newspaper ads and editorials, television commercials, political speeches, and the like. In the laboratory, an attempt is usually made to determine just what aspects of the communication process are effective in changing attitudes. The most extensive series of studies on attitude change was conducted at Yale University by Hovland and his associates (Hovland et al.,

1953). Their general procedure was to measure the attitudes of a group of persons, expose half of the group to a persuasive communication, and then remeasure the attitudes of all persons whose attitudes had been measured the first time. Any difference in degree of change between the persons exposed to the persuasive communication and those not receiving the communication was considered to be attitude change. Several important variables were identified, such as credibility of the source of the communication, the nature of the appeal, and the like.

The *communicator's reputation* is one variable that is related to attitude change. Generally speaking, a credible source is more effective in producing attitude change than a noncredible source; for example, a written communication was found to be more effective in changing attitudes of college students when the communication was attributed to Abraham Lincoln than when it was attributed to Karl Marx. However, differences in amounts of attitude change as a function of the communicator's reputation are usually temporary.

It is often assumed that *emotional appeals* are more effective than nonemotional or *rational appeals,* but at least one research study suggests that this belief is untrue. It was found that emotional and rational appeals were equally effective when the communicator was trying to make the attitude more favorable; when the attempt was to make the attitude more unfavorable, rational appeals were more effective than emotional ones.

An old adage states that there are *two sides* to every question and those who wish to change attitudes often assume that the most effective procedure is to present only arguments and information supporting their position. But is it? Research data show that one-sided communications are more effective than two-sided communications only when the audience initially agrees with the communicator (and the attempt is just to make the attitude more extreme); however, when the audience initially disagrees with the communicator, two-sided communications are more effective. We tend to see communicators who agree with us as credible and those who disagree with us an noncredible. It is probable that the two-sided communication to those who initially disagreed with the communicator made that person appear more credible. For example, it has been shown that a noncredible communicator who agreed with the audience regarding one topic was more effective in changing the attitudes of the audience on another issue.

Attitudes may also be changed by other procedures. For example, Lewin and his associates (1943) found that greater change could be produced by allowing persons to participate in a group discussion in which the relevant arguments were brought out than by a lecture presenting the same arguments. Similarly, if a person can be induced to act in ways that are contrary to his or her attitudes, the attitude is likely to change to become consistent with the actions. Presumably, *inconsistent cognitions* are psychologically unpleasant and the person adjusts the attitude to reduce inconsistency (Riess and Schlenker, 1977).

Attitudes and Behavior

The reason many persons want to change attitudes, of course, is because they believe that attitudes are related to overt behavior. For example, it is believed that the person who has a highly favorable attitude toward Chevrolets is more likely to buy a Chevrolet than the person who has an unfavorable attitude toward this type of automobile. Political candidates believe that their election depends on the attitudes that persons hold toward them. On the other hand, some social scientists have questioned the validity of these beliefs, because people often do not behave in ways that would be expected from their attitudes. This is a complex issue, because behavior is influenced by many factors and attitude is only one of these factors. To resolve the question of whether or not attitudes are related to behavior, several aspects of the situation must be considered. First, it is necessary to determine that the attitude and behavior *should* be related; an attitude cannot be expected to relate to all kinds of behavior. Second, both the attitude and the behavior must be *measured* with reliable and valid instruments. And, finally, it must be shown that strong determinants of *counterattitudinal behavior* are not present. Only investigations that meet these criteria can be accepted as evidence concerning the relation of attitudes to behavior.

When the evidence from studies meeting the above criteria is considered, it generally supports the conclusion that attitudes and behavior are related. For example, it has been shown that attitudes toward cheating are related to actual cheating (Corey, 1937), that attitudes toward the union are related to attendance at union meetings (Dean, 1958), that attitudes toward blacks are related to participation in civil rights discussions (Fendrich, 1967) and to agreeing to pose for a photograph with blacks (Linn, 1965), that attitudes toward breast feeding are related to success of breast feeding of babies (Newton and Newton, 1950), and many more (Ajzen and Fishbein, 1977).

To summarize, *attitudes* are generalized feelings, positive or negative, toward persons, objects, or issues in the individual's psychological world. They are derived from *evaluative concepts,* which are embedded in *evaluative beliefs* about the attitude object. Attitudes differ in *kind, content, precision, specificity, intensity,* and *saliency.* Attitudes may be *measured* by attitude scales designed to identify evaluative beliefs about the attitude object. Attitudes may be *changed* via procedures designed to change evaluative beliefs about the attitude object. When other determinants of behavior are not inconsistent with the attitude, attitudes *influence* relevant overt *behavior.* Attitudes play an unusually significant role in interpersonal attraction, as we shall see in the next section.

Interpersonal Attraction and Affiliation

It is a common observation that some persons are *attracted* to each other and seek *affiliation;* others are repelled by certain people and actively avoid association. Perhaps you have wondered what accounts for these attractions and repulsions, or perhaps you think you know the answer. Social psychologists may also believe they know that causes interpersonal attractions, but they seek to determine empirically whether they are correct. And it turns out that there is no single factor that determines who is attracted or repelled by whom. Instead, there are many conditions involved in interpersonal attraction and affiliation.

Proximity and Attraction

One of the first things that one finds is that inter-personal relationships (friendships, groups, and so on) tend to develop when individuals live in close proximity, make frequent contacts, and have occasion to interact often. For example, married couples assigned to a university housing unit merely by order of their applications made friends with those in nearby apartments much more frequently than with persons living in more distant apartments (Festinger, Schachter, and Back, 1950). In fact, couples who occupied apartments in the end of the building tended to be isolates. Similarly, various studies have shown that racial prejudice can be reduced by contact among majority-minority groups, although this effect is more likely to occur when the contact is (a) on an equal status basis, (b) between members of a majority group and higher status members of the minority group, (c) in a social climate that supports the contact, (d) of an intimate rather than a casual nature, (e) pleasant or rewarding, and/or (f) directed toward the achievement of common goals (Amir, 1969).

Proximity and contact usually lead to some form of interaction, and interaction provides the opportunity for individuals to learn about others. Whether or not *interpersonal attraction* results, and the degree of interpersonal attraction, depends on the characteristics of the persons involved in the interaction. When it is discovered that the other person has valued characteristics, that person becomes attractive.

Physical Attraction

Perhaps it is obvious that *physical attractiveness* is one factor that determines interpersonal attraction. In one interesting study, (Walster et al, 1966), males were randomly paired with females at a "computer dance." It was found that, regardless of the male's own attractiveness, the physical attractiveness of his partner determined how much he liked her, how much he wanted to date her again, and how often he actually asked her out again. Females responded in a similar way to their male dates. Attempts by the investigators to find

additional factors that might be related to attraction failed. For example, highly intelligent persons were not liked any better than persons having lower intelligence levels, nor were persons with exceptional social skills liked better than those with lesser social skills.

One might suspect that physical attractiveness is important only in the early stages of interaction and that its influence decreases as additional information about that person becomes available. This possibility has not been investigated directly, but related evidence suggests that physical attractiveness has some enduring effects. For example, the individual's first impressions of another affects his or her interactions with that person (Dailey, 1952), one's expectations influences one's behavior (Zajonc and Brickman, 1969), and physically attractive college women date more frequently than less attractive women (Berscheid et al, 1971).

Similarity and Attraction

Although physical attractiveness is important, it probably is not as important as similarity. Individuals are attracted to those who are similar to themselves, presumably because it is anticipated that interaction with similar others will be rewarding. That is, everyone needs social support for one's attitudes, beliefs, and opinions, and it is more probable that such support will be obtained from interaction with similar others than with dissimilar others.

As we mentioned earlier, attitudes play a significant role in interpersonal attraction, and *attitude similarity* is the most potent factor. For instance, Newcomb (1961) invited students to live in a house rent-free in exchange for participating in a research study. Seventeen men were selected for each of two years. Prior to moving into the house, all men were strangers. Periodically, the men completed a series of questionnaires and value inventories designed to measure attitudes and attraction. Initially, *proximity* was the primary determinant of attraction, but later in the interaction attraction was found to be a function of perceived similarity of attitudes.

The effects of attitude similarity on interpersonal attraction have also been investigated by Byrne and his associates. His technique was to ask individuals to express their attitudes toward a number of issues, ranging from relatively important things such as integration and God to relatively unimportant things like western movies and television programs. Later, participants were told that the tests had been given as a part of an interpersonal prediction study, that students in another class had taken the same test, and that they were now to be given each other's test with the name removed in the hope that they could learn about one another from this information. In fact, the tests had been prepared so that different groups of persons received tests that indicated that the other persons varied in degree of attitude similarity. In a number of studies (for example, Byrne, 1961; Byrne and Rhamey, 1965), it was found that degree of interpersonal attraction varied directly with degree of attitude similarity. This effect is depicted graphically in Figure 15-1.

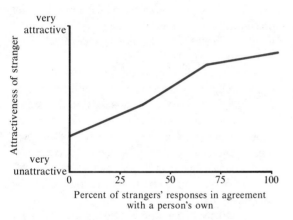

Fig. 15-1. Relationship between attitude similarity and interpersonal attraction.

Similarity also influences attraction in other areas. Persons are seen as more attractive when they have personality characteristics that are similar to those of the perceiver, at least with respect to self-concept, repression-sensitization, and the like. Similarity of economic status, race, sex, and ability have all been shown to be positively related to interpersonal attraction.

On the other hand, *complementarity* of personal characteristics sometimes leads to interpersonal attraction. For example, dominant persons often are attracted to submissive persons, those who need autonomy are attracted to persons who permit much freedom in interpersonal relations, and so on. Complementarity is most important for deep interpersonal relationships such as marriage and with respect to needs.

Affiliation and Attraction

Interpersonal attraction is, of course, one determinant of *affiliation:* persons want to be with those other persons to whom they are attracted. But interpersonal attraction is only one determinant of affiliation. Persons may choose to associate with others because they enjoy similar activities, because they have common goals that can best be achieved through joint action, or merely because they have a need for affiliation. The existence of a need for affiliation is demonstrated by an interesting study by Gewirtz and Baer (1958). Children ranging in age from three years ten months to five years three months were invited to play a game using toys. In one condition, each child was kept waiting alone for twenty minutes before playing the game; in another condition, the game was played as soon as the child reported to the laboratory. Children in the social deprivation condition were more responsive to social reinforcement (expressions of approval such as "good," "fine," and so on) than were children who were not deprived of social contact.

Affiliation may sometimes function as a means of reducing anxiety. In many situations, individuals state that being with others makes it easier to endure stressful or fearful situations. During war, soldiers find association with others makes combat more endurable; children find solace in the presence of friendly adults; police are less fearful when working in pairs or teams; in times of disasters such as earthquakes, hurricanes, floods, and the like, being with others has been found to be reassuring to the victims. In the laboratory, it has been found that persons who expect to experience electric shocks choose to wait with others more frequently than persons who do not expect electric shock. Thus, sharing adversity with others is one way of alleviating fear and anxiety.

In summary, *interpersonal attraction* is facilitated by situational circumstances such as *proximity, contact,* and *interaction.* These circumstances provide the opportunity for individuals to learn about each other. One may, through association, discover that another is physically attractive, that they hold similar attitudes, and so on. When another person is perceived to have similar attitudes, economic status, personality, race, sex, or other characteristics, he or she is usually as seen as being more attractive. Interpersonal attraction usually leads to *affiliation;* however, affiliation may serve other functions, such as satisfying a need for affiliation or reducing anxiety.

When persons affiliate, they occupy both physical and psychological space. The manner in which each person perceives "personal space" and how it is used, often determine whether the association will be congenial or conflictual. In the following section, we will consider this aspect of social behavior.

Personal Space

Social behavior is influenced not only by the foibles of individuals but also by the *physical environment* in which the behavior occurs. The shape of the room, lighting, furniture arrangement, the color of the walls, and similar aspects of the physical surroundings affect the person's mood and thus the behavior in relation to others. Many of you will recall the endless discussions during the Vietnam peace conference in Paris about the shape of the conference table. To many observers, this undoubtedly appeared to be exceedingly trivial, but the shape of the table and who sits where serve as indicators of relative social status. Even *affiliative behavior* (conversation, eye contact, and such) is often influenced by such minor things as the presence of pictures or sculptures in the room.

Perhaps more intriguing is the kind of social behavior that is the consequence of the person's orientation toward the space around him or her. It has been known for many years that animals establish territories and defend them against invasion, but the study of similar behavior in humans is relatively recent. Not only do persons establish *territorial* rights, but they also view certain areas around

their bodies as *personal* and *private.* These orientations to personal space significantly affect social behavior.

Territoriality

Many of you have observed that individuals tend to appropriate space and assume proprietary rights to it in almost all situations in which people meet together for an extended period of time. Students in the classroom usually sit in the same seat day after day and soon come to regard it as their own. If another student arrives first and takes that chair, the "owner" does not hesitate to tell the student that he or she is trespassing. And the "usurper" usually moves without question. In other words, not only do individuals assume rights to physical space and objects to which they have no legal right, but others tacitly accept their claim as valid. Such territorial claims may be maintained by the use of "markers," even when the person is not present. Placing a coat or purse on a chair, for example, indicates to others that the chair "belongs" to someone else.

When an individual assumes a proprietary right to particular geographical space or objects, congenial interpersonal behavior depends on the degree to which the other person respects the assumed territorial right. For example, if a person has adopted a particular chair as one's own and another person sits in it, conflict is probable. Even when the offender moves, some strain may be placed on the relationship.

The effects of *territoriality* on social behavior has been observed in a variety of situations. Many years ago, Whyte (1949) conducted an extensive study of the social structure of restaurants and found that territoriality was a significant factor determining social relations. For example, the kitchen workers held proprietary attitudes toward the kitchen area. When other employees entered the kitchen, the normal pattern of interaction was disrupted. If the outsider had lower status, the kitchen workers actively attempted to block participation in their activities.

The effects of territoriality were also observed in dyads living in isolation. As the length of isolation increased, members of the pair established strong preferences for a particular chair, bed, table, and so on. These "territories" were rigidly respected by both persons. Similarly, persons in retirement homes adopt territories and the relations with others vary with the degree to which their territorial claims are respected (Altman and Haythorn, 1967).

As suggested above, occupants of territories will ordinarily defend it against *invasion* by others. These defenses may be passive or active, depending on the person and the situation. For example, persons who wish privacy usually choose to sit at the end of a table rather than at the side; on the other hand, sitting at the side and in the middle is one way of discouraging others from sitting at the table. Placing tokens (items of clothing, books, and the like) on unoccupied chairs also serves as a passive defense against invasion. More active defenses include staring at intruders, shifting position, or openly asking the other person to leave.

Sometimes it is a group rather than an individual that assumes territorial rights to geographical areas. It is common knowledge that street gangs delimit their own "turf" and defend it to the death against rival gangs. More recently, the occupancy of vacant buildings by groups is an example of this type of territoriality. Residential segregation may also be considered one kind of territoriality. Although the boundaries of group territories are often invisible, they are sometimes identified by written signs, fences, hedges, or other barriers.

Failure to respect assumed territorial rights leads to conflict, but the existence of territories may also serve to reduce conflict when the boundaries are known and respected by others. Furthermore, it often serves to protect the individual against other people and provides some privacy that is otherwise unobtainable. The maintenance of *interperson distance* also serves this function.

Interperson Distance

Broadly speaking, both *territoriality* and *interperson distance* are aspects of *personal space* (Linder, 1976). However, the term "personal space" is more commonly applied to that area around the individual's body that is regarded as private. Unlike territoriality, personal space is not fixed in relation to a geographical area, but is carried about with the individual. The area that is identified as one's personal space is indicated by the distance that that person typically maintains relative to others. When personal space is identified by comfortable approach distances, it is smaller in relation to impersonal than to personal objects, it is smaller in relation to intimate than to less intimate others, it varies with the status of the persons and with the kind of interaction, and so on. Unwanted intrusions evoke negative reactions that vary from subdued expressions of displeasure to strong retaliatory actions, depending on the characteristics of the intruder and the circumstances under which the invasion occurs.

As we noted above, personal space is usually identified by measuring interperson distance; that is, the distance that the person typically maintains between himself or herself and others. You probably have noticed that some persons like to stand very close to others when engaged in conversation, whereas others like more distance between themselves and others. This is at least partly cultural; Latin Americans, for example, like to stand closer than North Americans. When members of these two cultures interact, an interesting phenomenon may be observed. The Latin American moves closer to the other in order to maintain an interperson distance that is comfortable, but this is too close for the comfort of the North American, who then retreats. This approach-retreat process may continue for some time, with the result that the pair may move across an entire room in their attempts to maintain comfortable interaction distances.

An interesting study of *interaction distance* was conducted by F. N. Willis (1966) who recorded the speaking distance between two persons under a wide range of circumstances. Forty investigators obtained data on 755 persons in such diverse places as homes, places of business, and halls of university buildings. When an investigator was approached by another person who began a conversation, the investigator remained at a fixed point and measured the nose-to-nose distance between himself and the other person with a tape measure. He found that women investigators were approached more closely than men, that persons the same age as the investigator stood closer than persons who were older, and acquaintances stood closer than strangers. Other investigations using somewhat similar techniques have yielded similar results, as can be seen in Table 15-1. It has also been observed that blacks stand further apart than whites when interacting with each other, and interaction distance increases with chronological age in all groups. The important point here is that the interaction distance varies with the *relationship* between the interacting individuals. When two interacting persons have similar interperson distances, the interaction is likely to be congenial, whereas when one person prefers to stand close and the other more distant, strain is placed on the relationship.

Table 15-1. Typical Interaction Distances as a Function of the Relations Between Participants

Relation	Distance (Centimeters)
Women-Men	54.8
Men-Women	62.1
Same Age	60.6
Different Ages	67.7
Acquaintances	60.5
Strangers	69.4
Friends	39.4

Invasion of Personal Space

Implicit in the several studies of interpersonal distance referred to above is the assumption that the distance an individual places another with respect to himself or herself and impersonal objects defines the limits of his or her personal space. We have seen how the boundaries of this space vary with the situation and the relationship of the person to others but personal space does not have regular boundaries, such as a circle around the person's body. Instead, personal space forms an irregular pattern about the person, with the interperson distance being greatest in front and least with respect to the person's back.

As we noted before, the intrusion of another into the personal space evokes discomfort, unease, and other negative feelings that are revealed in various defensive responses and ultimately in flight. Typical reactions include rubbing the face, breathing heavily, looking at watch, flexing fingers, and sim-

ilar kinds of behaviors. If these defensive reactions fail to produce an effect, the typical reaction is simply to move away (Sommer, 1969).

Usually, however, individuals avoid entering the personal space of another unless it is necessary to do so (Knowles, 1973). This effect is easy to observe in almost any public building that provides hallways where interactions may occur. For instance, it has been observed that persons will stop to drink at a fountain more frequently when no one is seated near it than when someone is seated nearby. Similarly, if two persons are carrying on a conversation in a hallway, passersby will usually detour around them rather than walk between the two conversing persons, even when it is very inconvenient to do so. In general, this tendency to avoid invasion of personal space is stronger with smaller interperson distances and with mixed sex groups than with larger interperson distances and same sex groups. There is the tacit assumption that groups have a right to the space they occupy and should not be intruded upon by others.

Functions of Personal Space

The personal space of an individual serves both personal and interpersonal functions. We have already seen how personal space can effect the emotional state of an individual and one's comfort in the situation. But personal space has important connotations for interpersonal behavior. One of the important functions of spatial relations among persons is the establishment and communication of status differences. In general, the high status person occupies the best position, and, conversely, the person who occupies the better position is seen as having higher status. For instance, when a table has obvious status positions, such as the head of the table, the high status person usually sits there, but when the table is square and therefore all positions equal, the positions occupied by high status persons usually place greater distance between them and lower status individuals. The leader sits at the head of the table, the professor at the head of his class, the politician before the crowd, and so on. It is possible that long familiarity with such situations has produced a cultural expectation of greater interperson distance between high and low status persons than between peers. We will see that the interperson distance-status relationship is found also in studies of the effect of seating arrangements.

Spatial Arrangements

The personal space of a person influences his relations with others, and this effect is in part demonstrated by the effects of *spatial arrangements* in groups. The spatial relations between two or more persons are determinants not only of the perception of status but also the patterns of participation, leadership activities, and the affective reactions of participants. For instance, when persons are free to choose their position in a group, their choices usually reflect the cultural influence of various locations. Persons who perceive themselves to have relatively high status in the group select positions that are in accord with this perception. It has been observed, for example, that jurors from professional and managerial groups usually select the chair at the head of the table more often than persons from lower status groups. If persons are instructed that they will be competing with another person who is already seated at the table, they usually choose to sit face-to-face with the other person. However, when they expect to be cooperating with the other person a side-by-side seating arrangement is usually preferred.

It is not difficult to see that certain positions created by seating arrangements are positively rewarding and others negatively rewarding. The rewarding values of spatial positions derive in part from their consequences for interpersonal behavior. Obviously, it is difficult to *interact* with another person at a great distance, and certainly interaction with a person one cannot see is less satisfactory than face-to-face interaction. For example, most people find a telephone conversation less satisfactory than a face-to-face conference, largely because the nonverbal parts of communication are not available during a telephone conversation. The significance of eye contact for social interaction is well known, because the direction of another person's gaze often serves as a guide for further interaction. For example, at points in an interaction where the speaking role

shifts from one person to another, the person who has been speaking typically ends an utterance by looking at the other person with a sustained gaze. When the other person begins to speak, he or she usually looks away. In this way, each person can signal to the other intentions and expectations and at the same time can determine whether the other has received and accepted the signals.

Spatial relationships between persons also influence the *flow of communication*. When members of a group are seated at a round table, there is a strong tendency for members to communicate with other persons across the table and facing them rather than with persons adjacent to them. Seating arrangement also has an effect on the quality of interaction. In general, the more distance between two persons the less friendly, acquainted and talkative they perceive each other to be.

We have already indicated that the leader typically sits at the head of the table, presumably because the leader has high status in the group. Therefore, it is not surprising to find a relationship between spatial arrangements and *leadership emergence*. When persons are assigned seating positions randomly, the person who sits at the head of the table emerges as the leader more frequently than would be expected by chance. Thus, seating arrangement determines, to a significant degree, the flow of communication and interaction among individuals, the status assigned to various persons, and the emergence of leadership. These effects are produced in part by the cultural patterns of interaction which typically place both persons in physical positions that correspond to their status positions. But, it also seems clear that spatial arrangements exert a more direct influence on the flow of communication, which in turn influences the person's chances of obtaining status in the group. Much of the behavior that occurs in group situations may be a consequence of these effects.

Behavior in Groups

A considerable amount of behavior that we call social occurs in *small groups* (Shaw, 1976). Our everyday interactions commonly involve such diverse groups as the family group, the work group, the social group, and so on. Groups serve many functions for the individual. We have already noticed that the presence of others often leads to the satisfaction of individual needs for affiliation and may help the individual achieve goals that cannot be achieved alone. We will also see that the *norms* or *standards of conduct* of the group provide a basis for determining appropriate behavior in otherwise ambiguous situations. It is probable that group interaction serves many more functions for the member, but it is quite obvious that much of an individual's behavior is a consequence of that person's group membership.

One of the first questions that the reader may ask is, "What is a group?" There is, unfortunately, no widely accepted definition of group, but it is clear that at minimum, a psychological group involves interaction between two or more persons. By *interaction* is meant that the behavior of each person influences and is influenced by the behavior of each other person in the group. Groups also are characterized by an organizational structure that includes a standard set of *role relationships* among the group members and a set of *norms* that regulate the functions of the group and of each of its members. Usually, groups also possess a *common goal*.

The initial event in group interaction is the establishment of a relationship between two or more persons. The formation of this initial relationship is, of course, necessary for group existence, but the process of group formation is a continuous one. The relationships among group members may often appear to be stable and indeed relatively little change may occur from day to day in some groups. In general, after relationships are established early in the life of the group, changes occur slowly. In this chapter, we will examine some of the factors determining group formation and development, the relative performances of individuals and groups, the nature of group structure, and leadership behavior.

Group Formation and Development

We have already learned about several factors influencing the attraction between two or more persons. And interpersonal attraction is, of course, an important variable in *group formation*. But individuals also may be attracted to a group because of the activities of the group. A person may join a bridge club, because that person likes to play bridge and because the social activities are pleasant. In many ways it is difficult to separate the activities of a group from its goals, and individuals may be attracted to a group, both because they enjoy its activity and because they value its goals. For example, a person may join the Chamber of Commerce because he or she has the same goal as other members of the Chamber of Commerce. Similarly, persons may join a church group because they believe in the religious goals of the group.

Sometimes an individual will join a group simply because of a belief that membership in the group will be *instrumental* toward the achievement of secondary goals. For example, a man may join a social club, because he believes that it will enable him to meet more young ladies. And, finally, an individual may join a group simply because of a need for affiliation. That person may simply enjoy being with other people. Thus, an individual joins a group and groups form for a variety of reasons. In any case, however, groups will form only if they serve some need of the individual members, and the group ordinarily breaks up when these needs are no longer being satisfied by the group.

Almost immediately after individuals begin interacting with each other, a *group structure* begins to emerge. We will be examining the nature of group structure and its effects on group behavior in a later section, but first it will be instructive to examine some of the differences between individual and group behavior.

Individual versus Group Behavior

A question that has interested social psychologists for many years concerns the differences between individual and group behavior. It is possible, of course, that each individual behaves in a group in exactly the same way that he or she would when alone, and that others in the group would have no effect on contributions to the group product. Actually, the individual's behavior is altered in a variety of ways by the *presence of others* in the individual's immediate environment. Many years ago, it was observed that bicycle riders pedaled more vigorously when other people were present than when they were riding alone. It has also been observed that behavior of a *passive audience* has an effect on other kinds of behavior. For example, if persons are asked to recall as many words as possible in response to a stimulus word, it is usually observed that more words are recalled when other people are present than when they are alone. This facilitating effect of an audience has been called "*social facilitation.*" A facilitating effect of an audience has also been observed with coacting audiences, that is, where several persons work on the same task in the same place, although each person works as an individual.

Although the presence of others often results in a facilitating effect, it is sometimes observed that no effect occurs or the presence of others has a negative effect for individual performance. It now appears that the presence of others serves to increase motivation of performing individuals and may facilitate highly learned activities but interfere with activities that require greater attention. For example, in one study (Zajonc and Sales, 1966), individuals practiced pronouncing nonsense words and then were given a difficult recognition text, either alone or in the presence of an audience. The amount of practice on each word varied. Individuals tested in the presence of others did relatively better on highly practiced words than individuals tested alone; however, on less well-practiced words, individuals tested in the presence of others did relatively worse than individuals tested alone.

Individuals versus Group Problem Solving. Perhaps the most interesting comparisons between individual and group performance are those relevant to *problem-solving* activities. Unlike the situations involving an audience, group problem solving requires interaction among group members. Investigators of individual versus group problem solving have used a variety of experimental designs as well as a variety of problems which subjects are asked to solve. The two most common designs are: (1) individuals are required to solve problems alone and the same individuals attempt to solve similar problems in groups, usually with order and problems counterbalanced,

and (2) one sample of individuals attempts a set of problems and another sample of groups attempts to solve the same set of problems.

The classic study of individual and group problem solving was conducted by Marjorie Shaw (1932). This study was conducted at Columbia University and students in social psychology served as participants. In the first half of the experiment, half of the participants worked in five groups of four persons each and the other half worked as individuals. In the second half, the roles of the participants were reversed. The problems in the first part of the study were puzzles, such as the cannibal and missionary problems. In this particular task, three cannibals and three missionaries cross a river in a boat that will carry only two persons. One of the cannibals and all of the missionaries know how to row the boat. However, the crossing must be arranged so that the cannibals never outnumber the missionaries. The problem is to determine how the crossing can be made in the fewest trips. The two other problems were similar in nature. The problems in the second half were ones that required the identification of the best location for a school and the best route for two school busses given the number of possible routes, the location and number of children to be picked up and the capacity of the busses. It was found that individuals produced fewer correct solutions than groups in both parts of the experiment, although groups usually required more time to solve the problems. In other words, groups produced more and better solutions but often at a cost in time, a cost which is much greater if time per individual is taken into account. In addition, Shaw noted that there was an unequal amount of participation by group members and that in the case of erroneous solutions, groups did not err as early in the process as did the average individual.

The relative superiority of groups with respect to accuracy was interpreted as being due to the reduction of incorrect suggestions and a checking of errors in the group. For example, it was found, that incorrect suggestions were recognized and rejected by someone in the group other than the one who made the error, a process that is not available to individuals working alone.

Many other studies have been conducted which

yielded results generally consistent with those re-ported by Shaw. The evidence thus strongly sup-ports the conclusion that groups produce more and better solutions to problems than do individuals, although the differences in overall time required for solution are not consistently better for either in-dividuals or groups. However, when the amount of effort invested, as measured by man-hours required for solution, is considered, individuals are found to be superior. In general, the relative supe-riority of group problem solving (in terms of accu-racy) may be accounted for by the following pro-cesses: (1) summation of individual contributions, (2) rejection of incorrect suggestions and checking of errors, (3) the greater influence of the ablest group member, (4) the social influence of the most confident member, (5) the greater interest in the task aroused by group membership, and (6) the greater amount of information available to the group. The degree to which each one of these fac-tors is operative probably depends on other charac-teristics of the group which will be discussed in subsequent sections.

An even more important aspect, perhaps, is the kind of task the group must complete. Tasks may be *additive, disjunctive,* or *conjunctive* (Steiner, 1972). When the task is disjunctive, the group must choose which of two or more alternative solu-tions is the correct one. On such tasks, the best performance of the group is usually no better than the performance of the most competent group member. Conjunctive tasks require that all members of the group complete the task individ-ually, as when all members of a scout troop must reach the top of the mountain they are attempting to climb. Here the performance of the group is lim-ited by the *least* capable group member. When the task is additive, the contributions of group members may be combined to produce a joint out-come. In such cases, group performance usually increases with increasing group size, up to some reasonable maximum number of persons. There-fore, whether one should employ groups or indi-viduals depends on the kind of task and whether one is more concerned about correct decisions or about cost in terms of man- or woman-hours.

Brainstorming.   Group behavior differs from in-dividual behavior in at least two other interesting ways. One of these differences is reflected in a procedure known as brainstorming. *Brainstorming* is a procedure in which groups attempt to produce new ideas by following a set of rules. These rules state that ideas are to be expressed without regard to quality, that no idea may be evaluated until all ideas have been expressed, and that the elaboration of one person's ideas by another is not only permit-ted but actually encouraged. In general, it is found that groups following the rules of brainstorming produce more good ideas than individuals working alone. The ideas expressed by group members ap-parently serve the function of stimulating the thought processes of other group members, thus resulting in a higher productivity by the group.

Individual versus Group Risk Taking.   The other situation in which individuals and groups differ is in the area of decision making under conditions of *risk.* For many years, it was assumed by most busi-ness people that group decisions are relatively con-servative in nature, whereas decisions made by in-dividuals are riskier. However, in 1961, a study by Stoner indicated that the opposite may be true. He compared the riskiness of decisions by individuals and groups using a choice-dilemma questionnaire. This questionnaire consisted of a series of state-ments regarding the probability of success, and subjects were required to indicate how much of a risk they would be willing to take in each case. The finding that groups often make riskier decisions than individuals (usually referred to as a *"risky shift"*) is generally supported by other research using the choice-dilemma questionnaire, although there is reason to believe that whether a risky or a conservative shift occurs may depend on the par-ticular task faced by individuals and by groups. When the risky shift does occur, there are several possible explanations for it. In general, a relatively risky decision by groups is most likely to result when (1) risk-relevant issues are being considered, (2) group members perceive themselves to be greater risktakers than their peers, (3) the initial opinions of group members are diverse, (4) the consequences of failure because of an incorrect decision are not too severe, and/or (5) the instruc-tions given the group are risk-oriented.

There are at least three processes that may ac-count for the risky shift phenomenon: *risk is a value,* the *most risky group member is more influential,* and *diffusion of responsibility.* In our culture, many persons value risk and feel that it reflects on their potential as a leader if they make risky decisions. And it is probable that persons who believe this way have more influence on group decisions than those who favor more conservative decisions. Furthermore, when a decision is made in a group, responsibility for the decision is diffused among the members of the group. Consequently, no single member can be held completely responsible for the decision if it turns out to be a bad one. This kind of diffusion of responsibility has been observed in crowd behaviors such as lynch mobs and other antisocial collectivities.

It is clear from the preceding discussions that individuals in groups do not behave in the same way that they do when acting alone. Consequently, it is important to examine the organization of groups and some of the factors that produce these differences in individual behavior. The most important factors for group behavior are the kinds of persons who are in the group (group composition) and organizational factors (group structure).

Group Composition

Everyone knows that individuals have different behavioral tendencies that are relatively consistent across situations and that these characteristics also influence the way the individual behaves in group situations (Shaw, 1976). Although personality characteristics are important determinants of behavior, the social psychologist is concerned with the relationships among personal characteristics of group members and the consequences of these relationships for interpersonal behavior. It is not the particular characteristic of an individual group member that is of interest here, but rather the relative characteristics of various persons who compose the group. These relationships are referred to as group composition. They include such group characteristics as group cohesiveness, member compatibility, and heterogeneity-homogeneity of group membership.

Group Cohesiveness. The term *group cohesiveness* is used to refer to the degree to which the group hangs together. Some groups are enthusiastic and appear to be deeply involved with the group and its goals. They are active, close to one another, loyal to their group, and morale is high. On the other hand, some groups show little enthusiasm for planning group activities, members are not involved with one another, they do not attend meetings of the group on a regular basis, and they are generally unconcerned about the group. These first groups would be called cohesive, whereas the latter would be noncohesive groups. Group cohesiveness, therefore, refers to the attractiveness of the group, the morale of the group, coordination of efforts of the group members, and similar characteristics. It is usually defined as the resultant of all the forces acting on the members to remain in or to leave the group (Festinger, 1950) and consequently includes all those factors contributing to interpersonal attraction that were discussed earlier in this chapter.

Group cohesiveness is reflected by many different behaviors of group members, and it is, therefore, not surprising that the measures of cohesiveness vary considerably from study to study. Perhaps the most common method of assessing cohesiveness is sociometric choice in which group members are asked to name the person or persons they would most prefer to work with in a variety of situations. The number of in-group choices is presumed to reflect the degree of cohesiveness of that group. Investigators have also used the difference in number of negative and positive choices, the relative frequency with which members use "we" and "I" in their discussions, the regularity of attendance at group meetings, and a variety of other indicators of group cohesiveness. These different measures of cohesiveness reflect different aspects of this group characteristic, but no single measure takes into account all aspects of group coherence.

The person on the street would probably assume that the cohesiveness of the group would be an important determinant of the group's *productivity:* the greater the cohesiveness the more productive the group. Students of group behavior also have made this assumption and numerous studies have been conducted to try to demonstrate this relationship. Unfortunately, the results of such studies have been highly inconsistent with some studies finding a positive relationship between cohesiveness and productivity and others finding a negative or no relationship at all. For example, positive relationships between productivity and cohesiveness have been reported for aircraft maintenance crews, military training groups, and industrial groups. On the other hand, studies of cohesiveness and productivity in laboratory situations have usually yielded inconclusive results. One of the factors that influences group productivity usually has not been considered when examining cohesiveness and productivity. This is the attitude of the group members toward the group goal. For the most part, investigators have assumed that the group members accept as their goal the task that is assigned to them. However, it seems likely that many group members do not accept the group goal that someone else assigns to them. This effect was demonstrated conclusively by a study by Berkowitz (1954) who found that cohesive groups are more effective in achieving tasks that they find acceptable than are low cohesive groups, but there is no relationship between cohesiveness and effectiveness in achieving tasks that they find unacceptable.

Group cohesiveness is also an important determinant of the amount of *communication activity* in the group. Cohesive groups tend to engage in a considerable amount of communication whereas noncohesive groups communicate relatively little. Differences in the pattern of communication within groups as a function of cohesiveness has also been observed. In general, members of high cohesive groups are active in seeking facts and attempting to reach agreement, whereas members of low cohesive groups tend to act independently.

As one might expect, cohesiveness is positively related to *member satisfaction* with the group. When the group is cohesive, the members are highly satisfied with its activities, with the kinds of decisions made by the group, and other aspects of group behavior.

In summary, high cohesive groups relative to low cohesive groups, engage in more social interaction, engage in more positive interactions, are more effective in achieving goals they set for themselves, and have higher member satisfaction.

Group Compatibility. A second aspect of group composition that is in some ways similar to cohesiveness is *group compatibility*. Group compatibility refers to the degree to which individual group members possess characteristics that make them compatible or incompatible with other group members. For example, if one member of a pair desires much affection and another person expresses little affection, the two pessons are likely to be incompatible. On the other hand, if one person has a need for affection and another has a need to express affection, the pair will be compatible. In other words, some combinations of interpersonal needs are presumed to produce compatibility and others to produce incompatibility. In general, the more compatible the group, the more effective it will be in the achievement of group goals. When group members are compatible, little time is spent in resolving interpersonal conflicts and they are able to devote most of their energies to the group task (Schutz, 1961).

Homogeneity-Heterogeneity of Group Membership. In the preceding discussion, there is the implicit assumption that the members of groups that are compatible or cohesive are heterogeneous with respect to characteristics. Although this is often true, it is not necessarily so. Sometimes homogeneity of personal characteristics is required for compatibility, for example, when two persons are both sociable. Furthermore, group cohesiveness and group compatibility are concerned with the particular kinds of relationships among group members. In some cases, it is simply the degree to which member characteristics are similar or dissimilar. This kind of relationship is usually referred to as *homogeneity-heterogeneity* of group membership. A homogeneous group is one in which the characteristics of group members are highly similar to one another, whereas a heterogeneous group is one in which member characteristics are highly dissimilar. Most group activities, of course, require a variety of skills and knowledges. Therefore, homogeneous groups tend to be less effective than heterogeneous groups, since the more heterogeneous the group, the more likely it is that the necessary abilities and information will be available in the group. Many studies have been conducted to test this general idea and the evidence is clear in showing that heterogeneous groups usually perform more effectively than groups that are homogeneous in this respect. When the group members have a variety of opinions, abilities, skills, and perspectives, the probability that the group will possess the characteristics necessary for effective group performance is enhanced, and, therefore, heterogeneous groups are usually more efficient than homogeneous groups.

The effectiveness of group activities and the relationship of these to group composition are influenced in part by the kinds of structural relations that are developed in the group. The kinds of organizational patterns that the group develops and the ways of getting things done that are adopted may exert a highly significant influence on group behavior. This aspect of the group is usually referred to as *group structure*.

Group Structure

When individuals meet together for the first time and begin to interact, consistent individual differences begin to appear (Shaw, 1976). Some persons speak more than others, some are listened to by other group members and some are ignored, some are more physically active than others, and some appear to elicit greater respect than other group members. These differences that develop among the members of the group serve as the basis for the formation of group structure. As the differences occur, relationships are established among members of groups so that there exists a pattern of relationships. The term *"group structure"* is the term that is usually used to refer to this pattern of relationships. Although the differences among the group members are highly complex and vary with respect to such things as *status, power, leadership,* and so on the various relationships among diverse parts of the group constitute a unitary integrated organizational structure.

Positions in Groups.

As the group structure develops different members of the group are relegated to different *positions* within the group. Each member occupies a position in the group and the pattern of relationships among the positions in the group constitutes one aspect of group structure. A typical group structure is depicted in Figure 15-2, which shows a group consisting of five positions: the supervisor of production, the foreman, and three operators.

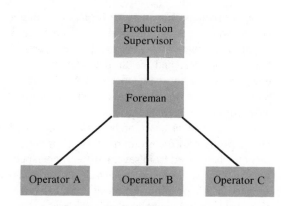

Fig. 15-2. A typical group structure of an industrial work group.

Social Status. Each position in the group is evaluated by the members of the group in terms of its importance or value. These evaluations determine the *status* of the occupant of the position. In almost all groups status differences exist so that the group structure is hierarchical in nature. In the diagram shown in Figure 15-2, the supervisor of production has the highest status in the group, the foreman has the second highest status, and the operators hold low status positions. Although positions are arranged in hierarchical order on the basis of status, it is common for two or more positions to have equal status in the group, as in the case of the operators in our example.

Social Roles. The occupant of each position is expected to perform certain functions during group interaction. The set of expected behaviors associated with a position within the group constitutes the *social role* of the occupant of that position. In our example, the supervisor of production is expected to lead the group, to decide on group goals, and to generally oversee the group functioning. The foreman is more directly concerned with production and supervises the actions of the three operators. The foreman determines which person will carry out which task, which machine they will work on, and so forth. The three operators are the ones who run the machines and actually carry out the activities that are concerned with producing the group's products. For instance, operator A might be one who wires an electrical panel, operator B might be the one who fastens the different parts of the unit together, and the third worker might be one who welds the parts together. Note that although the three operators have equal status, they have different roles in the group.

A social role is a set of behaviors associated with a position in the group but this set of behaviors may be viewed from several different perspectives. When we refer to *expected* behaviors associated with a position, we mean those behaviors expected by other members within the group. But, there is also a *perceived* role that refers to the set of behaviors that the occupant believes to be appropriate to enact, and the *enacted* role that includes the behavior which the occupant actually does carry out. The expected role is independent of the particular persons who may occupy the position, whereas both perceived and enacted roles depend in part on the behaviors of the particular individual who occupies the position. In general, an individual will enact those roles that he or she perceives to be appropriate. The degree to which the enacted role corresponds to the expected role will determine how effective the group may be.

In addition to the status accorded each position and the role associated with it, there are rules of conduct, called *social norms,* that specify acceptable behavior in the group. Some norms apply to all members in the group in the sense that everyone is expected to be governed by them, whereas other norms apply only to certain positions within the group. Social roles are norms that apply to particular positions, but not all norms are role specifications. Norms are established with regard to those aspects of the group activity that are of importance to the group. However, there are wide variations in the degree to which group members accept the norms of the group and in the degree to which group members may disobey norms without negative sanction. Once the structure of the group has been established, it is largely independent of the particular individuals who compose the group. In general, a position is accorded a particular status regardless of the person who happens to occupy it at the moment, the occupant is expected to carry out certain behaviors (role) regardless of who that

person is, and so on. Occupants may change the group structure by enacting behaviors that are inconsistent with the social role but in most cases the structure tends to be stable over time. That is, it is uncommon for a high status position to be demoted to a low status position within the same group.

Effects of Status. Status, roles, and norms exert a tremendously significant influence on social behavior. For instance, status contributes to a number of group processes and member behaviors. The high status person selects a spatial position in the group that is consistent with his or her status, conforms to the group norms more than low status group members, and has greater influence on the group's product than lower status group members. Although the high status person tends to conform more than the low status person, there are instances in which the high status person is permitted to deviate more than others in the group. This occurs when that person has made sufficient contributions to the group goals in the past that "idiosyncrasy credit" has been accumulated. It is probable that the high status person to a greater extent than the low status person is permitted to deviate from group norms in an attempt to aid in goal achievement.

Status differences also exert a powerful influence on the pattern and content of communications in the group. For instance, it has been observed that with increasing status differences, low status persons increase the total amount of communication addressed to high status persons, but the proportion of aggressively toned communication decreases. Low status group members tend to communicate more task irrelevant information than high status members and high status persons appear to be restrained from communicating criticisms of their own jobs to those persons of lower status. Furthermore, persons who are frustrated by high status individuals express relatively little verbal aggression toward the frustrating agent, as compared to persons who are frustrated by low status persons. In general, there is a tendency for communications to be directed upward in the status hierarchy and the content of messages directed toward high status persons are more positive than messages directed downward in the status hierarchy.

Effects of Role and Role Conflict. It is probably obvious that the person who occupies a particular position will behave in accordance with the role prescriptions of that position. But what happens when a person occupies two or more positions and the role prescriptions of those positions come in conflict? For example, a policeman may be expected to protect the property and lives of other members of the community, but in the role of father he is expected to protect his family. Under ordinary circumstances, the occupants of positions in different groups find no conflict because the different roles are enacted at different times. Under unusual circumstances, however, the occupant may be called upon to enact both roles simultaneously and *role conflict* results. When this happens, how the individual resolves the conflict is of great interest for group behavior. In general, it is expected that the person will elect to enact the role associated with the position in the group that he or she finds most attractive. This effect was observed in the disastrous oil fires that occurred in Texas City, Texas several years ago. At the time of this disaster, policemen were faced with role requirements that were obviously conflicting, namely, the policeman's role and the family member role. Except for one policeman whose family was out of town, all policemen resolved the conflict in favor of the family role (they went home to help their family to safety), presumably because they regarded this group as more attractive and more salient at the moment.

Effects of Norms. As we have indicated already, the role associated with a given position in a group is essentially a set of social norms or standards governing the behavior of the occupant of that position. But there are also standards of conduct or norms that apply to all or most members of the group regardless of the position that the member occupies. Such norms provide a basis for predicting the behavior of others and enable individuals to anticipate actions of others and to prepare an appropriate response. These rules serve as a guide for the group member's own behavior and therefore

reduce ambiguity, which many persons find intolerable.

There are several characteristics of norms that are important. First, norms are not established about every conceivable action that a group member might take, but only with respect to those actions that are of some *importance* to the group. For instance, groups do not ordinarily establish a norm concerning which hand a person shall use in writing. On the other hand, there are ordinarily norms governing the way one person responds to another member of the group. Second, norms may apply to every member of the group or they may apply only to specific individuals. The latter, of course, specifies the role of the person in the group. Third, norms vary in the degree to which they are *accepted* by the group. Some are accepted by almost everyone in the group, whereas others are accepted by some group members and rejected by others. And finally, norms vary in the *range of permissible deviation.* When a person deviates from the norm, some form of sanction is usually directed toward him or her varying from mild disapproval to the death penalty. Some norms require almost complete *conformity,* whereas others permit a sizeable deviation from the norm before sanctions are administered.

The degree to which a group member conforms to the norms of the group is therefore of critical importance for group actions. When group members conform to the norms, everyone in the group can accurately predict the behavior of other group members and the group is able to function smoothly. When group members deviate from the critical norms of the group, then group members are not able to predict the behavior of others and conflict and uncoordinated activity is likely to result. In fact, most members do conform to the norms of the group most of the time, but the amount of overall conformity varies greatly and is dependent on a variety of factors. In general, the amount of conformity behavior is determined by the personality characteristics of group members, the kinds of stimuli that are operating at the time, situational factors, and relationships among group members.

Personality factors refer to the characteristics of the individual group member that predispose him or her to behave in particular ways, in particular those that predispose the person to conform to the norms of the group. For example, authoritarian individuals are more likely to conform than nonauthoritarians, and submissive persons are more likely to conform than dominant individuals.

Stimulus factors refer to such things as task difficulty and ambiguity of the situation. In general, the more ambiguous the task facing the group member, the more likely he or she is to conform to the norms of the group.

Situational factors include such things as size of the group, unanimity of the majority opinion in the group, the structure of the group, and similar contextural variables. Conformity increases with the size of the majority up to at least four persons and the more unanimous the group in supporting the norm, the more likely that individual group members will conform. Conformity also tends to be greater in groups that have a centralized organization than in those that have a decentralized one.

Relationships among group members refer to such variables as the kind of pressure exerted, the composition of the group, how successful the group has been in the past, and the degree to which the individual identifies with the group. In general, conformity increases with increasing group pressure, with the degree to which the group has been successful in solving problems in the past, and with the degree to which the individual identifies with the group. Group composition has also been observed to affect conformity behavior. For instance, in racially mixed groups it has been observed that both blacks and whites conform more to a white majority than to a black majority.

To summarize, *conformity behavior* is pervasive and is determined by a variety of circumstances operating in the group. For the most part, conformity behavior has desirable consequences for the group, because it introduces order and consistency that permits the group members to accurately predict the behavior of others and, therefore, promotes coordinated group action. When a group member blindly follows the dictates of the group without evaluating the consequences of conformity, negative effects can result.

Communication Patterns. Role prescriptions and norms exert a tremendous influence on the behav-

ior of individuals in groups, as we have seen, but there are other influences that also operate to determine group behavior. Some of these are imposed on the group by the nature of the physical arrangements in the group. For instance, it is commonly assumed that a centralized *pattern of communication* is more effective and the arrangement of communication channels among group members are arranged in this way. Examples of centralized communication networks are shown in Figure 15-3, in which the circles represent positions within the group and the lines represent two-way communication channels between positions. In *centralized communication networks* one or a few positions have many communication channels, whereas other positions are limited in the number of channels available to them. In contrast, *decentralized communication networks* have the available communication channels fairly equally distributed among group members. Although it is commonly assumed that a centralized network is more efficient, research fails to support this contention as a general proposition (Shaw, 1964). As can be seen by examining Table 15-2, the complexity of the task determines whether a centralized communication network or a decentralized communication network is the more effective one. In general, a centralized network is more efficient if the task is extremely simple, whereas the decentralized network is more effective for complex tasks.

When the group task is simple, the primary problem is to assemble information in one posi-

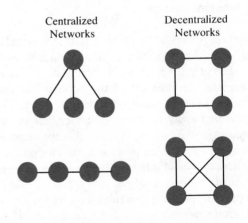

Fig. 15-3.   Typical communication networks.

Table 15-2. Percentage of Comparisons Showing Differences Between Centralized and Decentralized Networks for Simple and Complex Tasks

	Simple Tasks	Complex Tasks
Time to Complete:		
Centralized faster	78	0
Decentralized faster	22	100
Errors:		
Centralized made more	0	60
Decentralized made more	90	10
Satisfaction:		
Greater in Centralized	13	9
Greater in Decentralized	87	91

tion, at which time the proper solution to the task becomes obvious. When the task is complicated, however, it is important to have contributions from all members of the group. The free-flow of information (factual knowledge, ideas, technical know-how, feelings) among the various members of the group determines to a large extent the efficiency of the group and the satisfaction of its members.

The communication network also influences the *satisfaction* of the group members. For the most part, group members are much more satisfied in decentralized communication networks than in centralized ones. This is easily understandable in view of the fact that the decentralized networks provide them with greater sources of information and greater possibilities of interaction with other group members. On the other hand, a leader is much more likely to emerge in a centralized communication network than in a decentralized one, and the person who emerges as the leader is almost always the one who occupies the most central position in the network. Interestingly, that person is usually highly satisfied with his or her position in the group! As we shall see in the next section of this chapter, leadership has a marked influence on group behavior.

Leadership

The leadership role is one of the most important roles in a group. The position of leader is also one of the most valued positions in our society and one that has been of considerable interest both to the average person and persons in position of power. Everyone, of course, knows what a leader is and what is meant by leadership, but if you ask persons to define leadership, considerable differences of opinion emerge. Almost everyone agrees, however, that a leader is a person who exerts more influence in the group than other persons and who is able to get other group members to carry out desired activities and to generally abide by the leader's wishes.

The Trait Approach   In the early part of this century, it was believed that certain individuals were born leaders or at least that they had acquired certain traits and abilities that made them especially qualified for the leadership position. Consequently, the early studies of leadership concentrated on individual characteristics or traits. It was assumed that leaders had special traits that differentiated them from followers and that these traits could be identified, measured, and used to predict leadership effectiveness. Consequently, hundreds of studies were conducted in which leaders and nonleaders were identified, their characteristics measured, and attempts made to discover the differences between them. It was believed that if one could identify the unique characteristics of leaders, then one would be able to select leaders and place them in leadership positions, thus making the group more effective. After many years of research, it became clear that this conception of leadership behavior was highly inappropriate and the method of research had been extremely unproductive. However, these studies did yield some results of at least theoretical significance. They revealed that if a person is to be an effective leader that person must (1) have the necessary abilities to be a leader (such as intelligence, knowing how to get things done, insight into situations, and so forth), (2) the leader must possess characteristics that enable him or her to get along with other people in the group (such as dependability and exercising responsibility, cooperativeness, and so forth), and (3) the person must *want* to be a leader. Although these findings are of theoretical significance, they are of little practical value in selecting persons for the leadership role.

For example, many persons want to be a leader but are completely unqualified for the role.

Leadership Styles.   When it became clear that the trait approach to the study of leadership was ineffective, researchers turned to an investigation of leadership style. In particular, attention was directed to *autocratic* and *democratic leadership styles* (Lewin, *et al,* 1939). The autocrat is a leader who gives direction, issues orders, and exerts close control over all of the group's activities. The democratic leader is one who solicits the views of other group members, permits group members to share in the decision making process, and so forth. It was initially expected that democratic led groups would be more effective than groups led by an autocrat, but no consistent difference between the two types of leadership has been observed. On the other hand, members of democratic led groups are much more satisfied with the group, and there is less aggressive behavior and less hostility expressed in these groups than in autocratic led groups.

Fiedler's Leadership Theory.   The fact that there is no consistent difference between autocratic and democratic led groups in group efficiency is due in part to the circumstances under which the leadership occurs. The effectiveness of a group is a consequence not only of the leadership behavior but also of *situational factors* that relate to group performance. A theory of leadership proposed by Fred Fiedler (1967) attempts to incorporate leadership style and situational variables in the prediction of group performance. In Fiedler's work, leadership styles are identified by LPC (least preferred coworker) scores of the leader. The LPC score is based on ratings of the individual's least preferred coworker on a number of rating scales. The high LPC person perceives the least preferred coworker in a relatively favorable manner, whereas the low LPC person perceives the least preferred coworker in a relatively unfavorable manner. The high LPC person is presumably motivated primarily by a need for successful interpersonal relationships and only secondarily by a need for task completion. The low LPC person, on the other hand, is motivated primarily to be successful in task comple-

tion and only secondarily with regard to interpersonal relationships. According to the theory, the leader's LPC score will be related to group effectiveness in different ways depending on the *situation* in which the group finds itself. When the situation is highly favorable to the leader (that is, the leader has a position of power, the task is structured, and the personal relationships between the leader and members of the group are good) or when the situation is highly unfavorable to the leader (that is, the leader's position power is weak, the task is unstructured, and the personal relations between the leader and members of the group are poor) the low LPC or task-oriented leader is more effective. The relation-oriented leader performs most effectively when the situation is of intermediate favorability to the leader.

It is easy to see that the high LPC leader is essentially a democratic leader, whereas the low LPC leader is essentially an autocratic leader. The theory proposed by Fiedler thus specifies under what conditions the democratic leader will be more effective and under what conditions the autocratic leader will be more effective.

To summarize, the position of leader in the group is a critical one for group behavior. It is highly evaluated by most persons in our society, it influences the performance and satisfaction of group members, and is a highly significant determinant of group behavior. After many years of research, we still know relatively little about the contributions of personal characteristics, behavioral styles, and situational variables to leadership behavior and leader effectiveness.

Summary

Social behavior refers to behavior that is influenced by human beings and their products; it includes not only the behavior that is influenced by the presence and behavior of others, but also behavior that is influenced by the inventions of humans. Some important aspects of social behavior are person perception, attitudes, interpersonal attraction and affiliation, personal space, and behavior in groups.

Social perception concerns the effects of social

factors on perception and the perception of other people. Like other kinds of perception, social perceptions are selective and organized. When an individual first encounters another person, he or she seeks to learn as much about that person as possible, on the basis of which first impressions of the other person are formed. At the same time, the person is attempting to present himself or herself to the other person in such a manner as to cause the other person to see him or her in a particular way. The other person, of course, is engaged in similar processes. Thus, each attributes certain characteristics to the other, which may or may not be accurate. Person perceptions are often imprecise and may sometimes be grossly in error. When such gross inaccuracies occur, interpersonal conflict usually results.

Persons in all cultures develop attitudes about the significant persons, groups, and objects in their psychological world. An attitude may be defined as a relatively enduring system of affective, evaluative reactions toward a social object or class of social objects. Attitudes are the consequence of evaluative beliefs and associated evaluative concepts which are learned through the socialization process. Attitudes may be measured in several ways, the most common method being by means of attitude scales. Attitudes may be changed through a variety of procedures, such as the use of communication appeals. Attitudes are one of several classes of variables that influence behavior.

Some persons are attracted to each other and seek affiliation; others are repelled by certain others and seek to avoid associating with those persons. Interpersonal attraction is facilitated by situational circumstances such as proximity, contact, and interaction. Through association, one may discover that another is physically attractive, holds similar attitudes, and so on. When another person is perceived to have similar attitudes, economic status, race, sex, or other characteristics, he or she is usually seen as being more attractive than if characteristics are dissimilar. Interpersonal attraction usually leads to affiliation (or attempted affiliation).

Persons often appropriate space and assume territorial rights to it, even when they have no legal rights to the space. They also view the immediate area around their bodies as personal and private. These territories and personal spaces are defended against invasion; failure to respect another's territory or personal space leads to interpersonal conflict. Behavior is also influenced by the physical environment, such as size of room, seating arrangements, and communication networks.

A particularly significant kind of social behavior occurs in small groups. Behavior in groups is influenced by group structure, group composition, and other variables. The group structure is composed of positions, or differentiated parts of the group. Associated with each position is a role, that is, a set of behaviors that the position occupant is expected to enact. Each position is evaluated or assigned a status level by group members. Groups also establish norms or rules of conduct that guide the behavior of group members. All of these aspects of group structure influence group behavior in predictable ways. The behavior of groups also varies with the particular kinds of persons who compose the group.

Glossary

Attitude: A relatively enduring system of affective, evaluative reactions toward a social object or class of objects; a generalized feeling, favorable or unfavorable, toward persons or things in one's world.

Belief: A proposition that one accepts as true (valid, correct).

Communication network: The arrangement or pattern of communication channels among the positions in a group.

Conformity: The degree to which an individual's behavior corresponds to the norms of his or her group.

Group cohesiveness: The resultant of all those forces acting on group members to remain in or to leave the group.

Group structure: The pattern of relationships among the differentiated parts of a group.

Interpersonal attraction: The degree to which one individual is drawn to another person.

Attribution: A process by which characteristics, motivations, intentions, responsibility, and so on are ascribed to others.

Leadership: A process in which one group member exerts positive influence over other group members.

Personal space: The physical space surrounding each individual that he or she regards as personal and private.

Prejudice: An attitude that does not change when new and inconsistent evidence becomes available.

Social behavior: Behavior that is influenced by human beings and/or their products.

Social facilitation: The effect that the mere presence of others has on the behavior of other individuals.

Social norms: Standards that specify appropriate behavior in a group.

Social role: The behaviors expected of the occupant of a given position in a group by other members of that group.

Social status: The evaluation or prestige accorded a given position in a group.

Territoriality: The assumption of a proprietary orientation toward a geographical area by a person or by a group.

Suggested Readings

Calder, B. J., and Ross, M. *Attitudes and Behavior*. Morristown, N.J.: General Learning Press, 1973.

Hastorf, A. H., Schneider, D. J., and Polefka, J. *Person Perception*. Reading, Mass.: Addison-Wesley, 1970.

Kleinke, C. L. *First Impressions: The Psychology of Encountering Others*. Englewood Cliffs, N.J.: Prentice-Hall, 1975.

Linder, D. E. *Personal Space*. Morristown, N.J.: General Learning Press, 1974.

Rubin, Z. *Liking and Loving: An Invitation to Social Psychology*. New York: Holt, Rinehart and Winston, 1973.

Shaw, M. E. *An Overview of Small Groups*. Morristown, N.J.: General Learning Press, 1974.

Zimbardo, P., and Ebbesen, E. B. *Influencing Attitudes and Changing Behavior*. Reading, Mass.: Addison-Wesley, 1969.

16

Perspectives on Social Issues

Barry R. Schlenker and Lawrence J. Severy

Introduction

Most scientists make a distinction between *pure* versus *applied* research, each of which has its own unique goal. Pure, or basic, research tries to answer questions that may or may not have any apparent practical applications. Questions are explored to satisfy intellectual curiosity and to experience the thrill of unraveling one of nature's riddles (for example, Einstein was curious about the relationship between matter and energy; many psychologists are curious about the nature of human learning). Applied research, though, seeks to gain answers to specific practical questions that are important to people, and the scientific consequences of the work may not be of primary concern (for example, many engineers seek to perfect alternative energy sources, such as solar energy or nuclear energy, that would decrease reliance on other countries; many educators seek to develop classroom experiences that will maximize learning). These two goals, *explanation* versus *application,* often go hand in hand to supplement and reinforce one another. A breakthrough in pure research may lead to practical applications that were not initially imagined (for example, Einstein's theories were applied to the development of nuclear power; theories of learning can be applied to the classroom). Reciprocally, applied research may lead pure researchers to develop scientific theories to explain why the practical discoveries work as they do (such as a particular classroom experience that affects learning might be explored to deter-

mine why it is successful). In the long run, both science and the human condition can be advanced through both types of research goals.

Psychologists, like everyone else, are concerned about important social problems and believe that research will help us understand and, hopefully, solve, many of them. Much of this research has clearly applied characteristics, in that the researcher seems most concerned with the practical social consequences of the work. But pure research also plays an important role, in that we need to know why things happen as they do. For example, prejudice and discrimination are important social problems in today's world. How can we reduce discrimination in job hiring and pay practices? Will school bussing to achieve racial integration decrease or increase prejudice and hostility? These important applied research questions can be easily supplemented with numerous basic research questions. What is prejudice, and why does it seem to be a universal characteristic of humans? How does prejudice develop? Why are certain groups and not others chosen as objects of discrimination? Eventually, scientific theories of prejudice spring from answers to questions such as these, and the theories might help us to find ways to solve the social problems.

This chapter will explore six social issues that have received a great deal of attention from social psychologists. Obviously, many more social issues could have been selected, but we hope that this sampling will give you an idea of how psychologists approach social problems. We will begin with an examination of *prejudice* and *discrimination,* both as related to ethnic problems and to sexism. Prejudice, of course, also is manifested between groups that are rivals for scarce resources, such as between nations in conflict. Therefore, our second topic will be that of *social conflict:* what it is, what problems it creates, and how it can be reduced. A major problem in the contemporary world is that of the *population explosion,* our third topic. Overcrowding seems to produce numerous changes in our behaviors, not the least of which are feelings of deindividuation that can lead to aggression and violence. *Aggression* and *violence* will constitute our fourth topic and we will explore questions such as why do people resort to violence, and what effects does the mass media portrayal of violence have on our behavior? Our fifth topic will explore the opposite side of the coin—*helping behavior.* Finally, we will examine some of the social aspects of *sexual behavior,* including the effects of pornography on crime rates.

Prejudice and Discrimination

One of the most pervasive social problems in the United States continues to be that of racial injustice, and a high priority for social scientists is the identification of strategies to overcome it. As we are writing this, new chapters are being added to the social histories of Boston, Louisville, and Detroit that parallel the events that originally occurred in Little Rock, Arkansas, and Birmingham, Alabama with regard to forced desegregation and school bussing. In 1954, the United States Supreme Court decided in *Brown vs. the Board of Education* that "separate but equal" schools were, by their very nature, unequal. When white children attended one school and black children were only allowed to attend another, a form of *race discrimination* was being engaged in that could not and should not be tolerated. When psychologists use the term racial discrimination, they are describing instances in which the behavior accorded to individuals of one group is different from behavior accorded to individuals of a second group. For example, if one were to pay a male taxicab driver twice the tip for the same work and same trip as one would pay a female taxicab driver, just be-

cause one driver was male and the other female, one would be said to be discriminating against women in favor of men. (The idea of equal pay for equal work has been one of the prime demands of women's liberation.) Importantly, these behavioral differences are based solely on an individual's membership in a group and not on what the individual is like as a unique person. When a father of a white student from South Boston decides to aggress and act violently against black school children that are being bussed into his neighborhood school, he is engaging in such behavior not for reasons based on personal characteristics of those black children other than their being black.

Many individuals do not overtly display behavioral discrimination but engage instead in what is known as *prejudice.* Prejudice can be defined as a negative attitude toward an individual (or group of individuals) based solely on the individual's membership in a certain group. Groups can be identified on the basis of a number of characteristics—ethnic identity being the most prominent. It is conceivable that the white father who carries out aggressive acts toward black children has very negative attitudes about blacks in general. He may not know anything about the particular children he aggresses against or how wonderful they may be, but rather has formed a negative attitude based simply on their inclusion in an ethnic group known as black. Similar negative attitudes have been held at different times over the years towards Jews, Italians, Cubans, Indians, Chicanos, Irish, and so on. Even today, in different sections of our country, there is a differential ranking of negativeness towards certain groups. For example, in Denver and in some parts of the southwest, blacks are thought more highly of than are Chicanos who are at the bottom of the social status hierarchy.

A third concept that needs identification and delineation is that of *stereotype.* Accompanying negative attitudes are certain beliefs about individuals based on their membership in groups. These beliefs tend to be overgeneralized ideas that are not checked against individual characteristics to indicate when they are in error. For example, stereotypes regarding individuals representative of certain groups include: Latins are good lovers, fast talkers; blacks are lazy, musically-inclined, and dumb; Irish are pig-headed; and Jews are good with money. These stereotypes demonstrate the failure to see people as individual persons and respond to them accordingly (Figure 16-1).

A very important clarification is necessary at this point. Group membership does not have to be ethnic in nature to evoke stereotypes, prejudices, and discrimination. In fact, one of the more pervasive and popular current prejudices is *sexism*, or gender prejudice. Discrimination, prejudice, and stereotypes have affected women just as they have affected members of ethnic groups. For example, women receive less pay for the same work as men.

Discrimination in job hiring was so prevalent that the Supreme Court, on June 21, 1973, decided that no longer could newspapers accept nor publish help-wanted ads differentiated by sex. The recent push in hiring women in certain job classifications has closely followed the Federal mandates to hire blacks and other minority group members, again in occupations typically held by white males.

Much of the thrust of the women's liberation movement can be seen as a frontal attack on the prejudices and stereotypes pertaining to the "appropriate" place for a woman in this society. Is it in the home? Is it to have children? Is it to support

Fig. 16-1.   Stereotypes in action. Freeman F. Gosden and Charles F. Correll, both white, were stars of the immensely popular radio program, *Amos 'n Andy,* during the 1940s and 1950s.

the husband? Or, alternatively, is it to challenge for personal growth and accomplishment in the real world in a fashion exactly the same as has been described for men? The nonconscious pervasiveness of sexism has been well documented and can be identified in the writings of all major religious orientations, in our classic novels, on television, in the movies, and so on (Bem and Bem, 1970). Simply consider the number of major female stars holding series on television versus the number of males. As recently as 1974, there were only three female-lead continuing programs on U.S. television. The majority remain male, although the media is attempting to rectify the situation.

Sex prejudice, just like ethnic prejudice, is subject to cross-cultural variations. Margaret Mead (1949) in her classic work *Males and Females*, describes various New Guinea cultures wherein it is the female who is responsible, makes all the decisions, and is aggressive—with the males being docile, submissive, and homebodies. When cross-cultural variation such as this is found, the strong implication is that these orientations are learned phenomena.

At least five different factors have been identified as potential determinants of discrimination, prejudice, and stereotopy. They are as follows: *competition* and *exploitation, assumed belief dissimilarity, conformity, relative deprivation,* and the *prejudiced personality*. We will discuss each of these briefly in turn.

Competition and Exploitation

Competition and conflict between groups can produce hostility which results in prejudice and discrimination. Often, competition derives from economic considerations. When one's livelihood is threatened because members of another group move into the area and compete for jobs, the possibility of prejudice and discrimination increases. It has also been hypothesized that under frustrating economic conditions, people are likely to blame the members of an outgroup for their troubles and vent their frustrations on them. It has been claimed that blacks have frequently been used as scapegoats for economically stressed whites. In one

study, Hovland and Sears (1940) found a correlation between economic conditions in the South from 1882 and 1930 and the number of lynchings of blacks—as economic conditions became worse, more blacks were lynched, as economic conditions improved, fewer blacks were lynched. A. U.S. Department of Labor survey in 1969 conducted in four of our larger cities indicated that not a single black apprentice was employed in these cities in the mid 1960s in the occupations of plumbing, steamfitting, sheet metal work, painting, lathing, glazing, and stone masonry. Sex discrimination for occupational employment operates in a similar fashion with less than 1 percent of this country's engineers being female, prior to 1970.

Assumed Belief Dissimilarity

Many researchers speculate that prejudice is caused and fostered whenever someone believes that members of other groups "think differently" than they do, or somehow have different values. For example, many Americans believe that the "Oriental mind" is strange and foreign in comparison to western thought. Perhaps thinking that women have different values has led many officers of admissions to medical schools (and other professional schools) to hold down admissions of women into such professions. They may believe that women have different values and would simply want to get married and have children as soon as they finish their degree. Rokeach (1960) and his associates suggest that assumed belief dissimilarity accounts for many prejudiced social interaction patterns. According to this view, whites are prejudiced toward blacks largely because they believe blacks have different beliefs and values. Once shown that their beliefs and values are similar, prejudice would disappear. For example, a white should prefer to interact with a black with similar beliefs rather than with a white with different beliefs.

A contrasting point of view is taken by Triandis (1961) who suggests that "people do not exclude other people from their neighborhoods, for instance, because other people have different belief systems, but they do exclude them because they are Negroes." (See Chapter 17 for further discussion.) His concentration on characteristic cues such as color coding forces us to acknowledge a long social learning history portraying black as evil ("black as sin") and representative of the bad guys (wearing black hats) with white being on the side of law, order, and goodness (wearing white hats). At any rate, the belief that others have different values, beliefs, and ideals from your own might lead to differential treatment.

Conformity

It has been suggested that in some cases racial prejudice may serve some social adjustment function. If the norms of one's subculture encourage racial prejudice, then the more that one conforms to these norms, the better off one would be within that subculture, and the more prejudiced one would become.

Some extreme cases of this conformity effect have been found in coal mining towns where there is *rigid segregation of blacks and whites above the ground* in the town itself, and *total integration of black and white miners down in the mines*. Similarly, if a woman is conforming to what she perceives to be the appropriate behavior for a woman, namely, that of being submissive, docile, and homebound, she is increasing society's expectancies and prejudices for her gender's role. If, however, a male were to engage in such behavior, he would be frowned upon and seen as "strange."

Relative Deprivation

Whenever a group perceives that they are being rewarded in a fashion that is inequitable, they feel deprived. When they feel that the rewards given to members of their group are not fair in comparison to what other groups receive, they feel relative deprivation. It has been demonstrated that a growing feeling of relative deprivation among blacks in Los Angeles reached a critical peak just prior to the 1965 riots in Watts. When the deprivation became too great, it boiled over into insurrection.

Pettigrew and his associates report that in a study of whites' reactions to black mayorality candidates, whites who feel relative deprivation (with regard to blacks) are those least likely to vote for a

black for mayor (Vanneman and Pettigrew, 1972). A similar analysis of voting patterns for women candidates indicates that men who perceive women's liberation to have provided women with relatively more gains than men have received (that is, when relative deprivation is present), will be least likely voting for a woman.

Prejudiced Personality

There is a question as to whether or not there are certain people who can be described as having prejudiced personalities. During World War II, a concern developed for the profiling of antisemitic (anti-Jewish) individuals. A number of investigators identified a type of personality that can be characterized by antidemocratic tendencies, generalized loyalty to the ingroup and rejection of outgroups, rigidity, and rationalization. This personality type has been labeled the *authoritarian personality*. More recent description of individuals who are dogmatic, rigid, and cognitively simple expands the notion that there are people who are more prone to concentration on ingroup relationships and rejection of outgroup relationships. Clearly, these individuals would tend to be more prejudiced toward all outgroups.

Prejudice Reduction

Given that all these factors lead to both ethnic group and sex-role prejudice, discrimination and stereotypy, what can be done? Attempts have proceeded to alleviate both of these forms of prejudice via mass media campaigns, individual therapy, child-rearing practices, and forced changes of behavior. Clearly, socialization practices need to be altered so that better quality relationships between members of different ethnic groups are forthcoming. Bolstering women's images in mass media campaigns, changing child-rearing practices with regard to what is appropriate or inappropriate all have their impact.

Further, legislation and court decisions can have their effects. There are indications that forced behavioral interaction, as ordered by the Supreme Court decisions, can sometimes have a beneficial result. Probably the best laboratory examination of this question is provided by Stuart Cook (1970). Cook studied the conditions that are necessary in order for interpersonal contact and interaction to bring about changes in prejudiced attitudes. A number of factors were identified: (1) all participants in the situation must be of equal status, (2) cooperation and mutual interdependence must be encouraged, (3) social norms must be supportive of such interaction, (4) the situation should promote personal relationships and friendship formation, (5) individual attributes of the participants should contradict prevailing negative stereotypes, and (6) the situation should encourage participants to generalize their changed attitudes to other situations.

Cook deliberately created a situation in which all of the above conditions were met. The extremely comprehensive and time consuming project obtained results that are somewhat encouraging, although at the same time somewhat discouraging. About 40 percent of the subjects changed their attitudes in a quite positive direction as measured a month after the experience had ended. Unfortunately, a few changed in the opposite direction and became even more negative. In an attempt to see if personality factors could account for these changes, it was found that subjects with positive attitudes towards people in general and low cynicism tended to be those individuals who became less prejudiced. Later studies in "real world" settings such as "tough" state prisons essentially replicated Cook's findings. Racial attitudes do change during incarceration when situations are constructed along the lines delineated above. Further, the best personality predictor of change is positive attitudes towards people in general.

Social Conflict

Social conflict is a situation in which the goals of two or more parties are to some degree incompatible; all of the parties cannot achieve their desired goals at the same time. The incompatibility can occur over a clash in major goals, such as has occurred between the United States and the Soviet Union over conflicting ideologies. Or the incom-

patibility can occur even when people agree on major goals but disagree over minor ones. For example, you and your date might agree that your goal for the evening is to have fun together, but be in conflict about whether you would have more fun at a drive-in movie or at a dance. Whenever two or more people disagree about anything, the seeds for conflict exist. When major conflicts occur, such as between nations or between large groups, they can erupt into violence and bloodshed. Of course, these are the conflicts that we most often hear about. But even smaller conflicts can produce numerous difficulties—if a husband and wife have enough arguments, their marriage may dissolve or, in the extreme, one may murder the other.

Conflicts can have productive as well as destructive consequences. Two scientists may argue about which of their theories are most accurate, and as a result of their argument discover something that neither would have uncovered had the conflict not spurred them into action. Or a political minority may disagree with the policies of the majority, and as a consequence of the conflict, a new policy is formulated that gains strength from the views of both. The history of the United States is full of incidents where the positions of a minority third party in one election are implemented in slightly modified form by the victorious majority.

Stages of Violent Conflicts

All too often, conflicts get out of hand and result in an increasing spiral of violence. Certain consistent perceptual and behavioral changes take place during such conflicts, and they follow particular stages. First, when conflict is initially noticed by the participants, *tension* is shown. The participants begin to change their perceptions, both of themselves and of the "enemy." They tend to see themselves as the "good" guys, and the others as the "bad" guys. The actions of each party take on new meanings in the eyes of the other, as each begins to see possible threats in the other's behaviors. The tension and threat perception leads to the second stage, *rising preparedness* to deal with the perceived threats. In the case of larger groups, the preparedness can be shown by acquiring military weapons, which are felt to be necessary for "protection.'' In the case of a husband and wife, the preparedness may be evidenced by their thinking up rapier-like comments and put-downs to hurl at the other at the slightest provocation. If the parties cannot work out a peaceful solution to the conflict through talks and compromises, they are likely to enter the third stage of a conflict spiral—*open hostilities*. Threats are met with counterthreats, put-downs with still larger put-downs, and violence can erupt. These three stages, tension (with accompanying perceptual changes), rising preparedness, and finally open hositility, have been observed prior to most wars (see Pruitt and Snyder, 1969), and it is not hard to apply the stages to other, smaller conflicts. For example, the violence that erupted between police and demonstrators at the Democratic National Convention in Chicago in 1968 followed an identical pattern. The city officials and police perceived that political demonstrators would disrupt the tranquility of their city. Pamphlets written by some demonstrators, though largely peaceful in tone, were often interpreted by the police as a threat. The city prepared itself by calling out the army (in full battle gear, including rifles, flame throwers, and bazookas) and national guard, stationing armed personnel carriers in Soldier's Field, and even stationing firemen at each alarm box within a six block radius of the convention site. As all this was going on, perceptions were changing: demonstrators were viewed by the police as ''hippies,'' or ''anarchists,'' and police were viewed by the demonstrators as ''pigs'' or ''fascists.'' Finally, violence erupted, often with minimal provocation, with hundreds of policemen, demonstrators, and newsmen being hospitalized.

Perceptual Changes During Conflicts

Three types of perceptual phenomena can occur during conflicts: black-and-white thinking, double standards, and mirror images (Frank, 1967). Black-and-white thinking occurs when the participants to a conflict see things as ''either-or,'' ''for-us'' or ''against-us.'' Typically, this translates into seeing one's own position as ''right'' and ''good'' and the other party's position as ''wrong'' and ''bad.'' Two prevalent self-images that emerge are the *moral self-image* and the *virile self-image*. The

moral self-image amounts to each side viewing its own position as the only ''moral'' position a reasonable person could take, and certainly God and the fates must be behind it. No war was ever fought where the participants suspected that God might be on their opponent's side. In conflicts, though, it is not enough to be good and righteous, one must also be strong. The virile self-image describes the perception that one's own side possesses the strength, determination, and ''masculinity'' to triumph in the end. Wars are seldom fought when each party did not think it was powerful enough to win. Complementing these images is a negative view of the opponent, the *diabolical enemy image*. The opponent is viewed as evil incarnate, as barbaric, and as something less than human. Together, these forms of black-and-white thinking can facilitate violence. When one views oneself as moral and powerful, it becomes easy to justify any atrocity by claiming a high moral purpose. When opponents are viewed as diabolical, it becomes easy to rationalize why they must die; viewing them as less than human then makes it easier to kill.

Double standards are also easy to find in conflict situations. A *double standard* exists when the same action is evaluated differently depending on who performs it. Typically, parties to a conflict evaluate their own actions positively, but should the opponent do the same thing, the action suddenly takes on a different meaning and becomes negative. For example, placing United States military bases in Turkey next to the borders of the Soviet Union is viewed positively by most Americans, since it is felt that such an action is consistent with our peaceful intentions and promotes world safety. But should the Soviet Union place a military base in the Western hemisphere, Americans would see that action as hostile, aggressive, and anything but peaceful. Studies have shown that people do display double standards to a surprisingly large degree (see Frank, 1967).

Finally, *mirror images* are perceptions that exist on both sides to a conflict, but are opposite reflections of one another. For example, Americans view themselves as peaceful, well intentioned, rational, and trustworthy, and view people in the Soviet Union in the opposite ways. It should not come as a great surprise to learn that the Soviets hold exactly the same views, but in reverse. That is, they see themselves as peaceful, well intentioned, rational, and trustworthy, and view us in the opposite way.

Sadly, these types of misperceptions are almost necessary for survival once one does resort to violence as a means of settling conflicts. Unless one sees oneself positively and the enemy negatively, one might hesitate at a critical moment and be exterminated. Unfortunately, these perceptions often develop early in conflicts and color interpretations of ensuing events, making needless violence more likely to occur. When neither side to a conflict trusts the other, and when each interprets its actions positively and the other's negatively, it is difficult to get either one to move toward resolving the conflict. This is true whether the antagonists are nations, large groups such as labor and management, small groups such as street gangs, or even individuals.

Threats and Conflicts

Against a background of perceptual distortions, threats and punishments (whether real or imagined) will usually occur. When a party is in a conflict, dislikes and distrusts the adversary, and has the ability to threaten or punish that adversary, it requires a tremendous amount of restraint to refrain from inflicting the harm. In fact, as the magnitude of a conflict increases, people usually feel that they must use threats and punishments in order to get what they want. They feel that the adversary would never listen to reason or bargain in good faith, so they must use force. Unfortunately, if both parties have the ability to do harm, a threat by one usually produces resistance and counterthreat by the other. No one wants to lose face by appearing soft, compliant, and vulnerable. Soon such threats and counterthreats produce a conflict spiral of ever increasing magnitude.

It has been suggested that the mere existence of "weapons" (the ability to threaten and deliver harm) can present such a temptation that people in a conflict might actually be much better off without them. Instead of trying to harm one another, they would have to work together to resolve their dif-

ferences. To test this idea, Deutsch and Krauss (1960) constructed a trucking game that placed people on opposite sides in a conflict. Each of two people had control of a small, imaginary trucking company whose vehicles could be guided along routes via a control panel. The parties were in conflict, because the only route that each party could take to reach their goal and make a profit had room for only one truck at a time. If both parties tried to make a profit on every trip (they were to make twenty such trips), their trucks would meet head-on in the middle of the route, and they would lose a great deal of money. The only way to avoid such a confrontation was for one or both of the parties to use a longer, alternate route that guaranteed a small loss of money on that trip. The solution to this conflict was simple (at least from an objective standpoint): The parties should alternate their use of the short, profitable route, one time taking the short route and the next time taking the long route. However, each of the participants naturally would have liked to gain exclusive access to the short route. Into this conflict situation, the investigators manipulated the degree to which each person could threaten and harm the other. In one condition (bilateral threat), both parties were given the use of road gates that could block their opponent's use of the short route. In a second condition (unilateral threat), only one person was given the use of a road gate and the other person was "unarmed." And in a third (no threat) condition, neither of the parties had access to a road gate.

As hypothesized, the investigators found that the subjects were most cooperative and made the highest joint profits when neither one had the ability to threaten and harm the other. Subjects cooperated less, and jointly lost some money, when one of the parties had a gate. And, the subjects lost a great deal of money when both of them had threats. The investigators also found that when neither party or only one party had threat capability, they learned to cooperate over time and their profits increased. When both parties had threats, they were just as uncooperative (and were losing just as much money) at the end of the game as they were at the beginning. This experiment, and a number of others like it, provide evidence indicating that when conflicts occur, people are usually better off not having the ability to harm one another. Each side may feel that its weapons are for "defensive" or "peaceful" purposes, but ultimately, the temptation to use them becomes very great and a conflict spiral and mutual harm is likely to occur. Although no one should immediately advocate that the United States get rid of all its weapons solely on the basis of these experiments, they do give one pause to reconsider what the consequences of arms races and burgeoning defense budgets really can be.

Conflict Reduction

We have examined the stages that conflicts go through before they erupt into violence and considered some of the perceptions and behaviors that occur during conflicts. But probably the most important aspect of conflict is the practical question of how it can be reduced. Five different techniques, some of which are more effective than others, have been presented by various people. These include: (1) appeals to reason and brotherhood, (2) intergroup contact, (3) introduction of common goals, (4) pacifism, and (5) a strategy called GRIT. Examples of two of these techniques are shown in Figure 16-2.

Many people suggest that *persuasive appeals* to concepts like "brotherhood," "peace," and "harmony" might reduce conflict, and when very minute conflicts exist, they might be correct. However, when somewhat larger conflicts exist, appeals to reason are typically ineffective since no one then listens to reason. The misperceptions discussed earlier cause each party to distrust the appeals of an opponent, and a "neutral" third party is usually ineffective because each side feels that the neutral misunderstands the "real" issues involved. In an atmosphere of suspicion and misperception, it takes more to reduce conflict than just words.

An alternative approach is to try to bring the antagonists together in the same situation. Proponents of such *intergroup contact* suggest that it allows each side to see that the other is not really as bad as was thought. By talking together, they might find similar interests, and eventually work out their difficulties. Thus, "forced integration"

might be an effective way to reduce prejudice and conflict. Studies have shown that intergroup contact can sometimes effectively reduce hostilities. Unfortunately, it is not always effective. The parties can discover that they have even less in common than they initially thought, or they can use the opportunity to hurl insults at one another rather than talk amicably. Intergroup contact seems to be effective in reducing conflict only when the parties view one another as status and power equals. They can then talk on an equal footing, and possibly resolve differences. Otherwise, hostilities are likely to increase even further. During most large conflicts, the misperceptions that exist cause the parties to see each other as unequals, and therefore, intergroup contact has only minimal effectiveness in those situations where conflict reduction is most needed.

A third approach focuses on the effects that *working together on common goals* have on people. A popular theme of many science fiction novels is an invasion from outer space. Invariably, an author describes how the common goal of defeating the unfriendly invaders pulls people from all parts of the world together into a cohesive unit; worldly differences are forgotten to dispel the unworldly invader. Evidence indicates that the conflict-reducing effectiveness of the introduction of common goals (goals shared by the parties) is not mere science fiction—it can successfully reduce conflict. In one famous study conducted at a boys' camp at Robber's Cave, Oklahoma (Sheriff et al, 1961), investigators tried to reduce the conflict that existed between two rival boys' groups. They first tried to bring the boys together for intergroup contacts, such as eating together, viewing movies together, and so on. This only increased the hostilities, as the boys used the opportunities to hurl both insults and food at their opponents. The only way the investigators found to effectively reduce conflict was by introducing common goals that both groups had to work for in order to obtain. For example, when the camp's water supply was damaged (actually, it was sabotaged by the investigators to give the boys a common goal), the groups had to work together to fix it; they similarly worked together to repair a broken truck, to earn money for new camp movies, and so on. Over the

Fig. 16-2.
Two techniques of conflict reduction. The use of pacifism to bring attention to legitimate grievances was exemplified by the civil rights marches of the early 1960s. A strategy similar to GRIT was implemented by John F. Kennedy in his relations with Soviet Premier Khruschev.

course of several days, working together to achieve common goals reduced the conflict, and the group members left the camp as friends.

One important limitation of the use of common goals to reduce conflict is that the parties must discover, when working together, that they actually do have much in common and develop trust and liking. Otherwise, when the common goal is removed, the groups will be enemies again. This happened to the United States and the Soviet Union after World War II. Once the common goal of defeating Nazi Germany was accomplished, the two former allies became antagonists since their ideological differences still existed.

A fourth approach is that of *pacifism*. Pacifism is as much a strategy for behaving during conflicts as it is a means of settling them. Pacifism has been defined as "a very active effort to defeat, by means other than violence, a possessor of superior destructive power, and . . . it requires at least as much courage, discipline, and initiative as violent combat" (Frank, 1967, p. 259). It was brought to the attention of the world by Mohandas Gandhi, the great Indian leader, and was practiced in this country by Martin Luther King, Jr. during the Civil Rights protests of the 1960s. Pacifists hope to resolve conflict by steadfastly adhering to moral principles to demonstrate to the opponent that they have the strength to suffer for their beliefs. If successful, the pacifist will morally embarrass and demoralize the opponent and, instead of fostering increased violence, will inhibit violence. Clearly, pacifism must be judged as much on moral grounds as it is on the grounds of how effective a strategy it is for settling arguments. But the effectiveness question is one that has received the attention of social psychologists. Typically, experiments have found that pacifistic strategies result in a great deal of exploitation of the pacifist. Pacifism is most effective when communication between the parties occurs freely, when neutral observers are present who can condemn an opponent for exploiting the pacifist, and when the opponent does not have a number of "teammates" who urge that person to exploit the pacifist. However, even under these conditions, cooperation with the pacifist is not 100 percent. At present, it can be concluded that pacifism is a strategy that is morally satisfying for

many people and that, under the right conditions, can be somewhat effective in reducing conflict, but it does not always work.

A final strategy is called GRIT (Osgood, 1962), which stands for "Graduated Reciprocation in Tension-Reduction." Despite the impressive title, it is the ultimate in simplicity and common sense. In essence, it calls for one party to announce in advance an intention of making a cooperative gesture, and also stating a hope that reciprocation will be forthcoming. Advance notice is important, since without it, the other side is very likely to interpret the gesture as a trick or trap. The first gesture should be relatively small, such that if it is exploited, very little is lost. If the other side does respond to this combination of an appeal and a cooperative behavior, then the first side can make another, slightly larger gesture, that again might be reciprocated. This process can then continue until cooperation blossoms fully and the conflict disappears. If, at any stage, reciprocation does not follow, neither side will be much worse off than it was before. Although the gestures might initially be viewed with suspicion by the opponent, over time trust comes to replace hostility. This modest proposal, or something very close to it, was actually tried by the Kennedy administration and was producing results in reducing tension with the Soviet Union until Kennedy's death ended the project (see Tedeschi and Lindskold, 1976, p. 395).

Population Growth and Crowding

One contemporary social problem that many feel overshadows all other social issues is that of the world's increasing population growth. It is quite likely that population growth influences such diverse phenomena as prejudice, changing sexual mores, aggression and violence versus altruism, and international conflict. However, before such applications are attempted, the problem of population growth and increased crowding needs to be addressed as a problem in and of itself.

Even if one does not take an alarmist's position, (not predicting the end of the world as we now understand it by the doomsday year of 2030), it is evident that the earth's population is growing at an ever expanding rate (see Figure 16-3). One dramatic way of describing population growth is to attempt to assess the number of years that it would take for the earth's population to double. Each and every year it takes fewer and fewer years (according to projections) to double the entire population of the world. There are many writers who believe that the world is already overcrowded and cannot sustain life with adequate food provisions with the current population. Compound this belief with the statement that for every person on the face of the earth there will be an additional person in less than thirty-five years. In other words, *just thirty-five years from now the size of the world population*

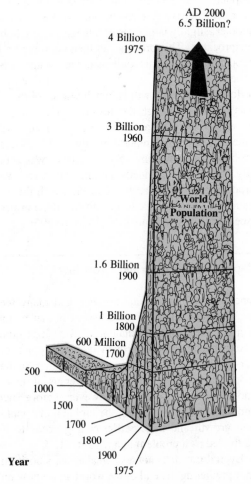

Fig. 16-3. Expanding rate of population growth. (Adapted from a chart © *National Geographic Society.*)

will be doubled. What are the implications for this tremendous increase?

The first and most obvious implication is that there simply will not be enough resources to provide the kind of quality life that most literate people expect. Pictures of food lines in Bangladesh, already the world's third largest country in terms of population, may be projections of the kind of life situation that will confront all countries within the foreseeable future. Let us be more optimistic, however, and hope that through both individual decisions and government policies, population growth will slow down and stabilize at closer to a *replacement* rate. For example, a Peking born novelist and surgeon, Han Suyin, reports that the most recent cry amongst women in the Peoples' Republic of China is "Have you taken your pill?" Reporting that family planning started in 1956 in Chinese cities, but only accelerated in the early 1970s in the communes where 85 percent of the people live, Dr. Han suggests that women "get together and decide how many children should be born that year on that particular street. Supposing that they feel that the street should have only five children that year and there are seven prospective mothers, there should be two volunteers to say 'I'll wait until next year.' If a woman disagrees, nothing is done to coerce her but someone else will have to sacrifice for her and she will feel bad about it" (Associated Press, June 21, 1975). Consequently, in a country where nearly a quarter of the earth's estimated 4 billion population lives, there is implementation of public policy to cut back on the birth rate. Even if such governmental policies are implemented, however, there are still very good questions that need to be addressed as to how increasing overcrowding and urbanization affect interpersonal behavior (the development of different personalities, development of aggression and violence, altruism, and so on).

Since the earth maintains a constant size and its population is growing, the result is that the number of people per any unit of area is also increasing. The number of people per unit area is known as *population density.* A concept that is related to density but carries important distinctions for psychologists is that of *crowding.* According to social psychological theorizing, crowding exists for any individual when the demand for space (the demand for interpersonal distance) exceeds what is available to them (see Chapter 15 for a discussion of interpersonal distance). For psychologists, the *feeling* of being crowded may be a more important determinant of behavioral changes than the actual number of people that exists in a particular unit of area density. Unfortunately, most studies addressing the issue have been studies of population density rather than crowding. These studies take two forms; (1) epidemeological (or demographic) in nature, and (2) laboratory studies. A look at these two different approaches provides insight to early findings regarding the response to population growth.

Demographic Perspectives

A brief overview of demographic findings obtained from around the world serves to introduce the complexity of issues involved. (*Demography* is the study of population dynamics as reflected in vital statistics such as: births, deaths, marriages, diseases, and so on.) For example, it has been reported that the consequences of urban housing in France are quite clear. Social and physical pathologies appear to double whenever the space available to people living in a particular area is below 8 to 10 square meters. Infantile deaths not due to biological or disease factors increase dramatically among South American children from larger families. In Hong Kong, overcrowding has apparently been found to produce superficial signs of psychological distress such as complaints, unhappiness, worries, and certain parental problems relating to controlling children. In Honolulu, several measures of density have been related to health problems and social disruption, such as death rates, tuberculosis, venereal disease, mental hospital admissions, illegitimate births, juvenile delinquency, and prison admissions. Lastly, research on crowded sections of Manila indicates that men tend to adopt one of three different forms of response that can be viewed as problematic. Some men become aggressive, some fantasize, and others become isolationist and plainly withdraw. Though cross-cultural variations are widespread, it is obvious that urban crowding and density have been related to social pathology in a number of different countries.

Most of the early research on population density dealt with the strong relationship between increased size of cities and increased crime rates. More recently, however, the studies on the nature of crowding have concentrated on more "psychological" factors. Let us examine one such study in an attempt to further delineate the problem.

Galle et al (1972) utilized 1960 census data and public record information in a study of seventy-five community areas in Chicago, Illinois. They found that there was a substantial relationship between crowding (or density) and social indicators, such as admissions to mental hospitals, family disturbances, juvenile delinquency, and so on. These investigators constructed measures and indicators reflective of a distinction they made between *interpersonal crowding* and what may be called *structural crowding*. Interpersonal crowding had to do with the number of people in a room, or the number of people we might face each day; whereas the structural crowding had to do with the number of living units per square mile or buildings per block. Galle et al found that it was interpersonal crowding that was most highly related to the social pathological variables of poor child care, high fertility, asocial and aggressive behavior, abnormally high death rate, and high mental hospital admission rates. In conclusion, there does appear to be a relationship between crowding and interpersonal problems. These investigators speculated that as the number of people that one must interact with increases that: (1) one has increasing social obligations and therefore must inhibit individual needs; (2) one is confronted with too much social stimulation—some which must be ignored; and (3) one faces a conflict for territory. However, socioeconomic factors contaminate some of these studies and make it difficult to draw conclusions. People who live in crowded conditions are usually from the lower classes in a society and may be part of a group that is discriminated against, while people who live in noncrowded conditions are usually from the upper and more fortunate classes. If a difference is found in a study that compares "crowded" and "noncrowded" conditions in a natural setting, is the difference produced by the effects of "crowded" versus "noncrowded," or by "lower class" versus "upper class," or by even other things? Because of these problems, many researchers have turned to laboratory studies that provide controlled conditions and allow one to independently examine the effects of each of these variables.

Laboratory Perspectives

One laboratory approach has been to do research with subhuman species. Reviews of the literature that include studies of about seventy different species suggest that there is disruption in social behavior as a result of increased density and crowding. The best known of these studies is that of John Calhoun (1962) in which he investigated Norway rats and their response to crowding. Calhoun coined the term "behavioral sink" to describe a condition that existed when crowding led to a severe disruption of social behavior with abnormal sexual behavior, interpersonal aggression, abusive displays of power, disregard for personal cleanliness, atypical eating habits, and so forth.

More relevant to our present discussion are laboratory studies dealing with human behavior. Here, discrepancies among research findings are, unfortunately, rampant. Some investigators have found increased aggressiveness among children when less space is available, while others have described the overall situation as one in which children become less aggressive and necessarily subdued in crowded situations. Similarly confusing findings have been obtained with regard to adults. Some researchers find that more disparaging remarks are made in crowded situations; while others report that there appears to be submission and less hostility expressed in small rather than large rooms regardless of the size of the group. The above studies have concentrated on variables related to interpersonal behavior and their association with crowding.

Another strategy has been to concentrate on the question of whether or not individual productivity is hampered by crowding. When individual subjects are given their own tasks that do not require cooperation and joint effort, when they are provided with their own working cubicles (no matter

how small), and do not have to share commodities, there does not appear to be a detriment in performance. However, this situation is not typical in today's world. We often need to share commodities, to work together in joint projects, and under these conditions, productivity does appear to be hampered. And, although productivity is important, the real question for psychologists regards the crowding effect on interpersonal behavior. This question is still unanswered through laboratory research.

Overload and Deindividuation

Another perspective for assessing the response to increased population growth is to concentrate on intrapersonal response. More specifically, what is the resulting implication for a single individual's personality in response to increased crowding and urbanization? Stanley Milgram (1970) has attempted to describe the psychological experience of living in the cities. He recognizes that cities are indispensible in complex societies, but there are a number of negative aspects of such life. He points out that an office worker in midtown Manhattan has the potential of meeting a quarter of a million people within ten minutes of wherever one is standing. Clearly, such a possibility is distinctly different from the situation confronting a rancher in the middle of Wyoming. These two living environments have implications for social behavior and developing personalities. Milgram employs the concept of *cognitive overload* to describe the experience faced by the urban dweller. According to his formulation, the individual simply has too many stimulus inputs. In response to this overload, less time must be given to each input; one adapts by disregarding certain low priority inputs; one assigns responsibility to others for certain tasks; one cuts down on the orbit of behavior so as to block off accessibility from others; and lastly, one develops specialized institutions created to absorb inputs that would otherwise fall on the individual. Milgram is suggesting that when one lives in the city, he or she is faced with too much going on. And, in response, the person does not pay attention to some people, lets others such as police, firemen, do things that he would normally be responsible for, hires secretaries to block accessibility, and creates programs such as social welfare to make sure that more jobs do not fall on the individual.

Another intrapersonal response to overcrowding and population growth has been termed *deindividuation*. Whenever people desire to not be identified, to draw back and "hide within the group," they are said to be deindividuating themselves. In contradistinction to the desire to stand out and to bring attention to oneself, deindividuation exists when one gets thoroughly emersed and nonrecognizable in a group. This nonidentifiability has been hypothesized as an explanatory cause of increased violence and aggression as well as a failure to help others when called on to do so. We will return to both of these possibilities when we discuss aggression, violence, and altruism. The point is, however, that it may be increasingly more difficult to remain "individuated" under crowded rather than noncrowded conditions. Becoming a part of a collective mob may have implications for increased antisocial interpersonal behavior and what might be described as more negative personalities.

What's the Right Number?

Throughout this section on population growth and crowding, we have concentrated on the potential problem created by having too many people in social settings. However, there is another side to the story. Consider the example provided us by the "new town" of Albertslund built in the mid 1960s outside of Copenhagen in Denmark. Albertslund is a town of approximately 10,000 people. Architects made every attempt to design and construct housing that would provide a minimum perception of crowding. Apartments were engineered to appear comfortable, were well designed in terms of traffic flow, were separated from other apartments, included their own patios, and, of course, had access to the outside. What happened to the social behavior of the Danish families living in these "private" apartments in the "well planned" town? Unfortunately, the opposite of what was desired happened. Many family disturbances occurred, and these were not unlike the disturbances we noted earlier in the social behavior of people in the crowded living conditions in Chicago and around the world. Further, in cases where couples had no children, there was a suicide rate among the wives that far exceeded the national norm. What had happened was that the planners had gone too far in psychologically-separating these Danish people from each other. In an attempt to provide privacy, they had created social isolation. Consequently, although it can be demonstrated that too many people create disturbances in social behavior, Albertslund suggests that too few people can also create tragedy. Social interaction, as well as privacy, needs to be available for those who choose it.

Results from the laboratory suggest that when individuals are provided with descriptions of certain social settings such as cocktail parties, studying for exams at libraries, football games, classroom lectures, and so on, they can, with remarkable consistency, identify what they consider to be the "right" number of people given the size of the room. This has led some such as Wicker (1974) to talk about the *manning* of a social setting. A basketball team is appropriately manned with five individuals. It is overcrowded with six and undermanned with only four. Analogous to basketball teams, many social situations are such that they imply to us the "correct" number of people. These norms of appropriateness regarding the right number of people must change if population growth continues, otherwise there are going to be problems. Either the norms are going to have to change or population growth and crowding must be curtailed.

Aggression and Violence

Stories of violence and aggression monopolize today's headlines. All indices of crime reveal drastic increases in street violence, and countries are spending ever-increasing amounts for weapons that can and have produced massive destruction. Why do people behave aggressively? What can be done to control aggression?

Aggression is a very difficult term to define. There does not seem to be any single type or class of behaviors that everyone would agree should clearly be termed "aggression." One of the simplest definitions has been advanced by behaviorists and focuses on the result produced by an action: Aggression is an action that produces harm or injury to another person or persons, and the harm can be either physical or psychological. Unfortunately, this definition leaves out many things that we would want to call aggression, and includes some that we would not. For example, suppose that a child throws a dart at a tree but misses and hits his sister; harm has been done, but we would not necessarily want to call the child "aggressive." Or, suppose that a sniper takes aim with a rifle but misses his victim; no harm has been done, but we would call the sniper "aggressive." For these reasons, most social psychologists include an intentional and motivational component in the definition: *Aggression is an intentional action whose goal is to inflict harm to another person or persons.* Even this definition is far from perfect, since intentions and goals are themselves very difficult terms to define, but most social psychologists adopt this as a starting point.

Three different theoretical positions on the nature of aggression have been taken by scientists. One position is that aggression is an instinctive aspect of human and animal nature, the second position is focused on genetic and physiological factors that can affect aggression, and the third position is focused on the psychological, social, and environmental factors that affect aggression.

Aggression as an Instinctive Part of Human Nature

In the seventeenth century, the social philosopher Thomas Hobbes wrote that life is "solitary, poor, nasty, brutish, and short." He professed a very pessimistic view of our nature, and felt that if left to their own devices, people would selfishly exploit and harm others, resulting in the extermination of the human race. Society, he felt, serves to keep people in line by devising laws that prohibit destructive behaviors. Social controls keep the cork in the bottle, and prevent aggression from overflowing.

Sigmund Freud similarly believed that aggression is instinctive—it is part of animal nature and is not learned. According to Freud, there are two basic instincts that are in constant conflict with each other. Eros, the life instinct, revolves around sexual drives and keeps a person and our species alive. Thanatos, the death instinct, aims to destroy life. If impulses from the death instinct are directed inward upon a person (which occurs when the death instinct outweighs the life instinct), self-injurious actions, suicide, and/or masochism could result. If the impulses are directed outward (which occurs when the life instinct outweighs the death instinct), violence, war, and/or sadism could result. The amount of energy that can be discharged in aggressive actions is fixed by instincts, so society can have no control over it. However, Freud believed that society can act to sublimate, or rechannel, this energy into socially acceptable forms of behavior. Thus, instead of cutting people up in street gang rumbles, a person can become a surgeon and save rather than take lives. Or a person can engage in athletic contests such as boxing or football to discharge aggressive energies. Freud's views have been largely rejected by scientists, because he was very unclear about what he meant by these instincts, predictions about behaviors are difficult to derive from his approach, and the same phenomena he sought to explain can be explained in simpler and less esoteric ways.

Another variant of the instinctive position has been taken by the Nobel-prize-winning scientist Konrad Lorenz (1966). Lorenz believed that aggression is instinctive, and that aggressive energies build up in an organism until they can be released by appropriate environmental triggers, or *releasers* (such as the sight of a male stickleback fish's red underbelly, that will trigger an aggressive attack in another male stickleback). Occasionally, aggressive energies will build up to the point where they overflow, and aggressive behaviors will then occur even in the absence of a specific environmental trigger. Thus, like a pressure cooker, aggressive energies build up over time, are released or overflow, and then build up again. Lorenz believed that all animals, except humans and rats, also have instinctive "stop" mechanisms that prohibit aggression from causing death in another member of the same species (for example, Lorenz believed that when two wolves fight, the loser bares his jugular vein to the victor, an action that could result in instant death if attacked but which instead serves to stop the attack long enough for the loser to vacate the premises). For humans, instinctive aggression will occur, but nature has taken no precautions to insure that fights to the death do not occur.

Lorenz's model of aggression has been severely criticized by many social scientists (see Montagu, 1973). Many feel that he made some inaccurate observations of animal behaviors (for example, intraspecies fights to the death *do* occur in many species besides humans and rats), that he failed to provide sufficient evidence to support the model, and that his indiscriminate generalizations from lower animal to human behavior are incorrect (since lower animals and humans differ in so many important ways). Wars, for example, are not caused because all of the individual soldiers suddenly build up aggressive energies and desire to kill; they are caused by very complex psychological, social, political, and economic factors. Perhaps most importantly, aggressive energies do not seem to build up over time and demand release. This is shown from studies of animals that are deprived of the opportunity to aggress. Later, they will not work to obtain the opportunity to aggress nor will they necessarily aggress when given the opportunity, as they should do if the model were correct. Although the merits and faults of the model are still being debated, many scientists totally reject the premise that aggression is instinctive.

Genetic and Physiological Determinants

Much current attention is being devoted to genetic and physiological factors that might underlie aggressive behaviors (see Johnson, 1972). It has been shown that by selectively breeding certain animals over numerous generations, one can develop either a highly aggressive or a highly pacifistic animal. Additionally, some reports have linked certain chromosome patterns to criminal behaviors in humans. These results certainly suggest that genetic characteristics can affect aggressive behaviors. Unfortunately, the data are not totally clear. Studies of chromosome patterns in humans have been criticized because of poor methodology and faulty conclusions. Studies that have examined selectively bred mice and rats have found that genes may not act by "forcing" the animal to fight, but instead lay a biological foundation that

allows the animal to be successful if it does fight. For example, rats bred to be aggressive are more active and less emotionally upset by stress than are "average" rats. If these animals get into a fight, they are likely to win, and the reinforcement of success makes it more likely that they will fight again. If the experimenter arranges for them to lose fights, they become less likely to fight again. Thus, at this point, all that can be concluded is that genetic patterns can affect aggressive behaviors, but it is not the case that genes alone "cause" aggression; environmental influences can drastically modify such behaviors.

Another approach has been to search for specific portions of the brain that control aggressive behaviors. Although there are places in the brain that do appear to be highly related to fighting behaviors (see Chapter 4), the picture is again unclear. Even when these "aggression centers" are removed from animals' brains, fighting behaviors can still occur; the whole brain seems to be involved in one way or another. Also, when such a "center" is electrically stimulated, the environmental cues that are present will determine the animals' reactions. For example, if a monkey is caged with an inferior monkey (one that it has beaten many times in prior fights), stimulation of a certain brain area will cause the first monkey to attack. However, if it is caged with a superior monkey (one that has beaten it in prior fights), stimulation of the same area will cause it to turn and run away. The same area thus causes both "fight" and "flight," depending on the environmental setting. The major conclusions that can be presently drawn from this research are that the brain does provide us with the capacity to behave aggressively, but whether or not this capacity is ever exercised depends on many other factors. Analogously, all "normal" people have the capacity to play a violin, but whether or not they learn depends on other personal dispositions and environmental experiences.

Psychological, Social and Environmental Determinants

Another major approach has been to examine the psychological, social, and environmental influences that affect aggression. The first important psychological theory of aggression is the frustration-aggression model (Dollard et al., 1939). We all know how frustrating many of life's experiences can be, and these can make us angry, hostile, and sometimes violent. Frustration is defined as the blocking or interference of a goal response which would otherwise have led to the accomplishment of a goal. For example, a person might want to go out on a date in his parents' car, but is thwarted because of their refusal to permit it. In its original form, the frustration-aggression model proposed that frustration *always* leads to aggression (either real or imagined), and aggression is *always* the consequence of frustration. Subsequent work has caused these invariant relationships to be modified, so that presently it is felt that frustration leads to arousal which *can* result in aggression, but does not necessarily *have* to.

The model also proposes that aggression does not have to take place against the original frustrating agent; instead, it can be *displaced* onto a substitute target. For example, the person who was frustrated by his parents may not aggress against them because they are powerful and could retaliate, so he hits his small brother to vent his frustrations. The more similar the substitute target is to the original frustrator, the more likely displaced aggression will be to occur. One interesting study (Hovland and Sears, 1940) that has been interpreted in terms of displaced aggression examined the relationship between the price of cotton and lynchings of blacks in the South between 1882 and 1930. Presumably, when the price of cotton was low, white Southerners would experience economic hardship and want to vent their frustrations onto a substitute target, such as blacks. It was found that as the price of cotton decreased, the number of lynchings of blacks increased, and vice versa.

One important concept for the model is *catharsis,* which is the reduction of aggressive drives that have been built up through frustration. To reduce aggression through catharsis, one engages in real or imagined aggressive episodes, thereby relieving the pressures of the frustrating experiences. For example, to vent frustrations, one might pin up a picture of their professor and fantasize wildly as they hurl darts at it, or one might watch a violent movie and fantasize about injuring one's enemies,

or one might play handball or football. This presumably makes one less likely to engage in subsequent aggression. Unfortunately for the model (and for this common sense notion), studies of aggression have indicated that aggressive thoughts and actions are more likely to increase subsequent aggression rather than decrease it. Playing football, for example, may be fun, but it does not make a person less aggressive in other activities; in fact, it might make him more aggressive.

The frustration-aggression model is important because it generated studies that showed that frustrating life experiences can often lead to aggression, some of which can be displaced onto substitute targets. But more is involved in aggression than frustration alone.

The second major approach under this heading is *social learning theory*. The theory stresses the fact that most social behaviors are learned responses to particular situations. One important type of learning is modeling, or imitation, in which a person learns the appropriate ways to behave by observing what others do. Albert Bandura (1973) and his associates have shown that aggression is often learned through modeling behaviors. By exposure to aggressive models, a child can learn that aggression is often an effective way of getting what one wants, and frequently copies the behavior.

There are numerous factors that affect how much imitation will occur. One of the most important of these are the *consequences to the model* for engaging in aggressive behaviors. For example, a child watches a TV western in which a character robs a bank, shoots several people, and rides off with his ill-gotten gains. How do you think this child's behavior would differ if the robber (a) was quickly apprehended by the sheriff, brought back for trial, and hung, versus (b) escaped with the loot, rode off into the sunset, and lived happily ever after with a lovely senorita in Mexico? As this example suggests, it has been found that when a model is rewarded for aggressive behavior, more imitation occurs than if the model is punished; punishment of a model can even decrease aggression in observers. The *qualities of the model* are another important factor. It has been found that attractive, respected, competent, high status, powerful models produce more imitation than those who have the opposite characteristics. Imagine your own differences in reactions and imitation if the Sundance Kid had been portrayed in the movie by Don Knotts rather than Robert Redford.

The instinct positions, it will be recalled, held out only minor hopes for altering the amount of aggression that occurs in society. Aggressive energies are thought to be fixed by nature, and all that society can do is to rechannel this energy into paths that are not destructive to society. The social psychological positions hold out the hope for much greater societal control. One way, however impractical it may sound, is to try to improve standards of living so that major frustrations do not occur. Another way would be to teach (both through direct rewards and punishments as well as through modeling) that aggression is inappropriate behavior that will not be condoned. We can avoid glamorizing aggression on the television and in movies. Some societies (such as the Hopi Indians and the Tahitians) have developed teaching techniques to the point where their people are very pacifistic and nonaggressive; they are slow to anger and view physical aggression as an inappropriate form of behavior.

Violence in the Mass Media

One much-debated social issue is the effect of violence as portrayed on television and in the movies on aggressive behavior. Three positions have been taken on this issue. The first is that watching mass media violence produces a decrease in aggression through catharsis or similar mechanisms, and hence is ''good'' for society. This position is compatible with the instinct model (Freud and Lorenz) and with the frustration-aggression model. The second position is that watching mass media violence produces an increase in aggression through imitation, and hence is ''bad'' for society. This position is advanced by social learning theorists. The final position, and one taken by many people in the television industry, is that the process is so complicated, that there should not be much of an effect one way or the other.

By and large, the results of numerous studies support the social learning theory position. Ex-

posure to violence usually increases subsequent aggression in viewers. One study even found a positive relationship between the amount of violence children watched on television when they were eight years old and the amount of aggression they displayed in their behaviors ten years later (Eron et al., 1972).

In another study, FBI crime statistics between 1960 and 1969, as shown in Figure 16-4, were examined to determine whether a relationship could be demonstrated between the occurrence of an infamous event that was much publicized on television and subsequent increases in crime (Berkowitz, 1970). It was found that crime rates drastically increased shortly after the assassination of President John F. Kennedy in 1963, and also after the famous Speck-Whitman murders in the summer of 1966 (Richard Speck brutally murdered eight nurses in Chicago, and Charles Whitman climbed atop a tower at the University of Texas and gunned down thirty-eight people, killing fourteen and even hitting an airplane). The FBI reported that they knew of no procedural reasons why such increases should have occurred, and the increases have been interpreted by many social scientists as the result of modeled aggression. Consider some specific examples of crimes illustrated

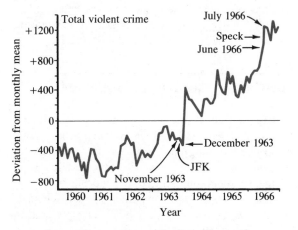

Fig. 16-4. Graph depicting the increase in crime rate after the assassination of John F. Kennedy. (Reprinted from The contagion of violence, by L. Berkowitz, in the *Nebraska Symposium on Motivation.* Copyright © 1971 by the University of Nebraska Press. Used with permission.)

by the above statistics. In November, 1966, an eighteen-year-old male walked into an Arizona beauty school and shot four women and a child. He later stated that he got the idea from Richard Speck's murder of the nurses and from Charles Whitman's shootings. A jealous husband finally shot his wife's admirer when he lost his fear of killing after watching Jack Ruby shoot Lee Harvey Oswald on television. He later commented, "I saw how easy it was to kill a man when Oswald was shot on TV." Numerous other incidents could be cited, indicating that children are not the only ones affected by mass media violence.

From such evidence, should one conclude that violence must be banished from the television screen? This question will be hotly debated for years to come. Clearly, total censorship of what can be shown would be intolerable in a free society. But to what degree, if at all, should the government control what can and cannot be shown? Another aspect of this issue is the type of individual we feel should exist in this or any other society. If the total elimination of aggression is our goal, then surely bans should be imposed on the portrayal of violence in the mass media. But is this a desirable goal? Most people feel that aggression and even violence are necessary under some conditions to defend ourselves against the unjust impositions of others. These questions are moral ones; they involve value judgments that are beyond the scope of what science can illuminate.

Bystander Intervention and Altruism

Our preceding two discussions have considered potential detrimental effects on social behavior due to overcrowding and the phenomenon of aggression and violence. We will now describe what many writers consider to be the opposite of aggression which is *altruism*. Many social scientists study when and why people either help or fail to help others when help is needed. Unfortunately, it is most often the case that the dramatic headlines and incidents that receive media attention are those instances where there is a failure to help. Research has also followed this avenue and concentrated on why people do not help. Perhaps the cause-célèbre for this area of investigation is the 1964 murder of

Kitty Genovese, a resident of Kew Gardens, New York. She was returning home from her job as manager of a bar at 3:20 the morning of March 13, 1964. After parking her car, she started walking across the parking lot and toward her apartment. Noticing a man at the far end of the lot, she became nervous and aimed for a nearby police callbox. She got as far as the street lights before the man grabbed her. She screamed "Oh my God! He stabbed me. Please help me! Please help me!" One would think at this point that fortune was smiling on Ms. Genovese—as many believe in the old adage that there is safety in numbers. It turned out that thirty-eight of Ms. Genovese's neighbors went to their windows to see what was happening. One shouted "Let that girl alone!" The attacker took off, only to return to continue his stabbing attack a few moments later. Again, lights went on in many apartments and the murderer got into his car and drove away.

However, he returned a third time. Kitty had crawled to the back of her building looking for safety and the killer found her slumped against the stairwell. This time the stabbing was fatal. One-half hour and thirty-eight witnesses later, Kitty Genovese was dead (Figure 16-5). The first call to the police was received at 3:50 A.M. and a patrol car was on the scene in less than two minutes. The neighbor who had made the call had first climbed to the roof of the building of the apartment to cross around and get a good look. He then went to the apartment of an elderly woman to ask her to make the call. Before he had done that, he had phoned a friend in Nassau County for legal advice. When questioned he simply said that he did not want to get involved (*New York Times,* 1964; Severy et al, 1976). The question that was focused on as a result of this unfortunate incident was "Why did thirty-eight people fail to respond? Why don't people get involved when help was clearly indicated?" This incident is certainly not isolated in our society and every several months, one similar in scope is reported by the national news media. In fact, exactly ten years after this incident, another attack of precisely the same nature took place in exactly the same apartment building in Kew Gardens, New York, and the same thing happened. The second girl also died while at least ten persons heard screams and did nothing.

Fig. 16-5.   Kitty Genovese and the scene of the attack on her.

Should I Help? Decisions

When social psychologists began to analyze these emergency situations, they focused on a sequence of decisions any bystander must make. John Darley and Bibb Latané (1969) suggested that: first, one must *notice an event;* second, one must *interpret* the *event as an emergency;* and third, one must *determine* one's own personal *responsibility to act.* After these decisions, the individual determines what kind of aid is required and how to act best according to one's perceived skills and abilities. Darley and Latané also differentiate between *direct* and *indirect* aid in emergencies. If someone has been stabbed, possibly the best that the average person can do is to call an ambulance or take the person to a hospital. In some sense this is indirect aid, whereas if one were a physician, then direct intervention would be possible. Medical procedures could be directly applied to the problem.

With considerations such as these guiding their laboratory research, Darley and Latané conducted a series of laboratory investigations to analyze more precisely what might be happening in the bystander situation. The first principle that they felt was operative has become known as *diffusion of responsibility.* They theorized that perhaps the reason no one helped Kitty Genovese was that thirty-eight people all thought and perceived that they were only 1/38th responsible if no one helped and, since there were thirty-seven others, someone had probably already helped anyway. This would seem to fly in the face of the adage that there is safety in numbers. The conclusion would have to be that the best way to guarantee help (if you are going to have an emergency) would be to have only one bystander. Laboratory research has indicated this may be true. A second principle emanating from the Darley and Latané research is what has been described as *pluralistic ignorance.* The possibility exists that the longer a group of people observe an event and decide not to help, the more it appears to all involved that, in fact, an emergency is not occurring and that help is not called for. In effect, everyone's doing nothing makes each person believe that no action is called for. Ambiguity in the emergency certainly is important, and this will be discussed again.

There is a sad and unfortunate side effect emanating from the bystander intervention phenomenon. Lerner (1970) suggests that when people see others suffer through no fault of their own, they experience a conflict. Either they must decide that the world is not such a fair place after all (which is something that most people do *not* seem to want to do), or, they must attempt to justify the victim's suffering through rationalization. Since many people choose to believe that they live in a "just world," what happens is that they come to believe that the victim deserves his or her fate and that they are basically bad anyway. Two negative results obtain under these conditions. First, someone is perceived to be bad when in fact they probably are not, and second, once perceived to be bad, there may be very little reason to help them. With all of the above principles in mind, it is now worth asking, "Are there any factors that have been demonstrated empirically to affect the speed of response, to actually increase the potential for help in emergency situations?"

Victim, Bystander, and Emergency Characteristics

In attempting to identify factors relevant to the increased potential of bystander intervention, one could consider (1) characteristics of the victim, (2) characteristics of the potential helper, and (3) characteristics of the emergency itself. For example, is it a child in need of help, or an adult? Is the potential helper an invalid or someone trained as a paramedic? Is the attacker meek or fierce in appearance?

What are a few of the factors that have been identified as affecting speed of response and the amount of help? First, as discussed above, the number of people present has been found to be quite important. When diffusion of responsibility occurs, there is less likelihood of help; when the numbers are small, there is increased potential for helping. Another factor that was mentioned above was that of pluralistic ignorance. Just how ambiguous is the situation? Researchers have found that whenever the situation is quite clear and there is no chance to make it ambiguous, when in fact the victim clearly asks for help and states the nature of the problem, help is increased. If asking for help increases actual aid, it is possible that when the victim is fairly dependent on the potential bystander, speed of help should be increased. Studies have shown that this is the case. When you see an emergency involving a person you know depends on you, you are more likely to intervene.

A number of other factors that have been identified as increasing the potential for help were investigated in an interesting subway car study by Piliavin et al (1969). These investigators took advantage of a situation in which there was a long run between two stops of a New York City subway. They had confederates dramatically fake a collapse in a subway car. In some of the conditions, the subject faked being drunk and in other conditions faked being ill. There was a tremendous amount of help offered in this situation and more so for the "ill" rather than "drunk" victim. It has been suggested that there are several reasons for the high incidence of aid. First, there was no ambiguity about whether or not someone should help. The person had collapsed right in front of the potential helpers. Second, this was a "closed" situation and clearly no one could escape. You could not avoid the realization that this emergency happened right in front of you in "your place" and that you could not get off the subway to avoid the situation. There was plenty of time to help, you were not pressed to go someplace else; in fact, you could not go someplace else. The situation was clearly one of low risk for the potential helper and lastly, when there appeared good reason such as being ill rather than just inebriated, help was readily available. It was also found that males and females helped at about the same rate.

Altruism

The question begins to focus on why people help. When put in a dilemma of self interest versus other interest, why should anyone be more concerned for the welfare of others than oneself? Maybe they are being altruistic. *Altruism exists whenever people help simply because the other needs it.* If you were to help for another reason (such as knowing that you will feel good, get a monetary reward, and so on), altruism would not be the appropriate description, but rather another form of "helping" behavior (such as cooperating, rescuing, and such). The fact remains that there are some individuals who immediately, on observation of an emergency, jump to the rescue. Secondly, there are others who appear to calmly deliberate and then decide to intervene. Lastly, there are individuals who simply refrain from any positive step at all. The question remains, then, "What are some of the explanatory factors for such behavior?"

Theoretical Perspectives

There are at least four explanations that have been offered to explain prosocial behavior.

Reciprocity. The principle of reciprocity suggests that people help because they feel that if they help when needed, the person whom they help may help them sometime in the future. This does not always have to be person specific but rather can generalize so that the person will say to himself or herself, "I'll help now and someone will help me when I need it. If I don't help now, then I may become recognized as someone who hasn't helped and therefore when I am in trouble they won't help me."

Social Learning. This position holds that one learns to help others by being rewarded for giving assistance and by being punished for ignoring emergency situations. Additionally, one can learn to help others through modeling or imitation of exemplars who themselves help others. Societies that teach their young to care about others and to offer assistance when others are in need will instill norms of social responsibility. These social responsibility norms should increase the chances that people will behave in a helpful manner.

Cost-Reward Frameworks. According to a cost-reward explanation, individuals tend to help whenever they perceive the relative reward to be more than the cost of engaging in helping behavior. The

most complex analysis of this more or less economic theory is described by Piliavin and Piliavin (1975). They analyzed costs and rewards *for helping* as well as costs and rewards *for not helping*. According to a four-cell matrix comprised of high and low costs for both helping and not helping, predictions can be made as to when individuals will be socially responsible and offer aid and when they will tend to avoid it. For example, when the cost for helping is very low, in fact, involves no risk, and the reward for helping is high, there will, of course, be help. When the cost for not helping is low (such as no one knowing that you did not help), and the cost for helping is high (such as a burly attacker carrying both a gun and a knife and looking for more trouble), the prediction would be that individuals would not intercede.

Sociogenic. The sociogenic explanation for helping behavior is based on the argument that the survival of the species is more important than the survival of any one organism in the species. In the long run, sacrificing one's life for others may help the species survive, and that protection is of first and foremost evolutionary concern. For example, a monkey may save its fellows by screeching and warning when a predator comes near—but at the same time, it makes itself stand out and increases its chances of being killed. Evolution might favor such altruistic genetic qualities, because groups that possess them will survive many predators, while groups without them might soon become extinct. Evolution, after all, does not demand that a desirable member of a species survives until old age—only that it survive long enough to procreate.

Whatever the reason, if there is an alternative to antisocial behavior that can be made more prominent by identifying factors that increase helping and by understanding why helping occurs, maybe tragic bystander nonintervention can be avoided.

Social Psychological Aspects of Sexual Behavior

The discussion and investigation of sexual behavior, long one of society's sacred cows with taboo status, is at last coming out into the open. Photos of nude females, that would have been considered lewd as centerfolds a decade or two ago, now adorn magazine covers for all to see, and females can now find sexually-oriented magazines that cater exclusively to them. *Playboy,* the long-time liberal leader in its field, is losing ground to its competition because of its relative conservatism. In the United States alone, about 600 million dollars per year is spent on books, magazines, and movies that are devoted primarily to sexual behaviors (*Report to the Commission on Obscenity and Pornography,* 1970). Alternative lifestyles, such as open marriage, nonmarriage, polygamy (more than one wife), polyandry (more than one husband), troilism (sexual activities involving three persons), bisexuality, and homosexuality, are openly discussed on television talk shows. To some, the loosening restrictions on sexual behavior are seen as the beginning of the end for our society. To others, it is viewed with delight, as a sign of the end of the Victorian era that should never have been imposed in the first place.

Sigmund Freud is considered by many in Western society to be one of the fathers of the modern sexual revolution. Freud shocked the world in the early 1900s when he proposed that during an early stage of their development (the phallic stage—ages 3 to 5), children unconsciously desire sexually their parent of the opposite sex. Freud believed that even in infancy, sexual impulses were active, which led to erotic feelings. Although many of Freud's specific beliefs about the sexual nature of child development remain unaccepted by psychologists, he opened the door to psychological discussions of sexuality.

Kinsey

One of the best known studies of sexual behavior was conducted by Alfred C. Kinsey and his associates in the late 1930s and early 1940s. The Kinsey Report (Kinsey et al, 1948), as it is popularly known, consisted of a large-scale opinion survey that examined the sexual behavior of over 5,000 American men, whose ages spanned 80 years. Interviewers were sent around to ask each respondent about 300 questions that pertained to their sexual

activities. Shortly thereafter, Kinsey and his associates (Kinsey et al., 1953) published a complementary volume that summarized the data from interviews with 6,000 females. Kinsey's samples of respondents were far from perfect, and were not totally representative of the entire population of the United States (for example, males were primarily from the East and Midwest, and rural areas and manual laborers were underrepresented). However, the studies were far and away the most ambitious ever undertaken on the topic. As they finally appeared, the volumes amounted to over 1,700 pages of imposing tables, graphs, charts, and commentary.

Among the many findings was the report that 83 percent of the males and 50 percent of the females reported having had premarital sexual relations. Of the 83 percent figure, the skeptical newspaperman and social satirist H. L. Mencken commented that all it shows is that most males are quite adept at lying about their sexual conquests. In a nutshell, this has been one of the major problems with such interview techniques: One can never be sure when a respondent is telling the truth. Many scientists, though, feel that although some of the responses could have been falsified by respondents, either intentionally or unintentionally, the data are largely valid. The reports also noted that 50 percent of the males and 27 percent of the females stated that they had had extramarital relations. Masturbation was reported by 92 percent of the males and 62 percent of the females. One finding of interest to college students was that male college graduates reported having fewer orgasms per week than did nongraduates. Additionally, premarital, extramarital, and homosexual behaviors were reported more frequently among noncollege graduate males than among college graduates. Male college graduates, though, were reported to have an increasing proportion of extramarital relations with age, while nongraduates reported a decreasing proportion. As compared to female college nongraduates, female college graduates reported a greater proportion of marital intercourse resulting in orgasm and masturbation, and a lesser proportion of premarital sexual behaviors. Like their male counterparts, female college graduates reported an increasing proportion of extramarital intercourse as they got older than did female nongraduates.

One of the most startling findings of the Kinsey Report, and one that briefly caused the validity of the data to be questioned, was that one-third of the males who replied admitted having one or more sexual encounter with another male. This is perhaps not as surprising as it first seems, when it is considered that 63 percent never engaged in homosexual behavior and only 4 percent preferred homosexual behaviors. About 2 percent of the females reported being exclusively homosexual.

Almost all recent interview studies, although smaller in scope than the Kinsey Reports, find that the incidences of premarital and extramarital sexual activity have increased. These increases appear caused by the widespread availability of birth control pills, a general loosening of sexual attitudes, and an increasing economic independence for females.

Masters and Johnson

The next major landmark in the study of sexual behavior was undertaken by Masters and Johnson (1966). In contrast to the Kinsey Report, this work consisted of laboratory studies of the physiology of the human sexual response. The implications of their work have led to the proliferation of numerous sex "clinics," which specialize in helping individuals and couples achieve more fulfilling sexual relationships and overcome sexual problems such as frigidity and impotence. Masters and Johnson's original clinic, in the Reproductive Biology Research Foundation in St. Louis, involved a two-week treatment that primarily aimed at correcting misinformation about sex and creating attitudes that allow one to view sex as a natural and appropriate behavior, more a "birthright" than anything else.

One of Masters and Johnson's books, *Human Sexual Response,* describes the work that they began in 1954 at the Washington University School of Medicine in St. Louis. By 1966, they had studied about 7,500 complete sexual response cycles in females and about 2,500 ejaculatory experiences of males. They developed special cameras and other measurement instruments that could record changes that took place during sexual relations in the female vagina. They found a basic pattern of changes that took place in both males and females during sexual activities. The first phase is an *excitement phase.* In males, an erection occurs and occasionally the nipples become erect. In females, the vaginal lining begins to moisten with a lubricating fluid, the breasts swell, and the nipples become erect. The onset of this phase is highly influenced by external cues as well as by fantasy activity. The second phase is the *plateau phase.* In males, the testes get larger and are pulled up into the scrotum. In females, the vaginal area fills with blood and muscles become more tense, causing a swelling of the outer third of the vaginal area, a reduction in the diameter of the vaginal opening, a retraction of the clitoris, and a distension of the upper portion of the vaginal cavity. The third phase is the *orgasmic phase.* In males, the penis begins rhythmic contractions, which usually culminate in ejaculation of semen. In females, muscles in the outer third of the vagina begin rhythmic contractions, as do muscles in other parts of the body, such as the anal sphincter, usually leading to orgasm. Finally, in the *resolution phase,* there is a return to unstimulated conditions, with the arousal level of males dropping off rapidly after orgasm, and the arousal level of females dropping much slower, often after several peaks of arousal as compared to the male's single peak.

Two of the conclusions from these studies have been well publicized and have important implications. First, it was found that the size and diameter of the male's penis was relatively unimportant for sexual satisfaction, since the vagina grips it almost irrespective of its size. Additionally, the size of penises varies much less when erect than when nonerect; smaller penises increase in size more than do larger ones. Second, they found no difference in females between a clitoral orgasm (produced by stimulation of the clitoris, such as during masturbation) and a vaginal orgasm. Until this time, many people, including Freud, felt that vaginal orgasm was far superior, and therefore females were dependent on males more than vice-versa. The clitoris is analogous to the male penis, and both sexes seem to be very much alike in their ability to experience sexual pleasure.

Influences on Sexual Behavior

In lower animals, sexual behavior is governed largely by sex hormones; reducing the level of hormones stops sexual activity even if a receptive partner is available. (See Chapter 6.) In higher animals, such as monkeys, apes, and humans, sexual behavior is largely controlled by the neocortex. Even castration will often not stop the sexual activity of a male member of these species, and for humans, there is no relationship between hormone level and sexual activity (see Baron et al., 1974). Similarly, the human female remains sexually active after menopause.

Learning plays a crucial role in human sexual behavior. Through classical conditioning, a previously neutral stimulus (such as a particular song) can become associated with sexual arousal and produce similar emotions when subsequently present (see Chapter 9). This is easily observed in couples who have favorite songs, movies, locales, perfumes, clothes, and so on, that have become associated with and come to evoke pleasurable thoughts and sensations. Occasionally, this process can produce "abnormal" sexual associations, called fetishes, in which objects such as shoes or handbags evoke sexual feelings. One method for "curing" fetishism is to reverse the process through desensitization, pairing the arousing object with something that is not sexually arousing, such as an electric shock, until it eventually loses its ability to evoke positive reactions.

Observational learning also plays a major role in the development of sexual preferences. By observing the behaviors of others (models), we learn what they consider to be appropriate or inappropriate actions and imitate them. Studies of imitative sexual behavior have shown that the activities of models can either inhibit sexual behaviors or disinhibit them (see Wiggins et al, 1971). For example, if a model closely examines all of the appropriate curves on a photo of a voluptuous naked female, observers will do likewise. But if the model seems anxious and guilty when looking at the photo and spends time gazing only at the background of the picture, observers will copy this behavior. Parental behaviors and the general sexual atmosphere of the family can drastically affect the attitudes and behavior of children. Children raised in sexually restrictive family atmospheres in which parents display high anxieties and guilt about sex are quite likely to have similar feelings when they mature. Conversely, a more permissive family atmosphere leads to more permissive sexual attitudes and behaviors in the children. Modeling studies also suggest that the sexual content of movies and TV can influence sexual attitudes, and this will occur whether the content is aimed at restrictiveness or permissiveness.

Cultural Differences

Since learning does play such a key role in human sexual behavior, it should not come as a surprise that the sexual preferences of the society into which one is born will drastically affect how one views sex. Sexual beauty, for example, is defined differently in different parts of the world. In some cultures, crosseyed girls are highly prized. In others, one's sexual attractiveness could depend on the size of one's breasts or buttocks, or legs. In some African tribes, the size of a female's clitoris and labia determine her sexual suitability, and female infants have these parts manipulated for long periods of time in the hope of enlarging them (which apparently works).

Some societies begin the sex training of their children quite early; in other societies, such training is condemned. In some societies, the woman is supposed to be passive, in others, she is the aggressor. Almost every type of sexual activity is condoned by one or another society. In some, heterosexual contacts prior to marriage are condemned, and males engage in homosexual activity until marrying, at which time such activity stops. In others, oral sex is considered one criterion for foreplay. The only type of sexual activity that is universally condemned is incest (sexual relations with members of one's family), although societies differentially define the family unit for incest (for some, it is only prohibited between parents and children, for others it is this plus brothers and sisters, for still others the taboo may include cousins). Even sexual positions that are favored vary from one society to another, and the position Westerners consider "normal" (man on top of the woman) is only favored by about one-third of the cultures that have been studied, although it is the single most popular position. Thus, what turns people on and what they do after they get turned on is subject to almost limitless cultural variations.

Individual Differences

Within any society, there are large variations in sexual attitudes and behaviors. Reactions to sexual materials (such as erotic photographs or movies) depend in large part on one's personality characteristics. It has been found, for example, that people do not simply differ along a positive-negative emotional scale in their reactions to such materials (see Baron et al., 1974). Instead, four types of reactions have been observed: liberal (materials evoke only positive emotional reactions), conservative (materials evoke only negative emotional reactions), ambivalent (materials evoke strong positive and negative emotional reactions), and indifferent (materials evoke weak emotional reactions). These types of people differ dramatically in their sexual attitudes. The conservative, for example, is most likely to call erotic material "pornographic" and is most favorable toward government censorship of sexually-related materials of all types. The liberal, on the other hand, labels very few things "pornographic" and only favors government restrictions for children. Those who are ambivalent display great anxiety and guilt about sexual materials. Individuals with high sex guilt have also been found to avoid sexual reading matter.

Sex Differences

Kinsey's studies indicated that males were very easily aroused by hardcore pornography and sexual themes, while females were not particularly aroused by these but were aroused by themes involving love, marriage, affection, and children. Women were thought to be passive recipients of sex, who put up with it to gain the love and affection they so desperately desired. Recent evidence, though, indicates that many of the females who were responding to Kinsey's interviewers may

have only been telling them what they wanted to hear. One of the first challenges to this traditional view was Masters and Johnson's discovery that the clitoral orgasm was as satisfying as the vaginal orgasm—women clearly did not need men to satisfy them. Masters and Johnson also provided fuel for women's libbers by demonstrating that women can have multiple orgasms over a short period while males are much more restricted. Females now seem to be more satisfied than males in terms of achieving and sustaining sexual pleasures. Other studies that involved showing people pornographic materials have found that males and females are both quite aroused by hardcore pornography. In fact, both sexes are more turned on by movies of petting and intercourse if the scenes are described as ones of couples who are interested in pleasure only, rather than if they are described as ones of couples who are in love (see Baron et al., 1974). When these data are combined with those on cultural differences that show that women often take the active and aggressive role in other societies, the traditional stereotypes crumble.

Pornography and Society

In 1970, a commission that was appointed by President Nixon reported its findings on the effects of pornography on society. The Commission's report is claimed by many to be a landmark in the area of sexual freedom, and it is also condemned by many as a pernicious attack on the very basis of Western society that would unleash a Pandora's box of evils. The conclusions of the Commission were so controversial that President Nixon and most of Congress ignored them, probably wishing that the Commission had never been established in the first place.

One of the major conclusions of the Commission was that they "found no reliable evidence to date that exposure to explicit sexual materials plays a significant role in the causation of delinquent or criminal sexual behavior among youth or adults." (*Report of the Commission on Obscenity and Pornography*, 1970, p. 169.) In its recommendations, the Commission strongly urged the launching of a "massive sex education effort" directed at all segments of society and all age groups. They felt that "much of the 'problem' regarding materials that depict explicit sexual activity stems from the inability or reluctance of people in our society to be open and direct in dealing with sexual matters" (p. 53). It also recommended that "federal, state, and local legislation should not seek to interfere with the right of adults who wish to do so to read, obtain, or view explicit sexual materials" (p. 57). To protect everyone's rights, the Commission recommended legislative regulations on the sale of such material to young persons who do not have parental consent and on the thrusting of such material on those who do not desire it.

An issue of the *Journal of Social Issues* (the official publication of the Society for the Psychological Study of Social Issues, a division of the American Psychological Association), was devoted exclusively to the topic of the effects of pornography on society (Wilson and Goldstein, 1973). Overall, the papers and data provide strong support for the conclusions and recommendations of the Commission.

These conclusions and recommendations will be hotly debated for years to come. Dissenting members of the Commission criticized both the morality of the recommendations as well as the data upon which the conclusions were based. Dissenting members complained that the majority members did not provide them with monies for office personnel and for gathering contradictory data. One psychologist who believed that the data could be interpreted to show that exposure to pornographic materials did increase deviant and pathological behavior wrote a reply for the dissenting members. Since statistical data can be interpreted in many ways, one's moral biases often will affect the conclusions one draws, whether for or against. The times are clearly changing, but they have not yet changed enough so that the mere mention of sex does not evoke controversy.

Summary

Throughout our discussion of the six social issues—prejudice, conflict, population and crowding, aggression, bystander intervention, and sexual behavior, it has been our intention to introduce the reader to the approach that social psychologists take when attempting to investigate and understand a particular social problem. As we mentioned in our introductory comments, often principles emanating from basic or pure research (such as a number of those described in Chapter 15) have been brought to bear to help explain and understand social problems. Simultaneously, taking an approach that has been described as applied, namely, attempting to tackle the present problems head-on often results in delineating new theoretical perspectives and new principles of interpersonal behavior that have implications for higher order theories and model building.

As one recalls each of the six issues we have chosen to discuss, although they appear superficially to be quite different, consider the fact that a number of rather basic principles were crucially related to more than one issue. For example, social learning orientations were clearly important in our discussions of prejudice, aggression, altruism, and sexual behavior. And in analyses of international conflict reduction and laboratory efforts aimed at prejudice reduction, similar concepts such as intergroup contact on equal status levels are advocated. Attitudes were important in our discussion of prejudice, population growth and crowding. Attributions of others' intent were particularly important in the conflict, aggression, and altruism sections. When one finds such regularities across a number of social problems, it becomes inviting to generalize from one issue to others. When solutions for old problems are known, one can often apply similar principles to new issues.

Glossary

Aggression: An intentional action whose goal is to inflict harm. Since intentions are difficult to measure, some psychologists adopt a behavioral definition which states simply that aggression is an action that produces harm or injury.

Altruism: Helping behavior that is motivated by another person's need rather than the anticipation of personal gain.

Applied research: See also *pure research*. Research designed to provide answers to questions of immediate practical relevance, irrespective of its impact on basic theories.

Authoritarian personality: A personality type associated with holding antidemocratic attitudes, a generalized loyalty to an ingroup and rejection of outgroups, cognitive rigidity, and rationalization.

Catharsis: The reduction of aggressive drives or energy that have been built up through instincts or frustration. Catharsis has been hypothesized to occur when one engages in real or imagined aggressive actions. Evidence fails to support the basic premise; aggressive actions usually do not decrease subsequent aggression.

Cognitive overload: A psychological state that exists when stimulus inputs exceed the individual's ability to cope with them. Cognitive overload has been hypothesized to occur frequently for city dwellers.

Conflict stages: Three stages accompany most conflict situations: tension is noticed, a rising preparedness occurs to meet the perceived threats, and open hostilities emerge.

Crowding: A personal feeling that occurs when the demand for interpersonal space exceeds the amount of space actually available. This psychological condition is to be distinguished from actual *population density*.

Deindividuation: A process of becoming emersed in and nonrecognizable in a group. The opposite of standing out and bringing attention to oneself.

Diffusion of responsibility: A phenomenon occuring in groups where the members minimize personal responsibility for costly actions that could occur.

Discrimination: See also *prejudice* and *stereotypes*. The differential behavioral treatment of an individual based solely on his or her membership in a particular group. Discrimination pertains to behaviors, while prejudice pertains to attitudes.

Frustration-aggression models: A model of aggressive behaviors which proposed that aggression resulted from frustration and that frustration produced aggression. It is now known that although frustration and aggression are often linked, frustration can produce behaviors other than aggression (such as regression) and that aggression can result from other causes besides frustration (such as social learning).

GRIT: The acronym for a conflict reduction strategy which stands for "Graduated Reciprocation In Tension-Reduction." One party unilaterally announces the intention to cooperate and does so, hoping for reciprocation by the opponent. The strategy aims to produce a cooperation spiral and minimize negative perceptions.

Kinsey report: A large-scale opinion survey which questioned respondents about their sexual beliefs and behaviors. It was the most ambitious project ever conducted on the subject.

Mirror images: Perceptions that exist on both sides in a conflict, but are opposite reflections of one another.

Pacifism: A conflict resolution strategy which involves an active effort to defeat an opponent by means other than violence. Pacifism can be effective under conditions where communication occurs freely, neutral observers are present who can morally condemn the use of violence, and the opponent does not have teammates who urge the use of violence.

Population density: The number of people per unit of area. See also *crowding*.

Prejudice: See also *discrimination* or *stereotype*. A negative unjustified attitude towards an individual or group of individuals based solely on the fact of their group membership.

Pure research: See also *applied research*. Research designed to test explanations of natural phenomenon irrespective of the immediate applicability to real world problems.

Stereotype: See also *prejudice* and *discrimination*. Unjustified generalizations about an ethnic group or its members.

Suggested Readings

Elms, A. C. *Social Psychology and Social Relevance*. Boston Little, Brown and Co., 1972.

Hamsher, J. H., and Sigall, H. *Psychology and Social Issues*. New York: Macmillan, 1973.

Severy, L. J., Brigham, J. C., and Schlenker, B. R. *A Contemporary Introduction to Social Psychology* New York: McGraw-Hill Book Company, 1976.

17

Cross-Cultural Psychology

Harry C. Triandis

Introduction

Approximately 90 percent of the world's psychologists are European and North American. Yet, only one-third of the population of the world lives on those continents. The psychology that is being developed in Europe and North America is largely based on observations of people who live there. Does it apply to the rest of the world?

Science aspires to be universal. However, if our "laws" are developed on limited populations, we may reach the wrong conclusions. For example, Freud noted that there was hostility between sons and fathers in early twentieth-century Vienna. Being an excellent scholar, he also noted a similar phenomenon in an ancient Greek myth. The Oedipus complex was proposed as a universal characteristic of man: Sons all over the world have a secret wish to sexually possess their mothers; their fathers are in the way; they develop a subconscious wish to kill them. Freud's method was to study the dreams of his patients, where he found much evidence of hostility toward fathers. However, fathers in Vienna did a lot of things besides have intercourse with their wives! One of these things was assuming the role of the family's chief disciplinarians. Freud chose to ignore this fact. Later, when anthropologists, such as Malinowski, found tribes where the father had a different role, it was discovered that hostility is directed toward the disciplinarian, and not the mother's lover. Malinowski found a South Pacific culture called the Trobrianders, where the mother's brother was the chief disciplinarian. Analysis of the dreams of these islanders showed the hostility directed toward the mother's brother and not toward the father. Thus, the Oedipus complex, if it has any validity at all, is limited to Western societies. The point of this example is that variables get "confounded" in natural settings. That is, cases that are high on one variable (that is, being a disciplinarian) are also high on other variables (such as sleeping with mother) and cases that are low on one are also low on the other. Fathers were *both* lovers and disciplinarians in 1900 Vienna. As a result, one may not be able to disentangle the causes of a phenomenon, until one studies other cultures where such confounding is not present.

Such considerations have led to the development of cross-cultural psychology. If our aspiration is to be a universal science, we must test our most significant findings in many contexts. Cross-cultural psychology offers many other advantages, which we will discuss later.

The data of psychology come from two major settings: laboratory and field. They involve comparisons across species (phylogenetic), age groups (developmental psychology), historical periods, and cultures. Studies may focus on a single individual (clinical) or groups of individuals (survey method.) They may involve manipulation of variables (experimental) or observations of phenomena as they occur in nature. They may involve only one or many dependent variables. Each of these contrasts generates special methodological problems. Cross-cultural psychology has developed a special methodology that takes advantage of the methodological developments in experimental, quantitative, and developmental psychology, but also includes special techniques unique to it.

Cross-cultural psychology as a field is very close to both psychology and anthropology. In fact, both of these disciplines are concerned with people—where do they come from, what makes them tick, what variations in behavior are found in different cultures and historic periods. There are however some differences. Anthropologists are extremely concerned with understanding the way people function in different cultures by using the concepts generated by the cultures themselves. They are interested in a culture-relative understanding of behavior much more than in predicting and comparing it across a spectrum of cultures. Psychologists are looking for the general laws of human behavior that transcend time and place. In the search for such universal laws, they are prone to miss some details.

One should not be fooled, however, by academic labels. There are anthropologists who think and act just like psychologists, and psychologists who think and act just like anthropologists. As the disciplines develop more and more specialization, it is quite conceivable that physical anthropology and physiological psychology will merge, as will cultural anthropology, cross-cultural psychology, and social psychology. Furthermore, some of the activities of cognitive anthropologists are very close to what some psychologists are doing.

For example, there is a group of anthropologists who ask people in different cultures to make judgments about the way various concepts are similar or different. To be more specific, they may present three names of diseases (in the native language, of course) and ask "Which one of these three is most different from the other two?" The equivalent study in English might involve a judgment concerning pneumonia, the common cold, and tuberculosis. The subject picks one of these three as being more different from the other two, than the latter are to each other. For instance, one person might pick the common cold as being different, because it is not as *severe* a disease as the other two. From such judgments, and using a complicated method called multidimensional scaling that was developed by statisticians and psychologists,

it is possible to find out what diseases "go together" in the minds of a particular group of people. For example, in the Western world, a common way of thinking about disease is to put contagious and noncontagious diseases into two separate groups. In other parts of the world, such as among some of the Indians who live in Mexico, the grouping is done according to whether the diseases are "hot" or "cold." There is an elaborate system for diagnosing into which of these two groups to place a particular set of symptoms, and many beliefs on how to "cure" diseases that belong to these groups. The anthropologists found the local "way of thinking" about diseases by using the kinds of judgments mentioned above. Many years earlier, George Kelly, a clinical psychologist, had used the same procedure to study the way people think about interpersonal relations. For example, if you think of your mother, your girl friend, and your most loved teacher, which one of these three is most different from the other two? From such judgments Kelly obtained the "way of thinking about people" of his patients and used that information to help them overcome their personal problems.

Now that we have taken a general look at cross-cultural psychology and how it is related to psychology and anthropology, we are ready to look a little more closely at the content of cross-cultural psychology.

Culture is the man-made part of the human environment (Herskovits, 1955). Most theoretical systems developed by psychologists specify a strong connection between environment on the one hand and behavior and experience on the other. Thus, culture is one of the major determinants of human behavior and experience.

It is unclear, however, exactly how culture relates to behavior. One can conceive of behavior as a consequence of particular schedules of reinforcement as was described in Chapter 9, and culture as a kind of summary of particular schedules of reinforcement that are likely to exist in the environment of a particular human group. Or, one can conceive of culture as a learned pattern of actions or "designs for living" which affects behavior. Many other conceptions have been proposed as well.

In this chapter, we will argue that the *ecology* (physical environment, climate, resources) surrounding a group of people is one of the determinants of certain aspects of their behavior and experience. (See Figure 17-5 on p. 559.) Thus, the *individual system* (perception, cognitive, behavior patterns) is, in part, a consequence of ecology. The individual system has some consequences (effects, influences) on the *interindividual system,* that is, the way people behave toward other people (such as the way people raise their children). Furthermore, the interindividual system influences the *sociocultural system,* such as the norms, roles, values, legal systems, and other aspects of culture. The sociocultural system then feeds back and modifies the ecology, individual, and interindividual systems, so that the attributes that characterize each of these systems are in a state of dynamic balance. By dynamic balance we mean that changes in one part of the set of relationships among these variables influences several variables in different parts of the whole.

Other influences could also have been included. For example, cultural diffusion, as when one culture influences another, and historical factors such as war and conquest, affect existing cultures in various ways. The Romans, for instance, acquired many aspects of Greek culture which were later transmitted to many western cultures. To take but one example, the Greek revival architecture of the nineteenth century, in the United States, was a Greek influence on American culture. As another example, the legal systems of states such as Massachusetts, Louisiana, and California are rather different and reflect elements of the legal systems of Britain, France, and Spain, respectively. Literally millions of such effects of cultural transmission on other cultures can be generated through comparative studies of human behavior in different societies. (See Figure 17-1).

When analyzing the way ecology, culture, and other factors influence behavior, we must be concerned also with what is universal. As we said earlier, science aspires to make the simplest possible statements about the most general phenomena. Thus, psychology aspires to make statements that can apply to all humans. Many such statements apply not only to humans but also to lower ani-

mals, to adults as well as children, to people of one historical period as well as another. Such statements usually apply to humans regardless of culture. When a phenomenon is robust, that is, obtained again and again, and stable across species (phylogenetic continuity), age groups (ontogenetic continuity), time (historical continuity), and society (universality), it usually has a physiological or other biological basis. Many psychological findings are of this kind. However, many other phenomena are not of this kind; they show a good deal of variation across time or society. In such cases, culture often plays a dominant role in determining the specific patterns characteristic of the phenomena.

To understand human behavior in its full complexity we need to study those situations where culture is an important determinant of behavior. This is one of the main concerns of cross-cultural psychology. In this chapter, we will first examine why cross-cultural psychology is worth studying. Then, we will touch on some special difficulties in carrying out cross-cultural studies. We will then focus on several examples that illustrate the connections between ecology, culture, and behavior.

An Early Cross-Cultural Project

We begin with an example that will point to both the utility and the problems of cross-cultural psychology. It is one of the earlier cross-cultural studies and suffers from many methodological weaknesses. Yet, its strengths are greater than its weaknesses, and it is useful as an illustration, particularly because it uses a very broad set of variables.

The study by McClelland (1961) attempts to answer the question: "Why are some countries (cultures) rich while others are poor?" (See Figure 17-2) McClelland uses an imaginative approach employing all of the ecosocial factors mentioned above. In the 1930s, Henry Murray developed a theory of personality, which included the idea that people have certain needs. One of these needs was the need for achievement. McClelland focused on this need, which he assumed was a "psychogenic need" and a universal attribute, which reflects a person's tendency to compete with standards of ex-

Fig. 17-1.
An example of cultural diffusion.
McDonald's in Tokyo, Japan.
(United Nations/John Orr)

cellence. A person high in nAch (need for achievement) gets aroused in competitive situations and
tries hard, prefers experts over friends when that
person chooses work-partners and takes "reasonable risks." And, most importantly, "reasonable
risk-takers" form the backbone of capitalism, as
we shall see.

The last point is important. When a person decides to undertake a new project, there are probabilities of success and failure attached to the project and also the *value* of the outcome can be small,
medium, or large. For instance, if one decides to
invest in a sure stock (high probability of success),
that persons is likely to get a small return for one's
money (such as 5 percent). Another person may
put the same amount of money in some gambling
project (such as horseracing) where that person
might have a very small chance of making a very
large (for example, 5000 percent profit) amount of
money. Neither of these two is taking what we
mean by the term "a reasonable risk." In short,
neither the sure bet nor the wild gamble are reasonable risks. By contrast, a reasonable risktaker
might invest in ways that are quite likely to succeed (but not sure) and make a good profit (perhaps
25 percent). Now, it is obvious that for entrepreneurial success (success in business enterprises) in

a competitive business world, the person who
takes reasonable risks is more likely to accumulate
capital, which that person can again invest and so
on until that person can buy a new industry and
create many jobs, thus contributing to general economic development. In short, the particular tendency of the high need achiever to take reasonable
risks can be associated with economic development, and hence there is a connection between
need achievement and economic development in
countries where there are many people with this
trait.

McClelland measures nAch by asking a person
to provide stories to a series of ambiguous pictures, taken from the Thematic Apperception Test
(TAT). Those who produce many competitive success themes in their stories are said to be high
nAch people. When scoring the stories that people
produce to the ambiguous pictures, when the story
refers to somebody doing something "great" that
helps others, it is not scored as nAch. Only themes
of achievement where the actor benefits himself
are scored as achievement themes. The more
achievement themes in the stories produced by a
given individual the higher the nAch score of that
individual.

McCelland used this approach in both experi-

Fig. 17-2.
In discussions of why some countries are rich and some are poor, we tend to forget the extreme variations within countries. Shown above are improvised shacks of the poor in the shadow of climate-controlled luxury towers of the rich in Bombay, India. We also tend to forget that in many cultures people are paid in services rather than money. Below is a laundry, also in Bombay, where the owner and his ancestors before him have for generations done the laundry of particular families, receiving in return such services as medical care and legal advice. Such interdependence creates problems when we measure the gross national product of a country, since only when money is exchanged do the economic indices reflect it. Nevertheless, in spite of such qualifications, there is value in studies of average income variability across countries. (United Nations/J. P. Laffonte and H. C. Triandis)

mental settings and surveys of the level of nAch in different groups. He found, for instance, that Protestants and Jews in the United States had higher nAch scores than Catholics. Taking a sample of predominantly Protestant countries (Norway and Sweden) and comparing it with a sample of predominantly Catholic countries (Belgium and Spain), McClelland found that the economic development of the Protestant countries, measured by the amount of electricity consumed per capita (kilowatt hours/capita) was higher than the development of the Catholic countries.

Using content analyses (a method that counts the number of times a particular idea is present in a text) of other kinds of cultural products, such as the books read to school children in many lands, the poetry and literature of a particular country during a particular period, the plays, epigraphs, and slogans of different periods and so on, he assembled evidence that (a) cultures differ in their level of n achievement, and (b) variations in nAch are systematically connected with cultural achievements. For example, the great period of ancient Greek civilization (fifth century, B.C.) was preceded by high levels of nAch in Greek cultural products (such as poetry and plays) while the decline before the Roman conquest was preceded by low levels of nAch. The British had two peaks of nAch, a generation before Queen Elizabeth the First and in the early nineteenth century, before the formation of the British Empire. The Spanish had a peak about thirty years before Christopher Columbus's voyage in 1492. The United States had its peak in the 1890s and we may now be entering a decline.

In short, taking cultural measures of two kinds (cultural products and economic achievements), McCelland found a covariation expected from the analysis which argues that high nAch *leads* to economic development.

One explanation is that when children are exposed to many achievement themes in cultural products, they acquire the idea that achievement is a good thing. This is particularly important when they encounter achievement themes in children's stories and primary school readers. McCelland did content analyses of such readers and found that when there were many achievement themes in the readers of one generation of children, there was a specially intense economic activity about twenty years later.

In another set of studies, McCelland found low but significant relationships between ecological (environmental, climatic) variables and the number of nAch themes in cultural products. For instance, he found that in environments that have moderate mean temperature (10°) and large temperature variations (large differences between summer and winter), the levels of nAch are high. In the tropics and in the polar region, it is low. In addition, McCelland and his students found certain kinds of childrearing patterns closely connected with high nAch. Specifically, when parents emphasize early independence training, and fathers have a small influence on childrearing, sons tend to be high in nAch. Presumably early independence training, such as learning to dress by oneself, to cross the street by oneself, to find one's way in town by oneself, and so on, means taking reasonable risks and getting rewarded for successful performance. A child who is over-protected does not take any risks and one that is neglected may take

high risks. Thus, it is the warm-autonomy-giving mother that will have the high nAch son. By contrast, as soon as the family is rich, where they can afford servants, slaves, and the like (depending on the historical period), children are likely to be overprotected (a slave might lose his head if the master's son gets in trouble), and hence nAch drops.

We can summarize much of what we said above by examining Figure 17-3. We see that the ecology is connected with an aspect of the *individual system* (parental need Achievement) which is connected with an aspect of the *interindividual system* (son's nAch and risktaking), which is connected with an aspect of the *cultural system* (economic development). Of course, we know that high economic development has implications for the ecology, such as pollution, possible changes in the microclimate, and so on.

One can quarrel with many aspects of McCelland's work. For example, the reliability of measures of nAch is often poor, his choice of variables (for example, Kilowatt hours/capita to measure economic development) can be challenged.

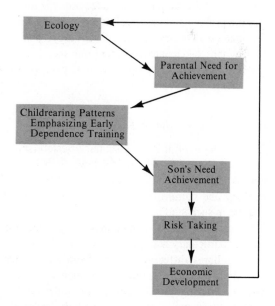

Fig. 17-3. Hypothetical relationships among the major sets of variables linking Need Achievement and Economic Development.

However, the overall coherence of the theoretical structure and the way the data hang together suggest that there is some validity in the argument, an argument that is bolstered by social philosophers such as Max Weber. On the other hand, it should be remembered that the argument applies to situations where competition and the free enterprise system require the taking of reasonable risks. Other forms of social organization, such as those found in the Soviet Union or China, would require different kinds of personal attributes for success. There is some doubt that the very concept of need achievement has universal utility. There are always problems with interpreting data based on a single measure and there are many unanswered questions about the extent to which cultural variables might modify the relationships as shown in Figure 17-3. For example, a person with high nAch in a culture where "reasonable risks" are dysfunctional (such as in a bureaucracy) may be less successful than a person who takes no risks; or, risks might be taken by groups rather than individuals, as is the case in Japanese industries and large business enterprises. In such cases, the theory needs the special kind of improvement that cross-cultural analysis can provide. In any case, this is a useful example to introduce both the utility and the problems of cross-cultural psychology, for the method of cross-cultural psychology, just as McCelland, takes into consideration sociological and anthropological factors as well as psychological theory.

Why Do Cross-Cultural Studies?

Cross-cultural studies are essential in establishing the generality of psychological laws or phenomena. At the same time, in order to understand how ecology and culture influence behavior, we must engage in such studies.

Several additional factors make cross-cultural studies particulary attractive:

1. Cultures differ very much from each other and thus provide "natural experiments" where widely differing environments can influence behavior (Strodtbeck, 1964). Some of these natural experiments allow variables to vary much more widely, and of course realistically, than is possible

even under ingeniously contrived laboratory conditions. The manipulation of variables is tied to very thorny ethical problems (American Psychological Association, 1973; Tapp et al, 1974), but we can observe differences that occur naturally and reduce the severity of such ethical concerns.

For example, psychologists have assumed for some time that exposure to a rich social environment with multiple stimuli, increases the intelligence of children, and conversely, exposure to a dull and unstimulating environment depresses the intelligence. It is not ethically acceptable to expose babies to a dull environment to see what effects this will have on their development. However, one can find situations where children are reared in this way. Hunt (1974) found an orphanage in Tehran, Iran, that did not provide much stimulation; children were left in their cribs with minimum contact with adults. Such children, he found, did not walk until age 3 (most normally raised children walk before 18 months of age) and did not develop language skills until very much later. Their language development and cognitive skills showed great deficiencies. By having tape recorders attached to the cribs, and activated when the child moved in the crib, Hunt was able to provide more exposure to language and to decrease the deficits. In this experiment, some children were left in their "normal" situation and other children were placed in an improved environment. That does raise an ethical problem, but since the resources of the world are limited, it is impossible to help everybody. Helping those who are selected randomly to be members of an experimental group helps some people, while, at the same time, advancing science. This kind of activity is ethically correct and only possible if we take advantage of opportunities that exist in different parts of the world, in natural environments.

2. We can understand somewhat how ecology influences behavior if we observe the frequencies, or intensities of behavior in different ecological settings. For example, we will see later that in some cultures, people conform to social pressures more than in others, and this makes sense when you study their ecology.

3. We can discover how different groups of people cut the "pie of experience" by studying

particular modes of categorization of experience. Studies of "ethnoscience" (for example, Romney and D'Andrade, 1964; Tyler, 1969) are examples. In such studies, an attempt is made to learn the way a cultural group experiences its natural environment, by looking at the way they classify botanical, animal, mineral, and other terms; or, as in the example given earlier, the way they think about diseases. Ethnoscience refers to locally developed science. It is quite important to learn how different groups of people think about the natural environment, because this reveals something about the way they think in general.

It is equally interesting to learn how people perceive the human-made part of their environment, or their "subjective culture" (Triandis et al, 1972). Here an attempt is made to discover, through an analysis of judgments made by samples of people from different cultures, the way people respond to the meaning of different words, roles, social behaviors, and values. Such work results in "maps" of experience that function as guides for behavior (Triandis, 1975). It can help in understanding why social behavior is different in different cultures, and also why people who come from different cultures have difficulties in interacting with each other. For example, a particular social behavior, such as inviting somebody to dinner, can be perceived quite differently by people from two cultures. In some cultures, this behavior implies that there is already much intimacy established, and the invitation is confirming the intimacy; in other cultures it implies very little, beyond a mildly friendly gesture. The perceived causes of such behavior can also be very different: in some cultures it can be seen as an attempt at building strong bonds of friendship, in others as simply doing what is required by one's role. Almost any social behavior can be viewed in such a discrepant way, and as a result, people who come from different cultures often misunderstand each other.

Still another interesting kind of study concerns how different ecological factors influence different types of "maps," and result in different subjective cultures. For example, people who live in crowded, agricultural environments tend to think that "good" is limited (Foster, 1965), while those who live in an open frontier are less likely to share this viewpoint, and more likely to think of "good" as an "expanding pie."

4. We can increase the range of variation on certain variables. One of the classic examples was presented by Whiting (1968). He pointed out that it is important to know what happens when mothers wean their children early, or late. In the United States, mothers wean their children very early (using a cup to feed milk, rather than their breasts). or somewhat later—at about 6 months of age. Some studies done in the United States had suggested that it is better to wean the child early, because children who are weaned at 6 months tend to show symptoms of anxiety in kindergarten and school. However, this idea seems to be correct only if we consider the restricted range of variation of weaning age found in the United States. When we look around the world, we find mothers who wean their children much later—as late as age 36 months. When we look at the children of these mothers, we discover that they are not anxious. In fact, the data show that the worst age for weaning is at 18 months. So, for the 0 to 18 months range, the relationship between age of weaning and anxiety suggests that the later a child is weaned the more anxious it will be; but if we look at the relationship for ages 18 to 36 months the reverse is true: the later a child is weaned the less anxious it will be. In other words, the relationship between age of weaning and later anxiety is curvilinear—an inverted U-shape. It is obvious that if we limit ourselves to observations in a restricted range, we would not know that. In fact, if we only look at a small range we might conclude that the relationship is positive (for age 0–18 months), or negative (for age 18–36 months). Neither of these statements is correct, and we can only know what is the true relationship if we have observations from the full range of 0 to 36 months. Such a range can usually not be obtained in any one culture; one needs to look at data from many cultures.

Above all, it should be remembered that a psychologist is a human being. The choice of problems, theories, and methods which characterize his/her research are strongly influenced by his or her culture. Distortions can enter into any point of the research process. Such distortions can, however, be discovered only if we do cross-cultural research. For example, if we tried to develop the science of meteorology just by taking observations from within the region situated within a mile of a major volcano, it is clear that this "volcanic meteorology" would be greatly deficient. In a similar way, our own culture distorts our observations (for example, it is not always true that volcanic dust contributes to the formation of rain drops; likewise, people studying interpersonal attraction in societies where interaction is not based primarily on tribal membership may assume that the basis of attraction in their society is universal) and complicates them (for example, one can get a better picture of many phenomena without the interference of volcanic dust). We get a much clearer view of human behavior when we have a clear understanding of what are universal processes.

For example, if McCelland had been able to study "achievement" in modern China, his contributions would probably have been much greater. It is unfortunate that political conflicts have prevented fruitful cooperation of Western psychologists with psychologists from socialist countries. One can easily see that much would be learned about the generality of human behavior if such collaboration were achieved. In such projects, the very definitions of the aims and goals, concepts and methods should be determined jointly and to the satisfaction of all, otherwise the project will be methodologically deficient, as will become apparent in the discussion that follows.

Special Methodological Problems

While there are obvious advantages in doing cross-cultural research, as outlined in the previous section, there are many difficulties. Methodological problems have been the focus of much cross-cultural writing (see Przeworski and Teune, 1969; Triandis et al, 1972, Chapter III; Brislin et al, 1973). Some of the more important problems can be summarized as follows:

The Emic-Etic Contrast. A serious problem in cross-cultural research is that an attribute important in one culture, but nonexistent or distorted in other cultures, might be made the central attribute

of a study. It is useful to distinguish universal (etic) attributes and culture-specific (emic) attributes (Pike, 1966). An example will help. Compare apples and oranges. Both are fruit and have some common (etic) attributes, such as price, weight, size, and color. However, they also have particular (emic) attributes, such as apple flavor and orange flavor. Note that *comparisons* can only be done on etic attributes. However, the description of the essential character of an apple requires the description and specification of apple flavor. A person who has never eaten an apple will never "understand" apples if that person is told only their price, size, weight, or color. In short, emic attributes are essential for the *understanding* of culture, but etic attributes are essential for the comparison of cultures. Some generalizations (for example, analogous to "large fruit are cheaper per unit of weight than small fruit") may be useful "laws," and use etic variables; these generalizations transcend culture. However, in order to understand how cultures "work" we must use emic variables. See Figure 17-4.

It is worth noting, here, that, traditionally, the perspectives of the anthropologist and psychologist have been somewhat different (Triandis et al, 1972). As mentioned earlier in this chapter, anthropologists want to do the best job of describing cultures, hence typically use emic variables and concepts. Psychologists are interested in generalizations of laws about human behavior; they typically use etic variables. However, there are many anthropologists who are interested in generalizations about human behavior (see Whiting, 1968; Naroll, 1970; Rohner, 1975) and many psychologists interested in describing specific cultures (see Triandis and Vassiliou, 1972; Triandis et al, 1975).

Our viewpoint is that *both* approaches are valuable and should be used under different circumstances. One way to tie the two approaches is to use etic constructs or ideas but make them operational with emic items. Essentially this approach requires that we start with a concept that is culture-general and find items that reflect cultural conditions to make it operational. For example, the concept of *social distance* exists in most cultures (Triandis et al, 1965). Suppose we ask if a

A.

Fig. 17-4.

Five different market places: (A) Bangkok's Floating Market, (B) Street vendors in Madras, India, (C) Ougadougou, Upper Volta, (D) San Cristobal de las Casas, Mexico, (E) Seattle, Wash. Note that each has some common (etic) elements and some culture-specific (emic) elements. (A, H. Triandis; B, C, United Nations; D, Jeffrey House; E, Jean Shapiro)

C.

D.

B.

E.

person "would exclude from the neighborhood" a particular type of person, say, a black person. This item makes sense in the United States, but not in Japan. In other cultures, we might ask if a person would allow a particular type of person to "touch his earthenware" (an item that makes sense in India, where there is the concept of ritual pollution, but makes no sense in the United States).

Now, suppose one has a sample of items that are appropriate for a particular culture. One can ask a sample of twenty people from that culture to look at each of the items and to rate it on an 11-point scale, as implying maximum social distance (10), minimal social distance (0), or some intermediate degree of social distance (a number between 1 and 9). If one has a sample of 100 or so items, some of the items will elicit good agreement from the 20 people, about where they belong on the social distance scale. For example, it is a good bet that "to kill" will be seen as belonging to positions 9 or 10 while "to marry" will be seen as belonging to positions 0 or 1. Other items will be shown to be ambiguous, that is, the twenty people may not agree among themselves on how to rate them. Such items can be eliminated from further consideration. Now, suppose one gets about 20 items that are clear and unambiguous, that have been placed on positions all along the 11-point scale (from 0 to 10). Then one has a set of items that are *locally standardized* and appropriate for use in that culture. But the "scale values" of these items, which are essentially the mean ratings of the items obtained in the particular culture, are etic measures, because they refer to an etic quality—social distance. This way one can get different scales in different cultures, such as the United States and Greece (Triandis and Triandis, 1962) or the United States, Germany, and Japan (Triandis et al, 1965), or the United States and Mexico (Davidson et al, 1976). There are elaborate techniques, developed by a famous psychologist called Thurstone, that allow one to check that the "scale values" obtained in each culture are reliable and form an "equal interval scale" (which means that the difference between, say, 8 and 6 on the scale is psychologically the same as the difference between 5 and 3: in both cases 2 scale units), which means the scale values and the scores obtained in each

culture can be analyzed by a wide range of statistical techniques, such as analysis of variance, to find out how people in the various cultures respond to different types of persons. (These scaling techniques are explained in a very readable book by Edwards, *Techniques of Attitude Scale Construction,* 1957). Such *local* standardization results in different scales (emic measures) in different cultures, yet the scales *reflect* etic variables which, in turn, permit comparisons.

Another approach is to use a broad sampling of item domains (for example all qualities that describe jobs) representative of each culture and a statistical procedure called factor analysis. If similar factors emerge in each culture, then etic dimensions (the similar factors) have been extracted. Yet the items that constitute the factors may be culture-specific. For example, in one culture the adjectives *good* and *clean* may hang together with several other "evaluative" adjectives defining a factor, while in another culture the adjectives *nectarlike* and *delightful* may define a factor. It is obvious that in both cases these adjectives express some sort of positive evaluation of a stimulus, yet the judgments are made on culture-appropriate scales (see Osgood, 1965, 1971; Triandis et al, 1968). We will return to a more complete discussion of this point when we review Osgood's research later in this chapter.

Cross-Cultural Equivalence. Ideally, we need to have equivalent stimuli, equivalent manipulations, equivalent samples of subjects, and equivalent response continua across two or more cultures. How to get equivalence is a highly technical problem that has been discussed in the methodological references mentioned earlier. Here we can only briefly mention the problem of translation, which is concerned with linguistic equivalence. Werner and Campbell (1970) have suggested a procedure that involves double translation with decentering. Suppose we start from English and want to translate to Thai. We first ask two bilinguals to translate an English text (call it E_1) into Thai (T_1). Then we ask two different bilinguals to translate the Thai text (T_1) into English (E_2). Now looking at E_1 and E_2 we will note probably some discrepancies. This happens because the Thai language may not have exactly parallel words for the English words and ideas of the original text. So when E_1 was translated into Thai, and became, T_1, it became a bit distorted; when T_1 was translated into English and we got E_2 the distortion was reflected in E_2. But, there is nothing sacred about E_1. If E_1 does not translate well into Thai, we can change it a bit to make it more easily translatable. How can we change it? Well, the differences between E_1 and E_2 give us a clue. Of course, we do want an English version that says what we want the text to say, and it is probable that E_2 is not perfectly satisfactory in terms of what we want to communicate. So, let us change it into E_3 which does say, in good English, what we want to say, but has a better chance of "mapping into" Thai, because it reflects some of the characteristics of the Thai language. So, now we start all over again. The E_3 version is translated into Thai by a bilingual, and gives T_3; then T_3 is translated into English by another bilingual and gives E_4. Suppose that E_3 is the same as E_4. That means that we have succeeded in getting a text that translates well into Thai. It is probable that T_3 will be a *good* Thai translation of the text. On the other hand if the E_3 and E_4 versions are different, we continue the process until we get two English versions that are the same. The Thai version that corresponds to the English version that does not change is the best translation.

Brislin, Lonner, and Thorndike (1973) give an example from a study by Brislin. He translated the Marlowe-Crowne Social Desirability Scale into Chamorro, a language of Guam and the Marianas Islands, in the Pacific Ocean. The process required first translation into Chamorro, then back translation into English, then review of the two English texts, then modification of the English and translation to Chamorro, then translation to English, and a second review. Again, some modification was required and translation into Chamorro and back translation into English. At that point, the English version agreed rather well with the previous English version. The changes in the wording are suggested by examining the original and final English versions. For example, the original included an item that was worded as follows: "I like to gossip at times." The final version included the following wording: "I sometimes like to talk about other people's business."

Experimenter or Tester Effects. It is well known that in some cases the experimenter or the tester has substantial effects on the way people respond to an experimental situation or a test. It helps to have experimenters or testers who are as similar to the people being studied as possible. Similarity in race, sex, age, language, and other variables usually helps. However, there are many complications. One such complication is that people who know they are in an experiment may respond to the experimental situation in very different ways. Some of them try to "help" as much as possible— that is, they guess the hypothesis and behave so as to confirm it; others try to "screw" the experimenter—that is, they guess the hypothesis and try to behave so as to disconfirm it; still others try to follow instructions as closely as possible, while others disregard them; many are apprehensive, that is, they feel that their abilities are being tested and try to behave in a way that will make them look "as good as possible." All of these effects are likely to bias the results. The way the experimenter is perceived increases some of these tendencies and decreases others. In general, if the experimenter is "unobtrusive" and the hypothesis impossible to figure out, the chances are that different people will respond with different biases, but the average responses will cancel out the biases so that the results of the study can be useable.

Cross-cultural researchers, when at all possible, use local experimenters or testers, who are not too different from the people being tested, to avoid some of these problems. Another approach is to use unobtrusive measures, that is, do the study in such a way that the people who are being tested do not know that they are participating in a study. However, this approach creates some serious ethical problems. People who participated may find out that they were "victims" of the experimenter, and protest. It is unethical because such people may become suspicious of any similar situations, and hence the work of one experimenter spoils the research site of future experimenters.

The ethically acceptable principle is that one can observe *public* situations, but not *private,* and one can only do so *passively*. If one is to *intervene,* then one must get permission from the people being tested. The concern here is that psychologists may acquire a bad reputation for observing private situations and the public might be angered, making all work in psychology difficult to perform.

When Do We Have a "Real" Cultural Difference?

Suppose you administered some measures to two cultural groups and you have obtained a difference. Is that difference "real?" The answer is: "Not necessarily." There are *many* competing (rival) hypotheses explaining why a particular difference may have emerged. For example, if cultures A and B differ in performance on a test, this might reflect differences in (a) familiarity with the instruments, (b) motivation, (c) response style (such as some groups of people like to always say yes; others always use the extreme position on a scale), (d) reactions to the experimenter (some like to please, others like to fool the experimenter; some cultures *require* that people lie to a stranger), (e) social desirability (some cultures may consider a particular answer "appropriate" and people may give that answer whether it is true or false), (f) reactions to anonymity (some cultures demand it, others reject it), and (g) mixtures of all of the above.

In some African cultures, "intelligent" means *slow* and *wise* (Wober, 1974). In the United States, intelligent means *quick* and *bright*. It follows that a *slow* response is more likely in Africa than in the United States if you tell a person you plan to measure that person's intelligence. In fact, an individual from an African culture would be surprised at the idea that timing a test, which is so often done in the West, has anything to do with intelligence.

Differences in familiarity with I.Q. tests, in reactions to time ("Why hurry?" says the South Pacific Islander), response style (answer all questions vs. guess those you do not know much about), reactions to experimenter (having a stranger of a different race test you), social desirability, and so on result in better scores for Westerners than for Africans. Yet when Africans are tested with the proper

instruments and under proper instructions, they do as well as United States citizens and other Westerners—(Cole and Scribner, 1974). So, if we obtain a cultural difference, does it really *mean* anything? To get around the obvious methodological problems mentioned above and to get around the obvious fact that such differences may not mean anything, there are two broad approaches:

(a) We can use several different methods for the measurement of the key constructs (Campbell and Fiske, 1959), varying instruments, conditions of administration, and so on, and then look for consistencies across instruments. If consistencies are noted, we can assume that the methodological problems, which operate unequally across methods, may not be the central factors in the obtained results.

For example, suppose you are interested in comparing "the effectiveness" of two samples of physicians. You might see how satisfied their patients are, how much respect they receive from their colleagues, how much respect they receive from their nurses, how many research papers they have published, how well known they are to other physicians in other countries, and, in addition, administer a test of medical knowledge. Now suppose that the 6 measures just mentioned correlate among each other, and suppose that one group of physicians is high on 5 out of 6, or even better 6 out of 6 of the measures, while the other group is low. Then the chances are that the two groups of physicians are indeed different, and one group is "better" or "superior." However, if some of the measures show one group higher than the other, and other measures show the opposite, or if the correlations among the 6 measures in one group of physicians are different from the correlations in the other group, we would not be justified in making any statement about the superiority of one of the groups of physicians.

Unfortunately, most psychologists doing comparisons of two or more groups have not used multimethod measurement, and, as a result, many of the statements that they have made are of doubtful validity. Furthermore, there is evidence that different measures correlate differently in different cultures, yet some psychologists have ignored this fact and made comparisons anyway. Such comparisons are not methodologically sound and should not have been accepted for publication.

The validity of a measure, as seen in Chapters 3 and 18, can be assessed in different ways. Among the most important are predictive, concurrent, and construct validity. Predictive validity refers to whether the measure predicts some other measure obtained at a later point in time, as when grades in high school are used to predict grades in college. Concurrent validity refers to having high correlations among several measures that supposedly measure the same thing. Construct validity refers to obtaining high correlations that are predicted from theory, as when we expect people who are intelligent to do well in school, to be successful in their professions, to have good judgment, to be able to learn new things quickly, and so on, and then find that our measure of intelligence correlates as expected with a variety of measures that reflect the expected consequences of being intelligent. In short, we would then have external checks or indicators that the "construct" indeed is meaningful.

In cross-cultural studies, only construct validity is truly defensible. This is because biases can equally affect both the predictor and the predicted measures, or all the measures that supposedly measure the same thing. For instance, in a society that is prejudiced against blacks, test scores that are developed on middle class white norms might correlate very well with grades, but part of the correlation may reflect the downgrading of blacks in *both* the tests and the assignment of grades. In the case of several tests that supposedly measure the same ability, the high correlations may be due to the same biases operating in each test.

While only construct validation is defensible, we must also take into account what it means to be successful in the *particular* culture, what it means to have good judgment in the *particular* culture, what it means to learn new things quickly in the *particular* culture, and so on. Suppose a person is brought up in a lower-class environment, in which most communication depends on context. The person may have learned to say, "Give me this book" (pointing to the book). Such a person may be very quick and effective in such communication, and hence intelligent *for that cultural setting*. But the very same person may be very ineffective if that person has to describe a book situated in a room in another town. A middle-class person is trained to deal with more abstract situations and has developed skills enabling that person to communicate such an idea, for example, "In room 329 Psychology Building, Champaign, Ill. USA, there is a desk next to the window, and the book is on the upper right-hand corner of the desk." Note that no one who can be effective in communicating when saying "Give me this book" would use the longer phrase that is needed when there is no context.

People who always communicate in situations where there is context simply do not develop the skills required for communication in situations without context. Note that a *skill* is required; it is like learning a foreign language. We do not call a person who does not speak Chinese stupid (if indeed such demeaning adjectives should ever be used), unless that person has been born and raised in China and does not speak Chinese. Similarly, it makes no sense to call a person stupid who has been raised in an environment where communications always *can be* context-dependent, just because that person cannot communicate in relatively context-free environments.

Of course, the inability to communicate in context-free environments is an impediment when such a person works in context-free environments, such as schools, white collar jobs, and so on. If a person wishes to operate in context-free environments, that person must acquire the new skills, like any person who plans to live in another country must learn the local language. Such learning must take place early in life, before the person goes to school, otherwise school will be a very hostile environment where failure is guaranteed.

The logic of construct validation has almost never been used by those engaged in cross-cultural measurements of abilities. In fact, we have no data on what it means to be successful in certain cultures. One could argue, for instance, that for some people, success is to convince others that one is a "holy person," and this is done by being able to live alone in a cave and to go without food for long periods of time. Such traits are obviously not reflected in our I.Q. tests. Thus, our I.Q. tests measure not intelligence, but the *probability of becom-*

ing successful in a middle class environment. We should keep these two ideas separate. What makes for success in one environment is not the same ability or skill that makes for success in another. A Nobel prize winning physicist dropped without equipment or preparation in the middle of Greenland would have less chance of surviving than an Eskimo who scores 80 on our I.Q. tests.

Of course, this does not mean that I.Q. tests are useless. They are practical and predict success in middle-class environments. The problem is that they have been oversold and overextended to other cultures, and we have been told that they measure "real" intelligence. Actually, they measure only some aspects of intelligence. Guilford (1967) has identified 120 abilities. Most I.Q. tests sample only some of them. Furthermore, what we call success is a very complex matter. Studies of the success of physicians (Taylor and Barron, 1963) identified no fewer than twelve independent aspects of this idea. A physician can be a success as a scientist, as a practitioner, as a public speaker, as a professional with a large practice, and so on. These aspects of success show very low intercorrelations. That is, people who are good on one criterion may be poor on another. One needs to obtain a very large number of ability measures to be able to predict all of these aspects of success, and even when all this is done, only about one-third of the variability in success (some people succeed and others do not) can be accounted by the ability measures. There are other factors—where a person is born, who are his (her) relatives, where did he (she) go to school, and a myriad of other factors, that determine two-thirds of the variability of success.

In other words, the concept of *intelligence,* which is a perfectly useful psychological concept, has been measured by procedures with limited validity. It is likely that future research in ability measurement will improve this situation. Similarly other concepts, such as personality traits, attitudes and so on have rarely been measured well, particularly in cross-cultural contexts. Most of these constructs are very complex, yet they have typically been measured by simple procedures, single measures. Only construct validation and multiple methods of measurement, which "triangulate"

and solidify findings, can be defended as sound procedures.

(b) We can keep changing the stimuli, conditions of administration or response continua until we get similar performance across cultures. In that case, we can be reasonably sure about what causes differences in performance, because these differences are explicitly tied to differences in the administration of the measurements (Cole and Scribner, 1974). For example, if Africans have trouble doing a categorization task (see Chapter 11) *except* when chairs, or some other concrete reminder, are used to remind them about different categories of sorting stimuli (such as put all red circles on *this* chair) we learn that such concrete methods of categorization are needed for good performance. People who depend on context, for thinking, may need such concrete reminders.

A Summary Methodological Statement. It is obvious that cross-cultural research faces some very difficult methodological problems. On the other hand, solutions to many of these problems are becoming available. In this section we introduced only a few of these problems and suggested rather briefly some of the solutions. The interested reader should consult some of the references mentioned earlier to obtain a more complete picture. We are now ready to turn to the substantive findings. Again only a brief sample can be given here. Reviews are available elsewhere (see Triandis et. al., 1972, 1973; Dawson and Lonner, 1974; Brislin et. al., 1975).

Some Substantive Findings

A Model of Cross-Cultural Findings

In Figure 17-5, we see the relationships among systems of variables. Ecology influences perception, cognition, and subjective (versus *objective*) culture, which is the way a group of people perceives its social environment. Furthermore, ecology has consequences for the motivation and social behavior of those who live in particular environments. The individual system, including the subjective culture of a cultural group, has influences

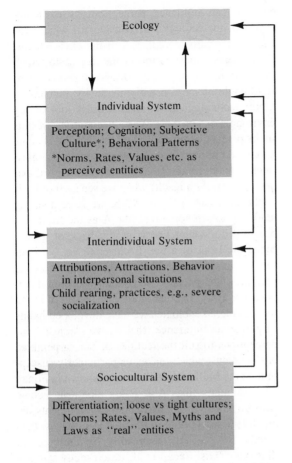

Fig. 17-5. Relationships among systems of variables in cross-cultural studies.

on the interindividual system, such as child-rearing practices typically found in a culture. The interindividual system, in turn, has consequences for the sociocultural system. Finally, the sociocultural system feeds back and modifies all the other systems, including the ecology. In the sections that follow, we will review some studies that illustrate these connections.

Ecology-Individual System

Ecology influences many aspects of the individual system, both biologically determined and learned. As an example of the influence of ecology on the biological system, consider Bornstein's (1973)

argument about cultural differences in color naming. The human eye is capable of discriminating about 7.3 million colors. But most languages have a very small number of color names. Some languages use the same name for green and blue, others for blue and black and still others use the same name for green, blue, and black. In short, in some cultures, people do not seem to differentiate green, blue, and black as much as in other cultures. If one draws a map of the world and places dots to show the location of the cultures where there is little differentiation of these three colors, there is a striking pattern: most of the dots are around the equator.

Bornstein presents arguments suggesting that the mechanism responsible for this phenomenon is yellow intraocular filtration. That is, exposure to a great deal of ultraviolet radiation, which is likely at high altitudes and near the equator, results in the development of a filtering system involving increased density of yellow pigmentation at the cornea, the lens, and other parts of the eye. The yellow pigment selectively absorbs short-wave radiation, before the light entering the eye has a chance to excite the blue and green receptor pigments specifically sensitive to that part of the visible spectrum. The consequence of the operation of this mechanism is *increased visual acuity*. In a way, it is as though people who live in regions where there is much ultraviolet light wear "natural dark glasses," that allow their eyes to see better, but reduce the contrast between the colors of the short-wave section of the spectrum.

Consider now an example where there is an interaction between the biological and the cultural systems. In some environments, it is functional for people to obey and conform, while in other environments it is not so important that people conform. For example, in a culture where food is obtained by poisoning a river, extreme coordination of action is essential if a successful catch is to be had. While some people drop poisonous plants in the river, others must have their nets ready to catch the fish. Obeying the chief who calls the signals and tells who is to do each job is essential if coordination is to be achieved. By contrast, in a culture, such as the Eskimo, where hunting is often an individual activity, conformity has little social value. It is not surprising, then, that we find much conformity in some cultures and little conformity in others, and generally the form of economic activity is related to the degree of required conformity.

Left-handedness is typical of a small portion of humans in every society. It is probable that in every society a small proportion are "naturally left-handed." A guess is that this is on the order of 15 percent of the population. In societies where conformity is not stressed, we note that left-handedness is found in 10 to 15 percent of the people; in societies where conformity is stressed we find less than *1 percent* left-handedness (Dawson, 1974). That difference is, of course, very striking. Everywhere in the world the right hand is considered "the correct" hand, but in some cultures the difference between the two hands is not stressed, while in others it is. Generally, the conformity-stressing cultures are the ones that impose the preferences of the majority on their left-handed minority, sometimes so strongly that *none* of the people are left-handed (such as lower-class Nigerians). So, here we have an example where a phenomenon is determined by biological factors (left *vs.* right hemisphere of the brain dominance), yet it is shaped by cultural factors. Furthermore, conformity becomes a value and is imposed in domains that have no special survival utility.

These examples suggest that both the physiological and the cultural systems that determine individual behavior may be determined by the ecology. In some cases, as in the example of left-handedness, some behavior pattern (conformity) becomes so valuable that it is applied inappropriately. Similarly, a biological trait useful in one environment may be undesirable in another. For example, blacks may have eyes that are very well adjusted to the light around the equator but may not be optimal for southern Scandinavia.

With this general introduction to the effects of ecology on the individual system, we now turn to some specifics about the way ecology influences perception.

Ecology→Perception. An important theoretical, methodological, and empirical achievement is a study by Segall et al (1966) which shows that the ecology can influence perception. A particular aspect of the ecology was considered, which was called the "carpenteredness" of the environment. By carpenteredness is meant the degree to which the environment has many orthogonal geometric or right-angle shapes, usually made by humans in highly technological cultures. A quick look at city environments, in most Western countries, results in the perception of many right angles. We become habituated to perceive most angles as right angles. Such a habit generally helps the accuracy of our perceptions. As a result, when we see a set of horizontal lines, as in Figure 17-6, we have a strong tendency to see horizontal line A as the front of a box and horizontal line B as the back of a box. Since the front of a box is closer to us, we infer that the line is smaller than the back line, which is seen as longer because we take into account that it is farther away. In other words, as a result of living in carpentered ecologies we have developed habits of perceptual inference (that is, we "adjust" our perceptions to suit the realities of our carpentered environment) which makes us particularly susceptible to the Müller-Lyer Illusion as shown in Figure 17-6. Actually lines A & B are identical. People who do not live in carpentered environments are much *less* susceptible to this illusion, that is, they cannot be "fooled" as readily by these visual illusions. Thus, Segall et al. tested many samples in many parts of the world and found Evanston (near Chicago, Illinois) residents to be exception-

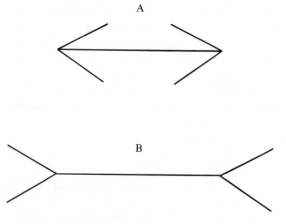

Fig. 17-6.   Müller-Lyer Illusion.

ally susceptible to this illusion; by contrast, African samples were much less susceptible. (Not everyone in the West is strongly susceptible, but the mean differences between carpentered and noncarpentered samples are consistent and dependable.)

An alternative interpretation of this phenomenon argues that those samples whose eyes are strongly pigmented are less susceptible to the illusion. (Pollock, 1970) Substantial literature has been generated around this issue (for a review, see Deregowski, 1979). It appears that both the carpentered world and the eye pigmentation hypotheses are valid.

Is the Cutting of the Pie of Perceptual Experience Arbitrary?   A major program to answer this question was reported by Rosch (1975). People all over the world respond to somewhat different stimuli as though they are identical, that is, they categorize. For example, there are many kinds of chairs in the world and no two chairs are completely identical (careful microscopic analysis will show at least differences in grain structures) yet we respond to most chairs as if they were the same. Categories are defined by conjunction of attributes. For example, an *animal* can be defined as a living thing that "reproduces" and "moves about." Now the question is whether these attributes are used according to a discrete or "digital" model to form categories, or is it more appropriate to use a continuous or "analog" model to understand the way categories are formed? For example, are things simply dead or alive, or are there degrees of being alive? Most psychologists and anthropologists have assumed that a digital model is correct (dead or alive) but Rosch shows that for many "domains" of meanings an analog model is more appropriate. Specifically, she argues that people form prototypes of categories and judge other events as a function (depending) of the object's distance from the prototype. Thus, within the category "bird," "robin" is a much better examplar (closer to the prototype) than is "turkey;" within the category "vehicle" a "car" is a better exemplar than a "bicycle." Rosch argues that people do not cut the pie of experience in arbitrary ways. Rather, there are prototypes that function like anchors in the formation of categories. This is particularly true for

"natural" categories such as colors, emotions, or shapes. For instance, for colors, one can use "focal colors" such as the best example of "red" or "green" (What is *pure* red, or *pure* green?). In one of Rosch's experiments, three-year-old American children oriented toward focal colors in preference to nonfocal colors and four-year-olds matched focal more accurately than nonfocal colors.

Taking advantage of the fact that some cultural groups do not have names for some colors, Rosch repeated her study among the Dani tribe of New Guinea. She found that, in spite of the fact that the Dani do not have a language with a color vocabulary, they remembered focal colors more accurately than nonfocal colors. They also learned a correct response to a focal color in a paired associate task more readily than a response to a nonfocal color.

Similar phenomena can be demonstrated for forms (for example, "good" forms are learned faster than "poor" forms; note that a circle is "better" than an ellipse) and for some semantic domains. Rosch argues that a category is most useful when, by knowing the category to which a thing belongs, the organism thereby knows as many attributes of the thing as possible. Natural categories have correlated attributes, so that there is much redundancy and objects can be categorized with little error. Once the object is correctly categorized, the organism "knows" much more about it (that is, knows many more attributes).

One problem with Rosch's work is that there is a confounding between the idea of a "best prototype" and the *number* of criterial attributes required to specify a category, in the sense that the prototypes require the processing of less information. For example, an ellipse is defined by two parameters a and b $(\chi^2/a^2 \pm y^{2j}/b^2 = 1)$ while a circle requires only one—the radius $(\chi^2 + y^2 = R^2)$. So what is "good" form is also a *simpler* form and hence can be learned more easily and remembered longer. Similarly, a focal red is less complex than a peripheral red. Nevertheless, the fact that natural categories have foci of least complexity which may be recognized as such *universally* is an important point. Categories, then, are not always arbitrary ways of cutting the pie of experience. Rather, they do take into account the complexity of the stimuli. The least complex examples are used as foci or prototypes of a category and this phenomenon is universal.

The Effects of Language on Thought. Just as the previous section rejects complete cultural relativism (the idea that thought is completely different in every culture) and describes some universal phenomena in the categorization of stimuli, so most of the recent work has rejected the view that language determines thought. An important advocate of this viewpoint was Benjamin Whorf, an anthropological linguist; the argument that language structure determines our perception of reality has become known as the Whorfian hypothesis. The strong version of this hypothesis is that language *determines* thought, while a weaker version is that it simply *influences* it. The hypothesis is almost impossible to test, since we can study thought processes mostly by using language. The way we instruct our subjects and the way they respond to verbal stimuli is supposed to reflect the way they think. A test of the hypothesis runs into problems of logical circularity since differences in language are supposed to affect something which is indexed by differences in language. For example, suppose language A has a grammatical category for elongated objects (such as sticks, pencils, knives) while language B does not. The Whorfian prediction is that people who speak A will think about sticks as being more similar to pencils than will people who speak B. But to find out if this prediction is supported, we must use words. We must ask people who speak A to rate the similarity of knife and pencil. The fact that the words belong to the same grammatical category can lead people from A to tell us they think of them as being more similar than people from B judge them to be. But, this finding tells us nothing about the actual "thought patterns." Since we do not have access to thought patterns but only to what people do or tell, we cannot test the theory.

It is well known that different languages have many or few names for particular domains. For example, the Eskimos have many names that designate different kinds of snow; the Arabs have almost 900 camel-related names; Americans have many names for cars (Ford, VW, "Vette," different years, and so on). What this tells us is that in some cultures, it is easier to discuss matters pertaining to one domain that it is to discuss other domains. A person who does not know that there is a difference between a Rolls-Royce and a Chevrolet, may be surprised to learn that one costs ten times as much as the other. After all, they are both *cars*. Similarly, a person who does not know about the use of different kinds of snow to build igloos, may find it difficult to see why an Eskimo might prefer one kind of snow to another. So, it is true that it is more or less difficult to talk about certain matters in certain languages. On the other hand, it is not true that it is impossible to discuss some matters. It may take a lot of time to explain the difference between the two cars mentioned, but one will eventually succeed. Thus, the difference occurs in the *ease* of coding and decoding information, but does not represent a radically different way of thinking.

There is a rich literature testing the implications of the Whorfian hypothesis. Most attempts to test it have had only modest success. To summarize sketchily, languages differ in the way they code experience and this results in some things being said better and being coded and decoded more efficiently in one language than in another. However, there is no evidence of fundamental differences in thought patterns across cultures. Almost anything that can be said in one language can also be said in other languages, though it may be much more difficult (requiring circumlocutions and much redundancy) to say it. The most difficult translations are in the fields of poetry and philosophy, because there, words are used to reflect special meanings and idiosyncratic aspects of the world view of a culture.

A related question concerns whether there is such a thing as "primitive thought." There are some differences between Western-trained individuals and those who have had little or no schooling, but these differences do not appear to be fundamental. People universally categorize, use opposites (bad-good), use associations, make implications, and solve problems. Thus, the basic *processes* of thought are the same. However, they are put together into *functional systems* (Cole and

Scribner, 1974) that differ from culture to culture. In other words, while the building blocks are the same, the buildings are different.

One of the striking differences is in the extent to which people use context in communication (and presumably in thinking). Consider an example: a male cat (or dog) approaches a door and utters a sound. A human interprets the sound: "He wants to go out." Communication has taken place. Now, the *same* animal utters the *same* sound next to its feeding bowl. The human interprets it: "He wants to be fed." Note the importance of context in communication. Now consider our own communication. I have written a chapter and you are reading it. The context is steady—a book. Yet you are reading about a range of studies, theoretical frameworks and methodologies, substantive findings and conclusions. In short, context is not involved much in our communication. This is typical of written communication. I cannot assume that you know what I know; I must spell out everything.

Between these two poles—the animal and our own communication—there are millions of human encounters that differ in the degree to which the context *can* be assumed. When two people know each other very well, they use their own special language. Context again is very important, not so much because of a common "here and now" but because of a common past. When a person uses a special word to a special person, communication may be the equivalent of thousands of words uttered in the past. By contrast, when we talk to total strangers, we often have to take much time to "introduce ourselves" and "define our terms" in order to be able to communicate without context. Now, in many cultures, people always communicate when they have a great deal of common context. In an African village people have grown up together, have common names for many inanimate things, have many common beliefs, and so on. Communication *can* assume knowledge of these names and does not require an explanation of one's basic beliefs. Thus, it takes a form that is elliptic (involves shortcuts) yet extremely efficient.

If you take such people out of their usual context and ask them to do something very unusual, their communication will become totally inadequate and you might interpret it as "primitive thought." But the fault is in the sudden change of context, not in the thought pattern. Consider the following example: Kpelle adults of Liberia were asked to communicate seated at a table. In front of each was a haphazardly arrayed pile of ten matched sticks made of different wood, of different shapes and sizes. A barrier was placed between the subjects so that they could not see their partner's sticks. The task was for one to describe a stick to his partner who was supposed to pick the twin stick from his array of sticks. Successful communication occurs when a person picks the "correct" stick. The Kpelle proved quite ineffective in their communication. Instead of using descriptions that would make one stick stand out in relation to all other sticks and thus be recognized by their partners (for example, the thickest straight wood), they used descriptions such as "one of the sticks," "a large one," "one stick," which do not communicate in that context (Cole, 1975). Note that when Kpelle communicate normally, they *do* have a great deal of context and their saying "one stick," when the context excludes any other interpretation, may lead to unambiguous communication. But, in the context of a psychological experiment, the situation was so remote from their experience that they failed to communicate. Note that this is not just an African phenomenon. It has also been observed in the United States as a difference in the communication effectiveness of lower-class and middle-class children. Lower-class children depend on context and do not do as well as middle-class children in communication tasks (Heider, 1971). Similarly, Bernstein (1961) has argued that the British lower class use particularistic rather than universalistic modes of expression. Particularistic talk is context-dependent.

It has often been argued that thought is "internal communication." So we can extrapolate these observations to thought patterns: A person who thinks about things that are in strong contexts may not have developed the skill to think abstractly. It should be stressed that it is a characteristic of the culture and ecology that leads to the use of a large or small amount of context in communication. We should not expect people who live in relatively constant environments to develop highly abstract thought simply because *they do not need it.* They do very well with concrete thought. So, rather than blame the people, we should blame their environments, if we must assign blame for a condition. Unfortunately, many social scientists have used the idea of a *deficiency* to characterize the cognition of ghetto blacks and members of the lower class. One can even consider the "etic-emic" contrast mentioned earlier and speculate that this sort of conclusion has been based on a blind "etic" (really a pseudoetic) analysis that has certain social and political overtones (Kamin, 1974). But difference does not mean deficit (Cole and Bruner, 1971). If one compares the environment of the ghetto, with its monotonous repetition of poverty and the dangers of exploring outside environments, with the globetrotting (actually or in fantacy) quality of middle-class environments, one can readily see that it is poverty, that is, the restriction of opportunities, and the discrimination of outsiders that make the black ghetto youngsters concrete thinkers. They are not deficient; their environment is. Their environment is the outcome of historical forces of economic exploitation that are continuing in the form of wage differentials, unfair hiring practices, and so on.

In summary, there are cultural differences in thought *patterns* but they are not fundamental. They reflect differences in *experience.* Different ecologies make different demands on the development of context-free thought. But the basic processes of human thought appear to be universal.

Ecology→Psychological Differentiation. An important body of research concerns the relationship between ecology and psychological differentiation (Witkin and Berry, 1975). The typical progression in psychological development is from less to more differentiation. As children become older, there is a separation of perceiving from feeling, thinking from action, and perceiving from thinking. With greater differentiation, what belongs to the self is separated from what does not and is external to the self. In the perceptual domain, greater differentiation shows itself in a tendency for parts of the visual field to be experienced as discrete from the field as a whole. Undifferen-

tiated perception involves a fusion of the parts of the perceptual fields, and a global experience. Several tests, such as the rod-and-frame test, the body-adjustment test, and the embedded figures test measure psychological differentiation (see Figure 17-7 for an example). The hidden objects tests you see in newspapers and party games require differentiation. There is usually much consistency in performance across these tests. For example, a person who is asked to align a rod located in a tilted frame with the vertical, often has difficulty ignoring the frame. The more susceptible that person is to the influence of the frame, the *less* dif-

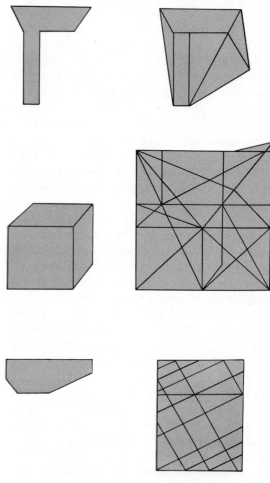

Fig. 17-7. Examples of problems like the ones in the Inbedded Figures Test. Find the figure to the left in the figure to the right. Trace it.

ferentiated that person is. A differentiated person can distinguish rod from frame and can ignore the frame when aligning the rod. People who are differentiated are called *field independent;* less differentiated people are called *field dependent.* Extensive research shows differences in the way the field dependent and independent respond to social situations. For instance, the field dependent are influenced by norms more strongly than the independent; they prefer to have people around them and close to them, while the field independent like to be left alone; the field dependent use repression as a typical defense mechanism, while the independent use other kinds of defense mechanisms. Of course, like nearly everything else in psychology, this "differentiation" dimension is not a simple dichotomy.

Ecology and culture have been found to be related to field-dependence and psychological differentiation. In some cultures, people survive very well without developing patterns of cooperation with many other people. For example, when the ecology allows people to survive who are migratory hunters, or fishermen, and/or gatherers of food that grows naturally (without human intervention), people do not need to develop much cooperation. Each hunter, fisherman, or gatherer is more or less on his or her own and gets along well without cooperating with other people. Usually in such cultures, there is little pressure for conformity to social norms. Such societies have been called "loose" (Pelto, 1968); they socialize their children for independence, self-reliance and achievement. Self-reliance training results in the child being away from home, exploring new and different sites, which makes for more differentiation. The result is children that are high in psychological differentiation.

By contrast, societies that are engaged in agricultural activites often have food accumulation (are wealthy) and a "tight" social structure. They impose the norms of the society on the children with considerable intensity. Social pressure and authority are important to ensure that planting is done on time, following carefully worked out rules. Children tend to be obedient and responsible rather than independent and self-reliant. Severe socialization tends to be related to field dependence (Witkin et al, 1974). In the Witkin et al study, six villages were selected in pairs situated in Holland, Italy, and Mexico. One village had people who used severe socialization practices and the other people used lenient socialization practices. Tests of the field dependence of high school students in these six villages showed that in each culture, the village that used severe socialization practices had children with a higher score on field dependence than the village that used more lenient socialization. Thus, there are three independent tests of the hypothesis that severe socialization leads to field dependence, and in all cases, the hypothesis was supported.

Much research on the determinants of field dependence suggests that the more information received by a child, the more stimulation, the more opportunities to see different things and visit different sites, the more field *in*dependent is the child. Women tend to be more field dependent than men, probably because they are more restricted in their movements and they spend more time indoors. The one exception to the sex difference pattern just mentioned is among Orthodox Jews. In that sample, women are more field independent than men. The explanation is that among Orthodox Jews, the males are supposed to engage in high level theoretical, theological, or conceptual analyses, while the women attend to the everyday activities—such as going to the market and paying the bills.

One can see that low differentiation may be functional (adaptive) when a society is agricultural. Many agricultural jobs (such as digging a long irrigation ditch) require cooperation. Cooperation often requires coordination of effort. Hence, chiefs and others are useful to organize and execute complex tasks. Thus, differentiation may be more adaptive for certain ecologies than for others. In short, many studies as reviewed by Witkin and Berry (1975), suggest that ecology does have an influence on psychological differentiation.

An important idea here is that the perceptual patterns, socialization techniques, social structures, institutions, political systems, and so on of a given culture have historically developed to ensure the survival of the cultural group. The process is similar to biological evolution, as described by Darwin. Remember the ideas of the theory of evolution: chance genetic events produce mutations; organisms resulting from some of these mutations are more successful in a particular environment, so those with the successful characteristics have a higher probability of survival and hence of having their genes transmitted to the next generation. Thus, the essential steps are variation, selection, and transmission. In a parallel way, social arrangements, such as socialization patterns, political systems, and so on keep changing. Some of the more successful forms win over and are selected by the new generation as better ways of doing things (Campbell, 1975). Again there is variation, selection, and transmission.

In the case of culture, things are more complicated because of cultural diffusion. People might adopt ways of doing things that are common among distant people, with very different ecologies, which are not particularly good for them. If this happens, the particular culture may suffer and may even become extinct. In any case, we should think of psychological characteristics found in different cultures and social arrangements as dependent on the ecology. What holds for these entities also holds for subjective culture.

Ecology→Subjective Culture.   Studies of subjective culture have examined how ecologies and/or cultures influence the way individuals in different cultures categorize experience, feel about different aspects of their environment, develop norms about the appropriateness of social behavior, and so on.

In studying social behavior cross-culturally, we can find connections between ecology and aspects of subjective culture. For example, Foster (1965) has pointed out that peasant societies have the view that "good" is limited. Thus, if something good happens to someone who is not related to them, they feel threatened. This may be a natural consequence of deriving "good" from the land. Since land is finite in most agricultural societies, when another acquires more land, one has less land at his disposal. By contrast the notion of an "expanding pie" is more likely to be found in the frontier. The point, then, is that there are natural connections between ecology and certain points of view. The concept of limited good is found not only in peasant societies but also in modern highly competitive

societies, such as one finds in southern Italy (Banfield, 1958) and Greece (Triandis and Vassiliou, 1972).

In Greek "Core Culture" we can find a conception of the social environment according to which the "ingroup" (family and friends and people concerned with one's welfare) is sharply contrasted from the outgroup (all others in the particular environment). Within the ingroup, mutual support and even self-sacrifice are prescribed. Toward the outgroup suspicious competition and distrust are appropriate. If something good happens to an outgroup member one feels threatened. Thus, the notion of limited good is found in that setting as well as in others.

Triandis and Vassiliou (1972) also point out that when an environment is highly unreliable, because of frequent wars or natural catastrophes, people do not develop a positive attitude toward planning. Greeks emphasize planning much less than Americans; they emphasize loyalty and enthusiasm much more than Americans. An anecdote will help illustrate this point. The American president of a college located in Greece complained about the way her Greek staff planned their activities. They may expect 500 people for a particular event and may not put out the chairs, microphones, and platforms until an hour before the crowd is to arrive. At that point a frenzy of activity takes place. An emergency is proclaimed! Everyone is expected to show loyalty to the organization by helping in the arranging of chairs. With great enthusiasm and effort the work gets done only minutes before the guests arrive. To an American, such lack of planning is difficult to understand. To a Greek, it makes excellent sense. The Greek would ask: "What if the event is cancelled? Why go to the trouble of setting up the chairs for nothing?" Now, it should be reasonably clear that for most Americans, the probability that the event would be cancelled is close to zero; not so for Greeks. When one lives in an environment where wars or other calamities frequently cancel events, one learns to hold different probabilities or expectations. Generally, for Greeks, all events are likely to be cancelled.

A similar point of view persists among the black ghetto unemployed in the United States (Triandis et al., 1975). Events in the ghetto are not well planned since little that one does leads to sure consequences. Most "good" is likely to be the result of random, mysterious, or lucky events. The connection between what one does and what one gets is weak. Thus a person feels controlled by external factors (Rotter, 1966) and distrusts the reliability of people and events in his (her) environment. In fact, Triandis and his associates have argued that in the ghetto there is "ecosystem distrust;" one does not trust any aspect of his or her environment to function predictably or to one's advantage. The point, once more, is that the ghetto is in many ways unpredictable. Unpredictability changes the perceived consequences of behavior. While the middle class sees approximately *zero* (it *won't* happen) or *one* (it *will* happen), probabilities connecting behavior and consequences (such as, if I graduate from college I will get a good job; if I go to the movies, I will not be killed), the ghetto black sees intermediate probabilities (maybe I'll get a job; maybe I'll be killed). Such chaotic expectations undoubtedly produce anxiety and distrust. However, the important point is that the social ecology *is* different and hence results in a different subjective culture (Triandis, 1975b).

One concern in this work has been with the relations between subjective culture variables and behavior (Triandis, 1975a). Briefly, it was suggested that the probability of an act depends on the number of times the act has occurred in the past history of the person (*habit*) and the person's self-instruction to carry out the act (*behavioral intention*). However, even when *habit* and *behavioral intention* have maximal values, the act may not occur if *facilitating conditions* are unfavorable. Under "facilitating conditions" are included the act-specific arousal of the organism (an organism that is not aroused may not act), the difficulty of the task, the person's ability relative to the difficulty of the task, and the person's knowledge of how to carry out the act.

Behavioral intentions are conceived as dependent on three sets of variables: (a) *Social* factors such as perceived norms, roles, the person's self-concept (such as, I'm the kind of person who acts that way) and interpersonal contracts (such as, We agreed to meet at such and such a place and time),

(b) The *affect* attached to the behavior itself, and (c) a *cognitive* factor reflecting the value of the perceived consequences of this behavior.

The value of the perceived consequences of behavior is conceptualized as the sum of the products of the probability of each consequence (Pc) times the value of this consequence (Vc). Mathematically, this would be $\Sigma Pc Vc$. Thus, for instance, a person may want to take a vacation but sees certain consequences such as the fatigue of getting to a place, the possibility of an accident on the way, the fun one might experience when there, meeting new people, and so on. Each of these consequences has a probability attached to it. Presumably the probability of fatigue is moderate, the probability of an accident is very low, the probability of fun very high and the probability of meeting new people moderate. In addition, each consequence has a value. Presumably fatigue has a negative value, an accident has an extremely negative value, fun an extremely positive value, and meeting new people a somewhat positive value. Now if we multiply each probability with the corresponding value and sum these products, we get an index that reflects whether the perceived consequences of taking a vacation are positive or negative.

Thus, another way of thinking about the relationship of ecology and subjective culture is to remember that behavior depends on *habits* and *behavioral intentions,* and the latter depend on *social, affective* and *cognitive* factors. The cognitive factors include the perceived consequences of action.

In environments that are "tight" (where people are required to do what others expect them to do), the social factors receive more weight than the cognitive factors. In environments that are "loose," there is more psychological differentiation and a greater emphasis on the cognitive factors. The greater emphasis on cognitive antecedents of behavior and information processing can also be deduced from other kinds of findings. For instance, when a child's father is absent, the child is likely to be reared by his mother. This results in less information flowing from the parents to the child than in the case when the father is present, since obviously mothers and fathers are not cognitively identical. Empirical findings (Witkin and

Berry, 1975) show that father-absent children are more field dependent and can be interpreted within such a theoretical framework.

We have already mentioned that tight environments result in more conformity. This is also consistent with greater emphasis on the social factors. In short, ecology, culture and subjective culture, and aspects of behavior are likely to be interrelated.

Osgood's Study of Affective Meaning. A major project, probably the largest cross-cultural study ever done reflecting aspects of subjective culture, focussed on the affective meaning of concepts. Almost thirty cultures are represented with the responses of monolingual males. Very briefly, the following steps were used independently in each culture.

1. One hundred subjects were asked to provide qualifiers of 100 "culture fair" substantives, such as HOUSE, FIRE, MOTHER, and POISON. Sentences such as "The . . . HOUSE" and "The HOUSE is . . ." were "filled in" by the subjects in their own languages. "Culture fair" substantives are substantives that are easy to translate, that is, when using double-translation (see p. 554–5), one easily retrieves the original term.

2. The 10,000 responses (100 people responding to 100 concepts) obtained in each culture were analyzed in terms of frequency and diversity (number of times the qualifier is elicited by different substantives). The qualifiers were then rank ordered according to a measure that reflects both their frequency and diversity. The 50 top ranked qualifiers were used in the next step.

3. Subjects were asked to provide the opposite of each term. If more than one opposite was frequently given, both were retained. The original terms and their opposites were made into 7-point bipolar rating scales, such as

good ———————————— bad.

4. New samples of males judged 100 concepts on 50 bipolar scales. The instrument used is called the *semantic differential.* It was developed by Osgood about twenty-five years ago, and is one of the most widely used instruments in psychology. A concept, such as HOUSE, GOD, MOTHER, or I

MYSELF is rated on a series of bipolar scales, such as the scale shown in the previous paragraph. So in this step, 100 different concepts were judged on 50 bipolar scales, which requires that information be obtained about 5000 judgments. Since the number of required judgments is too large (5000) the judgments were randomly assigned to 10 groups of 20 subjects, each subject completing 500 judgments.

5. The ratings given by each set of 20 subjects were summed. Thus a 100×50 matrix of numbers, reflecting 100 concepts × 50 scales was obtained.

6. The 50×50 table of correlations (each based on 100 observations) were subjected to a statistical technique called factor analysis. This technique reveals patterns of consistency in the way the subjects have responded to the 50 scales. It was found that *universally* three factors, or patterns of consistency, are reflected in these ratings. First, a factor labelled *Evaluation* (E) is reflected in the similar responses to scales such as *good, beautiful, nice, clean,* and so on. In each culture different terms might be involved (such as nectarlike) but the pattern of intercorrelations is unmistakable: good things tend to be beautiful, nice, and nectarlike; bad things tend to be ugly, bad, and poisonous. Second, a factor called Potency (P) reflected similar responses to scales such as *big, strong, heavy,* and *powerful.* Finally, an *Activity* (A) factor showed patterns of consistent responses to scales such as *active, quick, hot,* and *alive.*

Now, the meaning of any word can be represented by its coordinates on these three factors or dimensions. (Corresponding to the 7-point rating scales given above), using +3 to −3 scales, we might find that the E, P, A meaning of MOTHER is +2.5, +1.0, and −0.5 in a particular culture. This would mean that in that culture mothers are seen as very good, slightly strong, and very slightly passive. However, in another culture the concept might have a +2.0, −1.0, and −2.0 profile, meaning that mothers are seen as quite good, somewhat weak, and rather passive. Note, that over the complete set of 100 concepts the E, P, and A scores have intercorrelations approaching zero. Note also, that of the 50 original scales only 10–15 are strongly connected with other scales in ways reflecting the E, P, and A structure. In some cultures additional factors did emerge, but they were not found in any other cultures. Thus, these culture-specific (emic) factors are not suitable for comparison and only the etic E, P, and A factors can be used for that purpose.

7. The best bipolar scales (in the sense that they represent the three factors) were then used in a short (12-scale) form of the Osgood semantic differential. A much larger sample of concepts, usually about 600 concepts per culture, was then rated by new samples of subjects on this short version of this instrument.

Currently, the profiles of 600 concepts are available from some thirty cultures. In addition, a large number of other statistics such as the extent of disagreement, or the polarization of the judgments, when reacting to a particular concept in a particular culture, were recorded in the *Atlas of Affective Meaning* that will be published in ten volumes by Osgood and his associates in the next ten years. This makes for an extremely large data bank that allows an infinitely large set of studies to be done in the future.

As an example of the way the *Atlas* can be used, consider the following. Triandis (1973) was asked to write a paper on the meaning of *work* in different cultures. He started by reading the Human Relations Area Files. The complete files can be found in only twenty-two leading universities and libraries around the world, but abbreviated summaries (on microfilm) are available in many university libraries. They consist of verbatim extracts from ethnographies and other sources developed by anthropologists to describe different cultures. Reading under *work* and related concepts one notes that work has different meanings: in some cultures it was seen as a "necessary evil," a big bother, and a curse; in other cultures it was seen as a challenge and an opportunity to validate the self, to be useful to society, and to be creative. Why? One hypothesis was suggested by the observation that when the environment is very easy *or* very difficult, work might be less rewarding to the individual than when the environment is intermediate in difficulty. For example, if one only has to reach to a banana tree to get a banana which that person eats, "work" is not that challenging; similarly, if one has to chase a seal for miles under blizzard

conditions with low probability of catching it and getting a meal, work is a necessary evil. However, when work can be both pleasant and likely to result in satisfactions of most basic needs, one can feel quite positive about it. Thus, it was hypothesized that work will be positively evaluated in environments that are *not* too easy and *not* too difficult and will be seen as an evil in very easy or very difficult environments. Triandis turned to the *Atlas* to test the hypothesis. Some cultures provide environments that are extremely easy. Specifically, for the young males living in a postindustrial environment (for example, the United States, Sweden, France), who participated as subjects in Osgood's project, the environment is very easy. One can make more than $2.00 (minimum wage) by simply showing up in a factory. By contrast, the young people living in a less developed country such as India or Thailand often have to work very hard for minimum rewards or belong to extremely privileged groups for whom the environment is very easy. The prediction then is that Osgood's subjects in the very highly developed and much less developed environments will have less positive views of *work* than the subjects in environments intermediate in difficulty. The data supported the hypothesis. Young men from Greece, Iran, and Yugoslavia had the most positive attitudes toward work. This illustrates how the *Atlas* can be used to test different kinds of hypotheses.

While the Osgood procedures provide very interesting data that can help in the evaluation of many exciting hypotheses, it is important to point out some of their limitations. One limitation is that this project samples only male high school students. One could make the case that this is a very limited sample of humanity, particularly when we consider the fact that in less developed countries, the majority of the population is illiterate. Thus, the data are useful only if we are interested in the way "elites" in thirty cultures look at their social environment. Another limitation is that the semantic differential measures only one aspect of meaning—the connotative, affective meaning that is, the evaluative, potency and activity dimensions only. In some cultures, the concepts GOD and COCA COLA have identical profiles! Obviously, additional methods are needed to study the meaning of concepts. For this reason, Triandis et. al. (1972) developed the antecedent-consequent method, in which a concept such as PUNISH-MENT is presented with previously elicited perceived antecedents and consequences. A typical item might read:

> If you have Crime _____
> Deceit _____
> Disobedience _____
> Disturbance of the peace _____
> Mistake _____
> Then you have PUNISHMENT.

A respondent is invited to put a checkmark next to the concept that he or she thinks fits best. This indicates the perceived antecedents of PUNISHMENT. To obtain a consequence, a person is asked to respond to an item such as:

> If you have PUNISHMENT then you have:
> Anger _____
> Change of behavior _____
> Contempt _____
> Crime _____
> Dishonor _____

Again the subject checks one of these categories.

The frequency with which people from various cultures check the various categories reflects some aspect of the meaning of PUNISHMENT. For example, Americans see the antecedents *bad conduct, crime, defiance of the law, disobedience, lawlessness, naughtiness* more frequently connected with PUNISHMENT, than do other culture groups. Greeks see having *no God* specially connected with PUNISHMENT. Indians see *murder* and *theft* strongly connected, and the Japanese see *bad deeds, disturbance of the peace, immoral acts, injustice, sin,* and *unfair acts* so connected.

Turning to the consequences, we find Americans emphasizing *contempt, correction, dishonor, guilt, reform, resentment,* and *resistance*. Greeks emphasize *change in behavior, compliance, exemplification, justice, reasonableness, repentance.* Indians emphasize *hardship* and *imprisonment,* Japanese *introspection.* In short, we note some rather striking differences in emphasis. Now, of special interest is that most of the consequences perceived by Americans, Indians, and Japanese are affectively negative, but those perceived by Greeks are positive. We turn to the semantic differential data where we see that the E, P, and A profiles for the concept of PUNISHMENT (standardized across concepts so that Z − scores, see Chapter 3, varying from −3 to about +3 are recorded) which are as follows:

	Americans	Greeks	Indians	Japanese
Evaluation	−1.3	−0.5	−1.5	−1.7
Potency	−0.2	−0.4	+0.9	+0.2
Activity	−0.3	−0.1	−0.6	−0.8

We note at once that the cultures are similar in using average (around zero) potency and activity scores, but they differ on evaluation. Most cultural groups are *very* negative, but the Greeks are only *slightly* negative when evaluating PUNISHMENT. Looking at the differences in the consequences explains some of these differences. In fact, the unstandardized Greek score on evaluation shows that they see PUNISHMENT as slightly good. By contrast, the American data suggest nonacceptance of PUNISHMENT (resentment, resistance). This seems to be a real cultural difference, since other data are also consistent with the idea that Greeks believe the individual must be controlled by PUNISHMENT in order to function properly in society, while Americans tend to think that PUNISHMENT raises more problems than it solves. In any case, this study illustrates how the semantic differential can be supplemented with other kinds of data in an effort to understand the cultural differences that were obtained.

Finally, it is worth noting that closely related to the universality of the E, P, and A structure are several other kinds of universals. An example is that social behavior is perceived universally as varying along dimensions such as association vs. dissociation, superordination vs. subordination, overtness vs. covertness, and intimacy vs. formality. The first three dimensions correspond to the E, P, and A structure. Triandis et al (1968) noted that similar dimensions were also found in studies of emotional expression (see also Schlosberg, 1954; Triandis and Lambert, 1958), personality (see Leary, 1957), the behavior of mothers (see, Schaefer, 1959), the use of modes of address (for example, *tu* vs. *vous* in French) which depends on solidarity and intimacy (Brown, 1965), the social behavior of primates which exhibits solidarity (+E), aggression (−E), and pecking orders (+P) as discussed by Mason (1964) and many other phenomena. In short, the E, P, and A structure is not only widely valid, if not universal, but is also showing aspects of phylogenetic continuity and is *reflected* in many other kinds of data, including social behavior.

Much of the emphasis in this section has been on the universality of social behavior. But people live in different ecologies and this leads to cultural differences. See Figure 17-8 for an example. The following sections will emphasize such differences.

Fig. 17-8. Status, as reflected in superordination-subordination, is a universal dimension, but it takes different forms in different cultures. Shown here are *ubrellas* used in Thailand to indicate the relative rank of an official. The more "levels" of the ubrella, the higher the rank of the official. Such status symbols are found universally, even in supposedly egalitarian cultures like the United States. (H. C. Triandis)

Ecology → Abnormal Behavior

Many psychological disorders have a physiological basis that reflects the ecology. For example, in the Thule region of Greenland, the Polar Eskimos are exposed to very little sun, both because of the angle of the sun in the summer and the long periods of no sun in the winter. This condition may well result in lack of vitamin D which is necessary to help the organism pick up calcium from the diet, and hence there may not be enough calcium in the blood (Wallace, 1972). Low levels of calcium are associated with a so-called tetanic syndrome, which includes convulsions. In that region of the world, there is a form of hysteria called *Pibloktoq*. This disorder is characterized first by irritation, which then becomes an extreme excitement when the individual engages in many irrational and dangerous acts, such as swimming in icy water, followed later by convulsive seizures, after which the individual behaves again normally. While Freudians may find a number of interpersonal factors to explain this extreme reaction, Wallace presents a plausible argument that calcium deficiency significantly contributes to it. He also lists several culturally determined behaviors (customs) that appear designed to counteract calcium deficiency. For instance, these Eskimos eat certain birds that are high in calcium, use much vitamin D containing seal oil, breastfeed their children until the children are relatively old, and so on, all of which increase the chances that they will have enough calcium in their diet.

It is probable that some sort of disturbance in normal physiology is necessary before the predisposition for the disorder is created. This disturbance often results in anxiety and then in abnormal behavior. However, the exact form of the disorder is strongly influenced by cultural factors. For instance, the mythology of a particular region often is reflected in the kinds of beliefs expressed by patients. This can be seen in the case of another disorder called Windigo, which is found among the Ojibwa Indians. The patient in this case is consumed by a deep fear that that patient will eat human flesh. Corresponding to this symptom is a myth about a monster, with a heart of ice, that is called Windigo, that may enter one's body and force one to eat human flesh. The Ojibwa live in a part of the world where herds of animals are usually available for hunting. When these herds disappear, there is often a famine. Under conditions of famine, people may think of eating human flesh. (One might recall that when the plane carrying a soccer team crashed in the Andes a few years ago, as described in the novel *Alive,* the survivors did eat the bodies of their dead companions. If such behavior happens among people who for generations have not engaged in cannibalism, one can guess that the behavior is not that far-fetched among groups that have been cannibals.) One can also note that extreme famine conditions do break down many inhibitions, and if famine is a recurring phenomenon, the breaking down of inhibitions may become more and more probable. In any case, one can see that cannibalism is not so far-fetched a behavior in situations of famine. For a group often exposed to famine that has strong prohibitions against cannibalism, the anxiety that one's inhibitions might not prove strong enough (and one might break down and eat human flesh) is perfectly realistic. Furthermore, if one is to eat human flesh, one must be able to explain this strange and horrible behavior to himself; this can be done much better if one has a myth that explains the behavior in terms of possession by a monster. In short, given the ecology it makes sense that the culture has evolved the particular myth which is functional and helps people live with themselves after horrible actions. Given that the myth exists, the extreme fear that one might be possessed by Windigo is also understandable. In fact, one might expect that *any* extreme anxiety might evoke the myth. Such anxiety might occur when a physiological change makes a person feel very differently from the way that person usually felt, or when a major traumatic event has occurred. In short, the physiological change, or the traumatic event, may precipitate the anxiety which may then be explained in terms of existing cultural traditions, and result in culturally determined symptoms.

Thus, we find many examples of *symptom localization*. In Maylaya, there is a disorder called *Koro,* where a patient is consumed by extreme anxiety that his penis will disappear into his abdomen; in the Philippines there is a very high

frequency of running *amok,* where a person tries to kill as many others as possible. Running amok does occur in the United States (the last *major* case happened in Texas, when a disturbed man killed thirty-eight people from the top of the tower of the University of Texas), but the frequency in the United States is not as high as it is in Southeast Asia and the Pacific.

While many disorders have such localized distributions, there are many other disorders, such as schizophrenia, that are worldwide. Yet, the meaning of abnormal behavior may be quite different from culture to culture. In some cultures (such as the Soviet Union) disagreeing with the government results in hospitalization in a mental hospital rather frequently, while other cultures allow wide ranges of deviance before labeling a person sick.

In general, there is much evidence of similarity in *some* forms of psychopathology. Such similarity is an outcome of similar physiological processes. The specialists (clinical psychologists and psychiatrists) disagree on whether or not disorders are exaggerated versions of normal behavior or examples of behavior where the patient does exactly the opposite from what is culturally common. The evidence is meager, but tends to suggest that many disorders are caricatures of "normal behavior," frequently occurring in the particular culture.

A universal system for understanding disorders has been suggested by Phillips (1968) [and tested by Draguns et al (1971), and Nachshon, et al (1972).] It assumes that a disorder involves one of three roles and one of four spheres: the roles may involve turning self against self, turning against others, and avoidance of others. The spheres may be in behavior patterns (actions), emotions (affect), beliefs (thought), or physical symptoms (somatization.) Studies done in South America, Japan, and North America suggest that this typology describes the major varieties of disorders that occur in these cultures.

In short, there is a core of common elements characterizing abnormal behavior in many cultures. Each culture, however, shapes the disorders supplying cultural elements, permitting some behaviors in one culture that are unacceptable in other cultures, over- or under-emphasizing particular elements and increasing the chances that some behaviors will be considered abnormal in some cultures and simply unusual in others. Thus, both physiological and cultural elements shape abnormal behavior.

Individual System→Interindividual System

Subjective Culture and Attributions. There is an extensive literature suggesting that a strong attraction to a relatively narrow ingroup and a concept of limited good result in attributions of hostility to outgroups, excessive competition and suspicion of outgroups, and lack of attraction toward people who are perceived as outgroup members (Levine and Campbell, 1972). Many of the phenomena of discrimination and prejudice against outgroups can be related to such mechanisms of excessive positive evaluation of the ingroup to the detriment of the outgroup.

An important problem of social psychology is the specifications of the way cultural variables affect interpersonal relationships. An interpersonal relationship is satisfactory to the extent that each person does what the other expects him or her to do and the action is in itself rewarding. For example, receiving a compliment is more satisfying in itself than receiving an insult; however, when people receive a compliment when they expect to receive an insult, this action is in itself somewhat unpleasant because unexpected events have to be interpreted. Things get even more complicated in intercultural contexts, because what we expect does not necessarily happen and what happens is difficult to interpret. For example, in some cultures it is appropriate and required by good form for male guests to belch after dinner. An observer who does not know this custom might be at a loss to interpret this action. Why did the other belch? Because he has stomach cramps; because he is impolite; because he wants to insult the host; because he is bored; because he liked the food . . . ? Note that depending on the way the perceiver assigns a cause to the act, that is, makes an *attribution,* the act is evaluated one way or another. If the act is expected and evaluated positively, all is well; if it is neither expected nor evaluated positively, the relationship may suffer. Now, since people make different attributions in explaining behavior, because they use

different norms or values in different cultures, they ''misunderstand'' each other quite frequently. To improve interpersonal relationships one needs to develop similar expectations and make similar attributions. Triandis (1975a) argues that people have to learn to make *isomorphic attributions.* This idea corresponds to the situation where a person from one culture analyzes a social situation in similar ways as people from another culture. When people make isomorphic attributions, they expect and interpret the other's behavior in the same way as the other.

One way to develop isomorphic attributions is to live in another culture for a long time. However, that is expensive and impractical, in the case of diplomats, businessmen, and others who have to change cultures every few years. We need procedures that will train people to make isomorphic attributions in a short period of time. A procedure called a ''culture assimilator'' has been developed for that purpose (Fiedler et al, 1971). The procedure requires the presentation of 100 to 200 episodes involving social interaction in two cultures to a person from culture A learning about culture B. In each episode, one is asked to make an attribution about the behavior of a member of culture B. Each episode has been judged previously by samples of people from cultures A and B. These judgments involve making attributions. If an episode generates highly divergent attributions from members of cultures A and B, it is retained and followed by three attributions commonly made by members of culture A and one attribution commonly made by members of culture B. When members of culture A are faced with three attributions made commonly in their own culture, they are likely to select one of them as the ''correct'' answer. Turning the page of the training manual, they are told that their selection is incorrect and to try again. When they finally select the attribution commonly made by members of culture B, they are praised and given more information about culture B. Thus, they gradually learn to select culture B attributions, or explanations of the behavior of members of culture B.

The culture assimilator has been tested in different cultures and for different situations (Fiedler et. al., 1971; Weldon et. al., 1975). It has been shown that it does make attributions more iso-morphic, it increases the chances that a person will feel well adjusted in another culture, and it improves the chances that people from another culture will find the trained person less offensive.

An example of one culture assimilator item is shown below. On page X-1 there is an episode that describes a social situation where there is some sort of conflict. Page X-2 provides four explanations of the causes of the problem mentioned in the episode. The trainees are invited to select one of the four explanations. Depending on which one they select, the instructions direct them to turn to pages X-3, 4, 5, or 6. If the trainees select the cor-rect answer, they are given approval (told they are "correct") and an explanation about the relevant cultural pattern. If they select the wrong answer, they are told they are wrong and given some suggestions about where they may have gone wrong, and finally sent back to page X-1 to reread the episode and start all over again. On the other hand, if they do get the right answer, they are sent to page X-7 where they can find a new episode. After several episodes dealing with a particular cultural pattern are studied, the assimilator has a "summary" page where basic cultural principles are recapitulated and listed, just as they might be in a regular book.

Page X-1

Sharon Hatfield, a school teacher in Athens, was amazed at the questions that were asked her by Greeks whom she considered to be only casual acquaintances. When she entered or left her apartment, people would ask her where she was going or where she had been. If she stopped to talk, she was asked questions like "How much do you make a month?" or "Where did you get that dress you are wearing?" She thought the Greeks were very rude.

Page X-2

Why did the Greeks ask Sharon such "personal" questions?

1. The casual acquaintances were acting like friends do in Greece, although Sharon did not realize it.

Go to page X-3

2. The Greeks asked Sharon the questions in order to determine whether she belonged to the Greek Orthodox Church.

Go to page X-4

3. The Greeks were unhappy about the way in which she lived and they were trying to get Sharon to change her habits.

Go to page X-5

4. In Greece such questions are perfectly proper when asked of women, but improper when asked of men.

Go to page X-6

Page X-3

You selected 1:   The casual acquaintances were acting like friends do in Greece, although Sharon did not re-alize it.

Correct. It is not improper for ingroup members to ask these questions of one another. Furthermore, these questions reflect the fact that friendships (even "casual" ones) tend to be more intimate in Greece than in America. As a result, friends are generally free to ask questions which would seem too personal in America.

Go to page X-7

Page X-4

You selected 2:   The Greeks asked Sharon the question in order to determine whether or not she belonged to the Greek Orthodox Church.

No. This is not why the Greeks asked Sharon such questions. Remember, whether or not some information is "personal" depends upon the culture. In this case, the Greeks did not consider these questions too "personal." Why? Try again.

Go to page X-1

You selected 3:   The Greeks were unhappy about the way in which she lived and they were trying to get Sharon to change her habits.

No. There was no information given to lead you to believe that the Greeks were unhappy with Sharon's way of living. The episode states that the Greeks were acquaintances of Sharon.

Go to page X-1

Page X-6

You selected 4:   In Greece such questions are perfectly proper when asked of women, but improper when asked of men.

No. Such questions are indeed proper under certain situations. However, sex has nothing to do with it. When are these questions proper? Try to apply what you have learned about proper behavior between friends in Greece. Was Sharon regarded as a friend by these Greeks?

Go to page X-1

Conformity Needs→Severe Socialization

Individuals raised in cultures where conformity to social pressures and norms is associated with successful adaptation, often develop severe methods of socializing their children (see p. 565 also). A need felt at the sociocultural level can be internalized and expressed in particular child-rearing practices. An example can be drawn from the work of Kohn (1969) who found that among both Americans and Italians, the upper-middle-class values children who are self-reliant and creative, while the lower-class values children who are reliable and obedient. These viewpoints can be seen as functional. Obviously a physician who is self-reliant and creative is more "in role" than a physician who is obedient; conversely, a factory worker who is creative may be disruptive, while one who is reliable and obedient is just what his boss would like to have around. Here, variations in occupation (ecology) cause variations in needs (individual system) which cause particular child-rearing patterns (interindividual system).

Ecology → Sociocultural System

We mentioned earlier that aspects of the ecology, such as agriculture and food accumulation are often associated with severe socialization. Severe socialization is often associated with a highly differentiated social system. For example, the Eskimos depend on hunting and have a most equalitarian social system, while agriculturalists such as the Temne of Africa have a much more differentiated system, with chiefs located at different levels of a hierarchy. As we approach the state-form of political organization differentiation increases even more.

Sociocultural System → Individual System

A differentiated sociocultural system makes differentiated cognition much more probable, and indeed is much more important for individual survival. In fact, psychological differentiation is found more frequently in highly complex sociocultural systems than in simple ones (see Figure 17-9).

Cultures where Western contact is high, where education is given to children in well organized schools, where people live in cities and work in factories, rather than live in rural areas and work the land, have children that go through the series of stages of cognitive development postulated by Piaget (see Dasen, 1974), have more people who are favorable toward modernity (Inkeles and Smith, 1974), and have more young people showing cognitive development similar to that found in the Western world.

Psychological Modernity. Inkeles and Smith (1974) argue that there is a psychological state, which they call modernity, that can be found in all

Fig. 17-9. Some ecologies require that people use space economically. The Japanese, with over 100 million people in a relatively small area, have learned to make excellent use of space. Thus their gardens are small, but they represent large-scale landscapes; the bonzai (miniature trees) permit the landscape architect to represent a view from the top of a mountain while using only a few square yards of garden. Shown here is the principle of "tight" use of space on a street in Tokyo, where pedestrians cluster together, leaving the rest of the sidewalk empty. (H. C. Triandis)

cultures. It consists of openness to new experience, readiness for social change, a disposition to form and hold opinions about the major issues of the day, an awareness of the diversity of attitudes and opinions around oneself, having a good deal of information about what is going on in the world today, an orientation toward the future and the present rather than the past, a sense of efficacy, planning, and trust in the environment and valuing of technical skills, aspirations for high education and high occupational achievement, respect for the dignity of others, and an understanding of the way industry works.

Modernity is found in all cultures, to some degree. Inkeles and Smith developed a modernity scale that measures the attitudes and values incorporated in the modernity concept in several cultures. They then found the correlates of modernity. These include the amount of formal education, amount of experience in factory life, amount of exposure to the mass media, and the number of consumer goods possessed. These variables were correlated with modernity to about the same degree in Argentina, Chile, East Pakistan, India, Israel, and Nigeria. Other variables, such as the number of years of urban experience, did not correlate with modernity in all cultures (for example, India and Israel did not supply significant relationships), but they did correlate with modernity in the majority of cultures that were studied. One does not have to live in cities in order to be modern. For example, among agricultural workers, those who belonged to cooperatives were more modern than those who did not; the scores of people who belonged to cooperatives were slightly higher than the modernity scores of city dwellers working in factories.

Education is by far the most important determinant of modernity. For a 100-point modernity scale and rural origin factory workers, each year of education advances a person's modernity score by 1.6 units. Factory experience is also important, but each year in a factory advances a person's score by only 0.6 units. The predictor variables mentioned above explain only about one-half of the variance of the modernity scores; some of the variance may be due to local conditions not tapped by the study.

Interindividual→Individual Systems

Strong parental influence is often associated with less modernity. In traditional societies we find generally a much greater parental influence, adherence to group norms, and less modernity (McClelland, 1961; Inkeles and Smith, 1974).

Parental Acceptance-Rejection and Personality Development.   One of the key variables that distinguishes child-rearing behavior is the extent of parental acceptance vs. rejection. Rohner (1975) described parental acceptance as involving playing with, comforting, holding, cuddling, praising, caressing, hugging, and kissing a child, while rejection is characterized by the withdrawal or absence of warmth or affection. Parental withdrawal,

he hypothesizes, is universally an antecedent of hostility, aggression or passive aggression, dependence, negative self-evaluation, emotional unresponsiveness, a negative evaluation of the world, and emotional instability. Conversely, parental acceptance is related to low aggression, low dependence, positive self-evaluation and world view, emotional responsiveness, and stability. Using data from the Human Relations Area File (see p. 569 for description) Rohner found support for these hypotheses. Universally, rejected children tend to grow into adults who are hostile, insecure, dependent, who have feelings of low self-esteem and low self-adequacy, and who have a negative world view.

Sociocultural System→Interindividual System

In an extensive study of the behavior of children in different social situations, Whiting and Whiting (1975) examined data from six cultures. They distinguished cultures that are simple from cultures that are highly differentiated and complex; they also examined differences in children's behavior in cultures with nuclear and extended families. They found both of these attributes of the sociocultural system related to the behavior of the children. Specifically, in simple cultures, mothers tended to assign many child rearing duties to their children, and this resulted in children that were more willing to be nurturant, particularly when interacting with younger children. In complex cultures, children were less responsible for child rearing and were more likely to take than to give resources, such as love, status or goods. In cultures with nuclear families, children were more likely to behave intimately than in cultures with extended families. Hence, these data suggest that aspects of the culture do influence both child-rearing patterns and the typical behavior of children.

Child Rearing→Individual System

We have already mentioned that the severity of child rearing results in less psychological differentiation. Many other examples of a connection between child rearing and individual system variables can be mentioned. As noted in the previous section, Whiting and Whiting (1975) found that when parents assign many child-rearing roles to their children, these youngsters behave in more nurturant (giving) and more affiliative ways.

Individual→Ecology

High levels of affiliation have been found associated with less economic development, and less economic development results in fewer changes in the ecology. It is quite obvious that economic development is related to pollution, overutilization of resources, and other changes in the ecology.

Summary

In Figure 17-5 on p. 559, we presented a very abstract set of relationships between ecology and key variables that affect a person's behavior and experience. In the sections just concluded, we provided a number of illustrations that clearly show the abstract connections among the sets of variables of the theoretical framework can be specified more and more precisely. As cross-cultural psychology grows, we will be increasingly able to spell out the exact connections between ecology, culture, behavior, and experience.

This work will also have important practical consequences. As we learn more about this field, we will be able to reduce prejudice and discrimination, culture shock, differential rates of delinquency and crime associated with being a misfit in certain societies, marital conflict when spouses come from different cultures, and so on. The work will also help us improve teacher-pupil relations across cultures, international political relations, and generally help bridge the gaps between diverse peoples of the world.

Glossary

Construct validation of a measure: Finding sizable correlations between the measure and other measures that, as predicted from a theory, should correlate with it.

Content analysis: A procedure that counts the number of times a particular idea or theme is present in a text.

Culture: The human-made part of the environment.

Ecology: The physical environment, climate, and resources.

Emic: A concept or attribute that is defined with terms unique to a given culture; it is meaningful only within that culture.

Ethnoscience: A careful description of a system of beliefs developed by a preliterate ethnic group, that accounts for relationships within a domain of experience (such as, botanical terms, diseases, animals).

Etic: A concept or attribute defined with terms that have meaning everywhere in the world; it is meaningful in every culture and its meaning does not change from culture to culture.

Functional system: A set of basic cognitive processes, put together in a particular way by a group of humans.

Individual system: Basic psychological processes such as perception, cognition, and individual behavior patterns.

Isomorphic attributions: Situation when the attributions made by the observer are similar to the attributions made by the actor concerning the causes of the actor's behavior.

Multidimensional scaling: A procedure that allows the extraction of several dimensions determining human judgments concerning a particular topic.

Need for achievement: A psychological characteristic that is assumed to cause individuals to compete, be greatly concerned with, and try to, exceed a standard of excellence.

Psychological differentiation: The separation of perceiving from feeling, thinking, and action, with each of these processes becoming independent of the others.

Sociocultural system: The human-made part of the social environment, and the patterns of social interaction characteristic of a group of humans who speak a particular dialect.

Subjective culture: The way a group of people who speak a particular dialect, perceive the human-made part of their social environment.

Suggested Readings

Brislin, R. W., Bochner, S., and Lonner, W. J. *Cross-Cultural Perspectives on Learning*. New York: Sage, 1975.

Dawson, J. L. M., and Lonner, W. J. *Readings in Cross-Cultural Psychology*. Hong Kong: University of Hong Kong Press, 1974.

Triandis, H. C., General Ed. *Handbook of Cross-Cultural Psychology*. Boston: Allyn and Bacon, 1979.

18

Psychological Assessment of Individuals

Norman D. Sundberg and Joseph D. Matarazzo

Introduction

Variety is not only the spice of life, it is the basis for evolution, both biological and cultural. As human groups confront problems, it is the individual differences among group members which make it possible to overcome obstacles and create new solutions and opportunities. The development of society proceeds by sorting out individual abilities and interests befitting positions of all kinds—world leaders, workers, people taking care of children, and those occupying a park bench or a hideaway in the mountains. These same individual differences also provide society with many challenges such as how to help people who cannot learn well or who show severe abnormalities of behavior and thought.

That individuals differ from each other in height and weight, as well as in running, jumping, and throwing abilities must have been obvious to our most primitive human ancestors eons ago. The leaders of the Greek city-states of Athens and Sparta capitalized on these individual differences and selected their young men for military duty and athletic competitions from among those who gave evidence of high physical prowess. To a lesser extent, these ancient Greeks also paid attention to differences in quickness of mind in selecting those few fortunate Greek youngsters who would be given a formal education (Doyle, 1974). Befitting the different cultural conditions in that part of the world, Chinese emperors as early as 2200 B.C. had used other priorities, seeking to measure individual

differences in intellectual qualities. In ancient times, China instituted a system of competitive achievement tests akin to today's written Civil Service examinations. Every three years Chinese officials were examined to determine their fitness for continuing in public office, and were promoted or dismissed after three such examinations (DuBois, 1970). As civilizations flourished and declined during the next 4,000 years, the requirements of successive societies emphasized the need for physical prowess or mental achievement. As public education of the young became universal during the nineteenth century industrial revolution in Europe and the United States, schooling was no longer a luxury for the privileged few or the very ablest of the underprivileged class. Mass education, industrialization, and increasing size of social organizations required systems for quickly finding the special abilities and limitations of the large number of persons required to carry out society's daily activities.

In every field of human activity, there are needs to understand individual differences and treat people according to their particular needs and propensities. When an individual goes to a physician, that person expects the physician to conduct an individual examination and to determine the significance of the particular pattern of symptoms or problems. When a manager hires a secretary, that manager wants to conduct an interview and have information available to discern the individual's typing skills and personal manner of meeting strangers and coping with the demands of the office.

That part of psychology which brings together

knowledge about the vast array of such human variation is called *Differential Psychology* or *Individual Differences*. The closely related body of methods for measuring and using information for describing and deciding about individuals is called *Psychological Assessment*. Psychological tests are an important part of assessment, but the field is a broader one than tests; it includes interviewing, observation, study of personal records and products, and the processes of judging and combining information about people and communicating such information either to the client or to others. This chapter will cover the highly overlapping concepts and issues involved in the areas of both assessment and individual differences.

After a brief look at the basic methods of assessment, interviewing and observation, we will take up the most important concepts in psychological testing, reliability, validity, and norms, many of which were introduced in Chapter 3 of this text. We will introduce tests of ability, or maximum performance, and cover the personality testing approaches. Returning to intelligence testing, we will go into some depth about the history and current controversy surrounding intelligence testing. We emphasize the topic of intelligence, because the largest amount of research and theory concerning individual differences has gone into that area, and because of its importance for individual assessment and for current public policy decisions. Finally, we will conclude by illustrating how psychologists use assessment techniques in the study of individuals.

The Meaning of Assessment and Its Basic Methods

The word "assess" in a general way means to set or fix the value of something of worth—a piece of land, an art object. In a parallel fashion, psychological assessment is aimed at determining the personal characteristics of value for some purpose, such as counseling or psychotherapy, selection for a job or school, or research. The three purposes of psychological assessment are decision-making, image-making and theory-building. Psychologists use their skills and methods to help make important decisions about people, to develop impressions or understandings of persons, or to confirm or disconfirm hypotheses about personality, intelligence, or abnormality.

Assessment has always had a practical flavor to it, starting with the first use of the word for psychological purposes in *Assessment of Men* (Office of Strategic Services Staff, 1948). That book was a report of methods used to select men and women for special assignments in World War II—difficult and dangerous missions involving espionage and sabotage behind enemy lines. The psychologists in the project tested the strengths and weaknesses of the candidates by a series of ingenious methods such as stress interviews, role playing situations in which confederates tried to obstruct the candidates work, and all manner of tests. This project of the Office of Strategic Services was one of a series of large modern assessment programs, some later ones of which investigated the prediction of success in psychiatry, clinical psychology, Peace Corps work, graduate work, architecture and mathematics. Recently, large industries are making extensive use of assessment centers to select managers (see Bray et al, 1974). Along with the practical aspects of these assessment programs, there were also theoretical aims involving the testing of personality theories and trying out and validating new methodological approaches. Though these large-scale programs are of importance in assessment, we shall not go into them at length in this chapter but will confine ourselves to assessment procedures related to the study of the individual.

In assessing individuals, there are two basic processes that are fundamental: interviewing and observation. The best definition of an *interview* is an old one; it is "a conversation with a purpose" (Bingham and Moore, 1924). It involves face-to-face interaction between two people, one of them usually in the role of an expert or having a special position and the other usually in the role of a client, patient, or respondent. Assessment interviews are used by social workers, psychologists, and psychiatrists to obtain case histories, examine ways of thinking, and administer tests to patients and clients. They are used by personnel psychologists to obtain information relevant to a job decision. They are used by social science and other research workers to conduct surveys and carry out investigations into personality and other psychological characteristics. Interviews vary in the degree to which they are *structured;* they may be completely open as to the directions they may take or they may adhere precisely to a planned series of questions. Whatever the nature of the interview it is likely to be more successful if the interviewer clearly understands the *purpose* of the interview and its role in the whole assessment process.

We will not go into detail about the ubiquitous and flexible interview method here, but it should be noted that the critical student can ask the same questions of the interview as we will soon indicate should be asked of other assessment methods: How reliable is it? How valid is it for prediction, selection of people for jobs, and developing descriptions of people? In the recent period of skepticism about testing, many people would turn back to the interview as the sole means of evaluating job applicants. But, because of the great dependence of the interview method on the skill, memory and attitudes of the interviewer, there is much room for bias and inaccuracy. Research has shown that unsystematic interviews may be quite inadequate (Wiens, 1976). However, in the hands of a well trained professional, they can become reliable and valid (Matarazzo, 1979).

The second basic method of assessment is *observation.* We cannot meet or talk with a person but what we observe how he or she dresses, talks, responds to what we say or do, uses gestures, and exhibits a personal style. The interview tends to emphasize the verbal *content* of the information exchanged, though certainly the good interviewer is highly attuned to feelings. Observation inevitably emphasizes the nonverbal *manner* of the individual's actions. The behaviors we see are often so subtly taken in that we cannot explain what gives us a feeling that a person is cool or warm, or anxious and depressed (Harper, Wiens and Matarazzo, 1978). As with the interview, the purpose for which we intend our observation is important. Such a purpose will help determine the *structure for the observing situation* and the *structure for recording* the observations which is employed.

The observing situation can vary from the natural setting, in which an observer visits a home or follows a child around through its daily activities, to the highly controlled setting of the laboratory where only certain stimuli are presented to a subject and the response precisely recorded. The format for recording may vary from the loosely jotted down informal impressions of the clinician to a minute-by-minute record-keeping in a laboratory using a code for each behavior. Psychologists have made use of the technology of audio and video recording for clinical and research purposes, and highly detailed analysis can be made of such records. As with interviewing, the accuracy and usefulness of observation depends on the training and skill of the observer and the care with which purposes are clarified and techniques are developed ahead of time. Behavioral assessment, which will be discussed soon, makes much use of observation.

Psychological Tests and Testing

Psychological tests are not the only means for assessing individuals, but they are the most precise methods, and they provide a good introduction to the concepts and problems of assessment. A test is a *method for obtaining a sample of a person's behavior in a standard situation.* The sample of behavior may be the response to a question or instruction (such as, "What is the distance between New York and Los Angeles?" or "Say as many words as you think of that rhyme with 'cat' "); or a count of the number of occurrences of an error or other action (such as the number of errors in typing a certain paragraph); or a report of a perception (such as telling about the actions and feelings of people in a picture); or the answers to a questionnaire (such as checking "true" or "false" to the item "I like to tease animals"); or many other possibilities. Tests use different methods for obtaining the sample of behaviors, ranging from recording responses in individual interviews or observation to collecting responses from a large group filling out paper-and-pencil forms. Some tests are rigidly standardized. *Standardization* means that the items in the test, the instructions for administering and scoring it, and related concerns are all carefully prescribed and must be followed in order that each person examined has been examined under exactly the same conditions. Other tests, especially the projective personality tests described later in this chapter, require less rigid adherence to a standardized format of administration or scoring. The reason for having a standard situation is that the results must be compared with the results from other persons or with results from the same person or other occasions.

It should be clear then that in order for the results to be usable, the test materials, instructions and answer sheets and other recording and scoring materials must be the same for every individual. The administration of a test needs to be approximately uniform, but this is not always very easy. Considerable training is necessary before we can place much faith in what a beginning tester obtains. For example, consider the potential problems implied by the picture in Figure 18-1. The child is looking up with a puzzled expression on his face. How much should the examiner explain

Fig. 18-1. A psychological assessment situation.

about the test and the instructions? The good examiner will help the child feel more rather than less comfortable with the task, will repeat instructions if that is permitted, but will not give hints or suggestions. The distractions of the environment and the physiological and psychological state of the person need to be considered. A child, hungry and restless, and not too sure what this test is all about, is much more difficult to test than an older person who readily enters into the spirit of the examination. (However, the spontaneity and openness of the child offer special advantages for assessment, too.) The interviewing and testing of individuals requires *rapport,* a cooperative relationship of mutual trust and respect, between the test-giver and the test-taker. Even the testing of large groups requires this cooperative relationship and a sharing in order for the results not to be distorted.

Assuming that the conditions of testing are up to standard, there are certain technical qualities of tests that must be understood in order to evaluate their usefulness and to interpret their results. These technical concepts, *reliability, validity,* and *norms,* can be applied not only to tests but to the results of interviews, informal observations, and any scientific investigation. These concepts are basic to the process of measurement in psychology as explained in Chapter 3. The application of these concepts to psychological tests is spelled out in much more detail in such books as those by Tyler (1974), Anastasi (1976) and Cronbach (1970) and in *Standards for Educational and Psychological Tests* by the American Psychological Association (1974).

Reliability and Validity

Though often confused in everyday language, the concepts of reliability and validity are quite different. These concepts were introduced in Chapter 3, but can bear repetition and elaboration here. *Reliability* refers to the accuracy or consistency of the particular score obtained as a result of a test; in general it answers the question, "Would the person get the same score if the test or its equivalent were repeated?" Thus, for example, an IQ test is reliable if the same individual received a similar score when examined by three different psychologists, or by the same psychologist on three different occasions, with the same test or equivalent forms.

Validity refers to the relationship of that score to important matters outside the test itself; it answers the question "What is this test good for?" A valid test of intelligence is one that is determined to be measuring intelligence by criteria independent of the test itself; for example, the IQ score obtained relates closely to the same person's grade point average, or to success in intellectually demanding fields such as medicine, engineering, and so forth. Reliability is an internal question; validity is an external question.

No test score is absolutely free of variability or error. Any obtained score should be thought of as a *zone*—not a point—with many other possible scores lying close by. There is even some unreliability in using a bathroom scale to weigh yourself. The first time you step on the scale, you may obtain a reading of 145½ pounds; stepping back on the scale, you see it is 145 and another time 145½. Differences in your angle of vision, care in reading the scale, amount of clothing you are wearing, and slight differences in the mechanical components of the scale itself make the readings different. Your weight is different in the early morning than at night. Such degrees of unreliability may not matter for your purposes. However, a weight scale can be made to be very exact—much more exact than a psychological scale. Most psychological tests are somewhat affected by fatigue, distractions, momentary problems in remembering something, sense of trust in the situation, and emotional upsets—purely human matters that do not count for much with physical measurement.

A psychological test may have one scale or many. Scales are usually made up of a series of *items*. The score on the scale is usually the sum of ten to fifty items that are different in content, difficulty, and other characteristics. The variations in the person's attention, motivation, and attitudes as he or she goes through the test items combine to produce many sources of variability (unreliability) when item responses are totalled to give a score. Reliability of different measurements on the dif-

ferent tests of the same trait or on the same person on one trait over time is estimated exactly by the statistical procedure called *correlation* described in Chapter 3, and the numerical figure resulting is called the *correlation coefficient*. When the statistic is applied to the problem we are discussing, it is called a *reliability coefficient*.

One kind of reliability is called *equivalence* reliability. It is the relation between scores on two parallel forms of a test, which are supposed to be as similar as possible. In constructing these two forms of a vocabulary test, for example, the test maker would have tried out a large set of words on school youngsters and found the level of difficulty of each word. Then the test maker would have alternately taken different words of equal difficulty to make the two tests. One would then expect that a person would do about the same on one as on the other. Alternatively, equivalence reliability is obtained by breaking a single test down into two sub parts—such as by reconstituting and next correlating even numbered items with odd numbered ones. In this and various other ways the *internal consistency* of a test can be determined.

The second major kind of reliability is *stability*. Stability (or test-retest) reliability refers to the correlation between the same form of the test given two times with a few days or even weeks or months in between. A test may have different reliability coefficients for stability and equivalence. For instance, a vocabulary test given to fourth graders may have high stability, meaning Johnny ranked higher than Susie on both Thursday and Friday taking the same test, but when they were next re-examined with different sets of words, he came out lower and she higher. This last example would be unusual in well standardized ability testing inasmuch as ordinarily well constructed tests have reliability coefficients in the .80s and .90s for both stability and equivalence.

Reliability can be viewed as aiming to measure the degree to which a test score will *generalize* to other occasions, other situations, and other observers (Cronbach, 1970). It answers questions about the degree to which we can count on the measurement of a trait or quality. For example, is the score I get in a particular college course examination really representative and predictive of my performance in other tests at different times in this same course, or in other courses in this subject given by another instructor in this or another setting? In assessment test situations utilizing records of observations, there is a problem of the extent of the agreement or correlation between observers, and the term interobserver or *interrater reliability* is used. Such a situation might arise if two research workers were observing a child, Tommy, for aggressiveness on the playground on ten successive days. Each day the two observers (perhaps his teachers) independently watch Tommy during the morning recess and check a number between one and seven on a rating scale indicating their estimate of the degree of aggressiveness and hostility Tommy displayed. The two independent sets of ten ratings could then be correlated. A similar correlation could be run on two similarly obtained independent sets of ratings on fifteen different children observed by two observers on a single occasion. In any case, one important technical question to ask of any score, whether from a test, an interview or a psychological experiment, is "How *reliable* is it?" If different raters get a different rating on the same child observed at the same time, such a rating clearly is not reliable.

An even more important question is "How *valid* is it?" To have a perfectly consistent (reliable) test score or rating that has no relation to anything else is trivial. For instance, a very reliable count of the number of hairs on people's heads is highly unlikely to be of help if one is interested in intelligence or politeness (though we cannot be absolutely sure of this lack of relationship until it is tested empirically). Validity always refers to something outside the test itself—what is it good for? There are a number of ways of getting at validity, and all of these need to be considered in trying to understand what a test is measuring.

Content validity refers to the nature of the items with special reference to what they purport to measure or represent. If one wants a geography test, questions of personal philosophy and values would be irrelevant. If one wants to test personal religious beliefs, questions of geography typically are irrelevant. This kind of validity is usually evaluated by seeking consensus among judges who know the field involved. The content validity of a test of intelligence (or geography) is believed to be adequate when experts agree that it contains enough of the kinds of material generally believed to be related to intelligence (or geography). Although not usually evaluated statistically, a test's content validity could be estimated by checklists covering the defined domain of concepts and tasks. For instance, on a World Geography examination, we would expect that the test maker include items representing all sections of the globe, not just North America or Africa.

Criterion validity is the most important form of validity from a practical standpoint. It refers to the correlation between the test scores and an outside *criterion*—an accepted or desired standard. Criterion validity is of two kinds differing only in time when the criterion data are obtained. If the outside criterion data are available at the same time, we have *concurrent validity*. An example is the correlation of results from a new test of intelligence with the same persons' scores on another IQ test taken about the same time. The other kind is *predictive validity*. As the term implies, this kind of validity refers to the degree with which scores correlate with later events of importance. An aptitude test of clerical ability should be predictive of how well a typist will do on the job. The Scholastic Aptitude Test of the College Entrance Examination Board given to high school juniors and seniors should be (and actually is) predictive of grade point average in college (Cf. reviews in Buros, 1972). A personality inventory concerning maladjustment should be predictive of whether new recruits in the army will have psychological disturbances later on in their military careers. Figure 18-2 shows the results of a study of the validity of an examination taken in the tenth grade for predicting grades in the first year of college. The validity coefficient for the data in that figure is .55, which is typical for scholastic aptitude and intelligence tests in predicting subsequent school success. As validity coefficients go, this is high. Validity coefficients are typically much lower than reliability coefficients. It must be recognized that validity involves correlation with behavior outside the test which is influenced by many other things in the environment. (For the example in Figure 18-2, the reader well knows that interests, motivational

ITED Composite Score	Chances in 100 of Earning College GPA of			Expected Range of College Grades				
	2.0	2.5	3.0	F	D	C	B	A
29-30	97	86	62					
27-28	95	80	50					
25-26	91	70	40					
23-24	86	60	29					
21-22	78	49	19					
19-20	60	38	13					
17-18	59	28	8					
15-16	48	19	4					
13-14	38	12	2					
11-12	27	7	1					
9-10	18	4						
7-8	12	2						
5-6	7	1						
3-4	4							
1-2	2							

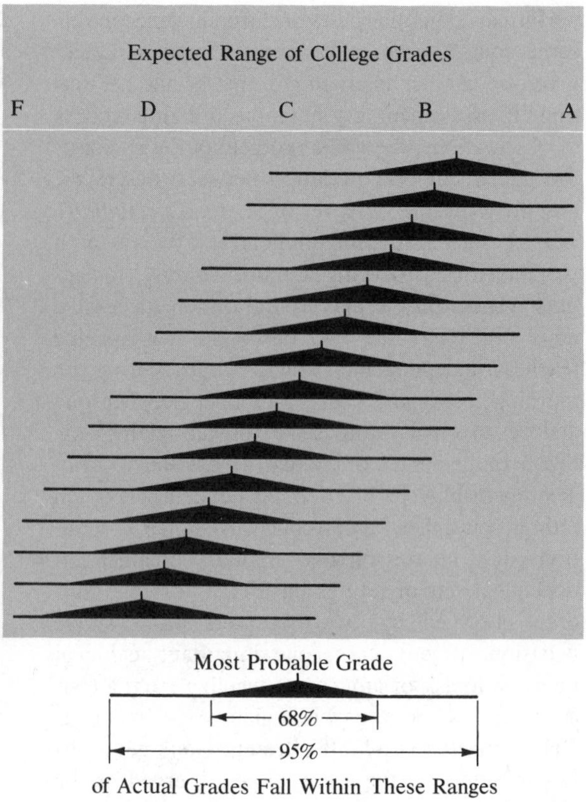

(For ITED Forms X-1, X-2, Y-1, Y-2)

N = 365   r = .55

For Students at U of O and OSC

Most Probable Grade

|← 68% →|

|← 95% →|

of Actual Grades Fall Within These Ranges

Fig. 18-2. Evidence about the validity of the Iowa Tests of Educational Development as measures of ability to do college work. (From J. S. Carlson and D. W. Fullmer, *College Norms*. Eugene, Ore.: University of Oregon Counseling Center, 1959, p. 11)

drive, study habits, partying, health, and choice of courses either enhance or lower one's college grade point average.) In the case of predictive validity, the longer the period of time between obtaining the test data and the later behavioral criterion data, the more likely intervening events will bring in irrelevant factors and the correlation will diminish. An IQ test predicts grades in school better for the first year than for subsequent years.

The final kind of test validity is *construct validity*. This refers to the theoretical meaning of the test—just *what* inferred quality or condition of the person is the test measuring? A construct is an idea or concept about the nature of persons. We use many constructs in psychology, such as intelligence, anxiety, aggressiveness, oral fixation, introversion, and ego strength. There is no single

clear criterion against which to validate a construct. The relevant empirical research, and theory or conceptual framework around the construct will suggest *indicators, correlates,* or *exemplars* of the presence of large or small degrees of the trait or condition. To illustrate, let us take "anxiety." No one has seen anxiety; nevertheless, it is a construct that is used in many theories of personality and motivation. (See Chapters 8 and 19.) In developing a questionnaire to measure anxiety, the psychologist would have to utilize several indicators predicted by theories of anxiety to show what the test was measuring. Possible indicators or exemplars of anxiety would be the following: objective measures of heartrate during exams, self reports of nervousness and uneasiness in many situations, quantitative measures of sweat on the palms such as palm prints which are known to relate to emotionality, and clinical ratings of the person interviewed made by a psychologist or a psychiatrist. The psychologist could correlate individuals' scores on the anxiety test with each of these outside measures. If the results with these independent indicators are positive, the psychologist could say that the test is measuring what theories based on prior empirical research indicate is meant by the trait of anxiety. In conducting this research, the psychologist would also want to make sure that the anxiety test was not contaminated by being highly correlated with characteristics which were quite different, such as intelligence or sociability. Thus, by finding out in many ways to what the test relates and does not relate, the test maker and test user build up their theoretical understandings of what the test measures—its construct validity.

Norms, Derived Scores and Other Comparisons

A test result has little meaning in and of itself. It needs to have some kind of framework against which to compare it. One needs to know not only reliability and validity, but comparative information when one begins to try to interpret the results of a test. The most common way to handle that problem is to develop *norms,* such as the descriptive statistics (that is, the mean, range of scores, and standard deviation) which are derived from the distribution of scores on a large sample of people. The reference group or sample must be similar to, or otherwise relevant for, the individual being tested. With well developed intelligence tests, for instance, the test is administered to several thousand people of different ages selected to represent the different regions and socioeconomic levels of the country. These results are then arranged in *norm tables,* which take into account, for example, that twelve-year-olds typically earn more points on an intelligence test than do typical ten-year-olds, whose scores in turn are higher than the typical 9, 8, 7, 6, and 5-year-olds on this same test. Because the total number of points earned by progressively older children and young adults increases until about age thirty where it levels off on most tests of

intelligence, the *raw scores* originally obtained from the administering of the test are converted on the norm tables into *derived scores* for each separate age group. The most common derived scores are *percentiles* and *standard scores*.

As was pointed out in Chapter 3, the normal probability curve mathematically describes the shape of the distribution of most measured psychological characteristics. Both percentiles and standard scores are depicted with the normal curve shown in Figure 18-3, the standard score (or Z) is the number of standard deviations from the mean. Thus, a person who obtains a result two standard deviations above the mean receives a standard score of +2; if he or she were a little higher, the score might be +2.3. To avoid using the + and − signs and decimal points or fractions, a number of standard score systems simply add an arbitrary amount for the mean and multiply by an arbitrary figure for the standard deviation. A common form is the T score (named to honor two early pioneers in psychological measurement, Lewis Terman and Edward Thorndike). It also converts scores on the obtained distribution into a normal distribution form. The T score uses an arbitrary mean of 50 which is combined with an arbitrary standard deviation of 10. The T score thus equals 50 plus 10 times the Z score. If John obtains a T score of 35 on a mechanical ability test, we know that he is one and one-half standard deviations below the mean. We know he did less well than on a clerical test on which his T score was 60, or one standard deviation above the mean. Thus, the T score pro-

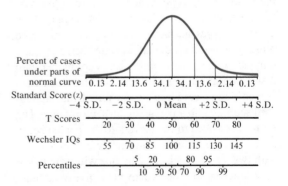

Fig. 18-3. The normal curve and various kinds of derived scores.

vides a common measuring stick. Individuals' raw scores on different tests with differing group means can all be converted to their relative equivalent on a common yardstick where the mean for the group on each test is set at 50, or any other arbitrary but agreed upon value. Thus, in a similar manner, the Wechsler IQs (called "deviation IQs") use an arbitrary mean of 100 and a standard deviation of 15, and the Scholastic Aptitude Test uses an arbitrary mean of 500 and a standard deviation of 100. There are quite a few other kinds of standard scores, all based on the distance from the mean in standard deviation units. The use of T scores and other standard scores makes it possible to place several different ability or personality subscales side by side to make a *profile* of many psychological characteristics, as we shall see later on.

The other principal derived score is the *percentile,* that is, the percentage of persons falling below a given raw score. The percentile is obtained by scoring the test, dividing the distribution of such scores into a hundred units, and ranking the scores from lowest to highest. Percentiles have the advantage of being commonly understood in the general population, but percentiles are not as useful statistically as are standard scores. Looking again at Figure 18-3 will tell you why. The percentiles tend to bunch up in the middle; the difference in score units between the percentiles of 40 and 60 is much less than is the difference between 80 and 99, so a constant meaning cannot be as readily assigned to different raw scores and certain statistics cannot be used. Nevertheless it is helpful to know the relationship between the two derived score systems. For instance, we know that 68 percent of the cases or scores normally fall between a plus and minus one standard deviation from the mean, and only about 2.3 percent of the cases are higher than 2 standard deviations above the mean. Thus, each person's raw score can be converted into a standard score or into a percentile on a *norm table.* The norms used need to be relevant to the person being tested. It is of little use to compare a five-year-old with twenty-year-olds; usually one will want to see how much he or she is like other five-year-olds. Similarly, norms for the ordinary American test

may be inappropriate for a child from a Spanish speaking home.

There are several ways for making comparisons which do not depend on the usual norms. As suggested earlier, one may compare a person with scores he or she made on the test at a different time or under different conditions. By comparing the two scores, one could say that a person has improved or become worse. Another way of making comparisons is to see how the person relates to some absolute or expected standard. If the state or county civil service examination requires a person to type 60 words a minute in order to be hired as a secretary, a new applicant's typing score can be judged against that standard. Expectations based on prior research may also be used for comparisons. Scores on a motor coordination test may be used to set levels of expectation of success in pilot training if the failure rate of pilots with differing motor coordination scores before training is known from a sample of previous trainees. In several ways, then, test findings can be *criterion-referenced* against some external, job-related standard. On the other hand, the procedure described earlier, when one uses comparisons relative to others' results only, as when comparing a person's score on a geography test against the mean earned on that test by his or her classmates, is called *norm-referencing.*

Assessment of Maximum Performance

Tests can be roughly categorized into two groups, as mentioned in Chapter 3. Procedures for eliciting an individual's ability aim to obtain the *maximum performance* from the person, and usually the answers are either right or wrong. Such tests are commonly called *ability* tests, but "maximum performance" covers a broader field, including tests of ability, aptitude, and achievement.

In contrast to such tests, other procedures try to elicit behavior or information that will reveal what the person actually thinks and does, whether or not he or she is trying to behave at his or her best. These assessment devices might be called techniques for eliciting *characteristic performance*, or typical or representative performance. These kinds of procedures are broadly called *personality* tests, but they include a wide variety of ways of obtaining clues to motivation and emotion, and the person's wants, attitudes, values, interests, and feelings. Answers are neither right nor wrong; they are just descriptive of that person.

To understand oneself or another person well, we need to know both abilities and personality—both maximum and characteristic performance. One author who has written extensively about both the science of individual differences and its application in counseling and clinical work, Leona Tyler (1974, p. 219), has expressed the idea concisely as follows:

When for any individual we have answered the two questions, "What can he or she do?" and "What does he or she want?", we have sketched the main outlines of his or her individuality (1974, p. 219).

In this section, we will briefly survey the tests of maximum performance. The most well known and widely used of all kinds of ability tests is that of *general ability,* or *intelligence.* It is a concept that applies to cognitive or thinking skills that permeate all mental activity; thus, it is often called general ability. We will delay detailed discussion of intelligence tests until a later section where we can tie in the important issues of heredity and environment and the controversies that rage about social policy in regard to testing. For the time being, we will simply point to the variety of ability tests that are available.

In addition to intelligence or general ability tests, there are many specific ability measures: For instance, clerical ability, language ability, tone discrimination, finger dexterity, and sensory-perceptual skills. Many kinds of abilities need to be assessed in some way for industrial work, such as assembly skills or mechnical ability.

In the general area of maximum performance assessment, we need to differentiate between three related kinds of testing that psychologists have carried out for many years—ability, aptitude, and achievement. *Ability* is the *actual power* to perform an action. One can picture a person carrying around many of these abilities. You probably have

the ability to high jump three to five feet, ride a bicycle or drive a car, play a musical instrument, or read a foreign language, even though you are not performing those activities at the time you sit reading this book. In contrast, *aptitude* is the *potential* for learning to perform a given task. You may not know how to fly an airplane, but a series of tests may show that you have the necessary aptitude or potential; that is, tests sampling the appropriate behaviors show that you can coordinate visual perceptions and motor activities similar to those required for learning to land a plane or do other flying activities. *Achievement* refers to the level of *accomplishment* or success in a given area. Someone who already has learned to fly may have attained the solo flight level; another may have reached higher levels of achievement, such as flying by instruments. In psychological and educational testing, there are many achievement tests— general reading, arithmetic, and language achievement, and all of the tests given in courses to measure knowledge of any area.

For those who are interested in particular areas of ability, aptitude, and achievement testing, textbooks such as that of Cronbach (1970) and Anastasi, (1976) are helpful. The major reference text for those working in psychological and educational testing is the series of *Mental Measurements Yearbooks* by Buros (1959, 1965, 1972, 1978, in press). These Yearbooks and others published by Buros list all the major tests currently extant; and they present critical reviews of all such tests published in English.

Assessing Personality

So far we have been talking about the assessing and testing of one's best or maximum performance. The subject taking an ability, aptitude, or achievement test is supposed to do the very best he or she can to get the right answers. But understanding an individual involves much more than knowing how well the person *can* do; we need to know what the person *wants to do,* what he or she typically *does do* in various situations and, more generally, what his or her thoughts and feelings are. In other words, we are interested not only in maximum performance, but performance that is *characteristic,* or representative, of one's typical personality or behavior repertoire. *Personality* refers to the individual's particular organization of characteristics with which he or she relates to the environment. Actually, personality is a broad term, and abilities can be thought of as part of personality; usually psychologists exclude the ability dimensions and reserve the term personality for the aspects of the person that reveal self-concepts, ways of relating to others, inner character, individual style, and especially the motivational and emotional components of a person's behavior.

There are many occasions and reasons for wanting to assess personality. As psychologists (and the rest of our society) have used a bipolar aproach and emphasized the assessment of retardation and genius in the sphere of intelligence, one also can roughly divide the bases for personality assessment into the negative and the positive. Psychologists, psychiatrists, social workers, and other paraprofessionals have responsibilities for understanding and helping people with abnormal or deviant behavior and feeling states. For instance, clinical psychologists diagnose mental and behavioral maladjustment such as schizophrenia, suicidal tendencies, anxiety neurosis, low self-esteem, antisocial behavior, abnormal fears, and sexual deficiencies. Psychologists along with professionals from other fields assist clients and patients in clinics, hospitals and private offices in understanding and improving their disturbed and disturbing behavior through psychotherapy and behavioral treatment. In such situations, assessment procedures emphasize the determination and differential sorting and descriptions of personal problems and of neurotic and psychotic thinking and behavior—the psychopathological side of personality.

On the more positive side of personality assessment is the need to determine, describe, and provide a perspective for understanding people's interests, values, personality strengths, and assets rather than their liabilities and pathologies. Vocational counselors, rehabilitation counselors, school psychologists, and industrial psychologists seek to learn about the personal needs and proclivities of normal individuals in order to help them develop career plans, choose training programs, obtain special educational programs, and be placed in satisfying and appropriate jobs. Often these kinds of professional psychologists make use of ability assessment, but typically, they also assess the interests, personal preferences, and habitual styles of people.

In addition, there are many research psychologists who are interested in both positive and less positive aspects of personality. For instance, the whole area of attitude measurement is closely related to personality. Over the years, many kinds of personality devices have been developed and have stimulated research. A study of Buros' books (Reynolds and Sundberg, 1976) indicates that in recent years, over one-half the publications on tests are concerned with personality, whereas a few decades ago intelligence, ability, and achievement publications were more prominent. Over the years that psychologists have been trying to assess and understand individuals, three major methods for studying personality and personal behavior have developed and flowered—*objective* techniques, *projective* techniques, and *behavioral* techniques. We will discuss each of these in turn.

Objective Techniques

Objective personality techniques are characterized by structured procedures for collecting responses; that is, they require a person to respond in a predetermined way, such as choosing "true" or "false," or marking one among several choices. They are called objective because they do *not* require that someone (the test giver) make a subjective judgment about how to categorize or rate the response. Almost all objective techniques are paper-and-pencil questionnaires or inventories. The first personality inventory was developed at the same time as the first group intelligence tests. The processing of masses of new recruits into the American military services in World War I required not only the assessment of intelligence, but also the detection of quirks of personality that might be troublesome in training or cause a breakdown in combat. Woodworth, a contemporary of the psychologists Terman and Goddard, who worked on early intelligence tests, put together a Personal Data Sheet that consisted of a set of questions aimed at revealing adjustment problems, such as "Do you feel sad and low-spirited most of the time?," "Are you often frightened in the middle of the night?" and "Have you ever lost your memory for a time?" (DuBois, 1970). The army psychologists found that recruits answering many of these questions in the unusual direction also were likely to show psychological problems and disturbance when examined more extensively by a psychiatrist or psychologist; so some concurrent validity was established.

After World War I, a number of personality inventories patterned after Woodworth's Personal Data Sheet were developed to detect maladjustment in college students or in people in general. Most of them were based on the erroneous assumption that people could or would openly reveal their personal problems on a questionnaire, and little was done to check what neurotic and psychotic patients actually said about themselves. However, starting in the late 1930s and early 1940s, Hathaway, a psychologist, and McKinley, a psychiatrist, developed personality scales based on the verbal behavior of psychiatric patients, in which they checked to see how well patients understood and cooperated with the questionnaire method. For the most part, they used an empirical method of test construction; that is, they selected items on the basis of statistical differentiation between the ways normals and patients answered them—rather than on the basis of professional judgment alone. The result was the publication of the empirically derived (as opposed to theoretically or rationally derived) *Minnesota Multiphasic Personality Inventory* (MMPI). This assessment device became the most widely used personality inventory, both for clinical and research purposes (Reynolds and Sundberg, 1976). Using 550 items, the test makers constructed the basic four "validity" (or test-taking attitude) scales and 10 clinical scales. The four validity scales alert the psychologist to unusual responses on the part of the patient or client in taking the test, suggesting that further inquiry be

made. The scales are the Question (?) or Cannot Say scale (the number of unanswered items), the L (or Lie) scale, the F scale (number of very infrequent or grossly deviant items answered), and the K or Correction scale (defensiveness). The ten clinical scales were composed of various combinations of the 550 items which Hathaway and McKinley found had empirically differentiated normal and abnormal groups. These 10 clinical scales were originally labeled Hypochondriasis, Depression, Hysteria, Psychopathic Deviate, Masculinity-Femininity, Paranoia, Psychasthenia, Schizophrenia, Hypomania, and Social Introversion. The original names, however, are less used now than the numbers (1–10) given each scale. Figure 18-4 shows an MMPI *profile*. The profile

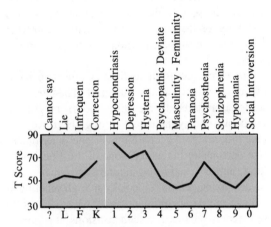

Fig. 18-4.   Minnesota Multiphasic Personality Inventory—profile of a neurotic person.

makes use of T scores with a mean of 50 and a standard deviation of 10. The more unusual or abnormal responses a person gives, the higher is his or her score. A score over 70 is usually considered indicative of considerable maladjustment, but the interpretation of the profile is not a simple matter, and the final result must be based on the *pattern* of the peaks and valleys, not just the absolute height of individual scales. The profile or pattern is depicted by the numbers of the highest scales; for instance, the three highest scales in the Figure are 1, 3, and 2. This profile can be compared with others in which 1-3-2 is the pattern, and clinical similarities between such patients studied. These profile patterns have been the subject of extensive research. Through relating common patterns to descriptive phrases and correlated diagnoses and prognoses, researchers have developed computer programs that produce automated interpretations of the test (see Graham, 1977). The MMPI is extensively used in psychiatric settings, such as mental hospitals and out-patient clinics, but also in medical, penal and employment settings, despite the many criticisms of the reliability (which is below .80 on several scales on a one week retest) and validity (which varies a great deal depending on the clinician interpreting the profile and also on the particular extra-test criterion against which the profile's validity is being investigated). A review of many research studies (Hedlund, 1977) has shown, however, that the original theoretical meanings of these scales, that is, their construct validities, are supported, though with low correlations.

There are scores of additional objective techniques for revealing maladjustment. The interested reader is referred to the Buros books or general textbooks on psychological testing. Here we will take time to briefly mention only one other objective personality inventory—one of the "positive" kind, aimed at exploring interests, not maladjustment. Young people, especially in high school and college, need to be thinking about what occupation or career to pursue. For such decisions, it is important to know not only something about one's abilities as revealed by school work and ability tests, but also the interests one has and how they compare with people already in the field. The psychologist, E. K. Strong, devoted his entire life to the measurement of vocational interests. In 1927, he published the first edition of the Strong Vocational Interest Blank. His basic test-making approach was an empirical one, not very different from that used in developing the MMPI later on. He asked a sizable group of men in different lines of work to answer many items about activities they liked or disliked. Then he compared the answers of men who were successful in particular occupations, such as law, medicine, engineering, and teaching, with men in general. By this method he was able to

obtain a set of items that empirically (statistically) differentiated between any given occupation and all the rest, thereby producing a scale for each occupation which he appropriately named "Lawyer," "Physician," "Certified Public Accountant," or whatever. The young man taking the test later on could thus find out how much his likes and dislikes were similar to those of men already successful in these differing occupations. Strong and others who succeeded him found that for the average male after age twenty-five, there was typically little change in interests; and people in a given occupation who obtained high scores on the relevant scale were likely to stay in it. Strong prepared a similar test for women, but found in the early years of his works that women's interests were less finely differentiated than men's. However, in recent years the men's and women's forms have been joined together in a greatly expanded and successful version that not only has empirical occupational scales, but theoretical scales as well; it is called the *Strong-Campbell Interest Inventory*.

Projective Techniques

The second approach to personality assessment is by means of projective techniques. The *stimulus material* the psychologist presents to the person being assessed is usually unstructured and ambiguous, such as ink blots or other vague pictures to which the subject is asked to give a response or make up a story. The approach is called *projective* because in interpreting the responses given, the psychologist assumes that the subject has projected ("thrown out") his or her inner feelings, thoughts and motives and residuals of prior idiosyncratic life experiences into the ambiguous task. The subject has organized perceptions of the unstructured material according to his or her own "private world." Given the immensely wide latitude possible for such responses, projective techniques have few standardized scoring methods or norms and require that the psychologist subjectively interpret the responses according to his or her own clinical experience as part of the assessment process.

The imagining of different forms in vague and ambiguous stimuli goes back a long way. Shakespeare in *Hamlet* talked about seeing different animals in clouds. One of the first persons to use such a procedure in a clinical way was Carl Jung, Freud's associate, who in about 1910 employed *word associations* to uncover a patient's "complex"—a set of interrelated fears and emotionally charged thoughts. Jung read a list of words one at a time, asking the patient to give the first word that came to mind in response. For instance, to the word "table" a common association would be "chair." Hesitations in response or unusual responses (such as "crying" or "disgust" to "table") would suggest emotional problems.

The best known and most widely used and published of the projective techniques is the *Rorschach* test. This is a set of ten inkblots similar to the one shown in Figure 18-5. Around the time of World War I in Switzerland, Hermann Rorschach found that hospitalized psychiatric patients showed large individual differences in the way they responded when asked to say what they saw in the inkblots. (The reader can demonstrate the variety of individual differences by showing Figure 18-5 to friends. Nearly everyone will see several things in the inkblot; each person will be somewhat different from the others.) Rorschach collected responses from hundreds of different kinds of patients and from normal people. He discerned differences not only in the content of the responses to the inkblots, but also in the use patients made of color (since several of the blots were colored), and the perception of movement, texture, and distance, and whether the patient responded to only a very tiny part of the blot or responded to the whole thing. Rorschach developed an extensive theory, which he published in 1921, about the relation of the reported perceptions to disordered thought. Though this young psychiatrist died shortly afterward, his ten inkblots and his theories lived on to stimulate the interest of thousands of professional people. Psychologists brought the inkblots to the United States in the 1920s and 1930s, and by the 1950s, the Rorschach test was being taught in nearly all clinical psychology and psychiatry training programs. It has accumulated more publications than any other psychological test (Buros, 1974), and it has generated a variety of similar procedures including the psychometrically sophisticated Holtzman Inkblot Technique, for which a computerized interpretation system is available.

The second most widely used projective device is the *Thematic Apperception Test* (TAT). It was developed by Henry Murray and Christiana Morgan at the Harvard Psychological Clinic in the mid-1930s. It consists mainly of a set of pictures and drawings of people in various situations to which the individual is asked to tell a story. One stimulus picture is described by the authors as follows: "On the floor against the couch is the huddled form of a boy with his head bowed on his right arm. Beside him on the floor is an object which resembles a revolver" (Murray, 1938). In clinical settings, stories told about this particular picture often bring out feelings about suicide, but some people perceive the situation very differently from others; for example, some respondents see the figure as a girl, whereas others do not perceive the object as a handgun or weapon. One examinee described the following to this same picture: "A young girl who has been out riding her horse all afternoon. She's home now, contentedly collapsed on the floor of her living room. Her riding stick is on the floor nearby." Murray worked out an elaborate theory about the way in which

Fig. 18-5.   Inkblot like those on Rorschach.

TAT stories reveal the individual's needs and perceptions of environmental pressures. The TAT has been widely used not only in clinical situations but also in research on the "positive" end of assessment—such as the work by McClelland (1961, 1975) on achievement motivation and power, and in programs for improving entrepreneurial thinking and motivational drives in developing countries.

Among the many other projective techniques are some widely used procedures that ask subjects to draw a person, to copy designs, to write the endings for incomplete sentences, and to construct scenes and stories from human figures and toys. Almost any activity, such as doodling or children's play, or the clothes we wear on a particular day, can be interpreted from the perspective of the *"projective hypothesis"*—namely, the idea that what a person chooses to see or do or wear reflects inner feelings, motives, hopes, and conflicts. Since projective techniques require considerable use of the examiner's subjective judgment in their coding and interpretation, there are many opportunities for unreliability to enter. After reaching a height of popularity with psychologists in the 1950s, there has been mounting criticism of the reliability and validity of projective techniques. As any reading of the Buros reviews of tests will indicate, professional opinion is now very critical of projective techniques, but the so-called objective techniques for personality assessment fare only a bit better. Personality is today still a complex and elusive area of study.

Behavioral Techniques

The newest of the three major assessment approaches is that of the behavioral techniques. They are called *behavioral* because they emphasize observable actions and reports of activities and are used mainly for the purpose of remediating or removing problem behaviors. A problem behavior might be a child's refusal and fear about going to school (school phobia), temper tantrums or bed wetting, or an adult's sexual dysfunction, overindulgence in alcohol, overeating, or lack of cooperation in a hospital program. Behavioral techniques are used with a wide spectrum of behavioral prob-

lems ranging from normal to psychotic. The behavioral techniques have largely grown out of the learning theories of B. F. Skinner which were explained in detail in Chapter 9. According to this theory, behavior, whether it is desirable or undesirable, is maintained by its rewarding consequences. If Susie finds that throwing a temper tantrum is one of the few ways to get her mother to pay attention to her and thus to get what she wants, she is likely to continue to have temper tantrums. If, however, Susie's mother ignores the tantrum or removes Susie from the place where she can attract attention, the tantrum behavior is likely to diminish, or extinguish and disappear completely. Skinner's ideas and those of other behavioral and social learning theorists have been applied to many situations, as other chapters of this book describe. Severely regressed patients in mental hospitals have been taught to take care of themselves and to enter into simple conversations by gradual steps of reinforcing only the desired behavior and ignoring the rest. Individuals have learned to manage their own "bad habits" such as cigarette smoking by either rewarding themselves for going without smoking or punishing themselves whenever they smoked.

But what does behavioral learning therapy have to do with assessment? At first glance it might seem to have little relationship, and it is true that very few tests or other standard procedures have been developed similar to those of objective and projective techniques. However, the careful attention to behavior itself has required the development of exact records with which to identify problems and against which to check improvement in a variety of behavior modification programs. Since behaviorists work only with *samples* of behavior and the changes in behavior, they cannot rely on attitudes, traits, or signs of inner feelings, as other assessment approaches do. The behavior modifier must establish what is the *baseline* occurrence of the problem behavior, that is, how often the temper tantrums occur, or how much an obese person weighs, before the treatment program is started. Then the psychologist or the client continues to keep records of the behavior throughout the treatment to see if it improves—somewhat like a physician uses a thermometer to keep a temperature chart on a patient in a hospital. If improvement does not occur, the psychologist may change the reinforcement procedure or some other part of the situation. In order for the treatment program to be shown to have worked, there must be assessment procedures to monitor the behavioral change.

In the 1960s and 1970s, a massive shift occurred among large numbers of clinical psychologists toward the use of behavior modification and learning procedures to help patients and clients with personal problems. Psychologists and other helping professionals became disappointed with the previously prevailing Freudian or psychoanalytic therapies which used largely projective assessment methods, and sought techniques to measure and record behavior directly; thus, a great many informal assessment procedures were developed. Primary among them are *observational techniques*. Trained observers might go into a child's home or classroom to make records of the occurrence of a problem behavior such as poor attention to school work or destructiveness—before, during, and after a treatment program. The observer would stay some distance away, usually unobtrusively in the back of the room, and record what the child was doing every 30 seconds. One highly developed procedure for use in the home is the Behavior Coding System (Jones et al., 1975). It has twenty-eight categories for recording the actions of the child and the mother, for example, CM (Command), CR (Cry), IG (Ignore), AP (Approval), and DS (Destructiveness). It has been shown that observers, including teachers and mothers, can learn to use this procedure readily and reliably. Positive changes from baseline behavior have been frequently documented in such programs (see Figure 18-7 on p. 613.

In addition to observational systems, behavioral psychologists have developed a number of other procedures to help with different phases of such treatment programs. *Problem checklists,* such as a list of fears or inappropriate social behaviors, may be used to identify behaviors which make for difficulty for a parent, teacher, or the client. In work with adults, *reinforcement checklists* may be used to find out what the client finds rewarding or punishing in daily life. The Pleasant Events Schedule (MacPhillamy and Lewinsohn, 1974), for in-

stance, is a long list of items such as "Talking with other people," "Taking a bath" or "Reading a newspaper" on which a new client gives a rating to indicate how strongly he or she enjoys an activity. These pleasant events then serve as target possibilities for everyday behavioral activities which the psychologist can encourage a depressed client to increase in a conscious way. Other areas of assessment related to the behavioral approach are measures of assertiveness, sexual orientation, and test anxiety. As yet, behavioral psychologists have developed few fully standardized assessment procedures, but it seems likely that many will appear in the coming years, inasmuch as there are common elements in the work of many behavioral treatment programs. Behavioral techniques face the same kinds of questions of reliability and validity as other assessment procedures. Of particular importance for observational approaches is the demonstration of interobserver agreement (or reliability). Because the observed behavior is the object of the investigator's study (providing a baseline against which to assess later change), there is a kind of intuitive or intrinsic validity to observation.

Nevertheless, in part because there are as yet no widely used standard behavior procedures, no definitive and generalized statements can be made about validity and reliability, although the general approach appears to be promising. As an assessment approach, it at least avoids much of the uncertainty caused by the high degree of subjective interpretation required by projective approaches. An increasingly sophisticated methodology is the likely result of the large amount of effort psychologists are putting into behavioral assessment (Ciminero et. al., 1977; Hersen and Bellack, 1976).

Comment on the Three Major Approaches and Additional Assessment Procedures

Table 18-1 (adapted from Sundberg, 1977) summarizes the characteristics of the three major kinds of personality assessment approaches. One of the most important of the differences between the three major personality assessment approaches is the manner in which they treat the data obtained

Table 18-1.   The Three Major Personality Assessment Approaches

	Behavioral Techniques	*Objective Techniques*	*Projective Techniques*
Primary Aim:	To determine anteced-ents and consequents of problem behavior	To develop test scores that relate to extra-test criteria of problem or solution	To elicit material of importance for inferring inner dynamics of person
Construction Methods:	Individually tailored data collection on problem behavior, counting, recording	Psychometric scale construction, norms, validity, reliability	Theoretical or impres-sionistic selection and interpretation of ambig-uous stimuli
Typical Stimulus Format:	Natural or contrived situations; interviews; few structured devices	Paper-and-pencil, self-reporting, verbal personality inventories, scales	Ambiguous, open-ended stimuli, both verbal and nonverbal
Typical Data Produced:	Observational reports, coded records, behav-ior counts	Choices on verbal items, scores, profiles	Perceptual reports, verbal narratives, observations, scores
Obtained Data Treated As:	Sample	Correlate	Sign
Degree of Subjec-tive Interpretation:	Low	Medium	High
Classifications and "Language" used:	Behavioral excesses, deficits and inappro-priateness; functional analysis; learning terms	Traits, diagnostic categories, psycho-metric terms	Subjective, idiosyncratic states; psychodynamics; perceptual-cognitive terms
Principal Theoretical Underpinning:	Behavioral learning theory, functional analysis; Skinner, Bandura	Trait and factor theories; psycho-metrics; Hathaway, Meehl, Cronbach, Cattell	Psychoanalysis, per-ceptual-cognitive theories; Freud, Murray, Rorschach
Examples of Assessment Instruments:	Few standard devices; Behavioral Coding System, Fear Survey Schedule	Many standardized inventories and scales; MMPI, Strong, attitude scales	Great variety; Rorschach, TAT, Sentence Comple-tion, Draw-A-Person, play situations

from assessment. As mentioned in the last section, the behavioral approach treats its data simply as a *sample* of the person's behavior. In strong contrast, the projective technique approach regards the subject's responses as a *sign* of more fixed and enduring inner motives, conflicts, and feelings. Most psychologists using projective techniques have been strongly influenced by Freud and psychoanalytic thinking, which, as described in other chapters, was very much concerned with the symbolic meanings of dreams and slips of the tongue as these related to relatively fixed personality traits and conditions. When a person reports seeing eyes or pointed objects on the Rorschach, the interpreter looks to the clinical history for evidence of possible sexual or aggressive meanings of these reports. In an intermediate position between treating assessment data as actual behavioral sample or as a more symbolic diagnostic sign, the objective approach tries to find extra-test and intermediately fixed *correlates* of the response. The objective approach emphasizes prediction to outside phenomena. For instance, on the MMPI a high score on Scale 8 (Sc or Schizophrenia) *with an appropriate supporting clinical pattern and history* could suggest that the person shows atypical or possibly even schizophrenic behavior in other ways and thus is likely to be diagnosed as schizophrenic.

There are advantages and disadvantages of all three approaches to personality assessment. The decision about the nature of the assessment procedure to use depends on the purposes the assessment psychologist has in mind—what he or she will do with the information after obtaining it. If a behavior modification program is to be used as the treatment of choice, the MMPI and Rorschach are likely to be of little value. If psychoanalytic therapy is to be used, something providing more than detailed counting of the occurrence of a problem behavior is needed (for example, the Rorschach or TAT are usually found to be more useful). Assessment should be closely tied to potential decisions about treatment, emotional education and retraining, or other possibilities being considered for the client.

The kinds of assessment procedures found under the three major approaches do not exhaust the broad array of possibilities for learning about individual differences in some systematic and standard way. For one thing, there are a number of *psychophysiological* assessment devices. Probably the best known of these is the polygraph, the so-called lie detector, which measures changes in heartrate, breathing, and skin perspiration as a person is interviewed or while a series of alleged crime-related words is read. It reveals only the emotional response of the person to questions, but used by an expert, it can be used as an aid in solving questions of guilt (although United States courts as yet do not feel the technique is valid enough to allow its results to be introduced as evidence). The electroencephalograph (EEG) is another psychophysiological assessment device; it records brain waves and is highly useful and regularly used by neurologists and others in clinical settings for detection of brain damage. Another kind of assessment area is that of *sociometry*. In sociometry, data are collected on all members of a group through such approaches as observation, reports of attitudes, or choices for partners in various activities. The resulting group interaction and attraction patterns can then be plotted. Another area of assessment lies between intellectual and personality assessment, the study of *cognitive style* (see Chapter 11). Procedures have been developed for studying how persons categorize objects, how they

are influenced by the context or field in working on tasks, and whether they tend to scan or focus in their thinking. Other assessment devices not covered above are general *rating scales* in a great variety of forms, adjective checklists, and other ways of recording impressions of persons.

Now, having finished an overview of testing techniques, we will return to the progenitor and best developed of modern tests, the intelligence test. We shall present the story of this type of test in considerable detail to illustrate some important points about individual differences and assessment. For example, the important debate about the influence of heredity vs. environment in producing individual differences has been fought to a considerable extent in the field of intelligence. This controversy is not just an academic matter. People see in the findings and in the attitudes about intelligence many implications for public policies concerning education, racial discrimination, job selection, and social relationships of a broad nature.

The Beginning of Intelligence Testing—Binet and Compassionate Pupil Placement of Slow Learners

Within the context of developments at the end of the nineteenth century cited at the beginning of this chapter, and foreshadowing what would happen in Great Britain and the United States later, certain teachers and administrators in the public schools of Paris discerned a compelling social need for separation of the masses of public school children requiring formal education according to whether they were fully educable, educable with special help in the public schools, or retarded to the point of being unable to benefit from public school placement or continuation. In light of today's raging controversy over the pros and cons of intelligence testing to which we shall return later, it is important to note that some seven or eight decades ago, these Parisian public school educators appealed to the young field of psychology for help with the humanitarian purpose of better classifying each child into one of these three groups in order to provide that child with the very best of learning environments. That is, they solicited classification of each child's human *potential,* not deficit. The teachers and administrators, in common with every parent, wished to place the child who could not keep up with others in a classroom geared to each child's learning or training potential rather than to his or her intellectual fraility.

Little or no further differentiation into subclasses of higher and higher ability was intended for the Parisian child who was fully educable. Such youngsters successfully navigated through each of the primary grades and thus received the minimum program of education mandated for preparation for citizenship. It was with the differentiation between those children of *below average* intelligence who were educable with additional special help from the public educational system and those who were not that teachers and the Minister of Public Instruction needed help. They also needed help in better distinguishing these two groups from the fully educable young child whose shyness or other personality makeup made him or her inaccurately appear to the teachers as marginally educable or retarded.

As these by products of the industrial revolution were unfolding, and by sheer coincidence, a leading Parisian psychologist, Alfred Binet, had been working for over two decades to develop a way of ascertaining the intelligence of children. Thus, not surprisingly, he and three colleagues were in a group that the Minister of Public Instruction appointed in November of 1904 to a special Commission whose responsibility it was to develop a method to identify and differentiate the fully educable, educable with special help, and the truly retarded child who could not benefit from public schooling and thereby better insure the provision of an educational and training environment best suited to their respective needs. The step-by-step solution to this challenge culminated in June of the next year, after decades of failure on three continents, in the successful development by Alfred Binet and Theodor Simon of the world's first standardized test for measuring intelligence. This solving of a social problem makes as fascinating reading as any good detective story. The interested reader will find this engrossing story described at some length by Wolf (1969, 1973) and sum-

marized in Matarazzo (1972). A social necessity thus became the stimulus for the invention of the 1905 Binet-Simon intelligence scale.

Galton and the Distribution of Human Ability with Special Reference to Genius

However, concern with the other (bright) end of the ability scale had not been totally neglected by the young field of psychology that began its modern development in the nineteenth century. Francis Galton, cousin of Charles Darwin, had given considerable thought to this aspect of the problem after the middle of the nineteenth century. Galton guessed and empirically demonstrated that the entrance examination scores (a forerunner of our own country's current Scholastic Aptitude Test) of young men applying to the Royal Military College at Sandhurst in 1868 distributed themselves symmetrically around the average score of all the applicants, with most students scoring at or near this middle and with fewer and fewer students scoring at each level as one moved away on both sides of this average. In his book, *Hereditary Genius: An Inquiry into its Laws and Consequences,* Galton (1869) showed with statistical clarity that societal eminence (which Galton equated with intellectual superiority) tended to run in families in generation after generation. Galton concluded that intelligence must, therefore, be passed on to each generation through heredity.

We shall not dwell here on the potential fallacy of such reasoning, except to point out that there was then and is now as much reason to believe that families such as the Roosevelts or Kennedys in our country pass on a potential for *eminence* through their higher access to social, educational, and other environmental resources for themselves and their children as well as through their supposed superior genetic endowment. What is important for this discussion is that almost four decades before Binet and Simon provided society with the first crude technology to measure mental ability objectively, Galton had predicted from his study of college entrance scores, college grades, and eminence, that such "mental ability" as was manifest in these indices, when assessed in large numbers of individuals, would be distributed in the well known bell-shaped distribution, just as were height, weight, and many other human attributes. It would be fifty years before Yerkes (1921) and his American colleagues would collect and be able to study the World War I distribution of Army Alpha intelligence test scores of 1,726,966 individuals and thereby fully confirm Galton's earlier insightful hypothesis.

Giftedness and Retardation: Classification by IQ Score Is Not Enough

By 1920, the powerful combination of Binet's ideas about the sampling of mental development through a series of intellectual tasks and Galton's ideas about statistical treatment of individual characteristics had become well established in the thinking of psychologists and, to a great extent, in the public in general. The term ''IQ'' standing for *Intelligence Quotient* became widely used, and the *IQ score,* despite its precise technical meaning in psychology, soon was unfortunately equated with *intelligence in general* by many people. The original IQ was the ratio of the mental age to the chronological age, multiplied by 100 to avoid decimals:

$$IQ = \frac{MA}{CA} \times 100$$

Mental age, a concept from Binet, refers to the number of age level tasks passed by a child. For instance, in the development of Binet-type tests, each item is assigned to an age level. That is, if a majority of eight-year-olds can pass an item, it is placed in the test at the eight-year-old level. If a child being tested passes all items at the eight-year level, he or she is said to have a mental age of 8; and if the child's chronological age is 8 also, the IQ is 100. If the chronological age of such a child being examined were less (such as 6), the IQ would be higher than 100 (133 in this instance). If the child were older than 8 (say 12), the IQ would be less than 100 (66 in this instance). In later years, the use of MA and CA has been replaced by statistical tables and the IQ has come to mean sim-

ply any score on an intelligence test which has been converted to a mean of 100 and a standard deviation of 15 or 16.

We should note that *intelligence* is a much broader concept than IQ alone. In order to assess intelligence, the practicing psychologist obtains not only the IQ, but also information about performance in real life situations and indications of ability to adapt and solve nonintellectual problems.

In introducing the new technology, Binet was clear on two points: First, his test should be used to enhance each youngster's own potential, and second, a child's *score* on the Binet-Simon scale, objective as it might be, was but one part of a required tripartite assessment of the intellectual-personal resources of such a child. Thus, before any educational or other social decision was made in regard to a Parisian child's ability, a comprehensive study consisting of a full (1) psychometric (today's IQ score), (2) pedagogical (classroom performance), and (3) medical examination should be carried out and the independently determined results collated into a single, integrated assessment of that child's intellectual ability.

Unfortunately, following Binet's premature death in 1911, these last two requirements of fully responsible assessment of intelligence (behavioral or adaptive success and the influence of a child's overall health status on an IQ score) would be all but forgotten in France and elsewhere during the next half century, as almost complete reliance came to be placed on IQ score alone. In the United States and Great Britain, some laws were passed specifying, for example, that an IQ under 70, without any additional supporting evidence was sufficient in and of itself as a legal requirement for the diagnosis of mental retardation. It would be the year 1959 before the American Association on Mental Deficiency (AAMD) would once again insist that these other two dimensions would have to be assessed along with IQ before a diagnosis of mental retardation could be given (Heber, 1959). Specifically, the AAMD statement required that a youngster or adult diagnosed as mentally retarded must be retarded both (1) in *measured intelligence* as assessed by an IQ test, and (2) in social-educational or social-occupational *adaptive behavior.* The wisdom of this latter requirement especially in school systems with large numbers of minority students is eloquently documented by Mercer (1973). She has shown that tests standardized primarily on Anglo (white American) children used in a mass administration in the public schools and in isolation of other corroborating evidence of the child's socio-adaptive behavior incorrectly diagnose as mentally retarded Mexican Americans and other minority children who function quite effectively at home, in school, and in the community at large.

During the half century after the first Binet-Simon Scale was introduced, many psychometric, albeit not necessarily humanistic, improvements were made by psychologists for objectively assessing an individual's intelligence quotient. In this country, numerous paper-and-pencil tests of mental ability were developed for mass use. Lewis Terman's widely used Stanford-Binet developed for professional use by clinical psychologists for face-to-face examination of individual children, originally published in 1916, was revised and improved in 1937, 1960, and 1972. For professional examination of adults, David Wechsler developed the individually administered Wechsler-Bellevue in 1939 and equally clinically-oriented Wechsler Adult Intelligence Scale in 1958. The latter is currently being updated and restandardized. Inasmuch as both these Wechsler Scales were found to be as highly useful with adults (effective age range 15 to 75 years of age) as had Terman's Revised Stanford-Binet with younger children, Wechsler developed two additional scales, the 1949 (revised 1974) Wechsler Intelligence Scale for Children (for ages 6 to 16), and the 1967 Wechsler Preschool and Primary Scale of Intelligence (for ages 4 to 6 and one-half years). All of the Wechsler scales consist of two major sections, verbal and performance, each with five or six subtests. Illustrations of three subtests of the verbal part and examples of the types of items which they might contain are:

Information: How many feet does a chicken have?
             Name three persons who signed the Declaration of Independence.
Comprehension: Why is it important to obey the stop signs on the street?
             What makes an airplane fly?
Similarities: How are a ball and an apple alike?
             In what way are a pencil and a typewriter alike?

Other verbal subtests are Arithmetic, Vocabulary, and Digit Span (the ability to repeat a series of numbers). The total number of correct answers on each of five of these six subtests is converted into a derived standard score to yield the person's *Verbal IQ*. Likewise, there are a series of five Performance subtests in which the subject works using his or her hands; Block Design (reproducing geometric patterns with colored blocks), Picture Completion (identifying the missing part in a picture), Picture Arrangement (putting several pictures in order to tell a story), Object Assembly (placing several pieces together to make a face or other object), and Digit Symbol (substituting a different symbol for each of a series of numbers, using a code). The result is converted to a standard score to yield a *Performance IQ*. The Verbal and Performance standard scores are also combined to yield a *Full Scale IQ*.

As stated above, concurrent with the developments of these clinical and individually administered assessment scales of intelligence for use in clinics, hospitals and some schools, there developed a vast technology and industry for the measurement by IQ score alone of the intelligence of *large* groups of school aged youngsters, military recruits, college applicants, as well as of a large percentage of adults seeking entry into or movement within America's job markets. Each of these tests yielded a bell-shaped distribution of IQ scores similar to the one predicted by Galton and shown in Figure 18-6.

Following the precedent established six decades ago by the early ratio IQ, the number 100 is arbitrarily assigned by psychologists to the *average* score on an IQ test given to a particular sample of individuals. In the development and standardization of an IQ test, as mentioned before, one simply takes the average raw score for such a sample, assigns it an IQ value of 100 and makes the standard deviation equal to 15 (roughly the standard deviation found on the early Stanford-Binet), using the theoretical Gaussian or normal probability curve proposed by Galton in 1869. With a large and representative sample, the actual results of well constructed tests like the Wechsler tests or the Stanford-Binet empirically fit closely the theoretically *expected* curve. The distribution of IQ scores of all the other individually adminis-

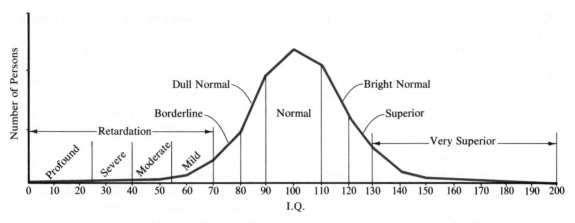

Fig. 18-6. The distribution of IQ scores in a large sample of individuals. (From Matarazzo, J. D. *Wechsler's Measurement and Appraisal of Adult Intelligence*. 5th and Enlarged Edition. Baltimore: Williams & Wilkins, 1972, p. 124)

tered or group administered tests, such as the Scholastic Achievement Test (SAT) or comparable tests for admission to graduate or professional schools, are similar to Figures 18-3 and 18-6 albeit with a mean of 500 instead of 100.

Wechsler, using his professional judgment decided that the 25 percent of the individuals on both sides of IQ 100, making up the middle 50 percent of the total sample and ranging from an IQ of 90 to 100, should be construed as falling within the "normal range" for measured intelligence as Figure 18-6 indicates. The remaining 25 percent below IQ 90, Wechsler called progressively Dull Normal, Borderline, and Mentally Retarded. This latter Retarded group more recently was further differentiated into the finer subclassifications of Mild, Moderate, Severe, and Profound retardation, each with its own boundaries of measured intelligence (IQ) as shown in Figure 18-6. As this figure also shows, Wechsler assigned comparable titles for individuals falling within the subcategories above an IQ of 100; namely, Bright Normal, Superior, and Very Superior.

It is important once again to underscore that the categories of *measured intelligence* by IQ test shown in Figure 18-6 are only one of the two components which professional psychologists, most college admissions officers, and a few of the more enlightened industrial companies that use such intelligence tests for basing practical decisions uti-

lize in assessing individual differences in ability. The other component is *performance* (that is, the day-to-day adaptive *use* of one's measured intelligence). Thus, if a child or adult who earns an IQ of 60 on a test like the Stanford-Binet is concurrently able to adapt and otherwise successfully function in a school training or work setting, he or she is *not* given the clinical diagnosis of mental retardation. Both measured intelligence and adaptive behavior must be defective for such a diagnosis; one dimension is not enough. Similarly, if a high school or college senior scores 750 (2.5 standard deviations above the mean) on the Scholastic Aptitude Test of the College Entrance Examination Board or the Medical College Admission Test, but concurrently presents a four-year high school or college grade point average of D (1.00 on a scale of 4.00), he or she would *not* be labeled as having superior general intelligence. *Performance and test results must go hand in hand, and where adaptive performance and measured intelligence are in conflict, the former (in these two instances successful training school or work history, or poor academic grade point average) is a more valid and meaningful measure of that person's "intelligence" than is his or her IQ score.* It is in great part due to the forgetting of Binet's admonition that demonstrated adaptive performance is as important as measured IQ in assessing intelligence that so much controversy has erupted in the IQ testing industry. Part of the controversy arises from the potential damage to people, especially children, when labels with negative implications are used by schools, hospitals, and agencies. Considerable effort is being made to lessen labeling effects and to make people aware of their hazards (Sundberg et al, 1978). Among such efforts is the development of procedures for assessing adaptive behavior and competences in the retarded (Lambert et al, 1975; Irvin et al, 1977) by means of inventories of skills and knowledge needed in daily living.

Measured Intelligence and Educational Potential: Validation of Binet's Approach

Remembering that Binet and Simon developed their 1905 Scale in part to identify the Parisian child's potential for education within one of three available public educational and training programs, the reader will not be surprised that both this 1905 Scale, and its most modern offshoots, have been remarkably successful in fulfilling this function. With all the current public clamor and outcry over the universal use of group tests of intelligence in this country's primary, secondary, and higher education systems, some of it justified (Matarazzo, 1972), one should also remember that each year, hundreds of thousands of parents of school aged children and young adults either request through the public school, or privately purchase, the services of a professional psychologist to carry out an individual assessment of intel-

lectual and related adaptive abilities of their offspring.

A large-scale, longitudinal study reported by Dillon (1949) gave substance to this conclusion of Binet and others about the value of testing. As can be seen in Table 18-2, Dillon started with 2,600 American youngsters in grade 7 who were administered intelligence tests and sorted into five groups based on their score on these tests. Thereafter, year by year, Dillon tabulated the number of these children who dropped out of school at various subsequent grade levels as a function of the youngster's IQ. Thus, as the table reveals, at initial testing, there were 400 out of the total of 2,600 seventh graders whose IQ measured below 85. By grade 9, a total of 93 of these 400 youngsters in this ability group had dropped out, leaving 307. The attrition in grades 9 and 10 was 241 additional youngsters leaving only 66 who entered grade 11. Of these 66, 52 dropped out in grades 11 and 12, leaving only 14 to graduate. As is shown in the last row, these 14 graduates constitute only 4 percent of the original 400 seventh grade youngsters in this lowest IQ group. The predictive validity of the IQ measure becomes apparent as one examines the increasingly lower rate of attrition for the seventh graders in each of the progressively higher IQ groups. Of the five respective groups which ranged in IQ from below 85 at one end to 115 and higher at the other end, the proportions of those *dropping out* before graduation was 96 (100 minus the 4 percent who graduated), 46, 37, 24, and 14 percent, respectively. In many other studies, IQ scores have been shown to predict the probable *college* grade point averages of students who are still in high

Table 18-2. IQ and School Attrition as a Measure of Adaptive Behavior for 2600 Seventh-Graders

	Intelligence Quotient				
	<85	85–94	95–104	105–114	115+
All students in Grade 7	400	575	650	575	400
Remainder entering Grade 9	307	545	636	570	398
Remainder entering Grade 11	66	374	493	492	369
Remainder continuing to graduation	14	309	412	437	344
% grade 7	4%	54%	63%	76%	86%

*Adapted from Dillon, H. J. *Early School Leavers: A Major Educational Problem.* New York: National Child Labor Committee, 1949.

school (Figure 18-2 on p. 586 is representative of such studies).

Role of Effort: An Important Perspective on IQ

Thus, these findings reveal that Binet and the thousands of psychologists since then who have been consulted by such school age children and their families had and still *have available in the IQ measure a highly useful instrument for identifying individuals at progressively greater potential risk* of school dropout who thus can be helped to achieve their educational aspirations by focusing their own attention, and that of their parents, on the second dimension that Binet concurrently underscored. This dimension is *effort*. Binet clearly identified this second dimension in the following admonition:

. . . A final remark, the most important of all. There exists a faculty which acts in a way opposite to the aptitudes (measured intelligence), it is general application to work. Whereas aptitudes give partial successes (in earned classroom grades), general application to work exercises a leveling action and assures success in all branches which are attacked (1909, translated in Varon, 1936, p. 50).

When, following Binet, one views the IQ score as only one aspect of global intellectual potential, rather than a fixed entity called inherited intelligence, then one can better understand why heredity, race, and station in life will be less relevant in the utilization of such an IQ finding than are such additional and equally important items of information such as the individual's level of personal drive or motivation, community resources for special or enriched education, and opportunities to be promoted to another employment situation or challenge. Every parent, teacher, and applied psychologist has known individuals who scored low on standardized tests of intelligence but who, through hard work and application, earned good grades in the classroom. If identified early by use of a well standardized and individually administered test of intelligence in conjunction with what quite likely was their progressively poorer

classroom performance, many of the early 1,100 out of the initial 2,600 seventh graders shown in Table 18-2 who failed to graduate from high school at the time of the study might have been counseled that they were at such risk and, hopefully, *helped to compensate* through greater effort and improved educational methods. It is because such individual counsel has been offered by the applied psychologist beginning with Binet that the practicing child, school, and clinical psychologists have been spared much of the criticism leveled against psychologists and their colleagues in the testing industry who make and market group tests of intelligence and achievement for mass administration in the classrooms and colleges, and the teachers and school officials who administer them. Since Dillon's 1949 study there have been many changes in American school policies. In more recent years, it has been common to pass children along through school with their peers even if they do not meet achievement standards, although such practices currently are being re-examined in many parts of our country. That is, if Dillon's study were repeated today, the results would likely be different; fewer school dropouts might be found. Still the general principle continues to be true: intelligence and scholastic aptitude tests can identify children *at risk* of doing poorly in school and alert the parents and the school to the need for preventive intervention. That such tests predict as well as they do despite the fact that most such predictive or postdictive studies have utilized primarily white, middle class samples of students is further evidence of their usefulness. When future studies take better account of the role socioeconomic and related variables play in determining academic performance in high school or college (see McClelland, 1973), such tests quite likely will have even more utility when used for individual career development and counseling.

Is Intelligence Unitary or a Composite of Specific Abilities?

Binet was a pragmatist. Although he did not know why, his crude, empirically-derived Binet-Simon Scale worked to reveal easily obtained and reproducible differences among individuals that were useful for better school placement. Binet did not involve himself in a controversy that had begun brewing in 1899 between two giants in the psychology of individual differences, Charles Spearman in London and E. L. Thorndike in New York City. These two began a debate in the scientific journals on the question of whether intelligence was an essentially unitary human characteristic or whether intelligence was a composite of many different, specific intellectual subparts.

Working in his laboratory at the University of London, Spearman was impressed by his analyses of the records of college students which showed high agreement between grades received in one subject and those received by that same student in other college subjects. Similarly, he was impressed that a given student's scores in a nationally administered arithmetic achievement test were similarly highly correlated with that student's achievement scores in a test of vocabulary, or of other abilities. Spearman thus postulated that there was a general intelligence factor, *g*, which underlay and determined how high or how low a student would score on any achievement test, or in a particular subject in the classroom, or on Binet's test.

At Columbia University, E. L. Thorndike's analyses of batteries of achievement test scores failed to show similarly high intercorrelations between pairs of tests. His research, plus that of others he cited, led him to postulate that intelligence was made up primarily of a number of independent, or poorly correlated, specific abilities, which he called *s,* each of which was sampled in different combinations by different mental tests.

The controversy between these two positions, the prepotency of a single unitary, global intelligence vs. many specific, not necessarily related facets of intelligence, raged for seven decades as later theorists (mostly university-based ones such as Thurstone) joined one side or the other, progressively using more and more sophisticated statistical and mathematical arguments and tests of ability to bolster their own side of the argument. Thus, for example, Guilford postulates a theory that intellect is made up of 120 different identifiable and measurable components. On the other hand, Cat-

tell and Horn postulate two major factors or components (fluid intelligence and crystalized intelligence), and Jensen postulates two still different components of intelligence (level 1 and level 2). Representing the other side today is Wechsler who, following Binet and Spearman, feels that intelligence is unitary, global, and inextricably intertwined in the person's total personal, physical, social, and cognitive being.

The reader need not be concerned here with the intricacies of the respective views of these modern theorists. (Textbooks on differential psychology, such as Tyler, 1974, contain detailed information for the interested reader.) Suffice it to state here that the field is still too young to have produced any definitive picture of the basic structure of that complex feature of the human mind, the measured component of intelligence. Well developed intelligence instruments since the work of Binet and Simon in 1905, *in the hands of a responsible and knowledgeable user who has the client's interest at heart,* provide very useful current information and have a high probability of predicting future performance. The interested reader will find many dozens of other successes and other measures of validity for the IQ measure reviewed at length in Matarazzo (1972). This success is clear despite the fact that even today no one can define "intelligence" clearly or explain in any theoretically well understood or precise manner why such individually administered and interpreted tests to sample some aspects of it work. This state of affairs is not uncommon in other disciplines. Thus, Roman engineers learned to build great bridges and aquaducts long before the underlying principles of physics were mastered; and medicine can recount similar empirical successes decades and centuries before biochemistry, microbiology, and related basic sciences provided first- or second-order explanations. Beginning with its introduction in 1905, Binet's scale was useful when assessed by the yardsticks of (1) general acceptability by experts (*content* validity), (2) low level, early *concurrent* validation (its results accorded with ratings of students' abilities by their teachers), and (3) low level *predictive* validity (young mental retardates in institutions, and educable youngsters of subnormal intelligence in the public schools acted at the levels predicted by the test results). In time this low order of concurrent and predictive validity began to manifest itself across the whole range of human capacity, namely, from mental retardation through the normal and finally through the gifted ranges. Despite all the current acrimony and debate about the use of such tests, the writers of this chapter know of no one, even the strongest critics of the use of such tests in the schools, colleges, or in industry, who has criticized their use when done by a responsible, well trained, and compassionate person who has the assessee's interest at heart and who provides the information to him or her and family for their own use.

Early Study of Nationality and Racial Differences in IQ

It is probably clear from the above that IQ or intelligence tests, in common with other tools such as the surgeon's scalpel, are themselves neither inherently good nor inherently bad. Therefore, an impartial evaluation of the social worth of such a tool is impossible in the abstract. Rather, the ultimate *use of the information* obtained from an intelligence test must of necessity be an integral part of such a tool when such a tool is subjected to scientific or social scrutiny. Unfortunately, in the debates that raged in the early 1920s, and the numerous important scientific discoveries regarding the IQ measure that were made by university scientists after that time, little attention was paid to this critical question of the use to which the results, especially those of mass group testing, would be put. Many publishers of tests also failed to lend financial support to needed research on such usage.

Terman imported Binet's test to the West Coast of the United States and restandardized it on a large sample of American children for use in America's schools in 1916. Within a year, he and his student Otis and others were helping the United States Government develop an offshoot of it for use in the selection and assignment of American recruits in World War I. Before long, Terman would be a strong proponent of the argument that IQ was inherited and, therefore, quite likely immutable to influence from the environment. Goddard,

another American psychologist, also imported Binet's test, for use in helping to identify and better serve mentally retarded persons in his position as Director of Research at the Vineland (New Jersey) Training School for Feebleminded Girls and Boys. Goddard's research with his mentally retarded patients also led him to conclude that mental retardation, as measured solely by IQ test, was inborn and followed the Mendelian law of heredity from one generation to another. Goddard soon became a spokesman for a eugenics policy (enacted into law by a majority of states) for the sterilization of the mentally retarded patient in what he regarded as a humane way to reduce the social burden and financial cost of this problem for future generations.

Additionally, early in this history, the United States Public Health Service invited Goddard to test the IQ of the teeming numbers of European immigrants who were coming to Ellis Island for processing before being admitted to the United States. Two years after Binet's death Goddard (1913), appearing to forget Binet's humanistically-oriented broader concept of intelligence, reported that some 80 to 90 percent of all Russian, Jewish, Hungarian, and Italian potential immigrants to this country who were waiting at Ellis Island were feebleminded. Not surprisingly, within only a short time (Goddard, 1917), many such immigrants identified by Goddard and his American IQ test were not being allowed to pass beyond Ellis Island but instead were sent back to their native lands.

It is probably an important historical fact which should be underscored today that Terman and Goddard were major architects in the development of the Army Alpha and Beta Tests during World War I (Yerkes, 1921). Both of these were group, paper-and-pencil tests for screening out retarded recruits or those who would need to be given special assignments. The Alpha was a verbal test and the Beta consisted of drawings and other nonverbal items. Although usually overlooked, among many other findings to come from the studies reported by Yerkes of the almost two million American draftees who served in World War I was a chapter on the IQ of 94,000 such draftees analyzed according to national origin. These findings showed that "In general, the (draftees whose national heritage derived from) Scandinavian and English speaking countries stand high in the list (of relative IQ), while the Slavic and Latin countries stand low'' (p. 699). No one today should be surprised at this finding given Goddard's studies a few years earlier of Slavic and Latin immigrants turned back at Ellis Island. It is interesting, however, that in the chapter following this analysis, Yerkes also reports an analysis of draftee IQ by length of each draftee's nationality group in the United States. In that chapter (p. 704) he presents clear evidence that, independent of their country of origin, foreign born Americans who had been longer residents in this country scored higher on the Army Alpha (or Beta) than did those who were more recent immigrants. Thus, one might expect (although Yerkes et al did not so note) that the Latins and Slavics who had begun their migrations at the turn of the twentieth century and their sons would be less acculturated to American ways, and tests, and therefore conceivably would score lower on these tests than would the sons and grandsons of the much earlier-arriving English speaking and Scandinavian immigrants.

As a prelude to a current controversy in intelligence testing of minorities, the very next chapter in Yerkes' book on findings from military testing in World War I was entitled ''Intelligence of the Negro.'' This first study of large groups of black and white citizens presented evidence that, on these Alpha and Beta tests, whites scored higher than did blacks. However, the book presented, without emphasis, internal evidence in the World War I data that environmental and other factors profoundly affected IQ score. For instance, Northern blacks, living in what later social scientist-critics presumed was at that time an educationally and culturally richer environment, scored higher than did Southern blacks. Additionally, albeit again not underscoring the *fewer* years of education completed by Southerners as compared to Northerners, both black and white, a few pages later Yerkes (p. 779) presented considerable evidence that Alpha Test score is highly correlated with years of schooling completed; the correlations ran about 0.70, a figure repeatedly confirmed in the succeeding fifty years.

It would be over a decade later before Brigham

(1930), renouncing his own earlier role along with Goddard, Terman, and Yerkes and others, would publicly state that review of these earlier studies shows that ''comparative studies of various national and racial groups may not be made with existing tests'' and that ''one of the most pretentious of these comparative racial studies—the writer's own—was without foundation'' (p. 165).

Heredity and IQ: Good Research, Debatable Interpretation

Although this voluminous 1921 report by Yerkes contains studies showing the relationship between IQ score and many other attributes in addition to those listed above, study of its 890 pages and hundreds of tables reveals no data on a comparison of the test scores of pairs of brothers or of fathers and sons. This no doubt was due to the limited numbers of such individuals as well as to the difficulty in cross referencing such a relationship among draftees. In any event, the American and British psychologists who returned to their university settings following World War I were not long in collecting and studying the correlation between the IQs of pairs of family members as well as between pairs of unrelated persons. As these findings were reported and subsequently bitterly debated by Terman and others, once again, as with race or nationality, *the factual, empirical findings did not, in and of themselves, engender the dispute.*

These factual findings gathered during the next several decades can be summarized fairly succinctly. If one picks at random and tests with an IQ measure a large group of *unrelated* persons and computes a correlation in the IQ scores of pairs of such unrelated persons, the obtained correlation is found to be zero (0.00). That is, pairs of unrelated persons, having no family or genetic history in common, show no similarity in IQ (nor in height, weight, eye color, or other such characteristics). Siblings, namely pairs of brothers and sisters, on the other hand, show a fairly sizable similarity in IQ; with a correlation of about 0.50. IQ's of parents paired with those of their children also show a correlation of .50. Fraternal twins (twins born of two different eggs) are merely siblings and thus, not surprisingly, empirically show a correlation in IQ of .50. On the other hand, identical twins (two individuals from the *same* egg) are, for all practical purposes, genetically the same individual. The correlation of IQ in pairs of such twins has been found empirically to be around .87 (a shade off a perfect correlation of 1.00). These results thus range from a correlation of 0.00 between pairs of unrelated persons, to a correlation of 0.50 between individuals with half their genes in common (a parent and a child or two siblings), to a correlation of .87 between pairs of genetically identical individuals. (For extensive discussion of these findings, see Tyler, 1965, 1974. Also see Chapter 7 in this text by Plomin and McClearn. For a recent confirmation of the correlation in IQ of siblings, see Matarazzo and Wiens, 1978.)

It certainly would appear from such empirical findings that "intelligence" is transmitted predominately through the genes. However, two other issues must be considered before this *interpretation* can be reached from these undisputed factual findings. First, intelligence and IQ or test scores are not synonymous as Binet repeatedly pointed out. Intelligence, as society understands it, is only partly reflected in IQ score. As discussed earlier, adaptive ability in school and at work, and motivation and a host of other personality factors also are critically important and must be taken into account in any comprehensive study of the genetics of intelligence as the layman and many scientists understand this concept.

The second issue is equally important, and it also grew out of empirical research carried out by university professors. The IQ of pairs of *unrelated* persons *living together* in the same household (adopted children, foster children, and others) correlates about 0.23 and not 0.00 as is the finding with pairs of unrelated persons living in separate household environments. This figure of 0.23 is almost the same as the correlation of 0.25 found for the IQ of a grandparent and a child (who share one quarter of their genes in common). Likewise, at the other end of genetic similarity, pairs of identical twins *reared apart* are found to correlate only 0.75 in IQ score and not the higher 0.87 found for pairs of identical twins reared together. These findings with pairs of unrelated persons reared together

(0.23 instead of the expected 0.00) and pairs of identical twins reared apart (0.75 instead of the 0.87 for those reared together) provided considerable ammunition during the 1920s and 1930s for psychologists with a strong *environmental* bias in their arguments with psychologists such as Goddard and Terman. However, these arguments were carried out almost exclusively in journals and made little impact on society in general. The same was true for the frequently confirmed empirical finding that, *on the average,* blacks scored approximately 13 points lower in IQ than did whites on IQ tests developed and standardized almost exclusively on middle class whites (Shuey, 1966; Baughman, 1971). This finding on apparent racial differences, like the IQ and inheritance findings, was of interest primarily to a few scholars, and it thus generated very little public acrimony (with a few notable exceptions whose voices were muffled) for most of the fifty years after Yerkes (1921) reported the first such finding.

It was not until Arthur Jensen (1969), a highly respected psychologist at the University of California at Berkeley, published what many could have expected would be another scholarly paper destined for similar musty library shelves that the earlier argument surrounding heredity and IQ was revived. In retrospect, the public outcry and vilification of this scholar from many quarters, described in the first person by Jensen (1972) and supplemented and placed in historical perspective by Cronbach (1975), was quite likely engendered more by Jensen's inferences for social policies in American society or implications attributed to him than by the merit and demerit of Jensen's largely empirically-based arguments themselves. Jensen's main argument was merely a modern restatement of Terman and Goddard's earlier view that intelligence, *by which Jensen specifically means IQ score,* is largely (albeit not exclusively) inherited. Although he has since added considerably more empirical support than can be reviewed here, the main underpinning of Jensen's arguments is found in the increasing magnitudes of the correlations from unrelated persons to identical twins summarized above. Jensen's 1969 monograph probably would have attracted the attention of only a few scholars had it not been for the millions of dollars of public funds that had been and were financing Head Start and other compensatory educational programs for the children of underprivileged American families, inaugurated by the Kennedy and Johnson administrations. Jensen's review suggested these programs, whose success was so desperately hoped for, had produced little benefit for the recipients.

Importantly, at the time Jensen's review appeared, the Vietnam War appeared to be exhausting the tax paying American public, and many socially-conscious people feared a large-scale curtailment of these programs by the incoming Nixon Administration. Journal editors and other members of the communications media, by giving wide coverage in the public press to Jensen's alleged attack on these programs, soon helped initiate a public debate on Jensen's carefully reasoned *personal* interpretation from the published research that IQ is mostly inherited. Jensen originally said very little about racial differences and IQ. However, in one section of his otherwise carefully buttressed arguments, Jensen (1969, p. 82) stated that "It seems not unreasonable . . . to hypothesize that genetic factors may play a part (in the 13 point difference in IQ between the black and white races)." This initially tepid hypothesis, a mere restatement of the earlier, generally held view, also was hucksterized by the press into an allegation that Jensen believed that blacks were inferior to whites in intelligence (note, not *IQ*, which Jensen clearly means). The uproar that followed after 1969 is eloquently described by Jensen (1972). The major thesis of Jensen's paper, the compensatory education issue, was almost forgotten in the loud debate on the racial issue. However, it should be noted that some experts deny the conclusions regarding compensatory education of Jensen's analysis; for instance, Zigler (1975) and Anderson and Messick (1974) argue that compensatory education in itself does have social value and that whether or not a child's IQ changes as a result of such compensatory education is not an important criterion or consideration.

Two lessons would appear to be clear from this controversy. First, the results of empirical findings must be *interpreted* within the context in which they are obtained. Specifically, experts whose scientific credentials and opinions Jensen respects

disagree with him that the *empirical* evidence summarized by us above and elsewhere is as yet sufficient to interpret that IQ is largely inherited, let alone that "intelligence" is inherited, or that the two races differ in intelligence. The carefully reasoned and buttressed arguments and interpretations of three such experts and others who disagree with Jensen were recently published and can be consulted by the interested reader (Loehlin et al, 1975). Today, many scientists are reluctant to conclude that IQ or other indices of intelligence as measured by what are still essentially American and middle class-oriented types of tests validated against white middle class school standards is largely inherited. The reason many scientists feel this way is because the developers of such tests simply have not examined IQ by appropriate norm-referenced tests for each specific cultural or subcultural sample, or in enough *different* subcultures of our own country, nor in enough other countries and cultures, nor in enough well-defined or well-controlled and varying environments in which either whites or blacks grow up within the same culture, to be able to conclude that the characteristics underlying IQ, and reflected in and measured by such tests, is largely inherited. That American blacks, disadvantaged whites and other poor, non-American youngsters from other countries can score as well on some types of assessment tests as do upper middle class American children is clearly being demonstrated by J. McVicker Hunt and his colleagues in a series of studies spanning the past decade, recently reaching publication (Hunt et al., 1975a; Hunt et al., 1975b; and Kirk and Hunt, 1975). (Chapter 17 of this text also describes a number of problems included in such cross-cultural or subcultural research studies.)

Interestingly, in a more recent study Jensen (1977) presents evidence that a very disadvantaged environment can, in fact, lower the IQ of black children. Specifically, Jensen found that, relative to their own younger siblings living in the same household, the IQs of black children showed a linearly-increasing decrement as they grew from age 5 to 16 years of age. Supporting a similar environmentalist position, Scarr and Weinberg (1976, 1977) have shown that black babies adopted by white parents shortly after birth earn IQs a number of years later that are (1) above average, (2) almost but not quite at the same high level as that of the natural white children reared in the same home, and (3) show correlations with their white adoptive parents' IQs and education that are well beyond the values of zero which would be predicted from a strictly hereditarian view. A longitudinal study on 26,000 pregnant, primarily poor American women and their later offspring (Broman et al, 1975) presents voluminous data on many factors, and in general supports both the hereditarian and environmentalist viewpoints. Many experts believe that causes underlying measured IQ and intellectual performance are too complex to be untangled by today's tools and methodologies.

One interesting sidelight that needs to be mentioned also is that *decisions made in constructing tests reflect assumptions and biases of the test developer*. By one simple decision that he may have felt was too self evident to even acknowledge, Binet appears to have decided that boys and girls were equal in measured intelligence. Consequently he, and every test maker since, have thrown out items which strongly favor one sex or the other, and current tests yield equal mean IQs. Fortunately this equality was easy to work out, despite demonstrated differences favoring girls on verbal tasks and boys on quantitative and spatial tasks (Tyler, 1974). Thus by a simple decision, Binet averted what today would be great outcry and public debate over sex bias in IQ tests. Would Binet have applied the same approach to racial differences if the Paris schools had held many nonwhite children in the early 1900s? We cannot say, of course, but it is true that there may be special kinds of learning in black American environments that are not available in white communities; one black psychologist (Williams, 1972) has constructed a test using ghetto vocabulary which clearly puts whites at a disadvantage (Matarazzo and Wiens, 1977). Making a truly culture-fair general intelligence test would be extremely difficult, and the many attempts to do so have so far failed (Anastasi, 1976).

Other Differences and Conclusions About Intelligence Testing

The empirical bases for interpretation of individual differences in IQ have been reviewed at length by Matarazzo (1972) and Tyler (1974). Here in brief are a few of the findings: IQ scores tend to be similar within families for both blacks and whites. Tests used solely within groups of disadvantaged students are useful in predicting school success (Cleary et al, 1975). Prenatal factors, especially those associated with very low or very high birth weight are closely related to measured IQ. Years of education and IQ are highly correlated, although which is cause and which is effect is still under debate. Aging does not appear to affect IQ score until well into the sixties, except on subtests that emphasize speed of performance; one psychologist (Schaie, 1974) even debunks the "myth" of decline with age in intact individuals. We must, of course, recognize that severe physical changes, such as those accompanying "strokes" and imminent death do result in considerable impairment. The relatively new area of study, neuropsychology, is developing ways of measuring mental function to assist neurologists in diagnosing brain disorders; current IQ measures and other behavioral measures of brain activity will some day be developed to a point where intellectual functioning can be more clearly differentiated and defined. Binet invented a crude technology that has been expanded and refined by many people since. Perhaps some of the present readers will sense the excitement of trying to understand humankind's crowning glory, the fully functioning mind, and assisting in improving brain-behavior relationships when they become disordered.

In concluding our discussion of intelligence testing, we will summarize a number of attitudes that currently seem important to us in understanding intelligence test results and their application to social practices and policy:

1. Intelligence is a broader concept than measured IQ. It includes general ability to adapt to real life situations.

2. Individuals are pluralistic and multitalented; so we need to test many aspects of the person. Many psychologists themselves see intelligence as made up of many abilities, some clearly cognitive, others more closely related to attitudinal-motivational and related dimensions.

3. One should not rely on a single intelligence test score for important decisions. For one thing, scores should be thought of as zones of possible

scores—zones that are relatively broad or narrow depending on the reliability of the test. A single test result applies best at the time of testing, and changes may occur over time. Confirmation of single results should be looked for in other tests or in repeated testing.

4. Interpretation of IQ scores must be related to the background of the individual—opportunities for education, language skills, and motivational supports for learning which are present in the home.

5. Results obtained on groups cannot be readily applied to an individual case. Individual differences within groups are always greater than differences between groups and the overlap between groups, such as found between blacks and whites, is very great. Thus, to stereotype all members of one group as low or high in intelligence is both incorrect and unfair. There are usually many more high scorers on tests than are given opportunities for access to the better schools or better jobs in which to show their abilities.

6. The scientific evidence is not conclusive about the relative effects of heredity and environment on intelligence; undoubtedly both contribute. Since at the present time we are much more able to influence and change environments than heredities, it seems important to concentrate public efforts on improvement of learning environments in the home, school, and work settings.

7. Research results do not automatically suggest public policy. Policy arises from values. If one assumes the value that society has responsibility for the well-being of all its citizens, then test results are to be seen as an opportunity to help. If areas of a city are found to have low achievement or ability test results, these findings should be a goad to look for assets in that area to build on and as a stimulus to seek out and introduce programs to improve the schools and other settings.

8. IQ scores are most relevant to, and predictive of, school success. They as yet have limited relevance to tasks unlike those in school. Thus, tests need to be developed which are more directly relevant to job success, and which take into account the special learning environments of minority group members, so that jobs can be better tailored to varying needs, backgrounds, and skills. This highlights the need for development of criterion-referenced instead of norm-referenced selection techniques.

9. Intelligence tests, used appropriately, can alert schools, parents, employers, and individuals themselves to the need for special efforts. In preventive programs in the community, persons "at risk" can be identified and given special assistance, be it in school or on the job.

10. In considering whether to use intelligence tests in public programs or to ban them, the decision-makers should weigh the tests carefully against alternatives. Often, tests will turn out to be the most fair and accurate way to provide information on individuals. If, in their anger with misuse of tests, critics should fall back on using the interview or other procedures, they need to justify the alternatives and evaluate them with at least as much care as has gone into present assessment devices.

Integration of Assessment Information in Individual Cases

We now need to return to the more general problem of assessment and the individual orientation with which we started out. After all of the discussion about different types of personality, interest, intelligence, and other types of tests and problems associated with psychological testing, we need to remember what the source of our interest is—providing assistance toward an understanding of people and providing help to each individual for making decisions of importance in his or her own life. The culminating activity of the work of a clinical psychologist, school psychologist, industrial consultant, or other psychologist using assessment procedures is to synthesize the results of a variety of data-gathering instruments and to communicate a useful picture to the individual patient or client directly or to the people who are to work with the client. Individual assessment involves much more than discrete acts of testing. It involves the development of an understanding of the person through interviewing, observing, collecting, and collating information from the life history and from psychological testing, and attempting to tie all of the findings together to assist the person toward becoming a more effective, satisfied, and fully functioning individual.

One of the sources of discontent with psychological tests, especially those group administered tests used in the schools and in industry by non-professionally trained personnel, is that they have been used for making decisions *about* individuals without knowing the person. When tests are used to make decisions *with* the person or his or her surrogates, with compassionate concern for that person as a human being, it is likely that there is less chance for a disappointing and anger-producing result. In fact, one of the trends in recent psychological assessment practices, in industry as well as in the clinic or schools, has been toward the development of tests that the client can use for gaining self-knowledge—exercises in self-understanding and self-management.

In today's usual clinical situation, a psychologist writes a summary report pulling together the information from the history, interview, observations, and tests. The three psychological reports that follow illustrate only a few of the many challenges that occur in clinical and consulting practice, and the ways that psychologists describe the results of assessment.

Report on Mrs. C., a New Patient
Seen by the Staff of a Mental Health Clinic

(condensed from Sundberg and Tyler, 1962, pp. 242–243)

Mrs. C. is a 44-year-old divorced woman. She was a practical nurse but is currently unemployed and living with her 60-year-old mother who helps take care of her two children. Her manner is noticeably reticent and depressive. She volunteers virtually no information, even when she is directly questioned. Her responses are guarded and cryptic. In the testing situation she was very cooperative, but her participation is more on the basis of submissiveness than of intrinsic interest in the proceedings. She was administered the Rorschach, Sentence Completion, Thematic Apperception Test, and the Minnesota Multiphasic Personality Inventory.

The Rorschach shows a basically hysterical type of personality structure, the presence of substantial obsessive trends and significant indications of paranoid pathology. Sexual maladjustment is clearly evident and the

indications of weakened reality contact seem to be related to the sexual problems. The patient is very resistant to attacking or even facing her basic problems, and this corroborates the impression one gets in attempting to interview her. There is a virtual absence of any insight. The MMPI shows significant peaks on the Hysteria, Paranoia, and Depression scales. This kind of pattern has been found to be common with neurotic patients, although a significant degree of paranoid involvement is suggested. The TAT is, for the most part, rather bland except for the presence of a considerable number of themes involving highly aggressive acts. The most salient and pervasive feeling that emerges is the paranoid one of a defenseless person in a hostile and brutal world in which violent aggressive forces are always lurking and may strike one or one's loved ones when they least expect it.

The Sentence Completion Test brings out most clearly the paranoid ideation which is suggested in the MMPI and Rorschach. She feels that she is extremely ill and that her condition is almost hopeless: I am very—"sick," and My greatest hope—"is almost gone." To further inquiries about these she says, "I feel that if my eyes, my ears, and my throat were thoroughly studied, they would find something wrong." Although a nurse, she is unable to explain how a local eye, ear, and throat condition could cause her to be so severely and hopelessly sick, and she shows no interest in attempting to explain it. She is confused and baffled by many inexplicable experiences she has had and projects motives and interpretations into many common daily occurrences; for example, from sentence completions, I want to know—"Why some people behave so strangely"; If only—"People would tell me the truth." In the inquiry on these items she replies, "None of these things are too important, but so many of them happened to me. For example, when by brother-in-law's leg was broken and I was present in the doctor's office, my brother-in-law remarked to the doctor, 'She's an excellent diagnostician,' referring to me. All the doctor said was, 'Well, I got you.' What did he mean by that? That's bothered and puzzled me ever since." In the same vein, What puzzles me—"Why one of the doctors talks about married men and men in high salaried positions." In the inquiry she responds, "The way he'd lower his voice or look at me when he'd get around to talking about those things. I don't know what his motive was, but I felt there was some reason behind it."

Along the same lines, and by dint of much probing, since the patient is very guarded in all her responses, additional evidence of paranoid ideation was elicited. She has visited fortunetellers twice. In both cases the fortunetellers told her about a particular man who would come into her life significantly. She relates many strange events which have happened around her house which she feels are all related to the return of this man into her life. She relates a recent experience in which she felt extremely good and symptom-free for a day or so, and she feels that this happened because she was given a massive dose of "dope" which was put in some coffee which was returned to her by a girl in a neighboring apartment who had borrowed some coffee from her. She is unable to account for these unusual experiences, but she feels that she is being used as a psychological experiment by someone who is causing these things to happen to her so that he can study her reactions to them.

Impression. On first impression derived from an initial interview, Mrs. C's superficial manner and guarded communicativeness conveys the picture of a person in good contact who is suffering from a reactive depressive state as a result of protracted and severe stress in a realistically difficult marital situation. The termination of the marriage in divorce and her stringent economic prospect of having to support her two children enhances this impression. On the basis of psychological testing and a searching and probing type of interview, however, evidence of substantial paranoid pathology, moving toward systematization, is elicited. It is felt that this patient is quite seriously ill, and the outlook is poor, inasmuch as her present uncommunicativeness makes her unavailable for a psychotherapeutic approach.

Case Summary from a Clinic, Concerning Billy Walker, Age 11

Referral Problem: Mrs. Walker sought help from the Clinic because the school would not accept Billy unless he had been seen professionally during the summer months. Billy is 11 years old, the second of four children. His older brother is 15 and the two younger sisters are 9 and 7; Mr. Walker does not live at home. His mother's main complaint concerned Billy's hitting her and his younger sisters. She also expressed fear of Billy and her inability to control him. Billy would not comply with requests to help around the home and as a result was rarely asked to do anything. Mrs. Walker did not seem very concerned with the school problem. The counselor at Larkin School, Mrs. Peters, said Billy's behavior had been a problem since he entered the school two years ago. Several attempts had been made to change his fighting with classmates, both boys and girls.

In an intake interview at the Clinic, Billy answered questions and talked freely about the behaviors that con-

cerned his mother and teachers. He said that teachers were unfair because other kids kept running to them all the time. He complained about things going on in his home. He didn't like the old house they live in, which is in a wealthy neighborhood. He said his older brother picks on him; he can't stay up as late as his older brother, and his younger sisters don't obey him. He said he "had to hit" his sisters about three or four times a day to get them to do what he asked. He did not see much wrong with his behavior, but agreed to work on it. He also told about some things he would like to do.

Intervention procedures: From data collected on hitting and noncompliance behavior in the home by trained observers, a decision was reached to work on the behaviors with the two younger sisters first. The plan was explained to both Billy and Mrs. Walker. Billy was to stop hitting his sisters; if he did hit, he was to be placed in "time-out" for five minutes. ("Time-out" is a procedure often used in behavior therapy; it involves putting the child in an isolated place, such as the bathroom, for a short time.) If he did not hit anyone the whole day, he was allowed to stay up for an extra half-hour at night to watch television. Mrs. Walker carried out the program, keeping a record, and the hitting dropped from approximately once every fifteen minutes to zero per day.

The next program concerned Billy's noncompliance with his mother's requests. Mrs. Walker was asked to give him instructions to do some household duties, for example, empty the rubbish, which he had not been asked to do before. If he did these, his mother was to reward him by permission to go on short bicycle trips and football games, go swimming, or get new shoes.

The program of behavior modification was a success and Billy carried out his assigned chores with ease. He became interested in other family members as friends rather than enemies and helped the younger children with various tasks. By the end of the summer, Mrs. Walker reported she felt Billy was under control and did not present any problems she was incapable of handling.

Follow-up: In Larkin school again in the fall, Billy did well at the beginning of the year according to monthly telephone conversations with Mrs. Walker. During the winter, Mrs. Walker called twice about reports that Billy was "talking back" and "sassing" his teacher. In a telephone conversation we had with the school counselor, we agreed that Mrs. Peters would talk with Billy and indicate the problem and tell him that if he misbehaved a school intervention program would have to be initiated. The counselor later reported that Billy did not want such a program in school. We agreed and his behavior changed, and no additional incidents were reported. Billy's academic achievement improved considerably; on a standard reading test he had placed at the 2.7 grade level in the fall but attained the 5.0 level the following May.

Attached are two charts on rates of hitting and non-compliance with requests (See Figure 18-7). These were based on observations made by observers visiting the home *before* and *after* the intervention period. It will be seen that the amount of hitting and noncompliance with mother's requests dropped during the period of treatment and remained at almost zero at the time of follow-up. (The authors wish to thank Dr. Gerald R. Patterson for the preceding case. Readers interested in more details about Patterson's social learning approach to family therapy may consult Patterson, 1974, and Jones, Reid and Patterson, 1975.)

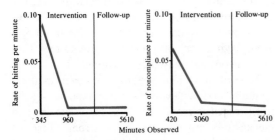

Fig. 18-7. Charts showing observed rates of Billy's hitting and noncompliance to mother's requests.

Report on the Managerial Potential of a 37-Year-Old Man

(slightly condensed from Matarazzo, 1972, pp. 499–501).

The writer was asked by the President of a large division of a national firm specializing in food products to evaluate a regional sales manager in the firm regarding his potential to assume the post of National Sales Manager for the company. Following establishment of the necessary rapport, the following initial history (changed in minor personal details) was obtained. The candidate was 37 years old, had been born in the Midwest in a very poor sharecropper household, the second from the last of six children. He dropped out of high school in the 11th grade, worked a few months, and joined the United States Air Force, serving four years as an Airman First Class working in aerial communications. He was discharged at age 21, took a full-time job nights and attended a two-year community college from which he

graduated several years later. At 23 years of age he married a girl he met in college and joined this national food products firm as a clerk. During the next 14 years he was transferred to sales and advanced from inside sales to outside sales in the same city, to responsibility for all sales in his state, and finally to sales manager for all 13 states in his region. Annual income also increased proportionally, from $3,600 the first year to $18,000 fourteen years later. His family grew to include two children, and the uprootings of residence his various promotions necessitated were described as providing no untoward hardship for him, his wife, or children.

Neither the history obtained in the opening phase of the appraisal nor the assessment procedures themselves revealed any indices of psychopathology. The global WAIS findings show a young executive of superior intellect, with Full Scale IQ of 137 (99th percentile), Verbal IQ of 133 (98th percentile), and Performance IQ of 138 (99th percentile). This absence of scatter among these three global indices was consistent, with the exception of the Block Design and Picture Arrangement subtests, with the comparable lack of intersubtest and intrasubtest scatter found in his performance on the 11 individual subtests making up these three indices. The relatively lower scores in Block Design and Picture Arrangement appeared to the examiner to reflect a transient situational anxiety. The results from the MMPI and the other clinical assessment instruments corroborate the suggestions from the WAIS alone that this is a highly intelligent young executive with minimal signs of psychopathology of the type which might impair his current or future effectiveness. That is, he is an excellent illustration of the point that, in the well-integrated person, measured intelligence (the superior global as well as inter-subtest WAIS results in this instance) and his past and current adaptive behavior (his 14 years of progressive advancement with his company) should go hand in hand.

At the end of the five-hour executive appraisal, the consulting psychologist, consistent with his promise to this client (made in the opening moments in all such executive industrial appraisals) to give such an opinion, informed him that in the personal-professional opinion of the psychologist, the candidate seemed well-qualified to accept the greater challenges associated with the potential promotion. The psychologist, sensing that rapport permitted such a candid question, then asked the client his own judgment of his capacity to carry out the new assignment. The answer was a forceful, but still low key, affirmative reply.

He was promoted to this position the next day with a sizable increase in salary and other perquisites. His life history to date is a good illustration that such high levels of measured intelligence are found frequently in persons of *modest* birth, family circumstances, and educational history. When nonintellective (personality and motivational) factors of the type possessed by this man were combined with the opportunities his life circumstances provided, his level of current, as well as predicted further success, is not difficult to understand.

Summary

The principal concerns of this chapter have been to explore how individuals differ from one another and how psychologists represent, study, and utilize such differences in professional work with their patients and other clients. Psychological assessment is the process of studying the person and his or her situation for the purposes of making decisions, producing descriptions, or testing theories. Differential psychology to which assessment is closely related is that part of psychology aimed, not at establishing general laws about human behavior, but at studying and explaining how individuals and groups differ from one another.

The most common procedures used in assessing persons are interviewing and observing. Both processes can be relatively unstructured and informal or structured and exact. One of the advantages of these procedures over psychological tests is the flexibility with which the examiner can scan wide areas of behavior and experience and then focus on particularly important details. However, in general, the more unstructured a procedure is the more it is subject to problems of reliability and validity.

Psychological tests are methods for obtaining a sample of a person's behavior in a standard situation. In addition to using standardized procedures, the examiner must also establish a cooperative relationship in order to achieve the best results from the assessment.

Reliability and validity are the two most important technical attributes of a test. These concepts can be applied not only to tests but also to interviews and any other measure one uses. Reliability refers to the accuracy or consistency of a particular score; it can also be viewed as the degree of generalizability of scores from one time to another, from one form of the same test to another, or from one observer to another. Related terms are stability, equivalence, and interrater reliability. Validity refers to how "good" the test is for accomplishing what the test user wants to do with it. An evaluation of validity includes answers to questions about the appropriateness of the content, the ability of the test to predict or correlate with an accepted outcome or criteria, and the adequacy of the test as a measure of constructs or theoretical relations.

Norms are the comparison standards for tests and usually involve percentiles or standard scores based on large samples of a relevant population. Norm-referencing is the process of comparing a single person's test results against similar test findings from a large sample of such individuals. Criterion-referencing is the process of relating such results to an expected standard of performance, not necessarily based on what others have done. Comparing an individual with an irrelevant group or a group with a very different background may lead to erroneous and biased conclusions.

Tests of maximum performance cover abilities, aptitudes and achievement; the person taking the test is asked to work as hard as he or she can and the answers are either right or wrong. Tests of characteristic performance attempt to represent what a person's habitual manner of doing things is and to delineate an individual's personality or behavior; on such tests, there are no particularly right or wrong answers. There are three main kinds of tests of characteristic performance—objective, projective, and behavioral.

Objective techniques cover the familiar paper-and-pencil personality inventories, called objective because the recording and scoring of the responses do not require the assessor's subjective judgments. The most widely used objective technique now is the Minnesota Multiphasic Personality Inventory (MMPI). Another widely used kind of inventory measures interests to help people understand their vocational inclinations. Objective techniques also include a wide variety of scales, inventories and questionnaires for measuring attitudes, values, and beliefs. Objective approaches have relied heavily for their development on psychometric theory and statistical techniques; they treat obtained responses as potential *correlates*—data to be correlated and otherwise manipulated to measure or indicate outside behavior or theoretical constructs.

Projective techniques cover a great many procedures which mainly use ambiguous or unstructured stimuli to elicit individualized responses such as reports of perceptions, stories, or associations. They are usually interpreted by assuming the person has "projected" inner feelings, conflicts, and misperceptions in the process of responding to the stimuli. The most widely used projective techniques are the Rorschach inkblots, Thematic Apperception Test, sentence completion test, drawings, and word association. Projective techniques depend heavily on the interpretative skills and theoretical leanings of the interpreter. They have been associated traditionally with psychodynamic or psychoanalytic psychology, and the interpreter regards the obtained responses as indices or *signs* of inner needs, conflicts, and conditions.

Behavioral techniques are a new and rapidly growing set of ways of sampling and analyzing behavior. Some depend on direct observation of behavior, others on self reports of occurrences of problematic or rewarding events in daily life. These techniques typically are used with behavior modification or social learning approaches to therapy. The assessor treats responses as *samples* of behavior without attempting to attribute any psychodynamic significance to them.

The second part of this chapter focused on the development and use of intelligence tests—how they started in 1905 with Binet's concern for assisting the schools of Paris to help pupils at different levels of ability, and how they related to Galton's search for a way to measure talent statistically and to relate it to heredity. The two most widely used tests which yield an intelligence quotient have been the Stanford Binet, originally developed by Terman in 1916, and the set of tests developed by David Wechsler starting in 1939.

Research has shown that the IQ score is very successful in predicting school success or failure (with correlation coefficients often around .50) and thus for identifying individuals "at risk" in educational environments. However, despite this repeated pragmatic success during many decades of usage, there are as yet no clear conclusions about what intelligence is; and there are many controversies about the proper use of IQ results. One dispute is whether intelligence is a single general ability, often called "*g*", or a composite of many specific abilities. Another raging dispute concerns the relation of IQ to race (and, earlier, nationality) and the closely related question of whether intelligence is a function of heredity or environment. Proponents of both positions abound. It is important that those who interpret individual IQs, and those who develop public policy regarding IQ testing do so carefully. IQ scores are a highly effective tool for a very specific purpose, identifying school children who may need extra help, academic, or motivational. They most clearly relate to school and school-related success and have limited applicability to proficiency in everyday adult life. Those who decry the use of tests altogether should question equally diligently the alternative techniques for making decisions about people; not using a test does not change the values of decision-makers, and using a less exact procedure such as interviewing may allow a great deal of bias to creep into an assessment.

As the last part of this chapter, we presented some typical assessment reports of individuals made by psychologists to illustrate how a variety of psychological tests and procedures are melded together with the interpreter's theories and knowledge of the person's background to produce recommendations for personal decisions and intervention treatment approaches. Because such decisions and plans are so important in the lives of individuals, and because assessment often requires subjective judgment, it is important that the professional psychologist or other assessor have considerable training and knowledge about the technical qualities of tests, a sense of compassion, and a high personal code of ethics.

Glossary

Ability: The actual power to perform a task, mental or physical, whether or not it was gained by training. To be distinguished from aptitude.

Achievement: Success in accomplishing a desired task. Usually applied to tests that measure past learning, such as tests of knowledge of history or mathematics.

Applied in the term "need: Achievement" to the need for purposeful effort or the gaining of desired ends.

Aptitude: The potential for performing a task after appropriate training or experience.

Assessment: The process of studying and evaluating an individual and that individual's situation for the purposes of description, decision-making, or research. May be applied to groups or larger systems. Closely related in clinical practice to psychodiagnosis for purposes of treatment or management.

Baseline: A record of the occurrence of a problem behavior before an intervention or treatment occurs in behavior therapy; used as a reference point for measuring later improvement.

Behavioral technique: An assessment procedure for sampling a person's activities in situations of interest usually for purposes of treatment of problem behavior. Examples are observational coding of occurrences of problem behavior and the surrounding events, questionnaires on problems, and reinforcing events.

Characteristic performance tests: Tests that ask the subject to present himself or herself as he or she characteristically or typically experiences situations, with no right or wrong answers to questions. Applicable to personality and interest tests. To be distinguished from tests of maximum performance.

Cognitive style: The mode by which a person organizes and classifies perceptions of situations or events; the way a person thinks in imposing order on a set of diverse test stimuli.

Concurrent validity: Evidence of the ability of a test to relate to other measures of the same quality or ability, for example, a high correlation between a new general test of intelligence with an old, widely researched, and established test.

Construct validity: Evidence that test results indicate that the test is measuring a theoretical concept or idea (such as anxiety or creativity) through a network of indicators hypothesized by the theory.

Content validity: Evidence that a test samples the domain of interest and covers the topics specified by the test developer.

Criterion-referencing: Comparing an obtained score from an individual with performances defined according to an outside criterion. The use of an absolute or defined standard rather than a comparison with others' performances, as is done in norm-referencing.

Criterion validity: Evidence that test scores relate to acceptable criteria, such as success on the job, or scores from an established test. Criterion validity may be either concurrent (that is, related to some other test or indicator measured at about the same time) or predictive (that is, related to some future outcome).

Derived score: A score resulting from a statistical manipulation of the original raw score. Examples: percentile or standard score.

Differential psychology: The branch of psychology that investigates the differences and similarities between individuals and groups and the causes and effects of such differences.

Equivalence reliability: The degree to which one form or part of a test correlates with another form or part supposed to measure the same thing.

"g": General intelligence, a pervasive ability to think well and behave adaptively in a wide variety of problem situations. Contrasted with specific abilities.

Intelligence: An individual's aggregate capacity to act purposively, think rationally, and deal effectively with one's environment. Defined by psychologists to cover an individual's relative standing on two quantitative indices (1) IQ or other index of measured intelligence and (2) an index of adaptive behavior (such as, two school grades behind age peers; or a four-year, high school grade point average of 3.6).

Intelligence quotient (IQ): An individual's relative rank expressed as a quantitative score (IQ) on a standardized test of intelligence. It is an index of his or her performance relative to a statistically established IQ of 100, higher scores being above average and lower, below average. Originally obtained by dividing a child's mental age as measured on a test by its chronological age and multiplying by 100.

Interview: "A conversation with a purpose" (Bingham and Moore, 1924). In assessment, a verbal interchange guided by the interviewer, designed to elicit certain information and feelings from the interviewee for the purposes of research or to aid in diagnosis or treatment.

Maximum performance tests: Tests that ask the subject to achieve at his or her highest level, using scoring for right or wrong answers. Applicable to ability, aptitude, and achievement tests. To be distinguished from tests of characteristic or typical performance.

Norm-referencing: Comparing an obtained score from an individual with norms, or a set of scores made by other individuals.

Norms: In regard to tests, a table or other set of scores provided by a large number of subjects which are used as a standard for comparisons in evaluating the results with new testees. Usually provided in the form of percentiles or standard scores. Must be distinguished from social norms or group norms, which are the expectations for behavior in an interacting group of people.

Objective technique: Personality tests requiring answers that can be scored without the use of judgment by an observer or clinician, such as a large number of personality inventories and attitude scales. (The term is also sometimes used only to refer to directly-measurable physical performance, such as number of As crossed in a page of random letters, or the work output using a machine.)

Percentile: A derived score using points that divide a ranked distribution into 100 parts based on counting from the lowest to the highest score.

Performance IQ: The index on the Wechsler Adult Intelligence Scale of a person's ability in nonverbal areas (for example, manipulate objects with his or her hands such as in copying designs by arranging blocks). Usually contrasted with Verbal IQ.

Predictive validity: The evidence that test scores correlate or otherwise relate to future events or outcomes of relevance to the test.

Projective technique: A procedure for revealing a person's characteristic way of thinking or behaving in a relatively unstructured or vague situation, with the assumption that the person "projects" his or her motives, conflicts and habitual perceptual experiences into the situation. Examples are the Rorschach inkblots and many forms of storytelling, association, and drawing.

Rapport: A cooperative and comfortable relationship between two persons, especially in a testing or interviewing situation.

Raw score: The original result from a person taking a test before it is converted into a comparative or derived score.

Reliability: "The degree to which the results of testing are attributable to systematic sources of variance." (American Psychological Association, 1974, p. 48). The accuracy, internal consistency, or generalizability of a test score, indicated usually by a reliability coefficient.

Sign: An indicator obtained on a test (often a projective technique) of an inferred underlying condition, such as a need or motive. Seeing test results as signs is contrasted to seeing such results as samples of behavior, or correlates or potential correlates of some other response or condition.

Stability reliability: The degree to which a test gives the same relative results with the same set of people at two different times, such as by test-retest methods.

Standardization: The process of establishing uniform procedures for administering and scoring a test and using test results. May refer specifically to the development of norms.

Standard score: Any derived score using the standard deviation of the criterion (or normative) group. For example, a standard score of -1.5 means one and one-half standard deviations below the mean. Standard scores often use arbitrary means and standard deviations to avoid decimals and negative numbers, for example, 35 would be -1.5 for a distribution with a mean of 50 and a standard deviation of 10.

Test: A method for obtaining a sample of a person's behavior or report of experience in a standard situation.

Validity: "The appropriateness of inferences from test scores or other forms of assessment" (American Psychological Association, 1974, p. 25). The meaning of a test score in reference to something outside the test itself; whether the test actually measures what it purports to measure.

Verbal IQ: The index on the Wechsler Adult Intelligence Scale of the individual's ability in verbal areas (such as to construe, manipulate, and define words and concepts). Usually contrasted with the Performance IQ.

Suggested Readings

Anastasi, A. *Psychological Testing.* 4th ed. New York: Macmillan, 1976.

Bray, D. W., Campbell, R. J. and Grant, D. L. *Formative Years in Business: A Long-Term AT&T Study of Managerial Lives.* New York: John Wiley, 1974.

Cronbach, L. J. Five Decades of Public Controversy over Mental Testing. *American Psychologist,* 1975, *30,* 1–14.

Matarazzo, J. D. *Wechsler's Measurement and Appraisal of Adult Intelligence.* 5th and enlarged edition. Baltimore: Williams & Wilkins, 1972.

Sundberg, N.D. *Assessment of persons.* Englewood Cliffs, N.J.: Prentice-Hall, 1977.

Tyler, L. E. *Individual Differences: Abilities and Motivational Directions.* New York: Prentice-Hall, 1974.

Personality

Franz Epting, Ted Landsman, and
Barbara Baldridge

Introduction

Personality is that area in psychology which is involved in the task of integrating the knowledge gained in all of the other specific areas of psychology (perception, learning, development, dreaming, remembering, and so on) in order that this knowledge can be seen as part of an individual's life. How can all this information be put together in order to make a whole person? The pull of this question is felt constantly by the personality psychologist. The total life of the individual must be dealt with from the beginning of life until its end. The component parts of the person must be brought together in such a way that we can understand how a person is organized and structured, how one develops one's life, how one moves through life first in one direction and then another, how one defends oneself in order to survive, and how one invents a life with enough joy in it to make it worth living. Even further, the field of personality attempts to specify what a person has been, what that person is presently, and what that person might become.

In many ways, every man and woman is an expert in the study of personality. When reading ''personality theory,'' they are constantly comparing it with what they know to be true about themselves and the other people in their lives. Putting forth a theory of personality is like having a whole population of critics present at every application or exposition of the theory. A person's grasp of what one's own personality is like and what others are like usually means a great deal as one goes about the business of making life decisions. The main difference between ''every person's'' theory and the theory of the experts (the personality theorists) is the fact that the experts have systematically written their ideas out in such a way that scientific procedures for validating these ideas can be applied.

The task of synthesizing information about persons in order to formulate a total personality theory is seen as a long range project. The immediate task of the personality psychologist is the study of ways to characterize people in such a manner that they will be recognizable over time and in different situations. Knowledge of personality characteristics should enable us to better predict the behavior and experiences of a person compared to instances where only the nature of the situation is known. For example, if a person is in a situation that requires a great deal of conformity, knowledge of personality characteristics will enable us to predict if in fact the person will yield; or if one does yield, how long it will take and the method of yielding one will choose.

These relatively enduring personality characteristics then provide the framework for holding together all the other aspects of the person's life. While this study of stabilizing characteristics is of great importance, the study of personality must also undertake an understanding of how people go about changing. To what extent do people change and what aspects of their personality are most susceptible to change? In addition, it is important to recognize that some of the personality dimensions we study (for example, anxiety, achievement need, self-actualization, authoritarianism, extraversion) may well apply to the whole population one might be interested in studying or may be restricted to relatively few people. They may apply to a given person at one time in life but not at some later date. In addition, these personality dimensions may be drastically modified by the nature of the different social situations with which a person must deal.

Range of Personality Theories

The size of the task that personality theory has undertaken means that every available source of information must be used. No one solution is likely to emerge which will be able to answer even a simple majority of the questions. For this reason, at the present time, a number of personality theories are being maintained and can best be viewed as alternative constructions or scientific models of what the person is like (see Chapter 1). All the different theories are, however, incomplete descriptions of what the authors of these positions hoped to achieve. One might almost think of these positions as additive; each theory giving us more information about people than we had before. More accurately, perhaps, these different theories are mixtures of attempts to explain the same human events differently, combined with attempts to explore entirely different events.

In presenting each of the theories, we shall attempt to convey only those aspects of each position that touch on its unique contribution. The focus will be on those events that the theory can best explain, thereby offering an illustration of its best contribution to personality theory. The theories will be presented in three main groups: *psychoanalytic, behavioristic,* and *humanistic.* These are very broad categories that will serve to organize the major themes shared by theories in each group. Subdivisions within each of these three major categories are provided along with an indication of theorists who serve as transitional figures between the major orientations.

Psychoanalytic Theory

The Freudian Revolution

In almost every academic generation in the recent past, Sigmund Freud has been the unflinching recipient of some specific, inordinately bitter criticism consonant with the spirit of that particular time. Psychoanalysis, in more or less its original form, nevertheless, has been maintained. It has shown remarkable durability. Historically, it is primary amongst the talking psychotherapies. Its early assertions and its sexual candidness, together with its fiery radicalisms, make it clearly of fundamental interest to the personality theorist.

Freud's theory of personality is deeply rooted in the pains and problems of the human being; this is perhaps his greatest contribution. Out of his theory grew most of the contemporary approaches to psychotherapy including client-centered therapy, Gestalt therapy, transactional analysis, rational-emotive therapy, and many of the techniques common to existential therapies. His theory remains as perhaps the most creative and daring series of statements in the history of personality theory.

Over the years, his theory has been made more scientific and researchable and more contemporary in terminology. Nevertheless Freud, in one manner or another, probably said a good part of it first. And what did he say?

Drive Theory. Freud proposed that the major drive motivating human behavior was essentially *libidinal* and erotic. This psychic energy labeled *libido* is aggressive, even destructive, violent, and in a sense uncontrollable, particularly as it is expressed and manifested in the original structural component of the personality, the *id.* While Freud never completed a catalogue of the instincts that he felt were fundamental to an understanding of human behavior and particularly to neurosis, the *libido,* as a sexual, procreational, and sometimes aggressive instinct (drive) was clearly the one that over the years has survived as a major part of many theories. This is in spite of the fact that Freud himself and many of his early followers attempted to soften the influence of this rather risky concept and generalize the libidinal energy into a more generally life-sustaining sort of drive.

Instincts were classified by Freud as life wishes (*eros*) and death wishes (*thanatos*). There is no doubt that Freud emphasized the life wish, the wish to survive and to continue as the more significant of the two. He also postulated, however, the existence of an unconscious wish to die, a concept that later played a major role in industrial research, with accidents as representative of such wishes.

A parallel set of principles govern behavior—the *pleasure principle* and the *reality principle*. Humans are motivated by the search for unregulated pleasure, raw and basic, sexual pleasure, physical and emotional pleasure. The relationship of this pleasure principle to contemporary behavioristic emphasis on the reward in learning should not be forgotten. Freud, however, recognized that the pleasure seeking behavior of the human had to be constrained by another principle, the *reality principle*. This principle suggested that man made compromises, choices, and so on to delay gratification and choose lesser pleasures when necessary to meet the social demands.

Structure of Personality. Three rather useful entities were presented as components of the personality or the mind: *id, ego,* and *super-ego.* Few concepts in the history of personality theory so quickly became household words. Thus, it behooves the student to separate the layman's meaning of these words from the professional meanings given them by Freud. The *id* represents the largest part of the personality and contains all the primitive, untamed urges and tendencies, including aggression, hostility, sexual, erotic, libidinal inclinations. It is governed heavily by the pleasure principle (as in the newborn baby) and represents the person seeking gratification, largely physical, crude, and unrestrained. The *super-ego,* on the other hand, represents the voice of conscience, inhibition, caution, morality, ethics, and so forth. It is the value systems introjected from moralizing parents and preachers and society as the infant progresses through childhood. It represents the refined restraints on primal urges, the drives to conform to society and to the needs of others. Mediating these two major systems is the *ego.* The concept of the

ego is perhaps the most misunderstood of Freud's terms. Ego, in the Freudian system, does not refer to the self or to selfishness but rather to the mediating procedures enabling the individual to balance the urges from the id and the super-ego into a pattern of satisfying but safe behavior. In some of the analogies that have sprung up over the concepts, the id is seen as the motor of a car, the ego is seen as the driver exercising control over the power system (presumably the libido is the gasoline), and the super-ego is seen as the traffic light or the police. An overly moralistic individual who might be beset by anxieties whose origins were a mystery to him might well be seen as having too strong a super-ego and too weak an ego and id. The violent, forceful, crude individual might be seen as having a strong id and a weak super-ego.

Infant Sexuality and Developmental Psychology. Freud's concepts of sexuality extend into infancy. He saw sexual urges and experiences not only as significant for the adult but originally placed great emphasis on sexual traumas in infancy. This concept was somewhat modified in later writings but was never minimized. Presumably all children proceeded through an orderly sequence of sexual stages: *anal, oral,* and *phallic.* These are presumed to occur in the first three to five years of life. In the *oral* stage the erogenous zone (the body zone of greatest pleasure) is the mouth. There seems to be little argument with this in contemporary child psychology inasmuch as this is a time when the child feels with the mouth, and feeding is the central attention of the child. In the second year of life, the *anal* stage is discovered, bowel training is important, the anus is the erogenous zone (the formation of the stubborn personality, for example, is seen in the child who is retentive in his bowel training or who refuses to release his bowels to please a highly attentive, pleading, overly anxious parent). The genitals themselves are the primary erogenous zone for the third phase, the *phallic* stage. One of the most important aspects of the phallic stage is the fact that it marks the time for the development of another concept that became a household word: the *Oedipus complex.* Named after the King of Thebes who married his mother, the Oedipus complex refers to an alleged sequence of wishes, on the part of the male child to have a full physical relationship including sex with the female parent and to do away with the male parent. He fears punishment from the father for these feelings in the form of castration—which becomes *castration anxiety*. The parallel pattern in the female child known as the Electra complex and results in penis envy—the girl's alleged wish to have a penis and her feelings of inferiority because she does not have one. It is this concept which is so repugnant to feminist movements.

A *latency period,* which extends from the sixth year to puberty, is said to follow at this point during which the sexual drives are more or less quiescent. This latency period is followed by the *genital stage* where intercourse, orgasm, and the normal sex life predominate in the motivational system of the maturing adult. One who fails for any reason to pass through each stage may become *fixated* at any one level and manifests this in neurotic symptoms characteristic of that particular phase; an example

might be the stubbornness of someone fixated in the withholding anal stage (see Figure 19-1).

The Unconscious. Perhaps the most accepted term of all the concepts which psychoanalysis presented in the early twentieth century was the *"unconscious."* Freud's early work in hypnosis convinced him of the reality of this "psychical" concept and he recognized that it would engender much controversy and be perceived by some as absurd.

"To most people who have been educated in philosophy the idea of anything psychical which is not also conscious is so inconceivable that it seems to them absurd and refutable simply by logic. I believe this is only because they have never studied the relevant phenomena of hypnosis and dreams . . ." (Freud, 1927/1960, p. 3).

This presentation of the mental life presupposes three levels of consciousness; the *unconscious,* the *preconscious,* and the *conscious* (see Figure 19-2). The conscious is not a controversial concept; the

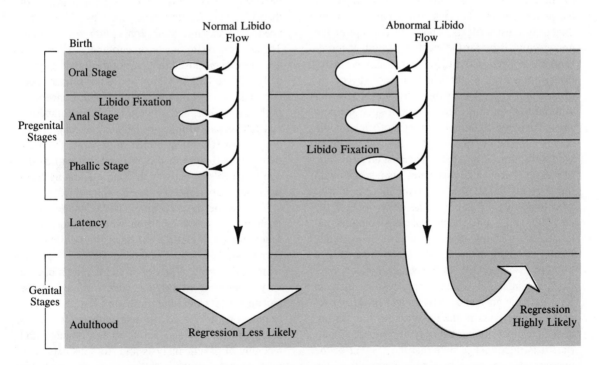

Fig. 19-1. Fixation of libido and model of regression. (From Joseph F. Rychlak, *Introduction to Personality and Psychotherapy: A Theory-Construction Approach,* New York: Houghton Mifflin, 1973, p. 55)

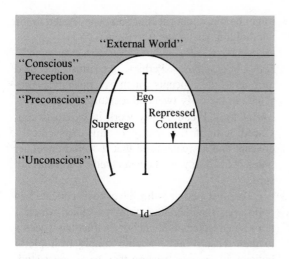

Fig. 19-2. Freud's structural model of personality. (From Joseph F. Rychlak, *Introduction to Personality and Psychotherapy: A Theory-Construction Approach,* New York: Houghton Mifflin, 1973, p. 34)

preconscious, which presumably included content not too heavily repressed and reasonably available to consciousness with a little effort on the part of the patient and the therapist, was soon to be abandoned by most analysts. Thus, the concept of the unconscious is by far the most important. It represents the collection of hidden fear, traumas, memories, unresolved issues which in one way or another control or influence the individual's behavior without his conscious knowledge of such happenings. There are countless examples of such unconscious motivation in everyday life—the student who finds himself in rebellion against an autocratic instructor, because he associates his neckties with those of his father; the man who chooses a wife who looks like his mother, the obsessions of the neurotic, and so on. The unconscious contains material repressed into it in the course of everyday living, information about self too uncomfortable to be kept in consciousness but which collects over time, and material which simply resides there in long past memory and collects over time. All repressed material is in the unconscious but the unconscious does not consist only of repressed material. It is important to note that the content of the unconscious was considered to be many times that of the conscious and much of psychoanalysis con-

sisted in explorations into the unconscious by the patient with the help of the skillful therapist.

Freud's history is one of audacity, courage in the face of enormous opposition, and great faith in himself and in his ideas. From a scientific point of view, perhaps his greatest contribution was his closeness to his original data. Very few of the researchers of his time were able to come as close to the deep, personal lives of people as he did in his clinical practice. Thus, his theories were based solidly in the most searching, intimate contact with real data. However, he also did little that today would be described as scientific research into the personality. Much of what he wrote was speculative, hypothetical, however brilliant and perceptive. His detractors fail to discover his own admission of such:

"In the present discussion (of Ego and Id) moreover, I am only putting forward an hypothesis: I have no proof to offer." (Freud, 1960, p. 34)

Ego Psychology. Before leaving our discussion of Freud and the psychoanalytic movement, it is necessary to concern ourselves with a group of theorists who felt that traditional psychoanalysts needed to expand their conception of the ego. These ego-psychologists or ego-analysts, as they are labeled, proposed that part of the ego is specifically built to handle vision and other sensory perceptions, learned muscular movement, conceptual problem solving, and other general developmental tasks. This part of the ego, labeled the *conflict free ego sphere* (Hartman, 1958), is separate from the defensive structure of the ego and that part of the ego that deals directly with conflicts arising from the id and super-ego.

Perhaps the most accomplished of the ego psychologists is Erick Erickson who expanded ego-functioning to include eight stages in the life cycle (Erickson, 1963). Each of these stages is seen as representing critical phases in the person's life—a very significant experience which influences the person's life from that time on. His theoretical foundations are based on data gathered from his study of children and adults in his practice and teaching of psychoanalysis and from his extensive work with American Indians.

His first stage begins with the task of establishing *basic trust* in others versus *basic mistrust*. This first stage corresponds to Freud's oral stage. The second stage is concerned with the amount of *autonomy* one is able to establish versus the *shame* and *doubt* one might develop. This would correspond to Freud's anal stage. In correspondence to Freud's phallic stage, Erickson posits the ego task of establishing *initiative* versus feeling *guilty* as a third stage.

Latency in the Freudian scheme is described by Erickson, in his fourth stage, as the time for finding *industry* in life versus producing in the person feelings of *inferiority*. The fifth stage *identity* versus *identity confusion,* occurring during adolescence, is perhaps Erickson's best known concept. He speaks of the person's need to enter into a *psychosocial moratorium* during which time the person explores different ways of living in order to find a suitable life plan. Erickson's book, *Identity, Youth and Crisis* (1968), provides insights that have been well received in the field of personality development.

Erickson spoke of the development of *intimacy* versus *isolation* as his sixth stage, occurring in young adulthood. In the seventh stage, occurring in the middle years (adulthood), the need to care for and maintain the well being of the next generation becomes the focal point of life. Erickson describes this stage with the terms *generativity* versus *stagnation*. With the eighth and last stage comes the problem of establishing *integrity* in one's life versus facing *despair,* as the person reaches full maturity and prepares for an end to life in old age. These last four stages of Erickson's theory can be seen as a differentiation and refinement of Freud's adult genital stage.

Neo-Freudians

The theorists discussed in this section are ones who have been very much influenced by Freud in the early formation of their theoretical work. Their concepts retain the psychodynamic quality of emphasizing the fact that early influences will be felt directly in the later life of the person and that pressures applied to one aspect of the person's life will result in a direct influence somewhere else in that person's system. They also generally accept the concept of repression and the other defense mechanisms used for protecting the person and keeping that person in some semblance of good order.

These neo-Freudians are united in their rejection of Freud's sexual libido theory (Sarason, 1966, 1972). They feel that some concept of psychological energy is necessary but that it is not necessary to maintain that the primary quality of that energy is sexual in nature. Most of the neo-Freudians (particularly Jung) expanded the general psychoanalytical theory to include an even wider range of events than Freud had proposed. In addition, the Neo-Freudians emphasize those events that are social in nature (with the possible exception of Jung), and they emphasize the role that social interaction has in influencing the personality of an individual.

Jung's Analytical Psychology. Carl Jung, an early associate of Sigmund Freud's, left the formal psychoanalytic movement because he felt the focus on the sexual nature of libido was too narrow. Jung's intention was to expand psychoanalysis in essentially a transpersonal direction. He was intensely interested in human creativity in the arts, literature, folklore, and themes of the occult. He, therefore, saw man's life as a part of all these events (Jung, 1963; Jung, 1964; Campbell, 1971).

His vehicle for accomplishing this is a concept that he called the *collective unconscious* in which he placed the learnings and residuals of past generations of man as an inherited part of each person's personality. A person is composed of all that has gone into constructing him, proceeding from the time of the evolution of the early forms of life up through each of the epochs of mankind which has led up to the present moment. Each person is more than a single individual; a person is specifically one's own unique inheritance, containing both the wisdom and pitfalls of the nature of that past.

The units of this past are called *archetypes,* that are constellations of the inherited characteristics that guide the life of the person. Two of the most important archetypes are the *anima,* the female aspects of men, and the *animus,* the masculine aspects of women. Because each of us has parents of both sexes, the characteristics of these people are within us. Jung advised that a man should not marry a woman who is antagonistic to the qualities of his anima. There needs to be a balance reached for the healthy person to exist. A woman should not be entirely passive, receptive, and caring. She should have some ways of expressing her more forceful, assertive, and aggressive nature. The same holds for a man in that he should allow for his tender feelings, even though his masculine qualities of forcefulness and aggressiveness remain his dominant features.

Consistent with his idea of balance, Jung posits the existence of the *shadow,* the other side of life. Because people usually give light to their best selves, the shadow is composed of the "evil" and darker side of life.

For Jung, the personality of an individual also contains a *personal unconscious* which consists of the personal experiences which have been removed from conscious awareness and an *ego* which restricts the conscious awareness of the person. The personal unconscious, however, is composed of *personal complexes* which are constellations of thoughts and feelings usually pertaining to a significant role figure, or dominant themes in organizing experiences. For example, repressed conflicting feelings might lead one to develop the role of a clown. During a rather fact-centered conversation, a person might find that, through his effort, the issues discussed are cast in the form of jokes. The collective unconscious, however, also influences the development of the complexes. They cannot be totally explained on the basis of past personal experiences.

Jung uses the term *persona* to refer to our public selves; the masks we wear for a social presentation of ourselves. Again, however, the collective unconscious influences the type of persona adopted. Finally, Jung used the term *individuation* to describe the process through which all these different aspects of the person are integrated in a new structural center for the person called the *self.* When the self has developed, the person is able to be truly wise in living. At this stage, the person has a fuller knowledge of what things in the world really mean, thereby enabling the person to develop even further than what a simpler knowledge of the world would allow. The total psychological structure is depicted in Figure 19-3.

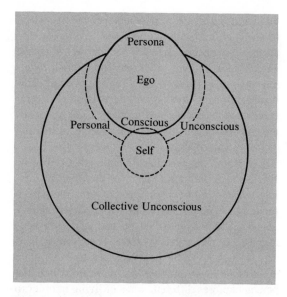

Fig. 19-3. Jung's model of personality structure. [From William B. Arndt, Jr., *Theories of Personality,* Macmillan, 1974, p. 313, which was adopted from Jolande Jacobi, *The Psychology of C. G. Jung,* Rev. Ed. (New Haven, Conn.: Yale University Press, 1962), pp. 27 and 126.]

Perhaps Jung's most direct effect on psychology has come through his study of individual differences. In pair-wise fashion, Jung proposes the existence of two basic attitudes (*introversion-extraversion*) and four psychological functions (*thinking-feeling and sensing-intuiting*). An *introvert* dwells on the life within himself; his own interpretations of the world. The *extravert* is primarily invested in the external world of other people and events. The *thinking-feeling* dimension refers to the way we process the information that we receive. A person disposed to *feeling* will reflect on how the information makes him feel, whereas a *thinking type* will try to relate the knowledge to other thoughts to see if it fits. The *sensing-intuiting* dimension refers to the way we receive information that we subsequently process. The *sensing type* reacts like a camera taking in the world as it appears, whereas the *intuiting type* represents the world as an abstract painter might, not as it appears on the outside but what lies behind it and gives it meaning. A summary of Jung's typologies are shown in Table 19-1. Work on these types has occurred largely through the development of a paper-and-pencil test (the Meyers-Briggs Type Indicator) based on Jung's two basic attitudes and four psychological functions. (Carlson and Levy, 1973; Levy et. al., 1972.)

Adler's Individual Psychology. Another early colleague and a close associate of Sigmund Freud, Alfred Adler, began to develop a theory that deemphasized the role of sexuality and emphasized the role of social goals (Adler, 1939; Ansbacher and Ansbacher, 1956). After leaving the psychoanalytic group, Adler developed his own theory which emphasized the uniquely individual pattern of life that is based on the types of goals the individual chooses. The emphasis placed on individuality and the active, creative choices the person makes, places Adler as an early developer of what was later to be called *humanistic* psychology.

For Adler, the person's life can be understood by examining the kind of life goals the person has chosen to pursue. These goals are lived, *as if* they were true and realistic ones. Basing his early theory on the philosophy of the *as if* developed by Hans Vaihinger (1925), Adler takes the position that the individual creates his own goals and acts as if these goals are externally real.

The dominant movement in life is from what he called "felt minus" to "felt plus." The person is born small and weak and feels the need to be strong and powerful. In the early stages of life, the person lives to overcome this position of inferiority. He used the term *inferiority complex* to de-scribe people who feel themselves to be extremely inadequate.

The movement in life is toward superiority or mastery and accomplishment. For Adler, this growth is in the direction of health only if the superiority is of a *social interest* nature and not selfish and self-serving. The person can only accomplish naturally and in a healthy manner the striving to "felt plus" by aiding the wellbeing and best interests of others. Adler felt that social interest is a natural state that the person evolves toward, but it is a very fragile condition and must be carefully nurtured. It is all too easy for the person to slip into a striving for selfish interest, thereby defeating himself in ever being able to develop into a truly healthy person.

The term *life style* is used by Adler to describe the unique pattern of the person's life. The life style is characterized and guided by the goals that the person has chosen. Personality change is accomplished by enabling the person to understand the nature of the destructive life style and the mistaken goals. The person is encouraged to adopt, instead, goals that are particularly high in social interest. Adler advised his patients who felt that they must worry, to worry themselves with how to be helpful to other people. It has been argued that Adler abandoned the *as if* (hypothetical) notion of life goals and substituted in their place life goals that have realistic (substantive) quality to them. He posited the concept of an evolutionary social reality that required an increasing social interest quality for healthy life goals (Rychlak, 1970).

Compared to other theorists, Adler uses very

Table 19-1. Jung's Eight Pure Types*

TWO ATTITUDES	FOUR FUNCTIONS			
	Thinking	*Feeling*	*Sensation*	*Intuition*
Extroversion: Oriented toward external events	Use of intellectual formulas based on objective facts	Judgments of pleasant-unpleasant determined by external standards	Realistic perception of external events	Penetration to essence of external events
Introversion: Interest in subjective experiences	Reflective reasoning about the subjective	Evaluation of pleasant-unpleasant based on subjective standards	Accurate, faithful experience of subjective factors	Creative elaboration of meaning of subjective states

* From Arndt, W. B. Jr. *Theories of Personality.* New York: Macmillan, 1974, p. 200.

few technical terms in his theory. It was Adler's intention to put forth a theory that could be read and used by the general public. His own interests centered around the problems of the common man. He was concerned with the industrial worker, the criminal, parents, children of troubled homes, and people having general marital problems.

The Social Theories of Horney and Fromm

Karen Horney and Erich Fromm were trained in orthodox Freudian psychoanalysis at the Berlin Psychoanalytic Institute, and both decided to depart from Freud's libido theory; both emphasized the social nature of man. Horney's expansion of psychoanalysis, however, was closely reasoned around the social life of the individual, while Fromm's emphasis was on the level of an institutional analysis of the social structure. (Sarason, 1972)

Karen Horney. For Karen Horney, the individual suffers from *basic anxiety* (Horney, 1945) which occurs as a consequence of the person's beginning life, surrounded by problems that are larger than his ability to cope. As a reaction to this basic anxiety, the person manifests three cardinal needs in the direction of social interaction: 1) the need to move toward people (need for affection); 2) the need to move away from people (the need for independence); and, 3) the need to move against people (the need for power) (Hall and Lindzey, 1970). In the healthy person, these needs are balanced and the person has realistic expectations concerning the ways to meet these needs. In the neurotic, however, one of these needs is dominant and leads the person to excessive behavior in order to either satisfy the need completely or to avoid it completely.

One of the most important contributions that Horney made to the psychoanalytic movement was to point out that a diagnosis of neurosis was only justified after having analyzed the social situation (Horney, 1937). If the particular society provides social sanction for the behavior, then that behavior is not psychodynamically determined, but rather, is simply a normal reaction of the person to the social situation. For example, if we observe a woman manifesting the classical hysterical symp-

toms of the dramatic display of emotions and, without awareness, has eroticized her language and her general body movements, and if that woman is from a small town in the deep south, we should not give a psychodynamic interpretation of her behavior. She is, in all likelihood, acting out what that society defines as "lady-like" behavior. If this same behavior were to occur in a woman from New England, then we may be more justified in using the psychodynamic explanation of a neurotic character development.

Erich Fromm. Being influenced by the social philosophy of Karl Marx, Erick Fromm's (1941, 1955, 1973) contribution to psychoanalytic thought has taken the form of a societal analysis of man's plight. For Fromm, man has a basic human nature that is manifest through the following five needs. First is the need for *relatedness* vs. *narcissism,* manifested in a search for truly productive love relationships with others. Second, the need for *transcendence* and *creativeness* vs. *destructiveness* is the need to reach beyond simple primitive interests to creative enterprises. Third, the need for *rootedness-brotherliness* vs. *incest* is the need to feel as if one belongs with others, to the family of mankind in something more than a superficial way. Closely related is the fourth need, the need for *identity-individuality* vs. *herd conformity*—knowing how to answer the question "Who am I?" as a specific individual person. The last need is the need for a *frame of orientation* and *devotion-reason* vs. *unrationality* which is a perspective the person evokes in order to establish trustworthy meanings for the events of life—a productive grasping of the world and one's place in it (Fromm 1955; Hall and Lindzey, 1970; Nordby and Hall, 1974). The modern societies that we have erected, however, are not at all well equipped to meet these needs. Man's plight, for the most part, is to feel alienated from his true human nature and to adapt a character structure destructive to himself and his fellow human beings.

People, however, have the creative ability to restructure society so that these basic human needs are met. Furthermore, man is free to choose either to oppose himself and adopt what Fromm (1964, 1973) termed a *necrophilous* orientation (a love for death and malicious destruction of others) or a *biophilous* orientation (a life-loving and creatively productive concern for others). Man has the ability to reshape societal institutions in such a manner that the basic human needs are met and harmonious relationships among all peoples can exist. Fromm described this new society as a *communitarian* socialism (Fromm, 1955).

Sullivan's Interpersonal Theory. Harry Stack Sullivan, a psychiatrist, was trained in both American empiricism and psychoanalysis. For him, the personality of an individual is viewed in terms of relationships with others. Personality is something that happens between people as they interact, rather than as an event which is primarily intrapersonal, that is, an event taking place within the person. The basic unit of personality is what Sullivan calls a *dynamism* defined as a "relatively enduring configuration of energy which manifests itself in characterizable processes in interpersonal relations" (Sullivan, 1938, p. 123). The dynamism is a patterning of relationships with people that characterize the person throughout his life. For example, a person who mistrusts others and is suspicious of them and their motives is said to have a dynamism of malevolence. A person who patterns at least part of his life according to lascivious relationships with others is said to have a dynamism of lust; the dynamism might be thought of as a habit (Hall and Lindzey, 1970). This concept has the advantage of placing the personality of individuals where it can be observed directly; it happens between people. In this way Sullivan can be seen as moving in the direction of the behaviorists by formulating an externally-oriented, objectively-observable base for studying personality (Rychlak, 1973).

For Sullivan, even when the events that he wants to discuss are internal events (for example, private thoughts), the nature of these private thoughts are basically social interactions which are internalized. The person is interacting with a fantasized social environment. Sullivan uses the term *personification* to describe the images of others that we carry around within us which are our codified abstraction of other people. For example, a woman might have personified her father as a person who could not be trusted and then used this personification in a projective manner in such a way that older males are reacted to as if they were untrustworthy. Personifications that are believed by the members of a social group are termed stereotypes, for example, the very big and/or muscular fellow who does not exercise very good judgment, "a meathead."

One of the most important dynamisms for Sullivan is the self-dynamism. This dynamism is built up as a result of our experiences with anxiety; it is designed to protect us from anxiety. Sullivan posited two motivational concepts—*satisfactions,* which are our biological needs, and *security,* which is our interpersonal need (see Figure 19-4). Anxiety is the feeling of discomfort felt when security is lacking. The self-dynamism protects us from feeling anxious and in some ways may be seen as a source of distortion in interpersonal relations. The healthy person is one who has a self structure loosened in such a manner that the person does not have to be rigidly self defensive.

Sullivan was particularly interested in the schizophrenic and the thought disorder present in such a person. This interest led him to formulate what he called modes of experiencing. These are the basic ways in which one takes the world in. First is the *prototaxic* mode where the experiences of the world are completely raw and unprocessed. It resembles Freud's id and is the undifferentiated and disjunctive events that are experienced by very young children and very disturbed people who are losing their grip on reality. The second mode is the *parataxic* mode, which is the first crude attempt to order events in life. Relationships are more or less assigned on the basis of chance momentary association. Even though the events are unrelated, they are seen as having a definite relationship. For example, if one becomes angry with another and that person at some point has an accident, the anger might be seen to be related to the accident. These thoughts are called *parataxic distortions* if they are preserved in adult life. The last mode and developmentally the most advanced is the *syntaxic mode,* in which a person begins to use symbolic thought and language in order to abstract the immediate situation in such a way that one can test his ideas with reality as perceived by others.

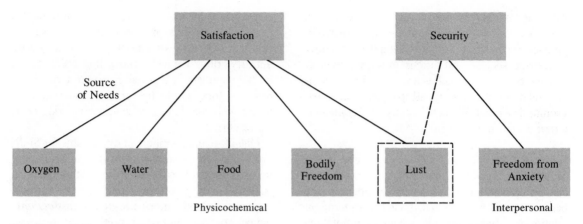

Fig. 19-4. Sullivan's system of needs. (From William B. Arndt, Jr., *Theories of Personality*, New York: Macmillan, 1974, p. 132)

Behavioristic Theory: Theories of Learning and Personality

These approaches to personality are based on the principles of learning gleaned from the work performed in experimental laboratories (see Chapter 9). In these laboratories, the study of animals provided a simplified situation where experimental manipulation could be accomplished with relative ease. The principles derived from this work were intended to provide information applicable to all living organisms including human beings. It is the intention of the learning theorists to build a theory based on the relationship between objective observable reactions of organisms (the response, R) and specifiable environmental events (the stimulus, S), in such a manner that orderly and predictable stimulus-response (S-R) connections could be formulated.

These applications have resulted in personality theories which are simpler in every respect when compared to other theories. They have fewer terms, they deemphasize inferred internal mechanisms, and they usually do not specify structural or developmental patterns. There is an attempt to define most terms in an objective, externally observable manner. In this respect, the learning theories stand in sharp contrast to the psychodynamic formulations which contained hypothetical terms like collective unconscious and super-ego.

It is not uncommon for the learning theorist to place major emphasis on personality change—how one set of troublesome behavior is eliminated and replaced by a more pleasing set of responses. This emphasis on change is no doubt a reflection of a kind of American optimism that is built into the environmentalist approach; a belief that if the proper environment is provided, a person can develop (change) in any desired direction (Rychlak, 1973).

There are many different approaches to learning in personality. However, this chapter will cover only examples from three major orientations: the traditional S-R theory of John Dollard and Neil Miller; the radical behavioralism of B. F. Skinner; and the position that has come to be known as social learning theory.

Dollard and Miller's Learning Theory of Personality

Taking their theoretical concepts from Clark Hull's theory of learning, John Dollard and Neil Miller (1950) formulated a theory of personality which attempted, among other things, to translate aspects of Freud's theory into learning theory terms. This venture was undertaken not because of any animosity toward Freud, but rather because these two men admired Freud's accomplishments and hoped that learning theory would aid in "tightening up" the psychoanalytic system so that formal experimentation could take place.

For Dollard and Miller, the personality of an individual is composed of complex sets of stimulus-response connections called *habits*. A habit is an inferred bond between the stimulus and the response, the strength of which is directly related to the *reinforcement* that the organism receives for producing the response to the particular stimulus. Those habits that receive the most reinforcement are maintained the longest. A reinforcement is defined as any event that will lead to a reduction in the strong stimulation (the *drive*) which aroused the organism initially and that increases the probability that the response will reoccur on future occasions. For any learning to take place, the organism must be motivated; a drive state must be present. Particularly when dealing with very young children, these drives refer to the biological drives of hunger, thirst, sex, and relief from pain. The concept of a reduction in drive is very similar to Freud's concept of the pleasure principle, because drive reduction is seen as a pleasurable event. It must be noted, however, that Dollard and Miller did not strictly adhere to a drive reduction hypothesis. They viewed sexual stimulations as reinforcing and saw some drive reduction as not necessarily pleasurable.

For example, after a short training period, a child who particularly likes sweets and has not received any in the last few hours (a motivated organism) hears the hall clock strike eight (the stimulus) and then trundles off to bed (the response), where he is comforted with cookies and hot milk (the reinforcement) for going to bed on time. In addition to particular S-R connections that have been reinforced, learning will *generalize* to other conditions that resemble the original learning condition. Through higher level concept generalization, the child will respond also to being told that it is eight o'clock, even if he does not hear the stimulus of the chimes.

Realizing that knowledge of the external stimulus and the external response is inadequate to handle complex situations, Dollard and Miller have allowed for the operation of internally-mediating processes which allow the organism to develop his own modification of the external stimulation. The external stimulus gives rise to an internal response which is said to have *cue* value for the organism. It

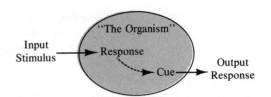

Fig. 19-5. Dollard and Miller's Learning and Personality model. (From Joseph F. Rychlak, *Introduction to Personality and Psychotherapy: A Theory-Construction Approach,* New York: Houghton Mifflin, 1973, p. 295)

serves as a signal that directs the organism to some action (English and English, 1958). The internal *cue* leads in turn to the external response, as depicted in Figure 19-5. The internally *response-produced cue* directs the response of the organism, not the external stimulus. The personality of an individual is manifest through these internal cues. It is obvious that the same external stimulus is responded to differently, depending on the different meanings (cue values) that the external stimulus has acquired.

The concept of *secondary reinforcement* and *acquired drives* were introduced into the theory in order to account for complex learnings that occur as the organism matures. For Dollard and Miller, anxiety is a learned or acquired drive used in learning the responses that are known as the defense mechanisms in Freudian theory. Repression, for example, is a response of stopping thought and memory when certain cues are detected. This response to the particular situation is reinforced by a reduction in anxiety, thus, the acquisition of the drive. Other acquired drives include achievement, affiliation, and conformity, to name but a few. These acquired drives, then, have their acquired or secondary reinforcers that will reduce these drives. Proportionally, these reinforcers might be 1) accomplishing things rapidly and well, 2) having other people attend to us, and 3) feeling the normative pattern of society fit snugly around our shoulders. These acquired drives and their reinforcers may then be used to shape complicated response patterns that form the fabric of the individual's personality.

Like Freud, Dollard and Miller emphasize early learning. For them, the first S-R connections are the most important. All further learning has to be based on this original learning and necessarily influences all further connections. The Freudian stages of development are treated as if they were special learning situations.

As important as any other aspect of the theory, Dollard and Miller were concerned with how S-R connections once established can be changed. The first method *extinction,* is accomplished by terminating the reinforcement that the organism is receiving. The child who is no longer attended to and fed in his room will soon not respond to the eight o'clock chimes by going to bed. The second method is to administer some aversive stimulation such as reprimand when the response occurs. A third method, *counter conditioning,* is accomplished by positively reinforcing a response that is antagonistic to the present response. When the chimes sound, we might continue to play with the child in the livingroom, thereby reinforcing a set of behaviors antagonistic to his running off to bed.

However, this last procedure of counter conditioning, when it is first started, will place the child in *conflict.* Dollard and Miller refer to this type of conflict as the most complex but most frequently occurring conflict for the human being—*double*

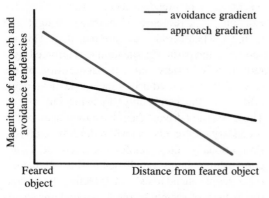

Fig. 19-6. Magnitude of approach and avoidance gradients as a function of distance from feared object. [From William B. Arndt, Jr., *Theories of Personality,* Macmillan, 1974, which was adapted from N. Miller, "Experimental Studies of Conflict," *Personality and the Behavior Disorders,* Ed. J. Mcv. Hunt (New York: The Ronald Press, 1944, I, 434.) p. 359.]

approach-avoidance conflict. This conflict occurs when an organism is both repelled by and attracted to two different goals simultaneously. The child is attracted to the cookies, but in order to get them, he must leave his play in the livingroom and go to bed. At the same time, the child is attracted to the play and attention being received in the livingroom but is repelled by the idea that continuing to play is delaying those nice big cookies.

The other types of conflict Dollard and Miller refer to are simpler in structure. Simple *approach-avoidance,* as shown in Figure 19-6, is a conflict created when an organism is both repelled by and attracted to a single goal. *Avoidance-avoidance* conflict occurs when the organism is attempting to avoid two undesirable outcomes. Finally, *approach-approach* conflict occurs when the organism has to decide between two desirable but incompatible outcomes.

Skinner's Theory of Operant Behavior

The theory developed by B. F. Skinner is by far the most parsimonious of all the behaviorist's positions. Skinner rejects the traditional explanations of behavior based on personality traits, motives, or psychodynamic interpretations. He argues that to explain an individual's behavior in terms of needs, drives, or inferred underlying processes such as the build up of "habit strength" as emphasized in the S-R formulation, is to explain nothing at all. Instead, Skinner proposes that we must analyze the functional relationships that exist between one's observable behavior and the environmental conditions and events that directly influence it. Only through such an objective and empirical approach can we hope to achieve and demonstrate "lawfulness" in behavior.

In order to understand the personality of an individual, we need to describe the conditions under which behavior occurs, the actual behavior emitted, and the consequences of such behavior. A description of these three terms make up what Skinner calls a *contingency of reinforcement.* The first term of the contingency represents antecedent events—the prevailing stimulus conditions of the environment which act, or have served in the past, as the occasion upon which a particular behavior is followed by reinforcement. Such stimulus events do not "elicit" a particular behavior in the Pavlovian sense, but rather "set the stage" for certain behaviors to be emitted and reinforced. Thus, an individual may be said to be rowdy, boisterous, and excited during a football game, but reverent, quiet, and calm during a religious service. In each case, particular behaviors are said to have come under the control of different stimuli in the environment, because in each environmental situation, different kinds of behavior have been differentially reinforced in that individual's past by the social community.

The future probability of a particular behavior—whether it shows an increase or decrease in the frequency of occurrence over time—depends on how that behavior operates on the environment such that reinforcement or punishment occurs as a consequence of that behavior. Unlike the conceptions of most learning theories, Skinner classifies the consequences of behavior as reinforcers or punishers depending on what functional relationship these response-contingent events or consequences share with the behavior emitted. Thus, reinforcement is defined not in terms of drive or tension reduction, but simply as a process or operation that will increase the future probability of that behavior.

In a very strict sense, the personality of an individual *is* the person's behavior, which in turn is determined by the interaction of that person's previous history of reinforcement and the prevailing contingencies of reinforcement in his current environment.

In Chapter 9, we saw how the techniques and principles of operant conditioning have been applied to shape relatively complex behaviors in lower animals, and how the rate and patterning of this behavior has been maintained and modified by appropriately arranging the schedule of reinforcement which controls it. It should not be surprising, therefore, to find that these same procedures have also been applied by clinicians in the successful treatment of behaviors generally attributed to personality disorders in man such as alcoholism, sexual perversion, and overeating, to name but a few.

Not only have these procedures been applied to overt public behaviors such as those indicated above, but they can be applied to private events such as "urges" or "desires." The assumption is that the same variables governing operant behavior apply equally to both public and private events. Particularly important in this area have been the behavioral programs developed that enable an individual to bring his behavior under stronger stimulus control by instructing him how to arrange his surrounding environment. Skinner (1948, 1971, 1974) has elaborated and expanded on this subject to also include the design for a better society as well as carefully spelling out the philosophical issues involved in this controversial direction.

The Social Learning Theories

Social learning theorists wish to explain the complexities of social life, while using the language and experimental orientation of the learning theories. Like Skinner, they want reinforcement tied to response contingencies rather than to hypothetical tensions or drive reduction. The social learning theorists, however, see the need to posit mediational processes in order to explain complex learning. In fact, the manner in which the social learning theorists treat mediational processes is similar to that of some of the humanistic psychologists and the ego-psychologists of the psychoanalytic group.

Recently, Walter Mischel (1973a, 1976) has listed a number of concerns of the social learning theorists that might well serve our purposes in examining these theories. They are concerned with *competencies* that people have to generate material that is appropriate to the situation in which they live. The individual is seen as *incoding* and *categorizing* material in a form not unlike a computer might go about the task of storing and retrieving information. The person's behavior in a particular situation is heavily influenced by what the person *expects* concerning the consequences that certain behaviors might have that he performs in a given situation, and what *expectancies* he has concerning stimulations or signs indicating the occurrence of related events. Additionally, there is a need to know how the person subjectively *values* these outcomes. Finally, there is a need to be concerned with the *self-regulation* system of the person, whereby he monitors and regulates his own behavior and brings it under his own control. This last concern is one that the social learning theorists share with all psychologists.

The first example of work in this field is the research on imitation by Bandura and Walters (1963), and Bandura (1973, 1977). Through their work, we have found that a great deal of *vicarious learning* takes place. Much of the learning that comprises the personality of the individual comes to be his through simply his having been able to observe an appropriate reinforcing model. This means that we learn the kinds of patterns of social behavior we manifest by observing and selectively imitating the actions of those around us. In this paradigm, reinforcement serves only to influence the performance of the learning and is not necessary for the new material to be acquired. For example, whether or not we are reinforced for aggressive behavior will influence whether or not we often overtly act aggressively. We have learned aggressive behavior simply by having observed someone being aggressive. In addition to research on aggressive behavior and phobia, this theory has stimulated some interesting research and theoretical speculation of the role of television on the personality structure of children and adults (Bandura et al, 1969; Liebert et al, 1973).

A second example of work in the field of social learning is the research of Julian Rotter (1966) and his colleagues. One of their main concerns has been with a personality dimension labeled "internality-externality locus of control of reinforcement" (I-E). Rotter has developed a paper-and-pencil measure for detecting the extent to which a person believes that the reinforcements that he gets are under his direct control. A person who scores high on this scale is manifesting the belief that chance or luck has a lot to do with the rewards he receives. A person who scores low on this scale is manifesting the belief or expectation that his own actions have a great deal to do with whether or not he receives rewards. The research with this instrument has been extensive and has generally confirmed theoretical predictions. It has been found that Externals are less perceptive of their environment when compared to Internals. Persons who score highly on externality generally come from the lower classes, particularly the black lower class. This is perhaps a realistic expectation for them to have. Internals are more likely to be found among the members of social action groups. With little reflection, it is easy to see how important this construct can be for persons trying to live effective lives in our very complex society (Rotter, 1966; Lefcourt, 1966; Rotter and Hochreich, 1975).

Humanistic Approaches to Personality

Generally, humanistic psychologists describe themselves as offering needed completion to the description of the person as it is stated in psychoanalytic and behavioristic traditions. There is usually a heavy emphasis on the conscious and deliberate *choices* that the person makes throughout that person's life. Optimally, these choices serve as *commitments* the person makes in order to guide the individual's life in a particular direction. With these choices and commitments made, the person is then seen as *responsible* for the kind of life that person leads. In terms of content, the humanists emphasize the passions and emotions that are most uniquely man's own. On the one hand, there is a concern with loneliness, dread, and despair and, on the other hand, there is a concentrated study of joy, exultation, elation, and religious transcendence.

This section will include an examination of the general class of theories that have been most concerned with the concept of the "self" (the self-theories), an experiential and phenomenological study of persons which nevertheless contains an access to traditional scientific methods (the personal construct theory of George A. Kelly), and the contributions of the existentialists which also includes the study of the truly healthy and superbly functioning individual.

Self Theory

Many of the earliest definitions of psychology (Hill, 1888) saw the discipline as "the study of the conscious self." Yet for perhaps as much as thirty years during which psychology was energetically establishing itself as a science, "the self" was exiled from respectable theory. Victor Raimy published a dissertation (Raimy, 1943) which, along with the writings of Rogers, (Rogers, 1951) seemed to reopen the role of the self in personality. Arthur W. Combs with Donald Snygg presented, at about the same time, a "phenomenological" theory of personality (Snygg and Combs, 1949) that was later revised and called a "perceptual" approach (Combs et al, 1975). All of these developed similar positions, centering about the phenomenal self or self-concept as the fundamental structure in personality theory.

According to this position, behavior of all human beings is lawful, and predictable in the sense that behavior is determined by the perceptions of the individual. Therapists, educators, or lay persons, for that matter, might better understand themselves or others were they able to determine the perceptions of the situation held by the other person. A child, who is withdrawn in a spelling class, can be understood if the teacher knows the child sees the class as a probable failure experience. A young adult, who has strong libidinal drives but who, however, sees all women as distant and pure as his own mother, could be expected to turn to homosexuality.

The central set of perceptions that most determine behavior is the perception of the self, or the self-concept. Thus, this self or self-concept is not synonymous with the "body," but is rather a set of not necessarily "real" perceptions of what one is like. It may be thought of as a highly organized system, that maintains its organization and consists in a sense of perceptions of the body (I am strong, I am tall), perceptions of other objects or persons which are identified by the subject as "self" (my car, my stereo set, my children, my spouse), value judgments concerning these aspects of the self (my children are good, I am bad), and ideological values (I believe in democracy, justice is important to me).

Some of the most frequently used methods for the investigation of the self-concept stress an overall *self-evaluation* which may be considered as a factor within the self-concept—indeed some regard the entire self-concept as a self-evaluation. However, a convenient model of the structure of

the self-concept is that it is organized into roles (I am a father, I am a student, I am a mother, I am a lumberjack) of varying degrees of importance or centrality to the individual.

If one can predict or understand behavior from all of the individual's perceptions, then that set of perceptions which is most useful in predicting behavior and which, in fact, does determine much of the individual's significant behavior, is the self-concept. Adults who see themselves as poor dancers may be expected to avoid dances. Children who see themselves as good athletes will go into new athletic contests with enthusiasm.

A large scientific literature has been built around the self-concept since Raimy's first study, which has been critically summarized in a multivolume work by Wylie (1974). Fitts (1972) has shown a narrowing of the self-concept in psychotic and neurotic patients. Engle (1959) has shown changes in the self-concept in pre- and post-adolescent girls paralleling the well known physiological changes in the body with changes in the self. Changes in the perceived self were the focus of the Rogers and Dymond (1954) investigations in psychotherapy. Positive changes in the self as perceived by the client were associated with client-centered psychotherapy.

Hall and Lindzey (1970) cite a long list of personality theorists who have utilized the self as a central concept including Adler, Allport, Angyal, Cattell, Freud, Goldstein, and Jung. They conclude: "clearly personality theorists today are characterized by an increased interest in the self and attendant processes" (p. 590). Historically, the self disappeared and has returned. The phenomenologists and the existentialists are primarily responsible for this. However, it is the growing body of research literature in the self which will assure its durable status in psychological science in coming generations.

A Motivational System: In contrast to the more complex Freudian drive systems, the self-theorists, particularly Combs, Snygg, and Rogers ordinarily favor a single motivational force—the need to maintain and enhance the phenomenal self, or to seek personal adequacy. Snygg and Combs (1949), and Combs, Richards and Richards (1975) insist that all behavior is explained in response to this drive, including seemingly self-destructive behavior. If one bears in mind that it is the phenomenal or perceived self that is involved, even externally inconsistent aspects of behavior may be seen as fitting this model. Thus, an individual who heatedly insists on a position which is known to be incorrect during a public argument, is maintaining or defending the "self." Butterfly, in Puccini's opera, is maintaining her "self" as a respectable woman by committing hara-kiri when her husband brings home an American wife. The student who seeks a higher degree, the social leader who throws a party for important people, and the beggar on the street corner are all enhancing themselves—as they each see their "selves." Under threat, the individual maintains the self; under challenge, one enhances the self.

Since first advanced by Lewin (1936), the concept of a "field" has been enlarged by the self-theorists to include the entire complex of perceptions comprising the individual's private world. In a second sense, all of the individual's behavior is related to the perceptions of the world about the *phenomenal field*. Rather than being seen as a field of forces, the phenomenal field is a field of meanings, and perceptions and feelings, personal meanings which the individual has for things, events, and ideas that comprise the individual's personal world. The concept has considerable value in teaching and in psychotherapy, since it places upon the therapist or the teacher the responsibility to attempt to see the world as the child sees it or as the client does in order to be able to facilitate the person's growth or learning.

The concept of *congruence* has become an important one in Rogers' system and has resulted in what Rogers refers to as a "general law." "The more that Y experiences the communications of X as a congruence of experience, awareness and communication, the more the ensuing relationship will involve: a tendency toward more mutually accurate understanding of the communications; improved psychological adjustment and functioning in both parties; mutual satisfaction in the relationship" (Rogers, 1961, p. 354).

Underlying the self-systems, particularly that of Rogers, is the emphasis on the meanings, values, and perceptions of the person, and also, the some-

times directly stated, sometimes implied assumption that individuals are independent, self-adjusting creatures (see Figure 19-7). These individuals should not be led (or misled) by therapists or teachers, but should be given the opportunity to grow, seek their own values, and their own destinies. Rogers originally referred to his system of therapy as "nondirective," but subsequently as "client-centered," and even more recently, as "person-centered." And a significant amount of evidence has been assembled over the years to support this position. Raskin (1952) demonstrated that successful clients become more and more reliant upon their own values rather than upon the values of others.

Supporting a possible contention that personality theories are a product of their political milieu, Rogers' system in a sense is a more "democratic" one compared with the authoritarianism of orthodox psychoanalysis. Rogers' system and the other self-theorists clearly pioneered the emphasis, even glorification, of the individual. Like psychoanalysis, it was born out of intimate relationships with

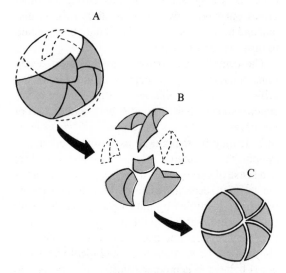

Fig. 19-7. Rogers' Person-Centered model of change. A. The self as poorly organized figure with denied and distorted symbolization. B. The loosening of self-structure over a course of psychotherapy. C. A reorganization and acceptance of self as organismically sensed at the completion of therapy. (From Joseph F. Rychlak, *Introduction to Personality and Psychotherapy: A Theory-Construction Approach*, New York: Houghton Mifflin, 1973, p. 433)

humans deeply in trouble. Rogers' drew heavily on his experiences in clinical and counseling work. In addition, however, Rogers much more than Freud, attempted to establish an empirical, experimental basis for his constructs. Although under heavy attack by Eysenck (1961, p. 707–708) and others, Rogers (1961), Rogers and Dymond (1954), and Seeman and Raskin (1953) have fostered a wealth of research literature, indicating an ability to generate testable concepts and hypotheses. In recent years, Rogers has expanded his theoretical system, originally developed in connection with psychotherapy, to include other human relationship problems such as marriage and personal power (1977). In 1978, he postulated a "formative tendency" at work at every level in the universe (Rogers, 1978).

Kelly's Personal Construct Theory

In developing personal construct theory, George Kelly (1955) hoped to promote an understanding of the person living and taking action in a world that is in a state of constant change and reorganization. He based his theory on a philosophical position he called *constructive alternativism* which implies that every fact that we now know might very well change as we gain new perspectives on our world (see Figure 19-8). We are limited only by our own creative imagination in our ability to change ourselves and subsequently the world in which we live. In other words, it is possible to

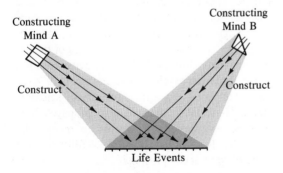

Fig. 19-8. Kelly's model of alternative constructions of the same life event. (From Joseph F. Rychlak, *Introduction to Personality and Psychotherapy: A Theory-Construction Approach*, New York: Houghton Mifflin, 1973, p. 476)

have a number of different interpretations of the world existing simultaneously without any immediate concern with which one is correct.

Kelly takes the position that people construct for themselves their own personal theory of the world and go about testing that theory through the kind of life they lead. In this way, *every person is a scientist*. A person evolves a set of personal dimensions in order to make sense out of the world. These dimensions of personal meaning are called *personal constructs* and are cast in a bipolar and dichotomous form. For example, a person might use the dimension kind-cruel in dealing with another and decide that another person is essentially kind with all the implications that has for how that person is to be approached. A construct is then a prediction about an event that is either *validated* or *invalidated* through the person's experiences. On the basis of experiences, the person then confirms predictions or reconstrues the event. For example, it may be decided that the whole dimension kind-cruel is inappropriate and that the other person can best be understood by applying the construct helpful-harmful.

In order to assess personal constructs, Kelly devised the *Role Construct Repertory Test* (Rep Test) that requires a person to consider some of the most important people in life in terms of how two of these people are alike and different from a third. This named quality becomes one end of the construct and the person supplies what is considered to be the opposite of this quality in order to generate the other end of a bipolar construct dimension. Taken in sets of three, the person usually is requested to produce about twenty construct dimensions. For example, when considering his sister, himself, and his wife, a man might decide that he and his wife are rather *outgoing* when compared to his sister. He then gives *shy* as the opposite of outgoing, thus producing the dimension *outgoing-shy*. Research using this instrument has led to empirical investigations in the areas of person perception, friendship, psychotherapy, and psychopathology to name but a few. (Bannister, 1963, 1977; Duck, 1973; Fransella, 1972; Fransella and Bannister, 1977; Landfield, 1971; Slater, 1976).

For Kelly, the world is constantly changing; therefore, there is no need for motivational constructs. The problem is to predict the direction of this movement and change. The direction is chosen by the person, as that person faces a world structured through sets of personal constructs. The person makes what Kelly called the *elaborative choice:* the person chooses that direction which offers the greatest possibilities for developing the person's own further understanding of the world. This can be in the direction of either taking in more varied kinds of events or investigating in more detail those events that directly confront him. In this way, the person is totally responsible for the kind of outlook on life that is assumed, and, therefore, has the possibility of making an increasingly more useful and creative approach to the world. Every vantage point in life gives one new possibilities for action. The external world never dictates the way in which we are to live, but rather holds us to the kind of questions we are able to ask about it.

Kelly was always striving for a new way to understand what the aim of psychology should be. The best objective might be to understand that people are in a constant state of becoming what they might be through behaving in such a way that a new "self" emerges. People actually make themselves up as they go along by undertaking things based on their present understanding of life events. One of the most well-known of the therapeutic techniques that Kelly developed is called *fixed role therapy,* where the person is invited to become a person with a different understanding of the world than is now possible and to enact this new understanding for a two-week period. It is through enacting a new position that people have the possibility of creating new alternatives in their constructural schemata. The person can then choose that alternative offering the greatest possibility for personal growth. Again we see the implications of Kelly's philosophical position of constructive alternativism.

The Existentialists and the Higher Level Model of the Person

In the third quarter of the twentiety century, there emerged in personality theory a new, free spirit that described itself as "the third force psychology." (The first and second forces were behavioristic psychology and psychoanalysis, respectively). Loosely allied and presenting varying degrees of a rather loose theory structure, third force psychology is composed of phenomenologists, existentialists, humanists, and the self-psychologists. These groups include Binswanger (1963), Buytendijk (1962) Moustakas (1961), and many others. Students, restless under the unpleasant constraints of orthodox psychology, flocked to these new thinkers and some permitted themselves unrestrained attacks on behavioristic psychology and highly imaginative, hardly testable constructs. It must be pointed out that the distinctions that distinguish humanists, existentialists and phenomenologists from each other will probably occupy the literature for another half century (Landsman, 1958). Some of the most distinguished of this group are Rollo May, A. H. Maslow, and Sidney M. Jourard. These psychologists will be discussed in more detail as representative of the third force.

The celebration of the human characteristics of the human being undoubtedly would be considered one of the greatest motivating factors for the third force generals. Smarting under the criticisms of orthodox psychology, they rejected the model of the person as described by the classical learning theories and elevated the science in their eyes to deal with a human just a "little lower than the angels" (Holy Scriptures, 1955, Psalm 8, Verse 5). Love, joy, ecstasy, even absurdity and anxiety were to be the subject matter of this expanded science of the human being.

If perception and the self-concept were central concepts for the self and the phenomenological psychologists (Landsman, 1961), then the study of *experience* is perhaps the common bond of the entire third force. From time to time, experience has been exiled from psychology (Landsman, 1974) as unsuitable, even impossible, for serious scientific study. Thus, the serious student of psychology must be forewarned that there are many who regard the efforts of the humanists as futile and that much of their accomplishments have flown in the face of more conservative psychological scientists.

Behavior is ordinarily considered to be the subject matter of psychology; *experience* for the humanists is equally pertinent though obviously a less quantifiable concept. Nevertheless, a significant number of the third force psychologists have been able to develop procedures that provide for the study of experience. Maddi (1961) studied the experience of ''unexpectedness'' that required subjects to predict whether the next page of a booklet in their hands would have on it a number or the beginning of a sentence. Maddi further studied the experience of variety and demonstrated that small degrees of variety are pleasant and large degrees are unpleasant. Lynch (1968) studied positive experiences and demonstrated that subjects report twice as many negative experiences as positive when asked to report intense experiences. The study implies a condition presently existing in persons which permits a greater experiencing of the unhappy and the negative and also implies, from the existential point of view, that there is a great well of positive experience, joy, and happiness which is largely untouched by humans in their present life styles. Horn (1977) has presented evidence that the integration of these negative experiences into the self is characteristic of high level functioning women.

Other key efforts in the humanistic-existential positions include a logical wrestling with two ancient philosophical mysteries: freedom and choice. Choice is considered in Sartre's (1956) existentialism as a fundamental characteristic of humanness. It is the person's absurd fate that choices must be made, and in making those choices, the animal becomes human. Many behaviorists see the human behavior as determined; that the person has no choices, or the choices the person has are determined. The person follows the dictates of an unpitying environment or of a mechanically predictable internal set of responses to pleasure or pain. The humanists, on the other hand, insist that the person does make real choices, has the freedom of will to do so, and that such a decision is a fundamental characteristic of humans. Thus, Jean Francois Steiner (1967), in his chronicle of the German death camp *Treblinka*, describes the dehumanizing effect of choicelessness on the victims—they seemingly had no choice but to be killed by their tormentors—until one person in the barracks hung himself. An electrifying change took place now that it was clear each person did have a choice—to be killed or to kill himself. From this,

other choices appeared—to be killed while attempting to break out. As each successive, though pathetic choice appeared, a rehumanizing of the prisoners emerged.

A characteristic of the existentialists which cannot be ignored is their impatience with the usual criteria of personality theory and for many, internal contradictions, or rather intramural contradictions, are commonplace. Thus, Combs and Snygg do, in a fashion, side with those who advocate a determinism in their humanism—that man is determined by his perceptions.

Almost a synonym for existentialism is ''being.'' ''Dasein'' or ''daseinsanalyse'' as applied to the work of Binswanger (1963) may be translated as ''being here'' or ''an analysis of being here.'' Paul Tillich (1952) wrote *The Courage to Be,* and Sidney Jourard (1971) edited a collection entitled *To Be or Not to Be.* Although a key word and key concept, being is defined only in the broadest terms. May's concept of ''being,'' includes ''becoming'' or potentiality, what the individual may become, and May suggests this may be a better, less literal translation of ''dasein.'' According to May, it illustrates the nonstatic nature of the concept, is not opposed to but is paired with nonbeing in that the knowledge of the possibility of nonbeing or death in itself increases the individual's consciousness of his own being. Illustrating the concept, May describes the ''I-Am'' experience of one of his clients:

Later on that night I woke up and it came to me this way, ''I accept the fact that I am an illegitimate child.'' *But* ''I am not a child anymore.'' So it is, ''I am illegitimate'' That is not so either: ''I was born illegitimate'' Then what is left? What is left is this. *''I Am . . .''*

What is this experience like: It is a primary feeling—it feels like receiving the deed to my house. It is the experience of my own aliveness not caring whether it turns out to be an ion or just a wave. It is like when a very young child I once reached the core of a peach and cracked the pit, not knowing what I would find and then feeling the wonder of finding the inner seed, good to eat in its bitter sweetness . . . (May, et al., 1958, p. 43).

May is responsible for the careful development of a number of concepts in humanistic psychology including a reconsideration of the meaning of "anxiety." Drawing heavily from Kierkegaard, May differentiates between normal and neurotic anxiety, terms heavily used in contemporary clinical and counseling psychology. He defines *anxiety* as:

The apprehension cued off by a threat to some value which the individual holds essential to his existence as a self. The threat may be to physical life itself, i.e. death; or to psychological life, i.e. loss of freedom. Or it may be to some value the person identifies with his existence as a self: patriotism, the love of a special person, prestige among one's peers, devotion to scientific truth or to religious belief (May, 1967, p. 72).

In May's system, normal anxiety is a necessary concomitant of growth and is realistic in that it does not exaggerate the threat while neurotic anxiety:

. . . is a reaction which is disproportionate to the threat, involves repression and other forms of intrapsychic conflict and is managed by various kinds of blocking-off activity and awareness (May, 1967, p. 80).

May is truly representative of the humanistic-existialistic phenomenological group in that his contributions are largely conceptual rather than experimental. He is generally acknowledged to be one of the finest scholars in the movement and draws heavily from the earliest thinkers in philosophical considerations about the behavior of man, including Nietsche, Husserl, Heidegger, and Kierkegaard. In addition, he has contributed to the thinking of, and has used the writings of, the contemporary existentialists including Sartre, Binswanger, Buytendijk, Boss, and others. His writings have been highly praised both for their literary quality and their psychological perceptiveness. *Love and Will* (May, 1969) was prominently mentioned for the Nobel Prize in Literature. He is an appreciator, though not a creator, of experimental approaches and has served as a stabilizing factor amongst some of the extreme positions in the third force psychology.

A preoccupation with high level personality, the superb person, or the "healthy personality" was an obvious outgrowth of the third force. Intimations of such conceptualizations preceded the development of existentialist psychology and were an inevitable extension of the mental health or mental illness mode for adjustment. Thus, Jahoda (1958) suggested the concept of the "mentally healthy" individual. Rogers (1961) utilized the term, "fully-functioning," Maslow (1971) preferred, "self-actualizing," and Landsman (1970) chose, "the beautiful and noble person," seemingly all to describe the same kind of personality. Jourard, (1974) favored the term "healthy personality" and placed a great emphasis on authenticity, openness or "transparency." Jourard's experiences as a psychotherapist and his own personal style of living convinced him that openness of self fostered high level functioning. He backed up his conceptualizations with a series of studies on "self disclosure" and his scale is widely used as an indicator of healthy personality. In addition, Jourard is one of the few third force psychologists who remained largely uncritical of the research concept. He and his students published a large number of studies on self-disclosure and touching, some of which were assembled in the volume entitled *Self-Disclosure* (Jourard, 1971).

Jourard was in the center of a group of psychologists and philosophers who were pioneers in the development of body psychology, in contrast to physiological psychology. This was a holistic view of the human body, not as a collection of organic parts, cells, tissues, nerves, bones, but as a whole experience for man, truly "the body of experience or the experience of the body." Thomas Hanna (1970) and others were strongly influenced by Jourard and he by them in this regard.

Utilizing two diagrams, one front and one rear view of the body, Jourard divided the body into 24 regions and in an ingenious test asked male and female unmarried students to indicate areas in which they have been touched (or seen) and by whom. The women in the group showed more experiences of touching and being touched by members of their family (mothers and fathers included) while the males seemed less "favored." In addition, the opposite sex friend seemed to do most of the touching in the Jourard study causing him to suggest that most regions of the young adult's body remain untouched unless he has a close friend of the opposite sex" (Jourard, 1968).

Jourard was firmly convinced that much of psychological research was badly biased because the subjects, usually college students, were not truly disclosing themselves to the experimentor. He reports a study by Powell (1963) in which "self-disclosure from the researcher was associated with significant increases in the subjects disclosures of both positive and negative self-references," (Jourard, 1968, p. 28), thus suggesting that more valid results would be obtained in even nonhumanistic research.

Jourard's conception of the healthy personality is embodied in the final revision of his major textbook, *The Healthy Personality:*

. . . a way for a person to act, guided by intelligence and respect for life so that his needs are satisfied and he will grow in awareness, competence and the capacity for love (Jourard, 1974, p. 28).

Thus, like almost all the contemporary humanists, he placed first the needs of the self as preliminary or "prerequisite" to the attainment of that state, and secondly a relationship to his fellow humans, one of caring and love.

Jourard's emphasis on openness and truthfulness, or transparency, will have set a pattern for much of humanistic psychology. Perhaps his own research places him in the ranks of the most productive in research among the third force psychologists. Yet, he did not let his concern about experimental approaches subdue his creativity, and he remains as one of the most innovative thinkers in the movement, even beyond his accidental death in 1974. One of his strongest arguments for use of "great literature" and dialogue as characteristic of high level functioning was posthumously published (Jourard, 1978).

Throughout the development of humanistic psychology, Abraham H. Maslow has perhaps been its most impressive figure. Maslow fashioned, piece by piece, a personality theory that permitted consideration of the highest capacities of the human. From an initial simplistic position that man is "good," Maslow later avowed:

It is too simple to say 'man is basically good' or 'man is basically evil'. . . . The correct way now would be to say 'Man can become good (probably) and better and better, under a hierarchy of better and better conditions. But it also is very easy, even easier for him to become bad or evil or sick, deprived of those fundamental 'conditions' and 'rights' (Maslow, 1972, p. 88).

While this illustrates Maslow's remarkable flexibility, it by no means changes his image as the major prophet of the movement to develop a picture of what it means to be healthy, superb, or in simplest terms, positive, in one's personality. His conceptualization of the high level personality was expressed as the "self actualizing" person, a term borrowed from Kurt Goldstein to whom Maslow had dedicated one of his volumes.

The self-actualizing person was originally seen as one moved largely by *metamotivation* and was characterized as having *"peak experiences."* The peak experience concept promises perhaps a major contribution in methodology, although no major methodological studies were produced by Maslow during his development of that concept. The peak experiences constitute those "most wonderful experience or experiences of your life; happiest moments, ecstatic moments, moments of rapture, perhaps from being in love or from listening to music or suddenly 'being hit' by a book or painting or from some great creative moment" (Maslow, 1962, p. 67).

One of the self-actualized persons named by Maslow was Eleanor Roosevelt, and later, Maslow was surprised to learn that she reported no peak experiences. Nevertheless, it does appear that the majority of those so designated do report these experiences; so, however, do many other humans with varying degrees of personal functioning. It appears that one may hypothesize that either the high level functioning person (1) experiences more of such experiences, (2) or more of them in critical periods of personality formation such as in early childhood or (3) experiences them as being of greater duration in real or phenomenological (perceived) time, and (4) finally experiences them more intensely.

Landsman (1968, 1974) has extended the concept to cover all positive experiences and has included the dimensions noted above, duration, intensity, and frequency. As Maslow indicated, they are likely to contribute to powerful changes in the personality. Although some efforts have been made to establish the significance of these dimensions in the creation of the high level functioning personality (Duncan, 1970: Rowe, 1970), this hypothesis shared by Maslow and Landsman cannot yet be said to have been decisively demonstrated.

The peak or positive experiences obviously contain considerable meaning to the person. Some examples taken from a collection of over 5,000 such experiences include the following positive experiences:

A 19 year old female student:

I do a lot of art work which always makes me ecstatic, but on one particular night one painting satisfied me greatly. Maybe it was not the painting in itself, but rather because I did it at night down by a beach. The atmosphere affected me greatly and influenced me and my painting. The air felt good, and even the mosquitoes I enjoyed. I think also that my subject matter influenced me, for it took me back to when I was younger. The water I painted actually had the feeling of movement, and I created the emotion I felt in myself on this canvas. Of course upon showing it to friends and relatives their approval gave me satisfaction, for I had created something that had pleased myself and the people I wanted to please.

A 35 year old male teacher:

Actually, I must report on two experiences, although they are similar in nature. In both cases I am an indirect participant. I refer to the births of my two children. My wife could not have the children normally, so an operation was necessary in both cases. She was extremely worried during the later months of pregnancy. Outwardly I tried to appear calm and unruffled and really thought that I was. I did not know the extent of my own concern for her safety, the newborn babies' normality, and things in general. It seemed as if I were in a state of suspended animation during both operations. When the doctor reported to me that everything was ok., and that mother and baby were doing fine, it seemed as if a great weight had been lifted from my shoulders. I became more aware of things around me, and even my breathing became easier.

Landsman (1974) refers to high level functioning as "the beautiful and noble" person and postulates not only peak or positive experiences having been involved in the creation of such persons, but also negative or unhappy experiences that the individual has somehow been able to turn into those having positive effects. For example, a male child who has known the early death of his father later learned to become the "man" of the family and felt that the experience made him a stronger, more

self-sufficient adult. Coan (1974) has suggested the term "optimal personality" and in addition has provided a limited survey of contemporary functioning (Coan, 1977).

Maslow's *metamotivation theory* is perhaps the best developed of his efforts to build a complete personality theory. Growing out of one of his best known earlier concepts, the hierarchy of needs, these range from the basic physiological and survival type needs to the growth or "being" related needs, those involving compassion and care for others, creativity and higher values. (Maslow, 1954).

The theory of metamotivation (Maslow, 1971) suggests that self-actualizing individuals have had their basic needs gratified and are now motivated by the higher need system, have some commitment or are devoted to tasks outside themselves, and also find that their innermost needs are in harmony with what the external world requires of them. Within the system is an implied vocational theory describing the self-actualizers as "vocation-loving" people whose intrinsic values guide their work rather than being means to other ends, such as money or status.

Gratifications cited by Maslow as characteristic of the self-actualizing people include:

Delight in bringing about justice
Delight in stopping cruelty and exploitation
They do not need to be loved by everyone
They avoid publicity, fame, glory . . .
They tend to enjoy peace, calm . . .
They respond to challenge in a job . . .

(Maslow, 1971, p. 308).

Throughout his approach, the concept of "B" or being values are contrasted with "D" or deficiency values, motivation, cognition, or needs. The B values, of course, are those involving metamotivation, growth producing, and growth fostering, while the "deficiency" needs are related to lower level adjustment and to physical and emotional survival. Maslow's original hierarchy of needs, in order from the most fundamental to the highest are: physiological, safety, belongingness and love, esteem, self-actualization, cognitive understanding, and aesthetic. The basic needs must be satisfied before the others.

Maslow's record with regard to the psychology of women seems to be relatively positive, although he could not keep himself from suggesting that there are women who are fully actualized by the housewife role (Maslow, 1971, p. 302) and others who have had various combinations of home life and professional work outside the home who could qualify as self-actualizers. Like Freud, he qualified his answers:

However, I should say that I feel less confident in speaking of self-actualization in women (Maslow, 1971, p. 302).

Maslow was certainly the major figure in the third force and led this revolution or onslaught against psychology as a behavioristic science. While this movement did not succeed in "overthrowing psychology," it did succeed in establishing new subject matter, new methodologies, and new, more creative thinking within personality theory. Maslow, in particular, opened the pathways to the study of the high level personality, despite the fact that he himself did not make significant methodological studies. Nevertheless, there is no doubt that his theories will provide the stimulus for a new era in personality research. While some argument could be made over the realization of that promise, he foresaw all of his hypotheses concerning motivation as being testable. Some of the research stimulated by this theory, while showing a true hierarchy of needs, does, however, suggest a simplification from the five levels suggested by Maslow to two or three levels (Mathes and Edwards, 1978).

Some Controversies in Personality Theory and Research

The images human beings have of themselves, their presuppositions about "the nature of human nature," and their common-sense conceptions of behavior have strongly influenced theory and research tactics. Are we generally rational or irrational but rationalizing, or both, or neither? Are our basic motives goal oriented, unconscious, and aimed at drive reduction? Does the social environment act to civilize our aggressive, egocentric, lustful nature? Does it frequently corrupt and distort our basic goodness, creativity, and freedom? Or does personality only exist in terms of interpersonal relationships? Are we unique, free, and unpredictable creatures of our own creation? Or is it only the illusion of freedom and dignity that we create?

It might be argued that these are not proper questions for a scientific psychology of personality, that such questions belong to philosophy, religion or art. Two radically different approaches to understanding the phenomena of personality agree that such questions have no place in a science of personality. Both positions agree that such questions cannot be resolved by objective, empirical data. On the one hand, Skinner (1971, 1974) suggests we keep the person and the science but throw out any traditional concept of the questions. On the other hand, existentialists (Binswanger, 1963; Boss, 1963) suggest we keep the person and the questions but throw out any traditional concept of science. Virtually all other personality theorists, implicitly or explicitly, first assume or presume an answer to most such questions and then attempt to give a scientific explanation to the data, that is, the behavior and experiences which constitute the subject matter of personality.

It would be convenient to be able to decide on scientific, empirical grounds whether or not such questions (rationality, freedom, and so on) should be included in a science of personality. Alternatively, it would be convenient if the data would "speak for itself," on the proper answers to such questions. Unfortunately, neither convenient possibility seems to be the case, and we are currently stuck on one or the other horn of a nonempirical dilemma.

The reason for the dilemma is simple. Those who agree about the incompatibility of such questions and science do agree that neither the questions, nor their answers, are empirical, and everyone else proceeds on the basis of assumptions (about the answers to the questions) that are not themselves empirically tested.

Practically speaking, there are two important results of this dilemma for a science of personality. The first result is that the theories often appear to be about qualitatively different species of animals.

If a visitor from a distant galaxy happened to have access to a standard work on personality theories, he could not be blamed for inferring that the Freudian, Rogerian, Skinnerian, and Kellian "persons" were critters as unrelated as kangaroos, eagles, toads, and butterflies.

The second problem is that different assumptions and theoretical concepts result in quite different research strategies and, most importantly, different data collection procedures. The empirical "facts" of behavior and experience do not interpret themselves, because what counts as a "fact" or "observation" to be explained depends on the theory and measurement procedure of the researcher (see Chapter 1). Personality psychologists simply do not agree on a common "unit" of study or procedure to measure the important variables in personality. An eight-year-old boy comes home from school and announces, "I'm mad at the teacher." Skinner would see this as *verbal behavior;* Kelly would say the child was actively *elaborating* his *construct system;* Rogers would take the statement as a *report* of the child's current *phenomenal field* and probably infer that the teacher had imposed *conditions of worth;* Freud might see the statement as the result of an *unconscious* displacement of the boy's aggressive feelings toward his father, feelings which find their origin in the child's unresolved *Oedipus complex;* Sullivan might speak of *dynamisms* and Maslow of *deprivation stages.*

Are You a Figment of Your Own Imagination?

Both the Skinnerian's and existentialist's positions start with a philosophical position about man's knowledge, known as *phenomenalism.* A standard dictionary (Webster, 1957) states a *phenomenon* is 1) any object known through the senses rather than through thought or intuition; 2) an observable fact or event; 3) any fact or event of scientific interest susceptible of scientific description or explanation. *Phenomenology* is a branch of science dealing with the description or classification of phenomena, or scientific description of actual phenomena with avoidance of all interpretation, explanation, and evaluation.

This position asserts that all we can know is that which is present directly in our perception. Hall and Lindzey (1970, p. 590) summarize the view of science that existentialist take:

Existential psychology is suspicious of theory because theory—any theory—implies that something that cannot be seen is producing that which is visible. For the phenomenologist, only that which can be seen or otherwise experienced is real. Truth is not arrived at by an intellectual exercise; it is revealed or disclosed in the phenomena themselves. Moreover, theory or any preconception, acts as a blinder for apprehending the revealed truth of experience. This truth can only be attained by a person who is completely open to the world. See what there is to see without any hypotheses or prejudgments is the existential psychologist's prescription for studying behavior (p. 590).

Unelaborated, this position is strikingly similar to the Skinnerian view. However, having agreed that what is present immediately in perceptions is the only "reality" we know and that we should avoid theory, inference, and hypothetical constructs, and that a true science is only capable of description of the phenomena perceived, an important difference occurs. Skinner assumes that perception is "of" the world as it is: "When operationism led to the study of the process of discrimination rather than of sensations, a person was regarded as looking at or listening to the real world. He was no longer reporting his perceptions or sensations; he was reporting stimuli. The world was back where it belonged" (1974, p. 86). It follows that if we avoid inference and do not talk about things we cannot directly see (purposes, drives, traits, concepts), and if we expose observers to similar environments or contingencies of reinforcement for the behavior of "seeing," then the observers will have the same description of the world. Further, this description is of the real world.

The existentialist rejects the view that we can see a real world directly. He would probably see such an assumption as an inference that goes beyond what is directly presented to our senses. In this view, each man creates his own subjective world; it follows that as each world is different, each description of an observer's world is different. Observers are unlikely to agree on general statements about *the* world or *all* men, much less *all* personalities. At best, what "true" science can do is help each man better describe his own world to himself.

Virtually all other personality theorists, implicitly or explicitly, adopt a position somewhere in between what might be called a radically objective phenomenology and radically subjective phenomenology. Such positions assume there is a world apart from our perception of it, yet they agree that it is not directly reflected in perception. The more "phenomenological" positions, such as those of Carl Rogers and George Kelly, tend to emphasize the ways in which "conscious" perceptions differ and stress this in their explanations of personality. As a consequence, their research techniques and methods are designed to investigate individual differences in each person's conception of himself and the world.

Many personality theorists who are not phenomenologically oriented would nonetheless contend that a person's conceptions of the world are important clues to his personality. For these positions, individual perceptions are interesting, because they are seen to be biased views of reality which reflect early developmental stages of growth or the operation of unconscious forces. Such distortions may or may not be seen as normal and healthy, depending on the theorist and the type of biased perception in question.

A stage-developmental theorist, such as Maslow, views distorted perceptions as a normal concomitant of growth. Although similar to the theories of Rogers and Kelly in emphasizing the person's point of view, Maslow does not see the person's subjective view as entirely unique to the individual. In these theories, a particular type of distortion correlates with each stage of growth, and all individuals are presumed to pass through the same stages in the same order. Knowing the person's private experience or viewpoint helps the researcher infer the person's point of view in the hypothesized developmental sequence.

Psychodynamic personality theorists, such as Freud, postulate active, unconscious forces which distort or bias each individual function of reality in both normal and abnormal ways. For the psychodynamically oriented theorists, some selective or distorted perception is seen as normal, necessary, and inevitable—a result of both current and childhood conflicts. Abnormal or disturbed individuals usually are seen as having pathologically exaggerated distortions of normal defenses and biases. For this type of theorist, a truly healthy person is one whose distortions of reality are minimal and who is generally aware of what those distortions are likely to be.

Research on psychodynamic personality poses its own special problems, since by definition, the workings of unconscious processes cannot be reported directly by the person, but always must be inferred by an observer. For instance, Freud thought that dreams were an especially rich source of unconscious material. But even though dreams are closer to the unconscious than ordinary waking states, dreams are also censored and dream symbols (*manifest content*) must be interpreted to reveal the *latent content* or true unconscious meaning of the dream.

Is there positive research evidence for unconscious processes? Many psychologists would give an alternative explanation of behavioral phenomena that a psychodynamically oriented person might explain *via* unconscious processes. Bandura (1969) has offered an explanation for cases of discrepancies between what people *do* (a husband beats his wife) and what people *say* ("I love you, dear") from the point of view of a social learning theorist:

Genuine disparities among different classes of behavior can be produced through the application of differential reinforcement. Thus, if hostile thoughts and verbalizations are approved or permissively accepted but overt aggressive actions are consistently punished, persons will readily verbalize aggressive feelings without exhibiting any of their motor equivalents. Similarly, by reversing the reinforcement contingencies one could effectively inhibit cognitive representations of behavioral manifestations (p. 590).

How Individual Are Your Individual Differences?

Are you really like a rat or a monkey or maybe Jonathan Livingston Seagull or Flipper? Can someone else predict what you will do with your life when you have not the foggiest notion yourself and secretly hope your parents are wrong?

No theorist exclusively intending to explain human personality would claim his theory is relevant to other species (nor would he see much reason to study other animals in order to understand persons); no one seriously attributes ids, archetypes, personal constructs, or traits to rats and pigeons.

Learning theory conceptions, on the other hand, did not start with the diversity and complexity of normal and abnormal human behavior. Such approaches purposely studied relatively simple animals in radically simplified laboratory environments. A chemist can analyze all complex matter from money to movie film to moonrocks once the basic elements of matter and their relationships are resolved in the laboratory. A learning theorist sees the range of the behavior of animals across animal species somewhat like the range of simple to complex chemical compounds. Complex human behaviors, like complex molecules, are built up from simple elements and relations. A rat pressing a bar and an artist sculpting a statue *appear* to have little in common except that they are both exhibiting behavior. From this view, a theorist does not need special explanations for human behaviors. Although most personality theorists claim persons require their own species specific theories of behavior and experience, they are far from agreement on the nature of that special human nature.

There is a second question about uniqueness, that is, are there general explanations for the phenomena of personality that hold true for all persons? The answer for all personality theorists to this question is an unqualified "yes." There is an unfortunate tendency to confuse the idiographic-nomothetic distinction with other dichotomies such as unique-general, subjective-objective, unpredictable-predictable.

A *nomothetic* statement or law is one that applies equally to members of the relevant class. For instance, "All trees have roots." Such a statement does not deny all the ways in which objects in the class (trees) differ; it simply ignores them and makes a statement about what they have in common. An *idiographic* statement, on the other hand, is a statement about an individual object (a particu-

lar tree) in a class (trees) and applies *only* to that particular one (the apple tree in my front yard).

All personality theories are nomothetic; no personality theorist claims that theory applies to some human adults but not others, or that the theory applies to human behavior only part of the time. Carl Rogers claims every person needs *unconditional positive regard;* Maslow claims every person has the potential to become *self-actualized;* Skinner claims every person is controlled by environmental stimuli; Kelly claims all persons behave in terms of their *construct system;* Allport claims all people have *traits;* and Freud envisions an id, ego, and super-ego in everyone. Even those bastions of individuality, the existentialists make statements like: ". . . man is *primarily* guilty. His primary guilt starts at birth . . . man's existential guilt consists in his failing to carry out the mandate to fulfill all his possibilities" (Boss, 1963, p. 270).

There is a sense in which all persons are unique. Looking at our apple tree again, we see that although all trees have roots, the particular root system of this tree (as well as its branches, leaves, fruit, flowers) is unique. The root system reflects the specific "life history" of the tree as it is affected by weather, soil conditions, and other flora and fauna in the environment. The fact that no particular tree has a root system exactly like that of any other tree does not mean lawful statements cannot be made about the relationship between annual rainfall, soil types, and root systems.

If theorists all assume there are general laws or principles of human personality, is all our behavior predictable or determined? Most personality theorists would agree that personality is determined by general laws and in principle predictable. They might add there are reasons we do not currently "do better" at prediction. The most obvious reason is "the state of the art;" we simply do not yet know enough about personality to know what general principles are in operation. That is, of course, why so many different theories continue to exist. Although each theory has its loyal adherents, no one theory can either logically or on the basis of unequivocal empirical data, convince the multitudes of skeptics in the scientific community.

The logic or internal consistency of a theory is a

necessary but not sufficient condition for the scientific validity of a theory. There must be empirical data that *both* support the hypotheses of the theory in question *and,* equally important, rule out plausible alternative hypotheses. All viable theories of personality have some research support, but none have unequivocally ruled out alternative, plausible (at least to *some* psychologists) explanations of the data.

Does Personality Grow Anywhere?

Is there a self-actualized person in your future? Will you ever escape toilet training? Would you really be happier if you moved to Tahiti?

The question of stability and change in personality over the lifespan is of central concern for many personality theorists. They differ with respect to the emphasis put on 1) long term effects of early experience, 2) conceptions of discrete stages or critical periods in development, and 3) whether or not there is a goal or ideal end state to growth and development.

Freud and Rogers differ on all three points; however, a combination of these positions is possible. Maslow postulates discrete stages of personality development but, unlike the Freudian case, once a stage has been successfully negotiated, it leaves no long term residue in normal personality. Like Rogers, Maslow hypothesizes an ideal end point of personality which he represents as the final developmental stage of self-actualization and metamotivation.

George Kelly's theory has neither an ideal end state of personality development nor a place for the lasting importance of early experience. Behavior is a result of the person's current *construction* of his world and change (represented as both *reconstruing* events and *extending* the construct system) is a constant, if not usually, dramatic part of normal life.

There is a sense in which a theory such as Kelly's is more optimistic about human personality than those postulating an ideal state. While Rogers, Maslow, and the existentialists frequently discuss human potential, they must also deal with the fact that, for most people, the potential is never realized. This leads to the curious outcome that full development is arrested (due to childhood experiences, adult defenses, nonsupporting environments, and so on) in the overwhelming majority of persons. On the other hand, hope for the perfectability of the individual is always possible because self-actualization is seen as a natural developmental process.

For learning theorists, stability and change in personality over the lifespan is a concomitant of stability and change in the environment. For Skinner, change in *operant behavior* comes about as the result of changing contingencies of reinforcement. Social learning theorists such as Rotter would see behavior change as a result of the person's changed *expectancy* for reinforcement. However, for Rotter (and other social learning theorists) changed expectancies are themselves a subjective reflection of changing environmental situations. Early childhood experiences (environments) have a long range effect on behavior, to the degree that the environment of the child is the same as the environment of the adult.

The Transituation Consistency of Individual Differences

Are you the same person today you were yesterday? Are you assertive with your friends but defensive with your father? Which you is the *real* you?

Although personality theorists have major disagreements about stability in personality over the lifespan and the origins of long term changes in the person's behavior, they all assume that there are stable, cross-situational individual differences in normal behavior. Personality, as a differentiated field of study in psychology, attempts to explain both why *persons respond differently* to the *same situation* and why an *individual* responds the *same way* in *different situations*.

For example, if introversion-extroversion is a stable individual difference dimension, it must be largely the case that in any *particular* social situation introverts and extroverts will behave differently and *across* the majority of social occasions introverts behave in an introverted way. If the cross-situational stability of individual differences was *not* the case, that is, a person's introverted behavior in one social situation is totally unrelated to introverted or extroverted behavior in any other social situation, then there would be no *stable* individual differences to be explained. Psychologists would be left with investigating the question of why persons behave differently in a given situation, but no explanation of these differences in terms of personality traits or dispositions would be possible.

There is reason to believe that in personality dimensions such as sociability, dependency, responsibility, honesty, and so on, there is much less cross-situational consistency in behavior than we assume in our day to day interactions with others (Jones and Nisbett, 1971). In ordinary life, we generalize far beyond "the data" (Passini and Norman, 1966). If a person is open and trusting with us and our mutual acquaintances, we usually assume that person is also open and trusting with all other people. Further, we make inferences about personality traits we have no knowledge of on the basis of the information we have. We may well feel that our open and trusting acquaintance would also be honest, considerate of the feelings of others, and reliable in an emergency, although we have no knowledge of how our friend behaves with respect to any of these qualities. There is a large and growing empirical literature (Schneider, 1973) on the common-sense assumptions that underlie our perception of the stability of the personalities of others.

In psychology, the assumption of cross-situational stability of personality traits has been challenged on specific empirical grounds (Bem, 1972; Fiske, 1974). Mischel (1968) has noted that personality tests designed to measure stable individual differences rarely do a very good job of predicting individual differences in specific situations, that is, the correlation between personality test scores and nontest behaviors is rarely greater than $r \pm .30$ (see Chapter 3). Such a low degree of relationship between test scores and nontest behaviors practically implies no psychologist would bet on whether or not, for example, someone with a high score on introversion would sit alone in the corner or be the life of the party at his next social get together.

The fact that standard personality tests typically do poorly when predicting a person's behavior in a specific situation does not *per se* invalidate the proposition that cross-situational consistency is present in the behavior of an individual. It does suggest that prediction of a *specific* nontest behavior *solely* on the basis of a global personality trait score is a bad idea. There are a number of reasons, to some degree tied to alternative theories about personality, as to why such a prediction strategy has not worked well.

The simplest reason is a methodological one. Accuracy in predicting nontest behaviors from individual differences in personality test scores is directly related to the validity of the personality test (see Chapters 3 and 18 for further discussion). If the test is a poor measure of a personality trait, predictions made on the basis of test scores will fare badly. For example, the failure to predict introverted and extroverted behavior at a party would surprise no one if the test consisted of items such as "How frequently do you wear lampshades?" The fact that the 'Lampshade Test' leads to poor predictions does not necessarily mean that there are not cross-situational consistencies in the behavior of introverts or extroverts. Unfortunately, it is the case that many studies of personality have used personality tests of questionable validity.

Given that a particular personality test is well designed and meets normal technical criteria such as those published by the American Psychological Association (1974), it may still do a poor job in predicting nontest individual differences if used incorrectly. One could argue that much of the data on the $r \pm .30$ relationships between personality test scores and nontest behaviors reflect the failure of test users to take personality *theory* seriously (Block, 1968).

In Rotter's social learning theory, the probability of a specific behavior (*behavior potential*) is determined by both a person's *specific expectancy* about the *consequence* of the behavior and the *reinforcement value* of the *consequence*. Faced with a new situation, a person *may not have a specific expectancy* for the outcome of a particular behavior. Rotter (1966) speculated that a person also develops a *general* sense of whether or not his predictions about the results of his behavior are confirmed. He hypothesized that in new, unfamiliar situations a person would behave in accord with this *generalized* sense of being able (or not being able) to predict or control one's outcomes.

The Internal versus External Locus of Control of Reinforcement scale (Rotter, 1966)—usually abbreviated I-E scale—was designed by Rotter to tap this *generalized* sense of the degree to which a person feels able to control his fate. Individual differences in I-E scale scores should lead to correct predictions about individual differences in behavior *only* in those situations which are new or unfamiliar to the person. Scores in the I-E scale are almost irrelevant in situations where the individual has a *specific* expectancy for the outcome of his behavior based on his own past experience. In this case, a correlation of $\pm$ .30 between I-E scores and predicted behaviors would be interesting, because the theoretically predicted relationship should be close to .00.

Studies using the I-E scale to predict nontest behaviors frequently overlook this point, that is, they do not determine whether or not individuals are familiar with the nontest situation. Predicting individual differences on the basis of I-E scores *without considering* the person's familiarity with the nontest situation is a total misuse of the I-E scale.

More generally, it could be argued that predicting cross-situational stabilities in behavior *solely* on the basis of individual differences in standard personality test scores is an exercise in misdirection from the point of view of any major personality theorist. Virtually all theorists who have conceptions of personality that are compatible with the use of standard personality tests would argue that any specific behavior is a result of the interaction between individual difference dimensions and situational factors. In the right situation, a timid man will be brave, a coward show courage, and a miser become generous.

A number of broad scale personality tests have been designed to test for individual difference dimensions conceptualized by Henry Murray (1938, 1959) as *needs.* However, while Murray's theory provided the basis for twenty different frequency measured *needs* (such as achievement, dominance and autonomy), it is the rare case (Stern, 1970) where predictions about behavior are made on the basis of Murray's *theory.*

Murray hypothesizes that behavior is the result of both *needs* and *press* or environmental factors.

He further distinguishes between *alpha press,* the objective environment and *beta press,* the situation as subjectively seen by the indivdiual. While predictions about cross-situational consistency in behaviors are frequently made from needs measured via the Thematic Apperception Test (Murray, 1943), Edward's Personal Preference Schedule (Edwards, 1959), The Adjective Check List (Gough and Heilbrun, 1965), or The Personality Research Form (Jackson, 1967), about the only predictions in accord with Murray's theory are made by Stern (1970). In Stern's work, *needs* are measured via the Activities Index and situations or environmental *press* by the College Characteristic Index.

Another commonly used, or misused, test is Cattell's Sixteen Personality Factor Questionnaire (Cattell et al, 1970). Test users often make behavioral predictions on the basis of test scores while ignoring Cattell's theoretical formula for specific behaviors. Each particular behavior in each particular situation is the outcome of a number of different personality traits *working together.* It is rarely the case that one trait dominates behaviors to the exclusion of others. In theory, then, the correlation between scores on any *one* of the sixteen dimensions and the behavioral criteria situation is expected to be low. Situational factors are represented in Cattell's multivariate theory by a mathematical factor that weights the contribution each of the sixteen traits made in terms of its relevance to the overall prediction situation.

Many personality theorists, of course, simply reject the idea that personality traits as measured by standard tests, are very useful or relevant for predicting specific behavior (Fiske, 1974). For example, Kelly would base predictions on the person's *construct system,* and Stage theorists would stress the individual's point in the developmental continuum.

As Mischel (1973b) notes, the general class of psychodynamic personality theorists (those such as Freud or Jung who give unconscious processes an important role in the explanation of behavior) need not be distressed by the inability of standard tests to predict cross-situational consistency in overt behavior. In these views, consistency in personality largely exists in current unconscious processes or unconscious residues of earlier experiences. Overt behavior only indirectly reflects these underlying dynamics. Further, unconscious processes usually work in irrational ways, so that what is functional consistency at the unconscious level may well be totally incoherent inconsistency at the level of overt behavior or rational consideration.

Summary

The theories of personality presented in this chapter were viewed as alternative constructions of the nature of persons. Encompassing both overt behaviors and personal experiences, each of these different theories are viewed, for the most part, as adding knowledge about persons from a particular viewpoint.

Starting with Freud's psychodynamic and conflict-oriented theory, the ego psychologists were then presented as an extension of this theory. The neo-Freudians: Jung, Adler, Horney, Fromm, and Sullivan were presented as offering alternative views while remaining within a psychodynamic orientation, particularly in the area of the defenses. With the exception of Jung, the neo-Freudians took the theory into the realm of social interaction. Jung's emphasis was instead in the area of transpersonal experience.

The second major orientation was described as behavioral, drawing from American learning theorists. In this camp, Dollard and Miller remained close to Freud's conflict model but translated the psychodynamic ideas into stimulus, response, and drive reduction language. Skinner, on the other hand, emphasized the overt response components in accounting for personality without emphasizing motivational terms like drive reduction. The social learning theories were seen as moving the emphasis from overt behavior to an analysis of cognitive processes.

The final theory section was devoted to the humanistic theorists with their emphasis on choice, commitment, and higher level functioning. Maslow, Jourard, Rogers, Kelly, May, Landsman, and others of this orientation emphasized the phenomenological approach of studying persons in their own personal terms rather than imposing the constructs of the psychologist. The potentials of human beings for full development of their abilities was emphasized along with an analysis of the meaning that sometimes comes from human suffering. The final section of the chapter was devoted to the issues and controversies present in these theories and research efforts in this field. An examination of unconscious motivation, growth orientations, individual differences, to name but a few, were issues discussed as the various theories were compared and contrasted.

Glossary

Anal stage—(Freud): The second psychosexual stage when the interests of the child are focused on the anal sphincter and the production of feces.

Anima—(Jung): That archetype in the collective unconscious dealing with female attributes found in the male.

Animus—(Jung): That archetype in the collective unconscious dealing with male attributes found in the female.

Archetypes—(Jung): Those constellations of thought and feelings which the person inherits from past generations; located in the collective unconscious.

Basic anxiety—(Horney): That feeling of horror showed by all people as a result of being helpless and defenseless as infants and young children.

Basic trust—(Erikson): The first stage in development indicating the first condition that must be satisfied at least minimally for identity and personhood to be completed.

Biophilous—(Fromm): The orientation that leads to life and productive enterprises.

Castration anxiety—(Freud): In the male, the fear of the father experienced at the onset of the Oedipal episode. The fear that the father will cut off the male child's genitals.

Conditions of worth—(Rogers): Those evaluations of others that the individual uses to evaluate his worth as a person.

Collective unconscious—(Jung): That aspect of the personality dealing with experiences that transcend the person's own personal experience and connect the person with the inherited past.

Constructive alternativism—(Kelly): The thesis that an event can be interpreted to reflect a number of different meanings.

Dynamism—(Sullivan): An organization of experience and behavior into a meaningful unit for understanding the personality of an individual.

Ego—(Freud): That aspect of the person dealing with rational thought and planning and control of the total personality system.

Elaborative choice—(Kelly): The movement in the direction of fuller development of the construct system.

Fixed role therapy—(Kelly): A therapeutic procedure in which the person is invited to take on the identity of another in order to elaborate present constructions.

Generativity—(Erikson): The need for a person to care for the next generation.

Genital stage—(Freud): Adult stage in psychosexual development revealing a unity of love and work in the well functioning person.

Id—(Freud): That aspect of the person dealing with the basic drives.

Individuation—(Jung): The process by which the person reaches self fulfillment. There is an integration of knowledge from all aspects of the personality.

Inferiority complex—(Adler): That unfortunate conclusion drawn by the person that the person is weak and incapable, which leads the person to seek superiority and domination of others.

Libido: A term used by both Freud and Jung to indicate the energy available for living. For Freud, this term implied sexual strivings.

Life style—(Adler): The term used to describe the particular path chosen by the person. The life style is guided by the person's goals, which may not be availble to conscious awareness.

Metamotivation—(Maslow): Motivations that transcend the biological and deprivation needs and project the person toward self-actualization; motivation related to higher level needs such as beauty.

Necrophilous—(Fromm): That orientation that leads to death and destructive impulses.

Oedipus complex—(Freud): Explanation of the attraction of the male child to the mother; seen as sexual and erotic. The male presumably fears castration from the father because of his competitive love for the mother.

Oral stage—(Freud): The first psychosexual stage when the interests of the child are focused on the mouth and oral cavity.

Parataxic—(Sullivan): Term for the child's crude thought processes that specify relationship between events by simple association and not by abstract reasoning. If present in adulthood, these cause difficulties.

Peak experiences—(Maslow): Experiences that the person has that enables that person to reach, momentarily, the height of potential. Experiences which are "oceanick," with an extremely high level of positive feeling, ecstacy, and enormous meaningfulness.

Persona—(Jung): The mask that is worn by the person for social interaction and social convention.

Personal unconscious—(Jung): That aspect of personality which is not now accessible to consciousness but is the result of past personal experiences.

Personification—(Sullivan): The stylized impression of others grown out of past experiences; a type of stereotyping.

Phallic stage—(Freud): The third psychosexual stage when the interests of the child are focused on the genitals.

Press—(Murray): An aspect of the environment that influences the individual's life.

Prototaxic—(Sullivan): The unordered, unorganized, undifferentiated thought processes of the infant and the very disturbed person.

Psychosocial moratorium—(Erikson): The period of relative inactivity during the identity phase when the individual engages in alternative life patterns.

Self-actualizing—(Maslow): The process of fulfilling one's potentials of high level functioning.

Self-concept—(Rogers and others): The person's perception of himself, the values, evaluations, roles, persons, and objects seen by the person as characteristic of himself.

Shadow—(Jung): Aspects of the personality which are the opposite of the manifest content of life. Since most people manifest their good side, the shadow contains the evil a person is capable of manifesting.

Social interest—(Adler): The plan to direct one's life in being helpful to others; seen as a movement in the direction of personal growth.

Super-ego—(Freud): That aspect of the person dealing with the moral decisions and aspirations.

Syntaxic mode—(Sullivan): Logical rational thinking of the well functioning adult.

Suggested Readings

General

Corsini, R. J. (ed.) *Current Personality Theories*. Itasca, Illinois: Peacock, 1977.
Hall, C. S. and Lindzey, G. *Theories of Personality*. 2nd ed. New York: John Wiley, 1970.
Hjelle, L. A. and Ziegler, D. J. *Personality Theories: Basic Assumptions, Research, and Applications*. New York: McGraw-Hill, 1976.
Rychlak, J. F. *Introduction to Personality and Psychotherapy*. Boston: Houghton Mifflin, 1973.
Sarason, I. G. *Personality: An Objective Approach*. 2nd ed. New York: John Wiley, 1972.

Psychoanalysis and Ego Psychology

Erickson, E. *Identity Youth and Crisis*. New York: Norton, 1968.
Hall, C. S. *A Primer of Freudian Psychology*. New York: New American Library, 1950.

Neo-Freudians

Ansbacher, H. L. and Ansbacher, R. R. (eds.) *The Individual Psychology of Alfred Adler*. New York: Basic Books, 1956.
Fromm, E. *The Anatomy of Human Destructiveness*. New York: Holt, Rinehart and Winston, 1973.
Hall, C. S. and Nordby, V. J. *A Primer of Jungian Psychology*. New York: Taplinger, 1973; New American Library, 1973.
Horney, K. *Neurosis and Human Growth*. New York: Norton, 1950.
Kelman, H. *Helping People: Karen Horney's Psychoanalytic Approach*. New York: Science House, 1971.
Mullahy, P. *Psychoanalysis and Interpersonal Psychiatry: The Contributions of Harry Stack Sullivan*. New York: Science House, 1970.

Personality and Learning Theory

Bandura, A. *Social Learning Theory*. Englewood Cliffs, N.J.: Prentice-Hall, 1977.
Lundin, R. W. *Personality: A Behavioral Analysis*. 2nd ed. New York: Macmillan, 1974.
Miller, N. E. Some Implications of Modern Behavior Theory for Personality Change and Psychotherapy. In P. Worchel and D. Byrne (eds.) *Personality Change*. New York: John Wiley, 1964.
Rotter, J. B. and Hochreich, D. J. *Personality*. Glenview, Illinois: Scott, Foresman, 1975.
Skinner, B. F. *About Behaviorism*. New York: Alfred A. Knopf, 1974.

Humanistic Psychology

Bugental, J. F. T. *Challenges of Humanistic Psychology*. New York: McGraw Hill, 1967.
Buhler, C. and Allen, M. *Introduction to Humanistic Psychology*. Monterey, Ca.: Brooks/Cole, 1972.
Chiang, H-M. and Maslow, A. H. (eds.). *The Healthy Personality: Readings*. 2nd ed. New York: D. Van Nostrand, 1977.
Jourard, S. M. *The Healthy Personality: An Approach from the Viewpoint of Humanistic Psychology*, New York: Macmillan, 1974.
Maslow, A. H. *The Further Reaches of Human Nature*. New York: Viking Press, 1971.
Misiak, H. and Sexton, V. S. *Phenomenological, Existential and Humanistic Psychologies: A Historical Survey*. New York: Grune & Stratton, 1973.
Nevill, D. D. (ed.) *Humanistic Psychology: New Frontiers*. New York: Gardner Press, 1977.

20

Behavior Pathology

Richard M. Suinn

Introduction

Seeing an event that does not exist, hearing sounds without cause, imagining things that are not true, behaving in ways that are bizarre—these are the principal topics of this chapter. Possibly ever since humans came into existence, some persons appeared with characteristics that were strange enough to cause other people to wonder about their uniqueness. Basic questions faced by psychologists include first defining and identifying the signs of behavior pathologies, and then developing methods for treatment. Historically, the field has been solely the concern of a branch of medicine called psychiatry, although currently psychiatrists, psychologists, and some paraprofessionals work with such problems. This chapter will briefly trace the history of psychopathology, discuss various definitions of pathology and factors which contribute to pathology, then present descriptions of some important types of modern pathologies and the various types of treatment currently available.

Historical Perspective

Anthropological findings, as shown in Figure 20-1, suggest that mental illness existed in early prehistoric humans. Trephining, a primitive form of surgery, consisted of cutting away pieces of the skull until the brain was exposed. Perhaps it was believed that this would enable the evil causing the

illness to leave the sick person. Human reactions to signs of mental illness have varied drastically over the centuries. During periods of religious fervor, a common belief was that abnormal behaviors were inspired by spiritual causes. Ironically, the spirit was viewed as benign in some cases, and as evil in other similar ones. Biblical writings have cited visions as favorable experiences associated with conversions to the faith. On the other hand, the Dark Ages were characterized by interpreting psychiatric symptoms as evidences of Satanic possession. *Stigmata diaboli,* now recognized as tactual

Fig. 20-1. Shown is archeological proof of an early form of treatment called trephining. Holes were made in the skull apparently to release the evil spirits believed to be causing the malady. (University Museum, Philadelphia)

anesthesias, were deliberately sought by zealous inquisitors using sharp instruments to jab a prisoner until a numb area was found. Even through the early eighteenth century, hospital services for the insane were little more than prisons. It was common to sell tickets to spectators who wished to be entertained by the sight of the mentally ill. In the fall of 1793 in France, Pinel spearheaded attempts at hospital reform. In the face of political pressure and ignorance, Pinel argued that the insane needed only ''Fresh air and . . . their liberty'' to recover, rather than chains, imprisonment, and neglect. His efforts began a slow trend toward a more humanistic, less fearful, approach in patient care.

The history of pathology has some interesting turns. Anton Mesmer induced changes in patients in groups and even on the stage. ''Mesmerism,'' as it was called, supposedly caused cures through readjusting the magnetic fluids in the universe and the human body through an instrument called the baquet. A specially appointed scientific committee determined that ''imagination without magnetism produces (results) . . . (while) magnetism without imagination produces nothing'' (Bailly, 1784). Mesmerism was eventually renamed hypnotism (Braid, 1843), and used as an explanation for the ailment known as hysteria. Hysteria has a long history as a mysterious malady involving paralysis, or anesthesia. The name itself derives from the belief that the illness was due to a travelling uterus, the Greek name for uterus being hystera. Liebeault (1886), founder of the French Nancy School of medical training, concluded that hysteria and hypnotism were both examples of the influence of suggestibility, with hysterical symptoms coming from autohypnosis. On the other hand, Charcot (1882) of the Salpetriere School of Medicine argued that both hysteria and hypnotic suggestibility were themselves signs of a basic organic rather than psychological abnormality, that is, that there was a physical rather than psychological cause.

As science matured, more and more new ideas were advanced. Janet offered the first psychological theory of neurosis. Mental symptoms were said to develop as the normal supply of mental energy was used up and not available for maintaining adjustment. Kraepelin (1883) devised an orderly classification of types of mental illness. This scheme was based on the disease entity model: certain symptoms group together which distinguish one disease from another, and each disease follows a predictable course once started. Thus, chicken pox is identified by certain signs and has a different sequence than scarlet fever. This application of the medical disease entity approach to mental illness was a significant step forward in convincing physicians that mental illness had a place in medical studies.

The twentieth century has produced some diverse views of man and mental illness. Sigmund Freud (1953) (see Figure 20-2) founded both a school of psychotherapy and a way of thinking about human problems. Psychoanalytic therapy relies on free association, dream analysis, emotional release through talking (catharsis), and an emphasis on understanding early childhood origins of current difficulties. Freud's theory sees humans as experiencing internal psychic struggles among conflicting inclinations. One result of such dynamic conflicts and early traumas is the development of repression, whereby experiences are driven into the unconscious. In mental illness, such unconscious materials have resurfaced to interfere with normal adjustment. By this view, human beings are at the mercy of deep, dark forces interacting in complex and often symbolic ways. Freud is credited with contributing a major breakthrough in both psychological therapy and in a theory of neurosis.

Another approach, behaviorism, has emerged in modern times to challenge psychoanalysis. While psychoanalysis grew out of Freud's contacts with patients in the Victorian era, behavior therapy originated out of data on learning. Pavlov (1904) identified classical conditioning as learning, whereby two stimuli are paired temporally, leading to a neutral stimulus being able to evoke the same response as the original stimulus. Thus, the cue ''Look out'' can evoke hand withdrawal in the same way that the sensations of a hot stove can. Thorndike (1905) and Hull (1943) studied instrumental learning as a form of learning, whereby new responses are acquired by reinforcement. Thus, humans acquire new habits because such be-

Fig. 20-2.
Sigmund Freud, the founder of psychoanalysis, was responsible for one of the most significant breakthroughs in modern times.

haviors have been followed by reward. Similarly, habits are extinguished when they are no longer associated with reinforcement. Children learn to speak, since speech leads to rewards such as approval from parents. Watson (1919) expounded the view that behaviors were the only worthwhile topics for study, thereby shifting the attention away from the unconscious, inner psychic forces so important to Freud. Laws from experimental research with animals on learning were applied to human pathology. Watson and Rosalie Raynor (1920) and later, Mary Cover Jones (1924) used the laws of learning to establish a full-blown phobia in a child and to cure a phobia.

Dissatisfactions with psychoanalysis and behaviorism have led some to humanism, which was described in Chapter 19. The humanists feel psychoanalysis to be too pessimistic and past-oriented, and behaviorism to be too technological and mechanistic. Among the humanistic leaders, Rogers (1961) and Maslow (1954) emphasize the value of self-actualization. Humans are viewed as constantly striving toward fulfilling their potential. A positive tone pervades theory and treatment,

with particular attention given to personal growth, inner resources, creativity, and love. Self-enhancement and actualization are promoted through group participation—for example, in encounter groups, training or T-groups, sensitivity groups, and marathon groups. As a relatively recent phenomenon, the humanistic approach is only gradually accumulating scientific support for its claims.

Some modern theorists have also attacked the traditional medical model of psychopathology previously offered. By viewing mental illness as a type of disease, early psychiatrists made psychopathology a legitimate topic for study by medicine. However, Szasz (1961) currently argues that this idea has lost its value, and indeed may even now be preventing further progress in understanding and treating abnormal behaviors. The major "myth of mental illness," he says, is that a mentally ill person truly possesses a disease and *is* sick in the same way as in physical illnesses. Rather, the symptoms of mental "illness" are simply maladaptive interpersonal behaviors expressing faulty attempts to deal with life stresses.

Definitions and Models of
Behavioral Pathology

Are seeing and hearing that which is not there, imagining that which is untrue, or acting in inappropriate ways, reasons to call one mentally ill? Defining mental illness has proven a truly difficult task, involving a variety of attempts at definitions or conceptualizations, each with its own contributions and problems. The earliest attempt might be called a *moral* definition, based on a model that suggests that abnormal behaviors are a reflection of evil. Thus, pathology reflects either Satanic possession from consorting with demon spirits, or punishment from God for immoral acts. Occasionally, this model accepts the possibility that a disturbed person is innocent of immorality, but has been chosen to suffer for other reasons, such as to atone for the guilt of others or as a test of purity.

Another approach involves the *cultural* definition: abnormality involves showing those traits that the majority agree to be unacceptable, or not showing those traits that the majority agree to be desirable. Thus, we might agree as a society that hallucinating is pathological. On the other hand, cultural norms do shift and require reflection on such cultural definitions. Homosexual behavior was once considered as clearly deviant, but the Gay Liberation movement has pressed for a more sympathetic view, arguing that homosexuals are no more pathological than heterosexuals. Drug usage was similarly looked upon as a symptom of pathology; however, current lifestyles have forced a distinction between drug use and drug abuse analogous to our conceptions of alcohol consumption.

The *psychodynamic* approach suggests that the symptoms are symbolically representative of internal emotional problems. Abnormality, therefore, is definable in terms of the nature and severity of these emotional conflicts. Proponents of this approach accept the fact that all persons experience conflicts; however, the mentally disturbed person has failed to come to grips with such problems in a healthy fashion. Pathology may be seen as an inability to resolve childhood issues which then carry into adulthood, the presence of severe emotional disturbances which interfere with functioning, or the reliance upon attempts to solve conflicts where the attempts themselves are unhealthy. Critics of the psychodynamic approach point out that it tends to isolate attention to the patient, thereby overlooking the environmental, social, or familial presses which may be contributing to the symptoms. Also, symbolic explanations of the conflict tend to be somewhat ambiguous; therefore, exact treatment recommendations are difficult to determine.

A *social problems* model has been offered which combines some aspects of the previous two approaches. Szasz (1961) argues that "mental illness"—a phrase he does not accept—really involves deviations from ethical, legal, or other social norms that stem from the stresses of everyday life. Hence, such behaviors are actually "problems of living." These problems are due to faulty learning and attempts to cope, leading to subjective feelings of discomfort, dissatisfying human relationships, and social rejection. The emphasis shifts to viewing pathology as an attempt to cope with daily problems which has failed. As such, the model fits into current analyses of the special stresses facing minority persons, who are under unique cultural pressures, but who are simultaneously prevented from learning useful methods to cope. A primary difficulty with the social problems model is its implication that few problems exist for which the patient holds primary responsibility. Thus, it implies that a change in society's standards or demands might easily lead to recovery from the pathology.

The *statistical approach* arose in an attempt to use mathematical methods to arrive at definitions. Whereas the cultural definition relies on consensus, arrived at by mutual agreement without data, the statistical approach arrives at consensus by an actual frequency tabulation. By the statistical approach, observers tally the actual numbers of times a behavior is shown in members of a society; the behaviors with the highest frequency are accepted as the norm. Eysenck (1970) has tested normal and pathological persons, scored their responses, and statistically plotted the answers. In its most refined approach, the statistical definition attempts to identify intercorrelated traits that seem to cluster together and that distinguish normals from non-normals. Then any person who shows the traits characteristic of the normal sample would be considered normal, and any person who shows the trait-cluster of non-normals would be considered pathological. Although more precise and objective in approach, the statistical method may still suffer from the same problems of the cultural definition. Specifically, the sample of "normal" and "non-normal" persons to be studied and tested must be selected on the basis of some other definition if the cluster approach is used. If the more simple frequency tabulation approach is used, then the difficulty is that some behaviors with high frequency may still be basically pathological. For example, heart disease and neuroses afflict large numbers of our society, yet neither would be considered "healthy."

A *legal* approach to defining mental illness has been necessitated by criminal law. Legal definitions are basically definitions of responsibility—the M'Naghten Rule (1843) used in the United States asks whether the criminal knew right from wrong, and is therefore responsible, and subject to punishment. Daniel M'Naghten killed the private secretary to Sir Robert Peel, the true intended victim. The *irresistible impulse* defense involves the idea that the criminal was compelled to the act and incapable of self-restraint, and again not responsible. Psychiatric experts dislike these legalistic approaches since they ignore emotional factors and the real factors often present in abnormality. For example, Sirhan Sirhan, the assassin of Senator Robert Kennedy, appeared to have brooded and reflected prior to the killing rather than having acted on sudden impulse.

Although the previous discussion points out that a single definition is probably never to be entirely satisfactory for identifying pathology, there are still some guidelines that help in recognizing abnormality. Some of these guidelines will be presented next, although none alone would be convincing evidence that a person would be clearly pathological. The guidelines actually involve certain characteristics of persons which would suggest pathology. *Subjective pain* may be reported involving tension, anxiety, severe conflict, or unhappiness, without due cause. *Disturbances of the emotions* may appear in exaggerated euphoria,

deep depression, or the absence of emotions appropriate to events. *Irrationality* may appear as disruptions of logical actions, such as incoherent speech, or behaviors that could be construed as self-destructive. *Disruptions* may appear in one or more of the "ABCs": Affect (emotions), Behavior, Cognition. Frequently, pathology is suspected when a person behaves in ways that are ineffective, inefficient, inappropriate, or inflexible. The person may experience a loss of control in the sense of being truly out of control, as in violent outbursts. Or the loss of control may be in terms of becoming so rigidly tied into maladaptive actions as to lose any sense of freedom of choice. Self-esteem is often defective, interpersonal adjustment deficient, and personal growth and development blocked or stifled.

Origins of Pathology

Genetic factors are often overlooked because of the difficulties in directly proving their role in mental illness. Yet, inheritance is a known factor in many medical ailments, such as in the bleeding disease, hemophilia. Kallman (1946, 1953) argued that schizophrenia and manic-depressive psychosis, two severe mental illnesses, follow family patterns expected from genetics. As in family physical traits, schizophrenia in one family member was more likely to occur in other family members. As shown in Table 20-1, the closer the blood relationship, the greater the incidence. Thus, the identical twin sibling of a schizophrenic patient is more subject to schizophrenia than a fraternal twin; a fraternal twin more subject than non-twin siblings; and, non-twin siblings more subject than half-siblings. Gottesman and Shields (1972) even found a close similarity between schizophrenic twins in the age that the symptoms first appeared, and in psychological test profiles of relatives.

Cultural factors have received some acceptance as possible influences on personality traits. Travelers often are impressed by the differing patterns of behaviors shown by people of different countries. The British seem invariably ruled by politeness to the point of routinely "queuing up," instead of crowding, even in the rain. The Japanese

Table 20-1. The Expectancy of Various Types of Mental Illness in Blood Relatives of an Afflicted Person

Family Relationship	MENTAL ILLNESS				
	Schizo-phrenia	*Manic-Depression*	*Childhood Schizo-phrenia*	*Involu-tional Psychoses*	*Senile Psychoses*
Monozygotic twins	86.2%	95.7%	70.6%	60.9%	42.8%
Dizygotic twins	14.5%	26.3%	17.1%	6.0%	8.0%
Full-siblings	14.2%	23.0%	12.2%	6.0%	6.5%
Half-siblings	7.1%	16.7%	—	4.5%	—
Step-siblings	1.8%	—	—	—	—
Unrelated gen. popul.	0.9%	0.4%	—	1.0%	<1.0%

Source: Adapted from L. Hurst, Classification of psychotic disorders from a genetic point of view. *Proceed. Second Intern. Congr. of Human Genet.* Vol. III. Rome: Instituto G. Mendel, 1963.

and the French seem to display a nationalistic pride, while the American appears to be competitive, achieving, and jealous of personal rights, such as the right to bear arms. Pathological traits also seem to reflect cultural origins. Eskimos have been afflicted with *pibloktoq,* characterized by fits of shouting, frantic activity, seizures, and coma. Malaysians have been subject to *latah,* involving a compulsion to mimic the actions of others. The Japanese may display *taijin kyofusho* through fear of meeting people, flushing, and feelings of inadequacy. In American studies, differing types of mental symptoms appear associated with different social factors, such as social stratification, religion, ethnic or minority membership, and marital status. As one proceeds lower on the socioeconomic scale, the incidence of severe mental illness tends to increase (Hollingshead and Redlich, 1958; Srole, et al, 1962). Schizophrenia, however, tended not to respect class but appeared to a large degree among persons of all classes. Psychoses appear more prevalent among Protestants (Frumkin and Frumkin, 1957), while Catholics seemed at one time to be more subject to alcoholism (Malzberg, 1936) and sex disorders (Hirning, 1945). Black men have been said to be characterized by fear of success (Horner, 1970); women appear in university counseling centers for help more than

men (Butler, 1975). Persons without a spouse by choice, divorce, or death show higher rates of illness than married persons (Taube, 1970).

Biophysiological factors cannot be overlooked as contributors to mental illness. In fact, mental symptoms can clearly be triggered as part of physical disease processes. Thyroid conditions can prompt anxiety reactions and mood swings; Addison's disease involving adrenal malfunctioning can lead to depression. Researchers have hoped to find a biochemical explanation for mental illness, perhaps directly linking a neurohormone, or the presence of a toxic factor to psychopathology. The apparent ability of some drugs to mimic psychoses, such as LSD, seemed to support the biochemical hypothesis. However, current findings are still very tentative and speculative. It is important to note that manic-depressive psychosis and some forms of schizophrenia may be proven to be biochemical/genetic in nature while others may be entirely psychological/cultural.

A purely *psychological* approach suggests that mental illness represents the outcome of certain specific life experiences, or the interaction between the person's adaptive characteristics and environmental stresses. One view would be that the mentally ill person has been taught certain pathological ways of acting, perhaps by parents. Indeed there is some evidence that the incidence of schizophrenia is much higher if one parent is or was also severely disturbed (Neale and Weintraub, 1975). Similarly, children of phobic parents tend to grow up fearful (Hagman, 1932). Another possibility is that the presence of a mentally ill parent produces chaotic child-rearing experiences, during a time when the child cannot cope. Hence, it is the trauma that prevents normal development. Some schizophrenics appear to have had families characterized by parental hostilities, role distortions, and conflicts (Fleck, et al, 1963). Another viewpoint is that mental illness occurs in persons who have failed to acquire the minimum skills needed to adapt. As long as they are protected from stress, they display a normal adjustment. However, symptoms develop when environmental stresses increase, for example, from the demands of an occupation, from marriage, parental responsibilities, or shifts in roles (Holmes & Rahe, 1967). Two million men were either rejected or discharged from military service during World War II for emotional disorders (Hadley et al, 1944), some probably due to breakdowns precipitated by pressures of wartime conditions. Other forms of stress which produce mental symptoms include: continuation of frustrations without solutions (Gantt, 1942), increasing conflict states without opportunities for escape (Miller, 1944), and certain need deprivations (Bexton et al, 1954; Harlow, 1958).

Types of Pathologies: Classifying Pathologies

Generally, mental illnesses are divided into two categories: the *functional* and the *organic*. Functional disorders are those primarily attributable to nonphysical, nonorganic causes; while the organic disorders are those for which a specific physical origin can be found. A phobia is typically considered a functional disorder, while the mental disorder caused by syphilis (known as general paresis) is classified as an organic one. As the reader can guess from the previous sections on genetic and biophysiological factors, it is still possible that future study may discover an organic basis for many disorders currently considered functional. The classification simply reflects the current viewpoint and the attitude that the functional disorders are best treated through psychological therapies rather than organic ones.

The classification system reflected in this chapter is that of the American Psychiatric Association. It has the longest history of acceptance among diagnosticians and is in current use by a majority of professionals in hospital institutions, mental health agencies, and private practices. This system is based on a *medical* model of illness, and assumes that common clusters of psychiatric symptoms exist to define a diagnostic category. Further, these clusters derive from the same or similar origins or causes. Thus, neuroses involve a milder cluster of pathological symptoms, probably due to psychological, learning, or sociocultural factors, rather than genetic or biochemical flaws, or organic damage. However, a *behavioral* model of illness has been offered as an alternative in recent years. This model emphasizes the identification of concrete behaviors as the basic unit of examination. Furthermore, behavioral classification systems tend to organize disorders into categories reflecting the learning factors involved in the disorders. For example, Bandura (1968) and Staats and Staats (1963) classified mental illnesses into: *behavioral deficits*—the absence of skills normally expected at a given age, such as delayed speech or social withdrawal; *defective stimulus control over behavior*—the inability of a stimulus, ordinarily associated with a response, to cue off this response, such as seen in alcoholism, where social constraints no longer seem influential in prompting abstinence; *inappropriate stimulus control of behavior*—the cuing of a response by a normally neutral stimulus, such as in a harmless animal triggering a fear response; *defective incentive systems*—the failure of an incentive system in guiding behaviors, such as in apathy and loss of motivation; *aversive behavioral repertoires*—the use of behaviors that have aversive effects on others, such as in sadism or criminal acts; and *aversive self-reinforcement systems*—the acceptance of evaluative standards that lead to self-depreciation rather than reward, such as in depression and suicidal acts.

Types of Pathologies: Neuroses

Neuroses generally involve the presence of fixed symptoms used to cope with tension and conflict. These symptoms are, for the most part, inflexible and rigid patterns of behaviors. In some cases, as in anxiety neuroses, the disorder reflects an inability to handle the stresses. In contrast with the psychotic, the neurotic can achieve a reasonable social, interpersonal, and work adjustment. The neurotic has some awareness of being or feeling maladjusted, although without necessarily knowing why. We will now discuss some common types of neuroses.

Anxiety Neurosis

The sufferer experiences apprehension, anticipates imminent danger, feels out of control. Physical symptoms include rapid heartbeat, muscle tremblings, constriction of the chest or throat, sweating, and difficulty in breathing. The feeling is that something is about to happen, something frightening, something one cannot cope with. In some, the anxiety builds to an extreme level of panic. The anxiety state may remain as a continuous unwanted companion, or it may come and go in waves as *anxiety attacks*. Anxiety neurosis may develop as a result of inadequate development of coping skills, thus leaving the person vulnerable. In some persons, the anxiety is passed on by a parental model who communicated fearfulness as a pervasive orientation. In others, the anxiety starts as a normal warning response to real threat, such as rejection, isolation, punishment, or loss of love. Although the real threat has now been removed, the patient may still suffer from a conditioned expectation.

Phobic Neurosis

In contrast to the diffuseness of the anxiety neurosis, phobias are triggered by specific objects or situations, such as heights. The phobia is an extreme, irrational fear. In some people, more than one fear may be present leading to severe restrictions in the person's life. Some theorists believe a phobia to be a symbolic representation of a more basic emotional conflict. Thus, a fear of open spaces may signify a fear of being sexually molested. Phobias may be learned through the association of a neutral object with a frightening experience. An attack by a vicious dog may develop into fear of anything furry. In many cases, a child adopts the same fear exhibited by a parent, retaining these fears in later life.

Hypochondriacal Neurosis

The hypochondriac is one with a preoccupation and exaggerated concern for health. For the neurotic, health is a serious business that must continuously be watched. Simultaneously, the hypochondriac is certain that his or her health is failing. A friend's passing reference to a supposed health hazard instantly leads the hypochondriac to taking excessive precautions. Mild physical symptoms are turned into major concerns and visits to physicians, quacks, faith healers, druggists, or anyone believed to profess knowledge about illness. In many ways, the imaginary illnesses of the hypochondriac serve a function. The hypochondriac is often a person who is fearful of interpersonal relationships, and who finds the narrow world of physical illness much more tolerable than the challenges of interpersonal interactions. A basically anxious person, the hypochondriac transfers these anxieties to bodily concerns. On occasion, the hypochondriac also gains some secondary rewards from the sympathy of others as well as the removal of responsibilities. Mechanic (1974) hypothesizes that "people who are unhappy, bored, or otherwise discontented may focus on symptoms that have a high prevalence in the population . . . as a means of managing life events . . . (and) indeed, may develop a career of such responses, managing their lives and others through a vocabulary of illness" (p. 93).

Hysterical Neurosis, Conversion Type

Although less frequent today, hysteria still does appear in patients. Unlike the hypochondriac who is *afraid* of becoming ill or disabled, the hysteric actually does experience a disability. This may be in a sensory or motor area, such as in hysterical blindness or paralysis. Where there is a loss of consciousness or memory, the disorder is called hysterical neurosis, dissociative type. Examples of dissociation include amnesia, somnambulism, and multiple personalities. Typically, a hysterical neurosis is suspected where the physical symptoms lack a medical origin, where survival reflexes are maintained (an hysterical convulsive will not typically fall in a dangerous area), where the symptoms are found to disappear under some conditions as during sleep or under hypnosis, and where the patient shows a curious blasé attitude known as *la belle indifférence*. Freud believed that hysteria was caused by severe repression, the act of driving emotionally charged conflicts into the unconscious. Symbolism may be present, such as in the case of the person who loses hand movement after feeling guilty about stealing with that hand. In this and other cases, the hysterical behavior is a way of solving a difficult conflict. An example is the rare patient who shows dual personalities, with completely independent characteristics (one often being unaware of the other's existence). By being two different persons, the patient may satisfy opposing needs and values without guilt. The dual personality differs from schizophrenia in that the latter is a much more severe syndrome.

Obsessive-Compulsive Neurosis

These involve either recurring thoughts (obsessions) or actions (compulsions) that interfere with normal activities (see Figure 20-3). The patient is under the control of the obsessions or compulsions, being forced to repeat them over and over. If the patient is prevented from engaging in the activities, anxiety and even panic develop. Thoughts may range from the trivial to the more frightening, such as the patient worrying that he himself *might* kill someone. Regarding compulsions, actions are repeated including even harmful ones. For example, one patient picked at her hair until she became bald; another washed his hands until the skin was raw. Many obsessive-compulsives come from perfectionistic, critical backgrounds. This leads to

Fig. 20-3. Obsessive-compulsive neurosis involves the need to repeat actions (compulsions) or thoughts (obsessions) to avoid anxiety. The handwashing compulsion is superbly illustrated in this scene from Macbeth. (Theatre Collection, New York Public Library)

the extreme type of self-criticism and self-monitoring seen in some obsessions or compulsions. The handwashing may be a ritualistic expiation of unclean actions or an attempt to clear one's conscience. Sometimes hostile impulses are controlled since the obsessions or ritualistic behaviors serve to block the carrying out of the hostile act.

Types of Pathologies: Psychoses

Psychoses are severely incapacitating disorders leading to serious impairments in personal, intellectual, and work adjustments. The psychotic may lack insight about being ill, can show a break with reality and a disorganization of personality function, and may display behaviors dangerous to others or self-injurious in nature. Symptoms may appear in affect, behavior, or cognition. Emotions, or affect, may be exaggerated or inappropriate, such as in depression or schizophrenia. Behaviors can involve sensory distortions, or hallucinations, that is, having sensory experiences without the presence of an external stimulus. Hallucinations tend most often to be present in schizophrenia, and may involve visions or sounds. Thought disturbances may be seen in excessive personalized fantasies (*autism*), irrational and rigid beliefs without basis (*delusions*), illogical and disconnected thought patterns (*flight of ideas*), or disorientation and confusion. Common delusions include *delusions of grandeur, delusions of persecution,* and *ideas of reference.* A delusion of grandeur entails a belief of being superior, for example, of being the new "Savior of the World," or a famous inventor. A delusion of persecution involves believing that others are out to harm or discriminate against you, as seen, for example, in the patient who felt the CIA was preventing him from obtaining employment. Ideas of reference involves a belief that others are referring to you or events are related to your life. One hospitalized patient was certain that even the most trivial news broadcast or article was a thinly veiled reference to her condition. The three major types of psychoses will be discussed next, the *affective disorders,* the *paranoid disorders,* and the *schizophrenic disorders.*

Affective Disorders

These are disturbances of emotion, or mood. In the *manic-depressive* psychosis, the patient experiences periodic feelings of extreme elation or deep depression. Some manic-depressives alternate cycles of elation-depression-elation, while others may shift from one extreme mood to a normal emotional state and back to the same extreme. These mood disturbances will terminate with or without treatment as the disturbance runs its course temporarily. Behaviors and cognitions may reflect the basic emotional state; thus, a manic person will

show euphoria by outbursts of exuberance, flight of ideas, and optimistic activities. On the other hand, the depressed person will show a slowing down of movements, a reluctance and disinterest in normal activities, and a glum outlook. A person in the manic phase may become so agitated in carrying out plans as to become a disturbance; in severe cases, the patient ends up thoroughly exhausted physically. In severe depressions, suicidal thoughts may be entertained, and the lethargy may reach a stuporous condition where the patient is oblivious to everything including food. The roots of manic-depressive psychosis may be in the early formation of a demanding conscience. The manic-depressive as a child experiences early parental warmth and unconditional acceptance, followed by a shift to an atmosphere of conditionality and high expectations. The later depression may represent the patient's self-punitive standards involving not working hard enough, not achieving more, not being more responsible, and so forth. Some analogue studies suggest that persons may even learn to think and behave in depressed ways if continuously exposed to uncontrollable life experiences that are traumatic. Seligman (1975) terms this "learned helplessness" and believes this happens in the milder forms of depression that are situationally caused. The euphoria of the manic phase may represent an escape defense, whereby the patient denies that anything is wrong and adopts a shallow facade of gaiety and sense of well-being. As indicated earlier, the possible role of genetic or biochemical factors cannot be ruled out as causative variables.

Paranoid Disorders

Unlike the affective disorders, the paranoid disorders are distinguished more by the cognitive disturbances than the emotional. The emotions are appropriate to the thoughts, but the thoughts are inappropriate to the situation. Typically, paranoid thoughts are persecutory in nature, usually involving organized delusions. Judgment in the delusional areas is impaired, hallucinations are rare, as are delusions of grandeur, although both have been known to occur. One type of paranoid disorder is *paranoia.* Patients suffering from paranoia are usually average or above average in intelligence, can superficially maintain everyday functioning, and possess highly systematized, involved delusions. If one accepts the patient's assumptions, then the delusion often appears loosely logical. Assuming that the FBI was monitoring his activities, one patient suspected that the occasional days that mail did not arrive was due to the agents sifting letters. He believed that the telephone company offered him only a party line so that he would become used to hearing others listening in. The rising price of gasoline was arranged so that he could not easily drive to pay telephones. The paranoid's beliefs are seldom completely unbelievable. However, he is too suspicious and wary to confide in others, ending up isolated and continuously under stress. Occasionally, the delusions lead to violent actions such as assassination. The paranoid is typically an insecure, self-condemning person raised in an atmosphere of parental neglect and rejection (Bonner, 1951; Schwartz, 1963). The paranoid becomes seclusive, loses the opportunity to share beliefs and validate them through other's opinions. In fact, the paranoid may be too sensitive to accept the feedback of others, and is even more driven into a private, distorted interpretation of the world. Distortion feeds distortion until a full-blown case of paranoia is the product.

Schizophrenic Disorders

Schizophrenia is characterized by withdrawal, isolation from reality, disturbance of emotional appropriateness, bizarre thoughts or behaviors, hallucinations, and delusions. Although *schizin* means split and *phren* means mind, schizophrenia is not synonymous with multiple personality; instead, the word emphasizes the splitting or impairment of the total personality structure. It has been recently suggested that one group of schizophrenic disorders are genetic or organic in origin, the process schizophrenias, while another are psychological, the reactive schizophrenias. Until more conclusive evidence is available, the more typical classifications of schizophrenias include *simple schizophrenia, hebephrenic schizophrenia, catatonic schizophrenia,* and *paranoid schizophrenia.* The simple schizophrenic shows a gradual, insidious develop-

ment of symptoms that are not dramatic enough to raise immediate concerns. Observers view the patient as being apathetic, listless, uninvolved in school or work commitments. There is a pervasive indifference to life and to people. Delusions and hallucinations are absent, but the person puts out only the most passive, sporadic and feeble attempts to adjust. Many marginal individuals, such as the vagrant, are suffering from simple schizophrenia. The hebephrenic schizophrenic is noted for immature actions, grimaces, giggling fits, uninhibited gesturing. Actions appear totally without sense, speech is garbled and full of self-created words with private meanings. Hallucinations are common. In many ways, the hebephrenic acts very much like a child in temperament, poor self-control, and behavior. The catatonic schizophrenic is most noticeable for motor symptoms. In the *catatonic stupor,* the patient, as shown in Figure 20-4, may stay in a fixed position for hours, or may retain a posture in which someone else puts that person, as though molded into a wax statue (*waxy flexibility*). Some catatonics will pass through the stuporous stage into a *catatonic excitement,* involving agitated, noisy, violent or destructive outbursts. A speech characteristic common to the catatonic is *echolalia,* the repeating of other people's sentences. Although the catatonic seems in a state of extreme isolation during the stupor, some former patients report being hypersensitive to surroundings during this condition. The paranoid schizophrenic is characterized by the persecutory delusions. It is the most common form of schizophrenia and combines the suspiciousness of paranoia with the deteriorated impairment of schizophrenia. Unlike paranoia, the paranoid schizophrenic suffers from vivid auditory hallucinations, an inability to function, and a grosser fragmentation of personality. Paranoiacs tend not to reveal willingly their pathological beliefs. A paranoid schizophrenic will write bizarre letters to newspapers, to the President, and may even seek a news conference. A great deal of effort has been exerted to identify possible genetic or biophysiological explanations for schizophrenia. The evidence in support of such explanations have included that on the process schizophrenia, as well as findings showing some abnormal EEGs (elec-

Fig. 20-4. In catatonic schizophrenia, a patient may hold a bizarre posture for long periods, as depicted here. (Ed Lettau)

troencephalograms) and abnormal endocrine function in some schizophrenics. Cultural factors have been examined because of the association between the incidence of schizophrenia and socioeconomic status, and the influence of different world societies in affecting the specific symptoms of the schizophrenic in their country. Psychological approaches have identified the traits of "schizophrenogenic mothers and fathers"; the former appearing to be rejecting, overprotective, aloof, subtly dominant, while the latter seeming to be detached, passive, and poor models. The family structure of the latter schizophrenic tends to be a destructive one, with distortions, miscommunications, and intrafamily conflicts.

Case History: Paranoid Schizophrenia

Henry B. was into his second semester in college when he first came to the attention of the author. Henry asked for an appointment to meet, since the author's previous book so accurately "described my experiences." He appeared a neatly dressed, outwardly friendly, but somewhat weary young man. He explained that he had been driving for hours from town to town, in a search for a sign that would answer his dilemma about school. Upon arrival at each community, he would let his "spirit" direct him to a locale that had the right intuitive "world feeling." Sometimes this locale was a meadow outside of the city, sometimes it was a darkened doorway to a bar which called to him, sometimes it was a fluorescent-bright department store at rush hour. Although no one directly spoke to him or even paid attention to him, Henry could often feel the "unspoken truths" pass from person to person about him, although these were unconsciously passed thoughts that only Henry could notice.

Henry's search was stimulated by his growing alienation from college, his former academic goals, his friendships, and his sense of disorganization to life. It was not a new experience that led to any concern, but rather a repetition of prior similar sensations of being aloof and separated from events and people. Always a bright and sensitive person, his sensitivity became even more severe as he tried to comprehend his world around him. He felt driven by an insight that all interactions were superficial and unreal, and that true reality lay below the surface. Everyone was an actor playing out a role, but only he was aware of the fact that roles were being played—even the actors themselves did not share this truth. This insight further increased Henry's sense of alienation and separateness, until his encounter with the author's book on abnormal psychology. The passage describing subjectivity in perception as having reality for the perceiver had an immense impact on

Henry. He took this passage as a direct reference to his own personal experiences. His first words to the author were, "Here I am, you know me."

Henry's return to town for the appointment was a high point for him after an extremely strenuous travel. He was now euphoric that he could share his "truths" with someone who could understand, and whose writings were a private signal for the meeting. In this euphoric state, Henry shared his private concerns that he was on the edge of a great revelation, but that no one would listen to him. His revelations were twofold. First that he was the only nonactor in the world, and that he could not wake other people into realizing their enforced roles. Second, that this reality was a form of punishment he had to bear as a test. In the same way that Jesus was to face isolation on the mountain, then alienation from his disciples Judas and Peter, and finally a glorious resurrection, so did Henry believe that his current experiences were a trial.

The author's writings were read with relief by Henry. Not only did he view them as a private message, but also as a sign that the trial was nearing an end. With this as an opening, the author encouraged Henry to accept further meetings to discuss his experiences. He had a modest chance for recovery through long term treatment. However, after minimal progress, Henry decided that counseling was another phase in his trial, and elected to again leave for another extended trip.

Types of Pathologies: Psychophysiologic Disorders

These disorders involve illnesses where bodily changes are attributable to emotional disturbance. Also known as psychosomatic disorders, they are believed to be a result of tensions and conflicts channeled to bodily organs. A simple analogy is the way in which some people describe anxiety as "that knot in my stomach." The psychophysiologic disorders tend to be more *organ specific,* in that the symptoms are displayed in accord with recognizable medical illnesses (for example, asthma, ulcers, high blood pressure, vertigo, cramps, hives). Whereas hysteria is noted for symptoms that often fail to exactly reproduce the

true symptoms of the medical ailment being imitated, the psychophysiologic disorders are often indistinguishable from known physical illnesses. There are several hypotheses about why a specific patient is more likely to develop one illness and not another, such as hives rather than migraine headaches. One is that this patient has a weakness in a specific organ and hence is predisposed to experience a dysfunction there. This may be due to an inherited, constitutional weakness or one that is the residual of a former bout with an illness of medical origin. Another hypothesis suggests that different emotional conflicts are automatically expressed through different organs; thus, persons in conflict over dependency needs would typically develop ulcers instead of asthma. It is also possible that the bodily symptom selected is a symbolic representation of the conflict, for example, the gasping of the asthmatic symbolizing a psychological call for help. Finally, it is speculated that certain symptoms derive because of the specific relationship between the tension and autonomic nervous system reactions. For example, continuous anxiety leads to release of stomach acid secretions, which in turn, may, cause ulcers. Although tentative, some associations among certain bodily illnesses and personality conflicts have been found. These are presented in the next section.

Peptic Ulcers

Ulcers are experienced as burning pains after meals, and may progress to hemorrhaging. The ulceration is due to the acid in gastric secretions damaging the stomach tissue; since these secretions are normally activated by food, the pains occur after eating. Dependency-independency conflicts are the most commonly examined as possible causes. The patient wishes to be cared for and protected, yet this is unacceptable to that person's self-image as self-reliant and assertive. The so-called ulcer personality typically is consumed by a pervasive drive to demonstrate competency. An intriguing study by Brady (1958) discovered that "executive" responsibilities can precipitate ulcers. Shock was delivered to two monkeys. The "executive" monkey could prevent the shock to himself or the other monkey by a lever; the other monkey had no such control. Results showed that "executive" monkeys suffered from ulcers so severe as to cause death, while the "nonexecutive" primate escaped any illness. Weiss (1968) failed to replicate Brady's hypothesis but instead showed that it is the "helpless" victim who develops more anxiety and hence ulcers.

Asthma

This illness involves bronchial spasms that prevent normal breathing. In many asthmatics, the origin is entirely nonpsychological and due instead to an allergy. However, even in these cases, emotional stress can sometimes act as triggers to an asthma attack (Stein, 1962). In the true psychosomatic asthmatic, psychological factors alone can prompt the illness, such as in the patient who went into a spasm upon seeing a flower she was "allergic" to, only to then discover that it was an artificial flower. A frequent explanation suggests that psychosomatic asthma is related to feelings of rejection. Fearing separation, feeling deprived, and experiencing anger, the patient expresses a suppressed rage or gasp for help in the asthmatic spasm.

High Blood Pressure and Heart Disease

Both of these ailments can be psychological in origin. In high blood pressure, also known as *essential hypertension,* continuing stress is suspected. Excessive anxiety over examinations (Bogdonoff, 1960) and exposure to natural disasters (Ruskin et al, 1948) have been shown to increase blood pressure. Many hypertensives have been described as hostile, overambitious, but controlled enough to appear superficially friendly and gracious. Additional data suggests an element of rigidity and an emotional isolation from others. A fascinating series of medical research studies has identified some other correlates of *coronary disease,* such as heart failure. The cardiologists, Friedman and Rosenman (Friedman et al, 1964; Rosenman et al, 1975), identified a Type A lifestyle as being associated with high risk of heart disease. Included in the lifestyle are a high drive to compete and succeed, self-imposed deadlines, rapid completion of physical and mental tasks, intolerance of delays,

and a tendency to work on several tasks simultaneously (for example, solving a problem mentally while eating breakfast). The relationship between the Type A behavioral style and high incidence of heart disease may be a function of the stress prompted by such behaviors (Suinn, 1975; Suinn and Bloom, 1978). Additionally, there is some apparent relation between stress and cholesterol level, such that cholesterol goes up (Friedman and Rosenman, 1974; Suinn et al, 1975); and cholesterol level is presumed to be a contributing factor to heart disease. Finally, severe life stresses seem to characterize the lives of persons just six months prior to their dying suddenly from heart disease (Rahe and Lind, 1971).

Types of Pathologies: Organic Disorders

This classification refers to those mental illnesses where damage to the brain is a known cause. Symptoms may include impairment of memory, emotions, intellect, judgment, or orientation. Where the damage is believed to be reversible, the term *acute brain syndrome* is used; where the damage is felt to be permanent, the term *chronic brain syndrome* is used. Organic brain damage can result from alcohol or drug abuse, head injuries, poisoning, deterioration from aging, tumors, or medical illnesses such as meningitis or syphilis. Symptoms are a function of the site of the brain damage; they are also influenced by the stresses facing the patient, and the patient's prior personality traits, psychological adjustment style, and motivational structure. In some cases, drastic changes in personality or behaviors may occur such that family and friends feel the patient to be acting like a total stranger. The organic, psychophysiological, hysterical, and hypochondriacal disorders might be compared briefly for the reader's interest. Both the organic and psychophysiologic disorders show medical symptoms that follow the expected pattern for such physical ailments; however, the origins of the former are primarily physical while the latter appear to be bodily illnesses primarily attributable to emotional origins. The hysterical neurosis, conversion type, involves medical symptoms too, but these symptoms fail to duplicate the symptomatology expected from true physiological or anatomical disease processes. Rather, the hysterical symptoms follow what the patient *believes* to be the expected symptoms that should develop based upon a limited or incorrect knowledge of anatomy or physiology. In hypochondriasis, the main sign is an excessive *concern* over becoming ill; typically, there are no real signs of actual medical illness or disability. Some important examples of organic disorders are discussed below.

General Paresis

The infectious disease, *syphilis,* is caused by a micro-organism called *treponema pallidum* and carries certain symptoms, such as the appearance of a small sore, followed by a dark skin rash over the body, followed by a long period of no signs, before the disease attacks the heart, the spinal cord, or the brain. *General paresis* results from this invasion of the brain. The incubation period from the onset of syphilis to the signs of brain damage may be anywhere from five to thirty years. Physical symptoms of paresis include pupils of different size, a slow pupilary reflex to light, tremors of the fingers or lips, slow and uncontrolled writing, and a shuffling walk. The patient slurs speech, for example saying "Meh-des Pis'ple" for "Methodist Episcopal." As the progressive attack of the syphilis organism proceeds, memory for events happening just a moment ago may be lost. Slovenliness and diminishing morality appear. Delusions may occur, either in a grandiose style, or in a depressed one. In the former, patients may perceive themselves as wealthy philanthropists; in the latter case, patients may be certain that their hearts are molding and deteriorating. The final stage of paresis involves loss of voluntary motion, lack of awareness or recognition, and a subhuman, vegetative existence. Fortunately, paresis is preventable by prevention of syphilis, and can be treated with penicillin. The Wasserman Blood Test detects syphilis.

Disorders from Trauma

Damage to the brain may occur through trauma, through a blow, or laceration. Concussions may result from playing football, from repeated punches in boxing, or from an accidental fall (see Figure 20-5). A direct laceration to the brain ruptures brain tissue from shrapnel, skull fragments, or other objects piercing the brain. Had President John F. Kennedy survived, the possibility of brain damage would have been of grave concern. Brain damage from trauma is suspected where there is loss of consciousness, disorientation, confusion, and headaches. With minor concussions, it is not uncommon for a person to return to activities while still suffering, such as in football players. Additional specific signs of brain damage are related to the exact site of the damage. For example, damage to the occipital lobe will lead to visual symptoms, while injury to the parietal lobe will lead to speech deficits (Penfield and Rasmussen, 1950). Certain general intellectual deficiencies signify possible brain damage, including an inability to understand concepts or abstractions, a compulsive repeating of actions, and occasionally an agitated reaction in the face of failure on intellectual tasks. In some cases, personality changes have been reported, such as increased seclusiveness, euphoria, and impulsiveness. It is difficult to determine whether these changes are directly related to the brain injury, or whether they are secondary to a personality maladjustment. A person better adjusted prior to the damage is less likely to show gross personality changes than the marginally adjusted patient.

Disorders of Aging

Aging of the brain occurs in the same way as aging of the body. *Senile psychosis* is one type of mental disorder that results from aging. Also called *senile dementia,* it is associated with brain atrophy involving actual shrinkage. Other changes also involve the appearance of senile plaques, areas of tissue degeneration seen as granular shaped tissue. In this dementia, memory for recent experiences is poor, time orientation is confused, and there is self-neglect. The patient dwells on past life events, becomes more and more set in doing things one way, and loses emotional stability, crying readily or bursting into anger. Behavioral regression can occur, whereby the patient acts childish and requires adult supervision. The *psychosis* connected with *cerebral arteriosclerosis* shares many symptoms common to senile psychosis, such as the

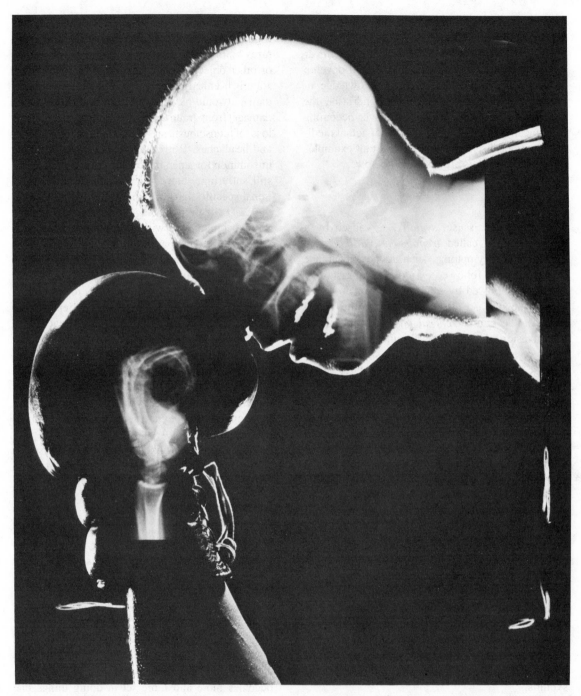

Fig. 20-5. Organic damage to the brain leading to abnormal behaviors can develop from a variety of causes, including the trauma from a hit to the head. (Howard J. Sochurek)

memory loss, carelessness with self-care, emotional instability, and deterioration in functioning. Cerebral arteriosclerosis is actually a medical condition characterized by obstruction of the blood vessels of the brain. The vascular wall has become thickened from fatty deposits and connective tissue. Additional signs of this ailment include headaches, faintness upon arising suddenly, temporary speech aphasia, and transitory weakness in the limbs. *Alzheimer's Disease* has been classified as similar to senile dementia, but appears at an earlier age. It may show up around fifty years of age and hence is sometimes referred to as a *presenile dementia*. It is relatively rare, apparently caused by neural degeneration. Symptoms include aphasia, orapraxia (inability to use objects correctly), restlessness, depression, delusions, and hallucinations. To compensate for memory loss, the patient may make up memories to answer questions (*confabulation*). Severe deterioration of normal physical functioning can take place in as short as five years from onset.

Epilepsy

Sudden disturbances of the normal rhythmic patterns of brain activity are associated with convulsions. The *grand mal seizure* may be preceded by an aura, a sensory experience, such as pressure moving up the body, or light flashes. In a grand mal, the seizure begins with the tonic stage involving muscles tensing so that the body is rigid, the head back, the jaws and hands clenched. The clonic stage follows as muscles alternately relax and contract, creating jerking motions. Within a few minutes a recovery phase of generalized muscle relaxation develops. The petit mal seizure involves brief (a few seconds) impairment of consciousness. The Jacksonian seizure begins with small muscle twitches in one limb, then progresses through the same side of the body, and finally spreads across the entire body. The seizure always begins in the same place for each attack for different patients. The psychomotor seizure is characterized by complex actions that are completed without awareness. Although the patient engages in the behaviors, and may look conscious, the patient is usually amnesic for the event. Such actions generally involve innocuous activities such as driving, attending a movie, or shopping. However, the lawyers for Jack Ruby, who shot the alleged assassin of President Kennedy, argued that Ruby may have done the shooting during an epileptic episode. In all three types of epilepsy, a loss of consciousness occurs with the corollary amnesia for events during the seizure itself. A majority of epilepsy sufferers follow a normal life without impairment of work, intellectual or social functioning (Himler and Raphael, 1945). Seizures are completely controllable with anticonvulsive medication in 50–60 percent of epileptics, and can be substantially reduced in a remaining 30 percent (National Epilepsy League, 1962). Medication, sometimes special dieting, and avoidance of conditions that prompt a seizure are also useful. Conditions that precipitate seizures include hyperventilating, alcohol, lights flickering, and emotional stresses. In severe cases, brain surgery is sometimes advised if the seizure can be traced to a specific brain site (Penfield and Erickson, 1941).

Types of Pathologies: Alcoholic Disorders

Alcoholism is listed fourth among health problems within the United States. Victims are characterized by excessive drinking, loss of control over drinking habits, and disturbances in mental, social, and economic functioning (Clark, 1966). Consequences of alcoholism (see Table 20-2) include ineffective job performance, financial drain, lowered esteem in the eyes of friends and family, and deteriorating physical health. The stomach and intestine can become irritated and painful, the liver may be damaged, the risk of heart disease can increase, and anemia or vitamin deficiencies may develop. Alcoholism is said to proceed through several stages: the *prealcoholic symptomatic* phase, the *prodromal* phase, the *crucial* phase, and the *chronic* phase. In the prealcoholic phase, drinking increases to a greater intake than just a few social drinks, although the drinking pattern still seems similar to that of social drinkers. The prodromal phase is noted for a change in attitude toward drinking, with alcohol being felt as a need

Table 20-2.   The Relationship of Alcohol Intake, Body Weight, and Driving Performance

Body Weight (lbs.)	Number of Drinks *											
	1	2	3	4	5	6	7	8	9	10	11	12
100	.038	.075	.113	.150	.188	.225	.263	.300	.338	.375	.418	.450
120	.031	.063	.094	.125	.156	.188	.219	.250	.281	.313	.344	.375
140	.027	.054	.080	.107	.134	.161	.188	.214	.241	.268	.285	.321
160	.023	.047	.070	.094	.117	.141	.164	.188	.211	.234	.258	.281
180	.021	.042	.063	.083	.104	.125	.146	.167	.188	.208	.229	.250
200	.019	.038	.056	.075	.094	.113	.131	.150	.169	.188	.206	.225
220	.017	.034	.051	.068	.085	.102	.119	.136	.153	.170	.188	.205
240	.016	.031	.047	.063	.078	.094	.109	.125	.141	.156	.172	.188

Under .05
Driving not seriously impaired

.05 to .10
Driving increasingly dangerous (.08 legally drunk in Utah)

.10 to .15
Driving dangerous (legally drunk in many states)

Over .15
Driving VERY dangerous (legally drunk in any state)

*One drink equals 1 ounce of 100 proof liquor or 12 ounces of beer.

to be filled, often secretively. Periods of amnesia or blackouts occur during intoxication. There is still an unwillingness to admit openly that the drinking is becoming a problem. In the crucial phase, the alcoholic suddenly realizes the extent of the problem and sporadically attempts abstinence, such as hiding liquor money. Yet the need persists, and control quickly dissipates once a drop is taken. Remorse, self-pity, excuses, and temporary promises alternate as outsiders express their rejection. By the chronic phase, the alcoholic no longer pretends to care about others, employment, money, or family troubles, but lives only to drink. Continued alcoholism results in certain psychotic conditions, such as *pathological intoxication, delirium tremens,* or *Korsakoff's psychosis.*

Pathological Intoxication

This rare, transitory, reversible condition is suspected in some criminal acts of violence. In some cases of pathological intoxication, outbursts of rage may lead to manslaughter, suicide, or rape. Equally likely symptoms are deep depression, anxiety, disorientation, hallucinations, delusions, or perceptual distortions. Primary signs include rigid-

ity of the pupils, sudden emotionality or behavioral change, mental confusion, and dramatic recovery. Recovery is usually rapid and the episode typically ends with sleep and amnesia. Pathological intoxication usually occurs in individuals with unstable personalities, and it is possible that the alcohol acts as a toxic trigger or an irritant prompting a type of brain seizure.

Delirium Tremens

The "d.t.s" are seen in tremors of the fingers and facial areas, irregular pulse rate, dilated pupils, and delirum. While delirious, the alcoholic is confused and disoriented, losing track of time, place, and people. Bizarre hallucinations develop, involving sensations of ants crawling under the skin, fantastic snakes slithering out of the walls, or strangling odors pervading the air. During moments of suggestibility, the patient may be led to "see" writing on a blank paper and even attempt to read it. Since the d.t.s occur during abstinence following a drinking binge, the delirium is a form of withdrawal symptom. Recovery usually develops within three to ten days, with symptoms sometimes recurring during the convalescence.

Korsakoff's Psychosis

This psychotic condition, named after its Russian discoverer, is characterized by confusion for time and place, anterograde amnesia, and a tendency to fabricate memories to fill in the gaps. Anterograde amnesia is the loss of memory for events that have just occurred. This amnesia, and the disorientation for time and place, is covered up by the patient's "recalling" events rather than admitting confusion. Superificially, the patient seems normal, is cooperative, and even pleasant during examination. The tendency to confabulate, or make up memories, reflects the lack of insight the patient has into the illness. If untreated, degenerative changes can occur in the brain and peripheral nerves. It is now believed that the primary cause of Korsakoff's psychosis is the vitamin deficiency common to alcoholics, especially a vitamin B complex, particularly thiamin deficiency. Since alcohol contains some calories, the alcoholic feels no need to maintain a balanced meal, but substitutes drinking for eating. The urge for alcohol supplants the need for food. Treatment for Korsakoff's psychosis, therefore, involves a high vitamin diet. The patient is usually restored to normal functioning within six to eight weeks, although in some cases amnesia continues and ethical values may be impaired.

Types of Pathologies: Drug Abuse

Addiction to drugs occurs in cases where there is an overwhelming need to have more drugs, an increased tolerance that requires a higher dosage for the same effects, and a dependence on the drug (World Health Organization, 1950). Dependence may be either *psychological dependence* or *physical dependence*. In psychological dependence, there is a heavy reliance on drugs for the emotional support or relief they provide. In physical dependence, there is a physiological alteration within the body which leads to the development of physical withdrawal symptoms upon abstinence. Since both types of dependency have serious effects on behavior, psychiatric work deals with both. The amphetamines, cocaine, peyote, LSD, psilocybin, and marijuana, are drugs that can lead to psychological dependence. Opium, morphine, heroin, barbiturates, some tranquilizers, and codeine, can produce physical dependence. Historically, attitudes toward drug usage have been influenced by cultural factors as much as by the behavioral effects of the drugs or of dependence. Morphine and heroin were introduced in the late nineteenth century as miracle drugs, but have since been more carefully controlled because of their addicting effects. Opium and peyote have been accepted parts of cultural activities or rituals in the Orient, Mexico, and by some Indian tribes. Various forms of marijuana have been used across the world because of its claimed relaxing effects. In the United States, use of heroin, cocaine, and opium are viewed as unacceptable by society; however, barbiturates "to help sleep" and tranquilizers "for the nerves" have become marketable commodities. Similarly, in the United States, LSD, amphetamines, and marijuana have become controversial issues as the rigid attitudes against drug usage continue to be questioned. Proponents of legalizing of marijuana, for example, distinguish between drug usage and drug abuse.

Because of the great variety of drugs, it is difficult to summarize the psychological effects of drug dependence. Similarly, matters are sometimes confused by the interplay between personality variables and drug characteristics. For example, some of the psychological effects of marijuana and LSD are a function of the user's expectations rather than a property of the drug itself (McGlothin and West, 1968). It is known that the withdrawal symptoms of heroin are agonizingly painful, and that tremendous social problems are associated with heroin addiction. Also, it is known that grave overdoses are the risks of barbiturate, amphetamine, and LSD abuse, including severe anxieties and psychotic conditions. Less definitive, although still worth considering, are the reports of intoxication effects from marijuana usage (McGlothin and West, 1968; U.S. Department of Health, Education, and Welfare, 1975), and chromosomal damage and hallucinatory relapses in LSD abusers (Louria, 1971). Other than introduction to drugs through medical purposes, modern users become involved for a variety of reasons.

The twentieth century youth, usually a male, better educated, from a higher socioeconomic class, raised in an urban environment (Berg, 1969), has adopted experimentation with drugs as a new generation experience. In some respects, it may be an approach toward seeking an identity, and a separation from parents. Drugs also offer a quick means of discovering new internal experiences through sensory and emotional stimulation.

Other patterns of drug involvement stem from the press of group membership. Subgroups using hallucinogenic drugs offer peer acceptance on the basis of shared drug activities (Scher, 1966). Initially, peer pressure is coupled with the extolling of the virtues of the drug experience, and the minimizing of the potential dangers. This sense of friendship and belonging and promise are powerful attractions for entry. Once addicted, the new group member then faces increasing isolation from the society at large, and becomes even more reliant upon the subgroup for acceptance. Threat of ostracism now comes into play as a powerful method for the drug users to further shape the values of the new member (Ausubel, 1961).

A more pathological cause for entry into drug abuse characterizes some addicts. These are the small proportion who use drugs as an emotional crutch. The neurotic may find that drugs relieve the unbearable anxieties, offering a more pleasant fantasy environment. For the psychotic, the hallucinatory experiences or the transcendent emotional impact of certain drugs may confirm existent delusional systems. Psychological dependence plays a crucial role in such addictions.

Drug abuse as a form of social deviance is common among narcotic addicts in the United States. In these cases, the user is typically from a low socioeconomic level, of a minority background, and lives in a metropolitan area (Murray, 1967). This type of drug addict experiences insecurity, social incompetency, lack of assertiveness, and a dependency alliance with the mother (Haertzen et al, 1963). The addict is infantilized and overprotected by the parent, and receives conflicting messages of both possessiveness and rejection. In turn, the addict feels ambivalent, both wanting the dependence yet wishing to strike out and be emancipated. In some cases, the parent procures the illegal drugs, expresses grief at the addictive condition of the offspring, while simultaneously attacking the youngster for being a personal and social blight. A corollary form of social deviance occurs in the users who are acting out their antisocial feelings through drugs. Drug usage becomes simply another part of the total pattern of rebelliousness, criminality, or delinquency (Vaillant, 1966). Many drug users grew up in slums, poverty, and fragmented family environments, and became alienated and hostile.

Types of Pathologies: Sexual Deviations

Sexual deviations may be classified in terms of *deviations of arousal,* or of *behavioral deficiency* (see Figure 20-6). The former involve being sexually aroused by a *deviant object,* by *deviant acts,* or *deviation in level of arousal.* Deviation of object choice includes fetishism (being aroused by inanimate objects), pedophilia (being aroused by children), bestiality (being aroused by animals), and necrophilia (being aroused by dead persons). Deviation in sexual acts involves being aroused by sadism (enjoying injury to others), masochism (enjoying self-injury), exhibitionism (enjoying being watched by others), or voyeurism (enjoying watching others' activities). Deviation in arousal level includes excessive sexual urge (satyriasis or nymphomania), or inability to become aroused (frigidity or impotence). With behavioral deficiency, there are normal arousal characteristics but deficiency in the sexual act. In vaginismus, the sexual act is obstructed because penile penetration is painful. Where sexual desire is present, but penile erection is lacking, impotency would be classified as a behavioral deficiency. Premature ejaculation would also be an example of male deficiency.

Case History of Sexual Dysfunction: Impotence

Victor J. was a successful businessman to all outward appearances. He had moved quickly into a management position in a retail chain of men's

Fig. 20-6. A transvestite is a person who dresses in the attire of the opposite sex and apparently derives personal gratification from such activity. Transvestites may appear in public and even give public performances. (Ellis Herwig/Stock, Boston)

clothing stores. He worked long hours, but did not begrudge the additional time, since it helped him meet crucial deadlines. The initial adjustment from retail sales to management was difficult. However, Victor quickly passed through any personal sense of being under stress, adapting to the higher pace and demands with his own matching outbursts of energy. His only threat to his orderly and controlled life was his mother. She extolled his success, even flaunted it, but constantly bemoaned his bachelor life. She said he should pick a suitable

mate to share in his success, some pretty girl who could also be as openly proud of his achievements as his mother was.

Victor was indeed an eligible bachelor, with many single and even some married women who enjoyed his company. Reasonably good looking, he had acquired the social graces of being attentive and flattering to women. Yet these social skills had been developed late in life, and served as a cover for his underlying sense of discomfort about his masculinity and acceptability. He had been slow in maturing physically, and even slower socially. The latter was due to his overly protective mother, who felt that "there is plenty of time for him to become interested in girls and leave his home." Victor had always been comfortable with his mother's presence, but lacked confidence when alone.

Upon leaving his family home at age 27 to live alone, Victor spent more and more time gradually testing out his social competencies. He dated one person at a time, forming a close alliance and breaking up only after intimacy threatened the relationship. On each occasion, an opportunity for sexual intercourse had presented itself, only to end unsuccessfully. Victor could not bring himself to even attempt penetration, although his partners were more than willing after heavy petting. Initially, it was simply that Victor was ignorant of what to do, and too embarrassed to ask help. Later, his embarrassment became mingled with his earlier feelings of inadequacy, and he began to dread sexual contact. Ultimately, he felt the pressure of demands that he perform, or at least what he thought were demands. Suddenly Victor discovered himself impotent, unable to become aroused sexually.

His most recent woman-friend, a slightly older woman, has been the most important person in his recent life. A calm and patient individual, she has gradually come to recognize Victor's dissatisfactions. Through her encouragement, she has taken him to attend human sexuality workshops. Instead of using professional sexual surrogates, she has accepted this role for Victor. After learning basic anatomy and physiology through training films, Victor and his girlfriend have practiced lying side by side undressed without the need for further action. As he has become more comfortable and felt less anxiety, Victor then learned that petting can take place without demands for further sexual performance. Also, he learned that mutual pleasure could be in itself valued. Throughout, he has been discovering an increased sense of warmth and loving communication toward his partner. Just recently, he was able to experience his first sense of potency and sexual gratification.

There are a wide variety of possible origins of deviations. Hormone imbalance has been explored in disorders of arousal, since there is some evidence that lower animals are directly influenced by the quantity of sexual hormones. Although there is some apparent relationship between arousal in women and menstrual cycle (Moos et al, 1969), the picture is very unclear in humans. Thus, hormonal activity seems to be only a vague contributor to understanding the transsexual, the person who believes that he or she is being trapped in a body of the opposite sex. Some theories have emphasized the role of social inadequacy. Fearing failure, the deviant person seeks refuge in object choices that are nonthreatening or incapable of acts of rejection, such as inanimate objects or animals. Deviant acts may also represent avoidance of rejection, or may derive from an early association between guilt feelings and sexual desires. Sadism, for example, may reflect a punitive act toward the sexual partner accused of being responsible for the deviant's unacceptable sexual desires. Masochism, of course, can be self-punishment for submitting to sexual temptations. Heightened guilt feelings, fear of punishment, excessive anxiety, can all act to inhibit arousal more directly and lead to impotence or frigidity. On the other hand, excessive sexual urges as in satyriasis or nymphomania may represent a symbolic attempt to prove one's worth or satisfy a deprived need to be wanted, if only for physical purposes. In one particular patient, the nymphomania was her expression of feeling unable to establish any meaningful interpersonal relationships. She, therefore, relied upon the simple, ritualized, and impersonal "relating" offered by sexual encounters. Psychoanalytic theorists trace most of such origins to unsatisfactory early interactions with parents. For example, sexual promiscuity may represent a rebellion against parental taboos toward sexuality, or an overcompensation

for a deprivation of parental love. Homosexuality in psychoanalytic theory may be due to a failure of the boy to identify with the male parent and this parent's masculinity.

From another viewpoint, homosexual behavior may be classified and understood in approach-avoidance terms. Homosexual behavior may involve the selection of the same-sex partner because of avoidance of opposite-sex persons. Such avoidance can, in turn, be because of fearfulness, or an absence of feelings of arousal or interest. Another possibility is that homosexual behavior in some individuals represents the approach toward same-sex partners as more stimulating or satisfying sexual objects. In closing, it should be noted that homosexuality has been removed from the American Psychiatric Association's list of abnormalities. This is partly because of criticism that previous definitions have relied too heavily on cultural definitions of abnormality. There is no doubt that homosexual behavior is maintained for a variety of reasons, some being personal preference with no overtones of pathology, while others turn to homosexuality for neurotic reasons.

Treatment Strategies: Medical

The study of mental illness is rooted in psychiatry, which is a branch of medicine. Additionally, the early classifications of mental pathology stressed the disease-entity approach. Hence, it is not surprising that a variety of major approaches to the treatment of mental illness have sought answers in medicine. Among these are *shock therapy, psychosurgery,* and *chemotherapy.*

Shock Therapy

"Shock" therapy, is more accurately called convulsive therapy; convulsions can be induced by the use of either drugs or an electric current. *Insulin shock therapy* was introduced by Sakel in 1927 on the premise that nerve energy is depleted during illness, and insulin could block further weakening of nerve cells. Although unplanned, convulsions occurred among some patients and Sakel observed that this seemed conducive to recovery (Sakel, 1933). Insulin shock involves the deliberate induction of a state of coma through daily increased doses of insulin injected intramuscularly. The coma, basically a state of hypoglycemia, is prolonged for 30 to 60 minutes and repeated daily for 30 to 90 treatments. During the treatment, bursts of activity may occur, including flailing, crying out, and convulsions. Risks are present, such as fractures from the convulsions, or even death from an irreversible coma. On the other hand, insulin shock therapy has been widely applied in the treatment of catatonic or paranoid schizophrenics, and patients with panic symptoms. Immediate improvement seems to occur in 44 to 68 percent (Staudt and Zubin, 1957) of treated patients, an improvement over the approximate 30 percent rate of recovery where no treatment is attempted. On the other hand, because of the risks and the tendency for patients to relapse within a few years, the use of insulin shock is recommended only after careful consideration, and is rarely used today.

Electroshock therapy (EST) or *electroconvulsive therapy* (ECT) was developed as an alternate approach to insulin by Cerletti during the early 1930s, and is the most commonly used convulsive therapy now in use. The first concerns of Cerletti was the possibility of electrocution or pain from the electricity, but experiments with cattle proved otherwise. These experiments were supported on the very first application on a human being, a schizophrenic patient referred by the police. EST relies upon passing a nondamaging alternating current across the temples (for example, 110 volts for .08 seconds). Convulsions are precipitated during the patient's unconsciousness. Treatment is carried out three times a week for a total of eight to twelve treatments. Side effects include temporary amnesia, occasional loss of identity, or fractures. While the fatalities from insulin shock may reach as high as one percent, EST fatalities are rare (.05 percent). EST is mildly successful with schizophrenia, but most effective with depressive symptoms. With manic-depressive psychosis, symptoms can be removed within three weeks as compared with the eight months it usually takes for spontaneous recovery (Thomas, 1954).

Psychosurgery

The early interest in the brain as the possible site of mental illness has remained with many surgeons.

Moniz, a neurologist, speculated that the prefrontal lobes suffered unhealthy nerve synapses. *Prefrontal lobotomy,* as shown in Figure 20-7, in-

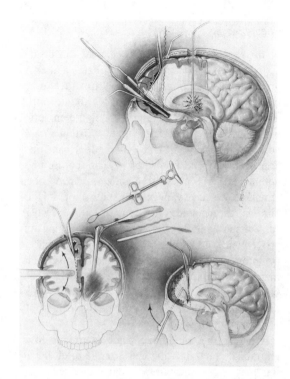

Fig. 20-7.   One form of treatment for mental disorders is surgery. A variety of methods are illustrated, whereby the connections between brain structures are separated and severed. (William Beecher Scoville)

volves the neurological severing of the fibers to the frontal lobes. The current belief is that the procedure isolates disturbing emotions, such that the patient is freed from experiencing the emotional conflicts or reactions causing the problem. This belief is similar to the use of lobotomy for intractable pain from cancer; the pain is still present, but the patient's subjective distress is diminished. Research has failed to either conclusively prove or disprove the value of psychosurgery as yet. When used with patients as a last resort in extreme cases not responding to other therapy, there seems to be gains not normally reached by such patients where other treatments had been tried. On the other hand, relapses are frequent, and it is recognized that the surgery is a permanent and irrevocable action. Side effects tend, therefore, to be permanent, such as occasional signs of brain damage impairment, personality changes, and sometimes loss of ambition.

Chemotherapy

In many ways, the twentieth century can be described as an era of drugs. Tranquilizers and energizers have revolutionized hospital treatment practices, enabling faster discharge rates and declining admissions. The tranquilizers reduce the anxieties experienced by a patient without creating sleepiness or sluggishness. Thus, the patient can function on the job, at home, or in school. The phenothiazine group of tranquilizers have been remarkably successful in the control of schizophrenia. In one study over nine hospitals, 75 percent of the patients treated showed important improvement, including changes in psychotic symptoms like delusions and hallucinations (Klerman et al, 1964). Other applications of the phenothiazines have been to control the manic symptoms of the manic-depressive and the hyperactivity of organic brain syndromes.

Whereas the tranquilizers aim at toning down emotional reactivity, the energizers aim at elevating reactivity. Energizers attempt to elevate the mood or stir a patient out of a depression. Stimulants such as the amphetamines were found to be of little value for this purpose. However, monamine oxidase (MAO)-inhibitors and the more commonly used imipramine compounds have been helpful as antidepressants. Where successful, such drugs tend to break the depressive gloom and enable the patient to again engage in more normal thoughts and activity level. However, the psychic energizer drugs are still not well understood and by no means should be considered a miracle cure for depression.

As alluded to in the earlier discussion on drug addiction, the effects of drugs are due to complex factors. Among these factors are the usual medical ones, such as the phsyical health of the patient, the rate of absorption of the drug, the weight of the patient, and other factors related to tolerance. At the same time, some psychological factors may well play a significant role, for example, the confidence of both the patient and the therapist in the drug's value, the basic personality pattern of the patient, and perhaps even the social atmosphere in which the drug is administered. As with all medications, several important issues need to be understood with regard to the role of chemotherapy in psychological problems. Many feel that the primary use of medication is to control the emotional reactivity of the patient, such that the patient can be led to confront and resolve the basic conflicts. Thus, drug treatment is for symptomatic control and does not directly serve as a cure. That is why psychotherapy and chemotherapy are often used together. A corollary issue is the possibility that some patients may become dependent on the relief provided by medication and never work at developing more adaptive behaviors. Or that the improvement in symptoms in the patient convinces family members that the "problem" exists in the patient, rather than in pathological behavioral interactions within the family structure. There is good reason to believe that some mental pathologies are actually reflective of familial dysfunctions in the family unit, rather than solely the patient's responsibility. For example, a very withdrawn patient may be defending against a spouse who is exhibiting pathological hostility. Delinquency or underachievement in academic work may be a symptom of the child's experiences of family conflicts. In summary, chemotherapy has made major contributions to the treatment of mental illness. Patients are more reachable, symptoms are often under sufficient control as to permit the development of better adjustment patterns, and, in some cases, a direct cure is actually a result. However, it would be a mistake to consider medication, shock, or surgery to be panaceas.

Treatment Strategies: Psychological

There is still a major belief that mental illness can best be understood from a psychological viewpoint. The symptoms are directly or indirectly the product of frustrations, conflicts, tensions, or traumatic experiences. These experiences may be longstanding or recent in origin. Furthermore, the symptoms may be a symbolic display of the patient's problems, or a display of the means being used by the patient to seek a resolution or display of the emotions associated with the problems. From this viewpoint, psychological factors need to be understood even in purely physical ailments. For example, confabulation might not be directly caused by central nervous system damage, but may be the patient's attempt to adjust to the memory loss caused by such damage. Similarly, the specific pattern prompted by pathological intoxication may be a function of the basic marginal personality pattern of the patient, with the alcohol acting as a trigger releasing, but not necessarily determining, the pattern. From this type of approach, a variety of more specific psychological treatment strategies have been developed, each with a different emphasis. Psychological therapies differ in the *time frame* considered important in treatment, in the *activities* believed to be needed for change to occur, in the *setting* in which change is produced, and in the specific therapeutic *intervention methods*. For example, psychoanalytic therapy stresses dealing with past childhood conflicts that need resolution before current adjustment can be effected; on the other hand, the humanistic approaches emphasize the client's capability of reaching toward future levels of adjustive potential. Regarding differences in activities, behavior therapy requires that the patient adopt actions, whereas client-centered therapy may accept verbal and emotional reflections by the therapist as sufficient to lead to change. In terms of the setting, the community mental health approach stresses that treatment must occur in the environment in which the patient lives, as opposed to only having therapy "happen" in the therapist's office. Finally, certain intervention methods may be characteristic of specific therapeutic strategies and not others, the most clear cut being the methods of behavior therapy versus the methods of psychoanalysis. Some of the major psychological treatment strategies are discussed below.

Psychoanalysis

Psychoanalysis is one of the oldest forms of psychotherapy used today, and derives from the ideas of Sigmund Freud (1955). Conflicts and traumas during early childhood experiences prevent the person from normal psychological development. In substance, a kind of stunted growth progresses with unacceptable impulses being driven underground (repressed) and neurotic defenses erected. The repression, or removal of conflicts from conscious awareness, is an insufficient solution, and such material resurfaces throughout life as symptoms or in dreams. Patients are incapable of helping themselves and, in fact, the defenses work against therapeutic attempts to uncover the problems. However, it is still possible to analyze the basic conflicts through *dream interpretation*. In addition, the patient tends to behave towards the therapist in ways similar to the patient's early reactions to parents as a child; this "transference" of emotions and behaviors from the parents to the therapist is, therefore, another useful source of analysis. Finally, the psychoanalyst can use *free association* to bypass the repression. Free association urges the patient simply to say whatever comes to mind, instead of monitoring or being cautious. Gradually, thread by thread, the analyst discovers the pattern underlying the symptoms. The therapist then proceeds to make use of all of the different materials to help the patient acquire insight into his or her pathology, and how it relates to earlier conflicts. The patient led by the therapist works through these earlier problems through verbal discussions, re-experiencing of emotions, and further removal of other defenses. Psychoanalysis is viewed as a long treatment process because of the time needed to reach the earlier origins of the symptoms, and because of the natural defensive resistance of the patient. A trained psychoanalytic therapist is typically schooled first as a medical doctor, then supervised in a psychoanalytic institute where he or she must also undergo personal analysis. Persons with nonmedical doctorates, such as a Ph.D. in psychology, may also be certified after additional psychoanalytic training. Psychoanalysis appears to have its greatest application for neurotic conditions, although some experimentation has been initiated with psychotics.

Client-Centered Therapy

This psychotherapeutic approach evolved from Carl Rogers' work with university students

(Rogers, 1951). In contradiction to psychoanalysis, Rogers believed clients to be "exquisitely rational" and goal oriented, instead of irrational, resistant, and defensive. Thus, rather than the therapist probing, searching for hidden material, and attempting to bypass the client's defenses, the client-centered therapist adopts a different role. This role is that of being nondirective, instead of analytic and interpretive. The therapist attempts only to provide the client with the accepting atmosphere needed by the client to gain confidence enough to begin steps toward self-actualizing. By communicating a warmth, empathy, and unconditional acceptance, the nondirective therapist encourages the client to become more open to experiences, including self-exploration. Client-centered theorists assume that self-perceptions form a core, the self concept, around which other experiences are evaluated. If the self concept is too narrow or distorted, other experiences may also be distorted or denied to awareness to prevent inconsistencies from reaching the self concept. The maladjusted person thus fails to function properly, because that person has incomplete or misleading information. A depressed person, for example, can accept only information that confirms the self perception of unworthiness and failure. It is the task of the therapist to enable the client to begin to perceive existing worthwhile traits, integrate these with other less positive traits, and formulate a more accurate and satisfying self-image. A more realistic, self-evaluative approach is adopted, and an optimistic outlook and release of growth potential evolves. Unlike the psychoanalyst, the client-centered therapist does not actually rely on special techniques, such as free association. Instead, the client-centered therapist does everything possible to *be client*-centered, and to respect the existence of an inner positive potential in everyone. Rather than applying certain techniques, the client-centered therapist strives toward overall goals of communicating positive regard for the client and a truly helping relationship.

Behavior Therapy

Behavioral approaches derive from a different set of data and a different conception of pathology than either psychoanalysis or client-centered ther-

apy. Behavior therapy relies on principles and laws established from laboratory findings on learning, rather than observations of patients. These laws are simply cross-applied to patient behaviors. The major premise is that pathology involves specific behaviors, that these behaviors have been learned, and that more adjustive behaviors can be acquired according to certain rules governing learning. Information on early experiences, conflicts, and traumas are not essential but may be interesting, since they lend an historical perspective to describing the learning history of the client. However, current changes in adjustment require that the client engage actively in new behaviors and that these new behaviors be emitted in the everyday environment with which the client must cope. Verbal discussions for insight, prolonged analyses of past experiences, grappling with the symbolic meaning of symptoms, or unguided talk in the therapy time, are all of secondary relevance to the principles of change accepted by the behaviorist. For example, talking about being different or understanding why one is behaving differently are insufficient conditions to prompt change in most clients. Instead, the client must have guidance in actually how to behave more adaptively, and must be faced with the proper incentive to adopt such new behaviors. The behavior therapist starts with basic principles regarding behavioral change, such as the rules of classical conditioning, extinction, operant conditioning, discrimination learning, and imitative learning (see Figure 20-8). Phobias, for example, are frequently acquired through classical conditioning, that is, the arousal of fear by one stimulus event in the presence of a neutral stimulus such that the neutral cue acquires fear-producing properties. Counter-conditioning is, therefore, a useful treatment approach to phobias. *Desensitization* (Wolpe, 1958), a form of counter-conditioning, pairs relaxation responses with the fear-producing cue, so that the relaxation becomes associated with that cue and replaces or counters the fear response. Diffuse or general anxiety is a response that a client can learn to reduce or eliminate through *anxiety management training* (Suinn and Richardson, 1970; Suinn, 1977). In anxiety management training, the client is trained to identify the early cues signalling anxiety arousal. The client then learns to

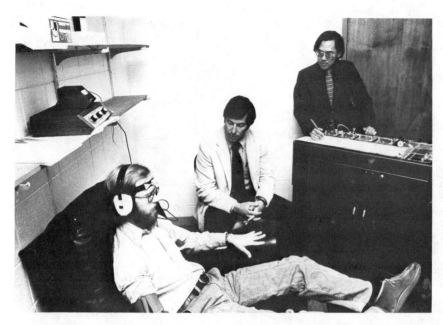

Fig. 20-8.
Biofeedback refers to a variety of methods, whereby recordings are displayed back to a person, giving information about bodily functions. The author (background) and a colleague illustrate the use of biofeedback for relaxation in order to control blood pressure. (Colorado State University Photography Laboratory)

use anxiety-reduction skills, such as self-initiated relaxation, to counter the anxiety responses. *Reinforcement* methods are applied to help psychotics acquire normal behaviors. It is assumed that the psychotic does not behave normally because the environment has rewarded that person for being pathological, and has not provided any incentives for being normal. In *token economy wards,* chronic hospitalized psychotics soon acquire normal interpersonal and occupational behaviors and extinguish abnormal activities when reinforcement is provided (Ayllon and Azrin, 1965). Similarly the conversion symptoms of hysterical neurosis may be viewed as serving a rewarding function, the reduction of anxiety from a now absent conflict. Using reinforcement, an hysterically blind patient regained sight through behavioral treatment without going into any discussion aimed at helping the patient to understand the origins or meaning of the symptom. (Brady and Lind, 1961). Adaptive skills have also been developed by principles of covert rehearsal (Suinn, 1976), and modelling (Bandura, 1969). Obsessive-compulsive behaviors have been eliminated by extinction procedures (Rachman et al, 1971), and sexual disorders successfully treated through a variety of learning approaches (Barlow, 1975).

Group Therapies

Critics of the individual therapy strategies suggest that changes can be enhanced through the proper use of groups. Patients are able to share their problems and solutions with one another, practice better ways of relating to persons other than the safe therapist, cope with social problems of alienation, and receive the emotional support and encouragement of others (see Figure 20-9). Moreno (1946) developed *psychodrama* to combine the advantages of group treatment with the desirable aspects of action in mock life circumstances. As in a drama, the patient acts out conflicts as well as possible solutions. Other stage participants join in to make the roles more realistic and to aid the patient in understanding the meaning of the conflicts. Sometimes another patient serves as an alter-ego to voice the hidden emotions or thoughts of the main character to promote insight. With the rise of the humanistic movement out of the beliefs of Rogers (1961) and Maslow (1954), groups with a different orientation have come on the modern scene. Both men share a belief in the dynamic potential existing in all persons, normal or pathological. Their premise includes the idea that even healthy persons are not always functioning fully. Hence, the self-

Fig. 20-9.   Sensitivity groups may use preliminary exercises to loosen inhibitions and increase spontaneity. (Ken Regan, Camera 5)

actualizing groups have been introduced, identified by differing names such as training or *T-groups, encounter* or *sensitivity* groups, *personal growth* groups, and *marathon* groups. The basic aims of such groups are to enhance the participants' ability to be more open to human and personal experiences, to become more creative, and to reach a higher level of life existence. Some groups may stress the desirability of expanded emotional growth, including the acceptance of deeper feelings toward oneself and others. Other objectives may involve increasing the capacity to be more spontaneous and appreciative of life experiences, sensory, intellectual, and emotional. Communication skills to open up better interpersonal understanding and honesty may also be an integral part of such groups. More study is needed to better understand the processes and effects of group methods. Personal reports from participants range from extremely positive feelings of significant

gains, to unfavorable reports of increased unhappiness and disillusionment (Jaffe and Scherl, 1969).

Community Mental Health

In one respect, the community mental health viewpoint is a philosophy of treatment rather than a specific strategy. It has been observed that hospitalization over long periods can lead to adverse effects on patients. By being removed from significant family members, from the responsibilities of normal life, and transported to a different lifestyle, patients sometimes develop apathy, loss of initiative, submissiveness, poor planning, and a constriction of interest (Wing, 1962). This pattern has been called *"institutional neurosis"* or *"institutionalism."* Partly in recognition of this, and partly because of the more general economic problems in hospitalization, the *mental health movement* has grown. The basic concepts involve returning the responsibility for care to the community, and minimizing the need for hospitalization. To achieve this, the following procedures have been encouraged: day hospitalization of patients who can return to their families overnight; night hospitalization of patients capable of maintaining a job in the day; halfway houses to aid hospital patients make the transition back into the community; use of mobile treatment teams to bring treatment to the patient instead of vice versa; and the establishment of crises programs to deal with immediate but short term emergencies such as suicide threats, pathological drug reactions, or family crises. The philosophy of treatment involves the belief that prevention of pathology has precedence over treatment, resolving immediate situationally caused problems has priority over depth analysis, solving current here-and-now problems is more important than attempting complete resolution of long standing pathologies. Hospitalization is viewed as appropriate for a limited group of patients, rather than as the routine solution for even psychotic patients. Psychopathology is accepted not as a maladaptive personality style, but as a series of immediate situational problems demanding solutions. It can be readily seen that the community mental health outlook questions the disease entity viewpoint, which tends to attribute illness to a process within the patient. Instead, treatment is organized to deal with all of the factors that can raise the level of the patient's performance. Such factors can include not only competency skills of the patient, but also family interaction patterns, environmental variables, and even the attitudes of the community and society toward the patient. As a relatively recent movement, the community mental health approach has stimulated much activity in the way of services. However, because of the rapid expansion of such services, proper evaluation has lagged somewhat, and it is difficult to determine the true effects of such services. Moreover, more research and evaluation is still needed to be able to specify the best means for effectively achieving the major objectives of the movement. Meanwhile, this quiet revolution is going on and will no doubt have a major impact on the history of psychopathology, its prevention, and its treatment. There is reason to be optimistic about the overall progress toward the reduction of the need for hospitalization. The census of patients in state hospitals in the United States increased every year from 1772 to 1957 at which date there were about 600,000 patients hospitalized. This upward trend reversed with the introduction of new drugs, open wards, and the community mental health approaches, so that today, the same census is about 300,000 patients. Although it is doubtful that mental illness or behavioral dysfunctions will ever be completely eliminated, such progress suggests that the scientific development of psychotherapeutic and medical therapies are having a substantial impact.

Glossary

Acute brain syndrome: An organic disorder involving damage to the brain believed to be reversible.

Anxiety neurosis: A neurosis characterized by apprehension and tension without an identifiable and realistic cause.

Behavior therapy: A type of psychotherapy involving principles based upon learning theory.

Catatonic schizophrenia: A type of schizophrenia characterized by motor inhibition or excitability.

Chemotherapy: A type of medical therapy involving the use of drugs.

Chronic brain syndrome: An organic disorder involving damage to the brain believed to be irreversible.

Client-centered therapy: A type of psychotherapy involving enhancing self growth through positive regard from the therapist.

Delusion: An irrational, rigidly held belief without basis in fact.

Dementia praecox: An outdated term referring to schizophrenia.

Epilepsy: An organic disorder involving seizures related to brain activity.

Functional disorders: Illnesses considered to be due to nonphysical origins, and attributable to psychological factors.

General paresis: An organic disorder due to syphilis and involving deterioration.

Grand mal seizure: A convulsion preceded by an aura, and involving a major type of convulsion.

Hallucination: A sensory experience without the presence of an external stimulus.

Hebephrenic schizophrenia: A type of schizophrenia characterized by immature, regressive, bizarre behaviors.

Hypochondriacal neurosis: A neurosis characterized by exaggerated preoccupation with health.

Hysteria: Now known as hysterical neurosis, conversion type, referring to the presence of somatic symptoms similar to actual medical disease but without a true physical cause, such as blindness. Typically, the hysterical symptom mimics, but is not identical, with a true physical disease.

Hysterical neurosis, conversion type: A neurosis characterized by physical symptoms mimicking a somatic disease, but without a true physical cause.

Hysterical neurosis, dissociative type: A neurosis characterized by loss of consciousness or memory such as amnesia, somnambulism, multiple personality.

Korsakoff's psychosis: A psychosis characterized by confusion, amnesia for recent events, and making up of details to fill memory gaps. Associated with alcoholism.

Manic-depressive psychosis: A severe form of mental illness involving euphoria and hyperactivity, and/or deep depression and motor retardation; in one version, these symptoms alternate cyclically.

Mesmerism: Original term for hypnosis, named after its identifier, Anton Mesmer.

Neuroses: Those disorders of a lesser level of severity than psychoses, whereby fixed symptoms are used to cope with tension and conflict. Includes anxiety neurosis, phobic neurosis, hypochondriacal neurosis, hysterical neurosis-conversion type, and obsessive-compulsive neurosis.

Obsessive-compulsive neurosis: A neurosis characterized by recurring thoughts called obsessions, or actions called compulsions which interfere with daily activity, since these repetitions demand completion.

Organic disorders: Illnesses considered to be due to specific physical origins such as infections, brain damage, and so forth.

Paranoia: A psychosis characterized by extreme suspi-

cion and delusions of being persecuted, occurring in a person who may otherwise function normally.

Paranoid schizophrenia: A type of schizophrenia characterized by delusions of being persecuted.

Pathological intoxication: An alcoholic disorder, transitory in nature, involving behavioral outbursts triggered by drinking alcohol.

Petit mal seizure: A convulsive starting with small muscle twitches in one limb, then progressing to include the entire body.

Phobic neurosis: A neurosis characterized by an irrational fear of specific objects or situations.

Psychoanalysis: A type of psychotherapy relying upon dream analysis, free association, and working through early life conflicts, and identified with Sigmund Freud.

Psychomotor seizure: A convulsion leading to complex actions without awareness.

Psychophysiologic disorders: A disorder where structural changes in the body are attributable to emotional factors. Originally called psychosomatic disorders, these include some forms of asthma, ulcers, and high blood pressure.

Psychoses: Those severe disorders usually requiring hospitalization, and involving major disturbances of reality contact, emotions, intellectual functioning, or behaviors. Included are schizophrenia, manic-depressive psychosis, and paranoia.

Psychosurgery: A type of medical therapy involving surgically isolating lobes of the brain.

Schizophrenia: A severe form of mental illness involving withdrawal, isolation from reality, emotional inappropriateness, bizarre behaviors, and hallucinations or delusions.

Senile psychosis: An organic disorder involving confusion, self-neglect, loss of emotional stability, and poor recent memory.

Sexual deviation: A class of disorder involving deviations of arousal or behavior deficiencies. Included are fetishisms, nymphomania or satyriasis, voyeurism, homosexuality, impotence.

Shock therapy: A type of medical therapy involving convulsions through electrical currents or drugs.

Stigmata diaboli: Physical signs presumed to confirm demon possession, such as anesthesia to pain.

Trephining: Primitive form of surgery involving cutting into the skull.

Suggested Readings

Josephson, E., and Carroll, E. *Drug Use: Epidemiological and Sociological Approaches*. N.Y.: John Wiley, 1974.

Leon, G. *Case Histories of Deviant Behavior*. Boston: Holbrook Press, 1974.

Morris, R. ed. *Perspectives in Abnormal Behavior*. London: Pergamon Press, 1974.

Plog, S. and Edgerton, R. eds. *Changing Perspectives in Mental Illness*. N.Y.: Holt, Rinehart, and Winston, 1969.

Suinn, R. *Fundamentals of Behavior Pathology*. 2nd ed. N.Y.: John Wiley, 1975.

Suinn, R., and Weigel, R. eds. *The Innovative Psychological Therapies: Critical and Creative Contributions*. N.Y.: Harper & Row, 1975.

References

Chapter 1

Braithwaite, R. B. *Scientific explanation.* New York: Harper & Row, 1953.

Carnap, R. *Philosophical foundations of physics.* New York: Basic Books, 1966.

Ferster, C. B., and Skinner, B. F. *Schedules of reinforcement.* New York: Appleton-Century-Crofts, 1957.

Guthrie, E. R. Psychological facts and psychological theory. *Psychological Bulletin,* 1946, **43,** 1–20.

Hempel, C. G. *Fundamentals of concept formation in empirical science.* Chicago: University of Chicago Press, 1952.

————. Philosophy of Natural sciences. Englewood Cliffs, N.J.: Prentice-Hall, 1966.

Holdstock, L. and Rogers, C. Person-centered personality theory, in Corsini, R. J. (Ed.). *Current personality theories.* Ilased, Ill. Peacock, 1977.

Jourard, S. *Self-disclosure.* New York: John Wiley, 1971.

Kagan, J. The maturation of cognition in early childhood, in Meyer, M.E. (Ed.). *Cognitive learning: The third western symposium on learning.* Bellingham, WA, 1972.

Kaplan, A. *The conduct of inquiry: Methodology for behavioral science.* San Francisco: Chandler, 1964.

Kosschau, R. A., Johnson, M. M., and Russo, N. F. *Careers in psychology.* Washington American Psychological Association, 1975.

Kuhn, T. *The structure of scientific revolutions.* 2nd ed. Chicago: University of Chicago Press, 1970.

Landsman, T. Psychology as the science of behavior and experience. Meeting of the American Psychological Association, Montreal, 1973.

Matarazzo, J. D. *Wechsler's measurement and appraisal in adult intelligence.* 5th ed. Baltimore: Williams & Wilkins, 1972.

Mpitsos, G. J., Collins, S. D., and McClellan, A. D. Learning: A model system for physiological studies. *Science,* 1978, **199,** 497–506.

Pap, A. *An introduction to the philosophy of science.* New York: Free Press, 1962.

Peterson, D. R. Is psychology a profession? *American Psychologist.* 1976, **31,** 572–581.

Popper, K. R. *The logic of scientific discovery.* New York: Harper & Row, 1968.

Quine, W. V. The scope and language of sciences, in *The ways of paradox.* New York: Random House, 1966.

Rogers, C. *Client-centered therapy.* Boston: Houghton Mufflin, 1942.

Rudner, R. S. The scientist *qua* scientist makes value judgments. *Philosophy of Science,* 1953, **20,** 1–6.

Sidman, M. *Tactics of scientific research: Evolutionary experimental data in psychology.* New York: Basic Books, 1960.

Soloman, R. L., and Corbit, J. D. An opponent-process theory of motivation: I. Temporal dynamics of affect. *Psychological Bulletin,* 1974, **81,** 119–145.

Turner, M. B. *Philosophy and the science of behavior.* New York: Appleton-Century-Crofts, 1967.

Chapter 2

Albrecht, F. M. The new psychology in America: 1880–1895. Unpublished Ph.D. dissertation, Johns Hopkins University, 1960.

Angell, J. R. The province of functional psychology. *Psychological Review,* 1907, **14,** 61–91.

Boring, E. G. *A history of experimental psychology.* 2nd ed. New York: Appleton-Century-Crofts, 1950.

Ebbinghaus, H. *Memory: A contribution to experimental psychology.* Translated by H. A. Ruger and Clara E.

Bussenius. New York: Teachers College, Columbia University, 1913 (1885).

Ellenberger, H. *The discovery of the unconscious: The history and evolution of dynamic psychiatry.* New York: Basic Books, 1970.

Fechner, G. T. *Elements of psychophysics,* Vol. 1. Translated by H. E. Adler, edited by E. G. Boring and D. H. Howes. New York: Holt, Rinehart and Winston, 1966 (1860).

Freud, S. *The interpretation of dreams.* 8th ed. Translated by J. Strachey. New York: Basic Books, 1955 (1900).

Harper, R. S. The first psychological laboratory. *Isis,* 1950, **41,** 158–161.

James, W. *The principles of psychology.* 2 vols. New York: Holt, 1890.

Köhler, W. Optische Untersuchungen am Schimpansen und am Haushuhn. *Abh. preuss. Akad. Wiss. Berlin,* Phys.-math. K1, 1915, No. 3.

———. *The mentality of apes.* 2nd ed. Translated by Ella Winter, New York: Harcourt, Brace, 1925 (1917).

Kuhn, T. S. *The structure of scientific revolutions.* 2nd ed., enlarged. Chicago: University of Chicago Press, 1970.

Müller, G. E., and Pilzecker, A. *Experimentalle Beiträge zur Lehre vom Gedächtnis.* Leipzig: Barth, 1900.

Peters, R. S. (Ed.). *Brett's history of psychology.* (Abridged ed.). New York: Macmillan, 1953.

Marx, M. H., and Hillix, W. A. *Systems and theories in psychology.* 2nd ed. New York: McGraw-Hill, 1973.

Sherman, M. The differentiation of emotional responses in infants. *Journal of Comparative Psychology,* 1927, **7,** 265–284; 335–351.

Thorndike, E. L., and Woodworth. The influence of improvement in one mental function upon the efficiency of other functions. *Psychological Review,* 1901, **8,** 247–261; 384–395; 553–564.

Titchener, E. B. *Experimental psychology: A manual of laboratory practice.* 2 Vols. New York: Macmillan, 1901–1905.

———. *A textbook of psychology.* Rev. ed. New York: Macmillan, 1910 (1909).

Watson, J. B. Psychology as a behaviorist views it. *Psychological Review,* 1913, **20,** 158–177.

———. *Behaviorism.* Rev. ed. New York: Norton, 1930 (1924, 1925).

Watson, J. B., and Rayner, Rosalie. Conditioned emotional reactions. *Journal of Experimental Psychology,* 1920, **3,** 1–14.

Watson, R. I. Psychology: A prescriptive science. *American Psychologist,* 1967, **22,** 435–443.

———. *The great psychologists.* 4th ed. Philadelphia: Lippincott, 1978.

Watson, R. I. Sr. Prescriptive theory and the social sciences, in Karin D. Knorr et al (Eds.). *Determinants and controls of scientific development.* Dordrecht: Reidel, 1975, pp. 11–35.

Wertheimer, M. Experimentelle Studien Über das Sehen von Bewegung. *Zeitschrift für Psychologie,* 1912, **61,** 161–265.

Wundt, W. *Principles of physiological psychology.* Intro. & Part I of 5th German ed. Translated by E. B. Titchener. New York: Macmillan, 1904 (1873, 1874).

Chapter 3

Flanagan, J. C. et al. *Design for a study of American youth.* Boston: Houghton Mifflin, 1962.

Green, D. M., and Swets, J. A. *Signal detection theory and psychophysics.* Huntington, N.Y.: Robert E. Krieger Publishing, 1974.

Meyer, M. E. *A statistical analysis of behavior.* Belmont CA.: Jones/Wadsworth Publishing Company, 1976.

Stevens, S. S. Mathematics, measurement and psychophysics, in S. S. Stevens (Ed.). *Handbook of experimental psychology.* New York: 1951.

———. Measurement, statistics and the schemapiric view. *Science,* 1968, 849–856.

———. *Psychophysics: Introduction to its perceptual, neural and social prospects.* New York: John Wiley, 1975.

Chapter 4

Butters, N. and Cermak, L. Some analyses of amnesic syndromes in brain-damaged patients, in R. L. Isaacson and K. H. Pribram (Eds.). *The Hippocampus, Volume 2.* New York: Plenum Publishing, 1975, pp. 377–409.

Dawson, R. G. and McGaugh, J. L. Drug faciliation of learning and memory, in J. A. Deutsch (Ed.). *The physiological basis of memory.* New York: Academic Press, 1973, pp. 78–111.

Dunn, A. The chemistry of learning and the formation of memory, in W. H. Gispen (Ed.). *Molecular and functional neurobiology.* Amsterdam, Holland: Elsevier, 1976, pp. 347–387.

Falck, B. Observations on the possibilities of the cellular

localization of monoamines by a fluorescence method. *Acta Physiologica Scandinavica,* 1962, Supplement 197, **56,** 1–25.

Isaacson, R. L. *The limbic system.* New York: Plenum Publishing, 1974.

Lashley, K. S. *In search of the engram,* in Symp. Soc. exp. Biol. N. 4. Cambridge, Eng.: Cambridge University Press, 1950, pp. 454–482.

Miller, N. E., Bailey, C. J., and Stevenson, J. A. F. Decreased ''hunger'' but increased food intake resulting from hypothalamic lesions. *Science,* 1950, **112,** 256–259.

Olds, J., and Milner, P. Positive reinforcement produced by electrical stimulation of septal area and other regions of rat brain. *Journal of Comparative and Physiological Psychology,* 1954, **47,** 419–427.

Teitelbaum, P. and Epstein, A. N. The lateral hypothalamic syndrome. *Psychological Review,* 1962, **69,** 74–90.

Wolgin, D. L., Cytawa, J., and Teitelbaum, P. The role of activation in the regulation of food intake, in D. Novin, W. Wyrwicka, and G. Bray (Eds.). *Hunger: Basic mechanisms and clinical implications.* New York: Raven Press, 1976, pp. 179–191.

Chapter 5

Adair, E., Stevens, J. and Marks, L. Thermally induced pain, the dol scale and the psychophysical power law. *American J. Psychol.,* 1968, **81,** 147.

Adler, F. *Physiology of the eye.* St. Louis: Mosby, 1965, pp. 585–603.

Amoore, J. Stereochemical theory of olfaction, in Schultz, H. *et al.* (Eds.). *Chemistry and physiology of flavors.* Westport, Conn.: Avi Publishers, 1967.

Andres, K. Der Feinstruktur der Regio olfactoria von makrosmatikern. *Z. Zellforsh.,* 1966, **69,** 140–154.

Beidler, L. A theory of taste stimulation, *J. Gen. Physiol.,* 1954, **38,** 133.

Békésy, G. von. *Experiments in hearing.* New York: McGraw-Hill, 1960.

———. Taste theories and the chemical stimulation of single papillae. *J. Appl. Physiol.,* 1966, **21,** 1.

Bessou, P. and Perl, E. Response of cutaneous sensory units with unmyelinated fibers to noxious stimuli. *J. Neurophysiol.,* 1969, **32,** 1025.

Borg, G., Diamant, H., Strom, L. and Zo Herman, Y. The relation between neural and perceptual intensity, a comparative study on the neural and psychophysical response to taste stimuli. *J. Physiol.,* 1967, **192,** 13.

Boycott, B., *et al.* Interplexiform cells of the mamma-

lian retina and their comparison with catecholamine containing retinal cells. *Proc. R. Soc. London.* 1975, **191,** 353–368.

Boynton, R. and Whitten, D. Visual adaptation in monkey cones: recording of late receptor potentials. *Science,* 1970, **178,** 1423.

Brown, J. L. Sensation, in Brobeck, J. (Ed.). *Best and Taylor's physiological basis of medical practice.* Baltimore: Wiliams & Wilkins, 1973, p. 168.

Cain, W. S. Olfactory adaptation and direct scaling of odor intensity. Unpublished Ph.D. thesis, Brown University, 1968.

———. Olfactory adaptation and direct scaling of odor intensity, in C. Pfaffmann (Ed.). *Olfaction and taste.* New York: Rockefeller University Press, 1969.

Chapman, L., Dingman, H. and Ginzberg, S. Failure of analgesic agents to alter the absolute sensory threshold for the simple detection of pain. *Brain,* 1965, **88,** 1011.

Davies, J. and Taylor, F. Molecular shape, size and adsorption in olfaction. *Proc. Int. Congr. Surface Activity,* 1957, **4,** 329.

Davis, H., *et al.* Temporary deafness following exposure to loud tones and noise. *Acta. Otolaryng.,* 1950, suppl 88, 1–57.

Davis, H. Peripheral coding of auditory information, in Rosenblith (Ed.). *Sensory communication.* New York: John Wiley, 1961, p. 121.

Daw, N., Berman, N. and Ariel, M. Interaction of critical periods in the visual cortex of kittens. *Science,* 1978, **199,** 565–568.

Dawson, W. Chemical stimulation of the peripheral trigeminal nerve. *Nature* (London), 1962, **196,** 341–345.

———. Thermal excitation of afferent neurones in the mammalian cornea and iris, in C. M. Herzfeld (Ed.). *Temperature, its measurement and control in science and industry.* Vol. III, New York: Reinhold, 1963.

———. Thermal stimulation of experimentally vasoconstricted human skin. *Percept. Motor Skills,* 1964, **19,** 775–788.

———. Is the brain behind the eye? Implications of Processing by the retina. *Invest. Oph.,* 1973, **6,** 398–399.

Dawson, W. and Perez, J. Unusual retinal cells in the dolphin eye. *Science,* 1973, **181,** 747–749.

De Valois, R. Analysis and coding of color vision in the primate visual system. *Cold Spr. Harb. Symp.,* 1965, **30,** 567–579.

Doving, K. B. Studies of the relation between the frog's electroolfactogram (EOG) and single unit activity in the olfactory bulb. *Acta. Physiol. Scand.,* 1964, **60,** 150–163.

Flock, A. Transducing mechanisms in the lateral line canal organ receptors. *Cold Spr. Harb. Symp. Quant. Biol.*, 1965, **30**, 133–144.

Fregly, M. The role of hormones in the regulation of salt intake in rats, in M. Kare and O. Maller (Eds.). *The chemical senses and nutrition.* Baltimore: Johns Hopkins Press, 1967, 115–138.

Galambos, R. and Davis, H. The response of single auditory fibers to acoustic stimulation. *J. Neurophysiol.*, 1943, **6**, 39–57.

Gasser, H. S. Conduction in nerves in relation to fiber types. *A. Res. Nerv. Ment. Dis. Proc.*, 1935, **15**, 35.

Gray, J. A. B. and Malcolm, J. L. Initiation of nerve impulses by mesenteric pacinian corpuscles. *Proc. Roy. Soc.* (London), 1950, **B137**, 96.

Graziadei, P. and Metcalf, J. Autoradiographic study of the frog's olfactory mucosa. *Amer. Zool.*, 1970, **10**, 559.

Guyton, A. *Medical physiology.* New York: Saunders, 1971, p. 1031.

Hardy, J., Wolff, H. and Goodell, H. Studies on pain. A new method for measuring pain threshold: Observations on spatial summation of pain. *J. Clin. Invest.*, 1940, **19**, 649.

Hecht, S., Schlaer, S. and Pirenne, M. Energy quanta and vision. *J. Gen. Physiol.*, 1942, **25**, 819.

Hensel, H. and Boman, K. Afferent impulses in cutaneous sensory nerves in human subjects. *J. Neurophysiol.*, 1960, **23**, 564.

Hensel, H. and Kenshalo, D. Warm receptors in the nasal region of cats. *J. Physiol.* (London), 1969, **204**, 99–112.

Hubel, D. and Wiesel, T. Binocular interaction in striate cortex of kittens reared with artificial squint. *J. Neurophysiol.*, 1965, **28**, 1041.

————. Receptive fields and functional architecture in two non-striate visual areas (18 and 19) of the cat. *J. Neurophysiol.*, 1965, **28**, 229.

Kaissling, K. and Priesner, E. Die Riechschwelle des Seidenspinners. *Naturwissensch.*, 1970, **57**, 23–29.

Kenshalo, D. R. Changes in cool threshold associated with phases of the menstrual cycle. *J. Appl. Physiol.*, 1966, **21**, 1031.

Kenshalo, D. R. and Nafa, J. The peripheral basis of temperature sensitivity in man, in Hertzfeld (Ed.). *Temperature–its measurement and control in science and industry.* Vol III, New York: Reinhold, 1963.

Kiang, N. *et al.,* in G. Wolstenholme and J. Knight (Eds.). *Sensorineural hearing loss.* London: Churchill, 1970.

Kuffler, S. W. Discharge patterns and functional organization of mammalian retina. *J. Neurophysiol.*, 1953, **16**, 37–68.

Le Magnen, J. Nouvelles données sur le phenouiene de l'exaltolide. *C. R. Acad. Sci.* (Paris), 1950, **230**, 1103–1105.

Loewenstein, W. R. Biological transducers. *Sci. Amer.*, 1960, **203**, 98.

Mark, D. and Maurice, D. Sensory recording from the isolated cornea. *Invest. Ophthal.*, 1977, **16**, 541.

Marks, W., Dobelle, W. and MacNichol, E. Visual pigments of primate cones. *Science,* 1964, **143**, 1181.

Melzack, R., Casey, C. Sensory motivational and central control determinants of pain, in Kenshalo (Ed.). *The skin senses.* Springfield, Ill.: Thomas, 1968.

Melzack, R., Wall, P. Pain mechanisms: A new theory. *Science,* 1965, **150**, 971.

Mountcastle, V. (Ed.). *Medical physiology.* St. Louis: Mosby, 1974, p. 836.

Mozell, M. M. Evidence for a chromatographic model of olfaction. *J. Gen. Physiol.*, 1970, **56**, 46.

Nafe, J. P. Pressure, pain and temperature senses, in Murchison (Ed.). *A handbook of general experimental psychology.* Worcester, Mass.: Clark University Press, 1934, p. 1037.

Ottoson, D. Analysis of the electrical activity of the olfactory Epithelium. *Acta. Physiol. Scand.*, 1956, **35** (suppl. 122), 1–83.

Pirenne, M. *Vision and the eye.* London: Pilot Press, 1948.

Polyak, S. *The retina.* Chicago: University of Chicago Press, 1941.

Riesen, A. Stimulation as a requirement for growth and function in behavioral development, in Fiske and Maddi (Eds.). *Functions of varied experience.* Homewood, Ill.: Dorsey Press, 1961, p. 57.

Sperry, R. Hemisphere disconnection and unity in conscious awareness. *Amer. Psychol.*, 1968, **23**, 723.

Stryker, M. and Schiller, P. Eye and head movements evoked by electrical stimulation of monkey superior colliculus. *Brain Res.*, 1975, **23**, 103.

Svaetichin, G. and MacNichol, E. Retinal mechanisms for chromatic and achromatic vision. *Ann. N.Y. Acad. Sci.*, 1958, **74**, 385.

Tucker, D. Olfactory, vomernasal and trigeminal receptor response to odorants, in Zotterman (Ed.). *Olfaction and taste I.* New York: Pergamon Press, 1963, pp. 45–69.

Von Noorden, G. and Middleditch, P. Histological observations in the normal monkey lateral geniculate nucleus. *Invest. Ophth.*, 1975, **14**, 55–58.

Wald, G., in *Handbook of physiology. Neurophysiology.* Washington, D.C.: *Amer. Physiol. Soc.*, 1959, Vol. I, Chap. 28, pp. 671–692.

Walls, G. The vertebrate eye and its adaptive radiation. *Bull. Cranbrook Inst. Sci.* Bloomfield Hills, Mich., 1942, **19**, p. 785.

Werblin, F. and Dowling, J. Organizations of the retina of the mud-puppy, Necturus maculosus: II. Intracellular recording, *J. Neurophysiol.*, 1969, **32**, 339–355.

Wersall, J., Flock, A. and Lundquist, P. Structural basis for directional sensitivity in cochlear and vestibular sensory receptors. *Cold Spr. Harb. Symp. Quant. Biol.*, 1965, **30**, 115.

Chapter 6

Alcock, J. The evolution of the use of tools by feeding animals. *Evolution,* 1972, **26**, 464–473.

———. *Animal behavior—An evolutionary approach.* Sunderland, Mass.: Sinauer 1975.

Allison, T., and VanTwyver, H. The evolution of sleep. *Natural History,* 1970, **79**(2), 56–65.

Beach, F. A. Experimental investigations of species-specific behavior. *American Psychologist,* 1960, **25**, 1–18.

Bitterman, M. E. The comparative analysis of learning. *Science,* 1975, **188**, 699–709.

Campbell, B. A., and Jaynes, J. Reinstatement. *Psychological Review,* 1966, **73**, 478–480.

Cullen, E. Adaptations in the kittiwake to cliff-nesting. *Ibis,* 1957, **99**, 275–302.

Darwin, C. *The expression of the emotions in man and animals.* London: Appleton, 1873. (Reprinted, Chicago: University of Chicago Press, 1965).

Dewsbury, D. A. Patterns of copulatory behavior in male mammals. *Quarterly Review of Biology,* 1972, **47**, 1–33.

———. *Comparative animal behavior.* New York: McGraw-Hill, 1978.

Dilger, W. C. The behavior of lovebirds. *Scientific American,* 1962, **206**(1), 88–98.

Garcia, J., Hankins, W. G., and Rusiniak, K. W. Behavioral regulation of the milieu interne in man and rat. *Science,* 1974, **185**, 824–831.

Hailman, J. P. How an instinct is learned. *Scientific American,* 1969, **221**(6), 98–106.

Harlow, H. F., Harlow, M. K., and Suomi, S. J. From thought to therapy: lessons from a primate laboratory. *American Scientist,* 1971, **59**, 538–549.

Henderson, N. D. Brain weight increases resulting from environmental enrichment: A directional dominance in mice. *Science,* 1970, **169**, 776–778.

Hinde, R. A. Interaction of internal and external factors in integration of canary reproduction, in F. A. Beach (Ed.). *Sex and behavior.* New York: John Wiley 1965, pp. 381–415.

———. *Animal behavior: A synthesis of ethology and comparative psychology* 2nd ed. New York: McGraw-Hill, 1970.

Hinde, R. A., and Tinbergen, N. The comparative study of species-specific behavior, in A. Roe and G. G. Simpson (Eds.). *Behavior and Evolution.* New Haven: Yale University Press, 1958, pp. 251–268.

James, W. *The principles of psychology.* New York: Holt, 1890.

Mayr, E. *Animal species and evolution.* Cambridge, Mass.: Harvard University Press, 1963.

McGill, T. E., Dewsbury, D. A., and Sachs, B. D. *Sex and behavior: Status and prospectus.* New York: Plenum Publishing, 1978.

Meyerriecks, A. J. Comparative breeding behavior of four species of North American herons. *Nuttall Ornitological Club Publications,* 1960, **2**, 1–158.

Miller, R. E. Experimental approaches to the physiological and behavioral concomitants of affective communication in rhesus monkeys, in S. A. Altmann (Ed.). *Social communication among primates.* Chicago: University of Chicago Press, 1967, pp. 125–134.

Money, J., and Ehrhardt, A. A. *Man & woman, boy & girl.* Baltimore: Johns Hopkins University Press, 1972.

Moyer, K. E. Kinds of aggression and their physiological basis. *Communications in Behavioral Biology,* 1968, **2**, 65–87.

Romer, A. S. *A shorter version of the second edition of the vertebrate body.* Philadelphia: Saunders, 1956.

Thiessen, D. D. Footholds for survival. *American Scientist,* 1973, **61**, 346–351.

Tinbergen, N. *The study of instinct.* Oxford: Oxford University Press, 1951.

———. On aims and methods of ethology. *Zeitschrift für Tierpsychologie,* 1963a, **20**, 410–429.

———. The shell menace. *Natural History,* 1963(b), **72**, 28–35.

Warren, J. M. Primate learning in comparative perspective, in A. M. Schrier, H. F. Harlow, and F. Stollnitz (Eds.), *Behavior of nonhuman primates: Modern research trends.* New York: Academic Press, 1965, pp. 249–281.

———. Learning in vertebrates, in D. A. Dewsbury and D. A. Rethlingshafer (Eds.). *Comparative psychology: A modern survey.* New York: McGraw-Hill, 1973, pp. 471–509.

Chapter 7

Baron, M., Gershon, E. S., Rudy, V., Jonas, W. Z., and Buchsbaum, M. Lithium carbonate response in depression. *Archives of General Psychiatry,* 1975, **32,** 1107–1111.

Bignami, G. Selection for high rates and low rates of avoidance conditioning in the rat. *Animal Behaviour,* 1965, **13,** 221–227.

Bovet, D., Bovet-Nitti, F., and Oliverio, A. Genetic aspects of learning and memory in mice. *Science,* 1969, **163,** 139–149.

Bruun, K., Markkanen, T., and Partanen, J. *Inheritance of drinking behavior, a study of adult twins.* Helsinki: The Finnish Foundation for Alcohol Research, 1966.

Buss, A., and Plomin, R. *A temperament theory of personality development.* New York: Wiley-Interscience, 1975.

Collins, R. L. Inheritance of avoidance conditioning in mice: A diallel study. *Science,* 1964, **143,** 1188–1190.

Collins, R. L., and Fuller, J. L. Audiogenic seizure prone (*asp*): A gene affecting behavior in linkage group VIII of the mouse. *Science,* 1968, **162,** 1137–1139.

Crowe, R. R. Adoption studies in psychiatry. *Biological Psychiatry,* 1975, **10,** 353–371.

DeFries, J. C. Prenatal maternal stress in mice: Differential effects on behavior. *Journal of Heredity,* 1964, **55,** 289–295.

DeFries, J. C., Ashton, G. C., Johnson, R. C., Kuse, A. R., McClearn, G. E., Mi, M. P., Rashad, M. N., Vandenberg, S. G., Wilson, J. R. Parent-offspring resemblance for specific cognitive abilities in two ethnic groups. *Nature,* 1976, **261,** 131–133.

DeFries, J. C., and Hegmann, J. P. Genetic analysis of open-field behavior, in G. Lindzey and D. D. Thiessen (Eds.). *Contributions to behavior-genetic analysis: The mouse as a prototype.* New York: Appleton-Century-Crofts, 1970, pp. 23–56.

DeFries, J. C., Hegmann, J. P., and Halcomb, R. A. Response to 20 generations of selection for open-field activity in mice. *Behavioral Biology,* 1974, **11,** 481–495.

DeFries, J. C. and Plomin, R. Behavioral genetics. *Annual Review of Psychology,* 1978, **29,** 473–515.

DeFries, J. C., Vandenberg, S. G., McClearn, G. E., Kuse, A. R., Wilson, J. R., Ashton, G. C., and Johnson, R. C. Near identity of cognitive structure in two ethnic groups. *Science,* 1974, **183,** 338–339.

Dobzhansky, Th. *Heredity and the nature of man.* New York: Harcourt, Brace & World, 1964.

Gottesman, I. I. and Shields, J. *Schizophrenia and genetics: A twin study vantage point.* New York: Academic Press, 1972.

Heston, L. L. Psychiatric disorders in foster home reared children of schizophrenic mothers. *British Journal of Psychiatry,* 1966, **112,** 819–825.

———. The genetics of schizophrenic and schizoid disease. *Science,* 1970, **167,** 249–256.

Horn, J., Plomin, R., and Rosenman, R. Heritability of personality traits in adult male twins. *Behavior Genetics,* 1976, **6,** 17–30.

Jarvik, L. F., and Erlenmeyer-Kimling, L. Survey of familial correlations in measured intellectual functions, in J. Zubin and G. A. Jervis (Eds.). *Psychopathology of mental development.* New York: Grune and Stratton, 1967, pp. 447–459.

Jencks, C. *Inequality: A reassessment of the effect of family and schooling in America.* New York: Harper & Row, 1972.

Jensen, A. R. How much can we boost IQ and scholastic achievement? *Harvard Educational Review,* 1969, **39,** 1–123.

Kety, S. S., Rosenthal, D., Wender, P. H., and Schulsinger, F. Studies based on a total sample of adopted individuals and their relatives: Why they were necessary, what they demonstrated and failed to demonstrate. *Schizophrenic Bulletin,* 1976, **2,** 413–418.

Kringlen, E. Schizophrenia in twins: An epidemiological-clinical study. *Psychiatry,* 1966, **29,** 172–184.

Kupfer, D. J., Pickar, D., Himmelhoch, J. M., and Detre, T. P. Are there two types of unipolar depression? *Archives of General Psychiatry,* 1975, **32,** 866–871.

Loehlin, J. C., Lindzey, G., and Spuhler, J. N. *Race differences in intelligence.* San Francisco: W. H. Freeman, 1975.

Loehlin, J. C., and Nichols, R. C. *Heredity, environment, and personality: A study of 850 twins.* Austin, Texas: University of Texas Press, 1976.

McClearn, G. E., and DeFries, J. C. *Introduction to behavioral genetics.* San Francisco: W. H. Freeman, 1973.

Mendlewicz, J., and Fleiss, J. L. Linkage studies with X-chromosome markers in bipolar (manic-depressive) and unipolar (depressive) illnesses. *Biological Psychiatry,* 1974, **9,** 261–294.

Nichols, R. C., and Bilbro, W. C. The diagnosis of twin zygosity. *Acta Genetica,* 1966, **16,** 265–275.

Perris, C. Abnormality on paternal and maternal sides:

Observations in bipolar/manic-depressive and unipolar depressive psychosis. *British Journal of Psychiatry,* 1972, **118,** 207.

Plomin, R., DeFries, J. C., and Loehlin, J. C. Genotype-environment interaction and correlation in the analysis of human behavior. *Psychological Bulletin,* 1977, **84,** 309–322.

Plomin, R. and Rowe, D. Genes, environment and development of temperament in young human twins, in G. Burghardt and M. Bekoff, *Ontogeny of behavior.* New York: Garland Publishing 1978.

Rosenthal, D. *Genetic theory and abnormal behavior.* New York: McGraw-Hill, 1970.

Scarr, S. Environmental bias in twin studies. *Eugenics Quarterly,* 1968, **15,** 34–40.

Schoenfeldt, L. F. The hereditary components of the Project TALENT two-day test battery. *Measurement and Evaluation in Guidance,* 1968, **1,** 130–140.

Shockley, W. Dysgenics, geneticity, raceology: A challenge to the intellectual responsibility of educators. *Phi Delta Kappan,* 1972, **53,** 297–307.

Skinner, B. F. *The behavior of organisms: An experimental analysis.* New York: Appleton-Century-Crofts, 1938.

Sprott, R. L., and Staats, J. Behavioral studies using genetically-defined mice—a bibliography. *Behavior Genetics,* 1975, **5,** 27–82.

Taylor, M. A., and Abrams, R. Acute mania. *Archives of General Psychiatry,* 1975, **32,** 863–865.

Wender, P. H., Rosenthal, D., and Kety, S. S. Cross-fostering: A research strategy for clarifying the role of genetic and experiential factors in the etiology of schizophrenia. *Archives of General Psychiatry,* 1974, **30,** 121.

Wender, P. H., Rosenthal, D., Rainer, J. D., Greenhill, L., and Sarlin, M. B. Schizophrenics' adopting parents: Psychiatric status, *Archives of Gen. Psychiatry,* 1978, in press.

Winokur, G. The division of depressive illness into depression spectrum disease and pure depressive disease. *International Pharmacopsychiatry,* 1974, **9,** 5–13.

Chapter 8

Adler, A. *The practice and theory of individual psychology.* New York: Harcourt, 1927.

Bolles, R. C. *Theory of motivation.* New York: Harper & Row, 1967.

Boring, E. G. *A history of experimental psychology.* New York: Century Co., 1929.

Boring, E. G. *The physical dimensions of consciousness.* New York: Appleton-Century-Crofts, 1933.

Broadhurst, P. L. Emotionality and the Yerkes-Dodson law. *Journal of Experimental Psychology,* 1957, **54,** 345–352.

Brush, F. R. (Ed.). *Aversive conditioning and learning.* New York: Academic Press, 1971.

Campbell, B. A., and Church, R. M. (Eds.). *Punishment and aversive behavior.* New York: Appleton-Century-Crofts, 1969.

Cappell, H., and Herman, C. P. Alcohol and tension reduction: A review. *Quarterly Journal of Studies on Alcohol,* 1972, **33,** 33–64.

Crowell, C. R. Conditioned-aversive aspects of electric shock. *Learning and Motivation,* 1974, **5,** 209–220.

Cunningham, C. L., Brown, J. S., and Roberts, S. Startbox-goalbox confinement durations as determinants of self-punitive behavior. *Learning and Motivation,* 1976, **7,** 340–355.

Davis, C. Self-selection of diet by newly-weaned infants. *American Journal of Diseases of Children,* 1928, **36,** 651–679.

Davis, J. D., Lulenski, C. G., and Miller, N. E. Comparative studies of barbiturate self-administration. *International Journal of the Addictions,* 1968, **3,** 207–214.

Deutsch, J. A., and Deutsch, D. *Physiological psychology,* Homewood, Ill.: Dorsey, 1973.

Dollard, J., and Miller, N. E. *Personality and psychotherapy.* New York: McGraw-Hill, 1950.

Dufort, R. H., and Wright, J. H. Food intake as a function of duration of food deprivation. *Journal of Psychology,* 1962, **53,** 465–468.

Fowler, H. Suppression and facilitation by response contingent shock. In F. R. Brush (Ed.). *Aversive conditioning and learning.* New York: Academic Press, 1971.

Freud S. The unconscious. In S. Freud (Ed.). *Collected papers.* London: Hogarth, 1948 (originally published in 1915).

Garcia, J., Ervin, F. R., Yorke, C. H., and Koelling, R. A. Conditioning with delayed vitamin injection. *Science,* 1967, **155,** 716–718.

Garcia, J., McGowan, B. K., and Green, K. F. Biological constraints on conditioning. In A. H. Black and W. F. Prokasy (Eds.). *Classical conditioning II: Current research and theory.* New York: Appleton-Century-Crofts, 1972.

Grossman, S. P. Role of the hypothalamus in the regulation of food and water intake. *Psychological Review,* 1975, **82,** 200–224.

Hamilton, C. L., and Brobeck, J. R. Hypothalamic

hyperphagia in the monkey. *Journal of Comparative and Physiological Psychology,* 1964, **57,** 271–278.

Harlow, H. F. The nature of love. *American Psychologist,* 1958, **13,** 673–685

Harlow, H. F., and Harlow, M. K. Social deprivation in monkeys. *Scientific American,* 1962, **207,** 136–146.

Hartlep, K., and Bertsch, G. Facilitation of licking by response-contingent electric shock. *Animal Learning and Behavior,* 1974, **2,** 196–198.

Hefferline, R. F. An experimental study of avoidance. *Genetic Psychology Monographs,* 1950, **42,** 231–334.

Hill, S. W. Eating responses of humans during dinner meals. *Journal of Comparative and Physiological Psychology,* 1974, **86,** 652–657.

Hoffman, H. S., and Ratner, A. M. A reinforcement model of imprinting: Implications for socialization in monkeys and men. *Psychological Review,* 1973, **80,** 527–544.

Hoffman, H. S., and Solomon, R. L. An opponent-process theory of motivation: III. Some affective dynamics in imprinting. *Learning and Motivation,* 1974, **5,** 149–164.

Hokanson, J. E. *The physiological basis of motivation.* New York: John Wiley, 1969.

Horney, K. *Neurotic personality of our times.* New York: Norton, 1937.

Hull, C. L. *Principles of behavior.* New York: Appleton-Century-Crofts, 1943.

————. *A behavior system.* New Haven: Yale University Press, 1952.

Isaac, W., and Reed, W. G. The effect of sensory stimulation on the activity of cats. *Journal of Comparative and Physiological Psychology,* 1961, **54,** 677–678.

Ison, J. R., and Krauter, E. E. Acoustic startle reflexes in the rat during consummatory behavior. *Journal of Comparative and Physiological Psychology,* 1975, **89,** 39–49.

Jakubczak, L. F. Frequency, duration, and speed of wheel running of rats as a function of age and starvation. *Animal Learning and Behavior,* 1973, **1,** 13–16.

Kent, M. A., and Peters, R. H. Effects of ventromedial hypothalamic lesions on hunger-motivated behavior in rats. *Journal of Comparative and Physiological Psychology,* 1973, **83,** 92–97.

Lawler, E. E. *Motivation in work organizations.* Monterey, Ca.: Brooks-Cole, 1973.

Lindzey, G., Winston, H., and Manosevitz, M. Social dominance in inbred mouse strains. *Nature,* 1961, **191,** 474–476.

Lindzey, G., Loehlin, J., Manosevitz, M., and Thies-

sen, D. Behavioral genetics. *Annual Review of Psychology,* 1971, **22,** 39–94.

Mackintosh, N. J. *The psychology of animal learning.* London: Academic Press, 1974.

McAllister, W. R., and McAllister, D. E. Behavioral measurement of conditioned fear. In F. R. Brush (Ed.). *Aversive conditioning and learning.* New York: Academic Press, 1971.

————. Role of the CS and of apparatus cues in the measurement of acquired fear. *Psychological Reports,* 1962, **11,** 749–756.

McClelland, D. C. (Ed.). *Studies in motivation.* New York: Appleton-Century-Crofts, 1955.

McClelland, D. C., Atkinson, J. W., Clark, R. A., and Lowell, E. L. *The achievement motive.* New York: Appleton-Century-Crofts, 1953.

McDougall, W. *Introduction to social psychology,* London: Methuen and Company, 1908.

McKearney, J. W. Fixed-interval schedules of electric shock presentation: Extinction and recovery of performance under different shock intensities and fixed-interval durations. *Journal of the Experimental Analysis of Behavior,* 1969, **12,** 301–313.

Miller, N. E. Learning resistance to pain and fear: Effects of overlearning, exposure, and rewarded exposure in context. *Journal of Experimental Psychology,* 1960, **60,** 137–145.

————. Learning of visceral and glandular responses. *Science,* 1969, **163,** 434–445.

Moss, F. A. Study of animal drives. *Journal of Experimental Psychology,* 1924, **7,** 165–185.

Mowrer, O. H. A stimulus-response analysis of anxiety and its role as a reinforcing agent. *Psychological Review,* 1939, **46,** 553–566.

Murray, H. A. *Explorations in personality.* New York: Oxford University Press, 1938.

Myer, J. S. Some effects of noncontingent aversive stimulation. In F. R. Brush (Ed.). *Aversive conditioning and learning.* New York: Academic Press, 1971.

Nachman, M. Taste preferences for sodium salts by adrenalectomized rats. *Journal of Comparative and Physiological Psychology,* 1962, **55,** 1124–1129.

Nation, J. R., Wrather, D. M., and Mellgren, R. L. Contrast effects in escape conditioning of rats. *Journal of Comparative and Physiological Psychology,* 1974, **86,** 69–73.

Nisbett, R. E., and Schachter, S. Cognitive manipulation of pain. *Journal of Experimental Social Psychology,* 1966, **2,** 227–236.

Novin, D., Wyrwicka, W., and Bray, G. A. (Eds.). *Hunger: Basic mechanisms and clinical implications.* New York: Raven Press, 1976.

Olds, J., and Milner, P. Positive reinforcement produced by electrical stimulation of septal area and other regions of rat brain. *Journal of Comparative and Physiological Psychology,* 1954, **47,** 419–427.

Orpen, C. A. Quasi-experimental investigation into the effects of valence, instrumentality, and expectancy on job performance. *International Review of Applied Psychology,* 1975, **24,** 71–78.

Pavlov, I. P. *Conditioned reflexes.* London: Oxford University Press, 1927.

Punzo, F. Oxygen deprivation as a drive state in an aquatic insect: Family Dytiscidae. *Animal Learning and Behavior,* 1974, **2,** 31–33.

Richter, C. P. Animal behavior and internal drives. *Quarterly Review of Biology,* 1927, **2,** 307–343.

———. Total self-regulatory functions in animals and human beings. *Harvey Lecture Series,* 1943, **38,** 225–239.

Rozin, P., and Kalat, J. W. Specific hungers and poison avoidance as adaptive specializations of learning. *Psychological Review,* 1971, **78,** 459–486.

Schachter, S., and Wheeler, L. Epinephrine, chlorpromazine, and amusement. *Journal of Abnormal and Social Psychology,* 1962, **65,** 121–128.

Siegel, P. S. The relationship between voluntary water intake, body weight loss, and number of hours of water privation in the rat. *Journal of Comparative and Physiological Psychology,* 1947, **40,** 231–238.

Singh, D. Preference for mode of obtaining reinforcement in rats with lesions in septal or ventromedial hypothalamic areas. *Journal of Comparative and Physiological Psychology,* 1972, **80,** 259–268.

Solomon, R. L., and Wynne, L. C. Traumatic avoidance learning: The principles of anxiety conservation and partial irreversibility. *Psychological Review,* 1954, **61,** 353–385.

Spence, K. W. *Behavior theory and conditioning.* New Haven: Yale University Press, 1956.

Steinbaum, E. A., and Miller, N. E. Obesity from eating elicited by daily stimulation of the hypothalamus. *American Journal of Physiology,* 1965, **208,** 1–5.

Strickler, E. M., and Wilson, N. E. Salt-seeking behavior in rats following acute sodium deficiency. *Journal of Comparative and Physiological Psychology,* 1970, **72,** 416–420.

Taylor, J. A. The relationship of anxiety to the conditioned eyelid response. *Journal of Experimental Psychology,* 1951, **41,** 81–92.

Terris, W., and Wechkin, S. Learning to resist the effects of punishment. *Psychonomic Science,* 1967, **7,** 169–170.

Thiessen, D. D. *Gene organization and behavior.* New York: Random House, 1971.

Thiessen, D. D., Owen, K., and Whitsett, M. Chromosome mapping of behavioral activities. In G. Lindzey and D. D. Thiessen (Eds.). *Contributions to behavior-genetic analysis: The mouse as a prototype.* New York: Appleton-Century-Crofts, 1970.

Thompson, W. R., and Melzack, R. Early environment. *Scientific American,* 1956, **194,** 38–42.

Thorndike, E. L. Animal intelligence: An experimental study of the associative processes in animals. *Psychological Review, Monograph Supplement,* 1898, **1,** No. 8.

Valenstein, E. S., Cox, V. C., and Kakolewski, J. W. The hypothalamus and motivated behavior. In J. Tapp (Ed.). *Reinforcement and behavior.* New York: Academic Press, 1969.

Valle, F. P. *Motivation: Theories and issues.* Monterey, Ca.: Brooks-Cole, 1975.

Veroff, J., and Veroff, J. B. Reconsideration of a measure of power motivation. *Psychological Bulletin,* 1972, **78,** 279–291.

Vroom, V. H. *Work and motivation.* New York: John Wiley, 1964.

Watson, J. B. Psychology as a behaviorist views it. *Psychological Review,* 1913, **20,** 158–177.

Watson, J. B., and Reyner, R. Conditioned emotional reactions. *Journal of Experimental Psychology,* 1920, **3,** 1–14.

Weinstock, R. B. Maintenance schedules and hunger drive: An examination of the rat literature. *Psychological Bulletin,* 1972, **78,** 311–320.

Woodworth, R. S. *Dynamic psychology.* New York: Columbia University Press, 1918.

Chapter 9

Anger, D. The role of temporal discriminations in the reinforcement of Sidman avoidance behavior. *Journal of the Experimental Analysis of Behavior,* 1963, **6,** 477–506.

Azrin, N. H. Some effects of two intermittent schedules of immediate and non-immediate punishment. *Journal of Psychology,* 1956, **42,** 3–21.

Azrin, N. H. and Holz, W. C. Punishment, in W. K. Honig (Ed.). *Operant behavior: areas of research and application.* New York: Appleton-Century-Crofts, 1966, 380–447.

Barker, L. M., Best, M. R., and Domjan (Eds.). *Learning mechanisms in food selection.* Waco, Texas: Baylor University Press, 1977.

Beecroft, R. S. *Classical conditioning.* Goleta, Ca.: Psychonomic Press, 1966.

Bolles, R. C. Species-specific defense reactions and

avoidance learning. *Psychological Review,* 1970, **77,** 32–48.

Brown, P. L. and Jenkins, H. M. Autoshaping of the pigeon's key-peck. *Journal of the Experimental Analysis of Behavior,* 1968, **11,** 1–8.

Church, R. M. Response suppression, in B. A. Campbell and R. M. Church (Eds.). *Punishment and aversive behavior.* New York: Appleton-Century-Crofts, 1969, 111–156.

Davis, H., and Hurwitz, H. M. B. Operant—Pavlovian interactions. New York: Erlbaum, 1977.

Dews, P. B. Free-operant behavior under conditions of delayed reinforcement. I. CRF-type schedules. *Journal of the Experimental Analysis of Behavior,* 1960, **3,** 221–234.

Falk, J. L. The nature and determinants of adjunctive behavior. *Physiology and Behavior,* 1971, **6,** 577–588.

Ferster, C. B. Intermittent reinforcement of a complex response in a chimpanzee. *Journal of the Experimental Analysis of Behavior,* 1958, **1,** 163–165.

Ferster, C. B. and Skinner, B. F. *Schedules of reinforcement.* New York: Appleton-Century-Crofts, 1957.

Garcia, J., Hankins, W. G. and Rusiniak, K. W. Behavioral regulation of the milieu interne in man and rat. *Science,* 1974, **185,** 824–831.

Gormezano, I. Investigations of defense and reward conditioning in the rabbit, in A. H. Black and W. F. Proskasy (Eds.). *Classical conditioning II: Current research and theory.* New York: Appleton-Century-Crofts, 1972.

Grice, G. R. The relation of secondary reinforcement to delayed reward in visual discrimination learning. *Journal of Experimental Psychology,* 1948, **38,** 1–16.

Harlow, H. F. The formation of learning sets. *Psychological Review,* 1949, **56,** 51–65.

Herrnstein, R. J. and Hineline, P. N. Negative reinforcement as shock-frequency reduction. *Journal of the Experimental Analysis of Behavior,* 1966, **9,** 421–430.

Homme, L. E., de Baca, P. C., Devine, J. V., Steinhorst, R. and Rickert, E. J. Use of the Premack principle in controlling the behavior of nursery school children. *Journal of the Experimental Analysis of Behavior,* 1963, **6,** 544.

Kalat, J. W. and Rozin, P. The role of interference in taste-aversion learning. *Journal of Comparative and Physiological Psychology,* 1971, **77,** 53–58.

Kelleher, R. T. and Morse, W. H. Schedules using noxious stimuli. III. Responding maintained with response produced electric shocks. *Journal of the Experimental Analysis of Behavior,* 1968, **11,** 819–838.

Kimble, G. A. *Hilgard and Marquis' conditioning and learning.* 2nd ed. New York: Appleton-Century-Crofts, 1961.

Kimmel, H. D. Instrumental conditioning of autonomically mediated responses in human beings. *American Psychologist,* 1974, **29,** 325–335.

Logan, F. A. *Incentive: How the conditions of reinforcement affect the performance of rats.* New Haven: Yale University Press, 1960.

Lovaas, O. I., Koegal, R., Simmons, J. Q. and Long, J. S. Some generalization and follow-up measures on autistic children in behavior therapy. *Journal of Applied Behavioral Analysis,* 1973, **6,** 131–165.

Lovaas, I. D. and Simmons, J. Q. Manipulation of self-destruction in three retarded children. *Journal of Applied Behavioral Analysis,* 1969, **2,** 143–157.

McKearney, J. W. Maintenance of responding under a fixed-interval schedule of electric shock presentation. *Science,* 1968, **160,** 1249–1251.

Miller, K. E. Learning of visceral and glandular responses. *Science,* 1969, **163,** 434–445.

Miller, N. E. and DiCara, L. V. Instrumental learning of heart-rate changes in curarized rats: Shaping, and specificity to discriminative stimulus. *Journal of Comparative and Physiological Psychology,* 1967, **63,** 12–19.

Morse, W. H. and Kelleher, R. T. Determinants of reinforcement and punishment, in W. K. Honig and J. E. R. Staddon (Eds.). *Handbook of operant behavior.* Englewood Cliffs, N. J.: Prentice-Hall, 1977, pp. 174–200.

Mowrer, O. H. *Learning theory and behavior.* New York: John Wiley, 1960.

Pavlov, I. P. *Conditioned reflexes.* Translated by G. V. Anrep. London: Oxford University Press, 1927.

Pierrel, R. and Sherman, J. G. Train your pet the Barnabus way. *Brown Alumni Monthly,* February 1963, 8–14.

Premack, D. Toward empirical behavior laws: I. Positive reinforcement. *Psychological Review,* 1959, **66,** 219–233.

Prokasy, W. F., Grant, D. A. and Meyers, N. A. Eyelid conditioning as a function of unconditioned stimulus intensity and intertrial interval. *Journal of Experimental Psychology,* 1958, **55,** 242–246.

Redd, W. H. and Birnbrauer, J. S. Adults as discriminative stimuli for different reinforcement contingencies with retarded children. *Journal of Experimental Child Psychology,* 1969, **7,** 440–447.

Rescorla, R. A. Pavlovian conditioning and its proper control procedures. *Psychological Review,* 1967, **74,** 71–80.

———. Second-order conditioning: Implications for theories of learning, in F. G. McGuigan and D. B.

Lumsden (Eds.). *Contemporary approaches to conditioning and learning.* New York: John Wiley, 1973.

Seligman, M. E. P. Chronic fear produced by unpredictable electric shock. *Journal of Comparative and Physiological Psychology,* 1968, **66,** 402–411.

———. *Helplessness: On depression, development, and death.* San Francisco: W. H. Freeman, 1975.

Seligman, M. E. P. and Hager, J. L. *Biological boundaries of learning.* New York: Appleton-Century-Crofts, 1972.

Sheffield, F. D., Wulff, J. J. and Backer, R. Reward value of copulation without sex drive reduction. *Journal of Comparative and Physiological Psychology,* 1951, **44,** 3–8.

Sidman, M. Two temporal parameters of the maintenance of avoidance behavior by the white rat. *Journal of Comparative and Physiological Psychology,* 1953, **46,** 253–261.

Skinner, B. F. The generic nature of the concepts of stimulus and response. *Journal of General Psychology,* 1935, **12,** 40–65.

———. *The behavior of organisms: An experimental analysis.* New York: Appleton-Century-Crofts, 1938.

———. Superstition in the pigeon. *Journal of Experimental Psychology,* 1948, **38,** 168–172.

Sokolov, E. N. *Perception and the conditioned reflex.* S. W. Waydenfeld (trans.) New York: Macmillan, 1963.

Taylor, J. A. The relationship of anxiety to the conditioned eyelid response. *Journal of Experimental Psychology,* 1951, **41,** 81–92.

Terrace, H. S. Errorless transfer of a discrimination across two continua. *Journal of the Experimental Analysis of Behavior,* 1963, **6,** 223–232.

Watson, J. B. and Raynor, R. Conditioned emotional reactions. *Journal of Experimental Psychology,* 1920, **3,** 1–4.

Weiss, B. and Laties, V. G. Behavioral thermoregulation, *Science,* 1961, **133,** 1338–1344.

Williams, C. D. The elimination of tantrum behavior by extinction procedures. *Journal of Abnormal and Social Psychology,* 1959, **59,** 269.

Wolf, M. M., Risley, T. and Mees, H. Application of operant conditioning procedures to the behaviour problems of an autistic child. *Behavior Research and Therapy,* 1964, **1,** 305–312.

Chapter 10

Anderson, J. R., and Bower, G. H. *Human associative memory.* Washington, D.C.: V. H. Winston, 1973.

Atkinson, R. C., and Shiffrin, R. M. Human memory: A proposed system and its control processes, in K. W. Spence and J. T. Spence (Eds.). *The psychology of learning and motivation,* Vol. 2. New York: Academic Press, 1968.

Averbach, E. The span of apprehension as a function of exposure duration. *Journal of Verbal Learning and Verbal Behavior,* 1963, **2,** 60–64.

Bartlett, F. C. *Remembering: A study in experimental and social psychology.* Cambridge, Eng.: The University Press, 1932.

Bousfield, W. A. The occurrence of clustering in the recall of randomly arranged associates. *Journal of General Psychology,* 1953, **49,** 229–240.

Bower, G. H. Organizational factors in memory. *Cognitive Psychology,* 1970, **1,** 18–46.

Bower, G. H., and Bolton, L. S. Why are rhymes easy to learn? *Journal of Experimental Psychology,* 1969, **82,** 453–461.

Bower, G. H., and Winzenz, D. Group structure, coding, and memory for digit series. *Journal of Experimental Psychology Monographs,* 1969, **80,** 1–17.

Bransford, J. D., and Franks, J. J. The abstraction of linguistic ideas. *Cognitive Psychology,* 1971, **2,** 331–350.

Brown, J. Some tests of the decay theory of immediate memory. *Quarterly Journal of Experimental Psychology,* 1958, **10,** 12–21.

Brown, R. W., and McNeil, D. The "tip-of-the-tongue" phenomenon. *Journal of Verbal Learning and Verbal Behavior,* 1966, **5,** 325–337.

Bruner, J. S., Goodnow, J. J., and Austin, G. A. *A study of thinking.* New York: John Wiley, 1956.

Cherry, E. C. Some experiments on the recognition of speech with one and two ears. *Journal of the Acoustical Society of America,* 1953, **25,** 975–979.

Cofer, C. N. Constructive processes in memory. *American Psychologist,* 1973, **61,** 537–543.

Collins, A. M., and Loftus, E. F. A spreading activation theory of semantic processing. *Psychological Review,* 1975, **82,** 407–428.

Collins, A. M., and Quillian, M. R. Retrieval time from semantic memory. *Journal of Verbal Learning and Verbal Behavior,* 1969, **8,** 240–247.

Craik, F. I. M., and Lockhart, R. S. Levels of processing: A framework for memory research. *Journal of Verbal Learning and Verbal Behavior,* 1972, **11,** 671–684.

Cronholm, B. Post-ECT amnesias, in G. A. Talland and N. C. Waugh (Eds.). *The pathology of memory.* New York: Academic Press, 1969.

Ekstrand, B. R. To sleep, perchance to dream (about

why we forget), in C. P. Duncan, L. Sechrest, and A. W. Melton (Eds.). *Human memory: Festschrift in honor of Benton J. Underwood.* New York: Appleton-Century-Crofts, 1972.

Ellis, H. C. *The transfer of learning.* New York: Macmillan, 1965.

————. *Fundamentals of human learning, memory, and cognition.* Dubuque, Iowa: Wm. C. Brown, 1978.

————. Stimulus encoding processes in human learning and memory, in G. H. Bower (Ed.). *The psychology of learning and motivation,* Vol. 7. New York: Academic Press, 1973.

Ellis, H. C., Bennett, T. L., Daniel, T. C., and Rickert, E. J. *The psychology of learning and memory.* Brooks-Cole, in press.

Ellis, H. C., Parenté, F. J., Grah, C. R., and Spiering, K. Coding strategies, perceptual grouping, and the "variability effect" in free recall. *Memory and Cognition,* 1975, **3,** 226–232.

Ellis, N. R., Detterman, D. K., Runcie, D., McCarver, R. B., and Craig, E. M. Amnesic effects in short-term memory. *Journal of Experimental Psychology,* 1971, **89,** 357–361.

Epstein, W. *Varieties of perceptual learning.* New York: McGraw-Hill, 1967.

Gibson, E. J. *Principles of perceptual learning and development.* New York: McGraw-Hill, 1969.

Hebb, D. O. *The organization of behavior.* New York: John Wiley, 1949.

Jenkins, J. J., and Russell, W. A. Associative clustering during recall. *Journal of Abnormal and Social Psychology,* 1952, **47,** 818–821.

Keppel, G., and Underwood, B. J. Proactive inhibition in short-term retention of single items. *Journal of Verbal Learning and Verbal Behavior,* 1962, **1,** 153–161.

Leask, J., Haber, R. N., and Haber, R. B. Eidetic imagery in children: II. Longitudinal and experimental results. *Psychonomic Monographs Supplement,* 1969, **3** (Whole No. 35) 25–48.

Light, L. L., and Carter-Sobell, L. Effects of changed semantic context on recognition memory. *Journal of Verbal Learning and Verbal Behavior,* 1970, **9,** 1–11.

Loftus, E., and Palmer, D. Reconstruction of automobile destruction: An example of the interaction between language and memory. *Journal of Verbal Learning and Verbal Behavior,* 1974, **13,** 585–589.

Martin, E. Stimulus meaningfulness and paired-associate transfer: An encoding variability hypothesis. *Psychological Review,* 1968, **75,** 421–441.

McLardy, T. Memory function in hippocampal gyri. *International Journal of Neuroscience,* 1970, **1,** 113–118.

Miller, G. A. The magical number 7 plus or minus two. Some limits on our capacity for processing information. *Psychological Review,* 1956, **63,** 81–97.

Montague, W. E. Elaborative strategies in verbal learning and memory, in G. H. Bower (Ed.). *The psychology of learning and motivation,* Vol. 6, New York: Academic Press, 1972.

Montague, W. E., Adams, J. A., and Kiess, H. O. Forgetting and natural language mediation. *Journal of Experimental Psychology,* 1966, **72,** 829–833.

Murdock, B. B. *Human memory: Theory and data.* Potomac, Md.: Lawrence Erlbaum, 1974.

Neisser, U. Visual search. *Scientific American,* 1964, **210,** 94–102.

Norman, D. A. *Memory and attention.* New York: John Wiley, 1969.

Paivio, A. *Imagery and verbal processes.* New York: Holt, Rinehart and Winston, 1971.

Peterson, L. R., and Peterson, M. J. Short-term retention of individual verbal items. *Journal of Experimental Psychology,* 1959, **58,** 193–198.

Piaget, J., and Inhelder, B. *The psychology of the child.* Translated by H. Weaver. New York: Basic Books, 1969.

Posner, M. *Cognition: An introduction.* Glenview, Ill.: Scott Foresman, 1973.

Posner, M. I., and Konick, A. F. Short-term retention of visual and kinesthetic information. *Organizational behavior and human performance,* 1966, **1,** 71–86.

Quillian, M. R. Semantic memory. Unpublished Ph.D. dissertation, Carnegie Institute of Technology, 1966.

Sperling, G. A. A model for visual memory tasks. *Human Factors,* 1963, **5,** 19–31.

Sternberg, S. Memory-scanning: Mental processes revealed by reaction-time experiments. *American Scientist,* 1969, **57,** 421–457.

————. High-speed scanning in human memory. *Science,* 1966, **153,** 652–654.

Stromeyer, C. F., and Psotka, J. The detailed texture of eidetic images. *Nature,* 1970, **225,** 346–349.

Thompson, C. P., Hamlin, V. J., and Roenker, D. L. A comment on the role of clustering in free recall. *Journal of Experimental Psychology,* 1972, **94,** 108–109.

Tulving, E. Subjective organization in free recall of "unrelated" words. *Psychological Review,* 1962, **69,** 344–354.

————. Theoretical issues in free recall, in T. R. Dixon and D. L. Horton (Eds.). *Verbal behavior and general behavior theory.* Englewood Cliffs, N. J.: Prentice-Hall, 1968.

Tulving, E., and Madigan, S. A. Memory and verbal learning, in P. H. Mussen and M. R. Rosensweig (Eds.). *Annual Review of Psychology*, Vol. 21. Palo Alto, Ca.: Annual Reviews, Inc., 1970.

Wickens, D. D. Encoding categories of words: An empirical approach to meaning. *Psychological Review*, 1970, **77**, 1–15.

Yates, F. A. *The art of memory*, Chicago: University of Chicago Press, 1966.

Chapter 11

Adamson, R. E. Functional fixedness as related to problem solving: A repetition of three experiments. *Journal of Experimental Psychology*, 1952, **44**, 288–291.

Adamson, R. E., and Taylor, D. W. Functional fixedness as related to elapsed time and to set. *Journal of Experimental Psychology*, 1954, **47**, 122–126.

Archer, E. J. Concept identification as a function of obviousness of relevant and irrelevant information. *Journal of Experimental Psychology*, 1962, **63**, 616–620.

Berko, J. The child's learning of English morphology. *Word*, 1958, **14**, 150–177.

Birch, H. G. The relation of previous experience to insightful problem-solving. *Journal of Comparative Psychology*, 1945, **38**, 367–383.

Birch, H. G., and Rabinowitz, H. S. The negative effect of previous experience on productive thinking. *Journal of Experimental Psychology*, 1951, **41**, 121–125.

Bloom, L. *Language development: Form and function in emerging grammars*. Cambridge, Mass.: M.I.T. Press, 1970.

Bloom, L., Hood, L., and Lightbown, P. Imitation in language development: If, when, and why. *Cognitive Psychology*, 1974, **6**, 380–420.

Bourne, L. E. Learning and utilization of conceptual rules, in B. Kleinmuntz (Ed.). *Memory and the structure of concepts*. New York: John Wiley, 1967.

Bourne, L. E., Ekstrand, B. R., and Dominowski, R. L. *The psychology of thinking*. Englewood Cliffs, N.J.: Prentice-Hall, 1971.

Bourne, L. E. Jr., and Haygood, R. C. The role of stimulus redundancy in the identification of concepts. *Journal of Experimental Psychology*, 1959, **58**, 232–238.

―――. Supplementary report: Effects of redundant relevant information upon the identification of concepts. *Journal of Experimental Psychology*, 1961, **61**, 259–260.

Bourne, L. E. Jr., and Pendleton, R. B. Concept identification as a function of completeness and probabil-

ity of information feedback. *Journal of Experimental Psychology*, 1958, **56**, 413–420.

Braine, M. D. S. The ontogeny of English phrase structure: The first phase. *Language*, 1963a, **39**, 1–14.

―――. On learning the grammatical order of words. *Psychological Review*, 1963(b), **70**, 323–348.

Braine, M. D. S. Children's first word combinations. *Monographs of the Society for Research in Child Development*, 1976, **41**, Serial No. 164.

Brown, R. W. *Social psychology*. Glencoe, Ill.: The Free Press, 1965.

Brown, R. *A first language: The early stages*. Cambridge, Mass.: M.I.T. Press, 1973.

Brown, R., Cazden, C., and Bellugi, U. The child's grammar from I to III; in J. P. Hill (Ed.). *1967 Minnesota Symposium on Child Psychology*, Minneapolis, Minn.: University of Minnesota Press, 1969.

Brown, R., and Fraser, C. The acquisition of syntax; in U. Bellugi and R. Brown (Eds.). The acquisition of language. *Monographs of the Society for Research in Child Development*, 1964, **29**, Serial No. 92.

Brown, R., and Hamlon, C. Developmental complexity and order of speech acquisition in child speech, in J. R. Hayes (Ed.). *Cognition and the development of language*. New York: John Wiley, 1970.

Bruner, J. S., Goodnow, J. J., and Austin, G. A. *A study of thinking*. New York: John Wiley, 1956.

Bruner, J. S. The course of cognitive growth. *American Psychologist*, 1964, **19**, 1–15.

Bulgarella, R. G., and Archer, E. J. Concept Identification of auditory stimuli as a function of amount of relevant and irrelevant information. *Journal of Experimental Psychology*, 1962, **63**, 254–257.

Cahill, H. E., & Hovland, C. I. The role of memory in the acquisition of concepts. *Journal of Experimental Psychology*, 1960, **59**, 137–144.

Carmichael, L. A., Hogan, H. P., and Walter, A. A. An experimental study of the effect of language on the reproduction of visually perceived form. *Journal of Experimental Psychology*, 1932, **15**, 73–86.

Carroll, J. B. (Ed.). *Language, thought, and reality, selected writings of Benjamin Lee Whorf*. Cambridge, Mass.: M.I.T. Press, 1956.

Cazden, C. Environmental assistance to the child's acquisition of grammar. Unpublished Ph.D. dissertation, Harvard University, 1965.

Chlebek, J., and Dominowski, R. L. The effect of practice on utilization of information from positive and negative instances in identifying disjunctive concepts. *Canadian Journal of Psychology*, 1970, **24**, 64–69.

Chomsky, C. *The acquisition of syntax in children from five to ten*. Cambridge, Mass.: M.I.T. Press, 1969.

Chomsky, N. *Aspects of the theory of syntax.* Cambridge, Mass.: M.I.T. Press, 1965.

Clark, E. V. On the child's acquisition of the meaning of *before* and *after. Journal of Verbal Learning and Verbal Behavior,* 1971, **10,** 266–275.

Clarke-Stewart, K. A. Interactions between mothers and their young children: Characteristics and consequences. *Monographs of the Society for Research in Child Development,* 1973, **38,** Serial No. 153.

Denny, J. P. Effects of anxiety and intelligence on concept formation. *Journal of Experimental Psychology,* 1966, **72,** 596–602.

Detambel, M. H., and Stolurow, L. M. Probability and work as determiners of multi-choice behavior. *Journal of Experimental Psychology,* 1957, **53,** 73–81.

Duncan, C. P. Attempts to influence performance on an insight problem. *Psychological Reports,* 1961, **9,** 35–42.

Duncker, K. On problem-solving. *Psychological Monographs,* 1945, **58,** No. 270.

Dunn, R. F. Anxiety and verbal concept learning. *Journal of Experimental Psychology,* 1968, **76,** 286–290.

Eimas, P. D., Siqueland, E. R., Jusczyk, P., and Vigonito, J. Speech perception in infants. *Science,* 1971, **171,** 303–306.

Ekstrand, B. R., and Dominowski, R. L. Solving word as anagrams: II. A clarification. *Journal of Experimental Psychology,* 1968, **77,** 552–558.

Ervin-Tripp, S. Imitation and structural change in children's language, in E. Lenneberg (Ed.). *New directions in the study of language.* Cambridge, Mass.: M.I.T. Press, 1964.

Freibergs, V., and Tulving, E. The effect of practice on utilization of information from positive and negative instances in concept identification. *Canadian Journal of Psychology,* 1961, **15,** 101–106.

Glanzer, M., and Clark, W. H. The verbal loop hypothesis: Binary numbers. *Journal of Verbal Learning and Verbal Behavior,* 1963, **2,** 301–309.

Glucksberg, S. The influence of strength of drive on functional fixedness and perceptual recognition. *Journal of Experimental Psychology,* 1962, **63,** 36–51.

Glucksberg, S., and Weisberg, R. W. Verbal behavior and problem solving: Some effects of labeling in a functional fixedness problem. *Journal of Experimental Psychology,* 1966, **71,** 659–664.

Harlow, H. F. The formation of learning sets. *Psychological Review,* 1949, **56,** 51–65.

Jacobson, E. Electrical measurements of neuromuscular states during mental activities. *American Journal of Physiology,* 1931, **97,** 200–209.

Jenkins, J. Language and thought, in J. Voss (Ed.). *Approaches to thought.* Columbus, Ohio: Bobbs Merrill, 1969.

Johnson, H. L. The meaning of *before* and *after* for preschool children. *Journal of Experimental Child Psychology,* 1975, **19,** 88–99.

Johnson, N. F. The psychological reality of phrase-structure rules. *Journal of Verbal Learning and Verbal Behavior,* 1965, **4,** 469–475.

Kaplan, I. T., and Carvellas, T. Effect of word length on anagram solution time. *Journal of Verbal Learning and Verbal Behavior,* 1968, **7,** 201–206.

Klima, E., and Bellugi, U. Syntactic regularities in the speech of children, in J. Lyons and R. Wales (Eds.). *Psycholinguistic Papers.* Edinburgh, Scotland: Edinburgh University Press, 1966.

Kohler, W. *The mentality of apes.* New York: Harcourt, Brace, 1925.

Kooistra, W. H. Developmental trends in the attainment of conservation, transitivity, and relativism in the thinking of children: A replication and extension of Piaget's ontogenetic formulations. Unpublished Ph.D. dissertation, Wayne State University, Detroit, 1964.

Krechevsky, I. "Hypotheses" in rats. *Psychological Review,* 1932, **38,** 516–532.

Laroche, J. L., and Tcheng, F. C. Y. *Le sourire du nourrisson.* Louvain, France: Publications Universitaires, 1963.

Lenneberg, E. H. Understanding language without ability to speak: A case report. *Journal of Abnormal and Social Psychology,* 1962, **65,** 419–425.

––––––. *The biological foundations of language.* New York: John Wiley, 1967.

Lenneberg, E. H., Rebelsky, F. G., and Nichols, I. A. The vocalization of infants born to deaf and hearing parents. *Human Development,* 1965, **8,** 23–27.

Levine, M. A model of hypothesis behavior in discrimination learning set. *Psychological Review,* 1959, **66,** 353–366.

––––––. Mediating processes in humans at the outset of discrimination learning. *Psychological Review,* 1963, **70,** 254–276.

Lewis, M. *Infant speech.* London: Routledge & Kegen, 1936.

Limber, J. The genesis of complex sentences, in T. E. Moore (Ed.). *Cognitive development and the acquisition of language.* New York: Academic Press, 1973.

McGuigan, F. J. *Thinking: Studies of covert language processes.* New York: Appleton-Century-Crofts, 1966.

McNeill, D. Developmental psycholinguistics, in F. Smith and G. Miller (Eds.). *The genesis of language.* Cambridge, Mass.: M.I.T. Press, 1966.

Malouf, R. A., and Dodd, D. H. Role of exposure, imitation, and expansion in the acquisition of an artificial grammatical rule. *Developmental Psychology,* 1972, **7,** 195–203.

Mayzner, M. S., and Tresselt, M. E. Anagram solution times: A function of letter order and word frequency. *Journal of Experimental Psychology,* 1958, **56,** 376–379.

Mednick, S. A. The associative basis of the creative process. *Psychological Review,* 1962, **69,** 220–232.

Menyuk, P. *Sentences children use.* Cambridge, Mass.: M.I.T. Press, 1969.

Menyuk, P., and Bernholtz, N. Prosodic features and children's language productions. *Quarterly Progress Report,* No. 93, M.I.T. Research Laboratory of Electronics, Cambridge, Mass., 1969.

Moerk, E. Changes in verbal child-mother interactions with increasing language skills of the child. *Journal of Psycholinguistic Research,* 1974, **3,** 101–116.

Messer, S. Implicit phonology in children. *Journal of Verbal Learning and Verbal Behavior,* 1967, **6,** 609–613.

Nelson, K. Structure and strategy in learning to talk. *Monographs of the Society for Research in Child Development,* 1973, **38,** Serial No. 149.

Nelson, K. E., Carskaddon, G., and Bonvillian, J. D. Syntax acquisition: Impact of experimental variation in adult verbal interaction with the child. *Child Development,* 1973, **44,** 497–504.

Osler, S. F., and Fivel, M. W. Concept attainment: I. The role of age and intelligence in concept attainment by induction. *Journal of Experimental Psychology,* 1961, **62,** 1–8.

Paivio, A. *Imagery and verbal processes.* New York: Holt, Rinehart and Winston, 1971.

Piaget, J. *Six psychological studies.* New Yrok: Random House, 1967.

————. *The origins of intelligence.* New York: International University Press, 1952.

Pollio, H. R. *The psychology of symbolic activity.* Reading, Mass.: Addison-Wesley, 1974.

Rheingold, H. L., Gewirtz, J. L., and Ross, H. W. Social conditioning of vocalizations in the infant. *Journal of Comparative and Physiological Psychology,* 1959, **52,** 68–73.

Ricciuti, H. N. Object grouping and selective ordering behavior in infants 12–24 months old. *Merrill-Palmer Quarterly,* 1965, **11,** 129–148.

Ricciuti, H. N., and Benjamin, J. Sorting behavior and conceptual thinking in preschool children. *American Psychologist,* 1957, **12,** 365.

Romanow, C. V. Anxiety level and ego-involvement as

factors in concept formation. *Journal of Experimental Psychology,* 1958, **56,** 166–173.

Routh, D. K. Conditioning of vocal response differentiation in infants. *Developmental Psychology,* 1969, **1,** 219–226.

Schlesinger, I. M. Production of utterances and language acquisition, in D. I. Slobin (Ed.). *The ontogenesis of grammar.* New York: Academic Press, 1971.

Schulz, R. W. Problem solving behavior and transfer. *Harvard Educational Review,* 1960, **30,** 61–77.

Sherman, J. A. Imitation and language development, in H. W. Reese (Ed.). *Advances in child development and behavior,* Vol. 6, New York: Academic Press, 1971.

Sinclair-de-Zwart, H. *Acquisition du language et developpement de la pensée.* Paris: Dunod, 1967.

Slobin, D. I. Imitation and grammatical development in children, in N. Endler, L. Boulter, and H. Osser (Eds.). *Contemporary issues in developmental psychology.* New York: Holt, Rinehart and Winston, 1968.

Smedslund, J. Concrete reasoning: A study of intellectual development. *Monographs of the Society for Research in Child Development,* 1964, **29,** Serial No. 93.

Smith, S. M., Brown, H. O., Toman, J. E. P., and Goodman, L. S. The lack of cerebral effects of d-tubocurarine. *Anesthesiology,* 1947, **8,** 1–14.

Snow, C. Mothers' speech to children learning language. *Child Development,* 1972, **43,** 549–565.

Staats, A. Linguistic-mentalistic theory versus an explanatory S-R learning theory of language development, in D. I. Slobin (Ed.). *The ontogenesis of grammar.* New York: Academic Press, 1971.

Thomas, D. R., Caronite, A. D., LaMonica, G. L., and Hoving, K. L. Mediated generalization via stimulus labeling: a replication and extension. *Journal of Experimental Psychology,* 1968, **78,** 531–533.

Thomas, D. R., and DeCapito, A. Role of stimulus labeling in stimulus generalizaton. *Journal of Experimental Psychology,* 1966, **71,** 913–915.

Thomas, W. I. *Primitive behavior.* New York: McGraw-Hill, 1937.

Tresselt, M. E., and Leeds, D. S. The Einstellung effect in immediate and delayed problem-solving. *Journal of General Psychology,* 1953, **49,** 87–95.

Vygotsky, L. S. *Thought and language.* Cambridge, Mass.: M.I.T. Press, 1962.

Walker, C. M., and Bourne, L. E. Jr. The identification on concepts as a function of amounts of relevant and irrelevant information. *American Journal of Psychology,* 1961, **74,** 410–417.

Weir, R. H. Some questions on the child's learning of phonology, in F. Smith and G. A. Miller (Eds.). *The genesis of language.* Cambridge, Mass.: M.I.T. Press, 1966.

Wolff, P. H. The natural history of crying and other vocalizations in early infancy, in B. M. Foss (Ed.). *Determinants of infant behavior,* Vol. 4, London: Methuen, 1966.

Chapter 12

Ames, Adelbert Jr. Reconsideration of the origin and nature of perception in situations involving only inorganic phenomena, in Ratner, S. (Ed.). *Vision and action,* New Brunswick, N.J.: Rutgers University Press, 1953.

Asch, S. E. Forming impressions of personality. *Journal of abnormal and social psychology,* 1946, **41,** 258–290.

Attneave, F. Triangles as ambiguous figures. *American Journal of Psychology,* 1968, **81,** 447–453.

Banks, M. S., Aslin, R. N. and Letson, R. D. Sensitive periods for the development of human binocular vision. *Science,* 1975, **190,** 675–677.

Boring, E. G. *Sensation and perception in the history of experimental psychology.* New York: D. Appleton-Century, 1942.

Bridgen, R. L. A tachistoscopic study of the differentiation of perception. *Psychological Monographs,* 1933, **44,** No. 197, 153–166.

Brunswik, Egon. *Perception and the representative design of psychological experiments,* Berkeley, Ca.: University of California Press, 1947.

Epstein, W. *Varieties of perceptual learning.* New York: McGraw-Hill, 1967.

Eriksen, C. W. and Collins, J. F., Some temporal characteristics of visual pattern perception. *Journal of Experimental Psychology,* 1967, **74,** 476–484.

Freeman, R. D., Mitchell, D. E., and Millodot, M., A neural effect of partial visual deprivation in humans. *Science,* 1972, **175,** 1384–1386.

Garner, W. R. *Uncertainty and structure as psychological concepts.* New York: John Wiley, 1962.

———. Good patterns have few alternatives. *American Scientist,* 1970, **58,** 34–42.

Gibson, E. J. *Principles of perceptual learning and development.* New York: Appleton-Century-Crofts, 1969.

Gibson, E. J. and Bergman, R. The effect of training on absolute estimation of distance over the ground. *Journal of experimental psychology,* 1954, **48,** 473–482.

Gibson, J. J. *The perception of the visual world.* New York: Houghton Mifflin, 1950.

———. *The senses considered as perceptual systems.* Boston: Houghton Mifflin, 1966.

Gottschaldt, K. Über den Einfluss der Erfahrung auf die Wahrnehmung von Figuren. I., *Psychologische Forschung,* 1926, **8,** 261–317.

Gregory, R. L. Visual illusions, in *Image, object, and illusion.* San Francisco: W. H. Freeman, 1974, 48–58.

Haber, R. N. Eidetic images, in *Image, object, and illusion.* San Francisco: W. H. Freeman, 1974, 123–131.

Hake, H. W. The study of perception in the light of multivariate methods; in Cattell, R. B. (Ed.). *Handbook of multivariate experimental psychology.* Chicago: Rand McNally, 1966.

Hake, H. W. and Eriksen, C. W. Effect of number of permissible response categories on learning of a constant number of visual stimuli. *Journal of Experimental Psychology,* 1955, **50,** 161–167.

Hake, H. W. and Rodwan, A. S. Perception and recognition, in Sidowski, J. B. (Ed.). *Experimental methods and instrumentation in psychology,* New York: McGraw-Hill, 1966.

Hammond, K. R. *The psychology of Egon Brunswik.* New York: Holt, Rinehart and Winston, 1966.

Hebb, D. O. *Organization of behavior.* New York: John Wiley, 1949.

Held, R. Plasticity in sensory-motor systems. *Scientific American,* 1965, 84–94.

Helm, C. E., and Tucker, L. R. Individual differences in the structure of color perception. *American Journal of Psychology,* 1972, **75,** 437–444.

Helson, H. *Adaptation-level theory.* New York: Harper & Row, 1964.

Hochberg, J. Effects of the Gestalt revolution: The Cornell symposium on perception. *Psychological Review,* 1957, **64,** 73–84.

Hubel, D. H. The visual cortex of the brain. *Scientific American.* Reprint No. 168 (November 1963).

Hull, C. L. *Principles of behavior.* New York: Appleton, 1943.

Hynek, J. A. *The UFO experience.* New York: Ballantine Books, 1972.

Ittelson, W. H., and Kilpatrick, F. P. Experiments in perception. *Scientific American,* 1951, Reprint No. 405.

James, W. *The principles of psychology.* New York: Collier, 1962.

Jones, L. E. Individual differences in women's perceptions of men's faces: Is beauty in the eyes of the beholder? Paper presented at the meeting of the Midwestern Psychological Association, Chicago, 1975.

Kohler, I. Experiments with goggles. *Scientific American*, 1962, Reprint No. 465.

Köhler, W. *Gestalt Psychology*, New York: Liveright, 1947.

Langdon, J. The perception of changing shape. *Quarterly Journal of Experimental Psychology*, 1951, **3**, 157–165.

Lichten, W. and Lurie, S. A new technique for the study of perceived size. *American Journal of Psychology*, 1950, **63**, 280–282.

Lippmann, W. *Public opinion*. New York: Harcourt, 1922.

Malpass, R. S. Recognition for faces of own and other race. *Journal of Personality and Social Psychology*. 1969, **13**, 330–335.

McCleary, R. A. *Genetic and experiential factors in perception*. Glenview: Scott, Foresman, 1970.

Posner, M. I., Goldsmith, R., and Welton, K. E. Perceived distance and the classification of distorted patterns, *Journal of Experimental Psychology*, 1967, **73**, 28–38.

Riesen, A. H. The development of visual perception in man and chimpanzee, *Science*, 1947, **106**, 107–108.

Rodwan, A. S. and Hake, H. W. The discrimination-function as a model for perception. *The American Journal of Psychology*, 1964, **77**, 380–392.

Rubin, E. *Visuell wahrgenommene Figuren*. Copenhagen: Gyldendalska, 1921.

Senden, M. von. *Space and sight: The perception of space and shape in the congenitally blind before and after operation*. Translated by P. Heath, London: Methuen, 1960.

Solley, C. M. and Santos, J. Perceptual learning with partial verbal reinforcement. *Perceptual Motor Skills*, 1958, **8**, 183–193.

Stevens, S. S., and Volkmann, J. The relation of pitch to frequency. *American Journal of Psychology*, 1940, **53**, 329–353.

Wallach, H. Brightness constancy and the nature of achromatic colors. *Journal of Experimental Psychology*, 1948, **38**, 310–324.

Warren, D. I. Status inconsistency theory and flying saucer sightings. *Science*, 1970, **170**, 599–603.

Watson, J. B. *Behaviorism*, New York: The Peoples Institute, 1925.

Weintraub, D. J. Rectangle discriminability: Perceptual relativity and the law of Pragnanz. *Journal of Experimental Psychology*, 1971, **88**, 1–11.

Chapter 13

Arkin, A. M., Toth, M. F., Baker, J., and Hastey, J. M. The frequency of sleep talking in the laboratory among chronic sleep talkers and good dream recallers. *Journal of Nervous and Mental Disease*, 1970, **151**, 369–374.

Aserinsky, E. and Kleitman, N. Regularly occurring periods of eye motility, and concomitant phenomena, during sleep. *Science*, 1953, **118**, 273–274.

Baekeland, F. and Lasky, R. Exercise and Sleep patterns in college athletes. *Percept. Motor Skills*, 1966, **23**, 1203–1207.

Dement, W. The effect of dream deprivation. *Science*, 1960, **131**, 1705–1707.

Foulkes, D. You think all night long, in R. L. Woods and Herbert B. Greenhouse (Eds.). *The new world of dreams*. New York: MacMillan, 1974.

Freud, S. *The interpretation of dreams* (1900). New York: Avon, 1965.

Hall, C. What people dream about. *Scientific American*, 1951, **184**, 60–63.

Hartmann, E. *The functions of sleep*. Clinton, Mass.: Colonial Press, 1973.

Jouvet, M. Biogenic amines and the states of sleep. *Science*, 1969, **163**, 32–41.

Jung, C. G. *Memories, dreams, reflections*. New York: Random House, 1961.

Kleitman, N. *Sleep and wakefulness*. Chicago: University of Chicago Press, 1963.

Loomis, A. L., Harvey, E. N., and Hobart, G. A. Cerebral states during sleep as studied by human brain potentials. *Journal of Experimental Psychology*, 1937, **21**, 127–144.

Oswald, I. and Priest, R. G. Five weeks to escape the sleeping pill habit. *British Medical Journal*, 1965, **2**, 1093–1098.

Oswald, I., Taylor, A. M., and Treisman, M. Discriminative responses to stimulation during human sleep. *Brain*, 1960, **82**, 440–453.

Snyder, F. The new biology of dreaming. *Archives of General Psychiatry*, 1963, **8**, 381–391.

Tune, G. S. The influence of age and temperament on the adult human sleep-wakefulness pattern. *British Journal of Psychology*, 1969, **60**, 431–441.

Webb, W. B. Sleep as an adaptive response. *Perceptual and Motor Skills*, 1974, **38**, 1023–1027.

Webb, W. B. and Friel, J. Sleep stage and personality characteristics of "natural" long and short sleepers. *Science*, 1971, **171**, 587–588.

Webb, W. B. and Kersey, J. Recall of dreams and the probability of stage 1-REM sleep. *Perceptual and Motor Skills*, 1967, **24**, 627–630.

White, R. M. Sleep length and variability: Measurement and interrelationships. Unpublished Ph.D. dissertation, University of Florida, 1975.

Williams, R., Karacan, I. and Hursch, C. *EEG of human sleep*. New York: John Wiley, 1974.

Chapter 14

Appleton, T., Clifton, R., and Goldberg, S. The development of behavioral competence in infancy, in F. D. Horowitz (Ed.). *Review of child development research*, Vol. 4. Chicago: University of Chicago Press, 1975.

Banks, M. S., Aslin, R. N., and Letson, R. D. Sensitive period for the development of human binocular vision. *Science*, 1975, **190**, 675–677.

Bayley, N. *Bayley scales of infant development*. New York: Psychological Corp., 1969.

Becker, W. C. Consequences of different kinds of parental discipline, in M. L. Hoffman and L. W. Hoffman (Eds.). *Review of child development research*. Vol. 1. New York: Russell Sage Foundation, 1964, pp. 169–208.

Bem, S. L. Sex role adaptability: One consequence of psychological androgyny. *Journal Personality and Social Psychology*, 1975, **31**, 634–643.

Binet, A. L'Etude experimentale de l'intelligence. Paris: Schleicher, 1903.

Binet, A., and Simon, T. Upon the necessity of establishing a scientific diagnosis of inferior states of intelligence. (1905) Translated and reprinted in W. Dennis (Ed.). *Readings in the history of psychology*. New York: Appleton-Century-Crofts, 1948, pp. 407–411.

Blum, Richard H., and Associates. *Horatio Alger's children*. San Francisco: Jossey-Bass Publishers, 1972.

Bogen, H. Experimental investigations on psychic and associative secretion of stomach fluids in the human, in Y. Brackbill, and G. G. Thompson (Eds.). *Behavior in infancy and early childhood*. New York: Free Press, 1967.

Brackbill, Y. Continuous stimulation and arousal level in infancy: Effects of stimulus intensity and stress. *Child Development*, 1975, **46**, 364–369.

———. The cumulative effects of continuous stimulation on arousal level in infants. *Child Development*, 1971, **42**, 17–26.

Broman, S. H., Nichols, P. L., and Kennedy, W. A. *Preschool IQ: Prenatal and early developmental correlates*. Hillsdale, N.J.: Erlbaum, 1975.

Bronfenbrenner, U. *Two worlds of childhood: U.S. and U.S.S.R.* New York: Russell Sage Foundation, 1970.

Burtt, H. E. An experimental study of early childhood memory: Final report. *J. Genetic Psychology*, 1941, **58**, 435–439.

Caldwell, B. M. The effects of infant care, in M. L. Hoffman and L. W. Hoffman (Eds.). *Review of child development research*. Vol. 1. New York: Russell Sage Foundation, 1964, pp. 9–87.

Chomsky, N. Review of "Verbal Behavior" by B. F. Skinner. *Language*, 1959, **35**, 26.

———. *Language and mind*. New York: Harcourt Brace Jovanovich, 1972.

Chukovsky, K. *From two to five*. Berkeley & Los Angeles: University of California Press, 1963.

Cohen, L. B. and Salapatek, P. *Infant perception: From sensation to cognition*. New York: Academic Press, 1975.

Condon, W. S. and Sander, L. W. Neonate movement is synchronized with adult speech: Interactional participation and language acquisition. *Science*, 1974, **183**, 99–101.

Darwin, C. A biographical sketch of an infant. *Mind*, 1877, **2**, 286–294.

Douglas, J. W. B. and Blomfield, J. M. *Children under five*. London: Allen & Unwin, 1958.

Fitzgerald, H. E. Autonomic pupillary reflex activity in relation to social and nonsocial visual stimuli. *J. Experimental Child Psychology*, 1968, **6**, 470–482.

Fitzgerald, H. E., and Brackbill, Y. Classical conditioning in infancy: Development and constraints. *Psychological Bulletin*, 1976, **83**, 353–376.

Flavell, J. H. *The developmental psychology of Jean Piaget*. Princeton, N.J.: Van Nostrand, 1963.

Freud, A. with Dann, S. An experiment in group upbringing. *Psychoanalytic study of the child*, 1951, **6**, 127–168.

Gibson, E. J. *Principles of perceptual learning and development*. New York: Appleton-Century-Crofts, 1969.

Hall, G. S. The contents of children's minds. *Princeton Review*, 1883, **11**, 249–272.

Harlow, H. *Learning to love*. San Francisco: Albion Publishing, 1971.

Hartup, W. W. Peer interaction and social organization, in P. H. Mussen (Ed.). *Carmichael's manual of child psychology*. 3rd ed. New York: John Wiley, 1970.

Holt, E. L., Jr., Davies, E. A., Hasselmeyer, E. G., and

Adams, A. O. A study of premature infants fed cold formulas. *J. Pediatrics*, 1962, **61**, 556–561.

Irwin, O. C. Infant speech: Effect of systematic reading of stories. *J. Speech and Hearing Disorders*, 1960, **3**, 187–190.

Krasnogorskii, N. I. An attempt to form artificial conditioned reflexes in young children, in Y. Brackbill and G. G. Thompson (Eds.). *Behavior in infancy and early childhood*. New York: Free Press, 1967.

Lorenz, K. Z. Imprinting. *The Auk*, 1937, **54**, 245–273.

Maccoby, E. E. *The development of sex differences*. Stanford: Stanford University Press, 1966.

Maccoby, E. E. and Jacklin, C. N. *The psychology of sex differences*. Stanford: Stanford University Press, 1974.

Maccoby, E. E. and Masters, J. C. Attachment and dependency, in P. H. Mussen (Ed.). *Carmichael's manual of child psychology*. 3rd ed. New York: John Wiley, 1970, pp. 73–157.

Makarenko, A. S. *Learning to live.* (Originally titled, *Flags on the Battlements*) Moscow: Foreign Languages Publishing House, 1953.

Mason, W. A., and Kenney, M. D. Redirection of filial attachments in Rhesus monkeys: Dogs as mother surrogates. *Science*, 1974, **183**, 1209–1211.

McNeill, David. *The acquisition of language: The study of developmental psycholinguistics*. New York: Harper & Row, 1970.

Molfese, D. L., Freeman, R. B., Jr., and Palermo, D. S. The ontogeny of brain lateralization for speech and nonspeech stimuli. *Brain & Language*, 1975, **2**, 356–368.

Moore, O. K. The preschool child learns to read and write in the autotelic responsive environment, in Y. Brackbill and G. G. Thompson (Eds.). *Behavior in infancy and early childhood*. New York: Free Press, 1967, pp. 340–352.

Polak, P. R., Emde, R. N. and Spitz, R. The smiling response to the human face. II: Visual discrimination and the onset of depth perception, *J. nerv. ment. Dis.*, 1964, **139**, 407–415.

Riesen, A. H. and Zilbert, D. E. Behavioral consequences of variations in early sensory environments, in A. H. Riesen (Ed.). *The developmental neuropsychology of sensory deprivation*. New York: Academic Press, 1975, pp. 211–252.

Scott, J. P., Stewart, J. M., and De Ghett, V. J. Critical periods in the organization of systems. *Developmental Psychobiology*, 1974, **7**, 489–513.

Sears, R. R., Maccoby, E. E., and Levin, H. *Patterns of child rearing*. Evanston, Ill.: Row, Peterson, 1957.

Shuey, A. M. *The testing of Negro intelligence*. 2nd ed. New York: Social Science Press, 1966.

Skinner, B. F. *Verbal behavior*. New York: Appleton-Century-Crofts, 1957.

Spiro, M. E. *Children of the kibbutz*. Cambridge, Mass.: Harvard University Press, 1958.

Wadsworth, B. J. *Piaget's theory of cognitive development*. New York: David McKay, 1971.

Watson, J. B., and Rayner, R. Conditioned emotional reactions. *Journal experimental psychology*, 1920, **3**, 1–14.

Wright, H. Psychological development in midwest. *Child Development*, 1956, **27**(2), 265–286.

Chapter 15

Ajzen, I., and Fishbein, M. Attitude-behavior relations: A theoretical analysis and review of research. *Psychological Bulletin*, 1977, **84**, 888–918.

Altman, I., and Haythorn, W. W. The ecology of isolated groups. *Behavioral Science*, 1967, **12**, 169–182.

Amir, Y. Contact hypothesis in ethnic relations. *Psychological Bulletin*, 1969, **71**, 319–342.

Asch. S. Forming impressions of personality. *Journal of Abnormal and Social Psychology*, 1946, **41**, 258–290.

Berkowitz, L. Group standards, cohesiveness, and productivity. *Human Relations*, 1954, **7**, 509–519.

Berscheid, E., Dion, K., Walster, E., and Walster, G. W. Physical attractiveness and dating choice: A test of the matching hypothesis. *Journal of Experimental Social Psychology*, 1971, **7**, 173–189.

Byrne, D. Interpersonal attraction and attitude similarity. *Journal of Abnormal and Social Psychology*, 1961, **62**, 713–715.

Byrne, D., and Rhamey, R. Magnitude of positive and negative reinforcements as a determinant of attraction. *Journal of Personality and Social Psychology*, 1965, **2**, 884–889.

Corey, S. M. Professed attitudes and actual behavior. *Journal of Educational Psychology*, 1937, **28**, 271–280.

Dailey, D. A. The effects of premature conclusion upon the acquisition of understanding a person. *Journal of Psychology*, 1952, **33**, 133–152.

Dean, L. R. Interaction, reported and observed: The case of one local union. *Human Organization*, 1958, **17**, 36–44.

Fendrich, J. M. A study of the association among verbal attitudes, commitment, and overt behavior in different experimental situations. *Social Forces,* 1967, **45,** 347–355.

Festinger, L. Informal social communication. *Psychological Review,* 1950, **57,** 271–282.

Festinger, L., Schachter, S., and Back, K. W. *Social pressure in informal groups.* New York: Harper & Row, 1950.

Fiedler, F. E. *A theory of leadership effectiveness.* New York: McGraw-Hill, 1967.

Gerwitz, J. L., and Baer, D. M. The effect of brief social deprivation on behaviors for a social reinforcer. *Journal of Abnormal and Social Psychology,* 1958, **56,** 49–56.

Heider, F. *The psychology of interpersonal relations.* New York: John Wiley, 1958.

Hovland, C. I., Janis, I. L., and Kelley, H. H. *Communication and persuasion.* New Haven: Yale University Press, 1953.

Jones, E. E., and Nisbett, R. E. The actor and the observer: Divergent perceptions of the causes of behavior, in J. W. Thibaut, J. T. Spence, and R. C. Carson (Eds.). *Contemporary topics in social psychology.* Morristown, N. J.: Silver Burdett, 1976, pp. 37–52.

Kelley, H. H. Attribution theory in social psychology, in D. Levine (Ed.). *Nebraska symposium on motivation* (Vol. 15). Lincoln, Neb.: University of Nebraska Press, 1967.

Knowles, E. S. Boundaries around group interaction: The effect of group size and member status on boundary permeability. *Journal of Personality and Social Psychology,* 1973, **26,** 327–331.

Lewin, K. Forces behind food habits and methods of change. *Bulletin of the National Research Council,* 1943, **108,** 35–65.

Lewin, K., Lippitt, R., and White, R. K. Patterns of aggressive behavior in experimentally created "social climates." *Journal of Social Psychology,* 1939, **10,** 271–299.

Linder, D. E. Personal space, in J. W. Thibaut, J. T. Spence, and R. C. Carson (Eds.). *Contemporary topics in social psychology,* Morristown, N. J.: Silver Burdett, 1976, pp. 455–477.

Linn, L. S. Verbal attitudes and overt behavior: A study of racial discrimination. *Social Forces,* 1965, **43,** 353–364.

Newcomb, T. M. *The acquaintance process.* New York: Holt, Rinehart and Winston 1961.

Newton, N., and Newton, M. Relationship of ability to breast feed and maternal attitudes toward breast feeding. *Pediatrics,* 1950, **5,** 869–875.

Riess, M., and Schlenker, B. R. Attitude change and responsibility avoidance as modes of dilemma resolution in forced-compliance situations. *Journal of Personality and Social Psychology,* 1977, **35,** 21–30.

Schutz, W. C. On group composition. *Journal of Abnormal and Social Psychology,* 1961, **62,** 275–281.

Shaw, Marjorie E. A comparison of individuals and small groups in the rational solution of complex problems. *American Journal of Psychology,* 1932, **44,** 491–504.

Shaw, M. E. *Group dynamics: The psychology of small group behavior.* 2nd ed. New York: McGraw-Hill, 1976.

Shaw, M. E., and Wright, J. M. *Scales for the measurement of attitudes.* New York: McGraw-Hill, 1967.

Sommer, R. *Personal space: The behavioral basis of design.* Englewood Cliffs, N. J.: Prentice-Hall, 1969.

Walster, E., Aronson, V., Abrahams, D., and Rottman, L. Importance of physical attractiveness in dating behavior. *Journal of Personality and Social Psychology,* 1966, **4,** 508–516.

Wells, G. L., and Harvey, J. H. Do people use consensus information in making causal attributions? *Journal of Personality and Social Psychology,* 1977, **35,** 279–293.

Whyte, W. F. The social structure of the restaurant. *American Journal of Sociology,* 1949, **54,** 302–308.

Willis, F. N., Jr. Initial speaking distance as a function of the speaker's relationship. *Psychonomic Science,* 1966, **5,** 221–222.

Zajonc, R. B., and Brickman, P. Expectancy and feedback as independent factors in task performance. *Journal of Personality and Social Psychology,* 1969, **11,** 148–150.

Zajonc, R. B., and Sales, S. M. Social facilitation of dominant and subordinate responses. *Journal of Experimental Social Psychology,* 1966, **2,** 160–168.

Chapter 16

Associated Press, June 21, 1975.

Bandura, A. *Aggression: A social learning analysis.* Englewood Cliffs, N. J.: Prentice-Hall, 1973.

Baron, R. A., Byrne, D., and Griffitt, W. *Social psychology: Understanding human interaction.* Boston: Allyn and Bacon, 1974.

Bem, D., and Bem, S. L. We're all non-conscious sexists. *Psychology Today,* November 1970, 22–26, 115–116.

Berkowitz, L. The contagion of violence: An S-R mediational analysis of some effects of observed aggression, in W. J. Arnold and M. M. Page (Eds.). *Nebraska symposium on motivation*. Lincoln, Neb.: University of Nebraska Press, 1970.

Calhoun, J. B. Population density and social pathology. *Scientific American*, 1962, 206, 139–148.

Cook, S. W. Motives in a conceptual analysis of attitude-related behavior, in W. J. Arnold and D. Levine (Eds.). *Nebraska symposium on motivation, 1969*. Lincoln, Neb.: University of Nebraska Press, 1970, pp. 179–231.

Deutsch, M., and Krauss, R. M. The effect of threat upon interpersonal bargaining. *Journal of Abnormal and Social Psycholoy*, 1960, 61, 181–189.

Dollard, J., Doob, L., Miller, N., Mowrer, O., and Sears, R. *Frustration and aggression*. New Haven: Yale University Press, 1939.

Eron, L. D., Huessmann, L. R., Lefkowitz, M. M., and Walder, L. O. Does television violence cause aggression? *American Psychologist*, 1972, 27, 253–263.

Frank, J. D. *Sanity and survival: Psychological aspects of war and peace*. New York: Vintage, 1967.

Galle, O. R., Gove, W. R., and McPherson, J. M. Population density and pathology: What are the relationships for man? *Science*, 1972, 176, 23–30.

Hovland, C. I., and Sears, R. R. Minor studies of aggression, VI: Correlation of lynchings with economic indices. *Journal of Psychology*, 1940, 9, 301–310.

Johnson, R. N. *Aggression in man and animals*. Philadelphia: Saunders, 1972.

Kinsey, A. C., Pomeroy, W. B., and Martin, C. E. *Sexual behavior in the human male*. Philadelphia: Saunders, 1948.

Kinsey, A. C., Pomeroy, W. B., Martin, C. E., and Gebhard, P. H. *Sexual behavior in the human female*. Philadelphia: Saunders, 1953.

Latané, B., and Darley, J. Bystander "apathy." *American Scientist*, 1969, 57, 244–268.

Lerner, N. The desire for justice and reactions to victims, in J. Macaulay and L. Berkowitz (Eds.). *Altruism and helping behavior*. New York: Academic Press, 1970, pp. 205–229.

Lorenz, K. *On aggression*. New York: Harcourt, Brace & World, 1966.

Masters, W. H., and Johnson, V. E. *Human sexual response*. Boston: Little, Brown, 1966.

Mead, M. *Male and female*. New York: Morrow, 1949.

Milgram, S. The experience of living in the cities. *Science*, 1970, 167, 1461–1468.

Montagu, M. F. A. (Ed.). *Man and aggression*. 2nd Edition. New York: Oxford University Press, 1973.

New York Times, March 26, 1964.

Osgood, C. E. *An alternative to war or surrender*. Urbana, Ill.: University of Illinois Press, 1962.

Piliavin, J. A., and Piliavin, I. M. *The good samaritan: Why does he help?* New York: MSS Modular Publications, 1975.

Piliavin, I., Rodin, J., and Piliavin, J. Good samaritanism: An underground phenomenon? *Journal of Personality and Social Psychology*, 1969, 13, 289–299.

Pruitt, D. G., and Snyder, R. C. *Theory and research on the causes of war*. Englewood Cliffs, N. J.: Prentice-Hall, 1969.

Report of the Commission on Obscenity and Pornography. New York: Bantam Books, 1970.

Rokeach, M. *The open and closed mind*. New York: Basic Books, 1960.

Severy, L. J., Brigham, J. C., and Schlenker, B. R. *A contemporary introduction to social psychology*. New York: McGraw-Hill, 1976.

Sherif, M., Harvey, O. J., White, B. J., Hood, W. R., and Sherif, C. W. *Intergroup conflict and cooperation: The Robber's Cave experiment*. Norman: Institute of Group Relations, University of Oklahoma, 1961.

Tedeschi, J. T., and Lindskold, S. *Social psychology: interdependence and influence*. New York: John Wiley, 1976.

Triandis, H. C. A note on Rokeach's theory of prejudice. *Journal of Abnormal and Social Psychology*, 1961, 62, 184–186.

Vanneman, R. D., and Pettigrew, T. F. Race and relative deprivation in the urban United States. *Race*, 1972, 13, 461–486.

Wicker, A. W. Undermanning theory and research: Implications for the study of psychological and behavioral effects of excess populations. *Representative Research in Social Psychology*, 1973, 4, 185–206.

Wiggins, J. S., Renner, K. E., Clore, G. L., and Rose, R. J. *The psychology of personality*. Reading, Mass.: Addison-Wesley, 1971.

Wilson, W. C., and Goldstein, M. J. (Eds.). Pornography: Attitudes, use, and effects. *Journal of Social Issues*, 1973, 29, No. 3.

Chapter 17

American Psychological Association. Ethical Standards for Research with Human Subjects. *Monitor*, May 1972.

Banfield, E. C. *The moral basis of a backward society*. Glencoe, Ill.: Free Press, 1958.

Bernstein, B. Social class and linguistic development: A theory of social learning, in A. Halsey, J. Floyd and C. Anderson (Eds.). *Education, economy and society.* Glencoe, Ill.: Free Press, 1961.

Bornstein, M. H. Color vision and color naming: A psychophysiological hypothesis of cultural difference. *Psychological Bulletin,* 1973, **80,** 257–285.

Brislin, R. W., Bochner, S. and Lonner, W. J. *Cross-cultural perspectives on learning.* New York: Sage/Halsted/Wiley, 1975.

Brislin, R. W., Lonner, W. J. and Thorndike, R. M. *Cross-cultural research methods.* New York: John Wiley, 1973.

Brown, R. *Social psychology.* New York: Free Press, 1965.

Campbell, D. T. Presidential address delivered on September 1, 1975 to the American Psychological Association in Chicago, Ill.

Campbell, D. T. and Fiske, D. W. Convergent and discriminant validation by the multitrait-miltimethod matrix. *Psychological Bulletin.* 1959, **56,** 81–85.

Cole, M. An ethnographic psychology of cognition, in Brislin et al. (1975), pp. 157–176.

Cole, M. and Bruner, J. S. Cultural differences and inferences about psychological processes. *American Psychologist,* 1971, **26,** 867–876.

Cole, M. and Scribner, S. *Culture and thought: A psychological introduction.* New York: John Wiley, 1974.

Dasen, P. R. Cross-cultural Piagetian Research: A summary. *Journal of Cross-Cultural Psychology,* 1972, **3,** 23–39.

Davidson, A. R., Jaccard, J. J., Triandis, H. C., Morales, M. L. and Diaz-Guerrero, R. Cross-cultural model testing: Toward a solution of the etic-emic dilemma. *International Journal of Psychology,* 1976, **11,** 1–13.

Dawson, J. L. M. Ecology, cultural pressures toward conformity and left-handedness: A bio-social psychological approach, in J. L. M. Dawson and W. J. Lonner. *Readings in cross-cultural psychology.* University of Hong Kong Press, 1974, pp. 124–149.

Dawson, J. L. M. and Lonner, W. J. *Readings in cross-cultural psychology.* Hong Kong: University of Hong Kong Press, 1974.

Deregowski, J. B. Perception, in H. C. Triandis and W. J. Lonner (Eds.). *Handbook of cross-cultural psychology, Volume 3,* Boston, Mass. Allyn and Bacon, 1979.

Draguns, J. G., Phillips, L., Broverman, K., Caudill, W. and Nishimae, S. The symptomatology of hospitalized psychiatric patients in Japan and the United States: A study of cultural differences. *Journal of Nervous and Mental Diseases,* 1971, **152,** 3–16.

Edwards, A. L. *Techniques of attitude scale construction.* New York: Appleton-Century-Crofts, 1957.

Fiedler, F. E., Mitchell, T. and Triandis, H. C. The culture assimilator: An approach to cross-cultural training. *Journal of Applied Psychology,* 1971, **55,** 95–102.

Foster, G. M. Peasant society and the image of limited good. *American Anthropologist,* 1965, **67,** 293–315.

Guilford, J. P. *The nature of human intelligence.* New York: McGraw-Hill, 1967.

Heider, E. R. Style and accuracy of verbal communications within and between social classes. *Journal of Personality and Social Psychology,* 1971, **18,** 33–47.

Herskovits, M. J. *Cultural anthropology.* New York: Alfred Knopf, 1955.

Hunt, J. McV. *Personal communication,* 1974.

Inkeles, A. and Smith, D. H. *Becoming modern.* Cambridge, Mass.: Harvard University Press, 1974.

Kamin, L. *The science and politics of I.Q.* Potomac, Ed. Erlbaum (Wiley), 1974.

Kohn, M. L. *Class and conformity: A study in values.* Homewood, Ill.: Dorsey, 1969.

Leary, T. *Interpersonal diagnosis of personality.* New York: Ronald Press, 1957.

LeVine, R. A. and Campbell, D. T. *Ethnocentrism: Theories of conflict, ethnic attitudes and group behavior.* New York: John Wiley, 1972.

Mason, W. A. Sociability and social organization in monkeys and apes, in L. Berkowitz (Ed.). *Advances in experimental social psychology.* New York: Academic Press, 1964, pp. 277–305.

McClelland, D. *The achieving society.* Princeton, N.J.: Van Nostrand, 1961.

Nachshon, I., Draguns, J. G., Broverman, I. K. and Phillips, L. Acculturation and psychiatric symptomatology: A study of an Israeli child guidance clinic population. *Social Psychiatry,* 1972, **7,** 109–118.

Naroll, R. "What have we learned from cross-cultural surveys?" *American Anthropologist,* 1970, **72,** 1227–1288.

Osgood, C. E. Cross-cultural comparability in attitude measurements via multilingual semantic differentials, in I. D. Steiner and M. Fishbein (Eds.). *Current studies in social psychology.* Chicago: Holt, Rinehart and Winston, 1965, 95–107.

———. Explorations in semantic space: A personal diary. *Journal of Social Issues.* 1971, **27,** 5–59.

Pelto, P. J. The differences between "tight" and "loose" societies. *Transaction,* April 1968, 37–40.

Phillips, L. *Human adaptation and its failures.* New York: Academic Press, 1968.

Pike, K. L. *Language in relation to a unified theory of the structure of human behavior.* The Hague: Mouton, 1966.

Pollock, R. H. Müller-Lyer illusion: Effect of age, lightness contrast and hue. *Science,* 1970, **170,** 93–94.

Przeworski, A. and Teune, H. *Logic of comparative social inequity.* New York: John Wiley, 1969.

Rohner, R. P. Parental acceptance-rejection and personality development: A Universalist approach to behavioral science; in Brislin, et al, 1975, pp. 251–271.

Romney, A. K. and D'Andrade, R. D. Transcultural studies in cognition. *American Anthropologist* 1964, **66,** Special Issue, 1–253.

Rosch, E. Universals and cultural specifics in human categorization, in Brislin, et al, (1975), pp. 177–206.

Rotter, J. B. Generalized expectancies for internal vs. external control of reinforcement. *Psychological Monograph,* 1966, **80,** No. 1 (Whole No. 609).

Schaefer, E. S. A circumplex model for maternal behavior. *Journal of Abnormal and Social Psychology,* 1959, **59,** 226–235.

Schlosberg, G. H. Three dimensions of emotion. *Psychological Review,* 1954, **61,** 81–88.

Strodtbeck, F. Considerations of meta-theory in cross-cultural studies. *American Anthropologist,* 1964, **66,** 223–229.

Tapp, J. L., Kelman, H. C., Triandis, H. C., Wrightsman, L. and Coelho, G. Continuing concerns in cross-cultural ethics: A report. *International Journal of Psychology,* 1974, **9,** 231–249.

Taylor, C. W. and Barron, F. *Scientific creativity: Its recognition and development.* New York: John Wiley, 1973.

Triandis, H. C. Culture training, cognitive complexity and interpersonal attitudes, in R. W. Brislin, S. Bochner and W. J. Lonner, *Cross-cultural perspectives on learning,* New York, Sage/Halsted/Wiley, 1975(a), pp. 39–78.

———. (Ed.). *Variations in black and white perceptions of the social environment.* Champaign-Urbana, Ill.: University of Illinois Press, 1975(b).

Triandis, H. C. and Lambert, W. W. A restatement and test of Schlosberg's theory of emotion with two kinds of subjects from Greece. *Journal of Abnormal and Social Psychology,* 1958, **56,** 321–328.

Triandis, H. C. and Triandis, L. M. A cross-cultural study of social distance. *Psychological Monographs,* 1962, **76,** No. 21 (Whole No. 540).

Triandis, H. C. and Vassiliou, V. Frequency of contact and stereotyping. *Journal of Personality and Social Psychology,* 1967, **7,** 316–328.

Triandis, H. C., Davis, E. E. and Takezawa, S. I. Some determinants of social distance among American, German and Japanese students. *Journal of Personality and Social Psychology,* 1965, **2,** 540–551.

Triandis, H. C., Feldman, J. M., Weldon, D. E. and Harvey, W. M. Ecosystem distrust and the hard-to-employ. *Journal of Applied Psychology,* 1975, **60,** 44–56.

Triandis, H. C., Malpass, R. S. and Davidson, A. Cross-cultural psychology. *Biennial Review of Anthropology,* 1972, 1–84.

———. Psychology and culture. *Annual Review of Psychology,* 1973, **24,** 355–378.

Triandis, H. C., Vassiliou, V. and Nassiakou, M. Three cross-cultural studies of subjective culture. *Journal of Personality and Social Psychology, Monograph Supplement.* 1968, **8,** 1–42.

Triandis, H. C., Vassiliou, Vl, Vassiliou, G., Tanaka, Y. and Shanmugam, A. V. *The analysis of subjective culture.* New York: John Wiley, 1972.

Tyler, S. A. *Cognitive anthropology,* New York: Holt, Rinehart and Winston, 1969.

Wallace, A. F. C. Mental illness, biology and culture, in F. Hsu (Ed.). *Psychological anthropology.* Cambridge, Mass.: Schenkman Publishing, 1972, pp. 363–402.

Weldon, D. E., Carlston, D. E., Rissman, A. K., Slobodin, L. and Triandis, H. C. A laboratory test of the effects of culture assimilator training. *Journal of Personality and Social Psychology,* 1975, **32,** 300–310.

Werner, O. and Campbell, D. T. Translating, working through interpreters and the problem of decentering. In R. Naroll and R. Cohen (Eds.). *A handbook of method in cultural anthropology.* New York: American Museum of Natural History, 1970.

Whiting, J. W. M. Methods and problems in cross-cultural research, in G. Lindzey and E. Aronson (Eds.). *The handbook of social psychology.* Reading, Mass.: Addison-Wesley, 1968.

Whiting, B. B. and Whiting, J. W. M. *Children of six cultures.* Cambridge, Mass.: Harvard University Press, 1975.

Witkin, H. A. and Berry, J. W. Psychological differentiation in cross-cultural perspective. *Journal of Cross-Cultural Psychology,* 1975, **6,** 4–87.

Witkin, H. A., Price-Williams, D., Bertini, M., Christinasen, B., Oltman, P. K., Ramirez, M. and Van Mell, J. Social conformity and psychological differentiation. *International Journal of Psychology,* 1974, **9,** 11–30.

Wober, M. Towards an understanding of the Kiganda concept of intelligence, in J. W. Berry and P. R. Dasen (Eds.). *Culture and cognition*. London: Methuen, 1974, pp. 261–280.

Chapter 18

American Psychological Association. *Standards for educational and psychological tests*. Washington, D.C.: APA, 1974.

Anastasi, A. *Psychological testing*. 4th ed. New York: Macmillan, 1976.

Anderson, S., and Messick, S. Social competency in young children. *Developmental Psychology*, 1974, **10,** 282–293.

Baughman, E. E. *Black Americans*. New York: Academic Press, 1971.

Bingham, W. V. D., and Moore, B. V. *How to interview*. New York: Harper & Row, 1924.

Bray, D. W., Campbell, R. J., and Grant, D. L. *Formative years in business: A long-term A T & T study of managerial lives*. New York: John Wiley, 1974.

Brigham, C. C. Intelligence tests of immigrant groups. *Psychological Review*, 1930, **37,** 157–165.

Broman, S. H., Nichols, P. L., and Kennedy, W. A. *Preschool IQ: Prenatal and early developmental correlates*. Hillsdale, N. J.: Lawrence Erlbaum Associates, 1975.

Buros, O. K. (Ed.). *The fifth mental measurements yearbook*. Highland Park, N. J.: Gryphon Press, 1959.

———. *The sixth mental measurements yearbook*. Highland Park, N. J.: Gryphon Press, 1965.

———. *The seventh mental measurements yearbook*. Highland Park, N. J.: Gryphon Press, 1972.

———. *The eighth mental measurements yearbook*. Highland Park, N. J.: Gryphon Press, 1978.

———. *Tests in print, II*. Highland Park, N. J.: Gryphon Press, 1974.

Ciminero, A. R., Calhoun, K. S., and Adams, H. E. (Eds.). *Handbook of behavioral assessment*. New York: John Wiley, 1977.

Cleary, T. A., Humphreys, L. G., Kendrick, S. A., and Wesman, A. Educational uses of tests and disadvantaged students. *American Psychologist*, 1975, **30,** 15–40.

Cronbach, L. J. *Essentials of psychological testing*. 3rd ed. New York: Harper & Row, 1970.

———. Five decades of public controversy over mental testing. *American Psychologist*, 1975, **30,** 1–14.

Dillon, H. J. *Early school leavers: A major educational problem*. New York: National Child Labor Committee, 1949.

Doyle, K. O., Jr. Theory and practice of ability testing in ancient Greece. *Journal of the History of the Behavioral Sciences*, 1974, **10,** 202–212.

DuBois, P. H. *A history of psychological testing*. Boston: Allyn and Bacon, 1970.

Galton, F. *Hereditary genius: An inquiry into its laws and consequences*. London: Macmillan, 1869.

Goddard, H. H. The Binet tests in relation to immigration. *Journal of Psycho-Asthenics*, 1913, **18,** 105–107.

———. Mental tests and the immigrant. *Journal of Delinquency*, 1917, **2,** 243–277.

Graham, J. R. *The MMPI: A practical guide*. New York: Oxford University Press, 1977.

Harper, R. G., Wiens, A. N., and Matarazzo, J. D. *Nonverbal communication: The state of the art*. New York: John Wiley, 1978.

Heber, R. A manual of terminology and classification in mental retardation. *American Journal of Mental Deficiency*, 1959, **64,** Monograph Supplement.

Hedlund, J. L. MMPI clinical scale correlates. *Journal of Consulting and Clinical Psychology*, 1977, **45,** 739–750.

Hersen, M., and Bellack, A. S. (Eds.). *Behavioral assessment: A practical handbook*. New York: Pergamon Press, 1976.

Hunt, J. McV., Kirk, G. E., and Volkman, F. Social class and preschool language skill: III. Semantic mastery of position information. *Genetic Psychology Monographs*, 1975(a), **91,** 317–337.

Hunt, J. McV., Paraskevopoulos, J., Schickendanz, D., and Uzgiris, I. C. Variations in the mean ages of achieving object permanence under diverse conditions of rearing, in B. Z. Friedlander, et al. (Eds.). *Exceptional infant*, Vol. 3. New York: Brunner/Mazel, 1975(b).

Irvin, L. K., Halpern, A. S., and Reynolds, W. M. Assessing social and prevocational awareness in mildly and moderately retarded individuals. *American Journal of Mental Deficiency*, 1977, **82,** 266–272.

Jensen, A. R. How much can we boost IQ and scholastic achievement? *Harvard Educational Review*, 1969, **39,** 1–23.

———. *Genetics and education*. New York: Harper & Row, 1972.

———. Cumulative deficit in IQ of blacks in the rural South. *Developmental Psychology*, 1977, **13,** 184–191.

Jones, R. R., Reid, J. B., and Patterson, G. R. Naturalistic observation in clinical assessment, in

P. McReynolds (Ed.). *Advances in psychological assessment,* Vol. 3. San Francisco: Jossey-Bass, 1975, 42–95.

Kirk, G. E., and Hunt, J. McV. Social class and preschool language skill: I. Introduction. *Genetic Psychology Monographs,* 1975, **91,** 281–298.

Lambert, N. M., Windmiller, M., Cole, L. and Figueroa, R. *AAMD Adaptive Behavior Scale—Public School Version.* Washington, D. C.: Amer. Assoc. Ment. Defic., 1975.

Loehlin, J. C., Lindzey, G., and Spuhler, J. N. *Race differences in intelligence.* San Francisco: W. H. Freeman, 1975.

MacPhillamy, D. J., and Lewinsohn, P. M. Depression as a function of levels of desired and obtained pleasure. *Journal of Abnormal Psychology,* 1974, **83,** 651–657.

Matarazzo, J. D. *Wechsler's measurement and appraisal of adult intelligence: 5th and enlarged edition.* Baltimore: Williams & Wilkins, 1972.

————. The interview: Its reliability and validity in psychiatric diagnosis, in B. B. Wolman (Ed.). *Clinical diagnosis of mental disorders: a handbook.* New York: Plenum Publishing, 1979.

Matarazzo, J. D. and Wiens, A. N. Black intelligence Test of Cultural Homogeneity and Wechsler Adult Intelligence Scale scores of black and white police applicants. *Journal of Applied Psychology,* 1977, **62,** 157–63.

————. Correlation of WAIS IQ in 10 pairs of brothers. *Journal of Consulting and Clinical Psychology,* 1978, in press.

McClelland, D. C. *The achieving society.* Princeton, N.J.: Van Nostrand, 1961.

————. Testing for competence rather than "Intelligence." *American Psychologist,* 1973, **28,** 1–14.

————. Love and power: The psychological signals of war. *Psychology Today,* 1975, **8,** 44–48.

Mercer, J. R. *Labeling the mentally retarded.* Los Angeles: University of California Press, 1973.

Murray, H. A. *Explorations in personality.* New York: Oxford University Press, 1938.

Office of Strategic Services Staff. *Assessment of men.* New York: Rinehart, 1948.

Patterson, G. R. Intervention for boys with conduct problems: Multiple settings, treatments and criteria. *Journal of Consulting and Clinical Psychology,* 1974, **42,** 471–481.

Reynolds, W. M., and Sundberg, N. D. Recent research trends in testing. *Journal of Personality Assessment,* 1976, **40,** 228–233.

Samuda, R. J. *Psychological testing of American minorities.* New York: Dodd, Mead, 1975.

Scarr, S. and Weinberg, R. A. IQ test performance of black children adopted by white families. *American Psychologist,* 1967, **31,** 726–739.

————. Intellectual similarities within families of both adopted and biological children. *Intelligence,* 1977, **1,** 170–191.

Schaie, K. W. Translations in gerontology—from lab to life: Intellectual functioning. *American Psychologist,* 1974, **11,** 802–807.

Shuey, A. M. *The testing of Negro intelligence.* 2nd ed. New York: Social Science Press, 1966.

Sundberg, N. D. *Assessment of persons.* Englewood Cliffs, N.J.: Prentice-Hall, 1977.

Sundberg, N. D., Snowden, L. R. and Reynolds, W. M. Toward assessment of personal competence and incompetence in life situations. *Annual Review of Psychology,* 1978, **28,** 179–221.

Sundberg, N. D., and Tyler, L. E. *Clinical psychology.* New York: Appleton-Century-Crofts, 1962.

Terman, L. M. *The measurement of intelligence.* Boston: Houghton Mifflin, 1916.

Tyler, L. E. *The psychology of human differences.* 3rd ed. New York: Appleton-Century-Crofts, 1965.

————. *Individual differences.* Englewood Cliffs, N.J.: Prentice-Hall, 1974.

Varon, E. J. Alfred Binet's concept of intelligence. *Psychological Review,* 1936, **43,** 32–58.

Wechsler, D. *The measurement of adult intelligence.* Baltimore: Williams & Wilkins, 1939.

————. *Manual for the Wechsler Adult Intelligence Scale.* New York: Psychological Corporation, 1955.

Wiens, A. N. The assessment interview, in I. B. Weiner (Ed.). *Clinical methods in psychology.* New York: John Wiley, 1976, pp. 3–60.

Williams, R. L. *The Black Intelligence Test of Cultural Homogeneity (BITCH): Manual of directions,* 1975. (Available from Robert L. Williams, Williams & Associates, Inc., 6374 Delmar Blvd., St. Louis, Mo., 63130.)

Wolf, T. H. The emergence of Binet's conception and measurement of intelligence: A case history of the creative process. *Journal of the History of the Behavioral Sciences,* 1969, **5,** 113–134; 207–237.

————. *Alfred Binet.* Chicago: University of Chicago Press, 1973.

Yerkes, R. M. (Ed.). Psychological examining in the U.S. Army. *Memoirs of the National Academy of Sciences,* 1921, **15,** 890 ff.

Zigler, E. Has it really been demonstrated that compensatory education is without value? *American Psychologist*, 1975, **30**, 935–937.

Chapter 19

Adler, A. *Social interest: A challenge to mankind*. New York: G. P. Putnam's, 1939.

American Psychological Association. *Standards for educational and psychological tests*. Washington, D.C.: American Psychological Association, 1974.

Ansbacher, H. L. and Ansbacher, R. R. (Eds.). *The individual psychology of Alfred Adler*. New York: Basic Books, 1956.

Bandura, A. *Aggression: A social learning analysis*. Englewood Cliffs, N.J: Prentice-Hall, 1973.

Bandura, A. *Principles of behavior-modification*. New York: Holt, Rinehart and Winston, 1969.

Bandura, A. *Social learning theory*. Englewood Cliffs, N.J.: Prentice-Hall, 1977.

Bandura, A., Blanchard, E. B., and Ritter, B. Relative efficiency of desensitization and modeling approaches for inducing behavioral, affective, and attitudinal changes. *Journal of Personality and Social Psychology*, 1969, **13**, 173–199.

Bandura, A., and Walters, R. H. *Social learning and personality development*. New York: Holt, Rinehart and Winston, 1963.

Bannister, D. The genesis of schizophrenic thought disorder: a serial invalidation hypothesis. *British Journal of Psychiatry*, 1963, **109**, 680–686.

Bannister, D. *New perspectives in personal construct theory*. London & New York: Academic Press, 1977.

Bem, D. J. Constructing cross-situational consistencies in behavior: some thoughts on Alker's critique of Mischel. *Journal of Personality*, 1972, **40**, 17–26.

Binswanger, L. *Being-in-the-world; selected papers of Ludwig Binswanger*. New York: Basic Books, 1963.

Block, J. Some reasons for the apparent inconsistency of personality. *Psychological Bulletin*, 1968, **70**, 210–212.

Boss, M. *Psychoanalysis and daseinanalysis*. New York: Basic Books, 1963.

Buytendijk, F. J. J. *Pain its modes and functions*. Translated by E. O'Shiel. Chicago: University of Chicago Press, 1962.

Carlson, R., and Levy, W. Studies of Jungian typology: I. memory, social perception, and social action. *Journal of Personality*, 1973, **41**, 559–576.

Campbell, J. *The portable Jung*. New York: Viking Press, 1971.

Cattell, R. B., Eber, H. W., and Tatsuoka, M. *Handbook for the sixteen personality factor questionnaire*. Champaign, Ill.: Institute for Personality and Ability Testing, 1970.

Coan, Richard W. *The optimal personality: An empirical and theoretical analysis*. New York: Columbia University Press, 1974.

———. *Hero, artist, sage or saint*. New York: Columbia University Press, 1977.

Combs, A. W., Richards, Anne C. and Richards, F. *Perceptual psychology: A humanistic approach to the study of persons*. New York: Harper & Row, 1976.

Dollard, J. and Miller, N. E. *Personality and psychotherapy*. New York: McGraw-Hill, 1950.

Duck, S. W. *Personal relationship and personal constructs: A study of friendship formation*. London & New York: John Wiley, 1973.

Duncan, C. W. A comparison of certain experiences of life stages of selected groups of self-actualized, modal, and low functioning college students. Unpublished Ph.D. dissertation, University of Florida, 1970.

Edwards, A. L. *Edwards Personal Preference Schedule*, New York: Psychological Corporation, 1959.

Engle, M. The stability of the self-concept in adolescence. *Journal of Abnormal and Social Psychology*, 1959, **58**, 215–221.

English, H. and English, A. *A comprehensive dictionary of psychological and psychoanalytical terms*. New York: Longmans Green, 1958.

Erickson, E. H. *Childhood and society*. 2nd ed. New York: Norton, 1963.

———. *Identity youth and crisis*. New York: Norton, 1968.

Eysenck, H. G. (Ed.). *Handbook of abnormal psychology; an experimental approach*. New York: Basic Books, 1961.

Fitts, W. H. *The self-concept and psychopathology*, in *Studies on the self-concept and rehabilitation*, Dede Wallace Center Monograph 4, March 1972.

Fiske, D. W. The limits of the conventional science of personality. *Journal of Personality*, 1974, **42**, 1–11.

Fransella, F. *Personal change and reconstruction: Research on a treatment of stuttering*. New York & London: Academic Press, 1972.

Fransella, F. and Banister, D. *A manual for repertory grid technique*. London & New York: Academic Press, 1977.

Freud, S. *The ego and the id*. Translated by J. Rivierre, Revised by J. Strachey, New York: Norton, 1960 (Originally published 1927).

Fromm, E. *Escape from freedom*. New York: Rinehart, 1941.

———. *The sane society*. New York: Rinehart, 1955.

———. *The heart of man*. New York: Harper & Row, 1964.

———. *The anatomy of human destructiveness*. New York: Holt, Rinehart and Winston, 1973.

Gough, H. C. and Heilbrun, A. B. *The adjective check-list manual*. Palo Alto, Ca.: Consulting Psychologists Press, 1965.

Hall, C. S. and Lindzey, G. *Theories of personality. 2nd edition*, New York: John Wiley, 1970.

Hanna, T. *Bodies in revolt*, New York: Holt, Rinehart and Winston, 1970.

Hartmann, H. *Ego psychology and the problem of adaptation*. New York: International University Press, 1958.

Hill, D. J. *The elements of psychology*. New York: Sheldon and Company, 1888.

Horn, M. L. Searching for knowledge: A research appraisal, in Nevill, D. D. *Humanistic psychology: new frontiers*, New York: Gardner Press, 1977, pp. 203–218.

Holy Scriptures Vol. II. Philadelphia: Jewish Publication Society, 1955.

Horney, K. *The neurotic personality of our time*. New York: Norton, 1937.

———. *Our inner conflicts*, New York: Norton, 1945.

Jackson, D. N. *Personality research form manual*. Goshen, N.Y.: Research Psychologists Press, 1967.

Jahoda, M. *Current concepts of mental health*. New York: Basic Books, 1958.

Jones, E. E. and Nisbett, R. E. The actor and the observer: divergent perceptions of the causes of behavior; in E. E. Jones et al. (Eds.). *Attribution: perceiving the causes of behavior*. Morristown, N.Y.: General Learning Press, 1971.

Jourard, S. M. (Ed.). *To be or not to be, . . . existential-psychological perspectives on the self*. Gainesville, Fla.: University of Florida Monographs, 1971.

———. *Disclosing man to himself*. New York: Van Nostrand Reinhold, 1968.

———. *Self-disclosures: An experimental analysis of the transparent self*. New York: Wiley-Interscience, 1971.

———. *The healthy personality: An approach from the viewpoint of humanistic psychology*. New York: Macmillan, 1974.

———. Education as dialogue, *Journal of Humanistic Psychology*, 1978, **18**, 47–52.

Jung, C. G. *Memories, dreams, reflections*. New York: Pantheon, 1963.

———. (Ed.). *Man and his symbols*. New York: Doubleday, 1964.

Kelly, G. A. *The psychology of personal constructs*. New York: Norton, 1955, 2 Vols.

Landfield, A. W. *Personal construct systems in psychotherapy*. New York: Rand McNally, 1971.

Landsman, T. Four phenomenologies. *Journal of Individual Psychology*, 1958, **14**, 29–37.

———. Discussion of papers by Patterson, etc. *Journal of Individual Psychology*, 1961, **17**, 29–42.

———. The beautiful person, *The Futurist*, 1970, **3**, 41–42.

———. Positive experience and the beautiful person. Presidential address, Southeastern Psychological Association, Roanoke, 1968.

———. The humanizer, *American Journal of Orthopsychiatry*, 1974, **44**, 345–352.

Lefcourt, H. M. Internal vs. external control of reinforcement: a review. *Psychological Bulletin*, 1966, **65**, 206–220.

Levy, N., Murphy, C., Carlson, R. Personality types among negro college students. *Educational and Psychological Measurement*, 1972, **32**, 641–653.

Lewin, K. *Principles of topological psychology*. New York: McGraw-Hill, 1936.

Liebert, R. M., Neale, J. M. and Davidson, E. S. *The early window: effects of television in children and youth*. New York: Pergamon Press, 1973.

Lynch, S. The intense human experience, its relation to openness and self concept. Unpublished Ph.D. dissertation, University of Florida, 1968.

Maddi, S. R. Unexpectedness, affective tone and behavior, in D. W. Fiske and S. R. Maddi (Eds.). *Functions of varied experience*. Homewood, Ill.: Dorsey, 1961.

May, R. *Psychology and the human dilemma*, New York: Van Nostrand Reinhold, 1967.

———. *Love and will*, New York: Norton, 1969.

———. Angel, E., and Ellenberger, H. F. (Eds.). *Existence*. New York: Basic Books, 1958.

Maslow, A. H. *Motivation and personality*. New York: Harper & Row, 1954.

———. *Toward a psychology of being*, New York: Van Nostrand, 1962.

———. *The farther reaches of human nature*. New York: Viking Press, 1971.

———. March 1, 1970, in *Abraham Maslow: A memorial volume by the International Study project with aid of Bertha Maslow*, Monterey, Ca.: Brooks-Cole, 1972.

Mathes, E. W. and Edwards L. L. An empirical test of Maslow's theory of motivation. *Journal of Humanistic Psychology,* 1978, **18,** 75–77.

Mischel, W. *Personality and assessment.* New York: John Wiley, 1968.

————. Toward a cognitive social learning reconceptualization of personality. *Psychological Review,* 1973(a), **80,** 252–283.

————. On the empirical dilemmas of psychodynamic approaches: issues and alternatives. *Journal of Abnormal Psychology,* 1973(b), **82,** 335–344.

————. *Introduction to personality.* 2nd Edition, New York: Holt, Rinehart and Winston, 1976.

Moustakas, C. *Loneliness.* New York: Prentice-Hall, 1961.

Murray, H. A. Preparations for the scaffold of a comprehensive system, in S. Koch (Ed.). *Psychology: A study of a science* Vol. 3. New York: McGraw-Hill, 1959.

————. *Thematic apperception test manual.* Cambridge, Mass.: Harvard University Press, 1943.

————. *Explorations in personality.* New York: Oxford University Press, 1938.

Nordby, V. J. and Hall, C. S. *A guide to psychologists and their concepts.* San Francisco: W. H. Freeman, 1974.

Passini, F. T. and Norman, W. T. A universal conception of personality structure. *Journal of Personality and Social Psychology,* 1966, **4,** 44–49.

Powell, W. J., Jr. A comparison of the reinforcing effects of three types of experimentor response on two classes of verbal behavior in an experimental interview. Unpublished Ph.D. dissertation, University of Florida, 1963.

Raimy, V. C. The self concept as a variable in counseling and personality organization. Unpublished Ph.D. dissertation. Ohio State University, 1943.

Raskin, N.J. An objective study of the locus of evaluation factor in psychotherapy, in W. Wolff and J. A. Precker (Eds.). *Success in psychotherapy.* New York: Grune & Stratton, 1952.

Rogers, C. R. *Client-centered therapy: Its current practice, implications, and theory.* Boston: Houghton Mifflin, 1951.

————. *On becoming a person: A therapists view of psychotherapy.* Boston: Houghton Mifflin, 1961.

————. *Carl Rogers on personal power.* N.Y.: Delacorte Press, 1977.

————. The formative tendency. *Journal of humanistic psychology,* 1978, **18,** 23–26.

Rogers, C. R. and Dymond, R. *Psychotherapy and personality change.* Chicago: University of Chicago Press, 1954.

Rotter, J. B. Generalized expectancies for internal versus external control of reinforcement. *Psychological Monographs,* 1966, **80,** 1, Whole No. 609.

Rotter, J. B. and Hochreich, D. J. *Personality.* Glenview, Ill.: Scott, Foresman, 1975.

Rowe, B. C. Humanistic dimensions in academic achievement. Unpublished Ph.D. dissertation, University of Florida, 1970.

Rychlak, J. F. The two teleologies of Adler's individual psychology. *Journal of Individual Psychology,* 1970, **26,** 144–152.

————. *Introduction to personality and psychotherapy: A theory-construction approach.* Boston: Houghton Mifflin, 1973.

Sarason, I. G. *Personality: An objective approach.* 1st ed. New York: John Wiley, 1966.

————. *Personality: An objective approach.* 2nd ed. New York: John Wiley, 1972.

Sartre, J. P. *Being and nothingness: An essay on phenomenological ontology.* Translated by H. E. Barnes. New York: Philosophical Library, 1956.

Schneider, D. J. Implicit personality theory: A review. *Psychological Bulletin,* 1973, **79,** 294–309.

Seeman, J. and Raskin, J. J. Research perspectives in client centered therapy, in O. H. Mowrer (Ed.). *Psychotherapy: Theory and research.* New York: Ronald Press, 1953.

Skinner, B. F. *Walden two.* New York: Macmillan, 1948.

————. *Beyond freedom and dignity.* New York: Alfred Knopf, 1971.

————. *About behaviorism.* New York: Alfred Knopf, 1974.

Slater, P. *The measurement of intrapersonal space by grid technique Volume 1: Explorations of intrapersonal space.* London & New York: John Wiley, 1976.

Snygg, D. and Combs, A. W. *Individual behavior: A new frame of reference for psychology.* New York: Harper & Row, 1949.

Steiner, J. G. *Treblinka.* Translated by H. Weaver. New York: Simon & Schuster, 1967.

Stern, G. G. *People in context: Measuring a person—environment congruence in education and industry.* New York: John Wiley, 1970.

Sullivan, H. S. Psychiatry: Introduction to the study of interpersonal relations. *Psychiatry,* 1938, **1,** 121–134.

Tillich, P. *The courage to be,* New Haven: Yale University Press, 1952.

Vaihinger, H. *The philosophy of "as if."* New York: Harcourt, Brace & World, 1925.

Webster's New International Dictionary Second Edition, Springfield, Mass.: G. C. Merriam, 1957.

Wylie, R. C. *The self concept,* revised edition, Vol. I, Lincoln, Neb.: University of Nebraska Press, 1974.

Chapter 20

Ayllon, T. and Azrin, N. H. The measurement and reinforcement of behavior of psychotics. *J. of the Exp. Analysis of Behav.,* 1965, **8,** 357–383.

Ausubel, D. Causes and types of narcotic addiction: A psychosocial view. *Psyhiat. Quart.,* 1961, **35,** 523.

Bailly, J. Rapport des commissaires chargés pare le roi, de l'éxamen du magnétisme animal. Paris: L'imprimerie royal, 1784.

Bandura, A. *Principles of behavior modification.* Holt, Rinehart and Winston, 1969.

Barlow, D. The treatment of sexual deviation: Towards a comprehensive behavioral approach. In K. Calhoun, H. Adams, and K. Mitchell (Eds.), *Innovative treatment methods in psychopathology.* New York: John Wiley, 1975.

Berg, Dorothy F. Extent of illicit drug use: A compilation of studies, surveys, and pools. *Bureau of Narcotic and Dangerous Drugs,* U.S. Department of Justice, 1959.

Bexton, W., Heron, W., and Scott, T. Effects of decreased variation in the sensory environment. *Canad. J. Psychol.,* 1954, **8,** 7076.

Bogdonoff, M., Estes, E., Harlan, W., Trout, D., and Kirshner, N. Metabolic and cardiovascular changes during a state of acute central nervous system arousal. *J. Clin. Endocrinol.,* 1960, **20,** 1333.

Bonner, H. The problem of diagnosis in paranoic disorders. *Amer. J. Psychiat.,* 1951, **107,** 677.

Brady, J. Ulcers in "executive" monkeys. *Scient. Amer.,* 1958, **119,** No. 4.

Brady, J., and Lind, D. Experimental analysis of hysterical blindness. *A.M.A. Arch. Gen. Psychiat.,* 1961, **4,** 331.

Braid, J. *Neurypnology, or the rationale of nervous sleep.* London: Churchill, 1843.

Butler, Martha. Client Evaluation of Counseling Center Functioning. Unpublished Ph.D. dissertation, Colorado State University, 1975.

Charcot, J. Essai d'une distinction nosographique des divers étes compris sous le nom d'hypnotisme. *Compt. rend. acad. Sci.,* 1882, 44.

Clark, W. Operational definitions of drinking problems and associated prevalence rates. Berkeley Drinking Practices Study, 1966 (unpublished).

Freeman, W., and Watts, J. *Psychosurgery.* Springfield, Ill.: C. C. Thomas, 1942.

Freud, S. *The standard edition of the complete psychological works of Sigmund Freud.* J. Strachey (Ed.). London: Hogarth Press, 1953.

Friedman, M., Rosenman, R., and Byers, S. Serum lipids and conjunctival circulation after fat ingestion in men exhibiting Type-A behavior patterns. *Circul.,* 1964, **29,** 874.

Friedman, M., and Rosenman, R. H. *Type A behavior and your heart.* New York: Alfred Knopf, 1974.

Fleck, S., Lidz, T., and Cornelison, A. Comparison of parent-child relationships of male and female schizophenic patients. *Arch. Gen. Psychiat.,* 1963, **8,** 1.

Frumkin, R., and Frumkin, M. Religion, occupation, and major mental disorders. *J. Hum. Rel.,* 1957, **6,** 98.

Gantt, W. The origin and development of nervous disturbances experimentally produced. *Amer. J. Psychiat.,* 1942, **98,** 475.

Gottesman, T., and Shields, J. *Schizophrenia and genetics, a twin study vantage point.* New York: Academic Press, 1972.

Hadley, E., et al. *Military psychiatry,* 1944, **7,** 379.

Haertzen, C., Hill, H., and Belleville, R. Development of the Addiction Research Center Inventory (ARCI): Selection of items that are sensitive to the effects of various drugs. *Psychopharmacologia,* 1963, **4,** 155.

Hagman, R. A study of fears in children of preschool age. *J. Exp. Educ.,* 1932, **1,** III.

Harlow, H. The nature of love. *Amer. Psychol.,* 1958, **13,** 673.

Himler, L, and Raphael, T. A follow-up study on 95 college students with epilepsy. Ann Arbor, Mich., *Amer. J. Psychiat.,* 1945, **101,** 760.

Hirning, J. Indecent exposure and other sex offenses. *J. Clin. Psychopath. Psychother.,* 1945, **7,** 105.

Hollingshead, A., and Redlich, F., *Social class and mental illness.* New York: John Wiley, 1958.

Holmes, T., and Rahe, R. The Social Readjustment Scale. *J. Psychosom. Res.,* 1967, **11,** 213.

Horner, M. The motive to avoid success and changing aspirations of college women, in *Women on Campus: 1970, a Symposium.* Ann Arbor, Mich.: Center for Continuing Education of Women, 1970.

Hull, C. *Principles of behavior.* New York: Appleton-Century-Crofts, 1943.

Jaffe, S., and Scherl, D. Acute psychosis precipitated by T-group experiences. *Arch. Gen. Psychiat.,* 1969, **21,** 443.

Jones, M. C. A laboratory study of fear: The case of Peter. *Pedagog. Sem.*, 1924, **31**, 308.

Kallmann, F. The genetic theory of schizophrenia. *Amer. J. Psychiat.*, 1946, **103**, 309.

———. *Heredity in health and mental disorder.* New York: Norton, 1953.

Klerman, G., Davidson, E., and Kayce, M. Factors influencing the clinical responses to schizophrenic patients to phenothiazine drugs and to placebo. In P. Solomon and B. Glueck (Eds.). *Recent research on schizophrenia*, Washington, D.C.: American Psychiatric Association, 1964, **97.**

Kraepelin, E. *Lehrbuch der psychiatrie.* Germany, 1883.

Liebault, A. Du Somneil et des états analogues considérés surtout au point de vue de l'action du moral sur le physique. Paris: Masson, 1866.

Louria, D. *Overcoming drugs, a program for action.* New York: McGraw-Hill, 1971.

M'Naghten's case. 8 Eng. Rep., 718, 1843.

McGlothin, W., and West, L. The marihuana problem: An overview. *Amer. J. Psychiat.*, 1968, **125**, 126.

Malzberg, B. New data relative to incidence of mental disease among Jews. *Mental Hygiene, N.Y.*, 1936, **20**, 280.

Maslow, A. *Motivation and personality.* New York: Harper & Row, 1954.

Mechanic, D. Discussion of research programs on relations between stressful life events and episodes of physical illness. In D. S. Dohrenwend, and B. P. Dohrenwend (Eds.). *Stressful life events: Their nature and effects.* N.Y.: John Wiley, 1974.

Miller, N. E. Experimental studies of conflict. In J. McV. Hunt (Ed.), *Personality and the behavior disorders*, New York: Ronald Press, 1944.

Moreno, J. *Psychodrama.* New York: Beacon House, 1946.

Moos, R. H., Kopell, B. S., Melges, F. T., Yalom, I. D., Tunde, D. T., Clayton, R. B., and Nomburg, D. A. Fluctuations in symptoms and moods during the menstrual cycle. *Journal of Psychological Research*, 1969, **13**, 37.

Murray, J. Drug addiction. *J. Gen. Psychol.*, 1967, **77**, 41.

National Epilepsy League, Special issue of *Horizon*, May 1962, 1.

Neale and Weintraub. Children vulnerable to psychopathology. *J. Abnormal Child Psychology*, 1975, in press.

Pavlov, I. *Lectures on conditioned reflexes.* Moscow and Leningrad: State Publishing House, 1904.

Penfield, W., and Erickson, T. *Epilepsy and cerebral localization.* Springfield, Ill.: C. C. Thomas, 1941.

Penfield, W., and Rasmussen, T. *The cerebral cortex of man.* New York: Macmillan, 1950.

Rachman, S., Hodgson, R., & Marks, I. The treatment of chronic obsessive-compulsive neurosis. *Behav. Res. Ther.*, 1971, **9**, 237–247.

Rahe, R., & Lind, E. Psychosocial factors and sudden cardiac death: A pilot study. *J. Psychosom. Res.*, 1971, **15**, 19.

Rogers, C. *Client-centered therapy.* Boston: Houghton Mifflin, 1951.

———. *On becoming a person: A client's view of psychotherapy.* Boston: Houghton Mifflin, 1961.

Rosenman, R., Brand, R. J., Jenkins, C. D., Friedman, M., Straus, R., and Wurm, M., Coronary heart disease in the Western Collaborative Group study: Final follow-up experience of 8½ years. *J.A.M.A.*, 1975, **233**, 872.

Ruskin, A., Beard, O., and Schaffer, R. Blast hypertension: Elevated arterial pressure in the victims of the Texas City disaster. *Amer. J. Mid.*, 1948, **4**, 228.

Sakel, M. Neue Behandlung der Morphinsucht. *A. Neurol. Psychiat.*, 1933, **143**, 506.

Scher, J. Patterns and profiles of addiction and drug abuse. *Arch. gen. Psychiat.*, 1966, **15**, 539.

Schwartz, D. A review of the "paranoid" concept. *Gen. Psychiat.*, 1963, **8**, 349.

Seligman, M. *Helplessness.* San Francisco: W. H. Freeman, 1975.

Srole, L, et al. *Mental health in the metropolis: The midtown Manhattan study. Vol. 1.* New York: McGraw-Hill, 1962.

Staudt, V., and Zubin, J. A biometric evaluation of the somatotherapies in schizophenia—A critical review. *Psychol. Bull.*, 1957, **54**, 171.

Stein, M. Etiology and mechanisms in the development of asthma. In J. Nodine and J. Moyer (Eds.), *Psychosomatic medicine.* Philadelphia: Lea & Febiger, 1962.

Suinn, R. M. The cardiac stress management program for Type A patients. *Cardiac Rehab.*, Vol. 5, No. 4, Winter, 1975.

———. Brock, L., and Edie, C. Behavior therapy for Type A patients. *American Journal of Cardiology*, 1975, **36**, 269.

———. Visuo-Motor Behavior Rehearsal for Adaptive Behavior. In J. Krumboltz and C. Thoresen, *Behavioral counseling methods.* Holt, Rinehart and Winston, 1976, 360.

———. *Manual: Anxiety management training.* Ft. Collins, Colorado: Rocky Mountain Behavioral Science Institute, 1977.

Suinn, R. M., & Bloom, L. J. Anxiety management

training for Type A persons. *J. Behav. Med.,* 1978, in press.

Suinn, R.M., and Richardson, F. Behavior therapy of an unusual case of highway hypnosis. *Behav. Therap. and Exp. Psychiat.,* 1970, **2,** 129.

Szasz, T. *The myth of mental illness.* New York: Holher-Harper, 1961.

Taube, C. Admission rates by age, sex, and marital status, state and county hospitals, 1969. Washington, D.C., Department of Health, Education, and Welfare, Statistical Note 32, 1970.

Thomas, D. Prognosis of depression with electrical treatment. *Br. Med. Journal,* 1954, *2,* 950.

Thorndike, E. *The elements of psychology.* New York: Serler, 1905.

United States Department of Health, Education and Welfare. *Marijuana and Health, 5th Annual Report.* Washington, D.C.: U.S. Government Printing Office, 1975.

Vaillant, G. A 12-year follow-up of New York narcotic addicts, *Arch. Gen. Psychiat.,* 1966, **15,** 539.

Watson, J. *Psychology from the standpoint of a behaviorist.* Philadelphia: Lippincott, 1919.

Watson, J., and Raynor, R. Conditioned emotional reactions. *J. Exp. Psychol.,* 1920, **3,** 1.

Weiss, J. Effects of coping response on stress. *J. Comp. Physiol. Psychol.,* 1968, **65,** 251.

Wing, J. Institutionalism in mental hospitals. *Brit. J. Soc. Clin. Psychol.,* 1962, **38,** 804.

Wolpe, J. *Psychotherapy by reciprocal inhibition.* Stanford, Ca.: Stanford University Press, 1958.

World Health Organization. *Expert committee on drugs liable to produce addiction. Second Report.* World Health Organization Technical Report Series No. 21. Geneva, Switzerland, World Health Organization, 1950.

Indexes

Name Index

Primary sources italicized

Subject Index

Primary definitions italicized